1968

THE LETTERS OF
PLINY

THE LETTERS
OF PLINY

A HISTORICAL AND
SOCIAL COMMENTARY

BY

A. N. SHERWIN-WHITE

Fellow of St. John's College
Oxford

OXFORD
AT THE CLARENDON PRESS
1966

Oxford University Press, Ely House, London W. 1

GLASGOW NEW YORK TORONTO MELBOURNE WELLINGTON
CAPE TOWN SALISBURY IBADAN NAIROBI LUSAKA ADDIS ABABA
BOMBAY CALCUTTA MADRAS KARACHI LAHORE DACCA
KUALA LUMPUR HONG KONG TOKYO

PRINTED IN GREAT BRITAIN
AT THE UNIVERSITY PRESS, OXFORD
BY VIVIAN RIDLER
PRINTER TO THE UNIVERSITY

PREFACE

THERE has been no general commentary on the nine books of Pliny's private letters since the eighteenth century, and even the admirable *Pliny's Correspondence with Trajan* of E. G. Hardy is now over seventy years old. There have been useful editions of single books and selections of letters, written mainly for use in schools, of which E. T. Merrill's volume in the Macmillan series was the best in any language. But the wide range of the private letters, which cover almost every aspect of Roman life except warfare, has discouraged learned commentators, myself not least. The range of the letters as sources is not only wide but deep. So many letters contain the principal evidence for a particular phase in the development of some social, political, or legal theme, that only an encyclopaedic knowledge of Roman history and society, and of modern opinion about them, could hope to satisfy the demands of specialists or to give proper guidance to the inquiries of students of each topic. Though the bulk of modern work primarily concerned with the content of the Letters is moderate, every treatment of the internal life of the earlier empire is apt to be concerned at some point with the Letters or their background, and every year produces new personal inscriptions or public documents that concern the matter of the much disputed chronology of the Letters. What then is the value of a commentary that only a modern Mommsen could hope to render satisfactory? At least it may bring within the compass of one book the essence of what is scattered so widely through the historical literature of the Principate that it is apt to elude even the best of Plinian bibliographies. It is also useful to place at the service of scholars who come to quarry in single letters, or groups of letters, or even in single paragraphs, a comparative elucidation of their meaning that is only possible after a long study of the whole collection. Because of this fragmentary approach the Letters are frequently misunderstood, despite the clarity of Pliny's Latin, since the illuminating parallel often lurks unnoticed in a letter about a different topic. After sixteen years of study I still continue to discover links and parallels within the letters that had hitherto escaped me.

The method of this Commentary therefore is to provide a self-contained discussion of each letter or group of associated letters. There is no general bibliographical list, in the modern fashion, of books and articles for the whole work. Such a list would be of scant intelligibility and little real use to most consultants. Instead, the commentary of each letter, and of each section of the introductory essays, contains its own citations of the most illuminating modern discussions. Much bibliography of sound but repetitive stuff has been omitted to make the work manageable. Besides, the study of Pliny has been plagued by amateurs who had nothing to say that had not been said before, or whose enthusiasm, like the worthy E. Allain's, exceeded their erudition and understanding. Pliny has also been the object of serious investigations, listed only in collections of doctoral theses, that unfortunately have never been published in print. These too it seemed pointless to include.

I was encouraged to attempt this task after the war by my former tutor Hugh Last, then Camden Professor. My original intention was to deal only with the political letters, but this proved an unsatisfactory limitation. The Commentary remains broadly historical, social, and economic. Though it widens its scope to cover the literary and semi-scientific interests that occupied Pliny's leisure hours, it excludes properly philological questions of grammar, syntax, and vocabulary, except where the elucidation of the context requires it. Even so the task has taken the spare time of some sixteen years.

The text printed is normally that of Professor Mynors's Oxford Classical Text. The rare occasions of disagreement with him are noted. My vast obligations to the written work of others will be apparent from the Commentary. I also owe a great deal to private advice and bibliographical aid from Mr. D. A. F. M. Russell, Professor Sir R. A. B. Mynors, Mr. P. A. Brunt, Mr. P. M. Fraser, Professor A. H. M. Jones, Professor A. Momigliano, and Mr. S. Weinstock. Professor Sir R. Syme and Professor E. Birley have sagely corrected some of my prosopographical fantasies, and Mrs. Radice gave me valuable topographical information. But the errors are all mine.

The book has taken a long time to prepare for printing and to correct in proof stages. Consequently it includes few references to the bibliography of the last two years.

A. N. SHERWIN-WHITE

St. John's College
1965

CONTENTS

MAPS

ABBREVIATIONS

The following abbreviations are frequently used throughout the Commentary.

Acta Ap.	*Acts of the Apostles.*
Act. Arv.	*Acta Fratrum Arvalium* in *CIL* vi.
AE	*L'Année épigraphique*, Paris.
A–J	F. W. Abbot, A. C. Johnson, *Municipal Administration in the Roman Empire*, Princeton, 1926.
Am. J. Phil.	*American Journal of Philology*, Baltimore.
Ap. Ty.	Philostratus, *De Apollonio Tyanensi.*
Asbach	I. Asbach, 'Zur Chronologie der Briefe des jüngeren Plinius', *Rhein. Mus.* xxxvi (1881), 38 ff.
Ashby, *Top. Dict.*	T. Ashby, S. B. Platner, *A Topographical Dictionary of Ancient Rome*, Oxford, 1929.
Bardon	H. Bardon, *La Littérature latine inconnue*, Paris, 1952–6.
B.C.	Appian, *Bella Civilia Romanorum.*
B.G.	Caesar, *Bellum Gallicum.*
C. Bosch	*Die kleinasiatischen Münzen der römischen Kaiserzeit* ii. 1, Stuttgart, 1935.
U. Brasiello	*La Repressione penale in diritto romano*, Napoli, 1937.
Bruns	C. G. Bruns, *Fontes iuris Romani antiqui*, Tübingen, 1919.
BSA	*Annual of the British School at Athens*, London.
BSR	*Papers of the British School at Rome*, London.
CAH	*Cambridge Ancient History*, vols. x and xi, Cambridge, 1934–6.
Carcopino	J. Carcopino, *Daily Life in Ancient Rome*, London, 1941.
CERP	A. H. M. Jones, *Cities of the Eastern Roman Provinces*, Oxford, 1937.
Charlesworth, *Documents*	M. P. Charlesworth, *Documents illustrating the reigns of Claudius and Nero*, Cambridge 1939.
Chilver, *Cisalpine Gaul*	G. E. F. Chilver, *Cisalpine Gaul, Social and Economic History*, Oxford, 1941.
Chrestomathie	L. Mitteis, U. Wilcken, *Grundzüge und Chrestomathie der Papyruskunde*, i–ii, Leipzig–Berlin, 1912.
Chron. Min.	*Chronica Minora*, ed. C. Frich, Leipzig, 1892.
CIG	*Corpus Inscriptionum Graecarum*, i–iv, Berlin, 1828–77.
CIL	*Corpus Inscriptionum Latinarum*, i–xvi, Berlin, 1863–1936.

Cl. Phil.	*Classical Philology*, Chicago.
Cl. Q.	*The Classical Quarterly*, London.
Cl. Rev.	*The Classical Review*, Oxford.
Cod. Iust.	*Codex Iustinianus* in *Corpus Iuris Civilis*.
D. or Dig.	*Digesta Iuris Romani* in *Corpus Iuris Civilis*.
Dio, Or.	Dio Chrysostomus, *Orationes*.
Ditt. Syll. or *D.S.*	W. Dittenberger, *Sylloge Inscriptionum Graecarum³*, i–iv, Leipzig, 1915–24.
Diz. Epigr.	E. de Ruggiero, *Dizionario epigrafico di Antichità Romane*, Rome, 1886–.
Domaszewski, *Rangordnung*	A. von Domaszewski, *Die Rangordnung des römischen Heeres*, Bonn, 1908.
D. Pen. R.	Th. Mommsen, *Droit pénal romain*, Paris, 1903.
Dörner, *Inschiften*	F. K. Dörner, *Inschriften und Denkmäler aus Bithynien* (Istanbule Forschungen 14), Berlin, 1941.
,, *Reise*	idem, *Bericht über eine Reise in Bithynien* (Öst. Ak. Wiss. ph.-hist. Kl. D. 75, 1), Wien, 1952.
DPR	Th. Mommsen, *Droit public romain* i–vi, Paris, 1889–93.
D–S	Ch. Daremberg, E. Saglio, *Dictionnaire des antiquités grecques et romaines*, Paris, 1877–1919.
Ec. Survey	T. Frank, *An Economic Survey of Ancient Rome*, vols. i–v, Baltimore, 1933–40.
E–J	V. Ehrenberg, A. H. M. Jones, *Documents Illustrating the Reigns of Augustus and Tiberius²*, Oxford, 1955.
Ep. de Caes.	Anonymous, *Epitome de Caesaribus*, printed in texts of Aurelius Victor.
Fast. Pot. or *F. Pot.*	*Fasti Potentiae*, in *AE* 1949, n. 23.
FIR	C. G. Bruns, O. Gradenvitz, *Fontes Iuris Romani*, Tübingen, 1909.
FIRA	S. Riccobono, *Fontes Iuris Romani Anteiustiniani*, i–iii, Florence, 1941–3.
FO	*Fasti Ostienses* in *Inscriptiones Italiae*, XIII. i, ed. A. Degrassi, Rome, 1947. See below pp. 734–6.
Fr. Vat.	*Fragmenta Vaticana* in *FIRA*.
Garzetti, *C., Inc.*	A. Garzetti, *Nerva*, Rome, 1950; numbers in the list of senators, certainly and uncertainly attributed.
GC	A. H. M. Jones, *The Greek City*, Oxford, 1940.
Gnomon Id.	*Forma Idiologi*, in *FIRA* i.
GS	Th. Mommsen, *Gesammelte Schriften*, i–viii, Berlin, 1905–13.
Guillemin, ad loc.	A.-M. Guillemin, *Pline le Jeune, Lettres*, Paris, 1927–47.
Hartleben	See L–H.
HE	Eusebius, *Historia Ecclesiae*.
IGRR	*Inscriptiones Graecae ad res Romanas pertinentes*, Paris, 1911–27, ed. R. Cagnat etc.

ILA	*Insciptions Latines d'Afrique*, ed. R. Cagnat, A. Merlin, Paris, 1923.
I.L.Al.	*Inscriptions Latines de l'Algérie*, i–ii, ed. S. Gsell, H.-G. Pflaum, Paris, 1922, 1957.
ILS	H. Dessau, *Inscriptiones latinae selectae*, Berlin, 1892–1916.
Index Verborum	Printed in Longolius, below, but now replaced by X. Jacques, J. von Oosteghem, *Index de Pline le Jeune*, Brussels, 1965.
Ital. agr.	V. A. Sirago, *L'Italia agraria sotto Traiano*, Louvain, 1958.
JB	*Bursians Jahresberichte.*
Jones, *Cities*	See *C.E.R.P.*
Jones, *Greek City*	See *G.C.*
JRS	*The Journal of Roman Studies*, London.
Lambrechts	P. Lambrechts, *La Composition du Sénat Romain*, Antwerp, 1936.
Lex Mal.	*Lex municipii Malacitani* in *FIRA*.
L–H	K. Lehman-Hartleben, *Plinio il Giovane, Lettere Scelte*, Florence, 1936.
Liebenam	W. Liebenam, *Städteverwaltung im römischen Kaiserreiche*, Leipzig, 1900.
Longolius	*Caii Plinii Secundi Epistolarum libros decem cum notis selectis.* G. Cortius, P. D. Longolius, Amsterdam, 1734.
Magie, *Romans*	D. Magie, *Roman rule in Asia Minor to the end of the third century after Christ*, i–ii, Princeton, 1950.
Marquardt, *Manuel*	J. Marquardt, *La Vie privée des romains*, Paris, 1892–3.
Merrill	E. T. Merrill, *Pliny, Select Letters*, London, 1903.
Monti, *Pliniana*	See p. 23.
O.C.T.	Plinius Minor, *Epistulae*, Oxford, 1963.
OGIS	W. Dittenberger, *Orientis Graeci Inscriptiones Selectae* i–ii, Leipzig, 1903–5.
Otto	W. Otto, 'Zur Lebensgeschichte des jüngeren Plinius', *S. B. Bayer. Ak. Wiss. Phil.-hist. Kl.* 1919, 1 ff.
Peter	C. Peter, 'Plinius der Jüngere', *Philologus*, xxxiii (1873), 698 f.
Pflaum, *Proc. Eq.*	H. G. Pflaum, *Les Procurateurs équestres sous le Haut-empire Romain*, Paris, 1950.
Pflaum. n.	idem, *Les Carrières procuratoriennes équestres sous le Haut-empire romain*, Paris, 1960–1.
Philol.	*Philologus, Zeitschift für klassisches Altertum*, Leipzig.
PIR	*Prosopographia Imperii Romani*, ed. 1, Berlin, 1897–8, ed. 2, 1933–.
P. Ox.	*The Oxyrhyncus Papyri*, London, 1898– .
Prete	S. Prete, '*Saggi Pliniani*', *Studi di Fil. Class. I*, Bologna, 1948.

Rangordnung	A. von Domaszweski, *Die Rangordnung des römischen Heeres*, Bonn, 1908.
RC	A.N. Sherwin-White, *The Roman Citizenship*, Oxford, 1939.
RE	*Paulys Real-enzyclopädie der klassischen Altertumswissenschaft*,[2] Stuttgart, 1894–.
RG	*Res Gestae Divi Augusti* in E–J.
Rev. Int. Dr. Ant.	*Revue internationale des droits de l'antiquité*, Brussels, 1948–.
RIC	H. Mattingly, E. A. Sydenham, *The Roman Imperial Coinage*, ii, London, 1926.
Rev. Hist. Dr. Fr.	*Revue historique de droit français et étranger*, Paris, 1922–.
Schultz	M. Schultz, *De Plinii epistulis quaestiones chronologicae*, Berlin, 1899.
SEG	*Supplementum Epigraphicum Graecum*, Leyden, 1923–.
SEHRE	M. Rostovtzeff, *The Social and Economic History of the Roman Empire*[2], i–ii, Oxford, 1957, revised by P. M. Fraser.
Sent. Pauli	*Sententiae receptae Paulo tributae* in *FIRA* ii.
SG (Eng. Tr.)	L. Friedländer, *Roman Life and manners under the early Empire* (translated by L. A. Magnus), i–iv, London, 1908–13.
SHA	Scriptores Historiae Augustae.
Stout	S. E. Stout, *Scribe and Critic at work in Pliny's Letters*, Indiana University publications, Bloomington, 1954.
Strack	P. L. Strack, *Untersuchungen zur römischen Reichsprägung des zweiten Jahrhunderts*, i, Stuttgart, 1931.
Studi Paoli	*Studi in onore di Ugo Enrico Paoli*, Firenze, 1955.
Syme, *Tac.*	R. Syme, *Tacitus*, Oxford, 1958.
Tab. Her.	*Tabula Heracleensis* in *FIRA* i.
T. A. Ph. A.	*Transactions and Proceedings of the American Philological Association*, Philadelphia.
Thes. L. L.	*Thesaurus Linguae Latinae.*
Tit. Ulp.	*Tituli ex corpore Ulpiani* in *FIRA* ii.
Vidman, *Étude*	L. Vidman, *Étude sur la correspondance de Pline le jeune avec Trajan* (Rozpravy Československé Ak. Věd. 70), Praha, 1960.
VL	A.-M. Guillemin, *Pline et la vie littéraire de son temps*, Paris, 1929.
von Arnim	H. von Arnim, *Leben und Werke des Dio von Prusa*, Berlin, 1898.
VS	Philostratus, *Vitae Sophistarum.*
Waddington, *Receuil*	W. H. Waddington, *Receuil général des monnaies grecques d'Asie mineure*, Paris, 1904–9. Second ed. Paris, 1925.

Weber, *Festgabe*   W. Weber, *Festgabe von Fachgenossen v. K. Müller*, Tübingen, 1922.

W–C   M. McCrum, A. G. Woodhead, *Select Documents of the Principates of the Flavian Emperors*, Cambridge, 1961.

WS   *Wiener Studien*, Zeitschrift für klassische Philologie, Wien.

Zaranka   J. Zaranka, *De Plinii epistularum . . . quaestiones chronologicae*. Dissertation, Louvain, 1949. See p. 23.

ZS   *Zeitschrift des Savigny-Stiftung für Rechtsgeschichte* (Romanistische Abt.).

BIBLIOGRAPHICAL SUMMARIES

Items appear annually in *Année Philologique* under the heading *Plinius Minor*. The following contain periodic summaries of writings in the twentieth century.

Bursians Jahresbericht: cliii (1911), 1 ff. (K. Burkhard).
ccxxi (1929), 1 ff. (M. Schuster).
ccxlii (1934), 9 ff. (M. Schuster).
cclxxxii (1943), 38 ff. (R. Hanslik).

Also R. Hanslik, *Anzeiger für die Altertumswissenschaft*, 1955, 8. 1 ff.
J. Beaujeu, *Lustrum*, vi (1961) 272 ff.

Note that in the commentary letter references to other letters in the same book are given in the form 'Ep. 23', while references to letters in other books are given by plain numbers, e.g. 'I. 23. 2', with Roman numerals indicating the book-number.

GENERAL INTRODUCTION TO
THE PRIVATE LETTERS

I. THE ORIGINS AND CHARACTERISTICS OF
THE LETTERS

Satura nostra tota est, was the Roman claim. They might have added *epistula quoque,* with justice so far as the surviving literature is concerned.[1] There is a chapter on the theory of letter-writing in a late Greek treatise, Demetrius, *De Interpretatione* 223–39, and the late rhetoricians have left behind two summaries of types of letters, the *formae epistolicae* and the *characteres epistolici,* with short examples of each type. The numbering of types is twenty-one and forty-one respectively (p. 42). But the surviving Greek letters are mostly addresses and long essays meant for publication, in the style of Isocrates, *Ad Nicoclem.* The Greek theorist recognized the letter as a by-form of literature akin to the dialogue, with a similar though simpler style (Demetrius, 223). But the Roman letter, as it emerges full-grown in the correspondence of Cicero and his friends, is the private letter of genuine intercourse, whether concerned with *res domesticae* or *res publicae.* Cicero in a passage of the Philippics brings out the characteristics of his own letters: 'quam multa ioca solent esse in epistulis quae prolatae si sint inepta videantur, quam multa seria neque tamen ullo modo divolganda' (2. 7). In several passages he finds the mark of private letters in the *iocus* and *iocatio,* and in the use of *sermo cotidianus* (*Ad Fam.* 2. 4. 1, 9. 21. 1; *Ad Att.* 7. 5. 5, 10. 11. 5) which seem to be the equivalent of τὸ λαλεῖν in the treatise *De Interpretatione.* But for serious matters the tone might be *severum et grave* (*Ad Fam.* 2. 4. 1). Cicero knows something of the theoretical types of letter catalogued by the later rhetoricians, and mentions three categories, the *promissio auxili*—characteristically unknown to the Greek lists—the *consolatio doloris,* and *litterae commendaticiae.* But apart from Book 12 of the *Ad Familiares,* which is a collection of the latter, his own letters to or from his friends would be hard to classify under any detailed scheme, except for a few, such as the well-known consolation of Sulpicius to Cicero on the death of Tullia.

[1] The basic discussion is H. Peter, *Der Brief in der römischem Litteratur* (Abh. Philol.-hist. Kl. d. Kgl.-Sächs. Ges. der Wiss. XX (1903)): ch. v is devoted to Pliny.

It is a great jump from the letters of Cicero to those of Pliny. The gap is not bridged by the metrical Epistles of Horace or by the letters in prose of Seneca to Lucilius. One or two of Horace's themes recur in Pliny's Letters, notably the 'invitation to a feast', and the 'enquiry to a man of letters overseas' (*Ep.* I. 3 and 5). These are not so remote from the manner and treatment of Pliny, not least in their brevity. But the rest are mostly letters of philosophic admonition with a gossipy social setting in which description plays a minor role, written in a rambling style very different from the concentrated method of Pliny. Peter, in his history of the Roman letter, omits Seneca altogether, and even Guillemin, who ransacks Latin literature in the search for predecessors, invokes Seneca seldom.[1] Seneca writes in a different tradition, continuing the vein of the Greek letter of admonition, the προτρεπτικός, and his letters make no claim to be considered as private correspondence. They belong with those defined by Artemon as 'half dialogue' (Demetrius, 223). Seneca claims that they are in the language of conversation, and rejects with disgust the notion of *accuratas . . . epistulas*.[2] Pliny's letters are not Senecan, though he adapts the letter of admonition to his own purposes (p. 42). But neither are they Ciceronian, though he claims a conditional comparison with Cicero (III. 20. 10 'veteribus', IX. 2. 2–3). Peter suggested that the true origin of Pliny's letter-type lies in the oratorical *egressus*, or formal digression, and that the immediate model was provided by the *Silvae* of Statius, a collection of occasional pieces in verse. Quintilian (*Inst.* 4. 3. 12), Pliny's master, characterized the *egressus* as concerned with: 'laus hominum locorumque, expositio rerum gestarum . . . etiam fabulosarum, descriptio regionum'. Statius first detached the *egressus* from oratory and gave it a life of its own in verse. This is true of many of the themes of Statius— the praises of Rutilius Gallicus and other notables, the description of the villa of Pollius, or of the Via Domitiana and the events of Domitian's seventeenth consulship (*Silvae* I. 4, 2. 2, 4. I, 3). Such themes recur in Pliny (p. 43–44). It may be added that conversely Statius borrowed an epistolary theme for his numerous Consolations, and once adopted the epistolary *iocatio* in his *hendecasyllabi iocosi* to Plotius Grypus. But apart from the metrical form there is a marked difference between Pliny's Letters and Statius' *Silvae* in length. The letters of a length comparable to many of the *Silvae* are exceptional (p. 4).

Martial comes to mind as an alternative influence. Guillemin rightly calls him the 'true master' of Pliny.[3] His influence may be

---

[1] Chiefly for the villa theme, *VL*, 142 ff.
[2] Sen. *Ep.* 75. I: 'quis enim accurate loquitur nisi qui vult putide loqui?'
[3] *VL*, 147 ff. Cf. R. Syme, *Tacitus*, 97.

seen not only in the style and language, where it is pervasive,[1] but
in the greater variety of topics, and in the comparative brevity of
most of the pieces. All three writers were experimenting in a new
form of literature, which may be better described as occasional
pieces than as essays in verse or prose. Martial was Pliny's protégé
(III. 21), while Statius, as Peter noted, is never mentioned by Pliny,
although echoes can be detected at least in the first villa-description
(II. 17 pref.).[2] This is hardly out of jealousy or dislike, since Pliny
has much to say about his forensic rival and enemy Aquilius Regulus.
Statius, unlike Martial, did not survive to balance his flatteries of
Domitian by flattering his successors. Hence he was out of fashion
and favour in the literary coteries of the period of the letters. Pliny's
direct copying of Martial is apparent in his books of verse, described
in IV. 14, VIII. 21, which have taken over from the letter its *iocatio*,
which plays a very subsidiary role in Pliny (p. 43).

Pliny defines his type of letter variously (I. I. I, VII. 9. 8, IX. 2. 3,
28. 5), as *epistulae curatius* or *curiosius* or *diligentius scriptae*,
and distinguishes them from the Senecan essay in epistolary form,
scholasticas litteras.[3] He and his friends were in the habit of exchang-
ing such letters (I. 16. 6, II. 13. 7, IX. 2. 1–3, 28. 5). Once a friend
proposes a subject for a letter of this type, and Pliny promises to
compose it (IX. 11. I n.). Certain principles of composition can be
inferred from Pliny. Each letter is normally confined to a single
theme.[4] There are few exceptions to this rule. Only three or four
times in the whole collection does Pliny introduce an alien topic or
notably change the subject. In II. 20. 9 he quotes the *lex scholastica*
that a theme should be illustrated by three examples. This defends
the unity of several letters where three different anecdotes illustrate
a common theme: II. 20, the captations of Regulus; III. 16, the
courage of Arria; VII. 27, the ghost letter, and perhaps the first part
of VI. 31, the trials at Centum Cellae. In two groups of letters he is at
pains to contrive a connexion where possible between alien topics.
The first group is concerned with travels. In V. 14. 1–6 the account
of Cornutus' career and that of Pliny's vacation are linked by a
reference to Pliny's official leave of absence from his own post. In IV.
13. 1–2 mention of the movements and occupations of Tacitus and
Pliny leads on to the subject of the schoolmaster of Comum, ibid.
3–11. So too in IV. 1 the account of Pliny's journey to Comum is
intertwined with that of the dedication of his temple at Tifernum.

---

[1] Cf. Guillemin, *VL*, ch. iii, for a detailed study: the parallels with Martial
are always the most convincing. For an extreme instance cf. IX. 7. 4 n.
[2] Cf. ibid. 125 ff.   [3] See I. I. I n.
[4] Cf. Guillemin, *VL*, 128, 130, 146–7, who, however, did not seriously consider the exceptions, which are significant for the genuine character of the letters.

These hardly count as exceptions to the rule of unity. The reference to travel is a regular form of opening and ending a letter, managed more briefly in, for example, I. 22. I, v. 6. I, VIII. I. I, 2. I.

The second group is more miscellaneous. Twice there is a brief and unexpected postscript acknowledging the receipt of a gift. In I. 7 it stands unrelated to the rest of the letter, but in VII. 21. 4 the intrusion is connected with the subject of the letter, Pliny's eyesight. Much more notable changes of subject occur in VI. 19, 31, VII. 6, VIII. 14, IX. 11, 28. In the first an account of Trajan's measures to check bribery is linked with that of a rise in the price of land, but the link is that of a genuine cause and effect (ibid. n.). The second describes three trials before the cabinet of Trajan, the hospitality of the emperor, and the building of the harbour at Centum Cellae. The three topics are linked only by the unity of the occasion, Pliny's visit to Trajan. In VII. 6 the report of a phase in the prosecution of Varenus is interrupted by the story of another criminal trial which bears only a strained similarity to that of Varenus. Pliny makes a formal apology for the change of subject (s. 6): 'quid enim prohibet, quamquam alia ratio scribendae epistulae fuerit, de studiis disputare?' In VIII. 14 a diatribe against the *servitus priorum temporum* is ingeniously linked to a technical discussion of the rules of division in senatorial debates, with which it has no genuine connexion. In IX. 11 the request of Geminus for a literary letter and the sale of Pliny's books at Lugdunum lack vital connexion. In XI. 28 three diverse topics—the vintage, a friend's visit, and an account of a speech of Pliny—are formally connected as the contents of three letters of which Pliny acknowledges receipt; possibly the *lex scholastica* may be invoked here.

With these limited exceptions Pliny sticks to the rule of the single theme. In II. 1. 12 he neatly makes a virtue out of this necessity: 'volui tibi multa alia scribere, sed totus animus in hac una contemplatione defixus est'.

A second rule forbids excessive length. In v. 6. 42–44 he insists that length should be appropriate to the subject, and in general he deprecates the long letter. In all but one of the few letters of exceptional length there is some apology for this, expressly in III. 9. 27, 37, v. 6. 41–45, IX. 13. 26, and indirectly in I. 20. 25, II. 11. 25, 17. 29. The exception is VIII. 14, a letter noted above for its lack of unity. The length of these letters does not fall below some five or six pages of text, and rises to about eight in v. 6. In an intermediate group of eleven letters of about three to four pages in length there is a touch of apology only twice, in III. 5. 20, IV. 11. 16, but none in I. 5. 8, IV. 9, VI. 16, 20, 31, VII. 27, VIII, 6, IX. 26. Yet surprisingly in VII. 9. 16 he apologizes for undue length after a somewhat repetitive exposition in less than three pages of a theme from which he does not seriously digresss.

The third rule concerns style—the colour and pattern of language and the tone of feeling. Pliny develops this beyond the doctrine of his master Quintilian, who remarked briefly that *oratio soluta* was suitable to letters unless they were concerned with philosophy or public affairs, and that letters should avoid hiatus and cultivate rythm (*Inst.* 9. 4. 19). Pliny states in VII. 9. 8: 'volo epistulam diligentius scribas. nam saepe in oratione quoque non historica modo sed prope poetica descriptionum necessitas incidit, et pressus sermo purusque ex epistulis petitur'. In I. 16. 6 he commends the letters of Pompeius Saturninus for their Plautian or Terentian simplicity of vocabulary. Peter (op. cit. 113) noted the connexion between the statements of Pliny and Quintilian about the poetic style appropriate in digressions (Ep. II. 5. 5; *Inst.* 2. 4. 3). Evidently Pliny intended a mixture of poetic vocabulary and simple language. How far he achieved it is not the subject of an historical commentary.[1] More pervasive than either aim is undoubtedly his ingrained technique as an orator, from which he could not hope to divest himself. In certain, but not many, letters, notably in descriptions of natural scenery, some poetical colour is obvious enough (VI. 20, VII. 27, VIII. 8, 17). The use of Vergilian language in the account of the building operations at Centum Cellae is merely the clearest instance (VI. 31. 15–17 nn.). The oratorical devices of the Panegyric dominate the account of the Vestal trial and the long letter about Pallas (IV. 11, VIII. 6), though Pliny there apologizes for the use of unsuitable language (VIII. 6. 17). More unexpected perhaps is the style of the argument on senatorial procedure in VIII. 14, which sounds more suitable to the Centumviral court of civil law, where Pliny spent a good deal of his professional career.

How far the use of *pressus purusque sermo* goes beyond the choice of plain words in factual narrative and quiet passages generally is questionable. Pliny's simplicity is decidedly studied. Passages may be taken, especially from the opening of letters, which at first sight promise simplicity, but artifice is soon apparent in the construction, if not in the vocabulary. A random sample, the opening of VII. 16, is characteristic. 'Calestrium Tironem familiarissime diligo, et privatis mihi et publicis necessitatibus implicitum. simul militavimus simul quaestores Caesaris fuimus. ille me in tribunatu liberorum iure praecessit, ego illum in praetura sum consecutus.' The commonest of nouns, only the most essential of adverbs and adjectives are used. But the cunning of the artist's hand appears in the order and arrangement.

---

[1] See Guillemin, *VL*, ch. iii, for an analysis of extensive poetical influences in Pliny's letters. But some of the parallels seem rather forced.

The letters to Trajan provide a fair comparison. The recommendation of Rosianus Geminus (x. 26) is very close to vii. 16. Or another random sample, from an official report (x. 31. 3), gives the same mixture of plain vocabulary and complex construcion: 'nam et reddere poenae post longum tempus plerosque iam senes et quantum adfirmatur frugaliter modesteque viventes nimis severum arbitrabar, et in publicis officiis retinere damnatos non satis honestum putabam'. Pliny is perhaps plain when there is no special reason to be otherwise, even in the literary letters, but he cannot be simple even in his official correspondence. It has been noted that in the more colourful passages he has a fondness for diminutives, and even invents some when they were not ready to hand, e.g. *columbulus, cumbula, metula, prominulus* in v. 6. 15 and 35, viii. 20. 7, ix. 25. 3.[1]

Pliny carries Quintilian's advice about the use of prose rhythm in letters to its logical conclusion. Both the private and the public letters follow the rules of oratorical prose for the *clausula*.[2]

This discussion of style demonstrates the extent to which the letters are literary compositions. Their formality is shown also by the frequent use of somewhat standardized opening phrases which affirm the subject of the letter. In the following list the types and their variants have been catalogued. Surprisingly little attention has been paid to this stylistic device hitherto. Guillemin (*VL*, 145) noted only the first two types.

vi. 18	rogas ut agam Firmanorum . . . causam.
vi. 27	rogas ut cogitem quid designatus consul . . . censeas.
i. 14	petis ut fratris tui filiae prospiciam maritum . . . .
iii. 15	petis ut libellos tuos . . . legam . . . .
iv. 26	petis ut libellos . . . emendandos . . . curem.
vi. 16	petis ut tibi avunculi mei exitum scribam . . . .
v. 13	et tu rogas et ego promisi . . . scripturum . . . quem habuisset eventum postulatio Nepotis . . . .
vii. 14	tu quidem honestissime, quod tam impense et rogas et exigis ut accipi iubeam . . . .

vii. 9	quaeris quemadmodum . . . putem te studere oportere.
ix. 36	quaeris quemadmodum in Tuscis diem . . . disponam.
vii. 15	requiris quid agam. quae nosti. distringor officio . . . .
i. 23	consulis an existimem te in tribunatu . . . .
vii. 18	deliberas mecum quemadmodum pecunia . . . salva sit . . . .

[1] In general see J. Niemirska-Pliszczyńska, *De elocutione Pliniana*, Lublin, 1955, the latest of a long series of studies on this theme, with bibliography p. 163. For the diminutives, ibid. 10, 14. Also, d'Agostino, *I diminutivi in Plinio il Giovane*, Turin, 1931. O.C.T. disallows *prominulam*, v. 6. 15 n.

[2] C. Hofacker, *De clausulis C. Caecili Plini Secundi*, diss. Bonn., 1903. Or, Th. Zieliński, 'Das Ausleben des Clauselgesetzes in der röm. Kunstprosa', *Philologus Suppl.* x (1907), 431 f.

I. 1   frequenter hortatus es ut epistulas . . . publicarem. . . .
II. 19   hortaris ut orationem . . . recitem. . . .
II. 16   tu quidem pro . . . reverentia admones me codicillos . . . .
IV. 17   et admones et rogas ut suscipiam causam Corelliae . . . .
IX. 1   saepe te monui ut libros . . . emitteres. . . .
V. 8   suades ut historiam scribam. . . .

IV. 13   salvum in urbem venisse gaudeo . . . .
IV. 16   gaude meo gaude tuo . . . nomine: adhuc studiis honor durat.
VI. 26   gaudeo et gratulor quod . . . filiam. . . . destinasti. . . .
VII. 23   gaudeo quidem esse te tam fortem. . . .
IV. 8   gratularis mihi quod auguratum acceperim. . . .
II. 11   solet esse gaudio tibi si quid acti est in senatu. . . .
VII. 32   delector iucundum tibi fuisse Tironis mei adventum. . . .

II. 17   miraris cur me Laurentinum . . . delectet. . . .
VII. 11   miraris quod Hermes . . . agros . . . addixerit. . . .
I. 9   mirum est quam singulis diebus in urbe ratio . . . constet. . . .
VII. 22   minus miraberis me . . . petisse ut. . . conferres tribunatum. . . .

VII. 30   torqueor quod discipulum . . . amisisti. . . .
VII. 19   angit me Fanniae valetudo. . . .
VII. 1   terret me haec tua . . . valetudo. . . .
IX. 22   magna me sollicitudine adfecit . . . valetudo. . . .
II. 9   anxium me . . . habet petitio Sexti. . . .

III. 8   facis pro cetera reverentia . . . quod petis ut tribunatum . . . .
VIII. 4   optime facis quod bellum Dacicum . . . scribere paras. . . .
VI. 34   recte fecisti quod gladiatorium munus . . . .
IX. 5   egregie facis . . . quod iustitiam . . . provincialibus . . . com-
          mendas. . . .

IX. 2   facis iucunde quod . . . epistulas . . . flagitas. . . .
IX. 24   bene fecisti quod libertum . . . .
VIII. 13   probo quod libellos . . . legisti. . . .
IX. 9   unice probo quod Pompei . . . morte . . . adficeris. . . .

VII. 6   rara et notabilis res Vareno contigit. . . .
VI. 22   magna res acta est omnium qui sunt provinciis praefuturi . . . .
VI. 15   mirificae rei non interfuisti. . . .
V. 4   res parva sed initium non parvae: vir praetorius . . . .
III. 14   rem atrocem . . . Macedo . . . passus est. . . .

I. 16   amabam Pompeium. . . .
IV. 12   amas Egnatium. . . .
VI. 8   Atilium Crescentem et nosti et amas. . . .
VII. 31   Claudius Pollio amari a te cupit. . . .
IV. 4   Varisidium Nepotem valdissime diligo. . . .
VII. 16   Calestrium Tironem familiarissime diligo. . . .
IV. 15   si quid omnino hoc certe iudicio facio quod Asinium singu-
          lariter amo.

IV. 1   cupis . . . neptem . . . videre . . . .
VIII. 10 quo magis cupis . . . pronepotes videre . . . .
IX. 10   cupio praeceptis tuis parere . . . .
VI. 6   si quando nunc praecipue cuperem esse te Romae . . . .

III. 21   audio Valerium Martialem decessisse . . . .
IV. 11   audistine Valerium Licinianum in Sicilia profiteri?
III. 7   modo nuntiatus est Silius . . . finisse vitam . . . .
V. 5   nuntiatur mihi C. Fannium decessisse . . . .
V. 14   secesseram in municipium cum mihi nuntiatum est Cornu-
          tum . . . .

I. 5   vidistine quemquam M. Regulo timidiorem . . . ?
I. 7   vide in quo me fastigio collocaris cum . . . .
V. 19   video quam molliter tuos habeas . . . .
VI. 13   umquamne vidisti quemquam tam laboriosum . . . ?
VIII. 8   vidistine aliquando Clitumnum fontem . . . ?

V. 17   scio quantopere bonis artibus faveas . . . .
VI. 19   scis tu accessisse pretium agris . . . ?
VI. 28   scio quae tibi causa fuerit impedimento quominus . . . .

IV. 5   Aeschinen aiunt petentibus . . . legisse . . . .
VI. 20   ais te . . . cupere cognoscere quos ego Miseni relictus . . . .
VII. 4   ais legisse te hendecasyllabos meos . . . .
VII. 28   ais quosdam apud te reprehendisse . . . .
IV. 7   saepe tibi dico inesse vim Regulo . . . .
IX. 26   dixi de quodam oratore saeculi nostri . . . .
IX. 19   significas legisse te . . . iussisse Verginium . . . .

I. 18   scribis te perterritum somnio . . . .
IV. 10   scribis mihi Sabinam, quae nos reliquit heredes . . . .
IV. 25   scripseram tibi verendum esse ne ex . . . suffragiis . . . .
V. 16   tristissimus haec tibi scribo Fundani nostri filia . . . .
VI. 5   scripseram tenuisse Varenum . . . .
VI. 7   scribis te absentia mea . . . adfici . . . .
VI. 25   scribis Robustum . . . iter peregisse . . . .
IX. 7   aedificare te scribis . . . .
IX. 40   scribis pergratas . . . fuisse litteras meas quibus . . . .

IV. 23   magnam cepi voluptatem cum . . . cognovi te . . . disponere
          otium . . . .
VI. 31   evocatus in consilium a Caesare . . . maximam cepi voluptatem . . . .
IX. 16   summam te voluptatem percepisse ex isto . . . genere venandi . . . .

These sixteen sets of stylized phrases, with minor variations,
reveal a formalization of the terms that naturally suggest themselves
to a writer when he introduces the principal subject of his letter. It is
remarkable that the most obvious letter-opening, a direct reference
to the receipt or dispatch of a letter or a book, of which there are
twenty instances, shows much less stylization.

I. 2   quia . . . adventum . . . prospicio, librum quem . . . . promiseram
exhibeo . . . .

II. 5   actionem . . . promissam exhibui . . . .

III. 13   librum quo . . . gratias egi misi . . . .

VII. 12   libellum formatum . . . quo . . . amicus . . . uteretur misi . . . .

VII. 20   librum tuum legi et . . . adnotavi . . . .

VIII. 3   librum quem novissime tibi misi . . . significas.

IX. 35   librum quem misisti recepi . . . .

I. 8   peropportune mihi redditae sunt litterae tuae quibus . . . .

I. 11   olim mihi nullas epistulas mittis . . . .

V. 11   recepi litteras tuas ex quibus cognovi . . . .

V. 21   varie me adfecerunt litterae tuae . . . .

VII. 13   eadem epistula . . . significat . . . .

VIII. 6   cognovisse iam ex epistula . . . debes . . . .

IX. 11   epistulam tuam iucundissimam accepi . . . .

IX. 17   recepi litteras tuas quibus . . . .

IX. 18   qua intentione . . . legeris libellos meos, epistula tua ostendit . . . .

IX. 20   tua vero epistula . . . iucundior fuit . . . .

IX. 28   post longum tempus epistulas tuas, sed tres pariter, recepi.

Of these eighteen instances only three from either group employ
a closely similar form—III. 13, VIII. 3, IX. 35 from the first, and
V. 11, IX. 11, 17 from the second. These six formal openings may be
added to the preceding list.

Altogether in the two sections there are some ninety-eight letters
out of the whole collection of 248 which use stylized openings. The
first three books account for only fourteen, or a seventh, of these
openings, in sixty-six letters or rather more than a quarter of the
whole collection. The middle four books, IV–VII, use them much more
freely: out of 118 letters precisely half use stylized openings. In
Book VIII they become rarer, with five formal openings out of twenty-
four, in much the same proportion as in I–III. Then Book IX, with its
miscellaneous forty letters, returns to a higher rate with some fifteen
stylized openings, according to the present lists. The figures, if not
statistical, are of some interest. They may suggest that the middle
books hold the highest proportion of letters consciously written for
publication, or that Pliny revised and wrote more according to
formula in these than in I–III and VIII.

When Pliny does not employ stylized openings and their variants, he
usually plunges straight into his theme with a specific statement, e.g.

I. 13   magnum proventum poetarum annus hic attulit.

III. 18   officium consulatus iniunxit mihi ut reipublicae nomine . . . .

VII. 24   Ummidia Quadratilla paulo minus octogensimo aetatis anno
decessit . . . .

VIII. 5   grave vulnus Macrinus noster accepit . . . .

But in certain letters he employs a less direct approach, beginning
with a general statement or proverbial remark, from which he proceeds to the particular. These openings are decidedly rare in the
early books. The earliest seems to be III. 16: 'adnotasse videor facta
dictaque virorum feminarumque alia clariora esse alia maiora'.
Possibly I. 17 also comes under the definition: 'est adhuc curae
hominibus fides et officium. . . '. There are only four other examples
of this type in III–VI: III. 20, VI. 21 and 24, and V. 17 which combines
a stylized opening with it. Then in VII and VIII there comes a spate of
them, nine in all. Surprisingly these are not distributed evenly
through the two books, but they come bunched together. Book IX
adds four others, better distributed.

VII. 25   quantum eruditorum aut modestia ipsorum aut quies operit ac
         subtrahit famae . . . .

VII. 26   nuper me cuiusdam amici languor admonuit optimos esse nos
         dum infirmi sumus . . . .

VII. 27   et mihi discendi et tibi docendi facultatem otium praebet.
         igitur perquam velim scire, ...

VIII. 2   alii in praedia sua proficiscuntur ut locupletiores revertantur,
         ego ut pauperior.

VIII. 18   falsum est nimirum quod creditur vulgo, testamenta hominum
         speculum esse morum, cum Domitius Tullus, ...

VIII. 19   et gaudium mihi et solacium in litteris, nihilque tam laetum
         quod his laetius tam triste quod non per has minus triste.
         itaque et infirmitate uxoris, ...

VIII. 20   ad quae noscenda iter ingredi, transmittere mare solemus, ea sub
         oculis posita neglegimus, ...

VIII. 21   ut in vita sic in studiis pulcherrimum et humanissimum
         existimo severitatem comitatemque miscere . . . qua ratione
         ductus, ...

VIII. 22   nostine hos qui omnium libidinum servi sic aliorum vitiis
         irascuntur quasi invideant, . . . ?

IX. 3   alius aliud; ego beatissimum existimo qui bonae . . . famae
         praesumptione perfruitur, ...

IX. 23   frequenter agenti mihi evenit ut centumviri laudarent . . .
         frequenter e senatu famam . . . rettuli . . . numquam tamen
         maiorem cepi voluptatem quam nuper, ...

IX. 27   quanta potestas quanta dignitas quanta maiestas . . . sit hi-
         storiae, cum frequenter alias tum proxime sensi. recitaverat
         quidam . . . .

IX. 29   ut satius unum aliquid insigniter facere quam plurima medio-
         criter, ita plurima mediocriter si non possis unum aliquid in-
         signiter. quod intuens ego, ...

Pliny seems to be deliberately developing a new style in the last
three books. In VIII. 20 the general thought is expounded for eleven

lines before he comes to the specific subject. In VIII. 22 the generalization is developed for the same length, and the specific instance is cut off short and left unspoken: 'quaeris fortasse quo commotus haec scribam. nuper quidam,—sed melius coram'. In IX. 3 the generalization continues for twelve lines, in somewhat similar fashion, and is briefly applied to the addressee.

II. THE AUTHENTICITY OF THE LETTERS AS CORRESPONDENCE

THE study of the letter openings gives some notion of the meaning of the term *epistulae curatius scriptae*, and some hints of the development of Pliny's technique. It also gives some tentative support to the argument, based on less subjective criteria, that on the whole the letters were composed in a chronological series approximating to the present order of books. It also leads naturally to the question of the authenticity of the letters as letters. Pliny presents the letters as part of a genuine literary correspondence. Modern scholars have taken no very coherent line about this. Some regard the letters as entirely fictitious, written for the books in which they appear. Peter saw little organic connexion between the contents of the letters and the persons to whom they are addressed. Others speak of the letters being written up for publication from simpler originals. These opinions emerged from the various discussions of the chronology of the letters. Mommsen held that the letters belonged in their composition to specific, successive periods (pp. 20 f.). His critics implied that the letters were being composed at widely varying dates and were later collected into books. Such a view has been taken again, in recent years, by Monti and Hanslik in studies of particular letters (cf. IV. 1, 11, V. 1, 3 nn.).

The more personal letters of advice on social, political, and literary problems, which Peter admitted were appropriate to their addressees —such as the letters to young protégés, Pedanius Fuscus, Ummidius Quadratus, and Rosianus Geminus (VII. 9, IX. 36, 40, VI. 29, VII. 1, VIII. 22) and earlier to Pompeius Falco and Iunius Avitus (I. 23, II. 6)— form a special group. They are highly polished specimens. Yet it is unlikely that their topics and occasions were entirely fictitious. It is certain that a praetorian senator called Maximus was sent on a special mission to Achaea, as in VIII. 24. The serious illness of young Geminus and the absence of the young advocate Fuscus from Rome on a long holiday need be no less genuine (VII. 9). So too the appropriate advice that each received. Anything is possible, no doubt, in the field of the imagination. But it would require an extraordinary ingenuity to invent so many convincing minor details for the setting of so miscellaneous a subject-matter as that of these letters. It must be reckoned at least a probability that Pliny was in the habit of advising or consoling his friends on occasion with appropriate *litterae curiosius scriptae*, and that these formed one basis of the collection.

A second group offers a firmer grip to the investigator. The letters dealing with Pliny's business affairs and domestic arrangements are full of precise and particular details that can hardly have been invented. They read as literary revisions of practical letters which have been polished in language and style and simplified by omission of the most technical and transient details. The instructions to an architect in IX. 39 to prepare a plan and buy materials for a small shrine lack the precise measurements necessary for the task, but otherwise give a clear account of the type of building required and the peculiarities of the site. So too the short letter of instructions to Pliny's agent at Comum to set up a Corinthian bronze with a dedicatory inscription (III. 6). Here the elaborate description of the bronze is an obvious expansion. The discussion of the prospective purchase of an estate, with a clear account of its condition, values, and previous mismanagement, and certain details about its necessary equipment, is hardly an invention (III. 19). So too the long description of Pliny's method of dealing with his vintage merchants with mathematical details, has the authentic ring (VIII. 2). There is a similarly convincing letter about an innovation in his system of agricultural leases (IX. 37).

These letters are close to the realities of correspondence. So too are the letters of recommendation for promotion written for equestrian friends and young senators in the public service, containing summary accounts of their careers, standing, and qualities. Both groups can be checked by comparison with certain of the letters to Trajan, which like the rest of Book X show no sign of literary revision, and have never been regarded as other than genuine letters. The account of Pliny's agricultural leases in X. 8 is put forward very much as in IX. 37, as the explanation of a necessary absence from Rome, and the agrictural situation is akin. The recommendation of Rosianus Geminus for senatorial preferment and of Suetonius Tranquillus for the *ius trium liberorum* (X. 26, 94) are generally similar in content to the recommendations of Arrianus Maturus and Cornelius Minicianus (III. 2, VII. 22), not least in their rather generalized descriptions of character and the absence of precise details about the men's careers. Equally comparable are the longer letters recommending Voconius Romanus to a consular legate for equestrian promotion, and to Trajan for senatorial status (II. 13, X. 4), which were written

within a year of each other. The private and literary letter has in
fact more to say about the candidate than the letter to the emperor.
A noteworthy feature of these letters of recommendation is the stress
laid on *studia*, the forensic and literary activity of the candidates.
This though stronger in the letter to personal friends is equally
present in the recommendations to the unliterary Trajan (x. 4. 4,
94. 1). Contrarily, the uncompromising brevity of x. 13, commending
Accius Sura to Trajan for a praetorship, may be compared to that of
iv. 4, commending Varisidius Nepos to Sosius Senecio for an equestrian commission. The latter has been thought cool and evasive;
more likely, it is merely very close to its original form.

The numerous brief notes, covering the receipt and dispatch of
letters and books, with a brief comment, or giving information about
the movements or occupations of the writer, seem to carry the signs
of authenticity. Though regularly distributed through the first six
books in threes or fours, they are a great deal commoner in the last
three, and form a quarter of the items in Book ix. One would hardly
sit down to invent this kind of thing—often described by scholars as
'fillers'—in excessive numbers, even if they may be considered with
Guillemin epigrams in prose.[1] It is notable that in this type of
note the introductory sentences or phrases are less stereotyped than
in the longer letters (p. 9). The following list excludes notes of
more than ten or eleven lines, except for the bracketed items, which
are notes of twelve to thirteen lines—while iv. 10 and vii. 10, though
very short, are excluded because of their special subject-matter—:
i. 1, 11, 21; ii. 2, 8, 15; iii. (12), 17; iv. 16, 18, 20, (26), 29; v. 2 (10),
(12), 15, 18; vi. 3, 9, 14, 28; vii. 2, 5, 7, 8, 13, 14, 15, (21), 23, 28, 32;
viii. 1, 3, 7, 9, 13, 15, (19); ix. 4, 8, 11, 14, 15, 16, 18, 20, 24, 32, 38.
This list supports the evidence on other grounds that in Books vii–
ix Pliny was becoming short, not of letters as such, but of *curiosius
scriptae* to make up his volumes.

There are a number of somewhat longer notes, akin to those just
discussed, which may represent worked-up versions of shorter
originals, developing a notion more fully, e.g. vii. 3, viii. 22, ix. 2.
Others seem so tightly packed that they may be close to their
original form. Thus in v. 11 Pliny says a good deal in a short space
to his grandfather-in-law about municipal benefactions. Again ix. 28,
discussing the miscellaneous contents of three letters from Voconius
Romanus, touches on topics as diverse as the harvest, a commission
to the emperor's wife, an invitation for a holiday, and literary
criticism. It seems unlikely that such a letter is a literary fiction.

These four groups—letters of advice, business letters, personal
recommendations, and notes of receipt and dispatch—establish a

[1] *VL*, 150; cf. ii. 15. 1 n.

claim to be considered as originating in genuine correspondence. What then of the letters of substance for which they form the setting, the *litterae curiosius scriptae* in the strictest sense, the long descriptions of character, of political and social events, of natural phenomena, and the rest? Were they written at the apparent date of composition, so far as this is determinable by their contents, or are they of later compilation? It is probably impossible to prove whether the long formal letters were written for separate circulation among literary friends or for collective publication. But there is no reason why Pliny should not have written long descriptions of his famous trials, for example, to his educated friends at Comum and elsewhere, who otherwise would depend for public news solely on what appeared in the *acta diurna* (v. 13. 8 n.), the contents of which can hardly have been on the scale or contained the personal bias of Pliny's versions. The private exchange of news, in plain or in literary form, is an obvious result of the broad distribution of the administrative class of the empire, and of its international origins and connexions.

The composition of the longer letters is so careful that most do not disclose their secret to the subtlest investigation. This in itself suggests that they were mostly written in their present form, and not as a recension of earlier compositions. But a few offer some clues to the investigator, notably three long political letters, I. 5, VIII. 14, IX. 13, and the shorter VII. 6.

The first describes the political situation in January 97, and an incident of the first day of that January. Pliny is considering the initiation of a charge against Aquilius Regulus, a prop of the former régime, but he remarks that he will wait for the return of Junius Mauricus from exile and take his advice. The whole letter is written in terms of the present moment. The verbal tenses are carefully managed to give the impression of a letter written soon after the incident of the first of January, and before the return of Mauricus. 'Exspecto Mauricum', Pliny writes twice, and also 'dum Mauricum venit'. But to the first phrase he adds a note (s. 10) 'nondum ab exsilio venerat'. This seems to indicate, as is commonly assumed, that the letter was revised later than its date of composition, when Book I was being put together for publication. Either the note was unnecessary for the recipient Romanus, who was in Italy, or the perfect tense should have been used. Pliny added a similar note in the similar context of IX. 13. 5 (below), but there it is appropriate because the story is being retold a decade later for the benefit of the addressee.

VIII. 14, addressed to the jurisprudent Titius Aristo, has already been mentioned for its peculiarities. It is one of the very few letters that extensively violate the rule of unity of subject. A technical discussion, filling three O.C.T. pages, of a single point in the rules governing senatorial debates, is preceded by an explanation in two pages of the reasons for Pliny's uncertainty. Pliny is elaborating with historical details his opening statement: 'priorum temporum servitus ut aliarum optimarum artium sic etiam iuris senatorii oblivionem quandam et ignorantiam induxit'. The section is an *egressus* in the rhetorical tradition, and appears absurd in a letter addressed to Titius Aristo, who was in a position to know all about the matter. Pliny's other historical and political narratives are addressed to persons to whom the information was new, as is several times emphasized: II. II. I, III. 4. I, 9. I, IV. II. I, 15, VI. 16. I, 20. I, IX. 13. I. The first part of VIII. 14 seems to be a clear example of the elaborate expansion of a much shorter original. The elaboration can easily be detected in its limits and pruned down without harming the sense of the rest (cf. Commentary, ad loc.). This discovery is the more interesting because VIII. 14 is the most certain instance in Books VII and VIII of a letter earlier than the apparent date of the book. It deals with an event of mid-105, the murder of a consul suffect, which should be some two years earlier than the general compilation date of VIII. No other letter betrays so elaborate a revision except VII. 6.

The digression in VII. 6 has already been mentioned (p. 4). Pliny adds a lengthy anecdote, about a different trial, taking twenty-two lines out of a total of fifty-six, to his account of a phase of the action against Varenus, with a formal apology to the reader. The digression seriously interrupts the narrative, which is resumed after its end, and it can be totally removed without leaving any jagged edges. The narrative closes neatly around the gap, and presents what may well be the original shape of the letter.[1]

In IX. 13 Pliny recounts for the benefit of the young Ummidius Quadratus the circumstances of his attempted prosecution of Publicius Certus in mid-97. It could be argued that the bulk of the letter belongs to 97, and that it was not published in I or II out of political caution—since Certus was a man of some political influence (s. II)—or because Pliny was satisfied with the publication of his speech against Certus. This is more probable, because Certus died apparently in 97 (IX. 13. 24), just after this publication. The reviser's hand may appear in the references to the death of Pliny's wife in ss. 4 and 13: 'quamquam tum maxime tristis amissa nuper uxore'. 'Bittius Proculus . . . uxoris . . . meae quam amiseram vitricus'. These notes were necessary for Quadratus in 107 because the wife lost in 97 had been succeeded by Calpurnia, whom Pliny had not yet

---

[1] Commentary, ad loc. The end of s. 6, 'multum me intra silentium tenui' could have been followed immediately by s. 14, 'consules, ut Polyaenus postulabat, omnia integra principi servaverunt'.

married in 97. So too in s. 5 'nuntia Arriae et Fanniae (ab exsilio redierant) consule te consule illas'—the parenthesis interrupting the flow of the speech suggests the hand of revision. But otherwise IX. 13 is a coherent whole. An attempt to prove similarly that v. 1 was written a decade earlier and subsequently revised, breaks down, and need not here be considered (Commentary, ad loc.). These are the only letters among the major pieces in which the touch of revision is so obvious, though III. 9 may be added to the list (below, p. 19) of possible revisions. Less certain indications of revision are noted in the Commentary on II. 15. 1, IV. 10. 4, 11. 5, V. 7. 3, VII. 9. 16.

LITERARY IMITATION

Another aspect of the historicity of the letters needs some attention. Pliny certainly writes under strong literary influences, both in the language and the content of the letters. Reminiscences of Vergil and of various subsequent writers of the imperial period are common enough. Themes from the letters of Cicero, the *Silvae* of Statius, and the lyrics of Martial recur. These influences are not generally the subject of this commentary. But Guillemin, in *Pline et la vie littéraire*, ch. iii ,musters them for an attack on the truth and accuracy of the letters. Because Pliny writes in the language of his predecessors on themes of Statius or Martial, the whole thing is taken to be a fiction. This seems a rather crude approach to the understanding of classical literature, though not without its parallel in the study of Tacitus, for example, in recent years. The influences are to be expected, but their purpose and effect is another matter. The extreme example is the criticism of Pliny's account of the building of the new harbour at Centum Cellae in VI. 31. 15–17. This is discussed in detail in the Commentary, where it is argued that Pliny simply uses Vergilian language to describe what he saw with his own eyes. The notion that the description is a literary commonplace applicable to any harbour is easily shown to be false from the narrative itself and from external evidence. So too the description of Pliny's two villas cannot be dismissed as literary reproduction of a stock theme, as with Guillemin (*VL*, 141 f). This might be said of the brief sketch of Caninius' villa in I. 3. But the accounts of the Laurentine and the Tuscan villas in II. 17 and v. 6 are altogether different in scale of detail and length from the limited and very selective snapshots in Seneca, Statius, and Martial, of certain aspects or features of the parks and palaces of their friends (see II. 17, pref.).

The account of the Tiber floods in VIII. 17 is similarly reduced to a literary pattern derived from Horace and used again by Tacitus (*VL*, 120). But as usual the individuality of Pliny's picture is more striking than the literary echoes (nn.), and comparison with the other scenic letters is reassuring. Against the accounts of Vesuvius, the spring of Clitumnus, and the islets of Vadimon (VI. 16, 20, VIII. 8, 20), no more can be alleged than echoes of occasional phrases in earlier writers. The only letters which closely resemble a type well established in previous literature are the two 'invitations to dinner', which exploit the stock comparison of the plain and the extravagant meal (I. 15, III. 12 nn.; *VL*, 135 ff.). Other attempts to establish the stylization of themes break down. Of the letters to his wife (VI. 4, 7, VII. 5) it is admitted that Pliny himself is creating the type out of various passages of Cicero and Ovid (*VL*, 138 f.). Others might prefer to say that Pliny used the obvious literary language to discuss the natural topics of Calpurnia's absence and illness. Very curiously Pliny's accurate summary of the main features of Trajan's second Dacian war (VIII. 4. 2 nn.) is regarded as stock treatment of the 'triumphal theme' (*VL*, 143 f.). But for the vast majority of the letters the establishment of stock themes is not even attempted.

A somewhat similar criticism was made by another scholar, rather paradoxically, of Pliny's report to Trajan about the Christians in Book X, where echoes of Livy are alleged (X. 96 nn.). The echoes turn out to be genuine but faint and dim, and in no way affect the historicity of the narrative. The question is much more subtle than such critics conceive. To a man immersed by long education and continued reading in his *native* literature, the appropriate language arose from memory's store at the prompting of the theme. It is doubtful whether this is a wholly conscious process. The notion that Pliny, like a modern student writing a Latin prose, looked up suitable parallel passages in Latin literature before attempting a particular composition, does not correspond to the advice which he gave to Pedanius Fuscus on the formation of style in VII. 9. He there recommends the practice of translation from the Greek classics as a preparatory technique, not for particular occasions but for the total linguistic culture of the writer, because (s. 2) 'imitatione optimorum similia *inveniendi facultas* paratur'. He speaks of 'copying and following' Demosthenes' speech against Meidias when he wrote his *De Helvidi Ultione* but with limitations: 'quantum aut diversitas ingeniorum . . . aut causae dissimilitudo pateretur' (VII. 30. 5) and *dumtaxat figuris orationis* (I. 2. 2). He claimed also to have copied Cicero's 'paintpots' in his colourful digressions (I. 2. 4). Yet though here and in I. 5. 11–12 he claimed Cicero among his masters, and refused to be content with *eloquentia saeculi nostri*, the Panegyric exists to show how far he is from being Ciceronian. The style of this eschews the use of Ciceronian periods, and has as one of its marked characteristics the emphatic use of a verb or verbal phrase at the opening of a sentence. The limitations of 'imitation' may be seen by considering the great difference, noted in the Commentary on II. 17, between Pliny's two 'descriptions of a villa' and that of Statius, despite an occasional verbal echo. The existence of literary influences detracts no more—nor less—from the historicity of the letters than from that of any other of the consciously erudite writers of the Empire.

THE ELABORATION OF THE EXTORTION LETTERS

Something may be gleaned from a comparison of the form of the letters about extortion trials, which are the largest group of letters with a common subject, a trial before the senatorial court. Despite the similarities imposed by the subject, there are notable differences of treatment. Both the trial of Marius Priscus and that of the associates of Caecilius Classicus are presented in two letters each, one lengthy and one short (II. 11–12, III. 4, 9). Letter II. 11 describes the accusation and double trial of Priscus in a single letter, while II. 12 adds as a postscript an account of the trial of his legate. But in Book III the shorter letter is concerned with the preliminaries to the main trial, which in the Priscus case are given in the long letter. The punishments are a great feature of each description. But whereas in II. 11–12 they are given formally with the names of the consulars or consuls designate who proposed them, in III. 9. 17–18, 22 only the substance of the sentence is given without the names of the movers. This is true also of the subsidiary trial for *praevaricatio* of Norbanus in III. 9, the leader of the original accusation, although Pliny names the consulars who gave evidence against him (ibid. ss. 29–34). This deliberate variation of method, characteristic of the Letters as a whole, is hardly accidental. In both accounts the narrative is clear and historical, but in the second the arrangement is less straightforward than in the former. Apart from the absence of names of the movers of motions, the order of events is altered so as to keep the trial of Norbanus until the end of the letter, though it took place between two parts of the main trial (nn. ad loc.).

In IV. 9, the trial of Bassus, Pliny combines the methods of II. 11 and III. 9. A single letter contains the whole story of the accusation, the trial, and an ineffective counter-accusation against the prosecutors, as in III. 9, while the sentences are given as in II. 11 with the names of the proposers.

The following conclusion may be hazarded. The Priscus letters may well be reports written shortly after the occasion, though it would be more natural for Pliny to have reported by itself the first part of the Priscus trial, which was separated by many months from his main trial. The second letter, about the subsidiary trial of Firminus, reports separately the events of a session of the Senate later than the condemnation of Priscus himself. Possibly II. 11 is an amalgamation of two news-letters about the different phases of Priscus' own trial. The main Classicus letter, III. 9, is so complex that it must be the product of leisured composition and written in deliberate contrast to II. 11.[1] But this consideration tends to guarantee the character of III. 4 as a genuine letter, especially as its contents are summarized at the beginning of III. 9, so that it is not necessary for the understanding of III. 9. Some details in III. 4 of Pliny's invitation to lead the case against Classicus closely echo a statement about his circumstances at this time in a letter to Trajan (x. 8): both refer to a visit to Tifernum, on official leave, to organize the building of a temple at his own expense. Also Pliny inserts in III. 4 a rather clumsy reminder of the title of his public office, unnecessary for his correspondent but essential in a publication: 'cum . . . in Tuscos excucurrissem, accepto *ut praefectus aerari commeatu*'. Contrarily, he obscurely refers to the present brief as 'munere hoc iam tertio' (s. 8 n.), although in this letter he has only mentioned one other of his two previous extortion cases. The statement would be clear to his friend and correspondent, but is obscure to the general reader. III. 4 then has all the signs of a genuine letter revised for publication.

The Varenus case is treated quite differently from the rest (v. 20, vi. 13, vii. 6, 10). Each phase of the prosecution is described in a separate letter of short or medium length. Since the case never came on for formal trial there was no occasion for a report like II. 11 or III. 9. The phases described in each letter were short procedural operations in the Senate or before the Princeps. The best parallel to v. 20 and vi. 13, which describe the manœuvres of the accuser and the accused in the opening phase, is the pair of letters v. 4 and 13 about the charge of *destitutio* against the advocate Tuscilius, handled in two sessions of the Senate. It cannot be maintained that Pliny was deliberately avoiding the use of long letters in these books: contrast the great length of the villa letter and the Vesuvius pair (v. 6, vi. 16, 20). Hence v. 20 and vi. 13 cannot be dismissed as fictitious epistles on that ground. It is noteworthy that the third Varenus letter (vii. 6) contains an unusual and deliberate digression (above, p. 15). This is an anecdote about an earlier criminal trial in which Pliny appeared, unconnected with Varenus. It is possible that since the Varenus case did not allow Pliny to present himself in the Ciceronian role that he assumes for himself in the trials of II–IV, he has

---

[1] The reviser's hand is revealed in s. 16: '*solet* dicere Claudius Restitutus qui mihi respondit . . . nunquam sibi tantum caliginis offusum, . . .', which was hardly written immediately after the event.

expanded this letter to make the most of his achievements. So too
in VII. 33 he resurrects the story of his advocacy against Baebius
Massa in the year 93, and in IX. 13 he resurrects the attempted prosecution of Certus in 97. In Book VIII, lacking a trial altogether, he
produced Ep. 14, the long procedural argument from the debate of
105, as a substitute.

This group of letters reveals the development of the technique of
managing a complicated subject in an *epistula curatius scripta*. These
letters have developed from genuine letters, and within limits Pliny
is faithful to the principle of authenticity. When there are no long
trials there are no long letters, and when there are no trials at all he
harks back to reporting events of an earlier period. But these latter
reports are dressed up in a possibly genuine contemporary disguise,
one as a submission of raw material to Tacitus for a volume of his
Histories, and another as a letter of explanation to a recent pupil.

III. CHRONOLOGY OF THE LETTERS

NATURE OF THE PROBLEM

PLINY, in the letter which forms a preface to Book I, states that
the order of the Letters is not chronological, 'non servato temporis
ordine', but that he took them as he found them: 'ut quaeque in
manus venerat'. Some of the early commentators, notably Masson,
assumed that this applied to all nine books, and that there was no
chronological order either in individual books or in the series as a
whole. Mommsen in his study of Pliny's life rudely reversed this
doctrine, holding that the nine books are in chronological order, and
that each book contains the letters of a specific period, in order
likewise. Pliny's remark was taken as a literary gesture intended to
give an air of artificial carelessness to the first volume. Mommsen
had two main arguments. First, it is easy to discern series of chronologically arranged letters about particular topics both within separate
books and divided between consecutive books. Second, in each book,
letters of which the content can be exactly dated fall within narrow
limits, and the dates that can be established thus for the nine books
are in chronological order. From these arguments Mommsen constructed the theory of 'book-dates'—that the letters in each book all
belong to the period of the datable letters, none earlier, none later.
On the general chronology thus established Mommsen based his
account of Pliny's life. It was because of certain difficulties that then
arose over the dating of some events in Pliny's career—and particularly the indictments of Classicus and Bassus—that two generations

of scholars criticized or rejected the rigidity of Mommsen's scheme, and raised fresh difficulties over the dating of a number of other letters. The more moderate, notably Schultz, held that though Mommsen's framework was generally correct individual letters in any book might be earlier than the date of the bulk of the letters of the book. Others, such as Asbach, suggested that the books were published in groups a good deal later than the apparent dates of composition, and hence that the spread of letters in each group —and book—was much wider than Mommsen's system allowed. The most radical, including C. Peter and Otto, abandoned the chronology of Mommsen, and returned to the position of Masson. For historical purposes, it may be observed, the more moderate criticism is as disturbing as the more radical, since no letter which is not internally datable need belong to the 'book-date'.

Two remarks may be made about the reaction to Mommsen. First, it was piecemeal and was concerned with particular letters. None of Mommsen's critics started from an analysis of the collection as a whole, and none seems to have had anything like Mommsen's knowledge of the letters. Second, as Merrill observed, the critics frequently contradicted one another in their arguments about particular letters. Fresh evidence from inscriptions and papyri that has accrued in the last twenty years, particularly in the calendars of Ostia and Potentia, has given the years of several consuls and suffect consuls mentioned in the Letters but hitherto undated, and the advance of prosopographical study has clarified the careers of many other officials who occur in them. The new evidence has tended to confirm the general scheme of Mommsen against his critics, and to overthrow some of their principal strictures. But it is still true that there are letters in the first three and the last two books that do not conform to the rigidity of Mommsen's chronology.

The remark in I. I on the lack of chronological order in the Letters, which had much weight with the critics of Mommsen, only counts against his type of chronological scheme if it can be proved that all nine books were published together. But this has not been maintained, still less proved, by any of the principal studies of the Letters. On the usual, and equally non-proven, theory of publication by triads (pp. 52 f.), the remark can only apply to the first three books. But the conjoint publication of I–III is decidedly uncertain, whatever may be held about the conjoint publication of the later books (p. 52). The most reasonable interpretation of I. I is that this remark refers only to the internal order of the letters in that book—and possibly in subsequent books—and not to the chronology of the successive books as wholes. The weakest point in Mommsen's system is the insistence that the internal order of letters in each book is chronological, although serial letters on the same topic are naturally given in serial order. Pliny may intend to warn his reader that unlike the editors of Cicero's Letters, which he allusively claims as his model, he has made variety of topic rather than chronology the guiding principle of the internal arrangement, so far as this was possible within groups of letters belonging to limited periods (pp. 46 f.).

The stream of criticism continued unchecked after Otto's article on the life of Pliny, through von Premerstein's discussion of the career of Julius Bassus—relevant to the dates of letters in Books IV–VII—down to more recent discussions by Hanslik, who alone showed a slight hesitancy in the face of the latest evidence, and Monti, who has attempted the positive redating of certain letters on internal evidence. Recently the school of Otto was challenged by Syme, who in an appendix of his *Tacitus* boldly and briefly reaffirmed the chronology of Mommsen, with minor reservations. But this discussion, though cogent, was not based on an exhaustive examination of the Letters as a whole.

Historians have generally paid little attention to the interrelationship of the letters that have no special historical significance. The miscellaneous character of the collection has discouraged the study of it as a whole. But in the course of such a study as the present a remarkable number of obscure links and connexions emerge, concerning the journeys and holidays, and the literary development of Pliny, which put the question of serial order and chronology in a new light. When this material is combined with the newer epigraphical information, the chronology can be established book by book on a sounder foundation. This is a lengthy task involving a large number of particular points. For clarity the following procedure has been adopted. The conclusions reached in the Commentary about the date and connexions of each letter are here summarized book by book; the detailed argument is to be found in the Commentary. The analysis seeks to show what can be reasonably established by an impartial critic about the compilation and publication dates of each book, without trying to defend or attack a particular thesis.

In this analysis the term 'book-date' means the period covered by the datable contemporary events described in the component letters of each book. This is not necessarily the same as the date of the compilation of the book in its present form, and still less of its publication. When such book-dates can be established, the question arises next whether letters in each book that lack not only dates but any sort of link with dated letters belong to the same period. Some ight is cast on this question, and on the allied question of publication, by a systematic inquiry, hitherto attempted incompletely and only by H. Peter, into the distribution of the letters by categories of subject-matter throughout the nine books. This second inquiry also helps to illuminate the literary method and purpose of Pliny in making this collection. A special section is devoted to the dates of the extortion trials, and the letters about them, which were the starting-point of the controversy about chronology, and which have been the object of extensive and contradictory discussion.

BIBLIOGRAPHY

TH. MOMMSEN, *Gesammelte Schriften* (Berlin, 1907), iv 366: *Hermes*, iii (1869), 31 ff.

H. F. STOBBE, 'Plinius' Briefe', *Philologus*, xxx (1870), 347 ff.

C. PETER, 'Plinius der Jüngere', *Philologus* xxxii (1872), 698 ff.

I. ASBACH, 'Zur Chronologie der Briefe des j. Plinius', *Rhein. Mus.* xxxvi (1881), 38 ff.

M. SCHULTZ, *De Plinii Epistulis Quaestiones Chronologicae* (Diss. Inaug.), Berlin, 1899.

H. PETER, 'Der Brief in d. röm. Litt.', *Abh. Sächs. Akad. Wiss. Phil.-hist. Kl.* xx (1903), ch. v. 101 ff.

W. OTTO, 'Zur Lebensgeschichte des j. Plinius', *Sb. Bayer. Akad. Wiss. Phil.-hist. Kl.* 1919, 17 ff.

A. VON PREMERSTEIN, 'C. Iulius Quadratus Bassus', ibid. 1934, 3, 72 ff.

R. HANSLIK, 'Der Prozess des Varenus Rufus', *Wiener Studien*, l (1932), 195 ff.; 'Zu Plinius' Ep. V. 1', ibid. lii (1934), 156 ff.; 'Die neuen Fragmente von Ostia, etc.', ibid. lxiii (1948), 133 ff.

S. PRETE, 'Saggi Pliniani', *Studi di filologia classica*, i (Bologna 1948), 84 ff.

S. MONTI, 'Pliniana', *Rend. Acc. Arch. Litt. Bell. Art. Napoli*, xxvii (1952), 161 ff.; xxviii (1953), 311 ff.; xxxii (1957), 90 ff.; *Ann. Fac. Litt. Napoli*, 1956, 69 ff.

R. SYME, *Tacitus* (Oxford, 1958), ii, Appendix xxi, 660 ff.

J. ZARANKA, *De Plinii Epistularum Novem Libris Quaestiones Chronologicae*. This doctoral dissertation from Louvain 1949 has not been published except in dactylographic form, and is otherwise known only in a brief summary of cardinal points in *Lustrum*, vi (1961), 285 f.

DATES OF CONSULAR ELECTIONS AND THE CHRONOLOGY OF THE LETTERS

In establishing the dates of particular letters, the mention of consuls designate—usually suffects—in senatorial debates gives a close approximation. The content of such letters must lie between the day of the formal *comitia consulum* for that year and the day on which that suffect consul entered office. Mommsen (*DPR*, ii. 251 ff.) assumed that January 9, the day given by the late calendar of Silvius (A.D. 448–9)—and confirmed by passages of Symmachus (*CIL*, i.² 256–7; *Mon. Germ.* vi. 1, Symm. *Ep.* i. 44) and in part by the fourth-century calendar of Filocalus—for the second *senatus legitimus* and the *comitia* of suffect consuls (and of praetors) was already established by the time of Trajan for the election of suffects for the current year. Hence he dated all letters of this sort to the calendar year indicated, and the sharpness of his chronology is the consequence. But if the election of suffects preceded the Kalends of January by many months a wider spread of time must be allowed. This consideration is fairly serious even for the chronological pattern which this commentary proposes. The suffect Tertullus in the trial of Priscus, which took place in January, gives the leading *sententia* over seven months before he was due to take office in September, though there were other senior suffects in the House (II. II. 19 n., cf. 12. 2). Hence considerable latitude is possible if the elections were in the previous year.

A factor not fully known to Mommsen now enters consideration. The discovery of the electoral Lex Valeria of A.D. 5 (E-J² n. 94 a) has clarified the terms *destinatio*, *destinare* used in the *Panegyricus*. They refer to the effective election of consuls (and also of praetors) which after A.D. 5 took place with the aid of the mixed body set up by the Lex Valeria and which by the time of Pliny—and probably a great deal earlier—was effected by the Senate, which simply ratified the list of consular candidates put forward by the Princeps. The term *designatus* is used in the Letters by Pliny in its original sense, for the magistrate formally elected in the *comitia populi Romani* in the Campus Martius after the preceding *destinatio* in the Senate. The distinction of procedure is apparent in three passages of the *Panegyricus*, describing the part taken by Trajan and the Senate in the elections of his third consulship. 'comitia consulum obibat ipse. tantum ex renuntiatione eorum voluptatis quantum prius ex destinatione capiebat' (77. 1). 'tu comitiis nostris praesidere ... tuo iudicio consules facti tua voce renuntiati sumus, ut idem honoribus nostris suffragator in curia in campo declarator existeres' (92. 3). 'vos proxime destinationem consulatus mei his acclamationibus approbavistis' (95. 2).

The date that matters for the chronology of Pliny is that of the final *comitia* at which the formal *designatio* took place. Mommsen accepted the January date from Silvius—which properly refers to the senatorial *destinatio* rather than the proceedings in the Campus—because Pliny's account of the elections of 100 seems to confirm it for the time of Trajan (*DPR*, ii. 253 n. 5). The elections that year took place as follows. The *consules ordinarii*, Trajan and Julius Frontinus, were elected at *comitia* held necessarily before the Kalends of January (*Pan.* 63, 66. 2). The election of suffects took place in January in two phases over which Trajan presided. First was the session of the Senate at which the nomination and 'destination' of candidates for all offices took place: this comes after the opening Senate of the New Year, held as is normal on 1 January (*Pan.* 66. 2, 67. 3). This election is described at length in *Pan.* 69–72. Pliny concentrates on Trajan's part—*nominatio* and *commendatio*—though in 71. 6 he briefly touches on the element of free election still left to the Senate. This phase is followed by the formal election in the Campus Martius in ch. 77 (above). There is a further reference in ch. 92. 3 (above) to the fact that Trajan presided over the election of Pliny and Tertullus, themselves suffects of 100. Hence the elections of January 100 included the suffect consuls of 100. By the date of the January session of the Senate at which Marius Priscus was tried, which is the third *senatus* of the month in the Panegyric's account, the electoral procedures were complete, and two suffects of A.D. 100 spoke as consuls designate (II. 11. 19, 12. 2).

Under the system established by Augustus there were two *senatus legitimi* in each month, on the Kalends and Ides (Suet. *Aug.* 35. 3; Dio 55. 3. 1). In the Calendar of Philocalus there are three in January, on the Kalends, the ninth, and the twenty-third, the last being for the quaestorian elections. If the later system of election days had already been operating in 100, the main elections at least would have been completed on the ninth in the Senate, and the trial of Priscus would take place on the Ides and following days.[1] The alternative, of putting it later in the month on a day otherwise unattested for senatorial business, is less likely. This account may be held to confirm the opinion of Mommsen that the suffect elections were already regularly held in January. It is substantially that of all modern scholars who have considered the matter in detail. Cf. the long study by M. L. Paladini, 'Le votazioni del senatus nell'età di Traiano', *Athenaeum* (1959), 3 ff. 'Il processo di Mario Prisco', *Rendic. Ist. Lombardo*, 92, 713 ff. Also Durry, *Pan.*, app. vi. But since Syme (*Tacitus*, 658 n. 2) has entered an objection on the score of lack of evidence, a new examination is required.

Trajan's first consulship as emperor at Rome was a special occasion, and the method of that year may not have been entirely normal. However, Pliny himself takes for granted the separation of the election of suffects from that of *ordinarii* (*Pan.* 63–64, 77). This separation may well have been established under the Flavians when it became the custom, especially under Domitian, for the Princeps to

---

[1] No difficulty arises from the fact that in the *Panegyricus* the confirmatory election by the *comitia centuriata* in the Campus (ch. 77) follows the mention in ch. 76 of the three-day session, which can only be the Priscus trial. Ch. 77 is a flash-back, as is indicated by its introduction: 'iter illi saepius in forum, frequenter tamen et in campum. nam comitia consulum', etc. Pliny completes the account of Trajan in the Senate in 69–76, and then switches to a new theme, 'Trajan in public'.

hold frequent consulships for the title's sake, only occupying office from the Kalends to the Ides of January (*Pan.* 65. 3; Suet. *Dom.* 13. 3), abundantly confirmed by the *Fasti* of Ostia and Potentia. It would be convenient for elections to be held on the ninth of January, so that a suffect could take office on the Ides. There was also a point of prestige in separating the consular election of the Princeps from that of commoners. It is unlikely that the *civilis* Trajan invented the separation.

A passage in IV. 15 is relevant but not conclusive. Pliny there urges his friend Minicius Fundanus, who, he believes, was to be *consul ordinarius* for the next year, to choose young Asinius Bassus, who had already been elected to a quaestorship, as his consular quaestor (ibid. 5–6 nn.). The quaestors who served at Rome took office on December 5 (Mommsen, op. cit. ii. 275, iii. 296 f.). It follows that the election of the *ordinarii* took place before that day; they alone had the option of choosing their quaestors, since these continued in office under the successive suffects (VIII. 23. 5, X. 26 nn.; Mommsen, op. cit. iv. 229 n. 1, 271 n. 3). It may also be inferred from *Pan.* 78–79, where Pliny urges Trajan to take a fourth consulship for the next year, that the elections of *ordinarii* did not take place before the September Kalends, the day of Pliny's speech.

For the Julio–Claudian period there is little evidence for the suffect elections, though Mommsen argued for elections in March and October–November. In January 40 the suffects were ready to take office on the twelfth and were probably elected before 1 January (Dio 59. 24. 2–7). A suffect of 59, T. Sextius Africanus, was designated during March of the same year (Arval *Acta*: ILS 229–30). No consuls had been appointed for the next year at the time of the death of Claudius on *III Id. Oct.* of 54. Before the death of Nero in June 68 the *destinatio consulum* for 69 had already been effected, and formal election of suffects had taken place before 1 January 69. (Suet. *Claud.* 46; Tac. *Hist.* 1. 6, 14, 77; Mommsen, op. cit. ii. 254 n. 1.) But perhaps the best evidence is the unnoticed statement in Tac. *Hist.* 3. 55, that after the disaster of Cremona at the end of October Vitellius *hurried on* the consular elections at Rome, which included the *destinatio* of the next year's suffects, while in other respects also his procedure was extraordinary. (Cf. Suet. *Vit.* II. 2; Tac. *Hist.* 3. 37.) It seems probable that down to 69 the consular elections were not regularly divided, and were usually held or completed in the last quarter of the year.

DATE OF OTHER ELECTIONS

In *Pan.* 69–72 it seems that the nomination and election of the annual magistrates above the quaestorship took place on the same day. Mommsen assumed that the quaestors, who are not there distinctly mentioned, were elected later, perhaps with the *vigintiviri*, on 23 January, the day given by the calender of Silvius (above). But in III. 20. 5 Pliny, describing the routine of the *dies comitiorum* in the Senate, speaks as if all magistrates were elected on the same day: 'dicebat ipse pro se (sc. candidatus) . . . testes et laudatores dabat vel eum sub quo militaverat vel eum cui quaestor fuerat vel utrumque si poterat'. The first category may refer to the candidates for the quaestorship. When in *Pan.* 69. 4–6 he speaks of Trajan restoring the descendants of noble families to senatorial office and rank, this should also refer to the first magistracy in the *cursus honorum*. Hence there probably was a single election day for these offices under Trajan, though phrases like *dies comitiorum* and *proximis comitiis* in III. 20. 3, IV. 25. 1, VI. 19. 1 are not decisive.

IV. CHRONOLOGICAL ANALYSIS OF THE BOOKS

BOOK I

FIVE letters are dated by historical context to 96–98 with strong probability, and fit the time of Nerva better than that of Trajan. Ep. 5, the fears of Regulus, was written between 1 January 97 and the return of Mauricus from exile. Ep. 12, the death of Corellius Rufus, cannot be separated dramatically by a long period from the death of Domitian, or by many months from that of Nerva, and it is now known that Corellius was not one of the *consules ter* of 100. Ep. 14, the betrothal of Mauricus' daughter, belongs to the period following the return of the exiles. Ep. 17, the anti-tyrannical gesture of Titinius Capito, is Nervan in colour and references, and fits the period of the first restoration of liberty. If Pompeius Falco was tribune in 97, as seems certain, then Ep. 23, about the tribunate, belongs early in that year, if not late in 96.

Four letters may be dated to the period before Pliny became prefect of the *aerarium Saturni* in January 98 by his freedom of movement and unfettered leisure, both of which were greatly constricted after his appointment. In Ep. 9 his daily round at Rome is not complicated by official duties; contrast Ep. 10. In Ep. 13, 'public recitations', and Ep. 22, 'illness of Titius Aristo', he is free to fix his departure from Rome without the necessity of official leave that limits his movements as prefect. So too in Ep. 7 he is enjoying an unrestricted absence from Rome in the autumn of a year that must be earlier than his prefecture for reasons connected with his activity as an advocate. The mention of April and October in these

letters suggests a whole year in which Pliny was not occupied in
official duties. Hence the period before 98 seems indicated for these
three letters. Two other letters, Ep. 4, his Tuscan journey, and Ep. 6,
his hunting, together with Ep. 7, might well belong to a visit to
Tifernum in the autumn of 97.

Several letters secure relative dates by references to Pliny's
literary or forensic interests. Thus Ep. 7 is shown by the mention of
Octavius' poems to be earlier than the further reference to these
poems in II. 10, where Pliny knows more about them. Epp. 8 and 16
are concerned with Pliny's first acquaintance with the man of letters
Pompeius Saturninus. In Ep. 8 Pliny has only a mere municipal
sermo to send him, delivered at Comum on a visit that cannot be
later than 97. Yet in Ep. 2 at least two more considerable works were
available, of which one seems to be the *De Helvidi Ultione* of 97 and
another the *Pro Patria* of II. 5. Hence Epp. 8 and 16 may be amongst
the earliest in the collection, while Ep. 2 should belong to late 97—
before his busy Prefecture began—and may coincide with II. 5 where
the *Pro Patria* is still being revised, though an early Trajanic date
cannot be excluded. Ep. 18, the dream of Suetonius, by its reference
to a private brief in which Suetonius and Pliny were acting together
should be earlier than Pliny's prefecture, which led him to abandon
private practice for the time.

An argument from distribution would suggest that Ep. 19, the
recommendation of Romatius Firmus, is earlier than the longer and
more exalted examples of this type in II. 9 and 13, both of which
may be Nervan.

Ep. 10, the portrait of Euphrates, cannot be earlier than January
98 since it describes Pliny's duties as prefect of Saturn.

The bulk of the letters are thus of Nervan date, but one (Ep. 10) is
later, and two or three others, though probably Nervan, might fall
in the early months of Trajan (Epp. 2, 14, 17) and so overlap with the
earliest letters of II.

BOOK II

This book contains three letters which by their historical context
belong to the Nervan period. Ep. 1, the death of Verginius Rufus,
depends partly on the date of Tacitus' consulship, which now can
hardly be assigned to any year but 97, and partly on indications
that Rufus did not survive Nerva. Ep. 7, the special honours of
Spurinna, is Nervan because Spurinna is not in Dio's list of those
thus honoured by Trajan. The recommendation of Voconius Romanus
for an equestrian post in the much-debated Ep. 13 should be earlier
than Pliny's recommendation of him to Nerva for senatorial status:

the difficulties of a Trajanic date for this letter are greater than those of a Nervan date. But the details of the candidature of Erucius Clarus in Ep. 9 fit 97 and 100 equally well, and a preference for 97 depends on the absence from Book x of a letter recommending Erucius to Trajan. Ep. 14, discontents of the Centumviral Court, should belong by its contents to the period before Pliny as prefect of Saturn discontinued his legal practice, though a post-Nervan composition date is not excluded, as also for Ep. 5, on the revision of his *Pro Patria*, which should, however, be earlier than the editing for publication of his speech of January 100 mentioned in Ep. 19.

Three letters connected with the condemnation of Marius Priscus (11, 12, 19) fall certainly in the year 100. Four other letters may belong to the period 98–100. A brief courtesy note (Ep. 8) seems to refer to his official duties of this time. Ep. 16, concerning an inheritance and the death of a man mentioned in I. 14, may reflect his experience as prefect of Saturn. Ep. 10, the exhortation of Octavius Rufus to publish his poems, must be later than the reference to them in I. 7. Ep. 18, education of the sons of Mauricus, is likely to be somewhat later than the betrothal of his daughter in I. 14, but both concern the first actions of an exile who returned in early 97; it is also earlier than III. 3, where the wanted schoolmaster has been discovered.

So out of twenty letters four or five belong to the period before Nerva's death (1, 7, 13, 14, and possibly 9), and only three are certainly of Trajanic date (11, 12, 19). Another four or five fit better in the post-Nervan period than earlier (5, 8, 10, 16, 18).

The comparison of I and II shows that there is an extensive overlap, but many more letters of II belong to the Mommsenian book-date of I than vice versa. The few certainly post-Nervan letters of II belong to the year 100 (11, 12, 19; so too 9, if Trajanic). Others possibly Trajanic have affinities with events or letters of the period before 98 (5, 10, 18). There are no exactly datable letters from the first two years of Pliny's prefecture of Saturn, 98–99; only one letter of substance (I. 10) and two short notes (II. 8 and 16) can on any grounds be referred to this period. This is not surprising when one considers Pliny's character and habits of work, his self-confessed *desidia*, his apparent slowness, and his preoccupation in 98–99 not only with his prefecture but also with the indictment of Marius Priscus and Caecilius Classicus (III. 4). Pliny after dabbling in literary letters before his appointment did very little in this line until the last months of his appointment, when his success in the Priscus case gave him something worth advertising. The bulk of the letters in II belongs to the last months of the Nervan period or to the year 100, whereas the bulk of I belongs to 96–97.

The omission from Book I of some Nervan letters of greater apparent interest than some included in this book, such as II. I, the record of Verginius Rufus, and II. 7, the honours of Spurinna, is easily explained. These are political letters, and Book II has a notably larger content of such letters (I, 7, 9, II, I2, I3, 20). After the accounts of Regulus and Corellius (I. 5 and I2), Pliny might prefer to avoid dangerous topics such as the Certus affair, described at length in IX. I3. The large amount of space in I given to literary topics is natural in a collection drawn from a period of *otium*. His developing interest in political themes in II reflects his circumstances and the increased confidence of the time.

Other omissions from I may be explained by the love of variety. The Centumviral letter II. I4 deals like I. I3 with the bad habits of the literary public. The vices of Regulus in II. 20, if this is an early letter, repeats the theme of I. 5. So too the single post-Nervan letter in I, the account of Euphrates (Ep. I0), is sole of its kind, like the sketches of Isaeus and Artemidorus in II. 3 and III. I9.

This analysis shows that, as one would expect, Pliny had many more literary letters available at the end of his vacation from public service during 96–98 than he could publish in one *libellus*. He made his first selection on principles of taste and caution, and combined what was left with the products of a fresh burst of activity in I00, when familiarity with office left him more leisure, to form a second volume.

Publication dates

It would seem from the previous analysis that Pliny may have published Book I at any time during or after, but not before, his tenure of the prefecture of Saturn. It is likely that his spare time in 98 or 99 before the Priscus and Classicus cases arose, when no other literary activity except the short Life of the younger Vestricius (III. I0. I) can be traced, was occupied with selecting and polishing this little collection—he was on full duty only in alternate months (X. 8. 3). The second book may have been compiled and possibly published in the middle or latter half of I00. There is no certain reference to his consulship in September–October I00, or to any event later than the trial of Priscus in January, whereas Book III includes some possible letters of late I00 and two or three references to his consulship (III. 6. 5, 9, I3. I, I8. I). As Pliny is careful to chalk up his own credits elsewhere—the prefecture of Saturn in I. I0, the augurate in IV. 8, the *cura Tiberis* in V. I4, and the tributes to his public service in the extortion trials (II. II. I9, III. 9. 23)—this silence is not accidental, and confirms the notion that the apparent compilation date of II is not later than the third quarter of I00, and that no letter of later than mid–100 is included. But whether the compilation dates are close to the dates of publication must be considered elsewhere (p. 54).

BOOK III

The chronology becomes less complex with III. Of twenty-one letters six can be dated firmly and another four with probability to the period of three or four years following Pliny's consulship in September 100. The known appointments of Vibius Maximus to the prefecture of Egypt, and of Neratius Marcellus to the governorship of Britain, and the chronology of Martial, date Epp. 2, 8, 21 to c. 102–3. The elections of Ep. 20 must be later than 100 by at least a year. References to the revision of Pliny's consular Panegyric account for Epp. 13, 18. The connexion of Ursus Servianus with the Dacian War may place Ep. 17 in 101–2. The little note Ep. 6, about the Corinthian bronze and the *honores* of Pliny, implies that he is now consular.

Unreal difficulties have been raised about Epp. 1 and 10, which describe Pliny's visit to the villa of Vestricius and his composition of a biography of Vestricius' son who died before Nerva. These have been set as early as 98 and as late as 104. But a date about the time of Pliny's consulship fits the various circumstances better than any other.

The letters about the trial of Classicus have caused most contention. Ep. 4, describing the acceptance of the brief, belongs to the end of 99. The trial itself, in Ep. 9, is certainly later than that of Priscus, but cannot be proved to be as late as 101; the evidence that it was before Pliny's consulship is inconclusive. A stylistic argument connects it fairly closely with the composition date of the Priscus letter (II. 11: pp. 18 f.). The reason for this partial overlap with Book II is clear. Pliny placed the Classicus letters in III because II had enough of this theme.

Four other letters fit well within the limits of the datable letters. Ep. 7, the death of Silius Italicus, is later than the return of Trajan to Rome in late 99, mentioned as no recent event (s. 6). The description of Julius Genitor the Latin *rhetor*, Ep. 3, and the letter addressed to him, Ep. 11, must be later than II. 18, where Pliny has not made his acquaintance; the whole tone of Ep. 11, and the reference to Pliny's distant praetorship, suggest the consular man. Ep. 15, in which Pliny is not yet a writer of poetry, is earlier than the long series beginning with IV. 14 describing his new hobby of versification. Ep. 14, the murder of a *praetorius*, should be earlier than the more notorious murder of the officiating consular Afranius Dexter in June 105.

Four letters are without close dating (5, 12, 16, 19). No letter is demonstrably later than the apparent book-date. Except for the first of the two Classicus letters, an exception which tests the rule, all the letters in this book seem to belong to the period from Pliny's consulship in 100 down to *c.* 103–4. No letter is certainly later than 103, and the presence of a letter of early 103 in IV (Ep. 9, trial of Bassus), though explicable on other grounds, may help to delimit Book III to the period from mid-100 to mid-103.

Compilation and Publication

It is apparent from the chronological analysis that Pliny in III is overhauling his production rate. Apart from Ep. 4 the book would seem to contain letters of the period between his consulship and his next post, the *cura Tiberis*, when he was free from official *occupationes*. It is possible that the book was prepared and published separately not only from II, as is often agreed, but also from IV, contrary to the view that III–VI were published together. The presence of Ep. 7, the death of Silius Italicus, of Ep. 14, death of Macedo, and of Ep. 21, the death of Martial, in the same book is surprising on grounds of distribution and variety if Pliny was already planning a fourth volume. Book IV is very light on deaths, having none of leading men; cf. IV. 2, 21. But this overloading was natural if Pliny had nearly exhausted his stock of good letters. The interval between III. 20 and IV. 25—the use of the ballot and its consequences a year later—suggests a clear interval between the two books. Alternatively it has been thought that Ep. 20 has been revised in knowledge of the incident described in IV. 25. If so, then III. 20 is to IV. 25 as IV. 29—the first of the Nepos series—is to its continuation in V. 4, and as V. 20, first of the Varenus letters, is to its continuation in VI. 5. In that case III, like IV and V, has its link forward with the next book, deliberately provided because III–VI were being published together.

BOOK IV

Consular dates set Ep. 17 (suit against Caecilius Strabo) and Ep. 29 (the opening of the praetorship of Nepos) in 105, and at last the much disputed trial of Julius Bassus, Ep. 9, is dated, to the confusion of Mommsen and his critics alike, to early 103. The mention of recent *consules designati* seems to date Ep. 12 (salary of a *scriba*), which is subsequent to III. 2 (of 103), before the end of 105. A fifth letter foreseeing the consulship of Minicius Fundanus—actually consul suffect in 107—mentions the quaestorian elections. The mechanics of the latter are such that no date later than January 106 is possible, and the circumstances of the consular Fasti at this time suggest that Pliny's forecast was upset by a year, so that the letter may be of January 105.

A second group of four letters cannot historically be earlier than 101–2, and may be much later: Ep. 8, Pliny's augurate, Ep. 22, his first session on the *consilium* of Trajan, Ep. 23, the retirement of Pomponius Bassus, and Ep. 25, the abuse of the ballot. Three of these letters are later than letters in III. Epp. 8 and 22 refer to new honours of Pliny not known at the date of III, and Ep. 25 is subsequent by not less than one year to III. 20.

By these arguments eight of the nine letters mentioned may be assigned to the period 104–5, leaving only Ep. 23 (Pomponius Bassus) possibly within the period of III. The book contains another seven letters which by their connexion with Pliny's private activities belong to a period later than III. Epp. 1, 13, 19, containing interrelated references to his marriage with Calpurnia and a visit to Comum, were dated by Otto to the period 100–1 following Pliny's consulship, and bulked large in his arguments about chronology. But Otto did not observe that these letters interlock with a series of no less than six in which Pliny touches on his new hobby of versification: 3, 13, 14, 18, 19, 27. The story of his dabblings is continued in the following books, but never mentioned in I–III, despite an obvious opportunity in III. 15. 2. This new pursuit was evidently taken up after the date of the letters in III. The versificatory series also includes three letters in which two new figures make their first appearance in the whole correspondence, Arrius Antoninus and his protégé Sentius Augurinus: 3, 18, 27. The group of seven letters must belong to a period later than III, and since the theme of versification is developed with fresh phases in later books—notably v. 3 and VIII. 21—there is good reason to assign this group in IV to the period established above for the exactly datable letters—104–5. An eighth letter may be added to this third group, Ep. 30, which records a visit to Comum that is reasonably connected with the visit in Epp. 1 and 13. This complicated argument may be illustrated by the following table.

Topic			Letter			
Marriage	1		13		19	
Comum	1		13			30
Verses	3		13	14	18	19	27
New men	3				18		27

Certain other letters fit the framework of IV. Thus Epp. 2 and 7 about the death of Regulus' son must be a good deal later than II. 20, where Pliny mentions Regulus' oath *per salutem filii*, which he does not here recall. The absence of a letter in III about the old rogue who so fascinated Pliny, and who appears four times in I–II, suggests that the material was not then to hand. Ep. 6 introduces Julius Naso, a youthful protégé of Pliny, who appears in VI. 6 and 9 as at the threshold of senatorial career. Pliny's young protégés seem always to appear at the correct moment in the series of book-dates to fit their careers: so too Falco in I. 23 or Salinator and Quadratus in VI. II.

Ep. 26 mentions the appointment to a proconsular province of a man who appears in office in VI. 19, providing a chronological link forward of some twelve months. Ep. II, the misfortunes of the exiled orator Licinianus, has been attributed to a year much nearer to Nerva's reign for no good reason. Pliny leaves vague the interval between Nerva's transfer of the man to Sicily and his opening of a school of rhetoric, the occasion of the letter. A veiled cross-reference to Licinianus in Ep. 24. 3 connects these two letters. Nothing dates either to the time of Nerva.

Thus IV seems to be a chronologically compact compilation. At least sixteen out of thirty letters cannot reasonably be detached from the setting of the book, and three or four others fit as well in IV as in III. The early letter, Ep. 9, the trial of Bassus, has been held over from III for the same reason that the first Classicus letter in III was held over from II. It would seem that apart from this Pliny was drawing on his contemporary production, and that the book contains the composition of a limited period. No letter except Ep. 9 is demonstrably earlier than 104 or later than 105.

Publication

The compilation date gives only the *terminus post quem* for publication. IV is the first book to contain a closely connected series continued in the next volume. The events of Nepos' praetorship fall within the first four months of 105, and seem to be in chronological order from IV. 29 through V. 4, 9, 13. Letters IV. 18 and V. 15—translation of the Greek verses of Arrius Antoninus—are also closely connected, as are IV. 20 and V. 5 by mention of the works of Novius Maximus. Since, as will appear, V has close links with VI and VI with VII, it is probable that IV, V, VI, and perhaps VII, about which a slight doubt arises, were published conjointly after the latest date in VI or VII, i.e. 107. This scheme fits the circumstances of IV. 15, which require that Fundanus' consulship in 107 should be assured by the date of publication.

BOOK V

Out of twenty-one letters five or six are datable with some exactness to 105–6. Three of these, Epp. 4, 9, 13, concern different episodes in the first four months of the praetorship of Nepos in 105, continuing IV. 29 in due order of time. Ep. 20 records the initial indictment of Varenus, now fixed to a year not earlier than 106. In Ep. 14, despite the specious arguments of Otto, the reference to Pliny's *cura Tiberis* cannot be earlier than 104–5. To this period may be attributed Ep. 19: the reference to the Egyptian journey and the return of Pliny's sick freedman links it with the sojourn of the recipient Arrianus as an official in Egypt *c.* 103–5 (III. 2, IV. 12).

Three letters dealing with Pliny's new verses, Epp. 3, 10, 15, are demonstrably later than corresponding letters in IV. An obscure reference to Pliny's poems in Ep. 8. 3, on writing history, may add this to the group. Cross-references justify the book-date for two other letters. In Ep. 5. 7 Pliny refers to the *libelli* of Novius Maximus, first received in IV. 20. The casual mention of Frontinus as dead in Ep. 1 makes this later than IV. 8, where his death was very recent; other reasons apart, it is unlikely that two references to this event in these adjacent books should both be misplaced in time.

Four other letters fit the context of V. Ep. 11, the second in the correspondence addressed to Calpurnius Fabatus, belongs to the period of Pliny's developing relations with the old man after the first letter to him, IV. 1. Two letters referring to a summer vacation on Pliny's Tuscan estate, Epp. 6 and 18, are later than the brief visit recorded in IV. 1. The death of Fundanus' daughter in Ep. 16 at the age of 12 or 13 would fit what is known of her father's age and career if placed in 105–6.

The book-date of Ep. 21 has been falsely impugned. The Pompeius Saturninus there alive is distinguished by his *patria* from the Saturninus of Comum dead in Ep. 7; the Julius Avitus whose death is recorded in Ep. 21 is distinct in many particulars from the Junius Avitus whose death comes in VII. 23, with whom some have sought to confound the former.

Book V, like IV, appears to contain a high proportion of letters exactly or reasonably attributable to a single period, and later than the preceding book. There are no letters that fail to fit a book-date of 105–6. It would be speculative to suggest that IV contains letters up to, and V later than, January–February 105. But the latest letter of V, Ep. 20, should be in the last quarter of 106, the season when extortion charges were usually initiated, if not in January–February 107. It is possible that for the sake of including an extortion letter, as in I–IV, Pliny has pre-empted a letter from the book-date of VI.

Publication

All the indications are against separate publication. As IV is linked to V by the Nepos series, so is V to VI by the Varenus letters.

BOOK VI

Six letters are dated closely by historical events to the end of 106 or to the year 107. Epp. 5 and 13 continue the Varenus affair, following v. 20 at close intervals, and a precise cross-reference to v. 20 dates Ep. 29 (on the duties of an advocate) to the same period. A consular date fixes Ep. 27 (on the speech of a designated consul) to early 107. The description of Trajan's judicial *consilium* at Centum Cellae in Ep. 31 is after the second Dacian War and probably in the summer of 107, since Ep. 10, describing Pliny's stay at Alsium on the way to Centum Cellae, is dated to 107 by a precise cross-reference to the death of Verginius Rufus.

Three letters, Epp. 11, 26, 29, are part of a group of nine letters scattered through vi–ix which introduce Pliny's young aristocratic protégés, Fuscus Salinator and Ummidius Quadratus, and are linked to the dated letters by the reference to the Varenus affair in Ep. 29.

Five short letters, Epp. 4, 7, 14, 28, 30, deal with a holiday that Pliny's wife and later himself took in Campania after an illness of Calpurnia. The series continues in vii. 5.

A second letter about Trajan's judicial Consilium, Ep. 22, is the first of a series referring to Calestrius Tiro's departure for and government of Baetica, continued in vii and ix. Neither of these latter two groups in vi–vii has a precise link with the book-dates, but both touch on Pliny's domestic life after his marriage to Calpurnia.

Six others fit the circumstances and date of the other letters. Two letters, Epp. 1 and 24, refer like v. 14 to a recent visit to Comum, and of these Ep. 1 being addressed to Tiro must by its content be earlier than his departure for Baetica. Epp. 6 and 9 describe the entry of young Julius Naso upon a senatorial career, with references to Pliny's poetry and to the career of Minicius Fundanus that help to support the book-date. The latest election scandals in Ep. 19 come at a reasonable interval after those described in iv. 25. The obituary of Regulus, Ep. 2, of whom there is no mention in v, cannot be far astray. The admonitory letter to Maximus, Ep. 34, is the first of three such addressed in the later books (vii. 26, viii. 24) to a younger Maximus, distinct from the elderly Maximus of other letters.

So, out of thirty-three letters nine cannot be separated from the book-date, while a place in this book fits twelve others very well. The close coherence of the middle books is again apparent, while the exacter dates fall neatly in either late 106 or the first half of 107. Pliny's movements also make a reasonable pattern—a journey to Comum at the beginning of the period of vi, possibly identifiable with a similar journey at the end of the period of v, is followed by a vacation in Campania presumably the following year. No fresh office is mentioned except his two brief sessions as judicial adviser to the Emperor (Epp. 22, 31). He has plenty of time for private practice (Epp. 2, 18, 23, 33), and *auditoria* (Epp. 15, 17, 21).

Publication

For reasons given above conjoint publication with at least IV and V is probable.

BOOK VII

In this book only three letters can be firmly dated: Epp. 6 and 10 continue the Varenus affair at a certain interval after the events of VI. 13; it is noteworthy that they are addressed to a different person from the recipient of the earlier series. Similarly Falco's army command in Ep. 22 fits his governorship of Judaea about 106–7. Ep. 3, touching the career of Bruttius Praesens, requires a date not earlier than 103–4, and Ep. 12, if addressed to Minicius Fundanus, may refer to his consulship in 107. Many other letters are closely integrated by serial connexions. The references to Tiro's proconsulship of Baetica link Epp. 16, 23, 32 to VI. 22. The Fuscus–Quadratus group is continued in Epp. 9 and 24, and intertwined with a new series, the first letters to Rosianus Geminus, Epp. 1 and 24, continued in VIII–IX. Another new acquaintance, Terentius Junior, makes his bow in Ep. 25, to recur in VIII and IX. Ep. 4, the history of Pliny's versification, comes at a reasonably long interval after the publication of his first volume in IV and before that of his second, in different metres, in VIII. 21. The letter to the absent Calpurnia, Ep. 5, is akin to those in VI. The offer of material to Tacitus in Ep. 33 for the history of Domitian comes neatly after the contribution for the reign of Titus in VI. 16 and 20. Another letter to Tacitus, Ep. 20, mentioning a book which might be the *Dialogus*, forms part of a series (VIII. 7, IX. 14, 23), comparing the merits of Tacitus and Pliny, that cannot be detached from the dates of the last three books. The criticism of the freedman Pallas and of the servile Claudian Senate in Ep. 29, continued at length in VIII. 6, though not datable, has never been suspected chronologically by the severest critics, and has certain links of theme with VI. 31.

Pliny's movements fit the serial order. The references to a distant visit to Comum and to a rise in land-values set Epp. 11 and 14 after VI. 1 and 19. The circumstances of his country holiday in Ep. 30. 2–3 are just those of the holiday of August–September 107 mentioned in IX. 37 and other notes of IX.

An ambiguous reference to *officium* in Ep. 15 might attribute this and Epp. 7, 8, which all concern the introduction of a certain Priscus to Pompeius Saturninus, to the period of Pliny's *cura Tiberis*; these notes have certain links with other letters in VII–IX about his forensic and literary activity at this period. Ep. 21, on Pliny's eye sickness, has been attributed to the period of his consulship or even of his prefecture of Saturn, on the grounds that in Ep. 21 Pliny addresses Cornutus Tertullus, with whom he had shared these offices formerly, as *collega carissime*. But this affectionate usage in an unofficial letter may better refer metaphorically to their tenure of similar *curae* at this time; Pliny had no occasion to resurrect a seven years' old file at this moment. Epp. 17, on recitations, and 31, about Claudius Pollio, like Ep. 20 above, have been assigned to the period 96–100 on grounds that are demonstrably false.

The letters of VII are thus of a piece with those of VI and VIII–IX. Some twenty-one or twenty-two out of thirty-one have connexions with the nexus of Pliny's life about 107. There are few indications of Pliny's public work apart from forensic activity, and the book might well coincide with the end of Pliny's appointment as *curator Tiberis*.

Publication

The continuous links with VI and VIII argue on the whole against separate publication. The links with VIII–IX are possibly closer than those with VI (Epp. 6, 16, 29, prefs.); hence a short interval in composition and separate publication of IV–VI and VII or VII–IX is possible, but is not required by anything in VII. See on IX below.

BOOK VIII

Only three letters can be firmly dated by historical references. Ep. 4, about a poem on the second Dacian war, is not earlier than 107, and Ep. 23, the death of Junius Avitus, is not earlier than the first quarter of 108, which is the latest date in the letters. Ep. 14, on the murder of the consul Afranius Dexter, may be as early as July 105, and is certainly earlier than the book-date. A fourth, Ep. 17, describing the floods of the lower Tiber, is evidently later than Pliny's retirement from the *cura Tiberis*. But a remarkably large proportion of the rest, by their subject-matter and addresses, are so closely associated with other letters in VII–IX that they can hardly be separated from the general date of this triad, though only a single letter directly continues a series begun in VII—Ep. 6, on Pallas, continuing VII. 29. The new groups of letters addressed to Geminus and Terentius Genitor continue in Epp. 5, 15, and 22. Ep. 7 carries on the comparison of the merits of Tacitus and Pliny from VII. 20 to IX. 14. The description of Pliny's second volume of verses, Ep. 21, is an undoubted novelty.

No less than five notes, Epp. 1, 10, 11, 16, 19, are interlinked by references to the illness or death of various members of his household, including his wife; elsewhere this theme recurs only in v. 19 and vi. 4. Two letters, Epp. 8 and 20, about the natural curiosities of Etruria hitherto unknown to Pliny, show him travelling on routes which he had not used before in order to oblige Calpurnius Fabatus, who has already appeared in vii. 16, 23, 32 as a man past the age for long journeys. These and other references to a journey to and a holiday spent on his estates, sometimes specified as Tuscan, in a year of poor harvest at the vintage season, occur in some five letters (1, 2, 8, 15, 20), which provide another link with vii and ix. There is no comparable group in i–vi. Four of these letters have other links with this period (1, 8, 15, 20, above). There is even less reference to public duties than in vii, and forensic occupations are seldom mentioned (cf. Ep. 9. 1, 12. 3, 21. 3).

Three letters have been unjustly suspected of an early date. Ep. 12, about the writings of Titinius Capito, refers to a different phase of his literary activities from i. 17, and the doubts about the interval between Calpurnia's marriage and her abortion mentioned in Epp. 10, 11 would be more serious if her husband had been less barren in his earlier life, or if the objection to the 'book-date' of this marriage could be sustained (above, p. 33).

Though Ep. 14, the murder of Afranius, cannot be as late as 107, its inclusion is no argument against the coherence of the rest of the book, in which some sixteen out of twenty-four letters seem to be in their right places. The excessive length of Ep. 14, for which the customary apology is not made, its lack of the unity of theme usual in the Letters (pp. 14 f.), and its markedly forensic style, may have secured its rejection at the compilation of Books v–vi, where it belongs by chronology. It was resurrected for viii when Pliny was beginning to run out of material, as the contents of ix demonstrate. Otherwise the book presents a united front, and is marked by considerable overlaps with vii and ix, so that its book-date is not far different from that of vii, though extending into 108.

Compilation and Publication

Conjoint publication with vii and ix seems most probable, whether or not vii–ix were published separately from iv–vi.

BOOK IX

This collection differs notably from the earlier books. The forty letters include only twelve of any substance. The rest are in the main short letters of thanks or advice, often very formal. Only one letter

(Ep. 37) is precisely datable, to August 107, and there are no fully serial letters continued from VIII, though Ep. 5 continues the Tiro series of VII. Two notes, Epp. 4, 8 (below), seem to connect with material in III and IV, and the lengthy Ep. 26 (below) may be a companion to II. 5. Hence at first sight IX might seem to contain a miscellany of letters from Pliny's files covering the whole period from I to VIII. But detailed study of subject-matter and addresses reveals a complicated nexus of links, involving absolute and relative dates, between many letters of IX and of VII–VIII. It is more likely that Pliny made up IX by combining some recent letters of real interest with the remnants of his polite correspondence from the period covered by VII–VIII together with a few older epistles to complete the roll.

Letters addressed to friends who appear only in the later books cover the Geminus, Fuscus–Quadratus, and Terentius Junior series (Epp. 11–13, 30, 36, 40). A set of nine letters and notes are interlocked with themselves and with letters of VII–VIII by a combination of specific references to prolonged rustic activities, sometimes defined as *in Tuscis* (10, 15, 36, 37, 40), to 'thin harvests' (16, 20, continued in 25, 28), and to the *retractatio* of certain speeches (10, 15, 28). Some of these nine have other indications of a late date in the circumstances of their addressees (15, 36, 40), or of Pliny himself (36, 40) including references to his latest versification (10, 16, 25). Thus in Epp. 36 and 40 Pliny's prolonged residence at Tifernum suggests that he is no longer *curator Tiberis*, and Pompeius Falco, known to have been overseas before 107–8, is at Rome in Ep. 15, and a possible consul. All or much of this group may be tied to the year 107 by the reference to the known consulship of Valerius Paulinus in Ep. 37 (on share-croppers).

Distinct references to Pliny's second volume of verses place the short courtesy notes Epp. 16, 25, and 29 just after VIII. 21. So too the versification of the reluctant Caninius Rufus sets the 'dolphin' letter, Ep. 33, and probably the brief note 38, no earlier than VIII. 4, of *c.* 107, where Rufus first brings himself to the act of writing. Equally the literary achievement of Passenus Paulus in Ep. 22 has advanced beyond the stage described in VI. 15, from elegiacs to lyrics.

A cross-reference to VI. 10, and the address to young Ruso, first mentioned in VI. 23, place the comparison of Frontinus and Verginius in Ep. 19 at least later than VI. Calestrius Tiro, *en route* to Baetica in VII, is now in mid-course of his annual proconsulship in Ep. 5. Two letters on the comparison of Tacitus and Pliny, Epp. 14 and 23, continue the theme from VII–VIII. Ep. 34, in which Pliny is training a new *lector*, should be later than VIII. 1, which records the serious illness and incapacity of his favourite reading clerk.

Weaker signs of a late date, but congruent with VIII, are the references to a life of literary leisure interrupted only occasionally by private or forensic *officia* (Epp. 2, 3, 6, 18; cf. also 25, 36, 40, already discussed).

These various connexions argue for the chronological coherence of some twenty-one or twenty-two letters, including eight of the twelve letters of substance (13, 19, 23, 28, 33, 36, 37, 40). Another four are more likely late than early (Epp. 2, 3, 6, 18). Of the remainder three would seem to belong to an earlier period. The mutual praises of Pliny and Sentius Augurinus in Ep. 8 and IV. 27 cannot be dissociated. Epp. 4 and 26 have not hitherto been suspected, but the description in 4 of a major speech which Pliny is revising fits exactly the *In Classici Socios* of III. 9. So too Ep. 26, a letter on style, has peculiar affinities with several letters on style in I–II, notably II. 5, which suggest an early date. But doubts which have been brought against Epp. 10 (to Tacitus on poetry), 13 (the trial of Certus) and 34 (above), rest on a superficial examination of their content.

Book IX has thus a very considerable overlap in material and chronology with VII–VIII, and the early element in it is not so considerable as is sometimes assumed. But criticism of Mommsen's chronology is here justified in so far as these three last books contain material of the same general period, spread from late 106 to mid-108. The assignment of the books to three different calendar years or annual periods cannot be maintained.

Publication and Compilation

There is a case for the contemporary publication of VII–IX, though the links are not as strong as those between IV–VI, and VII is evenly poised between VI and VIII. The separation of this group from IV–VI seems to be indicated by the implication in IX. 19 that Ruso has read VI. 10 in a published form, though the implication is disputable. It was seen above that the links between VI and VII do not preclude a break in the publication of the series, though the compilation of these books is likely to have been continuous.

SUMMARY OF RESULTS

This investigation suggests that the following book-dates can be established, with limited exceptions.

Books I–II. Late 96 to Sept. 100.
 III. Sept. 100 to 103, except Ep. 4 (99), Ep. 9 (mid-100).
 IV. 104–5.
 V. 105–6, except possibly Ep. 20 (early 107).
 VI. 106–7.
 VII. 107.
 VIII. 107–8.
 IX. 106–8, except Ep. 4 (100–1), Ep. 8 (104–5), Ep. 26 (96–98).

V. CLASSIFICATION AND DISTRIBUTION OF TYPES

THE chronology of the letters can be tested by the distribution of types of letter throughout the nine books. Classification by subject-matter also casts light on the nature of the letters. It is rendered easier by the literary convention that each letter must have a single subject (p. 3). Certain categories can be defined in general terms. For some of these there is ancient authority in Cicero and Quintilian, though the Latin writers, unlike the Greek rhetoricians, have not left a technical schema like the twenty-one types of the *formae epistolicae* (p. 1). Cicero in incidental references recognized the news-letter, the topic of *res domesticae*, the *promissio auxilii*, the *consolatio doloris*, and *litterae commendaticiae* (*Ad Fam.* 2. 4. 1, 4. 13. 1, 5. 5. 1). From Quintilian (4. 3. 12) comes a list of types of oratorical digressions which may be connected with the development of the literary letter (p. 2): 'laus hominum locorumque, expositio rerum gestarum, . . . descriptio regionum'. These eight types are easily recognized in Pliny, as the list below will indicate.

There is also the letter of advice, which originated in the Greek λόγος προτρεπτικός or παραινετικός, and has a long history down to the letters of Fronto to the young Marcus Aurelius. Statius provided Pliny with an immediate model in his addresses to Vitorius and Crispinus (*Silvae* 4. 4, 5. 2). This appears as a recognized form in Pliny, who develops his own usage of *sub exemplo praemonere* (II. 6. 6, VII. 1. 7 nn.). Among Plutarch's lost works there was an essay in letter-form on the question of 'ruling over Greeks'. The twenty-one types of the rhetorical tradition are all subtle variations of the letter of advice. Cicero's letters to his brother as proconsul of Asia belong to this category.[1] The *quaestio naturalis* was developed by Seneca in his essays, and appears in a shorter form in a small group of Pliny's letters, closely connected with Quintilian's *laus locorum*. Nepos (*Atticus* 20. 2) mentions the *quaestio poetica* and *de antiquitate* as epistolary subjects. These do not appear precisely in Pliny, but the numerous letters about *studia* are akin. *Antiquitas* is interestingly absent despite the existence of prototypes in Cicero, and the taste for it in the age of Aulus Gellius. But Pliny adapts for his letters the contemporary fashion of writing *exitus illustrium virorum* (V. 5. 3, VIII. 12. 5 nn.). Altogether there is ample ground for a classification of Pliny's letters by subjects. Pliny himself analysed his two books of lyrical verses, a form akin to his new pattern of letter-writing (pp. 2 f.),

---

[1] Cf. H. Peter, op. cit. 18 f., 21, 24. F. Zucker, *Philologus*, lxxxiv (1928), 216 ff. For the text of the Greek *formae* see *Demetri* ι′ . . . τόποι, V. Weichert (Leipzig, 1910). For Plutarch see the list of *Lamprias* 153 cited by Zucker, 219.

roughly by subjects: 'his iocamur ludimus amamus dolemus querimur irascimur describimus aliquid modo pressius modo elatius atque
ipsa varietate temptamus efficere ut . . . placeant' (IV. 14. 3; cf. VII.
9. 13 nn.).

There is ancient evidence for some thirteen types, largely corresponding with those distinguished in the following list. This is
shorter and simpler than the similar scheme of Peter, and it was
worked out independently. It goes beyond the ancient evidence
mainly in the attempt to distinguish between different types of *res
gestae*, but is economical in merging Quintilian's *laus locorum* and
descriptio regionum with the *quaestio naturalis*.

One category that is not included is the *iocus*. Cicero regarded
ioci and *iocatio* as characteristic of the letter (p. 1). But this is a
differential of mood and tone rather than of content. Pliny only
three times claims to be writing what is amusing in itself, in I. 6, 21,
and VI. 15. But the light bantering tone of *iocatio*, hardly rising to the
level of wit, pervades a number of the brief notes which have been
styled below as 'courtesy notes', though it is not confined to these.
The 'invitations to dinner' and the notes on hunting and gifts are
characteristic (I. 6, 15, III. 12, V. 2, VIII. 15). But the tone is apt to
deepen into seriousness or satire, as in the letters about Regulus and
kindred pieces (II. 6, 20, IV. 2, 7). The contents of the *epistulae iocosae*
of all sorts are too various to be included in a single category.[1] The
following account may be over-refined, but generally the letters fall
very easily into the categories listed for convenience. Illustrations
are given so far as possible from I–II.

I. Public affairs, *res gestae*

(a) Contemporary politics, e.g. senatorial debates, prosecutions, acts
    of magistrates and the emperor: I. 5, II. 11.

---

[1] For convenience the total list of these is given here. The more doubtful
examples are italicized; these are also the only letters of length, apart from
II. 10, which are both *iocosae* and of some substance.

I.	6, 11, 15, 21.
II.	6, 8, 10, 15, *20*.
III.	12.
IV.	*2*, 7, 26, 29.
V.	2, 10, 18.
VI.	15.
VII.	2, 3, 12, 13, *29*.
VIII.	7, 15.
IX.	7, 10, 15, 16, 25, 32, 34.

The paucity of such letters in the middle books III–VI is remarkable. They
contain at most nine against the same figure in I–II and seven in VII–VIII, with
one or two doubtful in each group. The large number in IX corresponds to the
peculiarity of this collection of mainly smaller pieces.

(b) Historical, e.g. political episodes of periods before the Letters
begin: III. 16.

(c) Anecdotes, social or political, distinguished from the above by
brevity, selectivity of focus, and gossipy tone: I. 17, II. 20.

(d) Centumviral court, operations of Pliny and his friends: II. 14.

II. Character sketches

(a) Full studies of notable men, *laudes hominum*: I. 10, II. 3.

(b) Obituaries, *exitus illustrium*, usually briefer, and having in later
books a formal tone of mourning: I. 12, II. 1.

III. Patronage, *promissio auxilii* or *commendaticiae*

Recommendation of young men to officials for promotion,
including notification by Pliny of his own personal benefactions:
I. 19, II. 13. Social introductions like VII. 7 are excluded.

IV. Admonitions, παραινετικός

Advice, praise and blame. Pliny comments on the actions of the
person addressed. This may overlap with *Anecdotes*, because Pliny
often advises *sub exemplo*, but is distinct in purpose: I. 23, II. 6.

V. Domestic, *res domesticae*

(a) Private business: material transactions, usually about land or
buildings, including municipal benefactions and testamentary
affairs: I. 21, II. 16.

(b) Intimate letters to friends and relations about, for example, treatment of slaves, children, and marriages, and social introductions:
I. 4, II. 18.

VI. Literary, including *quaestio poetica*

The composition, criticism, and publication of his own or his
friends' speeches and verses: I. 8, II. 19.

VII. Scenic, *laus locorum* and *quaestio naturalis*

Rare but characteristic: II. 17, IV. 30.

VIII. Social courtesy, including some *ioci*

Brief notes of invitations to dinner and replies, thanks for gifts,
greetings, receipts of letters, notes of departure and arrival: I. 6,
11, II. 2, 8. The type is akin to the *Literary* and *Domestic* by
contents, but is distinguished by its brevity and purpose, which is
informative, not discursive. But the distribution is so even that
the distinction is not of importance until Book IX.

The following table summarizes the distribution of types in I–IX,
which is discussed in more detail in the following sections. Brackets
are used to indicate the rare cases where there is doubt about the
category and the letter appears under two heads.

		Book I	Book II	Book III	Book IV
I.	Public Life				
(a)	Politics	5, 7	7, 11, 12	4, 9, 20	9, 12, 22, 25
(b)	Historical			16	11
(c)	Anecdotes	13, 17	20	11, 14	2, 7, 17, 29
(d)	Centumviral	(18)	14		16
II.	(a) Characters	10, 22	3	1, 5, (11)	
	(b) Obituaries	12	1	7, 21	21
III.	Patronage	19	9, 13	2, 8	4, 15
IV.	Admonitions	3, 9, (18), 23	6		(3), 23, 24
V.	Domestic				
(a)	Business	21	15, 16	6, 19	10, 13
(b)	Intimate	4, 14, 24	4, 18	3, 10	1, 19, 28
VI.	Literary	2, 8, 16, 20	5, 10, 19	13, 15, 18 (21)	(3), 5, 14, 18, 20, 26, 27
VII.	Scenic		17		30
VIII.	Courtesy	6, 11, 15	2, 8	12, 17	6, 8

		Book V	Book VI	Book VII	Book VIII	Book IX
I.	Public Life					
(a)	Politics	4, 9, 13, 20	5, 13, 19, 22, 27, 31	6, 10	14	
(b)	Historical		(16), (20)	29, 33	6	13
(c)	Anecdotes	1, 14	10, 15, 24, 25	(27)	18	19, 23
(d)	Centumviral		(2), 11, 18, 23, (33)			
II.	(a) Characters		(6)	19, 25, (31)		36, 40
	(b) Obituaries	5, 16, 21	(2)	24	5, 23	(9)
III.	Patronage		(6), 8, 9, 32			
IV.	Admonitions		29, 34	1, 3, (9), 26, 28	22, 24	5, 6, (9), 12, 17, 21, 24, 29, 30
V.	Domestic					
(a)	Business	7	3, 30	11, 14, 18	2	37, 39
(b)	Intimate	11, 19	4, 7, 12, 28	5, 7, 8, 15, 16, 21, 23, (31), 32	1, 10, 11, 16	7, 28
VI.	Literary	3, 8, 10, 12, 17	17, 21, (33)	4, (9), 12, 17, 20, 30	3, 4, 7, 12, 19, 21	1, 2, 26, (27), 34
VII.	Scenic	6	(16), (20)	(27)	8, 17, 20	33
VIII.	Courtesy	2, 15, 18	1, 14, 26	2, 13	9, 13, 15	3, 4, 8, 10, 11, 14, 15, 16, 18, 20, 25, (27), 31, 32, 35, 38

Note. Brackets indicate a letter which is listed elsewhere, but could fall into either category.

DISTRIBUTION IN BOOKS I–IV

If the letters of the first four books are analysed into types it becomes apparent that Pliny aimed at a varied distribution between the categories. Book I contains samples of all types except the 'Historical' and the 'Scenic' (I *b* and VII). Book II contains everything except the Historical. Book III lacks the Centumviral, the Scenic, and the Admonition (I *d*, IV, VII). Book IV is complete except for a full-length Character (II *a*).

The numerical distribution of types is interesting. In Books I and II the letters are evenly divided between the themes, as the analytical table shows. In Book I Politics, Anecdotes, and Characters have two apiece. The Domestic, Literary, Admonitions, and Courtesy have three or four apiece, the rest have singletons. As a whole the book has a relatively large number of short and unimportant letters on various themes. In Book II the latter are much fewer, but numerical distribution is otherwise similar to that of Book I. In Book III the gap made by the absence of three types is filled by a rich selection in types I and II, Politics, Anecdotes, Characters, and Obituaries, providing ten fine samples between them as against six or seven in Books I and II. The Literary (VI) remains much the same at four samples. In Book IV, which has 30 letters in place of 24–20–21 in I–III, for the same pagination, the fatness of the first two categories is maintained, but in different proportions. Politics and Historical (I *a* and *b*) have five samples, and Anecdotes four, but Character and Obituaries are reduced to a single short example (Ep. 21). The civil courts, though thrice mentioned, are the theme of a single letter, as in Books I and II (Ep. 16, cf. Epp. 17, 24). The Literary is stronger in numbers, at six, than in substance. Admonitions, after a gap in Book III, are up to three fair samples; the type does not normally run to length.

This analysis shows that though Pliny was devoted to the principle of variety in his selection, just as he insisted on it in his account of his volume of lyrics (IV. 14. 3 n.), yet distribution is neither automatic nor haphazard.[1] It is possible that if Pliny had too many of one particular type, he might exclude a sample and hold it over till the next book, as with the extortion letters in III and IV. On the other hand, the detailed analysis suggests that this did not happen very often. In Books III and IV Pliny does not hesitate to increase the number of a particular type, provided that there is no excessive similarity between the samples. The Obituaries of two poets, Silius Italicus and Martial, are published in the same book, III. 7 and 21,

---

[1] H. Peter made much of the cult of *varietas*, in the writers of this period, op. cit. 103 ff., as the basis of Pliny's arrangement.

though Pliny has no comparable letters in the rest of the collection. But one was a senator, a writer of epics and an Italian, the other a lyricist and a private citizen from the provinces. The same book contains two other Characters, but one is the exalted consular Spurinna and the other the procurator and historian Plinius Secundus. In Books I and II, where the distribution of types is most evenly maintained, he does not hesitate to include among Characters a statesman and a sophist or philosopher in each book, Corellius and Euphrates, Verginius and Isaeus. Of two Patronage letters in Book II, one is senatorial, the other equestrian (Epp. 9, 13).

These arguments suggest that in Books I–IV undated letters belong to the 'book-date' generally, and should only be suspected, if at all, when they have an exact counterpart in the preceding book. Thus the account of Verginius in II. I may have been left out of Book I because of excessive similarity to I. 12 (the death of Corellius); each was an elder statesman and a champion of *libertas* in his way. Certainly the trial of Bassus (IV. 9) was held over from Book III, to which it belongs by date, because the trial of Classicus was already in the book (III. 4, 9), which in turn may have been kept out of II by the trial of Priscus (II. 11).

The gaps tend to support the 'book-date' theory. One cannot publish what one has not yet written. The remark in Book I. 1 about hunting out more of his past correspondence might suggest that Pliny had a large store in his files. But Book I, for all its calculated variety, has an undue number of short and minor notes, which Asbach called 'fillers'. In the Literary section of I Pliny has no great speech ready for his friends (after the *De Helvidi Ultione*) and no great actions of his own in the courts to report as in II (I. 2. 8 nn.). But Book II has less need of 'fillers', and contains plenty of good things that might have come earlier if they had been ready, such as the two Patronage letters (II. 9, 13), both better than I. 19, or the villa letter, II. 17. So too the gaps in III might have been filled with the material available in IV, if the method of compilation was not chronological. Two or three samples of Admonition were then available, and the Centumviral and the Scenic likewise; IV. (3), 23, 24; 16; 30. Equally Pliny could have improved the balance of Books III and IV by postponing a sample of Character or Obituary from III to IV.

It is then probable that when an undated letter is of a type not represented, or feebly represented, in the preceding book, it belongs to its 'book-date'. It is unlikely that Pliny carried many letters of importance forward from book to book. Any such case needs specific proof. It is also possible, from the analysis of distribution alone, that the first four books were published separately from each other.

48   INTRODUCTION

In Book IV there first occur serial links between books. These become particularly strong from IV through to VII. Hence the compilation of V–VII may well be considered in relation to IV, but separately from I–III. In Book V the Historical, Centumviral, Characters, Patronage, and Admonitions are missing (I *b*, *d*, II *a*, III, IV). In Book VI there are no true Characters (II *a*). In Book VII there are no Centumvirals nor any Patronage, and the Scenic is doubtful. The gaps support the arguments advanced above, especially when the shorter duration of the book-dates of the middle books is taken into account.

Book V is stronger in Obituaries than IV, with three samples against one. Though similarly weak in Characters, it still maintains nine in the first two types, thanks to four letters in Politics. The Literary type is stronger in substance, though not in numbers, at five (V. 3, 8, 10, 12, 17). Book VI has thirteen more letters than V, and the increase comes precisely where V was weak, in Anecdotes, increased from two to four, Centumviral—no less than four, Patronage at four also, and a single long sample in the Historical—or two if both VI. 16 and 20 are put in the same category. Literature is surprisingly thin at two or three (VI. 17, 21 and possibly 33). The Domestic themes are fatter than usual at six in both branches together (V *a*, *b*). The increased number of letters is thus spread through all the types present in the books.

It seems probable that the peculiar features of Books V and VI are due to the chronological basis of the compilation. Pliny could have easily redressed the balance of the two books if he had been indifferent to dates. The marked increase in Centumviral letters may well correspond to a sudden outburst of activity in the Courts.

Book VII has a different distribution from VI in much the same total of letters. The four divisions of Public Life muster at most five letters after 14–17 in Book VI. Political affairs (I *a*) are reduced to two samples after standing at 4–4–6 in Books IV–VI. Anecdotes and Historical muster only two or three items after five or six in VI: Ep. 27, in form an Anecdote, is really a 'Natural Question'. The Centumviral disappears again as in Books III and V. Characters and Obituaries are strong at three or four, much as in Book V, after partial eclipse in IV and VI, but the type has evolved and is somewhat shorter than the set pieces of the earlier books (VII. 19, 24, 25, (31); cf. V. 5 and 21). Ep. 24, which is nominally an Obituary, contains two intertwined characterizations, of Quadratilla and her grandson. If public life is weak, private life is yet more strongly represented than in VI, with 11 or 12 samples in the two Domestic sections, five or six in Literature, and four or five Admonitions, an increase over Book VI in each category. The domestic letters include a new development of the Intimate (V *b*), the social introduction, Epp. 7, 8, 15, 31.

Though Pliny just manages to maintain his categories in VII with no absolute gaps, the balance is very different from that of the preceding five books. It is much closer to Book I in the large number of short unsubstantial letters on various themes: Epp. 2, 5, 7, 8, 13–15, 21, 23, 28, 32. Themes are frequently repeated or spun out in a series with a monotony hitherto avoided: Epp. 1 and 26 concern the moral effects of illness, 7, 8, 15 a social introduction, 16, 23, 32, Tiro's visit to Fabatus.

The marked variations in distribution between Books IV, V, VI, and VII argue even more strongly than in Books I–IV in favour of chronological compilation.

DISTRIBUTION IN BOOKS VIII AND IX

The impression first felt in VII that Pliny was running short of, or ceasing to compose, political types of letters is much stronger in VIII and IX. In Book VIII type I has only three samples in all its branches, of which Ep. 14 is certainly held over from an earlier date. Type II consists of two short obituaries (Epp. 5, 23). Type III, Patronage, is missing. The bulk of the letters, seventeen out of twenty-four, are provided by the Domestic (V *a*, *b*) with five samples, the Literary with six, and Admonitions with two, while the Scenic has the unusual score of three items. Though this book is no shorter of types than Book III, the balance of numbers has swung down decisively in favour of private topics.

In Book IX the scheme of representation collapses altogether. Politics and History are represented by Ep. 13, the Certus affair, which is resurrected as a subject from the period of Book I, though the letter itself is not of early date. There are two Anecdotes, but Centumvirals and Patronage are absent; Characters are represented by Pliny's account of his own country life (Epp. 36, 40), and Obituaries by the brief Ep. 9, which is partly an 'Admonition'. In Literature, only one of four samples has full substance, Ep. 26, which may be a reject from the period of Book I. The Domestic types have four items, and there is a good sample of natural curiosities or Scenic (Ep. 33). But the real peculiarity of the book lies in the remaining twenty-eight or so letters, which are short notes from a few lines to half a page, all falling neatly into the categories of Courtesy and Admonitions, and largely concerned with the exchange of books, brief news, moral sentiments, and specific advice. Only about five of these develop a theme to any extent: Epp. 5, 6, 17, 21, 30.

From the peculiarities of its contents Book IX might contain the remnants in Pliny's literary files from the whole period of the Letters. He certainly seems to have published in IX every scrap that his optimistic nature considered worthy of immortality. Whereas VIII can stand comparison with the earlier books, despite its lack of balance, IX contains a great deal of inferior material, among both the longer letters and the shorter, and includes more items than VIII that may have been rejected earlier: Epp. 4, 8, 11, 26, 32, 38 nn. But all these except Ep. 26 are very brief. Only a few, such as 13, 19, 23, 33, 36, 39, the bulk of the substantial letters, are unlikely to have been withheld earlier, or could have filled notable gaps in earlier books, and hence may be reasonably dated from this stand-point as later than the compilation of VII and VIII; cf. especially Epp. 13, 23. Evidence from the contents of the letters, however, somewhat diminishes the force of this argument against the book-date of IX (above, p. 39), and suggests that the bulk of the minor letters belong no earlier than the period of VI–VIII.

PLINY'S METHOD OF COMPILATION

Certain tentative conclusions emerge about the process of com-pilation. In each book Pliny sought to include a representative collection of the major themes, but he did not bind himself to an arithmetical proportion. The gaps and variations taken together suggest that each book contains the letters of a particular period, and that in the middle and later books he had some difficulty, and in the last book considerable difficulty, in completing his schedule. But in Books I–III he had in most categories plenty of material; it is likely that a few letters were held over from book to book on grounds of redundancy. The symmetry with which I and II each contain two Characters, one a sophist the other a statesman, is hardly accidental. But when in III the number of characters, living or dead—II *a* and *b*—increases out of proportion, with a sophist, two poets, and a scholar-official to one statesman, while certain categories are not filled, it is plausible to suggest that Pliny is coming to the end of his stock-pile. Similar tendencies in IV–VIII, noted above, reinforce this conclusion. In the central books Pliny was seldom using anything but contemporary material. Each book exhausted the letters of a determined period. Otherwise there could have been better balance and fewer or no gaps. There is, for example, a spate of Patronage letters in VI (3–4) and of Domestic in VI (6) and VII (11–12), because Pliny could not make up the volume without them. The length of time covered by each of the central books is not necessarily the same. If short of material Pliny might extend, or if rich in it, abridge his periods at will. Minor overlaps could arise between the books, but considerable post-dating is unlikely.

With VIII the warning flag goes up. The categories are barely filled, the balance alters markedly, though the interest of the material is on the whole maintained. Possibly recourse is being made to old material in one instance, and a shorter period of contemporary material covered. With IX this older material becomes more frequent. But it is apparent that by then Pliny's files did not contain much of value or substance, and that the nine books contain the sum total of his *litterae curiosius scriptae*. This conclusion should cause no surprise. Pliny was not a fruitful writer in any category. He was a slow worker who devoted a great deal of time to polishing and editing, and was easily put off from literary work by any *occupatio*. The total of his verse publication in the period covered by the Letters filled two slim volumes, despite much random scribbling: IV. 14, V. 15, VII. 4. 3-7, VIII. 21, IX. 10. 2 nn. His oratorical publications are more numerous, but not abundant. In I and II he has only two municipal orations to hand out after publishing his *De Helvidi Ultione*, and fobs a friend off with a speech that he had already heard (I. 2, 8, II. 5). The preparation of his *In Marium* and *Panegyricus* falls in the latter part of the year 100 (II. 19, III. 18). About this time comes his short biography of young Spurinna (III. 10). In IV. 5 he is reciting, as a preliminary step towards publishing, what may be his speech in the Classicus case. But in V. 8. 6 he is still busy editing his 'great speeches', or in 12. 1 reciting them. In VI. 33 he is editing a great Centumviral speech. In VII. 12 and 20 he is circulating an obscure work in prose. In IX. 4, 10, 15 he is still editing speeches from the past, but something new crops up in Ep. 28. The publication of at most fourteen or fifteen speeches, two short Lives, and two volumes of light verse, was no great effort for a period of about twelve years. In V. 8 the labour of editing these carefully written speeches was sufficient excuse for Pliny to refuse the attempt to write history. He rightly remarked that compared to his industrious uncle he was a very lazy man (III. 5. 19).

CONCLUSIONS FOR CHRONOLOGY

The evidence of the analysis of the distribution of types suggests that position alone is not a certain guide to dating in the first three books, except when a letter belongs to a category ill represented in the preceding volume. In Books IV–VII a letter should belong to the date of its book unless it can be clearly proved that it does not. In Books III–VII it is improbable that any letter is otherwise very far out of place. In VIII there is a probability that the letters mostly belong to a date later than those of VII. In IX there is a strong possibility that they do not, unless arguments from gaps can be advanced.

The analysis of distribution by itself does not clearly indicate whether the books were published separately. But the existence of gaps and changes of balance suggest that I–III and possibly IV were published individually, and that at least two groups were published separately after the publication of III.

VI. SEQUENCE AND DATES OF PUBLICATION

THE chronological analysis shows the absence of links between I–II and III, the existence of a weak link between III and IV, of strong connexions between IV–VI, and rather weaker links between VII–IX, with VII acting as a bridge between IV–VI and VII–IX, and a single positive argument for a break between the publication of VI and IX. The argument from distribution of types supports a similar conclusion. The evidence then points to three or four separate publications: I–II together or separately, III–VI or VII together, VII or VIII–IX together. But even III may be separate. Against this there stands the theory, unsupported by internal evidence, of publication of the nine books in three triads. This was first suggested by Asbach and supported systematically by H. Peter (op. cit. 105 ff.), whose argument was based, like the present scheme, on chronology and distribution of types. He held that each book contained a carefully varied selection of types which for that reason were not rigidly chronological in order, but which avoided numerous and excessive violations of a roughly chronological pattern. The violations were limited to the chronology of each triad. Thus III. 4 and 9, the Classicus letters, belonged to the book-date of II, but were within the scheme of I–III. The two notes to Arrius, IV. 18, V. 15, which he took to be in reverse order, belonged to the general date of IV–VI. Unfortunately this theory cannot account for the inclusion of the Bassus trial (IV. 9) in the second triad, since its date, 103, is now known to belong to the period of the first triad. Peter did not press his argument for the third triad, which he regarded as chronologically more miscellaneous.

Though putting great stress on Pliny's cult of *varietas*, he yet argued that the distribution of types was by triads rather than by single books. This is roughly true of the first two triads, but it does not help to prove Peter's case when the distribution by separate books is considered. If *varietas* rather than chronology is the keynote, why are individual books overloaded with certain types, and following or preceding books left short of them? The uneven distribution of patronage and admonitory letters—very clearly defined categories—

in IV–VI is an obvious example against Peter (p. 48). Again, he held that each triad had single examples of unusual types, such as the villa letters. But if IX. 7 is reckoned the equal of II. 17 and V. 6, then I. 3 with its brief description of Caninius' villa at Comum must be counted, and the principle breaks down. Equally the 'consiliar' trials have three examples in the second of Peter's triads (IV. 22, VI. 22, 31), and the scenic descriptions, if they are distinguished from the villa letters, have a very odd distribution by triads: they are absent from the first, appear twice or thrice in the second (IV. 30, VI. 16, 20), and have three fine samples in the third, all in one book (VIII. 8, 17, 20).

A curious argument which was based on the pattern of the names of the addressees hardly deserves mention. Peter claimed that in Books I–III and IV–VI with few exceptions the addressees are given *nomen* and *cognomen* on their first appearance, but only a single name, normally the *cognomen*, on subsequent appearances. This is not in fact true. The exceptions are too many for the establishment of a rule—for example Maturus Arrianus in IV. 8 and 12, Arrius Antoninus in IV. 3 and V. 15. Valerius Paulinus, IV. 16, V. 19, have both names on each appearance. Double names reappear in the first triad, e.g. Suetonius Tranquillus and Voconius Romanus in III. 8 and 13. The theory ignores the complexity of the manuscript tradition, including the fact that the index of the *codex Ashburnhamensis*, the principal source of double names, disappears after Book V.

Equally there is little weight in Peter's argument from the rough equality in lines of the books composing each triad, and the slight disparity of length between the three triads. This is supposed to prove that the books were compiled in threes. But it has never been suggested by the supporters of the book-dates that the books contain in each case the *total* production of letters in a given period, which would be unlikely to produce equality of length. Letters were certainly left over from I–VII and appear belatedly in VIII and IX. Pliny put in what he thought suitable to make up a book and the triadic variations are not great enough to be significant.

The triad theory, after the present detailed investigation of chronology and distribution—far more exhaustive than that of Peter—remains a possibility for I–VI, but has no positive evidence on its side. The case is no stronger than for the conjoint publication of IV–VII and VIII–IX. The triad is a fantasy born of a scholarly hankering after system where system is improbable, like the notion that Pliny wrote a book to be named after each of the nine Muses.[1] Everything in Pliny's methods of work tells against it. He was a slow and agonizing reviser and publisher of separate speeches and volumes

[1] W. C. Helmbold, *Cl. Phil.* xliv. 252.

of verse (p. 51; cf. I. 2, II. 5, III. 10, 18, IV. 14, V. 12. 1, VI. 33, VII. 4, 8, VIII. 3, 21, IX. 13, 24). There were no triads of hendecasyllabics, only single volumes. The separate publication of the *Silvae* of Statius, and of at least the first five books of Martial, appears from their prefaces and opening verses. These were Pliny's patterns. It is much more likely that Pliny proceeded cautiously with the publication of the earlier books, and only took the field in force when he saw that the new genre was popular. It is difficult to believe that I–II and III were all three being compiled at the same time on precisely the same principles. There are notable similarities between the contents of I and II. Not only is the pattern of distribution by types very similar in general (p. 46), but specific letters in I have their counterpart in II. Each book has its description of a Greek man of letters (I. 10, II. 3), its account of a speech of Pliny at length (I. 8, II. 5), and its letter about the children of Mauricus (I. 14, II. 18), its *exitus* of an illustrious 'lover of liberty' (I. 12, II. 1), its anti-Regulus story (I. 5, II. 20), its letter of personal discontents (I. 9, II. 14). Though there is a notable difference in the larger place given to living politics in II (II. 7, 9, 11–12 outweighing I. 5, 7, 17, 23), the overall similarity of I–II contrasts with their dissimilarity from III. This book is short of three types well represented in I–II (p. 46) and the letters, apart from the extortion letters, lack the family resemblance to predecessors noted in many letters of I–II. The accounts of Artemidorus and Vestricius Spurinna (Epp. 1, 11) are not precise counterparts of the Isaeus and Verginius Rufus letters, for example, in the manner of Books I–II. Book III has no satire of Regulus and lacks the very short notes frequent in I–II (p. 47). It is also free, with a single exception, from the unnecessary intermixture of letters of different periods that is notable in I–II. The only apparent exception, III. 4, turns out to have a very special reason for its inclusion in III instead of II (p. 47). Hence it seems probable that Books I–II were prepared and published earlier than III, and that Pliny revised his ideas before compiling III.

DATES OF PUBLICATION

The content of the books only provides each book or group with a *terminus post quem* for publication. Peter's dates of *c.* 104 and 107 for his first two triads are no more than that. It has been suggested, more positively by Syme (*Tacitus* 663), that none of the books was published before the death of the advocate Regulus *c.* 105, mentioned in VI. 2, who is much ridiculed in I–II and IV, on the ground that Pliny did not criticize living persons by name in the Letters, as Mommsen first observed (art. cit. 367 n. 3), or at least—it should be added—such as held high social status. His preference for anonymous satire is apparent (e.g. II. 6, VIII. 22, IX. II. I). Apart from Regulus, Fabricius Veiento in IV. 22 and IX. 13, 19, Javolenus Priscus in VI. 15, the wife, not named but identifiable, of Domitius Tullus in VIII. 18, and Julius Africanus in VII. 6. 11–13, come in for some criticism or ridicule. On this ground these, who are all except Africanus elderly persons, must be presumed dead by the publication dates of these books. Javolenus may not have survived until Hadrian's reign,[1] but Juventius Celsus, whose quarrel with Licinius Nepos is described with some asperity in VI. 5, outlived Pliny and the publication of the Letters. The argument only affects the first four books. Regulus is dead in VI. 2, and last mentioned alive in IV. 7. His is somewhat of a special case. No other high personage is satirized so severely by Pliny. In I. 5. 15–16, in the early months of Nerva, Regulus is regarded as still a dangerous political force. But he takes no part in the attack or defence of Publicius Certus later in 97, and remains in the background in the Priscus trial of 100 (II. 11. 22 n.). By the compilation date of I–II (99–100) he was no longer a force. Pliny after his consulship could afford to publish criticism of the decayed and ineffective praetorian senator if it formed part of the scheme of the letters to follow Martial in including satirical attacks on unpopular figures.

It is reasonable to argue from Pliny's self-comparison with Cicero (I. 5. 12, III. 20. 10, IX. 2) that Pliny did not consider publication before he reached consular status and something more, and before his reputation as a political orator was established—that is to say not before he held his first consular commission, the *cura Tiberis*, in or after 104, and not before his three big extortion cases, culminating in the defence of Bassus in 103. These various arguments point to Pliny's consulship as the *terminus post quem*, and to the period 104–5 for the earliest probable publication date for the first published books. But the omission of some form of IX. 13, the glorification of the attack on Publicius Certus, from I or II must still pose the question of an earlier publication of I–II. The subject would seem a first choice for Book II, where it would have formed an admirable counterpart to I. 5, unless Book II were published so early under Trajan that discretion still required the omission of so indiscreet a political letter. A clean break between the publication of I–II and that of IV–VI is indicated by yet another item concerning Regulus: the failure of Pliny in II. 20, where he refers to the perjury of Regulus *per salutem filii*, to give any hint of the boy's premature death recorded so unpleasantly in IV. 2. All in all, the publication of I–II and perhaps III

---

[1] See VI. 15. 2 n. He may also be the person mentioned anonymously in IX. 13. 11 (n.), and hence still alive after the publication of VI.

before, and of the middle books after the *cura Tiberis*, which kept Pliny busy between 104 and 106, is a reasonable hypothesis. The last two books, which are marked off, like I–II, by special characteristics, if not the last three, may have appeared late, and in a relative hurry, just before his departure to Bithynia, whether that was in 109–10 or later. No more can be asserted with any confidence.

VII. CHRONOLOGY OF THE EXTORTION TRIALS

SINCE doubts about the dates of the extortion trials in which Pliny was involved under Trajan were the starting-point of the attacks on the notion of a systematic chronology in the Letters, they merit separate discussion. The position has been changed considerably by the final stabilization of the dates of the trials of Bassus and Varenus in years that are far less remote from the 'book-dates' of the relevant letters in IV and V–VII than the dates proposed by the critics of Mommsen. The difficulties about the date of the trial of Classicus, described in III. 4 and 9, about which alone there is no new evidence, may now be more easy to resolve. For clarity's sake the following discussion avoids polemics with the earlier critics, much of whose work is now put out of date by new evidence. The detailed commentary on the Letters gives the bibliography and enlarges upon certain issues and finer points.

The evidence for the accusation and trial of Classicus and his associates is intertwined with that concerning the trial of Marius Priscus in II. 11–12. Though there is no difficulty for the chronology of Book II in the dating of Ep. 11, which is firmly fixed to January 100, with its sequel Ep. 12 in early February at the latest, there are certain peculiarities in the development of the Priscus affair that illuminate the chronology of the trial of Classicus. The understanding of certain aspects of the trials has also been altered since the days of the original controversy by fresh evidence concerning the procedure for extortion indictments in the Augustan *SC. Passienum* found in Cyrenaica. This has led to a reappraisal of extortion procedure in the Principate.

Priscus and Classicus were proconsuls of Africa and Baetica respectively in the same proconsular year (III. 9. 2 n.). The dating of this year, and of the formal accusation against Priscus, depends upon the date of Pliny's third letter to Trajan in Book X. In this Pliny as prefect of the Treasury of Saturn asks for leave to accept the brief against Priscus which the Senate had formally asked him to undertake. There can be no doubt that the private letters of Pliny to Trajan at the beginning of Book X are in at least rough chronological order; this is commonly accepted by all parties (pp. 62 f.). Equally there can be no doubt that the critics of Mommsen are right in maintaining that Ep. 3 A belongs to the year A.D. 98. The date follows from the dates of Epp. 5 and 8. In Ep. 5 he refers to his serious illness 'anno proximo', and Ep. 8. 3 refers to this illness as before the last illness of Nerva. This takes Pliny's sickness back into 97, between October, when he was active and in good health (I. 7. 4), and the end of the year, after which he was well enough to take up his appointment as prefect of Saturn in January 98 (pp. 75 f.). Hence Ep. 5, and those before it, belong to the year 98, and Marius Priscus and Caecilius Classicus were proconsuls in the year 97–98. Priscus must have been accused in the latter part of 98 following his return from his province in June or July. He was not finally brought to trial until sessions of the Senate in December 99 and January 100 (II. 11. 10 n. 'proximum senatum').

The reason for this long delay lay in certain peculiarities of the extortion procedure. Priscus had originally been accused only of the lesser forms of extortion, which could be judged in a fairly summary procedure by a judicial committee of the Senate, derived from or similar to that of the *SC. Passienum* (II. 11. 2 n.). Pliny and Tacitus his fellow advocate, revealed, at a session of the Senate later than the original indictment, that the charges concealed certain more serious offences, for which Priscus was trying to dodge the penalties by pleading guilty, in effect, to the lesser charges (II. 11. 2–3 nn.). The investigation into more serious charges of this kind required a more searching inquiry in the province than was customary to establish the lesser charges. The Senate therefore authorized the provincial *inquisitio*, but took the unusual step of proceeding in the meantime with the lesser charges also (II. 11. 4–5 nn.). This phase of the trial is dated by the mention of the consul designate Ti. Julius Ferox, who proposed this unusual dual procedure. His year is not yet known for certain. But recent intensive research into the Trajanic *Fasti* shows that he must either be a consul of the last months of 98, or, much more probably, after August in the latter part of 99, since it is likely that all the consuls of 98 are now known.[1] The debate in II. 11. 5, at which Ferox spoke, may have taken place, if not in 98, at any time in the earlier part of 99. There is no reason to assume, even if Ferox was not consul until the last months of 99, that the debate at which he spoke was just before his consulship, late in the year. Cornutus Tertullus, suffect consul in September 100, gave his *sententia* as designate consul at the trial of Priscus in January (II. 11. 19 n.).

After the condemnation of Priscus for his lesser offences the

---

[1] IX. 13. 23 nn. Syme, *Tac.* 71 n., 642, 665. An extra reason for preferring 99 as Ferox's year lies in his proconsulship of Asia in 116–17, the year after Bittius Proculus, who was probably consul in the last *nundinum* of 98.

provincial *inquisitio* was not unnaturally taken at a slow tempo, and Priscus was not arraigned on the criminal charges until December 99, a year or more after the initial accusation. This need cause little surprise, since the process of *inquisitio* was always lengthy; Tacitus mentions a case in which twelve months were allowed (*Ann.* 12. 43). So, the delay in the Priscus case arose for technical reasons after the *delatio nominis*. The intermediate decision against Priscus to proceed on both types of charge was taken either in the autumn of 98 or a few months later.

CLASSICUS

The date of the delation of Caecilius Classicus depends upon the combination of x. 8 and III. 4. In the latter Pliny tells how he accepted the brief against Classicus under pressure from the Senate, after the plaintiffs had asked for his appointment as advocate during his absence on a visit to his Tuscan estate. This visit agrees in its circumstances with that for which in x. 8 he sought leave of absence from his prefecture for the month of September. The year is left uncertain, and may be either 98, as most of Mommsen's critics urged, or 99. The year 98 would mean excessive compression of the petitions and events comprised in x. 3 A to 8, which would then all belong to the short period of July–August 98 (x. 7 n.). The year 99 is favoured by the chronology of the cycle of *locationes agrorum,* to which Pliny refers in another paragraph of Ep. 8 (5 n.). September 100 is excluded because Pliny was then consul at Rome. The leave certainly cannot be in 101, where Mommsen put it. Ep. 8 is placed between the two sets of notes in which Pliny recommends the various doctors who tended him in his illness of 97 and which belong to the second half of 98 and continue into 99 (x. 5, 7, 10. 2 nn., p. 63). Besides, the evidence is clear that Pliny did not continue his prefecture after his consulship (p. 77). The statement of Pliny in III. 4. 8 that this prosecution was his third task of this kind—'si munere hoc iam tertio fungerer'—suggests that Pliny accepted the brief later than that against Priscus. It does not suggest that the trial of Priscus was already finished.

For those who date Ep. 8 to 99 the objection arises: if Classicus was proconsul in 97–98, why was he not indicted, like Priscus, in late 98? The answer is that he may have been indicted then, but that Pliny was not brought into the case until later because of peculiar delays which arose through the sudden death of Classicus himself. Pliny in III. 4. 7 and 9. 5–6 suggests that Classicus' death, probably by suicide, anticipated his formal delation, and makes it clear that Pliny did not enter the case until after the death. There was considerable doubt, when Classicus died, whether a suit could be brought against the dead man's estate and whether the assistants and accomplices of Classicus could now be brought into the charge. As in the Varenus case (VII. 6. 1–2 nn.) the question of prosecution must have been reconsidered by the provincial Council of Baetica before it was launched again in the form in which it was presented to Pliny.

There is also good reason to think that the original indictment itself may have been launched later than that against Marius Priscus. The prime mover in the case was a provincial politician, Norbanus Licinianus, who, as Pliny briefly reveals, had himself been banished from the province by Caecilius Classicus when proconsul. The rules of relegation would prevent Norbanus from returning to his province and stirring up the case for several months after the end of the government of Caecilius (III. 9, 31 n.). Hence the September of 99 is altogether a more probable moment than that of 98 for the final delation and Pliny's acceptance of the brief. Thus the delay in the Classicus case arose before the final delation of the assistants, whereas that in the Priscus case arose after delation.

The date of the actual hearing of the Classicus case must remain open, since Pliny mentions the names of no consuls or designates. There is no reason why it should not belong to the latter part of the year 100, though the absence of the letter from Book II is no proof of this. It would probably have been excluded in any case in order to avoid reduplication of themes (p. 47). The detailed comparison with the Priscus case in III. 9. 2–4 may argue that both cases were in the air at no great interval. But a passage in *Panegyricus* (95. 1), which was delivered in September 100, has been wrongly used to prove that the hearing took place between the trial of Priscus in January 100 and Pliny's consulship in September 100: 'vos mihi in tribunatu quietis, in praetura modestiae, vos in istis etiam officiis, quae studiis nostris circa tuendos socios iniunxeratis, cum fidei tum constantiae antiquissimum testimonium perhibuistis. vos proxime destinationem consulatus mei ... approbavistis ...'. The *testimonium constantiae* has been taken to refer to the *senatusconsultum* in which Pliny's activity in the Classicus case was formally approved in similar terms (III. 9. 23). But the chronological run of the whole section shows that Pliny has in mind his credits won in the Massa case under Domitian (VII. 33), and the *SC.* inviting him to undertake the prosecutions of Priscus and Caecilius (X. 3A 2, III. 4. 3 'senatus-consultum perhonorificum . . .'.). These were all before his consular election, which is the latest of his credits in this passage: *proxime*. This paragraph, if it is to be pressed, tends rather to prove by its silence that the special credit of III. 9, 23 had not yet been won, and Classicus not yet been tried, in September 100, but it is better not pressed. Pliny is not given to silence over his own praises, but the conviction of fellow senators was not a theme on which to linger in the year 100; the destruction of the delator Massa in 93 was a very different matter.

The Classicus case, like the second charge against Priscus, involved the lengthy provincial *inquisitio*. Pliny stresses the complexity of the case, the number of the accused persons and also of the witnesses, who had to be brought compulsorily from the province; III. 9. 9; 12; 22; 24; 29. Only the authority of the Senate could set an *inquisitio* afoot; hence the full investigation could not be organized until after the formal delation, as is clear in the Varenus case (v. 20. 1–2). It is then reasonable that both in the Priscus and in the Classicus case about a year should elapse between the delation and the final trial. It is unlikely that the trial took place during Pliny's consulship, so that a date for III. 9 at the end of 100 is preferable. This is not so remote from the book-date of III even according to the scheme of Mommsen, and fits an alternative scheme in which III contains post-consular letters of Pliny. The presence of Ep. 4, thus dated to 99, in Book III is not surprising when its close connexion with Ep. 9 is considered, to which it forms an introduction.

JULIUS BASSUS

The interminable argument about the date of the indictment of Julius Bassus, whose case is described in IV. 9, which critics of Mommsen tried to date to 100–1, has been abruptly terminated by the dating of the suffect consulship of Baebius Macer, who intervened in the case as consul designate, to the second quarter of A.D. 103 (IV. 9, pref.). Bassus was known from coins to have been an early Trajanic proconsul, not later than 102 (ibid. 1 n.). The charges against him followed the shorter process without *inquisitio* (ibid. 5 n.). Hence it is likely that he was indicted like Priscus in the months following the end of his proconsulship, which may well belong to 101–2, and brought to trial quickly on the slighter charges, as Priscus had been, in the early months of 103 or at the end of 102, according to the date of the suffect elections for 103 (pp. 23 f.). The letter is a year earlier than the 'book-date' of Book IV, and the reason evidently lies in the principle of distribution, p. 47. The account of the trial of Caecilius has displaced IV. 9 from its chronological place in Book III.

VARENUS RUFUS

The initial indictment of Varenus is described in v. 20, and the peripeties of the accusation continue in a series through Book VI to Book VII; VI. 5, 13, VII. 6, 10. The case is linked to that of Julius

Bassus by the fact that Varenus was at one stage appointed by the Senate to undertake the accusation of Bassus, though in fact he did not finally appear in the case. Hence attempts were made to date the trial several years earlier than the 'book-date', close to that of Bassus, on the flimsy argument that Varenus departed to his own proconsulship of Bithynia before the Bassus case was heard. It is now extremely probable that the consul designate, Acilius Rufus, who spoke in the first phase of the Varenus case, is to be identified with a 'Rufus' whose consulship is dated by the *Fasti* of Ostia to the period March–May 107 (v. 20. 6 n.). If so, the delation belongs to late 106 or early 107. In any case the intervention of Licinius Nepos, the ex-praetor of 105, in vi. 5 excludes a date earlier than 106, a fact which might have been observed a great deal earlier in the course of this controversy. The date of Nepos is securely established by the connection of his praetorship with the consulship of Afranius Dexter in 105, long known from the Arval *Acta* (iv. 29, 2, v. 13, 4 n.). Alternatively, if Acilius Rufus is a consul of 106, he must have held office in the period September–December, or October–December, and the delation belongs to the months just following the return of the proconsuls in June 106 (*Fasti*, p. 736+).

These dates suggest that Varenus was proconsul in 105–6. This date agrees with a reference in Dio Chrysostom's Oration 48, in which, addressing the proconsul Varenus, he refers to the Dacians as the active enemies of Rome, i.e. to the second Dacian war of 105–6 (v. 20. 1 n.). The province or its Council seems to have been in a great hurry to start the action against Varenus, which Pliny describes in vii. 6. 1 as 'temere incohatam'. Hence a proconsulship ending in summer 106 followed by initial indictment in late 106 makes good sense.

It would now seem that far from the letters about Varenus being considerably earlier than their 'book-date', the first of them is, on either consular dating, the latest of the letters in Book v, and belongs rather to the 'book-date' of Book vi. It is apparent that Pliny, having managed to present a major case of extortion in which he was himself involved, in each book from ii to iv, now has recourse to his preliminary defence of the interests of Varenus to maintain this theme, though tenuously, through Books v to vii. The extortion letters in iii and iv are displaced by not more than a year forwards in relation to their 'book-dates', but the first of the Varenus letters may somewhat anticipate its proper chronological placing.

CONCLUSION

The extortion letters do not flagrantly violate the principle of book-dates; only iii. 4 and iv. 9 are positively out of line. A rational

explanation may be based on Pliny's avoidance of monotony in the
distribution of themes. The displacement of III. 4, which is introductory to III. 9, is venial. Book II already contained two letters on
the extortion theme, and Pliny had not yet invented the device of
splitting a series between two or more books. The earliest example
of such a series comes either with III. 20 and IV. 25 or IV. 29 and V. 4
(nn.). The extortion letters no longer provide a *prima facie* case
against the notion of book-dates. A more delicate analysis of chronology and themes may succeed in re-establishing a modified form of
Mommsen's chronology.

THE SC. PASSIENUM AND CHRONOLOGY

The question should be asked whether the rules laid down in the
Augustan regulations of the 'shorter process' for extortion trials
illuminate the chronology of Pliny's cases in any way. The *SC.
Passienum* (II. 11. 2 n.) enacted that after *delatio nominis* the consuls
or other magistrates should bring the plaintiffs before the Senate 'as
quickly as possible', and provide them with a *patronus* (1. 101–3).
Their plaints are to be given a first hearing by the Senate and a select
jury is to be provided on the same day (1. 106). These jurors are to
give sentence within thirty days (1. 134). In the first trial of Priscus
and in that of Bassus there is nothing to show how fast the special
jurors, after their appointment, proceeded with their work, which by
this date seems to approximate to little more than an assessment of
damages (II. 11. 2 n.). The preliminary hearing of the Augustan
procedure has developed, at least in the Bassus case, into a full
examination occupying four days, and the effective sentence is given
at its conclusion (II. 11. 2 n., IV. 9. 15). The delays that arose in the
Priscus case did not affect the charges under the shorter process
(above, p. 57). These were possibly handled with some despatch,
but the intentions of the *SC. Passienum* were no longer strictly
observed. It is clear in II. 11. 2–5 as in IV. 9. 16 that the session, at
which the decision to appoint jurors under the shorter process was
taken, is distinct from the session at which the delation was laid
before the House. Senatorial sessions were normally at intervals of
about a fortnight.

VIII. CHRONOLOGY OF THE PRIVATE LETTERS
IN BOOK X

THAT the private letters of Pliny to Trajan and Trajan's replies
(X. 1–14) are in roughly chronological order has been generally
accepted, except by Mommsen himself who was compelled by the

rigidity of his chronological system to attribute Epp. 8–9, perversely, to a period two years later than Epp. 10–11 (Stobbe, art. cit. 364; Otto, art. cit. 66–67; H. Peter, op. cit. 122). But there has been much dispute over the precise distribution of Epp. 1–11 between the years 98 and 99. There have also been doubts over the chronology of Epp. 12–14. Since these various doubts affect the chronology of certain letters in Books 1–1v and of certain events in Pliny's career, it is necessary to establish the dates of these letters on as independent a basis as possible.

There is no serious difficulty over Epp. 1–2, 4–7, and 10–12. In Ep. 1 Pliny formally congratulates Trajan on his accession in January 98. In Ep. 2 he thanks Trajan for the grant of a personal privilege *inter initia felicissimi principatus tui*. In Ep. 4 for the first time he asks Trajan to confer a favour on a friend. Hence this should be the first of the seven such letters: 'indulgentia tua . . . quam plenissimam experior hortatur me ut audeam tibi *etiam* pro amicis obligari'. The *beneficium* had been promised and left unfulfilled at the death of Nerva. The request should belong to the first part of 98. The series Epp. 5–7, in which he seeks citizenship for his physician Harpocras, is neatly dated to the latter part of 98—July to December—by the references to an illness which Pliny suffered in late 97 (Ep. 8. 3), as happening *proximo anno* in Ep. 5. 1, and by the naming of the prefect of Egypt Pompeius Planta, who is known to have entered office after June 98 (Epp. cit. nn.). Ep. 10, which contains a postscript to the Harpocras business, is dated to 99 by a reference to the forthcoming return of Trajan to Italy, where he had arrived by November 99 if not somewhat earlier in the year. In Ep. 11 Pliny asks favour for another physician, who may well have been stirred up by the success of Harpocras. Ep. 12, in which Pliny reminds Trajan that he had previously recommended a certain Accius Sura for a praetorship—as close attention to its contents reveals—is written after Trajan's return to Rome and subsequent departure, i.e. probably in 101 or 102; this may be inferred from the rule that the senators petitioned the emperor in writing only when he was absent from Rome (below, p. 64). Ep. 13, containing the request for the augurship, is subsequent to Pliny's consulship: 'dignitati ad quam me provexit indulgentia tua'. Ep. 14 congratulates Trajan on his victory in one of his two Dacian wars; a turn of phrase suggests that the first is meant, and with it the year 102–3: 'cum gloria imperii *novetur* et augeatur' (ibid. n.).

Since the serial character of the group is so strongly marked there is no reason to doubt that the remaining letters, 3 A–B and 8–9, are also in their correct places. This puts 3 A–B, concerning the delation of Marius Priscus, into a month of 98 later than the midsummer return

of the proconsuls. Epp. 8–9, which concern Pliny's request for leave
from his prefecture of Saturn, and through III. 4 affect the date of
his acceptance of the brief against Classicus, are sandwiched between
the two sets of letters about the physician Harpocras, separating those
of 98 from that of 99. The year 99 is indicated, though not conclu-
sively, by the chronology of the *locatio agrorum*, to which Pliny refers
in Ep. 8. 5 (n.). This was on either a quadrennial or quinquennial
rota, and the present turn should belong either to 97 or to 99, but not
to 98. That the year 99 fits better than the year 98 with the exigencies
of the Classicus trial has been demonstrated above, pp. 58–59.

Various minor objections which have been made against the dates
here indicated are discussed in the Commentary under individual
letters. Here only the placing of Ep. 10, the last 'Harpocras' letter,
need be mentioned. It is the immediate sequel to Ep. 7, yet comes
after Epp. 8–9 instead of before them. These two, about Pliny's
leave, are commonly thought to belong to the month of August,
whether in 98 or in 99, because Pliny refers in Ep. 8 to the termination of his present *menstruum*, or acting period, as officiating prefect
of Saturn, on the next Kalends of September. The assumption that
August is meant makes the conclusion of the Harpocras affair somewhat prolonged, even allowing for the technical difficulties that it
involved, since Pliny certainly raised the question first in 98. But
August is merely the latest possible month. The length of the *menstruum* is not known, and might, like that of the suffect consuls in
most years, be of three or four months' duration. It is possible that
the Harpocras letter is slightly displaced in serial order and should
be moved to follow Ep. 7, but the reference in it to the forthcoming
return of Trajan is decisive for 99 in any case. The suggestion that
this refers to a mere rumour is futile (Ep. 10 n.).

The difficulties raised by dating Ep. 8 to 98 are greater than those
raised by putting it in 99. All the petitions and affairs involved in
Epp. 3 A to Ep. 9 must then be crammed into July–August 98—since
3 A cannot be earlier than July—with the briefs against Priscus and
Classicus following hot on one another's heels; and an excessively
long interval must be posited between Ep. 7 (Harpocras, from
Trajan), which would be before August 98 on this supposition, and
Pliny's letter of thanks, Ep. 10, in the middle of 99.

The question arises, affecting certain other problems in Books I–II,
whether all Pliny's private letters to Trajan, written between 98 and
his departure to Bithynia in Ep. 15, have been included in Book x.
A control is provided by a statement of Tacitus in *Ann.* 4. 39. 4,
which indicates that in the time of Trajan it was the custom for the
gentry to request imperial favours in writing only when the emperor
was not available for a personal interview. He contrasts the present

with the former custom: 'moris quippe tum erat quamquam prae-sentem (sc. principem) scripto adire'. This is borne out by a phrase in Ep. 12, which shows that Pliny had first approached Trajan in the matter of Accius Sura in person, at a date between his return from the northern provinces (Ep. 10. 2) and the Dacian victory of Ep. 14; subsequently he sends a written reminder when Trajan may well be in Dacia. Consistently there are no private letters of the years between 100 and 110 at times when Trajan was certainly in Italy. There is nothing from Trajan's fairly brief absence on the second Dacian campaign, though it is possible that a second letter of congratulations has been lost or omitted. In the period of similar length covered by Epp. 15 to 121 Pliny only four times requests favours for himself or his friends (Epp. 26, 87, 94, 104), and once acknowledges a *beneficium* about which there is no previous request and which may have been a surprise to him (Ep. 51). Of these five instances three arose from the circumstances of his mission; they concern members of his staff—Caelius Clemens in Ep. 51, Nymphidius Lupus in Ep. 87, and Suetonius in Ep. 94. Since Trajan was not apparently continuously absent from Italy during the second Dacian war, it is quite possible that Pliny had no occasion to address him during that absence.

The only case before 100 in which there is the possibility of a miss-ing letter concerns the successful recommendation of Erucius Clarus to an emperor who may be either Nerva or Trajan (II. 9 nn.). The exact chronology is uncertain. Even if the emperor is Trajan, the favour may belong to the period after Trajan's return in 99, when Pliny would approach Trajan in person, as he did for Accius Sura (Ep. 12). The file of letters, then, is probably complete concerning matters of substance.

IX. SELECTION AND DISTRIBUTION OF CORRESPONDENTS

SOMETHING may be learned about the nature of the Letters, and about Pliny himself by considering the correspondents and their distribution through the books.[1] The series begins with twenty-three addresses in Book I, none of whom were politically men of great mark at the period of the book. At most three were consular, the advocate Cornelius Tacitus (suff. 97), the amateur poet Octavius Rufus (suff. 90), and probably the returned exile Junius Mauricus.

---

[1] The conclusions here given can be checked by reading the letter heads of each book against the list of contemporary persons p. 738, where the main facts are tabulated.

Several were junior senators, praetorian at most, whose distinction lay in the future: Fabius Justus (suff., c. 102), Minicius Fundanus (suff. 107), Pompeius Falco (suff. 108), Catilius Severus (suff. 110). Calestrius Tiro remained praetorian, but Sosius Senecio, Pliny's *amicus ante fortunam*, was to be favoured highly: cos. ord. in 99 and *bis* in 107. The connexion with Pliny is in every case through *studia*. Next come men of equestrian or municipal rank, none far advanced, if yet launched, in a public career, such as Septicius Clarus, Arrianus Maturus, Suetonius Tranquillus, and the most outstanding at the moment, though not destined for glory, Voconius Romanus, former president of the provincial Council of Spain. Lesser figures are the wealthy *studiosi*, Caninius Rufus of Comum and Pompeius Saturninus, and yet more modest are the land agent Plinius Paternus and the impecunious town councillor Romatius Firmus, both from Comum. There is also a lady, Pliny's well-connected mother-in-law Pompeia Celerina.

The mixture is characteristic, and persists. The next three books add each about a dozen new addresses. Book II among fourteen *novi* introduces only two senators of certain consular status, Domitius Apollinaris, recently suffect (97), and the legate Priscus, of uncertain identity. Possibly Nepos and Cerealis are suffects of 91 and 90 (Ep. 3, 19, prefs.). Valerius Paulinus (suff. 107) and Julius Valerianus are juniors, and Avitus is a young *laticlavius*. The equestrian and municipal grades include the wealthy Calvisius Rufus of Comum, the men of letters Lupercus and Caecilius Macrinus, another business agent Annius, and a needy lady, Calvina.

The *novi* of Book III contain two new consulars of the period, Cornelius Priscus (suff. c. 102–3) and Baebius Macer (suff. 103), and two more notable figures, Julius Ursus Servianus (cos. II 102) and Vestricius Spurinna, (cos. II 98 and III 100), props of the Trajanic régime. These two had close personal connexions with Pliny before the years of their second consulship. The other *novi* are obscure men, except for the equestrian Vibius Maximus, then prefect of Egypt, and include the professor Julius Genitor and a municipal *studiosus*, Cornelius Minicianus. Again there is a lady, the family friend Corellia, but of high rank.

The pattern is more brilliant in Book IV. Among thirteen *novi* there are five consular senators and two or three juniors. Julius Sparsus (suff. 88) and Novius Maximus (suff. 78) keep company with the distinguished administrator Pomponius Bassus (suff. 94), and the aged *bis consul* Arrius Antoninus (cos. II c. 97), both in retirement, and the leading man in the Trajanic régime, the ex-advocate Licinius Sura (cos. II 102 and later cos. III 107). The juniors are Sempronius Rufus (suff. 113), the senatorial candidate Julius Naso, and (probably) Statius Sabinus. The rest of the *novi* include the usual lady, aunt of Pliny's new wife, and the former's father Fabatus, and yet another municipal *studiosus* Cornelius Ursus. So far each book has produced a new correspondent of this type, destined to receive several letters about literary and public affairs and Pliny's public advocacy: Caninius in I, Caecilius Macrinus in II, Cornelius Minicianus in III, and now Ursus.

The first four books muster a considerable roll of correspondents. But after the second book the bulk of the additions tend to lose their place rapidly. Only three of the twelve *novi* of III appear more than once thereafter—Cornelius Minicianus, Julius Genitor, and—probably—Cornelius Priscus (III. 21, pref.). Three of those in IV similarly: Cornelius Ursus, Statius Sabinus, and probably Novius Maximus (IV. 20, pref.). But some eighteen of those in I–II muster a substantial number of letters apiece throughout the collection (see below, pp. 68–69).

After Book IV the pattern changes. Books V, VI, VII produce 7, 9, and 8 *novi* apiece. Book VIII has only three, and Book IX has nine or ten out of thirty-one or -two addresses. These *novi* include many senators—all those of VII seem to be such—in the same mixture of undistinguished men and able consulars as before. Calpurnius Macer (suff. 103), Bruttius Praesens (suff. 102), and Julius Ferox (suff. 98 or 99), all administrators of some note, but not men in the inner circle of the régime, rub shoulders with the new suffect Vettenius Severus (107), Claudius Restitutus and Lucceius Albinus, advocates of praetorian standing, and distinguished equestrians—the secretary Titinius Capito, the jurisprudent Titius Aristo, and the procurator Terentius Junior. But these senators make solitary appearances, and only the last two equestrians appear more than once. More persistent is the group of three junior senators, the undistinguished Rosianus Paetus, and two noble youths, Ummidius Quadratus and Pedanius Fuscus, whose letters form a significant element of VI–IX. Obscure figures still abound, notably in IX. There, out of nine or ten *novi*, the architect Mustius, Sardus, Venator, Colonus, and Sabinianus are men of an excessive obscurity, not solely due to lack of other evidence. The gloom is relieved by a consular, Pomponius Mamilianus (suff. 100), a senatorial poet, Sentius Augurinus, and two senatorial names of less certain identification, Ruso and Rusticus.

So far the *novi*. Comparison with the *veteres* is interesting. In Book V, out of twenty addresses thirteen are *veteres*, of whom six last appeared in IV, four in III, and three in I–II.[1] Of these same

---

[1] These are: IV: Fabatus, Arrius, Ursus, Novius, Sempronius, Paulinus; III: Spurinna, Suetonius, Annius, Calvisius; I–II: Saturninus, Apollinaris, Valerianus.

thirteen, seven originally appeared in the first two books: Saturninus, Suetonius, Paulinus, Apollinaris, Valerianus, Annius, Calvisius. Of the seven *novi* of v four reappear later: Aristo, Aefulanus, and Macer, as singletons, and Pontius Allifanus twice.

In vi out of twenty-six addresses nine *veteres* (excluding the uncertain Maximus and Priscus) first appeared in i or ii—Arrianus, Caninius, Romanus, Tacitus, Minicius, Tiro, Mauricus, Hispanus, Nepos—and four in iii or iv; but only two of the *novi* of v reappear: Pontius and Macer.[1] Of the nine *novi* of vi only two recur later— Pliny's wife Calpurnia, and the young noble Quadratus. The rest are a mixed bunch, including a consul designate, Vettenius Severus, two leading advocates, Lucceius and Restitutus, a farm tenant, Verus, a wealthy client, Triarius, and a needy gentleman, Quintilianus.

In vii out of the fourteen *veteres* (excluding Maximus, and Rufus of Ep. 25) seven last appeared in v–vi, five in iii–iv, and 2 in i.[2] Of these fourteen, eight go back to i–ii: Fabius Justus, Caecilius Macrinus, Saturninus, Caninius, Minicius (?),Tacitus, Septicius, Falco. Of the eight *novi* five do not reappear: Praesens, Ferox, Tertullus, all consulars, Celer and the elder Corellia.

In viii out of twenty-one addresses ten last appeared in vi–vii— Geminus, *Romanus*, Fabatus, *Caninius*, *Tacitus*, *Arrianus*, Cornelius Ursus, *Septicius*, Montanus, *Macrinus*. Eight last appeared in iv–v— Calpurnia, Minicianus, Aristo, *Paternus*, Aefulanus, *Calvisius*, *Gallus*, Sparsus. Of the three *novi*, the obscure young Genialis and the senator Fadius (?) Rufinus do not reappear in ix, but the procurator Junior does so. Two of the *novi* of vii reappear: Montanus and Geminus. Of the eighteen *veteres* the nine italicized go back to i–ii.

In ix out of twenty *veteres* (excluding Maximus) fourteen last occurred in vi–viii,[3] four in iv–v—Sabinus, Paulinus, Suetonius, Severus—two in i–ii: Titianus and Lupercus. But no fewer than thirteen of the twenty began in i–ii: Paulinus, Macrinus, Tiro, Calvisius, Romanus, Tacitus, Falco, Lupercus, Paternus, Titianus, Caninius, Suetonius, Saturninus.

The analysis of vii–ix shows the large part played by the *veteres* of i–ii—a gross total of thirty out of fifty-two *veteres*. These thirty cover, by repetitions, eighteen names, which contain the hard core of the persistent correspondents, notably those listed under ix above together with Justus, Minicius, Arrianus, Gallus, Septicius. Only

---

[1] iii–iv: Servianus, Ursus, Fabatus, Sabinus. Macer of v. 18 and vi. 24 could be different persons.

[2] v–vi: Pontius, Calpurnia, Saturninus, Minicius, Fabatus, Caninius,Tacitus. iii–iv: Macrinus, Falco, Sura, Genitor, and Cornelius Priscus, who receives either Ep. 8 or Ep. 19. i: Septicius, Iustus.

[3] Macrinus, Tiro, Calvisius, Romanus, Tacitus, Geminus, Junior, Quadratus, Falco, Genitor, Paternus, Caninius, Fuscus, Saturninus.

Minicianus, Cornelius Ursus, and Fabatus, among the *novi* of III–IV, and the three *adulescentuli* of VI–IX, Geminus, Quadratus, Fuscus, make a comparable contribution.

It emerges that Pliny was not greatly concerned to drag in illustrious names. The plain consulars, whether they make single or more frequent appearances in the roll, are not the greatest men of the age, but at the most persons like Tacitus and Minicius Fundanus who may hold an imperial legateship or attain, by the luck of the lot, to the titular distinction of the proconsulship of Asia. Catilius Severus, the most distinguished of them in later years, was an old friend of Pliny's praetorian days. Of the three great political men who appear in the Letters, Servianus, Senecio, and Sura, only the last has no known connexion with Pliny at an earlier stage of his career. The solidest part of the correspondence is addressed to old comrades; some are senators like Tacitus and Minicius, but more are of a lower rank, such as the two Rufi, Macrinus and Ursus. Youths beginning their public career, some obscure in birth, others noble, claim a large part. When Pliny picks a leading jurisprudent, to celebrate at length and then to address in two long letters, he chooses his intimate, the equestrian Aristo, and not his acquaintance the exalted consular Neratius or Javolenus Priscus. Pliny's closest colleague in public life was the consular Cornutus Tertullus. He like Aristo is celebrated in a single letter and later addressed in two personal letters, all in Books V and VII. The late and scanty appearance is remarkable. These close friends, like Servianus, were not devoted to literature; hence neither is a frequent recipient of *epistulae curatius scriptae*. Book VIII belongs to the most distinguished period of Pliny's career. Yet its correspondents are the most humdrum collection after Book I. The conclusion would seem to be that the selection of correspondents genuinely represents the circle of Pliny's friends in their various grades—the entourage of a provincial consular, the first of his family, who spent his career in civil administration and the courts of civil law.

X. THE FAMILY OF PLINY

THE personal background of Pliny is clear. His family belonged to the landed municipal gentry of Comum in the Cisalpine region of North Italy. His own inscriptions (pp. 732 f.) give his names as C. Plinius Luci filius Oufentina tribu Caecilius Secundus. Since he was adopted by his maternal uncle Gaius Plinius Secundus in later life, it follows that his father was a Caecilius and his mother came from the Plinii. Both families belonged to the municipal aristocracy of Comum, and more than one branch is known of each, though it is not possible to relate all the various Plinii and Caecilii to one another (cf. I. 21, pref.). His father may be L. Caecilius Gaii filius Secundus known from *CIL Add.* v. 745, who held the senior magistracy at Comum, as *ivvir iuri dicundo*, and initiated the building of a temple to the Eternity of Rome and Augustus in the name of his daughter Caecilia, presumably then deceased. The temple was completed by 'Caecilius Secundus filius', whose prenomen is unfortunately missing. He may well be our Pliny, before his names were changed by the later adoption. Mommsen found the father of Pliny in another man, L. Caecilius Luci filius Cilo, also a municipal magistrate, though of lower rank. His inscription, *CIL* v. 5279, mentions two sons, or possibly brothers, L. Caecilius Valens and P. Caecilius Secundus, and a concubine, 'Lutulla Picti filia'. But her Celtic names and apparent lack of citizen status suggest that the inscription belongs to a period too early for Pliny and his father, and there is no trace of a brother in Pliny's numerous references to his family affairs.

L. Caecilius Cilo should be a collateral relation: he cannot be a grandfather of the second Secundus in *Add.* v. 745 because the *praenomen* of the father of the elder Secundus in 745 was Gaius. Both inscriptions indicate the wealth of the family by the civic benefactions mentioned in them—*munificentia parentum* (I. 8. 5 n.).

That Pliny's uncle C. Plinius Secundus, came from Comum is stated in the Suetonius *Life* and is implied in I. 19. I where the father of an impoverished local decurion is described as 'et matri et avunculo meo mihi etiam familiaris'. It is not proved by epigraphical evidence, but the reference in *Nat. Hist.*, pref. 1—'Catullum conterraneum nostrum'—does not prove that the elder Pliny came from Verona, as some have believed (cf. *PIR*[1], P 373). His wealth is indicated by his equestrian career, and by the indirect evidence that Pliny derived his Tuscan estate, worth S.400,000 a year, from his uncle, who also owned lands in Campania (v. 6. 10, x. 8. 5 nn.; Pliny, *NH* 2. 180). Pliny's father died some years before A.D. 76, since Pliny was left to the care of a *tutor legitimus*, and the legal minority ceased at 14 (II. 1. 8 n.). His uncle seems to have adopted Pliny by a testamentary adoption after his death in A.D. 79, as was quite common; Pliny's frequent reference to his adoptive father as uncle rather than father may indicate this: only once does he speak of the Elder as *per adoptionem pater* (v. 8. 5 n.).

The adoption brought the change of name from Gaius or Lucius Caecilius Secundus to C. Plinius Caecilius Secundus. Pliny followed the contemporary fashion of retaining his paternal *nomen* unaltered instead of changing it to Caecilianus. His previous *praenomen* is unknown, but if he is the second Caecilius of *Add.* v. 745, or the third of 5279, he already had the same *cognomen* as his adoptive father.

Pliny's education followed the usual pattern. He studied under a *grammaticus* at Comum according to the implication of I. 19. 1 (n.), but went to Rome for his course of rhetoric, which he read under the great Quintilian, holder of Vespasian's chair at the Capital. He also studied under the Greek rhetorician Nicetes Sacerdos (II. 14. 9, IV. 13. 3 nn., VI. 6. 3). His first or second marriage may have brought him into relationship with the consular family of Pompeius Celer. His mother-in-law, Pompeia Celerina, owned numerous estates in Tuscany (I. 4 pref. n.). But his final marriage with Calpurnia brought him back to the family setting of municipal gentry. His wife's grandfather, the irascible Calpurnius Fabatus, had held equestrian posts in the imperial service under Nero, and like the Caecilii was capable of solid benefactions to the municipality. He owned lands in Tuscany and Campania as well as, presumably, around Comum (IV. 1, pref., V. 11, VI. 30, VIII. 20. 3). The number of Pliny's marriages is discussed under IV. 1 and X. 2. 2–3 nn. A curious controversy over this minor detail arose in connexion with the chronology of the letters. It concerns not so much the number of wives as the date of the marriage with Calpurnia. It is suggested in the Commentary that evidence not noticed earlier makes it now certain that the marriage was after Pliny's consulship. From this it follows, in X. 2. 2–3, that he married thrice. But nothing is known of the short-lived first wife (I. 18. 3 n.).

Well shod in worldly goods (II. 4. 3 n.), if not in the first rank for wealth, and connected with the Flavian administration through his uncle, whose procuratorial career was sufficiently distinguished, and two active consulars, Julius Frontinus (cos. suff. 74) and Corellius Rufus (cos. suff. 78), the young Pliny was well placed to attempt the senatorial career (III. 5, IV. 8. 3, V. 1. 5 nn.). His former guardian, the consular L. Verginius Rufus (cos. II 69), whose position in the civil war of 68–69 had been ambiguous, may have been of less immediate help (II. 1. 1 nn.). But yet another active Flavian consular, T. Vestricius Spurinna, was among Pliny's closer acquaintances (I. 5. 8, II. 7. 1–2, III. 1 nn.). His senior contemporary, T. Avidius Quietus, another Cisalpine senator, from Faventia (cos. suff. 93), was also at hand (VI. 29. 1 n.). Pliny's first steps in the public career would depend on the sort of assistance from powerful friends that he himself later gave to ambitious young equestrians, such as Erucius Clarus and Junius Avitus (II. 9. 1–2, VIII. 23. 2 nn.). One consular friend would secure him the *latus clavus* and election to his first magistracies as *candidatus Caesaris* (p. 73). Another would secure him the necessary preliminary commission which he held as a military tribune in the Syrian army (VII. 31. 2; cf. II. 13, III. 8 nn.). Meanwhile, the young Pliny launched himself into the life of an advocate, appearing in the Centumviral Court when he was eighteen years old, doubtless with the support of some senior counsel, just as in his later years he also assisted other young men to make their début (I. 18. 3 with IV. 24. I and V. 8. 8, VI. 23. 2 nn.).

There is no need to discuss at large the general background of provincial society in Cisalpine Gaul or political conditions in the time of Domitian and Trajan. The learned and unlearned reader alike will find a complementary discussion in G. C. F. Chilver, *Cisalpine Gaul*, ch. vi, and R. Syme, *Tacitus*, part i.

For the family of Pliny the basic discussions are W. Otto (partly followed here), 'Zur Lebensgeschichte des jüngeren Plinius', *S.b. Bayer. Akad. Wiss.* x (1919), 1–15, correcting Th. Mommsen, *GS*, iv. 394 ff. R. Syme, op. cit., ch. vii. M. Schuster's article in *RE*, 21. 1. 439 f. is derivative.

XI. THE OFFICIAL CAREER OF PLINY

THE known rules and customs regulating the careers of senators have been studied with considerable finesse by the prosopographical school of Roman history, following on the constitutional studies of Mommsen, whose analysis in the *Staatsrecht* laid the basis.[1] Pliny's own statements in the Letters and the Panegyric with the obituary inscription from Comum (below, p. 732), when interpreted in the light of the known rules, provide a tolerably precise account of his official career, which in most particulars was extremely normal. The precise chronology of his career was first established by Mommsen in accordance with his theory of book-dates, and later challenged by Otto on several major points as part of the general onslaught on the book-dates of Mommsen. But some of Otto's objections were fanciful, and his notions about the *cursus honorum* were inaccurate. Here a fresh reconstruction is attempted, which approximates in some particulars to the scheme of Mommsen, and makes the most of recent additions to knowledge.

Pliny was born before 24 August A.D. 62, since he was over 17 at the time of the eruption of Vesuvius on the same date in 79 (VI. 20. 5 n.). Candidates for the senatorial career normally secured the privilege of wearing the *latus clavus*, if they, like Pliny, were not the sons of senators, at or after the assumption of the *toga virilis*, which was usually around their sixteenth birthday, though sometimes the grant was not secured till nearer the age for the quaestorship (I. 9. 2, II. 9. 1, 14. 6 nn.; Suet. *Vesp.* 2. 2). They then proceeded to hold, first, one

---

[1] *DPR*, ii. 190 ff., 234 ff. Also *GS*, iv. 414 ff. Appendixes 17 and 18 in R. Syme, *Tacitus*, vol. ii, substantiate the latest refinements, particularly as to the age at which men commonly reached the quaestorship and consulship.

of the minor magistracies included in the Vigintivirate and, second, a military tribunate in a legion, usually only for a single season, between the ages of 18 and 20. Pliny's Vigintivirate is known only from the inscription. He held the particular post of *decemvir stlitibus iudicandis*, presiding in the Centumviral Court, in which he had already appeared as a junior advocate when only 18 years old, and where he was to spend a great part of his public life (I. 18. 3 n., V. 8. 8). Next, Pliny is found serving with a Syrian legion early in the reign of Domitian. This is mentioned in several letters (I. 10. 2 n.). His duties seem to have been limited to administration, and he saw no active service: VII. 31. 2, VIII. 14. 7. The Domitianic date comes from the latter passage: 'iuvenes fuimus quidem in castris sed cum suspecta virtus, inertia in pretio, . . .'. The precise year, often given as 81, is not known. Since he was in Italy during part of both his eighteenth and his nineteenth years, and since he was practising as an advocate in the latter year, it is difficult to fit in these two preliminary posts before his twentieth or twenty-first year (VI. 20. 5, V. 8. 8). The dates are not material. His entry upon his career may have been temporarily delayed by the death of his influential uncle in 79, but three consulars, Julius Frontinus, Verginius Rufus, and Corellius Rufus, all family friends, were at hand to help him forward (p. 71).

QUAESTORSHIP AND TRIBUNATE

Next came the quaestorship, which automatically admitted a man to the Senate, followed by the tribunate (alternative with the aedileship) and the praetorship. A passage in II. 9. 1 proves that in all these posts Pliny was one of the small group of candidates supported by the emperor's 'commendation', who were elected without contest. There, speaking about the election campaign of his protégé Erucius Clarus he writes: 'adficior cura et quam pro me sollicitudinem non adii quasi pro me altero patior'. The inference is supported by the fact that he served as one of the *quaestores Caesaris* (VII. 16. 2, Inscr.). These were regularly chosen from the *candidati Caesaris* (Mommsen, *DPR*, iv. 227). The date of Pliny's quaestorship does not materially affect anything in the Letters. It can be fixed only in relation to his praetorship, and depends on the application of VII. 16. 2, where he is speaking of his contemporary friend Calestrius Tiro: 'simul militavimus simul quaestores Caesaris fuimus. ille me in tribunatu liberorum iure praecessit, ego illum in praetura sum consecutus, cum mihi Caesar annum remisisset.' The effect of this depends upon the known rules about the magistracies. A man might not hold the quaestorship before he was 25 or the praetorship before he was 30. The tribunate or aedileship must be held in between, except in the case of patrician candidates who omitted this stage, and a clear interval of at least a year must be left between each office, unless a man had a special exemption (Mommsen, loc. cit.; Dio 52. 20. 1–2; *Dig.* 50. 1. 18, 4. 14. 5). The existence of this minimum interval is implied by the provision of the marriage laws, which allowed a year's reduction for each child of a candidate, but its exact length is not known, though it is commonly taken to be a single year (*Dig.* 4. 4. 2). The age limits of 25 and 30 also suggest this for the lower offices, though a *biennium* is possible at one stage: e.g. quaestor at 25, tribune at 27, praetor at 30. The single year best fits the datable careers, though these are few, and as Mommsen observed and others forget, the ready grant of remissions makes for uncertainty in any particular instance. The standard case is that of Agricola, who with two children secured the praetorship at 28, while apparently observing the annual breaks (Tac. *Agric.* 6; Syme, op. cit. 652; Mommsen, *GS*, iv. 414 n. 7).

Despite the doubts of Syme (loc. cit.) the passage in Pliny (VII. 16) makes sense only on the assumption that Pliny and Tiro both went through their career with the minimum intervals, minus reductions of a year each—though it does not imply that they started at the earliest moment. Otherwise there is no reason why Pliny should have caught up Tiro at the praetorship. Remissions worked in two ways. Either, as with Agricola, a man was enabled to stand for election before the minimum age, or, if he was a late starter, the minimum interval was reduced or abolished. Pliny, praetor not before 93, started late. His twenty-fifth year was 86–87, his thirtieth was 91–92. Even with a year's remission he was a year behind *annus suus*. The remission of a year after the tribunate could only help him if it reduced the legal interval. So too Tiro, starting at the same time reaches the tribunate a year early, by grace of children. If Pliny's praetorship was in 93, as is argued at length below (pp. 763 ff.), then he was tribune in 92 and quaestor in 90. So too Vespasian was aedile and praetor in successive years (Suet. *Vesp.* 2. 3, n., ed. Braithwaite). Mommsen quoted in illustration the remarkable case of *ILS* 2934: 'quaestori designato et eodem anno ad aedilitatem promoto'. The exceptional circumstance in Pliny's case was the continuous *suffragatio* of Domitian. Hence the rapidity of his rise from quaestorship to praetorship, after a late start for reasons unknown. Syme objects even to 89 for the quaestorship as too late, for no strong reason. Little is known about the precise dates of senators' early careers except for members of the imperial family. Even the cursus of Agricola is a reconstruction. The career of Ummidius Quadratus seems to be the only career in which the stages are unambiguously dated, and there is no evidence for any remissions ; his quaestorship in A.D. 14 was followed by the aedileship, undated, and the praetorship in A.D. 18. He, like Pliny, was a 'new man', *ILS* 972 nn.

Pliny's tribunate, in 92 on these arguments, is barely mentioned in I. 23 and *Pan.* 95. I. It was passed in formal inactivity, though an obscure passage may suggest that he used it to protect the rights of his equestrian friend Atilius (VI. 8. 3 n.).

PRAETORSHIP AND PRAEFECTURA AERARI MILITARIS

The date of Pliny's praetorship has been much disputed. In Appendix IX it is argued at length that A.D. 93, the year indicated at first sight by the anecdotes in III. 11 and connected incidents, and originally advocated by Mommsen, is the one year that fits all the circumstances of Pliny's life from 93 to 97. In this year he first took part in a public prosecution, acting with Herennius Senecio for the people of Baetica when they successfully accused Baebius Massa of extortion (VII. 33 nn.). At the end of the year certain of his acquaintance, including the same Senecio, were involved in a political affair, and condemned on charges of *maiestas minuta* (III. 11. 2–3 nn.). The business did not touch Pliny, though in later years he tried to secure some credit from his supposed risks and association with the heroes of the Domitianic purges (I. 5. 2–3, III. 11, VII. 27. 14). His career continued unimpeded.

The praetorship qualified a man for the first of the more serious posts in the service of the Princeps. The inscription reveals what the Letters and the Panegyric conceal, that after his praetorship Pliny held the *praefectura aerari militaris*. He probably vacated this post before the death of Domitian, if the last paragraph of the Panegyric may be pressed so far. There he claims that his career was checked after the purge of 93–94: 'si cursu quodam provectus ab illo insidiosissimo principe antequam profiteretur odium bonorum, postquam professus est, substiti'. References to his private life in the Letters which can belong only to 97 indicate that he was no longer holding public office in that year (pp. 767 f.). Since this prefecture was originally triennial in tenure (Dio 55. 25. 2), it is reasonable that Pliny should have held it from the beginning of 94 to some time in 96, if not till the end of that year.

PRAEFECTURA AERARI SATURNI

Much unnecessary fuss has been made about Pliny's tenure of this next post, the prefecture of Saturn, as one may conveniently call it ;

it was the Chest and Record Office of the senatorial administration
(I. 10. 9–10 nn.). The circumstances of his promotion are well documented. The date depends upon the combination of several passages
in the Panegyric and in x. 3 A and 8 with the story of the retirement
of his predecessor as related in IX. 13. In the course of A.D. 97 Pliny
launched a political attack in the Senate against Publicius Certus, for
the part that he took in assisting the condemnation of the younger
Helvidius Priscus in the affair of 93. While the new Princeps Nerva
discouraged the actual prosecution of Certus, the upshot was (ibid.
23), in Pliny's words: 'obtinui . . . quod intenderam. nam collega
Certi consulatum successorem Certus accepit'. Given the tendentious
character of Pliny's narrative in this letter, this probably means, as
Syme suggests (*Tac.* 658), that at the end of 97 both men vacated
their posts in the normal manner, but that Nerva passed over Certus
instead of awarding him the consulship, which was the usual reward
of the ex-prefects of Saturn. Bittius Proculus, Pliny, and his colleague
Tertullus, and also Catilius Severus, all secured this promotion in
this period (I. 22 pref.).

The successors of Bittius and Publicius were Pliny and his friend
Cornutus Tertullus, a fact which he is careful not to disclose in IX. 13.
In x. 8. 3, written to Trajan in the course of 99 (p. 64.), Pliny,
mentioning Nerva in the context, shows that he owed his appointment
both to Nerva and Trajan conjointly: 'delegati a *vobis* officii'. There
alone and in x. 3 A, 1 (n.), where he speaks of the same appointment
more ambiguously as due to *indulgentia vestra*, does he use the plural
pronominal instead of the universal *tuus*, as in the rest of Book x.
This should mean that he was appointed before the death of Nerva,
when Trajan was more or less co-regent, and was continued in office by
Trajan. Similarly, in *Pan.* 90. 6–91. 1 Pliny remarks: 'habuerat hunc
honorem periculis nostris divus Nerva ut nos etsi minus [notos?]
ut bonos promovere vellet . . . . nondum biennium compleveramus
in officio laboriosissimo et maximo cum tu nobis, optime principum,
. . . consulatum obtulisti . . .'. This should mean that Nerva made
the actual appointment to the prefecture of Saturn, and that two full
years had not elapsed when Pliny and Tertullus were nominated
suffect consuls by Trajan for a period of the year 100. Otto's suggestion (art. cit. 56) that Nerva intended to make the pair consuls is
absurd. Pliny's consulship in 100 was remarkably early even if he
had not been a 'new man'; cf. Syme, *Tac.* 657 n. 3. Syme boldly
suggests that the prefects entered office on 1 January—for which
there is no evidence[1]—and assumes that the consulars' list of 100
was drawn up before the New Year, to explain *nondum biennium*.

---

[1] Op. cit. 658. He suggests that the office followed the magisterial year; but
the *quaestores* whom the prefects replaced entered office on 5 Dec. IV. 15. 6 n.

But the description in the Panegyric of the elections at which Trajan presided in January 100 includes the formal *Comitia Consulum*, and seems also to cover the preliminary *destinatio consulum* (*Pan.* 92. 3–4, with 69, 71. 1, 72. 1, 77. 1, pp. 23 f.). The simplest solution is that Pliny and Tertullus took over their office as Prefects at a later day in January 98 than the day of the consular elections in January 100.

Merrill (in *Am. J. Phil.* xxiii. 405), stressing the force of *vellet* in *Pan.* 90. 6 (above) and misinterpreting a passage in *Pan.* 92. 1 (below), suggested that the pair did not take office till late in 98, when Proculus entered his consulship, because it was normal for the prefects of Saturn to continue in office till near the month of their consulships. But in the latter passage Pliny is harping on the exceptional favour which he and Cornutus Tertullus enjoyed in continuing in office thus. Merrill would in effect keep Proculus, but not Certus, in office until just before the *nundinum* November–December, and had to postulate that the vacant place of Certus was filled by a temporary substitute during most of 98. Had this been so, Pliny would hardly have held office a twelvemonth, let alone a *biennium* before the consulship came his way.

The date of the termination of Pliny's prefecture of Saturn affects the chronology of the prosecution of Caecilius Classicus in III. 4 and 9, and x. 8. Pliny makes a great fuss in *Pan.* 92. 1–2 about the fact that he continued in office right up to the beginning of his consulship: 'illud vero quam insigne quod nobis praefectis aerario consulatum antequam successorem dedisti. Aucta est dignitas dignitate, nec continuatus tantum sed geminatus est honor finemque potestatis alterius *altera* tamquam parum esset excipere praevenit.' From this statement Mommsen inferred that Pliny continued in office as prefect of Saturn right through his consulship and into the year 101. But the basic fact is given in the first sentence, and the rest is elaboration in the usual manner of the Panegyric. The *honor* would have been merely *continuatus* if they had passed from their prefecture to the recognized position of *consul designatus*. The next sentence, seldom noticed but less rhetorical, makes the point clear: 'tanta tibi integritatis nostrae fiducia fuit ut non dubitares te salva diligentiae tuae ratione facturum si nos post maximum officium privatos esse non sineres'. The word *post* is decisive. The pair held their prefecture after designation as consuls until the day before they entered upon their consulships. Trajan exempted them from the rule which required an interval between office and office, in which accounts could be cleared and any issues of malpractice could be brought forward. This rule has recently received fresh documentation in a new fragment of the *Sententiae Pauli* (*fr. Leidense* 11).

Pliny accordingly held the prefecture of Saturn from January

98 until the end of August 100 when he entered on his consulship (below). He refers to the duties of the prefecture in I. 10. 10–11, and mentions it in connexion with his prosecutions of Caecilius and Priscus in III. 4. 2–3 and X. 3 A. He asks for leave of absence from it in X. 8. It is also barely mentioned in V. 14. 5, in a summary of his career.

CONSULSHIP

The date of Pliny's consulship is established by passages in the Panegyric, which show that he was in office in September 100 when Trajan was *consul ter*; *Pan.* 60. 4–5, 92. 2–4. The only uncertainty touches the length of his tenure, since the consular list for 100 is not quite fully known. Pliny and Tertullus were succeeded by another pair at least, documented for December 100 (*ILS* 3619). Probably the consulships of the second half of 100 were bi-monthly, as apparently also in 97 and 98 (Syme, *Tac.* 642). But they might have been of only a single month; Trajan's third consulship was a special event, to be shared by as many men as possible. Another designate of 100, Acutius Nerva, speaks later than Tertullus in the debate of II. 12. 2 which took place in late January or early February. Hence, if Acutius spoke in order of seniority, there were two pairs after Pliny and Tertullus. Also in *Pan.* 92. 4 Pliny speaks of himself and Tertullus presiding only over the celebrations of September (*mensi*, not *mensibus*), not mentioning those of Trajan's day of adoption in October.[1] But he was possibly thinking of his own presidency in September, while Tertullus took over the *fasces* in October. As for Acutius Nerva, in II. 11. 2 the list of *sententiae* is not complete and the order may be stylistic. Hence the term of two months is to be preferred. The list for 100 was then as follows. Months not certainly known are in parentheses. See also Durry, *Pan.* 237, Syme, *Tac.* 643 n. 1. A very small fragment of *FO* (*AE*, 1954, n. 222) which may add an extra pair, and the colleague of Acutius Nerva, possibly implies monthly consulships for the colleagues of Trajan in January–April, but does not affect the last four months (G. Barbieri, *Studi romani*, i (1953), 371 f.).

Ian.–Feb.	Traianus III	Sex. Iulius Frontinus III
(Mart.–Apr.)	. . . .	T. Vestricius Spurinna III
Mai.–(Iun.)	L. Herennius Saturninus	T. Pomponius Mamilianus
(Iul.–Aug.)	Q. Acutius Nerva	. . . . . .ius Piso
Sept.(–Oct.)	C. Plinius Secundus	C. Iulius Cornutus Tertullus
(Nov.–)Dec.	L. Roscius Maecius Celer	Ti. Claudius Sacerdos

[1] I owe this point to Mr. F. Lepper.

CURATOR TIBERIS

The inscriptions show that after his consulship Pliny next became *curator alvei Tiberis et riparum et cloacarum urbis*. He refers obscurely to this office in V. 14, on hearing of the appointment of Tertullus to the *cura viae Aemiliae*: 'aliquanto magis me delectat mandatum mihi officium postquam par Cornuto datum video'. The reference to their previous offices—prefecture, consulship—in s. 5 makes all plain. Mommsen, working from the book-date, which on his system was 105, reasonably concluded that Pliny was the successor of Ti. Julius Ferox, who is testified holding this office in 101 and 103; *ILS* 5930; *CIL*, vi. 31550–1; *AE*, 1933, n. 97. The length of tenure at this period seems to be about three years. Messius Rusticus held the post from 121 to 124: *ILS* 5931; *AE* (1917–18), n. 108. But Otto, op. cit., tried to attribute letter V. 14 (with IV. 1 about Pliny's new wife) to 101, on very inadequate grounds (ibid., prefs.); he made Pliny a short-lived predecessor of Ferox, resigning after a few months because of supposed ill health. The seniority of Ferox as a consular makes this very unlikely, even if, as Otto assumed, the lot was still used to distribute this office, as under Tiberius Augustus (Dio 57. 14. 8). Sortitions, as with the proconsulships of Asia and Africa, seem to have been limited to the colleagues of a single year. In fact the post was now filled by imperial appointment: *mandatum*, as says Pliny, and Dio (loc. cit.) draws attention to this change (cf. V. 14. 2 n.).

Under a less precise chronology of book-dates than that of Mommsen it is likely that Pliny held the *cura Tiberis* from 104/5 to 106/7. Ambiguous references in VII. 15. 1 ('distringor officio' n.) and 21. 1 ('collega carissime' n.) may refer to this appointment. Otherwise it leaves no traces in VI–IX. The reference in III. 6. 6 (n.) seems to refer to private rather than imperial affairs: 'destino . . . si . . . officii ratio permiserit excurrere isto . . . . "ad paucos dies"': neque enim diutius abesse me eadem haec . . . patiuntur'. But if this referred to the *cura* it could equally well support the post-Ferox appointment coming in late 103 or 104.

AUGURATE

The date at which Pliny received the augurate depends on that of IV. 8 and X. 13. In the latter Pliny asks Trajan for one of two vacant priesthoods, either the augurate or the septemvirate. The note, from the serial order of X. 1–15, was written before the end of a Dacian war, mentioned in X. 14, which is more probably the first than the second. Pliny at the moment of X. 13 was holding no public office (cf. n.). In IV. 8 Pliny, replying to the congratulations of his friend

Arrianus Maturus, remarks that he had succeeded to the augurate left vacant by the death of Julius Frontinus, who had hitherto regularly recommended him for this priesthood. Arrianus had written to Pliny from Egypt, where he was holding an equestrian appointment no earlier than late 103 (III. 2 nn., IV. 12. 7 n.) Since the nomination of priests took place only once a year on a special day (II. I. 5 n.), there is no difficulty in accepting the book-date of IV. 8. The appointments were leisurely. Pliny may have applied in 102 and received his nomination in 103, and the congratulations of Maturus some months later in 104; IV. 8 nn. Hence the difficulties made by Otto (art. cit. 94 f.) against the date of Mommsen lack substance—the excessive interval as he supposed between the application in 101–2 and the conferment in 104. It hardly matters whether X. 14 refers to the second or the first Dacian war, since the request to Trajan in X. 13 for the augurate must belong in either case to the absence of Trajan in the first Dacian war, according to the custom (p. 64) that senators only made written requests to the Princeps when he was on a prolonged absence from Rome. For no scholar has ever suggested that IV. 8 belongs to a date later than Mommsen's.

LEGATUS AUGUSTI IN BITHYNIA

The only evidence in Book X for the date of Pliny's mission to Bithynia, where he was in office for a period covering parts of three calendar years (p. 529), is given by the reference to Calpurnius Macer as governor of Moesia Inferior, where Macer is known to have been in office in A.D. III–12 (X. 42 n.). This gives only an approximate correlation, because legates commonly held office for some three or four years. Syme (op. cit. 81) has suggested that a reference in IX. 28. 4 to Voconius Romanus refers to this post in advance, and contains an invitation to Romanus to join Pliny's staff in Bithynia: 'polliceris in fine cum certius de vitae nostrae ordinatione aliquid audieris futurum te fugitivum rei familiaris statimque ad nos evolaturum, qui iam tibi compedes nectimus quas perfringere nullo modo possis'. The language, however, is more appropriate to domestic affairs (nn.), and the dating of the letters in Book IX by book-date is sometimes hazardous. A more general argument from the rather haphazard character of Book IX (p. 50) might suggest that Pliny completed his publication of private letters in a certain hurry, because a forthcoming appointment required him to set aside literary work for a number of years to come. The decks were being cleared for action, and since only one letter in VIII or IX is certainly later than 107 (VIII. 2, 23, prefs.), nothing forbids the suggestion that Pliny went to Bithynia as early as 109.

The supposed omission from Pliny's obituary inscription of the titles of Trajan later than *Dacicus* has been taken to date Pliny's death before the assumption of *Optimus* in 114. But this part of the inscription is a restoration, and the absence of *Optimus* is conjectural, though probable. So this does not help to date Pliny's mission. It is likely that Trajan was in Rome during the period of the Letters, and that his departure for the eastern provinces in autumn 113 is a *terminus ante quem* for them. But though Trajan's presence in Rome may be inferred from x. 63, 65. 3, 68–69, which belong to Pliny's second calendar year in Bithynia, no reference from the letters of the third year, x. 100–3 onwards, indicates this. It is more decisive that there is no reference in the New Year congratulations of x. 35 and 100 to Trajan's assumption of the consulship in 112 for the first time since 103. This should fix Pliny's years to 109–11. The reference in x. 18. 3 to Trajan's building operations in Rome as incomplete, which were finished by the end of 111, supports an early date for the mission.

Technical powers. Pliny's position in Bithynia-Pontus is clear enough, though some have obscured it by equating him with the functionary known as *curator* or *corrector civitatium* that appears from Trajan on. This was an imperial official charged with the supervision of the finances of one or more cities within a province independently of the regular governor. Pliny combines the role of *curator* for *all* the cities of Bithynia-Pontus with the duty of overhauling the public life of the area as its regular governor, under the authority of the Princeps instead of the Senate. See the introduction to Book x, pp. 526 f., where the reasons for his mission are discussed. He was not commissioned to carry out a basic reconstruction either of municipal constitutions or of the machinery of Roman government. He was not, like a proconsul of Cyprus under Augustus, sent *ad componendum statum provinciae* (*ILS* 915), nor was he commissioned, like his friend Maximus in Achaea, *ad ordinandum statum . . . civitatium* (VIII. 24. 2 n.). Apart from specific instructions on some special points (Ep. 22. 1 n.) he was given rather loose directions to deal with any irregularities within the present system by making new regulations: 'ut ea constitueres quae ad perpetuam eius provinciae quietem essent profutura' (Ep. 117 n.). His position is not unlike that of Poppaeus Sabinus, whom Tiberius appointed in A.D. 15 as *legatus propraetore* of Achaea and Macedonia in place of the senatorial proconsuls when these provinces required assistance after the burdens imposed by the Illyrian wars of Augustus (Tac. *Ann.* 1. 76, 80).

Like Sabinus Pliny replaces a proconsul as an extraordinary appointment. That seems to be the only reason why his post is defined in the inscription as *legatus Augusti pro praetore consulari potestate.*

The last two words probably meant that he was attended by six lictors instead of the five normally allowed to the *legati Augusti pro praetore* in imperial provinces. His personal *dignitas* was proconsular. But Pliny makes it clear in Ep. 72 that his position otherwise was technically distinct from that of a proconsul. In the title of his successor Cornutus Tertullus the additional words are omitted (*ILS* 1024).

In addition to his special tasks Pliny is found in the Letters carrying out the ordinary duties of a Roman governor in civil and criminal jurisdiction (x. 56, 58, 65, 72, 81, 96), and in the maintenance of order (x. 19, 31, 74). For this he had the help of an assistant legate (x. 25 n.). But the equestrian procurators of the emperor and their adjutants were not, as has sometimes been held, subordinate to Pliny (x. 21. 1, 27 n.). As in other imperial provinces they were directly responsible to the Princeps in their particular spheres.

See Mommsen, *GS*, iv. 430 f.; Vidman, *Étude*, ch. iv. 42 f.; Rostovtzeff, *BSR*, xxii (1916), 18–19; Premerstein, *RE*, iv. 1647–8. For the *curatores* see Commentary on VIII. 24. 2.

His death. That Pliny died before Trajan, and probably before the end of his governorship, is the implication of the long inscription recording his career and his testamentary dispositions, since whatever the missing titles of Trajan may be in it, he is cited as a living emperor. It is unlikely that Pliny would have finished his work in Bithynia or been replaced before he had completed his second year of office, though a successor is not recorded until 113–14 (p. 84).

XII. THE TEXT OF THE LETTERS IN BRIEF

BOOKS I–IX

THE text of Books I–IX is known from three traditions which are now reckoned equipollent: the manuscripts of the Nine-Book series, containing all nine books with a few minor omissions, those of the Eight-Book series containing I–VII. 33 and IX, and those of the Ten-Book series, which though their source contained all ten books themselves contain only I–V. 6. These groups are designated in the O.C.T. system as α, γ, β. It has come to be accepted in recent years that the basic principle of reconstruction is that the coherence of any two traditions must be generally preferred to the readings of the third, provided that the rhythmical rules of the *clausula* or the Latin usages favoured by Pliny are not violated. This principle was widely argued and employed by S. E. Stout, *Scribe and Critic at work in Pliny's Letters* (Bloomington, 1954), and has been carried further in the O.C.T. edition of Sir R. A. B. Mynors, who corrects the numerous misapprehensions of Stout. The principal difficulty, which afflicted also the Teubner editions of M. Schuster, is to decide what is the best evidence for the γ or Eight-Book tradition. Further difficulties in applying the principle of agreement arise from the loss of the manuscript evidence for the Ten-Book tradition after v. 6, and the absence of VIII from the Eight-Book series. Though the Aldine edition derives from the earliest Ten-Book manuscript (now lost), its evidence is not altogether trustworthy (p. 84). In the Nine-Book series only one of the two manuscripts survives after v. 6, but some further evidence is provided by the recently distinguished, though not satisfactory, group of manuscripts known as θ. For a full and authoritative account of these matters the reader is referred to the O.C.T. introduction.

Considering the frequency of minor variations in the manuscripts it is remarkable how seldom uncertainty of readings affects the historical content. But sometimes a quite minor variation even of word order makes a decisive difference, as in IV. II. I. There the reading of $\beta\gamma$, *praetorius hic modo*, gives a different chronology from the previously favoured *praetorius modo hic*, which appears in a alone. My own preferences where historical points were involved were settled after study of Stout's *Scribe and Critic*, which is still the only systematic discussion of a large collection of variants on the principle of equipollency. They are generally in agreement with the decisions of the editor of the O.C.T., whose text is normally printed in the Commentary of I–IX.

The symbols used in the Commentary are those of the O.C.T., a for the Nine-Book series, β for the Ten-Book, and γ for the Eight-Book series. These correspond to Stout's X, Z, and Y, except that the group of Eight-Book manuscripts which comprise Stout's Y are not the same as those of the O.C.T. γ. Stout's own text (1962) has not been used.

BOOK X

The evidence for the text of Book X is far less satisfactory. The modern text derives principally from two printed editions: Avantius 1502 (*A*) and Aldus[1] 1508 (*a*). Both derive from a manuscript of Parisian origin containing the ten books. The letters now numbered 41–121 were first printed by Avantius, and also by Beroaldus[2] 1503 and Catanaeus[1] 1506, from a copy of these letters alone. But Aldus printed his edition of 1508 directly from the complete manuscript. This *Parisinus* was subsequently lost, but the Morgan fragment Π, containing II. 20. 13–III 5. 4 is thought to have come from it. Hence *Parisinus* was a manuscript of the sixth century. Some of its readings are however known from the manuscript additions (*I*) and numerous corrections (*i*) contained in a printed volume now in the Bodleian.

This book was made up by the scholar Budaeus, who thus completed his copies of the Avantius and Beroaldus 1498 text, which he had bound together. The invaluable evidence of Budaeus shows that Aldus copied his sixth-century manuscript with unusual carelessness, altering and rewriting what he could not be bothered to decipher. Hence the Aldine edition does not possess the primacy that one would expect. The agreement of '*A*' and '*i*' must normally be preferred to '*a*', and where '*i*' differs from both '*A*' and '*a*' it may be right. See O.C.T., preface 8. In the Commentary the O.C.T. text is printed except in corrupt passages, where a prototype reading is left in the citation.

Addendum to XI

An inscription published by Miss J. Reynolds in *Camb. Phil. Soc. Proc.* 1963, 189, dates the legateship of Pliny's probable successor Cornutus Tertullus to include the eighteenth year of Trajan, which should be the regnal year 115–16 rather than the tribunician year 113–14. Neither date decisively affects the chronology of Pliny's appointment, though the latter would favour the earlier chronology proposed above.

Addendum to II

Note as a final sign of the care taken in the revision of the Letters that only twice does a personal vocative of the recipient survive from the original version, in III. 10. I and VII. 21. 1, whereas in Book X Trajan frequently addresses Pliny as *Secunde* and Pliny normally uses *domine* of Trajan. Cf. also I. 15 *heus tu*, IV. 29 *heia tu*.

COMMENTARY ON BOOKS I–IX

BOOK I

1. *To Septicius Clarus*

Date. The latest in the book, written when the rest were ready for publication.

Address. C. Septicius Clarus, an equestrian of Pliny's generation who rose to the praetorian prefecture under Hadrian in *c.* 119, was brother-in-law of another literary equestrian, Erucius Clarus: 1. 16, pref., II. 9. 4 n. He was also connected with Suetonius Tranquillus, who dedicated his *Lives* to Clarus, Ep. 18, pref. He receives I. 15, VII. 28, VIII. 1.

The note resembles the prefatory letters attached to several volumes of Martial and of Statius' *Silvae*. But no other of the nine books has such a letter of dedication. In IX, Ep. 2 might have served for a preface, but is placed second. Books II, III, and V open with a fine set-piece. In VI and VIII a set-piece comes second. IV, VII, and IX, like I, begin with a string of shorter letters.

By dedicating the book to Clarus Pliny avoided offending any senator. Cf. II. 18. 5 (n.) for the touchiness of society: 'nec ignoro suscipiendas offensas in eligendo praeceptore'. It is notable that none of the recipients of Book I are men of mark. There are at most three consulars—Tacitus, and probably Octavius Rufus and Junius Mauricus, Epp. 6, 7, 14, prefs.—several junior and praetorian senators, such as Sosius Senecio, Catilius Severus, Pompeius Falco, whose distinction lay in the future, Epp. 11, 12, 13, 22, 23, prefs.; and several undistinguished equestrians with literary tastes, Epp. 2, 3, 5, 8, 16, 18, 19.

1. **epistulas si quas paulo curatius scripsissem.** Cf. VII. 9. 8 'volo epistulam diligentius scribas' and IX. 28. 5 'litteras curiosius scriptas'. Pliny refers to the composition of literary letters by the wife of Pompeius Saturninus and Voconius Romanus, Ep. 16. 6, and II. 13. 7. In IX. 2. 1–4 Pliny distinguishes his own letters, which he there compares to those of Cicero, after allowing for the difference of circumstances, from what he calls 'scholasticas . . . atque ut ita dicam umbraticas litteras'. So too in III. 20. 11 'habeant nostrae quoque litterae aliquid non humile nec sordidum nec privatis rebus

inclusum'. He is attempting something different from the literary
and philosophical essays in epistolary form of the Senecas. See Introduction, pp. 2 ff. Statius, in a list of literary genres (*Silvae* I. 3. 104),
includes 'seu tua non alia splendescat epistula *cura*'. Also Seneca,
Ep. 75. 1. Here *curatius* or *accuratius*, supported by γ and β against α,
and by the word-order, must be preferred to *cura maiore* of the α tradition (Stout, 54, 143). The O.C.T. is preferable, because closer to *cura*.

   **collegi non servato temporis ordine . . . sed ut quaeque in manus
venerat.** On the significance of this for the chronology of the letters
see pp. 21–2. Guillemin, ad loc., remarks that Pliny is disguising the
care with which he had arranged the sequence of letters in Book I
for effect and variety. So too in his volume of poems IV. 14. 3: 'ipsa
varietate temptamus efficere ut alia aliis quaedam fortasse omnibus placeant'. VIII. 21. 4 'liber fuit et opusculis varius et metris.
ita solemus . . . satietatis periculum fugere'. And in his speech *Pro
Patria*, II. 5. 8, 'ut universitatem omnibus varietas ipsa commendet'.
Pliny was the last man to publish anything carelessly, cf. Ep. 2 *et al.*

**2. ita enim fiet ut eas quae adhuc neglectae iacent requiram et si quas
addidero non supprimam.** This remark well fits Book II, which certainly contains some letters of the date of I. But since I was certainly
published separately from III–IX, and possibly also from II (p. 52),
there is no reason to apply anything in this note to the whole
collection.

2. *To Arrianus Maturus*

Date. Either the work here under preparation or that mentioned as
already published seems to be the *De Helvidi Ultione*. Also Pliny is
at leisure. Hence the period 97–98 is indicated before the prefecture
of Saturn, s. 3, 4 nn.

Address. Arrianus Maturus, an equestrian from Altinum, receives an
equestrian appointment in Egypt later, III. 2 n. The names are rare
in Cisalpine Gaul. Though Arrius is common, Arrianus does not occur
in the index of *CIL* v. The cognomen is also rare, but occurs twice in
inscriptions of Altinum, ibid., nn. 2169, 2266. Arrianus receives
letters about literature and politics, II. 11, 12, IV. 8, 12, VI. 2, VIII. 21.

   1. hunc rogo ex consuetudine tua et legas et emendes. Pliny has a
passion for revision and taking his friends' advice about it, cf. Ep. 8.
3–4, V. 3. 7–11 nn. He sends Arrianus his second volume of verses to
revise thus, VIII. 21.

   eodem ζήλῳ. Only four letters deal formally with the battle of
styles, I. 20, III. 18. 8–10, VII. 12, IX. 26, though I. 5. 11–12, 8. 3–5, 16.
3–4, II. 5. 5–7, 19. 5–6 touch on the theme. Quintilian's essay in *Inst.*

12. 10 discusses the development of Latin rhetorical style and its
contemporary manifestations. The Romans, using Hellenistic technical terms, distinguished principally the Attic and the Asian styles.
The former is characterized as compressed, precise, sharp, polished
('pressi', 'integri', 'acres', 'tersi', &c.) and abused as thin, dry, and
bloodless ('tenues', 'aridi', 'exsangues'); the latter is marked by
fullness, strength, richness, boldness ('abundantes', 'fortes', 'au-
dentes', 'sublimes', 'elati') and a love of startling or precious innovations ('pericula', 'flosculi'), and abused as inflated, wanton, headlong
('tumidi', 'luxuriosi', 'praecipites'). The contrast was too simple for
Quintilian, who complained that purists excluded even Demosthenes
from the Attic canon (cf. Pliny, I. 20. 4), condemned Cicero as Asianist, and confused the primitive Latin orators (*antiqui*), such as the
elder Cato and Gaius Gracchus, with deliberate Atticists such as
Calvus and Caelius among the contemporaries of Cicero. Quintilian
justly observed that the great masters had the best qualities of both
schools, and preferred to label Cicero as a 'Rhodian' from his connexion with the school founded by Aeschines. The old categories did
not fit the development of oratory in the Principate, when a new style
of forensic rhetoric was evolved by the political delators. Though
this had many Asian characteristics, notably its frequent use of
epigrammatic *sententiae*, its special quality was its cult of violence,
which seems alien to the true Asian mode and closer to the forcefulness of the 'Rhodians'. Cassius Severus was its main author, and it
may be best represented by certain political speeches in the Annals of
Tacitus (e.g. 16. 22). Aquilius Regulus, Pliny's *bête noire*, was a
contemporary exponent of this style (Epp. 5. 11, 20. 14 nn.)

Quintilian favours another threefold classification, also of Hellenistic origin: the *subtile*, the *grande ac robustum*, and the *medium ex
duobus* or *floridum*. He prefers the second of these, which is essentially
that of Cicero, and he interprets the third to fit a form of the contemporary style which contained a strong Asian element: 'medius
hic modus et translationibus crebrior et figuris erit iocundior, egressionibus amoenus, compositione aptus, sententiis dulcis, lenior
tamen'(*Inst.* 12. 10. 60). This, if carried to extremes, becomes 'vitiosum
et corruptum dicendi genus quod aut verborum licentia exultat aut
puerilibus sententiis lascivit aut immodico tumore turgescit aut
inanibus locis bacchatur aut casuris . . . flosculis nitet aut
praecipitia pro sublimibus habet' (ib. 73). These two sentences
illuminate much of what Pliny has to say about his own *stilus laetior*.
Pliny also owes much to Quintilian's advice that the best orator
uses the various styles as appropriate in each particular case (ib.
69): 'nec pro causa modo sed pro partibus causae'.

Many passages indicate that Pliny generally preferred a colourful and somewhat exalted style, I. 20. 17–22, III. 18. 10, VII. 12, IX. 26. But in a number of speeches written between 96 and 100 he experimented with a form of Atticism, as in the present case; so too in his *De Helvidi Ultione* (VII. 30. 5), in the library speech at Comum (Ep. 8. 5 n.), the *Pro Patria* (II. 5. 5–6 n.), an extortion speech, probably the *In Priscum* (II. 19. 5–6 nn.), and even, on his own evidence, in the Panegyric (III. 18. 8–10). The present letter, taken with IX. 26, where Pliny defends the grand style, suggested to Guillemin (*VL*, 95 f.) that Pliny round about the year 97 set himself to reform his style, hitherto markedly Asian, by adopting a more 'Ciceronian' tone (presumably the *grande ac robustum* of Quintilian). Others have inferred from the reference to Calvus (s. 2) that Pliny was turning completely 'Atticist'. Neither view quite fits the evidence. The suggestion that Calvus was at one time an exponent of the *grande ac robustum* cannot be maintained, s. 2 n. Though it is true that in the period of the Letters Pliny consistently cites Demosthenes, Aeschines, and Cicero as his models (cf. I. 5. 11–12, 20. 4, VII. 30. 4–5, IX. 26), yet in I. 5. 11–12 Pliny ascribes his imitation of Cicero to the earlier period of his career also, and in the present letter he is combining a new passion for moderate Atticism with his *previous* devotion to Cicero, s. 4. 'non tamen omnino Marci nostri ληκύθους fugimus'.

Perhaps Pliny's most characteristic judgements are in III. 18. 8–10, where while paying tribute to the stricter school he adds 'ac mihi quidem confido *in hoc genere materiae* laetioris styli constare rationem', and in II. 19. 6, where he admits that the stricter style was more serviceable for practical advocacy in ordinary courts. Regulus' criticism of Pliny as not 'contentus . . . eloquentia saeculi nostri' (I. 5. 11–12), his own outburst against the 'effeminate' style of certain young advocates in II. 14. 12–13, and his disclaimer in a discussion of poetic language (IX. 26. 7) 'nec nunc ego me his similia aut dixisse aut posse dicere puto; non ita insanio'—all suggest that he was never a full-blown Asian. His defence of the exalted style, as Guillemin remarked, is always relative to Atticist criticisms. Pliny's own statements indicate that he was an exponent of Quintilian's Mixed Style, and followed closely his advice to adapt one's style to the theme of the moment, and that his own Atticism was limited in extent. Pliny composed in *partes* and each *pars* might have its own style, II. 5. 1–2, 10–12. His friend Pompeius Saturninus seems to have adopted the Mixed Style in much the same fashion (Ep. 16) with a rather stronger dash of Attic salt.

The Panegyric itself, and fragments of Pliny's oratorical style in VIII. 6. 4 f., 14. 17 f., bear out what the Letters, especially I. 20 and IX. 26, suggest, that for Pliny style was largely a question of phraseology, the choice of words; this was characteristic of the newer

orators of the period (Marache, ch. v). In this he might make good
his claim to be a Ciceronian of sorts. But his construction of sentences
and paragraphs, though marked by a fine sense of balance, is seldom
periodic. The characteristic seems to be that a strong, self-contained
opening sentence affirms the theme, which is then elaborated in a
series of following clauses, cunningly balanced by various rhetorical
devices. The paragraph explains itself as it goes along, and can be
cut short at any point without shattering the construction; cf., for
example, *Pan.* 91. But the paragraphs are coherent, and are not
formed of explosive fragments in the late Tacitean manner. Perhaps
this is the *gravis et decora constructio* which Pliny admired in Pompeius Saturninus, Ep. 16. 2.

Some have sought for Pliny's oratorical style in the Letters at large.
Their main characteristic lies in a richness of vocabulary and the
elaboration of doublets, triplets, and cumulations of noun–adjective
and verb–noun combinations, which express his meaning ex-
haustively and describe every facet of an object. Such is the just
analysis of Norden (*Kunstprosa*, 319 ff.), summarized by Prete,
Saggi, 38 ff. Cf. E. Saint-Denis (*Révue universitaire* (1946), 17–18),
who observes that the Asian style was particularly popular with
young writers, citing II. 5. 5 (n.).

See Guillemin, *Vie littéraire*, &c., 87 ff., from whom the above
account is in part developed; Norden, *Die antike Kunstprosa* (1922),
251 ff., for the schools of style; D. A. F. M. Russell, *Longinus* (Oxford,
1964), xxxiv, for the Greek view of the three styles. F. Quadlbauer,
P. der Jüngere über den Begriff der erhabenen Rede, a dissertation
from Graz (1949), apparently stresses the Asian tendency in Pliny
(138 ff., 285 ff.); cf. Ep. 20. 1 n. R. Syme, *Tac.* 104 f., 323 f.,
331 f., gives a non-technical account of the accusatorial orators of
the Principate. R. Marache, *La Critique littéraire . . . et le . . . Goût
archaïsant* (Rennes, 1952), in a long study of the development of
rhetorical style in the Principate, practically ignores the evidence of
Pliny (cf. Ep. 16. 3 n.). He consequently underestimates the value
of the austere style in actual court-work. S. Prete, 'De Plinii . . . ad
Tacitum epistulis', *Giorn. It. Fil.* (1950), 77 f., and *Saggi Pliniani*
(Bologna, 1948), 32 f., gives a similar account to Guillemin's, and
stresses Pliny's love of *varietas*. Bardon, *Litt. Lat. Inc.* ii. 201–2, is brief.

**2. temptavi enim imitari Demosthenen semper tuum, Calvum nuper
meum.** Pliny hints at a new turn of style by using the word ζῆλος,
which means more than *sollicitudo* in a similar context, II. 5. 2.
Arrianus belongs to the moderate rather than to the extreme school
of Atticists called οἱ εὔζηλοι, who excluded practically every orator
except Lysias and the Latin *antiqui*. Cf. I. 16. 2–3, 20. 4, VII. 12,

and Quintilian 12. 10. 21. Since Quintilian groups Calvus with
Caelius, Pollio, and Caesar, while Cicero notes his *attenuata oratio* and
his fear of *vitia* (*Brutus* 283), it is unlikely that he began more floridly,
as Guillemin suggests (*VL*, 95). The elder Seneca (VII. 4. 6–8) compared Calvus to Demosthenes only for stiffness of composition.
Pliny in s. 4 *contrasts* Cicero with Calvus and Demosthenes.

eodem ζήλῳ. See VII. 12. 2 n. for κακόζηλοι and εὔζηλοι.

nam vim tantorum virorum 'pauci quos aequus' . . . adsequi
possunt. Quintilian stresses the *vis* and *impetus* of Demosthenes,
Calvus, and Cicero (10. 1. 115, 12. 10. 23 and 58). Pliny in s. 4 speaks
as if Cicero lacked this, and Calvus criticized Cicero as *solutus et
enervis* (Tac. *Dial.* 18. 5) while Cicero in turn criticized Calvus as
lacking force in delivery (*Ad Fam.* 15. 21. 4).

3. erat enim prope tota in contentione dicendi. This might refer to
Pliny's *De Helvidi Ultione*, which was full of *contentio* (IX. 13) and for
which Pliny read Demosthenes (VII. 30. 5). But the references in s. 4
suit better the *Pro Patria* of II. 5. 5–6. For *contentio* see also II. 19. 5,
in an extortion speech.

desidiae. In Ep. 8. 2 he is *desidiosus*. Since he does not plead
occupationes as in Ep. 10. 9–11—a favourite excuse—this letter
should fall in 97 between his prefecture of the *Aerarium militare* and
that of the Saturnian Treasury.

4. quotiens paulum itinere decedere non intempestivis amoenitatibus
admonebamur. The speech *Pro Patria* was full of 'descriptions of
places' in a style 'laetius . . . quam orationis severitas exigat', but
elsewhere it contained 'severity'. It too was a single volume, like
this (II. 5. 3–6).

ληκύθους. The metaphor is not quite clear. The usual citations are
Cicero, *Ad Att.* 1. 14. 3 'totum hunc locum quem ego varie . . .
soleo pingere, de flamma de ferro—nosti illas λ.'. Hor. *Ep.* 2. 3. 97
'tragicus . . . proicit ampullas et sesquipedalia verba'. Cf. ibid. 1. 3.
14 'an tragica desaevit et ampullatur in arte?' The formal rendering
'paint-pots' seems adequate.

acres enim esse non tristes volebamus. Cf. Ep. 16. 2 n. 'acriter et
ardenter nec minus polite', of the style of Saturninus. This suggests
the 'middle way' of Quintilian, which was also 'egressionibus amoenus' as here.

admonebamur. For the plural see Ep. 8. 3 n. 'nobis'.

5. confitebor et ipsum me et contubernales ab editione non abhorrere.
Suetonius and Voconius are among his literary companions at this
time, I. 24. 1, X. 4. 1.

editione. This and other forms of *edere* refer to the final placing of the much revised book in the hands of the *librarii* or *bibliopolae* to copy and sell. (T. Birt, *Kritik* . . . *des antiken Buchwesens* (Munich, 1913), 308.) Cf. II. 10. 6, V. 10. 2–3, IX. 13. 24. In V. 12. 1 he uses *publicare*. Martial briefly describes the bookshops of the Argiletum and near the Forum Julium in I. 66. 1–12, 117. 8–17. Little is known of the relationship between authors and publishers, except that the latter seem to have paid a lump sum for the right of copying, and acquired the ownership of the work. The satirists and the lawyers alike are surprisingly silent about these transactions. Martial, loc. cit., and 13. 3 mentions the profits and prices of booksellers as if they were of no concern to him. Hence the principal source of livelihood for needy authors seems to have been their patrons. But wealthy men, like Cicero earlier, and Regulus in IV. 7. 2, might finance their own publications, if they did not make them over to a publisher, as Cicero did to Atticus (*Ad Att.* 13. 12. 2). Pliny indicates in S. 6 and IX. 11. 2 that the distribution of his books was entirely in the hands of the *bibliopolae*. See Birt, op. cit. 308 f., 315 f. It seems from IV. 7. 2 that an outsize edition would be of a thousand copies.

6. libelli quos emisimus dicuntur in manibus esse. These are distinct from the writings above. The plural word fits the *De Helvidi Ultione*, for which he always uses the plural, IV. 21. 3, VII. 30. 5, IX. 13. 1, 24, whereas the present work is a single volume. The order of Pliny's works, published or edited in 96–98, seems to be: *Sermo de Bybliotheca*, Ep. 8 nn., *De Helvidi Ultione*, and *Pro Patria*. There follows an interval of public preoccupations, followed by the *In Marium Priscum* (II. 19) in 100 and the *Panegyricus* in 100 or 101 (III. 13, 18).

3. *To Caninius Rufus*

Date. There is no reason to doubt that this is the earliest of the seven letters to Caninius. Six of them touch on literature, and in four he urges Caninius to write seriously, but it is only in the ninth book that Caninius produced something, possibly a 'Dacian War' or the dolphin story, in verse, III. 7. 14, VIII. 4. 1, IX. 33. 11.

Address. Caninius is a wealthy landowner of Comum, much attached to his villa there, who never visits Rome. It is unlikely that he is the like-named Greek of Mytilene. *PIR²*, C 394; *IG*, xii. 2. 88. 19, 375. He receives II. 8, III. 7, VI. 21, VII. 18, VIII. 4, IX. 33, and possibly also VII. 25.

1. Quid agit Comum . . . quid suburbanum amoenissimum? quid illa porticus? For his lands at Comum see II. 8, VII.18. The terms for the various parts of this villa recur in Pliny's descriptions of his own villas, II. 17, V. 6. For the *porticus* see V. 6. 15 n. There is no evidence to locate this villa satisfactorily, though attempts have been made (cf. Sirago, *Ital. agr.* 42).

platanon. V. 6. 20, 'areolam quae quattuor platanis inumbratur'.

euripus. A water-course, Cic. *de Leg.* 2. 2; Sen. *Ep.* 83. 5. Compare those of the House of Loreius Tiburtinus at Pompeii (M. della Corte, *Case ed Abitanti di Pompeii²*, 311).

subiectus et serviens lacus. There may be a legal pun, derived from Statius, *S.* 2. 2. 73–74, 'servit sua terra fenestris'. But cf. V. 6. 23, 'piscinam quae fenestris servit et subiacet'. The *lacus* might be an artificial pool rather than the lake of Como. Cf. IX. 20. 2 n. But for villas overhanging the lake see VI. 24. 2, IX. 7. 3–4.

gestatio. See II. 17. 14, V. 6. 17 nn.

quod plurimus sol implet et circumit. Cf. II. 17. 8, 13, 23.

triclinia illa popularia illa paucorum. Such *triclinia* were not a grand feature of Pliny's country villas (II. 17. 5, 13, V. 6. 19), but he has a 'cotidiana amicorumque cenatio', and his Roman house could contain the audience of a *recitatio* in its *triclinium*, VIII. 21. 2.

cubicula diurna nocturna. II. 17. 22–24.

3. Quin tu (tempus enim) humiles et sordidas curas aliis mandas? Pliny likes to use this tone in literary correspondence, VII. 30. 3, IX. 15 *et al.*, but his anxious care for his own estates is not in doubt, II. 4. 3 n. Caninius also put first things first, s. 2, 'ut solebas . . . .'.

4. *To Pompeia Celerina*

Date. The letter describes a journey in Etruria which may well be the occasion of Pliny's protracted absence from Rome in Ep. 7, in the autumn of a year earlier than his prefecture of Saturn, and hence before 98.

Address. Pompeia Celerina is the mother of presumably his second wife, who died in 96–97. She is now married to Bittius Proculus, IX. 13. 4, 13. His third wife Calpurnia had no female relative alive closer than her aunt, IV. 19. 1, 6, VIII. 11. 1. Pompeia might be connected with the consular L. Pompeius . . . Celer, *PIR²*, F 544. For her wealth and friendship with Pliny see I. 18. 3, III. 19. 8, VI. 10. 1 nn.

1. Quantum copiarum in Ocriculano in Narniensi in Carsulano in Perusino tuo. The first three municipalities named are stages from south to north along the Via Flaminia, which Pliny would leave at Mevaunia to reach the fourth place, Perusia, on his way to his villa at Tifernum Tiberinum. From VIII. 8. 1 (n.) it appears that he did not ordinarily use the shorter route by Ameria and Tuder to Perusia.

copiarum. Domestic supplies are meant, as in II. 17. 26, VI. 28. 1, not produce of the farms.

in Narniensi vero etiam balneum. Pliny is surprised that the servants have it ready for his passing visit (Guillemin), cf. II. 17. 26, 'si forte balineum domi vel subitus adventus vel brevior mora calfacere dissuadeat.'

ex epistulis meis (nam iam tuis non opus est) una illa brevis et vetus sufficit. Guillemin, finding this difficult, suggests that *illa* is neuter plural, but the obscurity, if any, arises only from Pliny's revision; *una illa epistula* is a simple cross-reference to something in the preceding correspondence. No emendation is necessary, such as Wagenvoort's ingenious *exceptis epistulis*.

2. idem fortasse eveniet tibi si quando in nostra deverteris. Pliny later uses another villa of Pompeia at Alsium thus, and that of a friend in Campania, VI. 10. 28. Doubtless Pompeia kept these houses in commission to facilitate tours of management round her estates. The wealthy evidently used each other's villas instead of the uncomfortable public inns.

5. *To Voconius Romanus*

Date. The letter is dated to the first month of 97 by the reference to the ceremony of the praetors' new year, 10–11 nn.

Address. Voconius Romanus is a literary equestrian friend of Pliny from Saguntum in Spain, now resident in Italy, for whom he secured senatorial status and other privileges from Nerva and Trajan, II. 13, X. 4 nn. The letters to him cover most topics except estates' business, II. 1, III. 13, VI. 15, 33, VIII. 8, IX. 7, 28.

1. Vidistine quemquam M. Regulo timidiorem . . . post Domitiani mortem? After the death of Domitian, 16 September 96, there was a general attack in the Senate on the minor agents of his 'tyranny', the *delatores* of less than senatorial rank, IX. 13. 4 n. Pliny by the end of the year is nerving himself to join in the witch-hunt, but is looking for a more substantial victim and now picks on Regulus (cf. ss. 15–16). Finally in mid-97 he launches his attack on the praetorian senator Publicius Certus, as described in IX. 13.

M. Regulo. This man, M. Aquilius Regulus, is best known from Pliny's letters and, for his earlier career, from Tac. *Hist.* 4. 42. Sundry references in Martial add little of substance (1. 12, 82; 2. 74; 4. 16; 6. 38). Son of a ruined exile, he gained place and fortune by his ability as an advocate in both civil and criminal courts. Nothing is known of his senatorial career after his quaestorship (Tac. *Hist.*), but it is apparent from II. II. 22 that he did not pass beyond the praetorship, if so far (*pace* Syme, *JRS* (1953), 161). Between A.D. 64 and 68 as a young man he successfully prosecuted three consulars on capital charges, gaining much prize money, a quaestorship, and a priesthood from Nero, s. 3 n. But in 70 he was barely saved from condemnation as a vexatious *accusator* by his half-brother Vipstanus Messala. Thereafter he acted only for the defence in criminal trials, no Flavian victims being marked against him by Pliny, despite his ill-will (s. 2). He became the leader of the Centumviral bar under Domitian (IV. 7. 3–5, VI. 2, Martial 6. 38). *PIR²*, A 1005; Garzetti, *C.* 15; Syme, *Tac.* 101 f.

sub quo non minora flagitia commiserat quam sub Nerone sed tectiora. Like Fabricius Veiento (IV. 22. 4 n.) he ceased from *accusatio* after Nero, so that Tacitus and Pliny can name only Neronian victims. Few have noted this—Bardon ranks him among the Flavian delators (*Litt. Lat. Inc.* 201–2). But in Martial he saves *rei*.

In *Dialogus* 7–8 Tacitus gives the highest praise to Vibius Crispus and Eprius Marcellus as men who rise from social obscurity to high fortune and distinction in the imperial service 'sine commendatione natalium sine substantia facultatum'. He says not a word about their phase as delators, though they had been notorious under Nero (Tac. *Hist.* 4. 41–43). Such men could not begin to rise without the fall of others, but this was in the oldest tradition of Roman public life. The practice of accusation became disreputable only when professional advocates, bent on earning a regular income from the rewards given by the laws for successful prosecution, twisted the system for private profit or political advancement. Thus in Tac. *Ann.* 4. 68 six praetorian senators in search of a consulship trap an incautious *eques* into careless talk, on which they base a charge of treason. For the origins of professional delation under Tiberius see Tac. *Ann.* 1. 74, 2. 34, 4. 30. There arose also a host of minor figures concerned with the enforcement of the numerous *leges publicae* which formed the framework of the Roman social and criminal law. These provided the counter-victims when a 'tyrannical' Princeps was replaced by a friend of the Senate, but the higher figures usually survived; cf. IX. 13. 4, 21 nn. Quintilian defends the practice of *accusatio* so long as it is done for the public cause and not for profit (12. 7. 1–3). Regulus had offended against the feeling that men ought not to initiate delations save in self-defence, Tac. *Hist.* 4. 42: 'sponte accusationem subisse . . . nec depellendi periculi sed in spem potentiae videbatur'. So too Italicus Silius, III. 7. 3: 'credebatur sponte accusasse'. The only excuse was to plead imperial orders, Tac. *Ann.* 13. 43; Tac. *Hist.*

4. **40, 42.** But the professional delator could not be eliminated, because the Roman state had no other means of enforcing its laws, cf. II. 16. 3–4 nn. Their activity was controlled within limits by the rules about vexatious prosecution (*calumnia*, VI. 31. 12, VII. 33. 7 nn.), collusion (*praevaricatio*, III. 9. 29–33 nn.), *destitutio* or abandonment of a brief (v. 4. 2, 13. 2–5 nn.), and 'circumvention' (below s. 4 n.).

For a summary of the development of delation under Tiberius see Syme, *Tac.* 326 f.; F. B. Marsh, *The Reign of Tiberius* (London, 1931), 107 f.

sed tectiora. His technique is indicated by s. 2. and 4–6 nn.

2. Rustici Aruleni periculum. Junius Arulenus Rusticus, brother of Junius Mauricus (s. 15), was educated in Nero's reign in the tradition of political *libertas* current in the circle of the senator Thrasea Paetus, a staunch defender of senatorial privileges, whose condemnation for treason he sought to veto as tribune in 66 (III. 11. 3, 16. 10 nn.; Tac. *Ann.* 16. 26). As praetor in 69 he led a deputation of the Senate after the defeat of Vitellius to make peace with the advancing Flavian army, Tac. *Hist.* 3. 80. Under the Flavian régime he apparently followed the lead of Helvidius Priscus, Thrasea's son-in-law, in criticism and opposition, and was accused and condemned *c.* 93 with other members of this set, III. 11 nn. The charge against Arulenus was based on his praise of Thrasea and Helvidius in a biography of the latter, and on his interest in political philosophy, Suet. *Dom.* 10. 3; Tac. *Agric.* 2. 1; Dio 67. 13. 2. Yet despite this he seems to have been given a very belated consulship only a year earlier, if the entry in the Fasti of Potentia for 92—'Q. Arulenus Rust[icus]—refers to him, as Syme takes it (*Tac.* 83 n.) and not to a son of Cn. Arulenus Caelius Sabinus, consul in 69 and jurisconsult under Vespasian, whose relationship remains obscure. *PIR²*, A 1194. For the Cisalpine origin of Rusticus, and for his children, still in their teens, see I. 14. 1, II. 18.

exsultaverat morte. The younger Helvidius, Senecio, and Rusticus were executed, while those less deeply involved, such as Mauricus, Arria, and Fannia, were exiled or relegated, Tac. *Agric.* 45. VII. 19. 4–6, IX. 13. 5 nn.

Stoicorum simiam adpellat. A philosophic element enters into politics only under the Flavians, III. 11. 2 n., VIII. 22. 3 n. Thrasea Paetus heard philosophers, but did not act on their principles, to judge by his actions in Tacitus' Annals. Arulenus, who heard Plutarch (*de curios.* 15), had the great Stoic teacher Musonius Rufus in his company during the affair of 69, when he received his 'Vitellian wound' (Tac. *Hist.* 3. 80–81), and perhaps Dio Chrysostom, if the unknown victim of Domitian in Dio's *de exilio* 13. 1 may be identified with Arulenus. For Musonius see III. 11. 5 n.

3. **lacerat Herennium Senecionem.** For the senator Senecio and his misfortunes, fellow victim with Rusticus, see III. 11. 3, VII. 19. 5, 33. 4 n. He made too many enemies by poking fun at Regulus' oratory like Modestus below, defending Valerius Licinianus in the affair of the Vestals, and prosecuting the influential Baebius Massa, IV. 7. 5, II. 12–13, VII. 33. The basic charge against him was his composition of a life of the elder Helvidius Priscus, VII. 19. 5, 33. 7–8 nn.

Mettius Carus. He prosecuted Senecio and laid information against Pliny himself, VII. 19. 5, 27. 14 n. His career as an accuser was brief, beginning about 93 and ending before Domitian's death. Tacitus and Juvenal rank him with Baebius Massa and Catullus Messalinus among the terrors of the times, and Martial names him as a dangerous delator, Tac. *Agric.* 45. 1; Schol. *in Iuv.* 1. 36; Mart. 12. 25. Possibly he is the poet Carus of Mart. 9. 23–24; his death may be recorded in angry lines of 10. 77. *PIR¹*, M 402. His senatorial standing seems uncertain.

'**numquid ego Crasso aut Camerino molestus sum?**' **quos ille sub Nerone accusaverat.** Regulus made the most of his opportunities in the last years of Nero. He had a feud with the house of the Licinii Crassi, one of whom may have ruined his father, cf. II. 20. 2 n. 'marito inimicissimis'. He secured the death of M. Licinius Crassus Frugi, consul of 64, and maltreated, it was said, the corpse of his brother, L. Calpurnius Piso Licinianus, the heir and colleague of Galba, Tac. *Hist.* I. 48, 4. 42; *PIR²*, ii, C 300; *PIR¹*, L 131. Piso's father-in-law, the aged consular Q. Sulpicius Camerinus, and his son, made a second and third victim (*PIR¹*, S 713; Dio 62 (63). 18. 2). A fourth, about the same time, not mentioned by Pliny, was Sergius Cornelius Salvidienus Orfitus, consul in 51, and founder of one of the longest-lived of the noble houses of the Empire (*PIR²*, ii, C 1444; Tac. *Hist.* 4. 42; Suet. *Nero* 37. 1; Dio 62. 27. 1).

4. **cum recitaret librum non adhibuerat.** Pliny lets slip his complaisance under Domitian. He did not avoid the salon of Regulus in the ordinary course. So too he admits acting with Regulus as an advocate, Ep. 20. 14. Regulus' book would seem to be a hostile sketch in the tradition of Caesar's *Anticato*. For the fashion for biography, generally laudatory, see III. 10. 1 n.

capitaliter ipsum me apud centumviros lacessisset. Cf. v. 1. 7 n. 'ne ex centumvirali iudicio capitis rei exirent'. Regulus avoids initiating accusations, but provides the materials of a treason charge for others to exploit: 'periculum foverat'. Such behaviour might now be construed as an offence under that Lex Cornelia which established the crime 'coire convenire ne quis iudicio circumveniretur'. The law applied primarily to *iudices*, presidents of courts, and witnesses, and might be invoked when a charge of *calumnia* did not lie. Cic. *Pro Clu.* 148; *Dig.* 48. 8. 1 (Marcian); Mommsen, *D. Pen. R.* xviii (ii), 349 ff.

centumviros. For this court, mainly concerned with cases of inheritance, see II. 14, V. 9, VI. 33. 3 nn.

5. aderam Arrionillae Timonis uxori rogatu Aruleni. Timon must be one of Arulenus' philosopher friends. The name Arrionilla suggests that Timon married into the family of Thrasea and Arria. Compare the marriage of Musonia and Artemidorus, III. 11. 7. The emendation *Aristyllae* is unnecessary, and grounded only in a mention of the letters of one Timoxenus and Aristylla in Plut. *de praecept. coni.* 46.

rogatu Aruleni. Pliny's connexion went back to his youth, Ep. 14. 1.

nitebamur nos in parte causae sententia Metti Modesti optimi viri: is tum in exsilio erat, a Domitiano relegatus. Possibly the case concerned a provincial property which had come under the jurisdiction of Modestus as legate in Lycia; cf. x. 58. 3: 'sententia proconsulis'.

Trebonius Proculus Mettius Modestus, son of a Domitianic prefect of Egypt, Mettius Rufus. His career is obscure, but includes the government of Lycia. The like-named consul of 103, later proconsul of Asia, is probably his son rather than himself. *PIR*[1], M 355; Garzetti, *C.* 99; *FO*. The son was twice concerned in provincial decisions known from documents, *OGIS* 502, n. 4 (*CIL*, iii. 355); *DS*[2] 386.

nitebamur nos. Pliny appears as a witness in s. 6 and perhaps was not advocate in this case, despite *aderam* above.

exsilio . . . relegatus. Pliny elsewhere (VII. 19. 4, IX. 13. 5) fails to distinguish between exile and the less severe penalty of relegation; for these see II. 11. 19, IV. 11. 3 nn. The senior Rufus' name is possibly erased on Egyptian monuments; but there is little to connect the family misadventures with the conspiracies of either 89 or 93, as suggested by Pflaum n. 45.

6. quid de pietate Modesti sentias. The immediate question concerned the *pietas* of Modestus as judge, cf. 'impietatis reum' of an advocate VII. 33. 7 n.; but the implication was obvious, and presumably Modestus had been condemned for *maiestas minuta*.

8. apprehendit Caecilium Celerem, mox Fabium Iustum. Celer seems to be unknown outside Pliny, unless he is connected with the *praetorius* L. Caecilius Celer Rectus (*CIL*, ii. 190) from Olisipo, *PIR*[2], C 28–29. Perhaps he is the recipient of the letter on recitations, VII. 17.

Fabium Iustum. His connexion with barristers and oratory is shown by Tacitus' dedication of the *Dialogus* to him, and by VII. 2. 1, 'scripta nostra desideres'. He was *praetorius* in 96–98, suffect consul in 102, and governor of Syria by 109. The family might be of Spanish origin; the name recurs, like that of Celer, at Olisipo, *CIL*, ii. 214. These may be friends of the Elder Pliny, from his Spanish connexion, like Voconius Romanus (II. 13. 4, III. 5. 17, VI. 20. 5 nn.). *PIR²*, iii, F 41; Garzetti, *C.* 56; *AE* (1940) n. 210. Pliny addresses two short notes to him, I. 11 and VII. 2. Syme, *JRS* (1957), 131 ff., makes much of Fabius Justus, deducing imperial appointments from these two notes, otherwise untestified.

pervenit ad Spurinnam. The aged consular Vestricius Spurinna had much influence in these years, securing second and third consulships in 98 and 100. See II. 7. 1–2 and III. 1. 11–12 nn. Like other notables he was prepared to countenance the leading men of the previous reign, cf. IV. 22. 4–6 nn.

9. coimus in Porticum Liviae. Pliny's house was in the Esquiline district (III. 21. 5), and the Portico of Livia was not far off, on the Mons Oppius above the Clivus Suburanus (Ashby, *Top. Dict.* s.v.).

10. exspecto Mauricum (nondum ab exilio venerat). This helps to date the Regulus incident before the Certus affair of 97, which was after the return of the fellow exiles Arria and Fannia, IX. 13. 5. The second phrase seems to be an editorial addition by Pliny to the original version, cf. ss. 15–16.

The career of Junius Mauricus is not well known. Already a senator in A.D. 68–70 he first appears trying to abate the violence of the post-Neronian reaction against favourites and delators, remarking that men will live to regret Nero, Tac. *Hist.* 4. 40; Plut. *Galba* 8. Martial praised his *aequitas* in 5. 28. 5, and Pliny his common sense, s. 16 below. This earned him a place as a familiar of Nerva and on the *consilium* of Trajan, IV. 22. 3–6 nn. Hence also he was less deeply involved against Domitian than his brother Arulenus, and escaped the death sentence. Whether he was a consular is as yet unknown. His cognomen, in which the *i* is long according to Martial, may be Celtic, like Mariccus (Tac. *Hist.* 2. 61). The family was of Cisalpine origin, Ep. 14. 4 n. Three letters are addressed to him, two on family affairs, I. 14 and II. 18, and the short note VI. 14. *PIR¹*, J 504; Garzetti, *C.* 83.

11. paucos post dies ipse me Regulus convenit in praetoris officio. The ceremony at the installation of new magistrates was one of the many routine duties of public life at Rome, II. 1. 8, IV. 17. 6, IX. 37. 1. The praetors entered office on 1 January, which helps to date this letter.

Satrio Rufo. He supports Certus in the debate of 97, as a *praetorius* senior to Pliny (IX. 13. 17), but his career is not known (cf. Garzetti, *C.* 138) unless he is a connexion of the Flavian senator and officer of Potentia, known from a broken inscription as ' ( )atrio Q. f. Hor. Sep... TO (?)', *ILS* 2719. Municipal magistrates of this name are known from Iguvium and Teanum Sidicinum, *ILS* 5531, 9389.

eloquentia saeculi nostri. For this usage of *saeculum* see X. 1. 2 n. Regulus was an exponent of the 'new style' of the age of delators, cf. Epp. 2. 1–2 nn., 20. 14 n.

14. epistula quadam, quae apud Domitianum recitata est. The document was apparently read out at his trial. The phrase *apud principem* is commonly used of imperial *cognitiones*, with the emperor as sole judge, as in Tac. *Dial.* 7. 1: 'aut apud principem libertos et procuratores . . . defendere'. But trials of senators under Domitian were usually staged before the Senate as court, not *intra cubiculum*, cf. Tac. *Agric.* 45. 2 and IV. 11. 6 n.

15. locuples factiosus curatur a multis, timetur a pluribus. Compare Tacitus' description of the advocates Vibius Crispus and Eprius Marcellus under Vespasian, *Dial.* 7. 3–4: 'inlustres sunt in urbe non solum apud negotiosos et rebus intentos sed etiam apud iuvenes vacuos . . . potentissimi sunt civitatis ac . . . principes in amicitia Caesaris agunt feruntque cuncta'.

factiosus. Of an advocate, in IV. 9. 5: 'dicerem causas quibus factiosissimum quemque . . . offendisset'. For 'factiones accusatorum' cf. Tac. *Ann.* 4. 21, 6. 16. For the wealth of Regulus see II. 20. 13 n.

16. potest tamen fieri ut haec concussa labantur. Pliny is considering a direct accusation of calumnious activity: the *consilii huius* of s. 10. A similar situation arose in A.D. 70, Tac. *Hist.* 4. 43: 'spem caperet Helvidius posse etiam Marcellum (*sc.* Eprium) prosterni'. Pliny sees that Regulus could not be swept away as easily as the 'inimici dumtaxat minores' of IX. 13. 4. Mauricus evidently gave the same advice as he had given thirty years before—to let well alone, though not for fear of Regulus, since Pliny did not hesitate to publish two satirical letters about him in these years; cf. II. 20. When later in 97 Pliny opened a stronger case against Publicius Certus without support from Mauricus or the elder statesman Corellius Rufus, the general feeling of the Senate was expressed as 'salvi simus qui supersumus', IX. 13. 6–7, 15–16, 22.

6. *To Cornelius Tacitus*

Date. Not exactly determinable. The hunting may be connected with the visit to Tuscany of Ep. 4. The theme of the letter is repeated in a

different setting at a much later date in IX. 10. 1–2 nn. The two
notes, when carefully compared, are much less closely connected than
has been supposed by those who make IX. 10 the reply to this, s. 2 n.

Address. For the odd notion that this letter was written by Tacitus
see s. 2 n. The career of the future historian, like Pliny's, is of moderate distinction, so far as it is known. His praetorship in 88 was
probably followed by a legateship before his consulship in 97,
which led after the usual interval to a proconsulship of Asia (II. 1. 6,
IV. 13. 1 n.; Syme, *Tac.* 65 ff.). He was noted at this time as a successful advocate and perhaps as the author of the *Agricola,* published
late in 97 (ibid. 3). The publication of the *Dialogus* may be in 102 or
later (VII. 20. 1 n.). The six letters to Tacitus in I–VI are rather more
formal than the five in VII–IX, which form a interconnected series
(VII. 20, pref.). The former give the impression that Tacitus was not
one of Pliny's most intimate friends at this period, though no other
person is the recipient of so many letters as Tacitus in I–VI or in the
whole collection. Ep. 20 is an academic discourse. IV. 13 has several
formal touches (ibid., ss. 2, 10). VI. 9 is as between acquaintances.
The present note is only a literary conceit. So too the incidental
references to Tacitus in II. 1. 6, 11. 2, IV. 15. 1 lack intimacy;
Tacitus is never *noster.* Possibly Tacitus' request for the account of
the Elder Pliny's death and the Vesuvius eruption (VI. 16) which
the nephew alone could supply, led to the literary friendship that
emerges suddenly in VII. 20. Syme, *Tac.* 112 f., takes a somewhat
similar view of the relationship of Pliny and Tacitus, but misses the
distinction between the earlier and later group of letters and references.

1. **apros tres et quidem pulcherrimos cepi.** Pliny's references to his
hunting seem to be confined to the Tuscan estate, V. 6. 46, 18. 2,
IX. 10. 1, 16. 1, 36. 6. Hunting was possible at Comum, but fishing
was preferred, II. 8. 1, IX. 7. 4.

    ad retia sedebam. There are many illustrations of ancient hunting
in mosaics and sculpture. See the illustrations in J. Aymard, *Essai
sur les Chasses romaines* (Paris, 1951), or the magnificent reproduction in G. Jennison, *Animals for Show and Pleasure, etc.* (Manchester,
1937), p. 145. The nets, of great length, formed a curving trap into
which the beasts were driven and then slain with skill and danger.

    erat in proximo non venabulum aut lancea sed stilus et pugillares.
Cf. V. 18. 2, IX. 36. 6.

    By *pugillares* is meant either the usual waxed wooden tablets or
the recently introduced 'pugillares membranei'. Cf. Martial, I. 2, 14.
7, 184; T. Birt, in Müller's Handbuch, *Kritik . . . des antiken Buchwesens,* 260, 289 f.

2. **silvae et solitudo ipsumque illud silentium . . . magna cogitationis incitamenta sunt.** In IX. 10. 2 the notion that writing poetry is easier 'inter nemora et lucos' is attributed to Tacitus. Here Pliny initiates the thought, which was a commonplace (ibid. n.). He repeats it in Ep. 9. 6. So too with the conceit about Dinaa and Minerva in s. 3 and IX. 10. 1. Hence the notion of L. Hermann and others (*Latomus* (1955), 349 ff.) that either letter was written by Tacitus needs no serious discussion. Cf. IX. 10 nn. (Prete, *Saggi*, 80).

 cogitationis. Of composition as in IX. 36. 2: 'cogito si quid in manibus, cogito . . . nunc pauciora nunc plura ut . . . componi tenerive potuerunt'. The word is a favourite with Pliny. Here Pliny is composing prose. In IX. 10 it is verse. Here he writes *ad retia*, there *in via*.

7. *To Octavius Rufus*

Date. The reference to Pliny's absence from Rome in September–October should date the letter to September 97; his acceptance of a brief dates it before his prefecture of Saturn, ss. 3–4 n. The reference to the poems of Octavius sets it before II. 10, s. 5 n. There is no case for a late date, s. 2 n.

Address. This poetaster may be C. Marius Marcellus Octavius Publius Cluvius Rufus, suffect consul in 80, evidently a relation of the historian Cluvius Rufus, though Garzetti, *Inc.* 95, does not connect the two. *FO; CIL*, xvi. 26. He appears only here and in II. 10, a letter about his verses.

2. **fas est mihi . . . excusare Baeticis contra unum hominem advocationem.** Pliny has been asked to represent the province of Baetica and also the defendant in what would seem, from the reference to the Massa case in s. 2, to be an extortion case, though Pliny is not explicit. A province might need representation in any dispute before the Princeps, though in such cases the principals often spoke for themselves, IV. 22. 1–2. But in an extortion case a senatorial advocate was essential, II. 11. 2 n. This case cannot be identified with that of Caecilius Classicus, which was offered to Pliny when on leave from his prefecture of Saturn in September 98 or 99, III. 4. 2, X. 8. 6 nn. Details disagree. Classicus was dead before Pliny came into the case, and more than *unum hominem* were involved, III. 4. 7, 9. 6 (Asbach, 41, correcting Masson). The dates of the holidays also differ, 4 n.

 provinciam, quam tot officiis, tot laboribus, tot etiam periculis meis aliquando devinxerim. Pliny refers to the prosecution of Baebius Massa on behalf of Baetica in 93, which alone of his extortion cases involved him in *pericula*, VII. 33 nn. The plurals are no reason for dating this incident later than the Classicus case, as Asbach, loc. cit.,

sought to do. Pliny uses *pericula* of the Massa case alone in III. 4. 6.
Besides he is not yet *patronus* of Baetica as he was by the time of the
Classicus case, III. 4. 4 n., a stronger argument for refusing the
request of Gallus (Schultz, art. cit. 9 ff., against Asbach, loc. cit.).

fidei ... constantiae. The virtues of an advocate, III. 9. 23 n., v. 13. 2 n.

quam diligis a reference to some remark in the letter of Octavius.

4. me circa Idus Octobris spero Romae futurum. After his appointment in early 98 to the prefecture of Saturn he could only leave
Rome with official permission, *commeatus*. During his first such
leave, in September 98 or more probably 99, he was invited, at
Rome in the Senate, to prosecute Classicus, III. 4. 2, x. 8. But that
leave was for an exact month, and his return was required by 1
October to resume his turn as president of the Treasury, x. 8. 3; cf.
III. 6. 6, v. 14. 9 for the precision of leave. Hence this holiday must
precede his appointment, and should be in 97. The year 96 is probably
excluded by the circumstances of Domitian's death and Nerva's
accession in mid September.

Octobris. It seems to be normal at this period for indictments of
extortion to follow fairly closely on the return of the proconsuls in
July–August from their provinces. So too Classicus.

**eademque haec praesentem quoque tua meaque fide Gallo con-
firmaturum.** Gallus need not be the indicted man, but the *reus* must
have been one of the very first of the proconsuls who seized the
opportunity of Domitian's death to plunder their provinces in a
way that was rare in his lifetime, Suet. *Dom.* 8. 2: 'e quibus plerosque
post illum reos omnium criminum vidimus'. He must be the proconsul in office, June 96–June 97, if his indictment is to fall before
Pliny's appointment to the Treasury. Possibly Gallus is the pre-
torian senator Pomponius Gallus Didius Rufus and recipient of II. 17,
VIII. 20. See II. 17, pref.

5. quatenus tu me tuis agere non pateris. Pliny returns to this theme
in II. 10, where Octavius' verses are still being kept from the public,
though a few have leaked out.

6. accepisse me careotas optimas. The addition may be a literary
convention, cf. VII. 21. 4, 'gallinam ut a te missam libenter accepi'.
But Pliny gets the season right.

8. *To Pompeius Saturninus*

Date. Among earliest of the letters, written before any of Pliny's
Nervan works were ready (2 n.), and not long after Domitian's death
(17 n.). Yet the letter should be later than Ep. 16, where he appears
as a new friend.

Address. Pompeius Saturninus' career is unknown. He would seem
to be an equestrian advocate (VII. 15. 2). He is not to be identified
with the consul of *CIL* vi. 2018, who is Herennius Saturninus.
*PIR*¹, P 491. He is evidently a recent acquaintance of Pliny (Ep. 16),
as the tone of this letter also suggests. He is not from Comum nor
yet a Cisalpine (s. 2, 'municipes meos' n.), and hence is distinct from
the Saturninus of Comum reported dead in v. 7. The letters to or
about him concern literature and learned friends, I. 16, V. 21, VII.
7–8, 15, IX. 38. The absence of letters from II–IV suggests an absence
of Pompeius from Italy on a provincial appointment. The name
Pompeius Saturninus is remarkably rare in epigraphy, though not
so, it seems, to Pliny, Ep. 16. 1 n. The extant indexes of *CIL* supply
only about a couple of examples for all Italy and some four from the
west European provinces; even Africa, where Saturninus is a common
name, has only five Pompeii Saturnini.

2. nec me timide uti decet eo quod oblatum est. Pliny labours the
point. With his older friends he takes literary co-operation for
granted, e.g. I. 2. 1, II. 5. 2, III. 13. 1.

**non est tamen quod ab homine desidioso aliquid novi operis ex-
spectes.** So he has not yet composed his *De Helvidi Ultione*, of 97, nor
his *Pro Patria* mentioned in II. 5. 3. The *sermo* offered seems to have
been originally delivered in the latter part of 96 before the death
of Domitian, s. 17 n. Also, Pliny is out of office, as in Ep. 2.
6 n., *desidiosus* not *occupatus*. So the date should be at the turn of
96–97.

rursus vaces sermoni quem apud municipes meos habui. Had
Saturninus been a man of Comum or a Cisalpine, Pliny would have
written *nostros* instead of *meos*, cf. Ep. 14. 4 n. So too in VII. 15. 2
Saturninus' home is *rei publicae suae* not *nostrae*. Saturninus would
have heard this speech at a recitation of Pliny; cf. I. 13. 6, II. 10. 7,
19. 1 for his recitations at this period.

bibliothecam. He announced his scheme for *alimenta* at the same
time, s. 10. In his epitaph, which lists his benefactions in order of
time, these two are given as his first and apparently as his only
benefactions while alive. The cost of the library is given as S.1,000,000
and the *alimenta* (VII. 18. 2) cost S.500,000 out of the S.1,600,000
which he had given to Comum by the date of v. 7, while the epitaph
states that he also gave S.100,000 for the maintenance of the library.
This is his first large benefaction since his father's death. For his
relatively straitened circumstances at this period see II. 4. 3–4 nn.

3. qua soles lima. Pliny expects Saturninus to approve his style,
which in this speech was Atticist, s. 5. But cf. Ep. 16. 2–4. Pompeius
was a compromiser over style.

lima. The term sometimes has an Atticist tone, e.g. I. 2. 5, 20. 22; Quint. 12. 10. 17.

publicare. For publication methods see Ep. 2. 5.

nobis. Pliny's use of the plural in these sections, following the singular *me* and *meus* in the opening and closing sections of the letter, reflects his embarrassment at his own desire to boast and yet be modest. Ordinarily when Pliny uses *nos* there is a clear reference to a second person, as in the case of joint revision, Ep. 2. 6. Cf. II. 19. 8, V. 7. 1, IX. 28. 3. But the plural verb is singular in intent in IV. 14. 2–5, on the composition of poems: 'his iocamur', etc. Pliny's attitude is an advance on the classical behaviour of the Magnanimous Man, who claims his dues of praise: cf. II. 4. 2 n.

5. stilus ipse pressus demissusque. This speech is in Pliny's new Atticizing mode, Ep. 2. 1–2 nn.

munificentia parentum nostrorum. Probably this refers to the 'Templum Aeternitatis Romae et Augusti' built at the cost of L. Caecilius Secundus and dedicated by his son, Secundus, in the addition to *CIL*, v. 745 (p. 732).

8. ut subitae largitionis comitem paenitentiam caveremus. Cf. V. 11. 3, VI. 34. 2 for the reluctance which often accompanied large acts of municipal generosity, despite their frequency—it irked them but they did it.

10. annuos sumptus in alimenta ingenuorum pollicebamur. It was common to promise a second benefaction when completing the first, V. 11. 1: 'ut initium novae liberalitatis esset consummatio prioris'. The reason is given in II. 13. 9: 'haec beneficia mea tueri nullo modo melius quam ut augeam possum, praesertim cum ipse . . . dum priora accipit posteriora mereatur'. So too III. 4. 6. It is part and parcel of the patronage system, cf. x. 26.

alimenta. For the organization of Pliny's scheme, and of the big national schemes carried out under Trajan, see VII. 18 nn. They provided monthly or annual allowances for boys and girls of the municipalities concerned. Pliny follows imperial example—but whose? Asbach attributed the national scheme to Domitian's invention because of the indirect implication of Pliny, *Pan.* 28. 2: 'nullam alimentis crudelitatem redemisti'. The *Epitome de Caesaribus* 12. 4 attributes the large extension of *alimenta* at public expense throughout Italy to Nerva. Pliny speaks in x. 8. 1 of Nerva's exhortation of the citizenry to munificence. But the date of his own *alimenta* is Domitianic, if the argument based on s. 17 is correct. For the controversy see Garzetti, *Nerva*, 70 n. 2; Sirago, *Ital. agr.* 276 f.

debeant . . . reprimi. Pliny disliked public shows of an unintellectual kind, IV. 22, IX. 6.

11. ut . . . libenter educationis taedium laboremque suscipiat. This passage, with *Pan.* 28. 5–6, shows that the main motive in the alimentary foundations was not pure charity but increase of the population: 'hi subsidium bellorum ornamentum pacis . . . ex his castra ex his tribus replebuntur . . .', etc.

taedium. Here and in II. 7. 5, IV. 15. 3, Pliny expresses the objection of the wealthy classes: 'eo saeculo quo plerisque etiam singulos filios orbitatis praemia graves faciunt'. The 'plebes cui consulebatur' of s. 17 might have different feelings in the matter. Limitation of families is common enough in periods of expanding economy, especially in marginal wage-earning classes, when the production of luxuries tends to outstrip the means to acquire them. But the absolute aversion to children is an extraordinary thing in a class that had an excess of wealth and no lack of servants. Pliny stresses the financial aspect of a marriage in Ep. 14. 9 in a way that suggests that the serious expense lay in seeing children through a public career or into a good match: 'dignitas sumptuosa', II. 4. 3; 'ratio civilium officiorum necessitatem quandam nitoris imponit', VI. 32. 1.

16. non apud populum sed apud decuriones habui, nec in propatulo sed in curia. For another reference to the continuation of popular assemblies of a sort see IV. 7. 2: 'scripsit publice ut a decurionibus eligeretur . . . aliquis . . . qui legeret eum populo'. Pliny's avoidance of the assembly is characteristic of the period which saw the steady elimination of the popular element from municipal life throughout the Empire. See VI. 31. 3, X. 34. 1, 79. 3, 110. 1, 116. 1 nn. The Latin charters issued on a common model in the Flavian period show that the right of electing magistrates was retained by the popular assemblies at this time, and in places they survived to a much later age (Lex Malacitana, 51–60, in A–J, n. 65, or *FIRA*, i. 24; cf. A–J, p. 85; J. Toutain, *Cités romaines de la Tunisie* (Paris, 1896), 352 f.). But the effective power in administration belonged to the magistrates and Council.

sermonem. This word is often used by Pliny to distinguish a political speech from an *actio*. Cf. II. 11. 23: 'sermone quem ille habuerat in ordine Lepcitanorum'. Also III. 4. 4, V. 7. 5, IX. 13. 17.

17. plebem. See X. 79. 3 n. for the growing distinction between *plebes* and the curial class.

ne quam in speciem ambitionis inciderem. Pliny's caution by itself suggests that this occasion preceded the death of Domitian, during a visit to Comum in the late summer of 96. He usually visited his distant estates during the September–October recess from senatorial business (Suet. *Aug.* 35. 3); see I. 7. 4, VII. 30. 2, VIII. 2, IX. 37, X. 8. 4–5 nn.

9. *To Minicius Fundanus*

Date. Pliny's freedom from public business in this account of his life dates the letter before his appointment to the prefecture of Saturn.

Address. Minicius Fundanus should be a praetorian senator at this time, since he was ripe for the consulship in 105–6, IV. 15. 5 n. For his place in society and his interest in philosophy see IV. 15, V. 16. 8, VI. 6. 8 nn. Pliny's letters to him are about public life, not literature, cf. IV. 15, VI. 6. But VII. 12, on style, is probably not addressed to him.

1. **quam singulis diebus in urbe ratio aut constet aut constare videatur.** For a detailed description of the daily round of public life at Rome see Friedlaender, *SG* (Eng. Tr.), i. 209 ff.; J. Carcopino, *Daily Life in Ancient Rome*, 184 ff., 193 ff.

2. **officio togae virilis interfui.** The *puer* assumed the stripeless *toga pura* in place of the *praetexta* on reaching puberty. The occasion marked his coming of age, the end of *tutela*, and the acquisition of civil rights and duties. Lawyers fixed the age of puberty for technical purposes generally at 14 (cf. Gaius, *Inst.* 2. 113; *Lex Col. Gen.* 98; *contra* Ulp. *Tit.* 11. 28), but in practice the assumption of the *toga pura* varied in the Principate between the ages of 14 and 16 (cf. II. 14. 6), the latter age bringing it close to that of nominal liability for military service at 17 (*tirocinium*). The ceremony usually took place in the lad's home on the feast of Liberalia, 17 March, but Pliny here suggests that many other days were used. The ceremonies included sacrifices, registration on the tribal list under one's full name, the formal *deductio in forum*, and finally a feast. See Marquardt, *Manuel*: *Vie privée*, xiv (i), 148–57; *RE*, ii. 6, 1450 f.

sponsalia aut nuptias frequentavi. The earlier Republican ceremony of betrothal described by Aulus Gellius, *NA* 4. 4, from Servius Sulpicius, contained a legal contract between the two contracting parties who met face to face. Later, betrothals could be made less formally, by letter or intermediaries, and ceased to be enforceable at law, and might even be terminated by the action of a single party (Gellius, loc. cit. 3; Ulpian in *Dig.* 23. 1. 2, 4, 6, 10, 18; cf. Paulus, *Dig.* 45. 1, 134). The main legal interest was transferred to the question of dowries, but the engagement still established a degree of affinity within which marriage was forbidden (Ulpian, *Dig.* 23. 2. 12. 1–2; cf. 48. 5. 14 (13). 3). Socially, the *sponsalia* gave the girl a limited right of refusal to marry (Ulpian, *Dig.* 23. 1. 12). In general see Marquardt, op. cit. xiv (i), 48 ff.

nuptias. The essential ceremony was the 'deductio in domum mariti' which in classical law did not require the presence of the husband, who could act by letter or agent. Whatever legal form of marriage was used ('in manum', 'sine conventione', or the rare *confarreatio*), the ceremonies were much the same. After auspices and sacrifice the contract (*tabulae*) was signed and witnessed, and a feast took place in the home of the bride, whence she was carried to the husband's house. The maintenance of these ceremonies, barely indicated by Pliny is borne out by the parodies of Juvenal, 2. 119–21, 132–5; 6. 25–26, 200–4. Cf. Tac. *Ann.* 11. 26; Quint. *Inst.* 5. 11. 32; Marquardt, op. cit. 51–65; Carcopino, op. cit., 80 ff.

ad signandum testamentum. Cf. 11. 20. 10 n. for this. Seven witnesses were required, hence it became an occasion, cf. Martial, 10. 70. 7–8; Juvenal, 3. 81–82.

in advocationem. Merrill, ad loc., thought that Pliny used the term in the sense given by Pseudo-Asconius, *Div. in Caec.* 11, who distinguishes the *orator* from the *advocatus* who 'praesentiam suam commodet amico', either as a friend giving moral support or as jurisconsult. Possibly VIII. 21. 3 is an instance of this: 'forte accidit ut eodem die mane in advocationem subitam rogarer'. But everywhere else Pliny uses *advocatus* and *advocatio* solely of the pleader proper, as in Ep. 22. 6, 'multos advocatione plures consilio iuvat'; II. 11. 19, 19. 2, III. 4. 4, IV. 12. 4, &c. Pliny, despite his high opinion of forensic oratory, at times speaks slightingly of routine practice, as here, II. 14. 1, VIII. 9. 1. IX. 2. 1 nn.

in consilium. Senators with experience of the law were much in demand as assessors to magistrates such as the city prefect (VI. 11. 1) or *iudices privati* (I. 20. 12, V. 1. 5, VI. 2. 7), apart from the demands of the emperor (IV. 22, VI. 22, 31). Seneca complains of time thus consumed, *De Brev. Vit.* 7. 7.

3. quot dies quam frigidis rebus consumpsi. Martial, treating the theme in IV. 78, complains of some things omitted by Pliny: the morning *salutatio*, attendance on the inauguration of magistrates (cf. Ep. 5. 11 n.), and, what Pliny loved, the perpetual *recitationes* (Ep. 13 nn.).

4. aut lego aliquid aut scribo aut etiam corpori vaco. Compare his description of his daily life at Tifernum, IX. 36. For the Laurentine villa near Ostia see I. 22. 11, II. 17, IV. 6.

8. Atilius noster eruditissime. The hard-up Cisalpine, Atilius Crescens, a close friend of Pliny and a sharp wit but not a professional advocate (II. 14. 2, VI. 8 nn.).

10. *To Attius Clemens*

Date. After the accession of Nerva and the return of the philosophers, and almost certainly after Pliny's appointment to the *aerarium Saturni* at the beginning of 98, ss. 1, 9 nn. Hence after January 98 and probably the latest letter in the book.

Address. Attius Clemens, recipient of IV. 2 and possibly also of IX. 35, may be connected with any or all of the Attii or Accii (cf. the confusion Tuccius–Tullius in II. 11. 9) mentioned by Pliny, Accius or Attius Sura X. 12, the great Attius Suburanus VI. 33. 2 nn., or Accius Aquila X. 106, but is otherwise unknown. Syme supposes him a Narbonensian, where the name Attius is common, *Tac.* 802, n. 2. But see X. 12 n. for an upper-class Attius from Cisalpine.

1. urbs nostra liberalibus studiis . . . nunc maxime floret. So too in Ep. 13. 1. But Tacitus of the same period wrote in the *Agricola* 3. 1: 'ingenia studiaque oppresseris facilius quam revocaveris'.

2. sufficeret unum, Euphrates philosophus. Fronto (*Ho.*, p. 133 N., p. 115) says that the Stoic Musonius Rufus was *magister* of Euphrates and of Cocceianus Dio (see III. 11. 5 n., X. 81. 1 n. for these). Grimal oddly takes this to mean only that Musonius was superior to them. Euphrates' position at Rome resembles Dio's. Both men were at once 'philosophers' of moral and political theory, and 'sophists' or professional orators, who influenced the development of the Second Sophistic, the school of Greek oratory that had a great vogue in the second century A.D. (Philostratus, *VS*, I. 7, 25). But Euphrates like his pupil Timocrates was not included by Philostratus in his canon of the Sophists. Hence he was presumably more philosopher than sophist, though Fronto and Epictetus (IV. 8) commend his eloquence. Philostratus brings him in touch with Vespasian at Alexandria in an improbable anecdote in which he advises Vespasian about 'democracy' (*Ap. Ty.* 5. 33). One may compare Dio's claim to have declaimed his *De Regno* to Trajan (*Or.* 1. 9, 3. 2–3). Under Domitian Euphrates took part at Rome in the accusation of Apollonius of Tyana for magic (Philost. *Ap. Ty.* 7. 36, 8. 3; Euseb. *In Hieroclem* 29. 31; Jerome, *Chron.* under year 13–14 or 14–15 of Domitian). Apparently he left Rome at the last expulsion of philosophers in 93–94, returned under Nerva, and was still in Rome in 98. He took hemlock in 119 by the 'permission' of Hadrian, not it seems in a political affair (Dio 69. 8. 3; see *RE*, VI, c. 1215 'Euphrates'). P. Grimal, *Latomus* (1955), 370 ff., defends some of the less certain anecdotes in Philostratus, and argues from his *Ep.* vii that Euphrates returned to Syria in 97.

hunc ego in Syria, cum adulescentulus militarem, penitus et domi inspexi. Pliny also met the philosopher Artemidorus in Syria then, in an early year of Domitian before the philosophers expelled by Vespasian were again allowed in Rome, III. 11. 5, VIII. 14. 7. He was then serving as military tribune of Legio III Gallica, as his inscription reveals. Euphrates may have made Musonius' acquaintance in Syria, who certainly was there at that period, though he returned rather earlier, under Titus, III. 11. 5 n. For other references to Pliny as military tribune see VII. 16. 2, 31. 2, X. 87.

7. nullus horror in cultu. Stoics were expected to be *rigidi et tristes*, with long beards. Tac. *Ann.* 16. 22; Dio 65 (66). 13, 1 a. Epictetus (IV. 8. 15.) quotes a fragment of Euphrates against ostentation, and commends him for *not* flaunting the great beard that so impressed Pliny—despite the disapproval of his teacher Quintilian (12. 3. 12). The philosophers of this period were much concerned with the details of behaviour and incidentals of daily life. Cf. Musonius' sermons on food and clothing, furniture, and cutting the hair, *rell.* 18–21. Sufficiency and convenience are the keynotes. But Musonius insisted on the full growth of the natural beard as the mark of man. The reappearance of the beard in Roman society under the influence of Hadrian thus derives from the school of Musonius.

8. liberi tres, duo mares, quos diligentissime instituit. Musonius took the liberal side in his sermons on the themes 'should girls have the same education as boys?' and 'should women learn philosophy?', *rell.* 3–4. So too Pliny's philosopher friend Minicius Fundanus, V. 16. 3.

socer Pompeius Iulianus . . . ipse provinciae princeps . . . generum non honoribus principem, sed sapientia elegit. Compare the marriage of Musonius' daughter to Artemidorus, III. 11. 5. But most of the great names of the Second Sophistic came from high society. Apollonius complains that Euphrates forced his way into great houses, *Ap. Ty.* 8. 7. 11. Scopelianus of Smyrna, a contemporary of Euphrates, belonged to a family of Asiarchs (*VS* 1. 21. 2). Polemon, pupil of Timocrates, reached consular rank, like the millionare Herodes Atticus. Cocceianus Dio was a great man of Prusa, X. 81. 1 n. So Euphrates was probably not quite penniless. Apollonius makes him a successful man of business, decidedly mercenary, *Ap. Ty.* 5. 38, 6. 13, 8. 7. 11.

9. distringor officio, ut maximo sic molestissimo. In X. 9 his office as prefect of Saturn is described as *districtum* and in *Pan.* 91. 1 as 'laboriosissimo et maximo'. He had vacated his prefecture of the *aerarium militare* certainly not later than the date of the events described in Ep. 5, i.e. December 96, if not before the death of Domitian (p. 75), and received the prefecture of Saturn not earlier than the last month of Nerva, i.e. January 98. A date in 96 for this letter would not fit the return of the exiles, who took time to reassemble (I. 5. 10, 15, IX. 13. 5 nn.). The definition of his duties below fits the *aerarium* of Saturn much better than the *aerarium militare*. Hence everything favours the late dating of this letter and the identification of this post with the prefecture of Saturn (against Schultz, 11).

Pompeius Iulianus. Not otherwise known; and not necessarily of high Roman rank. *PIR*[1], iii, P 466.—Grimal, assuming that the children are still young, places the marriage in the 'eighties'.

10. **cognoscere iudicare, promere et exercere iustitiam.** The preceding description, 'subnoto libellos, conficio tabulas, scribo . . . litteras', might be referred to either of the public Treasuries. But this technical reference to jurisdiction fits well with the development of the duties of the prefect of Saturn in the Principate, who exercised administrative justice in interpreting the complicated rules of the inheritance tax dealing with pleas for exemption, &c. Cf. *Pan.* 36. 1, 'quam iuvat cernere aerarium silens et quietum et quale ante delatores erat', followed by a long account, 37–40, of changes made by Nerva and Trajan in the administration of the *vicesima hereditatum*. The prefects had a hand also in the administration of rules about the succession of *caelibes* and *orbi* under the marriage laws. Though such cases must have originally been settled by the relevant *Quaestio*, or jury court, a summary jurisdiction had developed by the time of Trajan whereby the prefect of Saturn adjudicated on claims to legacies and inheritances 'quod capere aliquis non potuerit', and delations were laid *ad aerarium*, *Dig.* 49. 14. 13–15. But on occasion the prefects had themselves to plead before a higher tribunal, IV. 12. 3 n. Cf. F. Millar, 'The *aerarium*', etc., *JRS* (1964), 33 f.

The prefects were also busied with the collection of fines under various *leges publicae*, such as the extortion law and the adultery law, II. 11. 19 'aerario inferenda', VII. 33. 4 nn., VI. 31. 6 'Iuliae legis poenis' n. They were responsible also for the handling of *vadimonia* in connexion with the farming of such *vectigalia* as were still under control of the Senate (Hirschfeld, *Verwaltungsbeamten*, 15; S. J. de Laet, *Portorium* (Bruges, 1949), 120, 364 f.).

Grimal (art. cit. 329) remarks that Euphrates' advice to Pliny reflects the theme of the middle Stoa that Justice is 'immanent virtue', and compares Cicero, *De Fin.* 3. 25.

11. *To Fabius Justus*

No evidence of date. For the advocate and senator Fabius Justus see Ep. 5. 8 n. This, and probably VII. 2, are the only letters to him. Both are of a type that is regularly scattered through the collection, and served as an epistolary visiting card, sometimes being distinguished by an aphorism, II. 15. 1 n. Letter IX. 32 resembles this note most closely in vacuity. Cf. also II. 2, III. 17, V. 18, VII. 2, 13. Slightly meatier are II. 8 and 15.

1. **at hoc ipsum scribe, nihil esse quod scribas.** Compare, with Schuster, Cic. *Ad Att.* 4. 8a. 4, and *Ad Fam.* 16. 26. 2.

  unde incipere priores solebant. The formula was reduced to initials in formal letters of acquaintances to Cicero, and not used in familiar letters. Cf. *Ad Fam.* 5. 9. 10 a.

2. **sine sollicitudine summa.** Syme (*JRS* (1957), 131) deduces, from Pliny's supposed fears, that Justus was on service as a legionary legate. But the language is not so strong as in III. 17. 3 and IX. 2. 4, and the inference is weak.

12. *To Calestrius Tiro*

Date. Since the death of Corellius cannot be much later than that of Nerva, and probably was earlier, the letter belongs to 97–98, s. 1 n.

Address. Calestrius Tiro, an exact contemporary of Pliny, is now a praetorian senator. He owns land at Ticinum and in Picenum, and probably hails from the latter region, V. 1. 1, VII. 16. 3 n. For his undistinguished career see VII. 16 nn. The letters to or about him mostly concern his proconsulship of Baetica (VI. 22, VII. 16, 23, 32, IX. 5) apart from this and a courtesy note, VI. 1. Evidently not a man of letters.

1. **decessit Corellius Rufus et quidem sponte.** Pliny has much to say about the activity of Corellius during the reign of Nerva and nothing afterwards, though opportunities are not lacking, as in III. 4. 1; the anecdote in ss. 7–8 would lose its point if Corellius long survived Nerva. Though he is certainly alive in mid-97 at the time of the indictment of Publicius Certus (IX. 13. 6), he would seem to have died not long after if not before Nerva. The notion of Asbach (art. cit. 43; *contra* Schultz, art. cit. 12) that Corellius was one of the consuls *bis* and *ter* of *Pan.* 61. 7 has been disproved by the *Fasti Ostienses*, which with the Panegyric show these men to have been Spurinna and Frontinus, II. 7. 1 n.

Corellius Rufus, born *c.* A.D. 30, is not mentioned till the Flavian

period, when he was suffect consul, rather late as a 'new man',
apparently in 78, and legate of Upper Germany about 82, but is not
known to have held any other office under Domitian (*ILS* 1995;
CIL, xiv. 4276. 2; *PIR²*, *C* 1294; Garzetti, *C*. 44). His sister married a
senior equestrian officer, Minicius Justus, who was an early supporter
of Vespasian in the Civil War, VII. 11. 4 n.; Tac. *Hist.* 3. 7. Corellius,
like Cornutus Tertullus and Julius Bassus, may have been one of
those friends of Vespasian and Titus who were dropped by Domitian,
and his anger that of a discarded official, IV. 9. 2, 17. 9, V. 14. 1–6 nn.
Pliny rates him with Frontinus among the *spectatissimi* of the last
years of Domitian, V. 1. 5. With Nerva he enjoys influence at court,
and is appointed to the Land Commission, IV. 17. 7–8, VII. 31. 4.
His long connexion with Pliny's family and the connexions of his
wife and sister with Comum point to a Cisalpine origin, s. 3 n., VII.
11. 3–5 nn. The Elder Pliny mentions an otherwise unknown
equestrian Corellius of Ateste, *NH* 17. 122; cf. ibid. 15. 94. The name
is rare among the upper classes, but occurs at this time in the region
of Beneventum among the *nomina* of the Neratii, one of whom may
have married a Corellia, s. 3 n. '*nepotem*'.

3. summa ratio ... ad hoc consilium compulit. Just like Titius Aristo
he coolly calculated the rival claims of family and his own sufferings,
Ep. 22. 8–10. The Stoics approved rational suicide. Corellius follows
the advice of Seneca, *Ep.* 58. 32–36, especially: 'morbum si sciero
perpetuo mihi esse patiendum exibo non propter ipsum sed quia
impedimento mihi futurus est ad omne propter quod vivitur'. So too
Marcus Aurelius, *Med.* 11. 3.

optimam conscientiam. Pliny uses the word of past deeds. Cf. Ep.
5. 8: 'conscientia exterritus', and Ep. 22. 5: 'omnia ad conscientiam
refert recteque facti ... mercedem ex facto petit'. In I. 8. 14, III.
20. 8, V. 1. 10, it is correlated with *fama*. He uses it more literally
in II. 11. 24. Cf. Trajan in X. 30. 2.

filiam uxorem nepotem. The rare cognomen borne by his wife and
daughter (s. 9, III. 3, pref.), Hispulla, which appears again as the
second name of Calpurnius Fabatus' daughter (IV. 19, pref.), points
to the Cisalpine connexion of Corellius. Possibly the wives of
Corellius and Fabatus were akin. So Syme (*JRS* (1949), 15). For
Pliny's friendship with the Corelliae see III. 3, IV. 17, VII. 11.

nepotem. The son of Corellia, born *c.* 89–90, cf. III. 3. 1 n. There
Pliny mentions but does not name his father. The boy may be Corel-
lius Pansa, consul of the year in 122, and the father one of the
Neratii of the Beneventum region mentioned above.

Corellius' son who presided at Pliny's praetorian games in 93 is
evidently now dead, VII. 11. 3.

7. **uxor quamquam omnis secreti capacissima.** Cf. the trusty wife of Spurinna, III. 1. 5, and of Macrinus, VIII. 5, and Serrana Procula, Ep. 14. 6. They were a feature of the region.

8. **'...ut scilicet isti latroni vel uno die supersim'.** Domitian was regarded as a 'brigand' because he confiscated the property of his political victims, and because he was apt to claim a share in the inheritances of wealthy men on flimsy grounds. Suet. *Dom.* 12. 1–2: 'praedaretur omni modo'. But this was due to public not private expenses: 'exhaustus operum ac munerum impensis stipendioque quod adiecerat (*sc.* militibus)'. Hence he was, ibid. 3. 2, 'inopia rapax'. How far this represents more than a caricature of the truth based on isolated instances is uncertain. See the note on Nerva's economies, II. 1. 9 n.

quod optabat. No senator was directly involved in the actual murder of Domitian, Suet. *Dom.* 17, Dio 67. 15–16, though the succession of Nerva was certainly prearranged, as Dio and the dates of his proclamation indicate. Domitian 'periit postquam cerdonibus esse timendus incipit'.

iam securus. For effect Pliny implies a much shorter interval than the year or nine months, which at least must have elapsed before the death of Corellius.

9. **communem amicum C. Geminium.** The variant reading in the Nine-Book tradition, German(i)um, cannot stand against the consensus of the other evidence (cf. Schuster, *app. crit.*). The man is unidentified, *PIR*², iv, G 143. He cannot be Pliny's friend T. Prifernius Geminus, VII. 1, pref.

Pliny normally uses two names to designate a new character if any ambiguity arise from a single name, but never the *tria nomina*. Some times, as here, he prefers prenomen–nomen to the more usual nomen–cognomen form, apparently for the sake of formality of one kind or other (I. 14. 6, 17. 1, III. 11. 4, IV. 8. 4, V. 3. 5, 5. 1, 5, VII. 24. 8), or in introductions (II. 9. 1, 4, IV. 4. 1, 17. 1.) The use of prenomen–cognomen is rare (I. 17. 2, III. 7, 12), mostly of historical figures.

10. **Iulius Atticus.** Four obscure men of this name are known, including a procurator and a writer on vines, *PIR*¹, J 116–19. Cf. also Tac. *Hist.* I. 35.

11. **implevit quidem annum septimum et sexagensimum quae aetas etiam robustissimis satis longa est.** But Spurinna beats this by ten years, and Pliny regards him as the ideal III. 1. 10–11. Generally Pliny looks forward to old age, contrary to the general opinion of the Latins, which Seneca sums up, *Ep.* 108. 28–29 as ʹsenectus

insanabilis morbus est '. Merrill has an excellent note, ad loc., on death
statistics in antiquity. The most useful evidence is that of Ulpian's
opinion, *Dig.* 35. 2. 68, that the expectation of life between 55 and 60
years was seven years, and beyond that five years. The Elder Pliny
gives a curious account of longevity, *NH* 7. 153–64, ending with the
statement that at Vespasian's census eighty-five males gave their
age as 100 or over. Since registration of births was established in
A.D. 4, for Roman citizens, by the Lex Aelia Sentia, and maintained strictly, Pliny's figure is acceptable, though the centenarians
of 74 were all born earlier than A.D. 4 (F. Schulz, 'Roman Registers',
JRS (1942), 78 f.).

12. meo Calvisio. His equestrian friend Calvisius Rufus of Comum,
II. 20, pref.

amisi vitae meae testem rectorem magistrum. For Corellius'
protection of Pliny see IV. 17. 4–7. Also IX. 13. 6: 'omnia ego semper
ad Corellium rettuli . . . in hoc tamen contentus consilio meo fui
veritus ne vetaret'. In V. 1. 5 Corellius sits as assessor to Pliny in an
arbitration. Pliny's connexion began when he was *adulescentulus*
(IV. 17. 6), and hence probably after he joined his uncle at Rome.
Oddly, Pliny does not here formally list the praises of Corellius, as
in IV. 17. 4–7, where he notes among more conventional qualities his
subtilitas; cf. IX. 13. 6, 'erat . . . cunctantior cautiorque'.

13. *To Sosius Senecio*

Date. April 97, s. 1 n.

Address. Q. Sosius Senecio, at this time no more than *praetorius*,
was son-in-law of the influential Julius Frontinus, who was soon to
be twice and thrice consul (IV. 8. 3 n.). Senecio later through the
friendship of Trajan became consul *ordinarius* in 99 and *cos. II* in
107, after a military governorship indicated in IV. 4. Otherwise his
career is obscure, though he may have held high command in the
second Dacian war, and he was one of three men to be honoured in his
own lifetime by Trajan with a public statue. Possibly he was a
member of Hadrian's clique (Dio 68. 16. 2; SHA, *Hadr.* 4. 2; *PIR*[1],
iii, *S.* 560; Garzetti, *C.* 141; Syme, *Tac.* 648). As a literary man he
was a friend of Plutarch, who dedicated works to him, and may have
sojourned in Greece (Plut. *Thes.* 1. 1; *Q. conv.* 4. 31, p. 666; *RE*, xxi.
1. 688). Like Minicius Fundanus (Ep. 9, pref.), he was in the forefront
of the contemporary Hellenizing tendency at Rome (cf. Syme, op.
cit. 505 f.). But though connected to Pliny through Frontinus and
his own son-in-law Pompeius Falco (Ep. 23, pref.) and Calvisius

Rufus (IV. 4. 1) Pliny addresses only one other note to him, a letter of commendation, IV. 4. His connexions suggest Cisalpine origin.

1. toto mense Aprili nullus fere dies quo non recitaret aliquis. Pliny's freedom of movement (s. 6) shows that he was not yet bound by official duties to the capital, as after his appointment to the prefecture of Saturn in early 98. So April 97 is the only possible date after the death of Domitian.

mense Aprili. There are *ludi* on not less than eighteen days. Cf. K. Latte, *Römische Religionsgeschichte*, München, 1960, 433. July and August were also suitable months for such parties, VIII. 21. 2 and Juv. 3. 9.

vigent studia. As in Ep. 10. 1 Pliny is fêting the new régime, which was felt to have restored life to letters by restoring liberty to men. Cf. VIII. 12. 1, 'Titinius Capito . . . litterarum iam senescentium reductor', and Tac. *Hist*. 1. 1, 'rara temporum felicitate ubi sentire quae velis et quae sentias dicere licet'.

2. plerique in stationibus sedent. There were many such public places where men congregated, cf. II. 9. 5, 'domos stationesque circumeo'— the porticoes of the imperial Fora, the great Baths, and for poets especially the library of the temple of Apollo (Mart. 5. 20. 8; Juv. 11. 3–4; Schol. on *Hor. Sat*. 1. 10. 38; Suet. *Nero* 37. 1). But the *recitationes* were private occasions given in private rooms to an invited audience, s. 4 n.

an iam recitator intraverit, an dixerit praefationem. The 'recitation' as met in Silver Latin writers is an innovation of the Principate, due according to the Elder Seneca to Asinius Pollio, who in the time of Augustus began to invite guests to the reading of his own works (Sen. *Contr*. 4, pref. 2; Isidore *Orig*. 6. 52). It became the popular form of initial publication, providing the cheapest and quickest means of making works known to the largest educated audience available before the invention of printing. Martial and Juvenal complain of the excessive number of recitations, and as literature became fashionable doubtless the custom encouraged the publication of much bad work. But Carcopino errs in attacking recitation as the basic cause of the decline of Latin literature on the ground that it encouraged the unduly rhetorical trend of literature. The causes of that lie deeper in the classical education itself. All classical literature was written to read aloud, and the recitation is the logical development of the Symposium and the public performances of classical Greece.

The formalities of the recitation are best known from Pliny, ss. 3–4 nn. For a general discussion see Carcopino, *Daily Life*, 193 ff.; *RE* (ii) 1, s.v. 'Recitatio', 435 ff.

praefationem. The custom was to introduce the work with preliminary remarks, sometimes published with it, like the prefaces of
Martial and Statius. Pliny rather disliked prefaces (IV. 5. 3, 14. 8,
V. 12. 3, VIII. 21. 3), unless there was a special reason for one, but
appreciated an apt example, as in the anecdote of IV. 11. 3. In a
technical *controversia* the preface explains the facts of the case to be
argued. See Bonner, *Roman Declamation*, 51–52.

evolverit librum. The awkward papyrus roll, cf. II. 1. 5.

3. Claudium Caesarem ferunt cum . . . audisset . . . clamorem.
Claudius gave his own recitations, Suet. *Claud.* 41. He was walking
in the great villa, the Domus Tiberiana, on the Palatine—the word
is not yet quite identified with the imperial 'palace'—and heard the
noise, but not as Merrill says from the Apollinine library, because it
was evidently a private party on which the emperor 'gate-crashed'.

Nonianum. The consular M. Servilius Nonianus, orator and historian, is known from Tac. *Ann.* 14. 19; Quint. 10. 1. 102; Tac. *Dial.* 23;
Pliny, *NH* 28. 29, 37. 81. He was the patron of Persius and of the
scholar Plotius Macrinus among others. *PIR*[1], S 420; Syme, *Tac.*
274, *et al.*

clamorem. Pliny sometimes preferred silent attention, sometimes not
(II. 10. 7, V. 3. 9, VI. 17), but was shocked by applause in Court (II. 14).

4. nunc otiosissimus quisque multo ante rogatus. See III. 18. 4 for the
forms of invitation: 'non per codicillos non per libellos sed si com-
modum et si valde vacaret admoniti'. The recitation was usually a
private affair of friends (III. 18. 4, V. 3. 11, 12. 1, VIII. 21. 3, IX. 34)
but could take place on a large and public scale 'quasi populum in
auditorium . . . advocarim' (V. 3. 11). Tac. *Dial.* 9. 3, 'domum
mutuatur et auditorium exstruit et subsellia conducit et libellos
dispergit'. But even so it was by invitation.

5. equidem prope nemini defui. So he testifies in numerous letters
about his own and others' recitations. It is his passion, like that of
Le Cousin Pons for dining out: I. 5. 2, Regulus. II. 10. 6, Octavius.
III. 10. 1, his life of Cottius. 18, his Panegyric. 15. 3, Silius Proculus.
IV. 7. 2, Regulus. 27, Augurinus. V. 3, his verses. 12, his speech.
17, Piso. VI. 15, Passenus. 17, anonymous. VII. 17, his speeches.
VIII. 21, his verses. IX. 27, an historian.

6. scribere aliquid quod non recitem. Pliny was not at this date a frequent reciter, II. 10. 7, 19. 1 nn. He may have read his *De Bibliotheca*,
Ep. 8. 2 'petiturus' n., and perhaps essays in the style of the rhetorical 'Suasoriae'. Later he used the intimate recitation before a select
gathering as a method of securing criticism and advice prior to
publication, III. 18, V. 3. 7–11, 12. 1, VII. 17.

14. *To Junius Mauricus*

Date. Not long after the return of Mauricus from exile in early 97 (s. 1 n., cf. Ep. 5. 10–11).

Address. For Junius Mauricus and his brother Arulenus Rusticus, and their condemnation in 93, see Ep. 5. 2, 10, nn.

1. **petis ut fratris tui filiae prospiciam maritum.** Mauricus might well be out of touch with the matrimonial market after his three years of exile. In II. 18 he asks Pliny's advice, more suitably, about a tutor for his nephews. Was Pliny expected to offer himself, a widower, at this date? The request might seem more probable while Mauricus was still in exile, but nobody would then want to marry a ruined man's portionless niece. Pliny saw more of the *clari adulescentuli* than most men, in his court practice, cf. II. 14, VI. 11, 23. Probably Mauricus spent some months in 97 restoring his sequestrated estates, cf. s. 9. But his presence at Rome under Nerva is indicated by IV. 22. 4.

filiae. Like her brother (II. 18) she must still be in her teens; cf. IV. 19, V. 16. 6 nn. on the marriage age. Arulenus' children are surprisingly young if he married at the usual age about the time of his quaestorship under Nero. Perhaps a second marriage is indicated.

3. **Minicius Acilianus qui me . . . familiarissime diligit.** This may well be the Acilianus whose death and inheritance are mentioned in II. 16. 1. Otherwise he is unknown. Though at least three consular families of Acilii are known at this period, Aviolae, Glabriones, Strabones, they show no connexion with this family from Brixia. *PIR²*, i, A 46–82; *PIR¹*, M 429; Garzetti, *C.* 100.

iuvenis iuvenem. See I. 19. 1, II. 13. 8 for similar relationship of patronage. Below Pliny calls him *adulescens*, and as an undistinguished *praetorius* he must be about 35 to Pliny's 36.

4. **Brixia . . . multum adhuc verecundiae . . . antiquae retinet.** Cf. Tac. *Ann.* 16. 5: 'remotis municipiis severaque adhuc et antiqui moris retinente Italia'. And ibid. III. 55: 'novi homines e municipiis et coloniis . . . in senatum crebro adsumpti domesticam parsimoniam intulerunt et quamquam . . . pecuniosam ad senectutem pervenirent mansit tamen prior animus'. Vespasian was a prime example 'antiquo ipse cultu victuque'. These passages illuminate the influences moulding the tone of Roman society in the Flavian age. This infiltration of a strait-laced element counterbalanced the excessive sophistication of the older Julio–Claudian aristocracy, whose influence lingers on in the more artificial parts of Martial's verses. It is remarkable that, except for the Fish Satire, Juvenal's instances of sophisticated vices are largely drawn from the age of Nero. See further VII. 24 nn.

nostra Italia. This implies that the family of Rusticus was Cisalpine in origin; so Chilver, *Cisalpine Gaul*, 104. But caution is necessary. Pliny uses *noster* of places and communes with the connotation of a common origin for the addressee, as in VI. 34. 1, 'Veronensibus nostris', meaning that Valerius there was also a northerner, whereas in VII. 22. 2 'regionis meae' means that the addressee was not Cisalpine. So too of Comum, to fellow Comenses, V. 7. 1, and of Rome, 'urbs nostra', I. 10. 1, IV. 22. 7, V. 6. 4. But of persons *noster* or *meus* usually means my or our mutual friend, and cannot be pressed for origins: 1. 9. 8, 12. 12, 16. 1, II. 14. 2, VII. 7. 1, 8. 1.

5. pater Minicius Macrinus. If this man is the Macrinus of VIII. 5 whose wife dies after thirty-nine years of marriage, then he is an old family friend of Pliny. But Minicius' wife seems to be already dead, as only an aunt is mentioned in s. 6. It is possible that the recipient of all the letters addressed to Macrinus, II. 7, VII. 6, 10, VIII. 17, IX. 4, on literary and political topics, is Caecilius Macrinus, addressee of III. 4. The 'Minicius' of VII. 12 may be Minicius Fundanus or Cornelius Minicianus, ibid., pref.

equestris ordinis princeps. The term is general, cf. 'provinciae princeps', Ep. 10. 8. Also III. 2. 2.

adlectus. Vespasian as censor in 73–74 had occasion to fill the gaps in the Senate caused by Nero's persecutions and the civil war, and did so 'honestissimo quoque Italicorum ac provincialium adlecto', Suet. *Vesp.* 9. 2. Pliny's friend Cornutus Tertullus was among these, V. 14. 4–6 nn. See A. W. Braithwaite, ad loc., *Divus Vespasianus* (Oxford, 1927), and *CAH*, xi. 10. Macrinus must have been over 30 at the time to be promoted to praetorian grade instead of quaestorian or tribunician.

quietem. Macrinus is one of several equestrians in this period who preferred the equestrian to the senatorial career. The example was set earlier by Annaeus Mela, brother of Seneca, in the time of Tiberius, who saw that as much power could be enjoyed in certain equestrian posts as by consular legates, Tac. *Ann.* 16. 17; cf. ibid. 12. 60 on the influence of equestrians. So too Cornelius Fuscus, the future praetorian prefect of Domitian, laid aside his *latus clavus* to pursue procuratorships, Tac. *Hist.* 2. 86. Pliny's Letters add Maturus Arrianus, II. 11. 1, III. 2. 4 and possibly Terentius Junior, VII. 25. 2 n. The motive is, in varying terms, always 'quietis amor', which means not the desire for slippered ease, *otium*, but a public career free from the political dangers of the senatorial career. Cf. Syme, *Am. J. Phil.* lviii, 'The colony of Cornelius Fuscus', 8 f. The phrase expresses the ideal of a civil service freed from politics. But Tacitus adds to the motives of Mela: 'simul acquirendae pecuniae *brevius iter* credebat per procurationes administrandis principis negotiis'. The procuratorial appointments were handsome and continuous, whereas senatorial salaries though larger were usually intermittent. Cf. the remark of a candidate of Fronto (*Ad Ant.* 9, p. 170 Naber), 'non procuratoris stipendii cupiditate optat . . . hunc honorem'. And there were many pickings in the ill-supervised imperial service, cf. Pflaum, *Les Procurateurs*, 165–9, who, however, sadly underestimates the value of the salary of S.100,000–300,000.

6. Serrana tamen Patavinis quoque severitatis exemplum est. Cf. Martial, 11. 16, 'tu quoque nequitias nostri . . . libelli . . . leges, sis Patavina licet'. Syme, *Roman Revolution* (Oxford, 1939), 485— and still in *Tac.* 202 n. 8—would explain thus the *Patavinitas* attributed by Quintilian to Livy as excessive priggishness, with his preface as an example, though Quintilian was speaking of vocabulary, *Inst.* 1. 5. 56, VIII. 1. 3.

contigit et avunculus ei P. Acilius. A maternal uncle, from whose family Minicius derives his cognomen, probably the addressee of III. 14, otherwise unknown. Age and *origo* forbid identification with P. Acilius Attianus of Italica, the praetorian prefect in 117 who helped to install Hadrian as emperor, Dio. 69. 1. 2.

7. quaesturam tribunatum praeturam honestissime percucurrit, ac iam pro se tibi necessitatem ambiendi remisit. Pliny's electoral letters (II. 9, III. 20, IV. 25, VI. 6, 9, 19. 1–2, VIII. 23) show that, apart from places reserved for imperial 'commendation' (II. 9. 1, X. 12 nn.), election to the lesser magistracies was still actively contested. Cf. Paladini, cited below, at immense length. This passage suggests that even the praetorship was involved in competition. Tibiletti has argued that there was little competition after the preliminary round for the twenty posts of the Vigintivirate. But there were never quite enough places to go round. The twenty ex-*xxviri*, plus candidates excused the office by the Princeps (II. 9. 1 n.), sought twenty quaestorships; twenty *quaestorii*, plus any recent *adlecti* (but less any patricians among the number), and the defeated candidates of the previous year, sought sixteen places as tribunes and aediles. In due course these competed, plus patrician ex-quaestors and any back-log, for the eighteen praetorships, the number to which the total had been raised by the time of Nerva (*Dig.* 1. 2. 32). Vespasian, *c.* 37–39, faced severe competition up to his praetorship (Suet. *Vesp.* 2. 3). In *Pan.* 69–75 Pliny confines himself to Trajan's part in the elections, but the activities of competitive candidates are hinted at in 76. 1 (Paladini, art. cit. 70 f.). The situation was also complicated from year to year by the irregular working of priorities under the system of marriage privileges (VII. 16. 2 nn.). See also III. 20. 4–5 nn. For

consular elections see IV. 15. 5 n. Further, Mommsen, *DPR*, iii.
232 f.; M. L. Paladini, 'Le votazioni . . . nel' età di Traiano', *Athenaeum*, xxxvii. 3 ff.; Tibiletti, *Principe e magistrati*, &c. (Rome, 1953), ch. iv.

9. cum imaginor vos . . . silendum de facultatibus puto. It is not clear whether this means that the Junii were excessively wealthy, or that as philosophers they despised money.

leges civitatis intueor quae vel in primis census hominum spectandos arbitrantur. More particularly the regulations which established financial qualifications for entry into the senatorial, equestrian, and even municipal careers (I. 19. 2, X. 4. 2 nn.).

et sane de posteris et his pluribus cogitanti. The rub lay not in the cost of educating children (Ep. 8. 11 n.) and providing dowries, but in seeing each son through a public career in a society that lacked the consideration of primogeniture. Lavish bribery was no longer necessary at elections, but extravagant treating continued (VI. 19. 1–2), and public games had to be provided during a magisterial career at considerable expense (VII. 11. 4). The cost of maintaining social style and municipal patronage, for sons and self, was not lessened by the early age at which the Lex Julia tended to enforce marriage; married sons might be entering the senate when a father was still in mid-career as a consular (VI. 26. 1, VII. 24. 3).

10. me putes indulsisse amori meo supraque ista quam res patitur sustulisse. Cf. VII. 28. 1: 'tamquam amicos meos ex omni occasione ultra modum laudem'.

15. *To Septicius Clarus*

Date. In a summer after the death of Domitian, ss. 2, 4 nn.

Address. For Septicius Clarus the equestrian see I. 1, pref.

1. promittis ad cenam, nec venis. dicitur ius: ad assem impendium reddes. The fiction is kept up throughout the note. Merrill imagined an action for damages under the Lex Aquilia, quoting *Dig.* 9. 2. 27. 5. But the metaphor is not so specific. For other letters on the *cena* theme see II. 6, III. 12.

2. paratae erant lactucae singulae, cochleae ternae, ova bina. This is *gustatorium* rather than *gravior cena*, v. 6. 37 n. But no antiquarian comment is required about the various foods, since Pliny makes no attempt to give a complete menu of either meal, or even to distinguish the courses, and adds nothing to the stock of knowledge on this topic. The 'comparison of feasts' was a favourite theme of the lighter writers. Martial, v. 78 is a fine example. Guillemin (*VL*, 136 f.)

traces the theme back through Horace, *Ep.* 1. 5. 1–11, Cicero, *ad fam.* 9. 16. 7, 20. 1, &c., to Catullus 13. 1–8. Since the vegetables are summer crops and no fresh fruit is mentioned, early or middle summer is indicated. Cf. Ep. 7. 6 for accuracy in such details.

halica cum mulso et nive. Pliny here betrays his ignorance of simple life. *Halica*, an ancient form of barley-water, was a poor-man's drink, but *mulsum*, even unchilled, was a rich man's delicacy: Martial, 13. 6, 'nos alicam, poterit mulsum tibi mittere dives', and 12. 81. It was a bottled mixture of new wine and honey, Columella, *RR*, 12. 41.

nive. Another extravagance, disapproved by the Elder, *NH* 19. 54. Snow was kept like ice in the eighteenth-century ice-wells, large blocks of ice not being available in the Apennines.

audisses comoedos vel lectorem vel lyristen. For the custom of recitation or music at dinners and feasts see also III. 1. 9, IX. 17. 3, 36. 4, 40. 2 nn. Pliny's tastes are shown by v. 3. 2: 'comoedias audio et specto mimos et lyricos lego et Sotadicos intellego'. In the theatre the mime and pantomime were fast driving out the production of classical plays, which tended to be limited to selected scenes and speeches. The recitation became the principal means by which the educated classes heard drama, as the contrast 'audio–specto' above indicates. See Friedlaender, *SG* (Eng. tr.), ii. 95–99, and iv. 255–6, who quotes M. Antoninus, *Med.* 12. 36 and Philostratus, *VS*, 1. 25. 3, for the last certain references to performances of whole plays. But M. Bieber, *History of the Greek and Roman Theater*, ch. xv, shows from the evidence of Pompeian frescoes that drama retained some popularity down to the age of Nero, when the new form of panto-mime was being evolved out of, or corrupting, the old forms of tragedy and comedy. See for pantomime VII. 24. 4 n.

comoedos. The entertainers were specialized in their callings. The *comoedus* recited plays of the New Comedy—Menander, Terence, and Plautus. The *lector* read poets, history, or oratory at choice. The *lyristes* is a soloist, but the very wealthy might own an orchestra, as in the anecdote of Macrobius, II. 4, 28, or a troupe of pantomimes like Quadratilla, VII. 24. 4–5. Pliny's Zosimus was exceptional in com-bining all three talents, v. 19, 3; contrast Sen. *Ep.* 27. 6.

3. Gaditanas maluisti. So too Martial promises a single flute-player instead of *Gaditanae*, who were singers and dancers, III. 63. 5, v. 78. 26. Pliny in IX. 17. 1–2 reproves a friend who complains of being offered 'scurrae cinaedi moriones' instead of the more cultured enter-tainment: 'equidem nihil tale habeo, habentes tamen fero'. See Carcopino, *Daily Life*, 223 f.

4. nusquam hilarius simplicius incautius. There is possibly a political reference in *incautius* to freedom from spies and suspicions as in IV.

9. 6 and IX. 13. 10. But the word is used in a more general sense also, cf. VIII. 4. 8.

adparatius. Gellius, *NA*, 13. 11, gives the rules for an elegant dinner among cultured folk, from Varro, who sets the number of guests between three and nine and regulates the topics of conversation and recitation, and the style of food. See Carcopino, *Daily Life*, 263 ff. For the contrast between the ordinary *comissatio* with ribald figures and the entertainments of the literary see also *RE*, iv, 'Comissatio', 618.

16. *To Erucius Clarus*

Date. The letter belongs to the period of Pliny's first familiarity with Pompeius Saturninus, and hence to about the same time as Ep. 8 (q.v.), i.e. 97.

Address. This Erucius should be the father, a practised orator, rather than the not less talented son, a junior senator at this time, II. 9 nn., since Pliny avoids the admonitory tone which he uses towards his young protégés, such as Avitus, Geminus, and the younger Maximus, II. 6, VII. 1, 26, VIII. 24. He is brother-in-law of Septicius Clarus, II. 9. 4 n. The *cognomen*, missing in the MS., is not in doubt.

1. amabam Pompeium Saturninum (hunc dico nostrum). See Ep. 8 for this otherwise unknown personage, who may be the 'doctus homo' of Ep. 20.

nostrum 'our mutual friend' not 'our friend from Comum', see Ep. 14. 4 n.

2. agentem . . . , nec minus polite et ornate . . . adsunt aptae crebraeque sententiae, sonantia verba et antiqua. In VII. 12. 4 *sonantia verba* are criticized as *tumida*, and in II. 19. 6 they are contrasted with *pressa*. Cf. also I. 20. 19, IX. 26. 5. So Saturninus' taste seems to be akin to Pliny's—Asian, but toned down by the Atticist school to some extent (3–4 nn.), much as in Pliny's experiment with a modified Atticist element described in Ep. 2. 1–4. Hence Pliny prefers Saturninus' fuller historical style, s. 4. On the stylistic controversy see Ep. 2 nn.

polite et ornate. Cf. IX. 26. 1, 'oratore . . . recto sed parum grandi et ornato'.

antiqua. Quintilian, 8. 3. 24–30, criticizes the excessive use of archaisms. They are not necessarily a mark of Atticism, since the new rhetoric of the Principate, which was mainly Asian in affiliation, searched them out for its own purposes. Cf. Marache, op. cit., ch. v, Ep. 2. 1 n.

sententiae. Roman rhetoric greatly developed the short aphorism, especially in the imperial age, when the aphorism *ex inopinato* had a great vogue. Quintilian discusses them in 8. 5 at length, and summarizes their effect: 'feriunt animum et uno ictu frequenter impellunt'. But like the *Ad Herennium* (4. 24–25) he deprecates excessive use of them as being the 'eyes' of a speech, not its 'limbs' (*Inst.* 8. 5. 33–34, 12. 10. 48; cf. S. F. Bonner, *Roman Declamation*, 54–55). Cicero (*De Or.* 1. 31, 2. 34) approves the aphorism in principle. Pliny's whole sentence echoes *De Or.* 1. 31: 'sapientibus sententiis gravibusque verbis ornata oratio et polita'.

3. senties quod ego, cum orationes eius in manus sumpseris, quas facile cuilibet veterum, quorum est aemulus, comparabis. Saturninus is an early representative of the new archaizing movement in Latin literature, best known from Aulus Gellius and Fronto, that revived the study of the pre-Ciceronian orators and writers, such as Gaius Gracchus and even Cato, as a quarry for vocabulary. Cf. Ep. 2. 1–2 nn., 20. 4. This tendency had some common ground with the contemporary Atticist taste in prose style, but there is a distinction. The archaizing style was grafted on to the Asian and modern style of the Principate—*eloquentia saeculi nostri*. Pliny's account of Saturninus shows that the archaizing style of which Fronto is the surviving exponent was already emerging before the time of Hadrian. Marache (op. cit., ch. v) fails to take notice of this evidence. The true Atticists were also attached to later models than Gracchus, such as Calvus, Ep. 2. 2: Saturninus was evidently no strict Atticist, s. 2, and by *veteres* Pliny may only mean the Ciceronian age as contrasted with *eloquentia saeculi nostri*, Ep. 5. 11.

4. idem tamen in historia magis satisfaciet vel brevitate . . . vel splendore etiam et sublimitate narrandi. nam in contionibus . . . pressior tantum et circumscriptior. Saturninus used a composite style, akin to Quintilian's *medius modus* (Ep. 2. 2 n.). These paragraphs might be a description of Tacitus. The whole letter illuminates the milieu in which Tacitus formed his historical style, and might have been adduced by Syme, *Tac.* ch. 17, for this purpose.

brevitate. The *brevitas* which Pliny discusses in Ep. 20, a letter to Tacitus, is sheer lack of length, not the stylistic quality.

splendore etiam et sublimitate. These suggest the Demosthenic touch, cf. IX. 26. 8 f., Quintilian, 12. 10. 23.

contionibus. In the speeches inserted into the narrative he showed the Atticist virtues which he did not fully exercise in his forensic speeches. Saturninus adapted his style to the theme, as recommended by Quintilian, 12. 10. 69–70. In V. 8. 9–10 Pliny notes the differences in style between history and oratory: 'haec vel maxime vi amaritudine instantia, illa tractu et suavitate atque etiam dulcedine placet', etc.

5. **praeterea facit versus quales Catullus meus aut Calvus.** The archaizing taste invaded versification also, IV. 27. 4, VI. 21, IX. 21. 1.

6. **legit mihi nuper epistulas; uxoris esse dicebat. Plautum vel Terentium metro solutum legi credidi.** These are 'epistulae accuratius scriptae' (I. 1 nn., II. 13. 7, IX. 28. 5) and their style is due to the cultivated taste of Saturninus and his erudite spouse, not to the 'incorrupta antiquitas sermonis' which women were said by Cicero (*De Or.* 3. 45) to preserve. Cf. a similar remark in Plato, *Crat.* 418B. Half-heartedly and needlessly—for Pliny could tell the difference—Bardon suggested that they were letters of Saturninus *to* a wife—*Lit. Lat. Inc.* ii. 198.

uxorem quam virginem accepit tam doctam politamque reddiderit. Compare Pliny's education of his own wife, IV. 19. 2 n., and the education of Minicia Fundana, V. 16. 3 n. But Juvenal satirizes *doctae nimis* in *Sat.* 6. 434–56 without sympathy. Guillemin remarks, ad loc., that the custom of early marriage meant that girls were but half educated at best when they married. Hence there is no occasion to suspect the phrase 'quam virginem accepit'. Pliny uses it again in VIII. 23. 7. It indicates the first marriage of a lady in a society in which divorce was frequent. Cf. Brakman, *Mnemosyne* (1925), 88, and Schuster, *app. crit.*

8. **etiam imagines conquireremus.** See IV. 28. 1 n. for the custom. Also Juv. 7. 29; Mart. 7. 44, 9 pref. (Guillemin).

17. *To Cornelius Titianus*

Date. Within the Nervan period, s. 1 n. Nothing suggests a Domitianic date, as oddly proposed by Hartleben, ad loc.

Address. Cornelius Titianus is known only from the address of this letter and of IX. 32, a formal note, where the *nomen* is not given. The variant 'Iccianus' in γ might, in the absence of α for this Letter, support the notion that the correspondent Cornelius Minicianus, of III. 9, &c., is intended, who is also the recipient of VIII. 12 where the subject is again Titinius Capito, and whose names may be misread again in the titles of VI. 31 and VII. 12.

1. **est adhuc curae hominibus fides et officium, sunt qui defunctorum quoque amicos agant.** Evidently Capito had been a protégé of the Junii Silani. Syme (*Tac.* 92 f.), failing to notice this sentence,

severely criticized Capito as a servant of the previous régime, for a false show of *libertas* unjustified by personal connexions. For the sentiment cf. IX. 9. 1.

impetravit ut sibi liceret statuam L. Silani in foro ponere. Cn. Octavius Titinius Capito is known from *ILS* 1448, found at Rome. After serving in Domitian's wars with distinction he became secretary of the combined departments *ab epistulis* and *a patrimonio*—apparently combined together—and continued to hold the former secretariat under Nerva and in the first years of Trajan, until he was promoted to be *praefectus vigilum* in late 101 or 102 before Trajan received the title *Dacicus*. He is the first of the equestrians known regularly to have held one of the great secretariats formerly found in the hands of imperial freedmen. It is possible that his literary aptitudes, which Pliny reckoned rare among the army-trained procurators of this period (VII. 25. 2–4), led to this appointment. So too the literary Suetonius held apparently the same *ab epistulis* office under Hadrian (Ep. 18, pref.). But the documents which the *ab epistulis* handled were like those of the prefect of Saturn (Ep. 10. 9 n.), *litterae inlitteratissimae*, reports and petitions of governors and officials (Statius, *Silvae*, 5. 1. 83 ff.). This post is distinct from that of the 'literary secretary', known as 'ab epistulis et ad responsa Graeca', who concocted the emperor's formal replies to loyal addresses and diplomatic replies to oriental kings on occasions that demanded a good Greek style, an office held by trained Greek rhetoricians such as Dionysius of Alexandria, who held the post in the same period down to Trajan that Capito was administrator *ab epistulis* (Suidas s.v. Διονύσιος). A. N. Sherwin-White, *BSR*, XV. 22 nn., 69–70; Hirschfeld, *Verwaltungsbeamten*, 363. Cf. Ep. 18, pref.; Pflaum, n. 60. Augustus had offered just such a literary secretaryship to the poet Horace (*Vit. Hor.* 45).

Capito is yet another of the Flavian figures associated with Nerva, like Fabricius Veiento, showing the connexion between Nerva and the entourage of Domitian: see IV. 22. 4 n. and VII. 33. 9 n. Pliny has much to say about Capito here and in VIII. 12, but addresses only V. 8 to him.

ab imperatore nostro. Nerva, who secured for Capito the award of *ornamenta praetoria* from the Senate (*ILS*, loc. cit.), is more probable than the absent Trajan. The action of Capito fits the period of the return of the exiles. In Books I and II Pliny uses *princeps* and *Caesar* indifferently for emperors alive or dead, but not *imperator*, which occurs commonly in the later books: I. 13. 3, 18. 3, II. 7. 1, 9. 2, 11. 10–11, 15, 13. 8, III. 5. 9, 18. 2, IV. 17. 8, 22. 4, 6, VII. 31. 4, VIII. 17. 2. Pliny would not have called Domitian *noster* in a publication after his death: cf. II. 9. 2, 'a Caesare nostro'.

statuam L. Silani. Probably the younger and more noteworthy of the two aristocratic L. Junii Silani Torquati, political victims of Nero. As a junior senator in 65 he might have been a contemporary of Capito. He was involved, with his teacher, the great jurisprudent L. Cassius Longinus, in the aftermath of the Pisonian conspiracy. His refusal to spare his executioner by a voluntary suicide rated with the saga of Arria, Tac. *Ann.* 15. 52. 3, 16. 7–9; *CIG*¹, 369; *PIR*¹, s.v.

in foro ponere. For control over this by the Princeps see II. 7. 1 n.; Suet. *Cal.* 34. 1; *CIL*, vi. 1438.

2. magna laude dignum amicitia principis in hoc uti. Equestrian officials were designated *amicus meus* in imperial documents, cf. x. 7, 'Pompeium Plantam praefectum Aegypti amicum meum', n. But by *amicitia principis* here, as in III. 5. 7 and IV. 24. 3—'illum civilibus officiis principis amicitia exemit'—Pliny means rather the upper crust of senatorial and equestrian administrators who formed the advisory council of the emperor. So too Tacitus, *Dial.* 8. 3, 'potentissimi . . . civitatis . . . principes in Caesaris amicitia agunt feruntque cuncta atque ab ipso principe cum quadam reverentia diliguntur'. Cf. J. Crook, *Consilium Principis* (Cambridge, 1955), 23 ff., who, however, misses the distinction between such counsellors and men like Pliny who were invited to sit as judicial assessors from time to time, IV. 22. 1 n.

3. quo studio imagines Brutorum Cassiorum Catonum domi ubi potest habeat. Public display of the regicides, as at funerals, was not allowed under Augustus and Tiberius, Tac. *Ann.* 3. 76. Private possession was permitted by Augustus, but indiscreet display within the home was charged against Silanus' fellow-victim Longinus, Appian, *BC* 4. 51; Tac. *Ann.* 4. 35, 16. 7; Suet. *Nero* 37. 1; Juv. 5. 36. Even under Vespasian it was reckoned dangerous to 'praise Cato', Tac. *Dial.* 3. 2, 10. 6.

By *imagines* Pliny means painted portraits, not sculptured busts or death masks, as in Tac. *Ann.* 3. 76. Cf. IV. 28. 1 n.

clarissimi cuiusque vitam egregiis carminibus exornat. Capito specialized in historical studies. In VIII. 12. 4 Pliny mentions his *exitus illustrium virorum*, and in V. 8 Capito encourages Pliny to write history. Bardon suggests rather literally that his verses were elegiac panegyrics set beneath portraits, *Lit. Lat. Inc.* ii. 221.

18. *To Suetonius Tranquillus*

Date. Before Pliny became prefect of Saturn, when he ceased from the private practice as an advocate here mentioned; x. 3 A.

Address. C. Suetonius Tranquillus, the biographer, was born of equestrian parents between A.D. 70–75: Suet. *Nero* 57. 2; *Otho* 10; *Dom.*
12. 2. He appears here and in X. 94. 1 as one of the *studiosi* who
gathered round Pliny, as around Tacitus, as their leader at the Bar
(IV. 13. 10). Pliny at this time negotiates the purchase of a farm for
him (Ep. 24), and later secures him admission to the *militia equestris*
(III. 8). This may have kept him out of Italy *c.* 103–6, though he did
not take the first commission offered (ibid.), since he reappears in the
correspondence only in V. 10. Later he accompanies Pliny to Bithynia,
if the ambiguous text of X. 94. 1 is to be trusted, and secures the
grant of marriage privileges with Pliny's help (ibid.). His career is
now better, but incompletely, known from the fragments of an
inscription found at Hippo Regius in Africa: *AE* (1953), n. 73. This
contains no mention of his *militia*, but it shows that he later
held the posts of *a studiis* and *a bibliothecis*—technical adviser on
forensic affairs, and head of the libraries at Rome—either in the last
years of Trajan or, less probably, in the first of Hadrian, before
becoming *ab epistulis* to Hadrian. Possibly he accompanied Hadrian
to Britain. His promotion owed something to Pliny's friend Septicius
Clarus, whose disgrace as praetorian prefect he shared in *c.* 121, and
to whom he dedicated his *Lives* (I. 1, pref., II. 9. 4 n.; Lydus, *De
Mag.* II. 6, p. 17).

His place of origin is not known. Hippo is possible, if the title
flamen, which comes early in the fragments, is a municipal office.
Ep. 24 may suggest that Suetonius at this time owned no land in
Italy. But the *nomen* Suetonius is very rare in Africa, and the city
may have honoured him for other reasons, perhaps as an advocate:
cf. VI. 18. 1. Pisaurum, where the *nomen* is common, is suggested by
Syme. The new inscription shows also that Suetonius served possibly
as *iudex selectus* in the Roman courts, and certainly as *pontifex
Volcani*. This is taken by some to be an error for the Roman priesthood known as *flamen Volcani*, but it might better be the well-
documented pontificate of Ostia, and indicate an Ostian origin for
Suetonius (Grosso). The secretariat *ab epistulis* has been assumed to
be the Palatine post, which in this period passed from freedmen to
equestrian personages, like the other great secretariats. SHA, *Hadr.*
11. 3 designates it as *magister epistularum*, anachronistically. But it
might be the literary secretaryship, often held by learned men such
as Dionysius of Alexandria, after or with the librarianship. Suetonius'
career recalls that of L. Julius Vestinus, who shortly afterwards held
a similar group of posts, including the charge of the libraries, the
studia, and the 'letters'. Later also Volusius Maecianus was *a libellis*
after the libraries' post. Cf. Ep. 17. 1 n.; *AE* (1924), n. 78; *CIG* 5900;
CIL, xiv. 5347–8.

The most systematic discussion of the evidence is now G. B. Town-send, *Historia* 1961, 99 ff., with Syme, *Tac.* 778 f.; F. Grosso, *Rendiconti Lincei* S. viii (1959), 263 f., and Pflaum, n. 96.

Only three other short letters are addressed to Suetonius, of which two concern literature: III. 8, V. 10, IX. 34.

1. scribis te perterritum somnio vereri. For the belief in dreams and visions see VII. 27. 1, 12–14 nn. Suetonius, like Fannius, V. 5. 4–5, is a believer. Tougher minds than Pliny's took them seriously, as did his uncle, who wrote his German Wars 'somnio monitus', III. 5. 4; cf. *NH* 25. 17. He leaves the question open in *NH* 10. 211, but remarks shrewdly: 'a vino et a cibo proxima ... vana esse visa prope convenit'.

rogas ut dilationem petam. Pliny and Suetonius are appearing together in a civil case before a *iudex privatus*, s. 6. So too Pliny offers a share in a case to his protégé Cremutius Ruso, VI. 23. 2. Suetonius as appears also from Ep. 24. 4, n., is only at the beginning of his career as advocate.

3. susceperam causam Iuni Pastoris, cum mihi quiescenti visa est socrus mea advoluta genibus ne agerem obsecrare. Junius Pastor may be the rich friend of Martial, IX. 22. Otherwise he is not identifiable, *PIR*[1], ii, J 520–21.

socrus mea. If the date proposed below is correct this is not Pompeia Celerina (Ep. 4 pref.) but the mother of Pliny's first wife. Pliny would have been married by the time he was 20, rather earlier than the normal age for young *laticlavii* to marry, cf. VI. 26. 1, VII. 16. 2, 24. 3. VIII. 23. 7 nn. He was unmarried and aged 17 in August 79, and could not be older than barely 20 in August–September 81. For the controversy over the number of his marriages see X. 2. 2 n.

contra potentissimos civitatis atque etiam Caesaris amicos. Pliny never gives Domitian his titles, observing the *damnatio memoriae*, in the Letters or the Panegyric, except in a contemporary quotation, IV. 11. 7 n. Hence this should be Titus—there is no hint of the terror of Domitian—and the case could be the *iudicium quadruplex* mentioned as a case of his youth (but *iuvenis* not *adulescentulus*) in IV. 24. 1. Such cases were rare, only one other occurring in the Letters, VI. 33. 3 nn., where he feels the necessity of explaining the term. He himself began to practise in the courts when aged 18, V. 8. 8; for youthful advocates see II. 14. 2, VI. 11 nn., 23. 2. But a date in the early years of Domitian is possible, and would meet the objection that the *socrus* of the letters should be the same lady throughout (Monti, art. cit., in IV. 1 pref.). A brief early marriage before the second and longer, which ends in 97, would be possible.

5, quod dubites ne feceris. Editors quote a longer version from Cicero, *Off.* 1. 30.

6. iudicium centumvirale differri nullo modo, istuc aegre quidem sed tamen potest. In an action before a single *iudex*, postponement of the opening of a case would be no inconvenience if the judge and contestants agreed, but the Centumviral court had a schedule of cases to work through. Adjournments *during* a Centumviral case might occur if the hearings were lengthy, v. 9. 1. The late rule of the *Sententiae Pauli*, v. 16. 17, allows a single postponement in lesser criminal cases; cf. the usage of Trajan in a criminal case, VI. 31. 9.

19. *To Romatius Firmus*

Date. This should be earlier than the longer and more socially interesting examples of patronage letters in II. 9 and 13, of which one at least is Nervan.

Address. Romatius is known only here and in IV. 29, where he is a *iudex selectus*.

1. municeps tu meus et condiscipulus. They went to the same *grammaticus* at Comum. It is apparent from IV. 13 that Pliny did not attend a *rhetor Latinus* at Comum, *pace* Otto, art. cit. 8.

magnae et graves causae cur suscipere augere dignitatem tuam debeam. Pliny was quick to adopt a patronizing attitude to his younger contemporaries of equestrian status when he had secured senatorial rank, cf. I. 14. 3, II. 13. 8 nn. Here the gap is greater, and his tone the more condescending. But the feeling of obligation towards his family's followers is genuine, and part of the patronal system, cf. II. 4, VI. 32.

2. esse autem tibi centum milium censum satis indicat quod apud nos decurio es. This passage is the only evidence for the amount of the property qualification for municipal councillors in Italy, the existence of which is indicated by the Republican Lex Municipi Tarentini 26–30 (W. Liebenam, *Städteverwaltung* etc., 234 f.). The figure may go back at least to the municipal reorganization initiated by Julius Caesar, and a passage in X. 110. 2 suggests that the figure of S.100,000 was introduced even earlier, on an Italian model, into Bithynia–Pontus by the Lex Pompeia. But the amount was probably not uniform throughout Italy, as with other details of municipal organization. In addition newly elected decurions were expected to make a voluntary contribution to public funds, the *summa decurionatus*, X. 112. 1 n.

This passage may also indicate that Pliny assumed that most local councillors were not worth much more than the minimum franchise, which was the value of only a moderate farm, such as that given for a pension to his nurse, VI. 3. 1 n.

ut te non decurione solum verum etiam equite Romano perfruamur, offerro tibi ad implendas facultates trecenta milia nummum. The equestrian property qualification had been set at a capital sum of S.400,000 in the later Republican period, if not earlier, in fixing the obligation to serve as a cavalryman, though the actual figure is not named before the date of Horace, *Ep.* I. I. 58, with reference to the Lex Roscia of 67 B.C. This sum is confirmed for the early Principate in the Elder Pliny's summary of a *SC.* of A.D. 23 and later literary references (*NH* 33. 32; Martial, 4. 67, 5. 38; Juv. 14. 326). From the present passage, as from Martial, 4. 67, where Gaunus asks a senator to add S.100,000 to his own estate of S.300,000, 'ut posset domino plaudere iustus eques', the question arises whether the term *eques Romanus* in the Principate meant merely the possession of the equestrian franchise, or whether all knights were registered in the eighteen *centuriae equitum Romanorum*, as holders of the 'public horse'—the 'equo publico exornati' of inscriptions—subject to the known imperial censorial reviews (*recognitio*) of the Order, and liable to take part in the annual *transvectio equitum* at Rome (Suet. *Aug.* 37. 1, 38. 3; *Gaius*, 16. 2; *ILS* 9483; Dion. Hal. *Ant. Rom.* 6. 13). The prevailing view due to Stein (below) is that all Roman knights in the Principate held the *equus publicus*. But Pliny, *NH* 33. 29–34, in his obscure discussion of the history of the Equestrian Order, implies that after the *SC.* of A.D. 23 and the Lex Visellia of 24 (*Cod. Just.* 9. 21. 1, 31. 1) about the wearing of golden rings, the term *eques Romanus* covered more than the members past and present of the *Centuriae*, and that all persons who could wear the rings were regarded as members of the Order: 'quod antea militares equi nomen dederant hoc nunc pecuniae indices tribuunt' (Pliny, loc. cit. 29). The qualification of the *SC.* included the equestrian franchise, three generations of free birth on the father's side, and whatever conditions were laid down by the Lex Roscia. For the Elder, whoever fulfils these conditions is a Roman knight. Hence it came about that a dual usage arose, and is apparent in numerous inscriptions, in the common distinction between those who describe themselves simply as *eques Romanus* and those who use the term *equo publico exornatus* (cf. also Brunt, cited below).

Yet there seems little point in Pliny giving Romatius so large a sum to secure a purely nominal title, like the modern English 'esquire', though he speaks as if the acquisition of the status would follow automatically. So too Seneca implied, *de ben.* 3. 7: 'iudex . . . quem census in album et equestris hereditas misit'. Since in IV. 29 Romatius appears as a *iudex* of the *decuriae iudicum*, the main public

service of those who held the 'public horse', it is likely that Pliny
meant to secure for Romatius equestrian status in this form. In
revising this note Pliny might well have omitted a technical reference
to the formalities of applying for the 'public horse'.

A passage in the *Tabula Hebana* (E–J² 94a) has been thought to
confirm the existence in the early Principate of a class of members
of the order who did not hold the public horse. In the arrangements
for the funeral of Germanicus in ll. 55–57 it reads: 'qui ordini
[equestri adscripti cla- *or* latum cla- *or* privatum eq- *or* neq. pub. eq.-]
uom habebunt qui eor(um) officio fungi volent et per valetudinem
perq(ue) domestic[um funus non impedientur, cum] clavo, ii qui
equom pub(licum) habebunt cum trabeis in campum veniant'. Here
the reference is to the active members of the centuries who are to
appear in military dress (*trabeis*) and to the elderly or retired members, mentioned in Suet. *Aug.* 38, who are to appear in civilian dress
(*clavo*). A reference to the young *laticlavii* (Staveley, art. cit. below)
does not fit the context, though the supplement *latum cla-vum* is
epigraphically possible. The supplement *privatum eq-uum*, which
implies two grades of knights, is a term of modern invention. Consideration of the dress worn by the knights suggests that *angustum
cla-vum* is a better solution than any of the above. The *trabea* was
the parade uniform of the *eques Romanus*, and the *tunica* with purple
stripe or *clavus* was his civilian garment, worn beneath the toga.
Cf. Tac. *Ann.* 3. 2; Suet. *Dom.* 14. 3; Mommsen, *DPR*, vi. 2, 113 f.
The use of the stripe by equestrians is first securely documented in
Augustan texts: Ovid, *Tr.* 4. 10. 35; Vell. Pat. 2. 88. 2.

For discussion see Stein, *Römischer Ritterstand*, ch. ii; Mommsen,
DPR, vi. 2, 84 f.; *CAH*, x. 186 ff.; E. S. Stavely, 'Iudex
Selectus', *Rhein. Mus.* (1953), esp. 253 n. 32; P. A. Brunt, *JRS*
(1961), 'The Lex Valeria', 76 f.; M. I. Henderson, *JRS* (1963),
61 f.

perfruamur. He is not expected to seek a place in the select officer
corps of the *militia equestris*, which required only a very small percentage of the numerous Order to maintain the supply of military
tribunes and auxiliary officers. Jury service was the only state
function performed by the average Roman knight, iv. 29 nn.

equestres facultates. Cf. x. 4. 5 for *facultatium splendor*, of equestrian wealth. The term *quadringenta*—a capital of S.400,000—is used
by Martial and Juvenal of a decent competency: Mart. 5. 25; Juv.
1. 106, 2. 117, 5. 132. Carcopino, who regards S.20,000 as a minimal
income for middle-class life at Rome, greatly exaggerates the cost of
living at this period (*Daily Life*, 66 f.). An estate of a million sesterces is regarded by Martial (4. 66) as a considerable fortune for a
municipal establishment.

20. *To Cornelius Tacitus*

Date. Undeterminable, but the letter may belong to the same period as those concerning Pompeius Saturninus, Epp. 8, 16. Cf. s. 1 n.

Address. For Pliny and Tacitus see Ep. 6, pref.

1. **frequens mihi disputatio est cum quodam docto homine et perito.** The parallel discussion on style in IX. 26 also starts from the criticism of an anonymous orator. This man may be the Atticist Lupercus, recipient of II. 5 and IX. 26, or Pliny's new friend, the advocate and man of letters Pompeius Saturninus of Epp. 8 and 16. That the anonymous man should be a fictitious character, as Prete suggested (*Saggi pliniani* 50 f.), is contrary to the character of the Letters. The theme is *brevitas*, which Pliny noted as characteristic of Saturninus' style (Ep. 16. 4). Here he is concerned with actual length and amplitude of treatment (ss. 14–16), but the two are connected (cf. Tac. *Dial.* 18. 4–6) and in ss. 20–21 he passes on to stylistic *brevitas*. Saturninus also was 'veterum aemulus', and something of an Atticist, Ep. 16. 2–3. 4. Arrianus Maturus is less probable, though an Atticist and archaist also, because Pliny implies that he was not a practising advocate, I. 2, II. 11. 1, III. 2. 2–4 nn.

brevitas. Pliny does not regard Tacitus as an exponent of this quality, s. 23. Hence the letter is not evidence for the development of Tacitus' style (cf. L. Hermann, *Latomus* (1955) 352 ff.). Length of speeches is again discussed, in similar terms, in VI. 2. 5–9, where it would seem that *brevitas* meant a speech that occupied less than two *clepsydrae*, i.e. half a Roman hour, s. 11 n. As a discussion of style this letter should be read with I. 16 and IX. 26. To *brevitas* Pliny opposes *magnitudo*, and extols its manifestation in *audacia* and *sublimitas*. F. F. Quadlbauer, in a partial discussion of Pliny's style, concludes that Pliny goes beyond the rules of Cicero and Quintilian in his demand for excessive fullness of style, with elaboration of detail and strain after effect, which produces an ornate style lacking effective 'pathos'. (*P. der Jüngere über den Begriff der erhabenen Rede*, Diss. Graz, 1949, 138 f., 285 f. Also, 'Die Genera Dicendi . . .', *Wiener Studien*, 71 (1958), 107 f.) Prete, op. cit. 55 f., finds in this letter an illustration of the very principle expounded in ss. 14–16: every line of attack is explored.

3. **oratio animo non ictu magis quam mora imprimitur.** Pliny exemplifies this in his account of Pericles, below ss. 17–19. The doctrine occurs in Longinus, *de subl.* 12. 2, for whom αὔξησις, amplification, consists of 'fullness' πλῆθος (*copia* s. 18), and produces its effect by persistence, ἐπιμονή. But Quadlbauer (*WS*, loc. cit.)

observes that Pliny conflates what Longinus distinguishes, 'fullness' and 'forcefulness', the ὕψος ἀπότομον of Pericles' thunderbolts. In IX. 26 Pliny gives a less strained account of the 'sublime', though there too (s. 5) he adds *plena* to *sublimia* and *audentia* as part of the same style.

4. Gracchis et Catoni Pollionem Caesarem Caelium, in primis M. Tullium oppono. For the cult of the *veteres* see Ep. 16. 3 n. The Augustan Asinius Pollio, quoted for a dictum in VI. 29. 5, was somewhat of an Atticist (Tac. *Dial.* 21. 7). Caesar the Dictator was much praised as an orator, Cic. *Brutus* 261 f. Caelius, Cicero's friend, is discussed with these in *Dial.* 21, 25.

5. idem orationibus evenit. Quadlbauer loc. cit. notes another similarity with a passage of Longinus (36. 3–4), who, however, distinguishes between natural creatures, including speech as part of man's nature, in which the beauty is improved by size, and artefacts, Pliny's *signa*, &c., in which exactness is preferred. These and other similarities with Longinus in s. 3 and IX. 26. 3, 6 n., do not suggest that Pliny knew the *De Sublimitate*.

6. contendat hos ipsos . . . pauciora dixisse quam ediderint. The critic does not maintain the thesis of the *eruditi*, discussed by Quintilian, 12. 10. 49 ff., that the published speech ought to be shorter than the original, as suggested by Guillemin (*VL*, 86). But Pliny in s. 9 takes up Quintilian's position, ibid. 51, almost in his own words: 'idem videtur bene dicere ac bene scribere neque aliud esse oratio scripta quam monumentum actionis habitae'. See further III. 18. 9 n.

7. quasi subscriptio quorundam criminum solis titulis indicatur. Cf. *pro Murena* 57 for an example, where the manuscript still reads, as then presumably, 'de Postumi criminibus, de Servi adulescentis', and nothing more. The *pro Vareno* is lost.

8. ait se totam causam vetere instituto solum perorasse. He says this in the *pro Clu.* 199, and comments adversely in *Brutus* 207 on the new custom of dividing a case between several advocates.

　　postea recisa ac repurgata in unum librum. Despite Pliny, Cicero implies in *Brutus* 91 and *Tusc.* 4. 55 that he published his speeches much as he delivered them. Asconius *in Corn.* 54 (62), says that Cicero turned his *pro Cornelio* into two published speeches, presumably in a format like that of the five Verrines. Nepos, quoted by Jerome, *Ep.* 72, adds that the published work was much the same length as the original. Pliny unfortunately followed the custom of enlarging speeches for publication, III. 18. 1, IV. 5. 4.

9. at aliud est actio bona, aliud oratio. Quintilian, 12. 10. 49 ff., dismisses these two views of publication. Pliny follows him very closely to the effect that the written text should be the *monumentum* (Quintilian) (cited s. 6 n.) or *exemplar* (Pliny) of the *actio*. See III. 18. 9 n.

10. ut in Verrem. See *II in Verr.* 4. 5 for this passage.

11. leges quae longissima tempora largiuntur. Cf. VI. 2. 6, 'nos legibus ipsis iustiores quae tot horas tot dies tot comperendinationes largiuntur'. There, as in II. 11. 14, IV. 9. 9 nn., the reference is to the rules of criminal jurisdiction. So too Tacitus remarks that the Lex Pompeia Iudiciaria of 58 B.C. first limited the length of speeches before criminal courts, *Dial.* 38. From VI. 2, 3, and 7 it is clear that in civil cases, about which he is chiefly concerned in this letter, the time assigned to speeches depended either on the *iudex* or the agreement of the parties.

12. usus magister egregius. He uses the phrase again in VI. 29. 4. The letter is full of proverbs, ss. 15, 30.

    frequenter iudicavi, frequenter in consilio fui. See Ep. 9. 2 'in consilium rogavit' n., VI. 2. 7 'quotiens iudico' n., for Pliny's activity as a civil judge and assessor; and for senatorial liability to jury service in the *quaestiones*, IV. 29. 2 n.

13. suae quisque inventioni favet. Guillemin compares Quint. 8. 3. 71.

14. dixit aliquando mihi Regulus, cum simul adessemus : '. . . ego iugulum statim video'. But Regulus liked plenty of time for his speeches, VI. 2. 3. For Pliny's professional association with Regulus see Ep. 5. 4–5 nn. From this passage, and from his preference in Ep. 5. 11 for the 'oratory of our times', it seems that Regulus used the violent style evolved by the school of Cassius Severus, Ep. 2. 2 n. Guillemin, op. cit. 104.

15. πάντα denique λίθον κινῶ. The proverb first appears in Euripides, *Heraclidae* 1002.

17. Periclen sic a comico Eupolide laudari. This passage from the *Demes* of Eupolis was much quoted in antiquity; cf. the references in Schuster's *apparatus*. Pliny gives only half the known verses. See Kock, *Com. Att. Fr.* i. 281 n. 94.

19. quae de eodem Pericle comicus alter. Aristophanes, *Acharn.* 531, also much quoted in antiquity. Cf. Quint. 12. 10. 24, 65, more briefly and without the Greek.

oratio . . . lata et magnifica. Cf. Ep. 10. 5, 'sublimitatem et lati-
tudinem'.

20. optimus tamen modus est. See II. 5. 13, 'ne modum quem etiam
orationi adhibendum puto in epistula excedam', and v. 6. 42, 'si
materiae immoratur, non esse longum'. But Prete (op. cit. 56–57)
reckons that Pliny tended to exceed the dictates of his theory.

21. ut illud 'immodice et redundanter', ita hoc 'ieiune et infirme'.
Pliny passes to brevity of style. For the battle of styles see Ep. 2. 2 n.
There he takes up the central position, as also in the composition of
his Panegyric, III. 13. 3–4, 18. 8–10. Guillemin (ad loc.) remarks that
Pliny here reflects the teaching of his master Quintilian in favour of
the mean (*Inst.* 2. 4. 4, 9, 12. 10. 66–72). But his real preference
as in VII. 12, IX. 26, is for the more florid aspects of this technique.
At heart he is Asianist.

22. illum Homericum. *Iliad* 2. 212, 3. 214, 222. Two of Pliny's
examples are also quoted—but not in Greek—in Quintilian's parallel
passage 12. 10. 64–65.

25. brevi epistula. See III. 9. 27 n. for the length of letters, and s. 20 n.
above.

21. *To Plinius Paternus*

The date and person addressed are not determinable, though the
names are known from the fragmentary inscription of a leading man
of Comum, L. Plinius Paternus Pusillienus (*AE* (1916), n. 116; cf. M.
Bertolone, *Lombardia romana* (Milan, 1939), ii, fig. 30). Three other
letters are addressed in the manuscript simply to Paternus, IV. 14,
VIII. 16, IX. 27. The rarity of the *cognomen* in upper-class society
suggests that the same man is meant, and he is likely to hail from
Comum. In the samples given by the index of Dessau, *ILS*, the name
is common among soldiers and in Celtic connexions, but only one
Italian and two provincial knights bear it before the third century:
ibid. 2727, 6932, 6983. Schulze, *Eigennamen*, etc., 192, who quotes
Etruscan by-forms and examples from Milan of *Paternius*, holds
that the latter form was mostly used by new citizens. The name does
not appear in the indices of Seneca, Tacitus, and Suetonius, but is
used by Martial of a mean and wealthy man, 12. 53. Such a one might
well advise about the choice of slaves, and need an indirect reproof
for meanness towards them, as in VIII. 16. The other two letters to
Paternus concern literature. He evidently belongs to the same circle
of society at Comum as Caninius and Calvisius Rufus, whose diverse
interests are combined in the letters to Paternus.

22. To Catilius Severus

Date. Pliny's movements fix this letter to a period before his appointment to the prefecture of Saturn, probably summer 97, ss. 1, 11 n.

Address. The man is one of those friends of Pliny addressed in Book I, such as Septicius Clarus and Pompeius Falco, Epp. 1, 23, pref., who, though at this time insignificant senators or knights, were destined to play a leading role in the history of the period, largely due, in these cases, to their connexions with Hadrian. L. Catilius Severus Iulianus Claudius Reginus, hardly as yet a praetorian senator, held a legionary command and some four administrative posts, including like Pliny the two treasuries, but no imperial province, before his consulship in 110. Yet later he took part in the Parthian campaigns and governed the military areas of newly annexed Armenia, and the Syrian province, between 116 and his second consulship in 120. About 137–8 he was *praefectus urbi*, and like other of Pliny's friends had hopes of the imperial throne (VI. 26 nn.). Possibly his son married Domitia Lucilla, grandmother of Marcus Aurelius, who reckoned Catilius among his forbears, VIII. 18. 2 n. His career is known largely from the restoration of two inscriptions, *ILS* 1041 (Antium) and *ILA* 43 (Thysdrus). His municipality is unknown. See *PIR²*, C 558; Garzetti, *Inc.* 40; Syme, *Tac.* 243; Dio 69. 21. 1, 75. 9. 6; SHA, *Hadr.* 5. 10, 15. 7, 24. 6–8; *Marcus* 1. 9. He receives III. 12 and possibly IX. 22.

1. diu iam in urbe haereo. As in other letters of this book (Epp. 7, pref., 13. 1 n.), Pliny's freedom of movement points to a date before his appointment to the *aerarium Saturni*, which limited greatly his ability to travel.

attonitus. A strong word used elsewhere by Pliny only in VI. 20. 7: 'volgus attonitum', of the effects of the Vesuvian eruption.

Aristonis. Titius Aristo is known from legal sources as one of the great lawyers of the day, a pupil of the distinguished Cassius Longinus (VII. 24. 8 n.), judicial adviser of Trajan, and correspondent of Neratius Priscus and Juventius Celsus, his rivals. Nothing is known of his career. He must have been older than Pliny to have heard Cassius, who died *c.* A.D. 70 (*Dig.* 1. 2. 2. 52). This letter implies (s. 6), contrary to the view of Mommsen, that he was not a senator, cf. *PIR¹*, T 197. Pliny consults him in VIII. 14 about senatorial procedure, but as a lawyer and an outsider. It has also been held that Aristo was not one of the small band of jurists, confined by Augustus to senators, who had the right of authoritative interpretation, *ius respondendi*, for citation in the courts of civil law. Yet he plays a considerable part in *Digest* texts, and Pliny speaks of him as of an oracle (W. Kunkel, *Herkunft* . . . *der römischen Juristen*, Weimar, 1952, 141 f.).

This letter, and v. 3, where Pliny defends his custom of writing and reciting his light verse, *lusus*, show marked respect.

2. quam peritus ille et privati iuris et publici. So too in VIII. 14. 1, with reference to *ius senatorium*, and in Gellius, *NA* 11. 18. 16. F. Schulze, *Roman Legal Science*, 46, 81 *et al.*, insists that the earlier jurisprudents down to the time of Hadrian paid no attention to constitutional and administrative law, but admits that after Hadrian lawyers were involved in its interpretation as members of the imperial *consilium*. But Pliny's account of Aristo, and the place of Pegasus and Javolenus Priscus as advisers of Domitian and Trajan, suggest that this is too sharp a distinction (cf. Schulze himself, op. cit. 103–4). The emergence of jurists interested in the rules of imperial administration was a gradual process.

mihi certe quotiens aliquid abditum quaero, ille thesaurus est. So in VIII. 14, and possibly over a question of personal status in X. 6. 1. This is the only specific reference in Pliny to the source of his legal opinions on cases; IV. 10. 1 and V. 7. 2 are vague. The work of the Roman Bar was divided between the *iurisprudentes*, who gave legal advice to the parties or sat as assessors to the civil *iudex*, and the advocates who represented the parties in court. Pliny's phrase suggests that clients consulted the jurisprudents through their advocates (cf. Schulze, op. cit. 111 ff.).

3. plerumque haesitat dubitat, diversitate rationum, quas acri magnoque iudicio ab origine causisque primis repetit discernit expendit. The very picture of a classical lawyer at work in a passage of the *Digest* weighing and dissecting his authorities. Roman lawyers, not being bound by precedent in the English sense, were involved in a yet keener analysis of the principles underlying their *exempla* (s. 2). These were not judgements, because in the Roman formulary system a judgement was factual in form, but the opinions of other jurisprudents dealing with similar cases. It was by accepting the legal opinion of one of the contending parties that the *iudex* decided how to answer the question set in the *formula* by the praetor who established the case. The *formula* itself was worked out in discussion with the parties and was based on a deal of legal argument. In theory the *formula* set a factual question to the *iudex*: 'si paret N. Negidium A. Agerio tot milia sestertium dare oportere, condemna'. But such a question could seldom be answered without much legal argument, needing the advice of jurisprudents on both sides. Hence the advocate who conducted the pleadings was bound to use and understand the language of pure law. Schulze, who is at pains to discount the influence of rhetoric and advocates on Roman law, underestimates this factor. Cf. S. F. Bonner, *Roman Declamation* (Liverpool 1949), ch. v and 45 f., and in general H. F. Jolowicz, *Historical Introduction to Roman Law*[2] (Cambridge, 1952), 576.

5. omnia ad conscientiam refert. See Ep. 12. 3 n.

6. non facile quemquam ex istis qui sapientiae studium habitu corporis praeferunt, huic viro comparabis. . . . in toga negotiisque versatur. That is, he did not behave like one of the contemporary professional philosophers or rhetoricians, such as Euphrates with his white beard, or the flashy Isaeus, I. 10. 6, II. 3. Pliny could not have written thus about a senator, to whom the very idea of *professio* was shocking and that of *negotia* normal, cf. IV. 11. 1–3.

istis. Catilius may be a lover of philosophers, as befits a friend of Hadrian. Pliny uses *iste* thus of the addressee in II. 10. 8, VII. 12. 5, VIII. 17. 6, but not always.

multos advocatione plures consilio iuvat. Schulze, op. cit. 108–9, is reluctant to admit that jurisprudents practised in court, and regards this as an exception, but quotes the parallel case of Paulus, *Dig.* 32. 78. 6. Aristo does worse, he even contributes to rhetorical studies, s. 1: 'litterae ipsae'.

8. nuper me paucosque . . . advocavit rogavitque. To commit suicide *e consili sententia* may seem a remarkable example of the Roman habit of taking multiple advice on every possible occasion, but follows from the fashion of rational suicide, Ep. 12. 3 n. So too the family of Corellius expected him to yield to advice, ibid. 9–10, and the Comensis took his wife's advice to end it all, VI. 24. 4. For the domestic council see also III. 4. 1, V. 1. 5 n.

si esset insuperabilis sponte exiret e vita. Corellius, I. 12, 9, Silius Italicus III. 7, 2, and Festus, in Martial, I. 78, took this line. But Aristo was allowed to survive, V. 3, VIII. 14. For the Stoic influence in this see Ep. 12. 3 n.

11. Laurentinum meum, . . . studiosumque otium repetam. See Ep. 9. 4 for his life at his villa at Laurentum. Here, as there, nothing suggests that Pliny had any official duties to occupy him.

23. *To Pompeius Falco*

Date. Early 97, if Falco is the tribune of IX. 13. 19, as fits.

Address. Pompeius Falco and his descendants are well known from a series of inscriptions, *ILS*, 1035–7, 1104–5; *CIL*, iii. 7537 *et al.*; *PIR*[1],

P 68; Garzetti, *C.* 134; Syme, *Tac.* 243, 510 n. These give him the remarkable name: Q. Roscius Coelius Murena Silius Decianus Vibullus Pius Iulius Eurycles Herclanus Pompeius Falco—and attest his later connexion with Q. Sosius Senecio (Ep. 13, pref.) whose daughter he married, and Sex. Iulius Frontinus (IV. 8. 3 n.), the lady's grandfather. His own names connect him with the wealthy Spartan dynastic family of C. Iulius Eurycles, powerful under Claudius, M. Roscius Coelius, a consul of 81, and the family of Silius Italicus (III. 7. 2 n.). His own origins and the source of these connexions are obscure. Since the genealogical inscription of Falconilla (*ILS* 1105) claims no senatorial dignity in the paternal line before Falco, he must have been the first senator of his family. His proper name before accretions was probably Q. Pompeius Sexti filius Falco. The importance of the Roscius element in the inscriptions suggests that his mother was a Roscia. From the Roscii comes the rare cognomen Murena; three senatorial Roscii Murenae are known, who may connect with the consul of 81, *PIR*[1], R 67, 69–71. This rare *cognomen* suggests that Pompeius Falco is the tribune Murena who intervened in the senatorial debate of 97 (IX. 13. 19; Syme, *Tac.* 76 n. 1). Shortly after, he commanded a legion and was decorated in the first Dacian war, governed Lycia-Pamphylia and Judaea before holding a suffect consulship in 108, according to a probable restoration of the *Fasti Ostienses* (VII. 22, pref.). In 116–17 he was governing Moesia Inferior, and under Hadrian Britain and Asia. He was still alive *c.* 141, Fronto, *Ep.* ii. 11. His descendants held exalted titular offices without real distinctions, including a great-grandson on whom the Praetorian Guard once sought to thrust the imperial power, Dio. 73. 8.

The pattern of his career resembles that of Catilius Severus, another administrator from the clique of Hadrian. Pliny knew him before his greatness, and may have met him in the house of Frontinus. The other letters to him give no impression of intimacy, IV. 27, VII. 22, IX. 15. He seems not to have been a Cisalpine nor yet a provincial, cf. VII. 22. 3 n., though his later names connect him with the Spartan Euryclids. The dedication at Cilician Hierapolis was due to a native legionary centurion who had served under Falco, *ILS* 1036.

1. **quid esse tribunatum putes.** In the Julio–Claudian period the tribunes exercised certain forms of civil and criminal jurisdiction that brought them into collision with the praetorian courts, and even used their *auxilium* against the *coercitio* of a praetor, Tac. *Ann.* 13. 28. The use of the veto is recorded from time to time, ibid. 1. 77. 3, 6. 47, 16. 26. 6; *Hist.* 4. 9. The use of *auxilium* in a senatorial debate is recorded in ibid. 2. 91, and implied in IX. 13. 9, where it is apparently

Falco himself who intervenes, perhaps taking Pliny's hint: Pliny also implies in s. 3 that tribunes still used their authority in lesser matters, as in VI. 8. 3: 'insolentiam cuiusdam tribunatum plebis inituri vereretur'. A late reference to the activity of tribunes occurs in SHA, *Severus* iii. 1.

2. ipse cum tribunus essem . . . abstinui causis agendis. This does not mean that he so abstained when holding any public office, as has been held (pp. 765+). The tribunate was a special case. When prefect of Saturn he also abstained from advocacy at first, for practical reasons, and then resumed practice in State cases, X. 3A. 1 n. It was a rule in the Empire that magistrates did not initiate criminal proceedings (*Dig.* 5. 1. 48 (Hadrian), 48. 5. 16, pref.; 2. 28), but the extension to advocacy seems to be Pliny's own idea. Advocacy by a tribune was known in the Republic: Cic. *pro Clu.* 74. Mommsen, *D. Pen. R.* ii. 40 n. 4.

3. si forte me adpellasset vel ille cui adessem. In the late Republic tribunician interference in civil jurisdiction was not uncommon: Cic. *pro Quinct.* 29; *Tull.* 38–39; Greenidge, *Legal Procedure of Cicero's Time* (Oxford, 1901), 290 f.

24. *To Baebius Hispanus*

Date. Neither the date nor the identity of the addressee can be determined. There are several equestrian and senatorial Baebii in this period, but none can be connected with this man. He may well be the Hispanus of VI. 25, q.v.

1. Tranquillus contubernalis meus vult emere agellum. For the biographer see Ep. 18, pref. The theme of the literary man's farm was established by Horace, *Epp.* I. 14, 16. 1–16; *Serm.* 2. 6. Martial also has his 'poet's farm', I. 55. This note is a business letter revised for publication, like several others, III. 6, 19, VI. 3, 30, VII. 11, IX. 39. It was customary for literary patrons to establish their protégés on small estates. So too Servilius Nonianus of Ep. 13. 3 sold his friend Martinus land below the market price, *Schol. ad Pers.* II. 1.

3. vicinitas urbis, opportunitas viae. Cf. the advantages of Pliny's Laurentine villa: 'decem septem milibus passuum ab urbe secessit . . . aditur non una via', II. 17. 2. In the Letters *urbs* nearly always means Rome, as in Epp. 9. 1, 10. 11, 13. 6, 22. 1. Sometimes he prefers *urbs nostra* as in I. 10. 1, V. 6. 4.

   modus ruris qui avocet magis quam distringat. The competition of estate management and *studia* is a constant theme, I. 3. 2–3, VII. 30, 2–3, IX. 15, 16, 36. 6.

4. scholasticis porro dominis, ut hic est. A valuable indication of
Suetonius' occupations, since Pliny uses *schola, scholasticus* of literary
'declamation' rather than forensic rhetoric, notably in II. 3. 5–6 n.,
20. 9, IX. 2. 3. Suetonius is not yet in continuous practice as advocate;
cf. his association with Pliny in Ep. 18. 1. See S. F. Bonner, *Roman
Declamation* 43. Della Corte suggests oddly that Pliny calls Suetonius
scholasticus in order to keep down the price of the farm (*Studi
. . . U. E. Paoli*, 91 f.).

BOOK II

1. *To Voconius Romanus*

Date. The letter is set in 97 by the necessity of dating the death of Verginius before that of Nerva, and by the consulship of Tacitus, ss. 3, 6 nn.

Address. For Pliny's as yet equestrian friend Romanus see Ep. 13 nn.

1. publicum funus Vergini Rufi. In a *funus publicum* the Senate voted the expense out of the *aerarium Saturni*, and magistrates presided instead of family or heirs. Cf. Tac. *Ann.* 3. 48, 'ut mors Sulpici Quirini publicis exsequiis frequentaretur petivit a senatu (Tiberius Caesar)'. So too members of the imperial family received a *funus censorium*, i.e. with dignities appropriate to a *vir censorius*, FO for A.D. 112. The custom was an invention of the late Republic, Sulla being the first person known to have been so honoured. Cicero gives the full formula for proposing the funeral of a *consularis*, and Appian describes the ceremonies, Cic. *Phil.* 9. 15–17; App. *BC* 1. 105–6; Plut. *Sulla* 38. Only the greatest men were so honoured, such as Trajan's friend Licinius Sura, Dio 68. 15. 3². See *RE(S)*, iii. 530 f., s.v.

2. triginta annis gloriae suae supervixit. The career of Verginius is known only from literary sources. Born *c.* A.D. 14 of an undistinguished equestrian family (Tac. *Hist.* 1. 52), he reached the consulship at the late age of 49, but as *ordinarius*. His fame came from his part in the civil wars of 68–69, when as legate of Upper Germany he refused to accept the repeated offer of the Principate from his troops, after he had, perhaps unwillingly, crushed the revolt against Nero led by Ti. Iulius Vindex, governor of, apparently, Gallia Lugdunensis (Dio 63. 25; Plut. *Galba* 10; Tac. *Hist.* 1. 8–9; see *CAH*, x. 739, 811). The offer was made after (Tac., Plut.) rather than before (Dio) the news of Nero's death arrived. Verginius left the choice of emperor to the Senate, and accepted Galba. Hence his epitaph in IX. 19. 1: 'imperium adseruit non sibi sed patriae'. He then met Galba in Gaul, who relieved him of his provincial command. After Galba's murder he supported Otho, who gave him a second consulship in 69 (Tac. *Hist.* 1. 77, 2. 49; *ILS* 241). After Otho's suicide troops again offered the Principate to Verginius, but he preferred to make friends with Vitellius (Tac. *Hist.* 2. 51, 68). It was, however, his first 'great refusal' at the height of opportunity 'pulso Vindice', that secured his fame. Pliny tells a tale of Verginius in IX. 19. 5 (n.) which may suggest that the friends of Nero thought him a traitor *quand même*. His social standing was very close to that of Vespasian, in whose shoes he so nearly stood. From 70 to 97 nothing is heard of him, and Garzetti (*Nerva* 53) may be right in suggesting that Nerva recalled him to office as a gesture to a set neglected by the Flavians. *PIR*[1], v 284. Garzetti, C. 147.

legit historias. Such as those of Cluvius Rufus, IX. 19. 5.

perfunctus est tertio consulatu. He was *cos.* III with Nerva in January 97, and *perfunctus* may mean that Verginius survived the period of his office, which was not more than three months in this year, and possibly only one month, as in 98 (*FO*).

summum fastigium. For the rare honour of a third consulship—no *privatus* ever received a fourth—see *Pan.* 60. 5: 'bellorum istud sociis olim periculorum consortibus parce tamen tribuebatur, quod tu (sc. Traianus) singularibus viris ac de te quidem bene ac fortiter meritis praestitisti.' Iulius Frontinus (IV. 8. 3 n.) and Vestricius Spurinna (Ep. 7. 1 n.) held third consulships in 100, and Licinius Sura in 107. Under the Flavians only the kingmaker Mucianus, the acute advocate and politician Vibius Crispus, and the foxy Fabricius Veiento (IV. 22. 4), were so fortunate; second consulships were somewhat less rare: Vespasian awarded some eight and even Domitian awarded not less than five, notably to politicians such as Nerva and Valerius Messalinus, and to Lappius Maximus Norbanus, his champion against the rebel Saturninus. Syme, *Tac.* 643.

3. Caesares quibus suspectus atque etiam invisus virtutibus. Tacitus calls Domitian *infensus virtutibus princeps* (*Agric.* 41), but Pliny may include Nero, who had eliminated the too capable Corbulo.

reliquit incolumem. This fits Nerva better than Trajan. Nerva had shown his friendship by the honours he gave Verginius. Pliny would have elaborated if Verginius had survived Nerva. Dio 68. 2. 4 seems to place his death before Nerva's. It has been held that Verginius was the *consul ter* mentioned by Pliny, *Pan.* 58. 1, as present *in senatu* early in 98 when Trajan refused a third consulship. But Verginius, even if then alive, was not in the senate house but in his bed, s. 9. That 'third consul' was Fabricius Veiento, IV. 22. 4, IX. 13. 19. For the old controversy see Asbach 44; Schultz, 12 f.; Otto, 20 f.

5. cum vocem praepararet acturus gratias. His accident happened at a rehearsal in his house, before the inaugural session of January 1, 97, not, as Garzetti (op. cit. 160) and others, at the session itself. It was the custom to give formal thanks either as consul designate or when taking up office, III. 18. 1, VI. 27. 1. Pliny seems to have done both.

6. saeculo. The term is a favourite with Pliny, and is used with a certain self-conscious rectitude for the Trajanic period to mark the beginning of an era of 'good' emperors. Cf. x. 1. 2, 'digna saeculo tuo', 97. 2, 'et pessimi exempli nec nostri saeculi est'.

laudatus est a consule Cornelio Tacito. This is the only date in the public career of Tacitus that depends on Pliny. Tacitus himself gives the date of his praetorship, A.D. 88, in *Ann.* II. II. The evidence of s. 3 suggests 97 for this year, and in the Fasti of 98, better known than 97, there is no vacant *nundinum* before July, and in all probability all the consuls of the second half of the year are known (p. 57). Besides, the agonies of Verginius cannot be protracted so long. So Tacitus was probably consul suffect in 97, and perhaps late in the year, like other forensic orators of this period: Pliny in September–October 100, C. Pomponius Rufus in September–October 98 (*FO*). Syme, *Tac.* 129 f.

Nothing is known precisely of other offices held by Tacitus except for a probable junior legateship, *c.* 89–93, and his proconsulship of Asia, *c.* 113. *RE*, iv. 1567 f.; *PIR²*, C 1467; Syme, op. cit., ch. vi. For the false inference of a second legateship see IV. 13. 1 n.

8. utrique eadem regio municipia finitima. By *regio* he means Transpadana generally, as in IV. 6. 1 and VI. 1. 1, 'ego trans Padum tu in Piceno', rather than the nominal *regio undecima* of the Augustan *regiones* identified by the elder Pliny with *Transpadana* (*NH* 3. 123). Cf. his use of *regio* in VIII. 2. 8, IX. 39. 2, X. 8. 5. In VII. 11. 5 his estates are located *circa Larium*, which like Comum lay in the *un regio decima*, Pliny, *NH* 3. 131; but see VI. 1. n., VII. 11. 5 n. Verginius came from Mediolanum, where the family name is well documented. Possibly the family was of Celtic origin, and enfranchised in the later Republic (Chilver, *Cisalpine Gaul*, 98–99). So too perhaps the family of Vestricius Spurinna, Ep. 7. 1 n.

agri. *ILS* 982 records a *saltuarius* of Verginius within the territory of Mediolanum. For Pliny's lands at Comum see II. 4. 3 n., VII. 11. 5 n.

ille mihi tutor relictus. Pliny's father must have died before A.D. 76 if Pliny was still within the age of *tutela*, which usually ended with nominal puberty at 14: I. 9. 2 n.; *Tit. Ulp.* II. 1, 28; Gaius, *Inst.* I. 144-5, 196. It is odd that Verginius rather than Pliny's uncle, with whom he was living in Campania in 79, was left as *tutor* (VI. 16, 20). Verginius spent his later years largely at Alsium in Tuscany, VI. 10. Neither man was well placed to administer Pliny's estate.

candidatum me suffragio ornavit. Pliny seems to have secured his early offices as *candidatus Caesaris*, Ep. 9. 1 n. But electoral support may have been needed for his praetorship. Pliny, loc. cit., uses *suffragium* of his recommendation of a man to the Princeps for *commendatio*. The word comes to have the looser sense of 'influence' in this period, cf. IV. 15. 13, X. 86 a, and G. E. de St. Croix, *British Journ. Sociology*, v (1954), 'Suffragium', 33 ff., who, however, underestimates the persistence of elections at this period. See I. 14. 7 n., III. 20. 5 n., VI. 6, VIII. 23. 2. M. L. Paladini (*Athenaeum*, xxxvii. 67 n., 210) notes that in the Panegyric the word *suffragium* is never literal.

die quo sacerdotes solent nominare. See IV. 8. 3 n. for the formalities of election to the great priestly colleges. After Verginius' death Frontinus supported Pliny, ibid., but finally Pliny had to canvass for himself, X. 13.

9. quinqueviros . . . qui minuendis publicis sumptibus iudicio senatus constituebantur. *Pan.* 62. 2 similarly describes this body. Dio 68. 2. 3 speaks of Nerva abolishing some horse-races, public sacrifices, and shows. Pliny here as in the Panegyric gives the official title. Those who have discussed, or invented, the controversy about the state of imperial finances from Domitian to Trajan have failed to observe that this Commission is irrelevant to the question. It was appointed by the Senate to deal with the expenses not of the empire at large, i.e. of the Fiscus, but of the limited field covered by the senatorial Treasury, the Aerarium Saturni. So much is shown by the word *publicis*, i.e. 'populi Romani'. Tacitus so describes a similar body concerned with non-imperial revenues, *Ann.* 15. 18: 'tres . . . consulares . . . vectigalibus *publicis* praeposuit . . . se annuum sescenties sestertium *rei publicae* largiri'. So too in 4. 12. 3, 'praefecti aerari *populo* vindicabant', and Ep. 16. 4 n. Hence the minor nature of the economies recorded by Dio. For the separation of Aerarium and Fiscus at this period see A. H. M. Jones, *JRS* (1950), 27 ff., with Pliny (*Pan.* 42. 1 *et al.*) as the definitive evidence. For the controversy over the finances of Domitian, Nerva, and Trajan: R. Syme, *JRS*, xx. 55–70, taking up Stein's article in *RE* iv. 143 ff.; C. H. V. Sutherland, *JRS* xxv. 150 ff.; J. Carcopino, *Points de vue sur l'impérialisme romaine* (Paris, 1934), 73 ff. Garzetti, *Nerva*, 60 ff., and Syme in his second thoughts (*Tac.* 630) come closest to the truth, that there was no crisis in the emperor's finances, but a shortage of cash in the Senate's chest and a show of economy for reasons of morale. Dio distinguishes between Nerva's restriction of court extravagance and the public economies on city festivals (68. 2. 2–3). See also F. Millar, *JRS* (1963) 29 ff., against Jones.

me huius aetatis per quem excusaretur elegit. Merrill remarks that Verginius was not recommending Pliny to take his place, but asking him to present his excuses. Pliny had not the standing yet for such a post. For the formula cf. III. 4. 3, 'excusare me et eximere temptarunt'.

2. To Paulinus

Date. Not determinable. This is the only letter in II which mentions an absence from Rome, but this is not identifiable with a particular occasion, s. 2 n.

Address. In IV. 16, V. 19, X. 104, the manuscripts and Index give the name as Valerius Paulinus. Here and in IX. 3. 37, as Paulinus. There is no reason to doubt, with *PIR* and Garzetti, that this is the man who speaks in the trial of Bassus as *praetorius*, IV. 9. 20 n. Since Paulinus had estates at Forum Julii (v. 19. 7) he may be identified with a son of that procurator of Narbonensis and native of Forum Julii who rallied the region for Vespasian in A.D. 69, 'amicus ante fortunam', Tac. *Hist.* 3. 43; hence the promotion of his son later, who is known from Pliny, the *Fasti*, and a diploma, as a suffect consul of 107. Cf. Syme, *Tac.* 63 n. 5. His death is recorded by X. 104. The letters to him concern literature, domestic and estate affairs. *ILS* 2003; *PIR*¹, V 105–7; Garzetti, *Inc.* 108, 152.

1. a te tam diu litterae nullae. This letter belongs to the genre of courtesy notes, I. 11 n.

2. ad villam partim studiis partim desidia fruor. This complete leisure suggests a visit to the Laurentine villa, where no estate duties distracted him, rather than the Tuscan estate with its active business, I. 9. 4–6, IV. 6. 2, VII. 30. 2–3 n. The tone suggests the slippered ease of 96–97 rather than the hasty holidays of 98–100, Ep. 17. 2, X. 8 nn.

    desidia. A fashionable term, I. 2. 6, 8. 2, 13. 5, &c. Tac. *Dial.* 4. 1.

    otio. So too in IX. 3, also to Paulinus, the theme is 'otium cum studiis' against *desidia*.

3. To Nepos

Date not determinable.

Address. Nepos receives two other long letters and a short note on varied topics, III. 16, IV. 26, VI. 19. The last two show him to be a senator and governor of a large province. In IV. 26 the Index gives his name as Maecilius Nepos. The gentile name is rare for senators and unknown for consulars at this date, though coins of a legate of Thrace *c.* 117–18 bear the shortened names MAIK NEP (*RE* xiv. 205; Stein, *Reichsbeamten von Thracia*, 14). Only three senatorial Maecilii

seem to be known in the next three centuries: *Dig.* 48. 18. 15. 1
(Pius); *ILS* 2621 (Gordian); *PIR*¹, M 35 (uncertain). Hence Mommsen
identified Pliny's friend with the consular, P. Metilius Nepos of
Novara. (Cf. Garzetti, *C.* 98; Groag in *RE* xv. 1400; Syme, *JRS* 1953,
151; 1957, 132 n. 6; *Tac.* 647.) But the evidence for this man's career
is ambiguous. P. Metilius Nepos, consul suffect in 91 (*F. Pot.* and
Arval records), might be the Nepos recorded in a fragmentary
diploma as legate of Britain before 98 (*CIL* xvi. 43), and he is very
likely the senior Arval Brother who appears as P. Metilius Sabinus
Nepos in the record for 105 and 118, where his death is noted
(*CIL* vi. 2075; *ILS* 5028). In the second citation the name Sabinus is
omitted, as in the *Fasti* of Potentia. The Ostian *Fasti* record as
suffect consul for 103 one']*etilius* ['. This has been variously restored
to show a second P. Metilius Nepos, presumably son of the first, or
the second consulship of the first Nepos. The case for two Metilii is
weak, given the short interval between the consulships, and the fact
that P. Metilius Secundus, son of Publius, was consul in 123 or 124.
Pliny's evidence in IV. 26. 2, if pressed, should refer to one of the two
consular proconsulships, Africa and Asia, for which the consul of 91
was ripe at the book-date, 105–6 or 106–7, indicated by IV. 26 and
VI. 19. If Nepos is not Maecilius, he should be the consul of 91.

But the correction of the text is neither certain nor necessary.
The Index of the Ashburnham MS., supported in III by the sixth-
century fragment *Π*, very rarely slips. In IV. 1 and V. 7 and 8, Fabius
for Fabatus, Calpurnius for Calvisius, and Caepio for Capito, are
intelligent substitutions expanding less familiar abbreviations. So too
with IV. 3, *ad Adrianum*. But in IV. 26 the Index has the address in
the abbreviated form, and the name is rare: 'ad Maecil. Nepotem.'
In III. 3 and III. 18 there is a positive error of a single letter—*Caerelliae*
for *Corelliae* and *Virium* for *Vibium*. A mistake over Maecilius–
Metilius remains possible but is not in keeping with the manuscript,
since the only explanation can be that the scribe, contrary to his
usage, has repeated the initial letters from the preceding entry,
which was *ad Maesium Maximum*. He repeats once elsewhere, but
correctly and in full: V. 13, *ad Terentium Scaurum* from Ep. 12.

Pliny's Nepos may be Metilius Nepos, but he cannot also be the
Sabinus of IX. 2 and 18, as has been suggested, because this involves
a change of *cognomen* in the form of address contrary to the usage of
the letters. IX. 2, pref.

1. **magna Isaeum fama praecesserat.** Isaeus was a professional orator,
not, like Euphrates (I. 10) and Artemidorus (III. 11), a philosopher.
He is reckoned among the canonical 'sophists' of the imperial era by
Philostratus, *VS* I. 20, whose account agrees with Pliny. He calls

him 'Assyrian', meaning that he came from north Syria, since Philostratus calls Antioch 'Assyrian' (*VS* I. 21. 4; *Ap. Ty.* I. 16). His social rank is not mentioned, but his pupil Dionysius of Miletus gained equestrian rank and office under Hadrian, *VS* I. 22.

summa est facultas copia ubertas. So Juvenal 3. 74: 'Isaeo torrentior'. Cf. v. 20. 4: 'est plerisque Graecorum . . . pro copia volubilitas'. Philostratus reckoned his style 'neither ornate nor dry but unexaggerated and natural'. This fits the 'mixed style' of Quintilian, cf. I. 2. 1 n.

dicit semper ex tempore sed tamquam diu scripserit. Cf. Philostratus: 'his discourses were improvised and yet prepared'. Likewise his pupil Dionysius, *VS* I. 22. 1. For the type of speech cf. Quint. 2. 4. 27; Cic. *ad Att.* 16. 6. 4.

praefationes tersae. For the use of the 'preface' see I. 13. 2 n., IV. 11. 3, VIII. 21. 3.

2. electionem auditoribus permittit . . . surgit amicitur incipit. This is the grand manner of the epideictic 'sophist', ready to speak on any side about any topic. Cf. IV. 11. 3, 'postquam se composuit circumspexitque habitum suum . . .'. An impressive moment, the performance begins.

3. crebra ἐνθυμήματα **crebri syllogismi.** This was an effective rhetorical use of the syllogism with suppression of parts. Quint. 5. 10. 1, 14. 1, 25, 8. 5. 9. Isaeus had a technique of his own, according to Philostratus, compressing the whole meaning of his theme into a compact phrase τὸ βράχεως ἑρμηνεύειν . . . καὶ πᾶσαν ὑπόθεσιν συνελεῖν ἐς βραχύ. (*VS* I. 20.)

5. adhuc scholasticus tantum est. Cf. I. 24. 4 n. Philostratus does not speak of him in forensic practice.

6. schola et auditorium et ficta causa. So too in I. 22. 6 Pliny contrasts court practice with literary rhetoric. He uses *schola* of *grammatici*, II. 14. 2, VIII. 7. 1, of the *rhetor Latinus*, II. 18. 1, III. 3. 3, and of a jurisprudent, VII. 24. 8. The *ficta causa* is illustrated by the *Controversiae* of the Elder Seneca.

8. Gaditanum quendam Titi Livi nomine . . . commotum. The story seems to be known only from Pliny.

10. illud Aeschinis. A favourite story of Pliny, IV. 5. For its history see Schuster's references. Cicero reveals that the speech was the *De Corona* (*de Or.* 3. 213). Demosthenes' own words (*Cor.* 313) about Aeschines are neatly put into Aeschines' mouth.

4. *To Calvina*

Date not indicated. The addressee is unknown.

1. **an adires hereditatem etiam viro gravem.** If an estate was burdened with debts one could refuse to accept the inheritance. In Roman law the natural heir had to declare his formal acceptance or *cretio*. The testator usually inserted a clause specifying a period within which this must be done. Or, as in intestate succession, the praetor could fix a period on request of the creditors. The formula of acceptance was: 'quod me heredem P. Maevius testamento suo instituit eam hereditatem adeo cernoque.' Gaius, *Inst.* 2. 164 ff.; *Tit. Ulp.* 22. 27–28.

2. **praeter eam summam quam pater tuus quasi de meo dixit.** He presumably means that the sum was due to him as a creditor. The letter is a remarkable document of Roman lack of delicacy. Pliny spares Calvina no detail. Compare IX. 17, and contrast his greater tact towards his equals, e.g. VII. 11, 14. But classical ethics, deriving from Aristotle, *Nic. Eth.* 4. 3. 1123b, instilled the view that the Magnanimous Man was conscious of his own virtue, cf. VI. 20. 17 n. Yet Pliny is aware that self-praise defeats its own purpose, I. 8. 14–15. Plutarch's contemporary essay *De laude ipsius* discussed the necessity and limits of self-praise.

    dixit. perhaps *addixit* would be better.

3. **donatio.** For the law of gifts see v. 1. 2–3 nn.

    sunt quidem omnino nobis modicae facultates. A minimal estimate of Pliny's resources may be attempted. From his Tuscan estates in 98–99 he draws an income of over S.400,000, x. 8. 5. At some 6 per cent for agricultural yields (VII. 18. 3 n.) this means a capital value of six or seven millions. Then in III. 19 he is able to find or borrow with expectation of easily repaying S.3,000,000 for an estate with a potential value of S.5,000,000, from which he may expect an eventual income of about S.300,000 a year. No exact estimate can be made of his Cisalpine estates, which at this period he reckoned unsatisfactory, Ep. 15. 2 n. But in VII. 11 he coolly takes a capital loss of S.200,000 on sale of a Cisalpine estate worth S.900,000, which was distinct from his family inheritance. So the total of his northern lands must have been substantial. The grand total may have been not less than twelve or fifteen millions, and his income between S.800,000 and a million. He took no professional income as a barrister (v. 13. 8, VI. 23. 1 nn.), but between 98 and 100 he received a salary of not less and probably much more than S.300,000 as Prefect of Saturn. Compared to such as Regulus, who hoped to complete a fortune of sixty millions, Pliny was in the second grade of wealth, Ep. 20. 13. But despite his complaints he did not do so badly. The highest known salaries of officials are the S.300,000 of the senior equestrians, and S.1,000,000 of the proconsul of Asia; Dio 79 (78). 22. 5; Tac. *Agric.* 42. 3, with Anderson's note. Purchasing power may be estimated in terms of the late eighteenth or early nineteenth century, reckoning the *denarius* somewhere between the silver franc and the silver shilling.

dignitas sumptuosa. Cf. VI. 32. 1, 'ratio civilium officiorum necessitatem quandam nitoris imponit'.

condicionem agellorum. See Ep. 15. 2 n.

frugalitate . . . ex qua . . . liberalitas nostra decurrit. This implies that all Pliny's benefactions were paid out of income or past savings. He never speaks of selling land except to oblige a friend, VII. 11. In III. 19 he is ready to face regular repayment of a large loan. So he must have made substantial annual savings. In the eleven years covered by the Letters his benefactions amount to over two millions: up to the date of v. 7. 3, S.1,600,000 to Comum, including the library, *alimenta*, and schools (I. 8, IV. 13, VII. 18), and S.550,000 to friends apart from Calvina here (I. 19, VI. 32, VII. 4). There is also the cost of the two shrines at Tifernum (IV. 1. 5, IX. 39) and his remission of a legacy of over S.150,000 to Comum (v. 7 nn.). So Pliny must have been saving some S.200,000 to cover his benefactions alone.

5. *To Lupercus*

Date. The *actio* mentioned in the Letter must have preceded Pliny's appointment to the Prefecture of Saturn, when he gave up private practice (Ep. 14. 1 n.), and the letter itself should be earlier than the second half of 100 when he was preparing his *In Priscum* and Panegyric for publication, s. 2 n. Possibly it is the work mentioned in I. 2; cf. s. s. 5 n.

Address. A long letter on style is addressed to Lupercus in IX. 26, who is else unknown, unless he is Martial's amorous man of letters, I. 117. Possibly Q. Valerius Lupercus Iulius Frontinus (*CIL* xii. 1859), from Narbonensis, may be connected through Pliny's friend Frontinus (IV. 8. 3 n.).

1. actionem et a te frequenter efflagitatam. It is tempting to identify this with Pliny's speech inaugurating his library endowment at Comum and promising to establish *alimenta*, I. 8. The reference in ss. 3, 5 would fit: 'ornare patriam et amplificare'. But Pliny calls the Comum speech a *sermo* and this an *actio* (ss. 1, 3, 10), a term which he strictly confines to forensic speeches, while using *sermo*

for non-forensic speeches, and *oratio* for both. Cf. I. 8. 2 n., 20. 9–10,
II. 19. 1. The only apparent exception is his speech in the Senate
against Certus, which he calls *actio* in IV. 21. 3, IX. 13. 24. But he
regarded that as a criminal indictment, IX. 13. 13. He calls the Comum
speech and the Panegyric *oratio*, but neither an *actio*: I. 8. 6, III. 13. 4.
Hence the identification of the present speech with the Comum
address does not fit. It was probably delivered in a civil suit about
municipal property like VI. 18. 1. The *descriptiones locorum* fit this.

**3. in ceteris actionibus . . . diligentia tantum et fides nostra, in hac
etiam pietas subicietur.** He is certainly referring to a forensic speech,
since these are the virtues of advocates, Ep. II. 19, III. 9. 23, V. 13. 2
et al. He also implies that he had no major speech in hand at this
moment, such as the *In Priscum* of Ep. 19.

dum ornare patriam . . . gaudemus . . . et defensioni eius servimus.
By *patria* he certainly means native borough as in I. 14. 4, III. 6. 4,
&c. The term *defensio* or *defendere* is sometimes used in a wider sense
than as the correlate of *accusare*, cf. IX. 19. 2, 7 and Ep. 9. 4: 'agendis
causis . . . quas summa fide . . . defendit', with reference to all types
of cases.

amplificare. The *alimenta* scheme could be meant, cf. VII. 32. 1
'cupio . . . patriam nostram . . . augeri . . . civium numero'. And there
are possible echoes of I. 8. 13, 'communibus . . . commodis . . . stude-
bamus . . . aliorum utilitatibus . . . servisse videamur'. So too the
'fastidium legentium' of s. 4 recalls the delicacy of the Comum
theme, I. 8. 14–15.

4. mediocritate. For the theme of brevity in speeches see I. 20.

**5. sunt enim quaedam adulescentium auribus danda . . . nam de-
scriptiones locorum non historice tantum sed prope poetice prosequi
fas est.** The speech appears to be in Pliny's new 'mixed' style, cf.
I. 2. 1–2 nn., and ibid. 4, 'quotiens paulum itinere decedere non
intempestivis amoenitatibus admonebamur: acres enim esse, non
tristes volebamus'. Evidently Pliny greatly enlarged the original
version, as later with his Panegyric, III. 18. 1.

adulescentium auribus. He means not the original audience of
jurors, who would be elder men, but his future readers (s. 6). Quintilian notes at length that the young have a natural preference for
the richer style, II. 4. 5–9, X. 1. 125, 130.

historice. For Pliny the historical style is between oratory and
poetry, and is concerned with *ornatio*, V. 8. 9–10, VII. 33. 3.

6. nos laetius fecisse. The reference is to style, not content. Cf. III.
18. 10, 'laetioris stili'. The Comum speech was in a restrained style,
I. 8. 5.

7. **diversa genera lectorum per plures dicendi species teneremus.** Quintilian gives advice to this effect at length, XII. 10. 69–72.

10. **per partes emendari.** For such literary dissection see VIII. 4. 6–7. Each part might have its own style, as advised by Quintilian, loc. cit., quoted in I. 2. 1–2 n.

6. *To Avitus*

Date depends upon the identification of the recipient with Junius Avitus, which would put the letter in 97–98, before his absence in Germany and Pannonia from 98–*c.* 100.

Address. Since this is a letter of advice this man is likely to be the young Junius Avitus, whose moral tutor Pliny claims to have been in VIII. 23. 2, rather than Julius Avitus with whom his connexion was less close, V. 21. Junius was on military service with Julius Servianus between 98 and 100–1, and later quaestor and aedile designate before his death reported in VIII. 23.

1. **homo minime familiaris.** Pliny's term for friend is *familiaris* or *amicus familiaris* (II. 13. 5, VII. 17. 11, IX. 34. 1, 37. 1) as distinguished from an acquaintance, *amicus*. For intimates he often uses *contubernalis*, I. 2. 5, 19. 1, II. 13. 5, X. 4. 1, or *sodalis* II. 13. 6, VIII. 21. 5. Cf. IV. 17. 2: 'est . . . mihi cum isto . . . non plane familiaris sed tamen amicitia'.

2. **sibi et paucis opima quaedam, ceteris vilia et minuta ponebat.** This unpleasing custom is recorded as early as the time of the Elder Cato, who like Caesar and Hadrian also disapproved, Pliny, *NH* 14. 91; Suet. *Iul.* 48; SHA, *Hadr.* 17. 4. It is a regular theme with the moralists, Juv. 5. 24 ff.; Mart. 1. 20, 3. 60, 4. 68, &c., and impressed Lucian as a characteristic of Roman senatorial society (*De mercede conductis*, 26).

aliud sibi et nobis, aliud minoribus amicis . . . animadvertit qui mihi proximus recumbebat. The traditional arrangement of dinner parties consisted of three couches each with three persons. Here more than one *triclinium* was set, since Pliny's neighbour noticed what was happening at another 'table'. Larger parties were accommodated by trebling or quadrupling the number of *triclinia*, Vitruvius 6. 7. 3, Athenaeus 2. 47; Carcopino, *Daily Life*, 265 f.; *RE* (2) vii, 'triclinium' 92 f.

nobis. Not Pliny's rare use of plural for singular, I. 8. 3 n., but 'those of us at his table', cf. 'nostris libertis' below. For Pliny's treatment of slaves and freedmen see IV. 10, V. 19, VIII. 1, 14. 12, 16.

gradatim amicos habet. Merrill saw the origin of this in the development of the *salutatio*. Some practical distinction became necessary with the steady increase of *clientelae*. The terms 'amici primi' or 'secundi' and 'admissio prima' or 'secunda' go back to the Gracchan period according to Seneca, *Ben.* 6. 33. 4–34. 5. Caesar distinguished the table of 'sagati palliative' from that of 'togati cum inlustrioribus provincialium', Suet. loc. cit. Pliny admits the distinction in VII. 3. 2: 'amicitiae tam superiores quam minores', but in IX. 30 as here demands fair treatment for *amici pauperes*.

3. etiamne libertos? The presentation of a dinner instead of a *sportula* in cash or kind is interesting. Private life follows imperial example. Nero replaced the public banquet by *sportulae*, and Domitian re-introduced the *cena recta*, Suet. *Nero* 16; *Dom.* 7. In Martial references to the abolition of the *sportula* are apparently limited to Book III, and it resumes its role later. Pliny never speaks as if he himself gave *sportulae*. See Friedlaender, *SG* (Eng. tr.), app. xiv; Carcopino, *Daily Life*, 171 f.; Marquardt, *Manuel*, xiv. 242 ff.

6. sub exemplo praemonere. An example softens the edge of advice and criticism, cf. VII. 1. 7, VIII. 22. 4, IX. 12. 2. Pliny also uses it in self-defence, V. 3. 3–6.

7. To Macrinus

Date. Before the death of Nerva, s. 1 n.

Address. The Macrinus addressed here and in VII. 6, 10, VIII. 17, IX. 4, is probably Caecilius Macrinus, addressee of III. 4, rather than Minicius Macrinus of Brixia (I. 14. 5 n., VII. 12 pref.). Four of the letters to Macrinus concern extortion trials, and the recipients of letters on this theme seem not to be senators, cf. II. 11, 12 pref. Otherwise the man is unknown. In VIII. 5. 1 (n.) he is elderly, not less than 60 years old in A.D. 100.

1. here a senatu Vestricio Spurinnae principe auctore triumphalis statua decreta est. There has been much ineffective discussion whether Trajan or Nerva is the emperor concerned. Garzetti, *Nerva*, 57 n. 6, summarizes the controversy. But no one has noticed that Dio 68. 15. 3², 16. 2, fails to mention Spurinna among the four consulars whom Trajan honoured with a public statue. Hence the Princeps must be Nerva. This honour appears to rank higher than that of the *ornamenta triumphalia*. Nominally Spurinna was being rewarded, like Plautius Silvanus Aelianus under Vespasian (*ILS* 986), for deeds neglected by the previous emperor, but his part in securing the succession of Nerva and later Trajan is indicated by the grant of a second consulship in 98 and a third in 100; cf. *Pan.* 60. 5–6 cited below, and I. 5. 8 n. He was one of the mainstays of the régime, like Verginius Rufus, Ep. I. 1 n., Julius Frontinus IV. 8. 3 n., and Arrius Antoninus IV. 3. 1 n., who also secured second or third consulships.

here. The closest indication of time in the Letters, and a sure sign that this letter originated as a genuine epistle.

principe auctore. The proposal could be made in person or by letter, but Pliny elsewhere makes it clear when the emperor communicates by writing, V. 13. 7–8, VI. 19. 3–4.

Vestricio Spurinnae. For his family origin see s. 3 n. His career is known in part. In the civil wars of 69 he was already an experienced soldier, and served Otho as legate, being probably already *praetorius*. Tac. *Hist.* 2. 11, 18, 23, 36. The date of his first consulship is unknown, but must precede his legateship of Lower Germany (below) under Vespasian or early Domitian. His other provinces are unknown (III. 1. 12 'provincias' n.). He reappears in history now, and was nominated with Julius Frontinus and Verginius Rufus to the Nervan economy commission (Ep. I. 9 n.), and with Frontinus to a second consulship held with the absent Trajan as colleague in April 98, followed by a third in 100. Two passages in the *Panegyricus* combined with the consular *Fasti* indicate this. *Pan.* 61. 7–62. 2: 'uterque nuper consulatum alterum gesserat a patre tuo . . . datum . . . hi sunt quos senatus . . . publicis sumptibus minuendis . . . elegit.' Ibid. 60. 5–6 states that Trajan gave third consulships to these same two men, *in toga meritis*. After his third consulship no more is heard of Spurinna in politics. Pliny describes his life in retirement in III. 1, and he is still alive at the date of IV. 27. 5, V. 17 (*PIR*¹, V 308; Garzetti, *C.* 148; Syme, *Tac.* 17, 35, 634).

2. Spurinna Bructerum regem vi et armis induxit in regnum. The date of this has been much debated. In *Germania* 33 Tacitus briefly tells of a Bructeran disaster inflicted by neighbouring peoples: 'nunc Chamavos et Angrivarios immigrasse narratur pulsis Bructeris ac penitus excisis'. Sixty thousand Germans fell in battle before the eyes of a watching Roman army: 'non armis . . . Romanis sed . . . oblectationi oculisque ceciderunt'. Possibly Spurinna's achievement followed this event, and hence only a show of force was needed ('ostentato bello'). But when? Otto and others (art. cit. 31) argued from s. 3 that the event was at the time of the younger Vestricius' death, and hence that Spurinna was legate of Lower Germany in 97. But the Panegyric shows that Spurinna's services to Nerva and Trajan were *in toga* (above), and there is little time available for such a legateship. In December 96 Spurinna was in Rome (I. 5. 8–9), and in 96–97 was a member of the Economy Commission. In April 98 he must be in Rome as consul, when his partner Trajan is absent. Too many other commanders are known in Germany at this time. Trajan before his adoption governed apparently Upper Germany, and thereafter was generalissimo of the whole area with Licinius Sura and Ursus Servianus as legates together or successively (SHA, *Hadr.* 2. 5; Dio 68. 3. 4; VIII. 23. 5 n.; *AE* 1923, n. 33; Garzetti, *Nerva*, 90).

Anderson argued from Tacitus' phrase 'nunc narratur' that the event took place in 98–99. But the silence of the Panegyric is decisive against this. The glory would have been Trajan's then, and *Pan.* 8. 2 can only credit Trajan and Nerva with a 'laurel from Pannonia', The *nunc* simply contrasts the situation of the Bructeri in the Flavian period with that given by his main and earlier source. It is more reasonable to attribute Spurinna's campaign, with or without the Tacitean story, to the Germanic wars of Vespasian or Domitian.

For the controversy see Mommsen, art. cit. 39–40; Otto, art. cit. 19, 30; *PIR¹*, V 308; J. G. Anderson, *Germania* (Oxford, 1938), ch. 33 n.; Garzetti, *C.* 148; Syme, *Tac.* 634.

3. et hoc quidem virtutis praemium illud solacium doloris accepit. From the parallelism of the two opening phrases Otto (art. cit. 31) concluded that the two events—the campaign and the son's death— were contemporary. But the parallel is only verbal. Smooth chronological transitions are a feature of Pliny's style, cf. Ep. II. 2–13, III. 9. 5–7, IV. 9. 2 n.

Cottio. In III. 10 Pliny mentions his *libellus* about the life of Cottius, without details. Here he is called both *iuvenis* s. 3 and *adulescens* s. 5, like Minicius Acilianus, I. 14. 3, 10. Like him he is probably already *praetorius*. His mother's name was Cottia, III. 10 pref. So this is a *cognomen*. It may well derive from the family of local rulers who gave their name to the Cottian Alps. Cf. *ILS* 94, 848; Strabo, iv, p. 204. An early Julio-Claudian proconsul of Baetica, A. Cottius, and his son who died as *aedilicius*, should be cognate, *ILS* 8343.

Spurinna is reckoned a Cisalpine by Chilver, *Cisalpine Gaul*, 103, because of this name and of his connexion with Sentius Augurinus in IV. 27. 5, which proves nothing. He may equally well have come from Narbonensis. His own names are Etruscan, and that should be the remote origin of the family. Cf. W. Schulze, *Lateinische Eigennamen*, 94, 254, 260.

amisit absens. Possibly Spurinna left Rome in 97 summer on a mission to Trajan in Germany, with the senior statesman Fabricius

Veiento, whose presence is recorded in these years at Colonia Agrippinensis, IV. 22. 4 n.; *PIR*[1], loc. cit.

5. ad liberos suscipiendos. See I. 8. 11 n.

7. in celeberrimo loco. Presumably one of the imperial *Fora* is meant.

8. *To Caninius Rufus*

Date. This note to 'a gentleman in the country' repeats more briefly I. 3, also to Caninius at Comum, but is later. Pliny is no longer a man of leisure as in many of the letters of Book I, but full of professional cares (ss. 2–3), and Caninius, earlier occupied with the management of his estates, is now free for hobbies. So the letter fits the period of 98–100 when Pliny could not quit Rome, or travel farther than a half day's drive to his Laurentine villa without official leave (I. 13. 1, 22. 1, II. 17. 2, III. 4. 2 nn.).

Address. For the equestrian Caninius Rufus of Comum see I. 3 pref.

2. quae sic concupisco ut aegri vinum balnea fontes. The theme is developed in VII. 1. Schuster compares Sen. *Tranq. An.* 10. 1.

3. maius in dies occupationum agmen extenditur. This may refer either to his private practice as in Ep. 14. 1 'distringor centumviralibus causis', before 98, or to his new duties as Prefect of Saturn, 'distringor officio . . . molestissimo' and the public prosecutions which accumulated during 98–100, I. 10. 9, II. 11 pref., and III. 4. 9 nn.

9. *To Domitius Apollinaris*

Date. Either late 97 or late 100 is arguable. Peter (art. cit. 704 f.) and Schultz (art. cit. 13) proposed the later date because of the chronological difficulty of fitting the career of Erucius into the reign of Nerva. But the absence from Book X of a petition to Trajan about Erucius, and the date of the consulship of Domitius distinctly favour the earlier dating, s. 2 n.

Address. The owner of this cognomen, unusual for a senator, is L. Domitius Apollinaris, known from IX. 13. 13 and a fragment of the *Fasti Ostienses* as suffect consul in the course of 97, and not, as formerly held, in January 98. The rarity of the name suggests that he is Martial's busy patron, the advocate Apollinaris of IV. 86, VII. 26, X. 30, XI. 15. This is confirmed by a coincidence between Pliny and Martial in V. 6. 45 (n.). But he is not to be identified by *nomen* alone with Martial's Domitius of Vercellae (x. 12). Just before his consulship he governed Lycia-Pamphylia. (*IGRR* iii. 559; *PIR²*, D 133; Syme, *JRS* 1954, 81; *Tac.* 631, 641.) Pliny and Apollinaris appear as warm friends in v. 6. 1–3 also, despite their opposition in the debate about Certus, IX. 13. 13.

1. **petitio Sexti Eruci mei.** This letter shows the liveliness of elections conducted since A.D. 14 in the Senate. Cf. I. 14. 7 n. and Paladini's article ibid., and also III. 20, IV. 25, VI. 6, 9, 19. The vote of the Senate was formally confirmed by the *comitia centuriata, Pan.* 92. 3.

    pro me. The qualification confirms what his holding the *quaestura Caesaris* suggests, that Pliny owed his earlier magistracies to the commendation of Domitian as *candidatus Caesaris*, though he speaks of personal convassing and support from Verginius and Corellius in Ep. I. 8 (n.), IV. 17. 6, perhaps for the praetorship (p. 37). Even for the *candidati Caesaris* the names were formally submitted to Senate and *comitia*. (Cf. Vespasian's *lex de imperio, ILS* 244 and *Pan.* 95. 2; Paladini, art. cit. 68.)

    Sexti Eruci. He is the first of his direct line to enter the Senate (s. 4 n.), though the *nomen*, which is connected with Spoletium, appears among the names of a suffect consul of 83, Terentius Strabo Erucius Homullus (*ILS* 1996; *CIL* xi. 4800, iv. 9. 15 n.). Later he appears among the more successful officers of the Parthian war, and seems to have become suffect consul in 117. (Dio 68. 30. 2; *Chron. Min.* i. 255; *PIR²*, E 96; Syme, *Tac.* 242; *Historia* 1960, 374.) He apparently secured no further employment under Hadrian, perhaps because of his uncle Septimius' disgrace, s. 4 n. He emerged again under Pius as *Praefectus Urbi* and consul for the second time in 146, when he died (*FO*). Aulus Gellius mentions him as a man of letters (*NA* 7. 6. 12, 13. 18. 2–3) and Fronto commends him (*Ad Antoninum Pium* 3. 3). He founded a successful consular family, *PIR²*, E 95–98. He exemplifies Pliny's knack of preselecting the leaders of the next generation.

    Sexti. For the use of *praenomen-nomen* see I. 12. 9 n. Here Pliny has to distinguish father and son with identical *cognomen*.

    mea dignitas in discrimen vocatur. For the convention see VI. 6, 9.

2. **ego Sexto latum clavum a Caesare nostro ego quaesturam impetravi.** Pliny played a similar part in the promotion of Voconius Romanus, Ep. 13, x. 4. 2 nn., 'a divo patre tuo petieram ut illum in amplissimum ordinem promoveret'. The first step in the promotion of a man of equestrian standing to the Senate was the grant of the right to the broad stripe on the tunic. Service in one of the posts of the vigintivirate and as a military tribune of a legion were normally required before the quaestorship, which gave admission to the Senate. But Pliny

mentions neither, whereas in the account of Junius Avitus' early career he mentions or implies both, VIII. 23. 2–5. Probably Erucius, whom Pliny calls *iuvenis* not *adulescens*, had already served as an angusticlave military tribune. For such promoted men the vigintivirate was sometimes omitted, if they were not very youthful, and the grant of *latus clavus cum quaestura* may have carried this dispensation. (Cf. Mommsen, *DPR* v. 204 n. 1.) Paladini, art. cit. 22 n. 52, suggests that Erucius was not *candidatus Caesaris* for his quaestorship, but the construction and balance of the sentence requires that 'a Caesare impetravi' be taken with both accusatives.

This sentence is the earliest unambiguous evidence for imperial control of the *latus clavus*, though Suet. *Vesp.* 2. 2, *Claud.* 24. 1 seem to take it back to the time of Tiberius and Claudius. (Cf. Mommsen, loc. cit., and *DPR* vi. 2. 61; D. M. McAlindon, *Latomus*, xvi. 253.) Dio 59. 9. 5, if reliable, also implies that Gaius controlled it. But Suet. *Aug.* 38. 2 refers to the sons of senators, not new men, and Ovid, *Tr.* 4. 10. 35, implies only that the use of the *latus clavus* by candidates was customary.

meo suffragio. For the metaphorical sense see II. 1. 8 n.

ad ius tribunatus petendi. The phrase means no more than nomination, cf. Paladini, art. cit. 206. A clear year's interval was required between the quaestorship and the next office, either the tribunate of the plebs or the aedileship, unless the candidate had secured special exemption by imperial favour or by the *ius liberorum*, VII. 16. 2 n. But Pliny is usually careful to mention such factors, Ep. 13. 8, cf. VII. 24. 3, VIII. 23. 7. So if the Caesar is Nerva, Erucius must have been quaestor in 97 and have proposed to stand in January 98 for the tribunate of 99. But he can only have owed his quaestorship to Nerva if the elections for 97 were held, or altered, after Domitian's death, or if a place fell vacant unexpectedly in the college of 97, as happened for the praetorship in an early year of Trajan, X. 12 n., 'cum locus vacet'. Usually the lesser elections seem to be held nearly a year ahead, IV. 15. 6 n.

The difficulty of identifying *Caesar* with Trajan lies in the absence of a request to Trajan on behalf of Erucius in X. 1–14, where all Pliny's letters to Trajan in his absences seem to have been carefully preserved. In X. 4. 1 Pliny clearly implies that Voconius was the first person whom he asked Trajan to promote after January 98. So Erucius' quaestorship would belong at earliest to the elections of 99 for 100, and his tribunician election—and this letter—to 101 for 102; or if after the return of Trajan then the years would be 100 for 101 and 102 for 103. The application for support to a consul of 97 favours the Nervan date. Senatorial affairs seem to be much influenced by the most recent consuls and consuls designate,

Ep. II. 19, IV. 12. 4 nn. Pliny writes to Minicius Fundanus with a similar request in a year close to his consulship, VI. 6.

nisi obtinet. Paladini (art. cit. 20 f.) inferred from this and from VI. 19. 1–2 that there was an interval between nomination day and election day. But there is no sign of this in *Pan.* 69–72, as Paladini's own analysis shows (art. cit. 77 f.). Nothing in this letter suggests that Erucius had yet made the formal submission of his name to the consuls.

4. pater ei Erucius Clarus vir sanctus antiquus disertus et in agendis causis exercitatus. The father is evidently of equestrian status, and lacking senatorial influence, cf. VI. 6. 4. He is recipient of I. 16.

habet avunculum C. Septicium. This man, whose cognomen was Clarus also, became praetorian prefect early in Hadrian's reign, after a career as yet unknown, with Marcius Turbo, replacing Attianus and Sulpicius Similis. Later he fell into disgrace in 122 and was dismissed along with the secretary *ab epistulis*, Suetonius Tranquillus, another of Pliny's friends: I. 18 pref.; SHA *Hadr.* 9. 5, 11. 3, 15. 2; *PIR*[1], S 302; Syme, *Tac.* 501, 779; *Historia* 1960, 367, 377. Both Pliny and Suetonius dedicated books to Septicius, I. 1 n.

5. domos stationesque circumeo. Cf. I. 13. 2 n. 'plerique in stationibus sedent'.

6. ostende modo velle te. So too at the election of VI. 6. 8, 'ea est auctoritas tua ut putem me efficacius tecum etiam meos amicos rogaturum'.

10. *To Octavius Rufus*

Date. Not to be widely separated from I. 7, where Pliny begs for a glimpse of Octavius' verses. A few have now been circulated against Octavius' will, but Pliny has still not seen the author's manuscript.

Address. See I. 7 for this undistinguished senator.

2. isdemque quibus lingua Romana spatiis pervagentur. Cf. Tac. *Agric.* 21. 2 for the spread of Latin in the western provinces: 'qui modo linguam Romanam abnuebant eloquentiam concupiscerent'. For the publication and sale of Latin books overseas see IV. 7. 2, IX. 11. 2. n.

3. ut errones aliquem cuius dicantur invenient. Martial complains persistently in his first book (29, 38, 52, 53, &c.) of a *plagiarius* who recites Martial's poems as his own. Pirated copies of Pliny's works got abroad, IV. 26. 1.

6. de editione . . . emittere. For the terms see I. 2. 5–6 nn.

7. cum dico vel recito. For the custom of recitation as an entertainment see I. 13 nn. Pliny was not yet a frequent performer, and apparently recited no forensic speech before his *In Priscum*, Ep. 19. I n. After that the habit grows on him, and he recites his *De Cottii Vita*, III. 10. 1, his *Panegyricus*, III. 18, and generally, VII. 17. He may earlier have recited his *Sermo de bybliotheca ad Comenses* I. 8. 2 n., and some formal compositions, I. 13, 6 n. For his later recitation of verses see V. 3, VIII. 21.

clamore. See I. 13. 3 for the different values of silence and applause.

11. *To Arrianus Maturus*

Date. Since the trial of Marius Priscus before Trajan and the Senate was in mid-January 100, ss. 10, 19 nn., the letter is of late January or February 100 (s. 1, 'per hos dies').

Address. For the literary equestrian Arrianus Maturus see I. 2 pref.

Arrangement. The commentary on this letter has been divided into two parts. The first deals with problems of law, procedure, and politics, the second and shorter with the persons, apart from Priscus himself.

Chronology. A summary of the discussion of the vexed problems of this affair in Introduction VIII is here given. The proconsulship of Priscus is fixed to 97–98, and his immediate indictment for the minor form of extortion, and the appointment of advocates (s. 2), to the second half of 98, by the references and dating of X. 3, where Pliny as Prefect of Saturn requests imperial permission to undertake the prosecution. The session of the Senate at which charges of *saevitia* were preferred (ss. 2–7) occurred either before November 98 or more probably early in 99, at a time when Iulius Ferox was consul designate (*Persons*, s. 5 n.). Then there was delay while evidence was gathered from Africa (ss. 5, 8). Meanwhile Priscus was condemned on the minor charges before a committee of the Senate (ss. 5, 12–13). The major inquiry was resumed in the Senate in December 99 (ss. 8–9), and then postponed to the sessions of January 100 described in the rest of the letter and Ep. 12.

2. Marius Priscus accusantibus Afris quibus proconsule praefuit omissa defensione iudices petiit. His career is known only from Pliny. A senator from Baetica (III. 9. 3), his consulship must have been in the eighties, before 86–96 when the continuous *Fasti* are known,

perhaps about 80 to judge by his proconsulship in the same year as
Classicus, which is fixed by the date of the prosecution to 97–98:
Marcus and Classicus were among the first of the numerous Nervan
governors who took advantage of the new régime, Suet. *Dom.* 8. 2.
Garzetti, *C.* 94.

accusantibus Afris. Cf. III. 9. 4. Not the whole province, as *Afri*
might imply, but *una civitas publice*—evidently Lepcis, s. 23—
multique privati. Pliny summarizes this phase very briefly. The case
would be brought before the Senate by the consuls, as in the Varenus
case, V. 20. 2, 'inducti in Senatum', and as provided by the *SC.
Calvisianum* (below): the first step was the assignment of advocates,
as in the Classicus case, III. 4. 2. Two sessions were taken up by
Pliny's reluctance to accept the brief, X. 3A. 2. Then at a third
session Priscus threw up his defence.

iudices petiit. As in the Bassus case, IV. 9, the procedure is derived
from that instituted by the *SC. Calvisianum* of 4 B.C., discovered in
Cyrenaica, *EJ* 311. 5; *FIRA* i. 68. 5. This established a new system
for extortion trials involving only material exactions. After preliminary investigation in the Senate such cases were to be referred to a
court of five senatorial *iudices*, elaborately selected, whose sentence,
given within thirty days of appointment, awarded singlefold restitution of monies taken. Charges involving a capital sentence were
excluded from this court's competence, and left to the *quaestio per-
petua*. In the Julio-Claudian period this system was modified by
the substitution of the Senate for the *quaestio* in all political charges
against senators. Hence charges of extortion involving what the
sources invariably call *saevitia*, and a penalty of exile or relegation,
came to be heard by the Senate, but the shorter process continued
for the less serious charges. The *iudices* here, and in the Bassus case,
IV. 9. 16, as in two Julio-Claudian cases, Tac. *Ann.* I. 74, 13. 52, are
the Court of the shorter process, though the procedure of the *SC.
Calvisianum* has been altered in details. Particularly, the Senate now
conducts an extensive preliminary investigation, and delivers a
general verdict, before the appointment of the special court, whose
function is limited to the assessment of the particular charges: IV. 9.
16 n., 'lege repetundarum Bassum teneri'. So too Pompeius Silvanus,
Tac. *Ann.* 13. 52, faced by a capital indictment for extortion, 'ilico
defendi postulabat', claiming the shorter process instead of the full
senatorial trial. It lay with the Senate to decide which form to follow,
as in the Bassus case, when the charges of *saevitia* were excluded
IV. 9, 1, 5 nn. By instructing his advocate to make no reply to the
charges Priscus hoped to secure the rapid allocation of *iudices*, and
so conceal more serious offences which had not been named in the
indictment.

adesse provincialibus iussi. Under the *SC. Calvisianum* the presiding magistrate assigned advocates to the provincials, but now the choice is made by the vote of the Senate. Apparently selected names were submitted to the lot, III. 4. 3, X. 3. 2 n. The duty could only be refused on set grounds; Pliny at first pleaded his Prefecture of Saturn as an excuse, III. 4. 3, X. 3. 2 nn.

excessisse Priscum immanitate et saevitia crimina quibus dari iudices possent. Cf. *SC. Calvisianum*, 99–100 ἐάν τινες . . . χρήματα πραχθέντες ἀπαιτεῖν βουληθῶσι χωρὶς τοῦ κεφαλῆς εὐθύνειν τὸν εἰληφότα. The *patroni* point out that an indictment under the shorter process does not lie. There has been much discussion about the legal basis of the capital charge. Some scholars hold that it was not under the law of extortion but under the laws controlling judicial bribery and murder, 'Lex Cornelia de sicariis' and 'ne quis iudicio circumveniretur' or else the 'Lex Iulia de vi publica', which forbade the physical punishment of Roman citizens by a provincial governor (s. 8 n.). M. I. Henderson suggested that offences of *maiestas* were implicit in serious extortion charges. Such views are based on the phrases in s. 3 'ne quid ultra repetundarum legem quaereretur', and s. 20 'repetundarum poenae quam iam passus esset . . . relinquendum'. But Pliny makes it clear that the charge was still the taking of money, s. 3 'pecunias accepisset', s. 5 'vendidisse', s. 8 'emisse', s. 19 'quae acceperat'. The difference lay in the circumstances of the taking, 'immanitate et saevitia'. In Ep. 19. 8 Pliny says that the offences had to be proved to be covered by the extortion law itself. Cf. the summary in *Dig.* 48. 11. 7 (Macer) 'lex Iulia de repetundis praecipit ne quis ob hominem . . . in vincula publica coiciendum . . . condemnandum absolvendumve . . aliquid acceperit', which is close to Pliny's words.

The same distinction between the shorter process with penalty limited to a fine and civil *ignominia* (s. 12), and trial for extortion *cum saevitia* before the full Senate inflicting sentences of exile or relegation (s. 19) is found frequently in the period covered by Tacitus' *Annales* and *Historiae*, the palmary instance being that of Pompeius Silvanus (above). Hence it would seem that the trial of criminal extortion before the full Senate was still under the general control of the *Lex Iulia repetundarum*.

For the controversy see A. von Premerstein, *ZS. Savigny, RA*, xlviii. 419 ff., and li. 431 ff.; J. Stroux and L. Wenger, *Abh. Bayer. Ak. Phil.-hist. Kl.* xxxiv. 145 ff.; F. De Visscher, *Les Édits d'Auguste* (Louvain, 1940), ch. viii; A. N. Sherwin-White, *BSR* xvii (1949), 5 ff.; *JRS* 1952, 43 ff.; M. I. Henderson, *JRS* 1951, 71 ff., esp. 87–88; F. P. de Fontette, *Leges Repetundarum* (Paris, 1954), ch. vii, summarizes the various views; J. Bleicken, *Senatsgericht*, etc. (Göttingen, 962) 37 ff.

3. deprecatusque est ne quid ultra repetundarum legem quaereretur.
Pliny's contemporaries seem to regard anything beyond the shorter
process as being beyond the scope of the extortion law, cf. ss. 4 and
20. Pliny dilates in VIII. 14. 1–10 on the general ignorance in the
Senate of public law and procedure. There are many instances of this
in the Letters, particularly in matters of extortion. See s. 5 n., III.
9. 6, 14, 32, IV. 9. 16, V. 20. 2. Possibly no case involving the full
procedure had occurred since that of Baebius Massa in 93, VI. 29. 8 n.
Suetonius, *Dom.* 8. 2, comments on their rarity under Domitian.

**4. aliis cognitionem senatus lege conclusam aliis liberam solutamque
dicentibus.** Cf. IV. 9. 17, 'licere senatui . . . et mitigare leges et
intendere'. The text suggests not that *another* law was being
invoked, but that the Senate had arbitary power. This view of the
Senate's powers, approved by some scholars (cf. Henderson, art. cit.
87–88; C. W. Chilton, *JRS*, xlv. 73 ff.) is rather extravagant.
Extortion like most political crimes was subject to a severe if not a
capital penalty, usually some form of exile (s. 8 n.). It became
common in the Principate of Tiberius for the Senate to vary the
penalties of *leges publicae*, to which it was not bound since they were
directed to the praetors and the *quaestiones*. The implication that the
Senate could increase penalties beyond the *poena legis* does not seem
to be true of the past. Cf. Tac. *Ann.* 3. 68, 4. 20, 14. 45. But the
Senate had been used to interpret the law in order to extend its
existing provisions to new offences (Cf. Tac. *Ann.* 3. 68, and Sherwin-
White, *BSR* art. cit. 19). The Senate certainly accepted the general
guidance of the *Lex Iulia*; Ep. 19. 8, quoted above, III. 9. 14 n., IV. 9.
7, 21. When the Senate flouts the letter of the law it is a scandal,
and to be corrected in proper form; III. 9. 29–32, V. 20. 6–7, VI. 5. 2
nn. In a senatorial trial the consul is technically the judge, using the
Senate as his *consilium*. He has nominally free *arbitrium* to order
things as he will, including the penalty, as in other forms of *cognitio
extra ordinem*, i.e. outside the forms of the *quaestiones perpetuae*. But
in practice they adhered to the *Lex*. Hence the composition of the
chapters in the *Libri Terribiles* of the *Digest* is under the headings
of the *Leges Publicae*.

See F. De Robertis, 'Arbitrium Iudicantis', *ZS. Sav.* 1939, 219 ff.,
and U. Brasiello, *La repressione penale in diritto Romano* (Naples,
1937), *passim*, expanding and correcting the sketch of Mommsen in
D.Pen.R. i. (xvii), 293.

5. Mario quidem iudices interim censuit dandos. The suggestion of
Ferox that both procedures should be followed was contrary to the
intention of the *SC. Calvisianum*, which made the two exclusive, as in
the Silvanus trial of A.D. 58; above, s. 2 n., Tac. *Ann.* 13. 52. Ferox

perhaps feared that an acquittal for *saevitia* might enable Priscus to escape the lesser charges.

evocandos. They are wanted as witnesses in the first place, s. 9 n. The Lex Iulia, like its predecessors, gave the prosecution the power of investigation, *inquisitio*, and of compulsorily summoning witnesses from the provinces, *evocatio*; III. 9. 29, VI. 29. 8, cf. V. 20. 7. But the *SC. Calvisianum* 139–41 limited *evocatio* under the short process to ten persons present in Italy, who presumably came voluntarily from their province. For Julio-Claudian examples see Tac. *Ann.* 13. 43, 52. The provincial summons thus indicates a charge of criminal extortion.

8. exilium equitis Romani septemque amicorum eius . . . ultimam poenam . . . arguebatur emisse. Within what limits could a provincial governor inflict corporal or capital punishment, in its various forms, on subjects who were Roman citizens? The Augustan *Lex Iulia de vi publica* asserted the general right of appeal of Romans in Italy and the provinces from the violence of magistrates: 'qui . . . necaverit necarive iusserit torserit verberaverit condemnaverit inve vincula publica duci iusserit' (Ulpian, *Dig.* 48. 6. 7; *Sent. Paul.* 5. 26. 1). So St. Paul invokes his privilege against the sentence of the governor (Acts xvi. 37, xxii. 25, xxv. 9–12). Claudius Aristion is tried by Trajan at Rome for offences in Ephesus, VI. 31. 3, and Pliny sends to Rome citizens accused of being Christians, but executes *peregrini* out of hand, x. 96. 3–4. Later instances of *provocatio* are recorded under Marcus Aurelius, *Dig.* 28. 3. 6. 9, A–J III. But Galba, as legate of Tarraconensis, crucified a citizen for murder, ignoring his claim to citizenship, and his action was represented as *immodica* but not as illegal; the man had hoped merely for a milder form of death-penalty, Suet. *Galba* 9. 1. Under Domitian a proconsul of Bithynia was in order in condemning Flavius Archippus *in metallum* for forgery, a punishment which the jurists reckoned as capital, and which involved *vincula publica*, x. 58. 2–3, 60. 1 n. Hence it seems that a governor might condemn citizens to such penalties in certain circumstances; possibly such powers were granted in the field of the *leges publicae*, the criminal laws about murder, forgery, adultery, kidnapping, *vis publica*, &c., as suggested by A. H. M. Jones, *Studies in Roman Government* (Oxford, 1960), 57 f. Such a grant is mentioned briefly in two passages of Ulpian and Papinian (*Collatio* 14. 3. 3; *Dig.* 1. 21. 1): 'qui . . . publici iudicii habeant exercitionem lege delegatam'. Since the sentences imposed by the *quaestiones* under such laws were not subject to appeal, provincial governors may have gained parallel powers by such a grant. So Jones. It might be suggested that such powers were originally conceded to diminish the pressure on the central court at Rome, or for the convenience of the parties, and were originally intended to be exercised solely in conjunction with juries modelled on the Roman *quaestio*, such as are testified in Cyrenaica and perhaps in Bithynia, x. 58. 1 n. The transfer to the personal *cognitio* of governors would be a later change. See also VI. 31. 6 for other limitations. See my *Roman Society* etc. 57 ff.

Hence Priscus might not have been acting beyond his powers in these cases, if he had not taken bribes. Towards ordinary provincials the governor had full powers of capital punishment, x. 30. 1, 96. 3. It was only under Hadrian that there began the tendency to assimilate the status of the municipal aristocrats, known as *honestiores*, to that of Roman citizens by granting them the same immunities, cf. *Dig.* 48. 19. 15: 'divus Hadrianus eos qui in numero decurionum essent capite puniri prohibuit' etc. The exemption then applied only to charges of murder. For its later extension see *Dig.* 48. 19. 2. 1, 9. 11–15, 27. 1–2, 28. 1–2, 38. 1–2; 22. 6. 2. G. Cardascia, 'L'apparition dans le droit d'honestiores', *Rev. Hist. Droit Fr.* 1950, 305 ff., 461 ff.

exilium. Governors had, at this time, unlimited power of expulsion from the province, both over Romans and *peregrini*, in the form of *relegatio*, which did not affect the *caput* of the accused, cf. III. 9. 32, x. 56. 2, 4; *Dig.* 48. 22. 4, 7. 3, 14. Hence Priscus may have been in his rights—apart from the question of *provocatio*—if by *exilium* Pliny means (as in I. 5. 5, VII. 19. 6 nn.) *relegatio*; he never uses the noun, though the verb is common in the Letters. Later checks were introduced. *Relegatio in insulam*, which confined the person, required imperial confirmation, and *deportatio in insulam*, which meant complete loss of rights, was reserved for the sentence of the emperor and his deputy, the urban prefect: *Dig.* 48. 19. 2. 1, 27. 1–2, 22. 6, 49. 4. 1. These rules were invented to prevent precisely such abuses of power as Priscus enjoyed. See in general Brasiello, op. cit., ch. x, esp. 273–92.

fustibus caesus, damnatus in metallum. These punishments were normal for all *peregrini*, but later tended to be confined to *humiliores*. *Dig.* 48. 19. 28. 2–5, 38. But a cudgelling was a form of *coercitio* rather than a true penalty, given, as to St. Paul, *pour encourager les autres*. It was used to deal with some types of theft and disturbance. *Acts* xvi. 22–23, xxii. 24; *Dig.* 48. 19. 10, 28. 3; Brasiello, op. cit., ch. xiv. 387 ff.

The sentence *in metallum* implied loss of liberty and civil rights, and ranked next to the death-penalty. Dig. 48. 19. 8. 4, 28 pref. See x. 31. 2 n. for its modifications, and Brasiello, op. cit. 373 ff.

strangulatus in carcere. This republican form of execution was rare in imperial times, when the tendency was to humanize the execution of citizens. Cf. *Dig.* 48. 19. 8. 1: 'animadverti gladio

oportet non securi vel telo vel fusti vel laqueo' (Ulpian). But crucifixion and burning were retained as *summa supplicia*, and served like
condemnation *ad bestias* for enemies of society, such as notorious
brigands, agitators, and traitors: *Dig.* 48. 19. 28 pref., 38. 2. Imprison
ment was irregular: 'carcer enim ad continendos homines non ad
puniendos haberi debet', ib. 48. 19. 8. 9.

The gravamen of the charge of *saevitia* against Priscus, apart
from the actual taking of monies, seems thus to lie in disregarding
the privileges of class, and treating citizens as *honestiores*, and
honestiores as *humiliores*, in so far as these distinctions were beginning
to emerge; cf. x. 79. 3 n.

9. Marcianus inductus est absente Prisco. Marcianus was not charged
with extortion because he had not taken but given money, and,
unlike Firminus (s. 23), he was not on the staff of Priscus, and hence
could not be made responsible as an associate, as in the Classicus
case, III. 9. 6, 14. His offence was under the law against judicial
corruption (above, s. 2 n.). Only senatorial and equestrian officials,
including members of the governor's entourage or *cohors*, and children or wives, could be charged with extortion. Mommsen, *D. Pen. R.*
iii. 9 f. On the death of Honoratus the question of the S.300,000 is
dropped, but the other matter, to which Marcianus and his account
books were witnesses, was continued, s. 23.

absente Prisco. Since his first condemnation he was no longer
entitled to attend the Senate unsummoned, s. 12.

iure senatorio. As in v. 4. 2, IX. 13. 7, the request is made to the
presiding consul during preliminary discussion before the opening of
the formal debate, and not 'sententiae loco'.

**10. princeps praesidebat (erat enim consul), ad hoc Ianuarius
mensis.** The reference to Cornutus Tertullus as designate consul in
s. 19, fixes the year to 100 and the day to a date in January after the
election of the suffect consuls of 100 described in *Panegyricus* 69–77,
since Tertullus was suffect consul in September–October 100. If the
election day was on 9 January, as in the later empire, then the trial
was probably on 13–15 January, the first three days available after
the ninth. The Kalends and Ides were the normal days of senatorial
meetings in the earlier Principate, but it is impossible to fit all the
business of January recorded by the Panegyric into less than three
sessions. The trial is placed out of order in *Pan.* 76, between the
election session of the Senate (ibid. 69–75) and its completion in the
Comitia (ibid. 77). See s. 18 n. Possibly the trial was held at an extraordinary meeting later than the Ides.

12. Stabat modo consularis. Condemnation by the shorter process involved loss of senatorial standing and offices, and certain disabilities before the civil law, *Dig.* 48. 11. 6. 1. For examples cf. IV. 9. 19; Tac. *Ann.* 12. 22, 13. 33, 14. 18.

septemvir epulonum. This was one of the four senior priesthoods held by senators as civic distinctions, IV. 8 nn.

14. duodecim clepsydris quas spatiosissimas acceperam sunt additae quattuor. The normal allocation to the prosecution was six hours (IV. 9. 9 n.), of which Pliny received three and Tacitus three, since four glasses were normally reckoned to the hour (Marquardt, *Manuel*, ii. 459 ff.). Pliny was allocated an extra hour, perhaps to deal with the extra complications, and the glasses were regulated to run more slowly, *spatiosissimas*, so that sixteen made nearly five hours. Merrill was misled by VI. 2. 5, which refers only to civil litigation, into saying that the allocation of time was at the discretion of the Senate. The proportion allocated to prosecution and defence was still the same as under the *Lex Pompeia* of 52 B.C. (Tac. *Dial.* 38. 2; Dio 40. 52. 2). But the regulating law of IV. 9. 9 is presumably the *lex iudiciaria* of Augustus, or the extortion law itself, which included regulations of this kind as early as the *Lex Cornelia*; Cic. *II in Verr.* I. 25; *pro Flacco* 82; Marquardt, op. cit. 461 f.

15. libertum meum post me stantem. The presence of secretaries does not seem to be testified elsewhere, except for an emperor (Dio 60. 16. 3).

gracilitas mea. The only reference to Pliny's physique, with IV. 9. 10, where he fears he may not last out two sessions of a trial. He had suffered a serious illness in 97, X. 8. 3 n., VII. 1. 4 n. But he was capable of speaking for seven hours non-stop when in form (IV. 16. 3).

16. nisi ut noctis interventu scinderetur. In s. 18 a speech is continued into the next day. In IV. 9. 14 lights are brought in to allow a speech to be completed before adjournment. The Republican custom of ending sessions at night-fall was translated into a schedule of fixed hours by the *Lex Iulia de senatu habendo*; Gellius, *NA* xiv. 7. 8; Dio 55. 3. 1–2, 58. 21. 2; VIII. 14. 19 n.

17. respondit Cornelius Tacitus. The order of speeches is as in the Bassus case, the reply for the prosecution following the speeches for the defence, IV. 9. 13. In the Caecilius case the order is left obscure, III. 9. 15–16.

18. itaque in tertium diem probationes exierunt. He uses *probationes*, as in IV. 9. 15, VI. 31. 5, VII. 6. 10, for the evidence, oral and written, as normally in Quintilian, not of a technical division of the speeches, as in *Inst.* 3. 9. 1. For the preparation of written evidence before trials see X. 74. 3 n.; *RE* (2), v, 'Testimonium', 1051 f. The technical term is *instrumenta* or *consignationes* (Quintilian 12. 8. 11–12)...

iam hoc ipsum pulchrum et antiquum, senatum . . . triduo contineri.
This is generally taken to be the threefold session mentioned in a similar passage of the *Panegyricus* 76. 1: 'iam quam antiquum, quam consulare, quod triduum totum senatus sub exemplo patientiae sedit' etc. He goes on to mention the technicalities but not the substance of a lengthy debate, 'consulti omnes atque etiam dinumerati sumus, vicitque sententia non prima sed melior'. There cannot have been two such debates in January 100, because of the silence of Pliny. But this session is the third in January described in the Panegyric. First comes the formal session of 1 January, *Pan.* 66–68. Next comes the day of the *ordinatio comitiorum*, 69–75, followed by this debate, and then the day of the *comitia consulum*, 77. That in turn is followed by an undated session at which Trajan is offered a fourth consulship, 78. No other sessions are described in the consulship or under the presidency of Trajan, who seems to have handed the *fasces* over to Iulius Frontinus at this point, *Pan.* 79. 5. So, if the two triple sessions are identified, Pliny has inverted the order of events in the Panegyric, because the suffect consuls of 100 have already been appointed before the present session.

19. Cornutus Tertullus consul designatus . . . censuit. The order of 'opinions' was fixed by the *lex de senatu habendo*', Gellius, *NA* 4. 10. 1 s. 16 n. The *designati* spoke in turn (but see Ep. 12. 2 n.), then the consulars and others in order of seniority, Mommsen, *DPR* vii. 153, 160 ff. In Pliny's accounts those below the consulars do not bulk large. Ep. 12. 2, III. 4, 3 (*praetorii*), IV. 9. 16, 20 (*praetorius*), 12. 4, v. 13. 4–6 (a tribune), 20. 6–7, VI. 5. 1–2 (*praetorius*), IX. 13. 13–15 (*praetorii*). No *praetorius* speaks in this debate, s. 22 n.

The statement of *Pan.* 76. 2, 'vicit . . . sententia non prima sed melior' means that Tertullus' proposal prevailed because it was the better not because it was the earlier of the two proposals.

aerario inferenda. The sums could not be restored because they had been criminally offered. *Dig.* 12. 5. 3, 'ubi . . . et dantis et accipientis turpitudo versatur non posse repeti'. The officers of the Aerarium Saturni had collected fines for extortion since early times, *Lex Acilia* 57 ff. For the duties of the prefects see I. 10. 10 n., IV. 12. 3.

urbe Italiaque interdicendum. They are spared the more serious form of relegation which assigned a place of residence, but the sentence is 'in perpetuum', cf. s. 20. Marius unlike Marcianus is not excluded from his native province, perhaps because as a senator his normal residence was in Italy. Cf. *Dig.* 48. 22. 7. 15, 'si cui urbe fuerit interdictum patria sua interdictum non videtur'.

20. Marcianum in quinquennium relegandum. For *relegatio in tempus* see *Dig.* 48. 22. 7. 2–3. None of these forms affected basic civil rights: 'sive ad tempus sive in perpetuum . . . relegatus et civitatem Romanam retinet et testamenti factionem non amittit'.

22. qui sellis consulum adstiterant in Cornuti sententiam ire coeperunt. The Senate divided by gathering in groups on the floor of the House (s. 21, *sequebantur*). See the formula in VIII. 14. 19, 'qui haec censetis, in hanc partem, qui alia omnia, in illam partem ite qua sentitis'. They were then counted, if necessary (*Pan.* loc. cit. *dinumerati*). Cf. the close of the debate in IX. 13. 20 n.

This passage does not mean that Trajan had indicated his opinion in favour of the severer penalty. He was too tender of the remnants of senatorial independence and too correct in the tenure of this consulship to do that; *Pan.* 76. 1–2, 78–79. Besides there was no great difference between the two proposals. Both left Marius stripped of his *dignitas* and of his gains, neither deprived him further of civic status or real estate. Hence Juvenal (1. 49–50) professed to regard the sentence as inadequate: 'exul ab octava (*sc.* hora) Marius bibit et fruitur dis iratis, at tu, victrix provincia, ploras'. The previous lines cannot refer, as commonly taken, to Marius: 'et hic damnatus inani iudicio. quid enim salvis infamia nummis?' For Marius had lost his *nummi*, and was, as Juvenal says, in exile. Juvenal is here listing examples.

23. sermone quem ille habuerat in ordine Lepcitanorum . . . stipulatus . . . quinquaginta milia denariorum probabatur. There is a straight charge of 'taking money', i.e. of simple extortion, against Firminus on the score of the 'scent money'. He had arranged the major matter with Marcianus on behalf of Priscus, but had not had that money for himself, which formed part of the grand total of S.700,000, taken by Priscus.

in ordine. Marcianus is a decurion of Lepcis, in the African Tripolis, which Firminus may have visited on assize, or to arrest the helpless *eques* of s. 8.

nomine unguentarii. This is a quotation from the account-books of Marcianus.

24. placuit censente Cornuto referri de eo proximo senatu. Probably Cornutus included this in his original *sententia,* or else the consul made a fresh *relatio* about Firminus. The next regular meeting of the Senate would be on 3 February, if this is the last of the meetings of the Senate in January, ss. 10, 18 nn.; Suet. *Aug.* 35, with Calendar of Philocalus; Mommsen, *DPR* vii. 104.

Commentary on Persons

1. quietis amore secesseris. Arrianus had avoided promotion to equestrian rank for the sake of a 'quiet life' in the political sense, I. 14. 5 n., III. 2. 4.

2. Marius Priscus. See above, s. 2 n.
   Cornelius Tacitus. Now consular, Ep. I. 6 n.

3. Fronto Catius. The career of Ti. Catius Caesius Fronto, consul suffect in September–December 96, the months of Nerva's succession, and dead by 117 (*Act. Arv.*) is little known, *PIR²* C 194; Garzetti, *C.* 37. Like Cerealis s. 9, Collega s. 20, and Regulus s. 22, who back him here, he was one of the cautious men who supported Domitian and Nerva alike. A persistent supporter of delinquent senators (IV. 9. 15, Bassus, VI. 13. 2, Varenus), as consul he checked the suppression of delators after Domitian's death, IX. 13. 4 n., Dio 68. 1. 3. His names connect him with the poet and orator Silius Italicus (III. 7. 1 n.) and the consul of 99, Memmius Senecio (*PIR* loc. cit., Syme, *Tac.* 88 n. 8). He may well be Martial's patron, 'militiae . . . togaeque decus', I. 55. 2.

5. Iulius Ferox. This man, Ti. Iulius Ferox, was *curator alvei Tiberis* from 101 to 104, *ILS* 5930 n., *AE* 1933, n. 97. His consulship must fall many months before January 100. In 98 all places are almost certainly taken, the only possible gap being for the last two months, IX. 13. 23 n. In 99 several places are vacant, p. 57. Later, between 105 and 109, he commanded an army, X. 87. 3 n., and was proconsul of Asia *c.* 116–17. Pliny addresses a formal note to him, VII. 13. *PIR¹* I 202; Garzetti, *C* 71.

   consul designatus. Early 99 now seems more probable than late 98 (above).

8. Vitellius Honoratus, Flavius Marcianus. Otherwise unknown. The latter name probably appears as the owner of forests in Dalmatia (*ILS* 5968), but our Marcianus is a decurion of Lepcis, s. 23. In a curious error Schuster, *RE* (2) ix. 391, makes Honoratus a recent proconsul of Africa.

9. Tuccius Cerialis consularis. The manuscripts are in virtual agreement, but he is M. Tullius Cerialis, suffect consul of late 90 (*Fast. Pot.*), Garzetti, *Inc.* 144.

16. Claudius Marcellinus. This figure is unknown, unless as father-in-law of the obscure praetorian senator Bellicius Sollers (V. 4, 1 n.), whose wife was a Claudia Ti. f. Marcellina, *ILS* 1031, 2710. *PIR²*

C 920. Not to be identified with Marcellinus of VIII. 23, who is probably the Aefulanus Marcellinus of V. 16.

17. Salvius Liberalis, vir subtilis dispositus acer. A magnate of Urbs Salvia, C. Salvius Liberalis Nonius Bassus, was adlected to the Senate and promoted rapidly by Vespasian, who admired his frankness, and Titus, Suet. *Vesp.* 13, *ILS* 1011. After his consulship, which was before 86 (*Fast. Pot.*), he fell foul of Domitian, like other friends of Vespasian (s. 19 n.), and was apparently exiled, III. 9. 33 n. In the Classicus case also he used his powers for the worse cause, III. 9. 36 n. (*PIR*¹ S 105; Garzetti, *C.* 137).

    dispositus. The passive is curious here, the word meaning 'well ordered' in III. 1. 2, 20. 4, V. 6. 40. But cf. III. 13. 3 for its rhetorical technical sense, 'disponere apte figurare varie'.

19. Cornutus Tertullus consul designatus. Another of Vespasian's recruits, who, less fortunate than Liberalis, did not even secure a consulship from Domitian. For his career and long connexion with Pliny, with whom he was consul in September–October of this year, see V. 14 nn.; also IV. 17. 9. He appears as the one just man both here and in the Certus debate, IX. 13. 15–16. Despite their long friendship Pliny addresses only two letters to him, both in VII. (21, 31). His tastes were evidently not literary, cf. VII. 31. 5 n.

20. Pompeium Collegam. Since he is not a senior consular this is probably Sex. Pompeius Collega, *cos. ord.* in 93 (*ILS* 9059) rather than Cn. Pompeius Collega, his father, legate of Galatia *c.* 75 (*ILS* 998, 8904; Jos. *BJ* vii. 3. 4); *PIR*¹ P 457; Garzetti, *C.* 119.

22. de Regulo questus est. For this now elderly advocate see I. 5. 1 n. He seems not to be a consular (*pace* R. Syme, *JRS* 1953, 161), and hence his *sententia* would come late and lack influence. So he works through another. This passage might imply that he had not even reached the praetorship. Only his *quaestura* is certainly attested. Syme presses the rhetorical reference in Tac. *Hist.* 4. 42 to prove both praetorship and consulship: 'quem adhuc quaestorium offendere non audemus, praetorium et consularem ausuri sumus?'

23. Hostilius Firminus legatus Mari Prisci. Otherwise unknown. As legate of a proconsul he would normally be of praetorian rank. The *nomen*, rare among senators of this period, recurs in the titles of T. Mustius Hostilius . . . Augurinus, a *praetorius* of this period from Patavium, Garzetti, *C.* 64. It is remarkable that neither of Marius' two other *legati*—three being the complement for the proconsuls of Asia and Africa—takes part in the case.

12. *To Arrianus Maturus*

Date. Continues Ep. 11 a fortnight later, ibid. s. 24.

Address. See Ep. 11 pref.

2. Firminus inductus in senatum respondit crimini noto. For the
charge see Ep. 11. 23. He had not been formally accused by the
provincials. Those who criticize the weakness of the Senate in handling this case should credit it with the punishment of Firminus.
Cf. s. 22 n.

Cornutus Tertullus censuit ordine movendum. The first proposal
amounted to partial *ignominia*, Ep. 11. 12 n. The increasing freedom
of the Senate's jurisdiction is apparent, Ep. 11. 4 n. Normally only
a censorial act by the Princeps could expel a member from the Senate,
Tac. *Ann.* 2. 48. 3, 11. 25. 5–6, 12. 52. 4. In effect the consuls were
being instructed to use the *censoria potestas* latent within their
imperium.

Acutius Nerva. Consul designate for a period of 100 before
Tertullus (p. 78), though Pliny does not give his title. He had not
spoken in the first trial, though senior to Tertullus; so too the *designati* for May–June 100, Herennius Saturninus and Pomponius
Mamilianus, were silent throughout, to say nothing of Spurinna,
about to be *cos.* III. It is unlikely that all these gentlemen were
absent in the year of their consulships. Pliny, *Pan.* 76. 2, says 'omnes
consulti' (Ep. 11. 18 n.). How did those who preceded Tertullus in
the *ordo sententiarum* (Ep. 11. 19 n.) make their agreement known?
From 'adsenserunt consules designati', s. 20, it looks as if the presiding consul was free to pick any of the *designati* to give the first
sententia, and Trajan showed his wisdom by starting with Tertullus
But the order here might be stylistic, to fit the continuation of the
paragraph—'quae sententia'.

Q. Acutius Nerva was shortly afterwards legate of Lower Germany
(*PIR*² , A 101), *c*. 101–3.

sortitione. The lot was normally used for the allocation of the
'public provinces' to the annual proconsuls from the beginning of
the Principate, Dio 53. 14. 1–4; Mommsen, *DPR* iii. 286 ff. Cf. VI.
22. 7. Firminus would be eligible for any of the nine or ten provinces
usually governed by *praetorii*. A similar attempt to exclude *infames*
from *sortitio* is recorded in Tac. *Ann.* 3. 69. 1. For Firminus and
Tertullus see Ep. 11, *Persons*, ss. 19, 23 nn.

6. diligenti tabellario dedi. Cf. III. 17. 2 and VIII. 3. 2, 'ut primum
diligentem tabellarium inveni'. The *cursus publicus* was available
only for official communications, X. 45, 120 nn.

13. *To Priscus*

Date. The chronology of this letter and its relationship to x. 4, in which Pliny in late 98 recommends Romanus to Trajan for promotion to senatorial status, have been much debated. Mommsen's date of 98 for it was assailed by M. Schultz (art. cit. 14 f.) and Otto (art. cit. 22), who assigned it to the lifetime of Nerva, while Asbach (art. cit. 44) argued for a date *c.* 104. Recently Syme briefly (*Tac.* 632, *Historia* 1960, 365 f.) and S. Monti at immense length (*Ann. Fac. Litt. Fil. Napoli* vi (1956), 69–106) have dated II. 13 later than x. 4, putting it *c.* 100–1 and *c.* 99 respectively. A short cut, depending on the reading and meaning of *statim* in x. 4. 4, is too uncertain to decide the matter briefly (s. 4, n.).

The main questions are the identification of the consular legate Priscus to whom the letter is addressed, and of the *optimus princeps* who granted Romanus the *ius trium liberorum* in s. 8, and whether Romanus in fact became a senator. Such promotion excludes a date later than x. 4 for II. 13. If II. 13 is earlier than x. 4, the reference to the grant of parental rights necessitates a Nervan date (s. 8 n.).

The most probable identification of Priscus seems now to be with Javolenus Priscus, when legate of Syria at a date between *c.* 95 and 101, when A. Julius Bassus took over the province. This excludes a date later than 100 for the request, since Priscus would not in 101 any longer be in a position to confer provincial posts, and favours a Nervan date, because the inscription (*ILS* 1015) which gives the career of Javolenus pointedly fails to mention the emperor who appointed him. Hence his appointment is likely to have been Domitianic, continuing into the reign of Nerva. In the context the identity of the *princeps* of s. 8 is uncertain; Nerva is as likely as Trajan (s. 8 n.). Since these arguments are indecisive, the question of Romanus' personal status is crucial. The present letter excludes the possibility that he was a senator at this moment. Information about the status of the recommended person was essential for the making of any appointment, and is given in all comparable letters, however briefly: III. 2. 4–5, IV. 4. 1, VII. 22. 2, X. 12, 26, 87. This letter strongly implies that Romanus is equestrian, and names no higher dignity than his provincial flaminate (s. 4 n.). Hence it should come before x. 4 unless Trajan refused, as Syme maintained, to grant Pliny's request. But this is extremely unlikely (s. 10 n.) in the case of a favour granted conditionally by Trajan's predecessor. Monti argued that Priscus would know that Romanus was a fellow-senator, and hence Pliny did not mention the fact. But considering Priscus' long absence from Italy this is not a plausible assumption. Monti also held that the absence of any reference in x. 4 to the recent flaminate of Romanus proved that this tenure, and hence II. 13, was later than X. 4. But X. 4 is the renewal of a request already made formally to Nerva and only held up on technical grounds; Pliny only summarizes the grounds of his previous recommendation.

Among minor arguments, there is no reason to maintain that Romanus must have acquired his *ius trium liberorum* later than Pliny—who gained it from Trajan in early 98 (X. 2 nn.)—and hence again that II. 13 is later than X. 4. This may well be the first, as it was the least, privilege that Pliny sought for Romanus. (See further s. 8 n.) There is equally little substance in the argument of Monti that the references to the inheritance and adoption of Romanus in s. 4 are remoter in time here than in X. 4. But it is probable, though this has not been remarked hitherto, from the reference to these two recent domestic changes in the man's family life in both letters in nearly identical language, that the two letters are separated by no long interval. The stress laid on the point would be absurd four or five years after the event.

The simplest solution of the various problems arising from the two letters is to date II. 13 before the death of Nerva.

Address. The statement in s. 2, 'regis exercitum amplissimum', indicates that Priscus was a consular legate of a province with more than one legion. Careful study of the lists of consular legates in Syme, *Tacitus*, App. 15–16, shows that only two consular Prisci are known to have held senior legateships between 90 and 107, Javolenus Priscus and L. Neratius Priscus, suffect consuls of 86 and 97, of whom the latter was legate of Pannonia not before 103 (ibid., nn. 16, 28), *ILS* 1015, 1033). Only one other Priscus, the elder Neratius in 87, is known to have held a consulship between 85 and 97, for which period the Fasti are complete except for some four places. The younger Neratius was long a favourite identification because his brother Marcellus gave a post to Suetonius on the recommendation of Pliny in these years (III. 8). But the term *longum tempus* (s. 2) effectively excludes him from consideration until about 104–5, to which period Asbach dated this letter. This cannot be a possible date in the present state of knowledge about the compilation of the Letters, and in the light of the close verbal and factual relationship of II. 13. 4 and X. 4. 4 (above). Hence the preference for Javolenus Priscus, but at the earlier date *c.* 97 rather than in 100–1 as urged by R. Syme (art. cit.). He had governed Upper Germany *c.* 90 and was proconsul of Africa not later than 102/3 (cf. Syme, App. 3, 23). He probably succeeded Lappius Maximus now testified in Syria as legate in 91 (*AE* 1961 n. 319) when this man became *cos.* II in 95. The suggestion (W. Reidinger, *Die Stadthalter . . . des Pannonien*, 1956, 58) that the *elder* Neratius governed Pannonia from 94–97 seems improbable, and would hardly have been made but for the mention of Neratius Marcellus in III. 8. Pompeius Longinus, legate of Moesia Superior in September 94 and of Pannonia in February 98, where he was succeeded by Julius Servianus and Glitius Agricola in the short space of 98–101, is likely to have been in Pannonia for two or three years before 98 (Syme, *Tac.*, App. 14, nn. 30, 20, 11). But at least two consular provinces are vacant in the records for 97—Syria and Moesia Superior, vacated by Pompeius Longinus' move to Pannonia— and probably Germania Inferior (cf. Syme, App. 15), if Javolenus was not yet in Syria. The elder Neratius remains a possibility, if he held one of these provinces, other than Syria. Even the elderly Novius Priscus, suffect consul in 78, with whom Pliny had connexions (IV. 20 pref., VI. 8), might be considered, since his coeval P. Calvisius Ruso was legate of Cappadocia as late as 105–7 (Syme, App. 14, n. 6). The identification with Javolenus Priscus, though the best on the external evidence, is doubtful, because VI. 15 suggests that Pliny was not well acquainted with him, and the present Priscus is among Pliny's personal benefactors (s. 1). Besides, Pliny had closer friends available among the consular legates of 98–101, if not of 97, notably T. Avidius Quietus and Neratius Marcellus in Britain, whither he proposed to send the scholarly Suetonius (III. 8), Servianus in Germany and Pannonia (VIII. 23. 5), Pomponius Bassus in Cappadocia (IV. 23 pref.).

The recipients of the other letters to Priscus must be divided between the later consular Cornelius Priscus (III. 21 pref.) and Novius Priscus (VI. 8 pref.). For the origins and career of Iavolenus see further VI. 15. 2 n.

2. regis exercitum amplissimum. So too in IX. 13. 11 a consular governor of either Syria or Cappadocia is indicated by the phrase 'ad orientem . . . amplissimum exercitum . . . obtinebat', which distinguishes the consular legates who controlled armies of two or more legions from the praetorian legates of such provinces as Judaea and Lugdunensis with one or none, and consular legates of such provinces as Tarraconensis and Dalmatia with a single legion. Eight such provinces existed at this time, the two Germanies, two Moesiae, Pannonia, Britain, Syria, and Cappadocia-Galatia.

hinc tibi beneficiorum larga materia. This passage, with III. 2. 8, IV. 4, VII. 22, shows that the governors personally appointed a number of their officers, such as *praefecti* and military tribunes, though doubtless these had to secure a general commission from the Princeps beforehand; Statius describes (*Silvae* 5. 1. 94 ff.) the *ab epistulis* secretary as advising: 'quis praecepisse cohorti, quem deceat clari praestantior ordo tribuni'. As late as Severus' reign such a nominee calls himself 'candidatus legati', *CIL* vi. 1410. Probably only a limited number were so appointed by the legates. Tac. *Ann.* 2. 55 carries the system back to the early Principate. This passage, with x. 85, 86 a–b, also shows that such appointments were not all made at the beginning of a governor's tenure. The advent of a new governor did not mean a total change of staff. This was one of the administrative improvements of the Principate, Mommsen, *DPR* iii. 305 f. For further technical details see iii. 8 nn. Cf. also E. Birley, *Roman Britain and the Roman Army*, 141 f.

longum tempus. The norm in the middle Principate was three to four years, but there was no fixed rule, as Agricola's seven seasons in Britain show, Dio 52. 23. 2; Tac. *Agric.* 9. 6; Mommsen, *DPR* iii. 298. Lengthier tenures, favoured in the early Principate, especially by Tiberius and Nero, later became rare. Tac. *Ann.* 1. 80, 12. 45, 14. 26; Suet. *Otho* 3. 2; *Galba* 9. 1. This discouraged close ties between commanders and armies, Dio, loc. cit. Pliny does not imply that Priscus had been exceptionally long in this command, but an appointee of 97 is clearly excluded if this letter cannot be later than 98, ss. 4, 8 nn.

4. is erit Voconius Romanus. pater ei in equestri gradu clarus, clarior vitricus, immo pater alius (nam huic quoque nomini pietate successit). The circumstances of Romanus *c*. 97–98 are known from this letter and x. 4, where Pliny secures him senatorial status from Trajan, though x. 4 adds no fresh personal information relevant to the problems of ii. 13. The identification of the family with the Voconii of Saguntum, known from the Spanish inscriptions *CIL* ii. 3865–6 was suggested cautiously by Hübner, ad loc., and more recently by A. W. van Buren (*Rend. Pont. Acc. Arch.* xv. 73–86). The first inscription merely names C. Voconius C. f. Gal(eria tribu) Placidus, magistrate of Saguntum. But the second commemorates the death of Popilia L. f. Rectina, wife of C. Licinius C. f. Gal. Macrinus Voconius Romanus. This links with the mention in ix. 28. 2 of a freedman of Romanus called Popilius Artemidorus, not noticed by van Buren, and of a friend of the Elder Pliny called Rectina in vi. 16. 8 n. That Voconius lost a wife is suggested by the grant of the 'ius trium liberorum', s. 8 n. The multiple names also suggest that the man, like Pliny's friend, was an adopted son. So our Voconius may be the very man of the inscription, rather than a relative. Pliny would meet the young Voconius in his uncle's house at Rome, while both were at school, s. 5 n. Voconius Placidus would seem to be the natural father, and Licinius Macrinus the adoptive, to judge by the use of names in the parallel case of Pompeius Falco, i. 23 pref.

For a general biographical treatment of Voconius Romanus see
M. Schuster's article in *RE* ii. 9. 1. 698–704, which, however, contains several errors.

huic quoque nomini pietate successit. The run of the sentence
requires that *vitricus* should be the subject of *successit*. Cf. also VIII.
18. 6 'successit in locum patris' for the usage. The β reading *huius*
cannot stand against the consensus of αγ. It would cause no hesitation as a bad correction if it did not give the same sense as X. 4. 4:
'Romani . . . eximia pietas . . . adoptionem a vitrico meruit', where
Pliny certainly attributes the *pietas* to the son, not to the father. But
there the point is that Romanus earned his adoption by his *pietas*
towards his relation, here that his stepfather showed a sense of duty
towards his wife by adopting her son. In the original draft ambiguity
would not arise, because Pliny would name all the persons. The
argument that the father's death is more recent in X. 4. 4 than here
is too refined to bear much weight: 'matris liberalitatem et *statim*
patris hereditatem et adoptionem . . . meruit'. See note ad loc.

in equestri gradu. So too in III. 2. 4, VII. 22. 2, Pliny is careful to
designate the exact status of those whom he recommends to strangers; cf. IV. 4 n. If the man was *laticlavius* he could only be offered a
military tribunate. Pliny here makes it clear that Romanus is
angusticlavius, to whom a wider range of posts was open. Hence the
letter is earlier than Pliny's request to Nerva for senatorial status for
Romanus—which may mean only the *latus clavus* and the opportunity
of standing for office (X. 4. 2 n.)—and cannot be later than 97. For
the notion that Trajan *refused* that request see s. 10 n.

ipse citerioris Hispaniae . . . flamen proxime fuit. This office, the
highest dignity in provincial life, combined the presidency of the
provincial council, composed of representatives of the provincial
boroughs, with the administration of the imperial cult and the
communal games, at the provincial capital. The post was annual
and elective, and very expensive, since the *flamen* was expected to
contribute handsomely to the ceremonies of his year. See *AJ* ch. xii
and nn. 62, 110, 140; *AE* 1947, n. 69 (or Bruns, *FIR* 29, 63; *CIL*
xiii. 3162; *FIRA* 22, 49). *RE* iv. 803, 'Concilium' 803 ff., suppl. iv
'κοινόν' 930 ff. For other references to the activities of the councils
in the Letters see III. 9. 4, VII. 6. 1 nn. Schuster very curiously took
the priesthood to be a salaried post given to Romanus by Domitian
on Pliny's request—ignoring *iudicium provinciae* (art. cit. 700).

Voconius was a wealthy man (X. 4. 5), but his election is remarkable
in that he seems no longer to be permanently settled in Spain. His
promotion is characteristic of the advance of the wealthy magnates of
the provinces towards senatorial status, cf. VI. 19. 4 n. Usually it
took two generations for such families to reach the Senate, the father

serving the Princeps as a procurator in the equestrian service, and securing the *latus clavus* for his son; the Roman citizenship was, of course, a prerequisite. But Pliny abandoned his scheme of securing Romanus merely equestrian promotion for the more ambitious plan of getting him into the Senate in a single stride when he realized how much influence he could enlist in the circle around Nerva, I. 5. 8, II. I. 8, 7. I nn. For general discussion of equestrian promotion see A. Stein, *Römische Ritterstand*, ch. iv.

5. ille meus in urbe ille in secessu contubernalis. Pliny moved to Rome for his higher education, and lived at his uncle's house during the latter years of Vespasian, I. 19. 1, VI. 6. 3, 20. 5. The two men are of an age, s. 8. It was normal for municipal magnates to enter the equestrian service in their early thirties, after holding municipal offices, cf. E. Birley, op. cit., 139 f.; Pflaum, *Procurateurs Équestres*, 210 ff. Romanus is a little old, but the opportunity arose only with the accession of Nerva. All these things depended on patronage as much as on merit.

in urbe. Schuster oddly thought this meant that Romanus was so poor that Pliny lodged him (*RE*, art. cit.). But *contubernalis* is a regular metaphor of literary friendships, I. 2. 5, X. 94. 1.

7. epistulas quidem scribit ut Musas ipsas Latine loqui credas. Some of these are mentioned in IX. 28. 5. For the type see I. I. 1 n., 16. 6. See III. 2. 2 n. for the qualities required in provincial appointments.

8. nuper ab optimo principe trium liberorum ius impetravi quod quamquam parce et cum delectu daret . . . indulsit. For this privilege see X. 2. 1, 94–95 nn. In X. 95 Trajan remarks of it: 'quam parce haec beneficia tribuam'. This was evidently a stock remark or policy, and the similarity does not identify the present *princeps* with Trajan. If II. 13 is earlier than X. 4 for the reasons given above, this must be Nerva. For X. 4 is Pliny's first and only letter to the absent Trajan on behalf of Romanus in the period 97–99, and he had no opportunity for an oral request during Trajan's absence (X. 4. 1 n.). Monti objected that the reference would be ambiguous if the unnamed Princeps was no longer alive at the time of writing. But Priscus did not need to know the name of the Princeps, he would assume that the living emperor was meant. Monti and others have assumed—in order to exclude Nerva—that if the emperor were dead at the time of publication, Pliny would have used *divus*. But that is impossible without the personal name, and in IV. 22. 4, written much later, he prefers *Nerva imperator* to the *divus Nerva* of VII. 33. 9.

optimo principe. Pliny applies this term to Nerva in Ep. 1. 3, to Nerva and Trajan in *Pan.* 7. 4, 88. 4–6, and to Trajan in IV. 22. 1.

It does not appear on the coins of Trajan before 103, and *Optimus* does not become an imperial cognomen until 114 (Dio 68. 23. 1; *RIC* ii. 249, 265; *ILS* 293–5 nn.) though it had been offered to him as early as 100 (*Pan.*, loc. cit.).

daret. The subjunctive is surprising. Pliny elsewhere uses the normal indicative with *quamquam*, e.g. VII. 9. 4, IX. 9. 3. The nearest parallels are III. 9. 29: 'iratus quod evocatus esset invitus . . . Norbanum . . . reum postulabat tamquam . . . praevaricaretur', and especially VI. 5. 3: 'fuerunt quibus haec eius oratio . . . displiceret quae . . . castigaret peractum'. These may be explained either as concealed indirect statements or as alleged causes or grounds, which comes to much the same thing. But this does not nullify the tense, as Otto thought, interpreting the word as 'dare se dixit'. Here, as with *displiceret* and *castigaret* in VI. 5. 3, the imperfect is deliberate. It means that Nerva, whether now alive or dead, said 'I was in the habit of giving but nevertheless . . .'. Too much weight has been laid on this word for the purposes of controversy.

9. haec beneficia mea. The most recent benefit is the grant of marital rights. Those who date X. 4 before II. 13 are compelled to include the grant of senatorial status among these *beneficia*, despite Pliny's silence, unless they deny, like Syme, that Trajan granted it.

10. tribuas ei quantum amplissimum potes. Cf. III. 2. 5: 'dignitati eius . . . adstruere . . . quod sit splendidum nec molestum'. The wide choice of office implies that Romanus is angusticlave: a *laticlavius* would require only a military tribunate. Syme (loc. cit.) suggests, improbably, that Trajan refused, in reply to X. 4, what Nerva had already granted in principle. He then dates this request later than X. 4 as Pliny's *pis aller* on behalf of Romanus. Syme assumes that Pliny was asking for the direct adlection of Romanus to the Senate, or his commendation as a *candidatus Caesaris*. There is no clear evidence in the seven letters addressed to Voconius that he was or was not a senator, any more than there is for Rosianus Geminus, another minor figure, in his six letters, though the fact emerges from X. 26. The absence of Romanus on his estates in IX. 7 and 28 does not prove that he lived permanently outside Italy, any more than the similar absence of Geminus in IX. 11. We should have a very obscure notion of the standing of Tacitus himself from the eleven letters addressed to him, where it is indirectly hinted only twice, in VI. 9. 1 and VII. 20. 3. Pliny never describes senatorial politics in letters to Romanus later than 100 (VI. 15, 33, VIII. 8, IX. 7, 28). III. 13. 1 may imply that he was not present in the Senate in September 100. The rule that emperors stood by the *beneficia* of their predecessors, whether

completed or not, suggests that Trajan must have fulfilled Nerva's
promise: x. 58. 10 n. There was no reason for Trajan to snub Pliny,
who was active in office at the time, and to whom he was ready to
give the honour of an early consulship and numerous other favours
(x. 2–13). An odd turn of phrase in x. 12. 1 (n.) means that Trajan
had granted senatorial advancement to men recommended by Pliny
before 101: 'quia tamen *in hoc quoque* indulsisti . . . rogo ut Attium
Suram praetura exornare digneris'. The reference can only be to the
promotion of Romanus or of Erucius Clarus (Ep. 9. 2 n.). Of these
two only the recommendation of Romanus is certainly Trajanic.
But it is possible, as Schuster suggested, that Romanus made no use
of his *latus clavus* (*RE*, art. cit.).

   That even Priscus refused promotion to Romanus—as Syme
(loc. cit.) suggests, adding insult to injury is most unlikely in view
of the general fear of causing *offensae*, Ep. 18. 5. On Syme's chronology the opposite is suggested by the absence of Voconius from
Rome in III. 13 and his omission otherwise from the letters until
Book VI. The over-ingenious might argue from the term *amplissimum*,
the appellation proper to the Senate and senators, that it was precisely for a senatorial post on the staff of Priscus that Pliny was
soliciting, and that Romanus was absent from 100 to 104 as the
comes of this legate. But this is against many points of interpretation
in this letter (ss. 4, 9, nn.).

14. *To Maximus*

Date. Pliny's activity in the Centumviral Court dates this letter as
no later than and perhaps just before his appointment to the prefecture of Saturn, i.e. late 97, ss. 1, 3, 14 nn.

Address. Pliny has several friends called Maximus. Here and in
seven letters of VI–IX no *nomen* is recorded: VI. 11, 34, VII. 26, VIII.
19, 24, IX. 1, 23. In five letters of III–V three different *nomina* occur,
Vibius III. 2, Maesius III. 20, IV. 25, Novius IV. 20, V. 5. The eight
undifferentiated Maximi seem to concern two persons. One is a man
of Pliny's age, with no clear senatorial connexions, interested in
literature and in Pliny's career: Ep. 14, VI. 11, VIII. 19, IX. 1, 23.
The other is younger, and a praetorian senator, with no such interests,
whom Pliny advises about conduct and career: VI. 34, VII. 26, VIII.
24. The present Maximus seems to be the 'elder' from s. 14 and the
other contents. Whether he is also Maesius or Novius is uncertain.
Novius is a man of letters, probably a senator, and possibly the
brother of the consular Novius Priscus: IV. 20 pref. Maesius is a
student of history and apparently not a senator. Vibius, an equestrian

official, may be excluded, because after his disgrace in 107 he is
unlikely to appear in VI–IX (III. 2 pref., IX. 1 pref.). There remains
'Maximus noster', of VI. 8. 4, who through his associations with
'Priscus' and Atilius therein might be uncertainly identified with
Novius Maximus and 'the elder' of this letter (s. 2 n.). For the
possible identification of 'the younger' with Quinctilius Valerius
Maximus see VIII. 24 nn. Novius seems the best identification of the
'elder': IV. 20 nn.

1. distringor centumviralibus causis. In X. 3A Pliny says that he
ceased to practise after becoming Prefect of Saturn, though he
accepts the state prosecutions against Marius Priscus and later Caecilius Classicus under pressure (III. 4. 2–4). This abstinence lasts
till after his consulship. There is no mention in III of private cases,
but in IV they are common (5, 14. 1, 16, 17. 1, 19. 3, 24. 1). So
this letter, like the *actio* of Ep. 5, should belong to the period before
January 98, a month in which jurisdiction was in recess, IV. 29 n.
The suggestion of Peter that it is much later than 100 cannot be
supported by the references to his age in ss. 3. 14 nn.

parvae et exiles. Pliny's dissatisfaction is not repeated in other
letters about the Centumviral Court. Usually he takes the greatest
pride in his work and pre-eminence there, IV. 16, 24, VI. 23, 33, IX. 23.
In IV. 24. 4 he attributes his political advancement to his Centumviral
reputation: 'studiis processimus, studiis periclitati sumus rursusque
processimus'. The tone of disgust is assumed as appropriate to the
incident and anecdote related. The Centumviral ranked at this time
as the principal court of civil law for an advocate seeking to make a
name, Tac. *Dial.* 38. 2. Cf. IV. 24. 3 n.

personarum . . . insignis. Cf. Ep. 11. 1, VI. 33. 2 for this description
of a big case.

2. ad hoc pauci cum quibus iuvet dicere ; ceteri audaces. Tacitus
called the schools of rhetoric 'ludum impudentiae', quoting Cicero
(*Dial.* 35. 1). In IV. 24 another explanation is given. Most of Pliny's
contemporaries turned from legal practice to careers in the public
administration. Pliny airs a different complaint in VI. 2. 5–6, about
the slackness of advocates who were not interested in rhetoric at all,
but wanted to settle their cases in the shortest possible time.

obscuri adulescentuli. Such as Pliny himself had been, contrasted
with the *clari* whom he was soon to patronize, VI. 11, 23. 2. He does
not usually show a 'new man's' contempt for his own origins, and is
tender to youthful follies in III. 1. 2, IX. 12. 2. Saint-Denis noted that
elsewhere Pliny was an admirer of youthful talent when accompanied
by respect, as in V. 17. 3, VI. 23, 26. ('Pline et la . . . Jeunesse', *Rev.
Universitaire*, 1946, 9 ff.)

Atilius . . . dixisse videatur . . . pueros a centumviralibus causis auspicari. Pliny himself began to practise in court at the age of 18, and introduces young men to it, I. 18. 3, V. 8. 8, VI. 23. 2. Quintilian approves the custom, though he deprecates an excessively early start for fear of *impudentia*, much as here (*Inst.* I. 8, 12. 6. 2).

Atilius is a man of letters but not an advocate (I. 9. 8 n., VI. 8. 6), and is a joint friend of Pliny and this Maximus. In VI. 8, addressed to 'Priscus', he is connected in less friendly fashion to 'Maximus noster', the heir of one Valerius Varus, who owed Atilius money; Pliny tries to persuade Priscus, who may be Novius Priscus, to induce his close connexion Maximus to give this money over to Atilius. That Maximus may be either the 'younger', or Novius Maximus and 'the elder', n. ibid.

ut ab Homero in scholis. Here the reference is to the courses of the *grammatici*. For Roman education see Ep. 18. 1, III. 3. 3, IV. 13. 3–5 nn.

3. at hercule ante memoriam meam. Only the humourless would claim with Peter (art. cit. 707) that Pliny is here speaking as an actual greybeard. Pliny here, as in III. 20. 5 and VIII. 14. 4, speaks of the age of Claudius as the 'good old days'.

nisi aliquo consulari producente. Pliny himself was thus introduced (IV. 24. 1 n.) and introduced others (above). For the custom, cf. also Tac. *Dial.* 34, cited VIII. 14. 4 n.

4. sequuntur auditores actoribus similes conducti et redempti. But contrast IV. 16, where a young man stands listening to a speech of Pliny for seven hours: 'adhuc honor studiis durat'.

in media basilica. The Basilica Julia was the home of the Centum-viral Court, V. 9. 1, VI. 33. 4 n.

5. Σοφοκλεῖς vocantur [ἀπὸ τοῦ σοφῶς καὶ καλεῖσθαι], isdem Latinum nomen impositum est Laudiceni. In Martial, 6. 48, the same pun on *laus* and *cena* is implied, 'quod tam grande sophos clamat tibi turba togata non tu, Pomponi, cena diserta tua est'. But Stout (p. 155), whom the Oxford text here follows, approves the text bracketed quoting K. Barwick (*Philol.* (1936), 441 f.) to the effect that Pliny added the explanation because of the 'frequent . . . mis-understanding of the word 'sophos' as a term of applause'. This is surely nonsense. Besides, Pliny never writes pointlessly in Greek. He quotes Greek frequently, and uses Greek words, e.g. I. 2. 1: 'eodem ζήλῳ scripsisse', or an impressive phrase as in Ep. 20. 12 and IV. 25. 5, VI. 8. 3. The ἀπὸ suggests an editor's hand. Pliny might have written *de* and *et* with Greek words between. But the point is made clear and neat by the Latin explanation. The Greek addition destroys the *urbanitas*.

Applause was shown by shouting rather than by clapping, s. 10,
IX. 23. 1.

6. qui nuper togas sumpserint. See I. 9. 2 n.—about the age of 17
or less.

ternis denariis ad laudandum trahebantur. A high fee, far above
a working man's wage or a soldier's pay of less than a denarius a day.
Elegant types were required.

8. nihil est quod tribunal ascendas. Distinguished visitors might be
invited to the platform among the *iudices*, IV. 16. 1, VI. 33. 4, Tac.
Ann. I. 75. 1.

9. primus hunc audiendi morem induxit Larcius Licinus. Larcius
Licinus was a Julio-Claudian advocate in the Asianic style who wrote
a *Ciceromastix*, Gellius, *NA*, xvii. 1. 1. For his career and connexion
with the Elder Pliny see III. 5. 17 n.

auditores corrogaret. In VI. 2. 3 Pliny approves the custom here
criticized.

praeceptore meo. In VI. 6. 3 Pliny names Quintilian and Nicetes
Sacerdos as his masters. The *Institutio* was written under Domitian,
and the date of Quintilian's death is inferred only from this passage.
For Pliny's fidelity to the principles of Quintilian see I. 2. 1 n., and
for echoes of the *Institutio* I. 20. 9, 19, V. 8. 10, IX. 26. 7, nn.

10. adsectabar Domitium Afrum. That is, as an adult admirer, not as
a pupil, cf. III. 11. 7, IV. 13. 10, VIII. 23. 5. Quintilian often quotes
Afer, the great Gallic orator, for whom see VIII. 18. 4 n. The incident
must be before A.D. 59, when Afer died (Tac. *Ann.* 14. 19).

audit ex proximo . . . clamorem. The Centumviral Court sat in
four sections, in different parts of the Basilica Julia, but not in
separate rooms (Quintilian 12. 5. 6). Afer, standing on the floor,
could not have seen through the throng what was the cause of the
noise, V. 9. 1, VI. 33. 3.

11. 'hoc artificium perit'. Compare Nero's 'qualis artifex pereo'.

12. pudet referre quae quam fracta pronuntiatione dicantur. For the
new style, avoided by Afer, and taught by the *phonasci*, see Quint.
9. 4. 31, 11. 3. 23. It went with the extremes of 'Asian' technique.
Tac. *Dial.* 26. 2: 'neque . . . oratorius iste . . . cultus est quo plerique
temporum nostrorum actores utuntur ut lascivia verborum et levitate
sententiarum et licentia compositionum histrionalis modos expri-
mant'. Cf. Quint. 12. 10. 73, quoted I. 2. 1–2 nn.

14. nos tamen adhuc et utilitas amicorum et ratio aetatis moratur.
This says the very opposite of what Peter (s. 3 n.) would have it.

Pliny means that he is too young to give up. He takes much the
same tone in III. 1. 11, IV. 23. 4—he admires the elderly. But he
continues to work in the Centumviral Court throughout the Letters
(s. 1 n.). In IX. 23, one of the very latest, he speaks as though his
career were at its height.

solito rariores. This might refer to his decision to abandon private
practice during his coming tenure of the prefecture of Saturn, s. 1 n.

15. To Valerianus

Date is not determinable, though there is an echo of Ep. 4. 3, s. 2 n.

Address. The name is given in v. 4 as Julius Valerianus. He is
apparently a senator (v. 4. 4), but is otherwise unknown. A like-
named knight is known from Noviodunum near Geneva (Syme, *Tac.*
802 n. 1; *CIL* xii. 2608). Evidently the family owned land and
possibly originated from the Marsian region. Nothing connects him
personally with Vicetia, mentioned in v. 4 and 13, letters about
politics which are also addressed to him.

1. quomodo te veteres Marsi tui? quo modo emptio nova? He owns
land in a municipality of the former Marsian tribal territory of the
central Apennines. Nothing suggests that he sold his old estate to
buy the new one, as Sirago imagines (*Ital. Agrar.* 45): the missing
verb is the same for both clauses.

**rarum id quidem ; nihil enim aeque gratum est adeptis quam con-
cupiscentibus.** Schuster (*RE* xxi. 1. 450) thinks that notes of this
kind were written simply for the sake of the aphorism; but both in
this sentence and the next the aphorism can be deleted without
disturbing the sense of the rest, and may well have been added in
the revision of an actual note of the visiting-card type, I. 11 pref.

2. me praedia materna parum commode tractant. His family estates
were at Comum, VII. 11. 5. The complaint is echoed in Ep. 4. 3:
'reditus propter condicionem agellorum . . . incertior'. The complaint is specific, and it may be that the early death of his father,
followed by that of his uncle, when Pliny was about 17, meant that
Pliny's estates suffered from the double disadvantage of prolonged
minority and absentee ownership. After his father's death Pliny
lived in Rome or Campania with his uncle, Ep. I. 8, III. 5. 12, VI.
16. 4. So too the farm which he gives to his old nurse, which is likely
to be in the north, had suffered from neglect in these years, VI. 3.
For evidence in Pliny of more general agricultural discontents see
III. 19, IX. 37, X. 8. 5 nn.

16. *To Annius*

Date. Later than I. 14 (s. 1 n.) and perhaps about A.D. 100–1, if the references to the Treasury imply that he is no longer prefect of Saturn (ss. 1, 4 nn.), and if the identification with III. 6 is accepted.

Address. Though the α and γ groups agree in reading Annianus against the Annius of the β group, the man is certainly Annius Severus, Pliny's agent and recipient of two other letters about inheritances or legacies, III. 6, v. 1. The opening phrase of s. 1 is akin to III. 6. 5: 'ut soles omnia quae a me tibi iniunguntur, suscipe hanc curam'. Cf. *PIR*² A 689.

1. **admones me codicillos Aciliani . . . pro non scriptis habendos.** Acilianus should be Pliny's friend and junior contemporary, the praetorian senator Minicius Acilianus, whom in I. 14 he recommended to Mauricus. This inheritance may be that mentioned in III. 6, where Pliny has taken possession at a date after his consulship.

codicillos. The use of separate *codicilli*, containing a short written statement extending a regular testament, came in during the Augustan period, *RE* iv, s.v. 174 ff. Pliny shows the usage in full swing, cf. Ep. 20. 5: 'poscit codicillos, legatum Regulo scribit'. VI. 31. 6. Also Tac. *Ann.* 16. 17.

confirmati testamento. The correct usage was to state in the will that *codicilli* whether already written or to be written in the future should be regarded as valid. Gaius 2. 270 a; *Dig.* 29. 7. 8 pref. The formula is given by Pliny's contemporary Juventius Celsus, ibid. 7. 18: 'si quid tabulis aliove genere ad hoc testamentum pertinens reliquero ita valere volo'. It was an innovation apparently due to this same Celsus to accept 'previous' codicils as valid, ibid. Pliny here shows that the later usage of accepting codicils *non confirmati* was not yet current, *RE* loc. cit.

2. **ut defunctorum voluntates . . . perfectas tuerer.** Twice elsewhere Pliny repeats this doctrine of equity, but it was largely foreign to contemporary Roman law; see v. 7. 2 n.

constat autem codicillos istos Aciliani manu scriptos. In later law, according to Mracian. *Dig.* 29. 7. 6. 1–2, a properly drawn codicil was valid even if not written or signed 'ipsius manu' though confirmation by will was always required in such a case. The Roman law generally preferred witnesses to signatures, Ep. 20. 10 n.

3–4. **delatori locus non sit. nam si verendum esset ne quod ego dedissem populus eriperet, cunctantior . . . esse deberem.** There is no puzzle here, *pace* Guillemin, ad loc. Trajan's abolition of political

delation (*Pan.* 34–35) had not ended the ordinary processes of public
law, which depended upon the intervention of private prosecutors
and plaintiffs. It is only in political contexts that *delator* is an
emotive word, I. 5. I n. If a valid legacy was not taken up it became
a *bonum caducum*, and like a vacant *hereditas* could be claimed for
the State. An action would be instituted by a private person on behalf
of the *aerarium Saturni*, under the appropriate law, who would
receive a proportion of the sum due as his reward. The *praefecti
aerari* did not themselves claim, but were the tribunal in most such
cases; *Tit. Ulp.* 17. 1, 28. 7, *Dig.* 49. 14. 2. 1–5, 13 pref., which latter
contains traces of the procedure of Trajan's time. But in the present
case, since the codicil is invalid, the estate retains the legacy and the
heirs benefit.

populus eriperet. Cf. *Tit. Ulp.* 28. 7, 'populo bona (*sc.* caduca)
deferuntur ex lege Iulia caducaria'. The *aerarium Saturni* was
properly *a. populi Romani*, hence the term *populus*, cf. IV. 12. 3,
'praefecti aerari populo vindicabant', and Ep. I. 9 'publicis sumptibus' n.

donare quod in hereditate subsedit. Pliny means to pay the whole
from his own part. For the law of gifts see v. 1. 2 n.

17. *To Gallus*

Date. No indication.

Address. This Gallus should be the man to whom the description of
the Vadimon lake is addressed (VIII. 20. 10 n.). He may be connected
through the elderly Pomponia Galla with the praetorian senator
Pomponius Gallus Didius Rufus, v. 1. 1 n. Possibly he appears in
I. 7. 4 as a proconsul of Baetica. But in IV. 17, in another context of
legal briefs, the Index gives the *cognomen* Clusinius to a Gallus.

Introduction. The two descriptions of the villas at Vicus Augustanus
(s. 1 n.) and Tifernum (v. 6) should be read together. They are
peculiar in extant Latin literature and form a characteristic innovation of Pliny, who elaborates a theme which Statius had indicated
in his panegyrical sketches of the villas of Pollius Felix and Manilius
Vopiscus, and of the bath of Claudius Etruscus: *S.* 1. 3, 5, 2. 2. Seneca
earlier had briefly indicated some features of the park of Vatia
(*Ep.* 55. 6–7). Martial touched the theme lightly in his verses on the
rustic villa of Faustinus, his own suburban farm, and the palace of
an anonymous millionaire: 3. 58, 4. 64, 12. 50. But none of these
does more than indicate some special feature or apartment, or the
general situation and prospect. Statius dilates on costly materials

and ornaments rather than the buildings themselves, and wanders into personal and mythological digressions. A few verbal echoes, especially of Statius, may be detected: ss. 6, 12, 13 nn., v. 6. 23 n. A few themes recur—the favourite *diaeta*, the noise of the sea, the heating system: ss. 9, 13, 20, 23 nn. But the differences far outweigh the resemblances overstressed by Guillemin, whose scepticism about the factual value of these letters is exaggerated (*VL*, 125 f. and 'Les descriptions des villas', *Bull. Ass. G. Budé*, 1928, 6 f.). Pliny's systematic description of the layout and his passion for exact detail are all his own. One could not even begin to reconstruct the villa of Pollius Felix. But with Pliny it has been attempted only too often. Pliny had an imitator in Sidonius Apollinaris, but even Sidonius' account of his *villa rustica* in *Ep.* 2. 2 is far less complete than that of Pliny. He seems to enlarge only where Pliny was brief, notably in describing his baths (s. 11, v. 6. 25 nn.).

Even Vitruvius in his account of domestic architecture has little to say about the residential parts of *villae rusticae*, as Winnefeld noted (see below, op. cit. 201), referring the reader back to his account of the town house: 'si quid delicatius in villis faciundum fuerit', ibid. vi. 6. 5. But the spacious country houses of the Flavian age had developed a long way from the urban architecture of the generation of Augustus; cf. H. Kähler, *Hadrian und seine Villa* (Berlin, 1950), 93 ff. Hence Vitruvius is of limited value as a guide to the scale and proportions of Pliny's villas, though more useful for the Laurentine than the Tuscan. The former is a glorified town house in its central block. But the latter is of a different type, for which the palace of Hadrian at Tivoli is a closer analogy, though on a far vaster scale than anything that Pliny could afford (v. 6. 15 n.). The best illustrations of Pliny should be found in sites at present being excavated in the area of Baiae. But it is the task of an historical commentary to explain the meaning of Pliny from unambiguous material, without adding to the number, already too great, of speculative reconstructions, of which few are based on a clear understanding of Pliny's Latin.

H. H. Tanzer, *The Villas of Pliny the Younger* (New York, 1924), surveys attempted reconstructions from the seventeenth to the twentieth century, and publishes many plans, including her own. But the notes are brief and the translation of the text inadequate. The best commentary on both letters is still that of K. Winnefeld in his paper, 'Tusci und Laurentinum des jüngeren Plinius' (*Jahrb. d. Kais. D. Archäol. Inst.* vi. 201 ff.). M. Rostovtzeff, 'Pompeianische Landschaften und römische Villen', ib. xix. 116 f., first connected Pliny with the evidence of wall-paintings. K. Lehman-Hartleben in a short archaeological commentary on selected letters (*Plinio il*

Giovane, Florence 1936, 43 ff., cited as L–H) contributed fresh material. These are the principal sources of the present commentary. A useful brief discussion of Roman rooms and houses and their development down to the Flavian period will be found in R. C. Carrington, *Pompei* (Oxford, 1936), chs. iii–v. More recent reconstructions are those of C. Pember, *Illustrated London News*, 23 Aug. 1947, whose model reposes in the Ashmolean Museum, Oxford, and of A. W. Van Buren, in *JRS*, 1948, 35 f., who defended his plan at length in *Rendiconti Pont. Rom. Acc. Arch.* xx. 165 ff. P. W. Lehmann, *Roman Wall Paintings from Boscoreale*, &c. (Cambridge, Massachusetts, 1953), makes several valuable comparisons with passages in Pliny. For gardens see P. Grimal, *Les Jardins romains* (Paris, 1943), ch. viii. Professor I. A. Richmond gave oral advice.

Reconstructions of the Laurentine villa have depended on the assumption that Pliny's account is reasonably complete and that obvious gaps, such as the lack of service quarters, can be supplied from Vitruvius. But Pliny's silences are not all detectable, and his claim in v. 6. 41, 44 to have described *omnes angulos* and *totam villam* is less justified for the Tuscan than for the Laurentine house, in which he at least mentions the living quarters of the staff (Ep. 17. 9). In neither account does he describe his wife's apartments or mention working quarters, except by implication or incidentally (Ep. 17. 9, 13, 23, v. 6. 30). But it is probable from Pliny's careful accuracy in other descriptive letters—notably the account of Centumcellae and of the *Fons Clitumni* in vi. 31 and viii. 8—that the description of the show-rooms and private apartments of the Laurentine villa is tolerably complete. Here he concentrates on the buildings, while in v. 6 it is the locality and grounds that receive the main emphasis, having twenty-one out of thirty-seven of the continuous descriptive paragraphs (ibid. 4–14, 16–18, 32–37, 40). In Ep. 17 the locality and grounds are given at most ten out of twenty-seven sections: ibid. 2–3, 14–15, 17–18, 25–28.

The pattern of the two descriptions is much alike—though the two villas are very different—with characteristic variations. In Ep. 17 the principal apartments and courts of the main block are described first, ss. 4–13, then the grounds and *cryptoporticus*, which is within the grounds and functionally part of them, ss. 14–19, and finally the detached pavilion, *amores mei*, ss. 20–24, lying at the far end of the grounds. In v. 6 the description of the main buildings (ss. 19–31) is sandwiched between that of the two sets of gardens and their related buildings—the lesser grounds in ss. 16–18 and the grand *hippodromus* in ss. 32–40, which include the account of a garden-house akin to the pavilion of II. 17, though smaller. The whole is enclosed, in both cases, in an account of the surrounding locality; Ep. 17. 2–3, 25–28,

v. 6. 4–14, 45–46. But v. 6 includes an apology for its excessive length, cunningly inserted into the description of locality, s. 41–44.

In Ep. 17 the main block is described in three parts. First the central axis of courts from the vestibule on the east through to the great *salon* which projects towards the sea on the west, ss. 4–5. Next, the left or south flank of the whole building, ss. 6–9—not just the left wing of the seaward front. Finally the right or north flank of the whole, ss. 10–13. The shore-line, which acts as an indicator, trends here roughly from north-east to south-west, cf. *JRS*, 1948, fig. 4.

In style the Laurentine villa is a mixture of a developed form of the Julio-Claudian town house, as exemplified in the larger establishments at Pompeii, with some of the embellishments, notably the gardens and the arcade leading to a detached pavilion, used on a grander scale in the Tuscan villa. (Cf. Rostovtzeff, art. cit.)

1. Laurentinum meum vel (si ita mavis) Laurens. The precise site, close to the shore (ss. 5, 12–13), has not been certainly identified, though much discussed. It must lie near the *vicus Augustanus*, close to modern Castel Fusano (s. 26). But Pliny does not give the precise orientation from that point (L–H). The site favoured by Lanciani at La Palombara still awaits proper excavation. Lanciani, *Mon. Lincei* (1903), 192 ff., pl. xiii; T. Ashby, *Roman Campagna in Classical Times* (London, 1927), 211 ff.; J. Carcopino, *Virgile et les Origines d'Ostie* (Paris, 1919), 171 ff., 183.

Laurens. For the notion that this is the only form of the adjective used by Virgil see Carcopino, op. cit. 261, who thinks that it refers to the territory of Lavinium. Certainly a Laurentum no longer existed, *RE* xii (i), 1008 f. Pliny's phrase may distantly echo Catullus 44. 1 —'o funde noster seu Sabine seu Tiburs', but in dragging in Cic., *Att.* 15. 13. 3 Guillemin, (*VL*, 145) abandons common sense in the hunt for stylization.

2. decem septem milibus passuum ab urbe secessit ut peractis quae agenda fuerint salvo . . . die possis ibi manere. The gentry seldom worked after the fourth or fifth hour of the Roman day, III. 5. 9 'Daily Routine' n. Pliny reckoned about twice this distance for a full day's leisurely travel, VI. 10. 1 n.

aditur non una via. For the roads see Lanciani, art. cit. 193 ff., Ashby, op. cit. 207 f., 214 f.

3. silvis via coartatur . . . multi greges ovium . . . quae montibus hieme depulsa herbis . . . nitescunt. Cf. s. 26, 'suggerunt adfatim ligna proximae silvae', and s. 28 'villa . . . praestat lac in primis; nam illuc e pascuis pecora conveniunt, si quando aquam umbramve sectantur'. This part of the Campagna was already out of cultivation and assuming the pastoral aspect which lasted until recent times. Cf. Ashby, op. cit. 211 f., Sirago, *Ital. Agraria*, 31–32. Pliny gives briefly an accurate account of the seasonal transhumance on which Mediterranean stock-breeding depends. If the woods and grazing grounds around the villa belong to Pliny, as Sirago supposes, he does not exploit them himself. Cf. IV. 6. 2: 'nihil . . . ibi possideo praeter tectum et hortum statimque harenas'. Possibly the *lac* came from payment in kind for use of grazing on the sandy lowland, and the timber from communal rights. But the description here concerns the last few miles of the route, s. 2, *iter . . . harenosum*, rather than Pliny's estate.

4–5. in prima parte atrium frugi . . . deinde porticus in D litterae similitudinem circumactae quibus parvola . . . area includitur . . . est contra medias (*sc.* porticus) cavaedium hilare, mox triclinium satis pulchrum quod in litus excurrit . . . undique . . . fenestras habet atque ita a lateribus a fronte quasi tria maria prospectat; a tergo cavaedium porticum aream porticum rursus mox atrium silvas et longinquos respicit montes. A series of three, not two, internal courts is being described, alined along an axis which runs from the western window of the dining salon to the vestibule (s. 15) of the *atrium*, cutting the base-line of the D. That the main axis of the villa is at right angles to the coast is suggested by the fact that all three sides of the salon have a seaward view. If the villa were at an angle to the coast, alined due east and west, as suggested by van Buren (art. cit.), the northerly window would not have a view of the sea but of the coastal villas, as in s. 21.

The term *cavaedium* is used by Vitruvius 6. 3. 1 as a generic term for different species of *atrium*; cf. Varro, *LL* 5. 161. The first *atrium* is as at Tifernum, *ex more veterum*; v. 6. 15. It cannot be a rare usage meaning the *vestibulum* itself (s. 15), despite van Buren art. cit. 173. Cf. VII. 19. 2.

H. Kähler (op. cit. 104) dilates upon the aesthetic aims of Roman architects in securing long perspectives that led through their buildings to link with the outer world. Professor Richmond remarks that the rich in their country houses realized the perspectives which they framed in the wall-paintings of their town houses.

tria maria prospectat. This salon corresponds, according to L–H, with the *oecus Cyzicenus* of Vitruvius 6. 3. 10. But that had two sets of windows only and faced north.

6. huius a laeva retractius paulo cubiculum est amplum, deinde aliud minus, quod altera fenestra admittit orientem, occidentem altera retinet; hac et subiacens mare . . . intuetur. To the left of the salon there are two rooms in line. The second has a westerly and a

southerly window, which looks across a stretch of coast to the sea.
Again, only if the villa is alined with the coast can the southerly
window catch the early sun.

7. angulus qui purissimum solem continet. It faces south, and gets
the main force of the midday sun. The Romans attached great
importance to the correct seasonal orientation of rooms and houses,
since warmth depended, as these letters indicate, much more upon
aspect than upon the inadequate heating system. Columella 1. 5. 5–8
and Vitruvius 6. 4 favour aspects adopted by Pliny in his two villas.

**8. adnectitur angulo cubiculum in hapsida curvatum, quod ambitum
solis fenestris omnibus sequitur.** The third and last *cubiculum* along
the shore must be set back from the line of the preceding one (as in
van Buren, loc. cit.), to allow for the southerly window of the latter,
if it is also on the seaward front. Its curved window should face from
north-east through south to south-west. It may be the first set of
the southern face of the villa. Cf. the apsidal room in the Villa dei
Misteri (Maiuri, cited s. 11 n., Tav. A).

   in bybliothecae speciem armarium insertum est. The only reference
to book-cases in either villa. But there is no mention of any other
furniture except in the garden pavilions, s. 21 and v. 6. 36–38, or
of any statuary (L–H, *ad* v. 6. 1).

   cubiculum. The word is used of any living apartment, and contrasts
with 'dormitorium membrum' s. 9, 'cubiculum noctis et somni' s. 22,
'dormitorium cubiculum', v. 6. 21.

9. adhaeret dormitorium membrum. This can only refer to a complex
of bedrooms, as L–H takes it, against Tanzer and many others.
This is implied by the reference to the servants' quarters in the next
sentence: 'plerisque tam mundis ut accipere hospites possint'. The
usage of *membra* in v. 6. 15 is ambiguous: 'multa in hac membra,
atrium etiam ex more veterum'.

   **transitu interiacente, qui suspensus et tubulatus conceptum vaporem
. . . digerit.** This is the system of piped hot air to which moderns
inaccurately apply the term 'hypocaust', s. 11 n., 23 n. For it see *RE*
vii. 2, art. 'Heizung', 2646 f.; G. Fusch, *Über hypokausten-heizungen*
(Diss. Hanover, 1910), 9. The corridor is 'hung over' the main heating passage from which wall flues distribute the heat, as in s. 23.

   reliqua pars lateris huius. The sets summarized in s. 9 should form
the southern and inland wing of the villa, stretching south-eastward
from the apsed *cubiculum* of s. 8.

10. ex alio latere cubiculum est politissimum. Pliny now starts on the
north side of the grand salon of s. 5. As far as the *calida piscina* of
s. 11 these rooms all seem to face the sea.

post hanc cubiculum cum procoetone. Three such chambers are
mentioned here and in s. 23. The *procoeton* is the opposite of the
zotheca or outward-facing alcove of s. 21 and v. 6. 38. Varro (*RR*,
2 pref. 2) comments on what in his day was a fad for using Greek
terms for apartments; but for Pliny they are merely technical,
cf. I. 3. I n.

11. inde balinei cella frigidaria spatiosa et effusa . . . adiacet unctorium, hypocauston, adiacet propnigeon balinei, mox duae cellae . . .
cohaeret calida piscina mirifica ex qua natantes mare adspiciunt.
The last statement suggests that all this section faces the sea, and
hence that the villa is not symmetrical, since there are only three
cubicula in the left wing.

The arrangement of the baths is not quite clear, because two sweat-
rooms, the *hypocauston* and the *propnigeon*, precede the hot-bath
rooms, and there is no mention of a *tepidaria cella*, or of a changing-
room, which cannot be the *unctorium*. At the Tuscan villa the order is
simpler: *apodyterium, frigidaria, media* or *tepidaria, caldaria*. v. 6.
25–26. That corresponds to the arrangement of a house-baths in
Vitruvius, though he adds (5. 10. 1, 5): 'laconicum sudationesque
sunt coniungenda tepidario'. Pliny here interposes two sweat-rooms
between his *frigidaria* and *caldaria*. The pattern is closer to that
given by Vitruvius 5. 11. 2, in somewhat ambiguous terms, for the
complicated layout of the baths of a Greek *palaestra*. There also the
tepidaria is missing and two alternative suites follow the *frigidaria*,
'elaeothesium-propnigeon' and 'laconicum-calda lavatio'. Hence
there may be two alternatives in the Laurentine baths: the dry
heat of the *hypocauston* and the damp heat of the *propnigeon* replace
the *tepidaria* and precede the hot-bath. Both as Vitruvius use the
same *frigidaria*. The parallel phrase *adiacet . . . adiacet* may mean just
this. Pliny's *hypocauston* then corresponds to Vitruvius' *laconicum
sudationesque*. The term usually means a room containing hot air,
as in s. 23. Cf. Ulpian, *D.* 17. 1. 16 'hypocauston et sphaeristerium'.
Vitruvius' description of heat-control in 5. 10. 5 shows that his
laconicum-sudatio is a dry-heat room (s. 23 n.). A small *laconicum* is
illustrated in A. Maiuri, *Villa dei Misteri* (1931), fig. 24. The term
propnigeon only recurs in Vitruvius and the *Notae tironum*, p. 184.
It is not the same as *praefurnium*, which is a type of furnace, *pace*
L–H and others. Cf. Forcellini, s.v., and A. Maiuri, *Casa del Menandro*
(1933), 221–2, fig. 100.

Pliny then has a more modern and elaborate arrangement of
baths at the Laurentine villa than at Tifernum. Sidonius, *Ep.* 2. 2.
4–5 expands some parts of Pliny's description, but casts no light
on technical problems. For typical small baths at Pompeii and

elsewhere see G. de A. d'Ossat, 'Tecnica costruttiva e impianti delle terme' (*Mostra della romanità*, N. 23), 8 ff. For further bibliography see L–H, op. cit., especially Krencker, *Die Trierer Kaiserthermen* (1929), 320 ff. Also Carrington, *Pompeii*, 51 ff.

adiacet . . . adiacet. Possibly the rooms stand out from the main building, as in many villas, for the convenience of service arrangements (Richmond).

mox duae cellae magis elegantes quam sumptuosae; cohaeret calida piscina. This is the hot section. The *tepidaria* cannot be discovered here because these rooms follow the sweat-rooms.

baptisteria. Cf. Sidonius, loc. cit. 8, 'piscina . . . seu graecari mavis baptisterium'. His largest pool contained some 40,000 gallons, and would measure some 30 by 40 by 4 feet. But Pliny's bath is not on this scale.

12. nec procul sphaeristerium quod calidissimo soli inclinato iam die occurrit. In v. 6. 27 (n.) the *sphaeristerium* is next to the *apodyterium*. It is a largish enclosure: 'plura genera exercitationis pluresque circulos capit'. Here, as at Tifernum, it is attached to the main block, not a separate building as in van Buren's plan, since it is sheltered from all but the afternoon or evening sun at the hour of exercise. Hence the court may be in the north range of buildings parallel to the servants' quarters in the south range, s. 9. In III. 1. 8 Spurinna took his exercise, with the ball, at the eighth hour in summer. Pliny followed his example, IX. 36. 3. Cf. Vit. 5. 10. 1: 'lumen habeant ab occidente hiberno . . . quod . . . tempus lavandi a meridiano ad vesperum est constitutum'. Columella 1. 6 recommends the same aspect. For the game cf. Statius, *S.* 1. 5. 57, 'strata solo referam tabulata crepantis auditura pilas', and Sidonius, *Ep.* 2. 2. 15.

12. hic turris erigitur, sub qua diaetae duae, . . . praeterea cenatio quae . . . mare . . . litus villas . . . possidet. The dining-room must face northwards along the shore, and the tower should hence be in the northern range, unless it is a detached building, as van Buren has it. There is no clear indication, except that Pliny does not use any of his connecting words, e.g. *adhaeret, adiacet, iungitur*. But *erigitur* may merely contrast the many-storied tower with the single floor of the rest of the villa. Mosaics and wall paintings often indicate towers as integral parts of country villas. See Lehmann, *Roman Wall Paintings, etc.*, 100 f., pls. xii–xvii; M. Borda, *La Pittura Romana* (Milan, 1958), 215, 258, 262; Rostovtzeff, art. cit. 125; cf. Martial 3. 58. 46, 'turre ab alta prospicis meras laurus'.

diaetae. Pliny uses this word for sets of apartments, whether in separate pavilions, as in ss. 20–23, or in the main block, as in v. 6. 20, 27–28. Grimal, op. cit. 275 f., is hardly right in suggesting that they were always isolated buildings. *Dig.* 24. 1. 66. 1, 29. 5. 1. 27 do not prove it. Lehmann, *Roman Wall Paintings*, 106–7, identifies them with certain elaborate structures in wall paintings.

possidet. This is the α γ reading where β has the easier *prospicit.* Guillemin and others defend the harder reading as a legal metaphor of a type used in similar contexts by Statius, *S.* 2. 2. 73–75, and Martial 4. 64. 8, and repeated by Pliny in 1. 3. 1 (n.) and v. 6. 23. (*VL* 126 f.)

13. est et alia turris; in hac cubiculum in quo sol nascitur conditurque. This tower is away from the sea front, and its unobscured prospect is east and west. It might be in either the northern or the southern range, if it is not a detached building. A clearer pattern can be detected if its *triclinium* may be identified with the *cenatio remota a mari* of s. 15, which also faces the gardens. If so, the tower lies at the east end or corner of the north range.

horreum. Store-rooms in upper stories are mentioned by Columella (1. 6. 9–10, XII. 52. 3) and others (L–H). The great heat made the top story of least value for living space. Lehmann, op. cit. 100 f., suggests that these *turres* represent a trace of the primitive farm-house.

turbati maris . . . sonum. Statius, *S.* 3. 2. 50, also dilates on this theme.

hortum et gestationem videt, qua hortus includitur. The formal garden lies within the circuit of the *gestatio* or walking ground. Pliny's descriptions here and in v. 6. 16–18, 32–40 add much to the knowledge of ancient ornamental grounds, for which L–H quotes Ruggiero, *Diz. Ep.* s.v., and Gottheim, *Geschichte der Gartenbaukunst*, i (1914), 87 f., 112 f., now replaced by Grimal, op. cit., who, however, confines himself to v. 6. Shrubs and topiary are the main elements here, as at the Tuscan villa, v. 6. 32, 36. The *gestatio* is a formal walk set in shrubberies and often connected with a colonnade. Grimal, op. cit. 269 f. For the measured tracks of the *gestatio* see III. 1. 4 'ambulat milia passuum tria', n.

15. adiacet gestationi interiore circumitu vinea tenera et umbrosa. Cf. I. 3. 1 'illa mollis et tamen solida gestatio'. Kukula's emendation of *via* for *vinea* is extremely logical, despite the agreement of all manuscripts. The *via* would form the boundary of the *hortus*, shaded by the mulberries. Cf. v. 6. 34 'viae plures . . . buxis dividuntur', in the *hippodromus*. A vineyard does not fit, and is excluded by s. 15 'terra . . . malignior ceteris'. In v. 6. 36–39 the garden pavilion is covered by a vine, not a vineyard. The Aldine *vinca* is no improvement, even if *vinca* is a plant of formal gardens (Pliny, *NH* 21. 68). A bed of periwinkle is no shady walking-place. Pliny means that his *gestatio* is shady on its inner circuit for hot-weather exercise.

hac . . . facie cenatio remota a mari fruitur, cingitur diaetis duabus a tergo, quarum fenestris subiacet vestibulum villae. This sentence gives the only firm indication of the relation of the *gestatio et hortus*, and consequently of the *cryptoporticus* and *xystus* in ss. 16–17, to the main building, if one assumes the identification of this *cenatio* with the *triclinium* of s. 13. Observe the cunning chiasmatic order of topics in 13–15: triclinium—hortus et gestatio—gestatio—hortus—triclinium. There is a similar cross-reference in v. 6. 27 back to an earlier-mentioned chamber. Pliny has completed the rectangle of his main building, and brought the reader back to the point of entry, the *vestibulum* of the first *atrium*, s. 4. The *cenatio*, at the eastern end of the north range, facing north (or more precisely N. by W.) overlooks the grounds which extend northwards from the villa, or north and south along the eastern, landward face. The two *diaetae* lie in the east front of the villa, filling in the space between the tower and the *vestibulum*. Beyond the latter comes the sector devoted to the servants, s. 9.

16. **hinc cryptoporticus prope publici operis extenditur.** The siting of the *cryptoporticus* in relation to the villa is not made precise. It is evidently a detached element that provides a covered way to the garden pavilion of s. 20; the Villa of the Papyri at Herculaneum has a similar arrangement, Grimal, op. cit., fig. 13. It borders the *xystus* and faces the sea across it. It is probably parallel to the coast since it alternately keeps off the south-westerly *Africus* and the north-north-easterly *Aquilo*. But does it extend to the north of the villa, lying between the *gestatio* and the sea, or to the south? The point of departure in *hinc* should be the preceding *vestibulum villae*. Not all scholars have observed that the garden of s. 16 (*ab horto*) strictly should refer to the second *hortus* of s. 15, 'pinguis et rusticus'. So too in s. 20 and 22. Pliny seems carefully to distinguish this from the *gestatio hortusque* in s. 18. Since the latter lay within the *gestatio* its wall could not be immediately adjacent to the pavilion, as in s. 22. Hence the garden which runs down to the pavilion is the 'kitchen garden', carefully screened from the ornamental *xystus* by the *cryptoporticus*. All this suggests that the pavilion lay at the southern end of the whole grounds, that the two sets of gardens formed a continuous belt from north to south, and that the *cryptoporticus* led from near the *vestibulum* south to the *diaeta* of s. 20. This is supported by the orientation of the latter, s. 23 n.

cryptoporticus. The term seems to be the invention of Pliny. It recurs in his imitator, Sidonius, who explains it, *Ep*. 2. 2. 10: 'quia nihil ipsa prospectat etsi non hypodromus saltem cryptoporticus meo mihi iure vocitabitur'. Pliny's corridor had walls and windows, where a normal portico had colonnades or arcades.

prope publici operis. A not uncommon phrase, cf. Vitruvius 6. 5. 2, though Guillemin (*VL* 126) reckons it an imitation of Statius, *S.* 3. 2. 31, 'porticus . . . urbis opus'. Sidonius copies it in turn, 2. 2. 5. The wall paintings show villas with galleries, covered and open, of astonishing length. M. Borda, op. cit. 213, 262. Lehmann, op. cit. pls. xii–xvii. There was a large gallery of this sort, but used only for storage, at the Villa dei Misteri (Maiuri, op. cit. figs. 36–38).

utrimque fenestrae, a mari plures, ab horto singulae sed alternis pauciores. This is the agreed reading of α β γ except that α omits *a* before *mari*, and β has *et* for *sed*. It is barely intelligible, as meaning 'on the garden side there is window for window, but fewer by every other one'. But it is better than the text of Schuster, derived from Postgate and Keil: '. . . ab horto pauciores scilicet alternis singulae'. In both *alternis* must be taken adverbially, as in v. 18. 2—'quae interdum alternis, interdum simul facio'. But there *vicibus* is easily understood. Here the usage is ambiguous; cf. IV. 30. 7, where he prefers to use the full phrase. Postgate's *scilicet*, derived from *sed* as a supposed misunderstanding of an abbreviation, is never used for parentheses by Pliny in I–IX, who prefers *nam* or *enim*, as in ss. 10, 25. It occurs only in I. 12. 8 and II. 6. 4 as an interjection in quoted conversations, though he used it for a parenthesis in x. 75. 1. The contrast *plures–pauciores* is Plinian: VIII. 16. 5, IX. 36. 2. The transposition of *pauciores* in Schuster is improbable. The manuscript variants in this letter tend rather to substitutions for difficult phrases, e.g. *possidet–prospicit* s. 12, *corruptus–salsus* s. 25. Possibly everything after *singulae*, or between *horto* and *pauciores*, is a gloss. Cf. Stout, op. cit. 155 f. and Ep. 14. 5 n. If every word is to be accounted for one might amend to: *singulas alternant pauciores*. 'Fewer windows take the place of each seaward one.'

Aldus printed *altius*, which L–H defends with VII. 21. 2: 'crypto-porticus . . . adopertis inferioribus fenestris'. But this suggests that the gallery had upper windows on both sides if this is the same gallery.

17. xystus violis odoratus. The *xystus* was in Latin usage a walking ground with alleys sheltered by shrubs and pleached hedges, not very different from a *gestatio* in its final development, Grimal, op. cit. 262 f., Vit. 5. 11. 4: 'hypaethroe ambulationes quas . . . nostri xysta appellant . . . faciunda . . . sic videntur ut sint inter duas porticus silvae aut platanones et in his perficiantur inter arbores ambulationes ibique ex opere signino stationes'. Cf. Suet. *Aug.* 72. 3, 'xystis et nemoribus'. At Tifernum Pliny (v. 6. 16) had 'ante porticum xystus in plurimas species distinctus concisusque buxo'. It is associated with the *gestatio* there and at Comum, ibid. 17, IX. 7. 4.

18. ante meridiem xystum post meridiem gestationis hortique proximam partem umbra sua temperat. Those who identify the *hortus* of s. 16 and s. 22 with the *gestatio hortusque* have no difficulty here about location. Otherwise the passage suggests that the *cryptoporticus* borders both gardens, or at least a part of the *gestatio-hortus*.

19. in capite xysti deinceps cryptoporticus horti, diaeta est amores mei. It lies at the outer end of all three elements, but not at the extreme verge since the southern window of the *heliocaminus* overlooks part of the *xystus*. It is not at the northern end of the whole estate, because all its windows which do not overlook the sea face south and none looks at the villa; cf. s. 21 'villae' n. The siting of the third *cubiculum* also requires this position, s. 23 n. This pavilion has often been compared to the Petit Trianon at Versailles, cf. Tanzer, op. cit. 145. Statius mentions similarly a favourite *diaeta*, *S.* 2. 2. 83 f.

20. in hac heliocaminus quidem alia xystum alia mare, utraque solem, cubiculum autem valvis cryptoporticum, fenestra prospicit mare. contra parietem medium zotheca . . . recedit. These two must both face west to the sea. Hence the *heliocaminus* is at the south-west corner of the pavilion, and—unless it projects, which is improbable— the *cubiculum* continues behind it, since the *zotheca* has a distant view south (s. 21). By *contra medium parietem* he means ' the middle of a wall', not 'the wall between door and window'; cf. s. 5 *contra medias* (*porticus*), v. 6. 20. The door in the north side gives access from the gallery, and is opposite the *zotheca* in the south wall. The corridor (s. 22) runs along the northern side of the block to give access to the bedroom and the third *cubiculum* which faces east and south, s. 22–23. The gallery is not directly attached to the pavilion entrance—*prospicit*.

For *heliocaminus*, a rare word, cf. Ulpian, *D.* 8. 2. 17, who equates it with *solarium*. Pliny seems to have adapted the term *zotheca*, and its diminutive in v. 6, 38, to the meaning of a bay or recess, whether angular or curved. Otherwise it means a cupboard or niche, as in Sidonius *Ep.* 8. 16. 3, 9. 11. 6, *ILS* 5449. It is not found in extant Greek texts. The 'Villa of Diomedes' at Pompeii gives a good example (Tanzer), for which see Carrington, *Pompeii*, 88, fig. 16. The Boscoreale paintings show a remarkable 'flying' alcove on an upper floor, Lehmann, op. cit., pls. xiv–xv.

21. specularibus et velis obductis . . . adicitur cubiculo. Calpurnia used a similar cabinet at her husband's recitations, iv. 19. 3.

a pedibus mare, a tergo villae, a capite silvae. Cf. ss. 3. 5, 12–13, 27. The woods lie to the east. The *villae* are those lining the coast. The singular *villa*, sometimes printed as an emendation, will not do. It causes difficulty about the doors, which must face the villa; besides, Pliny would seek the best possible view for his eyrie.

22. interiacens andron parietem cubiculi hortique distinguit. The bedchamber is on the east or landward side of the first *cubiculum*; the corridor along its outer northern wall gives access also to the *procoeton* of the third *cubiculum*, which has windows facing east and south, s. 24. For the curious meaning of *andron* see Vit. 6. 7. 5. The window of the second *cubiculum* is sheltered by the projection (s. 23) of the third from the assault of the rising sun: 'ne diem quidem sentit'(22).

23. adplicitum est . . . hypocauston . . . quod . . . fenestra suppositum calorem . . . effundit. Cf. v. 6. 25; 'cohaeret hypocauston et, si dies nubilus, immisso vapore solis vicem supplet'. These passages, with Statius, *S.* 1. 5. 58–59—'aedibus et tenuem volvunt hypocausta vaporem'—, explain the function of these hot-air chambers, called *cella hypocausta* in *CIL* vi. 1474. They either contain a separate furnace or receive hot air through a piping system, as in s. 9, from a furnace, for which the general term is *hypocausis*. (Cf. *Thes. L.L.* s.v.; *RE*, art. cit.) The *hypocausta* should be basements, as in most excavated examples, though Pliny's *adplicitum* and *cohaeret* suggest a chamber at the same level, with a furnace below (*suppositum*).

fenestra. Cf. the heating of a *laconicum* in Vitruvius 5. 10. 5: 'clipeum aeneum catenis pendeat per cuius reductiones et demissiones perficietur sudationis temperatura'. A flue in a wall or floor is indicated (Richmond).

procoeton . . . porrigitur in solem quem orientem statim exceptum ultra meridiem oblicum . . . servat. The most precise statement about orientation in the letters. It shows that the *diaeta* was alined parallel to the shore-line. The southern window, facing east of true south, would do just what is described in the last few words. It is impossible to put the gardens and the *diaeta* to the north of the villa, since its southern aspect would then be blocked by the *andron* lying between it and the garden to the south. Van Buren's plan, which does so, though its layout of the *diaeta* is reasonable in itself, inevitably makes this room face east and north, with not a trace of midday sun.

porrigitur. The room may project slightly, making the *diaeta* slightly L-shaped, s. 22 n.

Pliny probably gives a complete account of his *diaeta*, since it would need no service rooms. He would dine in the villa.

25. puteos ac potius fontes habet; sunt enim in summo. Lanciani, art. cit., confirms this from the present topography. Winnefeld, art. cit. 217 remarks that Pliny took special delight in the ornamental use of running water at Tifernum (v. 6. 36–40), and misses it here.

26. Ostiensis colonia. The considerable town and port of Ostia call for no comment here.

vicus. The village has been excavated and has the buildings of a little town. Lanciani, op. cit. 192 ff.; Carcopino, 183 ff., 250 f.; *RE*, XII. i. 1009; *CIL* xiv. 183.

si forte balineum . . . subitus adventus . . . calfacere dissuadeat. Cf. I. 4. 1, 'in Narniensi . . . etiam balineum (*sc.* paratum)'.

27. nunc continua nunc intermissa tecta villarum. Lanciani, *Mon. Linc.* xvi. 245, counted the traces of some 25 such villas along the coast north and south of Vicus Augustanus.

28. mare . . . soleas tamen et squillas optimas egerit. The fish of a sandy shore, flat-fish and shrimps.

illuc e pascuis pecora conveniunt. Cf. s. 3.

29. villulae nostrae. The diminutive is affectionate, but van Buren rightly remarks that, like most Roman houses, Pliny's was probably not very huge either in its separate apartments or its total size. Pliny claims size as a merit only of his *cryptoporticus*, s. 16. Cf. ss. 4, 6, 10, 11. Many reconstructions appear altogether too grandiose. Cf. earlier, Lanciani, loc. cit, though the villa which he excavated was altogether on a smaller scale than Pliny's.

18. *To Junius Mauricus*

Date. Fairly close to I. 14, where Mauricus' niece is being provided for, and earlier than III. 3 where the required schoolmaster has been found. So the letter is hardly in the wrong book.

Address. For Junius Mauricus, senator, recently returned from exile, see I. 5. 10 n.

1. ut praeceptorem fratris tui liberis quaererem. So too in I. 14 he finds a husband for the niece of Mauricus, who is fitting out his dead brother's family after his own return. One of these boys may later be the consul of 133, Q. Junius Rusticus, who turned Marcus Aurelius to the study of philosophy, *PIR*, s.v., III. 11. 3 n. This letter should be read with III. 3 and IV. 13, about the choice of a teacher of Latin rhetoric. The children, evidently boys, have finished with the *grammaticus* and need the services of a *rhetor Latinus*. They are probably about 13 years old, a year or two younger than their recently betrothed sister.

ex studiis. sc. 'eloquentiae', as commonly in the Letters. Cf. IX. 23. 2, 'nosti me, et quidem ex studiis'.

2. frequenti auditorio ... coram multis ordinis nostri. Set declamations, like those of Isaeus, and the extant *controversiae* of the Elder Seneca, composed as models or for practice, formed a large part of the course (Ep. 3. 6 n., IV. II. 1–3). See E. P. Parks, *Roman Rhetorical Schools* (Baltimore, 1945), 61 ff.; H. I. Marrou, *Histoire de l'éducation dans l'antiquité*[2] (Paris, 1950), ch. vi. Hence the appearance of the elder men in the 'school'.

auditorio. The rhetors like the *grammatici* kept school either in simple booths or under the colonnades and in the *exedrae* of the Roman Fora; cf. I. 22. 6 'porticus' n. Later Hadrian made the *Schola Fori Traiani* the official centre. Cf. Marrou, op. cit. 381, 554 n. 34; Carcopino, *Daily Life*, 198.

clare iocabantur, i.e. 'loudly'. The reading of β and γ groups is clearly better than the *loquebantur* of the α group (Stout, 156), even without the parallels in Schuster's *apparatus*.

posse fratris tui filios probe discere. Pliny makes less fuss than Corellia about the morals of the 'professor' (III. 3. 6).

3. cum omnes qui profitentur audiero, quid de quoque sentiam scribam. For this absolute use of *profiteri* compare IV. II. 1 n., 'audistine Valerium Licinianum in Sicilia profiteri?' Vespasian had established at Rome two public posts of Latin and Greek rhetoric with a salary of S. 100,000, Suet. *Vesp.* 18. 1. Quintilian was the first holder of the Latin *schola publica*. But Pliny implies that there were many teachers in private practice, and that there was much competition. Compare the *copia studiosorum* who flocked around Tacitus, themselves ready to 'profess', IV. 13. 10. Juvenal (7. 186, with scholiast) speaks of Quintilian making S. 2,000 a head a year, but there is little other evidence about fees; Marrou, op. cit. 380. For municipal schools see IV. 13 nn.

scribam. Pliny did not publish this second letter for the reasons given in s. 5.

5. suscipiendas offensas in eligendo praeceptore. Pliny is looking not for a private tutor, but for a school. There might be much competition among underpaid rhetors. Curious tales are told in a later age of professors at Athens capturing whole shiploads of newly arrived students by guile (Marrou, op. cit. 406 n. 89; Eunapius, *V. Prohaeresii* 485). But such could not trouble the peace of an eminent senator. Pliny is rather thinking of the patrons of the professors. Society was fussy in the extreme about *offensae*, cf. I. 5. 11, III. 9. 26, IV. 17. 11, IX. 27. 2.

19. *To Cerialis*

Date. During 100, if, as seems certain, the speech concerned is the *In Priscum*, s. 8 n. The reference to style supports this date, s. 6 n.

Address. This man may be Tullius Cerialis, the elderly consular who intervened in the Priscus trial, Ep. II. 9, rather than Velius Cerialis, recipient of IV. 21. His rank requires *obsequium*, s. 9.

1. hortaris ut orationem amicis pluribus recitem. faciam quia hortaris quamvis vehementer addubitem. Though Pliny had certainly recited speeches of a sort before (Ep. 10. 7 n.), this is apparently the first time that he has considered reciting a forensic oration. Even if his hesitation is only about this particular speech he is evidently not a frequent reciter as yet, cf. I. 13. 6. Hence in III. 18 he describes at length his next effort, the recitation of the Panegyric. After this no long descriptions are given until in VII. 17 he defends his practice to a critical friend. For IV. 5 and V. 12 are brief, and V. 3. 7–11 refers to verses. It is by no means certain that Pliny ever recited speeches made in civil actions, such as his *Pro Attia* (VI. 33), and that may be the cause of his hesitation here, IV. 5. 2, V. 12. 1 nn. Public speeches were more interesting.

2. impetum omnem caloremque . . . perdere. The case against recitation could hardly be better put than in this letter. Later Pliny found that the recital satisfied his passion for criticism and revision, and made increasing use of it for prose and verse. V. 3. 7–11, VII. 17. 5–10, VIII. 21. 4–5.

3. ii qui sedentes agunt. The custom was to recite sitting, even when a professional *lector* was employed, IX. 34. 2.

6. quem non potius dulcia haec et sonantia quam austera . . . delectant? For the taste of audiences see Ep. 5. 5 and III. 18. 9 nn. For the battle of styles, and Pliny's general preference for the richer 'middle' style see I. 2. 1–2 nn. But in preceding years he was experimenting with the more restrained style which he used in this speech, in parts of the Panegyric (III. 18. 8), and in those mentioned in I. 2 and II. 5—if they are distinct—of which the former also was *contentiosa*.

8. leges quas ut contrarias prioribus legibus arguebant. Pliny's comparison is rather forced. In fourth-century Athens the γραφὴ παρανόμων was the source of much political litigation, being concerned essentially with constitutional law; no particular proposal could be made in the Assembly that was contrary to a general rule of the constitution.

cum hac ipsa lege tum aliis colligendum fuit. This fits the *In
Priscum* (Ep. 11) much better than the *In Classicum* (III. 9). In the
former he had to show that acts of Priscus, criminal under another
law, were also criminal under the *Lex Repetundarum*, Ep. 11. 2,
'excessisse Priscum' n. In the latter he had only to show that the
subordinates of the proconsul were liable under the extortion law,
III. 9. 14–15 nn. So the *oratio*, as the order of the references to this
and to the Panegyric in the Letters also shows, must be the *In
Priscum*. Besides, the *In Classicum* involved a series of briefer separate *actiones*, not one long indictment, III. 9. 9, 18–19.

20. To Calvisius Rufus

Date. The letter fits the context of Books I–II, and cannot be later
than IV. 2, s. 5 n. Some critics have proposed a Domitianic date, on
the strength of Pliny's outcry against the times in s. 12, which
proves no such thing (n.).

Address. Calvisius Rufus, equestrian and decurion of Comum, was
Pliny's friend and business consultant, and connected also with
Sosius Senecio (IV. 4. 1, V. 7. 4). Possibly *CIL* vii. 324 records his
military tribunate in Britain. *PIR*² C 349. Letters to him deal with
politics, gossip, and business, but not literature: III. 1, 19, V. 7,
VIII. 2, IX. 6.

1. me priorum nova admonuit. The Verania story, told at length, is
the latest. The Blaesus story dates back to 93, s. 7 n.

2. Verania Pisonis . . . cuius marito inimicissimus . . . fuerat.
L. Calpurnius Piso Frugi Licinianus was a man of exalted family, as
his names indicate, whom political troubles kept out of office until he
was adopted, for no good reason save his family connexions, by the
emperor Galba in A.D. 69. The story of his adoption and murder by
the praetorian guard is told in Tac. *Hist.* I. 14–19, 34–44; Plutarch,
Galba 23, 27. Suetonius, *Galba* 17, implies that he had already been
named as adoptive heir in the will of Galba long before 69—hence the
choice. His wife Verania was daughter of the Neronian governor of
Britain, Q. Veranius, who earlier in life had been a noted enemy of
another Calpurnius Piso, the supposed murderer of Germanicus, *ILS*
240; Tac. *Ann.* 3. 10, 13, 17, 14. 29. Verania courageously secured her
husband's burial after his assassination, Tac. *Hist.* I. 47; Plut. *Galba*
28; *PIR*² C 300. She was interred with her long-dead husband, and
her name added to his memorial. *RE* ii. 8. 966.

Regulus. For his career and malpractices see I. 5. 1–3 nn. He had
secured the condemnation of Piso's natural brother under Nero, and

was reputed to have savaged the dead Piso's head, though Tacitus (*Hist.* I. 47, 4. 42) and Plutarch, loc. cit., tell the tale to reject it.

4. haruspicem consulam quem sum frequenter expertus. Compare VI. 2. 2, 'semper haruspices consulebat . . . a nimia superstitione'. Though Regulus starts by considering the lady's horoscope he was too cautious to patronize the astrologers, whose science was a forbidden art under the Principate, and contents himself with the *haruspices*, whose mysteries were of an official order and not politically dangerous, though later the lawyers couple them with the *mathematici* and *Chaldaei*, against whom a series of enactments had discriminated since a *SC* of A.D. 17 (Ulpian, *de officio proconsulis*, quoted in *Collatio* 15. 2. 1; cf. *Sent. Paul.* 5. 21. 3). Claudius had organized an official College of sixty *haruspices*, hoping to exalt them above the *externae superstitiones* of the time, Tac. *Ann.* 11. 15, and the emperors had their own *haruspices*, Suet. *Galba* 19. 1, Tac. *Hist.* 1. 27. Pliny shows that this official approval was still enjoyed by the profession, and though he disapproves of Regulus' superstition he regards it as genuine. The immense article in *RE* vii. 2. 2431 ff. tells all that can be known about *haruspices*.

5. poscit codicillos. See Ep. 16. 1 n.

per salutem filii peierasset. The boy's death is recorded in IV. 2. 7. This letter, and the publication date of the whole book, must be earlier than that. Pliny would not have missed his opportunity. The oath is, however, regarded as proper by the lawyer Paulus, *D.* 12. 2. 3. 4 (Merrill).

7. Velleius Blaesus ille locuples consularis. Perhaps the friend of Atedius Melior, known from Statius, *S.* 2. 1. 191, 3. 77. Martial appears to mention his death *c.* A.D. 93, 8. 38. The man is otherwise unknown. *PIR*[1] s.v. Syme suspects an adoptive connexion with Domitian's victim, Sallustius Lucullus, governor of Britain, who may also be the suffect consul of 89, P. Sallustius Blaesus. Suet. *Dom.* 10. 3; Syme, *Tac.* 648 n. 34. After the death of his son he was an obvious choice for *captatio*.

nuper captare eum coeperat. The whole letter, and its counterpart VIII. 18, illustrate the theme of *captatio*, known from Horace, *Sermones* 2. 5, Juvenal 3 and 12. 93–130, and many epigrams of Martial. The habit is discussed in Friedlaender, *SG* (ET), i. 212 ff. It first appears in the late Republic, and thereafter is constant in literature. It needs to be related to the Roman notion of *amicitia*. By assiduous attentions one qualifies for the title of *amicus*, and social custom ruled that all a man's friends must be recognized in his will by a legacy (cf. VII. 20. 6, 31. 5). To omit was to insult. Not many had the

courage of Blaesus or Domitius Tullus, as Pliny testifies in IV. 15. 3:
'plerisque etiam singulos filios orbitatis praemia graves faciunt'.
Besides it was not easy to distinguish *amicus* from *captator*. Pliny's
picture of Julius Naso could apply to a *captator*: 'paravit amicos,
quos paraverat coluit, me certe . . . ad amorem imitationemque
delegit', VI. 6. 5. So too Claudius Pollio is remembered in the wills
of the friends whom he 'cultivated' (VII. 31. 5). Pliny was then *orbus*
if not *caelebs*, and the characteristic of the *captator* was attention to
orbi. Perhaps V. 1. 3 gives the clue: 'non esse satis honestum donare
et locupleti et orbo'. The *captator* gives presents to entice legacies.
For *amicitia* see F. Schulz, *Principles of Roman Law* (Oxford, 1936),
233.

8. Regulo ne tantulum quidem. Public opinion was surprised because
Blaesus ought to have left Regulus something. So too there was
surprise when Tullus left nothing to his toadies and everything to
his daughter, VIII. 18. 2–3. Some even held that he was *ingratus*.

9. sufficiunt duae fabulae an scholastica lege tertiam poscis? Cf.
Quintilian 4. 5. 3, 'ne illos quidem probaverim qui partitionem ultra
tris propositiones extendunt'. Pliny observes this rule in other
anecdotal letters, III. 16, VI. 31, VII. 27.

10. Aurelia ornata femina signatura testamentum. Pliny speaks as
though Aurelia and Verania were free to make what wills they liked.
In law at this time women required the approval of their *tutor legitimus*, unless freed from *tutela* by the *ius trium liberorum*, and could
make a will only by the complicated process of *coemptio* whereby the
tutor legitimus was exchanged for a *tutor fiduciarius*. Gaius, *Inst.* I.
115 f., 194. But in practice they did what they liked, as always.
The *tutela* was nominal, and not required for a number of contracts,
and there were means of changing *tutores* or bringing them to heel
if tiresome. Gaius regarded the *tutela* of women as an anachronism,
and Hadrian abolished the formalities of *coemptio*, though the *tutela*
itself continued always in nominal existence. Ibid. I. 115 a, 173,
190; 2. 80 f., 118; *Tit. Ulp.* 20. 15. See Schulz, *Classical Roman Law*,
ch. v, 185 f.; W. W. Buckland, *Main institutions of Roman private
law*, 80 f.

    Aurelia. She cannot be identified, but might be a relative of the
consular Aurelii Fulvi, or of Aurelius Priscus, consul in 67. *PIR²*
A 1509–10, 1580.

    signatura. The chief guarantee was not so much the signature as
the seals of five to seven witnesses, Gaius 2. 104–5, 119, whose
presence was required so far as possible at the eventual opening of
the will, *Sent. Pauli*, 4. 6. 1.

12. ἀλλὰ τί διατείνομαι in ea civitate? Schultz, art. cit. 17, thought
that this letter did not fit the characterization of Regulus in I. 5. 1 as
'timidiorem post Domitiani mortem'. But he had recovered his
nerve, never very strong, by the year 100, Ep. 11. 22, and this
incident is not political. Asbach, art. cit. 47, and Otto, art. cit. 24,
took this gloomy judgement for a sign that the letter was written
before the death of Domitian. But Pliny voices similar criticisms in
IV. 15. 3, 8 and in V. 14. 6, letters certainly no earlier than 105.
Would he have voiced any complaint before the death of Domitian?

13. ex paupere et tenui ad tantas opes per flagitia processit. Regulus'
fortune, approaching S. 60,000,000, is still far below the wealth of
Vibius Crispus and Eprius Marcellus, acquired in the same way in
the previous generation, though characterized more mildly by
Tacitus, who sets it at two and three hundred millions respectively,
Dial. 8. 1; cf. I. 5. 1 n.

BOOK III

1. *To Calvisius Rufus*

Date. The three letters to or about Spurinna, II. 7, III. 1, 10, are connected by references to the death of his son Cottius, II. 7. 3 and Ep. 10. 1, and by a cross-reference to Pliny's visits to the villa in Ep. 10. 1; s. 1 n. A date after Pliny's consulship fits better than a date in *c.* 98 (as Schuster, art. cit. 18, 23), ss. 1, 11, 12 (nn.). Against the dating of Otto to *c.* 104 (art. cit. 25 f., 30 f.) see ss. 1, 10–11 (nn.).

Address. For Calvisius Rufus, equestrian of Comum, see II. 20 pref.

1. nuper apud Spurinnam fui. Cf. Ep. 10. 1, 'cum proxime apud vos fui'. It is reasonable to identify the two visits. It was a grand occasion for Pliny to stay with one of Rome's two most eminent consulars, and this was apparently his first visit to Spurinna's country estate, though he was earlier among the family protégés, I. 5. 8. This visit cannot be less than one, or more than some three, years after the death of young Cottius in Nerva's reign, II. 7. 3 n. The slow Pliny would need time to compose the biography (Ep. 10. 1 n.). In ss. 11–12 Pliny pictures himself as busy with official career and 'many labours'. Any date about 100–1, when Pliny was busy with public office and advocacy, would fit.

Otto sought to distinguish this visit from that of Ep. 10, on the score that Pliny does not here mention the *festi dies* of Ep. 10. 2, and that Spurinna is too cheerful in Ep. 1. But Pliny's visit lasted some time; he is describing Spurinna's routine, not his moods, and Spurinna evidently concealed his grief: loc. cit., 'ne vos festis diebus confunderem'.

Spurinnam. For the career and family of this *consul ter* see II. 7. 1–3 nn.

3. hanc regulam Spurinna constantissime servat. Spurinna's daily round should be compared with that of the Elder Pliny, Ep. 5. 8–13, which is urban, and that of Pliny himself, who modelled his country routine on Spurinna's, IX. 36, 40.

4. mane lectulo continetur. So too Pliny who keeps to his room studying much longer than Spurinna, IX. 36. 2. The Elder leaps forth before dawn, Ep. 5. 9. But in the country there are no *officia* to attend.

lectulo. Couch or sofa; he is not still under the blankets.

hora secunda calceos poscit. Shoes are for outdoors, cf. VI. 16. 5, IX. 17. 3. The twelve hours are counted from sunrise to sunset, and vary seasonally, but not so extremely as in northern latitudes. See Ep. 5. 8 n.

ambulat milia passuum tria. Cf. s. 7, 'ambulat mille', and IX. 36. 3, 'dein ambulo . . . iterum ambulo'. These set walks were taken so many turns round the *gestatio*, which was a standard fitting of the Roman *villa* (I. 3. 1, II. 17. 14, V. 6. 17)—like a passenger on an ocean liner's promenade deck. Cf. *ILS* 6030, 'in hoc pomario gestationis per circuitum itum et reditum quinquiens efficit passus mille'.

liber legitur i.e. by a trained reader, such as Pliny's Zosimus or Encolpius (V. 19. 3, VIII. 1. 2 nn.). For the use of the *lector* during exercise see Ep. 5. 10–11, 14–15. Pliny preferred mental composition at this phase, IX. 36. 3–4.

5. mox vehiculum ascendit. For the riding cf. IX. 36. 3, 5. Spurinna drives seven miles (s. 7) round the measured course of the *hippodromus* (for which see V. 6. 33). No wonder he needed company or a reader. The object was exercise, not pleasure. No one would drive for either on the *pavé* of the infrequent Roman highways, and the only lanes were narrow paths (*limites*) serving the peasant holdings; cf. I. 24. 4 'reptare per limitem unamque semitam'. But Pliny sometimes rode on horseback round his farms, 'pro gestatione' IX. 5. 3.

vehiculum. A very light carriage is indicated, such as the *mannuli iuncti* of IV. 2. 3 might draw.

uxorem singularis exempli. Cf. VIII. 5. 1 for the phrase. Worthy wives were a feature of the times (I. 12. 7, 14. 6, VI. 24. 2–4, VIII. 5, 18. 8–10) despite the strictures of Martial, and the suspicions of Carcopino, who takes the satirists at their face value, *Daily Life*, 84–100.

6. quantum ibi antiquitatis! quae facta . . . audias! Much of Tacitus' material in the *Histories* may well have come from such a source. Syme thinks Tacitus used Spurinna as a source, yet misses this passage: *Tac.* 177. By *antiquitas* Pliny means that Spurinna had the outlook and manners of the Italian provincial, like Erucius Clarus and Cornutus Tertullus, both *sancti et antiqui* (II. 9. 4, V. 14. 3), rather than the urban type. Tacitus also approved such qualities. See I. 14. 4 n., VII. 24. 3 n.

ne praecipere videatur. A politer fashion is replacing the brusque old Roman style of minding other people's business. Compare the mild tone of Pliny's letters of advice to Avitus, Geminus, and Maximus (II. 6. 6 n., VI. 34, VII. 26, VIII. 22, IX. 30), though on occasion he sharply rebukes a social inferior, IX. 17.

7. iterum residit. This seems to be the moment of siesta, taken by Pliny in summer, but not in winter, IX. 36. 3, 40. 2.

scribit enim et quidem utraque lingua lyrica doctissima. Spurinna shared this taste with other distinguished consulars, Arrius Antoninus and Verginius Rufus, IV. 3, 18, V. 3. 5. Pliny joins the band with his two books of verses, 'severos parum', V. 3. 2, IV. 14, VIII. 21. So too the obscurer Passenus Paulus, whose speciality was to imitate Horace, IX. 22. 2.

hilaritas. Merrill was shocked that Spurinna and Pliny wrote on 'amatory themes and not of the chastest sort', and attributed the sad fact to the ethical defects of the 'Roman race'. But their enthusiasm for light verse was a matter of fashion and convention followed slavishly by the most unlikely personages, including most of the emperors from Augustus to Hadrian. The fashion changed to favour prose in the post-Hadrianic age. See V. 3. 5, and Friedlaender, *SG* (ET), iii. 27 ff., 71 ff.

The qualities of *dulcedo, hilaritas,* and *suavitas* are much the same as those attributed to the epigrams of Arrius, IV. 3. 2, 4. The themes are listed IV. 14. 3: 'iocamur ludimus amamus dolemus querimur irascimur'; IX. 22. 2, 'amat . . . dolet . . . laudat . . . ludit'.

sanctitas scribentis. Here as in V. 3 Pliny repeats the stock defence, as old as Catullus (16. 5–8) and as recent as Martial (1. 4. 8): 'lasciva est nobis pagina vita proba'. There is a difference between *lascivia* and *hilaritas*; Quintilian, discussing *de ridiculo* (6. 3. 27–28), says 'id quod dicitur aut est lascivum et hilare . . . aut contumeliosum . . . lasciva humilibus hilaria omnibus convenient'. But *Ep.* I. 15. 4, VI. 30. 1, VIII. 11. 2, the term means no more than 'gay and cheerful'.

Four odes in the Horatian manner survive under the name of 'Vespruchius Spurinna', and dedicated to 'Marius' (*Anth. Lat.* 918–21.) They were published by the humanist K. von Barth in 1624 from a manuscript not otherwise known, and are commonly taken with other of his anecdota to be renaissance work. G. B. Pighi, *Aevum* (1945), 122 f., defends their genuinity. But one celebrates *nullis pauperies numinibus minor*. It is doubtful whether the potent thrice-consul was in any sense a poor man, with his well-equipped villa and his Corinthian bronzes.

8. ubi hora balinei nuntiata est . . . in sole, si caret vento, ambulat nudus. Spurinna here follows the rules of health prescribed by Celsus (1. 2), that exercise, whether by reading aloud, use of arms, ball, running or walking, should be followed by *unctio* and bath, and after a short rest by dinner. The bath is set later in winter to gain the warmest part of the afternoon. The Younger Pliny breaks up his afternoon, after riding, with repeated short walks, but the general sequence is the same, IX. 36. 3: 'iterum ambulor unguor exerceor lavor', followed by the *cena*.

in sole. So too the Elder Pliny takes the sun, Ep. 5. 10, VI. 16. 5.

9. adponitur cena. The Younger also mentions only the evening dinner in his daily round (IX. 36. 4), but the Elder takes two lighter meals before *cena*, one *interdiu* and the other *post solem*, Ep. 5. 10–11. Celsus prescribed *prandium* and *cena* for old men, but allowed the more vigorous of them to take only the single meal in winter. This is Spurinna's summer routine, s. 9.

sunt in usu et Corinthia. Vessels of the much prized Corinthian alloy, of which Pliny, *NH* 34. 5–12, gives an account. Pliny himself owned none, but gave a statuette to a temple at Comum, Ep. 6. 4 n.

sumit aliquid de nocte et aestate. It was more usual to end dinner before darkness, as did the Elder (Ep. 5. 13) and the Younger Pliny, who walked again after dining, IX. 36. 4. Trajan's banquets also extended into the night, VI. 31. 13.

frequenter comoedis cena distinguitur. See I. 15. 2 for these. Pliny kept them until after dinner, IX. 36. 4.

10. post septimum et septuagensimum annum. Spurinna's age, over 77, was regarded by Otto (loc. cit.) and Schultz (art. cit. 6–7) as an insuperable bar to a date *c*. 100 for this letter, assuming that the army command of II. 7. 1 (n.) belonged to the reign of Nerva. But the age itself is no bar to such an office. Galba governed Tarraconensis when 72, and Ummidius Quadratus was not less than 70 when he died as legate of Syria. Suet. *Galba* 23; Tac. *Ann*. 14. 26 with *ILS* 972. So the possibility of a legateship under Nerva is no reason to attack the 'book-date' of the letter.

11. ut primum ratio aetatis receptui canere permiserit. There is no argument here for a late date. Remarks of this sort occur in I. 10. 10–12, II. 14. 14, IV. 23. 4, but are absent from V–IX. The next section implies that Pliny was in mid-career. So a date later than his *cura Tiberis* is not required.

12. quoad honestum fuit, obiit officia, gessit magistratus, provincias rexit. By *officia* Pliny may mean imperial and public posts other than governorships and annual magistracies, as in I. 10. 9, III. 5. 7, 9, 18, V. 14. 2, rather than the duties of ordinary life, *civilia officia*, IV. 24. 3. Spurinna's only such known post is that of 'Vvir . . . sumptibus minuendis' under Nerva, II. 7. 1 n.

Stobbe (art. cit. 374) thought the omission of reference to Spurinna's third consulship was decisive for a date before 100. But Pliny does not mention even the second. Contrast II. 1. 2, IV. 3. 1. The omission is stylistic, to avoid repetition of II. 1 in III. 1.

provincias. No second province, after or before his German command, is known. But Pliny would hardly have written 'provinciam' here, cf. IV. 23. 2 n.

quoad honestum fuit. The parallel passage on Pomponius Bassus (IV. 23. 2–4) shows that there is no political reference here. Age alone is meant: 'se reipublicae quamdiu decebat obtulerit. nam et prima vitae tempora et media patriae extrema nobis impertire debemus'.

2. *Vibius Maximus*

Date. Not before late 103, from the date of Maximus' appointment to Egypt (below).

Address. This man is reasonably identified with the Vibius Maximus known from Statius, *Silvae* 4 pref. and 7, and Martial 11. 106, as an equestrian of literary tastes who after commanding an auxiliary *ala* in Syria was appointed to a post in Dalmatia—evidently as procurator —before 95, when Statius mentions him as in charge of mines there. He is also the C. Vibius Maximus known from Egyptian documents as prefect of Egypt from *c.* June–August 103 down to 107, when he was condemned on a serious charge and suffered *damnatio memoriae* and the erasure of his name from public monuments. Cf. A. Stein, *Die Prefekten von Aegyptus* (Bern, 1950), 50 ff.; *P. Ox.* iii. 471. The suggestion that it was this man's son who was so condemned is not soundly based, see IX. 1 pref. The further identification with the like-named *praefectus cohortis* serving in Dalmatia in 93–94 (*CIL* xvi. 38), favoured in *PIR*[1] V 389 and *RE* ii. 8. 2. 1975, seems to be excluded by the order of posts, since the holding of the cavalry command before the *praefectura cohortis* would be without precedent in this period; cf. the lists in Domaszewski, *Rangordnung*, 198 ff. But it is possible that Statius (4. 7. 47) incorrectly used *ala* to refer to a *cohors equitata*, though the wording is very precise—'signa frenatae moderatus alae'. Otherwise the rapid promotion of equestrians to the prefecture of Egypt is not unknown in this period (Stein, loc. cit.). The family may come from Dalmatia itself; an equestrian P. Vibius Maximus of Epitaurum is known in A.D. 71 (*ILS* 1991). Our man may have been *praefectus annonae* before his prefecture of Egypt (Syme, *Historia* (1957), 480 ff.; Pflaum, n. 65), but that cannot be his present post, because Arrianus goes overseas to his commission, s. 5 n. Vibius Maximus is probably not the recipient of other letters from Pliny: see II. 14 pref., IX. 1. Pflaum, loc. cit., cites the evidence in full, and doubts the condemnation, on inadequate grounds.

1. **quod ipse amicis tuis obtulissem, si mihi eadem materia suppeteret.**
For the formula cf. II. 13. 2. The words *nunc iure* suggest that
Maximus' appointment is recent.

2. **Arrianus Maturus Altinatium est princeps.** He is not known outside
Pliny, I. 2 pref. For the phrase cf. I. 8. 8 'ipse provinciae princeps'.
Altinum was a *municipium* of the Venetian district at the ancient
Po mouth. Martial, 4. 25, compares its comfortable palaces to those
of Baiae. *RE* i. 1697 s.v.; *CIL* v. i. 205.

   **loquor . . . de castitate iustitia gravitate prudentia. huius ego consilio
in negotiis, iudicio in studiis utor.** These qualities seem what is
required in a government official, unlike those put forward in other
of Pliny's letters of commendation (II. 13. 6–8, VII. 22. 2). Fronto,
Ad amicos, I. 5, stresses *studia* to prove that his candidate would be
a suitable member of a judicial *consilium*. For Arrianus' interest in
public affairs see II. 11, 12, and for his literary tastes I. 2, VIII. 21.

4. **caret ambitu; ideo se in equestri gradu tenuit, cum facile possit
ascendere altissimum.** Cf. II. 11. 1, 'quietis amore secesseris'. For
the political undertones of this see I. 14. 5 n. Reluctance to become a
senator was not confined to the period of Domitian.

5. **dignitati eius aliquid adstruere inopinantis nescientis, immo etiam
fortasse nolentis.** Cf. s. 6, 'quamvis . . . ista non appetat'. A curious
recommendation, enough to lose the petition. Perhaps the words
'inopinantis . . . nolentis' have been added in revision. They do not
affect the construction. Pliny knew that Arrianus 'wanted something',
but he had not been specific.

   splendidum nec molestum. No previous appointment of Maturus is
mentioned, so probably a military tribunate or prefecture is meant.
Otherwise he would be a suitable candidate for the headship of the
Alexandrine Library and Museum, often held by men of letters, like
the Roman librarianship, if this post was in the prefect's gift, cf.
I. 18, pref.

6. **grate tamen excipit.** So he did. In IV. 8 he is absent from Rome at
least, and in IV. 12. 7 is far away from Italy; he is back on his estates
in VI. 2. 10. Hence Syme's suggestion (art. cit.) that Arrianus became
adiutor to the *praefectus annonae* will not do. The three years' absence
fits a post in Egypt, where Pliny has friends at this time (V. 19. 6.)

3. *To Corellia Hispulla*

Date. The letter fits the book series well, coming after the death of
Corellius Rufus in I. 12, and after Pliny's hunt for a teacher of
rhetoric in II. 18, now found available, s. 5 n.

Address. She is the daughter of the consular Corellius, for whom see
I. 12 nn., and she is mentioned ibid. 3, 9. Pliny undertakes a case for
her in IV. 17.

**1. enitar ut filius tuus avo similis exsistat ; equidem malo materno,
quamquam illi paternus etiam clarus.** The son is evidently about 14
years old, ready to begin his rhetorical courses, II. 18. 1–2 n. Hence
he may well be Corellius Pansa, *consul ordinarius* in A.D. 122. This
combination of odd names suggests a connexion with the Neratii of
the Beneventum region, where a landowner called Neratius Corellius
is known at this period, and with the Vespasianic consul, M. Hirrius
Fronto Neratius Pansa, who might be the *avus paternus*. For the
use of the maternal *nomen* compare the case of Ummidius Quadratus
VII. 24. 2 n. (I. 12. 3 n.; *ILS* 6509, l. 14; *PIR*² C 1293). For *clarus* is
meant to imply senatorial status as in II. 14. 1, III. 8. 1, VI. 6. 3, 23. 2,
leading to the formal usage of *vir clarissimus*, VII. 33. 8 n.

   inlustri laude conspicui. For the connotation of exalted equestrian
rank in *illustris*, not elsewhere so used in the Letters, see Tac. *Ann.*
2. 59, II. 4, 35. (Cf. Stein, *Römische Ritterstand*, 96 ff., 101 f.)
Corellia's husband, and his brother, evidently died before achieving
senatorial status.

3. adhuc . . . praeceptores domi habuit. He has completed the 'grammatical' or literary phase of his education, at home, not like the
lads of Comum at a public school, IV. 13. 3. Quintilian (I. 2. 1–15)
discusses the pros and cons of private and public education, largely in
terms of moral influences, and takes the line followed by Tacitus
(*Dial.* 28–29), that the home influences were often as corrupting as
those of the school, thanks to the slackness of the parents and the
depravity of servants and instructors. The home education was
steadily giving ground to the schools in this period. Cf. E. de Saint-
Denis, *Rev. Universitaire*, 1946. 'Pline et la . . . jeunesse', 9 ff. But
evidently many children in the upper classes still continued to receive
their *grammatice* at home. Quintilian admits the advantages of the
private tutorial over the class, but regards it as wasteful of the
teacher's abilities (loc. cit. 9–15).

   **circumspiciendus rhetor . . . cuius scholae severitas pudor in primis
castitas constet.** This is not so much of a commonplace as it may seem
to the modern reader. Here and below, s. 5, 'in hac licentia temporum', Pliny admits the existence of horrid vices in the schools
(cf. IV. 13. 4, 'pudicius continerentur'), as darkly hinted by Juvenal
10. 224, 295 f.; earlier, Palaemon had a particularly bad reputation:
Suet. *Gramm.* 23. Pliny's version is more balanced, as usual, than the
satirist's, and his cure is a characteristically practical insistence on
careful choice of professors, as in II. 18 and IV. 13. His stress on the

moral purpose of education here and in II. 18. 4 is an expression of a contemporary reaction, which may not have been widely felt, against the prevailing view that the duties of a professor of rhetoric were merely technical (Saint-Denis, art. cit. 13). Seneca insisted in an unusual passage of *de tranquillitate animi* (3. 3) that the *praeceptor* was as much a minister of the state interest as the politician and the statesman. Pliny follows as usual the view of Quintilian (I. 2. 5, 2. 2. 1–5, 5): 'praeceptorem eligere sanctissimum quemque et disciplinam quae maxime severa fuerit'. For the Roman schools of rhetoric see II. 18. 1–2, IV. 13. 5 nn.

5. videor ergo demonstrare tibi posse Iulium Genitorem. Pliny now has his man to hand, for whom he was searching in II. 18. Ep. 11, the account of Artemidorus, is suitably addressed to his new acquaintance as a compliment.

paulo etiam horridior et durior. Pliny sometimes found him rather too much so, and rebukes him for his *rugae* and *stomachus* in IX. 17. For his devotion to his pupils see VII. 30. 1–2. He is not otherwise known.

A family tree of the Corellii might be as follows:

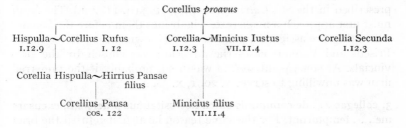

Corellius *proavus*

| Hispulla⁓Corellius Rufus | Corellia⁓Minicius Iustus | Corellia Secunda |
| I.12.9   I. 12 | I.12.3   VII.11.4 | I.12.3 |

Corellia Hispulla⁓Hirrius Pansae filius

| Corellius Pansa | Minicius filius |
| COS. 122 | VII.11.4 |

4. *To Caecilius Macrinus*

Date. The events described belong to October–November 99 (s. 2 n. and pp. 58–59). The letter itself is possibly later than January 100, s. 8 n. The theme is continued in Ep. 9.

Address. The *nomen* Caecilius depends upon *Π* and the index of B. For the probability that the same man, otherwise unknown, is recipient of all the letters addressed to Macrinus see II. 7 pref.

1. amici quos praesentes habebam. For the curious Roman use of a council of friends see I. 22. 8 n.

2. cum publicum opus mea pecunia incohaturus in Tuscos excucurrissem, accepto . . . commeatu. The circumstances exactly agree with X. 8–9, where he secures leave (*commeatu*) from Trajan for this very purpose, in September of a year that can be either 98 or 99. The latter fits better the chronology of X. 1–12 (p. 64). It is also unlikely that he would accept the second brief within a few weeks of the brief against Priscus (in 98), s. 8 n. The earlier date does not fit well with the development of events (below).

commeatu. See x. 8. 3, 6 nn. Pliny refers to official leave also in v. 14. 9, and possibly Ep. 6. 6 n.

ut praefectus aerari. He held office from January 98, see pp. 75–77. The words may be Pliny's addition when revising, for clarity.

legati provinciae. Cf. Ep. 9. 4, 'in Classicum tota provincia incubuit'. The indictment, as in the Varenus case, was set afoot by the *concilium provinciae*, VII. 6. 1 n. The African Classicus, of whom nothing is known outside Pliny, was proconsul in the same year as Marius Priscus, i.e. 97–98 (II. 11. 2 n., Ep. 9. 2). The indictment was projected earlier in 98–99, but delayed by the man's death, and pursued in a new form in late summer 99, when Pliny was brought into the case, Ep. 9. 5–6 nn. and p. 59. Such delays were not uncommon. Pompeius Silvanus was prosecuted in A.D. 58 for a proconsulship which he had held in 53–55, Tac. *Ann.* 13. 52; *AE* 1948, n. 17.

This letter, alone of those about the extortion trials, deals clearly with the first stage of an indictment. The procedure follows that prescribed in the *SC. Calvisianum* ll. 97–103 (II. 11. 2 n.). The *legati* must first approach a magistrate who brings them before the Senate, where they are assigned a *patronus* of their own choice. So too in the Priscus and Varenus cases the advocate was chosen by the provincials. At some point *sortitio* was used, probably if the preferred man was unwilling to serve: V. 20. 1, X. 3a. 2.

3. collegae . . . de communis officii necessitatibus praelocuti, excusare me . . . temptarunt. For the same reason he at first refused the brief against Priscus, X. 3a. 2. The *SC. Calvisianum* permitted such refusal only on specific grounds ᾧ ἐκ τῶν νόμων παραίτησις ταύτης τῆς λειτουργίας δέδοται. The usual ground for such *muneris publici excusatio* was sickness or holding some other public office, as here. *RE* XVI. i. 649 f.

collegae. Pliny's friend Tertullus was his fellow prefect of Saturn, V. 14. 5. The plural suggests that the prefects of the *aerarium militare* were grouped with those of the *aerarium Saturni*, on whom they must have been largely dependent—unless the quaestors are meant. Mommsen, *DPR* v. 307. Cf. VII. 21 pref.

4. legati rursus inducti iterum me iam praesentem advocatum postulaverunt. The present session and the authorization of the *inquisitio*, Ep. 9. 6, must be in October or November after Pliny's return from Tifernum.

Massam. For the career of Massa, his trial and condemnation for extortion in 93, and Pliny's part in it, see VII. 33 nn.

patrocini foedus. Since Pliny does not refer to this in 1. 7 when refusing an earlier Spanish request for his advocacy, it is likely that it was a recent arrangement. Formal compacts of *hospitium* and *patrocinium* continued throughout the Principate to be made between individual senators or even knights and municipalities or whole provinces. For examples see *ILS* 6095–114. These bound the senior partner to protect the interest of his *hospites* or *clientes*, cf. *ILS* 6100, 'C. Silius . . . civitatem Themetrensium liberos posterosque eorum sibi posterisque suis in fidem clientelamque suam recepit'. The formalities are described in *Lex Malacitana* c. 61, 'de patrono cooptando' (*A–J* n. 65). See Mommsen–Marquardt, *Manuel*, xiv. 229 ff. Pliny (s. 5) does not seem to distinguish between the lesser bond of *hospitium* and full *patrocinium*.

5. priores nostros etiam singulorum hospitum iniurias . . . exsecutos. A famous instance was Cn. Domitius Ahenobarbus' prosecution of M. Iunius Silanus in 104 B.C. 'propter unius . . . hospitis iniurias', Cic. *Div. in Caec.* 67.

6. quanta pro isdem Baeticis superiore advocatione etiam pericula subissem. Cf. I. 7. 2, 'provinciam . . . tot etiam periculis meis devinxerim'. He claims twice to have been in political peril in the years 93–96, first at the end of Massa's trial, and then at the hands of Mettius Carus, VII. 27. 14, 33. 7–8.

antiquiora beneficia subvertas nisi illa posterioribus cumules. For this tenet of Roman philanthropy see I. 8. 10, II. 13. 9 nn., V. 11. 1.

7. decesserat Classicus. Cf. Ep. 9. 5, 'accusationem . . . morte praevertit'. His death precedes the approach to Pliny, who is brought in only when the province has decided to sue the assistants of Classicus in his place.

8. si munere hoc iam tertio fungerer. This can only mean that the Classicus brief is his third extortion case, and that the Priscus case has been not merely initiated, as in 98, but substantially completed, as in December 99–January 100, before the composition of this letter: cf. Ep. 9. 2–4 nn. In VI. 29. 8–11 (nn.) Pliny groups the two Spanish cases together before the Priscus case for literary effect, not as a chronological series (despite Peter art. cit. 706–7).

5. *To Baebius Macer*

Date. No indication.

Address. Baebius Macer is the Macer praised by Martial *c.* A.D. 95–100 as a praetorian senator, in office as curator of the Appian Way and proconsul of Baetica (10. 18 (17) 6, 12. 98. 7; cf. 5. 28. 5). The like-named legate of Dalmatia is probably another man (ibid. 10. 78; Syme, *Tac.* 647), if this province was then consular. Macer's consulship was in 103 (IV. 9 pref.). He was opposed to the faction of Hadrian, held the prefecture of the City in 117 during Trajan's eastern campaigns, and incurred the suspicions of Hadrian when emperor. SHA *Hadr.* 5. 5; *PIR²* B 20; Syme, op. cit. 666.

Arrangement. The commentary has been divided into three parts for the literary work, public career, and daily routine of the Elder respectively.

The Books

1. libros avunculi mei lectitas. There is an extensive modern bibliography on the subject that so interested Baebius Macer. Le Bonnier, *Bibliographie de l'histoire naturelle de Pline l'ancien* (Collection d'études latines, série scientifique xxi, Paris, 1948). F. Münzer, 'Die Quellen des Tacitus für die Germanenkriege', *Bonner Jahrbücher*, civ (1899), 66 ff., deals also with the life of the Elder. Ch. Nailis, *Studie over de chronologie van het leven en de werken van Plinius*, &c. (Philolog. Stud. xiii–xiv), Louvain, 1943. Most recent is the article by various hands in *RE* xxi. i. 271 ff. This letter and references scattered through the Natural History are the main sources of information. Gellius, *NA* 9. 4. 13, 16. 1 speaks of the Elder's erudition.

2. quo sint ordine scripti. Difficulty arises only over the 'Life of Pomponius', below. Pflaum, n. 50, supposes that Pliny means publication dates: possibly so.

3. 'de iaculatione equestri unus'; hunc cum praefectus alae militaret . . . composuit. It is quoted in *NH* 8. 162, and possibly utilized by Arrian and Tacitus in some passages of the *Tactica* and *Germania* (F. Lammert, *Philologus*, Suppl., xxxi. 2. 48 ff.). It was probably written before A.D. 50 when Pliny was serving on the lower Rhine, s. 3 n. ('career').

'de vita Pomponi Secundi duo.' Quoted only in *NH* 14. 56 and perhaps 7. 80. The date of its composition, which affects that of the following two works, depends on the date of Pomponius' death, which is hardly to be placed as late as 60 on the strength of the loose reference in *NH* 13. 83 to an event happening 'some two hundred years after the death of Tiberius Gracchus', while Pomponius was alive.

For the development of Silver Latin biography of this commemorative kind see I. 17. 3, III. 10. 1, V. 5. 3, IX. 13. 1 nn.

P. Calvisius Sabinus Pomponius Secundus was an amateur of
poetry and drama whose plays, hissed by the mob, commended him
to the emperor Claudius, who despite his brother's opposition to the
Claudian succession made Pomponius consul *ordinarius* in 44 and
governor of Upper Germany in 50–51, and gave him 'triumphal
ornaments'. Tac. *Ann.* 11. 13, 12. 27–28, 13. 43; Jos. *Ant. Jud.* 19. 4.
5; Dio 59. 30. 3; *CIL* xiii. 5200–1, &c. For his earlier misfortunes
under Tiberius see Tac. *Ann.* 5. 8, 6. 18, and for his works, approved
by Quintilian (*Inst.* 10. 9. 8), cf. VII. 17. 11. Pomponianus, whom the
Elder gave his life to save, may be a son of this man, VI. 16. 11. *PIR*[1]
P 563: *RE* XXI. ii, s.v. 'Pomponius', n. 103; E. Ritterling, *Fasti
des röm. Deutschland* (Wien, 1932), 15 f.

**4. 'Bellorum Germaniae viginti' . . . inchoavit cum in Germania
militaret.** By its known content this could have been finished by 54.
Pliny may have begun it after the *de iaculatione* but not finished or
published it till after the *de vita Pomponi*, here listed as earlier. Its
main theme seems to have been the Germanic wars of the times of
Caesar, Augustus, and Tiberius. Münzer (art. cit. 78) and Gundel
(art. cit. *RE* 286–7) argue that Pliny closed the story with the campaigns of Corbulo in *c.* 47 (Tac. *Ann.* 11. 18–20), on which he may have
served, and did not include the campaigns of Pomponius described
in the biography. It certainly seems to have ended well before the
opening date of Pliny's *Historiae* (below, s. 6 n.). Though only quoted
directly once by Tacitus and Suetonius (*Ann.* 1. 69, *Gaius* 8. 1), it
has commonly been taken to be the source of the German wars in
the *Annals* 1–6. For a summary of discussions see *RE*, art. cit. 287.

Drusi Neronis effigies . . . commendabat memoriam suam. Drusus,
stepson of Augustus and father of Claudius, campaigned from 12 to
9 B.C., and died after reaching the Elbe. *CAH* x. 358. Dio 55. 1 gives
the story of his death. Gundel, loc. cit., takes this statement to mean
that Pliny wrote to rescue the glory of Drusus, and also his son Germanicus, father and brother of the reigning emperor, from the oblivion
into which pro-Tiberian writers, such as Velleius Paterculus, had
cast them. For so independent a character Pliny seems remarkably
prone to adulation of the ruling monarch, cf. s. 6 n.

5. 'studiosi tres', in sex volumina propter amplitudinem divisi. This
handbook of rhetoric is quoted by Quintilian (3. 1. 21, 11. 3. 143, 148,
and perhaps elsewhere anonymously), not always with approval,
and commended by Gellius who quotes a *controversia* from it (*NA* 9.
16, *RE*, loc. cit.). Eventually it was written under Nero, and is not
likely to have taken Pliny longer than the *dubii sermonis octo*.

divisi. This is one of the passages that misled T. Birt, *Antike
Buchwesen* (Berlin, 1882), 316, into the belief that authors usually

aimed at artistic units accommodated to the length of a single roll of papyrus.

'**dubii sermonis octo**' : scripsit sub Nerone novissimis annis cum omne studiorum genus . . . periculosum servitus fecisset. In *NH* pref. 28 he calls this 'libellos . . . de grammatica', and says that critics have been attacking it *iam decem annos*. Hence it was published by 68, and was probably begun after the conspiracy of Piso in 66, which involved many equestrians, and initiated the period of 'slavery', Tac. *Ann.* 15. 50, 71. The work was much utilized by later grammarians, and W. Aly (*RE*, art. cit. 294 f.) ranks Pliny as the last of the great grammarians of the earlier Principate, such as Probus, Palaemon, and Asconius, who had a living understanding of Roman history and the Latin language.

novissimis annis. This passage has some bearing on the vexed question of the supposedly 'good' *quinquennium Neronis*, though it does not seem to have been noticed in that connexion, e.g. by J. G. C. Anderson, *JRS* ii. 173, or F. Lepper, ibid., 1947, 95 ff.

6. 'a fine Aufidi Bassi triginta unus.' Cf. *NH* pref. 20: 'temporum nostrorum historiam orsi a fine Aufidi Bassi'. The Younger Pliny says least about the work of which we should like to know most. The current view is that the History began before the death of Claudius, perhaps in 47, though some take it as late as the death of Claudius, and that it ended in A.D. 71 with the Jewish war and Germanic revolt. The evidence is seldom clear. Tacitus quotes it for incidents of A.D. 55 and 65, and for the civil wars. Pliny himself quotes it for the earlier lives of the three Flavian emperors and for events of 67–68. (Tac. *Ann.* 13. 20, 15. 53; Tac. *Hist.* 3. 28; *NH* pref. 20, 2. 199, 232; H. Peter, *FRH*, 308–11.) The extent to which it was a main source of Tacitus is much debated. *RE*, art. cit. 292 f.; Syme, *Tac.* 180, 289 ff., 697 ff. Pliny is probably one of the historians criticized by Tacitus for undue attention to minor details of Roman life and for adulation of the ruling house, in *Ann.* 13. 31 and *Hist.* 2. 101. The work was completed some time before 77, but reserved for publication by his heir in order to avoid charges of *ambitio*, *NH* pref. 20.

Aufidi Bassi. A senior contemporary of the Elder, still alive *c.* A.D. 60, Seneca, *Ep.* 30. 1. Tacitus commends his eloquence, *Dial.* 23. 2, Seneca, loc. cit., his Epicurean calm, and Quintilian his book (*Inst.* 10. 1. 103), especially his description of German wars. He seems to have covered the period from the death of Caesar to the death of Caligula or the later years of Claudius, (Sen. *Suas.* 6. 18, 23.) Part was out by A.D. 38, date of the *Suasoriae*. See Münzer, art. cit., 78 and *RE* ii. 2290, XXI, i. 289. Syme, *Tac.* 697 ff.

'Naturae historiarum triginta septem', opus diffusum eruditum, nec minus varium quam ipsa natura. There were thirty-six books according to the list in the Preface, but the Elder did not count his Index, which still forms his first book. The Younger's comment best describes this more than encyclopaedic work, which alone would have earned for the Elder the title given bim by Gellius, loc. cit., 'aetatis suae doctissimus'. Pliny claimed, pref. 17, to have included 20,000 items worthy of attention, drawn from 2,000 *volumina*, and a hundred select authors. The preface is dated to the sixth consulship of Titus, A.D. 77, but a manuscript note to book xxxiv states that it was published after the Elder's death. The two Histories were evidently written between 70 and 77, no mean feat.

7. tot volumina . . . homo occupatus absolverit. Cf. *NH* pref. 18, 'homines enim sumus et occupati officiis subsicivisque temporibus ista curamus id est nocturnis', as in ss. 8–16.

illum aliquamdiu causas actitasse. Nothing is known of the Elder as a pleader. It is implied that this was in his youth.

17. electorumque commentarios centum sexaginta mihi reliquit, opisthographos quidem et minutissimis scriptos; qua ratione multiplicatur hic numerus. Usually a papyrus roll was only written on one side, except when the verso was used at the end to complete the text of a work that overran the estimate of its length, as in Juvenal I. 6. Otherwise this was a device of poverty, or as in the Elder's case, due to a kink of eccentric meanness. Cf. T. Birt, op. cit. 349 n. 2, and again in Müller, *Handbuch*, &c., i. 3. 301 f. Birt ingeniously conjectures that the text of the *NH* was likewise left as an 'opisthograph', by comparison of this passage with peculiarities of the book-reference in *NH* 14. 121 and 30. 12.

commentarios. This term is always used of documents in roll form. *RE* iv. 738; Birt, *Handbuch*, 285.

Career of the Elder Pliny

Too much has been made of supposed evidence for details of Pliny's career in the *NH* and the Letters by Münzer, art. cit., Pflaum, n. 45, and the author of *PIR*[1]. Ziegler, in *RE*, xxi. i. 276 ff., and Syme, *Tac.* 60 ff., show greater but still inadequate caution. Pliny speaks as an eyewitness of Lower and Upper Germany—*vidimus, novimus*—*NH* 12. 98, 16. 2–4, 17. 47, 31. 20, (but ibid. 25 is by report, *audivi*). So too of Africa Proconsularis—*vidi*, 7. 36, 17. 41, perhaps 18. 188—and Narbonensis, *vidimus* or *scimus* in 2. 150, 7. 78, 14. 43, 29. 53–54, where he was very well acquainted with Vasio Vocontiorum, 3. 124. Possibly also Belgica, but the passage is ambiguous, 7. 76; he witnesses the misfortunes of a procurator of, but not necessarily in, Belgica. He shows no personal knowledge by a *vidimus* or a *scimus* of the eastern provinces in the *NH*, despite Ziegler's plea that his account of Palestine shows the witness of his own eyes, art. cit. 279; *NH* 5. 70–73, 12. 111–13.

As for dates, he may well have served in Lower Germany with Corbulo during the campaigns among the Chauci, *c.* 47–50 (*NH* 16. 2 with Tac. *Ann.* 11. 18–19), and in Upper Germany with his friend Pomponius Secundus, legate in 50–51, Tac. *Ann.* 12. 27–28. To this period may belong the *phalera* found at Vetera bearing the inscription 'Plinio praefec' (*CIL* xii. 10026. 22). He was in Italy in A.D. 52, when he witnessed a naval spectacle of Claudius, *NH* 33. 63. His criticism of Pompeius Paulinus' extravagance as legate of Lower Germany *c.* 57 is not necessarily that of an eyewitness (*NH* 33. 143, *scimus*, not the stronger *vidimus*; Tac. *Ann.* 13. 53). The reference to Duvius Avitus in 34. 47 is to his praetorian legateship of Aquitania, not as is commonly taken, to his governorship of Lower Germany after Paulinus (Tac. *Ann.* 13. 54). Hence the evidence for a second military phase in Lower Germany *c.* 56–57 is rather weak. His brief account of the eclipse of A.D. 59 in Campania, where he had a villa, is possibly as an eyewitness, *NH* 2. 180, and he was certainly in Italy from *c.* 66 to 68, above, *Books* s. 5 n. He quotes a report from Narbonensis dated to A.D. 70 (14. 43), and refers to another report from Belgica dated to 74 (18. 183). This, with his reference to the adventures of a procurator of Belgica *non pridem*, 7. 76, would seem to exclude the possibility that Pliny himself was then in that office. His procuratorship of Spain was 'a few years ago' in 77 (19. 35, below s. 17 n.). He spent at least the last years of Vespasian and the first of Titus as prefect of the fleet of Misenum, VI. 16. 4 (*Ep.*). Pliny implies, s. 9 n. below, that his uncle spent a large part of Vespasian's reign in Rome.

The life included in the Suetonian *Corpus*, which adds no positive facts to the information in the Letters, save for a rumour about the cause of his death, speaks of *continuae procurationes*. The phrase only summarizes ss. 7, 9, 17. Suetonius, ed. Roth (Teubner, 1881), 300–1.

Münzer posits two periods of military service, and three posts, in Germany, 47–51 and *c.* 56–57, as above, then a period of inactivity unbroken until the accession of Vespasian, when he packs in no less than four procuratorships, in Narbonensis, Spain, Africa, and Belgica, into five years, followed by the *praefectura classis*. Ziegler accepts only the Spanish procuratorship as certain, but revives the thesis of Mommsen, rejected by Münzer (art. cit. 103), connecting the career of one '-inius Secundus' in an incomplete inscription from Syrian

Arad (*OGIS* 586, W–C n. 330) with the Elder, on the strength of Pliny's statement in *NH* pref. 3, that he served *in castrensi contubernio* with Titus. This man commanded an *ala Thracorum*, was an equestrian assistant on the staff of Titus in the Jewish war, then procurator of Syria, and next commander of a legion, presumably in Egypt. Ziegler, like Münzer, attributes all Pliny's procuratorships to the years 70–79. Both accounts fail to allow for the usual length of procuratorships, seldom less and often much more than three years, or for the statement in s. 7 that the Elder passed the middle phase of his life in official occupations. His known dislike of Nero is no proof that he did not hold office under him. A post in Africa is a probable addition to the Spanish post of s. 17 and the fleet command, since there is no known private connexion between Pliny and Africa. His visits to Narbonensis were due rather to his acquaintance among the gentry of Vasio, which included several knights and probably the senator Dubius Avitus (*NH* 34. 47, cf. *ILS* 979). His career may have consisted of a *praefectura alae* in Lower and a military tribunate (s. 3 n.) in Upper Germany, between 47 and 51, a period of service *c*. 56 when he may have been with the young Titus in Upper Germany (s. 4 n.), a procuratorship of Africa in the early years of Nero, a procuratorship in Spain before 66 or after 69, and the *praefectura classis* either from 70 or from *c*. 74 to 79; cf. s. 9 n. for his duties in Rome at this time, not so much *ex officio* but as *amicus Caesaris*.

The man of Arad is excluded by his too lengthy career after A.D. 70, by Pliny's personal ignorance of the East, and by the improbability that Pliny was procurator of Syria before the less important Spain, which must have come later in the inscription. Ziegler would restore the inscription to make him *adiutor procuratoris* to avoid this difficulty.

1. avunculi mei. So too in I. 19. 1, VI. 16, 20. In VI. 20. 10 he is 'uncle' on the day of his death. But in V. 8. 5 he is 'avunculus meus idemque per adoptionem pater'. Evidently the adoption was testamentary.

3. cum praefectus alae militaret. Born *c*. 24 he could well be on military service with Corbulo by A.D. 47, though an early beginning was far from the rule, II. 13. 5 n. Under Claudius this post preceded the military tribunate. Not more than two different posts were customary at this period, though the man of Arad must have held three. G. L. Cheeseman, *Auxilia of the Roman Imperial Army* (Oxford, 1914), 90 ff.; Domaszewski, *Rangordnung* 112 f., 122 f.

4. cum in Germania militaret. Pliny does not use this term of procuratorial service, cf. I. 10. 2, III. 11. 5, 20. 5, VII. 16. 2, etc. The Elder's *militia equestris* may have lasted many years if the period of duty in Germany *c*. 56 is accepted. It was probably here (and not in Palestine) that he served with the young Titus (above), who was certainly military tribune in one of the Germanies about A.D. 57–59, (Suet. *Titus* 4, Tac. *Hist.* 2. 77; Münzer, art. cit. 110), though this phase is still disputed by F. Stähelin, *Die Schweiz in römischer Zeit* (Bâle, 1948), 175 n. 2. The passage in *N H* preface 3 contrasts the obscure Titus of the fifties with the colleague of Vespasian, 'nec quicquam in te mutavit fortunae amplitudo nisi ut prodesse tantumdem posses et velles'.

7. medium temporis distentum . . . qua officiis . . . qua amicitia principum egisse. This sentence is responsible for the statement in the *vita* that Pliny held *continuae procurationes*, to which *officiis* refers, as in s. 18. Cf. Ep. I. 12 n.

amicitia principum. The *amici principis* formed the advisory circle, cabinet, or *consilium* of the emperor (I. 17. 2 n.), but there was at this period no specific post of *consiliarius*. Equestrian *amici* like Pliny held posts in the administration (s. 9, *delegatum . . . officium*), and attend the Princeps when required for advice, as they are found doing in Juvenal's parody, *Sat.* 4. See also IV. 24. 3 n., 'illum civilibus officiis principis amicitia exemit'. The number of equestrian officials available at Rome in the pre-Trajanic period was larger than Pflaum allows (*Les Procurateurs équestres* 80, 106). To the prefects of the *vigiles, annona*, fleet or fleets, and praetorian guard, with the head librarian and Greek secretary, Trajan added the imperial secretaries *ab epistulis* and *a rationibus*, offices now promoted to equestrian status, I. 17. I n., 18 pref.

9. ante lucem ibat ad Vespasianum imperatorem (nam ille quoque noctibus utebatur), inde ad delegatum sibi officium. Comparison with Suet. *Vesp.* 21 suggests that under Vespasian the formal *salutatio* was combined with or preceded by a kind of cabinet meeting: 'de nocte vigilabat dein perlectis epistulis officiorumque omnium breviariis amicos admittebat . . . postque decisa quaecumque obvenissent negotia . . . quieti vacabat'. He reads the correspondence, consults the *amici*, then makes his decisions. (So too J. Crook, *Consilium Principis*, 27–28.) Such discussions of policy are distinct from the judicial sessions of the imperial *consilium* described in IV. 22, VI. 22, 31, on which the Younger Pliny served. This appears very clearly in Dio's account of the morning work of Severus, 77 (76) 17. 1–2. He too began before dawn, consulted his cabinet, and later in the day sat in judgment. For the dawn session cf. also Dio 78 (77) 17. 3—Caracalla.

delegatum sibi officium. At the time of his death Pliny was prefect of the Misene fleet, VI. 16. 4, etc. It is there implied that his presence at Misenum was unusual—'erat Miseni classemque imperio praesens regebat'. Here it would seem that the Elder spent most of Vespasian's reign at Rome. Syme, op. cit. 61 n. 5, cautiously suggested that Pliny held the *praefectura vigilum* at this moment, before the fleet command.

17. potuisse se cum procuraret in Hispania vendere hos commentarios Larcio Licino. This man, a noted orator (II. 14. 9 n.), was governor of Hispania Tarraconensis when only of praetorian grade, though the province was usually held by a consular, 'a few years' before the date of *NH* 19. 35—a phrase which in *NH* 2. 18 refers to A.D. 59—and died in office, *NH* 31. 24. Münzer (art. cit. 109 f.) makes him successor of Ti. Plautius Silvanus Aelianus, legate c. 70–72. But a date after 70 is not certain, s. 9 n. For the family of Larcius see Ep. 14. 1. For other reminiscences of this visit see *NH* 19. 10, 20. 215, 22. 120, and Epp. II. 13. 4, VI. 20. 5.

procuraret. He was the ordinary procurator in charge of imperial finances.

Daily Routine

8. erat ... summa vigilantia. lucubrare Vulcanalibus incipiebat non auspicandi causa sed studendi. The Elder's routine differs greatly from that of Spurinna and his nephew, described in Ep. 1 and IX. 36, 40, who went to bed after dark and rose like most Romans at dawn, Ep. 1. 4, 9 nn. The wakeful Elder rose four or five hours before dawn, but went to bed early, s. 13 n.

vigilantia. His watchword was 'vita vigilia est', *NH* pref. 19. The Vulcanalia were on 23 August.

auspicandi causa. There is no difficulty here, though Merrill was puzzled, quoting Columella, *RR* II. 2. 98: 'religiosiores agricolae ... kal. Ian. auspicandi causa omne genus operis instaurent', and a similar passage from Ovid, *Fasti* 1. 165 ff., where the meaning is not parallel. Pliny means as usual just what he says—that his uncle did not wake up in the middle of the night like a consul or augur to take the auspices, which was properly done after a night vigil. Cf. Ennius 1 fr. 33 (Steuart), Plut. *Q.Rom.* 38; *RE* ii, 'auspicium', 2586.

hieme. Pliny, *NH* 2. 125, dates the beginning of winter to the setting of the Vergiliae, *III Id. Nov.*

ab hora septima vel ... octava. The variation was due not to human frailty, to which the Elder was seldom subject, but to the varying hour of sunrise, cf. Ep. 1. 8 n. The Roman measurement being by the solar hour, the twelve hours of day and night changed in length daily with the sun, but the inconvenience was not felt seriously in central Italy, and the equinoctial hour was used only for scientific purposes, Pliny, *NH* 2. 180, 18. 220–2, 326 f. A conversion table of the Roman hours at the solstices is given by Carcopino, *Daily Life*, 149 f.

9. quod reliquum temporis studiis reddebat. The clearest guide to the Elder's time-table is in Martial 4. 8. 1–8, who allots the first two hours to *salutatio*, the next three to *labores*, the sixth and seventh to siesta, the eighth to exercise, the ninth and tenth to *cena*. In VI. 16. 4–5, while at his Campanian villa, but on duty, the Elder has completed his bath, *gustatio* and siesta, exactly as in ss. 10–11, by the seventh hour. These operations followed his first meal, *cibum* s. 10, which in turn marked the end of his official work. If the first meal is to be put, with Merrill, at the end of the fourth hour, then his working day was not very long. Yet in *NH* pref. 18 he claims to have given his days to the emperor, and to have studied only by night. Perhaps he took for granted the exclusion of the hours of sunning, siesta, and bath, to which he certainly gave less time than Spurinna, the Younger Pliny, and Martial (Ep. I. 7–8 nn.); for he cuts out the hour of exercise altogether. On occasion he would seem, from the limitation in s. 10, 'si quid otii', to have worked on till siesta hour. But the official working day evidently seldom exceeded four hours, though a court case could, exceptionally, take up to seven hours, and the fortnightly sessions of the Senate could last all day, II. II. 18 n., IV. 9. 14, 16. 2. The emperor Domitian seems to have ended his working day, and turned to bath or siesta, at the sixth hour, Suet. *Dom.* 16. 2.

10. post cibum . . . aestate, si quid otii, iacebat in sole. Since this meal is distinct from the *gustatio* which follows his bath s. 11, the Elder followed the system of three meals, *ientaculum*, an ancient version of the continental breakfast, followed by a lunch (*gustatio, prandium*) which he took during the sixth or seventh hour (VI. 16. 4–5), and the usual *cena* at the ninth or tenth hour s. 13. For the Roman meals see Ep. I. 9, 15, II 6 nn. and Carcopino, *Daily Life*, 263 ff.

11. post solem . . . lavabatur, deinde gustabat dormiebatque . . . mox quasi alio die studebat in cenae tempus. Exactly as in VI. 16. 4–5. Hence his 'second day' lasted from the seventh to the ninth hour. For the bath before instead of after siesta and exercise, as was normal, Merrill quoted examples from SHA, *Alex.* 30. 5, Juv. II. 204. The emperor Severus followed a similar routine: after working— till midday—he took bath and exercise before *prandium*, followed by a sleep and discussion of *studia* until dinner (*cena*): Dio 77(76) 17. 1–4.

super hanc liber legebatur, adnotabatur. He was assisted by a *notarius*, as in s. 15, as well as the *lector*, to take down the Elder's reflections; cf. IX. 20. 2, 36. 2, for the technique. Thus he made his immense collections of select passages (s. 17 n. 'Works'). The Younger was brought up by his uncle in this habit, VI. 20. 5: 'posco librum T. Livi . . . excerpo'. Such anthologies had a special value when the book-form was the papyrus roll.

For the recitation of books at meals see IX. 36. 4.

13. surgebat aestate a cena luce, hieme intra primam noctis. Cf. Ep. I. 9 n. And so to bed, without waste of lights on mere pleasure. He slept some six or seven hours.

15. in itinere . . . ad latus notarius cum libro et pugillaribus. So too the Younger read or wrote in his carriage, IV. 14. 2, IX. 10. 2. There was no room for both *lector* and *notarius*, so one had to perform double duty, contrary to servile custom, V. 19. 3 n.

pugillaribus. The use of the *codex* notebook beside the papyrus roll is interesting, I. 6. 1 n., IX. 6. 1. For the use of the shorthand *notarius* see Seneca, *Ep.* 90. 25; Suet. *Titus* 3; Paulus, *Dig.* 29. 1. 40; Ausonius, *Epigr.* 146. Seneca speaks of 'verborum notas quibus quamvis citata excipitur oratio et celeritatem linguae manus sequitur'. For shorthand in antiquity see *RE* XI. ii, s.v. 'Kurzschrift'.

Romae quoque sella vehebatur. Use of carriages was forbidden in the city during the first ten hours of the day. Carcopino, *Daily Life*, 49; *Tab. Heracl.* 58–65; Suet. *Claud.* 25. 2.

6. *To Annius Severus*

Date. This letter, which has escaped the notice of Mommsen's detractors, who might have attributed it to 99, should be dated after his consulship, and possibly after his acceptance of the *cura Tiberis* in 104, not long before the date of IV. 1, ss. 5–6 n.

Address. For Pliny's agent Annius Severus see II. 16 pref.

1. ex hereditate quae mihi obvenit emi proxime Corinthium signum. Pliny apparently means that he bought the bronze with the proceeds of an inheritance (Merrill, Guillemin), not that he bought it in at the usual sale of an estate left to several heirs. The passion for Corinthian bronzes is regarded by Pliny with reluctant disapproval here and in Ep. I. 9 (n.).

quantum ego sapio. Petronius, *Cena* 50, robustly mocks the pretensions of amateurs of Corinthian bronzes, such as Martial's Mamurra who tested his bronzes by smell: 9. 59. 11.

2. effingit senem stantem. The realistic 'old woman' was a favourite type in late Hellenistic sculpture, originating apparently in the first century B.C. A. Lawrence, *Later Greek Sculpture*, 41. L.-Hartleben (op. cit. 69) cites a long list of examples, of which Lawrence, op. cit., pl. 68 c, and H. Stuart-Jones, *Cat. Sculptures in Palazzo dei Conservatori*, pl. 50, nn. 27–28, are close to Pliny's description.

3. aes ipsum quantum verus color indicat vetus et antiquum. For the subject see Pliny, *NH* 34. 5–12; *RE* iv. 1233; *D–S* i. 1507. The genuine article was supposed to be an alloy of bronze and precious metal, but the notion that it originated as a by-product of the sack of Corinth in 146 B.C. is a myth, repeated in garbled form by Trimalchio, in Petronius, loc. cit. In the Empire the term became a trade-name, and was applied to modern products, such as Pliny's specimen.

4. in Iovis templo. As at most municipalities this would be the principal shrine. No trace of it is known at Comum (M. Bertolone, *Lombardia Romana*, I. 328).

5. iube basim fieri . . . quae nomen meum honoresque capiat. Pliny reveals his true motive. He wants to make sure that his recent distinctions are publicly recorded at Comum. His career up to the prefecture of the *aerarium militare* would have been publicized on the walls of his library, I. 8. 2. This points to a date after his consulship when he entered the top class of the Senate.

The absence of practical details of size is a sure sign of the revision of a business letter for publication, cf. IX. 39 nn. and van Buren, *Cl. Rev.* 1905, 446 f.

6. destino enim, si tamen officii ratio permiserit, excurrere isto. Since there is no other trace of a visit to Comum between that of 96 (I. 8 pref.) and that of IV. I, after his second marriage, it is reasonable to identify this project with the latter. By *officii ratio* he may refer either to a public post or to private duties; cf. VII. 15. I n. 'distringor officio amicis deservio'; I. 10. 9, III. 5. 9, V. 14. 2. He speaks in s. 7 as if his duties were elastic and private, whereas if his *cura Tiberis* were meant he would need special leave, as in V. 14. 9. Otto might have used this letter, if the post-consulship date is accepted, to support his attribution of the *cura Tiberis* to 101 instead of 104 (art. cit. 91 ff.). But it would tell against his assumption that Pliny resigned the *cura* soon for bad health, because the letter implies that he had held it long enough to earn leave.

7. *To Caninius Rufus*

Date. A fair interval after late 99 (s. 6 n.). Hence the book-date is reasonable.

Address. For Caninius Rufus, equestrian dilettante from Comum, see I. 3 pref.

1. **modo nuntiatus est Silius Italicus . . . finisse vitam.** The author of the *Punica*, Ti. Catius Asconius Silius Italicus, whose names are revealed by epigraphy (*ILS* 5025; *Cl. Rev.* 1935, 216), was born not later than A.D. 29, and secured the distinction of being *cos. ordinarius* in 68, at an early age for a 'new man', as a reward for political services, ss. 3, 9 nn. His more virtuous contemporary Verginius Rufus had to wait till he was nearly 50 for the honour, II. I. 2. n. His place of origin is uncertain. Chilver (*Cisalpine Gaul* 109 f.) and Syme find Cisalpine connexions, perhaps maternal, in his names Catius and Asconius. But Pliny does not claim him for the north. Garzetti, *C.* 38; *PIR*[1] C 474; Syme *Tac.* 88 n. 7. The Titus Catius of IV. 28 is a much earlier figure.

2. **erat illi natus insanabilis clavus.** Merrill, disturbed by the notion that Silius killed himself because of a corn, which is Celsus' definition of *clavus*, supposes that Pliny means some kind of ulcer, which his uncle conjoins with *clavus* in *NH* 26. 142, and compares the story of the ulcerated man of Comum, VI. 24. But whatever the trouble, neither Pliny meant internal ulcers. Cf. *Thesaurus* s.v.

For incurable disease as a rational ground of suicide see I. 12. 3, 22. 8 nn. Silius, known to Epictetus (III. 8. 7) as a friend of philosophy, takes the Stoic line.

minorem ex liberis duobus amisit, sed maiorem . . . consularem reliquit. Martial refers to the consulship of the elder and the death of the younger son in 8. 66 and 9. 86, passages which Friedlaender, ad loc., dated to *c.* 93–94. The Fasti of Potentia give L. Silius Decianus a consulship in September 94, hitherto dated by a mildly erroneous *diploma* to 93. The same names appear on a water pipe of 102 (*CIL* xv. 7302). This should be the elder son, though Garzetti thinks that the son of Italicus should have the same names as his father (*C.* 39, *Inc.* 134).

3. **laeserat famam suam sub Nerone (credebatur sponte accusasse).** Silius began life as an orator, and like all the better men, practised in the Centumviral Court; Martial 7. 63. To have deliberately launched an accusation was regarded as the worst form of collaboration with 'bad' emperors, I. 5. I n.

Vitellii amicitia. Silius assisted Cluvius Rufus at the negotiations between Vitellius and the agents of Vespasian, Tac. *Hist.* 3. 65.

ex proconsulatu Asiae gloriam. Senatorial opinion attached great importance to these merely annual proconsulships, because they fell under senatorial control. Cf. the praise of Arrius Antoninus on the same score, IV. 3. 1. So too Tacitus praises C. Petronius' proconsulship of Bithynia, *Ann.* 16. 18, and Vespasian's government of Africa was supposed to have been remarkable, Suet. *Vesp.* 4. 3. The proconsulship of Silius fell *c.* 77, under Vespasian, *PIR*, loc. cit.

maculam veteris industriae laudabili otio abluerat. Cf. Martial 7. 63. 11, 'emeritos Musis et Phoebo tradidit annos'. He seems not to have begun the *Punica* before Domitian's reign, the earliest reference to him at work being *c.* 88, ibid. 4. 14; cf. *RE* (2) III. 81 f. (Klotz).

4. salutabatur colebatur. Merrill suggested that the formal *salutatio* was dropping out of fashion. But Pliny hardly bears this out here and in IV. 13. 3, VII. 3. 3, though he does not mention it among the daily round described in I. 9. For the custom see Friedlaender *SG* (ET), i. 382; Carcopino, *Daily Life*, 171 f.

5. scribebat carmina maiore cura quam ingenio. Pliny's devastating comment fits the *Punica* only too well. The short 'Latin Homer' is no longer attributed to him, *RE* art. cit. 91.

6. ne adventu quidem novi principis inde commotus est. This can only be Trajan returning from Pannonia to Rome in middle or late 99, to receive a tremendous welcome, *Pan.* 22.

7. magna Caesaris laus sub quo hoc liberum fuit. So too Trajan did not require attendance at the morning levée, *Pan.* 48. 2. Nero had been particularly offended at Thrasea Paetus for his prolonged absence from the Senate, Tac. *Ann.* 16. 22.

8. plures isdem in locis villas possidebat. All presumably in Campania, where he owned a former villa of Cicero, probably the *Cumanum*, Mart. 11. 48. Cf. *CIL* xiv. 2653; *PIR*, loc. cit.

multum ubique . . . imaginum. For the cult of *imagines* by scholars see IV. 28. 1, where the portraits of Nepos and Titus Catius are being sought after. Compare also Domitius Tullus' immense store of statues, VIII. 18. 11. Portraits of Vergil are mentioned in an anecdote about Caligula, who tried to destroy them all, Suet. *Gaius* 34. 2.

Vergili ante omnes cuius natalem . . . celebrabat, Neapoli maxime, ubi monimentum eius adire ut templum solebat. Martial mentions Silius' cult of Vergil and his birthday, in 11. 48. 50, 12. 67. Silius had bought the tomb and redeemed it from neglect. Statius shared this passion, *S.* 4. 4. 51 ff. Donatus (5. 5. 36) placed the tomb on the Via Puteolana before the second milestone.

9. postremus ex omnibus quos Nero consules fecerat decessit. Verginius Rufus, consul in 63, had died in 97, II. 1. 1–2 nn. It is not so surprising that by 100 all the Neronian consulars were dead. Though the minimum legal age was 33 (Mommsen, *DPR* ii. 236) the norm was nearer 40 (or higher), as with Silius himself, Pliny, and Tacitus (Syme, *Tac.* 654–5). For Roman longevity see I. 12. 11 n. Pliny does not count Arrius Antoninus, consul suffect in 69, who had been designated by 'Nero or Galba' and confirmed by Vitellius and Otho, IV. 3 pref., Tac. *Hist.* I. 77.

12. nuper L. Piso, pater Pisonis illius qui a Valerio Festo . . . occisus est dicere solebat. The first of these Pisones, whom Pliny does well to distinguish among the many Calpurnii Pisones of the early Principate, was L. Calpurnius Piso, son of the supposed murderer of Germanicus and consul *ordinarius* in A.D. 27. *PIR²*, C 293.

The second was the like-named *consul ord.* of 57. The tale is told in Tac. *Hist* 4. 48–50. He was proconsul of Africa in A.D. 70 when Valerius Festus was commander of the African legion. Festus first intrigued for Vitellius, then on the arrival of a Flavian emissary he arranged the murder of Piso in the interest of Vespasian. Festus' reward was rapid promotion, a consulship and three consular posts between 71 and 80. His full name, C. Calpetanus Rantius Quirinalis Valerius Festus, indicates a connexion by adoption with the obscure Claudian consular, C. Calpetanus Rantius Sedatus. See *ILS* 989 nn.; *PIR²* C 235, 294.

nuper. The date of Piso's remark is taken by Groag (*PIR*) to be later than the death of the son. But that is mentioned only for identification. Still, he would be over 75 by that date, the age of Silius, which is perhaps the point. The jurisprudent C. Cassius Longinus, consul in 30, survived to the beginning of Vespasian's reign, and Piso's remark should be after his death (VII. 24. 8 n.).

13. illae regiae lacrimae. For the story see Herodotus 7. 45, a popular yarn, cf. Sen. *brev. vit.* 17. 2.

14. quidquid est temporis . . . si non datur factis (nam horum materia in aliena manu), certe studiis proferamus. One of Pliny's rare complaints of the imperial autocracy, cf. Ep. 20. 12 n., IV. 24. 5. For the theme of *studiis proferamus* cf. I. 3. 3–4, V. 5. 7–8, IX. 3. 3.

8. *To Suetonius Tranquillus*

Date. The period 101–3 fits the reference to the army command of Neratius Marcellus, s. I n.

Address. Suetonius, the biographer, was now aged about 30, at the beginning of his rather leisurely procuratorial career; see I. 18 pref. After the letters and references in I–III he recurs only as recipient of V. 10 and IX. 34. Possibly he took up a military post outside Italy, despite his rejection of the present commission, between 102 and 105, though Pliny mentions none in his recommendation of the man to Trajan, x. 94, and the fragments of his inscription do not record it.

1. petis ut tribunatum, quem a Neratio Marcello clarissimo viro impetravi tibi, in Caesennium Silvanum . . . transferam. For the commissioning of officers by army commanders without direct consultation of the emperor see II. 13. 1 n. Suetonius jibbed at visiting Britain.

L. Neratius Marcellus, consul suffect in January 95 (*FO*), *curator aquarum* before 101, was legate of Britain by January 103. It was his first consular province if the headless inscription *ILS* 1032, from Saepinum, where the family belonged is correctly referred to him. Later he was *cos. II* in 129. *PIR*¹ N 43; Garzetti, *C.* 107. So Pliny's request fits the period *c.* 103—not necessarily the beginning of his tenure, cf. II. 13. 2 n.

transferam. With s. 4, 'neque . . . adhuc nomen in numeros relatum est', this suggests that Marcellus gave Pliny as it were a blank form, which had then to be registered at the proper place, either in the army list kept in the *officium legati* at provincial headquarters, or with the secretary *ab epistulis* at Rome, as Statius *S* 5. 1. 94 f. suggests (quoted II. 13. 2 n.).

Caesennius Silvanus is unknown, unless he is the like-named man of decent standing from Lanuvium commemorated in *ILS* 7212, II. 10–15; *PIR*² C 176. The well-known Caesennii are too aristocratic to need the patronage of Suetonius, *PIR*² C 170–4.

4. in numeros relatum. For the army list of the legions and other units see x. 29. 2, 'nondum distributi in numeros erant (tirones)', n.

9. *To Cornelius Minicianus*

Date. Any time in 100 after the hearing of the Priscus case (II. 11), except the period of Pliny's consulship, or early in 101 is possible for the hearing of the Classicus trial, and hence of this letter, s. 1 n. A date before the delivery of Pliny's Panegyric, September 100, cannot be proved, s. 23 n. See Introduction, pp. 58 f.. The letter shows signs of revision after the events ss. 2, 16 nn.

Address. Cornelius Minicianus was a wealthy equestrian bigwig from Bergamum in Cisalpine, advocate and man of letters, whom Pliny recommends later for a military tribunate, VII. 22. 2 n. Letters on public affairs (IV. 11) and about literature (VIII. 12), are addressed to him, possibly also I. 17, VI. 31, VII. 12 (prefs. ibid.)

1. possum iam perscribere. By *iam* he refers to the unusual length of time that the case took, with three separate *actiones* each occupying a senatorial session and hence spread out over some four weeks, ss. 12, 18, 19.

2. Caecilius Classicus . . . proconsulatum . . . gesserat, eodem anno quo in Africa Marius. Classicus is known only from Pliny. His proconsulship implies praetorian rank. African senators are rather rare at this period, when the Pactumeii of Cirta were the first African family to reach the consulship, *PIR*[1] P 24–26. No connexion can be made between Classicus and the senatorial family of Caecilii Aemiliani, from Africa in the later second century, *PIR*[2] C 17, 37, 87.

The date of the proconsulship is fixed by that of Priscus to 97–98, II. 11. 2 n., but the indictment is not completed until October–November 99 (Ep. 4. 2 n.). The delay is partly due to the death of the principal (s. 5 n.), and partly to the enforced absence from Baetica of the chief agent of the prosecution, Norbanus Licinianus, during 98, s. 31 n.

non minus violenter quam sordide. Against Classicus, as against Priscus, the charge is extortion with violence, and the procedure is before the full Senate, II. 11. 2 nn. The shorter process (ibid.) before a senatorial committee of *iudices* is never envisaged.

There is a deliberate contrast in the description of the two trials. Here Pliny says nothing about the precise charges, elaborated in II. 11. 8, 23, and in his account of the penalties and procedure avoids the formula *consul designatus censuit* and the names of the proposers, used in II. 11 and 12 throughout. He uses a long postscript to cover the subsidiary case of Norbanus ss. 28–35, instead of adding a second letter as in II. 12. Cf. Introduction, p. 18.

4. Marium una civitas publice multique privati reum peregerant, in Classicum tota provincia incubuit. The same distinction appears in *SC. Calvisianum* 97–98 (II. 11. 2 n.), ἐάν τινες τῶν συμμάχων . . . χρήματα δημοσίᾳ ἢ ἰδίᾳ πραχθέντες ἀπαιτεῖν βουληθῶσι repeated in l. 141. Prosecution could be set afoot by private persons, or separate municipalities, or by a resolution of the provincial Council to despatch legates, as in the Varenus case, VII. 6. 1. So too here, the whole province is acting, and Norbanus is the chief deputy, ss. 29, 31, Ep. 4. 2.

5. ille accusationem . . . morte praevertit. He would seem to have died before the formal indictment, which the emissaries had still to put forward when they approached Pliny after his death, Ep. 4. 2. The death caused delay and a change of tactics. The emissaries may well have referred back to the Council of Baetica. Compare the situation that arose in the Varenus case, VII. 6. 1–6, 10. 2–3, where the Council issued contradictory instructions.

6. provisum hoc legibus, intermissum tamen. The provision goes back to a clause of the Gracchan *Lex Acilia* 29 (*FIRA* i. 7): '[de iudicio in eum qui mortuus e]rit aut in exilium abierit'. Modestinus (*Dig.* 48. 2. 20) states that in his day only charges of extortion or of treason could be brought against a dead man's estate, even if his death anticipated delation. Scaevola limits such action to a year from the death of the principal, ibid. 48. 11. 2.

addiderunt Baetici quod simul socios ministrosque Classici detulerunt. These are the members of the proconsul's 'cohort', defined by Cicero, *pro Rab. Post.* 13, as 'tribuni praefecti scribae comites omnes magistratuum'. In the Republic they were immune from direct prosecution unless they were sons of senators, but sums could be recovered from such persons if the principal's estate proved inadequate to meet repayment; Cicero, loc. cit., and ibid. 8, 13, 37; Mommsen, *D. Pen. R.* iii, 9 ff. In the Julio-Claudian period equestrian procurators and governors were directly prosecuted; Tac. *Ann.* 4. 15, 13. 30, 14. 28. The new fragment of the *Sententiae Pauli* contains a rule of the *Lex Iulia* concerning equestrian officials (F. Serrao, *Il Frammento Leidense* (Milan, 1956), p. 33). The innovation was probably Augustan. In the later Empire prosecution of subordinates *ex cohorte* was normal; Marcian, *Dig.* 48. 11. 1. It may well be Pliny who established the precedent in this very case. He regards the change as a great novelty, quoting no precedent, while the accused thought they had a certain defence in their status, because the plea of superior orders was commonly accepted in other legal contexts, s. 14 n. Cf. Tac. *Ann.* 3. 17, where Piso's son is acquitted on a charge of treason for obeying his father.

inquisitionem. This term is connected with the *evocatio testium*, s. 29 and v. 20. 2. The procedure is as in ii. 11. 5, 8 (nn.). The Senate authorizes the *inquisitor* to make inquiries in the province with compulsory powers to bring witnesses and documents to Rome. Cf. *SC. Calvisianum* 95–96. This often took a long time, even as much as a year, Tac. *Ann.* 13. 43: 'inquisitionem annuam impetraverant'. Hence another cause of delay in the present case.

7. aderam Baeticis mecumque Lucceius Albinus. For his appointment see Ep. 4. 2–4. Albinus should be the son of the like-named procurator of Judaea and Mauretania, dead in 69 (Tac. *Hist.* 2. 58–59; Jos. *Ant. Jud.* 20. 9. 1; *PIR*[1] L 263–4; Garzetti, *C.* 91). His career is as yet unknown. Later he defends Bassus, iv. 9. 13. Recipient of vi. 10, probably. The family comes from Olisipo in Lusitania, *CIL* ii. 195.

9. ne gratia singulorum collata atque permixta pro singulis quoque vires omnium acciperet. The *rei* proved to enjoy a great deal of influence in the Senate, ss. 12, 25–26, 31–36. Compare the pressure exerted in the Nominatus case, v. 13. 2 n., 'monitum . . . ne desiderio senatoris . . . in senatu repugnaret'.

11. Sertorianum illud. Valerius Maximus, 7. 3. 6, tells the tale. The theme is that unity is strength.

12. Baebium Probum et Fabium Hispanum. They are otherwise unknown. That none of the *rei* was a senator is indicated by Ep. 4. 7.

13. sua manu reliquerat scriptum quid ex quaque re, quid ex quaque causa accepisset ; miserat etiam epistulas Romam ad amiculam. His regular account books were produced as evidence, as in ii. 11. 23, vii. 6. 2. The letters would be copies from his files, cf. i. i. 1 n.

iam **sestertium quadragiens redegi.** Four million sesterces is the largest sum mentioned in the extortion trials of Pliny, but it is only a tenth of the sum taken by Verres, Cic. I *in Verr.* 56, from a much smaller and poorer province.

14. ut constaret ministerium crimen esse. See s. 6 n. and, for a survey of the theme in history and law, D. Daube, *The Defence of Superior Orders in Roman Law*, Oxford, 1956 (Inaugural Lecture), who misses this contrary example.

15. esse enim se provinciales et ad omne proconsulum imperium metu cogi. Juvenal rubs in this 'fear of the rods', 8. 136: 'si frangis virgas sociorum in sanguine, si te delectant hebetes lasso lictore secures'. But these men were Roman citizens, not like soldiers directly under the authority of the proconsul, whose power of inflicting corporal punishment on citizens was still strictly limited, ii. 11. 8 n. Normally the plea was accepted (Daube, op. cit.). Pliny's success is all the more striking, and Restitutus' surprise was just.

16. solet dicere Claudius Restitutus, qui mihi respondit. This suggests the reviser's hand, or a longer interval after the event than s. 1 implies.

Restitutus may be another African—the names are known at Cirta, *CIL* viii. 7039—and is probably the recipient of vi. 17, about *studia*, and the advocate of Martial 10. 87. *PIR*² C 995.

17. bona Classici . . . placuit senatui a reliquis separari, illa filiae haec spoliatis relinqui. Only a capital sentence rendered the whole estate liable to confiscation, Callistratus, *Dig.* 48. 20. 1. A sentence of relegation carried no automatic financial penalty. Even for *capitis damnati* alleviations were made to benefit children. In Tac. *Ann.* 3. 68, when C. Silanus was sentenced *capitis*, a part of his estate was reserved for his son, cf. Tac. *Ann.* 4. 20. Later these exceptions were generalized into the principle that children had a right to a part of a condemned man's estate, Callistratus, loc. cit. Hadrian alleged expediency, *Dig.* loc. cit. 7. 3: 'ampliari imperium hominum adiectione potius quam pecuniarum copia malim'. Paulus called it justice (*Dig.* loc. cit. 7 pref.) 'rationem haberi liberorum ne alieno admisso graviorem poenam luerent'. See II. II. 8 'exilium' n., 20 n.

haec spoliatis. As in II. II. 19 only the *poena simplex* is intended, not the later fourfold restitution, Mommsen, *D. Pen. R.* iii. 28 f.

ut pecuniae quas creditoribus solverat revocarentur. This is an extension of the inquiry 'quo ea pecunia pervenerit', s. 6 n. The principle is later approved by Pius, that the children should not benefit by the crime of the father. Paulus quotes the rule that moneys acquired by extortion were not capable of legal transfer: *Dig.* 48. 11. 8 pref. and 20. 7. 4. The claims of Classicus' private creditors would still be good against the rest of the estate.

in quinquennium relegati. See II. II. 19–20 nn.

18. post paucos dies Claudium Fuscum . . . et Stilonium Priscum . . . accusavimus. The persons are unknown, though the names of the first recur later in the house of a consul of 169, *PIR²*, C 877. Despite Garzetti, *Inc.* 47, he cannot be a senator, s. 12 n.

post paucos dies. Sessions of the Senate were normally held on or about the Kalends and Ides of each month, II. II. 24 n.

tribunus cohortis. Since only the urban forces and auxiliary *c. miliariae* were officered by *tribuni cohortium*, this implies the presence of a unit in Baetica, like the urban cohorts stationed at Lugdunum in Gaul and at Carthage in Africa (*ILS* 2118, 2120). The tribunes of the urban forces were usually ex-centurions of the first grade, not men of equestrian birth.

Prisco in biennium Italia interdictum. This with the attendant loss of status (II. II. 12 n.) would ruin his hopes of promotion.

19. supererant minores rei . . . hunc in locum reservati, excepta tamen Classici uxore quae . . . non satis convinci probationibus visa est. The order of the later *actiones* is not made quite clear. He means that the third action included the *minores* and Casta, who was unlikely to be condemned and hence left to the end. There was no fourth action to deal with wife and daughter: s. 20 'in extrema actione' means 'at the end of my speech', not 'in my last and fourth speech'. The counter-charge against Norbanus (s. 29 n.) preceded the trial of Casta and daughter, 21, 34. Since 22–23 show that the hearing of the *numerosissima causa* was the last phase of the trial, the charge against Norbanus must have been made quite early on, cf. s. 29.

uxore. The sons of senators were always liable under the extortion law: *Lex Acilia* 2, cf. Tac. *Ann.* 13. 43. Ulpian quotes a *SC.* of A.D. 20 that made wives of proconsuls liable for their own offences,

presumably of extortion, *Dig.* 1. 16. 4. 2. In A.D. 21 it was proposed that
wives should not accompany husbands to provincial posts, because
of their propensity for extortion. In A.D. 24 the wife of a legate of
Germany was charged as her husband's associate in extortion and
treason. Tac. *Ann.* 3. 33–34, 4. 19–20. The tendency of wives to pecu-
late is a commonplace with Juvenal (8. 128) and Martial (2. 56).

non satis convinci. The evidence was alleged to have been concealed,
s. 29.

20. Classici filia. Presumably daughters were assimilated to sons
as members of the *ordo*. This seems to be the only reference to them
in an extortion case.

21. consilium a senatu petebam. Forewarned by the fate of Norbanus, Pliny protects himself against a charge of prevarication.

**22. hic numerosissimae causae terminus fuit ... relegatis aliis in tempus
aliis in perpetuum.** This refers only to the *actio tertia*, s. 19 n. The
persons are not named because they are small fry, but some of them
receive the heaviest punishment, as Pliny anticipated, s. 9.

**23. eodem senatus consulto industria fides constantia nostra ...
comprobata est.** Since this forms part of the *SC.* that terminated the
third action there is no room for a subsequent hearing of Casta.
Such a vote of thanks was customary, II. 11. 19, *Pan.* 95. 1. The latter
refers to the passing of such a *SC.* in January 100, at the end of the
Priscus trial, and is therefore not relevant to the date of this trial,
despite Otto, art. cit. 81 and Stobbe, art cit. 371.

25. quidam e iudicibus ipsis. i.e. some of the senators, who acted as
iudices, s. 2 n.

26. quantas etiam offensas subierimus. Pliny is very cautious about
offensae always, II. 18. 5 n., Ep. 4. 7.

27. tam longa epistula. How long is a long letter? Several of the
longest letters have some sort of apology for their length (I. 20. 25,
II. 11. 25, III. 5. 20, IV. 11. 16, V. 6. 41–45, IX. 13. 26), while a few do
not (I. 5, VI. 31, VIII. 14). See pp. 4 f.

28. facit hoc Homerus. Pliny has in mind Cicero's similar apology, *ad
Att.* 1. 16. 1.

**29. e testibus quidam ... Norbanum Licinianum, legatum et inquisi-
torem, reum postulavit tamquam ... praevaricaretur.** Norbanus, who
is known only from Pliny, was evidently a big man in Spanish
politics, though not a senator, and was the rival of such as Probus
and Hispanus, who like him had influence even at Rome, s. 12. But

after Domitian's death Norbanus' power waned and his enemies secured the proconsul's ear, who in 97–98 relegated Norbanus for a short period, ss. 31–33. On the expiry of this sentence Norbanus exploited the dissatisfaction felt against Classicus, becoming, like Theophanes in the Bassus case (IV. 9. 3), the *fax et origo* of the accusation, and took advantage of the extension of the case *in socios* to involve his private enemies in ruin. But at the last moment they cunningly turned the tables on him by exploiting the anti-Domitianic sentiment of the Senate. A truly Spanish intrigue. The internal politics of Bithynia, Asia, and Spain are much akin, see IV. 9. 3–5, VI. 31. 3, X. 58–59, 81 nn.

   evocatus. See II. 11.5 n.

   in causa Castae. To help the bigger fish the countercharge must have been made early in the hearings, long before the case against Casta was heard at length. How? Probably in the *prima actio* a statement was made about the whole series, from which it was argued that the case against Casta was being neglected. Perhaps the prosecution was already saying (s. 19), 'non satis convinci probationibus', or perhaps the delay in bringing her on sufficed.

30. est lege cautum ut reus ante peragatur tunc de praevaricatore quaeratur. So already in the *Lex Acilia* 75, and so too for the allied offence of *calumnia*, Marcianus *Dig.* 48. 16. 1. 3, who defines prevarication, ibid. 16. 1. 6, as 'quod proprias . . . probationes dissimularet' —as was here suspected—or else 'quod falsas . . . rei excusationes admitteret'. But such charges could only be brought against an *accusator*, which was the role of Pliny and Albinus. The leader of the provincial deputation has absorbed the accuser's duty of *inquisitio*, and tends to slip into his place altogether, as does Theophanes in the Bassus case, IV. 9. 3, 14.

31. non legati nomen non inquisitionis officium praesidio fuit. In the Augustan *SC. Calvisianum* the provincials appear only as petitioners before the Senate; the advocate assigned to them always acted as the accuser, and conducted any investigation in the province, s. 6 n. (Cf. Cic. *I in Verrem* 6; *SC. Calv.* 98–103.) By A.D. 58 the duty of *inquisitio* is regarded as a nuisance, Tac. *Ann.* 13. 43, and hence came by unknown stages to be transferred to the leader of the provincial deputation: 'electus . . . ad inquirendum'.

   legati nomen. cf. s. 36 n.

   tamquam Classici inimicus (erat ab illo relegatus). For the governor's power of *relegatio* see II. 11. 8 nn. Norbanus must have returned to the province at the end of his sentence, which can hardly have been for less than a year—irregular return is not alleged against him (cf. X. 56, 58). Here lies the best clue to the chronology of this case. If he were relegated late in 97, during Classicus' year (June or July 97–98), he could not return before a corresponding date in 98, precisely fixed by the expulsion order (Ulpian, *Dig.* 48. 22. 7. 17). Conversely the relegation of Norbanus excludes the possibility that the year of Classicus was 98–99. Mommsen cites from Cassiodorus a sole example of relegation for less than a year, *D. Pen. R.* 3. 324 n. 2.

32. dari sibi diem, edi crimina postulabat. Stout, p. 164, rightly remarks that the (virtual) agreement of *a* and *γ* against the additions and omissions in the *β* sources make the basic reading certain here; Schuster quotes an exact parallel in Tac. *Hist.* 2. 10. Besides, Norbanus is protesting against the irregularity of the procedure, not asking for time, as in the too ingenious addition *ad diluenda crimina*. Paulus (*Fr. Inst.* 2, in *FIRA* ii. 421) regards it as a very bad form of procedure indeed 'accipere nomen extra ordinem . . . ut oporteret eum respondere sine respectu loci temporis condicionis'.

33. apud iudicem sub Domitiano Salvi Liberalis accusatoribus adfuisset. This amounts to a charge of *calumnia*, and hence was relevant as to character in a case of *praevaricatio*. Norbanus would seem to have acted as secondary accuser, or *subscriptor*, in a criminal prosecution (*accusatoribus*). For *calumnia* see VI. 31. 12 n.

apud iudicem. As a senator one would expect Liberalis to be tried before the Senate, but if the case was non-political it might have been heard by a special inquisitor appointed by the Princeps, as in VII. 6. 8 and 10. Less probably the term refers to the *iudex quaestionis* of the ordinary criminal system, which seems not to have dealt with senators in this period. For the earlier career of Liberalis see II. 11. 17 n. A favourite of the elder Flavians, he may have been ruined by this charge. It has been argued that he was condemned and exiled from the absence of his name from the attendance roll of the Arval Brothers in 89–91, on which he had been present in 86–87. An earlier absence in 80–81 coincides with his known junior legateship in Britain, but by 86 he was a consular—since his consulship is before the beginning of the Fasti of Potentia—and his *cursus* (*ILS* 1011) gives no consular provincial post. He reappears in fragments of the Arval records for the later nineties, and again in 101 (*ILS* 5027–35). At an unknown date he refused the proconsulship of Asia. If not in exile he was evidently out of favour in Domitian's latter years like other friends of Vespasian and Titus, II. 11. 19 n., IV. 9. 2 n.

Pomponius Rufus. There are two distinguished consulars of this name at this time. Quintus, whose protracted career began in 68, after sundry commands was suffect consul in 95, legate of Lower Moesia in August 99, and legate of Tarraconensis in 105 (*AE* 1948, n. 3, *ILS* 1999, 2000, and 1014). The second, Gaius, bearing the

names Acilius Priscus Coelius Sparsus, who was consul at the end
of 98, and is not known as an active administrator, is more likely to
be the advocate appearing here and in the trial of Bassus, IV. 9. 3.
Pliny does not need to distinguish them, because only one was a
pleader. Their relationship to Pomponius Bassus (IV. 23 pref.) and
Pomponius Pius, consul in 98, remains uncertain. (See *RE* xxi, s.v.
Pomponii nn. 68–69; *PIR*¹ P 559–61; Garzetti, *C*. 125–7.)

Libo Frugi. His identity is not yet established; presumably he
descends from the consul of 27, M. Licinius Crassus Frugi and his
wife Scribonia, *PIR*¹ L 110, 130. His consulship being unknown may
be before *c*. 86, unless it fills one of the four vacancies in 93 or 99.

34. in insulam relegatus. This sentence (on which see II. 11. 19 n.)
greatly exceeded the normal penalty for prevarication and *calumnia*,
a ban on practice as an advocate, laid down in the *SC. Turpilianum*,
which regulated these offences, as in the case of Tuscilius Nominatus,
V. 13. 5 n. (*RE* iii, '*calumnia*', 1414 ff.). But Tac. *Ann*. 14. 41 gives
a parallel. So too Trajan's wholesale exile of delators, oddly described
in *Pan*. 35. Possibly such crimes, especially *calumnia*, were assimilated
in aggravated instances to the capital offence of procuring a condemnation ('coire quo quis . . . iudicio condemnaretur'): *Dig*. 48. 8.
1. 1.

35. usque ad extremum vel constantiam vel audaciam pertulit. The
SC. condemning him would authorize the consul to arrange his
expulsion by a named day: Ulpian, *Dig*. 48. 22. 7. 17.

**36. reliquos legatos graviter increpuit tamquam non omnes quos
mandaverat provincia reos peregisset.** The indifference of senators to
technical legality is again apparent. The charge amounted to
destitutio causae (see V. 13. 2 n.), but this could lie only after the
initiation of a case. So too in the Bassus case the provincial leader
was exposed to a counter-attack after the case was closed, and only
saved by the good sense of the consuls against the will of the House,
IV. 9. 20–21.

10. *To Vestricius Spurinna and Cottia*

Date. This letter belongs to *c*. 100–1, with Ep. 1, not to *c*. 97 with
II. 7 on the death of Cottius. See s. 1 n. and Ep. 1 pref.

Address. For the elder statesman Spurinna and his wife's family
see II. 7. 1 and 3 nn.

1. composuisse me quaedam de filio vestro. For the son's early death
in 97 and his status see II. 7. 3–5 nn. Pliny did not then contemplate
writing his life. It is implied by s. 2—'si in memoriam . . . reduxissem'

—that his death was not very recent. Pliny was a slow worker, slow to write, slow to recite, and slower still to publish (1. 2 nn.). Since 97 he had been busy with public duties, and in 99–100 busier still with his two great extortion cases and his consulship. Hence this Life might well belong to a period later than October 100.

There was a vogue in the Flavio-Trajanic period for short lives of the recent dead, in the style of Tacitus' *Agricola*, though it appears earlier with the Elder Pliny's life of Pomponius Secundus, and Julius Secundus' effort on Julius Africanus, Ep. 5. 3 n., Tac. *Dial.* 14. 4. Titinius Capito and C. Fannius specialized in death scenes as well as in whole lives, I. 17. 3, V. 5. 3 nn., VIII. 12. 4 nn. The obscure Colonus joins in the fun in IX. 9, and the procurator Pollio, VII. 31. 5. Under Domitian, Rusticus and Senecio had written lives of Thrasea Paetus and the elder Helvidius Priscus, I. 5. 2, VII. 19. 5 nn., Tac. *Agric.* 2. 1. Cf. H. A. Musurillo, *Acts of the Pagan Martyrs* (Oxford, 1954), 236 ff., for this type of 'martyr' literature. Also Bardon, *Litt. Lat. Inc.* ii. 207–9.

apud vos fui. For this visit see Ep. 1. 1, 5. Nothing therein contradicts the setting of it *festis diebus*, s. 2.

cum audisses recitasse me. Pliny's recitations before 100 were infrequent, I. 13. 6, II. 19. 1 nn.

2. quae in aliud volumen cogito reservare. As *volumen* means roll, not book (Ep. 5, 'Books', 5 n.), Pliny means only that he is going to enlarge his first draft, not write two 'books' on the theme.

11. *To Julius Genitor*

Date. A relative date is given by the address to Julius Genitor, a recent acquaintance, Ep. 3. 5 n., whom Pliny celebrates by inclusion in this volume. The tone of Pliny's reference to his own *pericula* and his praetorship suggests a time after his consulship, s. 2 'notabilius' n.

Address. For the rhetorician Julius Genitor, whom Pliny seems to rate as a new Quintilian, see Ep. 3. 5 n.

1. Artemidori nostri. Nothing is known of this pupil and son-in-law of the Stoic teacher Musonius Rufus (s. 5 n.) beyond what Pliny tells. He was evidently of the same kidney as Euphrates, I. 10 nn.

2. cum essent philosophi ab urbe summoti fui apud illum in suburbano et . . . fui praetor. This is the crucial sentence for fixing the much disputed date of Pliny's praetorship. The evidence is examined at length in Appendix IV, pp. 763 ff., where it is argued that only the year 93 fits all the evidence about Pliny's career in the period 93–97,

and that there was only one expulsion of philosophers in the
period after 90, dated variously to 93–94 and 95–96 by the different
versions of Eusebius' *Chronicon*, and recorded by Dio (67. 13. 3)
between 92 and 95, and without a date by Gellius, *NA* 15. 11. 3–5,
Suet. *Dom.* 10. 3.

   **pecuniam etiam qua tunc illi ampliore opus erat . . . mutuatus ipse
gratuitam dedi.** R. H. Harte (*JRS* xxv. 51 ff.) proposed an ingenious
but untenable solution of the problem, using the date given by Eusebius for an earlier expulsion of philosophers from Rome in 88–89 or
89–90. He sought to distinguish two chronological phases in the
present paragraph: the first, Pliny's kindness as praetor—supposedly
in 89—when he merely visited Artemidorus *in suburbano* at a time
when philosophers were expelled from the city of Rome only, and
the second, Pliny's loan made in 93–94, when they were expelled
from Italy also. This imports a most uncharacteristic obscurity into
Pliny's Latin, by referring *tunc* to an occasion different from the
immediately preceding sentence—*fui praetor*—to which it is linked,
not disjoined, by *etiam*. Pliny often compresses a narrative without
clear indications of the lapse of time, as in II. 11. 2–8 or III. 9. 2.
But he does not insert misleading adverbs. In VI. 20. 20 'nobis . . . ne
tunc quidem . . . abeundi consilium' *tunc* duly refers back to the
preceding statements. Cf. V. 1. 1, 6 nn. In s. 1 *meritum meum* implies
a single action, and the story means no more than that Artemidorus
was preparing to leave Italy, and hence in need of money, not that
he was permanently domiciled for three or four years outside Rome.
So too Epictetus left Italy after the great expulsion, Gellius, loc. cit.
Eusebius describes both expulsions as from Rome, without mention
of Italy. Gellius and Suetonius refer technically to an expulsion *urbe
Italiaque*, which Suetonius like Dio puts after the trial of Senecio.
Pliny like Dio and the source of Eusebius gives the main effect of
this expulsion—that the philosophers disappeared from Rome. Gellius
in the same section twice substitutes 'the City' for 'the city and
Italy'. He also alone preserves the technicality that the expulsion
was ordered by a decree of the Senate, not as in Eusebius by an
edict of the Princeps. See also s. 3 n.

   notabilius. There is a remarkable difference of tone between the
accounts of Pliny's adventures here and in I. 5. 5–7 and in *Panegyricus* 90. 5, 95. 3. In I. 5 he vaunts his rather sycophantic cleverness
in dodging an awkward question. In the Panegyric, as also in I. 7. 2,
III. 4. 6, he is the virtuous neutral, in danger only through proximity.
But here, as in VII. 33. 7–9, he claims to have outfaced the devil.
The change of tone, and the distant reference to his praetorship,
suggest the confidence of the consular man.

   philosophi. The expulsion of philosophers was an innovation of the Flavian Principate abandoned by its successors. The clique of Thrasea Paetus had made itself troublesome under Nero and in the first year of Vespasian by insisting upon the privileges of the Senate and the limitations of the Princeps' powers (Tac. *Ann.* 13. 49, 14. 48–49, 15. 20–21, 16. 21–22, 26–27; Tac. *Hist.* 4. 9, 40; Suet. *Vesp.* 15). But so far they did not preach a political philosophy, though as individuals they dabbled in Stoicism and Cynicism, as did such supporters of the Principate as Seneca. The gibes at Thrasea Paetus on this score are but passing cuts; compare Tac. *Ann.* 14. 57, 16. 22. Possibly during the reign of Vespasian the Stoic principle that the 'best man' should rule was invoked against Vespasian's determination to found a new dynasty, and Helvidius Priscus perhaps held that the Princeps ought to select and formally adopt as successor the most capable administrator of the day. Such a theory is expressed in a speech attributed by Tacitus to Galba on the occasion of the adoption of Piso in A.D. 69, Tac. *Hist.* 1. 16: 'loco libertatis erit quod eligi coepimus . . . optimum quemque adoptio inveniet', etc. Some phrases in *Panegyricus* 7 point the same way, as does the emergence of *Optimus* as an imperial encomium current already before the death of Nerva, 11. 13. 8 n. But the theory may only have been coined to adorn the fact of Nerva's adoption of Trajan; cf. Syme, *Tac.* 206 f., 233 f., who is sceptical as usual. Its only trace within the Flavian period is the anecdote in which Vespasian addresses to Helvidius his insistent remark about the succession, given by Suetonius as 'aut filios sibi successuros aut neminem'; Dio 65. 12. 1; Suet. *Vesp.* 25.

Otherwise the philosophers are said in Dio simply to 'attack monarchy', 'to teach things unsuitable to the times', 'to praise democracy', and also to criticize the personal behaviour of Titus. Marcus Aurelius summarized their teaching as 'equality before the law', 'free speech', and the 'liberty of subjects' (1. 14. 1). The assertion that Helvidius stirred up the mob and preached revolution is given only as an enemy's accusation, not as a fact, and recalls the conservative Dio Chrysostom's criticism of the radical Cynic tub-thumpers. The doctrine of Helvidius and his friends seems to have been a mixture of Stoic and Cynic thought in the style known a little later from Chrysostom's tracts *de regno*, addressed by the latter to Trajan, when, having fallen foul of Domitian, he made his peace with the Principate after the succession of his friend Nerva (Cassius Dio 65. 12. 1–2, 13. 1–3, 15. 5; Dio Chrys. *Or.* 32. 9. On Chrysostom see X. 81. 1 n.) Dislike of the personal arrogance of philosophers played an understandable part in the repression (Dio 65. 13. 1a). Compare phrases such as *intempestivam sapientiam*, etc., aimed at the set of Helvidius (Tac. *Ann.* 16. 22; *Hist.* 3. 81).

Two kinds of philosopher are to be distinguished, itinerant teachers of varying ideologies (such as Artemidorus and Euphrates) who were not usually Roman citizens, and members of the governing classes. The novelty lay in the political use of philosophy by the latter, and this may be due to the influence of Musonius Rufus, s. 5 n.

See Rostovtzeff, *SEHRE*[1], ch. iv. 109 ff., nn. 12–14, *CAH* xi. 8 ff., with different emphasis. C. Wirzsubsky, *Libertas as a Political Idea, &c.* (Cambridge, 1950, 138 ff., 147, 154 ff.), lays less stress on the philosophical element. Syme, *Tac.* 207 f., 233 f. (philosophy), 558 f. (Thrasea), is yet more sceptical.

mussantibus magnis quibusdam et locupletibus amicis. No doubt the cautious Corellius and Frontinus, or Verginius Rufus, raised eyebrows (II. 1. 8–9, V. 1. 5, IX. 13. 6). So too Musonius Rufus was rebuked for borrowing money, *fr.* 37. But his debts *ex pulcherrimis causis* are not due to the smallness of his estate, as Sirago absurdly suggests, op. cit. 50.

in suburbano. A villa like that of Suetonius, I. 24. 3.

3. atque haec feci ... septem amicis meis aut occisis aut relegatis. This sentence fairly conjoins all Pliny's acts and dates them to the time of the trial, *pace* Harte. The list of male victims agrees with that given by Tac. *Agric.* 45, which shows that the trial or series of trials was later than August 93. Pliny's statement ties all these events to his praetorship, and hence to September–December 93. Four months is ample time, despite Otto's doubts. The main trials after the conspiracy of Piso were finished in a fortnight (Tac. *Ann.* 15. 53, 69, 74), and the complicated Classicus case required only a month of the Senate's time for its three sessions, Ep. 9. 1 n.

Senecione. See I. 5. 3, VII. 19. 5, 33. 4 nn. for Herennius Senecio, who refused promotion after the quaestorship, his part in the accusation of Baebius Massa, and Carus' indictment of him, on a treason charge, for composing a life of the elder Helvidius.

Rustico. See I. 5. 2 n. for Q. Junius Arulenus Rusticus' earlier career, possible consulship, political opposition, and Stoic tendencies. His biography of Thrasea Paetus, and eulogy of the elder Helvidius, formed the basis of the charge, unless Suetonius is confused, *Dom.* 10. 3, Tac. *Agric.* 2. A descendant (II. 18. 1 n.), consul in 133 and 162, Q. Junius Rusticus, turned the young M. Aurelius to philosophy (*Ad seipsum*, I. 7. 2).

Maurico. For Junius Mauricus, brother of Rusticus, and most sensible man in this group, see I. 5. 10 n. He returned from relegation in 97, ibid.

Helvidio. The younger Helvidius Priscus, son of the elder by his first wife, not Fannia, lived in cautious retirement, but held all offices up to a consulship (before 86, since his name is not in *Fast. Pot.*) IX. 13. 1–3 n. He was charged with publishing a disguised criticism of Domitian's behaviour as a husband, Suet. *Dom.* 10. 4, *PIR*² H 60. In 97 Pliny sought to avenge his memory by attacking Publicius Certus, a senator who misbehaved as a juror at the trial, and later published his speech *De Helvidi Ultione* at great length, IX. 13. 2, 24 nn. For the descendants of Priscus see IV. 21 nn.

In all these cases the anecdotal sources relate only isolated elements of the charges against the accused. The elder Helvidius had formed a faction out of his friends and relatives against Vespasian, and formulated a theory of opposition (Dio 65. 12. 2, and above). But there is no evidence, except the expulsion of philosophers, that this set continued its former line under Domitian, though he made a clean sweep of the Helvidian coterie, late in his reign, after trying to placate them with high office or the offer of it.

Gratilla. Apparently the wife of Arulenus Rusticus, and possibly daughter of a senator Verulanus Severus (v. I. 8; Tac. *Ann.* 15. 3; *PIR*¹ V 288). She may be the Verulania Gratilia or Gratilla who sided with the Flavians at Rome in 69, when Rusticus was trying to mediate on the Vitellian side, Tac. *Hist.* 3. 69; cf. I. 5. 2 n. Possibly her protection saved the Junii brothers when the elder Helvidius was condemned, under Vespasian.

Arria, Fannia. This tedious pair, mother and daughter, inherited from the elder Arria, wife of that Caecina Paetus who after an unsuccessful conspiracy against Claudius was inspired to suicide by her example, a tiresome obstinacy and a traditional 'republicanism' that made them fit mates, Arria for Thrasea Paetus, and Fannia for the elder Helvidius. The ladies stood nobly by their husbands when Thrasea was executed and Helvidius exiled in the aftermath of the Pisonian conspiracy. Then in the affair of 93 both were involved with Senecio in the composition of the Life of Helvidius. They returned from exile in 97 and stirred up Pliny's attempted prosecution of Publicius Certus, the enemy of the younger Helvidius. Ep. 16, VII. 19. 3–5, IX. 13. 3–5, 15–16 nn.; Tac. *Ann.* 16. 34. Arria was dead and Fannia in a decline by the date of VII. 19. For their other family ties see Ep. 16. 2 n. All the facts about Fannia seem to come from Pliny, cf. *PIR*² F 118.

amicis meis. Pliny's direct connexion with the family of Helvidius seems to have been very slight before his accidental association with Senecio in the trial of Massa brought him into the circle, and made him the ladies' friend (VII. 19. 10, IX. 13. 3). But his friendship with the Junii was older, I. 5. 5, 14. 1 nn.

impendere idem exitium certis ... notis augurarer. In VII. 27. 14 he relates one of these portents, and claims to have been secretly

accused by Mettius Carus; he hints the same in IV. 24. 4–5. His
share in the too successful prosecution of Baebius Massa is the
supposed cause, VII. 33. 8–9. But the real ground of these boasts is
his feeling that he had not done enough for his friends, VII. 19. 10 n.:
'non feci tamen paria'.

5. C. Musonium socerum eius . . . cum admiratione dilexi. For other
oriental pupils of Musonius see I. 10. 1 'Euphrates' n. Musonius
Rufus, a Roman knight from Etruria, friend of the wealthy senators
Rubellius Plautus and Barea Soranus, was active in Roman society
between A.D. 60 and 65, was then involved in the conspiracy of Piso,
exiled to Gyarus, and returned under Galba, when he prosecuted his
rival P. Egnatius Celer, former accuser of Soranus (Tac. *Ann.* 14. 59,
15. 71; Tac. *Hist.* 4. 10, 40; Dio 62. 27; Musonius *fr.* 47). In his
harangues to the Flavian troops in 69, 'bona pacis ac belli discrimina
disserens', he was the first to apply philosophy to senatorial politics,
Tac. *Hist.* 3. 81. It may be through his influence, no *Graeculus* but
an upper-class Italian, that Stoic arguments were adopted by the
hitherto constitutionalist faction of Helvidius. Musonius was a
teacher rather than a writer, largely concerned with the morality of
private life, but he also discussed political themes such as the 'good
king', *rel.* viii, and the relation between governors and governed, *fr.*
31: 'they do not last long who towards their subjects are accustomed
to say not "it is my duty" but "it is in my power"'—an obvious
hit at Nero (cf. Suet. *Nero* 37. 3). As an opponent of Demetrius the
Cynic he survived the first expulsion of philosophers under Vespasian,
c. 74 or earlier, but was ejected later and recalled by Titus (Tac.
Hist. 4. 40; Dio 65. 13. 1–2; Jerome, *Chron.* under A.D. 79; Themistius
Or. 13. 173 c). For the dates see VII. 19. 4 n.

For the life of Musonius, with full citations of evidence, and his
brief essays, see O. Hense, *Musonii Rufi reliquiae* (Lipsiae, 1905)
pref., *PIR*[1] M 549. For his political and social theory, Goodenough,
'Political philosophy of Hellenistic kingship', *Yale Class. Stud.* i. 94;
M. P. Charlesworth, *Five Men* (Camb., Mass., 1936), 33 ff.

socerum eius. This would be a mixed marriage, between a provincial Greek and an Italian Roman citizen unless Artemidorus held
the Roman citizenship. But Pliny seems to use the proper names for
such gentry, cf. Claudius Aristion, VI. 31. 3, Fonteius Magnus, V. 20. 4.
His Greeks with single names would seem to be non-citizens,
Euphrates, I. 10, Isaeus, II. 3, Polyaenus, VII. 6. 6.

per aetatem. Pliny was not old enough to have heard Musonius until
about the time of his second exile. The date of his death is uncertain.

**Artemidorum ipsum iam tum cum in Syria tribunus militarem . . .
complexus sum.** So too he met Euphrates then, i.e. *c.* A.D. 81–2,

1. 10. 2 n. Musonius had been in Syria during his exile, s. 7 n., but returned before Pliny's tribunate. Hence the emphatic *ipsum iam tum*.

6. **ex omnibus qui nunc se philosophos vocant.** For the pullulation of bogus philosophers in Trajanic Rome see I. 10. 6–7 nn.

7. **a C. Musonio . . . gener adsumeretur.** The match may have been made during Musonius' second exile, when he visited Syria and conversed with local princes, *rel.* viii. I. 4–7. So too Euphrates married the daughter of a Syrian 'provinciae princeps', I. 10. 8 n.

12. *To Catilius Severus*

Not datable. For the still praetorian senator Catilius Severus see I. 22 pref.

1. **veniam ad cenam.** This note is in the same genre as I. 15, and shows Pliny's skill at variations, noted on a large scale in Ep. 9. 2 n. In I. 15 he dilates on the food and entertainment offered; here they are briefly summarized, and the theme is the length of the dinner, illustrated by a literary-historical parallel. Here he is the eager guest, there the host of an absent guest.

    Socraticis tantum sermonibus abundet, in his quoque teneat modum. Guillemin, ad loc., quotes M. A. Grant, *Ancient Theories of the Laughable* (Madison, 1924), for Socrates as the model of polite conversation in Panaetius and later. By *modum* he means in time, not decency, as the sequel shows.

2. **erunt officia antelucana in quae incidere impune ne Catoni quidem licuit.** For the *salutatio* in the first hour of day see Ep. 5. 9, 7. 4, and for the rising of ordinary folk before dawn see X. 96. 7 n.; Carcopino, *Daily Life*, 172.

    The story evidently derives from Caesar's *Anticato*. The younger Cato was known, like the Elder, for deep drinking—*vitium Catonis*, Plut. *Cato Minor* 6; Sen. *tranq. anim.* 17. 4, 9; Cic. *de sen.* 46; Martial 2. 89. Guillemin (*VL*, 119) notes the sequence in Horace Od. 3. 21 of *Socratici sermones* and drunken Cato, and sees Pliny's effort as an obscure imitation. But in Horace it is the elder Cato—'*prisci*'— not the younger.

13. *To Voconius Romanus*

Date. A good while after his delivery of the *Panegyricus* in September 100, s. I n., and before his recitation of the final version recorded in Ep. 18.

Address. For Pliny's Spanish friend, now a senator, see II. 13. 4 n.

1. **librum, quo nuper optimo principi consul gratias egi, misi.** The speech was delivered at a meeting of the Senate in September 100, at the special injunction of the Fathers that a public vote of thanks should be proposed to Trajan, *Pan.* 1. 2, 90. 3. For the month, ibid. 92. 4. Cf. Durry, ad loc.

Pliny's slow rate of work makes it probable that by *nuper* he means that many weeks or months have passed. Cf. II. 13. 8.

3. **ordo saltem et transitus et figurae.** Cf. Ep. 18. 8–10, about the Panegyric, where he notes that a select audience preferred *severissima quaeque*. These devices mark the 'middle style', cf. Quintilian 12. 10. 60, 'medius ... modus translationibus crebrior et figuris ... iocundior', etc. I. 2. 1–2 nn. On the difficulty of writing panegyrics see Ep. 18. 6–7 and VI. 27.

invenire praeclare . . . etiam barbari solent, disponere apte . . . nisi eruditis negatum est. The original version was less exuberant than Pliny's norm, Ep. 18. 1 n. In I. 20. 16 ff. and IX. 26 he does not prefer the tricks of the trade to the fine phrase and good delivery, though this came with difficulty to a man of his physique, II. 11. 15 n. The use of *barbarus* as the opposite of *eruditus*, as in Velleius 2. 73. 1, seems rare: *Thesaurus* II. 1739, 1743. Pliny uses the word twice elsewhere, but in its normal sense, VIII. 4. 3, 24. 4.

4. **ut in pictura lumen non alia res magis quam umbra commendat.** For Pliny's range of style in the *Panegyricus* see Ep. 18. 9–10. Cf. II. 5. 5. The observation about light was obvious to anyone who knew Hellenistic painting, and implies no deep knowledge of theory. Cf. Pliny, *NH* 35. 127, 131; Quintilian 12. 10. 4. Longinus (*de sublim.* 17. 2) and Plutarch (*de Herod. mal.* 28. 3) use the comparison, which may come direct from Cicero (*de Or.* 3. 101).

14. *To Acilius*

Date. Earlier than the account of the similar murder of the consul Dexter in 105 and later than September 100, ss. 1, 6 nn.

Address. Acilius may be the Cisalpine from Patavium of I. 14. 6, P. Acilius, rather than Acilius Rufus, consul in 107, V. 20. 6 n., or the consular orator Pomponius Rufus who included this among his many names, Ep. 9. 33 n. Index *Π* reads *Ad Patilium*. But possibly 'Atilius noster' of I. 9. 8, &c., is meant, who otherwise receives no letters, though thrice mentioned.

1. **rem atrocem . . . Larcius Macedo vir praetorius a servis suis passus est.** So too in 105 Afranius Dexter was slain while holding the consulship, and his household was involved, VIII. 14. 12 n. Cases were

sufficiently rare to merit attention. Tacitus comments at length on
the servile murder of Pedanius Secundus, *Ann.* 14. 42–45. Pliny's
great alarm, s. 5, and his silence, suggest that two contemporary
such murders were not yet known to him.

Larcius Macedo. Several senatorial Larcii are known in this period.
Two Vespasianic figures were of praetorian grade, Licinius and
A. Lepidus, and two consulars are known, A. Priscus (110) and M. Silo
(82) (Ep. 5. 17 'Career' n.; *PIR*¹ s.v.; Garzetti, *Inc.* 82–83; *FO*).
Possibly this man is the adopted son of a household favourite. His
own son, A. Larcius Macedo, governed Galatia and reached the
consulship under Hadrian: *AE* 1946, n. 178, 1954, n. 66; *PIR*¹ s.v.

servisse patrem suum. This, it seems, is the only case in the earlier
Principate where it is unambiguously stated that a senator's father
had been a slave, though the Claudian consular Curtius Rufus was
reputed the son of a gladiator, VII. 27. 2 n. Even Tacitus' general
statement, 'plerisque senatoribus non aliunde originem trahi' is hard
to substantiate; cf. Syme, *Tac.* 612–13; Tac. *Ann.* 13. 27, cf. 11. 24.
The Claudian censor L. Vitellius, father of the future emperor, was
supposed the descendant of a freedman, Suet. *Vit.* 2. For the technical process of *natalium restitutio* and the parallel grant of the *anuli
aurei*, whereby the stigma of servile birth was legally removed, see
VIII. 6. 4 n. Normally three generations of free birth were required
before promotion to equestrian and senatorial status.

3. concubinae . . . concurrunt. Carcopino is scandalized by this evidence for the harem life of wealthy Romans, *Daily Life*, 102.

4. ita vivus vindicatus ut occisi solent. For the wholesale execution of
the *familia* in such cases, including no doubt the odalisqs, see VIII.
14. 12 n. Execution was rapid. They do not wait for the runaways
to be found, cf. ibid. n.

5. vides quot periculis . . . simus obnoxii. Compare the speech of
Cassius the jurist in Tac. *Ann.* 14. 43–44 on this theme. Pliny's logic
seems to be scared out of him in the next sentence—'non enim
iudicio domini sed scelere perimuntur'—since he had stressed the
cruelty of Macedo in this instance.

6. dies feriatus patitur plura contexi. Hence Pliny will not be busy in
the courts. This suggests a date later than his Prefecture of Saturn
at least.

cum in publico Romae lavaretur. Cf. II. 17. 26, 'balinea meritoria'
were used by Pliny. This is a remarkably 'democratic' facet of
Roman social life. The ordinary price of admission, one *quadrans*,
excluded only the poorest (Horace *S.* 1. 3. 137; Sen. *Ep.* 86. 9;
Juv. 2. 152; cf. Carcopino, op. cit. 314 n. 41).

15. *To Silius Proculus*

Date. Earlier than the period of Pliny's versification, which begins with IV. 14, s. 2 n.

Address. Silius Proculus is not yet known. His names are shared by consuls of 94, Silius Decianus, and 109, Julius Proculus. He might be the writer of satires anathematized by Juvenal I. 20; *schol. Vall.*, *PIR*¹ S 514.

1. **petis ut libellos in secessu legam.** Cf. VII. 9. 1 'in secessu . . . studere'. Elsewhere Pliny always uses *secessus, secedere*, of life away from Rome, e.g. Ep. 21. 2, V. 14. 1, IX. 10. 2. So Pliny is about to go on holiday. The other references to absence from Rome in this book are in Ep. 4. 2—his hasty visit to Tifernum in 99—the projected dash to Comum in Ep. 6. 6, and the visit to Spurinna, Ep. I. 1, 10 1.

2. **poeticen ipsam religiosissime veneror.** But he does not claim to be a fellow practicioner yet, as in IV. 14, 27, V. 15.

3. **esse opus pulchrum nec supprimendum . . . si modo mihi non imposuit recitatio tua.** Pliny is rather cool in his praise for once, avoiding praise of the verses by praising the delivery. For the customs of formal recitation see I. 13 nn. Proculus evidently read only a selection of his many volumes.

16. *To Nepos*

Date determinable only as between the return of Fannia from exile in 97 (IX. 13. 5) and her expected death in VII. 19.

Address. For the literary senator Maecilius or Metilius Nepos see II. 3 pref. Index II is unfortunately without the name here.

2. **neptis haec Arriae illius quae marito . . . exemplum fuit.** The family of the elder Arria, wife of A. Caecina Paetus, and mother of the younger Arria, is not known, but she was connected to the satirist Persius Flaccus, who wrote her life. *PIR*², A 1113; Probus, *Vit. Pers.* For Fannia, her granddaughter and second wife of the elder Helvidius Priscus, see Ep. II. 3, VII. 19, IX. 13. 3 nn.

The story is told also by Dio 60. 16. 5–6; he adds only that Arria was a close friend of Messalina, who was foremost in harrying the conspirators (ibid. 15. 5). Other references are incidental. Her fame lived on in popular memory, as in the epitaph from Anagnia, *ILS* 6261,

3. aegrotabat Caecina Paetus. This man, consul suffect in 37, seems to be no relation of C. Caecina Largus, consul throughout 42, the year of Paetus' troubles, nor yet of the Vitellian general A. Caecina Allienus. *PIR²* C 101–3.

filius decessit. A second son survived, C. Caecina Paetus, to become consul in 70. *PIR²* C 104.

7. Scribonianus arma in Illyrico contra Claudium moverat. Tacitus' summary closely follows Pliny—'pater Scriboniani Camillus arma per Dalmatiam moverat'. Dio puts the events in 42. There was an urban conspiracy of many knights and senators headed by L. Annius Vinicianus, who stirred up L. Arruntius Camillus Scribonianus, legate of Dalmatia in command of two legions. (Dio 60. 15–16; Suet. *Claud.* 13. 2, 35. 2; Tac. *Ann.* 12. 52; Tac. *Hist.* 1. 89, 2. 75; *CAH* x. 671, *PIR²* A 701, 1140.)

The movement was over in fifteen days (Suet.), so Paetus must have been with Camillus in Dalmatia, whence the presence of his wife (cf. Ep. 9. 19). When the legions withdrew their support Camillus fled to Issa, and according to Dio died 'voluntarily'. But Tacitus, *Hist.* 2. 75, supports Pliny, and names the soldier who slew Camillus.

9. eadem apud Claudium uxori Scriboniani. It is remarkable that even so cautious a person as Pliny tells this tale in a way that glorifies open rebellion against an emperor who had not suffered *damnatio memoriae*. But Camillus had posed as a restorer of the old Republic, not as a claimant to the Principate. The family fêted its connexion with a daughter of Pompey the Great, *ILS* 976.

apud Claudium. The phrase often refers to trial *intra cubiculum*, common under Claudius. But Dio states that the trial took place before the Senate, with consuls presiding, in the presence of Claudius, who had resigned his consulship (op. cit. 10. 1, 16. 3).

uxori. Apparently one Vibia, Tac. *Ann.* loc. cit. She was relegated, but her son, also involved, was spared, Tac. *Ann.* ibid., Dio, loc. cit.

10. 'vis ergo filiam tuam . . . mori mecum?' This very situation arose in 66, when Thrasea, ever sensible, persuaded the younger Arria to live for Fannia, Tac. *Ann.* 16. 34. For Thrasea's politics see Ep. 11. 2, 'philosophi' n., and for his wife Arria, ibid. 3 n. His full names do not include Fannius—P. Clodius Thrasea Paetus. So his daughter was presumably called Clodia Fannia. Pliny's biographical friend C. Fannius (v. 5. 1) may be a connexion; the name is rare in society. *PIR²* F 112–18 gives only four post-Augustan Fannii, including Pliny's friends.

12. focilata. Pliny uses this rare word again in Ep. 14. 4.

13. unde colligitur quod initio dixi. Pliny is following the *lex scholastica* that required three instances to prove a point, II. 20. 9, hence the three obscure *gesta* of Arria. Traub (*T.A.Ph.A.* 86, 213 ff.) regards this as the first of Pliny's historical essays, followed by IV. 11, VI. 16, VII. 33, chosen to supplement the lack of political material from contemporary life noted in Ep. 20. 11. But the arrangement is more anecdotal, as in II. 20 and VII. 27.

17. *To Julius Servianus*

Date. The absence of Julius Ursus Servianus on official duties, s. 1 n., in a remote and dangerous place, may coincide with his legateship of Pannonia or with employment in the first Dacian war of Trajan. Either would fit a date *c.* 100–1. Ursus may have remained in Pannonia from 98 onwards until replaced by Glitius Agricola *c.* 101. VIII. 23. 5 n.

Address. Servianus was one of the pillars of the régime of Trajan, as appears in the incident recorded in VII. 6. 8. For his career see VI. 26 pref., VIII. 23. 5 n. Syme (*JRS* 47. 131) notes that this is the only indication of his presence in the Dacian war. Though only two short letters are addressed to him they reveal a special intimacy, cf. VI. 26. 3. It was he who secured Pliny the *ius trium liberorum*, X. 2. 1.

1. rectene omnia quod iam pridem epistulae tuae cessant? For this kind of 'courtesy note' see I. 11 n.

occupatus. As in IV. 26. 2 'occupatissimus maximae provinciae praefuturus', and in Ep. 5. 7, of the Elder Pliny's career, the word here connotes official duties. So too *occupationes*, I. 10. 10, III. 5. 18, X. 56. 1. But a wider connotation occurs in II. 2. 2, VI. 4. 1, *et al.*

tabellario misso. On postal arrangements see II. 12. 6 n.

3. timentem . . . pro capite amicissimo. Nowhere does Pliny express such strong fears for an absent friend, save for his sick wife, VI. 4. Contrast I. 11.

18. *To Vibius Severus*

Date. Probably some months later than his consulship, and some time later than Ep. 13, where the Panegyric is still being trimmed for publication. Possibly later than 102, if the final version of the *Panegyricus* is taken to refer to the Dacian victory of 102 (16, 17). Cf. *Lustrum*, vi (1961), 290.

Address. Vibius Severus comes from Mediolanum or Ticinum, IV. 28. 1 n., and is addressed on literary themes again in IV. 28 and perhaps

IX. 22. A like-named centurion of the Praetorians is known. *CIL* v. 5228, *AE* 1948, n. 68.

1. **officium . . . iniunxit mihi ut rei publicae nomine principi gratias agerem.** This repeats the substance of *Pan.* 1. 2. His personal thanks for his office are reserved for the end of the speech, 90. 3, the bulk of which is a *publica gratiarum actio*. If this took place with every change of consuls, it is not surprising that the Senate was easily bored, ss. 6–7. Verginius Rufus as consul for January 97 was preparing a similar speech, II. 1. 5, and this year Pliny's consulship was the third or fourth turn in the year's cycle. In addition the consuls designate regularly made proposals *in honorem principis*, VI. 27. 1.

eadem illa spatiosius et uberius volumine amplecti. For Pliny's habit of enlarging the published version of speeches see IV. 5. 4. Durry (*Pan.* 5 ff.) estimates that the original was only a third or a quarter of the final version. Any reader will notice how each chapter contains the elaboration of a single theme at great length. The original would contains the same number of themes much more briefly treated. So too of his speech *Pro Patria*, II. 5. 3: 'inde . . . liber crevit dum ornare patriam . . . gaudemus'.

2. **ut futuri principes non quasi a magistro sed tamen sub exemplo praemonerentur.** Pliny had in mind the sermons favoured by the political philosophers of the day, and their senatorial admirers, Ep. II. 2–3 nn. He himself evidently attempted more than was usual, but the Panegyric is factual and practical, very different from essays on the art of government such as Dio Chrysostom's speeches *de regno*, or Musonius Rufus' shorter sermon on kingly duty (*rel.* viii).

sub exemplo. Cf. II. 6. 6 n.

4. **cum amicis recitare voluissem non per codicillos . . . admoniti.** For the formalities of the *salon* see I. 13. 4 n. This seems to be only the second or third time that Pliny had recited a speech (II. 19. 1 n.), and is the only full account of his own recitals. The pros and cons of recitation are discussed in II. 19, V. 12, VII. 17.

ut adicerem tertium diem exegerunt. This passage is our best evidence for the length of recitals. Usually two sessions seem to be the most that could be endured, IV. 5. 2, VIII. 21. 4, IX. 27. 1. Works exceeding a single roll in length were seldom read in their entirety, Ep. 15. 3 n., I. 13. 2, IX. 27. 1. If he read the whole Panegyric in its present form, covering some 90 Teubner pages, the length of three books of the Letters, in three sessions, he can hardly have taken less than 1½–2 hours for each—*experto crede*—though Durry (op. cit. 8) and Syme (*Tac.* 94) allow only three hours for the whole job, and conclude that an hour was the normal length of a recitation. They underestimate the toughness of the Roman audience. But as Pliny originally intended only two sessions he probably read lengthy excerpts on each occasion. He certainly read the whole of his second and longer book of verses in two sessions, on the principle 'lego . . . omnia ut omnia emendem', VIII. 21. 4.

6. in senatu . . . ubi . . . gravari . . . puncto temporis solebamus. For the decline of the Senate's standards as a parliament see II. 11. 18, VIII. 14. 2–8 nn.

liberius ideoque etiam libentius scribitur. Pliny, like Tacitus, is satisfied with the restored but limited freedom of the Trajanic age. Cf. Tac. *Hist.* I. 1; *Agric.* 3. 1, 'sentire quae velis et quae sentias dicere'.

7. res . . . nunc ut vera ita amabilis. This is a fairly ingenuous testimonial to Pliny's belief in his approbation of Trajan expressed in the *Panegyric*, qualified only by the admission that it was a *laudatio*.

8. animadverti enim severissima quaeque vel maxime satisfacere. In Ep. 13. 3–4 he implies that the Panegyric combined richness of language with contrasting passages in a more restrained style, and hopes that it will succeed. Here he proclaims its success.

severissima. Here of style, as in v. 17. 2: 'exilia plenis severis iucunda mutabat', not of content as in II. 5. 6, v. 13. 8. Ordinarily Pliny champions the *stilus laetior*, which he realized suited his natural exuberance, I. 20. 20–22, II. 5. 5–6, VII. 12, IX. 26 nn. At most he gives a half-hearted support, as in I. 2, II. 19. 5–6, to the plainer style, but is ready as here to compromise. In actual forensic speeches, as in the original Panegyric, he had perforce to make some use of plainness, but enriches his speeches for publication. He apparently approves the 'middle way' of Quintilian rather than the full 'Asian' extravagance, and dislikes the simplicity of the *veteres*, see I. 2. 1–2 n.

9. Memini quidem me non multis recitasse quod omnibus scripsi. Guillemin (*VL* 83 ff.), using Quintilian's discussion of the publication of speeches (12. 10. 49 ff.), distinguishes between the ordinary reading public—here *omnibus*—of *mediocriter docti* (Ep. I. 10. 5) and the coteries of *eruditi* (II. 10. 5)—here *non multis*. The latter tended to be Atticist in taste, and objected to the publication of speeches in the form in which they were delivered to the general public or juries since these included *indocti* and *rustici*, for whom rhetorical tricks were necessary which a serious writer would disdain. 'At quod libris dedicatum in exemplum edatur, et tersum et limatum et ad legem ac regulam compositum esse oportere.' But Quintilian held that speeches should be published in full: 'neque aliud esse oratio scripta

quam monumentum actionis . . . editio habebit omnia'. Pliny in his
discussion of this theme in I. 20. 9–10 follows Quintilian. Here he
outdoes him in that he expands the original text (s. 1).

G.'s analysis is not exact. There are three audiences, the common audience of juries and assemblies, the *mediocriter docti* who are
not mentioned by Quintilian, and the *eruditi* mentioned by both.
The two latter both attend *auditoria*. Pliny is surprised that his
audience preferred Atticism, because in II. 19. 5–6, probably within
the last twelve months, when considering recitation of his *In Priscum*,
he noted a preference for the Asian style in the 'listening' public.
' Quotus quisque tam rectus auditor quem non potius dulcia haec et
sonantia quam austera et pressa delectant?' That was the casual
Roman audience whose habits are described in I. 13, and who flocked
to hear the voluble Euphrates and Isaeus (I. 10. 5–6, II. 3). The
present audience was more discriminating because it was hand-
picked (s. 4), and Pliny's literary friends were mostly Atticist; cf.
I. 2. 20, II. 5. 5, VII. 12, IX. 26. 13. Even Pompeius Saturninus
flavoured his 'Middle Way' with a strong dash of Atticism, I. 8. 3 n.,
16. 2–4.

**10. ac mihi quidem confido in hoc genere materiae laetioris stili
constare rationem, cum ea potius quae pressius . . . scripsi possint
videri accersita.** Pliny does not agree with the present verdict, and
this aside, though limited to *hoc genus*, i.e. the laudatory theme,
reveals his real preference. In II. 19. 6 he admits that for ordinary
court-work the stricter style was more useful. Certainly the final
version of the Panegyric contains much that is *elata et excelsa*, e.g.
30–31, 34–35. For Pliny's fluctuation between the Atticist and the
Middle style see I. 2. 1 n.

pressius et adstrictius. These are standard terms, I. 20. 21, II. 19. 6,
VII. 12. 4, IX. 26. 12. But *hilarius* and *exsultantius* are variants of
the stock epithets, not used again by Pliny. In Ep. I. 7 *hilaritas*
refers to the naughtiness of the content, not to the style.

19. *To Calvisius Rufus*

Date not closely determinable. Earlier than v. 6, where this estate is
in hand, and later than 100, because Pliny is at leisure, s. 4 n. The
reference to *socrus* does not help, s. 8 n. Sirago fantastically dated
this letter, and the purchase in it, to *c*. 110, on a misinterpretation
of s. 2 (n.).

Address. For Calvisius, compatriot from Comum and business adviser of Pliny, see II. 20 pref. Similar consultations occur in v. 7,
VIII. 2.

1. praedia agris meis vicina atque etiam inserta venalia sunt. The details in ss. 3 and 5 agree with the description of Pliny's estate at Tifernum Tiberinum with its topiary,i ts hunting facilities,i ts combination of woodland, vineyard, abundance of water and ploughland, v. 6. 8–9; 16–17, 32, 35, 46, IX. 36. 6. Even the weakness of the tenantry is parallel (IX. 37 nn.). Since the reference in s. 7 ('nec ibi quisquam' n.) excludes Comum, the home of Calvisius, the identification with the Tuscan estate is conclusive.

2. utraque eadem opera eodem viatico invisere. For the difficulty of administering scattered estates cf. I. 4. 1, VI. 30. 2, VIII. 20. 3.

sub eodem procuratore ac paene isdem actoribus habere. This is the land agent and his staff who administer the estate as a whole, not the servile manager of the home farm (*vilicus*). Cf. VI. 30. 4: 'rusticorum . . . praediorum administratio poscit durum aliquem et agrestem', etc. Sirago (*It. agr.* 114 f.) identified these agents with *exactores* of IX. 37. 3, oddly supposing that Pliny had no staff to manage his great estates until he introduced the share-cropping scheme in 107. But the term *actor* is used for any type of agricultural manager, including even *vilicus*, as Sirago's own citations show (op. cit. 180, e.g. Columella I. 8. 5; Scaevola, *Dig.* 20. 1. 32).

Nothing in this letter suggests that Pliny intended to introduce the share-cropping system of IX. 37 into this estate, or that he had yet turned his mind to it. Instead he assumes that he must follow the normal method of leasing.

3. sumptus atriensium topiariorum fabrorum. *Dig.* 33. 7. 12. 5 distinguishes between the *familia quae villam servat* including *fabri* for maintenance and those *ad usum rusticum parati*.

4. illa peregrinatio inter sua. As in I. 4. 1 Pliny speaks as a man with leisure to travel around: hence the date is later than 100.

5. silvis quae materiam et ex ea reditum sicut modicum ita statum praestant. For these woodlands see v. 6. 8 n. Pliny does not take the exaggerated view of the value of timber held by certain opponents of Columella (3. 3. 1–3, s. 7 n.) who puts the income of cutting timber at the high figure of S.100 per acre.

6. sed haec felicitas terrae imbecillis cultoribus fatigatur. nam possessor prior saepius vendidit pignora, et dum reliqua colonorum minuit ad tempus, vires in posterum exhausit. What is the system of land tenure? The *coloni* and *cultores* are evidently the same persons, peasants who provide their own equipment, which has been sold up and needs replacing. In VII. 30. 3, discussing the difficulty of letting

his farms, Pliny remarks: 'adeo rarum est invenire idoneos conductores'. T. Frank (*Ec. Survey*, v. 178 f., nn. 58–59) suggested that
by *coloni* Pliny here meant *conductores* of a kind known from the
inscriptions of the imperial estates in Africa, who were not working
farmers, but middlemen, who took up large blocks of land and
sublet to peasants called *coloni*. (For the system see IX. 37. 3 n.)
Frank based this partly on the system of *instrumentum* (below),
and partly on the usage of Columella, the main authority on agriculture in this period, who sometimes uses the two terms interchange-
ably (e.g. 1. 7. 1–6). But in Pliny, as in Columella, the system is
simpler than on the imperial estates. Pliny only uses *conductor* this
once. Elsewhere as here, in X. 8. 5, IX. 37. 2, he is dealing directly
with the actual cultivators, who are at once *coloni* by occupation
and *conductores* in their legal contract. This agrees with the usage in
contemporary legal texts cited below, and a passage in Gaius
(*Dig.* 19. 2. 25). See W. E. Heitland, *Agricola* (Cambridge, 1921),
317 f., 371 f.; *RE* iv, *conductio* 859 f., *colonatus* 486; Rostovtzeff,
SEHRE[1], 190 ff.; Sirago, *Italia agraria*, 155; E. Balogh, *Studi . . .
Paoli* (1956), 48.

Frank mistook the scale of operations. In VI. 3 a farm of less than
fifty acres is let to one man directly, and in VIII. 2 even the wine
merchants to whom Pliny sold the produce of the home farm operate
on a small scale. There is no room here for third parties between the
procurator of s. 2 and the farmers, though on occasion very big
landowners may have taken Martial's advice, 4. 64. 34: 'uni dedite
Setiam colono', cf. Columella 1. 7. 3. Sirago, op. cit. 154 f., finds
no evidence before the late second century for large-scale *conductio*
in Italy, even on imperial estates. He cites *ILS* 8555 for the earliest
imperial *colonus fundi* in Italy. Cf. Balogh, art. cit. 45, 48.

The bulk of Pliny's land is let in small parcels thus, under the
general control of the procurator. But a fair acreage around the villa
was retained under direct management of a *vilicus* and slave workers,
VIII. 2. 1 n., IX. 16, 20. 2. It was for such owners, interested in farming
their own land, but not able to live permanently on their estates,
that Columella wrote his book, which is about the *vilicus* system and
not tenancy-farming, though his ideal owner is a resident landowner
(1. 6. 1–3). The existence of this class of absentee owner is shown in
references of the lawyers of the first century and later to the visits of
such owners to their tenants' holdings at harvest time: *Dig.* 7. 8.
10. 4–12. 1. Columella makes it clear in 1. 7. 1–7 that the *colonus*
system was extensive and normal on big estates.

vendidit pignora. Pliny dealt more leniently, but not more successfully, with his tenants in arrears, by granting remissions of rent, and
finally changed the system to one of rents in kind, IX. 37, X. 8. 5 nn.

reliqua. Arrears of rent are a constant theme in legal texts. Cf.
Dig. 19. 2: 15. 4–5, 33 and at this period, *ILS* 6675, *c.* 43, at
Veleia, where the valuation is qualified by the words 'deductis reliquis colonorum et usuris pecuniae et pretiis mancipiorum'. Evidently the tenants were charged interest on their arrears.

**7. sunt ergo instruendi eo pluris quod frugi mancipiis; nam nec ipse
usquam vinctos habeo nec ibi quisquam.** This reading, which has the
decisive support of αγ against β (Stout, 83), has also the advantage of
making sense, which *plures* does not. The peasants had lost their
working equipment, including slaves, and Pliny must shoulder a
greater share than usual of the provision of farm tools. Vineyards
required one labourer to every seven acres (Columella, 3. 3. 8). The
contemporary lawyers Titius Aristo and Neratius Priscus discuss
such arrangements in a passage (*Dig.* 19. 2. 19. 2) which shows the
exactitude with which the schedules of equipment were drawn up:
'dolia utique colono esse praestanda et prelum et trapetum instructa
funibus, si minus, dominum instruere ea debere: sed et prelum
vitiatum dominum reficere debere . . . fiscos autem . . . ad premendam
oleam . . . colonum sibi parare debere', etc. Doubtless the rent varied
with the amount provided by the landlord. From Scaevola (*Dig.* 20.
1. 32, below) it would seem rare for owners to provide servile hands
on rented land, but *Sent. Pauli* 3. 6. 43–44 includes slaves in the
instrumentum fundi, and the Veleian Table refers to slaves included
in the assessment of lands worked by tenants, *ILS* 6675, *c.* 43.
There is nothing in the references to agricultural equipment to
prevent such arrangements being made in the letting of farms of
40 or 50 acres to small operators. J. Česka, *Listy Fil.* (1956), 24 ff.,
however, argued that Pliny's measure was exceptional. Sirago
(op. cit. 156 f.) summarizes the legal evidence for the conditions
and obligations of tenancy contracts.

vinctos. The revolution in land tenure has come far since the age
of the Gracchi, when the balance was swinging between the peasant-
owner and the chain-gang working large estates. Both have been
replaced by the tenant farming on a larger scale than the former
peasantry. The new *coloni* first appear in the Ciceronian age; cf. Cic.
pro Caec. 94, the earliest explicit reference, and Caesar, *BC* 1. 34. 2,
56. 3, where large numbers are indicated: cf. numerous references to
coloni in Republican lawyers collected by P. A. Brunt, *JRS* (1962),
71 n. 31. The servile labourer is ubiquitous but subsidiary, working
both on the home-farm under a *vilicus* and on the rented lands of the
colonus, but no longer competing with the yeoman. The description
of Scaevola, *Dig.* 20. 1. 32, may well be characteristic: 'eorum praediorum pars sine colonis fuit eaque actori suo colenda . . . tradidit

adsignatis . . . servis culturae necessariis'. So more briefly Martial implies both systems 2. 11. 9: 'nihil colonus vilicusve decoxit'. See *RE* iv, 'colonatus', 485–94. Sirago (op. cit. 151 f.) unduly minimizes the intermixture of methods on large estates.

nec ibi quisquam. [Česka (art. cit.) identified Pliny's *frugi* with the *soluti* whom Columella contrasts with *vincti* (1. 6. 3).] The area was evidently not familiar to Pliny's correspondent, and hence cannot be Comum. The system was described by Columella, 1. 7. 1, 9. 4. For Pliny's use of rustic slaves see IX. 16, 20. 2. Česka (art. cit.) avoids the implications of this statement, which implies a changing system.

posse emi sestertio triciens non quia non aliquando quinquagiens fuerint. Columella 3. 3. 8 and the Elder Pliny, *NH* 14. 48–52, give figures which indicate a normal price of S.1,000 per Roman acre for unplanted land and from S.2,500 to S.3,000 for vineyard under cultivation (Frank, op. cit. 149 ff.). Since a large part of this estate is not vineyard, an average price of S.2,000 might be assumed, which gives an acreage, based on the original value, of 2,500 *iugera*. What was the size of the individual farms? Of the smaller units recorded in the contemporary Table of Beneventum (*CIL* ix. 1455) about half fall between S.100,000 and S.50,000 and half between S.50,000 and S.15,000 in value. At Veleia the size of recorded units does not fall below S.50,000 (Frank, op. cit. 173 f.). In VI. 3 Pliny has given away a farm of S.100,000 value, probably of some 50 acres in mixed land. If this is a maximum size for a single *fundus* on Pliny's estates, Pliny may have been dealing with a group of fifty to seventy tenants, according to the amount of land which he works directly under the bailiff system. It is unlikely that he intended to work the whole, or a large part, of the estate directly, because this would involve a very heavy outlay on slaves, if there was no tenant and hired labour, at a price per head of up to S.8,000 (Frank, op. cit. 149, 235 n. 38). Reckoning with Columella one slave per 7 acres for vineyard, and less for ploughland, this would involve him in an extra outlay of half the purchase price or more, which he already had some difficulty in finding in cash. But he probably intends to work an area around the *villa rustica* by direct methods. He has a fair amount of produce from his own land to sell in VIII. 2.

verum et hac penuria colonorum et communi temporis iniquitate ut reditus agrorum sic etiam pretium retro abiit. Cf. VII. 30. 3, 'adeo rarum est invenire idoneos conductores'. This is the most specific of several passages in Pliny that may imply a general agricultural recession in Italy in the time of Trajan. His references to *locatio* reveal difficulties with *coloni* that persist from *c.* 94 to 107: VII. 30. 3, IX. 37, X. 8. 5 nn. Chilver (*Cisalpine Gaul*, 150 f.) dismisses much of this as the usual grumbling of landowners, yet follows Rostovtzeff (*SEHRE*[1] 189 f.) in thinking that the persistent failure of the small farmers may have been due to the over-production of wine in the Flavian period, and to provincial competition. The edict of Domitian, dated to 92 by Eusebius (*Chron.*), ordering the destruction of provincial vineyards and forbidding new plantations in Italy, is cited in support. But this was inspired by the fear of famine, and intended to expand cereal supplies rather than to protect Italian vineyards from competition, Suet. *Dom.* 7. 2: 'ad summam quondam ubertatem vini, frumenti vero inopiam'. So too Statius, *S.* 4. 3. 11–12: 'Cereri . . . reddit iugera'. The rule was being enforced in Africa in 117 (A–J 74, c. ii. 25), and was maintained nominally in the European provinces long after the crisis in Italy, if there was one, had ceased to matter. (SHA, *Prob.* 18. 8; Eutropius 9. 17. 2; *Lib. de Caes.* 37. 3.)

The Elder Pliny, before the death of Vespasian, indicates the sale of Spanish wine in bulk on the Roman market, and attempts to cut the cost of Italian production at Aricia evidently to meet competition (*NH* 14. 62, 71; 17. 213). He remarks: 'copiae potius quam bonitati studentium', and also 'vilitate reditum impendia superant'. Columella at this period argues against a popular view that pasture and forestry was more profitable than viticulture (3. 3. 1–2). But the complaint is as old as Varro (1. 8. 1): 'contra vineam sunt qui putent sumptus fructum devorare'. Probably they mean that vines were too speculative—unlike timber (s. 5) —and too dependent, as the Elder Pliny stresses, on skilful culture. The Elder, while telling stories of fantastic profits in the recent past, reports that the Caecuban vineyards failed 'incuria coloni locique angustiis', and the Falernan similarly (14. 48–51, 61–62). It is possible that the conditions on large estates, and the system of short tenancy, did not favour high-class viticulture in the ordinary way.

Pliny's own difficulties may have been sharpened by his unfortunate situation as a ward and minor for many years, and then as an absentee landlord. Two passages written before 100 suggest this, II. 4. 3, 15. 2 nn. Pliny here attributes the decline in value of this estate to the bad management of its previous owner. So too with the small farm mentioned in VI. 3. In both cases he expects good management to restore prosperity. In VIII. 2 he sells his vintage without difficulty despite complaints of 'abundantia sed par vilitas' (IV. 6. 1). The difficulties over *locatio* seem to have been confined to his Tuscan estate, and may be due to local conditions only. Pliny is never short of cash in these years despite his troubles, s. 8 and II. 4. 3 n. Yet the trouble persisted. Perhaps the real weakness lay in the shortness of tenure under the *colonus* system, with renewals and changes every four or five years, which discouraged the tenants from making major improvements. Columella remarks on the bad effects of frequent changes of tenure, I. 7. 3. For the length of tenures see X. 8. 5 n.

penuria colonorum. Largely out of this remark, repeated in VII. 30. 2, and a much less relevant remark in VI. 30. 3–4, Sirago (op. cit. 106 f., 174 f., *et al.*) has constructed a remarkable theory. Wine production, greatly expanded in the early Principate, in response to peace and prosperity in Italy, reaches a crisis in the Flavian period not through overproduction and provincial competition, but through a failure of production due to lack of labour. Hence the provincial wines take the place of Italian on the Roman market, as the consequence—and not the cause—of the Italian difficulties. But Pliny nowhere suggests that there was any shortage of ordinary working labour, including slaves, whom he here expects to find readily. The evidence of the new 'alimentary' foundations is at best ambiguous in this respect (VII. 18. 2 nn.). The evidence of Dio Prusensis in his *Euboicus* and elsewhere about depopulation in Greece cannot be used to illustrate the situation in Italy (*Or.* 7. 34, 33. 25, 27). Lack of labour might explain a change of crops, but not the economic distress itself, which must originate in terms of prices, supply, and demand. Besides, there is no evidence that the bulk of Pliny's tenants were concerned with viticulture, which occupied only a limited part of his Tuscan estate (s. 5 and v. 6. 8–11).

8. aliquid tamen fenero, nec molestum erit mutuari. He can pay a large part of the price by calling in his loans, and can later pay off whatever he needs to borrow out of income savings, cf. II. 4. 3 n.

socru. He freely uses her country houses, I. 4, VI. 10. I, and remarks 'non . . . tam mea sunt quae mea sunt quam quae tua'. This is Pompeia Celerina, mother of his first or second wife. The mother of Calpurnia was apparently dead, and is never mentioned in the family circle, IV. 19, V. 14. 8, VIII. 11.

20. *To Maesius Maximus*

Date. Later than 100 when Trajan presided over the elections, and probably January 103 or 104, a year before the continuation of the story in IV. 25; s. 2 n.

Address. The Indices give both names, the manuscript headings either omit the *nomen* or read *Mesius*. Contemporary senators bearing the *nomen* of Messius, Maesius, and Maecius are known, but none is called Maximus. No less than three *Maecii* held consulships in the years 98–101, and a fourth in the eighties (Garzetti, *C.* 92–93, 133;

Inc. 90; *PIR*¹ M 40, 46, 49; *FO*). But Pliny's man is probably not a
senator, since he misses two consecutive senatorial elections. Cf. *RE*
xiv. 282. Nothing links him to the other Maximi in Pliny, II. 14 pref.

1. meministine te saepe legisse . . .? He means, in accounts of republican history: Cic. *de Legg.* 3. 35, *de Or.* 2. 170.

2. omnes comitiorum die tabellas postulaverunt. On this occasion
the elections were apparently completed in one day, before he wrote
s. 9. So too in VI. 19. 1. Pliny nowhere suggests, in such letters as
II. 9, IV. 15, VI. 6. 9, 19, that the elections for annual magistracies
below the consulship were conducted in two parts, as is indicated
for a much later age by the Calendar of Silvius (*CIL* i. p. 335), on
9 January for aediles, tribunes, and praetors, and on 23 January for
quaestors (Mommsen, *DPR*, ii. 253 ff.). In A.D. 100 Trajan as consul
conducted all the elections including the *destinatio consulum* at a
single session of the Senate in January, and presided over the formal
appointment of the consuls at a *comitia populi* in the Campus on a
separate day, *Pan.* 69–74, 77. 1, 92. 3. (Cf. at length, M. L. Paladini,
Athenaeum, 37. 3 ff.) Hence there is no firm support for Mommsen's
view that the dual election dates of Philocalus were in force in the
age of Trajan, though it is probable that the elections were over
before the Ides. (See also Introduction III, p. 27.) The elections of
IV. 25 belong to a year, not a fortnight, later than the present occasion.
The years concerned may be 103 and 104 or 104 and 105. A year
when Trajan was consul is excluded by his evident absence here
(s. 12) and in IV. 25. In 103 he was consul but resigned on the Ides of
January. Since IV. 29 is concerned with the opening months of 105,
the years 104 and 105 are preferable.

   tabellas. Evidently voting had been oral before this change.
So Mommsen (cited below) and Paladini, art. cit. 12, who notes that
the change was carried out by the presiding consul. But he acted
on a decree of the Senate: 'in senatu . . . hoc . . . *placuit*', above.
The *Lex Valeria* of A.D. 5 introduced the use of wax tablets for the
centuries of knights and senators in the Comitia; how long this
lasted is not known (*Tab. Hebana* 18–19, E–J² n. 94 a.).

4. procurrebant omnes cum suis candidatis. For activity at elections
see I. 14. 7, II. 9. 5–6, VI. 6. 9, 19. 2; *RE* Suppl. vi. 780 f.; Mommsen,
DPR vii. 451 f.

5. supersunt senes ex quibus audire soleo. Such men as Vestricius
Spurinna and Arrius Antoninus are in mind, Ep. I. 6, IV. 3. Pliny's
golden age here, as in II. 14. 3, seems to be the time of Claudius if not
Nero, when the more frequent presence of the Emperor, now no
longer usual, tended to check blatant *ambitio*. Nero intervened to

appease such turmoils at the praetorian elections in A.D. 60, Tac. *Ann.* 14. 28.

testes et laudatores dabat vel eum sub quo militaverat vel eum cui quaestor fuerat, vel utrumque si poterat. A man's former legate or proconsul might be dead, or overseas, as Pliny in the commendation of Rosianus Geminus, X. 26, or out of Rome like Fundanus in VI. 6. 8. The relationship between quaestor and consul or proconsul was felt to be particularly close, IV. 15. 9 n.

quosdam ex suffragatoribus. Pliny here distinguishes the *suffragator*, the active campaigner, from the man who can speak from experience, as in IV. 17. 6 'suffragator et testis'. For the looser usage of *suffragium* as 'influence' see II. 1. 8 n.

6. natales competitoris aut annos aut etiam mores arguebat. The *Lex Visellia*, which excluded the descendants of slaves for three generations from the equestrian order, excluded them *a fortiori* from the Senate, I. 19. 2 n. Imperial grace could find a way round this difficulty (VIII. 6. 4 n.), though the Senate once protested against the origin even of a *candidatus Caesaris* (Tac. *Ann.* 11. 21). Hence occasional freedmen's sons crept into the House, Ep. 14. 1 n., VII. 27. 2 n.

annos. For the working of the *lex annalis* see VII. 16. 2 n. Augustus would seem to have fixed the minimum age for the quaestorship at 25, though the evidence is somewhat indirect. Dio 52. 20. 1; Mommsen, *DPR* ii. 235 n. 1; J. Stroux, *SB Bay. Ak.* (1929), 19.

mores. Disgraceful professions, and technical *ignominia* or *infamia*, barred men from public office (II. 11. 12 n.; *Tab. Herac.* 94–95, 104–6.). The emperors, like the republican censors, excluded *infames* and *indigni* on wider grounds from the Senate at the *lectio senatus*, Tac. *Ann.* 2. 48. 3; 11. 25. 5.

8. vereor ne procedente tempore ex ipso remedio vitia nascantur. Schultz, art. cit. 4, argued that Pliny's oracle was *post eventum*, and that this letter was written or rewritten at the time of IV. 25. This would argue for the joint compilation of III and IV. But the prophecy was easy, and Pliny may be using arguments put forward in the debate. He is not here anticipating the silly abuses of IV. 25, but that *gratiosi* will prevail in secret over *digni*, s. 6.

9. ut in reciperatoriis iudiciis. The virtue of the procedure before a group of *recuperatores* instead of the single *iudex privatus* lay in its swiftness, *RE* (2), i. 431; Cic. *pro Tull.* 10. This passage suggests that the lengthy *iudicis datio* of the ordinary procedure was cut down in the recuperatorial.

10. ut non numquam de republica loquerer cuius materiae nobis . . . rarior. Pliny makes similar remarks in II. 11. 1—'si quid acti est in senatu dignum ordine illo'—IV. 12. 3—'parva quaestio sed tamen quaestio', V. 4. 1, and IX. 2. 1–3, where he contrasts his situation as a letter-writer with Cicero's. These complaints about the unimportance of senatorial business are not confined to the later books, and hence cannot be used to prove any decrease of the Senate's activity under Trajan, which would seem rather to have been stabilized at the low level to which the Flavians had reduced it, VIII. 14. 2 n.

11. aliquid non humile nec sordidum. In v. 8. 9, this means 'court affairs' as contrasted with the splendid themes of history, cf. Traub, *T.A.Ph.A.* 86. 222 f.

12. sunt quidem cuncta sub unius arbitrio. So too in IV. 25. 5. Cf. *Pan.* 72. 1 'uni tibi in quo et res publica et nos sumus'. It is odd that Pliny's two most outspoken remarks about the absolute power of Trajan should be addressed to the same man. The position must have been generally recognized for Pliny to state it so frankly, unless he is trying to convey a delicate hint as in the Panegyric; cf. Ep. 18. 2, 'ut futuri principes . . . sub exemplo praemonerentur' etc. The Senate persisted in making things worse by referring even its few remaining problems to the Princeps; v. 13. 7–8, VI. 5. 2, 19. 3 nn. The public provinces tended to neglect the Senate and turn directly to the Princeps despite his efforts to check this: IV. 22. 1–3, VI. 31. 6, VII. 6. 1–6 nn.

solus omnium curas laboresque suscepit. The phrase uses the symbolism, which first appears on the coins of Trajan, of the emperor as Hercules: *RIC* ii, Trajan, 37, 49, 79; *RC* 278.

ad nos quoque velut rivi ex illo benignissimo fonte decurrunt. Paladini (art. cit. 16 f.) oddly refers this to the division of elections between Princeps and Senate. But it refers to the Senate's independent action taken in s. 2.

21. *To Cornelius Priscus*

Date. From the date of Martial's twelfth book this cannot be before 102–3, and the argument from distribution suggests that it is not later than the book-date, ss. 1–2 n.

Address. Cornelius Priscus, mentioned as *consularis* in v. 20. 7, may be the like-named proconsul of Asia *c.* 120–1. This suggests a consulship *c.* 103. The fragment of *FO* for 93–94—CORI—should refer to another man. (Cf. Syme, *JRS*, 1946, 163; *Tac.* 638.) But that this letter, and Ep. 5 to Baebius Macer, were included as delicate compliments to consulars is a fragile thesis. When Pliny wants to mention consuls in office he does so directly: VI. 27. 1, IX. 37. 1. Cornelius may be the Priscus of VI. 8, VII. 8. 19, but hardly the consular legate of II. 13 pref. Garzetti, *C.* 47; *PIR²* C 1420.

1. audio Valerium Martialem decessisse. This letter is the only evidence for the date of Martial's death, *PIR¹* V 77. Its presence in the same book as Ep. 7, on the death of Silius Italicus, and the absence of similar letters from IV, show that this letter has not been chronologically displaced, and suggests that III and IV were published separately. The next letter on this theme is V. 5. The position at the end of III may be due to desire for variety in the sequence.

2. prosecutus eram viatico secedentem. Martial refers first to his intended retirement to Bilbilis in Spain in 10. 104, last poem of a book dated *c.* 96–98 in its present form, after the adoption of Trajan by Nerva, ibid. 6, 7. He published 11 at Rome after the accession of Nerva, ibid. 2. 6, 4. 5, 7. 5. Book 12 was published from Bilbilis after the accession of Trajan in Jan. 98 (ibid. 8), and refers in the preface to his *triennium desidiae*, and to the consulship of Arruntius Stella (2. 10); this was either in October 101 or October 102 (*ILS* 6106; *PIR²* A 1151; *RE* x. 671 f.). Hence the usual view, that Martial left Italy in 98 and published Book 12 in 101 (Friedlaender, *Martial*, p. 67), needs correction, and the date of Martial's death could be as late as 104.

secedentem. Martial 12 pref. 'hac provinciali solitudine ... ubi ... sine solacio at sine excusatione secesserim'. Cf. Ep. 7. 6; Silius likewise 'ab urbe secessit'.

3. nostris vero temporibus . . . hoc in primis exolevit. Compare the complaint of II. 20. 12, that the biggest rewards go to *nequitia*.

4. qui sint versiculi. These appear in Martial 10. 20 (19), written from the book-date *c.* A.D. 96 when Pliny was only *praetorius*. The compliment is adequate, and not below Martial's standard for secondary figures; cf. 10. 37, on the jurist Maternus, and 10. 44, on Q. Ovidius, an elderly official.

5. ut domum meam Esquiliis quaerat. Martial bids his messenger cross the Suburra and pass the 'Lacus Orphei'.

6. at non erunt aeterna. Pliny's comment is as just as on Silius, Ep. 7. 5.

BOOK IV

1. *To Calpurnius Fabatus*

Date. The assignment of this letter to the book-date, which would give summer 104, was assailed by Otto (art. cit. 34 f., 84 n.2) whose arguments have been restated at length by S. Monti, 'Pliniana', *Rendic. Acc. Arch. Lett. Napoli* 1952, 161 ff. They date Calpurnia's marriage to 97 or 98, on a special interpretation, or misunderstanding, of x. 2. 2 (q.v. nn.). Hence Otto put the present visit to Comum in the summer after Pliny's consulship. The *longum tempus* of s. 1 is taken to be the interval between his appointment to the Treasury in 98 and the summer of 101. But there are no references in i–iii to Pliny's new marriage connexions, henceforward a frequent topic in iv–viii, and there are no visits to Comum mentioned in ii–iii except the project of iii. 6. 6, which may, but need not, refer to the present occasion, while two other letters in iv mention such a visit (Epp. 13. 3, 30. 1). These references to the marriage and to Comum tie up in Epp. 13. 1 and 19. 4 with mention of Pliny's new hobby of verse-writing, which is entirely absent from i–iii. This is decisively in favour of the book-date. It is hard to believe that Pliny kept silent about his verses for three whole books. Otto was rightly surprised that Pliny, freed from public duties since November 100, should not mention a visit to Comum until 104. The solution lies in the nature of the collection. Book iii, covering the longest span of any book, mentions the *secessus* of Pliny in Epp. 1, 4, 6, 10, 15. That sufficed. Pliny may have visited Comum and married Calpurnia at the earliest possible moment for legal reasons, without writing a literary letter about her until she was old enough to be of interest (Ep. 19 n.).

Otto also equated this visit with that of v. 14. 9, when Pliny was *curator Tiberis* (for Otto in 101). But there is nothing here to suggest that Pliny was on a hurried official leave, as there and in iii. 6. 6.

Address. The earlier career of L. Calpurnius Fabatus is known from his tombstone at Comum, *ILS* 2721, which shows that after a full equestrian military career his service ended rather abruptly with a minor regional governorship in Africa Proconsularis as 'praefectus nationum Gaetulicarum sex'. His career was cut short when he was involved, though not condemned, in the treason charges brought against L. Junius Silanus in A.D. 65, Tac. *Ann.* 16. 8. His birth can hardly have been later than A.D. 30. He was a magnate and local magistrate of Comum, owning lands also in Tuscany and Campania, VI. 30, VIII. 20. 3. He is an aged man in VII. 23. I, and dies in *c*. A.D. 110–11, X. 120. 2. For his family see Ep. 19. 1–2, V. 11. 1 nn. For his sharpness and irascibility see VI. 12, VII. 11, VIII. 10, 11. 3. *PIR²* C 263 adds nothing.

1. neptem tuam. The younger Calpurnia, daughter of Fabatus' son, who was now dead, Ep. 19. 1, V. 11. 1.

3. deflectemus in Tuscos. Tifernum Tiberinum lay off the direct north road, being to the west of the *Via Flaminia*, I. 4. 1, VIII. 8. 1 nn. For his Tuscan villa see V. 6.

4. oppidum est praediis nostris vicinum . . . quod me paene adhuc puerum patronum cooptavit. Possibly this took place at his uncle's death, from whom he may have inherited the Tuscan lands, since his parental estates were at Comum, VII. 11. 5. Pliny was then under 18, VI. 20. 5, and may not long have taken the *toga pura*, I. 9. 2 n. There were no limits on the age or number of *patroni* that a municipality might acquire. They were expected to act for the borough at Rome, as Pliny did for the province of Baetica of which he more recently became patron, and to act as local arbitrator. See III. 4. 4 n.

    cooptavit. In the charter of Malaca *patroni* were chosen by the decurions, a quorum of two-thirds being present. *Lex Mal.* 61, cf. *Lex Urson.* 97, 130.

    Tiferni Tiberini. The place, at Città di Castello, is known from a few inscriptions, which reveal the normal magistracies. The name is given in Pliny, *NH* 3. 114. It is to be distinguished from Tifernum Mataurense. There seem to have been no excavations. See *CIL* xi, p. 871; *RE* (2), vi. 940.

5. templum . . . cum sit paratum differre longius inreligiosum est. The work was first proposed by Pliny in 96–97, and set on foot in the visit of September 99, III. 4. 2, X. 8. 1–3 nn. Otto's argument (art. cit. 84 n. 2) that the building work would not have been protracted until 104 is uncertain. Pliny implied that the temple had been long ready.

6. erimus ero ibi dedicationis die quem epulo celebrare constitui. A public ceremony. The whole scheme was under the authority of the municipality, cf. X. 8. 2, unlike the rebuilding of the private shrine of Ceres in IX. 39. For the formalities of dedication see X. 49. 2–3 n., and for public feasts see D-S ii. 738.

7. filiamque tuam. For Calpurnia Hispulla see Ep. 19 pref.

2. *Attius Clemens*

Date. The theme of this letter is continued in Ep. 7. The book-date *c.* 104 well fits the age of Regulus' son. Born *c.* 87–88 (Martial) he would still be technically *puer*, yet old enough to manage his ponies and hounds, s. 3.

Address. For the obscure literary man Attius Clemens see I. 10 pref.

1. Regulus filium amisit, hoc uno malo indignus. It is a proof of the interval between the publication dates of II and IV that Pliny does not refer back to the bad omen of II. 20. 5 concerning the boy.

2. hunc Regulus emancipavit ut heres matris existeret. While under *patria potestas* the boy could not inherit, Gaius 2. 87. For the ceremonies of emancipation see Gaius 1. 132, 134; *Tit. Ulp.* 10. 1; Schulz, *Classical Roman Law*, 158, s. 272. The child was thrice sold by *mancipatio* to a third party, who manumitted him by a touch of a rod, *vindicta*.

   mancipatum . . . indulgentiae simulatione captabat. Schuster and O.C.T. The manuscripts are divided between the readings *mancipatum* and *emancipatum*, but αγ support the latter and only β the former. So Stout (op. cit. 170) is more logical in reading the latter. A remarkable fuss used to be made over this passage. But G. P. Shipp's explanation is the best—that Pliny is using the Livian dodge of repeating a compound word by its simple form, not referring to the mysteries of manication involved in the legal act. See *Cl. Phil.* 39. 117. In X. 4. 3 conversely he uses *emancipare* for *mancipare*.

   indulgentiae simulatione. This leads Carcopino (*Daily Life*, 79) to say that the youth died of over-indulgence!

   matris. Perhaps Caepia Procula, named 'M. Reguli (uxor)' in *CIL* xv. 7421, and presumably a sister or daughter of Eppuleius Proculus Caepio Hispo, a consular mentioned in Ep. 9. 16.

   captabat. The monstrous insult is not repeated in Ep. 7. For a similar case of emancipation 'hereditatis causa' see VIII 18. 4, which suggests that not all fathers were as ready as Regulus to free their children from *patria potestas*.

3. habebat puer mannulos multos. For the fashion among young men see IX. 12. 1: 'castigabat quidam filium suum quod paulo sumptuosius equos et canes emeret'. Cf. also Sallust, *Cat.* 14. 6; Horace, *A.P.* 161 f.

   luscinias. Martial 7. 87 records a curious collection of pets including snakes and monkeys as well as magpies and nightingales.

4. **omnes Regulus circa rogum trucidavit.** The idea was familiar from the literary tradition about the funeral rites of heroes, though in Homer Patroclus' pyre is honoured only by the sacrifice of cattle, *Iliad* 23. 165 ff.; cf. Virgil *Aen.* 11. 185 ff. Herodotus' account of the burial of the Scythian kings is closer, *Hist.* 4. 71. 4. Fundanus was less extreme in the extravagance of his grief, v. 16. 7.

5. **latissimum solum porticibus immensis, ripam statuis suis occupavit.** Cf. the statuary in the gardens of Domitius Tullus, VIII. 18. 11, and Hadrian's villa at Tivoli. Regulus was unique in preferriug statues of himself. For such gardens see Ashby, *Top. Dict.* s.v. *horti.*

6. **insaluberrimo tempore.** In summer, cf. v. 6. 1.

3. *To Arrius Antoninus*

Date. The book-date is certain. Three short notes in IV and V deal with an exchange of verses between Pliny and Arrius, a new friend in the book series, and a fourth refers to a common literary friend; Epp. 3, 18, v. 15, and Ep. 27. 5. Besides, Pliny's account of his own new interest in versifying begins with Ep. 14. The suggestion of C. Peter that the Arrius–Pliny series is not in serial order is unfounded so far as the content goes (Peter, art. cit. 704; Schultz, art. cit. 26). Here he first reads Arrius' verses, in Ep. 18 he translates some of them. In v. 15 he is still translating them.

Address. Arrius Antoninus' career is known solely from literary evidence. He was suffect consul in 69 and cos. II probably among the suffects of 97 (Tac. *Hist.* 1. 77; *Chron. Min.* (Frick) i. 381; Syme, *JRS,* 1953, 155). He was a member of the group of elderly consulars, such as his friend Vestricius Spurinna, who supported Nerva as emperor, II. 7. 1 n., IV. 27. 5. His remark apropos was famous: 'gratulare se ait senatui et populo provinciisque, ipsi autem nequaquam'. *Epitome de Caes.* 12. 3; SHA, *Pius,* 1. 4. He became maternal grandfather of the emperor Pius. *PIR*² A 1086; SHA, *Pius,* 1. 3, 4. His supposed origin from Narbonensis is a surmise; Syme, *Tac.* 605, 683.

1. **proconsul Asiae qualis ante te ... vix unus aut alter.** His proconsulship should fall before that of the elder Trajan in 79–80, who was consul *c.* 70–71, later than Arrius, and after that of Silius Italicus, consul in 68 and proconsul *c.* 77 (III. 7. 3 n.; *PIR*², loc. cit.; J. Morris, *JRS,* 1953, p. 80). For the attention paid to these annual proconsulships cf. III. 7. 3 n.

   aetate. His birth should fall between A.D. 30 and 35, and he must have been the eldest surviving consular after the recent death of Silius Italicus, 'Father of the House', III. 7. 9 n.

3. **cum Graeca epigrammata tua . . . legerem.** Spurinna also versified, III. 1. 7, and Pliny was beginning at this period, Epp. 14, 18, V. 15, and indeed translating Arrius' verses. All these letters fit together and illustrate Pliny's first dabblings, which VII. 4 describes at length.

legerem. Arrius did not recite his verses, cf. V. 3.

4. **quam dulcia illa quam** *amantia* **quam arguta quam recta.** The eight-and nine-book tradition αγ agree against the ten-book (β) reading *antiqua*, which is easily explicable by a haplography and subsequent amendment: 'quam (am)antia quam'. So Stout, op. cit. 170. Formerly there was an immense controversy. Certainly *antiqua* is out of place in a catalogue of poetic attributes; for the usual terms cf. I. 16. 5, III. 1. 7, VI. 21. 4–5, IX. 22. 2. But in all Pliny's usage of *amans* and *amantissimus* there is either an objective genitive—as in nine of eleven instances—or an implied object as in V. 21. 3 and IX. 28. 1 ('procul a fratre amantissimo', 'epistulas . . . recepi . . . amantissimas'). So too in VIII. 21. 5, cited by Schuster in support, 'hoc simplicius et amantius. amat enim qui se sic amari putat', the reference is to the author-audience relationship. But here *amantia* means simply *plena amoris*. The parallels are with the indicative usage, as in IV. 14. 3, 'his iocamur ludimus amamus', IX. 22. 2, 'amat ut qui verissime, dolet ut qui impatientissime'. A better amendment for sense might have been *amara*, as in the lists in I. 16. 5, 'quantum illis (sc. versibus) leporis dulcedinis amaritudinis amoris', and VI. 21. 5, 'non amaritudo non dulcedo non lepos defuit'. But a pair of 'soft' epithets is perhaps needed here to balance the pair of 'sharp' words. For the battle of texts, now ended by Stout, see the editions of Schuster and Guillemin. Worst of all was the irrelevant conflation of Postgate: 'antiquitatem amantia'.

4. *To Sosius Senecio*

Date. Not determinable, but later than 99, when Sosius as *consularis* qualified for a major army command.

Address. For Sosius Senecio, familiar of Trajan, see I. 13 pref. This present appointment cannot be identified.

1. **Varisidium Nepotem valdissime diligo, virum industrium rectum disertum.** The qualities here commended are much as in II. 9. 3–4, III. 2, but more briefly put. Though Guillemin, ad loc., finds the testimonial cool, and an example of the snub direct, it is no cooler than his commendation of Accius Sura to Trajan, X. 12. The man is otherwise unknown.

C. Calvisium. For the wealthy landowner of Comum see II. 20 pref.

2. **hunc rogo semestri tribunatu splendidiorem et sibi et avunculo suo facias.** For the method of these appointments see II. 13. 1–2, III. 8. 1 nn. Pliny usually describes the wealth and status of candidates carefully; cf. also III. 2. 2, VII. 22. 2, X. 4. But as the family was known to Senecio, *splendidiorem*, implying equestrian standing, sufficed (III. 2. 5).

semestri tribunatu. The term, well known from inscriptions, has not been adequately explained. Domaszewski (*Rangordnung* 41, 48, 130, cf. *RE* (2), vi. 2444) takes it as a low-grade tribunate at half-pay concerned with the command of legionary cavalry at headquarters. Mommsen (*DPR* i. 346 n. 2) refers it to the actual length of service. Mr. Birley similarly has suggested privately that the term refers to the campaigning season's length, but that the service was annual, as for *tribuni laticlavii*. The term is not identical with the latter—Varisidius is only of equestrian standing, and few of the known *semestres* are *laticlavii*. In *Tabula Heracleensis* 90 f. the *semestre stipendium* is contrasted with the annual. The size of the salary, S.25,000, known from *CIL* xiii. 3162, casts no further light, as the pay of other tribunes is unknown. But assuming that the other posts of the *militia equestris* were at S.50,000 a year, it makes sense that the procuratorial salaries began at S. 60,000.

5. *To Julius Sparsus*

Date. The letter corresponds in subject matter—recitation of a major speech—to II. 19 and III. 18, where the *In Marium* and *Panegyricus* are concerned. The present speech might be either the *In Classici Socios* or the *Pro Basso* (III. 9, IV. 9). The former was perhaps too disjointed for recitation, IX. 4 n. The date of the latter (Ep. 9 pref.) would fit admirably.

Address. Another letter about a speech is addressed to Sextus Julius Sparsus (VIII. 3). The *Fasti* of Potentia and *CIL* xvi n. 35 reveal him as a suffect consul of 88, and hence much senior to Pliny. He may be the wealthy friend of Martial 12. 57. Garzetti, *C.* 79.

1. **Aeschinen aiunt.** For the anecdote see II. 3. 10 n. It is unusual for Pliny to repeat a reference so precisely, though the point of the two citations is different, and the repetition indicates the interval between the publication of II and IV.

2. **orationem meam proxime doctissimi homines . . . per biduum audierint.** So too in III. 18. 4 (n.). The comparison with II. 19 and III. 18, and the Aeschines anecdote, suggest that a public rather than a civil law speech is meant. The *Pro Basso* lasted five hours, Ep. 9. 9,

which when extended (s. 4) might well need two days of recitation.
Though Pliny was proud of his seven hours' centumviral speech
mentioned in Ep. 16. 2, there is little evidence that he ever recited
private speeches, cf. II. 19. 1 n., unless V. 12. 1 refers to one such.
For the customs of the *recitatio* see I. 13. 4 n.

4. librum ipsum non tamen ultra causae amplitudinem extendimus.
See III. 18. 1 for Pliny's practice.

6. *To Julius Naso*

The book-date is not in doubt. This is the first and only note to
Julius Naso, a young man not yet in the Senate, whose elder brother's
death is mentioned in V. 21. 3, and whose candidature for the
quaestorship is described in VI. 6 and 9.

1. Tusci grandine excussi. Rare and disastrous at the vintage. For
weather as a topic see VIII. 17.

   in regione Transpadana . . . abundantia sed par vilitas nuntiatur.
See VIII. 2. 1–2 nn. for price variations.

2. nihil quidem ibi possideo praeter tectum et hortum. Cf. II. 17.
26, 28.

7. *To Catius Lepidus*

Date a little later than Ep. 2, on the same occasion.

Address. The man and his municipality (s. 6) are unknown. The
nomen Catius, which is common enough in Cisalpine (cf. Ep. 28. 1),
might connect him with Catius Fronto and Silius Italicus, II. 11. 3,
III. 7. 1 nn.

1. illum cera illum . . . auro ebore marmore effingit. Hartleben
(ad loc.) compared the luxurious busts from the treasure of Boscoreale
(*Mon. Piot*, V, pl. 2; cf. *CAH* x. 559). For the technique of waxwork
see VII. 9. 11 n. Here wax figures are clearly meant, and not the
preliminary stage of casting in *cire perdue*.

2. adhibito ingenti auditorio librum de vita eius recitavit. The 'book'
might be a lengthy *laudatio* in the style of a funeral oration, a
consolatio like Seneca's, or a full-scale life. For the new fashion of
biography see III. 10. 1 n. For Aquilius Regulus see I. 5. 1 nn.

   **eundem in exemplaria mille transcriptum per totam Italiam
provinciasque dimisit.** This is a rare example of private publication
at this period, when the book-trade seems generally to be in professional hands. It recalls Cicero's custom of reproducing his own works

before he made use of the facilities of Atticus, I 2. 5 n. The number evidently represents an out-size edition. Pliny does not indicate whether Regulus used his own slaves or contracted the work out. For the book-trade in the provinces see IX. II. 2 n.

transcriptum. T. Birt (*Kritik . . . antiken Buchwesens*, 309) suggested that large editions were commonly prepared by simultaneous dictation to a number of scribes, rather than by visual copying from a prototype, though he could quote no Graeco-Roman evidence either in this or his earlier books (cited ibid.), except (in a later discussion) the Pseudo-Acron scholium on Horace, *Ep.* I. I. 55: 'dictata propria dicuntur quae pueris a librario dictantur', and a less direct statement ibid. on I. 20. 19. His opinion was much disputed, and clarified by the analysis of types of manuscript errors, which can be shown to support the use of both methods. Cf. especially T. C. Skeat, *Proc. Brit. Ac.* xlii. 179 ff., who summarized and enlarged the controversy. But in it no use seems ever to have been made of this sentence. Pliny implies that in his experience direct copying was normal for the production of large editions: *trans.* In V. 10. 3 he uses the verb *describere* for the commercial process: 'describi legi venire volumina'. Here too the force of the preposition is more appropriate to copying than to dictation, though less emphatically so.

scripsit publice. He wrote to the municipal authorities (perhaps only where he was *patronus*, despite Pliny's generalization), of his own authority. Cf. v. 7. 5: 'haec ego scribere publice supersedi' with reference to the town council of Comum.

populo. Dio Chrysostom thanks the proconsul of Bithynia for permitting the holding of the town meeting to hear one of his discourses (*Or.* 48. 1). The holding of such meetings, save for elections, was now declining in Italy also, I. 8. 17 n.

3. **intentio quidquid velis obtinendi.** Cf. Pliny's judgement of Regulus in VI. 2. 7, 'ambitione ab omnibus obtinebas'.

quantum boni efficere potuisset. The context suggests that Pliny means practical rather than literary achievement.

4. **imbecillum latus, os confusum, haesitans lingua.** For a complementary list of oratorical qualities see VI. II. 2: 'decorus habitus, os Latinum, vox virilis, tenax memoria, magnum ingenium, iudicium aequale'.

5. **itaque Herennius Senecio mirifice Catonis illud.** For Senecio and his feud with Regulus see I. 5. 3. Quintilian gives the original version, 12. I. I.

6. **num aliquis in municipio vestro ex sodalibus meis . . . ut circulator in foro legeris?** A *circulator* is a showman, illustrated well by

Dig. 47. 11. 11: 'qui serpentes circumferunt et proponunt'. Petronius, *Cena* 47. 9: 'porcos, sicut in circulis mos est, portenta... facturos'.

municipio vestro. Evidently not Comum, or Pliny would have written *nostro*, but perhaps in the neighbourhood, because full of *sodales mei*.

ut ait Demosthenes. In *de Corona* 291.

8. *To Maturus Arrianus*

Date. Otto, art. cit. 94 ff., disputed the book-date on the unproven assumption that Pliny's application to Trajan for a priesthood (x. 13) belongs to c. 100 and was immediately successful. But Pliny would hardly have held back this letter if it had been available when he was arranging III. In the period of Book III he had less to boast about in public life, cf. III. 6. 5 n. See also s. 3 n., and x. 13 pref.

Address. For the equestrian Arrianus Maturus, and his absence at this time in Egypt on service, see III. 2. 2, and Ep. 12. 7 nn.

1. **acceperim auguratum.** In x. 13 he asked to be promoted either to be *augur* or *septemvir epulonum*, 'quia vacant'. These two posts ranked with the pontificate and the *quindecimviri sacris faciendis* as the most exalted of the Roman priesthoods held by senators, the *amplissima collegia* of Augustus, *RG.* 7. 3. Senators normally record their priesthoods in their *tituli* out of chronological order, along with the consulship and proconsulship of Asia or Africa, as the highest titular distinctions, so that Pliny's remarks about the honour are probably characteristic. They were the equivalent of modern titles and decorations. The four *collegia* included some sixty places for the 150–200 consular senators produced by the system of suffect consuls at this period. Sometimes new men might by special favour secure a priesthood before the consulship, as did Tacitus in 88, Tac. *Ann.* 11. 11, but usually they would have to wait like Pliny till they were consular. Sons of exalted families secured them much earlier, even as *quaestorii* or yet earlier, *ILS* 934, 955, 1127.

The augurate, like the pontificate, ranked slightly before the other two, Tac. *Ann.* 3. 64. Cf. *RE* 2. 2318 (Wissowa). Their chief concern in the Principate was with the *augurium salutis*, *ILS* 9337.

gravissimi principis iudicium. Cf. *iudicia principis* of a consular election, Ep. 15. 5, and, much earlier, *CIL* x 3903 (E–J 329).

2. **alia quamquam dignitate propemodum paria ut tribuuntur sic auferuntur.** Not the other priesthoods, which were all for life, but other imperial posts, *pace* Stout, op. cit. 172.

3. **successi Iulio Frontino principi viro qui me . . . inter sacerdotes**

nominabat. So too Verginius Rufus used to nominate Pliny for a priesthood, probably from his praetorship onwards, until his death in 97, II. 1. 8. Frontinus presumably since then. That Pliny waited so long despite such strong support shows the strength of the competition.

Sextus Iulius Frontinus, a senator possibly from Narbonensis, was in high office under Vespasian, Nerva, and Trajan, but apparently out of favour under Domitian, like Cornutus Tertullus (v. 14 nn.). After a praetorship in 70 and consulship in 73 or 74 he governed Britain *c.* 76–78, was *curator aquarum c.* 96–97, and held second and third consulships in 98 and 100 (Tac. *Hist.* 4. 39; *Agric.* 17. 3; Pliny *Pan.* 61–62; Frontinus *de aquis* pref.; *PIR*¹. s.v.; Syme, *Tac.* 790). Pliny in v. 1. 5 couples him with Corellius Rufus as the two *spectatissimi* of the age, and in the Panegyric indicates him and Vestricius Spurinna anonymously as securing repeated consulships 'for civic services'— possibly in connexion with the adoption and succession of Trajan (II. 7. 1–2 nn.). The date of Frontinus' death depends on this letter, to which the cross-reference in IX. 19 adds nothing. There is no reason—except the desire of critics to upset the chronology of the Letters—why he should not have survived till *c.* 104. The silence of his *Strategemata* about Trajan's Dacian Wars—urged by Otto—is irrelevant, since they mention nothing later than Domitian's German war of 88 (ibid. 1. 1. 8, 3. 10, II. 3. 23, 11. 7). He was author of the *de aquis*, and there is no serious reason to deny his authorship of the *Strategemata*. He is not known to be a Cisalpine, and the reason for Pliny's connexion is unknown but not obscure, from his friendship with other associates of Frontinus, including Corellius, Spurinna, and Pompeius Falco.

nominabat tamquam in locum suum cooptaret. Cf. II. 1. 8, 'illo die quo sacerdotia solent nominare'. The choice of the pontiffs and augurs had been subjected to forms of popular election in the later Republic, but was exercised by the Senate in the Principate, followed by nominal *comitia* of the people. Seneca, *de Ben.* 7. 28. 2, Tac. *Ann.* 3. 19; *Arval. Acta, ILS* 241. 70–75, and Pliny are the main sources. Cf. Mommsen, *DPR* iii. 32 ff. The Princeps exercised a right of commendation, to which Pliny owed his office, s. 1 and x. 13. So too Claudius commends in *Tab. Lugd.* c. 2. 11. After this election the chosen man was nominally *cooptatus* by his College, and installed in office, *inauguratus*, Suet. *Cal.* 12. 1; *RE*, loc. cit. 2318; Mommsen, *DPR* iii. 39.

5. ut sacerdotium idem, ut consulatum multo etiam iuvenior quam ille sum consecutus. Cicero was consul at 43 and augur at 53. Pliny is *c.* 43 in 104.

9. *To Cornelius Ursus*

Date. The publication of a fragment of the *Fasti Ostienses* which
dated the consulship of Baebius Macer (s. 16) securely to the second
quarter of 103 put an end to a long and complicated controversy.
The detractors of Mommsen, who had to a man put this trial in
100–1, were proved more wrong than Mommsen. But once again it
appeared that the extortion letters of Books III–IV were set slightly
behind the chronological sequence of the rest of their book, because
of Pliny's care for variety in the distribution of Letters, cf. III. 4, 9
prefs. No more need be said of the controversy, save that the light
was already becoming apparent to R. Hanslik (*Wiener Studien*, 50.
195 ff., 63. 133 ff.), who put Bassus' proconsulship later than most,
and that the reference to Baebius Macer in Ep. 12. 4 always implied
that his consulship was fairly close to that of Caecilius Strabo, consul
in 105. The trial is now firmly dated to the early months of 103,
and the letter with it.

Address. Cornelius Ursus receives the first three letters about the
Varenus case also: V. 20, VI. 5, 13, and probably VIII. 9 also. He
seems to be an equestrian member of Pliny's circle (V. 20. 8, VIII. 9),
like the other recipients of 'extortion' letters.

1. **causam per hos dies dixit Iulius Bassus, homo laboriosus et adversis
suis clarus.** This letter gives an account of the management of an
extortion case in which charges of *saevitia* were made but not pressed
(ss. 5, 16), and the issue was reduced to simple extortion, the very
reverse of the Priscus case, II. 11. 2 n. The *delatio nominis* had taken
place earlier, and the assignation of advocates, one of whom,
Varenus Rufus, withdrew from the case before the present phase
(V. 20. 1 n.). It is unlikely that the provincial *legatus* Theophanes had
conducted an *inquisitio* in Bithynia, as in III. 9. 6. This is not directly
stated, no personal witnesses are mentioned (s. 15 n.), and the
description suggests that the prosecution called no evidence except
of simple extortion (ss. 5, 15 nn.). When the case comes for trial the
hearing is prolonged because Bassus, unlike Priscus, defends his case
on all charges, and the verdict is limited to the reference of the details
to the *iudices* of the shorter process, s. 16 n.

　　Iulius Bassus. His proconsulship was always dated to the opening
years of Trajan by his provincial coins, which bear abbreviated
titles of Trajan including *Germanicus* but not *Dacicus*, which latter
elsewhere first appears at the end of 102. Though the proconsular
coins of Bithynia are erratic in their titulature, it is clear that the
year 100–1 or 101–2 would suit for the proconsulship, followed by

indictment in late summer 101 or 102. If there was a time-consuming *inquisitio*, indictment in late 101 is more probable. Bassus may be the governor whose cruelties were listed by Dio Chrysostom, *Or*. 43. 11 (s. 5 n.), but the uncertainty of the chronology of Dio's speeches makes Varenus Rufus as likely a candidate, despite von Arnim (*Leben . . . des Dio von Prusa*, 369 ff.). For the coins see W. H. Waddington, *Recueil gén.*[1] 239. 27–28; Bosch, *Münzen*, 88. His name appears as G. Iulius Bassus in a brief honorific inscription on the Flavian gate of Nicaea; *Ist. Forschungen*, IX. 46, n. 14.

The identification of our Bassus with a great soldier and administrator of the period, G. Iulius Quadratus Bassus, suffect consul in 105 after many legionary commands, and subsequently governor of Syria and Dacia about 116–17, was proposed with much argument and little plausibility by von Premerstein. This man's career is known from a long, but damaged, inscription at Pergamum. The identification is excluded by many considerations, notably that Pliny's man served as quaestor in Bithynia (s. 6), while every reasonable restoration of the inscription makes Quadratus quaestor —and not assistant legate—of Cyrene. That the document omits the proconsulship of Bithynia is perhaps less decisive. But the age and condition of Pliny's man (s. 22 'squalida senectus' etc.), and his narrow escape from *ignominia*, are all against the suggestion. Our man may well be a member of the same family (s. 4 n.) which also produced in this age another able administrator, C. Antius A. Iulius Quadratus, cos. II in 105. See A. von Premerstein, *SB. Bayer. Ak. Wiss.* 1934, 3 (Munich); R. Syme, *JRS*, 1946, 162 f.; Groag in *RE* (S.), vii. 311, N. 425 A; Garzetti, *C*. 67, 76; *AE*, 1933, n. 268. For Antius Quadratus see *ILS* 8819; Garzetti, *C*. 11.

laboriosus. Cf. VI. 13. 1, 'tam laboriosum et exercitum (*sc*. reum)'.

accusatus est sub Vespasiano a privatis duobus. Nothing more is known of this. An extortion charge is evidently meant; *privati* is used as in III. 9. 4, 'una civitas publice multique privati'. Bassus may have been *praetorius* and aged not less than 30 before A.D. 78.

2. Titum timuit ut Domitiani amicus, a Domitiano relegatus est. This is the earliest evidence of Domitian's dislike of Titus, cf. Suet. *Titus* 9. 3; *Dom*. 2. 3. His relegation must have been for a political charge, since Nerva did not recall criminals, Ep. 11. 5 n.

revocatus a Nerva sortitusque Bithyniam rediit reus. Bithynia was a praetorian proconsulship, and Pliny's silence shows that Bassus was praetor before his relegation. *Pace* Premerstein (op. cit. 73) he does not imply that Bassus secured his proconsulship at once, or under Nerva at all, but only that he held no other post between his recall and sortition. Ambiguity in marking intervals of time within a sequence is characteristic of Pliny's style, cf. II. 11. 2–8, V. 1. 1, IX. 13. 2–4 nn.

3. Rufo successit Theophanes, unus ex legatis, fax accusationis et origo. For the consular Pomponius see III. 9. 33 n. It is remarkable that one of the plaintiffs should speak as *patronus* in the Senate. He seems to be directing the case in s. 14, like Norbanus in the Classicus case, who, however, did not appear as a principal advocate, III. 9. 30 n., 35. Perhaps Theophanes took the place of the absent Varenus (v. 20. 1). He may well be of equestrian standing, like many wealthy Asiatics at this time. Theophanes is not otherwise known.

4. respondi ego. Pliny leads, as in all his extortion cases, II. 11. 14, 17; III. 9. 13–16.

ornamentis . . . quae illi . . . ex generis claritate . . . magna erant. Since no Julii Bassi of exalted station are known from Italy it is probable that Bassus was provincial. The remark recalls the ostentatious pride of Asiatic Greeks entering the Senate in this period, VI. 19. 4 n. So a connexion with the Pergamene house of Quadratus is possible, s. 1 n.

5. dicerem de conspiratione delatorum quam in quaestu habebant. The *delatores* are Bithynian figures. Dio Chrysostom, *Or.* 43. 6–7, satirizes the activities of provincial delators against himself—malicious prosecutions with an eye to blackmail, political attacks in public assemblies. He himself preferred not to act even as a defence advocate. Pliny here implies that there were *praemia delatorum* for successful prosecutions in provincial as in Roman courts, and in s. 20 that Theophanes hired or had been hired by others to stir up this prosecution. For the rival factions in Bithynia see VII. 6. 1–6, where the provincial Council is split into two groups, and X. 34, 58, 81; Dio, *Or.* 50. 3.

in aliis enim quamvis auditu gravioribus . . . etiam laudem merebatur. Dio, *Or.* 43. 11, lists the harsh acts of a 'bad governor', including sentences of exile and executions of refractory persons, who had doubtless been stirring up the riots which he frankly admits in *Or.* 46; such riots also caused the predecessor of Varenus to ban meetings of the assemblies, *Or.* 48. 1. Cf. von Arnim, op. cit. 374; it is now clear from the dates that Bassus cannot be this predecessor, though he may be the bad governor.

auditu gravioribus. Charges of *saevitia* are meant (II. 11. 2 n.). The accusers seem not to have made them good, and the Senate sets them aside, s. 16, deeming the case to be one of 'simple extortion'. Hence the power of *inquisitio*, essential to establishing charges of *saevitia* (III. 9. 29; V. 20. 2 nn.), is not even asked for.

6. fuerat in eadem provincia quaestor. See s. 1 n. Pliny's silence shows that his troubles under Vespasian did not arise from this office.

lex munera quoque accipi vetat. The extortion law forbade a senator in any official position to acquire any money or material object in any way whatsoever—*capere cogere conciliare*—including sale, with limited exceptions such as presents from close relatives, or perishable commodities for food. This latter rule was gradually modified and defined, from the small exceptions of the *Lex Acilia* to a global figure of a hundred *aurei* in the Severan age, and a distinction was drawn between small presents—*munuscula*—and handsome gifts, much as here. See *Lex Acilia* 2; *Dig.* 1. 16. 6. 3, Ulpian; 48. 11. 1. 1, Marcian; 6. 2, Venuleius. Mommsen, *D. Pen. R.* iii. 11 f. Possibly this very case first drew attention to the awkwardness of a strict interpretation of the older rule, when so many senators were coming to be drawn from the provinces. Cf. VI. 19. 4 n.

7. etiam principi dixerat sola se munuscula dumtaxat natali suo aut Saturnalibus accepisse. This was evidently in private conversation, not at the opening of the case.

For the Saturnalia see II. 17. 24 n. For 'birthday parties' the *locus classicus* is Horace *Carm.* 4. 11. Birthday festivities are mentioned only twice elsewhere in the private Letters, III. 7. 8 and VI. 30. 1. It is remarkable that the Italian Saturnalia are now recognized in the Greek capital city of Bithynia. For 'Romanization' in Bithynia cf. X. 39. 1–4, 112 nn.

9. e lege accusator sex horas . . . accepisset. See II. 11. 14 n.

10. verebar ne me corporis vires . . . desererent. Cf. his weakness in the Priscus case, II. 11. 15.

13. successit mihi Lucceius Albinus. They acted together in the Classicus case, III. 9. 7–8. See ibid. n. for Albinus, who is not consular, and below, s. 14 n.

14. respondit Herennius Pollio. The man is consular, according to Pliny, but unknown yet save from some tile-stamps, Garzetti *C.* 62. Perhaps a relation of L. Herennius Saturninus, a suffect consul of 100.

post duos . . . consulares. i.e. Rufus s. 3 and Pollio—his own advocates, not Pliny and Lucceius.

15. egerunt pro Basso Homullus et Fronto. The *cognomen* Homullus is rare among senators. He should be the suffect consul of 102, M. Iunius Homullus, later legate of Cappadocia-Pontus, a contemporary of Fronto, rather than the elder Terentius Strabo Erucius Homullus, consul in 83, *CIL* xvi. 47; *ILS* 1996; *PIR*[1] T 72;

Garzetti, *C.* 82; *Inc.* 138. He defends Varenus in v. 20. 6 and speaks in the Senate in VI. 19. 3.

The nine-book manuscript reads Titius before Homullus. This might be the remnant of a reading Catius Fronto or Fronto Catius as in II. II. 3.

For the consular Ti. Caesius Catius Fronto see II. II. 3 n.

quartum diem probationes occuparunt. The evidence in a case of simple extortion would be largely documentary, cf. II. II. 18 n., 23 n.

16. censuit Baebius Macer consul designatus lege repetundarum Bassum teneri, Caepio Hispo salva dignitate iudices dandos, uterque recte. The only difference between the two proposals lay in the voiding of *ignominia*, hitherto conjoined to any condemnation for simple extortion under the shorter process, II. II. 12 n. Pliny's explanation in s. 17 makes this clear. He could not have added *uterque recte* if Macer had found Bassus liable on the criminal charge of *saevitia.* Cf. de Visscher, op. cit. (II. II. 2 n.) 201, and Sherwin-White, *BSR* XVII, 20 ff. In II. 12. 4 Pliny takes a less favourable view of a similar proposal.

Baebius Macer. For his career see III. 5 pref. His proposal would fit Martial's 'honest Macer', 5. 28. 5.

Caepio Hispo. This is the man of many names, known—if the inscriptions are properly combined—as Galleo Severus M. Eppuleius Proculus L. f. Ti. Caepio Hispo, a Cisalpine who after the prefecture of the *aerarium militare* governed Baetica and Asia, and who may be the Proculus given as a suffect consul of 101 by the *Fasti* of the Latin *Feriae, CIL* xiv. 2243; Syme, *JRS*, 1946, 163; *PIR²* E 83; *contra* Garzetti, *C.* 144. For the evidence see *ILS* 1027; *CIL* v. 5813; *AE*, 1930, n. 77. Possibly the father- or brother-in-law of the iniquitous Regulus, Ep. 2. 2 n.

17. cum putaret licere senatui (sicut licet) et mitigare leges et intendere. This refers to the Senate as a judicial, not as a legislative body, and expresses the same notion as II. II. 4: 'aliis cognitionem senatus lege conclusam, aliis liberam solutamque dicentibus, quantumque admisisset reus tantum vindicandum'. The process whereby the Senate adjusted the penalties of the *leges publicae* when it undertook *cognitio* in the case of senators, in the place of the *quaestiones publicae*, develops steadily throughout the Principate. But this passage is not to be applied lightly to any case at any period. It is remarkable that in both places there are those who held that the Senate's duty was to administer the unaltered statute. The Senate's jurisdiction is not entirely *extra ordinem* (p. 163). See now J. Bleicken, *Senatsgericht und Kaisergericht* (Göttingen, 1962), 37–43.

et intendere. As the greater number of statutes had a capital penalty, it was normally a mitigation of sentence that was at issue, as here and in II. II. 19–20, 12. 2; cf. also V. 13. 4–5.

18. consurgenti ei ad censendum acclamatum est. In IX. 13. 19 there is a less friendly demonstration as a senator rises to speak; cf. also Ep. 25. 2, V. 13. 3. Ultimately this custom developed into the regular expression of the Senate's opinion by *acclamatio*. *RE* (S.), VI. 774.

20. Valerius Paulinus. If he speaks as consular, as some hold (*PIR*¹ V 107; Garzetti, *C.* 146; *Inc.* 152), he cannot be Pliny's friend, consul in 107, IX. 37. 1 n. But many *praetorii* speak in the Senate, cf. VI. 5. 1, for Licinius Nepos; IX. 13. 13 n., for five such. So no additions to the list are needed. For Paulinus' connexions see II. 2 pref.

arguebatur enim multa in accusatione fecisse quae illa ipsa lege . . . tenerentur. At first sight a charge of *calumnia* would seem to be afoot. But in imperial usage a charge of extortion also lay if a man took money *ob accusandum* (Venuleius, *Dig.* 48. 11. 6. 2). The reference is to the *quaestus* of the delators in s. 5. Theophanes may have been liable in his capacity as *legatus*.

21. hanc sententiam consules . . . non sunt persecuti. The consuls are still free to choose which *sententia* to put to the vote. Pliny's version is, however, incomplete, for it was also carried that Bassus' acts as proconsul should be invalidated, and his judicial decisions subject to retrial within two years, X. 56. 4.

Paulinus tamen . . . famam . . . constantiae tulit. For if Bassus' offences were merely technical, then the prosecution was malicious.

22. squalida senectus. He must have been not less than twenty-five years past his praetorship in 103, ss. 1, 2 nn., and not less than 55 years old—hardly the age and condition to be made a consul, as Premerstein would have him.

10. *To Statius Sabinus*

Date not determinable.

Address. The *nomen* is given only by the Ashburnham index. He should be the same Sabinus as the patron and native of Firmum, VI. 18 pref., and the man of letters and military commander of IX. 2, 18.

1. Sabinam quae nos reliquit heredes. For the formula cf. V. 7. 1. Sabina seems not to be the wife of Statius, but a relative.

2. contuli cum peritis iuris : convenit inter omnes nec libertatem deberi quia non sit data, nec legatum quia servo suo dederit. The freeing of slaves by testament, under the conditions of the *Lex Fufia Caninia*, made them Roman citizens of freedman status, Gaius 2. 42–46. The legacy was not valid because the testator failed to change the slave's status. Ordinarily a slave 'acquires' for his owner, and a legacy to a slave is valid but becomes the master's property. Sabina thus merely passed this legacy through the slave's hands back to the heir to whom she had already willed the substance of it. See Gaius 2. 86 ff.; *Tit. Ulp.* 22. 7 ff.; H. J. Roby, *Roman Private Law*, i. 195 f.; or more fully, W. W. Buckland, *Roman Law of Slavery* (Cambridge, 1908), 137 ff., 144 ff.

peritis. Such as Titius Aristo, I. 22. 1–2 n.

3. custodire defunctorum voluntatem quam bonis heredibus intellexisse pro iure est. For this unorthodox doctrine thrice approved by Pliny see II. 16. 2, V. 7. 2 nn.

4. fruatur legato quasi omnia diligentissime caverit. The change of subject from Modestus to Sabina is evidence of literary revision. The last two paragraphs have a more literary flavour than the first two. This sentence could follow more intelligibly after the end of s. 2, in the original version.

11. *To Cornelius Minicianus*

Date. Peter, art. cit. 707, argued for a date before 100 on the weak ground that Licinianus 'must' have taken to professional rhetoric soon after the death of Nerva, if not before. S. Monti, *Pliniana*, iii. 96 f., argued that the letter was written under Nerva, but not published until later because of its violent tone. But I. 5 is equally political and tendencious, and the evidence of dating is unprecise and in s. 2 has been misinterpreted. See ss. 2, 14 nn.

Address. For Cornelius Minicianus, Transpadane and procurator, see III. 9 pref., VII. 22. 2 n.

1. audistine Valerium Licinianum in Sicilia profiteri? The absolute use of *profiteri* recurs in II. 18. 3, of rhetoricians. Suetonius, *Nero* 21. 1, uses it of *citharoedi in albo profitentes*, and, *de gramm.* 9, of *grammatici*, and Quintilian of rhetors often.

praetorius hic modo inter eloquentissimos causarum actores habebatur. This does not mean that he had recently been praetor: *modo* qualifies the whole sentence. The contrast is between the former praetorian advocate and the present professor in exile. The Latin order has been misquoted by the advocates of the early date as *modo praetorius*—(cf. *Lustrum* vi. 300)—but even the formerly preferred reading of α, *praetorius modo hic*, must yield to the agreement of β γ.

2. in praefatione dixit. For the use of prefaces see I. 13. 2. In them the speaker sums up the main points of the theme or *controversia* on which he is going to elaborate.

facis enim ex senatoribus professores. Cf. Juv. 7. 197, 'si fortuna volet fies de rhetore consul' etc.. Licinianus is known only from Pliny, though mentioned without name by Suetonius (*Dom.* 8. 4), unless he may be identified with the elderly advocate and senator from Bilbilis, Lucius Licinianus, either the tutor or a close relative of the great consular Licinius Sura, celebrated by Martial I. 49, 61, IV. 55 (as in *RE* (2) viii. 52). But Martial speaks of his man as in permanent retirement at Bilbilis, and as a figure of the previous generation (I. 49. 41–42, 61). The suggestion of M. Griffin (*JRS*, 1962, 107) that he discreetly retired to Spain after the first Vestal trial, and later returned to Rome, will not do, because senators could not abandon Rome or even visit their provincial estates briefly (save in Sicily and Narbonensis) without the permission of the emperor. Dio 52. 42. 6; Tac. *Ann.* 12. 23. 2, cf. III. 7. 7 n. Besides, Martial's first book seems to precede the Vestal trial and subsequent German war of 83 first mentioned in II. 2. He would hardly twice flatter a suspected personage and refer to *Vestae virgineam domum* (I. 70. 3) in a book published just after the event. (For the dates see Xiphilinus in Dio 67. 3² and 4, with Jerome in s. 7 n.) There is no evidence that Pliny's Licinianus was involved in the first trial of Cornelia. The identification of the two is possible if he was not. Yet would Pliny risk offending the influential Sura, to whom a letter is addressed in this book, by mud-raking his former protector or parent?

3. Graeco pallio amictus . . . carent enim togae iure quibus aqua et igni interdictum est. For the contrast between *pallium* and *toga* see Cic. *de Rab. Post.* 25–27, and later Tertullian *de pallio* (*passim*). Before 90 B.C. the *toga* was the distinctive Italian, not merely Roman, dress. Marcian, *Dig.* 49. 14. 32, formalizes the connexion between the *toga* and citizenship. Pliny here gives the fully developed imperial doctrine whereby the interdict, and consequential *deportatio* with confiscation of goods (s. 13), replaced actual execution, and hence implied loss of citizenship. In the Republic the interdict simply drove a man out of the Roman state, and encouraged him to resign Roman status and seek the citizenship of another state. See Brasiello, op. cit. (II. 11. 8 n.), ch. iii. 61 ff., 98 ff. The voluntary exile was replaced by compulsory limitation of residence under Tiberius, if not earlier. Tiberius completed the compulsory loss of citizenship by forbidding exiles the right to make wills *quasi peregrini*. This prevented them from enjoying the citizenship of a provincial community. Brasiello, ch. x. 110, 298 ff.; Tac. *Ann.* 3. 38,

4. 13; Dio 57. 22. 5. Pliny here shows that deportation is still merely consequential to the interdict, and not a separate penalty as in later law.

5. **confessus est quidem incestum, sed incertum utrum quia verum erat.** Despite Pliny's innuendoes here and below—which s. 8 shows that he did not believe—the guilt of Valerius must have been generally conceded, since Nerva did not cancel his sentence. Suetonius, *Dom.* 8. 4, has no doubt of the guilt of the Vestals and implies that of Valerius, remarking only, as in ss. 12–13, that he withdrew before the case was completed against him. Juvenal 4. 5 ff. assumes the guilt of Crispinus also, the notorious but unidentifiable counsellor of Domitian. Similarly Tac. *Hist.* 1. 2, and more understandably the contemporary Statius *S.* 1. 1. 36. The story of the naughty Vestals is also told in Dio 67. 3 and the late chronographers, cf. *PIR²* C 1481. Monti, *Pliniana*, iii. 90 f., took the sole charge against Licinianus to be that of concealing the witness, s. 11, and hence exaggerated the difference between Pliny and Suetonius.

Domitianus aestuabat . . . in ingenti invidia destitutus. Because Cornelia and Celer continued to protest *tamquam innocens* to the end. Pliny resumes the thread in s. 11 with 'ardebat ergo Domitianus'. The whole letter is a remarkable example of special pleading. The reader goes away with a strong impression of the wickedness of Domitian, though even Pliny cannot assert the unequivocal innocence of the parties. Cf. H. W. Traub, 'Pliny's treatment of history' etc., *T.A.Ph.A.*, vol. 86. 214 ff., who stresses the Tacitean quality of Pliny's treatment, rightly.

6. **cum Corneliam Vestalium maximam defodere vivam concupisset.** There were two trials. At the first three or four Vestals were condemned, and allowed to perish by suicide, but Cornelia was acquitted. At the second she was retried and condemned, and punished *more veteri* (Suet. loc. cit.). Pliny turns Domitian's clemency against him. He could have buried them all. For the dates see s. 7 n. Suetonius includes these trials in the praiseworthy category of 'ius diligenter et industrie dixit'. Domitian's strictness is part of the new morality of the Flavian age, of which Pliny himself is a keen advocate, VII. 24 nn.

Corneliam Vestalium maximam. There were six Vestals, the senior bearing the title 'Vestalis maxima', Gellius *NA* 1. 12; Tac. *Ann.* 11. 32. For the organization of the College see D–S s.v. 752 ff. Suetonius names the Oculatae sisters and Varronilla, as well as Cornelia; this might well be Cornelia Cossa, who became a Vestal in A.D. 62, Tac. *Ann.* 15. 22. Vestals were usually chosen when under ten years old, and held office not less than thirty years. D–S 752; Tac. *Ann.* 2. 86.

The reading of β—*Maximillam* for *maximam*—cannot be supported against αγ and the text of Suetonius, loc. cit. (Stout, op. cit. 176). *PIR*² should be corrected on this.

defodere vivam. The punishment is described by Plutarch impressively in *Numa* 10. 4–7, and by Dion. Hal. *Ant.* 2. 67. 3–4, 9. 40. 3. Plutarch may have witnessed the scene. A solemn procession, led by the chief pontiff, or by the *promagister* of the College, taking the place of the Princeps, took the condemned Vestal, bound on a bier, to the neighbourhood of the Colline gate. There a subterranean cell was prepared, in which she was immured, containing a bench, food, drink, and a light.

saeculum suum. Cf. x. 1. 2 n., 'digna saeculo tuo'.

pontificis maximi iure . . . reliquos pontifices non in Regiam sed in Albanam villam convocavit. The Vestals were under the jurisdiction of the Pontifex Maximus, but not under his *patria potestas* (as Merrill said), because they were *sui iuris*, Gellius, *NA* i. 12. Cf. vii. 19. 1. This trial, which extends to the paramours, is a remnant of the sacral jurisdiction of the Pontiffs. Cf. the trial of 114 B.C., Asconius 40.

Regiam. The office of the Pontifex Maximus, Ashby, *Top. Dict.* 440. Pliny wishes to imply that the trial was *intra cubiculum*. But Roman jurisdiction was not tied to places, and Suetonius states that secret jurisdiction was not normal with Domitian, op. cit. 8. 1. Cf. I. 5. 14 n.

absentem inauditamque damnavit incesti. Merrill, ad loc., suggested that Cornelia was absent because this was merely the passing of a sentence. But it was a new trial, according to Suetonius, not the continuation of the first.

incesti. This was the normal charge, instead of *stuprum*, in case of Vestals. Cf. Isidore, *Or.* 5. 26. 24: 'incesti iudicium in virgines sacratas . . constitutum est'. So too Suetonius, Asconius, locc. cit.; Val. Max. 3. 7. 9, Cic. *de Nat. Deor.* 3. 74.

cum ipse fratris filiam incesto . . . occidisset. This choice story is repeated in Suetonius, *Dom.* 22. The charge of incest is repeated in *Pan.* 52. 3 without any particular details. Suetonius places the beginning of the affair during the reign of Titus.

7. qua sacra faciente vicit triumphavit. This is Pliny's only indication of date. Dio, loc. cit., puts the first trial about A.D. 83. The chronographer Jerome puts the condemnation of the three Vestals in Domitian's third year, 83–84, and that of Cornelia in his eleventh year, 91–92. The *Chronicon Paschale*, dating by consuls, puts the second trial in 89. Perhaps the reference in Pliny includes both the German triumph in 83 and the Dacian in 89. Hence *CAH* xi. 37 plumps for 90. It must be before the death of Senecio in 93–4, s. 12.

9. **carnifex.** His presence is surprising, since the ceremony is by way of a purification. Plutarch, loc. cit., mentions 'servants'. One expects the *calatores pontificum*.

10. **Celer . . . cum in comitio virgis caederetur, in hac voce perstiterat.** The man is unknown. Suetonius speaks of *stupratores*. The punishment was, again, traditional, Dion. Hal. 9. 40. 4. The use of the Comitium shows antiquity of custom, since this was the most ancient place of assembly of the Roman people. It adjoined the Curia Julia, and the *lapis niger* was found there. Ashby, op. cit. 134.

11. **in agris suis occultasset Corneliae libertam.** The witness of his crime, which was not limited to this simple interference with justice. Otherwise Nerva would not have maintained his sentence.

12. **locutus est pro absente Herennius Senecio tale quiddam, quale est illud.** For Senecio see I. 5. 3, III. 11. 3, VII. 33. 4 nn. As usual he is supporting the wrong side, against Domitian. The brevity of the Homeric announcement, *Iliad* 18. 20, was famous, cf. Quint. 10. 1. 49.

   pro absente. This may mean not merely that he has abandoned his defence, but that, as in the trial of Cornelia, it was normal to hear Vestal cases thus, though it is quite contrary to the usages of Roman criminal law.

   'Licinianus recessit', i.e. *a causa*, as in V. 13. 2.

13. **'absolvit nos Licinianus'.** This implies that there had been outspoken criticism of Domitian's action. Dio, loc. cit., states that one pontiff fainted during the examination of witnesses.

   si qua posset ex rebus suis raperet antequam bona publicarentur. The *publicatio bonorum* had become the normal consequence of the ordinary *capital* penalty, whether in the form of death or interdict, from the end of the Republic, and was total. Any remission was an act of grace. Usually in the early Principate exiles were allowed to keep a substantial sum, often one-twelfth of their estate, and concessions were made in favour of children. But evidently this had not yet become a rule. See Brasiello, op. cit. 105 ff., 117 n. 64; Tac. *Ann.* 3. 23, 68; 4. 20; Dio 56. 27. 2–3; *Gnomon idiologi* 36; Paulus, *Dig.* 48. 20. 7. 3.

14. **translatus est in Siciliam, ubi nunc profitetur.** Pliny does not imply that the two events were close in time, rather, by his *nunc*, he seeks to distinguish an interval; Schultz, art. cit. 24, sagely remarked that Valerius would use up his money first. In s. 1 *nunc* marks an interval of not less than eight years on any view.

15. **altius repetam.** Traub, art. cit. 213 ff., notes the skill with which Pliny combines the historical narrative of the trial with the contem-

porary anecdote about Licinianus in Sicily starting and ending with that, and sandwiching the Vestal story neatly between s. 5, 'fremebat . . . invidia destitutus', and s. 11, 'ardebat . . . infamia'. All is so managed as to give the letter the appearance of a genuine epistle. But ss. 1–3 and 14–16 could well form an original core, later expanded.

12. *To Arrianus Maturus*

Date. Between June and September 105, s. 4 n.

Address. For Arrianus Maturus, now on equestrian service in Egypt, s. 7 n., see I. 2 pref., III. 2 nn.

1. amas Egnatium Marcellinum. This is M. Egnatius Marcellinus, suffect consul in 116, *FO*, *PIR*² E 14, 24. A ten or eleven years' interval between quaestorship and consulship is normal enough, as in Pliny's own career.

2. scribam . . . qui sorte obtigerat. The use of *scribae* as magisterial clerks continued in the public provinces throughout the Principate as in the Republic, cf. VI. 22. 4. The scribes were a professional *ordo*, ranking just below the equestrian order in the Republic, and attached to the *aerarium Saturni*. They drew lots each year, like the quaestors themselves, for the various posts, cf. Ep. 15. 6 n.; Cic. *Cat.* 4. 15; Mommsen, *DPR* i. 397 ff.

ante legitimum . . . tempus. Before the opening of the proconsular year. It seems that the scribe only drew his salary from the moment of arrival in the province.

quod acceperat. The *aerarium* continued to authorize the *ornatio* or financial establishment of the public provinces each year, cf. Frontinus *de aquis* 100. The cash might be paid over in Rome or collected in the province; Jones, *JRS*, 1950, 23. Little is known of the pay of scribes, for which *merces* was the republican term. The Lex Ursonensis 62 gives S.1200 for municipal scribes of the top grade.

subsidere. Under the *Lex Iulia de residuis pecuniis*: 'tenetur is apud quem . . . ex pecunia quam accepit . . . pecunia publica resedit', Marcian, *Dig.* 48. 13. 5 pref. At the end of his office the magistrate is bound to balance his account with the *aerarium*. After this *professio* he is allowed a year to complete his payment before a criminal charge may be instituted, ibid. 11. 6.

3. reversus Caesarem deinde Caesare auctore senatum consuluit. Despite the separation between *aerarium* and *fiscus* completed by the Flavians (Jones, art. cit. 26 ff.; cf. Frontinus, *de aquis* 118), the Princeps continued to be regarded as the ultimate supervisor of the *aerarium.* Cf. Pliny, *Pan.* 36. 3: 'fortasse non eadem severitate fiscum qua aerarium cohibes'. Trajan elsewhere also is anxious to relax the imperial control over senatorial machinery established under the Flavians, cf. VI. 31. 6; VII. 6. 1, 6 nn. But officials and provincials within the senatorial sphere continued to turn to the emperor instead of the Senate, cf. Ep. 22. 1 n. The Flavians had done their work too well (*pace* F. Millar, *JRS*, 1963, 29 ff.).

parva quaestio. See III. 20. 10–12 for this theme: 'de re publica loquerer cuius materiae . . . rarior . . . occasio' etc.

praefecti aerari populo vindicabant. The terms *populus, publicus* commonly refer to the *aerarium* in the sense of 'state finances'. II. 1. 9 n. For the functions of the *praefecti* see I. 10. 9 n.

4. Caecilius Strabo aerario censuit inferendum, Baebius Macer heredibus dandum. These are senators giving their *sententiae*, not the advocates. Since Baebius Macer was senior to Strabo as a consular, IV. 9 pref., and yet Strabo spoke first, the latter should be consul designate according to the custom of debates, II. 11. 20; Pliny omits the designation in II. 12. 2, VI. 13. 5. He was consul suffect in September–December 105 (*FO*). Hence the debate falls neatly into the period after the return of the quaestors from the overseas provinces (cf. Ep. 15. 6 n.) after midsummer and before the Kalends of September. Hanslik, art. cit. 132 (*Wiener Studien*, 63). would have Strabo *consularis* and date the letter to 106, but this fails to explain the *ordo sententiarum*. In the midsummer of 106 Trajan was not in Italy.

For Macer see III. 5 pref. He is displaying his 'fairness' again. For Strabo see Ep. 17. 1 n.

7. laudis suae . . . peregrinatione laetetur. This suggests that Maturus is still in Egypt with Maximus, III. 2 nn., as in Ep. 8.

13. *To Cornelius Tacitus*

Date fits book. Pliny has recently married, s. 5 n., and visited Comum s. 1 n., and is finishing his volume of hendecasyllabics, s. 1 n. Probably in the autumn at the beginning of the Roman season.

Address. This is only the third letter in the collection addressed to the historian, who is not addressed in II, III, or V. For Pliny's relations with him see I. 6 pref.

1. salvum in urbem venisse gaudeo. Travel in Italy had its dangers, VI. 25. Tacitus has not come back from an overseas appointment, since his career as an advocate is in full swing, s. 10. Syme, *Tac.* 71, deduces from this passage and his omission from III, that he had just

held a provincial post. But he is absent from v also. The September–
October vacation, when senators were not required to be in Rome, is
over for both Pliny and Tacitus (*RE* (S.) vi. 766 f.; Suet. *Aug.* 35. 3).

**in Tusculano commorabor ut opusculum quod est in manibus
absolvam.** By *opusculum* he means his new slim volume of verses, as
in Ep. 14. 5, 10. The term is used for its successor, VI. 6. 6, VII. 9. 13,
VIII. 21. 4, but never for orations. He does not tell what this volume
is because that is not the subject of the letter.

in Tusculano. Guillemin is right in suggesting that this is a friend's
villa, because v. 6. 45 (n.) shows that Pliny did not own a villa at
Tusculum.

3. proxime cum in patria mea fui. For Pliny's recent visit to Comum
see Ep. 1. The force of *proxime* requires a short interval, cf. Ep. 16. 1.

salutandum. He could avoid the morning levée at his Tuscan villa,
IX. 36. 1, but not at Comum.

'studes?' As usual, rhetorical rather than 'grammatical' studies
are implied, cf. II. 18. 1, III. 3. 3–4. nn., which are companion pieces
to this letter.

Mediolani. For Milan as a regional centre cf. VII. 23. 1. For its
importance at this period see Chilver, *Cisalpine Gaul*, 53 ff., 120, 198.
In a later age St. Augustine held the chair of Latin rhetoric there,
Conf. 5. 13 (23).

4. aut pudicius continerentur. For the dangers of the *scholae* see III.
3. 3–4 nn.

**5. ego . . . paratus sum pro re publica nostra . . . tertiam
partem . . . dare.** Pliny is acting in the spirit of the times in encouraging education. The Flavians began the policy of advancing scholas-
tic education. Vespasian founded seats of Greek and Latin rhetoric
at Rome, and initiated the technique of indirectly subsidizing
municipal schools, in the first instance in the Asian province, by
granting personal privileges to the members of, apparently, the
teaching guilds, including *medici* and *grammatici*. Both fisca.
immunities and protection from personal injury are mentioned. The
latter lapsed later, but the former increased in scope in the second
century. Suet. *Vesp.* 18; Zon. 11. 17. Rescripts of Vespasian and
Domitian, *W–C* n. 458 (*AE*, 1936, n. 128); Marrou[1], op. cit. (cited
II. 18. 2 n.) 402 ff. Herzog regards the rescript as a general charter of
education, while Bardon sees no more than a grant of the right of
association—wrongly (cf. x. 34. 1, 96. 7 nn. for this theme). See
Herzog, *Berlin SB Preuss. Ak. Wiss.* (Berlin) 1935, 973 ff.; M. A.
Levi, *Romana*, i (1937), 361 ff.; H. Bardon, *Les Empereurs et les
lettres latines* etc. (Paris, 1940), 301. Earlier, E. Saint-Denis cited III.
3. 3–4 nn., 'Pline . . . et la jeunesse', 13 f.

qui nondum liberos habeo. The reference to his recent marriage is clear, Epp. I, 19. Earlier he had given up hope, X. 2. 2–3.

6. ne hoc munus ... ambitu corrumperetur, ut accidere multis in locis video. Pliny's meaning is clear from ss. 7–8; he fears nepotism in the choice of professors, not, as Marrou, op. cit. 405, the appearance of having acted to secure popularity. Intrigue among schoolmasters was regularly expected, II. 18. 5: 'nec ignoro suscipiendas offensas in eligendo praeceptore'. So too he tried to prevent the ruin of his *alimenta*, VII. 18. 2. Domitian had to check corrupt practices in the Flavian scheme by the rule that only *ingenui* were to be taught by the professors. How Trajan fulfilled the promise of *Pan.* 47. 1— 'quem honorem dicendi magistris ... habes'—is unknown.

multis in locis. This implies that municipal schools existed in the larger Italian municipalities, for 'grammar' if not for rhetoric. Gellius, *NA* 16. 6. 2 mentions such a school at Beneventum. Juvenal refers to them in the western provinces, 15. 111, and Tacitus mentions the school at Augustodunum for the Aeduan aristocracy, and another in Britain, Tac. *Ann.* 3. 43; *Agric.* 21. 2. Inscriptions add to the list from time to time. At Comum itself (*CIL* v. 5278) the municipality honoured a *grammaticus* with the *ornamenta decurionalia*. But the demand for the upper education would be naturally less intense outside the wealthiest classes than for the 'grammar' course. The Greek educational system of the eastern empire is well known through its connexion with the public *gymnasium* system, see Jones, *Greek City*, ch. 14.

As the numbers of the schools increased it became necessary to limit the application of the privileges granted by the Flavian rescript. Pius established a scale whereby cities rated in three grades, by size or municipal importance, and might maintain three, four, or five privileged rhetoricians and as many grammarians, *Dig.* 27. 1. 6. 2–3. Corrupt practices infiltrated early, and the emperors required the municipalities to apply proficiency tests.

7. si parentibus solis ius conducendi relinquatur. Pliny contemplates a private school. In municipal schools the local council made the choice, and a petitioner to the Princeps for the learned privileges had to produce his decree of appointment. Cf. Lucian, *Eunuchus* 3; *Dig.* loc. cit. 4; *Cod. Iust.* (Gordian) 10. 53. 2.

8. certe de suo diligentes erunt. Cf. VII. 18. 1: 'des agros: ut publici neglegentur'.

9. ita mox alieni in hunc locum confluant. The whole letter underlines the ease of communications in Italy, whether from Comum to Mediolanum, or to Rome.

10. ex copia studiosorum quae ad te . . . convenit. A *rhetor Latinus* is wanted, as in II. 18 and III. 3. An established man, such as Pliny's Julius Genitor (ibid.), would not leave Rome; hence a beginner is required. Pliny, like Tacitus, had his circle of *studiosi*, though he only tells about the *clari adulescentuli* (VI. 11, 23). Tacitus' circle evidently included obscurer persons who might welcome such a chance as this. The great orators, like the great jurisprudents, did not give regular instruction, but trained their followers by informal discussion, advice, and example, cf. VI. 11, 23, 29; VII. 9; IX. 13. 1; Schulz, *Roman Legal Science*, 122.

praeceptores. Pliny envisages a plurality of teachers throughout this letter, ss. 3, 9.

illi iudicent illi eligant. Probably the competitors would be asked to demonstrate their talents in an audition, like the *grammaticus* in Gellius, *NA* 16. 6. 1: 'a Brundisinis accersitus experiundum sese vulgo dabat', or like S. Augustine later at Milan, *Conf.* loc. cit.; Marrou, op. cit.[1] 406. Fronto, *Ep. ad amicos* I. 7, asks a provincial governor to secure a post in one of his cities for a *rhetor* from Rome.

As for pay, the professor at Athens received in the second century a salary of some S.40,000 a year, Philostratus, *VS* 2. 2, or twenty times the fee of a *grammaticus* at Teos in the Hellenistic age (Jones, op. cit. 222). Juvenal reckons a rhetor's pay at S.2,000 annually per pupil. But these are exceptional cases. See Marrou, op. cit.[1] 380, 403.

14. *To Plinius Paternus*

Date. The letters about Pliny's versification begin in IV and continue through to IX. The longer letters form an orderly series: here his first volume of hendecasyllabics is introduced, V. 3 gives his reply to criticism of it, VII. 4, 9. 9–14 is an account of its composition, VIII. 21 announces his second volume of verses. Interspersed are shorter references, IV. 13. 1—where the volume is not yet finished—18, 27. 3–4; VI. 6. 6; IX. 10, 16. 2, 34. 1. Certain cross-references tie these letters to the chronological framework of the books. ss. 8, 9 nn. In VII. 4. 3 he says that he gave up the writing of verses about the beginning of his public career, and took it up again *nunc primum*. There are no references to his verses in I–III, although his elder friends are mentioned as amateurs of the game, Spurinna in III. 1. 7, and Verginius Rufus, who died in 97, in V. 3. 5. It seems likely that it was his closer acquaintance with Spurinna and Arrius Antoninus, another dilettante, that led Pliny into this hobby at this time: 'exemplo multorum', VII. 4. 8, Ep. 3, 27. 5 nn. The total absence of any reference to his versification in I–III is in striking contrast to his parade of it from IV onwards.

Peter's attack on the chronological order of some of these letters (art. cit. 703) takes no account of these connexions and cannot be maintained; cf. Ep. 3 pref., VII. 4 pref., VIII. 1 pref., IX. 34 pref. Cf. also V. 3. 5 n. on Monti's attempt to date that letter to *c.* 98; and s. 4 n., on an attempt to make this letter contemporary with V. 3.

Address. For Plinius Paternus, a relation from Comum, see I. 21 pref.

2–3. accipies . . . hendecasyllabos nostros, quibus . . . iocamur ludimus amamus dolemus querimur irascimur, describimus aliquid. The style was worked out by Martial, who made the elegiac couplet and the hendecasyllabic verse his principal metres. His subjects are just those summarized by Pliny here and in VII. 9. 13, IX. 22. 2. For the fashion in these things see III. 1. 7 n. After various experiments, such as those of Ep. 18, he decided to publish 'unum separatim hendecasyllaborum volumen', VII. 4. 8. This seems to be the *opusculum* of Ep. 13. 1, completed after his visit to Comum.

in vehiculo. So too in IX. 10. 2 'in via . . . non nulla leviora . . . extendi'.

4. gravissimos viros . . . non modo lascivia rerum, sed ne verbis quidem nudis abstinuisse. Pliny elaborates this appeal to authority in V. 3. By *rerum* he means subject-matter, not personal behaviour. Pliny was evidently more allusive than the franker Martial. Even Spurinna indulged in *hilaritas*, III. 1. 7. Prete (*Saggi Pliniani* 22) thought this was written with knowledge of the criticism quoted in V. 3. But it was easy to anticipate, and is not here taken so seriously as in V. 3. Besides V. 3 is concerned with recitation, not here mentioned.

5. legem, quam Catullus expressit. Catullus 16. 5. Martial defends himself strongly on these lines in I pref., and counterattacks: 'epigrammata illis scribuntur qui solent spectare Florales'. After Catullus the remark became a commonplace. Editors quote Ovid, *Tr.* 2. 354; Martial I. 4. 8; Ausonius, epigrams, 9; Apuleius *Apol.* 11; and refer to G. R. Throop, *Wash. Univ. Stud.* i. 160 ff., 'The lives and verses of Roman erotic writers'. Pliny's defence may be relatively justified. See VII. 24 nn. for his prudery. The provincial Plutarch also disapproved of *lusus,Q. Conv.* 7. 8. 4.

8. longa praefatione. For Pliny's dislike of prefaces see Ep. 5. 4, V. 12. 3, VIII. 21. 3.

9. sive ut multi, poematia . . . vocare malueris. He may mean just Sentius Augurinus, who chose this term at this time, Ep. 27. 1. Pliny does not use the term again.

10. 'quaere quod agas.' Cf. the anecdote about Livius Drusus and the herald Granius, which turned on the idiom 'quid agis?', Cic. *pro Planc.* 33.

15. *To Minicius Fundanus*

Date. This has been much disputed. Since Pliny expects Fundanus to be consul 'next year', s. 5, and he was suffect consul in 107, Peter (art.cit. 708) and Otto (art.cit. 33–34) assigned the letter to 106, the suffects of 105 being already known to Pliny in Ep. 17. But they failed to note that Pliny was expecting Fundanus to be *ordinarius*, not suffect consul, for he is supposed to have a free choice of quaestors, s. 8 n. There is good reason to suppose that Fundanus' consulship was postponed from 106 to 107. In the years 105–7 there was unusual pressure on the consular list through the decision of Trajan to give second consulships to four leading men, Julius Candidus and Julius Quadratus in 105, and Licinius Sura and Sosius Senecio in 107, while the notables L. Ceionius Commodus and Sex. Vettulenus Civica Cerealis, men of family, were requiring 'ordinary' consulships also (106). Hence alterations may have occurred after the moment when Pliny first heard the rumour. Otto also argued that the letter could not have been published before the consulship of Fundanus was secured for fear of offending him by revealing his rebuff. But this confuses compilation and publication dates. The difficulty disappears if IV was *published* after the consuls of 107 were known (Schultz, art. cit. 24). Besides, the letter is flattering enough, whenever published.

So the book-date may stand. Even on Otto's view the letter need not be later than the election of quaestors in January 106 for 107, s. 6 n.

Address. Gaius Minicius Fundanus was one of Pliny's closer friends, I. 9, V. 16, VI. 6, reasonably identified, from his philosophical interests, with Plutarch's twice-mentioned friend of the same name, v. 16. 8 n. His earlier career, known from a fragmentary inscription republished by Syme (*Tac.* 801 n. 3), includes a legionary legateship and a senior priesthood, to which *CIL* vi. *falsae* 3205, may add the prefecture of Saturn. This would fit his presence in Italy in the period of IV–VI and make him a close successor of Pliny in that office. After his suffect consulship in 107 he is absent from the Letters. As proconsul of Asia *c.* 124–5 he received Hadrian's rescript about the Christians (Euseb. *HE* 4. 9). His name and tribe *Papiria* may indicate Cisalpine origin, not apparent in Pliny, but shared with other of Pliny's Minicii (Syme, loc. cit. Cf. I. 14. 5, VII. 11. 4).

1. Asinium Rufum singulariter amo. An undistinguished praetorian senator (s. 10), possibly the L. Asinius Rufus who was legate to the proconsul of Africa, Q. Pomponius Rufus, in 109–10, unless that is one of his sons: *AE* 1948, 3; Garzetti, *Inc.* 19–20. Syme suspects an African origin (op. cit. 800). Cf. also H. G. Pflaum, *Archeologia*, x (1958) 145 f., for men holding proconsular legateships before the praetorship.

3. eo saeculo quo . . . etiam singulos filios orbitatis praemia graves faciunt. Pliny does not restrict his comment to the age of Domitian, either here or in s. 8, or in II. 20. 12. For the *captatio* theme see ibid. 7 n.

est enim avus, et quidem ex Saturio Firmo. Since young Bassus, his eldest son, is not stated to be married, as often at the quaestorian age (cf. VI. 26. 1, VII. 24. 3, VIII. 23. 8), this means that Rufus has married a daughter to the unknown Saturius, who may be connected with the procurator C. Saturius of Asculum, governor of Rhaetia in 80 (Syme, *Tac.* 801 n. 1). This child may be the suffect consul of 148 (Pflaum, art. cit.).

5. tibi ominamur . . . in proximum annum consulatum. Either Pliny has heard a solid rumour, or has worked it out from the man's career. The prefecture of Saturn, if he held it (above), would be a clear tip. But the precise year could not be exactly predicted from the career, and Pliny is very precise.

6. concurrit autem ut sit eodem anno quaestor maximus ex liberis Rufi. The quaestorian elections, usually held early in the year, 24 January being later the regular date, have been completed, and Bassus is quaestor designate. Of the twenty quaestors two held the urban quaestorship in its few surviving duties, four were chosen to assist the consuls, two were taken by the Princeps, and the rest drew lots for public provinces outside Italy. Those serving at Rome entered office on the fifth of December following their election. (Mommsen, *DPR* iv. 229 f., 262.)

M. L. Paladini (*Athenaeum*, xxxvii. 33 f.) oddly translates this sentence to mean 'Bassus is competing to be quaestor this year'. This gives a strange meaning for *concurrit*, and would require *fiat* instead of *sit*. Pliny's inquiry was pointless if Bassus was not yet certain of the post. Cf. s. 13 n.

Bassus. No more seems to be known of the career of Asinius Bassus. *PIR*² A 1224.

8. diu pensitares, quem potissimum eligeres. Since Fundanus is to have the choice of quaestors Pliny must regard him as *ordinarius*. The choice of the four consular quaestors naturally precedes the sortition of the provincial quaestors, which took place not later than the beginning of the quaestorian year on 5 December (Mommsen, loc. cit.). The four consular quaestors remained in office throughout the year, serving the suffect consuls, but not chosen by them, like Junius Avitus: 'quaestor consulibus suis (et plures habuit) . . . utilis', VIII. 23. 5.

9. quem more maiorum in filii locum adsumas. For the traditional relationship see Cic. *ad Fam.* 13. 10. 1. Hence the horror when a quaestor accuses his proconsul, Tac. *Ann.* 1. 74. Cf. L. A. Thompson, *Historia*, 1962, 339 ff.

sapientes viri, ut tu. For Fundanus' philosophical line see v. 16. 8 n.

10. patre praetorio, propinquis consularibus. These kinsmen may be the more distinguished Asinii Marcelli, of whom one was consul suffect in 104, *PIR*² A 1233 f. The term *propinquus* covers both relations by blood and by marriage, Forcellini, *Lexicon* s.v. Cf. Suet. *Iulius* 1. 2; *Nero* 3. 1. Pflaum thinks the Pomponii Rufi (s. 1 n.) are meant.

11. si festinare videor ignosce. Pliny apologizes for writing long before the consular elections for *ordinarii*, held late in the year (p. 24).

13. cuius . . suffragio senatus libentissime indulgeat. For the influence of Fundanus see VI. 6. 8. Paladini, art. cit. 13, takes this paragraph to be a request for Fundanus' support at the quaestorian election of Bassus. But Pliny is here considering the candidature of Bassus at future elections after his quaestorship; 'illum . . . quaestorem . . . simus iuvaturi'. Paladini's suggestion would make the intention of the letter very obscurely expressed. Pliny's other electoral appeals are written in a very direct manner: II. 9, VI. 6.

16. *To Valerius Paulinus*

Date, uncertain. But the exceptional length of Pliny's speech suggests that this case might be the rare *quadruplex iudicium* of Ep. 24.

Address. For the praetorian senator Paulinus see II. 2 pref., Ep. 9. 20 n.

1. proxime cum dicturus apud centumviros essem. For the court and its arrangements see II. 14, V. 9 nn.

2. et quidem horis septem. nam tam diu dixi. The normal length of an advocate's speech in the Centumviral court was now apparently no more than an hour and often less, VI. 2. 5 n. Since court business usually started about the third hour of daylight and ended before the dinner hour—the eighth or ninth—Pliny took a whole court day. See III. 5. 9 n., Ep. 9. 14.

3. sunt qui audiant—instead of the hired claque described in II. 14. 4, the counterpart to this letter.

17. To Clusinius Gallus

Date. The consulship of Caecilius Strabo fixes the letter to the period January–August 105, s. 1 n.—much the same period as Ep. 12.

Address. The *nomen* Clusinius appears only here, in the Ashburnham index and in β. It is rare, but comparable to Salvius (II. 11. 17 n.) in being formed from a place-name. Cf. *RE* iv. 114. There is no need to emend it to the name of the known senator L. Cossonius Gallus (*PIR*² C 1541; Garzetti, *Inc.* 61, 70). Only two other letters are addressed to a Gallus, the descriptive pieces II. 17 and VIII. 20. A Gallus is also concerned in I. 7. 4 with Pliny's legal briefs, as here. Cf. II. 17 pref. One or other may be connected with the Pomponii Galli of V. 1. 1.

1. et admones et rogas ut suscipiam causam. For formalities of 'admonition' see II. 6. 6 n., 16. 1; VI. 18 is closer: 'rogas ut agam Firmanorum publicam causam'. There were no solicitors and barrister's clerks to arrange these things.

Corelliae absentis. Corellia Hispulla, daughter of Corellius Rufus, I. 12. 3 n. and III. 3 pref., where Pliny helps her to find a schoolmaster. He also helps her aunt the elder Corellia, VII. 11.

C. Caecilium. He is known, with his cognomen Strabo, from Ep. 12. 4, and as an Arval Brother in the Arval records from 101 to his death *c.* 117. His consulship is dated by *FO* to the September *nundinum* of 105. *PIR*² C 85. The use of the *duo nomina* is formal, cf. I. 12. 9 n.

2. non plane familiaris sed tamen amicitia. For the distinction see II. 6. 2 n., 'nam gradatim amicos habet', IX. 34. 1, 'familiaribus amicis'. Mere *amicitia* remains a relationship involving material interest, as in the Republic.

3. accedit huc dignitas hominis atque hic ipse cui destinatus est honor. For the hesitation to appear against a senator compare V. 13. 2, 'monitum . . ne desiderio senatoris . . . repugnaret'. But almost any social action involved the risk of 'subire offensas', s. 11, II. 18. 5 n.

4. ille vir quo neminem aetas . . . subtiliorem tulit. For the consular Corellius Rufus see I. 12 nn. By *subtiliorem* Pliny refers, as by *sapientissimi* s. 9, to the intellectual acumen if not to the philosophical interests of Corellius. Cf. Ep. 14. 7, II. 11. 17, I. 10. 5.

6. ille meus in petendis honoribus suffragator. Pliny was similarly supported by Verginius Rufus, II. I. 8 n. As *candidatus Caesaris* he had not so much need as others for the help of a *suffragator*. See III. 20. 5 for the custom. For attendance at the installation of new magistrates see I. 5. II, IX. 37. I nn.

in omnibus officiis nostris . . . conspiciebatur. This should refer to Pliny's prefecture of the *aerarium militare*, perhaps also to the occasion of his praetorian games before the death of Domitian.

8. cum forte . . . apud Nervam imperatorem sermo incidisset. He uses the same phrase in Ep. 22. 5 to introduce the story about Veiento at a dinner party of Nerva. The two stories show how informally the political *amicitia principis* worked. Promotions are settled at dinner. This may be the occasion when 'divus Nerva . . . nos . . . promovere vellet', *Pan.* 90. 6. Corellius appears eminent among the *amici* of Nerva.

9. sapientissimi viri. Pliny's usage of *sapiens* divides evenly between the technical sense of 'philosopher' and a wider meaning, cf. e.g., I. 22. 6, 23. 5; III. 7. 3, II. 5; IV. 14. 7, 15. 10.

Cornutum. For Pliny's colleague and friend Cornutus Tertullus see V. 14. 3–5 nn.

II. nova lis fortasse ut feminae intenditur. The allusion is obscure; its strangeness seems to lie in its being directed against a woman. The term *lis* excludes a criminal suit, suggested in *PIR²* loc. cit., as does the absence of the defendant, s. I. Women, despite nominal *tutela*, were competent in most actions of civil law, II. 20. 5 n.

18. *To Arrius Antoninus*

Date. This note continues Ep. 3, q.v., and is continued in V. 15. There is no reason to regard its contents as later than V. 3, which is equally about 'rivalling' the verses of Arrius, though translation is not there specified.

1. quaedam Latine aemulari et exprimere temptavi. He advises Fuscus Salinator on the value of this exercise in VII. 9. 1.

inopia ac potius ut Lucretius ait egestate patrii sermonis. Yet only those who have tried to translate Greek philosophical terms into Latin can complain of the 'poverty' of a language so rich in synonyms and subtle variants. Lucretius I. 832, III. 260. Cicero discusses the theme and defends the richness of Latin in *de Fin·* I. 2–3 (esp. 3. 10). It has been thought that *P.L.M.* iv n. 112 is one of Pliny's copies of Arrius: Prete, *Saggi* 30 f. 'huc mihi nos largo spumantia pocula vino ut calefactus amor pervigilare velit' etc.

19. *To Calpurnia Hispulla*

Date. From its content the letter is not much more than a year after Pliny's marriage to Calpurnia, first indicated in Ep. 1. Schultz, art. cit. 24–25, and Otto (art. cit. 36 n. 1) thought the tone earlier than fits Ep. 1, but the reference to Pliny's versification ties this to the other letters in this book, Ep. 14 pref. Pliny's comments on his wife cannot be assessed or dated by modern standards. She is still very young at the time of the miscarriage recorded in VIII. 10, and if married at the earliest moment might well have taken a year or two to develop the interests described by Pliny, whose own letters to her only begin in VI. Cf. V. 16. 2–3, on the education of girls.

Address. Calpurnia Hispulla is the sole surviving child of Calpurnius Fabatus, Pliny's grandfather-in-law, with whom she lived until she accompanied Pliny's wife and himself to Bithynia, Ep. 1. 7, V. 14. 8, VIII. 11. 3, X. 120. 2. Her second name may link her to the wife of Corellius Rufus, also Hispulla, I. 12. 10 n.

1. **patris amissi.** His death was probably recent, cf. V. 11. 1, VI. 12. 3.

2. **amat me, quod castitatis indicium est.** For the underlying notion cf. I. 14. 8 'facies liberalis . . . debet . . . castitati puellarum quasi praemium dari'.

3. **cum videor acturus . . . si quando recito.** Those who would push the marriage and this letter back to the period 99–100, when Pliny's career as an advocate was largely in abeyance, and his recitations rare, have not noticed this passage. Cf. II. 19. 1 n.

4. **versus quidem meos cantat.** This is decisive in favour of the later dating of the marriage Ep. 1. pref. Would Pliny let her read the naughty ones of Ep. 14. 4? He writes to her in amatory style in VII. 5.

6. **tuis manibus educatam.** It is evident here and in VIII. 11. 1 that her mother, never positively mentioned, is long dead.

7. **cum matrem meam parentis loco vererere.** Here lies the reason for this unambitious marriage, which does credit to Pliny's common sense—a provincial girl from his own circle, likely to have children. Pliny seems to know Hispulla better than her father, whom he addresses as a recent acquaintance in VI. 12, VII. 11.

    matrem. Plinia, the sister of the elder Pliny. Cf. VI. 16. 4, 20. 5, etc. Now dead, as the tense shows.

8. **gratias agimus, ego quod illam mihi, illa quod me sibi dederis.** This letter is often condemned as intolerable by modern standards,

but it reveals our great ignorance of Roman married life, of which it gives us a rare glimpse. At least Pliny looks to his wife as a possible intellectual companion; this sentence sets her as an equal partner to himself, and contains the germ of a surprisingly modern attitude.

20. *To Novius Maximus*

Date is not indicated, but there is a link with v. 5. 7, also addressed to Novius, s. 2 n.

Address. As in v. 5 the *nomen* is given by the Ashburnham index and F, one of the two β manuscripts. This man may well be a son or brother of the Flavian consular D. Novius Priscus (*cos. ord.* in A.D. 78; *AE* 1948, n. 56). In v. 5. 8 he appears as a man of Pliny's age, and if he is the Maximus of IX. 1, then he is the recipient of the letters addressed to the 'elder Maximus' (II. 14 pref.). He is also possibly the Maximus connected with a certain Priscus in VI. 8. 4.

2. est opus pulchrum validum acre sublime . . . in quo tu ingenii simul dolorisque velis latissime vectus es. The epithets, and the reference to *amaritudo* and *dolor* have a political colour, cf. I. 5. 4, III. 9. 3, V. 8. 10, VI. 8. 8. Hence this work may well be the violent attack of Maximus on his *inimicus* Planta mentioned in IX. 1, rather than the biography of a dead friend. He is addressed in v. 5 as one interested in political history. The work *in Plantam* had long been ready for publication in IX. 1, and Novius' books were still *inter manus* in v. 5. 7.

pulchrum. Possibly the higher qualities of *eloquentia* are absent, such as *splendor narrandi*, and *decora constructio*, I. 16. 2–4, but *sublimitas* ranks high, and *figuratum* means technical excellence, III. 13. 3, IX. 26. 5–6.

21. *To Velius Cerealis*

Date. The book-date fits the apparent age of the Helvidian sisters, s. 1 n.

Address. Velius Cerealis is as yet unknown—perhaps a connexion of the senator Velius Paulus, X. 58. 3 n. Hanslik identified him on no evidence with the versifier Cerealis of *Anth. Pal.* xi. 129, 144, who might be Martial's Julius Cerealis (*RE*, viii (2). 627). Mart. 10. 48. 5, 11. 52. The Cerealis of II. 19 pref. seems to be another man. The names recur at Assisi, for a freedman (*CIL* xi. 5421).

1. casum Helvidiarum sororum! utraque a partu utraque filiam enixa decessit. The daughters of the younger Helvidius Priscus, *consularis* when condemned in 93, IX. 13. 1–3 nn., might well be in their late teens by 105: *flore primo* s. 2. They have evidently been recently married, and these are their first offspring, s. 3.

3. actione mea librisque testatum est. For Pliny's attempted prosecution of Publicius Certus, who had abused his position at the trial of Priscus, and his *De Ultione Helvidi* see IX. 13 nn. Pliny's friend Tertullus was also a family friend, IX. 13. 16.

unus ex tribus liberis superest. This story illustrates the difficulty of maintaining the noble families in an age of inadequate medical science, even when deliberate limitation of family was not practised. Cf. Ep. 15. 3, V. 16. 1, and Pliny himself, X. 2. 3 nn.

This son is not yet known in the records, but the family names recur later in L. Valerius Helvidius Publicola (*PIR*¹ V 59) whose last cognomen recalls the family tradition of republicanism, and L. Valerius Messala Thrasea Priscus, *cos. ord.* in 196. Cynics will note the family alliance between the descendants of the notorious Catullus Messalinus (Ep. 22. 5 n.) and the worthy Helvidii. Pliny's silence on the names of the *optimi mariti* conceals this curious connexion.

22. To Sempronius Rufus

Date. Trajanic, s. 1, and after Pliny's consulship. Pliny appears on the *consilium* of Trajan in IV and VI. It was a glory to notify as soon as possible in the Letters. The rank of the addressee also fits. Hence the book-date seems suitable.

Address. Sempronius Rufus is known only as a suffect consul of 113 (*FO*). He would be a recent *praetorius* in 104–5. He receives V. 9, but probably not VII. 25 and IX. 38, despite *PIR*¹ S 273.

1. interfui principis optimi cognitioni in consilium adsumptus. This is the first of three letters—VI. 22, 31—describing Pliny's appearance on the administrative and judicial body known commonly, by modern scholars, as *consilium principis*. These letters are a principal source for the functioning of this body, which was a fluctuating group of experienced administrators and politicians, of both senatorial and equestrian rank, summoned by the Princeps for particular occasions, as in Juvenal's satirical account of the Fish Council of Domitian, *Sat.* 4, and as in the formula of Domitian's letter to the Falerienses: 'imp. Caesar . . . adhibitis utriusque ordinis splendidis viris cognita causa . . . pronuntiavi'. Even after the introduction of a grade of salaried legal experts in mid-second century, known as *consiliarii*, the *consilium* retained this informal character in its composition. See J. Crook, *Consilium Principis* (Cambridge, 1953), chs. iv and VIII, which supersedes earlier accounts, and the critical review of this in *JRS*, 1957, 252.

principis. The contrast with Nerva s. 4 shows that this must be Trajan.

gymnicus agon apud Viennenses ... hunc Trebonius Rufinus ... in duumviratu ... abolendum ... curavit. negabatur ex auctoritate publica fecisse. The novelty lay in the character of the festival, modelled like Domitian's *Quinquatria* on the Greek type of athletic and musical contest, instead of the Italian gladiatorial and beast show. Cf. the foundation by will of quinquennial games at Pontic Heraclea, X. 75. 2. The independent action of the annual magistrate, and the dispute as to the extent of his powers, are unusual in the records. The general tendency in the Empire was for the councils, membership of which was for life, to become the controlling element, X. 79. 1, 110. 1 nn. Most public activity was sanctioned by a *decretum decurionum*. The council of Vienna would have originally accepted this legacy by a decree, and the annual magistrate has set this aside by an act of *coercitio*. The question before Trajan was thus administrative rather than purely judicial. The principle at stake, justifying reference to the emperor, was the independence of the annual magistrate and the limit of his powers.

It is remarkable that this minor problem from a 'public' province should have been referred, presumably by the proconsul of Narbonensis, direct to the Princeps, and that Trajan did not refer it back to the Senate, as in Ep. 12. 3. See also VII. 6. 1–6, 10 and X. 65. 3 n. for the increasing interference of the Flavio–Trajanic rulers in the affairs of the public provinces.

celebrabatur. The O.C.T. reading *celebratur* is against the consensus of βγ and historical sense. The *agon* no longer existed. For the rare *clausula* cf. s. 5.

Trebonius Rufinus, vir egregius. Trebonii of magisterial rank are known at Narbo and Nemausus, and the name is known, of servile persons, at Vienna itself, *CIL* xii. 2014, 3142, 4394. The magistrates of Vienna were *duoviri* after the grant by Gaius of the status of a *colonia Romana*; formerly the commune was of 'Latin rights', ibid., pp. 218–19.

egregius. The epithet is not technical of rank, cf., for example, II. 11. 19, IX. 23. 4, X. 21. 1, 29. 1.

2. egit ipse causam ... tamquam homo Romanus. The absence of advocates was not unusual in the emperor's court, cf. VI. 22. 2 and 31. 3. At this date it was hardly surprising that a notable from Narbonensis was a skilled orator. Tacitus, *Agric.* 21. 2, notes the

spread of rhetoric even in Britain. But Pliny had not travelled in the
western provinces.

3. cum sententiae perrogarentur dixit Iunius Mauricus. For the
procedure cf. VI. 22. 5, 31. 12. The emperor gives sentence *e consili
sententia*, though he is not bound to accept the advice given. Crook,
op. cit. 109, holds that there was an adjournment for deliberation in
private, but this is not apparent in the Plinian evidence.

Mauricus. The presence of this restored victim of Domitian is
interesting, I. 5. 10 n.

4. cenabat Nerva cum paucis, Veiento proximus. See Ep. 17. 8 for a
similar anecdote about Nerva, possibly on the same occasion.

A. Didius Gallus Fabricius Veiento, who as a praetorian senator
knew his way too well round the court of Nero, and was disgraced in
A.D. 62 (Tac. *Ann.* 14. 50; Dio. 61. 6. 2), returned from relegation
later, and was an influential figure throughout the Flavian period,
when he held no less than three consulships; the second was in 80 and
the third probably in 82 or 83 and certainly before 90, since he was
mentioned as such by Statius in a lost poem about Domitian's Germanic
wars (Schol. Vall. on Juv. 4. 94; *PIR²* F 91; Syme, *Tac.* 5–6, 633).
Though the references of Pliny and Juvenal (*Sat.* 3. 185, 4. 113–29, 6.
113) are critical, they suggest, with his omission from the list of agents
in Tacitus, *Agricola* 45. 1, that like Aquilius Regulus (I. 5. 1 nn.), he was
not one of the delators of Domitian's reign, though he is commonly
taken as such (e.g. Garzetti, *Nerva* 50). Juvenal calls him *prudens* and
the hostile Victor (*ep. de Caes.* 12. 5) can only say: 'multos *occultis*
criminationibus persecutum'. Hence, as here and in IX. 13. 13, 19, he
retained his influence with Senate and Princeps under Nerva. He
may have had a hand in the succession of Trajan, if his mysterious
presence in Germany, recorded in *ILS* 1010, when already *cos.* III,
belongs to the year 97, when Trajan was in command of an army of
the Rhine, and not to the period of Domitian's German wars. *PIR¹*
and *PIR²* s.v. favour these rival theories; cf. Syme, *Tac.* 16 n. 7.

apud imperatorem Nervam. The order of words is the same in VII.
31. 4. Guillemin supposes this was to stress the chronology. But in
Ep. 17. 8, where there is equally a chronological point, he writes
apud Nervam imperatorem.

**5. Catullo Messalino, qui . . . á Domitiano . . . in optimum quemque
contorquebatur.** The well-born L. Valerius Catullus Messalinus, *cos.
ord.* in 73 with Domitian and *cos.* II in 85 (*F. Pot.*), is named by
Tacitus, *Agric.* 45, between the notorious delators Massa and Carus,
and by Juvenal, *Sat.* 4. 113–22, together with Veiento. He too is
generally taken for a *delator*, but both Tacitus and Pliny (s. 6)—

sanguinariis sententiis—attribute his deadly effect to his *sententia*, that is to his influence first within the *consilium* of Domitian (Tac. loc. cit. 'adhuc. . . . intra Albanam arcem') and later, during the years of 'terror', within the Senate, where his function was to complete the work of Massa and Carus by proposing ferocious penalties at the conclusion of trials. Hence Juvenal calls him *mortifer*. *PIR*[1] V 41.

6. si viveret. He evidently survived 93, Tac. loc. cit.

'**nobiscum cenaret**'. Syme, *Tac.* 6, thinks that Nerva was fishing for this answer, in order to check an unfortunate discussion.

7. placuit agona tolli, qui mores Viennensium infecerat. It seems odd that the Romans so disliked these contests, apparently much less vicious than their own sordid *ludi*. Friedlaender (*SG* Eng. tr. ii. 122 ff.) collects Julio-Claudian and contemporary passages to the same effect as Pliny, such as Tacitus' outbursts against Nero's games, *Ann.* 14. 14–15, 20–21. It was the homosexual tendency that was feared: '*degeneret . . . iuventus gymnasia et otia et turpis amores exercendo*'. The Elder Pliny held that Greek gymnastics were destroying the moral virtues of the Romans, *NH* 15. 19, 29. 26. Cf. Pliny, *Pan.* 13. 6. Even Martial, 7. 32, and Lucan, 7. 270, add their weight. Carcopino, *Daily Life*, 245, notes the unpopularity of Domitian's *Agon*.

Such contests were fairly common in the western provinces, especially in Narbonensis, where the Greek influence of Massilia was still felt, as at Nemausus and Arelate. Friedlaender, op. cit., IV App. 44, p. 268.

23. *To Pomponius Bassus*

Date. Bassus is in retirement. As his last known public office was in 101, there is no difficulty, but no precise argument, for the book-date.

Address. T. Pomponius Bassus is first known as *legatus proconsulis* to the father of Trajan in Asia in 79–80. His career is then checked under Domitian, like Frontinus' (Ep. 8. 3 n.), until his consulship in 94 (*FO*, not 93 as given in the diploma *ILS* 9053). Next he was legate of the military province Galatia-Cappadocia from 95 to *c.* 100. In 101 he is found organizing the Trajanic *alimenta* in central Italy. *PIR*[1] P 530; Garzetti, *C.* 123; *RE* xxi. 2, 'Pomponii', n. 39; *ILS* 5840, 6106, 6675, 8797. Pliny's summary s. 2 is just. His connexion with other Pomponii is obscure, III. 9. 33 n. No other letter is addressed to him.

1. disponere otium. The meaning of this is shown by Pliny's account of the life of Spurinna, summarized as *vita disposita* (III. 1. 2) and of his own customs in IX. 36.

multum disputare, multum audire. This, with *sapientia tua* above, suggests that Bassus, like Minicius Fundanus in Ep. 15, was an amateur of philosophy.

2. exercitus rexerit. The plural suggests a second military command, unknown as yet. But in III. 1. 12 ' provincias rexit' is used where only one is known.

quam diu decebat. In a similar context, III. 1. 12, he writes of Spurinna: 'quoad honestum fuit'. If Bassus was *praetorius*, as normally, when proconsular legate in 78–79 he might not be more than 56 years old at this time, a mere chicken compared to Spurinna, but some twelve years senior to Pliny.

3. ut ipsae leges monent, quae maiorem annis otio reddunt. Senators were freed from compulsory attendance at the House at an age fixed at 70 by the Augustan law *de senatu habendo*, and later reduced to 60. Dio 55. 3. 1–3; *SC. Calvisianum* (E–J n. 311) ll. 112 f.; Sen. *brev. vit.* 20. 4; *RE* (S) vi. 766 ff.

4. quando mihi . . . per aetatem honestum erit imitari istud . . . exemplum? For similar cries see II. 14. 14, III. 1. 11–12 nn.

24. *To Fabius Valens*

Date. The contents fit the book-date. The judicial case is probably that of Ep. 16, and a link is possible with Ep. 11, s. 3 n. The attempt of Monti to date this letter to 97, close to the return of the exiles, breaks down with the identification of the exiled advocate in s. 3 with Licinianus, who is still in exile in Ep. 11, at publication. Cf. ss. 4–5 nn. also. (*Pliniana* II. 315 f.)

Address. Fabius Valens is not known outside Pliny, but if Catanaeus's text of X. 86B is sound he served under Pliny in Bithynia as an equestrian officer. A connexion with the like-named legate of Vitellius in 69 is uncertain, Tac. *Hist.* I. 7 etc. *PIR*² F 69.

1. egisse me iuvenem aeque in quadruplici. The identification of the first case with that in which Pliny spoke for seven hours, Ep. 16, is reasonable. These quadruple cases were evidently rare, cf. VI. 33. 2–3. For certain complicated types of case the four panels of the court sat concurrently and together, ibid. nn., and such cases made a great stir. Pliny mentions only three in his whole career. The second

here mentioned may be identified with the great suit of Junius
Pastor when Pliny was *adulescentulus adhuc* and spoke 'contra
potentissimos civitatis', I. 18. 3.

2. solus eram qui in utroque dixissem. Pliny seems to have succeeded
Regulus as the doyen of the Centumviral Court, cf. VI. 12. 2, 'in
harena mea'.

3. quidam ex iis qui tunc egerant decesserunt, exsulant alii etc. In
this list not less than six personages are meant, if Pliny's plurals are
stylistic. The exile, still alive, should be Valerius Licinianus (Ep. 11.
1) whom Monti forgot; no known advocate was among the restored
exiles of 96–97. One or other of the retired men should be Regulus
himself, who can hardly have been absent from such a case, unless
VI. 2. 5 means that he never gave up. Fabius Justus, to whom
Tacitus dedicated his *Dialogus*, is a candidate for the general's place,
cf. I. 5. 8 n., VII. 2 pref.

    illum civilibus officiis principis amicitia exemit. This does not mean,
as *CAH* XI. 425, that *amici principis* enjoyed freedom from certain
public duties, but that they were too busy to practise in the Courts.
The phrase points to the growing specialization of the duties of those
advisers who formed the inner cabinet of the Princeps. Cf. Suet.
Titus 7. 2: 'amicos elegit quibus etiam post eum principes ut et sibi
et reipublicae necessariis adquieverunt'—such men as Nerva,
Fabricius Veiento, Frontinus, Spurinna, Ep. 22. 4 n., Ep. 8. 3 n.,
II. 7. 1 n. But the *amici* include also those holding posts in the equestrian public service, cf. X. 7 'Pompeium Plantam, praefectum
Aegypti, amicum meum' n., or earlier 'Otacilium Sagittam, amicum
et procuratorem meum', *FIRA* I. 72 (A–J 59). So too in Pliny's description of his uncle: 'impeditum qua officiis maximis qua amicitia
principum', III. 5. 7. He is thinking of some equestrian official, who
when not in a post overseas would attend the imperial consultations,
like the Elder Pliny, III. 5. 7, 9, 18. Perhaps Vibius Maximus is meant.
Now prefect of Egypt, he had deserted the Courts for a procuratorial career by 93, III. 2 pref. For a fuller discussion of the term see
Crook, op. cit. (Ep. 22. 1 n.), 23 ff.

4. studiis processimus, studiis periclitati sumus. Pliny makes much of
his supposed dangers under Domitian, especially in letters published
in III and later, and insists, as also in the published version of his
Panegyric (90. 5, 95. 3–5), that his career suffered a check. He claims
that he was involved in the troubles of the Senecio–Helvidius group,
and in danger from the delators Baebius Massa and Carus, in letters
addressed to such notable men as Licinius Sura and Cornelius Tacitus,
or to his private friends Voconius Romanus and Julius Genitor,

I. 5, III. II, VII. 27. 14, 33. 7–8. If this was all false, who was to be deceived? There was no personal advantage to be gained, since the clique that suffered under Domitian were not in power under Trajan, and Pliny owed his promotion to cooler heads such as Frontinus and Servianus Ursus, Ep. 8. 3, X. 2. I. Perhaps in the coteries for which Tacitus also wrote prefaces on the theme of *servitus* and *libertas* prestige attached to any who could claim any part in the 'resistance', however feeble. Cf. Titinius Capito's cult of Brutus and Cassius, I. 17. 3. Besides Pliny implies in a neutral instance, which did not affect him, that slight connexions with the disgraced could be dangerous, V. I. 8: 'et erant quidam in illis quibus obici et Gratillae amicitia et Rustici posset'. But it is not till after 100 that Pliny begins to take this attitude. The tone of I. 5 is different—there he shows how clever he was in dissociating himself from the victims of Domitian.

rursusque processimus. S. Monti (art. cit. 315 f., cf. V. I pref.) referred this promotion, and the letter, to the period of the 'return of the exiles'—late 96 to early 97. But Pliny's Nervan promotion to the prefecture of Saturn was not till January 98, which led on to his consulship in 100 under Trajan. Monti's arguments contradict each other, though he rightly saw that if the lawsuit of s. I was before Pliny's consulship, it must also have been before his prefecture of the Treasury, when he ceased from court work, X. 3A. I.

5. profuerunt ... bonorum amicitiae. Of the group of Domitianic victims in I. 5, VII. 33, IX. 13 only Arulenus Rusticus is ever said by Pliny to have helped him, and that only by private encouragement, I. 14. I. Pliny's real connexions were with the ladies, IX. 13. 3, 5. Cf. III. 16. 2, VII. 19. 9–10.

si computes annos, exiguum tempus. In VIII. 14. 10 *breve tempus* is used of a period of nine years. Pliny hints at a date after his consulship by renouncing the term *iuvenis* in s. I. When still *praetorius* he was content to admit it: 'ut iuvenis iuvenem', I. 14. 3.

7. praeceptis vel exemplis monere. II. 6. 6 n.

25. *To Maesius Maximus*

Date should be a year later than the corresponding letter about the elections III. 20, and should belong to the opening months of 105, like Epp. 12, 17, 29.

Address. For Maesius Maximus, who is probably not a senator, see III. 20 pref.

1. **proximis comitiis.** They were probably held in January, III. 20. 2 n.

in una vero pro candidatorum nominibus suffragatorum nomina inventa sunt. Unless the electors wrote all the names of their favourites on a single *tabella*, Pliny's plural *nominibus* must be literary. Cf. s. 4.

suffragatorum. See III. 20. 5 n.

2. **senatus . . . iratum principem est comprecatus.** Cf. VI. 5. 5, 'propitium Caesarem . . . precabantur'. It would seem that the votes were read out aloud one by one.

3. **qui . . . omnino in senatu dicax . . . est.** Cf. VIII. 6. 3, 'dicerem urbanos, si senatum deceret urbanitas'. The times have changed since Cicero made his sallies against Piso Caesoninus and Vatinius, perhaps through the influence of Stoic ideas of dignity, s. 4 n., but more through the general growth of decorum, Ep. 22. 7, VII. 24 nn.

4. **poposcit tabellas.** Stout, p. 191, wished to read *tabellam* as in *α*, despite the support of *βγ* for the plural, not understanding the system of voting. Pliny evidently means in ss. 1–2 that the same hand was responsible: 'ei qui scripsisset . . . ille tamen fefellit'.

se contemnit. Guillemin, ad loc., quotes Tac. *Dial.* 29 for the Stoic origin of this notion.

5. **cui . . . multum laboris adicit haec nostra . . . petulantia.** In III. 20. 12 he is similarly outspoken about the ineffectuality of the contemporary Senate.

26. *To Maecilius Nepos*

Date. The book-date is supported by the connexion between this letter, where Nepos has been appointed to a proconsular command, s. 1 n., and VI. 19. 6, where he is in a province. Since he has time to spare for the amendment of Pliny's *libelli*, the period of the year may be the opening months; proconsuls were expected to leave during April–May and to have taken over by July (Mommsen, *DPR* iii. 294; Dio 60. 17. 3; cf. 57. 14. 5). If the identification with Metilius Nepos is accepted the appointment was taken up later than 20 May 105 (*CIL* vi. 2075).

Address. For the obscurity of the *nomen* Maecilius, and the chance that the text means the consular Metilius Nepos see II. 3 pref. The reference in s. 1 (n.) to *maximae provinciae* is a chief argument for this identification.

1. **petis ut libellos meos . . . recognoscendos . . . curem.** The speeches of Pliny are meant, since Nepos is *disertissimus* (s. 2) and interested in oratory, II. 3.

recognoscendos. Cf. II. 10. 3, 'enotuerunt quidam tui versus, et invito te . . .'. Unreliable texts would seem to be common.

2. maximae provinciae praefuturus. In VI. 22. 1 *provinciis praefuturi* is used of proconsular appointments, and may be distinguished from *exercitus regit*, which seems to be Plinian for an imperial army command, cf. Epp. 23. 2, 24. 3, II. 13. 2, IX. 13. 11. By *maximae* the consular proconsulship of Asia or Africa may be meant, for which Metilius would be about due, as consul of 91, in *c*. 105–6.

27. To Pompeius Falco

Date. The reference to the verses of Pliny and Arrius Antoninus tie the letter to the book-date, Epp. 3, 14 prefs. The placing of this letter towards the close of IV recalls the placing of Martial's praise of Pliny at the end of III.

Address. Pliny's young senatorial friend Q. Pompeius Falco commanded a legion and a province, Lycia-Pamphylia, between 101 and *c*. 105, I. 23 pref. Pliny speaks as though Falco were out of Italy in s. 5.

1. audivi recitantem Sentium Augurinum. Q. Gellius Sentius Augurinus was proconsul of Macedonia, and hence still a praetorian senator, under Hadrian. *PIR²* G 135; *ILS* 5947 A. There is no proof that he was a Cisalpine from Verona, as *PIR* and Chilver, *Cisalpine Gaul*, 103, argue from *meus Catullus* in s. 4. The possessive pronoun used of persons does not localize them, I. 16. 1 n. In s. 5 *adfinis* may refer to either Arrius or Spurinna.

poematia appellat. Cf. Ep. 14. 9.

2. ipsum me laudibus vexit. Pliny requites him in a short note published in IX. 8, perhaps nearer the actual publication of his book, s. 5.

4. et Calvus veteresque. For the vogue see I. 16. 5 n.

5. quem tibi ut primum publicaverit exhibebo. For the distinction between recitation and publication see I. 2. 6, II. 10. 6 nn.

vivit cum Spurinna, vivit cum Antonino, quorum alteri adfinis, utrique contubernalis est. Both aged heroes wrote verses in retirement, III. 1. 7, IV. 3. Falco later had connexions with Antoninus Pius, grandson of Arrius Antoninus, I. 23 pref. There is no reason in style to make him *adfinis* of Spurinna. The phrase may be chiasmatic.

6. illud verissimum. From Euripides (Nauck) fr. *Phoenix* 809 (812).

28. *To Vibius Severus*

Date not determinable. The theme is similar to that of III. 6.

Address. The scholarly Vibius seems not to be a senator, III. 18 pref.
He may come from Mediolanum, s. 1 n., where his names are not
uncommon, *CIL* v. Index s.v.

1. **Herennius Severus, vir doctissimus.** Herennius, who is to be distinguished from Vettenius Severus of VI. 27, may be the consular
Herennius Severus, patron of the learned Philon and Hermippus,
whose consulship, though given in Suidas (s.v.) by Olympiad as
between 101–4, was apparently under Hadrian, *c*. 128 (*PIR²* H 116,
130). But such a man would be *adulescens* or *iuvenis* rather than *vir*
at the date of Book IV.

municipum tuorum. The biographer Nepos is called *Padi accola*
by Pliny, *NH* 3. 127, and the Cisalpine philosopher Catius is named
Insuber by Cicero, *ad Fam.* 15. 16. 1. Mommsen assigned both to
Ticinum, as being on the Po. But Mediolanum, once the capital of the
Insubres, is more probable (Strabo, v. 213; Pliny, *NH* loc. cit.).
Pliny there attributes Ticinum to the Laevi and Marici, who may be a
subdivision of the Insubres (*RE* xv. 1. 92, (2) vi. 847). Both were
Celtic communes with Latin Rights from 89 to 49 B.C., and then
became Roman municipalities.

Titi Cati. Though there is some confusion in the manuscripts, the
form of name seems to exclude the recently dead Flavian poet Ti.
Catius Silius Italicus, who had Cisalpine connexions, III. 7. 1 n. Since
Quintilian refers to the philosopher Catius (x. 1. 124) with mild
praise, the mention here is reasonable.

si sunt istic. Hartleben, ad loc., suggests family shrines and
tombs as a possible source, at least of busts based on funeral masks.

exscribendas pingendasque delegem. As in Pliny, *NH* 35. 90 f.,
paintings, not busts, are meant. For the custom of putting portraits
in libraries see I. 16. 8, III. 7. 8. Livy and Vergil were frequent, Suet.
Cal. 34. 2; Juv. *Sat.* 7. 29; Mart. 7. 84, 9 pref. But heads cast in
metal were commoner, Pliny, *NH* 35. 9–11 There were many cast
busts in the library at Herculaneum (Hartleben, ad loc., quoting
Comparetti, *La Villa Ercolanesi*, 1883). Friedlaender discusses the
development of portraiture and its uses briefly (*SG* Eng. tr.), ii. 276–7,
418.

3. **ne in melius quidem sinas aberrare.** Roman sculptured portraiture
is admired today for its apparent realism and fidelity. Pliny's comment is rare testimony to this artistic attitude; cf. his admiration

for a realistic bronze, III. 6. 2–3. Contrast Lucian, *Quomodo historia*
13: 'ugly men, and women especially, urge painters to paint them as
beautiful as possible' etc.

29. *To Romatius Firmus*

Date. This is the first of the series about the praetorship of Licinius
Nepos, v. 4, 9, 13, and belongs to February–March 105, s. 2 n.

Address. Romatius Firmus, decurion of Comum assisted to equestrian
status by Pliny in I. 19, is now a member of the *decuriae iudicum*,
s. I n.

I. cum proxime res agentur, quoquo modo ad iudicandum veni. The
jurors of the criminal *quaestio* system, and the judges of the civil
law, were provided by three equestrian *decuriae*, described in the
Tiberian *Tabula Hebana* (7–8) as 'equites omnium decuriarum quae
iudiciorum publicorum causa constitutae sunt', and two *decuriae*
with a lower qualification. The former, to which body Romatius
belongs, were known as *iudices selecti*—as commonly in inscriptions—
from the fact that the *decuriae* were recruited by the Princeps, not
the praetors. See Mommsen, *DPR* vi. 2, 131 n. 3, 139 ff., *D.Pen.R.*
i. 245 f., and the modifications proposed by E. S. Stavely, 'Iudex
Selectus', *Rhein. Mus. Phil.*, 1953, 203 ff. The principal sources are
Pliny, *NH* 29. 18, 33. 30–33; Suet. *Aug.* 32. 3; *Tib.* 41; *Gaius* 16. 2;
Claud. 15. 1, 16. 2; *Galba* 14. 3; Gellius, *NA* 14. 2. 1; Ulpian, *Dig.* 50.
5. 13.

This letter, with Gellius, loc. cit., 'a praetoribus lectus in iudices
sum ut iudicia . . . privata susciperem', suggests that praetors of all
courts drew up their own lists for the current year's service from
the *decuriae* (Mommsen, *DPR* vi. 2, 143; *D. Pen. R.* i. 245 n. 1),
though Stavely, art. cit. 213, thinks that Gellius refers to his enrolment in one of the two lower *decuriae* which were not 'select'. This
letter also proves, s. 2 n., that senators continued to form part of the
decury system.

2. Licinius Nepos praetor . . . multam dixit etiam senatori. Nepos has
drawn up his list, and the other praetors will soon be doing likewise,
s. 3 'non omnes praetores tam severi'. The members of the *decuriae*
(one of which was annually freed from duty) were bound to be
available, unless they had a special *vacatio muneris*, on pain of a fine
(Suet. locc. citt.).

Licinius Nepos. This new broom is known only from Pliny, since
dates make it unlikely that he is the M. Licinius Nepos, suffect consul in 127 (*FO*) and Arval in 139. His year coincides with the

consulship of Afranius Dexter, i.e. 105; v. 13. 4 n. Hanslik (*Wiener Studien*, 50, 196 f.), missing this, assigned Nepos to 104. For his further adventures see v. 4, 9, 13; VI. 5. His 'province' is clearly defined in v. 9. 3 (n.) as a *quaestio publica*. The courts sat for nine months of the year, with a vacation from November to January (Suet. *Aug.* 32. 3, *Galba* 14. 3). Hence jury lists would be drawn up in January or early February. *PIR*[1] L 150–1.

etiam senatori. This implies that senators were liable to service in the criminal juries, contrary to the generally accepted view of Mommsen that from Augustus onwards they were excluded from the *decuriae* (*DPR* vi. 2, 140 n. 2; cf. *RE* vi. 299; Staveley, art. cit. 205 n. 11). The new evidence of the *Tabula Hebana* (Jones–Ehrenberg, 94A. 5–15) quoted above would seem to support Mommsen: 'senatores itemque equites omnium decuriarum' etc., but is not decisive. But since Nepos was praetor of a criminal court, the reference here cannot be to any branch of the civil judicature. Further the *SC.* of 11 B.C. quoted by Frontinus, *de aquis* 101, rules that senatorial *curatores* had the privilege: 'iudiciis vacent privatis publicisque'. Dio too reports the Augustan ordinance that no court should be held during the time of senatorial meetings (55. 3. 2, cf. also 52. 20. 5). In the later *Strafrecht* Mommsen admitted the continued service of senators on criminal juries, but without adducing this or any fresh evidence, though the *SC.* was finally cited in a footnote to the *Contents* of the French edition of the *Staatsrecht* unnoticed by anyone (*D. Pen. R.* i. 244 f.; *DPR* vi. 2, 489 n. 1). This note suggested that the senatorial album was regarded as forming part of the general jury-list. Pliny's evidence shows this to be correct, and indicates that senators continued to be summoned for service in *quaestiones publicae*.

3. reducere eiusmodi exemplum. The use of the *multa* is a remnant of a cumbrous and obsolescent Republican practice. The fine was collected by a separate action before a jury court, Mommsen, *D. Pen. R.* iii. 375 ff. The continued power of magistrates to exact fines is testified under Augustus by another *SC.* quoted in Frontinus op. cit. 129.

30. *To Licinius Sura*

Date. The letter follows the visit to Comum, projected in Ep. 1 and completed in Ep. 13. Hence late 104 or early 105 is possible.

Address. L. Licinius Sura, to whom VII. 27 is also addressed, was the right-hand man of Trajan until his death in *c.* 110. Like Servianus (III. 17 pref.), he was a member of the Spanish group that supported Trajan, in whose elevation he played a great part, and later Hadrian.

He was a protégé of Domitian, and began like Pliny as an advocate. His first consulship is not dated, and his praetorian appointments are known, if at all, only from the headless inscription *ILS* 1022; they include the government of Belgica. After decoration in the Dacian war, in which he conducted a delicate mission, he held second and third consulships in 102 and 107. After his death *c.* 110 he was honoured with a public memorial (SHA, *Hadr.* 2. 10, 3. 10; Victor, *ep. Caes.* 13. 6; Dio 68. 9. 2, 15. 3–6; *CIL* ii. 4282; *CAH* xi. 221 f.; *PIR*¹ L 174; Garzetti, *C.* 89; *RE* xiii. 471; Syme, *Tac.* 73, 231, 790). Despite his military decorations his talents seem to have been in diplomacy and politics rather than war. He is not to be numbered among the 'marshals'. For his Spanish origin cf. Syme, *Tac.* 790. He erected buildings at Barcino and Tarraco, but hails from neither, and has relatives at Bilbilis (Martial, 1. 49. Cf. IV. 11. 1 n.).

1. **attuli tibi ex patria mea pro munusculo quaestionem altissima ista eruditione dignissimam.** Martial refers to the learning and eloquence of Sura before the days of his greatness (1. 49. 40, 6. 64. 13, 7. 47. 1). Julian states and SHA implies that Sura wrote Trajan's speeches (SHA, *Hadr.* 3, 11; Julian, *Caes.*, p. 327 B). Both Pliny's letters to him are about natural curiosities. The general interest in such subjects is shown also by VI. 16, 20, the Vesuvius description, and VIII. 20, the floating islets, but above all by the 'Natural History' of Pliny's uncle, and the 'Natural Questions' of Seneca. The Flavian consular Mucianus wrote a book of *Mirabilia*, and Bardon suggests that Sura did so likewise. But nothing here or in VII. 27. 1, 15–16 shows that a written work of Sura was known to Pliny (*Litt. Lat. Inc.* ii. 179 f., 183).

2. **fons oritur in monte.** The spring exists today exactly as described by Pliny, in the grounds of the 'Villa Pliniana' close by Torno on the eastern side of the lake. It was known to Leonardo da Vinci and to Catanaeus as Pliny's fountain (Longolius's ed., ad loc.). Its characteristics are described less accurately by the Elder Pliny, in *NH* 2. 232: 'in Comensi iuxta Larium lacum fons largus horis singulis semper intumescit et residit'. Apparently the phenomenon takes place every six hours, and there is a great noise of waters, which Pliny does not mention.

5. **spiritusne aliquis occultior os fontis et fauces modo laxat modo includit?** Guillemin waxes superior towards Pliny's speculations. But Catanaeus is more to the point; Pliny here follows his uncle's theory, originating in the Stoic notion of the world-spirit, that the world has its own breath, which causes natural phenomena: *NH* 2. 102 ff. This is put more precisely in Seneca, *Nat. Q.* 6. 16–17, who

holds that there are great reservoirs of air within the earth which cause earthquakes, and quotes Epicurus (ibid. 20. 7) for the notion of subterranean waters being thus moved. Besides this, the incidence of air pressure is not irrelevant, and Pliny's observation in s. 6 is creditable. A natural siphon is probably involved connecting the spring to a subterranean reservoir, which floods at a certain level. The whole passage bears on the failure of the ancients to develop experimental science.

9. **an latentibus venis certa mensura, quae dum colligit quod exhauserat, minor rivus et pigrior . . . profertur?** Here and in s. 10 Pliny applies a superficial knowledge of aqueducts to the question. He may have witnessed the checking of the water-supply at the central points, when the gaugings, *mensurae*, were taken; cf. Frontinus, *de aquis* 66 ff., who at least twice uses the word of the actual gauges (66, 69), though commonly he uses it in the abstract sense.

10. **an nescio quod libramentum abditum . . . quod cum exinanitum est, suscitat . . . fontem; cum repletum, moratur?** Another term from the water-works. A *librator* calculates levels of water (Frontinus, op. cit. 105), and *libramentum* is used by the Elder Pliny of the difference between the head and the foot of a supply, *NH* 31. 57 (cf. Vitruvius 8. 6. 6) and also of the level itself, ibid. 11. 173. In other contexts it is used as 'counterpoise', Livy 24. 34. 10; Tac. *Hist.* 3. 23. Forcellini, s.v., envisages a 'cavea . . . naturalis ad librandam ipsius fontis aquam ita ut haec per se ipsam defluere . . . possit'. Possibly Pliny combines the senses, and imagines a counterpoise that sinks when full to block the passage of water, and rises when empty to release it. Rudimentary, but at least practical logic. Pliny applies his theoretical interest in the movement of water to a practical problem in x. 61. Here, as in vi. 16, 20, viii. 8, 20, Pliny shows remarkable accuracy of observation, and intelligently comments on his observation. So too his account of ghosts and of the dolphin shows remarkable lack of exaggeration, vii. 27, ix. 33 nn. Cf. B. Radice, *Greece and Rome*, 1962, 163.

BOOK V

1. *To Annius Severus*

Date. The reference to Julius Frontinus as dead, s. 5, guarantees the book-date sufficiently, cf. IV. 8. 3 n. The events described are of A.D. 93–96, s. 8 n. But the occasion of the letter is the subsequent death of and legacy of Curianus, recent at the time of writing. R. Hanslik (*Wiener Studien*, 52. 156 f.) oddly dated the letter itself to 96, s. 12 n. S. Monti (*Rendiconti Acc. Arch. Lett. Napoli*, 1952, 173), admitted that the letter is not a re-issue of early date, though still trying to date Frontinus' death earlier than 104 in order to lower the date of this letter.

Address. For Pliny's agent Annius Severus of Comum see II. 16 pref.

This letter is a valuable document for stages in the development of several institutions of the Roman civil law, ss. 2, 3, 9, 10 nn. It is also an essay in Pliny's 'historical' style, though its subject is anecdotal (cf. IV. 11).

1. **Pomponia Galla exheredato filio Asudio Curiano heredem reliquerat me.** The tenses deserve study. Pliny switches abruptly from the recent event, the legacy, to the old story of the disputed *hereditas* with only the change of tense to indicate the distinction in time: 'legatum . . . obvenit . . . reliquerat'. He then begins the story of his own actions in a different sequence, ss. 2–3, passing from the imperfect, for the long-drawn-out discussion, to the perfect of specific action, ss. 5–6, 'adhibui . . . dixit . . . subscripsit', and back to the imperfect for the continued negotiations s. 7, 'adpetebat . . . cupiebant . . .'. Finally he passes to a narrative in present tense, for the last stage of the affair, s. 9: 'rogant . . . convenimus'.

The scene is set in Rome (ss. 5, 9), and the personages are the upper crust of society, not municipal bourgeoisie. Pomponia Galla may well be a daughter of the praetorian C. Pomponius Gallus Didius Rufus, and hence connected with A. Didius Gallus Fabricius Veiento, (IV. 22. 4), and the consular Pomponii of the period. Sertorius Severus is otherwise unknown. Garzetti, *Inc.* 119, 131; *C.* 122–7. Likewise Asudius, and his father.

2. **orabat, ut sibi donarem portionem meam seque praeiudicio iuvarem.** The power of gift save between relatives had been totally forbidden

by the Lex Cincia of 204 B.C., which, however, made no provision for annulment or sanctions. Hence lawyers built on its silences a system of legitimate gifts between strangers. The main effect of the Lex Cincia was to impose a maximum value on gifts, and to enable recovery in certain circumstances of gifts contrary to its provisions. In classical law gifts between strangers were valid if carried out with proper formalities. Pliny's letter helps to date the emergence of this classical doctrine, since Curianus meant to quote the proposed gift in court as a legal argument—*praeiudicio. Tit. Ulp.* 1. 1; *Fr. Vat.* 259, 298, 310–11; Schulz, *Classical Roman Law*, p. 566. Pliny refers to the legal formalities in connexion with his numerous gifts only in II. 4, 2, VII. 18. 2, X. 4. 2.

tacita conventione. A gift could be made on a condition, later known as *sub modo*, e.g. that the recipient should do something for the donor. Such condition was not itself enforceable, but the donor could reclaim his gift for non-fulfilment. *Fr. Vat.* 286; Schulz, op. cit. 568. But this secret agreement evidently was not to be put formally in writing. *Conventio* may be the original term for the post-classical *sub modo* which is otherwise unknown.

3. non esse satis honestum donare et locupleti et orbo. For the theme of *captatio* see II. 20 nn., IV. 15. 3 n. Asudius would not have been barred from his mother's inheritance as an *orbus* by the rules of the *Lex de maritandis ordinibus*, which applied only to strangers and distant relations. *Fr. Vat.* 216.

profuturum si cessissem. If Pliny failed to take up his inheritance (II. 4. 1 n.) his reluctance could be construed as evidence of a flaw in the title.

esse autem me paratum cedere si inique exheredatum mihi liqueret. Here and below, s. 6—'mater tua iustas habuisse causas irascendi tibi' —Pliny gives the earliest evidence for the emergence of the classical form of the *querela inofficiosi testamenti*. A second case is mentioned in VI. 33. 2. The rule was established in the Centumviral Court that the descendants of a person must be left not less than the fourth part of the share due to them in case of intestate succession, unless good cause for disinheritance could be shown. Otherwise a suit *inofficiosi testamenti* could be instituted against the named heirs. If this was successful they recovered not merely the fourth part but the whole of their intestate share; but they would have to sue all the heirs to secure this, each having to pay his due portion. Curianus means to sue all the heirs except Pliny, s. 6. Schulz, op. cit. 276; Paulus, *Dig.* 5. 2. 19; Ulpian 5. 2. 8. 8.

5. adhibui in consilium duos quos tunc civitas nostra spectatissimos habuit, Corellium et Frontinum. For these two consulars see I. 12,

IV. 8. 3 nn. Both are dead at the date of the letter, which can be no earlier than IV. 8, which records the death of Frontinus.

in consilium. Cf. s. 6, 'ex consilii sententia'. The forms of the domestic tribunal—so common in family affairs, I. 22. 8—follow those of the magisterial *consilium*, IV. 22. 3, VI. 31. 12 nn.

6. post hoc ille cum ceteris subscripsit centumvirale iudicium. Some two years elapse before this (s. 10 'biennium'); hence the indication of time (s. 1 n.). The term *subscribere*, normal in a criminal indictment, is used only here of the preliminary stage of a civil suit, which usually consisted of the *denuntiatio*, or giving of due notice, followed by the detailed statement of claim, *libelli datio*. Paulus, and rescript of Pius, *Dig.* 5. 2. 7. Wlassak, *RE* 3. 1946, takes the whole phrase to refer to the procedure by which both parties agreed to proceed in the Centumviral Court instead of by *formula* before the single *iudex* of the praetorian system. Martin (*Le Tribunal des Centumvirs*, Paris 1904, 107 f., 109 n. 2) regards it as the equivalent of the *litis contestatio* of an ordinary civil case, the procedure *in iure* before the *praetor urbanus* at which the issues were defined and referred to the Centumviral praetor (*pr. hastatus*) for judgment *in iudicio*.

7. metu temporum. verebantur . . . ne ex centumvirali iudicio capitis rei exirent. Compare the attempt of Regulus to trip Pliny into a dangerous statement in the case of Arrionilla, I. 5. 4–7. The elaborate arrangements of the Centumviral Court would provide a better setting for such attempts than the quieter atmosphere of the praetorian court. But Suetonius (*Dom.* 8. 1) notes that Domitian annulled *ambitiosas centumvirorum sententias*.

transigere cupiebant. The term recurs in Ulpian, *Dig.* 5. 2: 27 pref. and 29. 2. By such a settlement the validity of the will, and especially of its legacies, would not be disturbed, Roby, *Roman Private Law*, I. 215. Cf. Papinian, *Dig.* 5. 2. 15. 2.

8. Gratillae amicitia et Rustici. See III. 11. 3 n. The reference dates the whole story to the last three years of Domitian.

9. in aedem Concordiae. at the north-west corner of the Forum Romanum, Ashby, *Top. Dic.* 139.

'si mater' inquam 'te ex parte quarta scripsisset heredem num queri posses?' He would then have had his fourth part of the intestate succession, which for Curianus evidently amounted to a quarter of the whole estate, he being the sole direct heir.

'quid si heredem quidem instituisset ex asse, sed legatis ita exhausisset ut non amplius apud te quam quarta remaneret?' Here he makes a different point, referring to another legal fourth part, that allowed under the *Lex Falcidia* of 40 B.C. to all *heredes scripti*, or testamentary heirs, which in Curianus' case as sole heir would amount to a fourth of the whole. The law required that all such heirs should receive not less than the fourth part of the total estate, and provided for the scaling down of legacies in order to produce this part. Its application could be very complex, and the *Digest* has a great deal to say about it. The object was to protect heirs, and ultimately creditors of estates, who would suffer if heirs refused to take up unpromising inheritances (II. 4. 1 n.; *Dig.* 35. 2; Schulz, op. cit. 327 ff.; Gaius, 2. 227). Pliny's two arguments here show that the classical usage was now fully established. Curianus hopes to gain the whole (except Pliny's portion) if successful in his suit *inofficiosi*, but Pliny argues that he could not have counted for certain on more than the Falcidian fourth, even if he had not been disinherited.

10. scis te non subscripsisse mecum et iam biennium transisse omniaque me usu cepisse. Pliny seems to mean that he has acquired a double title, both as unchallenged heir, and if the will were invalidated, by the custom known as *usucapio pro herede*, whereby a third party could acquire an inheritance which the testamentary heir had not taken up. Roby, *Roman Private Law*, i. 212 n. 1, finds a double error here, in that the period for this *usucapio* required in classical law was only one year, two years being the period of ordinary *usucapio*, and that the argument was absurd, Pliny being the unchallenged testamentary heir. But Pliny ought to know the basic rules of his own game, as an advocate of the Centumviral Court. The sentence as a whole suggests that the Court had a rule at this period that no *querela inofficiosi* could be entertained more than two years after the heirs had taken possession, and that Pliny has merged this with a reference to *usucapio pro herede*.

The latter was evidently still a normal custom. From Hadrian on it survived only as a threat to induce reluctant heirs to accept inheritances, and restitution was readily granted against such *usucapio*. Gaius, 2. 52–58; Schulz, op. cit. 359.

offero pro mea parte tantundem. This was a 'factum antiquum' s. 11, because Pliny acted contrary to the *rem quocumque modo rem* principle that already marked Roman life in the second century B.C.; cf. Polybius, 31. 25. 9–10, 26. 9. 'No Roman willingly gives anything to any one.'

12. fraudare voluptate quam ipse capiebam. The joy is on account of the legacy, not of the arbitration story, as Hanslik supposed. Cf. S. Monti, art. cit. Hence this letter is not a 'reprint' of earlier date.

2. *To Calpurnius Flaccus*

Date. No evidence. Calpurnius Flaccus may be the suffect consul of 96, *CIL* xvi. 40, *FO.* The two persons in *PIR*² 265, 268 should be identified. He may have Spanish origins (cf. *ILS* 6946—a like-named *flamen provinciae*—and 7912) and hence belong to the Spanish connexion of Pliny's uncle, III. 5. 17, VI. 20. 5 nn., like Voconius Romanus I. 5 pref.; Garzetti, *C.* 31.

1. **nec urbis copiis ex Laurentino.** He had only a *hortus* at his Laurentine villa, IV. 6. 2.

3. *To Titius Aristo*

Date. The letter fits exactly into the series about Pliny's verses, which begins in IV. 14, and it is demonstrably later than that, s. 1 n. S. Monti sought to date it close to the death of Verginius Rufus in 98, because no other later versifier is mentioned in the catalogue of s. 5, but failed to observe Pliny's deliberate limitation of his list to the dead, and to exalted senators (*Pliniana* II. 313 f.). Other known writers of this category were still alive, and hence could not be named, s. 5 n.

Address. For the great lawyer Titius Aristo see I. 22 nn.

1. **reprehenderent quod haec scriberem recitaremque.** Pliny is now meeting criticism that had not been voiced at the time of IV. 14. The point to be met was not that his conduct was indecent in itself—which he met in IV. 14. 4—but that it was unbecoming in a senator. Hence his list of versifiers in s. 5 is limited to senators. Pliny himself considered that levity was unfitting inside the Senate House, IV. 25. 3 n. The same sense of propriety underlies the outbursts of Tacitus against Nero's athletic and dramatic activities. Cf. IV. 14. 4, 22. 7 nn.

2. **'facio, nam et comoedias audio'** etc. For Pliny it is a question of taste and fashion, not morality. An unprejudiced reader might observe that it was only this fashion that drove Martial remorselessly on in the same vein, in which his pen flows but feebly.

   comoedias audio. Guillemin, ad loc., observes that Pliny did not *see* comedies, though true drama continued to be performed, even if with increasing rarity, in the middle Empire, I. 15. 2 n.

   mimos. The Roman mime, after a literary phase in the hands of Laberius and Publilius Syrus, in the late Republic, became the main form of popular drama, in the shape of short character sketches, and playlets of considerable vulgar appeal and indecency. Friedlaender, *SG* (Eng. tr.), ii. 91 ff.; W. Beare, *The Roman Stage*² (London, 1955), 144 ff., 229 ff. For *pantomimi*, a distinct form, see VII. 24. 5 n.

Sotadicos. Despite the unanimity of the manuscripts, *Socraticos* is entirely out of place, and the emendation of Catanaeus must be read. Cf. Stout, 196. The context is quite different from that of 'Socraticis sermonibus' in III. 12. 1. The style, the coarsest form of *lusus*, originated with the Hellenistic writer Sotades, and owed its obscenity to Cynic influence. Quintilian (1. 8. 6) disapproved of them for the young: 'hendecasyllabi qui sunt commata Sotadeorum (nam de Sotadeis ne praecipiendum quidem est) amoveantur'. See *RE* iii. (2) 1207.

4. quantosque auctores sequar. Pliny's list in s. 5 is confined to senators, mostly distinguished also for oratory, of the post-Gracchan Republic, followed by two Julio-Claudian and one Flavian example. Many are most obscure as poets, and it is possible that Pliny drew his list from a literary history, or from an anthology of *scriptores erotici*, (Prete, op. cit. 23, and others). But the growing contemporary interest in the *veteres* might account for Pliny's knowledge, I. 16. 5, IV. 27. 4 nn. Gellius, in a similar context, *NA* 19. 9, quotes three of Pliny's worthies, Hortensius, Memmius, and Catulus. Ovid, in a list of amatory writers, names as poets, Memmius, Hortensius, and Servius Sulpicius from Pliny's list, *Trist.* 2. 433, 441. But verses by a Scaevola or the two Torquati are not mentioned in antiquity, and little or nothing is known of amatory verses by Sulla, Brutus, or Pollio. The list suggests the pedantic learning of Pliny's uncle.

The following summarizes what other references have been collected about the versification of Pliny's gentry. Cicero: cf. VII. 4. 4 n.; Quint. 8. 6. 73. Calvus, rival of Catullus: 11. 1. 24. Morel, *Fr. Poet. Lat.*, p. 84. M. Messala, Augustan: Virgil, *Catal.* 9. 39 f. Q. Hortensius, the orator: Catullus 95. 3.; Varro, *LL* 8. 14, 10. 78. M. Brutus, the regicide: Tac. *Dial.* 21. 6. Sulla, the dictator: Appian, *BC* 1. 97; Athenaeus vi, p. 261 c. Q. Catulus, the elder, consul of 101 B.C. apparently: Cic. *Nat. deor.* 1. 79. Lentulus, the consul of A.D. 26, Cn. Cornelius Lentulus Gaetulicus: Martial, 1 pref., Sid. Ap. *C.* 9. 259; *PIR*² C 1390. Seneca, the vizier of Nero: epigrams in the Anth. Lat.

By the Torquati Pliny means apparently the consul of 65 B.C., and his son, subject of Catullus' *Epithalamium*. By Scaevola he should mean the Gracchan figure, Scaevola the Augur. Sulpicius is Cicero's friend, the consul of 51 B.C. Memmius is the patron of Lucretius.

5. neminem viventium ... nominabo. He could have added to Spurinna the great Arrius, IV. 3, and Pompeius Saturninus 1. 16. 5, if the latter was a senator.

et proxime Verginium Rufum. This is Pliny's sole recent example; we only know his epitaph, VI. 10. 4. Pliny is careful not to name the living for fear of *offensae*, s. 5. Hence no word of the naughty Spurinna, III. 1. 7. Verginius with his three consulships should carry great weight, II. 1. 1. He was recent compared to Seneca, who precedes him in the list.

si non sufficiunt exempla privata. For the verses of Pliny's emperors see Tac. *Dial.* 21. 5; Suet. *Julius* 56. 7, *Aug.* 85. 2, *Tib.* 70. 2; Mart. 8. 70. 7; Suidas, s.v. Τιβέριος.

6. Neronem. See Tac. *Ann.* 13. 3, 14. 16; Mart. 9. 26. 9.

P. Vergilius. For the early ascription of some of the extant minor Vergiliana to Vergil as *lusus* see E. Fraenkel, 'Culex', *JRS*, 1952, 1 ff. Ovid apparently knew only *Aeneid* 4 and the Eclogues as amatory, *Tristia* 2. 533 f. (Merrill). Cf. Aus. *Cento* p. 206 (Peiper).

Cornelius Nepos. Nothing is known of the verses of the biographer.

Accius Enniusque. Passages in their plays are probably meant.

non quidem hi senatores, sed sanctitas morum non distat ordinibus. The remark is not so silly as Merrill thought, since the fuss was about Pliny's rank, s. 1 n. Compare Vespasian's remark: 'utrumque ordinem non tam libertate . . . quam dignitate differre', Suet. *Vesp.* 9. 2.

7. recito tamen. Pliny replies formally to the second part of the indictment.

8. has recitandi causas sequor. Pliny repeats this explanation in Ep. 12. 1.

quasi ex consilii sententia. A surprising application of the Roman principle of taking counsel, 1. 22. 8–9, Ep. 1. 5 nn.

11. quasi populum in auditorium, non in cubiculum amicos advocarim. Pliny kept his invitations select, III. 18. 4, VII. 17. 12, and his wife did not appear even at his prose recitations, IV. 19. 3, though matrons were not unknown at these occasions, Ep. 17. 5. Pliny tries to take the edge off the attack by insisting that his, unlike those of certain folk (1. 13. 1–2), were private affairs.

4. *To Juiius Valerianus*

Date. The letter belongs to the series about the praetorship of Nepos in 105, IV. 29 pref. It is continued in Ep. 13.

Address. Julius Valerianus is a senator, s. 4 *spectator*, but as yet unknown, II. 15 pref.

1. vir praetorius Sollers. The only candidate for this unusual *cognomen* is Ti. Claudius Alpinus Augustanus L. Bellicius Sollers, of Verona,

son of a Neronian procurator and later adopted by one Bellicius
Sollers, when he was in mid-career as an equestrian officer. As such
he took part in Domitian's Germanic wars, was later apparently
adlected to the Senate, and ultimately held the consulship at an
unknown date. (*PIR*² B 103; Garzetti, *Inc.* 46; Pflaum, n. 68; *ILS*
1031, 2710, 5968; *CIL* v. 3337.) His wife, Claudia Marcellina, should
be related to the advocate mentioned in II. II. 16. A connexion later
existed between Sollers and the family of Pompeius Falco, *ILS* 1104;
I. 23 pref. Hence his influence was not negligible, Ep. 13. 2.

a senatu petiit ut sibi instituere nundinas in agris suis permitteretur.
Cf. the late *SC*. 'de nundinis saltus Beguensis' (A–J n. 96). Control by
the Senate was made necessary by questions of public order. Suetonius
speaks of Claudius asking the consuls to license him to hold such a
market on his estates, *Claud.* 12. 2. Later even this authority passed
to the Princeps, *Dig.* 50. 11. 1 (Modestinus).

contra dixerunt legati Vicetinorum ; adfuit Tuscilius Nominatus.
The territory of Vicetia adjoins that of Verona. Sollers might own
land in both. The municipality objects to the diminution of its own
market by the new one.

Tuscilius Nominatus came from Ricina in Picenum, where he left
property to Trajan at his death, *ILS* 5675. Ep. 13. 2 suggests that
he is not a senator.

2. dixerunt se deceptos lapsine verbo an quia ita sentiebant. The
behaviour of advocates was controlled by special clauses in individual
leges publicae, and by the provisions of the *SC*. *Turpilianum* of
A.D. 61. Three forms of misbehaviour were recognized: frivolous or
vexatious accusation, *calumnia*, for which see VI. 31. 12; *praevaricatio*, or collusion with the other side, for which see III. 9. 29–34 nn.;
and *tergiversatio* or *destitutio*, the abandonment by an accuser of a
case once launched, which was specially the subject of the *SC*.
Turpilianum, for which the main source is *Dig.* 48. 16, though the
first steps to control it were taken by Claudius, *FIRA* i. 44, c. 11.
But this legislation primarily concerned advocates in criminal
procedure. In civil proceedings other considerations kept litigants
and advocates up to the mark—fear of losing one's *cautio* and other
poenae temere litigantium; see Wenger, *Institutes of the Roman Law
of Civil Procedure*, 279 ff., 331 ff. Here the principles of criminal law
are applied to an administrative inquiry as being a matter of *ius
publicum*. Nominatus is in effect charged with a kind of *praevaricatio*
or *destitutio*: 'non fidem sibi in advocatione sed constantiam defuisse',
Ep. 13. 2 n. He is criticized also for the taking of fees (below).

See further *RE* (2) 5, 'tergiversatio', 723 f., ibid. 3, 'calumnia',
1414 ff.; Mommsen, *D. Pen. R.* ii. 188 f.

interrogati a Nepote praetore. For Licinius Nepos see IV. 29. 2 n. As praetor of a criminal court he was the right man to take this matter up.

interrogati an tunc gratis adfuisset responderunt sex milibus nummum. The Republican practice, in the spirit of patronage, enforced by the old *Lex Cincia*, was that no fee was taken for advocacy. The more magnanimous, such as Pliny, still followed this custom, Ep. 13. 8–10. But custom, sanctioned by a Claudian *SC.*, also allowed a fee of S.10,000, the sum here paid in two instalments by the Vicetini; Ep. 9. 4 n. Violations of this rule were controlled by proceedings under the *lex repetundarum*, Tac. *Ann.* 11. 7.

Nepos postulavit ut Nominatus induceretur. He has not yet been formally accused, Ep. 13. 1. The consuls could compel any senator to attend by a fine, or any citizen by *coercitio*, cf. 11. 11. 8–9. Dio 55. 3. 2, Gell. *N.A.* xiv. 7. 10.

5. *To Novius Maximus*

Date. The cross reference in s. 7 to IV. 20 renders the book-date probable.

Address. For the elderly Novius Maximus see IV. 20 and s. 8 n.

1. nuntiatur mihi C. Fannium decessisse. The choice of his themes may indicate a connexion with the family of the Neronian statesman P. Fannius Thrasea Paetus (III. 11. 3 n.). For Pliny's use of the *duo nomina* see I. 12. 9.

2. decessit veteri testamento, omisit quos maxime diligebat. The Romans attached immense importance to testamentary succession. The Elder Cato is said to have reproached himself with only three things, one being that he once lived a single day without having made a will, Plut. *Cato Maior*, 9. 6; Cicero, *ii in Verr.* 1. 60, implies that Romans brought their wills up to date at frequent intervals. The *captatores* had their opportunities at these occasions, cf. 11. 20. In VIII. 18. 5 Pliny remarks as unusual that the wealthy Domitius Afer left a will eighteen years old, and contrary to his feelings.

3. scribebat tamen exitus occisorum aut relegatorum a Nerone. For the contemporary vogue in biographies, followed by Pliny and Tacitus, see III. 10. 1 n. The nearest parallels are the 'exitus illustrium virorum' of Titinius Capito (VIII. 12. 4) and VI. 20 itself. This literature is echoed in Tacitus, who in the *Annales* specializes in *exitus*; notably those of Thrasea and Seneca, and Soranus: 15. 60–64, 16. 21–35.

inter sermonem historiamque medios. By *sermo* Pliny may mean the style of non-forensic speeches, as in I. 8. 2 (n.), rather than that of conversation, as Merrill suggested quoting Horace, *Sat.* I. 4. 39 ff.

4. memoriam sui operibus extendunt. Cf. III. 7. 14, Ep. 8. 1–2.

5. iacere in lectulo suo . . . habere ante se scrinium. So too Pliny and his uncle worked *iacens*, III. 5. 10, IX. 36. 2–3. But they did not write their own manuscripts. The ancients were not well supplied with comfortable chairs.

primum librum quem de sceleribus eius ediderat. This is an early instance of the biographical method of writing by categories that dominates Suetonius. Compare *Nero* 19. 3: 'haec . . . laude digna in unum contuli ut secernerem a probris ac *sceleribus* eius de quibus dehinc dicam'. And *Calig.* 22: 'hactenus quasi de principe, reliqua ut de monstro narranda sunt'. Possibly Pliny gives the title of the book, as Münzer suggested. (*Klio*, 1901, 311; Bardon disagrees, *Litt. Lat. Inc.* ii. 208.)

7. pro istis quae inter manus habes. Pliny refers to the works submitted to him by Maximus in IV. 20.

8. dum suppetit vita, enitamur ut mors quam paucissima . . . inveniat. This is hardly the tone in which Pliny would address a young man. So too in Ep. 8. 7, to the elderly Capito: 'si rationem posteritatis habeas, quidquid non est peractum pro non incohato est'.

6. *To Domitius Apollinaris*

Date. The visit to Tifernum belongs to a year later than the brief call in IV. I. 3 and is clearly that of Ep. 18. 2 (n.).

Address. For the consular Domitius Apollinaris see II. 9 pref.

   For the pattern of this letter, and for the relevant bibliography, see II. 17 pref., adding G. F. Gamurrini, 'Le Statue della Villa di Plinio in Tuscis', *Strena Helbigiana*, Leipzig 1900, 93 ff. The description of the buildings and of their orientation is much less continuous and precise than in II. 17; see especially ss. 28–31 nn. Winnefeld, art. cit., is still the best discussion. For his and other attempted reconstructions see Tanzer, op. cit.

I. audisses me aestate Tuscos meos petiturum. That the villa was on his estates in the territory of Tifernum Tiberinum, modern Città di Castello, in the upper Tiber valley, is shown by the combination of III. 4. 2, IV. I. 4–5, and X. 8 nn. The distance from Rome, given as 150 miles in X. 8. 6, tallies. Gamurrini, art. cit., worked it out from the ancient itineraries and contemporary routes at 149

Roman miles. His identification of a particular site, the Campo di
Santa Fiora, in a locality known then as Colle di Plinio, depends on
the discovery of stamped bricks or tiles bearing what may be the
initials of Pliny, C P C S; *CIL* xi. 6689 n. 43. The site agrees in general
with Pliny's description of a gentle amphitheatre of foothills, ss.
7–8; two streams that flow down to the Tiber may be Pliny's *rivi*,
s. 11. Sundry fragments of masonry and decorative objects indicate
the presence of a villa, which has never been excavated. Gamurrini, art. cit. 95 f. But it should be remembered that Pliny owned two
villa buildings at Tifernum, if he completed the purchase proposed in
III. 19.

2. est sane gravis et pestilens ora Tuscorum quae per litus extenditur.
The malarial conditions of the marshes of the Tuscan coast are mentioned again by Sidonius, *Ep.* 1. 5. 8, in an obvious echo of Pliny—
'pestilens regio Tuscorum'. But there were favoured districts for
pleasaunces even here, cf. the villa of Verginius Rufus at Alsium, and
that of Trajan at Centum Cellae, VI. 10. 1, 31. 15.

4. laurum . . . interdum sed non saepius quam sub urbe nostra necat.
He means Rome, as in I. 10. 1, VIII. 20. 2. The *laurus* is the bay-tree,
Laurus nobilis, which behaves much the same in southern England.

8. inde caeduae silvae cum ipso monte descendunt. Cf. III. 19. 5,
'silvis quae materiam et ex ea reditum . . . statum praestant'. They
are coppice woodlands below the permanent forest of s. 7. The term
caedua silva is technical from Cato onwards (*de ag. cult.* 1. 7) and
apparently distinguishes timber used for firewood and lighter domestic
or agricultural purposes, as in II. 17. 26, from heavy building timber.
Pliny, *NH* 17. 151 includes many light trees as *caedua silva*. Cf.
Thes. L.L. s.v.

**8–10. has inter pingues terrenique colles . . . messem serius . . . per-
coquunt. sub his per latus omne vineae porriguntur . . . prata inde
campique . . . quos non nisi ingentes boves et fortissima aratra per-
fringunt.** The similarity with the estate described in III. 19. 5–7 is
apparent: 'agri sunt fertiles pingues aquosi. constant campis vineis
silvis'. The flourishing mixed agriculture is a warning against over-
simplified accounts of Italian farming and its supposed depression
at this period; ibid. nn.

10. nono demum sulco perdometur. The Elder Pliny notes: 'spissius
solum . . . sulco seri melius est in Tuscis . . . nono' (*NH* 18. 181).
This is probably from observation of this locality. The Younger
Pliny may well have inherited his original Tuscan estate from him.
Before the Plinies secured them, the lands around Campo di Fiora

had been owned by one Granius. Dated tiles of A.D. 7 and 15 suggest
that this is Granius Marcellus, the praetorian senator who appears
in an incident of A.D. 15, which may be connected with the statues
on this estate mentioned in X. 8. 1 (nn.) Cf. s. 1 n. *ILS* 8647. Tac.
Ann. 1. 74; Gamurrini, art. cit. 96 f.

12. **medios ille agros secat navium patiens omnisque fruges devehit in
urbem, hieme dumtaxat et vere.** Strabo (5. 2. 10, p. 227) notes that
the upper tributaries of the Tiber were used by small craft to bring
supplies downstream from Ocriculum. Pliny, *NH* 3. 53, says much
the same: 'Tiberis . . . tenuis primo nec nisi piscinis corrivatur,
emississque navigabilis, sicut Tinia et Clanis influentes in eum,
novenorum ita conceptu dierum, si non adiuvent imbres, sed Tiberis
propter aspera et confragosa ne sic quidem praeterquam trabibus
verius quam ratibus longe meabilis fertur'. By *urbem* here Rome is
meant, as in s. 4.

Since the Tiber cuts Pliny's lands, the estate must be in the main
valley. L-H quotes Livy 5. 54. 4 for Tiber–Rome transport 'ex
mediterraneis locis'.

13. **formam aliquam ad eximiam pulchritudinem pictam.** A map, as
in IX. 39. 5 (L-H).

15. **magna sui parte meridiem spectat, aestivumque solem ab hora
sexta, hibernum aliquanto maturius, quasi invitat in porticum latam
et prominulam. multa in hac membra, atrium etiam ex more veterum.**
This is the front facing towards the Tiber, which here flows from
north-west to south-east. From the description the villa must be
alined similarly, and face south-west rather than due south (L.-H.).
For orientation of villas see II. 17. 6 n.

This villa differs in type from the Laurentine. It is a porticoed
villa, dominated by its porticoed façade, which gives access to various
apartments—*membra*—including the *triclinium* s. 19, *diaeta* ss. 20–21,
two *cubicula* ss. 22–25, and possibly the thermal suite ss. 25–26.
The main block is linked by other porticoes to detached buildings
ss. 28–31. The type was first clearly distinguished by Rostovtzeff,
though Winnefeld realized that the layout was more open than that
of the Laurentine villa. The type appears in Pompeian landscape,
paintings, and its later developments have been discussed at length
by Swoboda. Rostovtzeff suggested that Vitruvius VI. 5. 3 in an
obscure passage refers to (an early form of?) this type: 'ruri ab
pseudourbanis statim peristylia, deinde tunc atria habentia circum
porticus pavimentatas spectantes ad palaestras et ambulationes'.
See Rostovtzeff, art. cit. 116–18; K. Swoboda, *Römische und roma-
nische Paläste*, Vienna 1919, 77 f. For illustrations, Borda, op. cit.

213, 262; Grimal, op. cit., pls. xxi. 3, xxvi. 1; Lehmann, op. cit., pls. 12–17.

magna sui parte. Not, as in s. 41, *maxima*, see s. 28 n.

For the *atrium*, remnant of an earlier building, cf. 11. 17. 4 'atrium frugi nec tamen sordidum'.

prominulam. Though supported by only one of the main groups of manuscripts, this should be right, *pace* Stout, op. cit. 199 f., and the O.C.T. The word is characteristic of Pliny who is partial to diminutives and apparently invented several, e.g. *zothecula* below s. 38, and *columbulus* IX. 25. 3. Cf. J. Niemirska-Pliszczyńska, *De elocutione Pliniana*, Lublin 1955, 9–18. Winnefeld objected that the portico lay behind the projecting *triclinium* and *cubiculum* of ss. 19, 23 (art. cit. 207 n. 12). But as a whole the portico thrust forward from the whole block, cf. s. 19 'quod prosilit villae'. The alternative reading *pro modo longam* is not very apt.

16. xystus in plurimas species distinctus. For this type of formal garden often set, as here and at the Laurentine villa, in front of a portico, see II. 17. 17 n.

demissus inde pronusque pulvinus cui bestiarum effigies invicem adversas buxus inscripsit. acanthus in plano. This shrubbery of topiary work lies below the *xystus*. The formal shrubs stand separately or in opposed lines, with a groundwork of acanthus, cf. s. 36 n. Possibly Grimal, op. cit., plate xix. 3, from Herculaneum, illustrates something like this. Pliny's gardens are full of topiary, ss. 17, 35.

17. ambit hunc ambulatio pressis . . . viridibus inclusa; ab his gestatio in modum circi. For the *gestatio* see II. 17. 14 n. Grimal, op. cit. 269 ff., notes that the different forms of formal garden with walks—*ambulatio, xystus*, and *gestatio*—all tended to the same pattern. The latter, with its measured miles, is the most considerable of these, while the *ambulatio* is a single 'broad walk'. Pliny's *gestatio* lies below the *ambulatio* at the park boundary.

ab his. For *abhinc*?

omnia maceria muniuntur. Such a wall was found by Gamurrini, art. cit. 96, at the southern margin between the two streams.

19. a capite porticus triclinium excurrit, valvis xystum desinentem et protinus pratum multumque ruris videt, fenestris hac latus xysti et quod prosilit villae, hac adiacentis hippodromi nemus comasque prospectat. The orientation is clear if the doors face outwards, perhaps through a pillared front continuing the style of the portico, resembling certain *diaetae* found in Pompeian paintings (Lehmann, op. cit. 106–7). Since the room at the other end of the portico gets most sun (ss. 23–24) the *triclinium* should be at the northern end. This locates the *hippodromus*, which is then seen through the right-hand or north-west window. For a villa of this type of façade see Swoboda, op. cit., fig. 38, p. 79, that of L'Hosté in Belgium.

quod prosilit villae. The portico and its adjuncts.

20. contra mediam fere porticum diaeta paulum recedit, cingit areolam. The front of the *diaeta* is set back from the line of the portico from which it is entered. The word means a special apartment of several rooms, which in this case surrounds two or more sides of a small court; II. 17. 12, 20 nn. Below, s. 27 n.

21. areolam illam porticum [aliam] eademque omnia quae porticus adspicit. This is M (for *a*). β reads *porticus alia*, γ omits. Winnefeld (art. cit. 208) rightly objected to *aliam*, which L-H tried to explain as the colonnade of the *areola* backing on to the grand portico. Pliny means much the same as in II. 17. 5: 'a tergo cavaedium porticum aream porticum rursus mox atrium silvas et longinquos respicit montes'. Hence *porticus* should mean the main colonnade, which is the point of reference from s. 16 to s. 20, and *aliam* obscures the sense. Its view—*eadem adspicit*—is the view of s. 15. There are minor variants in the manuscripts. Either delete *aliam* or read *illam* or Mynors's excellent *porticus alam*, though this is a conflationary reading.

22. nec cedit gratiae marmoris ramos insidentesque ramis aves imitata pictura. The obvious illustration is the mural painting of a similar subject in the Villa of Livia at Prima Porta, Grimal, op. cit., pl. xx, or Borda, op. cit., p. 212. Cf. also Grimal, pl. xiii, a scene from the Pompeian House of Romulus, and fig. 38, from the Auditorium of Maecenas at Rome. For the ensemble compare Statius, *S*. 1. 3. 36 f.: 'in picturata lucentia marmora vena mirer, an emissas per cuncta cubilia Nymphas?'

23. sed ante piscinam quae fenestris servit ac subiacet. Cf. I. 3. 1, 'subiectus et serviens lacus'. Grimal, op. cit. 271 stresses the interdependence of gardens and architectural elements. Guillemin takes the phrase for a legal metaphor imitating Statius, *S*. 2. 2. 73–74, *VL* 126 'omni proprium thalamo mare transque iacentem Nerea diversis servit sua terra fenestris'. Note that *ante* is adverbial.

24. idem cubiculum hieme tepidissimum quia plurimo sole perfunditur. The room windows face south-east and south-west rather than south-west and north-west.

25. cohaeret hypocauston et si dies nubilus immisso vapore solis vicem supplet. inde apodyterium balinei . . . excipit cella frigidaria. For the

hot-air room and its function see II. 17. 23 n., and ibid. 11 n. for the components of the bath-suite. Perhaps the hot-air room has a double function, warming the previous chamber or acting as the *sudatio* as required.

si natare latius aut tepidius velis in area piscina est. These bathrooms lie around an otherwise unmentioned court, and behind the portico if the *cornu* of s. 23 is its extremity. But the end of s. 28 suggests an alternative location, ibid. n.

The water is at air temperature; this was mainly a summer residence, IX. 36. 1.

26. frigidariae cellae conectitur media cui sol benignissime praesto est : caldariae magis, prominet enim. The *cella media* should be the usual *tepidaria*, cf. Vitr. 5. 10. 1 (Winnefeld, art. cit. 208–9). The *caldaria* may project, and face south-west with its windows, from the north-west face of the villa. But the location is far from clear.

magis. Tanzer mistranslated 'warmer than need be'. The sense is clear enough with *prominet*. The alternative *prominent*, equally well supported, makes less good sense.

in hac tres descensiones. Apparently a variant for *baptisteria*. Pliny, *NH* 20. 178, 'in descensione balnearum', fails to illuminate. *Thesaurus* equates it with ἔμβασις.

27. apodyterio superpositum est sphaeristerium. See II. 17. 12 n. It lies higher up the hill, rather than on an upper floor. There are several signs that the villa was built at different levels; cf. the stairs below and in s. 30, and s. 29 'in edito posita'. Winnefeld, art. cit. 210; Rostovtzeff, art. cit. 117.

non procul a balneo scalae quae in cryptoporticum ferunt, prius in diaetas tres. harum alia areolae illi in qua platani quattuor, alia prato, alia vineis imminet. The topography continues obscure. The steps lead up the hillside past a group of *diaetae* to a gallery which borders one flank of the hippodrome (s. 28). This arrangement of garden and gallery is normal, II. 17. 18 n. Grimal, op. cit. 269 f. The first *diaeta* must adjoin or overlook one flank of the *areola*, and perhaps also flanks the *area* of the bathrooms, s. 25, which may lie behind the *areola* and its *cenatio* (ss. 20–21). The second faces south-west and downhill to the meadows below, and the third faces uphill to the vineyards above the villa. They may be buildings of more than one story, though Pliny does not use the term *turris*; II. 17. 12 n.

28. in summa cryptoporticu cubiculum ex ipsa cryptoporticu excisum, quod hippodromum vineas montes intuetur. It is not easy to discern a pattern in the series of galleries and arcades described in ss. 28–31. The first, bordering the hippodrome, lies between that and the villa.

But whether it is parallel or at right angles to the great portico of s. 15 depends upon the meaning of *a fronte* below.

iungitur cubiculum obvium soli maxime hiberno. hinc oritur diaeta quae villae hippodromum adnectit. haec facies, hic usus a fronte. The first chamber has windows facing south-west, like the *porticus hiberna* in s. 31, but their relation to the gallery is not given. The *diaeta* should be at the opposite end of the gallery to the *scalae* of s. 27. This suggests that the gallery is parallel to the side, not to the front, of the villa. If so, then *a fronte* refers to the *cryptoporticus*, and in the next section *a latere* means 'to one side of the first cryptoporticus'.

But the phrase 'haec facies' etc. may represent the end of a phase of the whole description, as Swoboda (op. cit. 77 f.) takes it. Guillemin compares II. 17. 25, 'haec utilitas haec amoenitas', words which there sum up the whole account of that villa. If so, then the rationalization suggested above is wrong, since everything in ss. 15–28 would then be *a fronte*. But the close links between s. 28 and s. 29, the echo of *vineas intuetur* in 'non adspicere vineas sed tangere videtur', and the series of indicators, 'in summa', 'a fronte', 'a latere', suggest that the description is continuous, and that the latter terms all refer to the cryptoporticus.

For *cryptoporticus* see II. 17. 16 n.

29. a latere aestiva cryptoporticus in edito posita. This second gallery should lie higher up the hill, to one side of the first, perhaps at right angles to it, but not attached. Swoboda, loc. cit., is wrong in making *a latere* mean *behind* the villa, and regarding this gallery as a rear façade: *a tergo* would be required.

30. scalae convivio utilia secretiore ambitu suggerunt. These steps should lead down to the third, semi-subterranean gallery, as Winnefeld suggested.

subterraneae similis. This sounds more like the utilitarian *cryptoporticus* of the Villa dei Misteri at Pompeii, II. 17. 16 n.

31. post utramque cryptoporticum unde triclinium desinit incipit porticus ante medium diem hiberna, inclinato die aestiva. hac adeuntur diaetae duae. This fourth gallery leads away from the salon in the centre of the second gallery to isolated *diaetae*. It must face south-east if it is sunny in winter a.m. and shady in summer p.m., and hence be alined from south-west to north-east. Pliny expects shade in summer, not a sunbath, from his galleries, II. 17. 17–19.

32. longe longeque praecedit hippodromus. medius patescit. This is the most complicated of Pliny's garden-grounds, but differs only in shape and extent from the *xystus* and *gestatio*. Like them it combined

formal walks and formal shrubberies. See Grimal, op. cit. 265 and
plate xv, for a reconstruction. The so-called Stadium of the Palatine
is the best example, ibid., fig. 23, p. 266, and plate xvi. 1. Grimal
suggests that the fashion was set by Gaius and Nero, whose 'hippo-
dromes' were regular riding-grounds, whereas those of private owners
were only such in shape. But Martial expects his friend to use his
hippodrome for riding, 12. 50. 5. It does not take more than a circle
of fifty yards' diameter to make a riding-school. However, Pliny used
his for *ambulatio*, s. 40, and his rides in ix. 36. 5 were elsewhere.

   patescit. Grimal takes the garden to be walled, with a gate at the
narrow end opposite the semicircle.

33. rectus hic hippodromi limes in extrema parte hemicyclio frangitur.
Like that of the Palatine, it is curved only at one end, not being
intended for riding. The *limes* is the main outer path, lined on its
outer verge by the shrubberies described above.

   cupressis ambitur. For the use of cypress in topiary work see
Pliny, *NH* 16. 140.

   interioribus circulis (sunt enim plures). The path describes figures
of eight at the head of the garden. Cf. ii. 17. 15, 'interiore circuitu'.

35. alternis metulae surgunt alternis inserta sunt poma et in opere
urbanissimo . . . inlati ruris imitatio. Grimal, op. cit. 268, following
Guillemin, takes the *metulae* to be of stone and the *poma* to be actual
fruit trees. The intermixture of stone ornaments and shrubs is
frequent in Pompeian paintings (ibid., pls. iii, iv), but Pliny is still
describing his topiary work. It is all *imitatio*.

   brevioribus utrimque platanis adornatur. Grimal quotes Pliny,
NH 12. 13: 'et chamaeplatani vocantur coactae brevitatis'.

36. acanthus hinc inde lubricus et flexuosus. Cf. s. 16. This is *Acanthus*
mollis, not a plant capable of topiarism (Grimal, op. cit. 96 n. 3) but
used as a bedding plant, especially on banks and slopes. Pliny, *NH*
22, 76. It is only smooth compared to the other mediterranean
acanthus, *A. spinosus*.

   in capite stibadium candido marmore vite protegitur ; vitem quat-
tuor columellae Carystiae subeunt. Pliny's pergola may be illustrated
best from the paintings of the Villa Boscoreale (Lehmann, op. cit.,
pl. 22), and also from a Herculaneum scene (Grimal, pl. v. 2) where
the columns are of wood. There is little similarity between Varro's
big aviary, much quoted (*RR* 3. 5. 10–17), and Pliny's little garden-
house, except that both were used for picnics. The *stibadium* or *sigma*
is a semicircular dining-couch, cf. Sid. *Ep.* 2. 2. 11; *RE*, 3. 2481.

37. gustatorium graviorque cena margini imponitur, levior naucu-
larum et avium figuris innatans circumit. These toys bear comparison

with Varro's revolving dinner-table. For Roman *hors d'œuvres* cf. I. 15. 2 and Horace, *S.* 2. 4. 12 f.

38. alia viridia superioribus inferioribusque fenestris suspicit despicit-que. L-H rightly takes these to be windows of the same room; cf. VII. 21. 2 'cryptoporticus quoque adopertis inferioribus fenestris', etc. Nothing suggests that the building had two or more stories, as Grimal (277) has it, or that the windows were looking alternately at valley and mountains, as with Winnefeld, but they are on different sides, facing the rise and the fall of the site. The *cubiculum* is tiny, not a regular *diaeta*, and a single vine covers its roof. Its view is confined to the garden itself.

   mox zothecula refugit. II. 17. 21 n.

40. hic quoque fons nascitur simulque subducitur. The spring is enclosed as in IV. 30. 2, 'fons . . . excipitur cenatiuncula'. For a similar ensemble of spring, seat, and *cubiculum*—illustrated at the Villa Boscoreale—see Lehmann, loc. cit., Grimal, op. cit., pl. xxix. 1.

41. quae maxima ex parte ipse incohavi aut incohata percolui. Cf. s. 10 n. for the age of the villa, and s. 15, 'atrium . . . ex more veterum'.

42. titulum suum legat. L-H contrasts Cicero's view of such themes in *ad Att.* 12. 9, 'neque haec digna longioribus litteris'.

45. ego Tuscos meos Tusculanis Tiburtinis Praenestinisque praeponam. Pliny means that he prefers his provincial retreat to the fashionable resorts, where according to Martial (10. 30) Apollinaris owned villas. The passage is remarkably similar to Pliny's sentence:

> dulce Formiae litus . . .
> Apollinaris omnibus locis praefert.
> non ille sanctae dulce Tibur uxoris
> nec Tusculanos Algidosve secessus
> Praeneste nec sic Antiumque miratur.

The exhaustive list in IV. 6. 1 proves that Pliny owned estates and villas only in the three well-known localities: 'Tusci grandine excussi, in regione Transpadana . . . abundantia sed par vilitas . . . : solum mihi Laurentinum . . . in reditu'. These are the only villas mentioned as occupied by Pliny in the Letters. IV. 13. 1 *in Tusculano commorabor* is cited by Sirago to prove that Pliny owned estates in the localities here mentioned (*Ant. Class.*, 1957, 52; *It. Agr.* 33–34). But Pliny frequently stayed with friends on their estates, cf. VI. 14. 28, VII. 16. 2. The phrase in s. 45 is a cliché, recurring also in Martial, 4. 64, 32–36, where ownership is not implied as in 10. 30. Without *meis*, which is added by the minority of F against Mγ, and breaks the rhythm of the *clausula*, the text cannot be pressed against the evidence to attribute the ownership of this remarkable addition of estates to Pliny. Besides, *ego . . . meos* is deliberately emphatic.

46. studiis animum, venatu corpus exerceo. Cf. Ep. 18. 2, 'in Tuscis et venor et studeo', IX. 36. 6, 'venor aliquando sed non sine pugillaribus', also at Tifernum, IX. 10. 1 n. Possibly Pliny was keener on hunting than he cares to admit (Winnefeld, art. cit. 217).

mei quoque nusquam salubrius degunt. Cf. VIII. 1. 3, on the illness of Encolpius journeying probably to the Tuscan villa: 'salubritas caeli, secessus, quies, tantum salutis . . . pollicentur'.

7. To Calvisius Rufus

Date, not closely determinable, s. 3 n.

Address. For Pliny's equestrian friend and business adviser, Calvisius Rufus of Comum, see II. 20 pref.

1. nec heredem institui nec praecipere posse rem publicam constat. The idea that a corporation might possess a legal personality was slow to develop in Roman law, and in respect of municipalities never complete. See P. W. Duff, *Personality in Roman Private Law* (Cambridge, 1938), ch. 3. A municipality could not be *heres* because it could not perform the acts of a *persona certa*, who alone in classical law could become *heres* (Schulz, *Classical Law*, 259). Municipalities were already capable of holding property in the late Republic, and slowly they acquired the right to accept legacies, which were ratified on special occasions in the Julio-Claudian period (cf. Suet. *Tib.* 31; Tac. *Ann.* 4. 43; *ILS* 977). Then Nerva granted the right to all boroughs, apparently throughout the Roman empire, and a Hadrianic *SC.* later smoothed out difficulties. *Tit. Ulp.* 24. 28: 'civitatibus omnibus quae sub imperio populi Romani sunt legari potest idque a divo Nerva introductum'. Later this was extended to include *fideicommissa*, Paulus, *Dig.* 36. 1. 27 (26), and possibly under Marcus they received the right of inheritance from their own freedmen (Ulpian, *Dig.* 38. 16. 3. 6; *Tit. Ulp.* 22. 5; Duff, op. cit. 88 n. 6; *Cod. Iust.* vii. 9. 3). But the rule against ordinary inheritance was firmly maintained, *Tit. Ulp.*, loc. cit.: 'nec municipia nec municipes heredes institui possunt quia incertum corpus est'. See X. 75. 2 n. for the position of provincial communes under these enactments, and the use of *fideicommissa* in this sphere.

Pliny's statement thus agrees with the legal texts, and adds the information that a legacy in the form of *praeceptio* was not valid under the Nervan rule. This is because, as Gaius, 2. 217–19, maintains, only a *heres* can receive by *praeceptio*. Cf. X. 75. 2 for an instance. It was a form devised to enable a testator to leave a particular object to an heir, since ordinarily an inheritance was divided up on a cash settlement between joint heirs. Saturninus wanted to make sure that the municipality received a certain sum, instead of the uncertain share of what was left after legacies and creditors had been paid (cf. Ep. 1. 9 n.). Pliny confirms for this period the doctrine of Gaius, that only a properly qualified heir can receive by *praeceptio*. A rival view tended to assimilate *praeceptio* to ordinary legacies. This is shown by Pliny to be not yet current. It was supported by a ruling of Hadrian (Gaius 2. 221) and ultimately prevailed, since Justinian's law freed the 'preceptor' from all the conditions of heirs (*Cod.* 6. 24. 13; cf. Mommsen, *GS* iii. 194 f.). The disadvantage of the system was that if the estate cut up well the 'preceptor' might receive less than his quota, in this case the fourth part, would have given him.

Why Saturninus used the form of *praeceptio* instead of a straight legacy or a *fideicommissum* is not apparent. Possibly having learned that the ordinary inheritance was invalid he was badly advised about the validity of the *praeceptio* form. It is unlikely that the bequest would reduce the total net value of the remaining estate below the figure of a quarter laid down by the *Lex Falcidia*. In such cases the legacies were scaled down to increase the value of the estate to the heirs (Gaius, 2. 227).

Saturninus. This is an unknown man from Comum, not Pliny's literary friend Pompeius Saturninus, who, as is evident from 1. 8. 3, 16 and VII. 15. 2, was not from Pliny's native place. Schultz, art. cit. 28 f., 33, failed to observe this, and wrongly identified the two.

quadrantem reipublicae nostrae deinde pro quadrante praeceptionem quadringentorum milium dedit. Saturninus evidently first used the formula *heres esto* and then added *praecipito* etc. This agrees with Gaius against the rival school which required only the formula *L. Titius praecipito*.

2. mihi autem defuncti voluntas (vereor quam in partem iuris consulti quod sum dicturus accipiant) antiquior iure est. Pre-classical lawyers were generally literal in the interpretation of documents, upholding the strict form of words against the obvious intentions of testators. The classical lawyers of the Principate continued mainly in this tradition, though perhaps with less extreme rigour. Then in the post-classical period there was a marked reversal of doctrine, and the *voluntas testatoris* was accepted as a principle of interpretation, greatly modifying the classical system. It is much disputed how far this doctrine can be detected in the earlier period. It appears occasionally even in the Republican period at an early date in the famous

causa Curiana described by Cicero (*Brutus* 145 ff.), and later in a
dispute between Servius and Tubero about the interpretation of
terms by reference to common meaning and intention (*D*. 33. 10. 7. 2:
cf. Bonner, *Roman Declamation*, 46–48). Before Pliny, Quintilian,
7. 6. 1, generalizes to the effect that 'scripti et voluntatis frequentissima inter consultos quaestio est'. It seems that the manifest intention of a testator might occasionally be preferred to the most literal
interpretation of an ill-chosen phrase, but that consideration of
hypothetical intentions was rigidly excluded. See F. Schulz, *Principles* etc., 210 ff., *Roman Legal Science*, 76 f., 132 f., 295 f., and bibliography cited. The chief defendant of Roman 'equity' is J. Stroux
'summum ius summa injuria', *Festschrift Speiser-Saragin*, Leipzig,
1926.

Pliny here, and in II. 16, IV. 10, shows something of the social and
moral forces that slowly produced this transformation in the spirit of
Roman law, and also the strength of the professional opposition to
his views. The doctrine of *voluntas* had powerful friends in the administration. Trajan applied it to the *form* of soldiers' wills: 'ut quoquo
modo testati fuissent rata esset eorum voluntas', Ulpian, *D*. 29. 1. 1,
citing a *caput ex mandatis*. The accompanying comments of the
lawyers show how awkward they found his rule.

**3. cui de meo sestertium sedecies contuli, huic quadringentorum
milium paulo amplius tertiam partem ex adventicio denegem?** This
is the only indication of date in this letter, and a poor one. His last
major benefaction was the alimentary scheme, *c*. 97–98, followed
recently by the endowment of the schoolmaster. But the costs
cannot be exactly apportioned, I. 8. 10 n., IV. 13, VII. 18. 2 n.

The arithmetic of the shares is sufficiently clear. Since Comum
was named as heir to a fourth part, Pliny and Rufus shared nine-
twelfths between them. If Rufus was *e quincunce* there would be
four-twelfths left for Pliny. The two share the invalid inheritance in
the proportion of their shares. Four-ninths is *paulo amplius tertiam
partem*. Cf. Sirago, op. cit. 40 n. 5. If Saturninus calculated his values
correctly the whole estate was worth about S.1,600,000. This would
be a poor fortune for a society figure such as Pompeius Saturninus,
but a decent estate for a municipal squire. Cf. I. 19. 2 n.; Martial 4. 66.

scio te quoque iudicio meo non abhorrere. Pliny coolly takes the
acquiescence of Rufus for granted. This, with the abrupt beginning, is
a sign of revision. The letter was evidently in reply to a tentative
proposal of Rufus, and the original may have read less awkwardly
in this respect.

4. parce tamen et modeste. Cf. I. 8. 5–7 for Pliny's care in dealing
with the town council of Comum.

5. **scribere publice.** cf. IV. 7. 2.

6. **malignitati interpretantium exponitur.** Was he afraid of gossip about *captatio*?

8. To Titinius Capito

Date. Pliny's references to his poems, to the revision of speeches, and to the novelty of a Flavian history, ss. 4, 6, 12 nn., variously support the book-date. Peter's argument, art. cit. 708, that this letter must be later than VI. 2, 18, 23, where Pliny is still active in the courts, is not cogent, since Pliny revised speeches for publication throughout his forensic career, s. 6 n.

Address. For the retired imperial secretary Titinius Capito and his interest in history see I. 17 pref., VIII. 12. Sidonius Apollinaris, *Ep*. 4. 22. 2, referred to this letter as addressed to Tacitus, but since he confuses the two Plinies in *Ep*. 4. 3 this is no reason to dispute the address in the manuscript (Mommsen, *GS* iv. 441 n. 5; Prete, *Saggi*, 64 n. 1).

1. **me autem nihil aeque ac diuturnitatis amor et cupido sollicitat.** Here and elsewhere the letter contains distant echoes of Cicero's letter to Lucceius about the history of his own consulship, *ad Fam.* 5. 12, as ibid. 1: 'neque enim me solum commemoratio posteritatis ad spem quandam immortalitatis rapit sed etiam illa cupiditas' etc.

    diuturnitatis. Longolius remarked long ago that Pliny never claims *aeternitas* for himself. Compare his doubts about Martial, III. 21. 6, and the qualification in II. 11. 1.

3–4. **hoc satis est quod sola historia polliceri videtur. orationi enim et carmini parva gratia nisi eloquentia est summa : historia quoquo modo scripta delectat.** This implies that having tried the first two he will now try the third, and thus dates this letter after the publication of his hendecasyllabics, IV. 14 pref. Again Pliny's modesty rings true. He has no illusions about the value of his cherished speeches, although he pins his chances of fame to them, Ep. 5. 7–8, s. 6. He rates them far below those of Tacitus, VII. 20. 4, VIII. 7, and knows that he is no Demosthenes, VII. 30. 5.

    historia quoquo modo scripta delectat. This was an unusual attitude towards written history in antiquity, and goes beyond Cicero, loc. cit. 5, 'ordo . . . annalium mediocriter nos retinet . . . at viri . . . excellentis . . . casus habent admirationem'. Perhaps Pliny is thinking of his uncle's work, which he mentions at once in s. 5. It is not his own notion of the best historical style, as ss. 9–11 show. In

VII. 33. 10 (n.) he asks for embellishment, but adds 'nec historia debet egredi veritatem'. In IX. 13. 14 he claims to have written his account of the attack on Certus 'cuncta ipsorum verbis'.

5. avunculus meus idemque per adoptionem pater historias . . . scripsit. The adoption, only mentioned here, was several years after his father's death, and probably testamentary, since there is no word of it in VI. 16. 20, and Verginius Rufus was his legal guardian, II. 1. 8. For the Elder's histories see III. 5. 6, 'Books', n.

6. has . . . destino retractare. In I. 2, 8, and II. 5 we hear of the careful preparation of such speeches for publication. After that we hear of the recitation of three speeches, his *In Priscum* and *Panegyricus*, which was not forensic, and an unidentifiable third, II. 19, III. 13, 18, IV. 5 nn. In IV he is generally preoccupied with his poems, Ep.14 nn., and puts off the editing of his *Pro Basso* IV. 9. 23. Then comes this intention, which is put in hand in Ep. 12 and frequently in the last three books: VII. 12, 17; VIII. 3, 15. 1, 19. 2; IX. 10. 3, 15. 2, in addition to his preparation of verses (VII. 4, 9, VIII. 17, 21). In VI there is no such reference, but he sends a big new speech to Romanus (VI. 33). The letter thus comes perfectly well in its place in the series of Pliny's references to his own writings. The speeches *In Caecilii Socios* and *Pro Basso* might be chiefly in his mind.

7. quidquid non est peractum pro non incohato est. Cf. Ep. 5. 7–8.

8. unodevicensimo aetatis anno dicere in foro coepi. This would be in A.D. 79–80, the year after his uncle's death, cf. VI. 20. 5. His earliest effective appearance was in the case of Junius Pastor, when he was *adulescentulus adhuc*, I. 18. 3. His own protégés begin at a rather later age, VI. 11. 1 nn., but Septimius Severus gave a public *declamatio* when 17, SHA, *Sev.* 1. 5, and Pliny complains long and loud of 'boys' appearing in the Centumviral Court, II. 14. Quintilian preferred that men should not practise in court before their quaestorship, i.e. about the age of 25 (12. 6), but made no fixed rule.

9. habet quidem oratio et historia multa communia, sed plura diversa . . . narrat illa narrat haec sed aliter. In II. 5. 5–6 he puts the historical style between oratory and poetry, and in I. 16. 2–4 he approves Saturninus' speeches for *acritudo* and *ardor*, and his histories for *suavitas, splendor*, and *sublimitas*. Pliny is on the side of his master Quintilian (10. 1. 31 ff.) in regarding history as more poetical than oratory, especially in its vocabulary and figures of speech. Hence in the following comparison *haec* must refer to oratory and *illa* to history, though they have not always been so taken. So too Syme, *Tac.* 202 n. 3; H. W. Traub, 'Pliny's treatment of history' etc., *T.A.Ph.A.* 86, 221 n. 27.

10. hanc saepius ossa musculi nervi illam tori quidam et quasi iubae decent. Quintilian, loc. cit. 33 is decisive: 'licet . . . in digressionibus uti vel historico . . . nitore dum . . . meminerimus non athletarum toris sed militum lacertis opus esse'.

11. ut Thucydides ait. But Pliny reverses the famous judgement of Thuc. I. 22. 4. History is a possession, and therefore must be, for Pliny, more, not less, ornate.

12. vetera et scripta aliis? parata inquisitio sed onerosa collatio. Guillemin hesitated over the meaning of *collatio*, 'mise en œuvre' or 'comparaison'? But only the latter is possible from Pliny's usage. Cf. II. 19. 8, 'leges . . . aliarum collatione convincere'; IV. 5. 2, VI. 16. 16. The meaning must be that the comparison of the previous writers with each other is a trouble, not the comparison of Pliny's work with that of his predecessors, as Prete thought (*Saggi*, 77 n. 1, against Nissen, *Rhein. Mus.* XXVI. 501).

intacta et nova. Pliny can only be thinking of the Flavian period. The subject is available. Hence he has not yet heard of or received any volume of the Histories of Tacitus, or been approached by him, as in VI. 16, 20, VII. 33. Syme (*Tac.* 117) oddly takes the opposite view, and detects the first hint of the Histories being noised abroad in Pliny's failure to take up the suggestion of Capito. Mommsen also thought that Pliny was put off by Tacitus' success (*GS* iv. 441). This is doubtless true, but Pliny would not have rushed suddenly into this or any literary labour.

graves offensae. So the anonymous writer in IX. 27 found. Tacitus, taking up what Pliny left undone, found the same difficulty, *Hist.* I. 1: 'neque amore quisquam et sine odio dicendus est'. Cf. the preface to the *Annales* of Tacitus: 'res florentibus ipsis ob metum falsae postquam occiderant recentibus odiis compositae sunt'.

14. praesternas ad quod hortaris eligasque materiam. Guillemin (*VL* 132) finds this obscure without the assumption that Pliny has in mind Cicero's request to Atticus for historical information (*Ad Att.* 16. 13 (c) 2). She oddly imagines that Capito is to put the imperial archives at Pliny's disposal. But Capito was no longer Secretary by 102, and Pliny means 'choose me a subject' (I. 17. 1 n.).

9. *To Sempronius Rufus*

Date. At the beginning of the year of Nepos' praetorship, s. 6 n., hence *c.* February 105, cf. IV. 29 pref.

Address. For the senator Sempronius Rufus see IV. 22 pref.

1. descenderam in basilicam Iuliam. The basilica was at the south side of the Forum Romanum, Ashby, *Top. Dict.* 78. The Centumviral Court regularly met there, Mart. 6. 38. 5–6.

proxima comperendinatione. This term retains its technical sense of adjournment until the day-after-next, as in Gell. *NA* 14. 2. 1, in all classical citations in *Thesaurus* s.v., which quotes no classical example of a looser or metaphorical meaning. Hence it seems that the Centumviral Court regularly met every other day. Cf. VI. 2. 6, 'leges . . . tot comperendinationes largiuntur'.

2. sedebant iudices. decemviri venerant. obversabantur advocati. silentium longum. tandem a praetore nuntius. This letter, with VI. 33. 2–6, is the principal source for the administration of the Centumviral Court. Augustus had placed it under the direction of the *decemviri stlitibus iudicandis*, in place of ex-quaestors, and the general supervision of the praetor known as *ad hastam* or *hastarius*, from the *hasta* which was the sign of the court (Suet. *Aug.* 36; Gaius 4. 16), who first appears in a Tiberian inscription, *ILS* 950. The court, now composed of 180, not 100, jurors, sat usually in four sections (VI. 33. 3 n.). Hence the function of the praetor was administrative, as here, rather than judicial. The court was only concerned with proceedings *in iudicio*, since the establishment of cases *in iure* which preceded the hearing *in iudicio* took place before the *praetor urbanus*. Mommsen, *DPR* iii. 258 f.; O. Martin, *Les Centumvirs* etc., ch. 2. 22 ff.

3. causa dilationis Nepos praetor, qui legibus quaerit. Licinius Nepos, praetor in 105 (IV. 29 pref.), was certainly not himself the praetor of the Centumviral Court, as Mommsen suggested in *DPR* iii. 255 n. 1, ignoring s. 5. Elsewhere Mommsen argued that he was the *praetor repetundarum*, because of his interest in the illegal payment of advocates here and in Ep. 4. 2, which fell under the cognizance of the extortion law, and because of his criticism of an amendment of the extortion law in VI. 5 (*D.Pen.R.* i. 237 n. 4, iii. 2 n. 3). But his activity is compatible with any sphere of jurisdiction, and Pliny's phrase *legibus quaerit* certainly points, with *accusatores* and *reos*, to his presidency of one of the criminal courts, of which the function was defined as *quaerere de eo qui* etc. Probably the growth of the criminal jurisdiction of the Senate, for certain forms of crime involving the upper social classes, had led to the grouping of two or three of the obsolescent *quaestiones* under a single praetor to deal with offences affecting lower ranks of society.

admonebat accusatores. The following section shows that this means that he would exact the oath laid down in the *SC.* in his own court, not that he was warning parties in other courts. Nepos is exercising the right of a Roman magistrate to draft his own rules of procedure under the guidance of a *senatusconsultum*.

4. hoc omnes qui quid negotii haberent iurare priusquam agerent iubebantur nihil se ob advocationem cuiquam dedisse promisisse cavisse. This is likely to be the Claudian *SC.* briefly summarized in Tac. *Ann.* II. 7: 'capiendis pecuniis posuit modum usque ad dena sestertia, quem egressi repetundarum tenerentur', Mommsen, *D.Pen.R.* iii. 2 n. 3. It is evident from s. 6 and from Epp. 4. 3, 13. 6–9 that no recent action had been taken in the matter to which Nepos' attention was drawn during the Nominatus affair, Ep. 4 nn.

quid negotii. Pliny summarizes. The *SC.* covered the whole sphere of court work, Tac. *Ann.* II. 6–7.

his enim verbis ac mille praeterea. The verbosity suggests Claudian authorship, cf. the wordy *SC.* in honour of Pallas, VIII. 6, and other Claudian documents (Charlesworth, *Documents* etc.) (C. 2–5)).

permittebatur pecuniam dumtaxat decem milium dare. Cf. Tac. *Ann.*, loc. cit., and Ep. 4. 2. For a discussion of the payment of advocates see E. P. Parks, *Roman Rhetorical Schools* (Baltimore, 1945), 56 ff. It was not by fees of this order that Regulus amassed his sixty millions (II. 20. 13), which would require 6,000 cases in thirty years at the legal rate!

5. praetor qui centumviralibus praesidet, deliberaturus an sequeretur exemplum. Each praetor is free to take his own line. The matter is finally taken further by a *SC. ex auctoritate principis*, Ep. 13. 8 n. The Centumviral praetor might hesitate to apply the procedural rules of the criminal courts in his own sphere, when certain rules, such as those concerning *praevaricatio* and *calumnia*, did not apply to both; Ep. 4. 2 n.

6. initurus magistratum iura cognovit, senatusconsulta legit. So in VIII. 14. 2–3 Pliny complains of the *iuris senatorii oblivio* that had grown up under the autocracy of Domitian. The time is near the beginning of the Court year, which began in January or February, IV. 29. 2 n.

10. *To Suetonius Tranquillus*

Date. Subsequent to IV. 14; Pliny's hendecasyllabics have now been published and are in circulation, s. 2 n.

Address. For the biographer Suetonius' career see I. 18 pref.

1. hendecasyllaborum meorum fidem, qui scripta tua communibus amicis spoponderunt. Pliny has foretold a volume by Suetonius, originally in a poem read at a private recitation (cf. Ep. 3. 11).

The implication favours a volume of verses, rather than the lost prose work *De Viris Illustribus*, suggested in *RE*. (2) 4. 598, but no poems are mentioned in the list of his works given by Suidas s.v. or the longer list in Bardon, *Litt. Lat. Inc.* 206, save possibly '*Prata*'. His *Lives* appeared under Hadrian. Cf. also Fr. della Corte, 'Suspiciones II', in *Antidoron U. E. Paoli*, Genoa 1956, 93 f.

ne cogantur ad exhibendum formulam accipere. A complicated legal joke, drawn from the process of the *interdictum exhibitorium*. The praetor issued a set form of words for the production of a thing or person by the defendant, and later issued an ordinary *formula* which bade a *iudex* condemn the defendant to pay a certain sum if it appeared that he had not produced the thing in question. Schulz, *Classical Roman Law*, 59 ff. Pliny's *formula* could refer to either stage of the process.

2. sum et ipse in edendo haesitator. Cf. I. 2. 5–6, 8. 3; IV. 9. 23; V. 3. 7–10 *et al.* Evidently Pliny's volume is now published and for sale. For the stages cf. Ep. 12. 1, 'recitaturus oratiunculam quam publicare cogito'. For publishers, I. 2. 5 n.

3. describi legi venire volumina. By *legi* he does not mean 'corrected', and certainly not recited with a view to revision, after Pliny's own custom (as Birt, *Kritik . . . des antikes Buchwesens*, 313) but literally as in VII. 4. 9, 'legitur, describitur'. Not all copies were acquired by sale.

11. *To Calpurnius Fabatus*

Date not determinable exactly, but not earlier than IV. 1, the first letter addressed to Pliny's new *prosocer*, Calpurnius Fabatus of Comum, for whom see ibid. pref., and below.

1. te porticum sub tuo filiique tui nomine dedicasse. The presentation and endowment of public buildings is among the commonest acts of municipal munificence in the Roman Empire. The building by a certain L. Caecilius Secundus, who may be Pliny's father, in honour of a dead daughter, and the dedication, possibly by Pliny himself, of a 'templum Aeternitati Romae et Augusti cum porticibus et ornamentis', at Comum is an apposite illustration (below, p. 732 n. 4). Fabatus, as a local *flamen divi Augusti*, would be familiar with it, and inspired to imitation.

dedicasse. Cf. IV. 1. 5–6, for the ceremony.

in portarum ornatum pecuniam promisisse, ut initium novae liberalitatis esset consummatio prioris. For the idea see I. 8. 10. The promise would be made at a meeting of the Council, of which Fabatus was a member; cf. Ep. 7. 4 for the procedure. The known *Porta* of Comum is of later date. M. Bertolone, *Lombardia Romana*, ii. 207. A gateway of the 'triumphal' type is probably intended. For the development of these in the early Principate see I. A. Richmond, *JRS*, 1933, 149 ff.

2. memoriam soceri mei. His death, before Pliny's marriage to Calpurnia, seems to have been fairly recent, IV. 19. 1, VI. 12. 3.

3. semel incitata liberalitas. So not all were so generous in money matters as Pliny; cf. VI. 34. 2 n. Fabatus was pretty close, and never spent a penny on his borough until now, cf. VI. 30, VII. 11, VIII. 20. 3, but he was devoted to the idea of a male heir, like most men of money, VIII. 10. 3.

12. *To Terentius Scaurus*

Date. The book-date is slightly supported by the cross-reference to Pliny's proposed *retractatio* of his speeches in Ep. 8. 6 (n.). This is the only recitation of a speech in V and VI.

Address. The man might be the Hadrianic grammarian, Q. Terentius Scaurus, who commented on Horace (*PIR*[1] T 71; Gell. *NA* 11. 15. 3), but is more likely to be the parent or close relation of the two consulars, D. Terentius Gentianus, suffect consul in 116, and D. Terentius Scaurianus, first governor of Dacia (*PIR*[1] T 56, 68; *FO*; *ILS* 1046, 2004; *AE* 1944, 57–58; *CIL* iii. 1443).

1. recitaturus oratiunculam quam publicare cogito. Pliny's use of prose recitations is described at length in II. 19, VII. 17. He may here be referring modestly to one of the *magnas et graves causas* which he proposed to revise in Ep. 8. 6. For the use of the diminutive cf. Ep. 20. 8, IX. 10. 3, 15. 2.

3. quem iam nunc oportet ita consuescere ut sine praefatione intellegatur. For prefaces, and Pliny's dislike of them, see I. 13. 2, IV. 5. 4, II. 3, 14. 8. By *ita consuescere* he means, much as in VIII. 21. 2, that the book must 'get the habit' before publication, not that it is a mere literary exercise on a stock theme.

13. *To Julius Valerianus*

Date. The letter, continuing Ep. 4, belongs to early 105, s. 4 n.

Address. For the senator Julius Valerianus see Ep. 4 pref.

1. egit ipse pro se nullo accusante. The informality of senatorial trials is indicated. There is no formal accusation, yet he is certainly on trial, of a sort, s. 4. Cf. the indictment of Norbanus contrary to the rules in III. 9. 30–32.

2. ne desiderio senatoris . . . de gratia fama dignitate certantis . . . in senatu repugnaret. The senator is Bellicius Sollers, Ep. 4. 1 n. The passage shows the influence of the *potentissimi* and their cliques on such occasions, just as in the trial of Classicus, III. 9. 9 n. Yet here as there the better cause just manages to prevail.

The implication is clear that Nominatus himself was not a senator.

alioqui maiorem invidiam quam proxime passurum. This with *tam pertinaciter* above refers to the first session of the inquiry, not described by Pliny, who mentions only its adjournment, Ep. 4. 1.

3. erat sane prius . . . acclamatum exeunti. For these informal demonstrations see IV. 9. 18 n.

4. absolutus est sententia designati consulis Afrani Dextri. This man is known only from Pliny, and from *FO*, as the suffect consul of May–July 105, who was murdered by his slaves in June, VIII. 14. 12 n. The date, which is crucial for the sequence of many letters in IV–VI, sets this letter before May. Possibly he is brother of another consular, P. Afranius Flavianus; Garzetti, *Inc.* 6, *C.* 4; *PIR*² A 442.

liberandum, i.e. *poena*.

5. adsenserunt omnes praeter Flavium Aprum. is interdicendum ei advocationibus in quinquennium censuit. This was the usual penalty under the *SC*. *Turpilianum* for *destitutio*, Ep. 4. 2 n. Such penalty might be for a varying number of years. Ulpian, *Dig.* 48. 9. 9 pref.; Paulus, ibid. 16. 2.

Flavium Aprum. If the reading of Aldus—'Flavium'—is not a guess, this man may be the unknown father of M. Flavius Aper, consul in 130. The senatorial standing of the family may derive from the praetorian senator and orator of Vespasian's time, M. Aper, a man of Gallic origin, known from Tacitus' *Dialogus*, 7. 1, 10. 2. *PIR*² A 910, F 206, 208; Syme, *Tac.* 799. But M reads *Fabium*, and has some support from the γ reading, which suggests that their original reading was 'F. Aprum', i.e. Fabius rather than Flavius; cf. Stout, p. 208, Fabius Postuminus, IX. 13. 13 n. No Fabii Apri are known as senators. A *Fulvius* is also possible; cf. Fulvius Gillo, Fulvius Rusticus, VII. 3 pref., IX. 13. 13 n. For senatorial Flavii not connected with the house of Vespasian compare L. Flavius Fimbria, consul of 71, *PIR*² F 269.

5. prolata lege de senatu habendo iurare coegit e republica esse quod censuisset. This is the Augustan law of 9 B..C, which minutely regulated senatorial procedure, in such points as the *ordo sententiarum*, the schedule of sessions, the size of the quorum, and compulsory attendance. Dio 55. 3. 1; Suet. *Aug.* 35. 3; Gell. *NA* 4. 10. Pliny quotes it again in VIII. 14. 19 for the rules about dividing the house.

iurare. There was no provision for enforcing relevance to the question in debates, which allowed filibustering by the device of *egredi relationem*, VI. 19. 3, IX. 13. 9, 18 nn. This oath may have been devised as a partial check on factious senators, as here. Tiberius once took it, Tac. *Ann.* 4. 31: 'amovendam in insulam censuit tanta contentione animi ut iure iurando obstringeret e republica id esse'. Its meaning is shown by a clause in the *Lex de imperio Vespasiani* which enabled the Princeps to do 'quaecunque ex usu reipublicae . . . esse censebit'. This was the basic duty of a Roman magistrate, cf. Gell. l.c. 8. No exact Republican precedents exist for an oath of this sort, while Tac. *Ann.* 1. 74, 4. 21 refer only to senators giving their *sententiae* in senatorial trials. Cf. *RE* (S) vi. 769.

6. exprobrare enim censenti ambitionem videbatur. In Pliny the word *ambitio* has the general sense of currying favour, without any undertone of corruption; cf. III. 9. 10, 'tum . . . ambitio dominatur cum sub . . . specie severitatis delitescere potest'. Also I. 14. 5, V. 14. 2, VI. 2. 6 *et al.*

Nigrinus, tribunus plebis, recitavit libellum disertum. For the function of tribunes in the Principate see I. 23 nn., and for the reading of speeches VI. 5. 6. Nigrinus intervenes again in Ep. 20. 6 on the side of legality. Nepos set a fashion that was followed by Nigrinus and also by Homullus in VI. 19. 3. The man is C. Avidius Nigrinus, who rapidly became suffect consul in 110 and later legate of either Dacia or Moesia under Trajan. For a short time he was in high favour with Hadrian, but was soon involved in the 'conspiracy of the four consulars', and executed. *PIR*² A 1408; Garzetti, *Inc.* 25; Syme, *Tac.* 669; *ILS* 2417; SHA, *Hadr.* 7. 1, 23. 10; Dio 69. 2. 5–6. His father is the like-named Nigrinus, proconsul of Achaea, X. 65. 3 n., brother of Pliny's acquaintance T. Avidius Quietus, VI. 29. 1 n., whose like-named son Quietus was consul suffect in 111, the year after our Nigrinus, and survived his unlucky cousin to become proconsul of Asia in *c.* 126 (*PIR*² A 1409). The family, which came from Faventia in Cisalpine, evidently owed much to the favour of Hadrian in the time of Trajan. Details of their careers are still obscure, cf. *PIR*² s.v., for which the evidence in *FO* about their consulships appeared too late.

questus est venire . . . praevaricationes, in lites coiri. A new phase has begun in the development of professional advocacy. Contemporaries of Tiberius had blamed not the emperor but the *factiones accusatorum* for the first outburst of vexatious delation, which battened on the social legislation of Augustus, Tac. *Ann.* 2. 34, 4. 21, 6. 16. When Claudius had tried to check the *accusatorum regnum* (*FIRA* i. 44) the advocates redressed the balance by increasing their fees in civil litigation, which Claudius checked in turn by legal limitation of fees, Ep. 4. 2 n. Trajan too had checked unrestricted delation by his famous purge of vexatious delators (*Pan.* 34–35). Hence advocates are trying new rackets.

ex spoliis civium magnos . . . reditus. See the debate in Tac. *Ann.* 11. 6–7 on the morality of payment for advocacy. The professionals claimed that they were men of peace: 'nulla nisi pacis emolumenta peterent'. The others maintained: 'ne fidem quidem integram manere ubi magnitudo quaestuum spectatur'. And so it proved.

7. recitavit capita legum. For the various enactments involved see Epp. 4. 2, 9. 4 nn.

petendum ab optimo principe ut . . . ipse tantis vitiis mederetur. This is one of three examples in the Letters where the Senate goes out of its way to invite imperial interference in its few remaining spheres of independent business, cf. VI. 5. 5, 19. 3–4. Also IV. 25. 5, IX. 13. 22 for a similar tendency. The Princeps is not present at this debate, though certainly in Italy until June 105 (*FO*).

8. pauci dies et liber principis severus et tamen moderatus. The Senate evidently adopts Trajan's proposal as the basis of a *SC*. In IX. 13. 22 they present a proposal to Nerva, which he suppresses. A Trajanic amendment to the *SC. Turpilianum*, in conjunction with the Senate, is attested in *Dig.* 48. 16. 10. 2, but casts no light on the present proposal.

leges ipsum ; est in publicis actis. Cf. VII. 33. 3. There are several references in Tacitus' *Annales* to the *acta diurna*, a gazette which was circulated in Italy and even in the provinces, containing an account of events at Rome, great and small, such as public works, state funerals, and evidently, as here and in VII. 33. 3, a summary of senatorial proceedings: *Pan.* 75. 1; Tac. *Ann.* 12. 24, 13. 31, 16. 22; Suet. *Cal.* 8. 2; Pliny, *NH* 7. 60, 8. 145. The latter had not been published as such since Augustus stopped the custom initiated in 59 B.C., Suet. *Caes.* 20. 1; *Aug.* 36. Cf. A–J 96. 1–2.

There is no occasion to distinguish between the *diurna*, or in full, *acta diurna populi Romani*, or *diurna urbis* popularly, and a more exalted set of *acta publica*, themselves distinct from the *acta senatus*, as do Syme (*Tac.* 120 n.) and others. The adjective *publica* is the equivalent of *populi*, cf. II. 1. 9 n., and their content seems identical with that of the *diurna urbis*. *RE* i. 287 ff.

quam me iuvat quod in causis agendis non modo pactione dono munere verum etiam xeniis semper abstinui. Pliny never reckons fees as a source of income, II. 4. 3 n. Even Regulus did not make all his fortune by advocate's fees, II. 20. Pliny's phrase indicates that it was not usual to make a direct demand for a fee. The *SC*. did not allow even the legal fee to be exacted beforehand, Ep. 9. 4 n. The lesser advocates concerned with minor cases would be satisfied with far less than the maximum permitted fee, which represents about a year's income for the middle classes that formed the majority of the municipal councils of Italy, I. 19. 2 n.

pactione. Cf. Ep. 9. 6, 'reprimit foedissimas pactiones'. Quintilian disapproved of such arrangements, but thought that while the wealthy should take no payment for advocacy, others might in moderation (12. 7. 8–11).

14. *To Pontius Allifanus*

Date. This letter is one of the pivots of Otto's theories, though to the unprejudiced eye Pliny's reference to his present tenure of the *cura Tiberis*, assumed not before 104 on the obvious meaning of the evidence, supports the book-date. Otto, art. cit. 34, identified this visit to Comum, s. 8, with that mentioned in IV. 1 and 30, and shifted all to the year 101, s. 8 n. But a second, separate visit to Comum, one or two summers later, which may be identified with that in VI. 1, makes equally good sense, and avoids creating a difficulty about Pliny's *cura*. Peter, art. cit. 708, detecting echoes of *Pan.* 90–92 in the account of Tertullus' career, anticipated Otto's dating. But references to Pliny's earlier career are no proof of an early date, any more than in the similar references to Pliny and Calestrius Tiro in VII. 16, or Rosianus Geminus in X. 26. See ss. 2, 5, 6, 8 nn.

Address. Two other letters, VI. 28, VII. 4, indicate similar connexions of Pontius with Campania and literature, ss. 8–9. For the cognomen derived from locality compare Aefulanus Marcellinus, Ep. 16 pref. Pontius Fregellanus in Tac. *Ann.* 6. 48, and M. Aefulanus, *PIR*² A 115. Syme remarks that the numerous Pontii of Campania needed distinctive *cognomina* (*JRS*, 1949, 13). L. Pontius Allifanus is now known as the son of a like-named proconsul of Cyprus whom he accompanied to his province *c*. A.D. 60 (*SEG* 18. 588.) Hence he was probably himself a senator and close contemporary of Tertullus, the subject of this letter. There was never any occasion to amend the *cognomen*, with P. Lambrechts (*Rev. Belg. Phil.* 1936, 125 f.).

1. nuntiatum est Cornutum Tertullum accepisse Aemiliae . . . curam. The career of C. Julius Cornutus Tertullus is known from *ILS* 1024, found near Rome, and references in Pliny. Already *aedilicius* in

A.D. 73–74, when adlected to the Senate *inter praetorios* by Vespasian and Titus, he held only the post of proconsular legate of Crete-and-Cyrene, and the proconsulship of Narbonensis under the Flavians. As a friend of Titus he may have been out of Domitian's favour, or like Bruttius Praesens preferred to idle (VII. 3); his friendship with Helvidius seems to have been non-political (cf. IV. 9. 2 n., IX. 13. 16). In 97 he is resident in Rome (ibid.). Then he shares with Pliny the prefecture of the treasury and the consulship, in 98–100. After a few idle years he returns to office in this *cura viae*, is commissioner for the census of Aquitania, succeeds Pliny in Bithynia, and holds the titular crown of the public career with the proconsulship of either Africa or Asia *c.* 117 (*PIR*¹ s.v.; Syme, *Tac.* 82 f.). His origin is uncertain, though his family names recur at Perge in Pamphylia. His public life, parallel to that of Pliny, shows the emergence of a civilian type of senatorial career pursued by men of non-military abilities. It is comparable to the procuratorial career of the *advocati fisci* which appears later in the century. *PIR*¹ T 187; Garzetti *C.* 70. (See p. 84 for the date of his Bithynian appointment *c.* 115.)

Aemiliae viae curam. This usually means the great Aemilian Way from Ariminum to Placentia, not the short coastal route from Pisae to Vada built by M. Aemilius Scaurus in 109 B.C. (Chilver, *Cisalpine Gaul*, 33, 41). The trunk roads were maintained by the Princeps at this period, who appointed the senatorial supervisors. The other known *curatores Aemiliae* were praetorian, not consular men like Tertullus. Hence Syme (op. cit. 71 n. 6) suggests that he was a commissioner for *alimenta*, a duty often conjoined to a *cura viae*. (Cf. *ILS* 1005, 1175; Statius *S.* 3. 3. 102; Mommsen, *DPR* v. 382 f.; *RE* iv, 'curator', n. 2, 1781 f.)

2. honor . . . ultro datus. As distinct from personal sollicitation, as Pliny's augurship, or the recommendation of a friend, as Pliny for Accius Sura, X. 12, 13.

mandatum mihi officium. This is the 'cura alvei Tiberis et riparum et cloacarum' of the inscription, *ILS* 2927, a consular appointment which Pliny held at the normal moment. He succeeded Ti. Julius Ferox, known from several inscriptions as curator from 101 to 104, II. 11. 5 n. Hence a date in 104–5 fits for Pliny's appointment, to which he may possibly refer in III. 6. 6. That Pliny held the office for a brief tenure, terminated by illness, in 101, as Otto has it, before Ferox, who was two years his senior as consular, is extremely improbable even by itself.

The curator was in charge of drainage, artificial and natural, in the Roman area. In the Julio-Claudian period there was a board of four praetorian curators with a consular president, but under the

Flavians a single consular curator replaces the board, cf. *ILS* 5925–9. The sewers were added to the charge in this period; the words *et cloacarum* appear first in the title of Julius Ferox. From Claudius onwards the post, first created in A.D. 15, came under the full control of the Princeps. *RE* iv. 1790 f.

4. una dileximus omnes . . . in utroque sexu aemulandos. The women of the Helvidius group are meant, Anteis, Arria, Fannia, whom Tertullus supported in lukewarm fashion in the Certus affair, IX. 13. 16. His ward, ibid., the daughter of the younger Helvidius, was now dead, IV. 21.

5. collega . . . in praefectura . . . fuit, fuit et in consulatu. tum ego qui vir . . . esset altissime inspexi. Cf. *Pan.* 90–92. For Peter and Otto these references meant that the offices were very recent. But *tum* suggests a decent interval of years as against his favourite *proxime* or *nuper* of close intervals, like *tunc* in I. 10. 3 (at least sixteen!), III. 11. 2, V. 1. 5, or *tum* in IX. 13. 4.

aetatis maturitate. Tertullus would be some fifteen years older than Pliny. As *aedilicius* in 74 he would not be less than 27 years old.

6. tandem homines non ad pericula ut prius verum ad honores virtute perveniunt. Remarks of this sort occur in firmly dated letters of the period 105–6 (VIII. 14. 2–3, IV. 15. 8), and are no indication of an early date.

8. eram cum prosocero meo, eram cum amita uxoris, eram cum amicis diu desideratis. For Otto this *diu* must be the same as *post longum tempus* in IV. 1. 1, and both must refer to Pliny's absence from Comum between 97 and his consulship, while *desiderati* echoes the *incredibili quodam desiderio* of the same passage. But this polite passion could inspire Pliny more than once, and when he was less busy it was probable that he would visit Comum more than once. It is possible to identify the visit projected in IV. 1 and completed in IV. 13 and 30, with this visit, so long as it is not placed in 101; but it is likely that the references spread through IV, V, VI to Comum refer to more than one visit. It seems as though one summer in the period of IV–VI was spent on the Tuscan estate, Ep. 6. 1 and 18 nn., separating a visit to Comum in perhaps 104 from a second visit in *c.* 106.

For the separate argument of Otto that *duobus matrimoniis meis* in X. 2. 2, written in 98, refers to Pliny's marriage with Calpurnia at that date see note ad loc.

audiebam multum rusticarum querelarum. rationes legebam invitus et cursim, aliis enim chartis aliis sum litteris initiatus. Between letters of *c.* 98 and 106 (II. 4. 3, 15; X. 8. 5; to VII. 30. 2; VIII. 2) Pliny has

little to say about agricultural troubles on his own estates—III. 19
and VI. 3 concern those of other people, and IV. 6 is only a complaint
about the weather and a bumper harvest. But in the last four books
there are frequent complaints; in VII. 30. 2–3; VIII. 2, 15. 1; IX. 15.
1, 16. 1, 20. 2, 36. 6, 37. Thrice Pliny adopts the disdainful pose of a
man of letters to conceal his keen interest in the management of his
estates, here to Pontius, and in IX. 15, 36, to Pompeius Falco and
Fuscus Salinator, all three devotees of the Muses (IV. 27, VII. 4, 9).
Contrast the shrewdness of his letters of business to intimates such
as Calvisius Rufus, III. 19, VIII. 2, Caninius Rufus, VII. 18, and
Valerius Paulinus, IX. 37. Ordinarily Pliny did not expect to talk
letters to the squirearchy, cf. VII. 25. 4: 'Athenis vivere hominem
non in villa putes'. The presence of only two letters (VII. 21, 31) to
Cornutus Tertullus himself is doubtless due to the man's lack of
interest in *studia*, suggested by VII. 31. 5 (n.).

9. **includor angustiis commeatus.** Cf. X. 8. 6, where Pliny requests
leave for a month's absence from Rome during his prefecture of
Saturn, and possibly III. 6. 6 n.

15. *To Arrius Antoninus*

This note continues the little series to the elder statesman and
literary man, Arrius Antoninus, IV. 3, 18. Pliny has now finished
translating Arrius' verses, and repeats his earlier compliment in
similar terms. Considering the slow rate of Pliny's work there is no
difficulty about the appearance of this in V. Some six months may
separate the two. Pliny was evidently anxious to please his illustrious new friend, thrice mentioned in as many letters in IV (with
IV. 27. 5).

16. *To Aefulanus Marcellinus*

Date. No specific indication. Fundanus as a consul of 107 was likely
to have a first child of 13 years old in about 105–6 since the ordinary
age of senatorial marriage was about 24, VIII. 23. 5, and for the
consulship about 40.

Address. Aefulanus Marcellinus is not otherwise known, but may
be a connexion of Fundanus' wife, s. 4 n., and is probably the
recipient of VIII. 23, on a similar theme.

1. **Fundani nostri.** For Minicius Fundanus, consul in 107, see IV.
15 pref. and 5 n.

2. nondum annos XIIII impleverat. This child's urn and epitaph were found in the family tomb at Monte Mario outside Rome, *ILS* 1030. 'D. M. Miniciae Marcellae Fundani f. v(ixit) a(nnos) XII m(enses) XI d(ies) VII.' It is better to accept the discrepancy than to correct the manuscripts, which all agree on the same figure, given in numbers.

3. ut praeceptores pro suo quemque officio diligebat! As a girl she would have a private tutor for the 'grammar' phase of Roman education, as did the grandson of Corellius, III. 3. 3 n. This was the usual limit of women's education (Friedlaender, *SG* (Eng. tr.) i. 230). But Pliny's letters are full of educated ladies, even if they have not studied rhetoric, such as the wife of Pompeius Saturninus, I. 16. 6, Corellia Hispulla, III. 3, Calpurnia Hispulla, IV. 19, and the mother of Calpurnius Piso, Ep. 17. 5, while Pliny's own wife was being brought up to the ancient equivalent of novel-reading, IV. 19. 2–4. The general position of women as property-owners in Roman society, and the virtual elimination of the *tutela* (II. 20. 10 n.), implies that education was widespread among women of the middle and upper classes, even if the formidable Ummidia Quadratilla was exceptional, VII. 24. Juvenal satirizes such learned ladies in *Sat.* 6. 434 ff., but the education of women had its champions in the philosophers. Musonius Rufus in his fourth sermon maintained that women should have the same education as men, even in philosophy, and Plutarch treated the education of women in a lost work. Fundanus, as a student of philosophy and a friend of Plutarch, would follow such advice. Cf. M. P. Charlesworth, *Five Men* (Camb., Mass., 1936), 41 f.; *RE* xxi. 1. 702. Carcopino, *Daily Life*, 84 ff., seeks to discount such evidence for the respectability of Roman ladies.

ut parce custoditeque ludebat! Here witty conversation, as in Ep. 3. 2, 'rideo iocor ludo', not the writing of naughty verses, as in IV. 14. 3. Pliny did not object to his wife reciting his *lusus* in private, IV. 19. 4, and here implies that feminine conversation was by no means always domestic.

4. sororem patrem adhortabatur. The omission of the mother suggests that she was dead. She may be the Statoria M.f. Marcellina, whose epitaph was also found in the family tomb, *CIL* vi. 16632. Both ladies were alive at the time of Plutarch's *De cohibenda ira*, 455 F.

6. iam destinata erat egregio iuveni iam electus nuptiarum dies. Friedlaender, op. cit. I. 232 and App. 18, put the usual age of marriage for girls between 13 and 16, the legal minimum being 12 (Pomponius, *Dig.* 23. 2. 4). Engagements, *sponsalia*, could be at any age, but usually were at the marriageable age and completed within the year (Modestinus, ibid. I. 14; Gaius ibid. I. 17; cf. VI. 26. I n.). The lawyers all insist that the consent of the girl is required for an engagement, but consent was narrowly interpreted; an objection could only be sustained: 'si indignum moribus vel turpem sponsum ei pater eligat', Ulpian, ibid. 1. 12. Pliny insists on good character in future husbands, and prefers good looks as well, 1. 14. 8, VI. 26. 1.

8. se ab ineunte aetate altioribus studiis artibusque dediderit. This is the main ground for the identification of Pliny's man with Plutarch's friend, whose philosophical interests appear from his place as the main speaker in the *De coh. ira*. He is also mentioned in *De tranquillitate animi* 464E. As a young man he attended the Stoic Musonius Rufus, but was never a Stoic doctrinaire (*De ira* 453 D), preferring like Plutarch a form of Platonism, according to Groag's interpretation in *RE* xv. 1825 f. Cf. also ibid. xxi. 1. 691.

10. memento adhibere solacium, non quasi castigatorium . . . sed molle. This astonishing warning reminds the modern reader of the frequent harshness of Roman *amicitia*, with its duty of *praeceptio* (II. 6. 6 n.). Pliny softens this in most of his admonitory letters (e.g. VII. 26, VIII. 22, IX. 30), though he is rough with Julius Genitor, IX. 17, and himself endured severe letters from Titius Aristo and his grandfather-in-law, V. 3. 1, VI. 12. 3. Guillemin contrasts Pliny's humanity with the severity of Sulpicius' consolation to Cicero, *ad Fam.* 4. 5. Seneca wrote in a rough fashion about a friend mourning a lost child, with philosophical self-satisfaction (*Ep.* 99. 1–5 etc.).

multum faciet medii temporis spatium. Merrill collected the classical bibliography of Time the Healer, which characteristically begins with Menander, fr. 652 (Koerte), and enters Latin literature through Terence, *Heaut.* 422.

17. To Vestricius Spurinna

Date, not exactly determinable, but the address of a letter on this theme to Spurinna fits well with the reference to him as a patron of young men of letters in the similar letter IV. 27. For Spurinna, now an octogenarian consular, see II. 7. 1, and for his poetic interests III. 1. 7.

1. si nobiles iuvenes dignum aliquid . . . faciant. Presumably here and in *Pan.* 50. 3, 69. 6, Pliny uses this term in the republican sense, of the old consular families. Syme, *Tac.* 577 f., waxes most indignant at Pliny's condescension, though even in the earlier Principate the surviving Republican nobles played an undistinguished part in affairs, and the work of the empire was done by men like Pliny. The true *nobiles* of the Principate were the families of the new consulars, such as the Ummidii and Pedanii, whose young men Pliny encourages in VI. 11, 23.

fuisse me hodie in auditorio Calpurni Pisonis. This man or his brother (s. 5) should be the consul *ordinarius* of 111, C. Calpurnius Piso, though Pliny implies that he is rather young for this to be possible. His father was probably the suffect consul known from *F. Pot.* for 87 (and *CIL* vi. 2065. 31724) C. Calpurnius Piso Licinianus, who may be the conspirator Calpurnius Crassus Frugi relegated for plots against Nerva and Trajan: Dio 68. 3. 2, 16. 2; SHA, *Hadr.* 5. 6; *Ep. de Caes.* 12. 6; *PIR²* C 259, 281, 285; Garzetti, *C.* 32; Bardon, *Litt. Lat. Inc.* ii. 231. The father links these Pisones with the numerous but now nearly extinct Julio-Claudian family, from which so many conspirators or political victims were drawn. The second *cognomen* suggests a connexion through Galba's ill-starred heir, L. Calpurnius Piso Frugi Licinianus, rather than other of the Neronian unfortunates; see I. 5. 3, II. 20. 2, III. 7, 12 nn. Perhaps this Piso was one of those *nobiles* promoted by Trajan at the election of 100, *Pan.* 69. 4–6. See also *CIL* vi. 2055, 64. 31724.

auditorio. See I. 13 nn. for the system of recitations.

2. recitabat καταστερισμῶν eruditam sane luculentamque materiam. We owe the recovery of the Greek title to the acumen of Aldus, rather than to his ten-book manuscript, who alone of the early editors penetrated the mysterious meaning of the letters TACTAE PIGMON to which the Greek had been reduced in the eight-book tradition. Later Aldus' restoration was confirmed by codex M. Stout, p. 66.

4. quod sibi maiores sui praetulissent. If this implies that Pisones had been men of letters, this would seem to be known only of the Augustan politician, L. Piso, consul B.C. 15, and City Prefect from A.D. 13 to 32. He is named as a man of letters by Porphyrio (*Commentarii* 344 Meyer), to whom Horace sent his *Ars Poetica*. *PIR²* C 289.

5. gratulatus sum optimae matri, gratulatus et fratri. The absence of the father, if alive, is suggestive of his disgrace.

18. *To Calpurnius Macer*

Date. The same year as Ep. 6, s. 2 n.

Address. P. Calpurnius Macer Caulius (or C. Aulius) Rufus, now known as suffect consul in 103 (*FO*), governed Moesia *c.* 109–12, when Pliny was in Bithynia, X. 42 n. He should be identified with the Macer of VI. 24, and hence be a Cisalpine (ibid. 2 n.). *PIR²* C 273; Garzetti, *Inc.* 36.

1. **habes uxorem tecum habes filium.** The son may be P. Calpurnius
Atilianus Atticus, *cos. ord.* in 135, whose mother may have been
named Atilia. *PIR²* C 250, cf. *CIL* iii. 12496.

2. **ego in Tuscis et venor et studeo.** In Ep. 6. 1 he intends to spend a summer on his Tuscan estate, with hunting and writing to amuse him, ibid.
46. A similar holiday is mentioned in VII. 30. 2–3; VIII. 1–2, 20. 3;
IX. 15; and is described at length in IX. 36. His duties as *curator
Tiberis* prevented prolonged holidays at both places in the period
c. 104–6, Ep. 14. 9. Hence three summers should be allocated to the
Comum and Tuscan visits of books IV–VI, Ep. 14. 8 n., unless he
ceased to be *curator* before the Tuscan holiday, which would enable
the Comum visit of VI. 1 and 24 to be put in the same year as it. His
custom of spending time in winter at Tifernum, IX. 40, must be
after the termination of his public duties.

et venor et studeo. For this conceit see I. 6. 1 n.

19. *To Valerius Paulinus*

Date. Support can be urged for the book-date from the reference to
the freedman's return from Egypt, s. 6 n.

Address. For Pliny's literary friend, now *praetorius*, see II. 2 pref.

1. **quam molliter tuos habeas.** Pliny and Paulinus were exceptional
in giving their household freedmen a standard of life approaching
their own, as in meals, II. 6. 3–4 nn. Exhortations of self-control,
such as Plutarch attributes to Pliny's friend Fundanus, in *De cohibenda ira* 459 c, 460 a, etc., show how uncertain was the treatment of
dependants in the average household. Pliny's liberality towards his
slaves in the disposition of their earnings was not the general custom,
VIII. 16 nn. Seneca's discourse on the friendly treatment of slaves
and *humiles amici, Ep.* 47, *De clementia* I. 18, was rather ahead of the
age, though the Principate saw a steady advance in the defence of
the human rights of slaves. Cf. Carcopino, *Daily Life*, 56 f.; R.
Barrow, *Slavery in the Roman Empire* (London, 1928), 49 f., 151 f.

2. **infirmitas liberti mei Zosimi.** Evidently consumption, s. 6. For a
similar case see VIII 1.

3. **ars quidem eius et quasi inscriptio comoedus.** The intense specialization of servile duties is well known. Normally a *lector* would be
responsible for reading 'orationes et historias et carmina', cf. VIII. 1.
2, but ability with the zither would be expected only of the *citha-
roedus.* Cf. I. 15, 2, 'audisses comoedos vel lectorem vel lyristen'.
Friedlaender, op. cit. (Eng. tr.) ii. 341 ff.

6. **ante aliquot annos . . . in Aegyptum missus . . . rediit nuper.** It is reasonable to suggest that he went out under the aegis of Pliny's friend Vibius Maximus, prefect of Egypt from mid-103 onwards, or of the equestrian procurator Maturus Arrianus who served under Maximus, was still out of Italy at the time of IV. 12. 7 (n.), and had returned in VI. 2. See III. 2 nn.

7. **quae Foro Iuli possides.** Probably Valerius Paulinus, like Tacitus' friend Agricola, hailed from this Roman colony in Narbonensis.

esse ibi et aera salubrem et lac eiusmodi curationibus accommodatissimum. The treatment of tuberculosis by fresh air and milk diet was well known to the medical science of antiquity, and is described by Celsus and Galen, who notes that there were many relapses, as in the case of Zosimus. Celsus 3. 22; Galen 12 (Kühn). 191. Cf. Pliny, *NH* 28. 54, 125, 31. 62, 163. Egypt is recommended by Celsus and the Elder Pliny, but it is the sea voyage, not the climate, that they have in mind. For a summary of the evidence see Friedlaender, op. cit. i. 321. Fannia, VII. 19. 3, is another case. These have been discussed by F. M. Leon, *Journal of History of Medicine*, xiv (1959), 86–88.

8. **scribas tuis ut illi villa ut domus pateat.** For the custom see I. 4, VI. 10. 1 nn.

20. *To Cornelius Ursus*

Date. Late 106 or early 107 on the present evidence, s. 6 n. The trial of Varenus used to be one of the most disputed dates in Pliny. But the establishment of the year 103 for the trial of Bassus, with which that of Varenus is connected, has destroyed the principal argument in favour of an early date for the Varenus case urged by Premerstein; IV. 9 pref. Until the dating of Acilius Rufus' consulship to 107 is certainly established (s. 6 n.) the possibility of 106 remains open. The reference to the ex-praetor of 105, Licinius Nepos, in the debate of VI. 5 excludes—and always excluded, though only Hanslik perceived it—a date earlier than 106 for the sessions of the Senate recorded by Pliny; the consulship of Acilius also excludes 105. For Hanslik see *Wiener Studien*, 63, 133 f.

Address. For Cornelius Ursus, recipient also of the Bassus letter, see IV. 9 pref. The case continues in VI. 5, 13, VII. 6, 10.

1. **breve tempus a Iulio Basso, et Rufum Varenum proconsulem detulerunt, Varenum quem nuper adversus Bassum advocatum . . . acceperant.** This passage was supposed by the detractors of Mommsen to anchor the Varenus case to within a year of the Bassus case,

excusably, for Pliny often uses *nuper* in the sense of *proxime* (e.g. VII. 26. I, VIII. 22. 4, IX. 23. 2); *breve tempus* in III. 9. 26 means a period of months, though it means nine years in VIII. 14. 10. Varenus did not act in the Bassus case according to IV. 9. His absence might have been due to his designation as future proconsul of Bithynia, (Hanslik, loc. cit.), or simply to ill health. But if he were designated early in the year 103, his proconsulship must have been 103–4, and the delay in initial indictment until some time in 106 is not explicable by anything in Pliny. His proconsulship is only known from Pliny and Dio Chrysostom whose oration xlviii was addressed to him in office; Dio's reference to the 'cursed Dacians' (ibid. 6) fits better the period 105–6, when the second Dacian war of Trajan broke out with unexpected suddenness, than 103–4. The absence of Trajan from Rome at a later stage of the Varenus debates, VI. 13. 2, may also belong to the period of the war. For the possibility that Varenus is also the 'bad governor' censured in Dio *Or.* 43. 11, see IV. 9. 5 n. Nothing else is known of Varenus' career, Garzetti, *Inc.* 154.

2. **inducti in senatum inquisitionem postulaverunt.** The Varenus letters describe the first phase of an extortion trial, touched allusively in II. 11. 2; III. 4. 2–3, that precedes the substantive proceedings described in the accounts of the Classicus and Priscus trials, III. 9, IV. 9. The procedure is much as laid down in the *SC. Calvisianum* (II. 11. 2 n.), by which, after *nominis delatio* before a magistrate, the provincial representatives were brought into the Senate and supplied with advocates (III. 4. 2–4 nn.). The provision of advocates is not here mentioned, but there is a later reference to it in VII. 6. 3. Next the provincials unfold their case, and make it apparent that they are bringing charges of *saevitia* against Varenus, to establish which they require the usual authority to seek out and bring witnesses from the province, III. 9. 6, 29, II. 11. 5 nn. The trial would eventually take the form of a criminal indictment before the full Senate instead of the 'shorter process' for financial restitution before a select committee.

Varenus petit ut sibi quoque defensionis causa evocare testes liceret. This was a complete novelty, s. 7 n., like the remission of *ignominia* in the Bassus case, IV. 9. 16 n.

recusantibus Bithynis cognitio suscepta est. The primary question, as the *sententia* of Acilius shows, s. 6, was not the request of Varenus, but whether the charges were serious enough to justify the longer form of trial, with its attendant process of *inquisitio*. Compare the parallel case in Tac. *Ann.* 13. 52: 'Silvanum magna vis accusatorum circumsteterat poscebatque tempus evocandorum testium. reus ilico defendi postulabat'. But Varenus, unlike Marius Priscus and

Silvanus, prefers the longer process, doubtless because he knows what is afoot in Bithynia to ruin the prosecution, VII. 6. 1–6.

3. liber offensis . . . caret. For the political passions raised by these cases see III. 4. 7, and 9. 26 'quantas . . . offensas subierimus'.

4. respondit mihi Fonteius Magnus, unus ex Bithynis. In addressing the Senate here, and in VI. 13. 2. VII. 6. 2, 6, the provincial representative encroaches on the function of the official advocates. So too in the Caecilius and Bassus cases, III. 9. 29 f., IV. 9. 3, 14 nn., it appears, as here, that the *inquisitio* is now regularly carried out by the provincials themselves, who had in their *Concilia* a ready instrument, VII. 6. 1 n. Magnus is not otherwise known.

est plerisque Graecorum ut illi pro copia volubilitas. Pliny's assessment of the rhetor Isaeus is more favourable, II. 3. 1–3. Pliny is freer than most of his contemporaries from the Roman dislike of *Graeculi*, I. 10, II. 3, X. 40. 2 nn.

5. Iulius Candidus non invenuste solet dicere. This is more probably the distinguished consular, Ti. Iulius Candidus Marius Celsus, *cos.* II. in 105, than the younger Ti. Iulius Candidus Caecilius Simplex, because the shortened *nomina* appear thus in official documents as the proper names of the elder (*FO* and *ILS* 1374). Both men occur throughout the Arval records of Trajan's reign (cf. *ILS* 5028, 5046), and the younger continues till A.D. 145. *PIR*¹ I 162, 164; Garzetti, *C*. 68.

si M. Antonio credimus. The orator of the age of Marius, and Cicero's great predecessor.

6. postero die dixit pro Vareno Homullus. The continuation of the session was now no longer, as in the year 100, so rare as to make Pliny comment, II. 11. 16, 18; IV. 9. 15 n.

For the identification of the first speaker with M. Junius Homullus see IV. 9. 15 n. He is acting as advocate, not giving his *sententia*, because the division begins with the vote of the consul designate. Nigrinus likewise is the official advocate of the prosecution, cf. VII. 6. 2. For his short but brilliant career see Ep. 13. 6 n.

censuit Acilius Rufus, consul designatus. A fragment of *FO* gives . . . *Rufus* as consul for the first 'suffect' period of March–May in 107. The assumption that this is Acilius is probable but not certain (Hanslik, art. cit. 133; Syme *JRS*, 1946, 163). Rufus is a remarkably common senatorial cognomen even among the limited circle of Pliny's friends. A son of Accius Rufus, a suffect of 90 (*F. Pot.*), or of one of the two Pomponii Rufi (III. 9. 33 n.) is possible. As consul of the second *nundinum*, Acilius, if it is he, was one of the two senior

A a

designates present from the suffect-consular elections onward—in late 106, if these were held before the new year—and from January onwards in 107, in any case. The *ordinarii* of 107, Sura and Senecio, as Trajan's chief advisers, never take part in senatorial debates. The new date means that Varenus was formally indicted in late 106—at the end of the travelling season—and that the present phase is before March 107. For the date of suffect elections see pp. 23 f.

Acilius is commonly identified with an undistinguished praetorian senator from Sicily (*CIL* x. 7344; *PIR²* A 78; Garzetti, *C.* 2). The procurator of the like name, *ILS* 1376, is shown by a difference of tribe to be no relation.

7. Cornelius Priscus consularis. See III. 21 pref. for the uncertainty as to the date of his consulship, probably *c.* 102–3.

rem nec lege comprehensam nec satis usitatam, iustam tamen. For the further debates about this see VI. 5. 2. It certainly was not envisaged in the *SC. Calvisianum*, or practised in the cases recorded by Tacitus' *Annales*. Quintilian (5. 7. 9) excludes the possibility: '(genus testium) eorum quibus in iudiciis publicis lege denuntiari solet . . . accusatoribus tantum concessum est'. Possibly the *lex ambitus* allowed it, VI. 5. 2 n. But the power of the provincial *Concilia* at this time might make the proposal equitable; cf. Tac. *Ann.* 15. 20–21, on the 'novam provincialium superbiam'.

21. *To Pompeius Saturninus*

Date. Apart from the vain attempt to identify the dead Saturninus of Comum (Ep. 7. 1 n.) with the living Pompeius Saturninus, and the dead Julius Avitus of this letter with the dead Junius Avitus of VIII. 23, s. 3 n., there is no argument against the date of the book for this letter. It was written in late summer during one of the holidays mentioned by Pliny in this book, s. 1 n.

Address. For the literary Pompeius, who was not from Comum, see I. 16 and Ep. 7. 1 nn.

1. statim ut venissem. Pliny's absence from Rome, and the recent return of the quaestors from their provinces, s. 3, point to a date in late summer, when Pliny was out of Rome, either at Comum or more probably—because he seems to envisage a quick return—at Tifernum, Epp. 6. 1, 14. 1, 18. 2.

2. Iulius Valens graviter iacet. As yet unknown, evidently an elder man.

3. Iulius Avitus decessit dum ex quaestura redit, decessit in nave, procul a fratre amantissimo, procul a . . . sororibus. Asbach's identification,

art. cit. 47, of our man with the second dead ex-quaestor, Junius
Avitus in VIII. 23, is impossible. Julius is unmarried, childless,
leaving brother, sister, and mother behind him. Junius has a young
wife and child, and neither brother nor sisters. Julius was a provincial
quaestor, Junius an urban quaestor, and already aedile designate,
ibid. 5–8. The brother is in all probability Julius Naso, VI. 6. 8 n.
The family is unknown. The provincial quaestors returned at the
end of the proconsular year, in June or July; cf. IV. 12. 4, 15. 6 nn.
Possibly like other of Pliny's friends these Julii came from Olisipo in
Lusitania, where a Julius Avitus is magistrate in 121. *CIL* ii. 186;
cf. I. 5. 8, iii. 9. 7 nn.

5. quo ille studiorum amore flagrabat. Junius Avitus too was among
Pliny's pupils, but was less accomplished, VIII. 23. 3–4, and more
the man of action. Schultz, art. cit. 27, remarked that Junius was the
more intimate friend, to judge by the tone of the two letters.

BOOK VI

1. *To Calestrius Tiro*

Date. Calestrius Tiro, the subject or recipient of the interlinked group of letters, Ep. 22, VII. 16, 23, 32, and IX. 5, has not appeared in the correspondence since I. 12. His imminent departure for the proconsulship of Baetica in Ep. 22 etc., provides a *terminus ante quem* for this note, and the reference to Pliny's Cisalpine visit gives a crossbearing on Ep. 24 and V. 14. Hence the book-date is well supported. For the praetorian Tiro's earlier career see VII. 16 nn. It would seem from s. 1, and the negative evidence of I. 12 about another Cisalpine, that his *patria* lay in Picenum, not Cisalpine, though he may have owned land at Ticinum, VII. 16. 3.

> **ego trans Padum.** Sirago attempts (*It. agr.* 28) to distinguish between Pliny's estates *circa Larium* (VII. 11. 5) and those in *regio Transpadana* (IV. 6. 1) on the assumption that Pliny refers there and in II. 1. 8 (*regio eadem*, of Mediolanum and Comum) to the Augustan division of Italy into *regiones*. He wrongly thought that Comum borough and Lake Como lay in different *regiones*; see vii. 11. 5 n. Here Pliny has not the *regiones* in mind, though Picenum was in fact an Augustan *regio* (Pliny, *NH* 3. 110), and he was probably staying in his lakeside villas, mentioned in IX. 7.

2. *To Arrianus Maturus*

Date. The book-date fits. The subject, Aquilius Regulus, was last mentioned as an old man in IV. 2 and 7. The recipient Maturus is now back in Italy (s. 10) from the travels of IV. 12. 7. There is a possible cross-reference in s. 10 to troubles of Pliny known from other letters in VI–VIII.

Address. For the equestrian Arrianus Maturus see I. 2 pref. and III. 2. 2 nn.

> **1. soleo non numquam in iudiciis quaerere M. Regulum.** For the elderly advocate, M. Aquilius Regulus, see I. 5. 1–2 nn. Quaestor about A.D. 66–67, he might be aged about 65 at his death, which was evidently a year or so before this letter, s. 5.

> **2. habebat studiis honorem, . . . scribebat quamvis non posset ediscere.** So too in IV. 7. 3–4 Pliny reluctantly admires his forceful

performance in the courts. He there remarks that Regulus had no memory. He does not mean that he read his speeches, but that he prepared them carefully.

quod oculum . . . circumlinebat, . . . quod candidum splenium in hoc aut in illud supercilium transferebat, quod semper haruspices consulbat . . . a nimia superstitione. These tricks were done for luck, as Merrill observed, not to frighten the judge or judges, who were not likely to be moved by such dodges in this age, though a strong *vultus* was helpful (v. 7. 6). The point of the devices is far from clear. The patch (*splenium*) is stuck presumably on the side of his face towards the tribunal. For Regulus' devotion to *haruspices* see II. 20. 4–5, 13. Martial mentions the use of face-patches in 2. 29. 9–10, 8. 33. 22.

Stout, p. 45, would retain the manuscript reading *animi superstitione* in place of the early emendation *a nimia*. But the preposition is necessary, and repeated, in MV, with *magno honore*. An adjective is wanted to balance *magno*; cf. X. 96. 8, 'superstitionem pravam immodicam'.

a possessore. It seems that the defendant always stands to the left of the judge. Quintilian, in a long description of the movements of the advocate, does not illuminate this, II. 3. 88–144.

3. una dicentibus. Pliny had acted with Regulus, though the phrase may refer to appearing on either side in the same case. I. 20. 14, II. 14. 2.

audituros corrogabat. Pliny discusses the origins of this custom in II. 14. 9–11, which he there deplores, and here approves.

4. sub eo principe sub quo nocere non poterat. But in I. 5. 1 (n.) the relative innocence of Regulus under Domitian can be detected.

5. invaluit consuetudo binas vel singulas clepsydras, interdum etiam dimidias, et dandi et petendi. Pliny is speaking here, as in ss. 7–8, of private suits, where it was left to the two parties to fix the length of speeches (s. 7) by arrangement with the judge or president. Thus in IV. 16. 2 Pliny speaks in a Centumviral case for no less than seven hours. But in criminal cases there were fixed rules (below).

6. nos legibus ipsis iustiores quae tot horas . . . largiuntur. Cf. IV. 9. 9 n. 'cum e lege accusator sex horas accepisset', and I. 20. 11, II. 11. 14 n. This refers primarily to the criminal jurisdiction and the *quaestio* system, for which the procedure was controlled either by the individual *leges publicae* or by the Lex Iulia Iudiciaria.

ambitione ab omnibus obtinebas. This recalls his 'intentio quidquid velis obtinendi', IV. 7. 3.

7. quotiens iudico, quod vel saepius facio quam dico, quantum quis postulat aquae do. Cf. I. 20. 12, 'frequenter iudicavi frequenter in consilio fui'. The single *iudex* of the praetorian court was assigned by the *praetor urbanus* for each particular case, and was not a trained jurisprudent. He depended for legal knowledge on the advice of some specialist whom he invited to join his *consilium*. The procedure of the civil courts was evidently much less strictly controlled by statute than that of the *quaestiones*. See v. 4. 2 n.

8. satius est et haec dici quam non dici necessaria. Pliny believed in fullness, I. 20. 14–15.

9. amore communium. The usage is unusual, and unparalleled in Pliny, but in I. 8. 13 'communibus . . . commodis' means *publicis*. Cf. Seneca, *Tranq. Anim.* 3. 1, 'communia privataque'.

10. leviora incommoda quod adsuevi. This could refer to his wife's illness, Ep. 4, the grouchiness of Fabatus, Ep. 12, his freedmen's illnesses, V. 19, VIII. 1, 16, or money, VIII. 2, or a combination of them as in VIII. 19. 1.

3. *To Verus*

The date, and the identity of Verus cannot be determined.

1. agellum quem nutrici meae donaveram colendum suscepisti. For the formalities of *donatio* see V. 1. 3, X. 4. 2 nn. The farm was evidently meant to provide the nurse with a pension, like the lands given to legionary veterans, or that given by Pliny for his alimentary endowment, VII. 18. 2. The nurse would be at least a freedwoman, since she had the right of ownership.

erat cum donarem centum milium nummum. From the land-prices given by Columella, which vary from S.1,000 per Roman acre for rough land to S.3000 for productive vineyard, the farm may be reckoned at about 40–50 *iugera* (Columella, *RR* 3. 3. 8; Frank, *Ec. Survey*, v. 149 ff.). Since Columella reckons one vine dresser to 7 *iugera* of vineyard, this farm could be managed by a man with his family and a few slaves, if he were a working *colonus* of the type known from III. 19. 6–7, IX. 37. 2–4. But since Pliny honours Verus alone among his tenants with the publication of a letter, he is probably a *conductor* of higher station managing more than this one farm, and more akin to the manager sought in Ep. 30 for the Campanian estate of Fabatus: 'rusticorum . . . praediorum administratio poscit durum aliquem et agrestem', or the retired procurator of VII. 25. 3, 'ut diligentem agricolam intuebar, de his locuturus in quibus illum versari putabam'.

postea decrescente reditu etiam pretium minuit quod nunc te curante reparabit. Bad management, not economic crisis, is the immediate trouble, as on the big Tuscan estate, III. 19. 6–7 nn.

4. To Calpurnia

Date. This note, and its counterpart Ep. 7, are linked to Epp. 28 and 30 by the references to a visit to Campania; VII. 5 belongs to the same series. So the book-date presents no difficulty. If the visit to Comum belongs to 105–6 (Ep. 1) this might come in the early summer of 107.

Address. For his wife Calpurnia see IV. 1. 1 and 19.

1. occupationibus meis . . . quae me non sunt passae . . . proficiscentem te valetudinis causa in Campaniam prosequi. Pliny is busy with court cases in this book, Epp. 5, 11, 12, 13, 18, 23, 33, and also with his duties on the imperial Council, Epp. 22, 31, and even with politics, Epp. 6, 9, 19. But his movements suggest that he is no longer *curator Tiberis*.

The illness cannot be the pregnancy of VIII. 10–11, of which Calpurnia was unaware. This is the first time that Calpurnia has left Pliny's house without him, cf. VII. 5. 1: 'non consuevimus abesse'. To this separation we owe Pliny's three letters to her.

Guillemin (*VL* 138 f.), noting Pliny's theme of the 'excluded lover' in Ep. 7, and other touches which reflect the language in which Ovid addresses his wife in the *Tristia* (e.g. III. 3. 15–18, IV. 3. 23–24), remarks that Pliny established the theme of conjugal love in Latin literature, by combining the Ovidian strain with reminiscences of Cicero's affectionate inquiries about the health of Terentia (e.g. *ad Fam.* 14. 2. 2–3). But she exaggerates the formality of the letters to Calpurnia, and their debt to Cicero. Pliny unlike Cicero has nothing to say about his business and public affairs to his wife; cf. *ad Fam.* 14. 4. 4–5, 5. 1–2. The letters to Calpurnia are very unlike those to Terentia.

5. To Cornelius Ursus

Date. About a fortnight later than v. 20, which it continues (s. 1 n.), and hence late 106 or early 107.

Address. For the unknown Ursus see IV. 9 pref.

1. scripseram tenuisse Varenum ut sibi evocare testes liceret. See v. 20. 1–2 nn.

quibusdam iniquum et quidem pertinaciter visum, maxime Licinio Nepoti. The active praetor of 105 (IV. 29, v. 4, 9, 13 nn. and prefs.) is now out of office, but still full of zeal. His intervention indicates a date later than 105 for the trial of Varenus (v. 20 pref.), since senators below the rank of praetor unless in office (v. 13. 6) do not give *sententiae* in the debates recorded by Pliny (cf. II. II. 19, 22; 12. 2; IV. 9. 16, 20; IX. 13. 13 nn.), and Nepos' activity begins with his entry to the praetorship in IV. 29.

sequenti senatu, cum de rebus aliis referretur, de proximo senatus consulto disseruit. The next normal meeting of the Senate would be about a fortnight later, II. II. 24 n., III. 9. 18. Hence V. 20 and VI. 5 are very close in time, and Books V and VI should be continuous.

Nepos follows the procedure of 'egredi relationem', to which Pliny refers in Ep. 19. 3: 'sententiae loco postulavit ut consules . . . peterent' etc., and IX. 13. 8: 'sententiae loco dices si quid volueris'. A senator could thus raise any issue under cover of his *sententia*, however irrelevant to the question before the House. It is a means by which a senator not in office can try to initiate a proposal. Tacitus, *Ann.* 2. 37–38, records an earlier instance in the Principate. But a new procedure was arising whereby a senator could make a *postulatio* to the consuls before they began the business of the day, II. II. 9, IX. 13. 7 nn. See *RE* (S) vi. 769 f.; Mommsen, *DPR* vii. 133.

finitam . . . causam. Cf. Ep. 13. 4. 're . . . peracta quod pluribus placuisset . . . tuendum'.

2. addidit etiam petendum a consulibus ut referrent sub exemplo legis ambitus de lege repetundarum. Nepos' proposal is to regularize the position by a general enactment. But why the reference to the *lex ambitus*? From Pliny's usage of *sub exemplo* the point of the comparison should lie in the substance of the proposal (e.g. I. 18. 5, II. 6. 6). Nepos, the expert in criminal law (IV. 29 etc.), has found an analogy in the texts of the *lex ambitus* that will meet the case. But Quintilian states that the *reus* never enjoyed this privilege (V. 20. 7 n.) in criminal cases. The sentence might mean that the consuls were to make a proposal about changing the extortion law just as they had already done about bribery, referring to the proposals made in Ep. 19. 3, which effected just such a change, but with the concurrence of the Princeps. Nepos' object as always is to get the Senate to do things themselves. This interpretation would imply that there was a slight chronological disorder in the arrangement of the letters within VI, though not within a series of interrelated letters.

a consulibus. Possibly the *ordinarii* of 107, Sura and Senecio, V. 20. 6 n., Ep. 13. 2, 5.

4. Iuventius . . . Celsus. He may be the younger of the two like-named lawyers, P. Iuventius Celsus (T. Aufidius Hoenius Severianus), later adviser to Hadrian and *cos.* II in 129, SHA, *Hadr.* 18. 1. His career is not known in full, but he was praetorian legate of Thrace before 114, and may have been consul in one of the vacant places of the list for 114 or 115, perhaps at the end of 115, where the tail fragment of *F. Pot.*, 'I IVV', apparently precedes the list for 116 (p. 736). He can hardly be the adulator of Domitian in Dio's anecdote (67. 13. 3–4); that may be his father. He became head of the Proculian school of law, rivals of the Cassian (VII. 24. 8 n.), with or after Neratius Priscus. See Garzetti, *C.* 84. W. Kunkel, *Herkunft . . . der R. Juristen*, 146; Schulz, *Roman Legal Science*, 105, 229. *PIR*¹ I. 590.

respondit Nepos rursusque Celsus. Celsus as magistrate had the right to speak independently of the *ordo sententiarum*, but not to give a formal *sententia*, cf. Tac. *Ann.* 3. 17. The consequent *altercatio* is unusual, since Nepos should only speak *sententiae loco*. So too in the debate about Publicius Certus the order was interrupted by the senior consular Fabricius Veiento, who had already spoken once, IX. 13. 19. Tacitus records a similar *altercatio*, led by a praetor, in *Hist.* 4. 6. The irregularity could only take place with the approval of the presiding magistrate, or the help of the tribunes (IX. 13. 19–20). See Mommsen, *DPR* vii. 125 ff., 130 n. 2, 175.

5. cupiditate audiendi cursitabant. For movement about the floor of the House during sessions see IX. 13. 10, Tac. *Ann.* 11. 6.

ambobus interdum propitium Caesarem, . . . precabantur. Cf. IV. 25. 2 'senatus . . . ei . . . iratum principem est comprecatus'. It is assumed that the issue will be referred to the Princeps, as in Ep. 19. 3 and V. 13. 7. Both claim his support. Trajan is not present, being possibly in Dacia at this time. Cf. Ep. 13. 2 n.

6. Celsus Nepoti ex libello respondit. For prepared speeches see V. 13. 6. Celsus must have been taking notes during Nepos's first oration.

6. *To Minicius Fundanus*

Date. The book-date is trebly supported by the reference to Pliny's verses, by a connexion with v. 21, if Julius Naso is the brother of Julius Avitus, s. 6 nn., and by the reference to the elections also mentioned in Ep. 19. These might be the elections of January 107, and the letter belong to the previous autumn when everyone was out of Rome (s. 8, cf. Ep. 9. 1).

Address. Minicius Fundanus, for whom see I. 9, IV. 15 prefs., would be consul designate if the letter belonged to early 107, but it is not known how long beforehand the electoral campaign began. The absence of both Fundanus and Tacitus (Ep. 9. 1) from Rome points to the preceding autumn when senators enjoyed a recess in September–October (Suet. *Aug.* 35. 3; Tac. *Ann.* 2. 35. 1). Both Pliny's substantial electoral letters are addressed to men about the time of their consulships, cf. II. 9 pref.

1. petit honores Iulius Naso, petit cum multis. For the electoral proceedings see II. 9, on the candidature of Erucius Clarus. The phrase suggests that this is Naso's first step on the ladder, and presumably the quaestorship, which admitted to the Senate, is meant rather than the vigintivirate or minor magistracy which preceded the quaestorship. The quaestorship would not be competitive, if there were only as competitors the twenty ex-vigintiviri. But usually the Princeps would put forward by *commendatio* his favoured candidates, who do not always seem to have been required to hold the vigintivirate, if they were given, like Erucius Clarus, *latum clavum cum quaestura*, II. 9. 2 n. Hence the twenty *vigintivirales* would outnumber the vacant places, on these occasions. The only other references to individual vigintiviral elections are Tac. *Ann.* 3. 29. 1, SHA *Did. Jul.* 1. Mommsen, *DPR*, ii. 200 f., iv. 226, 299.

Julius Naso, probably the father of Julius Avitus (s. 6 n.), is only known from Pliny, IV. 6 pref. Syme, *Tac.* 801, takes him for a Gaul, but there is no evidence; IV. 6 shows that he is not from Cisalpine.

quos ut gloriosum sic est difficile superare. This letter, with II. 9, indicates the reality of senatorial elections at this period, despite the reservation of places for the imperial candidates 'sine repulsa et ambitu designandos', Tac. *Ann.* 1. 15; *ILS* 244. 10–15 (*Lex de imperio Vespasiani*).

2. rursus mihi videor omnium quae decucurri candidatus. Cf. II. 9. 1 n., 'quam pro me sollicitudinem non adii'. Pliny was *candidatus Caesaris* for some if not all of his offices.

3. solebat tamen vixdum adulescentulo mihi pater eius . . . monstrari. Pliny, as a quaestor of *c.* A.D. 90–91, would be less than twenty years older than his protégé. The father evidently died before Pliny completed his studies, i.e. before he was 18 (v. 8. 8).

quos tunc ego frequentabam, Quintilianum, Niceten Sacerdotem. Pliny names his professors of Latin and Greek rhetoric respectively. For the great Quintilian see II. 14. 9. Nicetes was not greatly approved by Tacitus, or even by Greek opinion, including that of Pliny's pet Isaeus (Tac. *Dial.* 15. 3; Philostratus, *VS* I. 19–21). It is suggested in *PIR*¹ N 61, that Pliny is naming three, not two, professors, because Philostratus does not give the second name of Nicetes. This is improbable but not impossible. In the *Dialogus* only *Sacerdos* is in the manuscript, and *Nicetes* is due to emendation. The man may have had a long Roman name, such as Ti. Claudius Sacerdos Nicetes. Pliny's custom with Greeks is to use a single name, or if they are Roman citizens, to use the Roman gentile name with Greek cognomen, e.g. 'Claudius Aristion', Ep. 31. 3; IV. 9. 3; V. 20. 4; VII. 6. 6.

vir alioqui clarus et gravis. Pliny cannot find much to say about

him. He was a senator, s. 4, but not of consular rank, not *clarissimus*,
cf. Ep. 11. 3, 23. 2. He does not seem even to have been a good
orator.

5. amicos, quos paraverat coluit. This is the technique of the social-
political *amicitia*, which easily degenerated into *captatio*, but Pliny
is more than a political friend, cf. Ep. 9. 1.

6. primis etiam et cum maxime nascentibus opusculis meis interest.
By *opusculis* he means his poems, IV. 13. 1 n. The extent of time
suggested by *primis* and *ante* indicates a fair period since Pliny first
renewed his Muse, as revealed in IV. 13.

primis. The manuscripts divide curiously over this. The αγ manuscripts agree on *primis*, but β has *primus*, which gives a meaning
that is hardly true.

nuper amissi. The circumstances are very close to those of the
death of Julius Avitus in V. 21, who also died fatherless, at an early
age, leaving one brother, and as a *quaestorius* would be senior to
Naso, and hence an *adiumentum*. For the use of *nuper* of fairly short
intervals see VIII. 20. 3 n.

8. ea est auctoritas tua. See IV. 15. 3 for his reputation, which would
be greater if he were now consul designate.

7. *To Calpurnia*

For date and circumstances see Ep. 4.

1. libellos meos teneas. She is said to read his speeches in IV. 19. 2.

2. torqueat. A word of the 'amatory' style, Ep. 4. 1 n.

8. *To Priscus*

Date not determinable.

Address. Priscus is hard to identify. He may be the person introduced
to Pompeius Saturninus in VII. 7. 1, 8, 15. 3, or the recipient of
VII. 19, or the consular Cornelius Priscus of III. 21, or the imperial
legate of II. 13, or a combination of them. But his relationship to
Maximus in s. 4, his friendship with Atilius, and that of Atilius with
the scholarly Maximus of II. 14, suggest a possible identification of
Maximus and Priscus with Novius Maximus, recipient of IV. 20, V. 5,
another scholarly figure, and his kinsman the elderly consular
Novius Priscus. Cf. IV. 20 pref.

1. **Atilium Crescentem et nosti et amas.** A man known for his wit, he appears as the friend of Minicius Fundanus and 'Maximus', I. 9. 8, II. 14. 2. Nothing connects him with Martial's Atilius, IX. 85. From the reference to *oppida nostra* s. 2 he is a Cisalpine from Milan, or less likely the more distant Bergomum.

2. **oppida nostra unius diei itinere dirimuntur.** In II. 17. 2 seventeen miles is a short half-day on an easy carriage road, and from Ep. 10. 1 (n.) Pliny does the seventy-odd miles from Rome to Centum Cellae in two stages, stopping at Alsium.

   modestia, quies, securitas eius. For the political significance of *quies* see I. 14. 5. Atilius is a man of equestrian standing who might have entered public life; cf. VII. 31. 1, 'vir alioqui rectus integer quietus ac paene ultra modum . . . verecundus', of an equestrian.

3. **cum insolentiam cuiusdam tribunatum plebis inituri vereretur idque indicasset mihi.** This incident might be set at the time of Pliny's own tribunate, but Pliny does not imply this. The tribunes exercised a jurisdiction in Italy of which little is known, I. 23. 1 nn. Paladini (*Athenaeum*, xxxvii. 28) suggested rather oddly that the incident referred to elections.

4. **debuit ei pecuniam Valerius Varus. huius est heres Maximus noster, quem et ipse amo, sed coniunctius tu.** The personal connexion between Priscus, Maximus, and Atilius suggests that this is the 'elder Maximus' of II. 14 and certain others where no *nomen* is recorded, and also that this is Novius Maximus (pref.). Otherwise the present Maximus might be identified, less probably, with the 'younger Maximus' of Ep. 34, who had a Cisalpine wife and was equally hard to part from his cash. A third possibility, that he is the senator Sex. Quinctilius Valerius Maximus of Alexandria Troas—who may be the Maximus of VIII. 24 (pref.), sent to Achaea—inheriting the name Valerius from Varus along with the estate, is less likely, since the present Maximus is connected with Cisalpine through Atilius if not through Ep. 34.

5. **ut Atilio meo salva sit non sors modo verum etiam usura plurium annorum.** Maximus will pay up the capital but not the interest, and Atilius is not anxious to sue, even with Pliny as advocate. Perhaps the claim was more moral than legal. Hence the fear of s. 8, 'cum contumelia damnum'. There was no legal claim to repayment of interest unless this had been specifically stipulated at the time the loan was made. Roby, *Roman Private Law*, ii. 70–73; Buckland, *Text-book of Roman Law*,[1] clxxxviii. 545.

5–6. nullus . . . nisi ex frugalitate reditus. nam studia . . . ad voluptatem tantum et gloriam exercet. Atilius, like Pliny, does not take fees (v. 13. 8), or limits his exercises to *suasoriae*. Pliny does not expect his social equals to make money by teaching rhetoric, IV. 11. 1, 13. 10.

9. *To Cornelius Tacitus*

Date and circumstances as for Ep. 6. For Pliny's correspondence with the advocate-historian Tacitus see Ep. 16 pref. Books VI and VII contain five letters to him.

1. si te Romae morante ipse afuissem. This may be the autumnal recess, Ep. 6 pref.

10. *To Albinus*

Date. The summer of 107 is indicated by the reference to Verginius Rufus' death ten years before, and the connexion with Ep. 31, ss. 1, 3 nn.

Address. The man is probably the Spanish advocate Lucceius Albinus, III. 9. 7 n.

1. cum venissem in socrus meae villam Alsiensem, quae aliquamdiu Rufi Vergini fuit. Pliny would stay a night here on his way to or from the imperial conference of Ep. 31. Alsium was just half way between Rome and Centum Cellae, and an easy day's journey of thirty to thirty-five miles from either. So too he uses his mother-in-law's houses in 1. 4. This is his only known visit to the Tuscan coast, which was a favourite zone for residential villas despite its bad reputation for health in v. 6. 2. Cf. Ep. 31. 15 n. and *RE* i. 1639.

socrus. For Pompeia Celerina, mother of his first or second wife, see 1. 4 pref., III. 19. 8 n. The identification is certain because the mother of his third wife Calpurnia is not alive at this time, loc. cit. and IV. 19. 6 n. Her estates are all in the Etruscan region. She had bought this from the heirs of Rufus after his death; nothing in the letter suggests that it was a recent purchase, or that it can be identified with the later imperial villa in this locality, as Sirago imagines on inadequate grounds (*It. Agr.* 38, 301).

For the career and death of Verginius Rufus see II. 1 nn.

hunc enim colere secessum . . . consueverat. Cf. II. 1. 8: 'ad omnes honores meos ex secessibus accucurrit'. Senators from Cisalpine, like Pliny, needed a country house near Rome. Cf. II. 17. 2. Hence the frequent changes of owner of these suburban estates.

3. inertia eius cui cura mandata est. The heir, not the contractor, seems to be meant, as in s. 4, 'ille mandaverat caveratque'. The neglect was probably due to the fact that the heir sold the estate, though the sale did not cancel his obligation.

post decimum mortis annum. Since Verginius died in A.D. 97 (II. I. 6 n.) the tenth year must be 106–7, and the year of narration (*post*) is firmly fixed to 107. This fits Ep. 31, which is dated after the return of Trajan from the second Dacian War.

cinerem sine titulo sine nomine iacere. Dio 68. 2 4 states that this epitaph was inscribed on the tomb. Either this was finished in due course, or the sources have inaccurately summarized Pliny's statement. The phrase became famous, and recurs in Justinus-Trogus 6. 8. 5.

4. divinum illud et immortale factum. For the story of his refusal of the imperial position after he defeated the rebellion of Vindex against Nero see II. I. 2 nn.

C. Julius Vindex, a native of Aquitania, is usually taken to have been *legatus propraetore* of the imperial province of Gallia Lugdunensis. But since his activities covered Vienna, and Lugdunum was hostile to him, he might have been proconsul of Narbonensis. Tac. *Hist.* I. 65; Dio. 63. 22. I², 24. Suet. *Galba* 9. 2 excludes the legateship of Aquitania. Plutarch calls him στρατηγός in Gaul (*Galba* 4) which may mean *legatus*, cf. *Otho* 5.

'**imperium adseruit non sibi sed patriae.**' Cf. Suet. loc. cit., 'Vindicis litterae hortantis (sc. Galbam) ut humano generi assertorem ducemque se accommodaret'. The offer was made to Verginius before the death of Nero (Suet. *Nero*. 47. I with Dio 63. 25. 2–3). Dio says that Rufus would not let the soldiers offer the power to anyone because it belonged to the Senate and People, and persuaded them to submit the question to the Senate. Coins of the claimants of the period make much use of such terms as *adsertor libertatis, libertas restituta* (Mattingly and Sydenham, *Rom. Imp. Coinage*, i. 182 f.). Verginius, in the anecdote told by Pliny in IX. 19. 5, claims: 'ideo me fecisse quod feci, ut esset liberum vobis scribere quae libuisset'. This freedom meant only the liberty enjoyed by senators under a well-conducted Principate. In Dio's version though Rufus was in effect loyal to Nero his intentions were disloyal, but prevented by the precipitate action of his army. His reluctance to accept the offer may only have been due to his consciousness of his weak personal claims, as Tacitus hints: 'merito dubitasse Verginium equestri familia ignoto patre', Tac. *Hist.* I. 52. Vespasian had similar doubts, ibid. 2. 76. For the theme of *libertas* see Wirzsubski, *Libertas as a Political Idea* etc. 160 f.

11. *To Maximus*

Date. This letter introduces a distinguished pair of young men, not yet senators, who appear in a group of nine letters of VI, VII, and IX. The details of their careers given by Pliny fit the book-dates, cf. Ep. 26. 1, VII. 24. 2 nn. The group is linked to the book-date of VI by a reference to Pliny's defence of Varenus Rufus, Ep. 29. 11.

Address. The identity of Maximus should be sought among the elder Maximi, since the theme of the letter is the praise of the young; cf. V. 17, addressed to Spurinna. The man must be one who 'favours Pliny's praise', like the Maximus of IX. 23. 6, and a *studiosus*. Hence Novius Maximus, IV. 20, V. 5 pref., is probable, if Vibius Maximus can be regarded as unmentionable after his political disgrace (III. 2 pref.). See II. 14 pref.

1. **adhibitus in consilium a praefecto urbis.** For the magisterial *consilium*, and Pliny's appearance on them, see I. 20. 12, IV. 22. 1 nn.

The development of the jurisdiction of the City prefect is an obscure topic. Tac. *Ann.* 6. 11 sketches the original function of the prefect as a police magistrate, apparently acting as the representative of the Princeps, to deal with the lowest classes of offenders: 'qui coerceret servitia et quod civium audacia turbidum nisi vim metuat'. Under Nero his jurisdiction attracted the attention of professional prosecutors, and collided with the authority of the praetorian *quaestiones*, Tac. *Ann.* 14. 41. Among the disturbances of A.D. 69 a senator involved in a treason charge was accused in exceptional circumstances before the City prefect, Tac. *Hist.* 2. 63. Statius, *S.* i. 4. 10–13, shows that in the Flavian period the prefect's authority extended outside Rome to cases originating in the municipalities of Italy. Pliny here indicates that the court was now attracting advocates of the aristocratic tradition instead of professional hacks. In the earlier phase one would hardly expect advocates even to appear in this court of summary jurisdiction. The limitation of its power to a hundred miles from Rome is of a later age. This would seem to be the only reference to the *consilium* of the City prefect. See Mommsen, *DPR* v. 361 ff.; G. Vitucci, *Ricerche sulla Praefectura Urbi* (Rome, 1956), ch. ii, who misses this passage.

Fuscum Salinatorem et Ummidium Quadratum. For their families and subsequent careers see VII. 24. 2 n. and Ep. 26. 1 n. Both moved in the highest circles and were later associated with Hadrian, and supported by other of Pliny's friends, notably Ursus Servianus and Catilius Severus. At this time neither seems to be older than 25. They have only just reached the age of marriage, and neither is a

senator, though both were to reach the consulship by 118 in minimal
time, like the distinguished young Avidius Nigrinus (v. 13. 6 n.).

**2. os Latinum, vox virilis, tenax memoria, magnum ingenium,
iudicium aequale.** Contrast the catalogue of an orator's faults in IV. 7.
4: 'imbecillum latus, os confusum, haesitans lingua, tardissima
inventio, memoria nulla . . . ingenium insanum'.

   me ut rectorem . . . intuebantur. He guides their studies and lives
alike, VI. 29, VII. 9, IX. 36, 40.

   constantia salva. The phrase is odd but cf. IX. 1. 3, 'salva sit tibi
constantiae fama'; X. 31. 1, 'salva magnitudine tua'.

**3. quid enim . . . publice laetius quam clarissimos iuvenes nomen et
famam ex studiis petere?** He implies that this is rather rare, as in
V. 17. 1, 'si nobiles iuvenes dignum aliquid maioribus suis faciant'.
After the early Principate the great orators tend to be 'new men', as
Tacitus remarks at length in connexion with Eprius Marcellus and
Vibius Crispus in *Dialogus* 8. 3: 'quo sordidius et abiectius nati sunt
. . . sine commendatione natalium sine substantia facultatum . . .
per multos iam annos potentissimi sunt civitatis ac donec libuit
principes fori' etc. So too Domitius Afer was a new man from Gaul
(II. 14. 10 n.), M. Regulus the son of a ruined man, and Tacitus and
Pliny themselves were 'new'. This situation may be contrasted with
the situation under Claudius when the new men still had to contend
with the noble scions of wealthy houses, Tac. *Ann.* 11. 6–7. This withdrawal of the nobility from the Forum had in part political causes,
in the *pericula* of public life which specially attended on the well-
born, but it weakened public life itself by the absence of men of
good example.

12. *To Fabatus*

Date is not closely determinable.

Address. For his grandfather-in-law Calpurnius Fabatus see IV. 1 pref.

2. Bittio Prisco. He might be a relative of the consular Bittius
Proculus, a connexion of Pliny by marriage, IX. 13. 13, since the
name is very rare in prosopography, *PIR*² s.v. The manuscripts
agree in reading Bettius, the early printed editions introduced
Vectius or Vettius, and Aldus made it Bittius, which is the epigraphical form.

3. ut ais 'aperto pectore' scripsisti. He writes in this strain again to
Pliny on a business matter, VII. 11. 1. In Ep. 30 and VII. 16 Pliny is

seeking to oblige the hasty old man again. In VIII. 10–11 he is expected to be very cross about Calpurnia's miscarriage.

tuo filio. The date of his death cannot be fixed, cf. V. 11. 1 n.

13. *To Cornelius Ursus*

This continues Ep. 5 not less than a fortnight later, ss. 2, 5 nn.

2. Bithyni senatusconsultum apud consules carpere ac labefactare sunt ausi atque etiam absenti principi criminari. Encouraged by the criticism of Nepos (Ep. 5) about this *SC.*, they went to the consuls after that session. Their application to Trajan seems to have been of their own initiative, as in VII. 6. 1. Trajan is either absent from Italy on his Dacian war, or simply out of Rome, as in a similar context, V. 13. 8: 'pauci dies, et liber principis'. The absence of Trajan from the Senate is taken for granted; cf. IV. 12. 3; V. 13. 7–8; VI. 5. 5, 19. 3–4; VII. 6. 6, 14. Pliny only once indicates his presence, II. 11. 10, in the special circumstance of his first consulship at Rome as Princeps, of which so much is said in the Panegyric. The consuls might be the *ordinarii* of 107, Licinius Sura and Sosius Senecio, men well acquainted with the mind of Trajan. V. 20. 6 n.

ab illo ad senatum remissi non destiterunt. As in IV. 12 Trajan is careful not to interfere in the few affairs which the Senate is prepared to manage itself. In Ep. 31. 6 he apologizes for similar interference with the affairs of the criminal courts.

egit Claudius Capito irreverenter. This should be one of the provincial deputies, as in V. 20. 4. This meeting of the Senate may be the next scheduled occasion after the debate of VI. 5 (ibid. 1 n.).

respondit Fronto Catius. For this consular and advocate see II. 11. 3 n. He speaks as advocate, not 'loco sententiae'.

4. re . . . peracta quod pluribus placuisset cunctis tuendum. Nepos in Ep. 5. 3 was unpopular for seeming to disregard this principle.

5. Acilius tantum Rufus et cum eo septem . . . in priore sententia perseverarunt. Since Rufus gives a *sententia* he is still consul designate, as in V. 20. 6.

14. *To Mauricus*

The visit to Formiae is probably to take place during Pliny's journey to join his wife in Campania mentioned in Epp. 28, 30. The recipient is the now elderly Junius Mauricus, last mentioned in IV. 22. 3. For him see I. 5. 10 n.

15. *To Voconius Romanus*

Date, not determinable, but earlier than IX. 22, recording later poems
of Paulus. For the Spanish senator Voconius Romanus see I. 5 pref.,
II. 13 nn.

**1. Passenus Paulus, splendidus eques Romanus . . . scribit elegos.
. . . est enim municeps Properti.** A brief dedicatory inscription from
Asisium gives his names as C. Passenus Paullus Propertius Blaesus,
ILS 2925. The fantastic theory of M. L. Hermann and others (cf.
RE 18. 4. 2094), that he was the author of Propertius' fourth book
or part of it, need not be discussed here. *PIR*¹ P 105.

**3. est omino Priscus dubiae sanitatis, interest tamen officiis, adhibetur
consiliis.** Pliny means that the man was rather odd, cf. s. 4 *deliratio*,
and IX. 26. 1, 'oratore . . . recto quidem et sano sed parum grandi'.
This man, like Titius Aristo (I. 22 nn.) and Neratius Priscus (II. 13
pref.), was among the most distinguished lawyers of the Flavio-
Trajanic period, succeeding Caelius Sabinus as head of the Sabinian
school (*Dig.* I. 2. 2. 53; see VII. 24. 8 n.). His public career included a
legateship in Britain and Numidia, and after a consulship in 86 the
government of Upper Germany under Domitian, and that of Syria
c. 95–*c.* 100 (II. 13 pref.). Later he served on the *consilium* of Trajan
and must have survived until *c.* 120, since he taught Julian, born
c. 100–3. His names in full were C. Octavius Tidius Tossianus L.
Iavolenus Priscus. He may come from central Italy rather than from
the Dalmatian colony of Nedinum where one of his inscriptions was
found. See *RE* xvii. 1830 f. (n. 59); Schulz, *Roman Legal Science*,
104, 337; Kunkel, *Herkunft . . . der römischen Juristen*, 138 f.; *ILS*
1015, 9089; *CIL* xvi. n. 36. *PIR*¹ O 40; A. M. Honoré, *Gaius* (Oxford,
1962), 49.

ius civile publice respondet. The interpretation of private law had
in the Republic been left to unofficial experts, who gave their
opinions, *responsa*, on request, the value of their opinions depending
on their reputations. Augustus only altered this system in that the
most eminent lawyers were licensed to give their opinions *ex auctoritate principis*. The precise effect of this change is in dispute; it
would seem not to have prevented other persons from practising as
advisers also. Pliny's phrase shows that the system is still in being.
Later Hadrian's inclusion of leading jurisconsults as permanent
members of his *consilium*, together with the codification of the
Praetorian Edict, tended to transfer the law-making functions of the
great jurisconsults to the *consilium*. Naturally there was always
room for lesser lawyers to expound within the framework of the

system. See Schulz, *Roman Legal Science* 49 ff., 112 ff.; Crook, *Consilium Principis*, 57 f., 58 n. 2 (for recent bibliography); Kunkel, op. cit. 281 ff. Oddly Kunkel in his index does not include Iavolenus among the official jurisprudents.

4. aliena deliratio. Pliny does not show the fear of giving offence that often restrains him elsewhere from criticizing the living by name, VIII. 22. 4, IX. 11. 1, 29 nn., and Introduction, pp. 54 f.

16. *To Cornelius Tacitus*

Date. This letter, like VII. 33, was written, in its original form, to provide Tacitus with material for his *Historiae*, to which VII. 20 and VIII. 7 refer less certainly. None of the four letters contains a certain indication of date; hence the chronology of the Histories, for which these are the main evidence, depends upon the value of the book-date. Thus Schwabe in *RE* iv. 1575 dates the compilation and publication of the Histories on Pliny's evidence to 104 onwards. So too Syme, who finds the first hint, perhaps wrongly, in v. 8. 12 (n.): *Tac.* 117. That the letters to Tacitus in VI–IX form an interconnected series that cannot be separated from the chronological framework of the later books is argued in I. 6 and VII. 20 prefs.

Address. For Tacitus see I. 6 pref.

1. avunculi mei exitum. For the elder Pliny see III. 5 nn. He accepted the prefecture of the fleet at Misenum in the latter years of Vespasian.

4. erat Miseni classemque imperio praesens regebat. Misenum had been the main base of the west Italian fleet, *classis Misenensis*, since Augustus, but the fleet had been commanded by freedmen, instead of equestrians, from the time of Claudius until A.D. 69. Tac. *Hist.* I. 87, 2. 100; J. C. Starr, *Roman Imperial Navy* (New York, 1941), 32. This passage, with III. 5. 9—'ante lucem ibat ad ... imperatorem ... inde ad delegatum sibi officium'—suggests that the headquarters of the fleet administration were at Rome. Starr, op. cit. 30, 35, seems not to have noticed this connexion. The duties of the prefect were mainly bureaucratic, since the fleet served mainly as an imperial transport service.

imperio. Pliny uses the term loosely here. The prefect had not the powers of an imperial legate. He needed only enough authority to maintain discipline in a peaceful establishment. Any major offence could be referred to other officials at Rome, such as the *praefectus urbi*, holding the power of capital punishment. In *Sententiae Pauli*

5. 26. 2 **the fleet prefect** is grouped with military tribunes and prefects of *auxilia* in this respect. Cf. Starr, op. cit. 31, 35.

nonum Kal. Septembres hora fere septima. The day 24 August, depends upon Pliny. The year, A.D. 79, is known from Dio (Xiphilinus) 66. 21, who places it in the first year of Titus, and from Eusebius and other chronographers. The hour, counted from sunrise, would be between 2 and 3 p.m. Cf. III. 5. 8 n., 'Routine'.

mater mea. See Ep. 20. 4 n. for Pliny's family circumstances at this moment. Plinia is dead by the date of IV. 19. 7 n.

apparere nubem inusitata et magnitudine et specie. In the account of Xiphilinus (Dio 66. 21–24), which gives a fair description of the first phase of what seismologists call a Vesuvianic type of eruption, the catastrophe begins with preliminary rumblings and a tremendous explosion, the volcano hurling out great rocks followed by torrents of flame and smoke. Pliny's observation evidently begins at this moment, when subterranean steam has cleared the vent of the material choking it. None of Pliny's household appears to have noticed the noise of which Xiphilinus makes so much.

A summary of subsequent eruptions in antiquity may be found conveniently in Smith's *Dictionary of Greek and Roman Geography*, s.v. The next recorded eruption was in A.D. 203, Dio 76 (77). 2, and the worst after 79 was in 472, Marcellinus, *Chron.* (*ad annum*). For a list of eruptions in modern times see *Admiralty Geographical Handbook of Italy* (Oxford, 1944), i. 474 f. Dio, 66. 21. 2–4, describes the volcano in his own day in terms that applied equally well to it before the great eruption of 1943–4. For a modern account see *Handbook*, 471 ff. E. T. Merrill gave a bibliography in *Am. J. Arch.*, 1918, 304 ff.; 1920, 262. Cf. also G. B. Alfano–J. Friedlaende, *Die Geschichte des V.* (Berlin, 1929), 11 ff. Earlier, J. L. Cobley, *Mount Vesuvius* (London, 1889).

5. **usus ille sole ... gustaverat iacens studebatque.** Pliny's routine is as in III. 5. 10–11 n., 'Routine', filling the day between the end of his public duties and the hour of dinner.

Vesuvium fuisse postea cognitum est. Strabo (v, p. 247), speaking as an eye-witness, shows that in his own day the top was relatively level, and that the prehistoric crater was worn down and filled in. Cultivation reached far up the mountain side, but he noted evidence of volcanic activity. So too the source of Diodorus 4. 21. 5. The ironical silence of Pliny, *NH* 3. 62—'Herculaneum, Pompei haud procul spectato monte Vesuvio'—confirms Strabo's implication that the thing was believed harmless. The mountain had had a strategic role in early wars (Livy 8. 8. 19), and had been the base of the bands of Spartacus (Appian, *BC* 1. 116; Vell. Pat. 2. 30. 5).

formam non alia magis arbor quam pinus expresserit etc. The flat-headed Mediterranean or stone-pine is meant. Others have made similar observations, and modern physics has made this pattern of explosion cloud only too familiar.

6. recente spiritu evecta dein senescente eo destituta. Here, as in the account of the spring at Comum, IV. 30. 5–10, Pliny shows himself a worthy pupil of his uncle. His speculation is as careful as his observation, despite his refusal to seek field experience. His account contains none of the nonsense about giant spectres imported into the story by Dio (loc. cit. 22. 2).

7. liburnicam. For the vessels of the Roman fleet see Starr, op. cit. 51 ff.

8. accipit codicillos Rectinae Tasci imminenti periculo exterritae. The names are not in doubt, though the manuscripts variously divide the constituent letters, and the γ group read Casci rather than Tasci. Pliny uses the ordinary formula for the name of a wife, as in II. 20. 2, 'Verania Pisonis'. The unusual name Rectina recurs in the family of Voconius Romanus, II. 13. 4 n., another family friend. The husband's name is Tascius; cf. for example, IX. 13. 13, 16 where the weight of manuscripts support *Publici* and *Helvidi*, and IX. 2. 2 for *Tulli*. The ingenious emendation '*Caesi*'—i.e. Caesius Bassus, poet and editor of Persius known to have perished in the disaster—is unnecessary. More likely Pomponianus, s. 11, is the same man.

9. quadriremes. The main fleet, cf. Starr loc. cit.

11. iam navibus cinis incidebat . . . iam pumices etiam. The dust and stones predominate in this account, ss. 14, 16, Ep. 20. 16. The main products of the Vesuvian type of eruption are 'steam, dust and stones, sometimes accompanied by lava'. *Handbook*, loc. cit. 471. Campania was spared in 79 the streams of lava that devastated the region in 1943–4. L-H, ad loc., quotes Sogliano, *Rendiconti Acc. Napoli*, xv (1901), 91 ff.

iam vadum subitum ruinaque montis litora obstantia. The rising of the sea-bed is more accurately attributed in Ep. 20. 9 to terrestrial movement. This is the reason for Pliny's change of course, which R. M. Haywood failed to understand (*Cl. Weekly*, 46. 1).

'Pomponianum pete'. Probably a son of the Elder's friend and protector Pomponius Secundus (III. 5. 3 'Books'), who had changed his name by an act of adoption and become Tascius Pomponianus.

12. Stabiis erat, diremptus sinu medio. The width of the inner bay of Stabiae separated Pliny, who was somewhere in the neighbourhood of Herculaneum, from Stabiae. The Sarno delta has advanced the ancient shore-line some two miles westwards from Pompeii. Cf. Sogliano-Jacono, *Mem. Lincei*, 1925, 244. (L-H ad loc.)

si contrarius ventus resedisset. Cooler air pouring into the hot centre from seaward makes a great sea rise, s. 17, too strong for the crews of the vessels of Pomponianus or the quadriremes. Hence many failed to escape by sea. This wind kept the worst of the dust and stones away from Misenum. Cf. Ep. 20. 13.

deferri in balneum iubet. He coolly completes the routine interrupted in s. 5.

14. diaeta. A special apartment, see II. 17. 20 n.

exitus negaretur. These circumstances account for the bodies found in the excavations, of those that failed to escape. *Not. Scavi*, 1914, 205 ff., 257 f.

17. iam dies alibi, illic nox omnibus noctibus nigrior. This is the second day, 25 August, following the night described in ss. 13–16.

19. crassiore caligine spiritu obstructo clausoque stomacho, qui illi natura invalidus . . . erat. He was perhaps asthmatical, whence the heavy snores of s. 13, and died the more quickly, like the victims of London 'smog'. There is nothing mysterious about the cause of death, even if Pliny's diagnosis is not medically sound in detail, as Haywood held, art. cit. The lungs, not the wind-pipe, were troubled.

20. ubi dies redditus (is ab eo quem novissime viderat tertius). The morning of 26 August.

corpus inventum integrum inlaesum opertumque. A careful investigation was made to see that he had not been murdered by his frightened slaves when Pomponianus and the others ran away, s. 18; Ep. 25. 4. This suspicion is voiced by the Suetonius *Life* (for which see III. 5, p. 220), in a version which makes the Elder ask his slave to kill him. The *Life* has at least one inaccuracy, in dispatching Pliny in a *liburnica*, not a quadrireme (s. 9).

21. interim Miseni ego et mater—sed nihil ad historiam. Guillemin, ad loc., sees the reviser's hand in this phrase, which is neatly taken up in Ep. 20. 1.

22. omnia me quibus interfueram quaeque statim, cum maxime vera memorantur, audieram, persecutum. Pliny received immediate news at Misenum of his uncle's death from Pomponianus and the slaves, Ep. 20. 20. Both letters are a remarkable testimony to the solid factual element that underlies the much adorned historical and biographical products of this age. Pliny must have questioned his informants very carefully to secure the details given in ss. 11 and 18 about the physical phenomena. Haywood's complaints (art. cit.) are

unfounded, ss. 11, 19 nn. That there is no account of the activity of
the ships is not surprising or misleading; some at least are still with
Pliny (s. 17). The letter is confined to the *exitus* of Pliny.

17. *To Restitutus*

Date not determinable. Pliny regularly sets one or more descriptions
of recitations in this place, cf. I. 13, III. 18, V. 17, VII. 17, VIII. 12,
IX. 27, but in II. 14 a variant replaces the type, while IV. 27 comes
rather late.

Address. The man should be Claudius Restitutus, the senator and
advocate who appeared against Pliny in the trial of Classicus, III.
9. 16 n.

1. in cuiusdam amici auditorio. See I. 13 nn. for the custom.

2. surdis mutisque similes. The silence of expectancy was to be
approved, and could be construed, II. 10. 7, V. 3. 9. But these fellows
gave no signs at all, like the bored audience of I. 13. 1–2.

3. totum diem impendere. Pliny split his own recitations into short
sessions of two or three hours, III. 18. 4, VIII. 21. 4. Guillemin quotes
Juv. I. 4 and Martial 10. 70. 10 in favour of literal interpretation, but
these were instances of the monstrous: 'impune diem consumpserit
ingens Telephus'. Pliny's own speeches might run to seven hours,
IV. 16. 3.

18. *To Sabinus*

Date not determinable, but the reference to Pliny's *occupationes*
agrees with the contents of VI, s. 1 n.

Address. Sabinus, addressed as Statius Sabinus in IV. 10, appears as a
military man and man of letters in IX. 2, 18. There is no difficulty in
identifying all as one man. He seems to be a patron of Firmum,
whence he originates, s. 2 n. In *CIL* ix the name appears only twice
among the scanty inscriptions of Firmum, ibid., nn. 5370, 5406. The
identification with Metilius Sabinus Nepos proposed by Syme for
Sabinus in IX. 2 will not do here, since the next letter is addressed to
Nepos. Cf. II. 3 pref.

1. quamquam plurimis occupationibus distentus. See Ep. 4. 1 n.

2. familiaritatem nostram. See II. 6. 1 n., IX. 34. 1, 37. 1 for this
degree of friendship.

    pro patria petenti. He may well be *patronus*, like Pliny at Tifernum;
see III. 4. 4–5, IV. 1. 4–5 nn. for the obligations involved.

3. splendor ipsorum. In the empire *splendidissima* became the fixed epithet of colonies, cf. for example, *ILS* 6623, 6818, 6835. Firmum originated as a Roman settlement with Latin status in 264 B.C., became a *municipium civium Romanorum* at the enfranchisement of Italy in 90 B.C., and took its title of colony from a draft of veterans in the triumviral period. *RE* iv, art. 'Colonia', nn. 27, 65.

19. *To Nepos*

Date. The letter is about the elections recently held, to which Epp. 6 and 9 refer as a future event, and which certainly belong to a later year than those of IV. 25, s. 1 n. It is addressed to a man, apparently absent overseas, who was last mentioned in IV. 26 as about to depart to a provincial appointment. Hence the book-date fits the circumstances. See also IV. 26 pref. for the possibility that it is post-105.

Address. For the senator Maecilius, or less probably Metilius, Nepos see II. 3 pref., IV. 26 pref. The absence of the man, who is in a province, s. 6, at the great moment of the elections, makes the identification with Maecilius of IV. 26 probable. The young Varisidius Nepos of IV. 4 is not known among Pliny's correspondents, any more than Licinius Nepos, IV. 29. 2, who does not seem to be a friend of Pliny.

1. proximis comitiis honestissimas voces senatus expressit : 'candidati ne conviventur' etc. These may well be the elections of Epp. 6, 9. The scandal that arose is different in its details from the election troubles of III. 20. 3–4, IV. 25. 1, and represents an ingenious development of tactics to meet the limitations imposed on canvassing by the introduction there made of secret ballots. No elections are mentioned in V. If those of IV. 25 belong to 105 (ibid. nn.), then these may be those of two years later, early 107.

The dodges are meant to avoid the open violation of the *lex ambitus*, and are the products of the *circuli* and *immodicus favor* described in III. 20. 4, 7.

pecunias deponant. For the meaning cf. X. 96. 7, 'ne depositum . . . abnegarent'.

3. Homullus . . . usus hoc consensu senatus sententiae loco postulavit, ut consules desiderium universorum notum principi facerent. For Homullus, consular and advocate, see IV. 9. 15 n. This shows an early stage in the development of passing a *SC.* by *acclamatio*, without a formal debate and vote. Cf. IX. 13. 7 n. The informally expressed opinions (s. 1 *voces*) lead to a regular proposal; this occurs at any stage of business. The habit is growing, as the frequency in Pliny's short selection of debates shows: III. 20. 2; IV. 9. 18, 25. 2; V. 13. 3.

A similar proposal to bring a matter to the notice of the Princeps was made after the earlier electoral scandal, and after the discussion of advocates' fees, IV. 25. 2, V. 13. 7. Contrast the attempt of Licinius Nepos to confine the Senate's business to the Senate, Ep. 5. 2.

4. sumptus candidatorum . . . ambitus lege restrinxit. The new regulation was probably ratified by *SC.*, cf. v. 13. 8 n., but the use of the *SC.* for legislation becomes ever rarer under Trajan and Hadrian, and is replaced steadily by the appropriate form of imperial 'constitution'.

ambitus lege. Cf. Ep. 5. 2, 'sub exemplo legis ambitus'. There were many laws against electoral corruption in the violent politics of the late Republic, later summed up by the *Lex Iulia ambitus* of 18 B.C. Little is known about this. Modestinus says of it: 'haec lex in urbe hodie cessat quia ad curam principis magistratuum creatio pertinet'. Pliny's electoral letters (II. 9; III. 20; IV. 15, 25; VI. 6) show that this stage has not yet been reached, though it is not far away. For the *Lex Iulia* see Dio 54. 16. 1; Suet. *Aug.* 34. 1; Tac. *Ann.* 15. 20; *Dig.* 48. 14; *Sent. Paul.* 5. 30a. 1; *RE* xii. 2365 ff.

eosdem patrimonii tertiam partem conferre iussit in ea quae solo continerentur. The proposal was renewed by Marcus Aurelius, who required the investment of only a quarter of a man's estate in Italy, SHA, *Marcus* 11. 8: 'ut . . . senatores peregrini quartam partem in Italia possiderent'. Mommsen, *DPR* vii. 75–76, took this to refer only to the minimal senatorial census of a million sesterces. Hence, perhaps, the future emperor Septimius Severus owned only a small house in the City and a single farm (*fundus*) in Venetia, SHA, *Sev.* 4. 5.

iussit. This proposal is attributed by Pliny to the initiative of Trajan. Sirago (*It. Agr.* 272 f.) supposes that it originated in the Senate, and that the whole purpose of the *consensus senatus* was to induce Trajan to sanction a dodge which would check the fall in value of Italian land. Nothing of this is in Pliny. The Senate left it to Trajan to make specific proposals. This regulation was intended to deal with the third point raised in 5. 1, by diminishing the amount of uninvested capital in the hands of candidates, and hence limiting the scale of corruption. This took the form, not of gifts, but of loans— *pecunias deponant*—doubtless to influential senators in need of liquid assets. Sirago notes Pliny's own lack of such funds in III. 11. 2, 19. 8.

deforme arbitratus (ut erat) honorem petituros urbem Italiamque non pro patria sed pro hospitio aut stabulo quasi peregrinantes habere. Cf. the phrase from the Marcus 'life' above. The measure was made

necessary by the steady increase in the numbers of senators from
the provinces, both of the Romanized western empire, and from
Trajan onwards of the hellenized East. This phenomenon has been
studied at length by Stech, 'Senatores Romani etc.', *Klio* Beiheft x
(1912); Walton, 'Oriental Senators in the Service of Rome', *JRS*,
1929, 38 ff.; P. Lambrechts, *La composition du Sénat romain A.D.*
117–192 (Ghent, 1936), and 'Trajan et le récrutement du Sénat',
Ant. Class. 1935, 108 ff.; Syme, *Tacitus*, chs. 42–44; M. Hammond,
JRS, 1957, 74 f., summarized for the period A.D. 64–235.

Senators had always been required to make their domicile at
Rome. Being required in theory to be permanently available, they
were able to leave Italy only with leave given in the form of a *libera
legatio*, originally by the Senate and later by the Princeps. But a
general dispensation of Augustan date allowed senators to visit
estates in Sicily freely, and this was extended by Claudius to senators
of Narbonensis. Tac. *Ann.* 12. 23; Dio 52. 42. 6–7, 60. 25. 6; Suet.
Claud. 23. 2. These rules were never further relaxed down to Dio's day,
but evidently were neglected in practice. Cassius Dio owned a villa
in Campania, but his main estates were in Bithynia, whither he
retired in old age. Dio 77 (76). 2. 1 with 80. 5. 2. Hence the lawyers
later maintained that senators had two 'domiciles'—the city of
Rome and their place of birth. Paulus, *D.* 1. 9. 11.

5. concursant ergo candidati. The legislation was after the elections,
as in III. 20, and came into force at the next occasion; hence these
must be next year's crop of candidates.

quoque sint plura venalia efficiunt. The effects of this may be seen
in the increased value of an estate of Pliny recorded in VII. 11.

6. hoc vendendi tempus tam hercule quam in provinciis comparandi.
Strictly speaking Nepos as a provincial governor was forbidden to
buy land, or any costly object, while in office, in his own province;
Mommsen, *D.Pen.R.* iii. 17 f.; *Dig.* 1. 16. 6. 3, 18. 1. 46.

20. *To Cornelius Tacitus*

Date. This continues Ep. 16 directly, picking up 16. 21 in s. 1.

**2. reliquum tempus studiis (ideo enim remanseram) impendi, mox
balineum cena somnus.** Pliny takes his ordinary bath later than the
Elder took his *frigida*, Ep. 16. 5; his daily round in IX. 36 is closer to
that of Spurinna (III. 1 nn.) than to that of his uncle.

3. praecesserat per multos dies tremor terrae. So too Dio 66. 22. 3.
For the 'customary earthquakes' compare the great shaking of
A.D. 63, Tac. *Ann.* 15. 22; Sen. *Q. Nat.* 6. 1. 1–3.

illa vero nocte ita invaluit. The night of 24 August, when the Elder was at Stabiae, Ep. 16. 13.

4. inrupit cubiculum meum mater. The residence of Pliny and his mother in his uncle's house suggests that Pliny's father was dead. His mother too was dead long before the date of II. 15, and possibly not long after 79, cf. IV. 19. 7 n. Her name is presumably Plinia.

resedimus in area domus quae mare a tectis modico spatio dividebat. The house is within the town of Misenum, and built by the shore, ss. 6–8. It is not clear why Merrill, ad loc., suggested that the house lay 'towards the eastern end of the promontory of Misenum just beyond the town'. The *aperto loco* of s. 6 is simply the *area*. L.–H. (ad loc.) takes it to be a terrace above the sea.

5. agebam enim duodevicensimum annum. This passage determines Pliny's age. He is past his seventeenth birthday at this moment in 79, and hence was born between 24 August 61 and 24 August 62.

excerpo. A habit of his uncle, III. 5. 10, 17.

amicus avunculi qui nuper ad eum ex Hispania venerat. For the Spanish connexions of the two Plinies see II. 13. 4; III. 4. 4, 5. 17; and Ep. 16. 8 nn.

6. iam hora diei prima. About 6–7 a.m. on 25 August, some time before his uncle's death, Ep. 16. 17.

8. egressi tecta consistimus. They pass along the neck of land to the north of the town, till they reach the ground rising up to the hill behind Baiae, whence they look down to the promontory and to the island of Capri beyond, s. 11.

9. mare . . . tremore terrae quasi repelli. Ep. 16. 11 n.

nubes atra et horrenda ignei spiritus . . . in longas flammarum figuras dehiscebat. This corresponds to the 'flammae flammarumque praenuntius odor sulpuris' of Ep. 16. 18.

11. nec multo post illa nubes descendere in terras, operire maria. This seems to be the phase when the Elder perished in the great dust cloud. Hartleben, ad loc., suggests that the wind swung round from the north to north-east and east, driving the clouds seawards.

13. iam cinis, adhuc tamen rarus. Cf. s. 16, 'cinis rursus, multus et gravis'. Stabiae and Misenum lying somewhat to windward (Ep. 16. 12) of the focal point escaped the worst of the precipitation that buried Pompeii and Herculaneum.

14. vix consideramus, et nox. The 'night' is due to the *caligo* of s. 13, which dissipates in s. 18, restoring daylight. Then comes the night of 25–26 August, in s. 19.

15. **nusquam iam deos . . . aeternamque illam et novissimam noctem mundo interpretabantur.** Dio 66. 23. 1 and 5 follows fairly closely. (I owe the substance of the following comment to Mr. D. A. F. M. Russell.) The idea of the world ending in a catastrophe of fire and flood is a common theme in Stoic thought (E. Zeller, *Die Philosophie der Griechen*,⁵ 1963, iii. 1. 155 n. 2), perhaps drawn from a Platonic passage, such as the *Politicus* myth (272 ff.) or Timaeus 22. It recurs frequently in Seneca, e.g. in *Cons. ad Marciam* 26. 6 and *Q. Nat.* 3. 27. 1, and the dramas: *Thyestes* 832 f., *Hercules Oet.* 1100 ff. Of these the Thyestes passage is closest to Pliny, with chaos overwhelming gods and men. In *Ep.* 9. 16 Jupiter survives while the world crumbles and the gods are 'merged into one'. More commonly the gods abandon the world, as in the Little Apocalypse of the Hermetic *Asclepius*, 24–26; cf. A. D. Nock's notes 201–4 in the Budé *Hermetica*, ii. This notion, in a primitive form, is as old as Hesiod, *Works* 197 f., 220 f. Pliny does not share these beliefs.

nec defuerunt qui fictis mentitisque terroribus vera pericula augerent. Dio, loc. cit., speaks of 'those who thought that the giants were rising again in revolt, for at this time many of their forms could be discerned in the smoke, and also a sound of trumpets was heard'. Seneca, *Q. Nat.* 6. 2–3, gives a like account of the terror during the earthquakes of A.D. 63.

17. **possem gloriari non gemitum mihi, non vocem parum fortem in tantis periculis excidisse.** This is in the tradition of the Magnanimous Man, who does not hide his own virtues, cf. II. 4. 2 n.

19. **suspensam dubiamque noctem.** 25–26 August.

20. **nobis . . . ne tunc quidem . . . abeundi consilium, donec de avunculo nuntius.** This is early morning, 26 August, when the old man's body was found. Ep. 16. 20.

haec nequaquam historia digna. Cf. Tac. *Ann.* 13. 31, 49, on themes fit for history. Tacitus objects to the commonplace. Pliny means that his party did nothing outstanding. The great disaster soon became a literary theme, appearing in Silius Italicus (17. 594), Valerius Flaccus (3. 208), Statius (*S.* 4. 4. 79–85), then Plutarch, *Pyth. Or.* 9, and Martial (4. 44), and after Pliny in Tacitus (*H.* 1. 2; *Ann.* 4. 67).

21. *To Caninius Rufus*

Date, cannot be determined. For the equestrian Caninius Rufus of Comum see I. 3 pref.

1. **mirer.** This remarkable instance of attraction is defended by Stout, p. 218, and others, from Cic. *De or.* 3. 16.

non tamen, ut quidam, temporum nostrorum ingenia despicio. So too Tacitus, *Ann.* 3. 55, 'rebus cunctis inest quidam velut orbis . . . nec omnia priores meliora sed nostra quoque aetas multa laudis et artium imitanda posteris tulit'. Cf. v. 17. 6, 'faveo enim saeculo ne sit sterile et effetum'.

neque enim quasi lassa et effeta natura nihil iam laudabile parit. Columella energetically rebutted this doctrine in terms of agriculture, *RR*, pref. 1–2. So too Quintilian 1. 1. 1. For the doctrine see Lucretius 2. 1150 ff. It depends on a belief in the creation and ultimate destruction of the universe. Cf. also Sall. *Cat.* 53. 5.

2. nuper. Here used with the sense of *proxime*; contrast III. 7. 12.

Vergilium Romanum paucis legentem comoediam ad exemplar veteris comoediae. Pliny evidently means the pre-Menandrian school, though pure Aristophanic comedy can hardly have been possible, even under Trajan. So too Seneca wrote 'old' tragedy. As always in Pliny the drama is for recitation only, I. 15. 2, III. 1. 9, v. 3. 2 n. So too Maternus in Tacitus, *Dialogus* 2–3, recites his tragedies. The terms 'New' and 'Old' Comedy must go back to Alexandrine scholarship. They are used in the singular by Plutarch, *Q. Conv.* 7. 711 F; *Lucullus* 39. 1; Antoninus, *Mem.* 11. 6. Aristotle used them in the plural, *EN* 1128ª22. Suetonius *Aug.* 89. 1 uses *vetus comoedia*.

Vergilius Romanus is as yet unknown. Unlike Calpurnius Piso, v. 17, he is not a youth.

4. mimiambos. Romanus would seem to have imitated the literary form of Herodas rather than the Latin mimes of Laberius, cf. Beare, *Roman Theatre*, 231. These too are not for acting. Cf. Bardon, op. cit. 218.

Menandrum . . . aemulatus. Bardon notes the curious inscription of M. Pomponius Bassulus of Aesculum who also (under Hadrian?) composed Menandrian comedies. *CIL* ix. 1164. (*Litt. Lat. Inc.* ii. 217.)

5. fictis nominibus decenter, veris usus est apte. He follows the advice of Martial, 1 pref.: 'de illis queri non possit quisquis de se bene senserit, cum salva infimarum quoque personarum reverentia ludant (libelli)', Guillemin, ad loc. Such a satirical comedy was a very rare bird in Latin literature (Schuster) though Senecan tragedy had done likewise.

22. To Calestrius Tiro

Date. This is the first of the series referring to Calestrius Tiro's proconsulship of Baetica, VII. 16, 23, 32; IX. 5, which all come in chronological order. There is a cross-reference to the present occasion in Ep. 31. 2, which is dated after the Dacian wars, s. 2 n. So the suggestion of Peter, art. cit. 709, that the series should be dated back to about 99–100, in the erroneous belief (s. 7 n.) that Tiro must have been proconsul five years after his praetorship, is invalid. The letter should fall between the return of Trajan from Dacia in late summer or autumn of 106 and the seasonal departure of proconsuls to their provinces the following April, s. 7 n.

Address. Calestrius Tiro, addressed first in I. 12, reappears in VI. 1, perhaps after an absence on service overseas. He is still a praetorian senator, VII. 16 nn.

2. Lustricius Bruttianus cum Montanium Atticinum, comitem suum, in multis flagitiis deprehendisset, Caesari scripsit. Atticinus flagitiis addidit ut quem deceperat accusaret. The personages are unknown. The former may be a connexion of the consular Bruttius Praesens, VII. 3. He is shown to be a proconsul by the comparison with Tiro, and also by the reference to *scriba*, s. 4; cf. IV. 12. 2.

For an assistant to accuse his proconsul was always regarded as very improper, cf. IV. 15. 9–10 nn., X. 26. 1; Tac. *Ann.* I. 74.

Caesari scripsit. It is characteristic of the period that the proconsul in unusual circumstances consults not the Senate but the Princeps. Cf. Ep. 31. 3, IV. 22. 1, VII. 6. 1 nn. But Ep. 31. 6 shows how reluctant the Princeps was to interfere with the ordinary working of criminal justice.

recepta cognitio est ; fui in consilio. Pliny dilates not on the main charges against Atticinus but on the special *scelus* that emerged during the hearing, s. 4. This probably fitted no exact definition, but amounted to a gross form of *calumnia*, to charge one's friend on the basis of forged documents. Cf. VII. 33. 7, 'impietatis reum', n.

This is Pliny's second session on the imperial *consilium*. Cf. IV. 22. 1 for the formula. From Ep. 31. 2, 'principis iustitiam . . . in secessu *quoque* . . . inspicere', it appears that Pliny attended both in Rome and at Centum Cellae in this period. Pliny's evidence suggests that senators were invited to attend particular sessions rather than for a fixed period.

egit uterque pro se, egit autem carptim . . . quo genere veritas statim ostenditur. So too in IV. 22. 2, 'egit ipse causam', but advocates appear in Ep. 31. 11. The procedure *carptim* was introduced under Nero, but never became the sole procedure; Crook, *Consilium Principis*, 111; Suet. *Nero*, 15. 1. Pliny's accounts show that at this time the process of *cognitio extra ordinem* before the Princeps and his assistants was simpler and quicker than the procedure of the ordinary courts, one reason for its rapid extension. Cf. VII. 6. 8–10 nn.

4. ita regessit ut dum defendit[ur] turpis, dum accusat sceleratus probaretur. The text is in some confusion. *regessit* is better than the well-supported *recessit*, which could only mean 'retired from the case', as in IV. 11. 12, V. 13. 2. But *defendit*—like *accusat*—is preferable to the passive, which is due to a simple dittography from *tur-pis*. Atticinus had no advocate.

interceperat commentarios interciderantque. He first abstracts the proconsul's records, and then alters them to fit his charge: hence he is *sceleratus*. The verb *intercidere* has special associations with forgery, *Dig.* 11. 3. 1. 5; 48. 10. 4. At a later date the forgery of official documents was brought under the *lex Cornelia de falsis*, Marcian, *Dig.* 48. 10. 1. 4 (under Severus). For proconsular records and archives see X. 31. 4 n.

crimine suo. He was attempting some form of extortion charge, since the *integritas* of Bruttianus was involved, s. 5 n.

5. statim de Atticino perrogavit. i.e. 'sententias', IV. 22. 3 and Ep. 31. 12. He then gives his verdict *e consili sententia*.

damnatus et in insulam relegatus. The Princeps is responsible in virtue of his *imperium* for the sentence, which is formulated on the advice of his assessors. The punishment, which is the extreme form of *relegatio* (II. 11. 19 n.), is less than the capital penalty of the *Lex Cornelia de falsis*, which would require *deportatio*, and *bonorum publicatio*. IV. 11. 13; *Dig.* 48. 10. 1. 13, 33.

integritatis testimonium . . . constantiae gloria. For the contrast *integritas–avaritia* applied to a public official see VII. 31. 1; *constantia* is the usual commendation of an advocate, III. 9. 23, V. 13. 2 n.

7. te sortitum provinciam praemonerem. The province is Baetica, whither he proceeds in VII. 16 and is established in IX. 5. It was one of the proconsulships reserved for praetorian senators. There is no clear evidence of the normal interval between praetorship and proconsulship, the five years rule being merely a minimum interval, Dio 53. 14. 2; Mommsen, *DPR* iii. 288 f.

Since proconsuls were expected to set out in April they must usually have been appointed during the preceding winter, IV. 26 pref. So too the legate Corbulo in late A.D. 54 for 55, Tac. *Ann.* 13. 6–8.

23. *To Triarius*

Date and addressee are not determinable. But the reference to Ruso fits the later books, s. 2 n.

1. 'non gratis tu?' Pliny never took fees, v. 13. 8–9. The allusion to such *pactiones* is maintained throughout the letter: 'exigam . . . paciscor . . . obliga . . . spondeo'.

2. ut simul agat Cremutius Ruso. i.e. as Pliny's 'junior'.

hoc mihi . . . iam in pluribus claris adulescentibus factitatum.
Ummidius Quadratus and Fuscus Salinator may serve as examples,
though in Ep. 11 Pliny is not actually appearing with them. Pliny
had himself so assisted in his youth, I. 18. 3, but speaks in II. 14. 2–3
as if the custom of 'leading' juniors had gone out.

Cremutius Ruso, addressed in IX. 19, is otherwise unknown, but
the implication that he is *clarus* suggests that he is connected with
the Augustan man of letters, Cremutius Cordus. The *cognomen* alone
cannot link him to the better-known Calvisii Rusones, with whom
Pliny's friend Frontinus was connected, *PIR*² C 350, 1566.

4. brevi producturus alios. Cf. II. 14. 3, 'aliquo consulari producente'.

24. *To Macer*

Date. The recent visit to Comum links the letter to Ep. I and V. 14,
possibly dating it to the summer of 106.

Address. The man may either be the Cisalpine Calpurnius Macer,
the future legate of Moesia, addressed in V. 18 (pref.), or the consular
Baebius Macer, orator and student, addressed in III. 5 (pref.). This
letter makes him a fellow Cisalpine, if not a compatriot, of Pliny, s. 2.
Calpurnius is more probable, since Pliny has a habit in IV–VI of
introducing new figures with two or three letters each, such as
Sempronius Rufus, IV. 22, V. 9, and Pontius Allifanus, V. 14, VI. 28,
VII. 4.

2. per Larium nostrum. In II. 8. 1 and VII. 11. 5 (nn.) this implies
that the other person is a compatriot of Pliny, though here 'ne mihi
quidem qui municeps' (s. 5) casts doubt on Macer being a *Comensis*.

cubiculum quod in lacum prominet. Pliny's own villa had such a
room, IX. 7. 3.

5. non quia minus illo clarissimo Arriae facto, sed quia minor ipsa.
For Arria see III. 16 nn. For the contemporary view of marriage see
VII. 5 n., and for other devoted wives VIII. 5, 18. 8–10.

25. *To Hispanus*

Date. The letter is connected with Ep. 24 by its subject-matter of
'strange deaths', but is otherwise undatable.

Address. The man may be the landowner Baebius Hispanus addressed
in I. 24 (pref.). Possibly he was the *praefectus vigilum*, and guided
the investigation into the disappearance of Robustus. But see s. 5 n

1. **Scribis Robustum . . . cum Atilio Scauro amico meo Ocriculum usque commune iter peregisse.** These personages are unknown, but Atilius Scaurus might well be the brother of Pliny's close friend Atilius Crescens, Ep. 8. 1. The distance is about a day's journey from Rome.

3. **huic ego ordinem impetraveram.** Centurions were recruited either from soldiers who had seen long service in the non-commissioned ratings of the Roman army, as *beneficiarii* and *principales*, or from men of decurional rank in their municipalities who were appointed direct to centurionates. Appointments were made by the Princeps after application had been made through the secretary *ab epistulis*, on the recommendation of an army commander, or, as in this case, of an influential person (Statius, *S.* 5. 1. 95; Juv. 14. 193). Compare *CIL* viii. 217: '. . . in legione III Augusta librarius (tesserarius optio signifer) factus (ex suffragio) leg(ati Augusti centurio) '. Pliny's man would seem to belong to the second category, like the man in Frontinus, *Strat.* 4. 6. 4: 'adulescentem honeste natum . . . angustiarum rei familiaris causa deductum (ad longiorem ordinem)'. Cf. Suet., *de gramm.* 24; Dio 52. 25. 7. Domaszewski, *Rangordnung*, 71 f., 80 ff., Parker, *Roman Legions*, 199 f., 214; E. Birley, *Roman Britain and the Roman Army*, 121 ff.

profisciscenti, i.e. to Rome, where all appointments were made. So too the club of the *optiones* at Lambaesis gave each member S.8,000 when he went off to his commission: 'ad spem proficiscens': *CIL* viii. 2554.

quadraginta milia nummum ad instruendum se. The centurion must fit himself out at his own cost with expensive items such as the 'golden rings' and the *vestis candida*. Domaszewski, op. cit. 81. Metilius was not a pauper, since he owned slaves, s. 4. Pliny's gift was probably to meet maximal requirements—compare his generosity in I. 19. 2. The professionals at Lambaesis could not reach this standard if they had to make up the S.8,000 out of their own savings, since a leading legionary would earn on the Flavian rates no more than S.3,600 a year. Domaszewski, op. cit. 71; Parker, op. cit. 216; Suet. *Dom.* 7. 3. Metilius Crispus is otherwise unknown.

4. **a suis an cum suis.** Compare the fate of Macedo, III. 14.

5. **accersamus Scaurum ; demus hoc tuis, demus optimi adulescentis honestissimis precibus qui . . . patrem quaerit.** The son of Robustus has visited Ocriculum and reported to Hispanus, who wants Pliny to put pressure on Atilius to return to Rome. Pliny and Hispanus seem to be in the same place (s. 1, 'ut Scaurus veniat nosque . . .'). The affair seems private; *tuis* hardly means 'your officers'.

Pliny's choice of the two stories suggests that such incidents were rare. He cannot produce a third to fulfil the *lex scholastica* of II. 20. 9 n.

26. *To Julius Servianus*

Date. The letters about the young Fuscus, like those about the young Quadratus, are confined to VI–IX, and cannot be separated from the book-dates. Ep. II. 1 n. and pref.

Address. For the Spanish origins and early career of L. Julius Ursus Servianus see VIII. 23. 5 n. He was one of Trajan's trusty supporters, being *cos. II ord.* in 102 with the great Licinius Sura. He married a sister of Hadrian, Domitia Paulina, whose daughter is here of marriageable age (SHA, *Hadr.* 1. 2). Of great influence under Hadrian, he was *cos. III* in 134, but perished in 136 on a charge of conspiracy, aged 90. (s. 1 n.; Dio 69. 17; SHA, op. cit. 8. 11, 15. 8, 23. 2, 25. 8; *PIR*¹ J 417; Garzetti, *C.* 81.) The notion that Servianus was the persistent enemy of Hadrian under Trajan (*CAH* xi. 222) depends only on an incident of A.D. 98: see VIII. 23. 5 n. For most of Hadrian's reign he was a trusted support.

1. **Fusco Salinatori filiam tuam destinasti.** Cn. Pedanius Fuscus Salinator appears as Pliny's pupil in Ep. II. 1 n. He is probably about the same age as his recently married friend Quadratus, i.e. not yet over 25, VII. 24. 3 n. For his connexion with Barcino in Spain see, for example, *ILS* 5486; Syme, *Tac.* 785 n. 4. Having married this girl, who was a niece of Hadrian, he shared an early consulship with him as Princeps in 118, and afterwards showed too openly his hopes of succession, lost favour and died (SHA, op. cit. 23. 2). Later the aged Servianus tried to secure the succession for a son of this marriage, born about 118. Both perished (Dio loc. cit.; *PIR*¹ P 142, 144; Syme, *Tac.* 247, 600).

filiam tuam. She is mentioned as *filia Serviani* in the will of Dasumius Tuscus in 108. *FIRA*, 3, n. 48. 8–10. Probably she was now not more than 15 years old, since *sponsalia* were not usually made before the twelfth year, cf. V. 16. 6 n.

pater honestissimus. The elder Pedanius Fuscus, consul before 86, proconsul of Asia in a year *c.* 98–102, and a consular legate under Trajan: X. 87. 3 n.; *PIR*¹ P 143–6; Garzetti, *C.* 114. Possibly he is Martial's advocate Fuscus, who is too old for the son, I. 54, VII. 28. Their patrician standing goes back to Vespasian rather than Claudius, under whom the first consular Pedanius appears. Syme, *Tac.* 479.

ipse studiosus. Cf. Ep. II, VII. 9.

3. **nepotes tuos ut meos vel liberos vel nepotes ex vestro sinu sumere.**
The tone of the passage, with that of III. 17, shows that Pliny, for
whom Servianus secured the *ius trium liberorum* from Trajan in 98
(X. 2), was an intimate friend. Pliny was not so remote from the ruling
circle as is sometimes thought. If there are not many letters to such
men as Servianus and Catilius Severus, the reason is indicated in
VII. 25. Not all these gentry had literary tastes. If the tone of the
Court was set by Trajan, then drinking, boys, and field sports would
predominate, cf. *Pan.* 33, 81; *Ep. de Caes.* 13. 4; SHA *Hadr.* 2. 7, 3. 3.
Pliny sought to develop a taste for the last of these pursuits, I. 6,
IX. 10.

27. To Vettenius Severus

Date. The identification of the recipient with C. Vettenius Severus,
suffect consul in May–August 107, dates this letter to the first weeks
of 107, s. 1, 5. (*FO* and *ILS* 2002; Garzetti, *Inc.* 158.)

1. **quid designatus consul in honorem principis censeas.** Evidently
at the first Senate after the elections, which for suffects were almost
certainly in January (pp. 23 f.; cf. IV. 15. 5 n.), the new *designati* in
their first *sententia* were expected to make some honorific proposal.
According to Pliny, *Pan.* 55, Trajan usually declined them.

2. **designatus ego consul omni hac . . . specie . . . adulationis abstinui.**
This occasion was distinct from the *gratiarum actio* or Panegyric
delivered on the day on which he entered office. It should be the
session of *Pan.* 78, at which others urged Trajan to take a fourth
consulship.

   non tamquam liber et constans. He did not take the tone of a
Helvidius.

3. **non dissimulatione et silentio praeterii.** There was a general conspiracy to forget the past at that period; IX. 13. 7: 'salvi simus
qui supersumus' was the watchword.

5. **recentia opera maximi principis.** The final conquest of Dacia,
completed in 106, is meant as in VIII. 4. 1, not his building programme
which was hardly yet under way: 'quae tam recens . . . in verissimis
rebus tam fabulosa materia'.

28. To Pontius Allifanus

Date. The letter belongs to the series about the visit of Pliny and his
wife to Campania (Epp. 4, 7, 30; VII. 5) and cannot be separated from
the book-date. Cf. Ep. 4 pref.

Address. For Pontius Allifanus see V. 14 pref.

1. adventum meum in Campaniam. Pliny evidently joined his wife for a brief period, and stayed on the Campanian estate of Pontius mentioned in V. 14. 9.

tantum mihi copiarum . . . nomine tuo oblatum est. For the custom cf. I. 4. 1 n., a companion-piece.

29. *To Ummidius Quadratus*

Date. The letter belongs to the Fuscus–Quadratus series (Ep. 11 pref.), and is attached to the period 106–7 by the reference to the Varenus case, s. 11 n. There is no reason to date it earlier than Ep. 11, s. 3 n.

Address. For Pliny's aristocratic young protégé, Ummidius Quadratus, see Ep. 11. 1 n. and VII. 24. 2–3 nn.

1. Avidius Quietus qui me unice dilexit. T. Avidius Quietus of Faventia, alive at Rome in 97 (IX. 13. 15) and now dead, who had been a legionary legate before 82, proconsul of Achaea under Domitian, suffect consul in 93 (*F. Pot.*), and legate of Britain in 98 (*CIL* xvi. 43), and his brother Nigrinus (X. 65, 3 n.), founded a consular family prominent under Trajan. The former's son, T. Avidius Quietus, suffect consul in 111, was outstripped by the nephew, C. Avidius Nigrinus (V. 13. 6 n.), who was one of the four consulars executed in Hadrian's interest after his succession. Once again Pliny's connexion with the inner circle of the régime is apparent, Ep. 26. 3 n.

Pliny's indication of the philosophical interests of Quietus suggests that Plutarch's friends Quietus and Nigrinus were the elder pair. (*De sera numinis vindicta* 548 B, *De fraterno amore* 478 B, *Q. conviv.* 2. 5.) Cf. *RE* xxi. 1. 691. All four men were governors of Achaea, and seem to have taken a special interest in Greek affairs; see *SIG*³ 827; *OGIS* 502.

It is possible that Pliny's Quietus is a yet older man, father of the first consular, and only of praetorian rank, since he speaks in the debate of 97 apparently just before Tertullus (IX. 13. 15). But there Pliny is listing separately the only two who spoke against Publicius Certus. Pliny's style of reference excludes the coexistence at this moment of two elder senators with the same names, cf. III. 7. 12 n. See *PIR*² A 1407–10; Garzetti, *C.* 22; Syme, *Tac.* 51 f., 669.

ut multa alia Thraseae (fuit enim familiaris). Since Thrasea perished in 66 (Tac. *Ann.* 16. 21 ff.) Quietus must have been a very young member of his circle, even if as a 'new man' he did not secure his *honores* early in life. As a family friend he supports the interests of Arria and Fannia in 97, IX. 13. 15 n.

3. ad haec ego genera causarum . . . addam . . . claras. Pliny's very characteristic amendment shows that he quite misunderstood the principle of Thrasea, who deliberately excluded such cases unless they were covered by his definition in other respects.

hos terminos, quia me consuluisti, . . . statuo. Pliny claims in Ep. 11. 3 to be the *exemplar* of Quadratus. The suggestion that this letter must be earlier than the début of Quadratus at the Bar in Ep. 11 (Schultz, art. cit. 29 f.) is absurd. The question only arose when Quadratus had started to practise.

4. multos parvo ingenio . . . ut bene agerent agendo consecutos. He is thinking of Regulus, IV. 7. 3–5.

5. illud . . . Pollionis. For the Augustan orator see I. 20. 4.

6. mollitia frontis. This account is given by Dionysius Hal. *Isocrates*, I, p. 535. Compare the defects of Regulus, loc. cit. But Quadratus had *decorus habitus*, VI. 11. 2.

7. necessitati quae pars rationis est parui. Conversely in I. 12. 3, 'summa ratio . . . sapientibus pro necessitate est'. He is again widening Thrasea's ruling.

egi enim quasdam a senatu iussus, quo tamen in numero fuerunt ex illa Thraseae divisione, hoc est ad exemplum pertinentes. In II. 11. 1 he claims that the Priscus case was 'personae claritate famosum, severitate exempli salubre'. But here there is a touch of apology for having anything to do with accusations, cf. I. 5. 1 n. In fact the responsibility lay with the provincials for initiating charges of extortion, not with the advocates assigned by the senate (*iussi*), II. 11. 2 n. In III. 4 he similarly explains away his acceptance of the brief in the Classicus case.

8. adfui Baeticis contra Baebium Massam : quaesitum est an danda esset inquisitio; data est. The case was in A.D. 93, and Pliny seconded Senecio, VII. 33. 4 n. For *inquisitio* see III. 9. 29, V. 20. 2 nn. Massa, like Priscus later, evidently sought to secure trial by the short process, and so avoid the maximum penalties, II. 11, 2 n.

adfui rursus isdem querentibus de Caecilio Classico. III. 4, 9. It has been argued that Pliny's order of cases here is chronological, and hence that the Classicus case preceded that of Priscus, despite the order of Pliny's letters, and against this that Pliny is grouping the two Spanish cases together (Stobbe, art. cit. 359; Asbach, art. cit. 41 n. 1). Neither is right. The order is rhetorical, combining a crescendo with a chiasmus for effect: 'adfui . . . data est . adfui . . . poenas luerunt . accusavi . . . relegatus est. tuitus sum . . . remansit. dixi pro . . . impetratum est'. The last phrase neatly corresponds with the first.

9. accusavi Marium Priscum. The responsibility for converting the case into a full-scale criminal indictment for *saevitia* was that of the advocates; hence *accusavi*, II. II. 2–3.

10. tuitus sum Iulium Bassum. IV. 9.

11. dixi proxime pro Vareno postulante ut sibi invicem evocare testes liceret : impetratum est. V. 20. 2 and 7, 'impetravimus rem'. This letter must be later than V. 20 and perhaps than Ep. 13, but earlier than VII. 6 and 10, where the charge against Varenus is in process of being abandoned. For the use of *proxime* of a short interval see e.g., IV. 16. 1.

30. *To Calpurnius Fabatus*

Date. The letter belongs to the series of the Campanian holiday, and is close to Ep. 28 pref.

Address. For the aged Fabatus see IV. 1 pref. He never travels far from Comum in these years, cf. VII. 23. 1, VIII. 20. 3.

2. villa Camilliana quam in Campania possides. So too in VIII. 20. 3 Pliny inspects the property of Fabatus at Ameria.

3. attendimus ergo ut quam saluberrime reficiantur. Pliny is concerned also for the whole estate, s. 4. Absentee ownership is at work, for a *villa* would have its own maintenance staff, III. 19. 3 n.

4. rusticorum autem praediorum administratio poscit durum aliquem . . . cui nec labor ille gravis. Compare his comments on the rarity of the scholar-squire Terentius Junior, VII. 25. 2–6. The passage speaks for the growing separation of town and country interests at this period, to which Pliny persistently subscribes, perhaps insincerely yet significantly for the tastes of his audience, IX. 15, 2 n. He is not here talking about the scarcity of peasent tenants, as in III. 19. 7, VII. 30. 3. Fabatus wants to lease the whole estate, not a single farm, to a man of substance.

5. tu de Rufo honestissime cogitas. fuit enim filio tuo familiaris. At least two of Pliny's equestrian friends bear this cognomen, Calvisius and Caninius, both of Comum, of whom the former was certainly a man of business (III. 19, VIII. 2). But probably a third is meant. For the death of the younger Calpurnius see IV. 19. 1.

31. *To Cornelianus* (?)

Date. The letter is after the return of Trajan from Dacia, ss. 8–9, and the scene is laid in summer, s. 15. Hence mid-107 is probable.

Address. The name Cornelianus occurs nowhere else in the collection. Possibly it conceals the equestrian Cornelius Minicianus, to whom descriptions of public affairs are addressed in III. 9, IV. 11. Cf. I. 17, VII. 12 prefs. for other possible misreadings of his name.

1. evocatus in consilium a Caesare nostro ad Centum Cellas (hoc loco nomen). The letter contains the longest and most detailed description of the judicial activity of the Princeps and his *consilium*, and is supplemented by IV. 22, VI. 22, and VII. 10. It is the second such appearance of Pliny at this period, as indicated by the cross-reference in s. 2, *in secessu quoque*, cf. Ep. 22 pref.

The development of Centum Cellae, the modern Cività Vecchia, as a convenient supplement to Ostia for the corn supply of Rome, and the origin of the town, was apparently entirely due to Trajan's construction of an artificial harbour there. The place was unknown to the Elder Pliny (*NH* 3. 51), as also to Strabo. Its name was evidently unfamiliar to the Younger Pliny's audience. The site must have lain in the territory of Castrum Novum, seven kilometres to the south, and have replaced Pyrgi, which in Strabo's day was the harbour of Caere (Strabo, v p. 226). Cf. S. Bastianelli, 'Centum Cellae' etc., *Italia Romana*, s. 1, vol. xiv (1954), 11 f. Meiggs (*Roman Ostia*, 58 f.), discusses Trajan's development of Ostia and Centum Cellae at the expense of Puteoli.

evocatus in consilium. For the formula compare IV. 22. 1, 'in consilium adsumptus'. It would seem from Pliny that the *consilium* was specially constituted for each occasion, though doubtless jurisprudents such as Titius Aristo and Iavolenus Priscus (I. 22. 2, Ep. 15. 2) were in frequent attendance at judicial sessions, anticipating the Hadrianic reform whereby they became permanent members (Crook, *Consilium Principis*, 59). Thus in *Dig.* 37. 12. 5 a decision of Trajan is ascribed to the advice of Titius Aristo and Neratius Priscus. The composition of Trajan's *consilium* must have been much like that of Domitian's in Juvenal's parody (*Sat.* 4), with politicians, administrators, and lawyers of the court circle, both equestrians and senators, in attendance, though Pliny does not mention any equestrians. The distinction between judicial and administrative business is not well marked. Here and in Ep. 22 the cases all concern criminal law, but IV. 22 is a matter of municipal powers. The procedure is very simple, differing little from that of any Roman magistrate taking the customary advice of friends before making a decision. Compare the formula of Domitian's letter *ad Falerienses* (A–J n. 63; Bruns, n. 82): 'imp. Caesar . . . adhibitis utriusque ordinis splendidis viris cognita causa . . . pronuntiavi'. Also Suet. *Tib.* 55: 'super veteres amicos et familiares viginti . . . e numero principum civitatis depoposcerat velut consiliarios in negotiis publicis'. The number present in the cases attended by Pliny is not given, and elsewhere is only twice known—eleven in Juvenal and thirty-six in a Claudian document. See at length Crook, op. cit., chs. iv and viii, and for numbers, 59 n. 3.

Crook holds that there was only one *consilium*, but in practice it was differently constituted for different kinds of affairs. Pliny was not required when foreign affairs were being discussed.

2. fuerunt variae cognitiones. One case is heard each day before the hour of dinner, and probably before the period of exercise and bath. If Trajan started work as early as Vespasian, this would allow a good six hours to the working day, cf. iii. 5. 9 n., 'Career'.

3. dixit causam Claudius Ariston, princeps Ephesiorum, homo munificus et innoxie popularis; inde invidia. The man is known from several inscriptions of Ephesus as thrice Asiarch and Archiereus of Asia, holding the presidency of the provincial Council about A.D. 90–95 and again about 110, and as chief magistrate of Ephesus itself. *PIR*², C 788; *AE*, 1898, n. 66, 1906, nn. 28–29. His family, like many leading Greeks of Asia Minor, received citizenship from Claudius or Nero. Pliny's thumb-nail sketch sums up the violent local politics of the cities of the Asian province, known in more detail from Pliny's letters to Trajan (x. 58, 81, 110), and from the municipal speeches of Dio Chrysostom. See A. H. M. Jones, *The Greek City*, chs. xi, xx, and especially pp. 180 f. A similar brief glimpse is given by Pliny's account of Julius Bassus' troubles, iv. 9. 4–5. Ariston may have been giving some of those vast public banquets to the citizens 'quasi per corpora, non viritim singulos' which so alarmed Pliny and Trajan in Bithynia, x. 116–17. For the lavish outpouring of private fortunes on municipal affairs at this time see Plutarch, *Praecepta rei publicae gerendae*, 31, and Dio Chrys. *Or.* 46. 3.

popularis. The Roman government discouraged in every possible way the popular element in the municipal administrations of Asia Minor, both in the political assemblies and in the social organizations, x. 34, 93 nn., and tried to limit political power to local councils of a plutocratic type, x. 112–15 nn. At Ephesus the local council was in full control by the time of Hadrian; Jones, op. cit. 177 f., 183.

delator immissus. Probably a charge of *vis publica* was put forward; this charge was widely interpreted in the second century and applied in the provinces, cf. Marcian, *Dig.* 48. 6. 1–3, 'lege Iulia de vi publica tenetur . . . qui turbae seditionisve faciendae consilium inierint'. Ulpian, ibid. 6–7, referred to it in his *de officio proconsulis*, quoting a rescript of Pius. The case would come to the Princeps on *provocatio*, as Ariston was a Roman citizen, cf. x. 96. 4 n. For the vogue of delation in adjacent Bithynia see IV. 9. 5: 'dicerem de conspiratione delatorum quam in quaestu habebant', and x. 58. 2, 81. 1–2 nn.

4. nupta haec tribuno militum honores petituro . . . maritus legato consulari, ille Caesari scripserat. The husband is a *laticlavius*, and the rank of his wife is probably the reason why the governor referred the case to the Princeps, although he had power to adjudicate over both parties, since the penalties of the *Lex Iulia de adulteriis* were not capital. So Ulpian later, *Dig.* 48. 5. 16(15). 4: 'si quis in provincia in qua agit adulterium commiserit accusari poterit nisi sit ea persona quae ad praesidis cognitionem non spectat'.

By *legato consulari* is meant a consular holding one of the senior legateships. In common use the term ὑπατικός already appears at this date for 'army commander', Michigan Papyri viii. 466, l. 26.

5. Caesar excussis probationibus centurionem exauctoravit atque etiam relegavit . . . reliqua pars ultionis. This part of the affair has been concluded before the present trial, and it would seem that the Princeps dealt with the centurion without referring the case to his *consilium*. Pliny seems surprised at the relegation of the centurion, which is part of the normal penalty, s. 6. Perhaps with persons of low rank exile was not usually imposed; the Princeps in his *cognitio extra ordinem*, not being bound by the text of the *lex*, might have been satisfied with the dismissal of the centurion. Later, soldiers convicted of adultery were automatically dismissed the service. Ulpian, *D.* 3. 2. 2. 3.

maritum non sine aliqua reprehensione patientiae amor uxoris retardabat, quam quidem etiam post delatum adulterium domi habuerat. This case shows how strictly the harsher provisions of the adultery law were enforced at this time. The law required the husband to divorce the erring wife, and expected him, without compulsion, to prosecute her as well. For sixty days he, with the wife's father, had the prior right of prosecution, after which third parties might intervene. Ulpian, *Dig.* 48. 5. 4 pref., 16 (15). 5. But if the husband discovered the facts himself and failed to prosecute, then he was liable to a charge of *lenocinium*. This provision was aimed at discouraging the complacent husband; if a third party wished to prosecute in such circumstances he must first prove *lenocinium* against the husband. Ulpian, loc. cit. 2. 2 and 27(26). This sanction was softened later by exceptions: 'si patiatur uxorem delinquere non ob quaestum sed . . . quandam patientiam vel nimiam credulitatem', ibid. 2. 3 and 30(29). 4. If the charge of *lenocinium* failed, no further proceedings could be taken. Such is the doctrine of Ulpian, cf. *CAH* x. 446. But this qualified protection of marriages which were not hopeless was not favoured by Trajan: 'reprehensione patientiae'.

6. admonitus ut perageret accusationem. He cannot be compelled, only advised to prosecute his wife, cf. above. But the circumstances were peculiar in that the husband had already initiated proceedings, s. 5, and then changed his mind when he had got rid of the centurion.

legis poenis relicta est. According to the late *Sententiae Pauli* 2. 26. 14 the penalty for wives was a fine of half the dowry and a third of their property together with relegation *in insulam*; for men, the same apart from the dowry. That the sentence of relegation was normal in the early Principate is shown by Tac. *Ann.* 2. 50, 85; 4. 42. Such relegation was not necessarily *in perpetuum*, but women were forbidden remarriage, *Dig.* loc. cit. 12 (11). 13; Tac. *Ann.* 6. 49.

ne omnis eius modi causas revocare ad se videretur. Cf. Pliny, *Pan.* 77. 4: 'pleraque ad praetores remittebat'. The case, involving a lady of senatorial rank, might have gone to the Senate rather than to the *quaestio*.

7. Iuli Tironis codicilli, quos ex parte veros esse constabat, ex parte falsi dicebantur. The charge is under the *Lex Cornelia de falsis*. *Codicilli* were either a supplement to a normal will, or a less formal document which was held to be valid when certain circumstances prevented the drawing of a regular testament. Cf. II. 16. 1 n. Wills and codicils might be drawn up by a second party, or by the testator, or by both, cf. Ep. 22. 3. *Dig.* 29. 7. 6. 1: 'codicillos et plures quis facere potest et ipsius manu neque scribi neque signari necesse est'. The warranty depended on the witnesses, as for a will, who were summoned at the opening of the document to recognize their marks, *Sent. Pauli* 4. 6. 1.

Julius Tiro and the others are unknown.

8. heredes . . . petierant ut susciperet cognitionem. Tacitus, *Dial.* 7. 1 notes that charges against the freedmen and procurators of the emperor were commonly heard *apud principem*, as here. Senecio, however, does not seem to be in the service.

9. 'nec ille Polyclitus est nec ego Nero'. For the notorious freedman of Nero see Tac. *Ann.* 14. 39, Dio 62 (63). 12. 3.

10. omnes heredes agere cogerentur, cum detulissent omnes, aut sibi quoque desistere permitteretur. They already fear the countercharge of frivolous accusation, *calumnia*, with which Trajan presently threatens the absentees, s. 12. The passage illustrates the place of the *calumnia* process in controlling the Roman system of private delation. So too the emperor Claudius had complained of those who failed to complete prosecutions which they had initiated, and left their *rei* 'in albo pendentes'. He ruled that in such cases a charge of *calumnia* should lie against the prosecutors unless they could plead a valid excuse. *BGU* 611 (Charlesworth, *Documents*, C. 3, col. 2). Less serious forms of the offence, called *tergiversatio* and *destitutio*, were regulated by the *SC. Turpilianum* of A.D. 61, see v. 4. 2 n. The usual penalty for *calumnia* was civil disability, *ignominia*, which put a stop to the career of an advocate. *Dig.* 3. 2. 1, 48. 2. 4. But sometimes a sentence of relegation was imposed *extra ordinem*, Tac. *Ann.* 13. 33; Pliny, *Pan.* 35; *RE* iii. 1416 ff.

11. advocatus Senecionis. For the permissive use of advocates in this court see Ep. 22. 2 n.

12. isti enim queri volunt quod sibi licuerit non accusari. The necessary emendation from the manuscript *accusare* is due to Guillemin. With *accusare* the remark is pointless and obscure. The accusers were not complaining. Trajan had at first conceded their request. Then the *rei* complained of being left under suspicion. *Isti* should refer to the *rei*, not to the accusers, in each place. If the passive *accusari* is read, all is at once clear, and the remark has point: 'Those fellows are making a fuss at being let off without a charge.' The passive is common enough with *licet*, though rarer than the active. Keil, reading *quaeri* (M) for *queri*, felt the difficulty. (Guillemin, *Mnemosyne*, 1929, 54.) The only defence of the manuscript would be to argue that the non-appearance of the others could be twisted to prove the *calumnia* of those who persisted. The incident reveals an interesting fear of the influence of the officials over the *Optimus Princeps*.

ex consili sententia iussit denuntiari heredibus ... aut agerent aut singuli approbarent causas non agendi. Trajan makes every one happy. For the procedure compare Ep. 22. 5 'de Atticino perrogavit', and IV. 22. 3. Roman magistrates were not bound to follow the numerical majority of their *consilium*, though they usually did so, but might take what seemed the best advice tendered, or none of it. Cf. Crook, op. cit. 5. Even in the Senate, where counting was used, the magistrate was not bound to carry out the advice given. Mommsen, *DPR* vii. 223 ff. Cf. Suet. *Nero* 15. 1 for an imperial attitude.

Crook, op. cit. 109, suggests that the proceedings before the *consilium* always fell into two parts, the hearing of the pleas and evidence being followed by a private deliberation before the sentence is pronounced. The only evidence for this is in the account given by Josephus of the discussion about the settlement of Judaea after the

death of Herod, when the embassies were dismissed before Augustus
retired to deliberate; Jos. *AJ* 17. 317. There is no trace of this
adjournment in Pliny's three accounts, and the implication here is
that opinions were taken and sentence given straightway in the
presence of the parties.

13. erat modica si principem cogitares. Plutarch, *Quaest. Conv.* 7.
712 A, remarks that at an imperial banquet, probably of Domitian,
each guest had a separate wine steward.

15. villa pulcherrima cingitur viridissimis agris. This villa has not
been systematically excavated, though its site, called Belvedere,
was established by diggings in the early nineteenth century, Bastianelli, op. cit. 60 f., fig. 5. It lay on high ground, a kilometre inland.
Bastianelli's sketch-map shows seven or eight other villas along this
stretch of the *pestilens ora Tuscorum* (v. 6. 2). That of Verginius
Rufus lay to the south, Ep. 10. 1.

    fit cum maxime portus. Cf. s. 1 n. Trajan's harbour is also described
by Rutilius Namatianus, *de red.* 1. 239–45, and is well known from
the antiquarian evidence of the architect Collicola, who drew plans
of the ruins at the time of its reconstruction in about 1727. The three
accounts agree as to the general design, though Pliny is incomplete,
doubtless because he saw the works at an early stage of construction.
The plan was an adaptation of that already followed by the architects
of Claudius and Trajan at Ostia-Portus: cf. Suet. *Claudius* 20. 3;
Dio 60. 11. 4; R. Meiggs, *Roman Ostia*, 153 ff.

    An outer basin was sheltered by the moles and 'island', as de-
scribed by Pliny, and there was an inner pentagonal basin, not in
Pliny but mentioned by Rutilius. Pliny may be inexact in some
lesser details, but he is attempting to describe what he saw, including
the stone-laying vessel (s. 16). Guillemin suggested unconvincingly
(*VL* 118) that Pliny's description is a literary cliché without factual
value, after the style of Vergil's description of Carthage (*Aen.* 1.
159 ff.) used also by Livy (26. 42. 8) and Lucan (2. 616–18). There are
verbal echoes of Vergil, (s. 16 n.), but the other parallels are not
detailed. For a summary of the archaeological evidence, and for
the bibliography of Centum Cellae, see Bastianelli, op. cit. 36 f. and
Fig. 2, and his reconstruction on plate iii. Also K. Lehmann-Hartleben,
'Die antiken Hafenanlagen des Mittelmeeres', *Klio* B. xiv. 192 ff.,
and plan 33 ibid. Paribeni, op. cit. fig. 15, gives the plan of Collicola.

    sinistrum brachium firmissimo opere munitum est. Rutilius,
loc. cit. 239, 'molibus aequoreum concluditur amphitheatrum'. This
is the eastern and longer mole, about 400 metres long, cf. Hartleben,
op. cit. 194.

16. in ore portus insula adsurgit. Rutilius 240, 'angustosque aditus insula facta tegit'. His *tegit* is more exact than Pliny's 'in ore'. The island was not between the two moles, as at Portus, but overlapped their two ends, the design being unsymmetrical. Hartleben, loc. cit., remarks that the scheme improved on Portus in meeting the needs of the site. Even after the destructive Saracen sack in A.D. 828, the ruined works protected the basin from silting up until the restoration in the eighteenth century.

inlatum vento mare obiacens frangat. This is the chief echo of Vergil, *Aen.* I. 159: 'insula portum efficit obiectu laterum, quibus omnis ab alto frangitur, inque sinus scindit sese unda reductos'.

ingentia saxa latissima navis provehit contra; haec alia super alia deiecta ipso pondere manent. Vitruvius 5. 12 describes the technique of submarine construction. For the building of an artificial island at Ostia, the engineers of Claudius apparently used a sunken ship as a substructure: Suet. loc. cit.; Pliny, *NH* 16. 202.

The text is obscure, though the rhythm favours the O.C.T. *provehit contra*, which must be supposed to mean 'brings them up to the island'. Hartleben defends 'contra haec': the *ingentia saxa* are the bottom course, and the *alia super alia* the upper courses. Stout, op. cit. 222 f., supports this with v. 6. 20 and IX. 39. 6, but the parallel is not exact; the meaning of *contra* is there 'over against' or 'opposite': 'contra templum (*sc.* ultra viam) . . . porticus explicabuntur'. Cf. also II. 17. 5. Emendations—*onera, pondera*—do not convince, especially with *pondere* recurring seven words later. The difficulty lies not in the text, but in Pliny's abbreviation or misunderstanding of the report of the architect, to whom he had been talking, since he knows what was to be done next (s. 17), though he confuses this also.

17. saxis deinde pilae adicientur, quae procedente tempore enatam insulam imitentur. This is obscure. An openwork arcading or pier to extend the island at either end, or to finish off the structure above sea level, might be meant: Hartleben, op. cit. 169, 193. Possibly these are the *turres* of Rutilius: 'attollit (insula) geminas turres bifidoque meatu faucibus artatis pandit utrumque latus'. Hartleben, op. cit. 1936, ad loc. took this sentence to refer to the action of the water eroding the stonework. But Pliny is describing the building operations and their effect.

habet nomen auctoris. Presumably 'Portus Traiani', like the Ostian harbour, or 'Portus Ulpius'. But there is no evidence. Hitherto only Portus Iulius, Agrippa's Campanian harbour, and Herod's Portus Augustus are known in this style: Hartleben, op. cit. (*Klio*) 297.

vel maxime salutaris. Hartleben (1936) quotes the *titulus* from Trajan's port at Ancona: 'accessum Italiae ... portu tutiorem navigantibus reddiderit'. *CIL* ix. 5894.

per longissimum spatium litus importuosum. There was no shelter from the Tiber to Portus Herculis under Mons Argentarius; cf. Rutilius, op. cit. 279, of the coast north of Centum Cellae: 'litus fugimus Munione vadosum'. His next harbour is Portus Herculis. Strabo mentions only Pyrgi, and the Elder Pliny only Telamon, north of M. Argentarius, along this stretch, s. 1 n.

32. To Quintilianus

Date is indeterminable. Scholars have generally rejected the identification of this Quintilianus, who is an advocate (s. 2), with the great master of rhetoric, who was wealthy, and had no surviving children about A.D. 96 (Juv. S. 7. 188; *Inst.* vi *prooem.* 4), and who seems to be dead in II. 14. 9 and Ep. 6. 3, despite the existence of a Tutilius, s. 1, who was an advocate or rhetorician in the generation of Martial, mentioned by Quintilian as already dead; Mart. 5. 56. 6; *Inst.* 3. 1, 21. Cf. *RE* (2) vii. 1613 f., 'Tutilius'.

1. tuam filiam Tutili neptem. The grandfather could be Martial's man. His granddaughter might well marry another professional advocate, though the undertones of the letter (*continentissimus* etc.) could point to the Stoic philosopher, Tutilius of Cortona, known from *ILS* 7779, as suggested by Bücheler, *Rhein. Mus.* 1908, 194. Other Tutilii include a Spanish family with consuls in A.D. 135 and 183.

ratio civilium officiorum necessitatem quandam nitoris imponit. So too Pliny assists the centurion in Ep. 25. 2, 'ad instruendum se ornandumque'. By *civilia officia* he means practice as an advocate in the courts, as in IV. 24. 3, where the term is contrasted with the imperial service. For the expensiveness of public life see I. 8. 11 n.

Nonius Celer is evidently not of exalted family, and hence not connected with any of the consular Nonii.

33. To Voconius Romanus

Date is not determinable unless the dead octogenarian of s. 2 or the father of Suburanus in s. 6 can be identified with the Attius Suburanus, consul II in 104 and possibly dead thereafter.

Address. For Pliny's old friend Romanus, the Spanish senator, or knight from Spanish Saguntum, see II. 13. 4–9 nn.

2. est haec pro Attia Viriola et dignitate personae et exempli . . . iudicii magnitudine insignis. Contrast II. 14. 1 on the Centumviral Court, 'raro incidit vel personarum claritate vel negotii magnitudine insignis (causa)'. But its prestige remained high, cf. the praises of Rutilius Gallicus and Vitorius Marcellus, advocates before they became military men, Statius, *S.* I. 4. 24, 4. 4. 44. Sidonius, *Ep.* 8. 10. 3, refers to this as Pliny's most famous speech, outdoing even his Panegyric, but he seems only to be quoting Pliny's own words.

femina splendide nata . . . exheredata ab octogenario patre intra undecim dies quam illi novercam . . . induxerat, . . . bona paterna repetebat.

The *nomen* of the lady, and the *cognomen* of her kinsman, read as Suburanus in s. 6, suggested to Mommsen that she is the daughter of Sextus Attius Suburanus, Trajan's praetorian prefect who was elevated to the consulship in 101, and to a second consulship in 104, VII. 6. 10 n. But she is more probably this man's sister or niece. Pliny would hardly have referred to so great a man in so colourless a phrase, or to his daughter as merely *splendide nata*, i.e. of equestrian standing (V. I. I, Ep. 15. 1, 25. 1). Sextus Suburanus could hardly have been 80 in *c.* 106, since he was a very junior procurator in about 83. Cf. *PIR²* A 1370. Possibly the octogenarian is the father of Sextus also, who is now dead after likewise disinheriting his son (s. 6), also called Suburanus.

exheredata. The suit was a *querela inofficiosi testamenti*, on which see V. I. 3, 9, 10 nn. These usually arose when an emancipated child was disinherited without just cause, and the commonest case was as here, according to Gaius (*Dig.* 5. 2. 4): 'quod plerumque faciunt (*sc.* patres) . . . novercalibus delenimentis . . . corrupti'. Pliny evidently made much of the 'eleven days' to prove his case.

3. sedebant centum et octoginta iudices (tot enim quattuor consiliis colliguntur). This figure excludes the presiding *decemviri stlitibus iudicandis*, v. 9. 2. The passage is the main evidence for the nature of a *iudicium quadruplex*. Such cases were uncommon, I. 18. 3, IV. 24. 1 nn. Ordinarily a single panel of the *centumviri* sufficed, though Quintilian mentions a *iudicium duplex* (*Inst.* 5. 2. 1, 11. 1. 78). It seems from s. 5 that in a fourfold court each panel decided separate issues. The multiple procedure was probably used when more than one person sued more than one party. This would arise mostly in cases of disinheritance, in which there were often several joint heirs, as passages from the *Digest* suggest, s. 5 n. Here the *noverca* is only heiress to the sixth part, s. 6.

colliguntur. This is against the suggestion of Wlassak that the *centumviri* were not a court but a panel from which *iudices* were assigned to particular cases, *RE* iii. 1938.

4. ex superiore basilicae parte qua feminae qua viri . . . imminebant. In the Basilica Julia, where the court sat (v. 9. 1), there was a gallery supported on the double row of columns around the central space, from which Caligula once threw money to the populace, Suet. *Gaius* 37. 1; Ashby, *Top. Dict.* 78 f. Women are unexpected in a place of state business, though they attended theatres.

5. duobus consiliis vicimus totidem victi sumus. Ulpian, speaking of the *querela inofficiosi*, *Dig.* 5. 2. 24, says: 'evenire plerumque adsolet ut in una atque eadem causa diversae sententiae proferantur. quid enim si fratre agente heredes scripti diversi iuris fuerunt?' Another child might be among the defending heirs, and the plaintiff might succeed only against the weakest defendant, as here the stepmother. Cf. the cases cited by Papinian, *Dig.* 5. 2. 15. 2 and Paulus, ibid. 19. But unless the defendant sued all the heirs he could not secure the whole of the share due to him. If successful against all, he received the total due to him by the rules of intestate succession, otherwise only a proportion of this. Cf. v. 1. 9 n.

Wlassak, (loc. cit.), takes these words to mean that the four cases were conducted separately, but at the same time. If so, Pliny can only have spoken before one section, and the words in s. 3, 'sedebant centum et octoginta iudices', are misleading.

6. victus Suburanus qui exheredatus a patre singulari impudentia alieni patris bona vindicabat. The correction by Catanaeus and Budaeus of the manuscript from *Suberinus* to Suburanus is cogent, but the man's exact identity and relationship are uncertain. Most simply he could be the son of the recently deceased consular Suburanus, and so nephew of Attia, and grandson of the old man. In *PIR*[2] he is taken to be the nephew of the latter. Unless he was in the direct descent he could hardly be a bar to the claims of Attia. He appears to be making a rival claim under the *querela inofficiosi*, which was nominally open to all those in the line of the intestate succession (Ulpian, *D.* 5. 2. 6 pref.). In later practice cognates other than brothers were discouraged from suing under the *querela*. But this man cannot be a brother of Attia because their fathers are different; an act of adoption cannot be invoked to remove this difficulty, because the suit would not lie if Suburanus were no longer in law the descendant of the old man, but the adopted son of a stranger. This second 'disinheritance' is incidental to Pliny's case.

9. ut repente in privati iudicii formam centumvirale vertatur. In a *querela* suit the Court had to adjust the will in dispute. Complicated calculations were involved when the will was partly invalid. Ordinarily the issue of invalidity did not involve this kind of redistribution of shares, but would lead to the application of the rules of intestate succession.

34. *To Maximus*

Date depends on book. The admonitory letters to Maximus are confined to VI–IX, cf. VII. 26, VIII. 24.

Address. The present Maximus may be Valerius (?) Maximus of Ep. 8. 4 (n.), identified by his Cisalpine connexions and his meanness, s. 2 n. He is distinct from the elderly scholar Maximus of Ep. 11, VIII. 19, IX. 1. See Ep. 11 pref. For the career of this younger Maximus, and his possible alternative identification with Sextus Quinctilius Valerius Maximus, from Alexandria Troas, see VIII. 24 pref. It is not clear that he as well as his wife hails from Verona (s. 1 n.). Hence a connexion with Martial's Maximus of Verona is not established (1. 7, 7. 73).

1. **recte fecisti quod gladiatorium munus Veronensibus nostris promisisti a quibus olim amaris.** The tone is that of elder to younger man. Cf. the admonitions of Titius Aristo to Pliny, and of Pliny to Rosianus Geminus, V. 3. 1, VII. 1, etc. Maximus shares Pliny's disapproval of games, IX. 6, and has written to defend his *constantia*, s. 2.

Veronensibus nostris. Cf. I. 14. 4 n., 'Brixia ex illa nostra Italia'. Maximus does not necessarily himself come from Verona, but may have been made honorary magistrate or patron there, cf. IV. 1. 4 n.

cuius memoriae aut opus aliquod aut . . . hoc potissimum, quod maxime funeri, debebatur. For the connexion of gladiatorial combats with memorials to the dead cf. the *ludi* given in honour of Sulpicius Rufus, on the proposal of Cicero, *Phil.* 9. 16. Carcopino, *Daily Life*, 208 nn. Fabatus was content to honour his dead son with an *opus*, V. 11. 1–2.

2. **tam liberalis in edendo fuisti.** The Maximus of Ep. 8. 4 is rather close with his money. This may be Pliny's way of encouraging him to be generous, as with Fabatus, V. 11. 1 n.

3. **vellem Africanae quas coemeras plurimas . . . occurrissent.** Pliny may well have picked out this letter for publication because of the parallel with the letters of Cicero and Caelius about beasts for the aedilician games, *ad Fam.* II. 11. 2, VIII. 8. 10, 9. 3. But the reference is too circumstantial to be an absolute invention. It would seem ('tu tamen meruisti' etc.) that the people of Verona had complained of Maximus' meanness in not producing lions.

BOOK VII

1. *To Rosianus Geminus*

Date. The book-date is probable. This is the first of a series in VII–IX of admonitory letters addressed to Geminus, who does not appear earlier. (VII. 24; VIII. 5, 22; IX. 11, 30.) It is connected by subject with two other letters in VII, Epp. 21, 26, in which Pliny discusses his own morbid states. The theme does not recur in the letters.

Address. Pliny recommends Rosianus Geminus to Trajan in X. 26. He had been *quaestor consularis* to Pliny in 100, and seems by *c.* 109 to have held the praetorship and possibly a legionary command (ibid. nn.). His presence at Lugdunum in IX. 11 does not prove that he was then imperial governor of Lugdunensis. He is associated with Ostia, where patronal lists of A.D. 140–50 give his names as T. Prifernius Paetus Rosianus Geminus, and the same for his son, consul in 146 (*FO*). Possibly Pliny's friend was born Sextus Rosius Sexti filius Geminus and adopted by T. Prifernius (Paetus), suffect consul in 96. Two equestrian procurators called Prifernius Paetus are known in the time of Trajan (*ILS* 1350, 8863), of whom one hails from Reate, which was the family home rather than Ostia or Lugdunum, where they are otherwise unknown. It does not seem that Pliny's recommendation helped Geminus immediately; rather late in life he became proconsul of Achaea, consul (*c.* 125) and proconsul of Africa *c.* 142, if he is the Rosianus Geminus of *ILS* 1067, where he appears as the father-in-law of his proconsular legate, the African jurisconsult Pactumeius Clemens. He thus belonged to an active family of municipal Italians connected like Pliny with provincial senators. See *PIR*[1] P 690–2; Syme, *Tac.* 83 n. 5; *Historia*, 1960, 368; Lambrechts, n. 469.

1. terret me . . . tua tam pertinax valetudo. This may be the illness of a friend to which Pliny refers in a rather different strain, in Ep. 26.

vereor tamen ne quid illi etiam in mores tuos liceat. In Ep. 26, Pliny observes 'optimos esse nos dum infirmi sumus'. But there he is thinking of the great human passions. Here he refers to the minor self-control of the sick-room. The two letters are complementary.

4. perustus ardentissima febre. This may refer back to Pliny's serious illness of A.D. 96, X. 5. 1, 8. 3, 11. 1 nn. He does not date the reference closely. But in Ep. 21 he is suffering from an eye infection, possibly after a fever.

utque tangeret. To feel his pulse, as Guillemin.

5. balineo praepararer. In Ep. 26. 2 the sick man's two longings are as here for a bath and a drink: 'balinea imaginatur et fontes'.

7. ut in posterum ipse ad eandem temperantiam adstringerer. This anticipates Ep. 21. 3: 'balineum adsumo quia prodest, vinum quia non nocet', and conversely Ep. 26. 4: 'ut tales esse sani perseveremus quales nos futuros profitemur infirmi'.

2. *To Justus*

Date. The reference to his literary *nugae* in s. 2, which mean his poems, fixes the letter later than IV. 14.

Address. This man may be either Fabius Justus, now a consular, and last addressed in I. 11, or the elderly and less distinguished Minicius Justus mentioned in Ep. 11. 4. No other letter is addressed to the latter, but Ep. 12, addressed to a Minicius, at first sight reads like the continuation of this note, s. 1 n. Syme (*JRS*, 1957, 131 ff.) sees references to the military duties of Fabius Justus, who was later legate of Syria, from 109 on, in the words *occupationibus* and *exercitam*, and conjectures an earlier consular legateship *c.* 106 from Pliny's words. These words equally can refer to private activities, (s. 2. n.). But the balance of probability favours Fabius, who enjoys the advantage of possession, in that he is a known addressee. The 'Minicius' of Ep. 12 is either Minicius Fundanus, or Cornelius Minicianus, ibid. pref.

1. simul et adfirmes te adsiduis occupationibus impediri et scripta nostra desideres. The main reason for connecting this letter with Ep. 12 is that Minicius there too suffers from *occupationes*, and is sent a book by Pliny. But that is an oratorical composition, borrowed for a friend's use not here mentioned, and this is a volume of poems. He calls them *nugis* in s. 2, a word which only recurs in the Letters in his description of his hendecasyllabics in IV. 14. 8. The appeal of a military man for reading matter recurs in the note to Maecilius Nepos, IV. 26, and that to Sabinus, IX. 2, where the word *occupationes* occurs with a military significance, ibid. ss. 1, 4.

2. aestatem inquietam vobis exercitamque transcurrere. The reference fits a soldier better than a landowner, who might indeed be more busy in winter than in summer with his ploughing and sowing. But *exercitam* in Pliny has not a military flavour. Pliny's only other use

of the past participle is in VI. 13. 1, of the accused Varenus, 'laboriosum et exercitum'. He is rather fond of the verb in connexion with
occupationes of all sorts, cf. II. 14. 1, VI. 8. 6, VII. 9. 12, IX. 7. 2 *et al.*

3. *To Bruttius Praesens*

Date. There is no precise indication. But the career of Praesens
suggests a year not earlier than 103–4, s. 2 n.

Address. This man's chequered career has been recently revealed
by an inscription from Mactar in Africa, *AE*, 1950, n. 66. After
serving as military tribune in Domitian's last war C. Bruttius
Praesens L. Fulvius Rusticus advanced to the praetorship, but after
that secured no advancement until he served with distinction as a
legionary legate in Trajan's Parthian campaigns, as is confirmed by
Arrian, *Parthica* fr. 85. He soon returned to Italy to become *curator
viae Latinae*, but was back in Cilicia as an imperial legate before the
death of Trajan. As legate of Cilicia he must have witnessed the
transactions that secured Hadrian's succession. Under Hadrian his
career was accordingly brilliant, though not overcrowded. After
a belated consulship he governed the military provinces of Moesia
and Cappadocia, and, as is revealed by an inscription from Palmyra,
Syria *c.* 136 (*AE*, 1938, 137). Under Pius he held a second consulship,
in 139. His family held many distinctions in the following century,
and his granddaughter became the wife of the emperor Commodus.
He himself was the son of a praetorian senator, now known as
governor of Cyprus from *AE*, 1950, n. 122. *PIR*² B 161–4, now
need corrections. G. Picard, *CRAI*, 1949, 298 ff.; R. Syme, *Historia*,
1960, 374 f.

1. **'ipse enim' inquis, 'Lucanus, uxor Campana'.** An inscription of
Praesens' son from Volcei in Lucania gives the family tribe as Pom-
ptina, appropriate to Lucania. *ILS* 1117. Other family connexions and
possessions are recorded in South Italy at Amiternum, Venusia, and
elsewhere. *CIL* ix. 338, 425 n., 4232.

The testament of his wife is mentioned in an inscription of
Amiternum, *CIL* ix. 4512. Another lady of the family is named in a
document from Capsa in Africa, *CIL* viii. 110.

2. **ubi dignitas honor amicitiae tam superiores quam minores.**
Pliny's chaff exactly fits the indications of the new inscription that
Praesens was a man who cared little for advancement until a lucky
chance in 117 enabled him to reach consular rank unexpectedly and
belatedly, apparently in 124 (Picard, art. cit.). As military tribune
not later than 93 he should have been praetor by about 104. Compare
the careers of Pliny and Calestrius Tiro, Ep. 16 nn. Pliny implies

that Bruttius has completed the *cursus honorum*, and expects nothing more. If he were still seeking the praetorship he would not so neglect the Senate.

amicitiae . . . superiores. Cf. II. 6. 2 n., 'minoribus amicis, nam gradatim amicos habet' The distinction here is of rank, not of wealth as in IX. 30. 1.

quousque calcei nusquam? Pliny makes no reference to the fines by which the *lex Iulia de iure senatorum* sought to enforce the attendance of senators, Gellius, *NA* xiv. 7. 10; *RE* (S) vi. 766 ff. The long absence of Silius Italicus, III. 7. 6, and the excitement when Licinius Nepos fined an absentee, IV. 29. 2 n., suggest that the law was freely neglected.

The senatorial shoe was a high red sandal, distinguished by its lacings (*lora, corrigiae*), and in the case of patricians by an ivory buckle (*lunula*). Mommsen, *DPR* vii. 63 ff., discusses it at length.

toga feriata. Compare Martial, I. 49. 31, 'lunata nusquam pellis et nusquam toga'.

4. *To Pontius Allifanus*

Date. The book-date fits. The publication and circulation of the volume of poems is known from IV. 14, V. 3 and 10. The occasion of this letter is a query of Pontius subsequent to the publication, not a criticism of a copy circulated previously: s. 3, 8 nn. Hence the argument of Peter (art. cit. 703) and Schultz (art. cit. 31–32), revived by Prete (op. cit. 90), that *nunc primum* in s. 3 means that this letter is contemporary with IV. 14, V. 3, will not do, s. 3 n.

Address. For the senator Pontius Allifanus see V. 14 pref.

1. hendecasyllabos meos. See IV. 14 for their first appearance.

2. quattuordecim natus annos Graecam tragoediam scripsi. About A.D. 76, at the age when he was finishing the course with his *grammaticus* and beginning rhetoric, II. 18 nn. Seneca might be his model.

3. e militia rediens in Icaria insula ventis detinerer. For his military tribunate in Syria about A.D. 81 see Ep. 31. 2; also I. 10. 2, III. 11. 5, VIII. 14. 7 nn. As Icaria lies between Delos and Samos he was evidently returning by Corinth. For winds see X. 15 n.

expertus sum me . . . hendecasyllabis nunc primum. It is very forced to take this to mean 'I have just finished my first efforts', as do Peter and the rest. Pliny quite naturally says 'this is my first effort in this line'. Besides, ss. 8–9 make it plain that the book was published and in circulation.

legebantur in Laurentino mihi libri Asini Galli de comparatione

patris et Ciceronis. Gallus seems to have started the reaction against Ciceronian style, which was carried forward by the *Ciceromastix* of Larcius Licinus, II. 14. 9, III. 5. 17 nn. Claudius before he became emperor joined issue with Gallus. Suet. *Claud.* 41. 3: 'composuit . . . Ciceronis defensionem adversus Asini Galli libros'. Gellius, *NA* 17. I, shows the niggling nature of some of the criticisms. Quintilian (*Inst.* 12. I. 22) and Seneca (*Suas.* 6. 15, 27) show that Guillemin is wrong in suggesting, ad loc., that the Asinii criticized Cicero's poetry. The father of Gallus, Asinius Pollio, consul in 42 B.C., a partisan of Antonius, orator and historian, himself disliked Cicero (Sen. *Suas.* loc. cit.). For his career see R. Syme, *Roman Revolution*, Index s.v. His son Gallus held a high but uneasy position under Tiberius, and perished in prison in A.D. 33, Tac. *Ann.* I. 12, 76–77, II. 32–36, VI. 23.

epigramma Ciceronis in Tironem. Quintilian quotes another, *Inst.* 8. 6. 73, and Pliny lists Cicero among the writers of *lusus*, V. 3. 5. But the items and collections variously attributed to Cicero may be pseudepigrapha. *RE* (2), Cicero (Fragmente), vii. 1259, at length. The subject-matter is notably absent from Cicero's letters and essays, though there was no reason for Cicero to hide what Catullus did not blush to publish.

Tironem. Pliny adds nothing to our knowledge of Cicero's secretary.

4. meridie (erat enim aestas) dormiturus. Cf. IX. 40. 2, 'in Laurentino hieme . . . meridianus somnus eximitur'. This too was at the Laurentine villa, s. 3.

6. cum libros Galli legerem. To these verses, and the couplets in Ep. 9, may be added two couplets attributed to Pliny in the Palatine anthology: *PLM*[1], iv. 103; Prete, op. cit. 30. See IV. 18 n.

8. in itinere. Cf. IX. 10. 2, 'in via . . . leviora . . . extendi'. He copied his uncle's habit of working while riding, III. 5. 15.

This visit to the Laurentine villa, distant only a few hours from Rome, cannot be identified. II. 17. 2 n.

9. describitur. 'Copies are being made', IV. 7. 2 n. For publication method see also I. 2. 5–6 nn.

nunc cithara nunc lyra personatur. This means 'in public and at home', the zither being the concert lyre. G. B. Pighi, *Aevum* xix. 116. n. 4.

5. *To Calpurnia*

The letter continues the series of VI. 4 and 7, written to his wife Calpurnia in Campania, where Pliny visited her in the summer holiday recorded in VI. 28 and 30. Guillemin (*VL* 140–1) regards the

letter as a fictitious piece in which Pliny adopts the stock phrases of
the *amator exclusus*. But the tone of the letter does not differ from
that of VI. 1, addressed to the respectable Calestrius Tiro, and VI. 4
and 7, where Pliny is the anxious husband rather than the passionate
lover, and which have a core of circumstantial truth. The three letters
are a valuable document for social history. They blend together, for
the first time in European literature, the role of husband and lover,
and like other letters of Pliny cast a favourable light on the attitude
of his social equals to marriage, cf. I. 14, IV. 19, VI. 24, VIII. 5, 18. 8–9.

6. *To Macrinus*

Date. The letter is later than VI. 13, which it continues. Hence it is of
late 106 or 107.

Address. Probably Caecilius Macrinus, to whom another extortion
letter (III. 4) is addressed, is meant rather than Minicius Macrinus
of Brixia (I. 14. 5). See III. 4 pref. The earlier letters about Varenus
were addressed to Cornelius Ursus. The change of addressee corresponds to a change of subject. Epp. 6 and 10 are about the *voluntas
provinciae*.

1. **adest provinciae legatus, attulit decretum concilii ad Caesarem.** The
provincial emissary leads a second deputation. It is remarkable that
no copy is addressed to the Senate itself. For the increasing tendency
of the local authorities in public provinces to by-pass the Senate see
IV. 22. 1 n. For the part played by the provincial councils in organizing charges of extortion see III. 9. 4 n. The councils were formed of
representatives from each self-governing community of the particular province, but details of organization varied from province to
province. (See A–J ch. xii; *RE* iv, 'Concilium', 803 ff., and S, iv,
'κοινόν', 929 ff. For Bithynia, ibid. 932; Magie, *Roman Rule in
Asia*, ii. 1607 f.) Each part of the double province of Bithynia-
Pontus had a separate council. Pliny's letters show that the councils
provided a focus for the politics of the provinces, cf. III. 9. 31, IV. 9.
3, 5 nn. Evidently there were two factions in the *concilium* on this
occasion. A group favourable to Varenus revised the earlier decision
when his enemies had sailed for Italy on the first embassy. Compare
the disagreement in the Gallic council about a prosecution in A.D.
235, A–J n. 140. 3. Tacitus tells in *Ann.* 15. 20 the story of the Cretan
Timarchus who boasted that he could control the verdict of the
Cretan council on its governors.
    nos. Pliny and Homullus, V. 20, 6.

2. idem ille Magnus. A member of the first embassy, v. 20. 4 n. Nigrinus is the senator Avidius Nigrinus, advocate of the Bithynians, v. 20. 6 n.

per hunc a consulibus postulabat ut Varenus exhibere rationes cogeretur. Cf. II. II. 23, III. 9. 13 nn. This passage shows that the production of account books by the accused was compulsory. So too Cicero had access to the accounts of Verres, *ii in Verr.* i. 36. Magnus assumes the function of the *inquisitor*, like Licinianus in the case of Classicus, III. 9. 29. Nigrinus makes his request either before the tribunal of the consuls, s. 14, as in Ep. 33. 4, or at the preliminary business of the Senate, but not in a *sententia*. For this procedure cf. IX. 13. 7 n., also II. II. 9, V. 4. 2, VI. 5. 2.

3. advocatus a senatu datus. Pliny does not make it clear in v. 20. 2 that he had been officially assigned to Varenus. Accused senators had formerly arranged their own defence. The date and motive of this innovation is obscure. Pliny takes it for granted as the usual thing. Perhaps in the imperial Senate, which lacked the solidarity of the republican House, some senators might find it difficult to secure the best representation, especially as some advocates of Pliny's standing still observed the tradition of giving their services free (v. 13. 8). The concession is in the spirit of that granted to Varenus in v. 20: the two parties must be equal to one another.

5. potest et mihi quod est melius liquere. Guillemin, ad loc., thinks that there is an obscure pun on the formal expression of acquittal 'non liquet'. The editors of the Eight-Book tradition were puzzled and interpolated the text.

6. Polyaenus causas abolitae accusationis exposuit . . . ne cognitioni Caesaris praeiudicium fieret. By withdrawing a prosecution the accuser rendered himself liable to a charge of *destitutio* or *calumnia* in some degree; v. 4. 2 n., VI. 31. 12 n. In s. I Pliny speaks of the prosecution as *temere incohatam*.

The case is referred to the emperor to decide not the issue of extortion, but the question of procedure, as to whether the provincial council could withdraw its charge. This is apparent in s. 14 and in Trajan's remark in Ep. 10. 2: 'erit mihi curae explorare provinciae voluntatem'. If the Senate allowed the case to go forward the decision of the emperor would be forestalled.

Polyaenus may be a connexion of the Claudius Polyaenus who was a big man at Prusa in the time of Claudius, and other notable Polyaeni in Bithynia. x. 70. 2 n., *PIR*[1] P 423.

8. quamquam alia ratio scribendae epistulae fuerit. The apology is due because he breaks the convention that a letter should be about one topic only. Compare the convention against long letters, III. 9. 27 n., Introduction, p. 4.

mater amisso filio . . . libertos eius eosdemque coheredes suos falsi et veneficii reos detulerat ad principem, iudicemque impetraverat Iulium Servianum. There are many points of procedure here and in the following sections. Two distinct capital charges were involved under the *lex Cornelia de sicariis et veneficiis* and the *lex Cornelia de falsis*. Normally these would have gone, after *delatio nominis* before a magistrate, to the appropriate *quaestio* or jury court, according to the rules laid down by the *lex Iulia iudiciorum publicorum*. *Dig.* 48. 2. 3 gives the formula: 'consul et dies. apud illum praetorem vel proconsulem Lucius Titius professus est se Maeviam lege de adulteriis deferre quod dicat . . .'. Why then does this case come before the Princeps in the first instance? Probably because the accuser was a woman. The classical rule was that a woman could not make accusations under the *leges publicae* except in special circumstances. Pomponius in *Dig.* 48. 2. 1: 'non est permissum mulieri publico iudicio quemquam reum facere nisi . . . parentium liberorum . . . mortem exsequatur'. Papinian adds (ibid. 2. 2 pref.) 'idem et in lege Cornelia testamentaria senatus statuit'. Vespasian allowed minors to prosecute in similar circumstances (ibid. 2. 2. 1). The exceptions to the rule were evidently developed gradually, as here, by the action of Princeps or Senate. Hence this woman took her case to the Princeps, who allowed her the privilege.

But a second difficulty arises. Why did the emperor assign a special judge to the case instead of referring it to the proper *quaestio*? In VI. 31. 6 and 8 Pliny makes it plain that Trajan normally avoided encroaching on the jurisdiction of the praetorian courts. It seems that the question before Servianus was still procedural, because ultimately the case is heard by the *quaestio* (s. 9). The clue should lie in the rules that forbade multiple accusations. The *lex Iulia iudiciorum publicorum* laid it down that no one might accuse more than one person at the same time (*Dig.* 48. 2. 12. 2) with the exception 'nisi suarum iniuriarum causa', and there was an undated *SC.* to the effect: 'ne quis ob idem crimen pluribus legibus reus fieret'. Quintilian (3. 10. 1) states that at this period double charges were admitted in the jurisdiction of the Senate and the Princeps but excluded in that of the *quaestiones*: 'quod nunc in publicis iudiciis non accidit quoniam praetor certa lege sortitur'. This rule had been re-affirmed in the time of Titus. Suet. *Tit.* 8. 5: 'vetuit . . . de eadem re pluribus legibus agi'. So the woman was seeking a dispensation from an old and recently reaffirmed principle of the criminal law. Servianus is appointed to decide whether the circumstances alleged justify the dispensation. He appears to have allowed it and sent the case to the *quaestio*. That is the only meaning that the following sentence can bear. (For the procedural rules see Mommsen, *D. Pen. R.* ii. 37 f., 48 f.)

Iulium Servianum. The mention of Servianus and Suburanus together, two great Trajanic figures, shows that these events take place under Trajan rather than under Domitian or Nerva, when these men were not so close to the Princeps. If both judges must be senators, then the trial should fall not before 101, s. 10 n. For the career of Servianus, consul II in 102, see VI. 26 nn., VIII. 23. 5 n.

9. finem cognitioni quaestio imposuit, quae secundum reos dedit. This obscure phrase implies that the *cognitio* of Servianus was followed by a trial before the regular *quaestio*, which dealt conjointly with both charges. Pliny uses *cognitio* freely both in the sense of jurisdiction outside the praetorian system, strictly *cognitio extraordinaria*, e.g. VI. 31. 8, and more loosely for administrative and procedural inquiries, as in s. 6 above and IV. 22. 1, V. 20. 2.

10. adfirmavit se novas probationes invenisse. Renewal of a criminal charge after acquittal must have been very rare. It is explicit in the legal texts from the Gracchan *lex Acilia* (c. 56) down to the late *Sententiae Pauli* (1. 6 b 1) that a man could not be charged again with the same offence after acquittal. Ulpian derives the rule from decisions of Pius, *Dig.* 48. 2. 7. 2–3. The topic is not discussed at length in the *Digest*, though the forms of criminal appeal (*Dig.* 49. 1–12) and the renewal of abandoned charges (ibid. 48. 16. 4–18) and *restitutio damnatorum* (48. 23) are discussed at length in the penal books. Mommsen, *D. Pen. R.* ii. 132 ff. Equally the revocation of a sentence was very rare, and allowed only, after reference to the emperor, in special circumstances, such as the discovery of new evidence: Callistratus, *Dig.* 48. 19. 27. For the origins of appeal in criminal cases and its connexion with the emperor see *RE* ii. 208 ff. But this case has nothing to do with *provocatio*, which concerned only a *reus* in this period. See my *Roman Society and Roman Law*, 68 f.

praeceptum est Suburano. The earlier career of Sextus Attius Suburanus Aemilianus is known from a Syrian inscription, *AE*, 1939, n. 60 (W–C, n. 334). He served after earlier commissions as the *adiutor* of the elder Julius Ursus when prefect of the corn supply and then of Egypt, between 81 and 84, before Ursus became a senator and consul in 84 (Dio 67. 4. 2, *FO*). Later Suburanus was procurator of Judaea and then of Belgica, possibly when Trajan was legate of Upper Germany in 97–98. He emerges as Trajan's first praetorian prefect, being connected with Trajan doubtless through Ursus Servianus, and was promoted to be consul in 101 and *cos*. II in 104, as oue of Trajan's intimate advisers (Dio 68. 16. 1; Victor, *de Caes.*

13. 9; Pliny, *Pan.* 67. 8; *ILS* 5035; *PIR²* A 1366; Pflaum, n. 56). For his family and possibly his father see VI. 33. 2 n.

vacaret. If he is busy with an official post, as Groag thinks (*RE* x. 884), his consulship of 101 rather than his praetorian prefecture is indicated. It is unlikely at this date that an equestrian would be given capital jurisdiction at Rome over persons of substance. But if the point was purely procedural—to see if the new evidence was sufficient to justify a retrial by the *quaestio*—the earlier post is possible. If so, this would, with an anecdote about highwaymen in Seneca (*Clem.* 2. 1), be the earliest evidence for the judicial activity of the praetorian prefects. Otherwise it is first testified, by a single instance, under Commodus. Mommsen, *DPR* v. 256 n. 2, 258 f. Cf. x. 57. 2 n.

11. Iulius Africanus nepos illius oratoris quo audito Passienus Crispus. The elder Africanus, an orator approved by Quintilian (10. 11. 118), was already dead by A.D. 75, the dramatic date of Tacitus' *Dialogus* (14. 4, 15. 3). He was junior to Passienus Crispus, an immensely wealthy orator and politician under Tiberius and Claudius, who was dead by A.D. 48 (Suet. *Nero* 6. 3; *Schol. Iuv.* 4. 81; *PIR¹* P 109). The younger Africanus could well be *iuvenis ingeniosus* in Trajan's early years.

11. adsignatumque tempus implesset. For the division of time between advocates see VI. 2. 5 n.

14. hactenus [non] tacui. All manuscripts have an unwanted negative. Its removal seems necessary to meaning and rhythm alike. For the clausula 'hactenus tacui' compare Ep. 1. 6, 'vultumque composui'. So deletion is better, with Guillemin and O.C.T., following an early correction.

7. *To Pompeius Saturninus*—8. *To Priscus*

Date. Letters 7, 8, and 15 are interconnected by their theme, and linked to the book-date by a reference either to Pliny's *cura Tiberis* or to his legal preoccupations, in Ep. 15. 1 n.

Address. There is no reason to doubt the identification of Saturninus, who is given to *studia* (s. 2) and not obviously a senator, with the orator and author Pompeius Saturninus. See 1. 16 nn. and v. 21 pref. There is no reason to drag in the consular Herennius Saturninus, as does Garzetti, *C.* 63. Pliny's Saturninus never appears to be a senator, but rather an equestrian big-wig concerned with local affairs, Ep. 15. 2.

1. **et proxime Prisco nostro et rursus . . . gratias egi.** It is not easy to identify the Priscus of this series. He may be the literary consular Cornelius Priscus of III. 21 or the legate of II. 13, or a third party, possibly Novius Priscus VI. 8 pref. But he need not be the Priscus of Ep. 19.

2. **te negotiis distineri.** These lawsuits seem to be in the interest of his municipality if they are the 'reipublicae suae negotia' of Ep. 15. 2.

9. *To Pedanius Fuscus*

Date. The letter, like Ep. 24, belongs to the Fuscus–Quadratus series, and hence to the book-date. See VI. 11, 26, 29 prefs. and s. 1 n.

Address. For the distinguished career of the young Pedanius Fuscus Salinator see VI. 26. 1.

1. **quaeris quemadmodum in secessu . . . putem te studere oportere.** Schultz (art. cit. 29–30, 34–35) argued absurdly that as Fuscus is still Pliny's pupil in this letter (as also in VI. 26) it must be earlier than VI. 11, where he appears in this first case. Pliny is not a schoolmaster, but a friend advising his young admirers in the Roman tradition of *praeceptio.* Cf. VI. 23. 2. Like Tacitus he has his 'copia studiosorum quae ad te ex admiratione ingenii tui convenit', IV. 13. 10. Roman orators did not give up 'study' when they had had their first brief, witness Pliny himself, to say nothing of Cicero after his *pro Roscio Amerino.* Fuscus wants advice on how to make good use of his leisure away from Rome, but does not know how to work in isolation. Hence he consults Pliny. Quintilian also advises the trained orator to improve his style by certain exercises, 10. 5, 6.

For the formula 'quaeris quemadmodum' compare IX. 36. 1 and 40. 2.

in secessu. Cf. V. 14. 1, 'secesseram in municipium'.

2. **ex Graeco in Latinum . . . vertere.** Cf. Quintilian 10. 5. 2 on translation from Greek prose into Latin.

6. **nova velut membra peracto corpori intexere.** Cf. II. 5. 11, 'quaedam .. . per partes emendari possint' etc.

7. **scio nunc tibi esse praecipuum studium orandi.** This is as much in favour of a date after as before he savoured the delights of forensic battle.

8. **diligentius scribas.** For the literary letter see I. 1. 1 n.

saepe . . . prope poetica descriptionum necessitas incidit, et pressus sermo purusque ex epistulis petitur. Pliny in his *Pro Patria* speech

made much use of the 'poetic' style, II. 5. 5. For the *purus sermo* of
the epistolary style cf. I. 16. 6, where he is thinking of Terence and
Plautus. Pliny's own descriptions of the Fountain of Clitumnus, the
Vadimonian Lake, and Vesuvius, are poetic enough, but hardly
Terentian. VI. 16, 20; VIII. 8, 20.

9. fas est et carmine remitti. See V. 3 in general. Merrill compares
Cicero's arguments in the *pro Archia*. The reference to Pliny's *lusus*
gives a *terminus post quem* with reference to IV. 14 but, *pace* Schultz,
loc. cit., does not equate the date of this letter with IV.

10. lusus vocantur. For the word see IV. 27. 3, 'interdum versibus
ludo', and V. 3. 4 where he uses *lusus* more widely than Tacitus,
Dial. 10. 4, and Martial 4. 49. 2, who limit the term to *epigrammata*.

11. ut laus est cerae. The simile might be from the casting of bronzes
by the technique of *cire perdu* (L-H, ad loc.). But IV. 7. 1
suggests actual working in wax for permanent use: 'illum cera . . .
illum aere illum argento . . . effingit'. Pliny, *NH* 35. 153 and Juv.
Sat. 7. 238 seem to refer to the same process.

13. recipiunt enim amores odia iras. So too in IV. 14. 3, 27. 1.

16. vel istud ipsum quod coeperas scribis? The obscurity of the reference indicates at once the reviser's hand and the genuine core of a real
correspondence. Introduction, pp. 13 f.

Guillemin calls this letter Pliny's *Institutio oratoria*. With Ep. 4,
IX. 36 and 40, it is among the most autobiographical of Pliny's
Letters. But it is not concerned with the training of a *student*. Saint-
Denis, art. cit. 15 (III. 3. 3–4 n.), citing H. Lion, 'Plinii . . . epistulae
quid ad pueros educandos aptum praebeant' (diss. 1875), noted that
Pliny does not provide the material for a handbook of education.

10. *To Macrinus*

Date. This continues Ep. 6 in late 106 or early 107.

1. acta causa hinc a Polyaeno, inde a Magno. These are the leaders
of the rival Bithynian deputation, v. 20. 4, Ep. 6. 2, 6.

2. erit mihi curae explorare provinciae voluntatem. The question was
procedural, whether the province could be allowed to withdraw its
previous resolution to prosecute. Varenus was not involved at this
inquiry, Ep. 6. 1–6, 13 nn.

3. ne rursus provinciae quod damnasse dicitur placeat. The silence
of VIII and IX suggests that the prosecution was abandoned. The

series of extortion trials closes on a note of restored confidence. The major abuses of power (Priscus, Classicus) fell within the short and weak reign of Nerva. The Bithynian prosecutions were frivolous adventures, largely motivated by personal considerations, cf. IV. 9. 5 and VII. 6. 1 nn.

Only three other high personages are known to have been disgraced in the reign of Trajan. The consular Laberius Maximus, who was involved in political charges, is the only senator known to have suffered the capital punishment of *deportatio*, x. 74. 1 n. C. Calpurnius Crassus, who had made trouble under Nerva, repeated his follies, Dio 68. 3. 2, 16. 2; SHA, *Hadr.* 5. 5. Vibius Maximus, prefect of Egypt, was condemned for maladministration, III. 2 pref., IX. 1 pref. See *CAH* xi. 196, 203 n. 2.

11. *To Calpurnius Fabatus*

Date. The reference to his last visit to Comum, s. 5 n., supports a date in 106–7. The letter may also show the sequel of an event reported in VI. 19, s. 2 n.

Address. For Pliny's grandfather-by-marriage see IV. 1 nn.

1. miraris quod Hermes . . . hereditarios agros, quos ego iusseram proscribi, non exspectata auctione pro meo quincunce . . . Corelliae addixerit. So too in VI. 12. 3–5 Fabatus is free with his advice to Pliny. Here he is protecting the interest of his granddaughter and her future children.

The legal situation is complicated. When there was more than one heir to an estate, as here, if the heirs were not prepared to hold the estate in common, or to divide it by private agreement, it was divided up between them by an arbitrator in a *iudicium familiae erciscundae* (Buckland, *Textbook of Roman Law*, 315; Gaius 2. 219; *Sent. Paul.* 1. 18). Then the heirs may sell their own portions if they choose, cf. s. 7: 'mihi licuit omnino non vendere'. Pliny and his coheirs, however, after the division of the estate, agreed to sell it as a whole. Pliny, mindful of his promise to Corellia, informed her of the coming sale, but his freedman exceeded his instructions and engaged Pliny to sell the land to her, s. 6. Pliny now stands by his freedman's action at the expense of his promise to the coheirs. This was less unfair to them by Roman usage than it sounds to English ears, because Roman law strongly defended the right of partners in a joint enterprise to break up the partnership at short notice (Schulz, *Principles of Roman Law*, 149 f.). Also, the freedman may have been held to be acting as Pliny's legal agent (s. 6 n.). But Pliny defends his action not on legal but moral grounds: 'maiore officio iubente', s. 2.

ex septingentis milibus. The valuation would be that accepted at
the arbitration *familiae erciscundae*. Since Pliny was heir to five
twelfths, the total valuation was between sixteen and seventeen
hundred thousand sesterces. This is about the value of the estate to
which he and Calvisius were joint heirs in v. 7. But the existence of
several coheirs shows that the two are not the same.

adicis hos nongentis milibus posse venire. Ep. 14. 1 shows that the
higher figure comes from the price paid at the auction of the twentieth
part that fell due to the *aerarium militare* under the inheritance
tax: 'ex nongentis quanti a publicanis partem vicesimam emisti'.
The rest of the estate had not yet been sold. The higher price may
be due to the stimulus given to Italian land prices by the recent
enactment of Trajan mentioned in vi. 19. 5–6.

**2. cupio . . . coheredibus meis excusatum esse quod me ab illis . . .
secerno.** Schulz, op. cit. 159, presses this to suggest that coheirs in
general were not expected to sell separately. But Pliny only apologizes because he had made a specific promise s. 7, as Schulz sees,
ibid. 150.

3. Corelliam . . . diligo, . . . ut matri meae familiarissimam. For Pliny's
relationship with this family see I. 12, III. 3, IV. 17. The friendship of
Corellia with Pliny's mother may be through the wife of Corellius,
Hispulla. For the like-named, and probably related, Calpurnia
Hispulla, daughter of Calpurnius Fabatus, was a junior intimate of
Pliny's mother, IV. 19. 7.

4. sunt mihi et cum marito eius, Minicio Iusto, . . . vetera iura. This
ancient veteran was already *praefectus castrorum*, a senior post, in
A.D. 69 when he supported the Flavian cause, Tac. *Hist.* 3. 7. He and
Corellia must now be between 70 and 80 years old, cf. I. 12. 11 n.
He was still alive in 108 at the date of the *Testamentum Dasumianum*,
in which he figures, *FIRA* 3. xlviii. 20. His son is evidently dead.

ludis meis praesederit. The praetors were responsible in the Principate for the organization and ultimately the main cost of *ludi* at
certain major festivals. Little is known about the allocation of
games to individual praetors. This is Pliny's only reference to his
games. It is not clear why he did not preside himself, as was usual.
Possibly he was ill. (Mommsen, *DPR* iii. 271 f.; Dio 54. 2. 4, 17. 4,
61. 31. 7; Tac. *Ann.* 1. 15.)

5. cum proxime istic fui. Pliny's last visit to Comum was mentioned
in v. 14 and vi. 1, probably in the summer of 105. His wife's long
illness and the visit to Campania (vi. 4, 7, 28, 30; Ep. 5) exclude a
second visit to the north in the period covered by vi and vii. The
holiday of vii. 30 fits Tifernum better than Comum.

exceptis maternis paternisque. The last time these were mentioned,
Pliny regarded them as more a source of trouble than profit, but
professed a family devotion to them, II. 15. 2. The suggestion that these
estates are distinct from other paternal estates in the *regio undecima*
or *Transpadana* (VI. 1. 1 n.), and lay in the *decima regio*, is improbable.
The eastern shore of lake Como ('Larium nostrum') was the boundary of the two *regiones*. Cf. R. Thomson, *The Italic Regions*, 136 f.
Pliny *NH* 3. 131. Sirago (*It. agr.* 28) misunderstands the situation:
Comum and the lake lie west of the boundary.

**6. vides quam ratum habere debeam quod libertus meus meis moribus
gessit.** The passage illuminates the development of the legal capability of agents. The lawyers were slow to enlarge the power of the
agent to bind his master. Neratius at this time defended the innovation that a *procurator* could acquire by sale, i.e. buy, for his master,
Dig. 41. 1. 13 and 3. 41. Gaius seems barely to admit the power of the
procurator to alienate (11. 64). Here Fabatus thinks that Pliny is not
bound to confirm the acts of his freedman. Ulpian carefully distinguishes between the properly appointed *procurator* and a mere
messenger, *Dig.* 3. 3. 1. 1. Pliny's man was probably in the latter
category. In classical law a *procurator* gave a bond to the effect that
his master would ratify: 'caveat ratam rem dominum habiturum'.
Fr. Vat. 333, 336. See Buckland, op. cit. 202, 277.

12. *To Minicius* (?)

Date. There is a link through the *libellus* (s. 1) with Ep. 20. If the
recipient is Minicius Fundanus, the date is mid-107. The letter is
not the continuation of Ep. 2, addressed to Justus, because the
books mentioned are different, and the circumstances, s. 1 n.

Address. The manuscripts, which agree, must if correct refer to
Minicius Fundanus, recipient of I. 9, IV. 15, VI. 6 and portrayed in
V. 16. 7–9. He was consul in May–August 107, which fits the book-
date, and Pliny was appropriately absent from Rome in August 107,
if *occupationes* in s. 5 is taken to refer to Fundanus' office (with
Syme, *JRS*, 1957, 131). But his *studia* were in philosophy (IV. 15. 10,
V. 16. 8 n.), not rhetoric, which is never the main feature of the letters
concerning him, and barely mentioned once, in VI. 6. 3. The elderly
Minicii, Macrinus and Justus, of I. 14. 5 and Ep. 11. 4, are not
connected with *studia* or directly addressed in the Letters (Ep. 2
pref.). But a more probable recipient than Fundanus is Cornelius
Minicianus, who alone among the possible recipients is devoted to
oratorical *studia* and receives letters about them: Ep. 22. 2 n., III. 9,

IV. 11, VIII. 12. He too had *occupationes* suitable to s. 5. The textual alteration would be minimal.

1. libellum formatum a me, sicut exegeras, . . . misi. This is the only formal discussion of style between I. 20 and IX. 26, which gives Pliny's opinion of the Atticists at greater length, q.v. Pliny's new book is evidently not the volume of verses sent to Fabius Justus in Ep. 2, but a work of or about rhetoric. It may be the same as he sends to Tacitus in Ep. 20.

quo amicus tuus. No mention of this in Ep. 2. He might be Atilius Crescens, a common friend of Pliny and Fundanus given to rhetorical exercises, I. 9. 8, VI. 8. 6. Or anyone.

2. οἱ εὔζηλοι optima quaeque detrahitis. Quintilian criticizes the affectations of the *cacozeli*, the extreme of contemporary Asianism in oratory (*Inst.* 8. 3. 55–58) distinguished from the opposite pole of the *antiquarii* (Suet. *Aug.* 86. 2). Cf. also Longinus, *de subl.* 3. 3; Pseudo-Demetrius, *de eloc.* 239. For Pliny's own efforts in the restrained style see I. 2. 1–2, 8. 5; II. 5. 5–6, 19. 5–6 nn.

4. ut tibi tumidius videretur quoniam est sonantius. Compare IX. 26. 5: 'visus es . . . adnotasse quaedam ut tumida quae ego sublimia' etc.

5. haec ut inter istas occupationes aliquid aliquando rideres. For the convention compare Ep. 2. 1 n., IV. 26. 2, IX. 2. 1, where the *occupationes* are official. Hence a reference is possible to the consular duties of Minicius Fundanus. In I. 9. 7 Pliny urged him to leave the 'occupations' of private life at Rome. But the phrase could refer more pointedly to the duties of Minicianus as a *rectissimus iudex*, Ep. 22. 2.

6. mihi viaticum reddas. Cf. III. 17. 2 for the phrase. For the use of private messengers see II. 12. 6, VIII. 3. 2.

13. *To Julius Ferox*

There is nothing to be said about this courtesy note, which is presumably addressed to the consular Ti. Julius Ferox, whom Pliny succeeded in the *cura Tiberis*. Cf. II. 11. 5 n.

14. *To Corellia*

For the date, persons, and subject see Ep. 11, which this continues.

1. ex nongentis quanti a publicanis partem vicensimam emisti. Cf. Ep. 11. 1–2. This passage shows that the *publicani* collected the inheritance tax not in cash but in land, which they then sold. The heir could buy it in. Guillemin, ad loc., suggests, reasonably, that it was the twentieth part of Pliny's share that Corellia had bought from the tax farmers, not that fraction of the whole estate.

The passage also shows, with *Pan.* 39. 5, that this tax was still collected by tax-farmers, and that the imperial bureau of *procuratores XX hereditatum* simply supervised the tax-farmers and represented the Treasury in dealing with them. M. Rostovtzeff, 'Geschichte der Staatspacht', *Philologus*, ix. 383 f.

15. *To Pompeius Saturninus*

Date. This continues the series of 7 and 8, and possibly belongs to the period of Pliny's *cura Tiberis*, s. 1 n.

Address. For Pompeius Saturninus see Ep. 7 pref.

1. **distringor officio amicis deservio studeo interdum.** This triple phrase has given a deal of trouble. Schultz (art. cit. 33) and Otto (art. cit. 39), reasonably comparing I. 10. 9, 'distringor officio maximo', and X. 9, 'tam districtum officium', unreasonably referred this *officium*, not to his *cura Tiberis*, which is possible, but to his presidency of the *aerarium Saturni* in 98–100. Unreasonably, because as Otto was fond of insisting in other contexts, Pliny while at the Treasury abandoned his private practice (X. 3A. 1), here implied by *amicis deservio*. The phrase is apparently disjunctive, and can reasonably refer to the *cura Tiberis*. But it is worth noting that throughout VII–IX Pliny complains that his forensic duties interfere with his literary work. This is the most compact of several references, and could be equated with VIII. 9. 1: 'multa me negotia amicorum nec secedere nec studere patiuntur ... ut amicitiae officium deseratur'. Cf. Ep. 5. 1, VIII. 21. 1–3. 1 n., IX. 2. 1, 25. 3 he uses *distringere* of his civil cases.

Pliny very rarely uses *officium* in the singular without a defining adjective, participle, or noun, except in the most abstract sense. Cf. I. 5. 11, 9. 2; III. 5. 9; V. 14. 2; VI. 18. 1, with definition, and I. 17. 1, VII. 23. 2 without. The closest parallel, if the sense is public office, is III. 6. 6, 'si ... officii ratio permiserit', where this meaning is probable in the context. There is a possible second reference to his *cura Tiberis* in this book in Ep. 21. 1, 'collega' n.

2. **rei publicae suae negotia curare et disceptare inter amicos laude dignissimum est.** This seems to refer to the legal suits with which Saturninus was busy in Ep. 7. 2. Saturninus, like Pliny in II. 5. 3, is busy with the defence of his municipality. It has been suggested that Saturninus was one of the new Trajanic *curatores rei publicae*, whose main duty was to supervise municipal finances by exercising

a veto over certain forms of local expenditure. See *CAH* xi. 219 f.,
468 f. But Pliny's phrase is not technical, and men were not, for
obvious reasons, appointed *curatores* of their own municipalities. For
Trajanic examples of *curatores* see *ILS* 5918 A, 6725; Ep. 22. 2 n.
The attribution of this innovation to Nerva, on the strength of *Dig.*
43. 24. 3. 4 is absurd. The Nerva there mentioned is the jurist, not
the emperor.

suae. This is another indication that Pompeius Saturninus did not
come from Comum, I. 8. 2 n.

3. Prisci nostri contubernium. See Epp. 7–8, and for such introductions compare Ep. 31, where Pliny introduces Claudius Pollio to
Cornutus Tertullus.

16. *To Calpurnius Fabatus*

Date. Before April, in the year 107. This is the second of five letters
referring to the proconsulship of Tiro as imminent (VI. 22, Epp. 23,
32) or in course (IX. 5). The series is attached to the book-dates by
the probable dating of the interconnected VI. 10, 22, and 31 to 107
(prefs.). The series fits easily into the sequence of VII–IX. Tiro would
leave Italy in or after April 107, and still be in office in 108, at the
time of IX. 5 (s. 3 n.).
   For the month see s. 3 n.

Address. For Calpurnius Fabatus see IV. 1 pref. and nn.

1. Calestrium Tironem familiarissime diligo. His career is known only
from Pliny (*PIR*² C 222; Garzetti, *C.* 30). He may originate from
Picenum, where he owns land, VI. 1 pref. If he were a Cisalpine Pliny
would probably have written 'Calestrium nostrum' here and
'Calvisium nostrum' in I. 12. 12. He may own land at Ticinum,
s. 3 n. The consul of 122 and possible legate of Lycia should be his
son. *AE*, 1942–3, n. 84; 1958, n. 199.

2. simul militavimus simul quaestores Caesaris fuimus. He served as
military tribune with Pliny in Syria, early in Domitian's reign,
I. 10. 2 n. etc. As *laticlavii* they would be in different legions. This is the
only reference to Pliny's quaestorship outside his inscription, which
reads *quaestor imp.* With II. 9. 1 this shows that both were *candidati
Caesaris* also and elected without contest: 'quam pro me sollicitudinem (sc. petitionis) non adii'. The emperor normally chose his
commendati to be his personal quaestors. Little is known of their
duties except that they read out the emperor's speeches or letters
to the Senate. (Mommsen, *DPR* iv. 227 f., 272 f. Cf. Tac. *Ann.* 16. 27.)

ille me in tribunatu liberorum iure praecessit, ego illum in praetura sum consecutus cum mihi Caesar annum remisisset. The date must be calculated back from Pliny's praetorship. Otto (art. cit. 50) rightly remarks that this passage shows that the two were promoted with the minimum intervals, once their careers had begun. Syme, *Tacitus*, 653, ignores this argument. Hence, if Pliny was praetor in 93 (pp. 763 f.) they were quaestors in 90, and tribunes in 91 and 92 respectively. Pliny evidently enjoyed great favour, as the nephew of Vespasian's trusted friend (III. 5. 9) and supported by other worthies (IV. 24. 5), as he admits in *Pan.* 95. 3. But he did not begin his career at the earliest possible age, being quaestor when he was about 27. For a general characterization of politics at this period of his career see VIII. 14. 7–9.

liberorum iure. Cf. II. 13. 8, X. 2. 1 nn. The *lex Iulia de maritandis ordinibus* allowed a remission of as many years as a man had children in the interval between annual magistracies. Pliny's letter shows that this could be invoked only once for each child, not at each stage. (Mommsen, *DPR* ii. 191 f., 237 f.; *CAH* x. 452; Ulpian, *Dig.* 4. 4. 2; Dio 53. 13. 2; Gellius, *NA* 2. 15. 4.) For the tendency to marry at the right moment for the *cursus*, cf. Ep. 24. 3, 'intra quartum et vicensimum annum maritus et si deus adnuisset pater'.

3. hic nunc pro consule provinciam Baeticam per Ticinum est petiturus. Peter, art. cit. 709, argued that this proconsulship should be nearer Tiro's praetorship than fourteen years. The minimum interval was five years, but there is little regularity in practice. Tiro's frequent illnesses may account for the gap (s. 2). Compare the career of Cornutus Tertullus, v. 14 nn. Mommsen, *DPR* iii. 288 f. By a Claudian rule proconsuls were supposed to leave Italy before mid-April, IV. 26 pref.

per Ticinum. The route by the *Via Aemilia* was much longer than the coastal *Via Aurelia*. Tiro was in no hurry (Ep. 23), and may be visiting an estate, like Pliny in X. 8. 5. The sea-route from a peninsular port was not used, doubtless because of the prevalence of contrary winds in summer. *Geog. Handbook of Italy*, i. 411 and fig. 69.

4. vindicta liberare, quos proxime inter amicos manumisisti. Fabatus had already freed some slaves by the informal, *minus iusta*, method of manumission. This secured for them the intermediate status of *Latini Juniani*, created by the *lex Junia*, and guaranteed them some but not all the rights of full freedmen citizens for their lifetime. It notably excluded the right of testamentary disposition, cf. X. 104–5 n. Fabatus now wishes to promote them to full freedmen status by formal, *iusta*, manumission in the presence of a magistrate. This double process is called *iteratio* by Gaius (*Inst.* I. 35; cf. Ulpian,

Tit. 3. 4). In it the lictor touches the person with his rod, *vindicta*. Gaius regards manumission by a statement among friends as the commonest form of the informal process. Marcian states that a proconsul could only use his *imperium* outside his province for 'iurisdictio non contentiosa', *Dig.* 1. 16. 2. See in general Gaius 1. 17, 22; *CAH* x, ch. xiv; Buckland, *Roman Law of Slavery*, 533 ff., 548 ff.

17. *To Celer*

Date. No precise indication. Peter, art. cit. 709 f., argued that the letter belonged to the period when Pliny first took up recitation, indicated by II. 19 (s. 2 n.). But s. 14 shows that it is now a regular custom with him. In s. 4 he is defending a fashion, not his own first occasion of public recitation. The letter is in its right place in his discussions about recitation, s. 1.

Address. The man may be his friend Caecilius Celer who is connected with advocates, I. 5. 8.

1. sua cuique ratio recitandi. Pliny here elaborates the two reasons already given in v. 3. 7–9 and 12. 1: 'ut sollicitudine intendar' and 'ut admonear'. Earlier he was more conscious of the disadvantages of reciting speeches already delivered in court, II. 19, III. 18, IV. 5. Since then he has combined his persistent passion for revision, I. 2, 8. 3–4; II. 5, with recitation and turned his *auditorium* into an editorial committee. So too with poetry, v. 3, VIII. 21. 4–6.

2. reprehenderent quod orationes omnino recitarem. Pliny first recited speeches in 100 or 101 on the advice of Cerialis, beginning with his *In Marium* and *Panegyricus*, II. 19, III. 18. But previously he had recited some type of composition, II. 10. 7 n. The objection lies in the novelty which Pliny claims to have originated or revived s. 4, 'num ergo culpandus est ille qui coepit?' The numerous recitations by other persons in the Letters are limited to the three categories here cited as acceptable for recitations—history, drama, and poems: history, IV. 7, VIII. 12. 4–5, IX. 27; poetry, I. 13, II. 10. 6, III. 15. 3, IV. 27, V. 17, VI. 15; drama, VI. 21. Only VI. 17 is unspecified. So Pliny's example was not universally popular, despite the vogue for *suasoriae* in the schools of rhetoric. Compare Suet. *Aug.* 89. 3: 'recitantis . . . audiit nec tantum carmina et historias sed et orationes et dialogos'. (Cf. Schuster, *Wiener Studien*, xlvi. 234 f.; Prete, *Saggi*, 69 f.)

9. cum surgis ad agendum. Here Pliny is speaking of speeches in court before the vulgar mob, *pullatos*, not in an auditorium where the reader sat while performing, II. 19. 3.

11. Pomponius Secundus, hic scriptor tragoediarum. For this Claudian figure see III. 5. 3 n., 'Books'.

12. non populum advocare sed certos electosque soleo. Cf. v. 3. 11 n.

13. quod M. Cicero de stilo. Schuster quotes *de Or*. I. 150, 'stilus optimus et praestantissimus dicendi effector ac magister'.

14. non deterreor sermunculis istorum. Pliny is less perturbed than by Aristo's criticism of his recitation of *lyrica*.

18. To Caninius Rufus

Date. There is a possible connexion between the selection of this business letter for inclusion in VII and the appearance of the legends ALIMENTA ITALIAE and RESTITUTIO ITALIAE on coins of Trajan beginning in 107/8 and continuing through to 111/12. There was no mention of the *alimenta* on coins of the period 98–100 when they were first set up. Pliny is drawing attention gently to his part in the imperial scheme by reviving the memory of his own foundation, which, like that of Trajan, was now ten years old. Cf. P. L. Strack, *R. Reichsprägung des II. Jahrh.* i. 188–90; *RIC*, II Trajan., nn. 93, 105, 230 with 459–60, 470–3, 604–5. The first coins of the series are dated by the form of the obverse legend and stylistically.

Address. For this equestrian from Comum see I. 3 pref.

1. numeres reipublicae summam : verendum est ne dilabatur. Fears such as these prompted Trajan to invent the office of *curator rei publicae*, and to send Pliny on his mission to Bithynia. So too Pliny feared that his school benefaction might be ruined by corruption, IV. 13. 6. Cf. the failure of an endowment scheme in x. 70.

2. pro quingentis milibus nummum quae in alimenta ingenuorum ingenuarumque promiseram. The earliest known benefaction of this kind occurs at Atina in the Neronian period (*ILS* 977), where S.400,000 was left to the municipality 'ut liberis eorum ex reditu dum in aetate(m) pervenirent frumentu(m) et postea sesterti(a) singula millia darentur'. But Pliny's scheme, based on a rent-charge, closely resembles the large-scale *alimenta Italiae* established by Nerva and Trajan, best known from the 'alimentary tables' found near Beneventum and at Veleia, and dated between 101 and 104 (*ILS* 6509, 6675). The date of Pliny's scheme is fixed to *c*. 97 by his description in I. 8. 10–11; nothing in this letter suggests that it is a recent endowment. The motive is given by Nerva's exhortation *ad munificentiam*, and the first imperial endowments had been made by Nerva; x. 8. 1. Victor, 12. 4. See in general *CAH* xi. 210 ff.; *Diz*.

Epigrafico, s.v. 'alimenta'; F. de Pachtère, *La table hypothécaire de Veleia*, Paris, 1920; V. Sirago, *Italia agraria*, 276 ff.

At Veleia the boys received S.16 a month, and the girls S. 12, and there were seven boys to each endowed girl. But in the private benefactions known in any detail the numbers of the sexes are equal. All these schemes were limited to the free-born, and aimed at the maintenance of the native Italian stock; 1. 8. 10–11. While the motive is mainly charitable in the private schemes, Trajan evidently had an eye to army recruitment, as the disproportion of the sexes indicates. Trajan's extension of the corn doles at Rome to an extra 5,000 children is described thus in *Pan.* 28. 5–6: 'hi subsidium bellorum . . . publicis sumptibus aluntur . . . ex his castra ex his tribus replebuntur'. Cf. now R. Duncan-Jones, 'Purpose of . . . the *alimenta*', *BSR* 1964, 124 f.

agrum ex meis longe pluris actori publico mancipavi ; eundem vectigali imposito recepi, trecena milia annua daturus. Pliny regains the ownership after a permanent charge has been made on the land. In the state schemes landowners received a non-repayable grant of up to 10 per cent. of the value of their estates. The interest at the rate of 5 per cent. became a permanent charge payable to the local authority. Pliny pays at a higher rate—6 per cent. on the original sum—though still at half the normal rate on ordinary loans, x. 54. 1 n. The *actor* is the agent of the city of Comum.

3. semper dominum a quo exerceatur inveniet. An owner, not a tenant, is meant, cf. s. 4 'pretium'. Pliny envisages the possibility of a sale. Hence the ingenious suggestion of Sirago (op. cit. 291), that Pliny lets the land as *ager vectigalis*, will not do. Such tenancies were often lifelong, and even inheritable, but they were not alienable private property; cf. ibid. 164 f. Besides, Pliny in that case would have given away the capital value of the land, not just the S.500,000 or 'a little more'.

4. me plus aliquanto quam donasse videor erogavisse cum pulcherrimi agri pretium necessitas vectigalis infregerit. Strictly the price ought not to sink by more than the intended value of the gift, unless the average yield on land investment was reckoned to be less than the 6 per cent. charge with which Pliny saddled the land. But the existence of a fixed due which could not be cut in bad seasons (*necessitas*) might well discourage purchasers and diminish the value of the whole.

For a brief discussion of interest rates see Carcopino, *Daily Life*, 66. G. Billeter (*Geschichte des Zinsfusses*, etc., Leipzig, 1898, 182 ff.) assumes that Pliny's 6 per cent. was a normal rate of yield on secure long-term investment at this time, and quotes similar cases from Columella (*RR* 3. 3. 9), who allowed 6 per cent. on the purchase price of a young vineyard in the expectation of higher ultimate yields, and from Pliny, *NH* 14. 56, who called this rate *usura civilis ac modica*. But generally Billeter's evidence points to 5 per cent. as the ordinary rate in the first century A.D. for security of this kind, as in the alimentary loans and in Persius 5. 149–50. So possibly Pliny's capital drop is due to his setting too high an interest rate.

19. *To Priscus*

Date. Later than IV. 21 by some years, ss. 8–9 n. So the book-date fits loosely.

Address. For the difficulty of identifying Pliny's Prisci see Ep. 7. 1 n.

1. angit me Fanniae valetudo. contraxit hanc dum adsidet Iuniae virgini . . . (est enim adfinis), . . . ex auctoritate pontificum.

Fannia was the daughter of the Neronian senator and defender of 'liberty', Thrasea Fannius Paetus, and of the younger Arria, and became the second wife of the elder Helvidius Priscus, champion of 'liberty' under Vespasian; III. 11. 3 n., 16. 2 n. She was married by A.D. 66 and born not later than about 53. Considering the close relationships of this group it is likely that the Vestal Virgin Junia was a sister of the brothers Junius Arulenus Rusticus and Junius Mauricus: I. 5. 2, 10, 14. 1–2 nn. One of these men may have married another daughter of Thrasea or Helvidius at some time—*adfinis*; but Rusticus' surviving wife was Gratilla, III. 11. 3, V. 1. 8. *PIR*² F 118.

The Vestals were under the disciplinary charge of the College of Pontiffs, IV. 11. 6 n.

3. insident febres tussis increscit. Cf. the case of Zosimus, another tubercular patient, V. 19. 7 n. Pliny is accurate in observation as ever; IV. 30 nn.

4. bis maritum secuta in exsilium est, tertio ipsa propter maritum relegata. Helvidius was first condemned when a junior senator for his connexion with Thrasea and relegated in A.D. 66, Tac. *Ann.* 16. 29, 33. He returned after Nero's death, and was praetor in 70. Tac. *Hist* 4. 53. His persistent opposition to the principles of Vespasian's Principate led to his second exile, probably at the time of Vespasian's first expulsion of philosophers, before A.D. 75; III. 11. 3 nn.; Dio 65. 12. 1–3; Suet. *Vesp.* 15. On each occasion the sentence was technically not exile, which means *deportatio in insulam* with loss of all civic status (IV. 11. 3, 13 nn.), but the lesser penalty of *relegatio*; cf. Suet. loc. cit. Pliny uses the incorrect term for stylistic reasons, as in s. 6. Helvidius was put to death while out of Italy, apparently against the wishes of Vespasian, possibly through the excessive zeal of Titus, then praetorian prefect; cf. Suet. loc. cit. and *Titus* 6. 1; Dio 65. 16. 3.

The date of Helvidius' death is not given by Dio. Xiphilinus mentions only the events of his praetorship in 70, in the continuous narrative, ibid. 12. 1, and the rest comes from the Excerptor, ibid. 12. 2. It may have been in connexion with the illegal return of the Cynics in or after 75–76, recorded by Xiphilinus (Dio 65. 15. 5). *Contra* Braithwaite, Suet. *Vesp*. ad loc., who puts the death between 71 and 75.

5. nam cum Senecio reus esset . . . quaerente minaciter Mettio Caro an rogasset, respondit : 'rogavi '. This passage is the sole source for the accusation of Fannia. For Senecio see Ep. 33. 4 n. His trial is known also from Dio 67. 13. 2, Tac. *Agric.* 2, 45, and from I. 5. 3. Dio adds that Senecio had offended by failing to pursue his career beyond the quaestorship. A similar complaint had been made earlier against Thrasea Paetus: 'publica munera ⟨patres⟩ desererent, eorumque exemplo equites Romani ad segnitiam verterentur', Tac. *Ann.* 16. 27. Mettius Carus was the accuser, I. 5. 3. The obscure charge brought by Baebius Massa, after his own condemnation for extortion in 93, had been manœuvred out of court by Pliny, Ep. 33. 7–9 nn.

These events are dated later than August 93 by Tac. *Agric.* 44. 1, 45. 1. See p. 763 and III. 11. 3, Ep. 33. 7 nn.

5. an sciente matre : 'nesciente '. But Arria was relegated with Fannia just the same, IX. 13. 5. For the other victims of this year see III. 11. 3 n.

6. ipsos libros quamquam . . . abolitos senatusconsulto . . . servavit. There was a special measure ordering the destruction of the books, as in the case of Cremutius Cordus, Tac. *Ann.* 4. 35, in addition to that proposing the capital penalty and consequent *publicatio bonorum* for Senecio himself.

metu temporum. Cf. IX. 13. 3 for the phrase. Did Pliny have a hand in the execution? He was in office at the time, III. 11. 2–3 nn. And Tacitus admits, *Agric.* loc. cit.: 'nostrae duxere Helvidium in carcerem manus', where *nostrae* means senatorial. The books were burned by the *tresviri capitales*, ibid. 2.

8. domus ipsa nutare . . . videtur, licet adhuc posteros habeat. In IV. 21. 3 Pliny deplores the death of two daughters of the younger Priscus, leaving infants behind, and the survival of only a single son. These descendants of the elder Priscus stem from his first wife, mother of the younger Helvidius; Fannia had no known children

(IX. 13. 3). Pliny is writing a year or two after the deaths of IV. 21,
or he would have made more of the theme.

9. matrem rursus videor amittere. The date of the death of Arria
is uncertain. She was alive in 97 when she returned with Fannia
from exile, IX. 13. 5. She is not mentioned in III. 16, and may be
already dead then.

10. habuerunt officia mea. Pliny owed a Roman debt of gratitude to
the family group. Arulenus Rusticus had encouraged him as a young
man, I. 14. 1. Cf. II. 18. 5, IV. 24. 5: 'profuerunt nobis bonorum
amicitiae'. But his connexion with the Helvidii is not clear. In IX.
13. 3 he refers to *friendship* with Arria and Fannia, and rather less
with the younger Priscus. Pliny's persistent but improbable claim
to have been under a cloud in 95–96 may well cover the feeling that
he had not been a loyal friend in 93.

   ego solacium relegatarum. Pliny's connexion with Junius Mauricus
in 96 before his recall is established by I. 5. 15–16. In 14 and II. 18
he advises about the children of Arulenus Rusticus. Then in concert
with Arria and Fannia he concocts the attempt to prosecute Publicius Certus, who took sides against the younger Priscus at his trial,
IX. 13.

11. in his eram curis cum scriberem ad te. For the tense cf. VIII. 23. 9.
Both seem examples of the epistolary imperfect, despite Stout (*Cl.
Weekly*, xlii. 139 f.), who thinks that Pliny is commenting on the
completed letter. But that would require a perfect tense. Yet the
tense does not by itself prove that this was written as a genuine letter.

20. *To Cornelius Tacitus*

Date. The chronology of this letter has been much discussed, because
it contains evidence about a book of Tacitus, which is nearly ready
for publication, and which may be either the *Dialogus* or the Histories.
The themes of this letter are continued in VIII. 7, IX. 14 and 23, all
addressed to Tacitus, which in turn have links with other letters in
VII–IX, which effectively date the group to the period *c.* 106–7, ss. 2, 4,
5 nn. Hence Schuster's proposal to attribute this letter (with IX. 10,
also to Tacitus), to *c.* 96–97 is invalid. The book-date should be
retained, as by Wagenvoort who saw that Pliny would gladly have
published the letter-series to Tacitus earlier if it had existed. (M.
Schuster, *Wiener Studien*, xlvi. 234 ff. *Contra*: Prete, *Saggi*, 69 ff.,
H. Wagenvoort, *Mnemosyne*, xlvii. 360, followed by R. T. Bruère,
Cl. Phil. 1954, 166 ff., and Syme, *Tac.* 672.)

Address. For Tacitus see I. 6 pref.

1. librum tuum legi. So too in VIII. 7 Tacitus has sent Pliny a book 'ut discipulo discipulus'. Since Pliny has been sending Tacitus material for his *Histories* in VI. 16, 20 and Ep. 33, at first sight these books would seem to be volumes of the *Histories*, as Schwabe thinks, *RE* iv. 1575. Schuster and Wagenvoort prefer to identify them with the *Dialogus*, because it was the only work of Tacitus, they think, which Pliny was competent to criticize; because only *orationes* were ordinarily circulated instead of recited, according to Ep. 17. 2; and mainly because in IX. 10. 2, another letter to Tacitus, Pliny is supposed to be quoting a passage from the *Dialogus*. None of these grounds hold. Pliny was a critic of history, and was prepared to write it himself, and history was not regarded as very distinct from oratory, I. 16. 4, V. 5, 8, VIII. 12, IX. 27. Pliny and others circulated poetry as well as oratory; IV. 3, 14, 18; VIII. 4. 6. Pliny regularly recited speeches, II. 19, III. 18, V. 12, and others; Ep. 17. 2 gives only a partial opinion on the recitation of speeches. Again, the letter IX. 10, but for which the suggestion about the *Dialogus* would never have been made, does not refer directly to any book of Tacitus, and has no direct links with this present letter. If the present *liber* is the *Dialogus*, then the second book, in VIII. 7, must be a volume of the *Histories*. The circumstances of VIII. 7 show that the two books are different (ibid. n.). It is much more likely that both are volumes of the *Histories*, mentioned to elaborate Pliny's connexion with the historian of whose future fame he is convinced, Ep. 33. 1. Schuster's argument that *liber* must refer to a complete work, as, e.g., in VIII. 21. 4–6, is undermined by IX. 13. 1, 26, where Pliny uses the plural *libri* of his work *De Helvidi Ultione*, called *libelli* in I. 2. 6 and Ep. 30. 5. In IX. 1. 1 the book of Maximus is called *libri in Plantam*.

Pliny's evidence, then, places the publication of the Histories no earlier than 107–8, and cannot be used with any confidence for dating the *Dialogus* (IX. 10 nn.). Syme, *Tacitus* 672, would link the publication of the *Dialogus* with the consulship of Fabius Justus in 102, to whom it was dedicated. Recent comparative studies have suggested that the *Dialogus* is imitated by Pliny in the *Panegyricus*, and hence earlier than its final publication *c.* 102–3 (III. 18 pref.). Cf. *Lustrum*, vi. 298 for a summary.

2. si qua posteris cura nostri. The theme is taken up in the short note to Tacitus, IX. 14.

3. duos homines aetate dignitate propemodum aequales. Tacitus was praetor in 88, Pliny in 93, both as new men. Pliny reached the consulship faster, in 100, than Tacitus in 97. Of the four great priesthoods, Tacitus secured the quindecimvirate during if not before his praetor-

ship, Pliny the augurate after his consulship. Tacitus is likely to
have been five or six years the senior, II. I. 6 n.

4. equidem adulescentulus . . . te sequi. He means, as an advocate.
The theme is taken up in VIII. 7.

    et erant multa clarissima ingenia. Such men as Fabricius Veiento,
Aquilius Regulus, Pompeius Saturninus, and the worthies of Tacitus'
Dialogus. The remark is a little absurd, if the anonymous book was
all about them.

5. una nominamur. This is neatly illustrated by the story in IX. 23.

6. quin etiam in testamentis . . . eadem legata . . . accipimus. In the
will of Dasumius, A.D. 108, they are bracketed precisely thus, *FIRA*
iii, n. 48, l. 17. The social etiquette of the legacy was intensified in
this period of peace and wealth in a high society small enough to
be closely acquainted. *Captatio* is merely the most disagreeable aspect
of this custom, II. 20, V. I, VIII. 18.

21. *To Cornutus Tertullus*

Date. Otto, art. cit. 37, supposed this letter to be out of series because
Pliny calls Tertullus his *collega*, and they were not strictly *collegae*
after their joint tenure of the prefecture of Saturn and their consulship. The term would not be exact for the relationship of the *curator
alvei Tiberis* and the *curator viae Aemiliae*, offices which they may
still be holding at the book-date, v. 14 nn., although the prefects
of Saturn and those of the *aerarium militare* seem to have been
official *collegae*, III. 4. 3 n., and Macer, *D*. 48. 3. 7 uses the term of a
group of governors. But Pliny is not writing officially. He uses the
term out of tenderness (*carissime*) towards the holder of what in v.
14. 2 he called a *par officium*. The letter is a counterpart to Epp. I and
26, and might have been picked out of an old file to point the moral
of Ep. I. 7: 'ut . . . ipse ad eandem temperantiam adstringerer'.
But a contemporary letter would be more apt. The book is very
well supplied with letters about illness without the necessity of a
flash-back, Epp. I, 5, 19, 26.

Address. For Pliny's old friend Cornutus Tertullus, who is addressed
in the Letters only here and in Ep. 31, see II. II. 19 n. and V. 14 nn.

I. carissime. The rare vocative suggests a genuine letter, cf. III. 10. I.
    huc tecto vehiculo . . . perveni. Either the Tuscan or the Laurentine
villa may be meant. Both had baths and *cryptoporticus* (s. 2), II. 17.
11, 16; v. 6. 24, 29. A short journey is implied by the hen, s. 4.

lectionibus difficulter sed abstineo solisque auribus studeo. Private reading is not customary in the Letters, save for exercise, IX. 36. 3; but VI. 20. 5 may be an example. Elsewhere the use of a *lector* is implied. Even the Elder Pliny used a *lector* for serious study, III. 5. 10–11. Cf. Ep. 4. 3, I. 16. 6, III. 1. 4, 8. Pliny takes tablets, not rolls, out hunting. I. 6. 1 n. The phrase *in manus sumere* indicates the awkwardness of reading rolls by oneself (VIII. 3. 3, 9. 1, IX. 22. 2).

3. balneum adsumo quia prodest, vinum quia non nocet. Cf. Ep. I. 4–5, 26. 2.

custos adest. One of his private doctors, cf. VIII. 1. 3.

22. *To Pompeius Falco*

Date. The facts of Falco's career sufficiently fix the date of this note to *c.* 106–7.

Address. For this successful senator, a new man, and an Italian (s. 3 n.), see I. 23 pref. He was tribune probably in 97, and held two army commands under Trajan, the praetorian legateship of Judea, which alone fits this letter, and the consular legateship of Moesia *c.* 116–17. The known *fasti* exclude a consulship between 109 and 113, and his name is now restored in the *Fasti Ostienses* for 108 (p. 736), though there is a vacant place in 107, when his father-in-law Sosius Senecio was *consul bis*. He may have ruled Judaea from 105 to 107, since earlier he was busy in the Dacian war of 101–2 and governed the province of Lycia-Pamphylia.

1. ut in amicum meum conferres tribunatum. Here as in IV. 4 he names the grade required, though Minicius seems to have received a prefecture instead. There was still a certain flexibility in the *militia equestris*, though it was becoming normal for officers to hold all three posts at this period, i.e., two prefectures (*cohortis*, *alae*) and a military tribunate.

2. Cornelius Minicianus ornamentum regionis meae. He is the addressee of III. 9, IV. 11, and VIII. 12. Like Voconius Romanus and Arrianus Maturus he was no chicken when he entered the equestrian service, II. 13. 4, III. 2. 2 nn. From IV. 11. 15 it seems that he was a youth at the time of the Vestal affair, some twenty years ago. His career is known from *ILS* 2722. He hails from Bergomum, where he held municipal offices, as also at Mediolanum, and he was nominated *curator reipublicae* for the Municipium Otesinorum; cf. Ep. 15. 2 n. for this post. He evidently secured from Falco the prefecture of the Palestinian unit *cohors I Damascenorum*, and was later military tribune in the African *legio III Augusta*, and *praefectus fabrorum*

in an unknown province, apparently after his military posts. Up to
the death of Trajan he held no procuratorship: *PIR*² C 1406. For
the Palestinian unit see Cheeseman, *Auxilia*, 162 (under Hadrian).

natus splendide abundat facultatibus. For these qualifications and
for equestrian *splendor* see VI. 33. 2, X. 4. 5 nn.

rectissimus iudex. His interest in political crimes is shown by III.
9 and IV. 11. But here Pliny refers to civil jurisdiction. The merits of
jurors of the large *quaestiones* could hardly be known. Civil judges
were either taken from the *decuriae* or chosen among men of like
standing by consent of the parties. Wenger, *Institutions of Roman
Civil Law Procedure* (New York, 1940), 59 f., 138.

3. cum propius inspexeris hominem. Falco does not know this star of
the north because he himself is not a Cisalpine, though his son's
names show Cisalpine affiliations, *ILS* 1104. The family inscriptions
come from Tarracina, Tibur, and Capua in Italy. *ILS* 1036 was set
up by a client of Falco at Cilician Hierapolis-Castabala.

23. *To Calpurnius Fabatus*

Date. This forms part of the series Epp. 15, 32. Pliny here replies to
Calpurnius' acknowledgement of Ep. 15, the substance of which can
be gathered. These three notes can hardly be other than genuine,
if rewritten, documents.

2. non debet . . . exigere officium quod parenti suo remisisset. The
courtesy was due to the proconsul, not to the man.

24. *To Rosianus Geminus*

Date. The letter belongs to the group in VI–IX about the young men
Ummidius Quadratus and Fuscus Salinator, and also to the group in
VII–IX addressed to Rosianus Geminus, s. 9 n., VII. 1 pref. Hence it is
doubly secured to the book-date.

Address. For Pliny's young senatorial protégé Rosianus Geminus see
VII. 1 pref.

**1. Ummidia Quadratilla paulo minus octogensimo aetatis anno
decessit.** Evidently born about A.D. 26, she is the daughter of C.
Ummidius Durmius Quadratus of Casinum, whose long career
reached from a quaestorship in A.D. 14 to the governorship of Syria,
where he died in office, himself a septuagenarian, in A.D. 60. Cf. Tac.
Ann. 14. 26; *ILS* 972; *PIR*¹ V 606. *RE* (2) 9. 600 f. adds little in
many words.

2. decessit honestissimo testamento. For the phrase see v. 5. 2, and for the theme compare VIII. 18, the counterpart to this letter— 'bad man makes good will'.

nepotem familiarissime diligo. Pliny's friendship for young Ummidius is shown in VI. 11, 29, IX. 13. 1. Little is known of this C. Ummidius Quadratus except that he was consular colleague of Hadrian in 118 at an early age, and that he was high in court society as a member of the faction of Catilius Severus, which provided Hadrian with several ministers, only to fall into disfavour, like Catilius, late in the reign (SHA, *Hadr.* 15. 7; *PIR*¹ V 603). It is possible that his son was the Ummidius Quadratus who married Annia Cornificina, younger sister of the future emperor Marcus Aurelius; this man is called 'the son of Severus' in certain Greek verses found at Ephesus (*PIR*¹ V 601; Hicks, *Greek Inscr. in the Brit. Mus.* iii, p. 189; SHA, *M. Antoninus*, 1. 8, 7. 4). Our man, as grandson of Ummidia was not in the male line, and must have taken the family names by an act of adoption. His natural father may have been a Severus, as in the Greek inscription of the son. This suggests the family of Catilius Severus, with whom he was politically connected. Cf. Syme, *Tac.* 670.

It may be noted that Pliny always uses *nepos* in its strictest sense, so that Ummidius cannot be a grand-nephew in the male line. Cf. I. 14. 2, VI. 26. 3, VIII. 18. 2.

3. intra quartum et vicensimum annum maritus. For the early marriages of *laticlavii* see Ep. 16. 2 n., VI. 26, VIII. 23. 7. He anticipated the *Lex Julia* by two years.

vixit in contubernio aviae delicatae. The tastes of this formidable lady were those of Nero's court: 'noverat *illa* luxuriam imperii veterem noctesque Neronis'. Pliny's comments reflect the change of tone that was spreading through senatorial society during the Flavian period, as the Julio-Claudian nobility was steadily being replaced by straight-laced types 'remotis e municipiis severaque adhuc et antiqui moris retinente Italia'; Tac. *Ann.* 3. 55, 16. 5. The same attitude is apparent throughout Tacitus, and especially in the overtones of his study of Nero.

delicatae. The connotation varies from the wanton, as in Suet. *Vesp.* 3 'uxorem . . . Statili Capellae . . . delicatam olim', to the merely idle and luxurious, as in IX. 32: 'scribere . . . nolim . . . tamquam delicatus'; cf. Suet. *Cal.* 43, 'segniter delicateque'. Pliny implies only that Quadratilla enjoyed all the luxurious frivolities of the age, s. 5 n.

4. habebat pantomimos . . . effusius quam principi feminae convenit. Contrast Titus, playing Henry the Fifth to his Falstaffs, Suet. *Tit.* 7. 2: 'quosdam e gratissimis delicatorum . . . artifices saltationis

. . . non modo fovere prolixius sed spectare omnino in publico coetu supersedit'. Pliny disapproves of the pantomime in *Pan.* 46. 4: 'effeminatas artes et indecora saeculo studia'. In IX. 6. 3 he is shocked at *graves homines* who attend the races. Tacitus similarly quotes with approval regulations of Tiberius designed to prevent senators from associating publicly with actors, *Ann.* I. 77.

The Roman pantomime drama of the Principate was a combination of tragedy, opera, and ballet, in which the leading part was played by the *pantomimus*. This was a highly trained actor who united the social and dramatic role and temperament of a modern prima donna and prima ballerina, and was supported by chorus, *corps de ballet*, and orchestra. Pliny here used *pantomimi* in the plural for the whole troupe. See in general Carcopino, *Daily Life*, 223 ff.; M. Bieber, *History of the Greek and Roman Theatre*,[2] 165 f., 232 ff. A member of Quadratilla's troupe may be recorded in an inscription from Puteoli, *ILS* 5183; ibid. 5628, from Casinum, shows that her enthusiasm led her to build an amphitheatre there.

5. cum mihi commendaret nepotis sui studia. Pliny was specially invited to supervise the young man's introduction to the law and the law courts, as the leading advocate of the day. He does not seem to have been a family friend (s. 2, 'neptem parum novi'). Possibly his friend Catilius Severus made the arrangement. (I. 22 pref.).

in illo otio sexus. Carcopino, op. cit. 90 ff., 181 ff., remarks that the women of wealth were usually quite unoccupied. They could not enter public life, and the extreme organization of servile labour deprived them of domestic occupation.

lusu calculorum. For the ancient forms of draughts, chess, and backgammon, see Carcopino, op. cit. 252; D–S ii. 414 f., iii. 992 f.; *RE* xii. 980 f. If by *calculi* he means the last-named, then Ummidia preferred the least intellectual of the three.

semper se nepoti suo praecepisse abiret. Guillemin, taking too seriously Juvenal 6. 60 f. on wanton women and actors, absurdly suggested that Ummidia did not want Quadratus to witness her amours. Even when playing backgammon? The new puritanism spread its net wide. Earlier legislation against gambling in public was maintained and extended by the Principate. Carcopino, op. cit. 250 f.; *Dig.* II. 5; Juv. I. 88 f.

6. proximis sacerdotalibus ludis. Cf. Ep. II. 4, IX. 6. The phrase is too loose for exact dating. 'Games' meant either races, or gladiators, or as here, dramatic shows. The season of *ludi* ran from April to November, and by this time covered some 150 days. Cf. Carcopino, op. cit. 203 ff.

productis in commissione pantomimis. Quadratilla had not hired them out, as Merrill suggested, but entered them for a competition, at some occasion like the *Quinquatria*, organized on the lines of a Greek festival. The term *commissio* is used in a similar context in Suet. *Aug.* 89. 3. The abolition of public performances of pantomimes by Domitian, reimposed by Trajan, cannot have lasted long, *Pan.* 46. 1–3.

7. per adulationis officium in theatrum cursitabant. Merrill compared the claqueurs described in II. 14. 4–13, who were actually hired. These too are 'auditores actoribus similes', and so deserve a *corollarium*.

8. domus aliquando C. Cassi, huius qui Cassianae scholae princeps et parens fuit, serviet domino non minori. C. Cassius Longinus, consular and jurisprudent, governed Syria as legate in A.D. 49–51, and was exiled by Nero in 65. He returned to Rome in 69. (Tac. *Ann.* 12. 11–12, 16. 7–9; *PIR²* C 501; Kunkel, *Herkunft der . . . röm. Juristen*, 130 f.) His severity is illustrated in Tac. *Ann.* 13. 48, 14. 43–45.

There were two 'schools' of law in the early Principate, the Proculian and the Cassian. Their foundation is carried back by Pomponius two generations further, through the Tiberian lawyers Nerva and Masurius Sabinus, to the Augustan rivals Antistius Labeo and Ateius Capito; *Dig.* 1. 2. 2 (47–53), cf. Tac. *Ann.* 3. 75. F. Schulz (*History of Roman Legal Science*, Oxford 1946, 120) asserted that the tradition of Pomponius is a false reconstruction, and that Pliny's words show that the Cassian school had no existence until Cassius gathered the pupils of Masurius around himself. This puts too much weight on Pliny's words. He does not say that Cassius founded the school, but that he was its head and protector, as the emperor was of the State. Pliny does not mention the predecessors of Cassius because the context did not require it. He is merely seeking to compliment young Quadratus. He is certainly not quoting a tradition learned in his boyhood before the death of Cassius. He is unlikely to be an accurate source for the history of Roman law, with which he was not always in sympathy, cf. v. 7. 2 n. A. M. Honoré, *Gaius* (Oxford, 1962), 18 f., indicates the continuity of Cassius and Proculus with their predecessors, and argues that organized teaching began only with Cassius and Proculus. It is often stated that the Cassian school was more rigid in its application of rules than the Proculian. Schulz (op. cit. 122) denies that there was any fundamental distinction of method or principle between these or any Roman jurisprudents of this or the later 'classical' period. Honoré (op. cit. 36 f.) maintains that the Proculians gave more weight to equity and less to pure reason as a ground of decision than did the

Cassians or Sabinians, who were 'conservative, rational, republican', and attached to principles and institutions more than were their rivals. But the opinions of the pre-classical lawyers are mostly known in short citations that are hard to judge as a whole. Certainly in the debate about slaves recorded in Tac. *Ann.* 14. 43–45 Cassius did not tend to leniency. In 13. 48 his severity as an arbitrator was too much for the contestants. In Pliny's time the jurists Javolenus Priscus represented the Cassians, and Neratius Priscus and his friend Titius Aristo the Proculians, I. 22 nn., VI. 15. 2–3 n.

scholae. Very little is known about the organization, if any, of these 'schools'. They were probably very similar to the schools of rhetoric in their arrangements; II. 18. 1–2 nn.

9. implebit enim illam Quadratus meus et decebit. The reading of the last word is not in doubt. Both α and β give it, against γ. For the personal usage cf. VIII. 6. 3, 22. 1: 'eos . . . lenitas deceat'.

cum tantus orator inde procedet. This should date the letter after VI. 11, where Quadratus makes his first bow in the courts.

25. *To Rufus*

Date. This is the first of three letters involving Terentius Junior, cf. VIII. 15, IX. 12. He is evidently a new acquaintance, whom Pliny may have visited at Perugia on the Tuscan visit of Ep. 30. 2–3. Hence the book-date is secure.

Address. This should be Caninius Rufus, or Octavius Rufus, both men of letters (I. 3, 7 prefs.), since Pliny never writes to Calvisius Rufus, II. 20 pref., or Sempronius Rufus, IV. 22 pref., on literary themes.

2. Terentius Iunior . . . procuratione . . . functus . . . paratis . . . honoribus . . . otium praetulit. This man is probably C. Terentius Junior, known as a landowner of Perugia from *ILS* 6120. He can be added to the list of gentry who in the Flavian period preferred equestrian *quies* to the senatorial *pericula*, cf. I. 14. 5, III. 2. 4 nn. His was the more unusual case of a man offered promotion to the Senate in mid-career, like Attius Suburanus, Ep. 6. 10 n. His young son, IX. 12. 2, might be the suffect consul of A.D. 146 (*FO*), though the praenomen is different. The senatorial promotion of Junior after a single procuratorship is surprising; but he may be connected to the consular Terentii of Pliny's time through the senator L. Terentius Homullus Junior, *CIL* ii. 5084; *PIR*[1] T 57–58; Garzetti *Inc.* 138. The Flavian procurator of Bithynia, Terentius Maximus, may be his brother, X. 58. 5 n.

3. ille me doctissimo sermone revocavit ad studia. In VIII. 15 Pliny sends him books, and in IX. 12 a gentle letter of admonition. Pliny expresses less surprise at the tastes of his other literary procurator, Claudius Pollio, Ep. 29. 5. It was not his profession but his retirement to the country that led Pliny astray. The combination recalls the ex-procurator of the Graian Alps who composed the charming iambics to Silvanus found at Aîme, *ILS* 3528.

6. cultu pagano. See X. 86B. 2 for the contrast *paganus–miles*.

26. To Maximus

Date. The discussion of illness links this with Ep. 1 and Ep. 21. (s. 1 n.).

Address. This should be the 'younger' (Valerius) Maximus, rather than the scholar Maximus, because of the admonitory tone, VI. 34 pref.

1. nuper me cuiusdam amici languor admonuit. Possibly this friend is Geminus, sick in Ep. 1, if it is not himself, ill in Ep. 21. The treatment of the theme is different. In Ep. 1 the sick man is advised against intemperance in small things. Here he is described as free from the great passions.

2. ne sermonibus quidem malignis . . . attendit. Pliny blames gossip in I. 9. 5, VIII. 22. 4. For its prevalence cf. Ep. 33. 8, VIII. 18. 3.
    balinea imaginatur et fontes. Cf. Ep. 1. 4–5, 21. 3.

4. tibi mihique praecipere. Cf. VIII. 24. 1 for the qualified *praeceptio*.

27. To Licinius Sura

Date. The letter is probably after the end of Pliny's *cura Tiberis*, and at least after the end of the first Dacian War, in which Licinius Sura was on Trajan's staff, since both men now enjoy leisure, ss. 1, 15.

Address. For the career, erudition, and curiosity of Trajan's right-hand man Sura see IV. 30 nn.

1. esse phantasmata et habere propriam figuram numenque . . . putes. A material explanation of dreams and visions was given by Democritus of Abdera, who regarded them as physical emanations or εἴδωλα that penetrated the pores of the dreamer; Diels, *Fragm. der Vorsokratiker*, ii Dem. 166. Lucretius elaborated a similar 'atomic' explanation in his doctrine of *rerum simulacra*, 4. 45 ff., 84 ff., 721 ff. A similar view recurs in Plutarch, *Brutus*, 37. Pliny's alternative to this is the physiological and psychological explanation of Aristotle,

who attributed dreams to the physical or mental state of the patient.
See E. R. Dodds, *The Greeks and the Irrational*, 117 ff.; Aristotle
Div. p. somn. 463ᵃ ff.

2. quod audio accidisse Curtio Rufo. The best commentary on this
letter is provided by the collection of ghost and bogy stories in
Lucian's *Philopseudes*. The feebleness of many ancient ghost stories,
judged by modern standards, may be due in part to the material
factor of the classical environment. The relatively small size, and the
compact building, of houses even of the wealthy classes, and the
preponderance of urban life, did not allow the free development of the
'haunted house' and 'lonely castle' themes dear to the ghostly
literature of the nineteenth century.

The story of Curtius Rufus is told with minor variations by
Tacitus, *Ann.* 11. 21.

tenuis adhuc et obscurus. He made his way at first *acri ingenio*,
then attracted the attention of the emperor Tiberius, was given the
praetorship by commendation, and was later consular legate of
Lower Germany *c.* A.D. 47. But the date of his consulship and
proconsulship of Africa are unknown. Tacitus, loc. cit., and *PIR*²
C 1618.

comes. Tacitus calls him *sector quaestorius*, which is probable,
since he was not yet a senator. He places the incident at Hadrumetum.

inclinato die spatiabatur in porticu. The time is just after midday,
as Tacitus confirms. The hour, when the streets were empty and
everyone at siesta, is suitable for a Mediterranean ghost story,
cf. v. 6. 31. Merrill notes three midday visions in Lucian, op. cit. 22,
and *Acts of the Apostles*, 10. 9 f., 22. 6.

Africam se futurorum praenuntiam dixit. The 'genius Africae' is
not testified, but elsewhere *genius provinciae* occurs, *CIL* iii. 10396;
RE vii. 1168. Or else the popular Romano-African version of the
Phoenician Tanit or *dea caelestis* is meant. (Toutain, *Cités romaines
de la Tunisie*, 214 f.)

5. erat Athenis spatiosa et capax domus. Lucian tells a similar story
about a Pythagorean philosopher Arignotus and a house at Corinth,
in a more extravagant vein. Pliny, unlike Lucian, suspends disbelief.
Other stories of *revenants* are listed by M. P. Nilsson, *Greek Religion*
(Oxford, 1925), 100.

6. mors sequebatur. Lucian kills them off the morning after the vision.

7. philosophus Athenodorus. This may be intended for the well-
known late Republican Stoic teacher from Tarsus, and friend of
Augustus, though he is not otherwise connected with Athens, *PIR*²
A 1288.

iubet sterni sibi in prima domus parte. The house is, as it should be, on the Greek plan, with θάλαμος on the front court, separated by the passage or μέταυλος from the servants' quarters and inner court or garden (Merrill).

9. stabat innuebatque digito similis vocanti. Lucian obscures the point with mumbo-jumbo. The ghost assumes Protean shapes, and Arignotus masters it by Egyptian spells. Pliny's independent version would not disgrace the annals of a psychic research bureau.

11. adit magistratus. Not, as in Lucian, the owner of the house. Pliny gets this point right. The burial of an unknown man could only be done by the representative of the community, who would also be concerned at the improper burial of a corpse within the city precinct or its removal. Cf. *lex coloniae Ursonensis* (A–J, n. 26) 73; x. 68 nn.

12. illud affirmare aliis possum. Pliny observes the *lex scholastica* which required three examples to illustrate a point, II. 20. 9 n.

14. nihil notabile secutum nisi forte quod non fui reus. Pliny believed in dreams at least, cf. I. 18. 2, v. 5. 5–6, and he had investigated the evidence of these visions to his own satisfaction. The portents affected his own self because the boys were his own property. So Aelius Aristides adopted the dream of his valet, when seeking treatment in the temple of Aesculapius at Pergamum, in an anecdote quoted by Dodds, op. cit. 109. Aristides *Or.* 48. 9, II. 396. 24 (ed. Keil).

in scrinio eius datus a Caro de me libellus inventus est. Pliny claims to have braved the wrath of Baebius Massa in defence of Senecio, and to have befriended Artemidorus the philosopher at a dangerous moment, under Domitian; Ep. 33. 7–9, III. 11. 2–3, IV. 24. 4–5. That friendship might have given ground for attack, but Domitian knew young Pliny too well to bother. For a possible explanation of these curious claims of Pliny to a near miss of martyrdom see Ep. 19. 10 n. Pliny was in favour with Domitian until the end, despite his claim in *Pan.* 95. 3–4, whatever view is taken of the dates of his praetorship and prefecture of the military treasury, pp. 763 f. Syme notes that at this time Pliny's friend Capito was Domitian's secretary, but *ab epistulis* not *a libellis, Tac.* 82, n. 3. Cf. I. 17. 1. For Mettius Carus the *delator* see I. 5. 3 n., Ep. 19. 5.

28. *To Septicius Clarus*

Date not determinable. The equestrian Septicius Clarus, to whom I. 1 is dedicated, has not appeared since I. 15, and reappears again only as the recipient of VIII. 1. For his career see II. 9. 4 n.

1. **ais quosdam apud te reprehendisse.** For this formula in similar replies to *admonitio* see V. 3. 1 and Ep. 17. 1–2, also letters addressed to *amici pares* or *superiores*.

tamquam amicos meos . . . ultra modum laudem. Cf. VI. 17. 4, VIII. 24. 10 for Pliny's justification (Merrill, ad loc.), but in I. 14. 10 he guards against it. Guillemin (ad loc.) finds a model for this note in Horace, *Serm.* I. 3. 41–42.

There is no reason to assume that the criticism was of the content of earlier volumes of the letters, rather than of his actual habits, as in V. 3 and Ep. 17. Hence there is no argument here for the separate publication of previous volumes of the letters, as was suggested by Schultz, art. cit. 3, and Otto, art. cit. 27 f.; *contra*, Prete, op. cit. 84 f.

29. *To Montanus*

Date. The note may be linked by its theme, the abuse of powerful imperial freedmen, with VI. 31. 9–11, where Trajan publicly proclaims his aversion from such creatures. It is continued at great length in VIII. 6, but there is no other evidence of precise date.

Address. Both letters about Pallas are addressed to Montanus, who cannot be the rascally Montanus or Montanius Atticinus of VI. 22. 2. No other senator of this name—if the man is a senator, as VIII. 6. 17 implies—seems to be known in this period, save the consul of 81, T. Junius Montanus, and Juvenal's yet elder man, 4. 107, 130.

2. **monimentum Pallantis ita inscriptum.** M. Antonius Pallas, freedman of the mother of the emperor Claudius, Antonia the Younger, and *a rationibus* to Claudius, retired in A.D. 55 and died seven years later, Tac. *Ann.* 13. 14, 14. 65. The sepuchral inscription of a like-named man found in this zone may belong to a later age, *CIL* vi. 11965. *PIR²* A 858.

Tombs were usually set outside the city gates along the roads, as at Rome and Pompeii. Burial within cities was forbidden, cf. Ep. 27. 11 n. The date of this journey is uncertain. He would not pass this way to Tuscany or Campania or Comum or Ostia.

huic senatus ob fidem pietatemque erga patronos ornamenta praetoria decrevit. According to Tac. *Ann.* 12. 53 the occasion was oddly insignificant, the drafting by Pallas of a *SC.* about relations between free women and slaves. But the full text in VIII. 6, and the rider of Scipio given by Tacitus, show that this was a general reward for the public services of Pallas: 'quod . . . se . . . inter ministros principis haberi sineret'. The main decree was proposed by the notable Stoic, Barea Soranus, consul designate, at the instigation of the empress

Agrippina according to Pliny *NH* 35. 201, the date being 23 January 52. A subsequent decree ordered the first to be set up in a public place, VIII. 6. 13 n. The day was the eve of Claudius' *dies imperii*, and possibly the decrees marked Pallas' completion of ten years of service. Tacitus uses much the same words to summarize the decree as are in the inscription.

honore contentus. So too Tacitus: 'contentum honore Pallantem intra priorem paupertatem subsistere'. He was worth some 400 millions at the time of his death, according to Dio 62. 14. 3. The phrase is modelled on the epigraphical formula used for the presentation of statues: 'honore contentus impensam remisit'.

3. quam essent mimica et inepta quae interdum in hoc caenum, in has sordes abicerentur, quae denique ille furcifer et recipere ausus est et recusare. Pliny's indignation, here and in VIII. 6, is shared by Tacitus and his uncle. None of them seem to perceive, except perhaps Pliny in VIII. 6. 3, that there was a satirical twist to these wordy resolutions. Cf. the words of Scipio in Tacitus: 'quod regibus Arcadiae ortus veterrimam nobilitatem usui publico postponeret'. Pliny suspects *urbanitas*—'si senatum deceret urbanitas'. His generation of senators, drawn from a less exalted level of society than the Julio-Claudian aristocracy, was more afraid of the competition of the freedman element, whose descendants were now rising to high position in the senatorial and equestrian orders, III. 14. 1 n. This development was barely perceptible to an earlier generation. Pliny's violent language, exceeding even his abuse of Regulus, recalls Juvenal's outburst against the Greek element at Rome, largely of freedman origin, 3. 60 ff.

30. *To Julius Genitor*

Date. This letter can be dated to the late summer of 107 with great probability on the evidence of Pliny's journey to his estates and the *locatio praediorum* in s. 3. The reference to Pliny's speech *De Helvidi Ultione* provides a link with the contemporary letter to Quadratus, IX. 13. 1. The date proposed by Zaranka *c.* 98–100 (cf. *Lustrum*, 1961, 285–6) overlooks the fact that Pliny had not made the acquaintance of Genitor at the period of the publication of this speech, s. 5 n.

Address. For this professional *rhetor Latinus* see III. 3. 5. Pliny did not know of him at the date of II. 18.

3. accedunt querelae rusticorum qui auribus meis post longum tempus suo iure abutuntur. instat et necessitas agrorum locandorum. In IX. 37. 1–3, dated precisely to July–August 107, Pliny is occupied with a similar difficult *locatio* and troublesome tenants. Since the cycle of

lettings was normally for five years, it is likely that the two letters
refer to the same occasion. The estate may be identified with that of
Tifernum. His last recorded visit was that of v. 6. 1, 14, 18. 2. In
VI visits are recorded only to the north, to Campania and to Alsium,
VI. 1, 4. 10, 24, 28, 30. In VII. 11. 5 he has been to Comum and in
Ep. 25 to Perugia. Then in VIII (1, 8, 20) he is in Tuscany and in IX
visits Tifernum where he complains of the *querelae rusticorum* keeping
him from his books just as here (15. 1, 20. 2 n., 36. 6). There is no
specific reference in VIII or IX to any visit to Comum (cf. IX. 7 pref.).
So the *longum tempus* may well be the interval between a visit in
105 summer and 107 summer, and the present visit be identified
with the Etruscan holiday of VIII and IX.

locandorum. See X. 8. 5, IX. 37 nn. for the *locatio* of 98–99 and
that of 107. Evidently Pliny let his farms on a schedule of four or
five years, five being the normal period in Italy, IX. 37. 2 n.

conductores. For the normal system of cash rents see III. 19. 6–7
nn., and for Pliny's adoption of rents in kind, IX. 37 nn.

5. libellos meos de ultione Helvidi. In IX. 13. 1 Pliny's young admirer
Quadratus has just been reading the *De Ultione*. Probably he studied
with Genitor, like young Corellius (III. 3), on the advice of Pliny,
though by now it would be as *contubernalis*. It is not odd that Genitor
should not have discussed the *De Ultione* earlier, since he was not an
acquaintance of Pliny at the time of its composition and publication;
cf. I. 2. 6, 18. 1–2 nn., III. 3. 5 n.

non ut aemularer. For another attempt to imitate Demosthenes
about the same date see I. 2. 2–3 n.

31. *To Cornutus Tertullus*

Date. At least post-Nervan, and later also than his consulship, ss.
1, 3 nn.; otherwise no clear evidence. Peter's argument (art. cit. 709)
that it was written while Nerva was alive, because the career of
Pollio is given only down to Nerva, is due to a careless reading of
ss. 3–4, as Otto saw (art. cit. 30). Zaranka has dated it *c.* 98–100
(*Lustrum*, vi. 286). But the reference to Nerva as *imperator* and to
Corellius as *noster* does not prove that they were still living at the
composition date (ss. 3–4 nn.). Since Pliny and Tertullus were
confined to Rome as colleagues, except for rare and short leaves of
absence, from January 98 to October 100, the letter must be at least
post-100. At the book-date Tertullus' duties as *curator Aemiliae*
would take him out of Rome, and Pliny was free to take long holidays
after the termination of his *cura Tiberis*, v. 14. 1, 9 nn. The letter
thus fits the book-date, and not the period 98–100.

1. **Claudius Pollio amari a te cupit.** An inscription from Rome (*ILS* 1418) gives his name and career as: 'Ti. Claudius Pollio proc. Aug. XX hereditatium, proc. Alpium Graiarum, flamen Carmentalis, praef. gentium in Africa, (pr)aef. alae Flaviae milliari(ae)'. This confirms Pliny, ss. 2–3, but gives no date. His career was evidently completed under Domitian, s. 3, 'postea promotus ad amplissimas procurationes . . . otium *nunc* patitur. quod quidem paulisper . . . intermisit' etc. A senatorial relation, probably a son, of this man is named among the Arval brothers under Hadrian and Pius, *AE*, 1947, n. 59; Pflaum, n. 54.

By *amari* Pliny means that Pollio wants to be admitted to friendship as an *amicus familiarior*. Compare the introduction of Priscus and Saturninus in Epp. 7, 8, 15.

vir alioqui rectus, integer, quietus. He is another of the political neutrals, cf. I. 14. 5 n., Ep. 25. 2. Hence Pliny amplifies below: 'numquam secundis rebus intumuit'. Though promoted by Domitian he did not trouble the *boni*.

2. **hunc cum simul militaremus . . . praeerat alae miliariae.** They served together in Syria, about A.D. 81; Ep. 16. 2 n. His military career was unusual in that he held neither a *praefectura cohortis* nor a military tribunate, one of which was commonly held before the *praefectura alae* in the Flavian period (III. 2 pref.). Instead he held a semi-military post as district officer in Africa, which probably involved the command of one or more cohorts, as in the case of Calpurnius Fabatus, IV. 1 pref. But the sole command of an *ala* occurs in other careers of this period, e.g. *ILS* 1392; Pflaum, loc. cit., p. 124 n. 4, and n. 56, Attius Suburanus.

ego iussus . . . rationes alarum et cohortium excutere . . . magnam quorundam . . . avaritiam . . . inveni. In VIII. 14. 7 he speaks of this experience: 'fuimus quidem in castris, sed cum suspecta virtus . . . nusquam imperium nusquam obsequium, omnia soluta, turbata'. Domitian, it seems, had good cause to suspect the virtue of his Syrian officers, if not that of the legate. Pliny evidently specialized in accountancy from the beginning of his career, and hence naturally proceeded later to the prefectures of the two Treasuries, and to his special mission in Bithynia. His tribunate was the usual, so-called *tribunatus semestris*, held by young men without military ambitions and served at headquarters, IV. 4. 2 n.

alarum et cohortium. The *auxilia*, self-contained and independent units, commonly formed half the armed strength of a military province, and were frequently used as the main striking force of a Roman expeditionary corps, as in Agricola's battle of the Mons Graupius, Tac. *Agric.* 35. 2. The distinction between *auxilia* and *legiones* steadily diminished as the legions came like them to be recruited in the provinces. In general see Cheeseman, *Auxilia of the Roman Imperial Army* (Oxford, 1914), chs. 2–3.

foedam . . . avaritiam. Faking the military accounts is at least as old as Julius Caesar's story of the false returns of strength made by his Gallic cavalry commanders in *BC* 3. 59. 3–4. The first of the 'quiet men', Annaeus Mela, saw the opportunities open to an equestrian official, Tac. *Ann.* 16. 17: 'adquirendae pecuniae brevius iter credebat per procurationes administrandis principis negotiis'. Domitian checked for a time the peculations of the higher officials, Suet. *Dom.* 8. 2. But H. G. Pflaum remarks that it is significant that *integritas* was the virtue that provincials most prized in their laudations of equestrian officials: *Les Procurateurs équestres* etc. (Paris, 1950), 165 f.

3. postea promotus ad amplissimas procurationes. As governor of the Graian Alps he ranked as *centenarius*, i.e. with a salary of S. 100,000, and as head of the inheritance-tax office he was *ducenarius*, which for nearly all procurators was the top grade. His three posts should have filled from nine to twelve years together, so that his retirement might be placed in about A.D. 93, unless he held another post after the date of the inscription. Cf. Pflaum's lists, op. cit. 322 f. and 337 n. 54.

nunc otium patitur quod quidem paulisper . . . intermisit. The date is at least post-Nervan. He has completed his assignment with the land commission and resumed his *otium*, like Pomponius Bassus, IV. 23. He has had time to write his life of Annius also. Any date after his final retirement is possible, but not demonstrable.

4. a Corellio nostro ex liberalitate imperatoris Nervae emendis dividendisque agris adiutor adsumptus. For the consular Corellius see I. 12 nn. He must be dead at the date of this letter's composition since he died before Nerva (I. 12. 8), while the land commission was at work, which has now finished. Otherwise Pliny usually confines *noster* to living persons, though he uses it of Cicero, I. 2. 4, 'Marci nostri'. For an anonymous member of this commission, who cannot, however, be Corellius, see *CIL* vi. 1548.

Dio 68. 2. 1 records that Nerva placed senators in charge of a fund of S.60,000,000 for the purchase of land and its distribution to 'very poor citizens'. Nothing is known of the results of this, but an inscription records the title of a *colonia Minervia Nervia Augusta* at Scolacium, unless *Nervia* is mere dittography, *CIL* x. 103; and the *Liber Coloniarum* records the restoration of land to the people of Verulae by Nerva (*Gromatici Vet.*, p. 239 Lachmann). Between 97 and 100 three colonies were founded in the confines of Numidia, two of them under Nerva, *ILS* 469, 496; *CAH* xi. 192; Garzetti, *Nerva*, 74 f., 79 n. 4; T. S. R. Broughton, *Romanisation of Africa Proconsularis*, 126, 128 ff.

imperatoris Nervae. The phrase does not mean that Nerva was still alive at the time of writing, cf. IV. 17. 8, 22. 4, which omit *divus*. On the order of words see IV. 22. 4 n.

adiutor. Equestrian assistants of senatorial and equestrian officials are so designated, but the post is commonly at the beginning of a career. Thus Attius Suburanus began his career as *adiutor* to a prefect of the corn supply, and a prefect of Egypt, VI. 6. 10 n. According to Pflaum (op. cit. 49), these were personal appointments, filled by the office-holders like military tribunates. Pliny's statement confirms this.

5. supremis iudiciis . . . Anni Bassi. A senator who as legionary legate was active in the Flavian march on Rome in A.D. 69, and thereby earned a premature consulship in 70, Tac. *Hist.* 3. 50. He should be the son of the like-named proconsul of Cyprus in A.D. 52, not the same man as *PIR*² A 637 has it. Cf. Garzetti, *C.* 8.

For the seriousness with which legacies were regarded as a sign of friendship, II. 20. 7–8 nn.

librum de vita eius. For the fashion of biography of minor figures see III. 10. 1 n.

studia quoque . . . veneratur. The remark is curiously apologetic and not stressed. Pliny's letters to and about Tertullus never refer to literary matters, which were perhaps not to his taste.

32. *To Calpurnius Fabatus*

This is the last of the series about Calestrius Tiro's visit to Fabatus. See Ep. 16 nn.

1. cupio . . . patriam nostram . . . augeri . . . civium numero. Pliny does not object to the increase of the foreign element within the Roman community, which it was the purpose of the Augustan legislation on manumission to hold in check. Other contemporaries found it less desirable. Tacitus gave publicity to the speech of the lawyer Cassius on the servile peril, *Ann.* 14. 43–44, and Juvenal denounced the *urbs Graeca* of Rome in *Sat.* 3. 60 ff. But these refer to Rome itself. Sirago (*Italia agraria*, 122 f.) suggests that it was imperial policy to increase the working population by liberal use of manumissions, and connects the edicts against castration of slaves with this object under Domitian and Nerva (Suet. *Dom.* 7. 1; *D.* 48. 8. 6). But here, as in VIII. 16, it is the household rather than the rustic slaves who are intended.

2. te meque et gratiarum actione et laude celebratos. The context suggests that this refers to a decree of the Council rather than to the spokesman of the freedmen. Compare I. 8. 17: 'plebem ipsam . . . limine curiae . . . discreverim ne quam in speciem ambitionis inciderem'.

Ut Xenophon ait. *Mem.* 2. I. 31.

33. *To Cornelius Tacitus*

Date. The reference to the *Historiae* of Tacitus supports the book-date. In VI. 16 he was dealing with the reign of Titus, and has now reached the latter years of Domitian. The letter is also in series with VIII. 7 and possibly with Ep. 20.

Address. For Tacitus see I. 6 pref.

I. auguror, nec me fallit augurium, historias tuas immortales futuras. Pliny has been stirred by a first reading of a volume of the *Histories* —either that mentioned in Ep. 20 or that in VIII. 7—to which he had already contributed the material on Vesuvius, IV. 16, 20. The present events concern the years A.D. 93–94, which Tacitus has not yet reached, but is approaching.

inseri cupio. Pliny accepts a similar proposal in IX. II. I but Martial twice rejects such, 4. 31, 5. 60.

3. diligentiam tuam fugere non possit, cum sit in publicis actis. Pliny takes it for granted that Tacitus will consult archives, including the news bulletin circulated by the emperors. For this see V. 13. 8 n. Though Pliny is not explicit, he implies that Tacitus was not in Rome at the time of this incident, though he was certainly present at the trial of Senecio, *Agric.* 45. 1–2, having returned after the death of Agricola, ibid. 5.

4. dederat me senatus cum Herennio Senecione advocatum provinciae . . . contra Baebium Massam. The date is fixed by Tacitus' statement, loc. cit., that Massa was already accused but not condemned for extortion at the moment of Agricola's death in August 93. It appears from VI. 29. 8 (n.) that Massa was accused of extortion in the aggravated form *cum saevitia*, because the procedure of provincial *inquisitio* was allowed against him; cf. III. 9. 29 n. For the appointment of advocates see II. II. 2 n. Herennius was connected with the set of Helvidius Priscus, and was later charged with treason and condemned to death; I. 5. 3, III. II. 3, Ep. 19. 5 nn. He was of Spanish origin (s. 5), and is only known from literature. Dio adds the fact that he sought no office after his quaestorship (67. 13. 2). In this he followed more drastically the example of Thrasea Paetus, who held no public position after his consulship. Such behaviour was a political strike against the Princeps, who depended upon the upper grades of the senatorial class for his senior administrators, cf. Tac. *Ann.* 6. 27 and 16. 27: 'patres arguebat quod publica munia desererent' etc. *PIR*² H 128.

Baebium Massam. Cf. III. 4. 4 n. Already an equestrian procurator in Africa and hence not a young man in A.D. 69, he secured pro-motion to the Senate from Vespasian as a reward for his part in the murder of the Vitellian follower L. Piso, Tac. *Hist.* 4. 50. He did not reach the consulship, the praetorian province of Baetica being his last post. Tacitus numbers him among the dangerous delators of the period (ibid.), and Juvenal associates him with Mettius Carus, *Sat.* 1. 35–36. His proconsulship cannot have been later than 92–93, and might have been a year or two earlier; delay was possible as in the cases of Marius and Classicus (II. 11. 2, 8–10 nn.; III. 9. 5 n.). His condemnation meant that Massa was not one of the agents of terror in the last and worst period of Domitian. Martial 12. 28 (29). 2 briefly refers to his disgrace. *PIR*² B 26.

damnatoque Massa censuerat ut bona eius publice custodirentur. Condemnation on a serious extortion charge involved repayment, relegation, and partial loss of civic status, II. 11. 12–13, 19 nn.; III. 9. 17–18 nn. Steps might be taken, as in the Classicus case, to protect the estate in part while satisfying the plaintiffs, III. 9. 17 nn. The *bonorum publicatio* which went with a full capital punishment (IV. 11. 13 nn.) was not normally applied to *relegati*, though excep-tions occurred under Domitian (*Dig.* 48. 22. 1). The financial pro-vision proves that Massa was merely relegated, since his goods were not confiscated, only protected, whereas, if he had remained in Italy, the step would not have been necessary. He would then have provided pledges to the *Aerarium*, much as in the procedure laid down by the old *Lex Acilia* (57–58), and would only have been sold up if he failed to satisfy the plaintiffs. Cf. Mommsen, *D. Pen. R.* 3. 26 f.

ne bona dissipari sinant quorum esse in custodia debent. The *Lex Acilia*, loc. cit., charged the quaestors with the duty of seizing and selling the goods of condemned persons who defaulted. Pliny's phrase suggests that guardians were now appointed by the consuls for *relegati*; consuls were generally responsible for allocating other *tutores*, IX. 13. 16 n. Hence Senecio fears that Massa may make off with the movable assets, as Licinianus was allowed to do (IV. 11. 13 n.), or that the valuations might be fudged in some way, with the connivance of the guardians.

5. dispice num peractas putes partes nostras senatus cognitione finita.
Pliny's doubt was just. The exaction of penalties was not the duty
of the advocate, but of the magistrates. The *Lex Acilia* made detailed
provision for the exaction of fines (ibid. 57–62), though it depended
upon the initiative of the plaintiff to collect his portion from the
aerarium Saturni. Senecio shows the officiousness of a follower of the
elder Helvidius.

nulla cum provincia necessitudo nisi ex beneficio tuo. Pliny later
became a patron of Baetica, but apparently not until about A.D. 97,
I. 7. 2, III. 4. 4 nn. His uncle's connexions were with Tarraconensis,
III. 5. 17.

ipse et natus ibi et quaestor in ea fui. His origins are those of a
numerous band of senators in the earlier Principate, such as the
family of Seneca, Trajan himself, and Licinius Sura.

7. venimus ad consules. Here as in s. 4 'consules postulationibus
vacaturos' the reference is to the consuls sitting in their administrative role on their tribunal, as in Ep. 6. 2, not presiding over the Senate.
Hence Massa, though no longer a senator, could be present. A period
of grace was allowed before an exile was required to leave Italy, cf.
III. 9. 34–35 n., IV. 11. 13 n.

**Massa questus Senecionem non advocati fidem sed inimici amari-
tudinem implesse impietatis reum postulat.** This has been taken to
be the charge on which Senecio was condemned, as if *impietas* meant
maiestas. Otto had doubts, art. cit. 45, because Mettius Carus is
named as the actual accuser of Senecio, and the charges were quite
different, I. 5. 3 n., Ep. 19. 5. Besides, a condemned man lost the
capability to act as an *accusator*, or even as a witness (cf. Venuleius
on the *lex repetundarum, Dig.* 48. 11. 6. 1). But he could at the end of
his trial raise questions of procedure, particularly in the form of a
charge of *praevaricatio* or of *calumnia*, III. 9. 29–30 nn., V. 4. 2 n.,
VI. 31. 12 n. So Eprius Marcellus turned the tables on his accusers
in Tac. *Ann.* 13. 33: 'ut quidam accusatorum eius exilio multarentur
tamquam insonti periculum fecissent'. Senecio's officious action had
given Massa a chance to suggest that he was activated by malice
and had exceeded his duty as an advocate. This gives point to Pliny's
reply—that he himself must be guilty of the opposite offence to that
imputed to Senecio, *praevaricatio*, since Massa has not included him
in the charge. The situation is as odd to Pliny as that in III. 9. 34:
'accidit . . . res contraria . . . ut accusatore praevaricationis damnato
rea absolveretur'.

The word *impietas*, used only this once in the Letters, is exact
for a failure of duty to a client, though *fides* is more common in this
connexion, e.g. V. 13. 2: 'non fidem sibi in advocatione . . . defuisse'.

Pliny uses *pietas*, with *iustitia*, of Titius Aristo's loyalty to his clients in I. 22. 7. In I. 5. 5–6 the question 'quid de pietate Modesti sentias?' referred to the man's function as *iudex*; ibid., n. In VI. 22. 4 the treachery of a quaestor in accusing his consul is called *summum nefas*. Cf. also Ep. 29. 2, 'pietatem erga patronos', though the words are not Pliny's; IX. 9. 2, towards a father; X. 8. 6, in official duty.

8. quae vox . . . statim excepta . . . est. This and the following imply that Massa's ruse was not successful.

9. Divus quidem Nerva . . . non mihi solum verum etiam saeculo est gratulatus. This is the earliest evidence of Nerva's attention to Pliny, mentioned also in the story of IV. 17. 8–9, which brought him preferment to the prefecture of Saturn. The incident also indicates the role played by Nerva behind the scenes during the Principate of Domitian. As one of the inner circle of the régime, like Fabricius Veiento (IV. 22. 4 n.), he conveys to Pliny the assurance that he had done the right thing.

10. haec . . . notiora clariora . . . tu facies . . . nec historia debet egredi veritatem. Compare Pliny's unusual opinion in V. 8. 4: 'historia quoquo modo scripta delectat'. In IX. 13. 14 he claims to have told the story of the debate about Publicius Certus 'ipsorum verbis'. But here Pliny is nearer to Cicero's idea of history—that it ought to glorify deeds—given in his letter to Lucceius, *ad fam.* V. 12, especially 3: 'te rogo ut et ornes ea vehementius etiam quam fortasse sentis et in eo leges historiae neglegas'. The Romans paid lip service to the 'laws of history' in their prefaces, disclaiming *gratia*, as Cicero says Lucceius did. So too Tacitus in all three of his historical books. So too Cluvius Rufus in the anecdote of IX. 19. 6: 'scis Vergini quae historiae fides debeatur' etc.

BOOK VIII

1. *To Septicius Clarus*

Date. The letter is linked by cross references to the series about the sickness of Pliny's wife and servants (Epp. 10, 11, 16, 19). The date may be summer 107 if this journey can be identified with the visit to Tifernum in IX. 37; s. 1 n.

Address. For Septicius Clarus see I. 1 pref. Pliny's equestrian friend reappears in VII. 28 after a long absence from the Letters.

1. iter commode explicui excepto quod quidam ex meis adversam valetudinem ferventissimis aestibus contraxerunt. This should be the visit to the healthy Tuscan villa (s. 3) which he mentions in Epp. 8 and 20, IX. 15, and probably also in VII. 30. 2, Ep. 2, IX. 37, which may date all these references to summer 107.

For the sickness of his wife and servants at this period see Epp. 16. 1, 19. 1.

2. Encolpius quidem lector . . . sanguinem reiecit. Compare the illness of Zosimus and his treatment, V. 19. Encolpius may be the reader whose first reading of Pliny's verses is described in IX. 34.

quis deinde libellos meos sic leget? Verses are probably meant, as Peter suggested (art. cit. 704), because Pliny usually recited his own speeches.

3. ad hoc salubritas caeli secessus quies. In v. 6 Pliny praises the healthiness of Tifernum, especially ibid. 46: 'mei quoque nusquam salubrius degunt'.

2. *To Calvisius Rufus*

Date. The letter is written after Pliny's return from his Tuscan estates in the autumn of probably 107, s. 1 n., Ep. 1. 1 n. The suggestion of Sirago that the letter belongs to a year later than the introduction of the share-cropping scheme in 107, and hence to 108 or 109, is not proved by the contents, s. 1 n.

Address. Several letters about business affairs are addressed to Calvisius Rufus of Comum, notably III. 19 about the same estate.

1. alii in praedia sua proficiscuntur ut locupletiores revertantur ego ut pauperior. He is back in Rome, and from Tifernum rather than Comum because all the certain references in VIII–IX are to Tuscan journeys (VII. 30. 3 n.) and there is no reference to *patria* here. Cf. especially IX. 15. 3, 39. 1.

vendideram vindemias certatim negotiatoribus ementibus. invitabat pretium et quod tunc et quod fore videbatur. spes fefellit. The buyers are middlemen, who buy the crop 'on the vine', as in Pliny, *NH* 14. 50. Pliny disposes of what grew on that part of the estate which he worked directly with a bailiff, on the system described in Columella's book. He refers to this in IX. 16. 1: 'vindemiae in manibus', IX. 20. 2: 'ipse . . . vindemias colligo'. The greater part of his land was, however, let to tenant farmers, III. 19. 6–7 n. T. Frank, *Ec. Survey*, v. 178, maintains that vineyards were generally worked on the direct system. But the passage from Titius Aristo and Marcellus quoted in III. 19. 7 n. shows that this was not so. Hence Sirago's ingenious suggestion (*It. agr.* 118) is possible, that these transactions refer to the period after Pliny introduced the share-cropping plan in 107 (IX. 37), and had large quantities of produce from rents in kind to sell. But Pliny could not sell his tenants' crops before the collection and division of the harvest. It is evident that there was a considerable interval between the bidding and the collection. The quantities involved are not so large as Sirago supposes. The total rent of the Tuscan estates amounted to some S.700,000 (X. 8. 4 with III. 19. 7). The land under direct cultivation of vines might well total a ninth or tenth of this, and call for half a dozen contractors at S. 10,000 to S.15,000, the sums indicated in ss. 4–5. Pliny would then lose some S.10,000, rather than up to S.100,000 on Sirago's supposition. The largest sum mentioned by Pliny corresponds to no more than some seventeen acres, s. 6 n.

Frank, op. cit. 258, suggests from Pompeian evidence that *negotiatores* stored their wines in the *cellae vinariae* of estate-owners whose crop they had bought. But he thinks that middlemen were rare, and that villas usually made their own wine. The *cella* of the Villa Boscoreale held 84 *dolia* which each could contain about 315 gallons, ibid. 264. Cf. also Day, 'Agriculture in the Life of Pompeii', *Yale Cl. Studies*, iii. 190 f.

invitabat pretium. The expected margin disappeared. The reason may appear from comparison of Ep. 15, where Pliny reports the prospect of a light harvest, with IX. 20, where it turns out better than expected: 'vindemias graciles quidem uberiores tamen quam exspectaveram'. So too in IX. 16. 1 'vindemiae in manibus . . . exiguae'. The buyers bid in hope of a scarcity price which did not materialize. The opposite case is recorded in IV. 6. 1 'abundantia sed par vilitas'.

3. partem octavam pretii quo quis emerat concessi. There was not a total collapse of prices. Pliny's double remission amounted to less than 16 per cent in the case quoted in s. 5, and this evidently sufficed to keep the dealers in business. The depreciation is about what one might expect in the situation noted above.

6. cum reputarem quosdam ex debito aliquantum . . . quosdam nihil reposuisse. Pliny writes after the harvest, when the money was due, in October. He returns to Rome at a similar season in I. 6. 4.

For a discussion of the evidence of Columella and the Elder Pliny on prices and yields see Frank, op. cit. 149 f. Columella, 3. 3. 10, expected at least S.300 per *culleus* (524 litres) of wine, and three *cullei* to a Roman acre of good vineyard. The production margin was wide, since yields sink as low as one *culleus* and rise as high as seven per acre (Pliny, *NH* 14. 52). On Columella's figures the largest unit in Pliny's sale was a plot of some seventeen Roman acres, producing fifty *cullei*, worth 15,000 sesterces. It would need a great many bidders at this rate to deal with the whole vineyard area of the estates on Sirago's supposition.

3. *To Sparsus*

Date is not determinable, save for a possible link with VI. 33. The addressee is presumably Sextus Iulius Sparsus, a literary consular last addressed in IV. 5.

2. contra istum librum faveo orationi quam nuper in publicum dedi. Neither work seems to fit the book of Ep. 19, which is unpublished, and with which he is somewhat dissatisfied. One of the two may well be his *pro Attia*, VI. 33, and the other the *librum* of VII. 20. 2.

4. *To Caninius Rufus*

Date. A moment in *c.* 107 is indicated, after the Dacian victories of Trajan have become well known, s. 2.

Address. Pliny's literary friend from Comum, despite his urgings in I. 3, II. 8. 1, III. 7. 15, has not yet produced a work. But in IX. 33. 1 his 'poetic ability' is established.

1. quae tam recens tam copiosa . . . et quamquam in verissimis rebus . . . materia? Trajan's second Dacian war was completed by the autumn of 106, when the *Fasti Ostienses* record the displaying of the head of the dead king Decebalus at Roma. The continuous story of the two wars is known only from the epitome of Xiphilinus and the excerpts of Cassius Dio (Dio 68. 6–15), and from the narrative reliefs on Trajan's Column. Trajan published his own account of the war, of which only a brief phrase survives. The story must have become known quickly from Trajan's *epistulae laureatae* to the Senate. For the Column see C. Cichorius, *Die Reliefs der Traiansäule*, Berlin, 1896–1900. For its bibliography see *CAH* xi. 889, and especially G. A. Davies, *JRS* vii. 74 ff.

elata. The correction of Budaeus for *lata* is clearly right. This is not a list of synonyms.

fabulosa. The strangest incident recorded is the message sent to Trajan by the Buri, supposedly inscribed on a great mushroom, Dio, loc. cit. 8. 1.

2. dices immissa terris nova flumina. In the second war Decebalus is said to have diverted the River Sargetia, and buried his treasure in its bed, where Trajan discovered it. Dio, loc. cit. 14. 4.

novos pontes fluminibus iniectos. Especially the great stone bridge over the Danube described by Dio, loc. cit. 13, as one of the wonders of the world. This and other bridges are visible on the Column; Cichorius, op. cit., pl. 71. 91.

insessa castris montium abrupta. Dio mentions the capture by Trajan of hill fortresses in 9. 3, during the first war. They appear frequently on the Column.

pulsum regia . . . regem nihil desperantem. The capture of the capital Sarmizegethusa and the withdrawal and suicide of Decebalus formed the climax of the second war (Dio, loc. cit. 14. 3), figured also on the Column, cf. Paribeni, *Optimus Princeps*, i, fig. 30. By *nihil desperantem* Pliny refers to the king's twenty years of resistance to Rome, rather than (as Merrill) to the Stoic doctrine of suicide as an act of *constantia* as in I. 12. 9, III. 7. 2. Worldly despair and moral *constantia* were not contradictory in the ethic of suicide. Cf. I. 22. 9–10, VI. 24. 3–4.

Ignoring the precise details, Guillemin (*VL*, 143–4) unconvincingly regards this section as a literary commonplace based on such passages as Horace, *Epist.* 2. 1. 252–4—'terrarumque situs . . . dicere et arces montibus impositas et barbara regna, tuisque auspiciis totum confecta duella per orbem'—or Ovid, *Pont.* 2. 1. 37 f., about conquered lands, to which it has a general similarity.

actos bis triumphos, quorum alter ex invicta gente primus alter novissimus fuit. Dio mentions the first triumph, and the immense games that followed the second war, ibid. 10. 2, 15. 1. Pliny ignores Domitian's triumph *de Chattis Dacisque*: Suet. *Dom.* 6. 1, Dio 67. 7. 4, 8. 1.

3. barbara et fera nomina, in . . . Graecis versibus non resultent. Like Arrius Antoninus (IV. 3. 3), he writes in Greek. But for this remark one would assume a Latin poem. In Dio the name 'Dekebalos' has all its vowels short.

4. datur Homero et mollia vocabula et Graeca ad levitatem versus contrahere extendere. It is not clear why Merrill, ad loc., thought that Pliny regarded Homeric Greek as a distortion of Attic. The ancients had the full texts of Sappho and Alcaeus to familiarize them with the dialects. The variations of Homeric forms amongst themselves justifies the remark.

5. iure vatum invocatis dis et inter deos ipso. Since Vergil, *Georgics* I. 24, and Horace, *C.* 3. 5. 2, the hailing of the emperor in verse as a deity had been a harmless convention.

7. non posse perinde carptim ut contexta, . . . placere. Pliny likes dissecting the carcass, II. 5. 10.

5. *To Rosianus Geminus*

Date. The letter belongs to the Geminus series, which is confined to VI–IX. So the book-date is safe.

Address. For Pliny's young senatorial protégé, Rosianus Geminus, see VII. 1 pref.

1. grave vulnus Macrinus noster accepit : amisit uxorem singularis exempli. This might be Minicius Macrinus, the elderly equestrian of Brixia described in I. 14. 5–7. The age fits him, but no wife is mentioned in I. 14: an excellent *avia* takes her place, as if Minicius' wife were dead already. Hence this Macrinus may be better identified with Caecilius Macrinus, the probable recipient of all the letters addressed to Macrinus, cf. III. 4 pref.

   vixit cum hac triginta novem annis. From the book-date, he married her about A.D. 68, and would himself be born not much later than 43. Hence Caecilius, if it is he, is now an old man. Equally Minicius Macrinus was not less than 30 in A.D. 73–74 and had a son already praetorian in A.D. 97. Caecilius in the Macrinus letters is certainly not younger than Pliny, who seeks his advice with marked respect, III. 4. 2, 9.

3. dum admittere avocamenta . . . possit. Compare his remarks on the death of Fundania, V. 16. 10–11, and Ep. 23. 1. Though Pliny writes many letters about the deaths of friends, he never writes a letter of consolation such as he suggests to Marcellinus in V. 16. 10.

6. To Montanus

Date. The letter continues VII. 29.

Address. Montanus is possibly the consular Junius Montanus. See ibid. pref.

2. postea mihi visum est . . . ipsum senatus consultum quaerere. inveni. He would find it not *in actis publicis*, as in VII. 33. 3 n., which might not give the whole text, but in the senatorial archives kept by the *curator actorum senatus* or *ab actis* and consulted by historians, as by Tacitus, *Ann.* 5. 4, 15. 74. Cf. *RE* i, 'Acta', 287 f., iv, 'Curatores' 1795 f.; *ILS* 1032, 1062. Cf. A–J 96, 'libro sententiarum in senatu dictarum'. It is noteworthy that Pliny did not consult any written history.

non dico illi veteres Africani Achaeici Numantini sed hi proximi Marii Sullae Pompei. The time interval between the victory of Scipio Aemilianus in the Numantine war, 133 B.C., and the first consulship of Marius, who had served in the army of Scipio at Numantia, is much less than Pliny implies. Scipio never took the cognomen Numantinus.

3. dicerem urbanos si senatum deceret urbanitas. Cf. IV. 25. 3, 'qui . . . omnino in senatu dicax et urbanus . . . est'. But the unthinkable is probably true, and the excessive flattery was satirical, cf. VII. 29. 3 n.

procedendi libido. Cf. IV. 24. 4, 'studiis processimus', of a senatorial career.

4. Pallanti servo praetoria ornamenta offeruntur. VII. 29. 2 n. So too *ornamenta quaestoria* were given to the freedman Narcissus, Tac. *Ann.* 11. 38. These decorations did not confer a seat in the Senate, and Pliny exaggerates in calling Pallas *praetorius* below, and *servus* here.

censent . . . compellendum ad usum aureorum anulorum ; erat enim contra maiestatem senatus si ferreis praetorius uteretur. A *SC.* of A.D. 23 forbade the wearing of golden rings to all persons save those who had the equestrian census, the right to sit in the seats reserved for equestrians at the theatre, and whose family had been free-born for three generations, Pliny, *NH* 33. 32. A *Lex Visellia* of the next year confirmed this, but, according to *Cod. Iust.* 9. 21, allowed an exception for special grants by the Princeps. It is disputed whether the grant of the golden rings to distinguished freedmen, several times recorded in the early empire, in connexion with the grant of equestrian status, was technically equivalent to the legal process later known as *natalium restitutio* (e.g. Tac. *Hist.* 1. 13, 2. 57; Suet. *Galba* 14. 2). This deleted the servile stain, and so eliminated the *poena* *legis Viselliae*. Certainly the *lex Visellia* came to be so interpreted in a later age. Ulpian quotes Hadrian's authority for this interpretation of the grant of the rings, *Dig.* 40. 10. 6. Pallas' brother Antonius Felix, who went through the equestrian *cursus* in the ordinary way, may have secured his promotion like this; his career began before the offer of rings to Pallas (Suet. *Claud.* 28; Tac. *Ann.* 12. 53–54). Whatever the legal position, the grant of rings was an outward and visible sign of a promotion that was impossible without some form of *natalium restitutio*. For the controversy see Mommsen, *DPR* vi. 2, 115 ff.; A. Stein, *Römische Ritterstand*, 35 ff.; A. M. Duff, *Freedmen in the Early Roman Empire* (Oxford, 1928), 214 ff., who exaggerates the value of the *Codex* passage as a summary of the original law.

ferreis. The freedman Trimalchio in *Petr.* 32. 3, who hankered after equestrian dignity, wore rings of gold-plated iron, and of solid gold with iron studs.

7. custodis principalium opum. The functions of the *a rationibus* in the Flavian period are described by Statius *S.* 3. 86 ff. in terms of the receipt and expenditure of the revenues from imperial provinces and of revenues allocated from the public provinces.

8. voluisse quidem senatum censere dandum ex aerario . . . centies quinquagies. This passage has not been discussed in the more recent articles about the relations between *aerarium* and *fiscus* in the earlier Principate. Its implications support the contention of A. H. M. Jones that until Vespasian the *aerarium Saturni* remained the central bank for the concentration and redistribution of all surplus provincial revenues (*JRS* xl, 1950, 22 ff., with bibliography). The sum of S.15,000,000 was equivalent to the revenue of one of the smaller provinces. Cf. T. Frank, *Ec. Survey*, v. 6 f., 51 f. If the *aerarium Saturni* contained extensive surpluses in the time of Claudius it is unlikely that the greater part of the Roman revenues were already segregated into a separate imperial *fiscus*, and the *aerarium Saturni* reduced to the narrow scope apparent at the accession of Nerva (II. 1. 9 n.). The contrast between the term *custos principalium opum*, used of Pallas, and *publicarum opum egestione* applied to the *aerarium*, in s. 7, illustrates the position. As *a rationibus* Pallas administers the emperor's finances, but the public moneys which he handles, apart from the revenues collected in the military provinces and spent on the spot, come from the general surplus collected in the *aerarium* from the non-military provinces. These would be placed at the emperor's disposal by standing arrangements made, or reconfirmed, at each emperor's accession. See Jones, art. cit. 24. But over and above these funds there were still under Claudius considerable sums in the *aerarium* available for specific allocations, as on this occasion. In A.D. 62 it seems, from an obscure passage in Tac. *Ann.* 15. 18. 4, that the proceeds of the considerable indirect taxes of Italy, and possibly throughout the provinces, still went into the *aerarium*, apart from those that went to the separate *aerarium militare*. Cf. F. Millar, 'The Aerarium', *JRS*, 1964, 33 ff.

13. ea quae x Kal. Februarias, quae proxime fuissent, in amplissimo ordine optimus princeps recitasset, senatusque consulta de iis rebus facta in aere inciderentur, idque aes figeretur ad statuam loricatam divi Iulii. The speech of Claudius, and the *SC.* quoted in ss. 4–9, were made on this day, 23 January, but the second *SC.*, quoted in 10 and 13, belongs to the next session of the Senate.

The locality where the 'praepositi rerum eius curae' work is evidently 'ad statuam loricatam'. This gives the address of the *fiscus* office at Rome. The reference helps to explain the duties of an official known as *procurator a loricata*, or *ad loricatam*, and another, sometimes conjoined with him, called *ad Castoris*. *CIL*, vi. 8688–92. Mommsen, ibid., referred them to the charge of a safe-deposit in the vault of the temple of Castor, known from republican times (Cic. *pro Quinctio* 17; Juv. 14. 260–2). Hirschfeld thought that the vault was the actual bank of the *fiscus*, after the separation of this from the *aerarium*, and that the *a loricata* was the head cashier of the *fiscus* (*Verwaltungsbeamten*, 4, n. 4). Since the *statua loricata* probably stood in front of the temple of Divus Iulius, it is more probable that both temples housed the offices and vaults of the *fiscus* (Ashby, *Top. Dict. Rome*, 498). The statue seems to be known only from this reference.

The inscriptions cited above show that the *a loricata* and *ad Castoris* were servile or freedman posts in the earlier period. The post then emerges as equestrian under Trajan in the career of L. Vibius Lentulus, who after holding the Mint, and two provincial procuratorships, was either *a rationibus loricatae*, or more probably first *a loricata* and then *a rationibus*. This inscription, though imperfect, establishes the connexion between the *loricata* and the *rationes* suggested by Pliny's letter. *AE*, 1913, 143a; 1924, 81.

7. To Cornelius Tacitus

Date. This letter is closely connected with VII. 20 and IX. 23, in which Pliny takes pride in his close relationship with Tacitus, and for the first time exchanges compositions for revision.

1. ut discipulo magister. Cf. VII. 20. 4 'te sequi, tibi longo sed proximus intervallo'; IX. 23. 3 'nomina nostra quasi litterarum propria'.

There is no trace of this theme in the earlier letters to Tacitus, I. 6, 20, IV. 13, where it might have been expected.

2. num potui longius hyperbaton facere? The letter reads like an apology for the bolder tone of VII. 20. Perhaps Tacitus had sent Pliny a cool reply.

in librum tuum. This should be distinct from that received by Pliny in VII. 20, since here he sends nothing of his own. Probably it is a second roll of the *Historiae*, cf. ibid. s. 1 n.

8. *Voconius Romanus*

Date. This letter and Ep. 20 both concern travels of Pliny in parts of Etruria which he had not visited before, though not far off the route from Rome to Tifernum, s. 1. They can hardly be dissociated from each other or from the book-date (Ep. 1. 1 n.).

Address. For Voconius Romanus, Pliny's Spanish friend and possibly a senator, see I. 5 pref.

1. vidistine aliquando Clitumnum fontem? . . . quem ego . . . proxime vidi. Taken with Ep. 20, where Ameria and Lake Vadimon are new to him, this confirms the impression given by 1. 4. 1 that Pliny whether travelling to Comum or to Tifernum always took the main route of the Via Flaminia, and branched off at Mevaunia for Perusia and Tifernum. Hitherto he had used neither the more direct route along the Via Amerina or Annia by Ameria and Tuder to Perusia, nor the easterly branch of the Via Flaminia that leaves the main Flaminia at Narnia, crosses the Clitumnus bridge between Spoletium and Trebiae, and rejoins the Flaminia at Forum Flaminii (or Mevaunia?). Caligula when he went to visit the Clitumnus springs took the main Flaminia to Mevaunia, Suet. *Cal.* 43. 1, and Honorius came from the north by Mevaunia (Claudian, *vi cons. Hon.* 500–14). Pliny may have taken the detour on this occasion to avoid exceptional traffic on the Flaminia, cf. Tac. *Hist.* 2. 64, 'vitata Flaminiae viae celebritate'. He does not seem to have ever gone out of his way to seek out scenes of natural beauty.

His description is original and independent, despite the fact that the Clitumnus was almost a commonplace in Latin literature, from Virgil, *Georgics* 2. 146, Propertius 2. 19. 25, 3. 22. 23, Statius, *Silvae* 1. 4. 128 f., and Silius 4. 545 f., down to Claudian, loc. cit. The numerous citations are mainly concerned with the famous white oxen, the one thing that Pliny does not mention.

2. modicus collis adsurgit antiqua cupresso nemorosus. Suetonius and Propertius barely refer to this wood, locis citt.

hunc subter exit fons et exprimitur pluribus venis. The modern situation is, or was till recently, very much as described. Wilamowitz-Moellendorf remarked that it was the volume of water maintained throughout the summer that made this inconsiderable stream, set in a valley of no unusual beauty by Italian standards, one of the lesser wonders of Italy (*Reden und Vorträge* (Berlin, 1925), i. 333 f.). Compare Pliny's comment on the summer shrinkage of the upper Tiber at Tifernum, v. 6. 12. The Fontaine de Vaucluse in Provence enjoys a similar fame. For an account by a traveller in the nineteenth century see G. McN. Rushforth, *Guardian*, 24 January 1900, 135 ff. (quoted by Merrill, ad loc.). Earlier see R. Venuti, *Osservazioni sopra il fiume Clitunno*, Rome, 1753.

fons. The stream itself is but an affluent of the Tinia, a major tributary of the Tiber.

venis. The neighbouring village is still called Le Vene.

numerare iactas stipes. The custom was frequent in antiquity, as at the Trevi fountain in Rome, of casting coins into a sacred stream as a thank-offering to the deity for restored health. At Oropus also it was associated with an oracle, as here (s. 5). Cf. Pausanias, I. 34. 4, with Frazer's note, and Suet. *Aug.* 57. 1.

3. iam amplissimum flumen atque etiam navium patiens. An exaggeration to stress his point that the stream rapidly deepens. But literary Latin is short of words for small boats, cf. 'nauculam' III. 16. 9, Ep. 20. 5. The Tinea, however, carried small barges, Strabo, 5. 2. 10, p. 227. Probus on Virgil, *Georg.* 2. 146 called it 'a fonte navigabilis'.

5. adiacet templum priscum et religiosum. The little church of S. Salvatore on the river bank is no longer identified with this temple. It is now supposed to have been built out of the material of an ancient mausoleum, of which some inscribed stones survive. (Cf. *CIL*, xi. 4817, 4846, 4904; *RE* iv. 57.)

stat Clitumnus ipse amictus ornatusque praetexta. The figure was covered with a real toga; so too an ancient statue of Fortuna at Rome, Pliny, *NH* 8. 197. Cf. Frazer's note on Ovid, *Fasti* 6. 570 and Varro, *Vit. Pop. Rom.* 17. The scarlet-bordered toga was the formal dress of magistrates and priests, Mommsen, *DPR* ii. 45 ff. The statement of Vibius Sequester (Riese, *Georg. min.*, p. 148) that the cult name was Juppiter Clitumnus is thought by Wissowa (in *Lexicon der gr. und röm. Mythol.* i. 912) to mean that the sky god manifests himself locally. Compare Juppiter Appeninus and Juppiter Cacunus, *ILS* 3073, 3076.

praesens numen atque etiam fatidicum indicant sortes. Pliny is too brief to be quite clear, but such methods were usual at several Italian shrines, notably the great temple of Fortune at Praeneste.

The method is described by Cicero, *Div.* 2. 86. Oracular sentences were written on slips of wood or metal and shaken together until one emerged or was picked out. Virgil's Sybil was to use similar methods, *Aen.* 3. 443–6, 6. 74; 'foliis tantum ne carmina manda, ne turbata volent' etc. *RE* 13. 1455 ff.; Wissowa, *Religion und Kultus²*, &c., 260; Hartleben, op. cit., quotes an illustration on coins; Grueber, *Coins of the Roman Republic* etc., III, pl. 44, nn. 23–24.

sparsa sunt circa sacella. The *Itinerarium Hierosolymitanum* indicates a posting station on the high road called Sacraria, eight miles from Spoletium and four from Trebiae, at the Clitumnus site— the modern Le Vene.

sunt minores capite discreti. Eight or nine are now reckoned.

sed flumini miscentur quod ponte transmittitur. The mention of the bridge and the *hospitium* below shows that the Flaminian branch crossed the river at the confines of the grove.

6. in superiore parte navigare tantum, infra etiam natare concessum. For similar taboos see Ep. 20. 5: 'nulla in hoc navis, sacer enim'. Also Tac. *Ann.* 14. 22. 6.

balineum Hispellates quibus illum locum divus Augustus dono dedit publice praebent. The locality was separated from the territory of Hispellum by that of Fulginiae and Trebiae. This grant may be connected with the veteran settlement of a *colonia Iulia*, presumably of the Triumviral period (*CIL* xi. 2, p. 766). For the public bath cf. II. 17. 26, 'balinea meritoria'.

7. leges multa . . . omnibus columnis omnibus parietibus inscripta. Merrill and Hartleben took these to be graffiti, which are rare or non-existent in Italian shrines, though common in the East; but they may equally be inscriptions of the type 'votum solvit libens merito'. In Ep. 6. 1 *inscriptio*, and in IX. 19. 1 *inscribi* refer to formal inscriptions. Possibly Pliny himself made a presentation to Hispellum, if the fragmentary *CIL* xi. 5272 refers to him, but at Hispellum.

9. *To Cornelius Ursus*

Date. This scrap has been dated back to the period of I–III on the ground of Pliny's *occupationes*. But his troubles are concerned with *negotia amicorum*, not public employment. These recur frequently enough in the last three books. See Ep. 21. 3, IX. 2. 1, and IX. 25. 3: 'nunc me rerum actus modice . . . distringit'. A little earlier he was very busy with such affairs, VI. 4. 1, VII. 5. 1, 15. 1 n.

Ursus is not the great Servianus (III. 17 pref.), but Cornelius Ursus, recipient of the extortion letters, IV. 9, V. 20, VI. 5, 13, commonly called Ursus in the titles. His absence from I–III also excludes an early date.

10. *To Calpurnius Fabatus*

Date. The cross-references in Epp. 1, 16. 1 and 19. 1 to the sickness of his wife and his servants link this letter and Ep. 11 to the book-date. The attribution of these two letters to *c.* 107, three or four years after the ordinarily accepted date of Pliny's last marriage, roused the indignation of Otto (art. cit. 40). Calpurnia miscarried sooner, according to him. Yet Pliny was a notoriously barren man, x. 2. 2–3, iv. 13. 5. Besides we know little about the working of the child-marriage system. The ceremonies sometimes took place even before the twelfth year, though marriage was not legally recognized until that year. See v. 16. 6 n.; also Ulpian, *Dig.* 24. 1. 32. 27. Two medical opinions in Pliny's day were against early matches (Friedlaender, *SG* (Eng. tr.), i. 232, app. 18). Soranus gave 15–40 as the best years for conception, while Rufus favoured 18 as the earliest year. Hence a prudent man wanting children might wait for the best season, especially if his wife was not very strong (vi. 4. 7), as Augustus did, Suet. *Aug.* 62. 1. Pliny, protected by the *ius III liberorum*, could afford to wait. Cf. s. 1 n.

Schultz, art. cit. 36–37, assumed without reason that Calpurnia's miscarriage was the same as the illness that sent her for convalescence to Campania in vi. 4, 7, 28, 30. None of these wholesale derangements of the series are necessary, and the connexion of Ep. 1 with Pliny's journey to Tifernum may help to date the group in viii to 107.

Address. For Calpurnius Fabatus, Pliny's wife's grandfather, see iv. 1 pref.

1. neptem tuam abortum fecisse. Note the remarkable contrast between Ep. 10 and Ep. 11, both telling the same story. To Fabatus Pliny begins with the brutal fact, and the letter is entirely concerned with the prospects of an heir and the excuses of Calpurnia. To the aunt he breaks the news gently, the fact comes only in the eleventh line, and he is chiefly concerned for his wife's health. Carcopino, *Daily Life*, 89–90, is shocked at the harshness of Ep. 10 and Ep. 11. 3. But the harshness is in Fabatus, not Pliny.

dum se praegnantem esse puellariter nescit. Cf. Ep. 11. 2, 'culpa aetatis'. Pliny, *NH* 10. 154, is the closest parallel: 'Iulia Augusta prima sua aetate . . . gravida . . . usa est puellari augurio'. Livia, as she then was, was at that time aged 15. An age above 17, the upper normal limit for *puer*, is unlikely here.

3. pronum ad honores iter . . . et non subitas imagines relicturus. The concept of Republican *nobilitas* dies hard. The *novus* is still ashamed of himself.

11. *To Calpurnia Hispulla*

Date and circumstances as Ep. 10. The lady is Pliny's wife's aunt, IV. 19 nn.

3. excusa patri. Pliny finds the tough old man hard to manage at times, cf. VI. 12, VII. 11.

12. *To Cornelius Minicianus*

Date. Schultz, art. cit. 37, connected this letter with I. 17, which also mentions historical works of Capito, assuming that this was the first time that Pliny attended a recitation of Capito. But Pliny does not say that, and the references to Pliny's own recitations and occupations fit a later date better, ss. 2, 3, 4 nn.

Address. The man is the literary equestrian of VII. 22. 2 n., III. 9, IV. 11.

1. recitaturus est Titinius Capito. For this literary procurator see I. 17. 1, V. 8 nn.

litterarum iam senescentium reductor. In I. 10, 13, 16 Pliny regards literature as flourishing, not decaying.

2. domum suam recitantibus praebet. Cf. I. 13 nn.

mihi certe si modo in urbe defuit nunquam. Since Pliny hardly ever recited before the year of his Panegyric and *In Marium*, this is strong against an early date, II. 19. 1, VII. 17. 1–2 nn.

3. nunc quia mihi omne negotium omnis in studiis cura. This fits the circumstances of the latest letters, Ep. 9 pref., much better than an early date.

4. scribit exitus inlustrium virorum. So too Fannius wrote *exitus occisorum*, V. 5. 3. In I. 17. 3 Capito wrote in verse about *clarissimi cuiusque vitam*. The topics differ, as much as Pliny's account of his uncle's life in III. 5 differs from that of his death in VI. 16. As Pliny does not specify, the *exitus* may well have been in prose. In V. 8 Capito urged Pliny to write *prose* history. Cf. Bardon, *Litt. Lat. Inc.* ii. 221.

13. *To Genialis*

Neither the date of the letter nor the identity of this young admirer of Pliny can be established.

1. a disertissimo viro discere. He means the father of Genialis.

14. *To Titius Aristo*

Date. Afranius Dexter was found dead, according to the *Fasti* of
Ostia, on 24 June 105 (see below, p. 735). The punishment of his
household would not normally be long delayed: compare the speed
shown in a similar case, III. 14. 4 n. There were circumstances in this
case that might have caused a certain delay, as there was an element
of doubt about the cause of death, s. 12 n. But it is impossible to
date the letter later than the end of 105. The reason why Pliny did
not publish it earlier may well lie in its lack of unity of theme,
pictorial quality, and incident. Its forensic argumentation is alien to
the style of the Letters, except in discussions of literary theory.

The letter bears clear traces of revision and expansion. Its style
in ss. 1–3 and 12–26 is much barer and more argumentative than
is normal in the letters. Favourite devices like double synonyms and
triplets are less in evidence. The letter ends abruptly, and there is
no apology for its unusual length. The main subject is badly interrupted by the historical excursus in ss. 4–10 of things as well known
to Aristo as to Pliny. In this section Pliny's epistolary style reasserts
itself. The section may well be an addition meant to brighten up an
otherwise dull, technical letter. Sections 7–10 are particularly
irrelevant; s. 10, 'quo iustius peto', could easily continue after s. 3;
or s. 12, 'referebatur de libertis', might follow s. 1. In the core of
the letter there are one or two obvious additions to the original text
such as s. 12, ' "quis?" inquis; ego, sed nihil refert'. Pliny may have
resurrected this letter because, as has often been noted, he is rather
short of political material in the last two books.

Had not the date of Dexter's death been known, this letter would
certainly have been dated much earlier than 105 by the critics of
Mommsen on the strength of *breve tempus* in s. 10: cf. v. 20. 1 n.

Address. For the great lawyer Titius Aristo see I. 22. 1 n., V. 3. 1.
The excursus on the internal history of the Senate helps to confirm
the impression that Aristo was not himself a senator.

1. **cum sis peritissimus et privati iuris et publici.** So too in I. 22. 1.
Pliny's stress on public law, i.e. knowledge of the criminal, political,
and administrative law of the *leges publicae*, is interesting. Schulz
exaggerates the distaste of Roman jurisprudents for this type of
legal inquiry, and perhaps dates too late the origins of the science of
administrative law in attributing it to the second half of the second
century (*Roman Legal Science*, 81, 138 f.).

2. **priorum temporum servitus . . . iuris senatorii oblivionem . . .
induxit.** Pliny's account of the extortion trials shows this weakness,

in the continual abuse of procedure and penalties: II. II. 5, 12. 2; III. 9. 30–32; IV. 9. 16–17; V. 20. 2 nn. Hence Licinius Nepos as praetor tried to restore strictness of procedure to senatorial business: IV. 29. 2–3; V. 4. 2, 9. 3–6; VI. 5. 1–2 nn.

4. erat autem antiquitus institutum. To what period does Pliny attribute this golden age? The general tone of the passage fits that of the anecdotes about the second century B.C. preserved in Valerius Maximus, the period of *illi veteres* in Ep. 6. 2. The sons of senators hardly continued to serve in the ranks (s. 5) after the Marian army reforms. The passage has a general resemblance to the account of the training of young orators by apprenticeship in Tac. *Dialogus* 34. 1, which refers to the late Republic: 'ergo apud maiores nostros iuvenis ille qui foro . . . parabatur . . . deducebatur a patre . . . ad eum oratorem' etc.

5. honores petituri adsistebant curiae foribus. Valerius Maximus tells of this kind of thing in 2. 1. 9, 2. 7. But the custom was revived by Augustus, Suet. *Aug.* 38. 2: 'liberis senatorum . . . quo celerius rei publicae adsuescerent . . . curiae interesse permisit'.

6. quae distinctio pugnantium sententiarum. Guillemin, ad loc., referred this to the division of the two parts of a single *sententia* of which one was approved and the other not, as in Cic. *pro Mil.* 14. But the metaphor of the battle, as in ss. 21 and 26, fits better the obvious case which Pliny has in mind in s. 12.

quae exsecutio prioribus aliquid addentium. The putting of a rider to the vote. Guillemin rightly compares IV. 9. 20–21: 'hoc amplius censuit . . . sed hanc sententiam consules . . . non sunt persecuti'. The consuls are free to choose which *sententia* they put to the House. For *exsequi* cf. V. 9. 3, VII. 33. 4.

7. at nos iuvenes fuimus quidem in castris, sed cum suspecta virtus. In this passage Pliny links the oppression of the Senate under Domitian to phases of his own career. He describes the Senate as *trepidam et elinguem* in s. 8 before his quaestorship, and thus attributes a reign of terror to the period before 90. This continues after he entered the Senate, *iam participes malorum* s. 9, until the end of the reign. But Tacitus confines the worst of the Senate's troubles to the time after the death of Agricola in August 93; *Agric.* 44–45; cf. VII. 33. 4 n. Since the military conspiracy of Antonius Saturninus in 89 was the turning-point for the worse in the reign, there is not much exaggeration in Pliny's account; cf. *CAH* xi. 27; Gsell, *L'Empereur Domitien*, 260 ff.

suspecta virtus. Cf. Tac. *Agric.* 1. 4, 41. 1: 'infensus virtutibus princeps'.

ducibus auctoritas nulla, nulla militibus verecundia. Pliny refers to
the Syrian army in which he served as military tribune *c.* A.D. 81.
But the discipline of that force, which seldom faced even the
prospect of war, was notoriously lax, cf. Tac. *Ann.* 12. 12, 13. 35.
Pliny never saw the active armies of Rhine, Danube, or Britain.

**8. cum senatus aut ad otium summum aut ad summum nefas
vocaretur.** Cf. *Pan.* 54. 4, 'de ampliando numero gladiatorum aut de
instituendo collegio fabrorum consulebamur . . . nunc menses etiam
. . . nomini Caesarum dicabamus'. The only major function remaining
to them seems to have been that of a court in political trials—the
summum nefas. It is only by comparing this letter and the *Panegyricus* passage with the accounts of the Senate's duties in the letters
about Trajan's reign, that one secures any clear impression of what
happened to the Senate's administrative powers under Domitian.

9. iam participes malorum multos per annos. In fact barely six years
for Pliny, whereas the *breve tempus* of restored liberty in s. 10 had
lasted nine years at the time of writing. Hence his apology in s. 10:
'nam tanto brevius' etc.

**12. referebatur de libertis Afrani Dextri consulis, incertum sua an
suorum manu, scelere an obsequio perempti.** The treatment of the
familia when a *dominus* was murdered is a theme with a long history.
Republican custom demanded the execution of all the slaves in the
house on the principle expressed by Modestinus, *Dig.* 29. 5. 19: 'cum
dominus occiditur auxilium ei familia ferre debet . . . quod si cum
posset non tulerit merito de ea supplicium sumitur'. The matter was
first regulated by the Sullan law about murder. This seems to have
excepted from the general punishment slaves manumitted in the dead
man's will, unless they showed guilt by running away (Gaius, *Dig.*
ibid. 25. 1). A *SC. Silanianum* of A.D. 10, expanded by a subsequent
enactment in A.D. 57, withdrew this exemption, Tac. *Ann.* 13. 32;
Dig. loc. cit. When in A.D. 61 the City Prefect Pedanius was
murdered by a slave the resident *familia* of 400 was executed after a
debate in the Senate; the jurist Cassius insisted on the necessity of
severity if owners were to be protected, but a proposal to include
resident freedmen was rejected by the Princeps, Tac. *Ann.* 14.
42–45. So too in the present case the treatment of slaves and freedmen is separate. Popular opinion in the Senate grows less not more
humane, while the imperial lawyers tend to a certain leniency in
elaborating the rules. The motion here resisted by Pliny was a
revival of the harsh proposal of A.D. 61 for the punishment of actual
freedmen. For a short discussion see A. M. Duff, *Freedmen of the
early Roman Empire.* 63. For Afranius Dexter see v. 13. 4 n.

incertum. There was a possibility of suicide with servile assistance (*obsequio*). Originally the law did not apply to suicides, but it was extended on the ground that it was the duty of a slave to prevent his master's suicide if possible, Ulpian, *Dig.* 29. 5. 1. 18, 22. Pliny's wording leaves it unclear whether the punishment depends on establishing the fact of murder, as later. The *Fasti Ostienses* read 'exanimis inventus est'. This cannot have been set up before the end of the year in its original form. Possibly inquiries were protracted, as, for example, by the hunt for runaway slaves. In the similar case in III. 14. 4 the facts were in no doubt, and punishment followed swiftly.

hos alius . . . post quaestionem supplicio liberandos, alius in insulam relegandos. It seems that Pliny was the senior consular to make a proposal, which accordingly had the priority when it came to a division, if the consuls were prepared to accept any of them; ss. 14–15, 22. Cf. II. 11. 19–22, where the *sententia* of the consul designate, who always had the precedence in the *ordo sententiarum*, is put before that of a consular. On this occasion the *designati* must have remained silent.

Investigation was necessary to establish the facts, cf. Ulpian, *Dig.* 29. 5. 1. 24: 'liquere debet scelere interemptum ut senatus consulto locus sit'. Ordinarily this would be a matter simply for the court of the City Prefect. Pliny's proposal, affecting all freedmen, closes a loophole in the Neronian *SC.*, which while allowing the punishment of those manumitted by testament made no provision at all for investigation among actual freedmen. Pliny would allow the use of torture as a means of inquiry, but not any indiscriminate punishment of the freedmen. Paulus, *Dig.* 29. 5. 10. 1, seems to refer to the present case: 'sub divo Traiano constitutum est de his libertis quos vivus manumiserat quaestionem haberi'. The wording shows that the enactment did not emanate from the Princeps himself.

in insulam relegandos. For the diverse forms of punishment, relegation, deportation, and death, see II. 11. 19, IV. 11. 3, 13 nn. Pliny is not always technically exact in his use of terms (cf. I. 5. 5, VII. 19. 4 nn.), but here he correctly uses *relegare* throughout. The capital penalty, whether in the form of execution or of the later *deportatio in insulam*, was a stage beyond *relegatio in insulam*, which did not extinguish the civil *caput* of the condemned person. There is here no mention of the interdict which effected that, and which was still in use at this period (IV. 11. 3). The use of deportation as a *substitute* for the interdict belongs to a later period; cf. Brasiello, *Diritto Penale*, 292 ff., 308 ff.

15. servos supplicio adficiendos censuisset. This was merely the routine application of the law. If one of the questions at issue was that of suicide (s. 12 n.) it would seem that the Senate decided to disregard the distinction between murder and suicide and united in agreeing on the punishment of the slaves in either case. At a later date some qualified protection was given to slaves involved in the suicide of a master, Ulpian, *Dig.* 29. 5. 1. 22. One must assume that the conscientious Roman suicide, such as Corellius Rufus and Titius Aristo himself (I. 12, 22. 8), took good care not to involve their slaves, by sending them out of the house.

19. lex . . . iubet : 'qui haec censetis in hanc partem, qui alia omnia in illam partem ite qua sentitis '. He is quoting the text of the *lex Iulia de senatu habendo*; v. 13. 5 n. Festus gives the Republican form similarly, s.v. 261 M.: 'qui hoc censetis illuc transite, qui alia omnia in hanc partem'. This passage, with II. 11. 22 and IX. 13. 20, is the best evidence for the method of voting in the imperial Senate, and shows that the system has not changed from the Republican. Each *sententia* is voted on separately by the whole house (Mommsen, *DPR* vii. 181 ff.; Moore, *RE* (S), vi. 766 ff.; Greenidge, *Roman Public Life*, 271).

dirimi debere sententias. Pliny wants to alter the rules. Unless the two rival *sententiae* are voted on together, there is nothing to stop his rivals from combining against him, before their own *sententiae* are put to the vote. He says this fairly clearly in s. 14 and s. 17. But he can only make the *lex Iulia* support his case by sophistical arguments; hence the fog of words in ss. 20–22.

20. num ergo dubium est alia omnia sentire eos qui occidunt quam qui relegant? No doubt! But the law envisaged the single *sententia* at issue, and no extraneous parties.

nonne videtur ipsa lex eos qui dissentiunt in contrariam partem vocare? A very thin argument to put to a jurisprudent. For Pliny means disagreement *inter se*, but the law means disagreement *ab hac sententia*.

23. nisi dicente sententiam eo qui relegat, illi qui puniunt capite initio statim in alia discedant, frustra postea dissentient ab eo cui paulo ante consenserint. Now the supposition is that the death party support the exile party as such, and by carrying the *sententia relegantis* place their own *sententia* out of consideration. Pliny poses as the protector of his opponents' interests. No wonder his adversaries complained of the clouds of confusion by which Pliny paralysed their arguments, III. 9. 16. In fact the other parties only intended to co-operate against Pliny. Throughout this letter Pliny treats Aristo to a display of forensic rhetoric that might be little to the taste of an austere jurist.

24. obtinui quidem quod postulabam. Only indirectly, as he at once reveals. He is still in his forensic vein, attributing his opponents' change of front to the fear that Pliny *might* obtain his request.

nescio an iure certe aequitate postulationis meae victus. Pliny betrays the badness of his case by his *nescio*.

25. tum illi quoque . . . reliquerunt sententiam ab ipso auctore desertam. It was much as in the Priscus trial, when the supporters of Collega's proposal abandoned him, II. 11. 22.

26. tenuitque ex duabus altera tertia expulsa. Pliny does not give the final result, but the passage of Paulus, cited s. 12, suggests that Pliny gained the day.

The intransitive use of *teneo*, in sense of 'last' or 'hold on', is not uncommon, Forcellini, s.v., nn. 36–39; here the implied object is perhaps *locum*.

15. *To Terentius Junior*

Date. This note is closely connected with VII. 25, where Pliny mentions a newly discovered literary friend, Terentius Junior, with whom he here begins a literary correspondence. The reference to a poor harvest also helps to secure the book-date, s. 1.

1. scripseras tam graciles istic vindemias esse. This should be the poor harvest of Ep. 2. 1 and IX. 20. 2. Terentius' estates were in Pliny's region, at Perugia, VII. 25. 2 n.

2. sit modo unde chartae emi possint [quae si scabrae bibulaeve sint, aut non scribendum] aut necessario quidquid scripserimus boni malive delebimus. The bracketed words have no support except the Aldine edition. Rand defended them in *Harv. Stud.* 1923, 182. The second *aut* might suggest an omission, but Pliny uses a solitary *aut* in the sense of 'or else' in Ep. 24. 1 and 1. 10. 3. The shorter text makes a poor joke, but it is less feeble than the longer version, and is in line with a similar witticism of Cicero about using palimpsest for lack of new papyrus: *ad Fam.* 7. 18. 2. It is the existence, not the quality, of the papyrus that is in question. Pliny himself used waxed tablets for composition (1. 6. 1): hence *delebimus*. He will have to erase his compositions if there is no papyrus for the final version made by his copyist.

16. *To Paternus*

Date. This is one of the series interconnected by the illness theme, Ep. 1 pref.

Address. Plinius Paternus is a literary friend, probably from Comum, 1. 2 pref.

1. confecerunt me infirmitates meorum, mortes etiam et quidem iuvenum. Cf. Ep. 19. 1, 'infirmitate uxoris et meorum periculo, quorundam ... morte turbatus'. This may connect with his journey to Tifernum in August 107, Ep. 1 pref. The death may be that of Encolpius, ibid. For his solicitude for his personal servants see v. 19.

facilitas manumittendi. Pliny did not limit his free slaves to the inferior status of Junian Latins. In x. 104, when left rights in Junian Latins, he hastens to secure them citizen status. His attitude is remarkable among Romans. The motives of acquisition and ostentation are somewhat in abeyance.

permitto servis quoque quasi testamenta facere. Again he is in advance of contemporary law and custom, as in the question of *voluntas* in wills, IV. 10. 2, V. 7. 2 nn.

2. servis res publica quaedam et quasi civitas domus est. Seneca similarly says of slaves (Ep. 47. 14): 'domum pusillam rem publicam esse'. The underlying thought is as in Tac. *Ann.* 14. 27. 4: '. . . ut consensu et caritate rem publicam efficerent'. Pliny is here speaking of his domestic staff, not his agricultural slaves at Comum (as Sirago, *It. agr.* 120 f.), or of any staff at Comum, since he is probably writing from Rome to a landowner of Comum.

3. nec ignoro alios eiusmodi casus nihil amplius vocare quam damnum, eoque sibi magnos homines et sapientes videri. He similarly objects to meanness in patrons, II. 6 nn. By *sapientes* he means 'philosophers', as in V. 16. 8 n.

17. To Macrinus

Date. The letter seems to be after the end of Pliny's *cura Tiberis*, and hence to belong to the autumn of a year not earlier than 107, s. 1 n.

Address. Probably the literary correspondent Caecilius Macrinus, of III. 4, etc., rather than Minicius Macrinus of Brixia: III. 4 pref., Ep. 5. 1 n.

1. num istic quoque immite et turbidum caelum? Pliny writes from Rome or its neighbourhood. He has seen the floods below and above the city, ss. 2–3. But oddly he says nothing about the havoc within the city itself. The reference in *istic* depends on the identity of Macrinus.

1.–2. Tiberis alveum excessit et demissioribus ripis alte superfunditur quamquam fossa ... exhaustus. Pliny writes with the knowledge of a *curator Tiberis*, but without any official connexion with the matter. So a date later than 106 is probable. The floods are due to autumnal

rains. There is no mention of ruined crops, and the ploughmen are out
in the fields, s. 4.

2. providentissimus. For *providentia* on the coins of Trajan see *RIC*, ii.
'Trajan', nn. 28, 358 f., 514, 663 f. Cf. VI. 19. 3; X. 54. 1, 108. 2.
P. L. Strack, *R. Reichsprägung*, i. 45 f.
  fossa. Pliny does not indicate the site of this. A fragmentary
inscription, *ILS* 5797, from the territory of Ostia, dated 102 or later
by the titles of Trajan, reads: 'fossam [fecit q]ua inun[dationes
Tiberis a]dsidue u[rbem vexantes rivo] peren[ni instituto arceren-
tur].' Claudius earlier dug dykes in connexion with his new harbour,
ILS 207. R. Meiggs (*Roman Ostia*, App. iii. 488–9) remarks that there
is no trace of a canal above Rome, and hence favours the identification with the Fiumicino channel below the city, replacing the
channels of Claudius. Trajan's dyke seems to be separate from his
harbour, which was not completed apparently until 113 (Meiggs,
loc. cit.). Pliny's silence about flood damage in the city itself suggests that the dyke succeeded at this time in keeping the city dry.

3. Anio . . . adiacentibus villis velut invitatus retentusque. Compare the
description of the Pomptine shore II. 17. 27: 'litus ornant . . . nunc
continua nunc intermissa tecta villarum'.

**4. alibi divitum apparatus et gravem supellectilem, alibi instrumenta
ruris.** Pliny gives a general picture of a richly adorned country-
side, intensely exploited and populous. For the panoply of villas see
II. 17, v. 6. For *instrumenta*, III. 19. 7 n.

5. etiam decussa monimenta. In Horace, *C*. I. 2. 13–16, the Tiber
in flood destroys 'monumenta regis templaque Vestae'. Guillemin
(*VL* 120 f.) sees an echo in Pliny here, and from a few other turns
of phrase—rivers blocked by landslides, collapse of buildings, men
trapped by floods—alleges that Pliny is employing a literary commonplace in this description, repeated by Tacitus in *Hist*. I. 86 and
briefly in *Ann*. I. 76. But the differences outweigh the resemblances.
Pliny's *monimenta* are tombs, as in II. 10. 4, III. 7. 8, VI. 10. 2, and his
disaster is rural, those in Tacitus urban.

18. *To Rufinus*

Date. There are no close indications of time.

Address. Rufinus is addressed only here. He is probably the senator
L. Fadius Rufinus, mentioned in IX. 23. 4 n., a suffect consul of 113.

1. Domitius Tullus longe melior apparuerit morte quam vita. This
reference leads to a maze of consular prosopography. The names and
careers of this man and his brother Lucanus are known from a

number of inscriptions, particularly *ILS* 990–1, and references in Martial. (*PIR*² D 152, 167; Garzetti, *C*. 52; Syme, *Tac*. 794.) The pair were rapidly promoted by Vespasian, and served, often conjointly, in the Flavian wars and administration. Pliny casts no light on their public careers, but helps to date the birth of Tullus to a year before A.D. 41, s. 5 n. Tullus, the younger of the two, was praetor designate when Vespasian, probably in A.D. 73–74 as censor, gave the two patrician status. The reason for the special favours which the two enjoyed is not known; but if not *boni viri*, they were certainly *locupletes*. Their consulships, as yet undated, fell in the early years of Domitian, and they possibly served in his Germanic wars; otherwise their services were then confined to the senatorial province of Africa. Tullus may have secured a second consulship as a supporter of Nerva if he is the Cn. Domiti(us) . . . of the *Fasti Ostienses* for the Ides of January 98. His names were Cn. Domitius Sex. f. Afer Titius Marcellus Curvius Tullus. The first three came from his adoptive father, s. 5. Martial (1. 36, 5. 28. 3) calls the two men 'Curvii fratres'. So the natural father was presumably Sextus Curvius Tullus, a man possibly known from *CIL* vi. 16671. Their place of origin is uncertain, possibly Narbonensian (Syme). They are commemorated in several Italian municipalities, none of which is Cisalpine. The elder brother was dead by *c*. 94 (Martial, 9. 51).

2. cum se captandum praebuisset. See in general II. 20 nn.

reliquit filiam heredem . . . prosecutus est nepotes . . . legatis, prosecutus etiam pronepotem. This is the elder Domitia Lucilla, 'Cnaei filia', *PIR*² D 182; Syme, *Tac*. 792, 793, nn. 7–8. She married a member of an old consular family, P. Calvisius Tullus Ruso, himself consul in 109 (*PIR*² C 357). Her daughter, the younger Domitia Lucilla, who is one of the *nepotes*, married a son of the Hadrianic *ter consul* M. Annius Verus (*cos*. 97, 121, 126) and bore the future emperor Marcus Aurelius in 121. Hence the *pronepotem* of s. 2 cannot be Marcus himself. Cf. SHA, *Marcus*, 1. 3–4, 6. 9). Possibly the match with Ruso was the elder Lucilla's second marriage, and the *nepotes* came from an earlier union with Catilius Severus (or his son), reckoned among the ancestors of Marcus in SHA, loc. cit., and Dio 69. 21. Ruso would be about 25, and likely to marry, in *c*. 94–95. In 87 he was still *puer*, and Lucilla must have been born many years before the death of Lucanus in *c*. 94 if she is already a grandmother. The family money secured these marriages for the daughter of a sordid house.

The names of both Lucillae occur on stamped tiles *ILS* 8652–5.

3. sit frustratus improbas spes hominum, quos sic decipi pro moribus temporum est. Ummidia Quadratilla left an equally satisfactory will,

VII. 24. 2. Pliny is not always so favourable to the spirit of the times, cf. II. 20. 12, IV. 15. 8 nn.

4. nam Curtilius Mancia perosus generum suum Domitium Lucanum . . . sub ea condicione filiam eius . . . instituerat heredem si esset manu patris emissa. The father-in-law of Lucanus was consul in 55 and legate of Upper Germany in 56–58: Tac. *Ann.* 13. 56; *PIR²* C 1605. He was apparently the owner of great estates in Africa Proconsularis (A–J, 74; *FIRA* i. 100). Possibly unaware of the peculiar legal condition of Lucanus' affairs, Mancia failed to specify that Domitia should be freed altogether from *manus* and left under the nominal charge of a *tutor*. (Cf. II. 20. 10 n.; Gaius, I. 132–4, 142–5.) So she was transferred from the *manus* of Lucanus to that of Tullus, and by the operations of the *consortium bonorum* was subject to the *manus* of both (below). For a parallel dodge see IV. 2. 1–2 n.

ita circumscripto testamento consors frater in fratris potestatem emancipatam filiam adoptionis fraude revocaverat. This is explained by the workings of *consortium bonorum* revealed by the 'new fragments' of Gaius, printed as III. 154 A. There was an old legal form, *erctum non citum*, by which brothers held their inheritance in common instead of making the usual division, and which gave rise to an analogous partnership between strangers created by a *legis actio*. Both forms were obsolete in Gaius' day, and modern textbooks exclude them from the discussion of classical law. (Cf. Schulz, *Classical Roman Law*, 550; Buckland, *Main Institutes*, etc. 276, R. Monier, *Manuel élémentaire*⁴ etc., 2. 176 f. F. de Zulueta, *JRS*, 1935, 18 f.) But Pliny here reveals that two of the richest consulars at Rome were using the *consortium* in all its niceties some thirty years earlier, or less. For on it depended the trick. The partners of the *consortium*, according to Gaius, bound each other mutually by all their contractual operations, e.g.: 'unus ex sociis communem servum manumittendo liberum faciebat et omnibus libertum adquirebat' etc. So Tullus, by adopting his brother's daughter, brought her again under the communal *manus*. This Mancia forgot, showing the rarity of the custom. Cf. W. Kunkel, *Heidelberger Akad. Wiss.*, *Jahresheft*, 1955–6, 45.

Martial celebrates the 'concord' of the brothers (1. 36, 3. 20. 17, 5. 28. 3), and their names appear together on stamped tiles, *ILS* 8651 etc. Pliny does not seem unduly shocked, but Lucilla resented the trick, s. 7.

5. Domitius Afer . . . reliquit testamentum ante decem et octo annos nuncupatum, adeoque postea improbatum sibi ut patris eorum bona proscribenda curaverit. Another seamy yarn. The great orator from Narbonensis (II. 14. 10 n.) died in A.D. 59, and hence must have adopted the Curvii brothers in 41–42 (Tac. *Ann.* 14. 19; *PIR²*

D 126). His attack on the elder Curvius is not recorded elsewhere, and perhaps fell in the early years of Claudius, before the beginning of the present narrative of Tacitus.

For the Roman dislike of an 'old' will cf. v. 5. 2, 'decessit vetere testamento' n.

7. sed haec quoque hereditas Afri . . . transmittenda erant filiae fratris . . . ut conciliaretur. The will of Lucanus was evidently full of conditions designed to secure that the whole estate of both brothers passed ultimately to Lucilla, who had evidently been on bad terms with her tricky parents. The two brothers were possessed by a passion for property that recalls the most sordid of Balzac's characters.

8. accepit magnam pecuniam uxor optima et patientissima. This distinguished lady, evidently a second wife, is not yet identified. Her name is purposely omitted, as in Ep. 22. 4. The letter still maintains its Balzacian tone in the next anecdote.

11. amplissimos hortos . . . instruxerit plurimis . . . statuis. Compare the gardens and statues of Regulus, IV. 2. 5.

19. *To Maximus*

Date. The letter belongs to the 'sickness' group, Epp. 1, 10, 11, 16 prefs.

Address. This should be the 'elder' and 'learned' Maximus, II. 14 pref., who is distinct from the 'young' Maximus of Ep. 24 and VII. 26. Though interest in *studia* appears in II. 14, III. 20, VI. 11, IX. 1. 23, among the letters to a Maximus, collaboration is mentioned only here and in IX. 1 (s. 2).

1. infirmitate uxoris et meorum periculo. Cf. Ep. 16. 1.

20. *To Gallus*

Date. Pliny may well have visited Ameria on the journey to Tifernum indicated in Epp. 1 and 8.

Address. Gallus, recipient also of the account of the Laurentine villa II. 17 (pref.), may be Clusinius Gallus of IV. 17, an obscure figure.

1. ad quae noscenda iter ingredi transmittere mare solemus. We seldom hear of an *iter cognoscendae antiquitatis* undertaken for itself alone. Even in the famous case of Germanicus' visit to Egypt 'cura provinciae praetendebatur', Tac. *Ann.* 2, 59. Senators could not travel about the world except under the licence of a *legatio libera*.

It is much discussed whether the Elder Pliny's visits to provinces were limited to official appointment, III. 5, 'Career' nn. Provincials like Strabo seem to have done more 'scientific' travelling than the official classes. Nero's visit to Greece proves the rule. Romans when officially in Egypt liked to visit and 'hear' Memnon. Yet Pliny implies an active tourist interest in s. 2. Here Pliny elaborates in fourteen lines a theme that he dismisses with five words in Ep. 8. 1, 'ego—paenitet tarditatis—proxime vidi'. Travel in antiquity, though extensive, usually had a professional or religious motive. Cf. Friedlaender (Eng. trans.), i. 316, at length.

2. in urbe nostra. Rome, as in v. 6. 4 etc.

3. ipse certe nuper . . . audivi pariter et vidi. The adverb is used of recent events in Ep. 22. 4, II. 14. 6, VII. 26. 1, IX. 23. 2. For his reported evidence see ss. 6–8.

exegerat prosocer meus ut Amerina praedia sua inspicerem. So too he asked Pliny to inspect his Campanian estate in VI. 30. He was now declining in strength, VII. 23. Ameria lay off Pliny's usual route to Tifernum, Ep. 8. 1 n.

mihi ostenditur subiacens lacus nomine Vadimonis. The site of the great battle with the Etruscans in 310 B.C. (Livy 9. 39, Polybius 2. 20) is identified with the little lake of Bassano near Orte, now much shrunken. It is mentioned by the Elder Pliny, *NH* 2. 209, and by Seneca, *Q.Nat.* 3. 25. 8, in discussions of floating islands, which evidently interested the *scriptores curiosi* of the age, though neither had visited it. For a nineteenth-century description of the lake see Dennis, *Cities and Cemeteries of Etruria* (1883), i. 142 ff. Also *RE* (2) vii. 2053. It is noteworthy that Pliny does not mention the battles connected with the lake,—and also that he is not acquainted with his uncle's description of such islets. Cf. IX. 33. 1 n.

4. undique aequalis. The volcanic origin of the lakes of southern Etruria is apparent in their regular outlines.

color caerulo albidior viridior et pressior. Schuster emended this text, which gives good sense, into 'viridi ora pressior'. Pliny means that the colour is a deep dull green instead of a Mediterranean sky-blue. Cf. Sen. *Q. Nat.* 3. 2. 2, 'purae sunt (sc. aquae) turbidae caeruleae luridae'.

sulpuris odor saporque medicatus, vis qua fracta solidantur. Seneca (ib. 3. 25. 9–10) describes similarly the lake Cutiliae, 'aquae gravitas medicatae et ob hoc ponderosae', and attributes the formation of floating islands to the cohesive effect of the sulphurated water: 'fortasse enim leves truncos frondesque in lacu sparsas pinguis umor apprehendit ac vinxit'. He compares the crust found around sulphur springs: 'ubi purgamenta aquarum coaluerunt et spuma solidatur'. The scientific tendency does not go beyond accurate observation.

5. nulla in hoc navis, sacer enim. Cf. Ep. 8. 6 for the taboo.

6. interdum iunctae copulataeque. Seneca speaks only of a single island. Pliny here is reporting what he heard rather than saw, s. 3.

9. idem lacus in flumen egeritur quod . . . specu mergitur. Another wonder. Seneca has something to say about disappearing rivers, op. cit. 3. 11, 16, also Curtius Rufus, 6. 4. 5–6.

10. nam te quoque ut me nihil aeque ac naturae opera delectant. This taste for natural wonders, which Pliny shared with his uncle, produced Seneca's *Natural Questions* and his uncle's *Natural History*. Pliny contributes IV. 30 Larium, VI. 16, 20, Vesuvius, VII. 27, ghosts, and IX. 33, the dolphin of Hippo, as well as this letter and Ep. 8, the fountain of Clitumnus. In these Pliny shows himself exact as an observer and recorder, and cautious and unexaggerated according to his lights. His speculations are seldom silly, cf. IV. 30. 9–10 nn.

21. *To Maturus Arrianus*

Date. The letter requires a late date, because in VII. 4 the volume of hendecasyllabics was still his latest book. In IX. 16 and 25 two interconnected notes show him busy with the first draft of a volume of poems in the autumn of a year that is probably 107. So a date in or after July 107 is possible for this letter, ss. 2, 4.

Address. For the literary equestrian Maturus Arrianus of Altinum see I. 2 pref.

2. graviora opera lusibus iocisque distinguo. This letter should be read with other defences of his versifying, IV. 14, V. 3, VII. 9. 9–14.

Iulio mense, quo maxime lites interquiescunt, . . . amicos collocavi. So too his first book was recited to a select private party, V. 3. 11. The choice of day was difficult, because the civil courts sat continuously, with numerous but irregular interruptions for holidays. The calendar allowed from 200 to 230 days for judicial work in the second century, according to the calculations quoted by Carcopino, *Daily Life*, 203–6. Between the absence of friends in the courts on business days, or in the amphitheatre on festal days, a time was hard to find. In I. 13 April is a favoured month for recitations.

3. mane in advocationem subitam rogarer. Cf. I. 9. 2 and Ep. 9. 1 for these sudden calls. The courts began work very early in the day,

and lasted normally till the fourth hour; Martial, 4. 8. 2, 8. 67. 3. Siesta
and *cenae tempus* further diminished the day. So even short books
might take several days to read, as here (s. 4 n.). In VI. 17. 3 *totum
diem* of a recitation is an evident exaggeration. See III. 5. 9 n.

quod mihi causam praeloquendi dedit .Pliny rather disliked 'prefaces' that had no excuse, IV. 5. 3–4, 14. 8; V. 12. 3. On prefaces see
also I. 13. 2, IV. 11. 3 nn.

4. liber fuit et opusculis varius et metris. This clearly distinguishes the
book from his earlier volume confined to hendecasyllabics, IV. 14. 8,
VII. 4. 3 (Schultz, art. cit. 32–33). He had as a young man in 81–82
tried his hand at elegiacs, but not published them, VII. 4. 3, 7.

liber. This may suggest that the book was longer than his *libellus*
of hendecasyllabics, which filled only a single roll, VII. 4. 8.

recitavi biduo : hoc adsensus audientium exegit. So too his Panegyric took a third day by request, III. 18. 4, and the reading in IX. 27
needed two days but lost his audience.

lego . . . omnia ut omnia emendem. Pliny wrote verses by committee,
V. 3. 7–11.

6. adhuc museteum librum. The same metaphor is used of these poems
in IX. 16. 2: 'pro novo musto . . . versiculos . . . ut primum videbun-
tur defervisse mittemus'.

22. *To Rosianus Geminus*

Date. The letter belongs to the Rosianus series, confined to VII–IX,
see VII. I pref.

Address. For the now praetorian senator Rosianus Geminus see ibid.
Of the six letters to this protégé three are letters of example and
advice, cf. VII. 1, IX. 30, as here.

3. Thrasea crebro dicere solebat, 'qui vitia odit homines odit'. For
the Neronian statesman Thrasea Paetus see III. 16. 10 n. The theme,
common in Latin literature, is Stoic, but is characteristically softened
by Pliny. Cf. Seneca, *de ira* 2. 8. 1, 28. 1; *de tranquill. anim.* 15. 2;
Tac. *Hist.* 4. 74. 3.

4. nuper quidam—sed melius coram, quamquam ne tunc quidem.
Guillemin compares Cicero's warning against gossip in *de off.* I. 134:
'cum studiose de absentibus detrahendi causa . . . contumeliose . . .
dicitur'. Pliny gives Rosianus a delicate lesson. The story is not taken
up in any other letter.

23. To Marcellinus

Date. The date is fixed to a year later than 107 by the mention of the young Avitus in the will of Dasumius, signed between May and August 108, s. 1 n.

Address. The senator and advocate Claudius Marcellinus (II. 11. 16 n.) is less probable than Aefulanus Marcellinus, recipient of the similar letter v. 16.

1. ex morte Iuni Aviti. The identification with the like-named man in the will of Dasumius seems certain: *CIL* vi. 10229 20; *PIR*¹ J 472. The will mentions other members of Pliny's circle including himself, Tacitus, and Minicius Justus. They have a common friend in Servianus, whose daughter is among the co-heirs. The will uses the same name forms as used in this letter, single nomen and cognomen. Hence there cannot have been two senatorial Iunii Aviti at this date. For the false attempt to identify our man with Julius Avitus of v. 21 see ibid. nn.

2. latum clavum in domo mea induerat, suffragio meo adiutus in petendis honoribus fuerat. The young man was of equestrian origin, and at the beginning of a senatorial career, like Erucius Clarus and Julius Naso, II. 9. 2 n., VI. 6 nn.

By *suffragio* Pliny here and in s. 6 refers to the actual election. For the metaphorical sense of *suffragatio* see II. 1. 8 n.

me quasi magistro utebatur. Cf. VI. 11. 2 for parallel cases.

3. rarum hoc in adulescentibus nostris. Pliny's attitude to youth is usually friendly, IX. 12. 1 n., but cf. II. 14, IV. 15. 8.

4. semper ille aut de studiis aliquid aut de officiis vitae consulebat. Pliny's silence about the quality of his *studia* is eloquent. By *officiis vitae* he here distinguishes what in IV. 24. 3 he calls *officia civilia* from the service of the emperor. He advises Avitus about social behaviour in II. 6.

5. Serviano . . . quem legatum tribunus . . . ex Germania in Pannoniam transeuntem . . . ut comes . . . sequeretur. L. Julius Ursus Servianus, the great consular, friend of Trajan and Hadrian, was born *c.* A.D. 46–47 of an unknown father, Servius, and (apparently) adopted later by Julius Ursus, who became praetorian prefect of Domitian, and was promoted consul in 84 (Dio 67. 4. 2, 69. 17. 1, *P. Berl.* 8344). All that is certain about his early career comes from this passage and from SHA, *Hadr.* 2. 6. These show that he was consular legate of Upper Germany in January 98, when he prevented the young Hadrian,

serving as military tribune, from taking the news of Nerva's death
privately to Trajan, then at Colonia Agrippinensis in Lower Germany: cf. *Pan.* 9. 2–5, Victor, *Ep.* 13. 3, Eutropius 8. 2. 1. Hence
Servianus' consulship is better attributed to 90, when the *Fasti* of
Potentia give Ser. Julius Servianus among the suffects, than to 98,
when the *Fasti* of Ostia give another Julius Ursus as suffect in March
98. The difference of praenomen, if not a mere error of the cutter,
may reflect some later testamentary disposition; that of Servianus
was certainly Lucius by the end of his life (*ILS* 4271): so too the
cognomen Ursus, not used by Pliny, appears in his later inscriptions.
Otherwise many difficulties arise, particularly that in Pliny's
account Servianus does not return to Rome for the period of his
consulship. Consulships were rarely if ever held in absence except
by emperors up to this period (R. Syme, *JRS* 1958, 1 ff.). It is not
likely that by *legatum* Pliny meant only a legionary commander,
since *comes* implies service under a provincial governor, as in VI.
22. 2. The adoptive son of Ursus should have secured a consulship
long before he was 52; one in 90 is already late enough.

Servianus probably went to Pannonia with Trajan, who visited the
upper Danube area in 99, and he may have remained there until
the opening of the first Dacian war, in which he evidently served,
being replaced in Pannonia *c.* 101 by Glitius Agricola (III. 17. 3 n.).
For his marriage to the sister of Hadrian, and his political role under
Trajan and Hadrian, see VI. 26, VII. 6. 9 nn. His Spanish connexions
strongly suggest that he was himself of Spanish origin, as was his
son-in-law Pedanius Fuscus, VI. 26 n. See *PIR*[1] J 417, which needs
amendment. Garzetti, op. cit. 89 f., 134 n., C. 81; Lambrechts, op. cit.
74; Syme, *Tac.* 17, 52, 603 f., 636.

ut comes. Pliny implies that he ceased to hold a military
tribunate when he went to Pannonia, though prolonged military
tribunates are not uncommon, as in Trajan's own career, *Pan.*
15. 1–3.

quaestor consulibus suis (et plures habuit) . . . utilis. For the consular quaestors see IV. 15. 6–8 nn. This passage shows that the quaestors
of the *consules ordinarii* continued to serve under the suffects for
the rest of the year.

qua vigilantia hanc ipsam aedilitatem cui praereptus est petiit.
If he was designated aedile in January 108 for 109, he could have
been quaestor any year before 108. His recent marriage suggests that
he had married for the sake of his public career, about the time of
his quaestorship, as was common, VII. 24. 3 n. The interval of some
eight or nine years between a military tribunate *c.* 98–99 and a
quaestorship *c.* 107 is very similar to that in the career of Pliny
himself.

9. in tantis tormentis eram cum scriberem ⟨ut⟩ haec scriberem sola.
Despite Stout the addition of *ut* is essential, its omission being
without precise parallel in Pliny's usage. Stout, op. cit. 173, rightly
remarks that Pliny omits the *ut* in jussive and final constructions only.

    eram. Surely an epistolary tense? Cf. VII. 19. 11 (n.), 'in his eram
curis cum scriberem ad te'.

24. *To Maximus*

Date. There are no exact indications. The usual identification of
Maximus would exclude a date before *c.* 104–5, s. 8 n. His mission
is more probable in any case after the second Dacian War, s. 4 n.

Address. The tone of the letter shows that this is the 'younger
Maximus' addressed in similar style in VI. 34, VII. 26, who is possibly
Maximus the heir of Valerius Varus in VI. 8. 4. The further identi-
fication, widely accepted, with Quinctilius Valerius Maximus of
Troas is doubtful, s. 8 n.

1. non ut praecipiam . . . admoneam tamen. Cf. VII. 26. 4 for the half
apology, half directive, fitting from a senior consular to a recently
promoted praetorian senator. So too Cicero to his brother when
proconsul of Asia, *ad Q. Fr.* 1. 1. 18, 36. Pliny closely echoes but
modifies Cicero's blunter approach to Curio, *ad Fam.* 2. 1. 2.

**2. cogita te missum in provinciam Achaiam, illam veram et meram
Graeciam, in qua primum humanitas, litterae, etiam fruges inventae
esse creduntur.** F. Zucker (*Philologus*, lxxxiv (1928), 209 ff.) drew
attention to the echoes of Cicero's language on the same theme,
in his letter of advice to his brother as proconsul of Asia, *ad Q. Fr.*
1. 1, which must be regarded as Pliny's prototype here. Cf. especially
ibid. 27 'ei generi . . . a quo ad alios pervenisse putetur humanitas',
and ib. 6, 'genere . . . quod est ex hominum omni genere humanissimum'.
Pliny also echoes *pro Flacco* 61–62, 'florem legatorum . . . ex vera atque
integra Graecia . . . Athenienses unde humanitas doctrina religio
fruges iura leges ortae putantur' etc. Zucker rightly remarks that
Pliny spoke as a member of the philhellenic circle of Sosius Senecio
and Minicius Fundanus. Cf. I. 9 pref., 13 pref., V. 16. 8 n. He compares
this letter to Statius' *Protrepticon* to Maecius Celer, *Silvae*, iii. 2,
traces the type back to Isocrates' address *ad Nicoclem*, and compares
the title of a lost book of Plutarch: ὑποθετικὸς ἢ περὶ αρχῆς (cited from
the list of Lamprias, 153 in *RE* xxi. 700).

    missum ad ordinandum statum liberarum civitatum. Pliny quotes the title of Maximus' commission, s. 7. He was sent, like Pliny later, 'ex senatusconsulto et ex auctoritate principis'. Cf. s. 9, 'iudicio missus'. He is to take the place of the annual proconsul of Achaea as imperial legate with *imperium*, s. 6. A special commission was required because the *civitates liberae* were usually exempt from the governor's control, and there was the possibility of disputes about status of cities, as happened in Bithynia (x. 47, 92–93). Subsequent commissioners were limited in their function to the particular job, and bore such titles as *corrector et curator*, *logistes*, or 'legatus ad rationes civitatium putandas', *ILS* 1066–7, 8826. Maximus is the first certain example, if the Domitianic commissioner given by Philostratus (*VS* I. 19) is an anachronism. The mission of Maximus belongs to the same category as Pliny's special legateship in Bithynia, and Trajan's institution of municipal comptrollers, *curatores civitatium*, in Italy (VII. 15. 2 n.). All these experiments show the same paternalism towards local self-government, the same desire to protect the municipalities of the Empire from their own mismanagement. This gradually assumed a form of bureaucratic control during the second century A.D. that distinguishes the Late Empire from the Principate. See A. H. M. Jones, *Greek City*, 136 ff.; Abbot and Johnson, *Municipal Administration*, 90 ff., 189 ff.; *RE* iv, 'curator', n. 10, 1806 ff.; *CAH* xi. 219 f., 468 f. Also Introduction, pp. 526 f.

liberarum civitatum. Pliny understands this to include *civitates foederatae*, as in his own mission, x. 92 n., if *foedere* below is to be pressed. These two categories of community originated in the pre-provincial period of Roman power in Asia, in the earlier second century B.C. Within the provincial system they became the most privileged class of community, with a status that could only be altered by decree of the Senate, or later the emperor. The *c. foederata* was nominally an autonomous community associated with Rome through a mutual treaty which regulated the rights and duties of either party, whereas the privileges of a *c. libera* were conceded solely by Rome. The most valuable of these were: independence from pro-consular jurisdiction, freedom from billeting of troops, and from military requisitions, and freedom from Roman taxation, *immunitas*. The latter required a separate grant, which was not made to all 'free cities'. See A. N. Sherwin-White, *Roman Citizenship*, ch. vi; Abbot and Johnson, op. cit. ch. v; Jones, op. cit. 115 ff., 131 f. For a list of the free cities of Achaea see Jones, op. cit. 129, and n. 63. They were remarkably numerous, but apparently Athens was the only *civitas foederata*, ibid. 17–18.

Nero during his tour of Greece granted free status, with *immunitas*, to all the cities of Achaea, but Vespasian revoked the general grant, limiting the status to those that held it before Nero's act, as this letter seems to indicate. See Braithwaite, Suet. *Vesp*. 8. 4; Pausanias vii. 17. 2; Ditt. *Syll*.³ 814 (A–J, n. 56).

3. nihil ex cuiusquam dignitate nihil ex libertate . . . decerpseris. It is not made clear what ills Maximus was meant to cure, but the analogy with Pliny's mission suggests that financial mismanagement was the main concern. If there had been any general crisis in the province Maximus' mission would not have been limited to the free States. Possibly the continuous Balkan wars had upset their equilibrium, as in A.D. 14; Tac. *Ann*. 1. 76, 12. 62–63. This consideration points to a date after the second Dacian war. Possibly also the situation had been left unclear in details after Vespasian's action. Changes of status were not infrequent, as Tacitus notes of Rhodes, *Ann*. 12. 58: 'prout externis bellis meruerant aut domi seditione deliquerant'.

4. umbram. Documents, such as A–J, nn. 90–92, 121, show how little 'freedom' was left to Athens and Sparta in the later second century, when it was possible to appeal from their courts to the Princeps. Trajan shows a 'correct', but not a liberal, attitude towards the privileges of Amisus in x. 93 nn.

8. onerat te quaesturae tuae fama quam ex Bithynia optimam revexisti, onerat testimonium principis. From this, Maximus has been identified by Groag and others with the provincial quaestor commended by Trajan in A.D. 100 (*Pan*. 70. 1) for organizing the finances of a certain great city, and both further identified with the man Sextus Quinctilius Valerius Maximus, known from *ILS* 1018, an inscription of Alexandria Troas: 'lato clavo exornato a divo Aug. Nerva quaestori Ponti et Bithyniae', who should have been quaestor about the same time. But the ground of this identification is otherwise very weak. Groag supposed that the man in the Panegyric was a friend of Pliny. Pliny's Maximus may be connected with the name Valerius through the reference in vi. 8. 4, where a *Maximus noster* is heir to Valerius Varus. But the characters in vi. 8 appear to be Cisalpine (ibid. nn.), whereas Quinctilius Maximus and his descendants were natives of Alexandria Troas (*ILS*, loc. cit., Philostratus, *VS* 2. 1. 11, p. 559; *PIR*¹ Q 19–24). Better evidence for the identification might come from an inscription of Sparta (*IG* 5. 1. 380), in which a statue is dedicated to Trajan as Parthicus, i.e. not before 116, and a Quinctilius Maximus is mentioned in a broken passage, possibly as authorizing expenditure. But the date is too late for our man. The inscription might be Hadrianic and refer to a son of Quinctilius. Hence the accepted identification is better left in doubt. Our man, however, is likely to be the Maximus mentioned by Arrian as a *corrector* in an episode at Nicopolis (*Epictet*. 3. 7). For the accepted view see

M. N. Todd, *Anatolian Studies presented to W. H. Buckler* (Manchester, 1939), 333 ff., who restated the case advanced by Groag, *Jahresh. österr. arch. Inst. Wien.* B. xxi–xxii. 435. Also *PIR*[1] J.

testimonium principis. This may mean that the man was *candidatus Caesaris* for the following magistracies. The term is associated with commendation and *suffragatio* in *Pan.* 91. 3, IV. 15. 13. (Paladini, *Athenaeum*, xxxvii. 37.)

BOOK IX

1. *To Maximus*

Date. The letter is later than 100, when Pompeius Planta was alive, and earlier than *c.* 107, when Vibius Maximus fell into trouble, on the doubtful assumption that these are the personages involved in this letter. Otherwise there is little ground for dating it. The identification of Planta is more probable than that of Vibius (below).

Address. The recipient should be identified with the 'elder Maximus' of II. 14, VI. 11, VIII. 19, and Ep. 23. This man—if he is one person— may be either Maesius Maximus of III. 20, IV. 25, or Vibius Maximus, the equestrian, of III. 2, or the senator Novius Maximus of IV. 20 and V. 5. See II. 14 pref. Vibius Maximus is known to have had literary interests, but has only been brought into the discussion because of Planta. Both men were prefects of Egypt. Vibius in 103 followed Minicius Italus who succeeded Planta *c.* 100. It is unlikely that they indulged in diatribes about their official duties. From the erasure of the name of Vibius on surviving documents in Egypt it seems that he was condemned for malpractices and suffered *damnatio memoriae* after his governorship, which ended in 107, despite the doubts of Pflaum, nn. 58, 65. It is possible that a version of the speech of an advocate attacking him is preserved in *P. Oxy.*, iii. 471. It is unlikely that Pliny would publish a letter addressed to him after his condemnation. See III. 2. pref.

A recent attempt to show that the *damnatus* was a later, Hadrianic prefect, of the same name, son of Pliny's friend, is unconvincing. J. Schwartz (*Chronique d'Égypte*, xxvi, 1951, 254–6) and Hanslik (*RE* (2) viii. 1976), thought that the earlier man's names were deleted in error, but this interpretation of the principal item of evidence (*AE*, 1952, n. 159) is not the natural way of taking it, and the deleted name, essential to the case, cannot be read with any certainty. Cf. R. Syme, *Historia*, 1957, 480 ff. For the deletions of Maximus' name on several monuments see *RE*, loc. cit.

More probably our man is Novius Maximus, whose work, activated by *dolor*, IV. 20. 2, and still under preparation in V. 5. 7 (*inter manus*), fits the description below. Novius was expected by Pliny to take an interest in the Neronian histories of Fannius, and it is possible that his relative, the Vespasianic consular Novius Priscus (IV. 20 pref.), was criticized in the history of Planta, s. 1 n.; a friend of Seneca,

he had earlier been exiled after the Pisonian conspiracy, Tac. *Ann.*
15. 71.

1. **libros quos vel pro te vel in Plantam . . . composuisti.** The uncommon cognomen makes the identification with the equestrian Pompeius Planta, prefect of Egypt 98–100 (X. 7 n.), reasonable. The
scholiast of Juvenal 2. 99 mentions an account of the Civil Wars of
69 written in this period by a Pompeius Planta. The difficulty that
the scholiast seems to date this later than Tacitus' own *Historiae* is
not very serious. Guillemin, ad loc., suggested that Planta may have
criticized some of the heroes of Pliny's circle, such as Arulenus
Rusticus. Novius Maximus evidently shared the admiration of
Fannius for such persons. Hence the note of *dolor*. Pompeius and
Novius would know and criticize each other's work from recitations
and circulations, cf. IV. 20. Vibius Maximus' known work, finished
before 95, was an epitome of republican history, from Livy and
Sallust (Statius, *S.* 4. 7. 54–56). For the *scholium* see *RE* xxi. 2283.

4. **hoc perfice quod nobis qui legimus olim absolutum videtur.** In
IV. 20 the whole work of Novius Maximus has been read, apparently
twice, by Pliny, who stresses the element of *dolor* and *amaritudo* in
the book.

   This note gives the impression that Maximus has for long been a
man of leisure, certainly not that he has just come back from long
occupationes in Egypt pursued by vengeful provincials. The references
to the younger Maximus in VI. 34, VII. 26, VIII. 24 do not fit the
implications of this letter, which agree with the circumstances of
the 'elder' in VIII. 19. 2 and Ep. 23. 6.

2. *To Sabinus*

Date. The theme is continued in Ep. 18, also to Sabinus. The reference to Pliny's activities in s. 1 closely resembles that in a number
of letters in VI–IX, which have sundry other connexions with the
book-series; cf. VII. 30. 2, VIII. 9, 21. 3 and Epp. 25. 3, 35. 1. Though
free from official duties, sporadic briefs pursue him in town and
country. Hence the late date is probable.

Address. The identification of the recipient with Statius Sabinus of
Firmum, IV. 10 pref. has been questioned by R. Syme (*JRS*, 1957,
132 n. 6), who, assuming that the military duties mentioned in s. 4
refer to a senior post, would identify our man with the consular
P. Metilius Sabinus Nepos. But if this man appears in the Letters
he appears as the Nepos of II. 3, III. 16, VI. 19, and under the form
Maecilius Nepos in IV. 26. See II. 3 pref. It is against the usage of

Pliny and his MS. that the name should appear here in the form of
Sabinus, which would imply that Pliny wrote Metilius Nepos in the
earlier Letters and changed to Metilius Sabinus here and in Ep. 18.
Besides, letters to Nepos and Sabinus are consecutive in VI. 18–19,
which does not occur for the same recipient after II. 11–12. The
names of Nepos in common use were Metilius Nepos, as appears in
the Arval record of his death, *ILS* 5028. Hence either Metilius or
Nepos should appear in Pliny, not Sabinus. The man is rather old
to be summoned to the standards again after his consular appointment in Britain ten years earlier. Altogether the identification does
not fit, and Statius Sabinus, serving as a praetorian legate of a province or a legion, is preferable.

3. nisi forte volumus scholasticas tibi . . . litteras mittere. Cf. III. 20.
10–11: 'de republica . . . cuius materiae . . . rarior quam veteribus
occasio . . .. Habeant nostrae quoque litterae aliquid non humile.'
Pliny is trying to write genuine news letters in literary form, and
rejoices, as in II. 11. 1, when something great offers itself. The letters
of Seneca may serve as an example of *scholasticae litterae*, such as
Pompeius Saturninus, or his wife, may have written, I. 16. 6. Cf. pp. 2 f.

4. cum arma vestra, cum castra, . . . pulverem, soles cogitamus. This,
with *tuas occupationes* s. 1, indicates a military commission, in some
more than Mediterranean clime, such as the Syrian, Cappadocian,
or Numidian zone. A legionary or provincial legateship is probably
indicated by *occupationes*, rather than the lesser duties of a military
tribune; cf. IV. 26. 2, VII. 12. 6, Ep. 25. 1.

3. *To Valerius Paulinus*

Date not determinable. The recipient should be Valerius Paulinus,
the consul of 107, II. 2 pref., addressed also in Ep. 37. The *otium*
theme is touched lightly in the first note to him, II. 2. 2.

1. nisi praemium aeternitatis ante oculos, . . . otium placeat. For the
theme cf. I. 3. 3–4, III. 7. 14–15, V. 5. 4–7 nn. Pliny is not attributing
otium to Paulinus, or he would have written *istud*, as in I. 3. 3.

2. ad vilitatem sui pervenire. The phrase is Senecan, cf. *Ep.* 121. 24,
'in nullo deprehendes vilitatem sui'; *De Clem.* I. 3. 4.

4. *To Macrinus*

Date. There is no exact indication of date, but the speech in question
is probably a revised version of his *In Caecilii Socios*, s. 1 n. There
is no trace of the final publication of this earlier, cf. IV. 5. 4 n. In

v. 8. 6 he was considering the revision of certain of his *graves causae*, and is so occupied in the late note, Ep. 15. 2, as well as Epp. 10. 3, 28. 5. But an earlier date is not excluded.

Address. The first letter about the trials of Classicus (III. 4) was addressed to Caecilius Macrinus, and the last two about the case of Varenus to apparently the same Macrinus; see III. 4, VII. 6 prefs.

1. immodicam orationem . . . nam singulis criminibus singulae velut causae continentur. The speech concerns a criminal case, and hence one of the extortion trials. The description exactly fits the multiple character of the *In Caecilii Socios,* with its numerous *rei,* III. 9. 9, 12, 22. He had written about its origins in III. 4 to Macrinus. Since he did not deliver a set speech on the main charge in the abortive Varenus case, that is excluded (VII. 6. 3).

5. *To Calestrius Tiro*

Date. This continues the series referring to the appointment of Calestrius Tiro to the proconsulship of Baetica, probably in the spring of the year following Trajan's return from the Dacian conquest, i.e. 107. Since Tiro is now established in his province, a date in 107–8 is likely. See VI. 22 pref.

Address. For the earlier career of Tiro see VII. 16 nn.

1. egregie facis. inquiro enim. Pliny as patron of Baetica was bound to take an interest in its welfare, III. 4. 4 n. His connexion with the province reached back to his accusation of Baebius Massa under Domitian (VII. 33. 4) and was invoked in the time of Nerva (I. 7).

2. ne gratiae potentium nimium impertire videantur . . . malignitatis famam consequuntur. So Julius Bassus by his severity stirred up the hostility of *factiosissimum quemque,* and Caecilius Classicus was accused by a notable whom he had exiled, III. 9. 31, IV. 9. 5. Marius Priscus conspired with one set of *potentiores* against another, II. 11. 8. Tacitus remarks upon the phenomenon: 'ut solent praevalidi provincialium et opibus nimiis ad iniurias minorum elati', Tac. *Ann.* 15. 20. See further, on political feuds in Bithynia, X. 58. 1, 81 nn.

3. ut discrimina ordinum dignitatumque custodias. The lawyer Callistratus remarks, *Dig.* 1. 18. 19 pref.: 'mandatis adicitur ne praesides provinciarum in ulteriorem familiaritatem provinciales admittant: nam ex conversatione aequali contemptio dignitatis nascitur'. Increasing attention was given to the distinctions of class in the second century, notably in widening the gap between the municipal upper classes, or *honestiores*, and the mass of the people, the *humiliores*. This is well documented in the sphere of criminal punishment. Beginning with an enactment of Hadrian which exempted municipal councillors from any form of physical execution (save for parricide, *Dig.* 48. 19. 15), the whole curial class was gradually freed from all degrading forms of punishment. See further x. 58. 3 n., and, for example, Ulpian, *Dig.* 48. 19. 9. 11–12. In general, G. Cardascia, 'L'apparition dans le droit des classes d'*honestiores* et d'*humiliores*', *Rev. Hist. droit fr. et étranger*, 1950, 305 ff. The phenomenon appears at a higher social level in the immense pride taken by provincial Roman citizens in gaining equestrian and senatorial rank. The 'genealogical tree' of Oenoanda is a remarkable document of this; *IGRR* iii. 500; Sherwin-White, *Roman Citizenship*, 243–4.

nihil est . . . aequalitate inaequalius. Cf. II. 12. 5: 'numerantur . . . sententiae non ponderantur'. Very Roman sentiments.

6. *To Calvisius Rufus*

The date remains open. For the equestrian Rufus of Comum see II. 20 pref.

1. circenses erant, quo genere spectaculi ne levissime quidem teneor. The number of days on which racing was held in the Circus is too great to allow of identification, cf. Carcopino, *Daily Life*, 203 f., 212 ff. For a general discussion see Friedlaender's classical description in *SG* (Eng. tr.) ii. 19 ff., *RE* iii. 2571.

Pliny follows the lead of Cicero in his intellectual snobbery, *Off.* 2. 57; *pro Arch.* 13; *ad Fam.* 7. 1. 2. The letter may be Pliny's model, as earlier editors suggest. So too Seneca, *Ep.* 7. 4.

2. nunc favent panno. The usual race was between *quadrigae* hired by the promoter, who might be the emperor or an annual magistrate, from the professional riding schools or *factiones* which organized the sport. The number of these rose from two under the Republic to six under Domitian, but was later fixed at four. They were distinguished by their coloured shirts—*mussata, albata, prasina*, or *veneta*. Pliny implies, but does not state, that this enthusiasm was dependent on gambling, though this was nominally forbidden, cf. vii. 24. 5 n.

agitatores illos equos illos quos procul noscitant. Caligula had his favourite jockey and horse, which he greatly honoured even if he did not make it his consul, Suet. *Cal.* 55. 2–3. So too Commodus, Dio 74. 4. Dessau collects records of horses and riders, *ILS* 5288 ff., such as 'Aquilo, out of Aquilo' which won 130 first prizes, 88 seconds, and 37 thirds, ibid. 5295.

3. apud quosdam graves homines. Pliny makes similar strictures against Ummidia Quadratilla for favouring pantomime actors 'effusius quam principi feminae convenit', VII. 24. 4 n. Tacitus was similarly offended by the memory of Nero's efforts as an amateur *auriga, Ann.* 14. 14.

7. *To Voconius Romanus*

Date. Indications point to a fairly late date. The last visit to Comum is mentioned in V. 14, VI. 1, 24. 2, VII. 11. 5, but not elsewhere in VIII–IX. Here a visit is merely implied. Hitherto there has been no mention of building operations at his villas, for which before his retirement from the *cura Tiberis* he had little time or perhaps money, after the acquisition of the big estate in III. 19, cf. II. 4. 3 n.

Address. For Pliny's Spanish protégé Voconius Romanus see I. 5 pref.

1–2. ego ad Larium lacum. huius in litore plures villae meae. Plurality at one place seems to be rare (I. 4. 1 n.), and testifies to Pliny's accumulation of estates, as in III. 19. 2. There are no serious identifications possible of Pliny's villas around Comum; cf. the silence of M. Bertolone, *Lombardia Romana* (Milan, 1939), ii. 183 ff. For the speculations of an earlier age see Sirago (*It. agr.*), 26, nn. 8–9.

3. altera imposita saxis more Baiano lacum prospicit. For villas similarly situated at Comum see I. 3. 1 and VI. 24, the suicide's jump. Perhaps Pliny implies that Romanus had his villa *ad mare* at Baiae.

4. recta gestatio. For this and the *xystus spatiosissimus* see II. 17. 14, 17 nn.

ex hac ipse piscari. Cf. Martial, 10. 30. 16–19, for fishing out of windows 'a cubili lectuloque'.

8. *To Sentius Augurinus*

Date and Address. Since this note refers to the circumstances of IV. 27 where Pliny commends the verses of Sentius Augurinus and quotes a poem about himself, Schultz, art. cit. 37, referred it to the same date. But the note is a reply to a letter from Augurinus on reading Volume Four, and hence of somewhat later date, according to the publication date of that volume, which may have been issued together with several of the subsequent books. As with Epp. 4, 34, and VIII. 14, the early letters of these last two books are not earlier than the dates of IV, except for Ep. 26 (pref.) and less probably Ep. 38.

9. *To Colonus*

The date and the persons of Colonus and Pompeius Quintianus are equally uncertain, s. 1. The rare *cognomen* appears in upper-class society in *P. Ox.* xxii. 2349. 26, for L. Peducaeus Colonus, prefect of Egypt under Vespasian, and possibly the father of Pliny's friend.

1. Pompeii Quintiani morte tam dolenter adficeris. There is a possible connexion with the family of an equestrian official, Claudius Quintianus, *epistrategus* in Egypt about A.D. 131, and that of the consular senator Ti. Claudius Pompeianus, who was *cos.* II in 173. If so, the family is of oriental origin from Syrian Antioch, *PIR*² C 973, 975, 991–2. The names are borne by a legionary veteran of Marcus Aurelius from Africa (*AE*, 1946, nn. 65–66), but Pliny's man belongs to the upper social stratum, s. 2, 'miseros tuebatur'. He appears not to be a senator, and not a very young man—*iuvenem* not *adulescentulum*, s. 3.

    defunctorum obliviscuntur. Cf. I. 17. 1: 'sunt qui defunctorum quoque amicos agant'.

2. qua pietate cum dissimillimo patre vivebat. So too Quadratus and his grandmother, VII. 24.

3. cuius praedicatione putas vitam eius ornari . . . posse. It was not unknown to write the biographies even of young men, cf. III. 10. 1. The parallel usage in VII. 31. 5—'cuius memoriam tam . . . extendit ut librum de vita eius . . . ediderit'—and VII. 33. 2 shows that it is a book, not a funeral sermon that is required of Pliny.

10. *To Cornelius Tacitus*

Date. Connexions of theme and locality link this note with Epp. 15, 28, 36, where he is also busy in the country with revision of speeches and hunting, ss. 1, 3 nn. Those letters are interlinked with Epp. 16, 20, 37, VII. 30, VIII. 15. Hence a date in the summer of 107 or 108 seems secure. An early date, before *c.* 104, is excluded by the reference to Pliny's versification, s. 2 n. The date is of interest because the note has been connected with the *Dialogus* of Tacitus, and its much-discussed publication date, through a supposed cross-reference about poetry and solitude in s. 2. Schultz, art. cit. 38–39, following A. E. Lange, who originated the idea in his 1814 edition of the *Dialogus*, connected this note with I. 6, also addressed to Tacitus, which is similar in contents to this, with a similar statement about solitude. Schuster, Wagenvoort, and others, including Syme (*Tacitus*

672), linked this association with the possible reference to the *Dialogus*
in VII. 20 (q.v. pref.) though only Schuster argued that all these
letters and the *Dialogus* were written before A.D. 100. This whole
concatenation is unproved, and the main premise, that the *mot* about
solitude and poetry was an original thought of Tacitus, is false,
s. 2 n. On this set of arguments depended also the curious idea of
C. Landi and others that this letter was written by Tacitus in answer
to Pliny's I. 6, or vice versa (*Athenaeum*, 1929, 501 f. Cf. I. 6. 2 n.).
Prete, *Saggi*, 78 ff., summarizes the controversy over these letters.
Cf. also *Lustrum*, vi. 298. At most I. 6 and IX. 10 may suggest that
the *Dialogus* was published between the dates of the two, since in
I. 6 Pliny originates the great 'mot'.

Address. See I. 6, 20, prefs., etc., for a discussion of the friendship of
Pliny and Tacitus.

**1. sed aprorum tanta penuria est, ut Minervae et Dianae, quas ais
pariter colendas, convenire non possit.** Though the Diana–Minerva
notion appears in I. 6, the circumstances are different. There it is a
mot of Pliny, not Tacitus. Pliny caught a great bag of game, and
served both goddesses. Here the phrase comes from Tacitus, Pliny
takes nothing, and only Minerva is served. There Pliny was writing
ad retia, here *in via*. So the two notes are not closely linked even on
this ground. Things are just as in V. 18. 2, 'ego in Tuscis et venor
et studeo quae interdum . . . simul facio, . . . utrum sit difficilius
capere aliquid an scribere', and in Ep. 36. 6, 'venor aliquando sed
non sine pugillaribus . . . quamvis nihil ceperim'. Hence this note
fits the context of the later books better than that of I. 6.

2. ea garrulitate qua sermones in vehiculo seruntur. So too in IV. 14. 2
and VII. 4. 8 it is his habit to compose light verse while travelling.
**his quaedam addidi in villa cum aliud non liberet. itaque poemata
quiescunt quae tu inter nemora et lucos commodissime perfici putas.**
This reference excludes a date earlier than Book IV, where his
versification appears as a new hobby (IV. 14, 27. 3, VII. 4 nn.). The
argument for the *Dialogus* arises from the similarity between the
present phrase and *Dialogus* 9. 6, 12. 1, and the belief advanced by
Schuster (art. cit.) that the thought is otherwise unknown in antiquity. But the idea is clearly expressed and developed in Quintilian
(*Inst.* 10. 3. 22 f.): 'qui credunt aptissima in hoc nemora' etc. In
I. 6. 2 it is Pliny who formulates and presses upon Tacitus the notion,
repeated in I. 9. 6, that woods and solitudes are 'magna cogitationis
incitamenta'; Tacitus himself regards it as a commonplace of poets:
'ut ipsi dicunt' (*Dial.* 9. 6). Horace comes close to this idea in his
praise of country life as the nursery of philosophy, *Serm.* 2. 6. 60–74.

(Cf. L. Herman, *Latomus*, 1955, 349 ff., and as long ago as 1899, Valmaggi, *Riv. Filol.* 27. 233.)

Pliny is here quoting Tacitus back to himself not from a book but from a letter or conversation about writing out of doors, *praeceptis tuis*—containing the Minerva–Diana *mot*, which does not appear in the *Dialogus*. Scholars mistakenly assume that ancient authors knew only those books which have come down to us. A more probable reference to the *Dialogus* occurs in Ep. 23. 2–3.

quiescunt. i.e. as the poems receive no serious attention they do not thrive, despite the solitude.

putas. This word can hardly bear the burden of proving, as Schuster and Wagenvoort wished, that a book is meant, though *ais* (s. 1) often has this meaning. But Pliny never uses *praeceptis* for the literary word; cf. I. 18. 5, III. 1. 6, IV. 19. 6, 24. 7.

3. oratiunculam unam alteram retractavi ; quamquam id genus operis inamabile. Exactly as in Ep. 15. 2, on his Tuscan holiday: 'retracto . . . actiunculas quasdam, quod . . . frigidum et acerbum est'. In Ep. 28. 5 he has edited another speech. In V. 8. 6 he announced a general intention of revising several of his major speeches. He has now begun, as already in Ep. 4.

11. *To Rosianus Geminus*

Date and Address. As the six letters to Rosianus Geminus begin only at VII. 1 the question of date is not crucial. The suggestion of Otto, art. cit. 41, and Merrill, ad loc., that this is the earliest is possible, s. 1 n. But it is unlikely that Geminus, who was as a senator bound to reside at Rome, was writing from Lugdunum as from his home, s. 2 n., and as a stranger to Pliny. Geminus was out of Rome on other occasions in the correspondence, cf. VII. 24, IX. 30.

For Geminus' career see VII. 1 and X. 26 nn. He should be a praetorian senator by the date of this book. Pliny had known him since his quaestorship in 100, when Geminus was his consular quaestor.

1. aliquid ad te scribi volebas quod libris inseri posset. Cf. VII. 33. 1, 'illis (sc. historiis tuis) . . . inseri cupio'. Either Geminus wanted material for a book of his own, like Pliny's contributions to the *Historiae* of Tacitus (VI. 16, 20, VII. 33), or more probably he wanted the publication of a letter addressed to himself in Pliny's collection. If so, the letter is earlier than the rest of the series to Geminus, which begins in VII. 1. Merrill, Guillemin, ad loc., Prete, op. cit. 86 n. 4, take different sides, but miss the parallel passage.

sunt . . . in hac offendicula nonnulla. For the risk of giving offence

in almost any matter see II. 18. 5 n. Pliny expects a braver attitude
in others, if not in himself. In Ep. 27 he objects to the hushing up of a
scandal. Pliny can be indiscreet where those of junior status are
concerned, as in the cool praise of Geminus' friend Nonius, Ep. 30.
But in VIII. 22. 4, also to Geminus, he suppresses an anecdote for the
fear of giving offence. That could be the *materia* mentioned here.

2. bybliopolas Lugduni esse non putabam. In the late Republic there
were apparently no bookshops at Verona (Catullus, 68. 27 f.).
But Martial knew that his verses were read at Vienna (7. 88) in
Narbonensis, and the spread of Latin rhetoric in North Gaul and
Britain is well documented: Tac. *Agric.* 21. 2; Martial, 11. 3. 5; Plut.
defect. orac. 2; Juv. 15. 111. Pliny's surprise contrasts with his own
suggestion that Octavius Rufus' verses will be read as far as the
bounds of the Latin tongue, II. 10. 2. For Lugdunum was a Roman
colony of the Second Triumvirate, and capital of the Three Gauls.
But Pliny had never visited any western province. This reference
seems to be the earliest direct evidence for bookshops in the west
outside Rome. See T. Birt, *Kritik . . . des antiken Buchwesens*
(Munich, 1913), 311.

Since Geminus cannot be living permanently at Lugdunum, as a
Roman senator, he has either reported the news to Pliny after a
vacation in Gaul, or passed through the city on public business.
As X. 26 refers to his *commilitium* outside Italy, he may have served
as a legionary legate with the armies of the Rhine.

For an account of the book trade see Friedlaender, *SG* (Eng. tr.),
iii. 36 ff.

quibus peregre manere gratiam . . . delector. Cf. IV. 12. 7, 'laudis
suae . . . peregrinatione laetetur'.

12. *To Terentius Junior*

Date. The note is later than VII. 25, where Pliny describes his new
friendship with the ex-procurator Terentius Junior, to whom he here
addresses a letter of *admonitio*. Hence the note belongs to the general
date of VII–IX.

1. castigabat quidam filium suum. The same polite technique of
indirect precept is used towards Avitus, II. 6, Maximus VII. 26,
and Geminus, VIII. 22. For the horses and dogs of gilded youth
see IV. 2. 3 n.

numquamne fecisti quod a patre corripi posset? The theme is the
commonplace 'homo sum', as in VIII. 22. 3. Cf. for the faults of youth
Horace, *AP* 162. But Saint-Denis (III. 3. 3–4 n.) suggests that Pliny

shows considerable tolerance for the young—provided that they are respectful (II. 14. 2 n., VIII. 23. 3).

2. filium tuum. For this young man and the family of Terentius see VII. 25. 2 n.

13. *To Ummidius Quadratus*

Date. The letter belongs to the interlinked series in VI–IX addressed to the young men Fuscus Salinator and Ummidius Quadratus, who are first mentioned in VI. 11. 1. Like VI. 29 and VII. 9 it is concerned with their education as advocates. Pliny had high hopes of both.

Address. For Ummidius see particularly VI. 11. 1, VII. 24. 2–3 nn.

This letter, with I. 5. 1–4, III. 11, VII. 19 and 33, provides the contemporary evidence for the prosecution and trial of the friends of Senecio in A.D. 93. There is nothing in it to suggest that it was originally composed in the period before 100 and re-addressed. See also s. 24 n.

1. legisti libros quos de Helvidi ultione composui. Helvidius Priscus the younger, consular son of the like-named critic of Vespasian, was involved with Herennius Senecio and Arulenus Rusticus on an obscure charge of treason in the multiple trial of late 93; see I. 5. 2–3, III. 11. 3 nn. The book was published before the end of 97; see s. 24 n.

quae . . . extra libros. In the accounts of trials Pliny is careful to say little about the content of his actual speeches already published.

rei cui per aetatem non interfuisti. Quadratus was aged 23 at the date of VII. 24. 3.

2. occiso Domitiano statui mecum . . . esse magnam pulchramque materiam insectandi nocentes. Pliny first had thoughts of attacking his senior rival, the advocate Aquilius Regulus, in January 97, I. 5. 15–16. As in the Republic, so in the Principate an accusation was a means of securing political advancement, despite the growth of a fee-earning class of professional advocates. See I. 5. 1 n. Also V. 4. 2, 9. 4, 13. 8 nn. Garzetti minimizes the intentions of Pliny, and suggests that he never meant to do more than create a stir (op. cit. 50). Certainly the technical charge against Certus remains obscure, s. 2.

The date of Domitian's death was *a.d. xiv Kal. Oct.*, according to the *Fasti Ostienses* and Suetonius, *Dom.* 17. 3. *CAH*, xi. 33, gives September 16 in error.

in senatu senator senatori praetorius consulari reo iudex manus intulisset. The precise charge against Publicius Certus, who is named

in s. 13, is obscure. It is frequently stated in plain error (e.g. *CAH*
xi. 30, *RE* xxiii. 2, 1903) that Publicius was the accuser of Helvidius.
The trial of Senecio and his friends took place before the Senate, so
that all the senators were *iudices*, cf. Tac. *Agric.* 45. 1–2. Possibly
the violence of Certus might be construed as criminal under the law
ne quis iudicio circumveniretur, cf. I. 5. 4–6 n. Tacitus, loc. cit., 'mox
nostrae duxere Helvidium in carcerem manus', refers to the responsibility of the magistrate concerned for the formalities of execution,
cf. VII. 19. 6 n. Possibly Certus had proposed the *sententia* of condemnation: 'cruentae adulationis', s. 16. But Pliny does not say so.

Pliny withholds the name effectively in this account as he did in
the actual debate, but the story was well known to the audience of
the Letters. The man seems to be unknown outside Pliny. *PIR*[1]
p. 777.

3. metu temporum nomen ingens paresque virtutes secessu tegebat.
Since Helvidius held a consulship in the early years of Domitian
(III. 11. 3 n.) the implication of Pliny is rather misleading, as in his
account of Domitian's early years in VIII. 14. 7–8 nn. For the phrase
metu temporum see V. 1. 7, VII. 19. 6.

**Arria et Fannia, quarum altera Helvidi noverca altera novercae
mater.** Less confusingly, Fannia was the daughter of the great critic
of Nero, Thrasea Paetus, and second wife of the elder Helvidius,
while Arria was her mother and wife of Thrasea. For these very
political ladies see III. 11. 3 nn. Pliny's admiration of the family is
expressed also in III. 16 and VII. 19.

4. pro se quisque inimicos suos dumtaxat minores . . . postulaverat.
Pliny's first plan, of attacking Regulus, was hatched at the beginning
of 97, s. 2 n. His action against Certus may belong to the second or
third quarter of 97, before Domitius Apollinaris entered his consulship (s. 13 n.), and many weeks before the adoption of Trajan in
September.

redditae libertatis. Cf. the dedication at Rome, *ILS* 274, 'libertati
ab imp. Nerva . . . restitutae senatus populusque Romanus', and the
titles of the Nervan coinage such as *libertas publica*, *RIC* ii, 'Nerva',
nn. 7, 19, 31, 36.

dumtaxat minores. Men of less than senatorial rank are meant,
s. 21. But many even of these escaped, to be exiled by Trajan in
the purge of delators at the end of 99, so curiously described in
Pan. 34–35. Dio 68. 1. 1–2 speaks of slaves and freedmen conspiring
against their masters, but slaves could not act in court. The notorious
Palfurius Sura was one of this group of *minores*, Suet. *Dom.* 13. 1,
Juv. 4. 53. The *Panegyricus* passage shows that their activities
included an extensive exploitation of the social legislation of the

Principate as affecting property rights and wills: 'nulla iam testa-menta secura nullus status certus, non orbitas non liberi proderant' (ibid. 34. 1–2). In addition to political charges: 'auxerat hoc partium avaritia'. In v. 1 Pliny describes the unforeseen difficulties that might lurk even in a plain civil case, ibid. 7: 'verebantur ... ne ex centum-virali iudicio capitis rei exirent'. For an example of this see I. 5. 5–7.

oppresserat. Evidently by trial in the Senate, s. 21, accompanied by such clamours as presently greet Veiento, s. 19.

tum maxime tristis amissa nuper uxore. This was his second wife, the daughter of Pompeia Celerina and stepdaughter of Bittius Proculus, s. 13. See I. 4 pref. and, for the argument about the number of Pliny's wives, X. 2. 2 n. She evidently died in early 97, before the consulship of Domitius, s. 13, and after the return of the exiles (I. 5. 15). Cf. S. Monti, *Pliniana* 1952, 166 f.

mitto ad Anteiam. nupta haec Helvidio fuerat. She married again, s. 16, 'vitrico'. Anteia might be a connexion, though hardly a daughter, of the Julio-Claudian consular, P. Anteius Rufus, victim of Nero in A.D. 66. Tac. *Ann.* 16. 14.

luctus limine contineret. Pliny was observing the ritual *novemdial* of Roman mourning (Monti, loc. cit.; Mommsen-Marquardt, *Vie privée*, i. 443–4.)

5. **ab exilio redierant.** Hence later than 1 January 97; I. 5. 11, 15.

consule te ... an velitis adscribi facto. Cf. I. 5. 15–16 for Pliny's similar consultation of Junius Mauricus in his abortive plan against Regulus. Pliny could not technically associate the ladies in his accusation, if there was a formal charge, because women could not normally act as prosecutors; cf. VII. 6. 8 n. Perhaps he wanted them as witnesses, though this hardly seems necessary in so well-witnessed an affair.

6. **omnia ego semper ad Corellium rettuli.** For Pliny's friendship with the elderly consular Corellius Rufus, and his death in 97, see I. 12. 1, IV. 17. 6, V. 1. 5 nn.

veritus ne vetaret. He had evidently already been checked by Mauricus in the Regulus affair.

7. **venio in senatum, ius dicendi peto.** This passage shows the develop-ment of the new custom of informal discussions, on special requests or *postulationes* (as in II. 11. 9), before the regular session of the Senate opened under the rules of the *lex de senatu habendo*. (Mommsen, *DPR* vii. 133 f.; O'B. Moore, *RE* (S) vi. 769 f.) The new practice was a more effective way of introducing private members' business than the old procedure by which a senator might digress while giving his *sententia* on the official *relatio*, as in VI. 19. 3 (*egredi relationem*).

Both systems are in use in this debate, s. 9 n. Mommsen found earlier examples of the new technique in Tac. *Ann.* 11. 6, 13. 26.

undique mihi reclamari. Cf. s. 19 and IV. 9. 18. In the later Principate such *acclamationes*, following a *relatio*, were taken to signify the sense of the House, and replaced the formal division; VI. 19. 3 n., Moore, loc. cit.

'**salvi simus qui supersumus**'. This fits the nervous tone of the House, ss. 10–11 and 21. Contrast the staunch attitude shown on the accession of Vespasian towards the Neronian delators in Tac. *Hist.* 4. 10, 40–44. Corellius made it his prayer: 'ut . . . isti latroni vel uno die supersim', I. 12. 8.

9. 'sententiae loco dices . . . '. 'permiseras', inquam, 'quod usque adhuc omnibus permisisti' . . . aguntur alia. The consul withdraws his permission to Pliny to speak *extra ordinem*. Hence the pluperfect in Pliny's reply: 'You had only allowed . . . '. Pliny is to speak on the matter in his *sententia* during the debate on whatever topic— *alia*—the consul put to the House. For *egredi relationem* see Mommsen, *DPR* vii. 121 n. 2. The outstanding example is Cicero's seventh Philippic. Cf. also Tac. *Ann.* 2. 38.

10. 'notabilem te futuris principibus fecisti'. 'esto', inquam, 'dum malis'. The whole section 10–11 shows the uncertainty felt about the prospects of Nerva in 97 before the adoption of Trajan. The age of Trajan and the Antonines came without premonitions. Despite Pliny's rejoinder the general expectation was that future emperors would be *mali*.

11. lacessis hominem iam praefectum aerarii et brevi consulem, praeterea . . . quibus amicitiis fultum! Cf. s. 23. This prefecture normally led to the consulship, as with Pliny and Tertullus, and also Neratius Priscus and P. Tullius Varro in this period, *ILS* 1033, 1047. The friendships of Certus are sufficiently indicated by the list of his defenders, ss. 13, 17, of whom Veiento and perhaps Nerva himself (s. 22) were the most formidable, apart from the anonymous legate.

nominat quendam qui tunc ad orientem amplissimum [et famosissimum] exercitum non sine magnis dubiisque rumoribus obtinebat. This man might be either the legate of Syria or that of Cappadocia with Galatia-Pontus. It has been suggested by R. Syme (*Philologus*, xci. 244) that Javolenus Priscus, probably then legate of Syria, is meant; cf. Garzetti, *Nerva*, 38 n. 6. But no support should be drawn from the words *et famosissimum*, which are an Aldine addition with no justification. Though Pliny uses *famosus* in its neutral sense, he uses it only twice in the Letters, and each time of a legal case (cf. II. 11. 1, VI. 23. 1). Here, as in II. 13. 2, he wrote simply *amplissimum* *exercitum*, to indicate that the man was a consular legate with more than one legion at his command. See II. 13 pref. for Priscus.

13. iam censendi tempus. dicit Domitius Apollinaris consul designatus. Mommsen (*DPR* vii. 133 n. 2) thought that a magistrate now brought forward Pliny's affair for discussion. But in s. 8 the presiding consul refused to do this. The ordinary debate proceeds, and the interested parties in turn take up the affair of Proculus: 'nondum . . . nominatum . . . suscipiunt'. They are all speaking 'off the question'.

Domitius Apollinaris. A fragment of *Fasti Ostienses* (p. 734) shows that this man was consul suffect in the course of 97, probably sometime between May and August, and not in January 98 as formerly appeared; see II. 9 pref. The absence of any other consul designate from the list of speakers might suggest that the debate was held fairly late in the year. But it was common form as in II. 11. 20 that 'adsenserunt omnes consules designati'. The affair must be dated before the adoption of Trajan in September, cf. ss. 10–11.

The debate follows the rules laid down by the *Lex Iulia de senatu habendo*. The consul designate speaks first, followed by the senior *consularis*, Veiento, and the other consulars, and then the praetorian senators in order of seniority; cf. II. 11. 19 n. But Pliny in his narrative separates those who spoke for Proculus from those who spoke against him. Avidius Quietus, a consular of 93, would precede Postuminus, a consular of 96. Hence Pliny corrects his narrative in s. 18: 'haec illi quo quisque ordine citabantur'. Pliny himself then speaks after Tertullus who was many years his senior as a praetorian senator. It is noteworthy that no less than four praetorians spoke, in addition to Pliny.

Fabricius Veiento. A power under Domitian, who gave him a third consulship, he was still influential under Nerva, and naturally protected the supporters of the previous régime. See IV. 22. 4 n.

Fabius Postuminus. Consul suffect in May 96, he was later legate of Moesia (103) and probably proconsul of Asia, *PIR*², F 54. Garzetti, *C*. 57. The reading is a correction of Aldus's *Posthuminus*, for the Postumius of the Eight-Book tradition. The reading Maximinus in M suggests that another name has been altogether lost.

Bittius Proculus . . . uxoris . . . meae . . . vitricus. Consul in 98, s. 23, and son of a consular of Vespasian, he appears frequently in the Arval records from 101 to 120 as Q. Fulvius Gillo Bittius Proculus, but his career is mostly unknown. *PIR*² F 544, Garzetti, *C*. 58. Here the M codex (with θ) has the right reading, the rest producing forms of Vettius, for Bittius. Proculus has at some time married Pompeia Celerina, herself of distinguished family; s. 4 n., I. 4 pref.

post hos Ammius Flaccus. Therefore a praetorian senator. The *nomen* is as yet unknown among senators before the late second century, and might be a textual error, as in other names in this letter. But the MSS. do not disagree about it. *PIR*² A 561–2.

14. in libris habes ; sum enim cuncta ipsorum verbis persecutus. In VII. 33. 10 he does not expect Tacitus to be literal in writing history, so long as he does not 'egredi veritatem'. In V. 8. 4 Pliny is even satisfied with *nuda rerum cognitio* in historical writing. Here he only means that as in I. 5, VII. 33, he did not totally rewrite the comments.

15. dicunt contra Avidius Quietus, Cornutus Tertullus. The consular Quietus defends the memory of Helvidius because of a long-standing family connexion mentioned in VI. 29. For his status see ibid. 1 n.

For Pliny's friend Cornutus Tertullus, shortly to become prefect of Saturn with Pliny, see II. 11. 19, V. 14. 1 nn. He was also a friend of the cautious Corellius Rufus (IV. 17. 9), and takes here a less hazardous line than Pliny.

Arriae et Fanniae ius querendi non auferendum nec interesse cuius ordinis quis sit. Presumably the objection had been raised that the ladies were not senators, though wives and daughters of senators had been long regarded as members of the order in the wider sense, and as such had been tried on charges of extortion. Cf. III. 9. 19–20 nn. An outsider could only secure a hearing through a senator, as did Musonius Rufus in his attack on delators in A.D. 70, Tac. *Ann.* 4. 10. Women as such did not normally have the right to initiate a prosecution: see VII. 6. 8–9 nn.

16. datum se a consulibus tutorem Helvidi filiae. The younger Helvidius left two daughters and a son, all young children in 93, IV. 21 nn. There is no reason to suppose (with Merrill) that Anteia was the mother of only one of these. The administrative task of *tutela* was always regarded as a nuisance the consuls would not ask Tertullus to undertake for more than one child.

Women were nominally under *tutela* for life, unless they secured exemption by the *ius trium liberorum*. But in practice the *tutor* did not exercise his powers over adult women. See II. 20. 10 n. Schulz, *Classical Roman Law*, 180 f.; Gaius, *Inst.* I. 190.

vitrico. Like Pompeia Celerina, above s. 13, she remarried, as the legislation *de maritandis ordinibus* required her to do, nominally within two years of the husband's death; Ulpian, *Tit.* 14. She seems to have done so with some haste, unless an earlier *tutor* had died. Like the marriages of young senators about the time of their quaestorships (VII. 24. 3, VIII. 23. 7, etc.), these remarriages testify to the effectiveness of the sanctions of the marriage legislation.

a consulibus. Claudius lightened the burden on the urban praetor,

by charging the consuls with the duty of providing guardians to
those in need, Suet. *Claud.* 23. 2. But the praetor continued to officiate
in the matter at times, until both were replaced under Marcus by a
special *praetor tutelarius.* Schulz, op. cit. 170.

si poena . . . remittatur, nota . . . inuratur. They would be satisfied
with a *sententia* like that delivered over Tuscilius Nominatus, ex-
pressing disapproval but with no penal consequence, v. 13. 4. But
this does not satisfy Satrius Rufus, who rightly presses for a formal
verdict.

17. tum Satrius Rufus. For his abilities and a possible identification
see I. 5. 11 n. He speaks as a senior praetorian.

18. venitur ad me, consurgo. If one did not rise when cited, evidently
the *locus sententiae*, s. 8, passed to the man next in seniority.

**19. incipit respondere Veiento ; nemo patitur . . . et statim Murena
tribunus : 'permitto tibi . . . dicere'.** Veiento behaves as though he
were an advocate in a regular trial, but he is speaking out of turn.
Hence the uproar, and the appeal to the tribune. From the tribune's
veto and *auxilium,* still occasionally practised in the Julio-Claudian
period and later, there had arisen a right of intervention against the
presiding magistrate. Cf. I. 23 nn., and ibid. 2: 'qui iubere posset
tacere quemcunque'.

Murena. This should be Pompeius Falco, tribune in about 97, who
is the only senator known to bear this name at this time, I. 23 pref.

20. consul citatis nominibus et peracta discessione mittit senatum.
First the consul completes the taking of *sententiae*; cf. s. 18, 'citabantur'. Then a division takes place formally, on the *sententia*
apparently of Pliny. Cf. II. 11. 22, VIII. 14. 19 nn. for the technical
terms. The others have made speeches (ss. 13–17, *dicit* etc.) but have
made no formal proposal (*censuit*). Hence the consul presumably
put Pliny's *sententia* to the vote. This must have been a proposal that
the conduct of Certus should be subject to an investigation, provided
that the Princeps concurred, s. 22 n.

citatis nominibus. This implies that all the senators, not just the
consulars and praetorians, were formally asked for their opinions.
In *Pan.* 76. 2 it is noted as unusual in the Priscus case that 'consulti
omnes atque etiam dinumerati sumus'. The majority express briefly
agreement or the reverse with a prior *sententia,* as in II. 11. 20–21.
Cf. Mommsen, *DPR* vii. 173.

**21. intermissum iam diu morem in publicum consulendi . . .
reduxissem.** For a parallel compare again the events of A.D. 70 in
Tac. *Hist.* 4. 10. 40–44.

22. relationem quidem de eo Caesar ad senatum non remisit. It is not easy to gather just what Pliny had proposed, or why the emperor was involved. Pliny's action is like that of Musonius in A.D. 70. Musonius first stated his complaint against P. Celer before the Senate, which then voted that the case should be heard, and a day was accordingly assigned for the trial. Musonius, though not a senator, was allowed to state his own case, but Pliny states the case on behalf of the plaintiffs, being women, and presumably proposes the indictment of Certus. This then requires the sanction of Nerva. Why? Mommsen (*DPR* vii. 133 n. 2) compared Tac. *Ann.* 13. 26: 'consules relationem incipere non ausi ignaro principe perscripsere tamen consensum senatus'. But here the formal vote had been taken, and the matter is not legislative, as there, but judicial. Such control over the judicial function of the Senate did not exist in the Julio-Claudian period. Perhaps the earliest instance is that of Julius Bassus under Vespasian: 'accusatus est sub Vespasiano a privatis duobus, ad senatum remissus'; IV. 9. I. But there the case apparently originates before Vespasian, not the Senate. The nervousness of the consul may explain the reference to the Princeps, as Mommsen suggested op. cit. 137, but the examples in the Letters of such reference are administrative or legislative, not judicial; v. 13. 7, VI. 5. 5, 19. 3.

relationem . . . non remisit. Nerva sends back no proposal of his own. What he had just received was not a *relatio* but a *SC*. The term 'remittere senatusconsultum' appears in the clause of Vespasian's *Lex de imperio* which empowers the Princeps to hold and preside over meetings of the Senate, and to 'make' *senatusconsulta*. The present phrase ought to mean that the Princeps could veto or revise a *relatio* before its passing, rather than revise *SC*, as Moore (*RE* (S) vi. 772) interprets the *Lex de imperio*. The whole procedure is like that in the Letters cited above where the Senate, through the consuls, presents the Princeps with a problem, who then formulates a solution as a *relatio* for the Senate to adopt as a decree. The cases in Tac. *Ann.* 3. 10 and 52 quoted by Moore, loc. cit., differ, because there was no substantive decree of the Senate, and Tiberius merely refused to make certain proposals; in Suet. *Tib.* 61. 6 the details are not clear. In the Julio-Claudian period the Princeps' control over delations was effected by the use of his veto; Tac. *Ann.* 3. 70. I, 13. 43. 5. Bleicken does not discuss Pliny's evidence in this connexion (*Senatsgericht und Kaisergericht*, 1962, 64–65).

23. collega Certi consulatum, successorem Certus accepit. The names of Vettius Proculus and Julius Lupus appear as suffect consuls for the November of an unknown year in a suspected inscription (*CIL* vi. 616 *falsae*), which like other forgeries may contain genuine elements. (Cf. IV. 15 pref., Syme, *JRS*, 1953, 154. For Bittius/Vettius cf. s. 13 n.) The latest fragments of the Ostian *Fasti* show that fresh consuls held office in the last two months of 98, though the end of 97 is also possible for Proculus. Either year fits what is known of his career in relation to other consulars of the period (*PIR²*, loc. cit.; Syme, *Tac.* 642). But it is reasonable to suppose that the two prefects did not vacate office before Pliny and Tertullus took their places in January 98. The implication that Certus was dismissed before his time is not to be read into the sentence. Pliny evidently preferred not to underline the success of his scheme for self-advancement in this context (s. 2). There was always disrepute in favouring any *periculum senatoris* (III. 4. 7).

24. editis libris Certus . . . morbo decessit. This work is mentioned as out in I. 2. 6 (n.), but not again until IV. 21. 3, while the preparation of Pliny's subsequent speeches for publication is regularly indicated in due order, I. 8. 2; II. 5. 1, 19. 1; III. 10. 1, 13. 1, 18. 1. Hence the *De Helvidi Ultione* was published before the date of the first book of letters, and Certus dead before 98. The reason why the subject of this letter was not employed in Book I or II is evidently that its theme overlapped too extensively with his recently published book. Hence he preferred to include the Regulus affair in Book I. 5, and this is revived as an historic incident for IX.

14. *To Cornelius Tacitus*

The note is connected with VII. 20 and VIII. 7 by its theme, the fame of Tacitus and Pliny, and by verbal echoes.

1. posteris an aliqua cura nostri nescio. Cf. VII. 20. 2, 'si qua posteris cura nostri' etc. It has been remarked that this note reads like Pliny's rejoinder to a reply of Tacitus to VII. 20, in which Tacitus took the line 'mihi non plaudo'.

15. *To Pompeius Falco*

Date. Pompeius Falco, absent on a provincial command between 105 and 107 (I. 23 pref., VII. 22 pref.) is now back in Rome, and there may be a reference to his consulship, held about 108, s. 3 n. The note is one of several in IX that refer to a country holiday, twice with mention of the Tuscan estate, in the summer of 107 (Ep. 37. 1) and possibly also of 108. These notes refer to various combinations of the topics of boredom of country life, revision of speeches, harvest, and hunting, ss. 1, 2 nn. Altogether the chronological unity of the group seems probable.

**1. at hoc ne in Tuscis quidem : tam multis undique rusticorum libellis
. . . inquietor.** The theme is repeated exactly in VII. 30. 3 and Ep. 36. 6,
where a Tuscan sojourn is fully described. In Ep. 37 he explains at
length his remedy for these complaints. A Tuscan visit is the setting
also of VIII. 1, 8, 20 (prefs.).

2. retracto enim actiunculas quasdam. So too in Ep. 10. 3—which
brings in the hunting theme—Epp. 28. 5, 36. 2.

3. rationes quasi absente me negleguntur. He takes the same tone
with his young aristocratic friend Fuscus Salinator, Ep. 36. 6, and
also in Ep. 20. 2. With his intimates he does not conceal his serious
interest in estate management, as in III. 19 and VIII. 2 to Calvisius
Rufus and Ep. 37 to Valerius Paulinus. So too in an official, non-
literary letter to Trajan, X. 8. 5.

   pro gestatione. i.e. instead of taking a turn round his exercising
paddock, V. 6. 32–36.

   tu consuetudinem serva nobisque . . . urbana acta perscribe. If
Falco was consul suffect in late summer 108, as suggested by a
fragment of the Ostian *Fasti* (VII. 22 pref.), his presence in Rome
during the vacation season would be explained, and Pliny's remark
apposite, though *consuetudinem* suggests a non-official connexion.
By *acta* he means the *acta diurna urbis*; V. 13. 8 n.

16. *To Pomponius Mamilianus*

Date. This note, with its sequel Ep. 25, links with VIII. 2, 15, Epp. 20
and 28, by the references to a poor harvest and also with VIII. 21 by
the reference to Pliny's new volume of verses, ss. 1–2 nn. Ep. 25
has other links with letters in VII and VIII, s. 2 n. The whole of this
group thus fits the period 107–8, while the grape harvest mentioned
here and in Ep. 20 may well be that of the Tuscan visit in Epp. 15 etc.

Address. In Ep. 25 Mamilianus is in command of an army, and hence
has been reasonably identified with the consular T. Pomponius
Mamilianus, suffect consul in 100 and a relative of Pliny's elderly
friend T. Pomponius Bassus, IV. 23 pref. An uncertain text suggests
that he might be legate of Britain; if so, perhaps at this moment;
CIL vii. 164; *PIR*[1] M 92–93; Garzetti, *C.* 124. Syme, *JRS*, 1957,
132 n. 7 thinks he was only a legionary legate in the inscription.

1. nobis . . . vindemiae . . . exiguae. Cf. Ep. 20. 2, 'vindemias graciles'.
Ep. 28. 2, 'modicas . . . vindemias'. The same situation is implied in
VIII. 2. 1–2 nn., and stated in VIII. 15, which is demonstrably a late
letter. The harvest is likely to be the same in each case, and is probably
that of 107, when he was on his estates in August–September,
Ep. 37. 1.

2. devehemus tamen pro novo musto versiculos tibique mittemus. This promise is repeated in Ep. 25. 1, where the dispatch of his *lusus et ineptias* is held back by court occupations. The reference exactly fits the second volume of his verses, described in VIII. 21. 6 as *adhuc musteum librum.* Pliny there recited it to a select company in the July of a year when he was busy in the courts, and promised to send it to Arrianus after lengthy revision. The recitation should be in the July preceding the *exiguae vindemiae* of this letter. The renewed promise of Ep. 25 should belong to the last part of the same year; Pliny is still occupied in the courts, though less so, ibid. 3.

17. *To Julius Genitor*

This letter of admonition to the *rhetor Latinus* Julius Genitor, last addressed in VII. 30, has no indication of date.

1. scurrae cinaedi moriones. These were specialists in verbal humour —witty, salacious, and clownish respectively. For the specialization among entertainers see V. 19. 3. In I. 15. 3 dancing girls take their place.

2. vis tu remittere aliquid ex rugis? So might Calvisius Rufus have replied to Pliny on reading Ep. 6 on racing, and Pliny was no less severe on Ummidia for keeping *pantomimi* in VII. 24. In III. 3. 3 Genitor is described as 'emendatus et gravis, paulo etiam horridior'. Pliny takes a rather rougher tone with him than in his letters of admonition to his friends of higher social grade, such as the equestrian Terentius Junior, Ep. 12. 1 or the senator Geminus, Ep. 30, VII. 1, or young Avitus, II. 6.

    nihil tale habeo. But in V. 3. 2 he admits his pleasure in literary debauchery: 'specto mimos et lyricos lego et Sotadicos intellego'.

3. lector aut lyristes aut comoedus. For the custom and the combination see I. 15. 2, III. 1. 9, IX. 36. 4 nn.

4. demus igitur alienis oblectationibus veniam ut nostris impetremus. For the general theme of 'homo sum' see Ep. 12, VIII. 22. 2–3.

18. *To Sabinus*

For the identification of Sabinus with Statius Sabinus of IV. 10 see Ep. 2 pref. He had there asked for letters. Here he is sent apparently a selection of Pliny's speeches. The two notes are not closely connected.

2. per partes tamen et quasi digesta. So also in II. 5 and in Ep. 4 Pliny sends a speech to be read and revised in sections.

19. *To Ruso*

Date and Address. The late appearance of Cremutius Ruso, the
young advocate of VI. 23. 2, among Pliny's protégés, and the cross-
reference to VI. 10 in s. 1, indicate a late date. Syme, *Tac.* 802, on no
evidence, seeks to identify this Ruso with P. Calvisius Ruso Julius
Frontinus, consul in 79, or his son, presumably because of the family
connexion. But there is no hint that Pliny's Ruso was connected with
Frontinus, who is not called *tuus*.

1. **significas legisse te in quadam epistula mea iussisse Verginium
Rufum inscribi sepulcro suo.** The reference is to VI. 10, a letter dated
to 107. Ruso has seen a published copy, or a copy not sent to him by
Pliny himself. Hence VI may have been published before the compilation date of IX; cf. Asbach, art. cit. 49 f., Otto, art. cit. 27 n.
Prete (op. cit. 84 f.) objects that Ruso might have seen an unpublished
version, but this begs the question of what is meant by publication.
1. 2. 5–6, II. 10. 3 nn.

For the part played by Verginius, the *ter consul* of 97, in the rising
of Galba and the events of 68–69 see II. 1. 2 n. The couplet and the
anecdote below cast some light on the attitude of Verginius, otherwise mainly known from late sources. The epitaph is ambiguous. It
can be interpreted as combining two notions, first that Verginius
saved the Empire for Rome by defeating the rebel Vindex, and
second that after the defeat of Vindex, he left the choice of ruler to
his country—without any hidden implication. For the second view
see VI. 10. 4 n. The first interpretation, which reads overmuch
between the lines, supports the conclusion which has been drawn
from the brief references in the *Historiae* where Tacitus classes
Vindex with the earlier Tiberian rebel Sacrovir, and refers to the
rising of Vindex as a war 'inter legiones Galliasque': I. 89, IV. 57.
But there is nothing in the fairly full version of Dio, given in the
epitome of Xiphilinus (Dio 63. 23–25), or in the coinage propaganda
of the time, to suggest more than that Vindex was trying to replace
Nero by Galba, which is the interpretation found in Plutarch's
Galba iv–v. Even the late and garbled version of John of Antioch
(fr. 91, quoted in the Loeb *Dio*) suggests only that Verginius, Vindex,
and Galba planned to divide the western provinces amongst themselves, with Vindex receiving not Gaul but Spain. Probably the
epitaph was deliberately ambiguous, and hints at Rufus' excuse for
allowing his troops to destroy the forces of Vindex, that under cover
of supporting the claims of Galba they were seeking 'empire' for the
Gauls. Dio states that the troops acted without orders from Rufus
after Rufus and Vindex had made a secret agreement against Nero,

which may be represented in the version of John of Antioch. The anecdote which Pliny gives below suggests that Cluvius Rufus did not accept the excuses of Verginius. See *CAH* x. 810; C. M. Kraay, *Num. Chron.*, 1949, 129 f.; P. A. Brunt, 'Vindex and the Fall of Nero', *Latomus*, 1959, 531 f.; J. C. Hainsworth, *Historia*, 1962, 86 f.

melius rectiusque Frontinum quod vetuerit omnino monumentum sibi fieri. This is C. Julius Frontinus, twice and thrice consul in 98 and 100, friend and champion of Pliny. For his career see IV. 8. 3 n. where he is recently dead. Frontinus' instructions, evidently in his will (cf. VI. 10. 4), show great independence of mind in an age which was excessively devoted to the ceremonial of burial. From emperor to slave none lay without his memorial and formal epitaph. Pliny was indignant in VI. 10. 3 at the thought that Verginius might come to lie 'sine titulo sine nomine'. Trimalchio took tremendous care for his monument: Petr. 71. The wording here and in s. 6 suggests that Frontinus wished to dispense altogether with a funerary structure, the sense of *monumentum* in the passage cited from the *Cena*. In VIII. 6. 1 *monumentum* is distinguished from *titulus*: 'monumentum Pallantis sub hac inscriptione'. Cf. VII. 29. 2. Presumably Frontinus like Verginius was cremated; VI. 10. 3.

2. utrumque dilexi. Both advised and advanced him, but Rufus had been his guardian and was a closer friend, s. 5; cf. II. 1. 8–9, IV. 8, V. 1. 5.

5. familiariter . . . dilectus. A genuine, not just a political, friend. Cf. II. 6. 1 n. for the terminology of friendship.

semel omnino . . . de rebus suis hoc unum referret. So Rufus is not the source of Tacitean history, unlike the more garrulous Vestricius Spurinna; III. 1. 5: 'quae facta quos viros audias'.

Cluvium locutum. This consular, orator, and historian is mentioned by Tacitus among his sources for the reign of Nero, *Ann.* 13. 20, 14. 2. Possibly consul in 39 or 40, he was a blameless friend of Nero in the emperor's later and worse years; Tac. *Hist.* 4. 43, Suet. *Nero* 21, Dio 63 (62). 14. 3. Like Verginius he took part in the civil wars of 69, holding Hispania Tarraconensis first for Galba, and then, despite suspicions of his personal ambitions, for Otho and Vitellius, suppressing from Spain the attempted rising of Lucceius Albinus in Mauretania. He joined Vitellius on the march to Rome, where he later witnessed the ineffective compact between the defeated emperor and Flavius Sabinus, Tac. *Hist.* 1. 8, 76; 2. 58–59, 65; 3. 65; *PIR*[2] C 1206; Syme, *Tac.* 178 f., 293 f.

si quid in historiis meis legis aliter ac velis. Cluvius, as a supporter of Galba, may well have criticized Verginius' part in the events of 68 whereby Vindex was destroyed, Nero nearly saved, and Galba nearly ruined; II. I. 2 n. Cf. Tac. *Hist.* I. 8: 'Germanici exercitus ... tarde a Nerone desciverant nec statim pro Galba Verginius'. As an innocent friend of Nero, Cluvius was well placed to blame Verginius for standing too long on Nero's side, or alternatively if he accepted the 'official version', for betraying Nero. At least the anecdote suggests that Dio's version of the battle of Vesontio is not the whole truth. Similarly, Syme, *Tac.* 179, Hainsworth, art. cit.

The story, with a passage from Plut. *Otho* 3, shows that Cluvius' work extended through and possibly beyond the events of A.D. 68. Cf. Syme, *Tac.* 675. Practically nothing is known otherwise about the extent and content of his History.

The tone of the remark of Cluvius suggests that he was senior to Verginius. If he is the consular Cluvius mentioned by Josephus in A.D. 41 (*Ant. Jud.* 19. I. 13) he would be over 60 in A.D. 68.

historiae fides. For truth and history see VII. 33. 10 n.

ideo me fecisse quod feci ut esset liberum vobis scribere. The reference is to his 'grand refusal', which could be taken as a manifesto in favour of legality and liberty, rather than to the defeat of Vindex. See VI. 10. 4 n.

20. *To Venator*

The note belongs to the group referring to a bad harvest, possibly that of 107, and a visit to his estates, probably Tifernum. See Ep. 16 pref. and s. 2. But autumn 108 is not excluded. The addressee is unknown.

2. ipse cum maxime vindemias, graciles quidem, uberiores tamen quam exspectaveram, colligo. The circumstances are very like those of the harvest of VIII. 2. 1–2. *Pace* Chilver, *Cisalpine Gaul*, 153 n. 2, it is not a *good* harvest.

gustare de lacu mustum. The vat, not the lake, as Chilver in mistake, op. cit. 151 n. 5. Hence the scene is not fixed at Comum.

obrepere urbanis qui nunc rusticis praesunt meque notariis et lectoribus reliquerunt. The situation is as in Ep. 15. 2 and 36. 6, which refer to the Tuscan estate. There may also be a reference to the new system of rent-collection and tenure established in 107, Ep. 37. 3, which involved the use of a new staff of collectors, 'ex meis aliquos operis exactores . . . ponam', as Sirago (*Italia agraria* 119) also suggests. But the Latin is more appropriate to the vintage of Pliny's home farm under direct management (VII. 2 n.). He did not 'collect' his tenants' harvest, but took his share after it was gathered in.

21. *To Sabinianus*

The date and recipient of this note and its sequel Ep. 24 are not
determinable. The theme is akin to Ep. 12. The note has often been
compared with St. Paul's *Letter to Philemon*. But as Merrill remarks,
ad loc., the grounds that Pliny urges are very different from St.
Paul's.

1. **libertus tuus cui suscensere te dixeras venit ad me.** His offence
does not emerge, but he had been expelled from the household.

3. **ne torseris illum.** This is metaphorical, as always in Pliny; cf. VI.
7. 3, VII. 12. 4, 19. 9, *et al.* A master could not subject his freedmen to
physical punishment like a slave. Save for a limited power of expulsion from Rome itself, they were no longer under discipline. Cf. Tac.
Ann. 13. 26, 'quid . . . aliud laeso patrono concessum quam ut
centesimum ultra lapidem . . . libertum releget?' See A. M. Duff,
Freedmen in the Roman Empire, 40 ff.

22. *To Severus*

Date. A fair interval separates this letter from its companion VI. 15.
There Passennus has published only elegiac verses. Here he has published *lyrica* also. The argument against the book-date is very feeble,
s. 2 n.

Address. Five Severi occur in the Letters. Perhaps the scholarly
Herennius Severus of IV. 28. 1 is the most likely, with his passion for
minor figures of literature, rather than the recipient of the same
letter, Vibius Severus. The consular Vettenius (VI. 27) and the agent
Annius Severus (III. 6) have no particular claim. Catilius Severus is
not excluded, but the abbreviating MSS. of I. 22, III. 12 omit Severus,
not Catilius, in the address.

1. **in litteris veteres aemulatur, . . . Propertium in primis.** For Passennus
Paulus see VI. 15. 1. By the *veteres* Pliny elsewhere means the
Republican rather than the Augustan writers, I. 16. 3. Cf. IV. 27. 4.

2. **si elegos eius in manus sumpseris.** For Peter, art. cit. 39–40, this
meant that Severus had not read the poems, and hence the date of
this letter must be close to that of VI. 15. An evident *non sequitur*.

nuper ad lyrica deflexit, in quibus ita Horatium . . . effingit. The
term *lyrica* or *lyrici*, is used by Pliny only of the verses of Spurinna
elsewhere, III. 1. 7, or quite generally in V. 3. 2, VII. 17. 3. He does
not apply it to his own verses, in IV. 14, V. 3, VIII. 21.

amat ut qui verissime etc. The definition is that of his own *lusus*, IV. 14. 3, but less stress is laid on *petulantia*. Passennus doubtless imitated the greater decency and reticence of the Augustans. So too perhaps did Spurinna, III. 1. 7 n.

23. *To Maximus*

Date. Despite the doubts of Peter, art. cit. 40, the letter is later than VII. 20 and VIII. 7 on the same theme—the equal and equable rivalry of Pliny and Tacitus, s. 2 n.

Address. This Maximus is likely to be the 'Elder Maximus', from his interest in literature and from the turn of phrase in s. 6. See Ep. 1 pref.

1. frequenter . . . centumviri consurgerent. The supreme standing of this Court at Rome is shown by Pliny's comparison of it with the Senate in the next sentence. He is here more complacent about the Court than in the dissatisfied account of II. 14. For some of his great occasions see IV. 16, VI. 33.

2. cepi voluptatem . . . nuper ex sermone Corneli Taciti. Tacitus evidently retailed the story to Pliny after their correspondence about their own reputations, of which this is his best example: VII. 20, VIII. 7, Ep. 14. Pliny would surely have published it sooner if it had been available.

sedisse secum circensibus . . . equitem Romanum. Knights and senators had special seats in the Circus Maximus, as well as in the theatre, since a dispensation of Claudius; Suet. *Claud.* 21. 3, Pliny, *NH* 8. 21, Carcopino, *Daily Life*, 214.

Italicus es an provincialis? The question nicely illustrates the extension of equestrian status among wealthy provincials, cf. Juv. 7. 14, 'faciant equites Asiani . . . et Cappadoces faciant equitesque Bithyni'. For the theme see Stein, *Römische Ritterstand*, 383 ff., or more briefly Sherwin-White, *Roman Citizenship*, 243. Syme, arguing for the Narbonese origin of Tacitus, suggested that some nuance of pronunciation indicated that Tacitus was not an Italian of the peninsula, and prompted the question (Syme, *Tac.* 619). The order of questions prevents the conclusion that since Pliny was an *Italicus* then Tacitus must be *provincialis*.

nosti me et quidem ex studiis. As commonly in Pliny *studia* means forensic oratory. Cf. IV. 16. 1, VI. 2. 2, 11. 3.

3. Tacitus es an Plinius? The use of a single name is not surprising in a limited context, though it is remarkable that Secundus was not used for Pliny. The anecdote is illustrated by Tacitus himself in

Dialogus 7. 4, which may refer to this event. 'Advenae quoque et peregrini iam in municipiis et coloniis suis auditos (sc. *oratores*) cum primum urbem attigissent requirunt ac velut adgnoscere concupiscunt.'

4. recumbebat . . . super eum municeps ipsius . . . cui Rufinus demonstrans me. The story casts a curious light on Roman social customs. They were all reclining at the same table, yet they had not been introduced—unless this is the normal Roman introduction.

The man may be L. Fadius Rufinus, suffect consul in 113, rather than one of the Fabii Rufini of Albula in Latium preferred by Guillemin, ad loc.; *PIR*² F 100. The Aldine reading supports M's Fadius against the Fabius of γ. Pliny implies that the stranger came from a remoter part of Italy than Latium. The term *vir egregius* is applied by Pliny alike to leading senators, junior senators, and knights; II. II. 19, IV. 22. I, V. 16. 6, *et al.* It has not yet its later connotation as an honorary title of knights.

5. illum anus Attica ita noscitavit. The tale is told by Cicero, *Tusc.* 5. 103, and others.

6. nec ullius invides laudibus et faves nostris. He says something similar about the 'Elder Maximus' in VI. II. 4: 'teste te peto ut omnes qui me imitari tanti putabunt meliores esse quam me velint'.

24. *To Sabinianus*

This continues Ep. 21, q.v. Pliny improves the occasion with a little letter of admonition.

libertum . . . in domum . . . recepisti. For the expulsion of ill-behaved freedmen see Ep. 21. 3 n.

25. *To Pomponius Mamilianus*

For date and circumstances see Ep. 16. Mamilianus has now received the promised volume of verses.

1. turba castrensium negotiorum. Pomponius is a consular legate, Ep. 16 pref. Cf. *aquilas*, s. 3.

3. nunc me rerum actus modice sed tamen distringit. This fits the circumstances of VIII. 21. 3, where Pliny's recitation of his new volume of verses was delayed by duty in the courts. In several other letters of VII–IX Pliny is still sporadically active in the courts, but not in administration. See Ep. 2. I n.

continendos cavea. Pliny has not yet published them. In VIII. 21 the recitation was a preliminary to revision.

26. *To Lupercus*

Date. This letter enlarges a literary theme touched in II. 5, the only
other letter to the obscure Lupercus. The extensive quotation of
Greek is paralleled only in I. 20; s. 6 n. Technical discussion of prose
style is rare outside I and II. The only two examples in III–VIII are
short—III. 18. 8–10 and VII. 12. So too the comparison of history
and oratory in V. 8. 9–10. In the period 96–98 Pliny was certainly
studying Demosthenes, who is much quoted in ss. 8–9, for his *De
Helvidi Ultione*: I. 2. 2, VII. 30. 5 nn. Hence Schultz, art. cit. 41, may
be right in attributing this letter to the date of II. 5, though it need
not be an immediate sequel of that (s. 5 n.). Its excessive use of
quotation may have excluded it from earlier publication.

Address. Lupercus is unknown, but may come from Narbonensis,
II. 5 pref.

2. debet . . . orator erigi attolli. Pliny supports the case of the more
exuberant school against the admirers of plainness, as in I. 20.
20–22, II. 5. 5–8, VII. 12. But s. 7 shows that he is not in favour of the
extreme 'Asianists', and adheres on the whole to the 'middle way'
of Quintilian. See I. 2. 1–2 nn. for a discussion. Equally, he is
defending himself not against the extreme Atticist of s. 1, but against
Lupercus, who is less Asian than Pliny (s. 13). He is not maintaining
a 'moderate Atticist' position, as Guillemin thought, s. 7 n. (*VL*
95 f. Cf. Prete, *Saggi Pliniani*, 61, *contra*.)

3. eloquentiam nihil magis quam ancipitia commendant. Pliny is close
to the doctrine of Longinus, *De Subl.* 33. 2, that average abilities
take no risks and never reach grandeur, while great abilities risk a
fall in daring the heights, and ibid. 35. 5 that only the unexpected
astonishes. Cf. F. Quadlbauer, *Wiener Studien*, 1958, 107 f. For other
similarities with Longinus see s. 6 and I. 20. 5 n. D. A. F. M. Russell,
Longinus (Oxford, 1963), xli, notes the similarity in overall treatment
between this letter and the *De Sublimitate*, and supposes a common
source, which could be Pliny's own professor of Greek rhetoric,
Nicetes. It is likely that Pliny was as faithful to him as he was to the
teaching of Quintilian.

    qui per funem in summa nituntur. For the simile cf. Horace,
Ep. 2. 1. 210:

> 'ille per extentum funem mihi posse videtur
> ire poeta meum qui pectus inaniter angit' etc.

5. in scriptis meis adnotasse quaedam ut tumida. This was the criticism which he expected from Lupercus in II. 5. 5–8. But these writings

are not necessarily the same as the half-finished oration there sent to Lupercus. In this letter Pliny defends fullness of verbal expression; in I. 20 fullness of argument is the theme—two aspects of the same style.

6. ut Homerum potissimum attingam. The same passage is quoted as an instance of grandeur by Longinus, *De Subl.* 9. 6. Quotation of Greek is relatively frequent in I and II, in which twelve letters contain Greek phrases or words: I. 2, 5, 7, 9, 12, 18, 20; II. 3, 11, 12, 14, 20. But in III–VIII Greek appears in only seventeen letters altogether, and thrice elsewhere in IX: 1, 13, 23. Single words and short or half-finished quotations are the norm, running to a couple of lines of Greek only in seven letters: I. 7, 18; II. 3; IV. 7, 11, 27; V. 20. The usage is most frequent in letters about forensic matters, e.g. in I. 7, 18, II. 3, IV. 7, but occurs in many other contexts. So I. 20 and this letter are exceptional in this respect, which may be another argument for an early date.

7. incredibilia sint haec . . . an magnifica. This topic must be pursued in the commentaries of the writers *de sublimitate.*

  laxandos esse eloquentiae frenos. This sufficiently summarizes Quintilian's criticism of Latin Atticism, and his approval of a fuller and more forceful style, expressed at length in *Inst.* 12. 10. 12–15, 35–37, 63–65.

27. *To Paternus*

The date of this note is not determinable, unless the suggestion in s. 2 n. is acceptable. In IV. 14 Paternus receives Pliny's first letter about his book of verses. He should be Plinius Paternus of I. 21 pref.

1. numen . . . historiae. For Pliny's views about history and its truth see V. 8, VII. 33. 10 nn.

  partemque eius in alium diem reservaverat. For serial recitations see III. 18. 4. The phrase suggests that he was reading excerpts.

2. ecce amici cuiusdam orantes obsecrantesque ne reliqua recitaret. On the danger of writing contemporary history see V. 8. 12–13 n. 'graves offensae, levis gratia'. The narrative evidently concerned the Flavian period, and the attitude is as in the debate about the misdeeds of Publicius Certus: 'salvi simus qui supersumus' (Ep. 13. 7). Fabia long ago (*Rev. Phil.* 1895, 8) and Syme recently (*Tac.* 120), have seen a reference to Tacitus and his *Historiae* here. The remark in his preface is a defence against this style of criticism: 'incorruptam fidem professis neque amore quisquam et sine odio dicendus est'. Tacitus was not the only historian writing in this decade (I. 16. 4),

but v. 8. 12 suggests that he was the only person writing in the years
105–7 about the Flavian age.

For Pliny's cautious silence as to names compare VIII. 22. 4 and
earlier II. 6. 1.

28. *To Voconius Romanus*

Date. The letter connects both with the harvest series and with the
closely linked series about revision of speeches, ss. 2, 5; Ep. 10 pref.,
15 pref. It is later than Epp. 16 and 20, since Pliny is back in Rome
from the country, ss. 1–2 n. A date late in Pliny's career is indicated
by the proposed biography in s. 3.

Address. For Romanus, Pliny's Spanish friend and protégé, see I. 5 pref.

1. post longum tempus epistulas tuas . . . recepi. In Ep. 7 he quotes a
letter received from Romanus who was then, as here, away on his
estates.

**iniungis mihi iucundissimum ministerium ut ad Plotinam, sanctis-
simam feminam, litterae tuae perferantur.** Pliny and Plotina, the wife
of Trajan, are evidently both in residence at Rome. Pliny has easy
access to the 'Palace'. Another of his literary friends, Suetonius,
was on good terms with the wife of Hadrian, SHA, *Hadr.* 11. 3. But
Romanus is not a member of the *factio Plotinae*, mentioned ibid. 4.
10 (as *RE* (2). ix. 701), since he is in need of an introduction.
Equally the suggestion that he is the Voconius to whom Hadrian
addressed the verses quoted by Apuleius, *Apol.* 11, lacks confirmation.

sanctissimam. Not exactly a title, but as in III. 3. 1, 10. 3, V. 3. 3,
the connotation is *sanctitas morum*; cf. *Pan.* 83. 5, 'quid . . . (uxore)
illa sanctius quid antiquius?' and X. 1. 1, 3A. 3, of Trajan. Little is
known of the origins of Pompeia Plotina, who is possibly a Narbonensian from Nemausus; Syme, *Tac.* 604. Her name appears late, after
III, on the coins of Trajan, with the title Augusta, and sometimes in
association with Vesta. *RIC* ii, pp. 297–8.

2. commendas Popilium Artemisium. Evidently a freedman, by his
cognomen. The wife of the Voconius Romanus from Saguntum was
called Popilia. So this man is likely to be a freedman of the family,
II. 13. 4 n.

indicas etiam modicas te vindemias collegisse. communis haec mihi.
For this light harvest see Ep. 16 pref. From Ep. 7 Romanus' maritime
villa seems to be in Campania, though his principal estates were in
Spain, X. 4. 2.

3. multa te . . . nunc scribere quibus nos tibi repraesentes. Evidently
Romanus is attempting some sort of biography of Pliny. The fashion
was strong in this period, though the subjects were not usually taken

from among the living; III. 10. 1 n., Ep. 9. 3 n. But perhaps Romanus was proposing only to write one of his 'literary letters' about Pliny, s. 5 n.

nos. Pliny commonly uses *nos* only in the literal sense, 'my friends and I', 'my wife and I', 'you and I'. But in talking about his speeches in several letters he uses plural for singular; cf. I. 8. 5–17, II. 5. 6–7, 11. 11, III. 9. 23. In the latter two instances, but not in the former, he may be including fellow advocates.

repraesentes. A rare word in Pliny. Only used by him again in IV. 19. 1, since VIII. 6. 7 is a quotation.

4. cum certius de vitae nostrae ordinatione aliquid audieris . . . te . . . ad nos evolaturum qui iam tibi compedes nectimus. Syme (*Tac.* 81. 659) took this to mean that Pliny was expecting an imperial appointment, presumably the Bithynian post, and proposes to take Romanus with him. There is a technical meaning of *ordinatio* as the list of official appointments (Suet. *Dom.* 4. 2). In an official context in X. 58. 10 the sense is non-technical. By Pliny himself *ordinare* and *ordinatio* are used non-technically for the arrangements of private affairs. The clue lies in III. 1. 2: 'me... vita hominum disposita delectat . . . senibus placida omnia et ordinata conveniunt'. Cf. Ep. 37. 1, 'necessitas locandorum praediorum . . . ordinatura'. X. 8. 6, 'status ordinationem', of business affairs. So, in Suet. *Vesp.* 21 *ordinem vitae* refers to Vespasian's daily routine. The tone of the whole sentence better fits a private visit than an official mission. The bonds are Pliny's affection, as in the very similar passage in Ovid, *Ep.* 19 (20). 85–86 (Guillemin, *VL* 123). In Pliny *vita* lacks the specific connotation of public *officia*, and sometimes contrasts with that: III. 1. 11, 20. 5; VII. 3. 5, 9. 13; VIII. 22. 3. In VIII. 23. 4 *de officiis vitae* is used to give a special meaning, where *de vita* would be quite general. Here Syme's sense would require *de officii nostri ordinatione*; cf. I. 10. 9, 'distringor officio', III. 6. 6, 'officii ratio', V. 14. 2, 'mandatum officium', for his imperial posts. Pliny cannot be *threatening* Romanus with the grievous bonds of business, as in the metaphor of II. 8. 2–3.

5. orationem pro Clario . . . visam uberiorem. For Pliny's revision of his speeches at this period see Ep. 10. 3 n. For his habit of expanding the original version see III. 18. 1. The name and identification of this litigant are uncertain. The Eight-Book MSS. (γ) read *proclamo*. Aldus printed *pro Clario*. *Damo* and *Clanio* have been read, and Stein (*PIR*² C 747) suggested the obscure senator L. Clartius or Ciartius. Pliny seldom uses the gentile name singly thus, except for 'pro Vareno' in a similar context, VI. 29. 11. Within the circle of the Letters the person is more likely to be one of the Erucii or the Septicii, both being Clari; II. 9. 1, 4 nn.

adicis alias te litteras curiosius scriptas misisse. For the phrase for 'literary letters' see I. 1 n. Guillemin, op. cit. 133 f., relies greatly on this passage to distinguish between such letters and normal correspondence. In II. 13. 7 Pliny says that Romanus wrote letters, 'ut Musas ipsas Latine loqui credas'. But the three letters received by Pliny, s. 1, were all 'elegantissimas', and must have been much like the shorter letters of Pliny's collection, such as this very one.

29. To Rusticus

Date. The book-date fits. Pliny apologizes for writing outside his métier; the reference should be to his volumes of verse. Of these Rusticus has already received one, and has just been sent the second, with this covering note, s. 2. The tone is very much as in his references to his verses, IV. 14. 8–10, VII. 4. 1, 4, VIII. 21. 1, very different from the confidence with which he discusses his oratorical works, cf. VI. 33, VII. 20.

Address. This might be Fabius Rusticus, the historian of Nero, who appears from the will of Dasumius to be alive in 108 (*CIL* vi. 10229). But nothing supports this much-favoured identification (cf. *PIR²* F 62; *RE* vi. 1865 f.; Syme, *Tac.* 179, 293). Bruttius Praesens, of VII. 3, also had Rusticus among his names. The young Junius Rusticus (II. 18. 1 n.) is not so probable, since the tone suggests an older man. Messius Rusticus, consul in 114, is as likely as any—and the family of Fulvius Rusticus, senator a generation later, hailed from Comum or Milan. (Cf. *RE* vii. 279, n. 106; *PIR²* F. 557.)

30. To Rosianus Geminus

Date. Like Ep. 11, this belongs to the Geminus series, which is confined to VII–IX; cf. VII. 1 pref. Geminus is not necessarily at this moment in Gaul, as in Ep. 11.

1. Nonium tuum. The name is an early correction for the *non sum* of the very defective MS. tradition at this point, confirmed by θ. There might be a punning reference to the elderly consular C. Nonius Bassus Salvius Liberalis; II. 11. 17, III. 9. 33 nn. Nonius Celer of VI. 32 is too poor to fit. Two other consular Nonii are known at this time —L. Flavius Silva Nonius Bassus, consul in 81, and L. Nonius Torquatus Asprenas, consul in 94; *PIR¹* N 123, *PIR²* F 368. But it is unlikely that the ever-tactful Pliny would risk offending such men; cf. Ep. 27. 2 n., II. 18. 5 n. Pliny deliberately avoids a clear identification.

qui sit vere liberalis. The theme is frequent in the Latin moralists. The Roman meanness in money matters (v. 1. 10 n.) yielded but slowly to a more generous attitude under the influence of Stoic humanity. Guillemin, ad loc., quotes, among others, Cic. *de off.* 1. 16–17, Sen. *de ben.* 1. 4. 2, 4. 20. 3. But Pliny's own example is more impressive, even if well advertised, because realized in hard cash; I. 19, II. 4. 6, VI. 32.

patriae. Not all Pliny's friends were equal to him in the public munificence which is so marked a feature of municipal life in the Principate. Old Calpurnius Fabatus was decidedly reluctant, and so was one of the Maximi; v. 11 nn., VI. 34. 2.

2. aliena corripere. *Captatio* is but one facet of this unattractive aspect of Flavio-Trajanic society; II. 20, VIII. 18 nn. See Juvenal's account of the *pauper homo*, S. 3. 126–89.

31. *To Sardus*

Neither the date of the note nor the identity of Sardus can be established. The note is in the general style of Ep. 8. Bardon supposes the book to be a history of Nerva and Pliny's actions in 97; he also identifies Sardus with the author in Ep. 27. But it is much more likely to be a treatise on oratory. (Bardon, *Litt. Lat. Inc.* ii. 203.)

32. *To Titianus*

Again undatable. The recipient is presumably Cornelius Titianus, recipient of I. 17. It is the emptiest of these courtesy notes in the whole collection; cf. II. 8, 15.

33. *To Caninius Rufus*

Date. The book-date is secured by the connexion between this letter and VIII. 4, s. 1 n. There is no reference to Caninius writing verses before VIII and IX, though Pliny has been busy exhorting him to literary activity for a long time; I. 3. 3–5, III. 7. 14–15.

Address. For Caninius Rufus, equestrian of Comum, see I. 3 pref.

1. incidi in materiam veram sed simillimam fictae dignamque isto . . . poetico ingenio. Cf. Pliny's description of the theme proposed by Caninius in VIII. 4. 1: 'quae tam . . . poetica et quamquam in verissimis rebus tam fabulosa materia?' Caninius has been consulting Pliny in his search for a poetical theme in recent history. The two letters cannot be widely separate in date.

is tamen auctor cui bene vel historiam scripturus credidisses. This well fits Pliny the Elder, who tells a shorter version of this dolphin story in *NH* 9. 26 among his collection of dolphin yarns, ibid. 24–32. But there are considerable differences in minor details, s. 3 n., and only one verbal echo, s. 9 n. Pliny contradicts his uncle on a major point in s. 9, and implies that several versions were known: *constat*. Some of Pliny's details occur in the Elder's other dolphin stories, and Pliny may have concocted this version by a skilful combination. Possibly he is concealing from Caninius the fact that the story was already in writing. But he certainly has a separate and longer source than the *NH*. One doubts whether Pliny could have endured to read his uncle's immense and inelegant book.

quid poetae cum fide? What Pliny and all the world since has doubted and disbelieved has been shown to be possible in modern times. T. F. Higham, in *Greece and Rome*, 1960, 82 ff., published a fully authenticated account of a dolphin in Hokianga Harbour, New Zealand, in 1956, which behaved just like Pliny's beast, playing with the swimmers and allowing children to mount and ride it like Arion. This is shown on a photograph and vouchsafed by 'many credible witnesses'. The facts give a sharper interest to this and all other dolphin stories, of which a great collection may be studied in R. N. Hill, *Window in the Sea*, London, 1956.

2. est in Africa Hipponensis colonia mari proxima. adiacet navigabile stagnum. ex hoc in modum fluminis aestuarium emergit. The elder Pliny names Hippo Diarrhytus without any of this description, which exactly depicts the great lagoon of Bizerta connected, as it still is, by a narrow tidal channel to the open sea.

colonia. There was a veteran settlement of Julius Caesar. *CIL* viii. 25417.

3. omnis hic aetas piscandi . . . natandi studio tenetur, maxime pueri. The description of the seaside sports and the specification of boys are not in the Elder, who mentions boys in his other dolphin stories. Pliny's elaboration in 4–8 is his own. He omits the feeding of the dolphin from a man's hand, *NH*, loc. cit., and adds the calling of it by name, found in another of the Elder's stories; s. 6 n. Though the Elder speaks of pairs of dolphins in general, he does not provide this one with a mate. The landing of the monster also comes in a different story in *NH*.

6. appellant. The Elder speaks of dolphins responding to the name of Simo, loc. cit. 23, 25, 30.

7. ibat una (id quoque mirum) delphinus alius. For pairs cf. *NH* loc. cit. 33.

8. in terram quoque extrahi solitum ... in mare revolvi. This exceeds the yarns in the Elder, loc. cit. 27, where dolphins come to land for love, but perish on the dry shore. These tales are made up from the stranding of dolphins.

9. constat Octavium Avitum ... in litus educto ... superfudisse unguentum. The Elder names the proconsul Flavianus, and dates the event *inter hos annos*. Tampius Flavianus, legate of Pannonia in A.D. 69, was later proconsul of Africa; Tac. *Hist.* 2. 86, *ILS* 985. This part of the story evidently has a germ of truth in the anointing of a stranded dolphin at Hippo during Vespasian's reign by the governor of the province or his deputy. Hence the greater degree of coherence between the two Plinies at this point.

Octavius Avitus is not otherwise known, unless he is the commentator who wrote about Vergil's verse-endings, *PIR*[1] O 20–21.

religione prava. This is our Pliny's own comment. Compare his view of the Christians as a *superstitio prava immodica*, x. 96. 8 and VI. 20. 15 n.

novitatem odoremque in altum refugisse ... post multos dies visum languidum ... mox ... priorem lasciviam ... repetisse. This is fairly close to the version in *NH*, though 'odoris novitas' is the only common phrase: 'sopitus ... odoris novitate fluctuatusque similis exanimi caruit hominum conversatione ut iniuria fugatus per aliquot menses. mox reversus in eodem miraculo fuit'.

10. confluebant omnes ... magistratus, quorum adventu ... modica respublica ... sumptibus atterebatur. The Elder has the same ending in very different words. By *magistratus* Pliny means the Roman governing hierarchy rather than the local magistrates of the African municipalities, who could not compel hospitality in the same fashion. The Elder speaks of 'iniuriae potestatum in hospitales'.

34. To Suetonius Tranquillus

Date. The date of this note has been impugned (Peter, art. cit. 704, Schultz, art. cit. 33, Otto, art. cit. 41, and Zaranka; *contra*, Prete, *Saggi*, 94 n. 1) on the ground that the phrase in s. 2, 'est enim tam novus lector quam ego poeta', could only refer to the earliest period of Pliny's versification, i.e. to the period of IV–V, *c.* 105. But at any time between 105 and 108 Pliny, a veteran of oratory with a quarter of a century's experience of the courts behind him, could call himself a 'new poet'. His second slim volume is first mentioned, in unpublished form, in VIII. 21. In IX. 25 similarly he remarks: '*incipio* ... ex hoc genere studiorum ... etiam gloriam petere'. Both in VIII. 21 and in v. 3 he makes it clear that his regular practice was to recite for himself. This is the first mention of a doubt in the matter. The objection that Pliny had plenty of experienced *lectores* who would by this time be accustomed to his poems is not relevant. Pliny is afraid that the servant will be disturbed not by the novelty of the poems but by the occasion, a large gathering of friends. He is a trained reader: 'melius (scio) lecturum'. Hence the letter is in its logical place in the series. Pliny after reciting in person the first readings of his latest poems (VIII. 21) is going to make a change. Possibly also this letter is later than the sickness of Encolpius, recorded in VIII. I, s. I n.

Address. For the biographer Suetonius see I. 24 nn.

I. recitaturus familiaribus amicis. For Pliny's methods on these occasions see V. 3. 7–11, VIII. 21. 2–4. Pliny's gatherings were select, but they still filled a reception room set with benches.

Pliny had been losing his best readers recently through illness, and may have switched to one whose speciality was in some other branch of literary performance, a *comoedus* or *lyristes*. Cf. V. 19. 3, VIII. I, 19. I. There is no particular reason to identify this man with the sick Encolpius of VIII. I.

35. *To 'Atrius'*

There is no indication of date, but the reference to *occupationes* fits other letters of this period; cf. Ep. 2. I n.

Address. The Eight-Book MSS., which alone survive here, read either Appius or Atrius. Aldus printed Oppius. Likewise in the heading of I. 10, where the true reading is certainly Attius, one of the same group of MSS. reads Atrius. Hence Keil here proposed Attius, that is, Attius Clemens, who in I. 10 and IV. 2 appears as a man of letters just as here. This seems likely to be correct. Guillemin preferred Appius, which was printed in the earliest editions, before Aldus. But there is no other example of a prenomen surviving in a letter-heading. Conceivably Appius Annius Trebonius Gallus, *consul ord.* in 108 might be meant (Garzetti, *Inc.* 10).

36. *To Pedanius Fuscus*

Date. This belongs to the Fuscus–Quadratus series which begins in VI. II. The letter, which is continued in Ep. 40, is closely connected with VII. 9, another letter of instruction to Fuscus, s. I n. Details here and in Ep. 40 agree with other references to Pliny's life at Tifernum in VII–IX, ss. 5–6 nn. Hence the book-date is assured.

Address. For the young nobleman Fuscus see VI. 11. 1, 26. 1 nn. For this type of letter, an account of *ordinatio diurna*, Guillemin invoked the brief passage in *ad Fam.* 9. 20. 3 as a Ciceronian parallel, but Cicero's principal item, the *salutatio*, is absent, though another may be detected s. 5 n. (*VL* 132). For the type cf. III. 1, 5. 8–15 nn.

1. **quaeris quemadmodum in Tuscis diem aestate disponam.** In VII. 9 Pliny begins 'quaeris quemadmodum in secessu . . . putem te studere oportere', and here continues the 'instruction to a young man' on a broader canvas.

in Tuscis. See V. 6 for his Tuscan villa.

His day is divided into two parts—morning activities up to the midday siesta, ss. 1–3, then the period of exercise and *cena*, ss. 3–4.

evigilo cum libuit plerumque circa horam primam. Compare the beginning of his uncle's daily routine at Rome, and that of Spurinna in the country, III. 1. 4, 5. 9. Pliny's corresponds to neither exactly, but is naturally nearer Spurinna's.

For the Roman hours, counted from sunrise to sunset, see III. 5. 8 n., 'Routine'.

2. **cogito ad verbum scribenti emendantique similis . . . notarium voco et . . . dicto.** For his practice of revision at this period see Epp. 10. 3, 15. 2 nn. For the distinction between *scribere* and *dictare* see Ep. 28. 3. Merrill (ad loc.) rightly took this to mean that Pliny composed as much as he could memorize before sending for his secretary. The passage illuminates the practice of Silver Latin prose writing, its concentration on *partes* and patches, the composition in short sections, and lack of architectonics; cf. II. 5. 9–11, VII. 9. 5–6, IX. 4. Pliny's *Panegyricus* bears the marks of this, in the technical brilliance of its sections and the tediousness of the whole.

3. **ubi hora quarta vel quinta . . . in xystum me . . . confero, reliqua . . . dicto. vehiculum ascendo.** Pliny spends his morning more studiously than Spurinna, who did not put pen to paper until after the *vehiculum* and *ambulatio*, III. 1. 5–7. He now walks about in his colonnades and avenues, and drives around the 'hippodrome'. For these features of his Tuscan villa see V. 6. 16, 27–29, 32.

paulum redormio deinde ambulo. The time of siesta arrives, as in III. 5. 11, VII. 4. 4, and is followed by a walk, either on the avenues or on the special *ambulatio* or promenade of V. 6. 17 for a change.

Pliny makes no mention of any early meals, such as his uncle took, III. 5. 10–11, either here or in the account of Spurinna.

clare et intente non tam vocis causa quam stomachi lego. As in Celsus I. 8: 'si quis vero stomacho laborat legere clare debet'. He recommends a course of reading, special exercise, and a drinking

diet. The *phonasci* took care of this weakness. Suet. *Aug.* 84. 2, *Nero*
25. 3. Quintilian, II. 3. 19 f. suggests that their treatment resembled
that of Celsus. For Pliny's weakness see II. II. 15: 'voci laterique
consulerem'.

4. **iterum ambulo ungor exerceor lavor.** The afternoon routine is
exactly as with Spurinna, and as there is followed by the *cena*, III. 1. 8.
Pliny had a special *sphaeristerium* for this exercise, v. 6. 27.

**cenanti mihi si cum uxore vel paucis liber legitur ; post cenam
comoedia aut lyristes.** The limitation suggests that at more formal
functions the more elaborate performances replaced the *lectio*
(Guillemin, ad loc.), as at Spurinna's house-party, III. 1. 9. The Elder
Pliny preferred the reader at dinner, III. 5. 11. Elsewhere the custom
varies, Ep. 17. 3, I. 15. 2. Despite all this professional entertainment,
the Romans, like the British, did not altogether avoid conversation
at dinner, cf. IV. 22. 4–6. For another oddity about Roman dinner
parties see Ep. 23. 4.

mox cum meis ambulo quorum in numero sunt eruditi. Some of
these are mentioned in v. 19. 3, VIII. 1. Pliny ends dinner before the
hours of darkness, like his uncle, III. 5. 13 n. But Spurinna continued
his dinner into the night, III. 1. 9 n.

5. **si diu iacui vel ambulavi.** These are the activities of ss. 2–3. He is
iacens as long as he is in his *cubiculum*.

equo gestor. Still in the park, in the special 'gestatio in modum
circi', v. 6. 17. A country ride was a great rarity, Ep. 15. 3.

interveniunt amici ex proximis oppidis. Cf. Cicero, loc. cit. 'veniunt
etiam qui me audiunt'.

6. **venor aliquando sed non sine pugillaribus.** He regularly hunted at
Tifernum, v. 6. 46. For the strange combination see I. 6, v. 18. 2,
Ep. 10. 1 nn.

**colonis . . . quorum . . . agrestes querelae litteras nostras . . . com-
mendant.** For this theme, and its recurrence in several notes of the
period see Ep. 15 pref. Perhaps this sentence refers to the *salutatio*,
which Cicero puts in its usual place, the early morning.

37. *To Valerius Paulinus*

Date. The letter is dated to August 107 by the consular reference in
s. 1.

Address. There is no reason to doubt the identity of Pliny's intimate
friend, whose death is indicated in x. 104, with C. Valerius
Paulinus, suffect consul for September–December 107, according to
ILS 2003, and the Ostian *Fasti.* Ep. 13. 15 n., II. 2 pref., p. 736.

1. **nisi te kalendis statim consulem videro.** Cf. I. 5. 11, where Pliny
attends the installation of the praetors on 1 January. The letter was
evidently written during August, not long before the occasion when
Pliny was away at his Tuscan villa on the visit to his estates mentioned in Ep. 15 (pref.) and elsewhere in VII–IX, notably VII. 30. 2
(below).

**cum me necessitas locandorum praediorum plures annos ordina-
tura detineat.** Compare VII. 30. 2, 'instat et necessitas agrorum
locandorum perquam molesta: adeo rarum est invenire idoneos
conductores'. The occasion should be the same, because of the long
interval between the *lustra*. The circumstances are also like those of
Ep. 15. 1, where the Tuscan estate is named. The condition of the
estate recalls that of his Tuscan estate in X. 8. 5, and of that in III. 19,
which also seems to be Tuscan (ibid., s. 5 n.). The curious reading of
the surviving MSS. might suggest that the words *in Tuscis* or something similar have fallen out here. They read *Tuscan(i)orum* for
locandorum, which comes from Aldus and the correction of Budaeus
in I. But *locandorum* cannot be retained if it is a substitute, and the
passage makes no sense without it. Hence the MS. reading must be
explained as due to a dittography of the last syllable of *necessitas*.
The literary adjective is *Tuscus* or *Tuscanicus*, not *Tuscanus*. The
phrase *necessitas ordinatura* is odd and unparalleled in Pliny; it gives
a better rhythm and worse sense than *ordinaturum*.

For the normal system of letting to tenant farmers, *coloni* or
conductores, and the meaning of these terms, see III. 19. 6–7 nn.

2. **priore lustro quamquam post magnas remissiones reliqua creverunt.**
In X. 8. 5, best dated on other grounds to A.D. 99 rather than 98,
Pliny remarks of his Tuscan estate 'continuae sterilitates cogunt
me de remissionibus cogitare'. In III. 19 the new estate of which he
contemplates purchase is burdened with *reliqua colonorum*. In IV. 6. 1
we hear of 'abundantia sed par vilitas'. In VIII. 2 Pliny records a
heavy fall in the price of the grape harvest. Conditions have thus
been somewhat adverse persistently from the period 95–99 down to
107. In the contemporary alimentary 'table' of Veleia allowance is
made in the land valuation for overdue rents; *ILS* 6675 s. 43.

priore lustro. Since the year is 107, the *locatio* of X. 8 should be that
of 99, since two *lustra* have passed, and the year 97 certainly will not
fit the circumstances of that letter. So Pliny was letting his farms
on a four-year, not a five-year cycle, unless the cycles for the two parts
of his Tuscan estates did not coincide; for though legal sources give
five years as the norm in Italy, they also speak of lettings *per
plures annos*, and the elder Pliny uses *lustrum* of the four-yearly
cycle of leap-year. Paulus, *Dig.* 19. 2. 24. 2–4, 34. 3. 16, 45. 1. 89;

Balogh, *Studi . . . Paoli*, 48 n. 6; *RE* iv, 'colonatus', 487; Pliny, *NH* 2. 122. The suggestion of Sirago (op. cit. 109) that Pliny was anticipating the end of a five-year cycle by one year contradicts s. 1.

3. medendi una ratio si non nummo sed partibus locem ac deinde ex meis aliquos operis exactores custodes fructibus ponam. He proposes in place of a cash rental a system similar to that in use at this time on the large imperial estates in Africa Proconsularis, and known from four lengthy inscriptions. Of these the first is of Trajanic date, A.D. 116–17, the letter to the procurator of the *Villa Magna*; A–J 74, 93, 111, 142, or *FIRA* 1. 100–3; Bruns, 86, 114–16. There the tenants are share-croppers who pay a proportion of their produce in kind, *partes tertias* of all threshed grain, and, in pressed product, of all olives and grapes A–J 74 (i. 25–30). The *partes* are collected by contractors and their stewards, independent middlemen like tax-farmers, who make their account with the emperor's agent, the *procurator saltus*. The only difference between this system and Pliny's proposal is that Pliny's agents are not independent middlemen, but his employees. This difference is the result of the smaller scale of Pliny's estates. With the help of his land-agent he let the farms directly to the working *coloni*; see III. 19. 2, 5–7, VI. 3, VII. 30. 3 nn. The new system placed a greater burden on the staff because the rent had to be measured in raw material, not just counted in coin.

Columella speaks only of cash rents and minor services in kind (1. 7. 1–2). In Italy there is no trace of the partiary system between Cato, who mentions it in his *de agri cultura* (16, 146–7), and the period of Pliny, when it first appears briefly mentioned or implied in Tacitus, *Germania* 25. 1, and possibly Martial 13. 121 (cf. Balogh, *Studi . . . Paoli*, 1956, 45 n. 6. Sirago, op. cit. 110). It recurs as a new means of dealing with an agricultural crisis in the *Euboicus* of Dio Prusensis (*Or*. 7. 34–37), which should belong to the same decade as this letter. Sirago (op. cit. 174 f.), noting at least one close parallel between Dio's proposals and the Trajanic regulations, in the offer of rent-free tenure for a period of years to those who bring neglected land into cultivation, suggests that Dio learned his ideas during his sojourn (*c*. 97–98) at Rome from the advisers of Trajan. Since Pliny seems to regard himself as initiating a new scheme, the coincidence is hardly accidental. All three documents show the same approach to the agricultural problem of the age. But the African system is not nearly so new as the use of it by Pliny and Dio in Italy and Greece. The *lex Manciana* quoted as the basis of the Trajanic document may be a schedule of rules laid down by a landowner of the earlier Principate, or by a commissioner of Vespasian, possibly the Neronian consular Curtilius Mancia of VIII. 18. 4; for large estates in Africa were confiscated in Nero's last years (Pliny, *NH* 18. 35; *Ec. Survey V* 43 n. 25). Later the partiary system appears in Gaius and Paulus as a less usual alternative to the cash rent. (*Dig.* 19. 2. 25. 6, 47. 2. 26. 1).

et alioqui nullum iustius genus reditus quam quod . . . annus refert. Cf. *Dig.* 19. 2. 25. 6: 'partiarius colonus . . . damnum et lucrum cum domino . . . partitur'. Chilver (*Cisalpine Gaul*, 152) remarks that 'unless the tenants could maintain a proper standard of living out of their net produce and its sale it did not matter how they paid their rents'. This is mere modern benevolence. The partiary system protects the tenant against the vagaries of the market in difficult years. In a year of low prices or of low yields the cash tenant has to sell an unduly high proportion to pay his rent, and is left, like Pliny's tenants, without any standard of living at all. The share-cropper still has to realize his own share of the crop if he is growing a cash-crop, but if he is a subsistence farmer he is enabled to survive on his two-thirds for food and seed, provided his plot is of reasonable size. The proper criticism is that métayage tends to discourage improvements, since these profit the landlord without any contribution on his part. But the system protects the peasant from the disastrous vagaries of the Mediterranean climate, and enables the cultivating population at least to survive. In some zones métayage has persisted over long periods of time. In Syria, where it prevails and the peasantry are exposed to every form of exploitation by landowners and creditors, the vast majority of tenants are said to change their lands seldom, although the usual form of contract is annual tenancy. See *Syria*, 'Admiralty Geographical Handbook Series', BR 513, p. 267, quoting S. B. Himadeh, *Economic Organisation of Syria*, Beirut, 1936; R. Thoumin, *Géographie humaine de la Syrie centrale*, Paris, 1936.

Ultimately the colonate system may have helped to depress the Italian peasantry by Julio-Claudian standards, but it had its value as a stabilizing factor. The new system of share-cropping tenancy is thought by Rostovtzeff and others to have led by an inevitable evolution to the colonate of the Late Empire, in which the peasant is a kind of serf, tied to the soil by imperial enactment. But the general history of share-cropping elsewhere suggests that this would not have happened if other factors had not existed, notably the declining prosperity in the period of the barbarian invasions coupled with the growing demands of the imperial government upon the peasant as the ultimate producer of all wealth. In Pliny's time the *coloni* are impermanent; they continually flit, as s. 2 shows: 'ut qui iam putent se non sibi parcere'. Cf. VII. 30. 2. The landlords have no defence against their defalcations except the ordinary *pignoris capio*,

III. 19. 6 n. See Rostovtzeff, *SEHRE* 321, 472 ff.; Seek, art. 'colonatus', *RE* iv. 483 ff.; H. F. Pelham, *Essays*, Oxford, 1919, 275 ff.

4. at hoc magnam fidem . . . numerosas manus poscit. The series of rescripts to the African share-croppers shows both the complexity and the corruption of the administration of great estates by these methods.

in veteri morbo. Pliny's letters, however much is allowed for the habitual grumbles of landowners, show that something is wrong with Italian agriculture at the level of the working farmer. Pliny, by the standards of his age, was a long-sighted and benevolent landowner. Yet even he could not keep his peasants prosperous. The fact remains that the big owners continued to flourish, evidently at the expense of the peasants. The implication is that the margin of profit on Italian products had shrunk sufficiently to trouble the peasant whose holding was not adequate in size; the millionaires merely registered a decline of a point or two in their percentage income. The possible causes of this decline are discussed in III. 19. 7 n.

38. *To Pompeius Saturninus*

The book-date fits if the author of the book mentioned is Caninius Rufus, whose experiments in versification are mentioned in VIII. 4 and Ep. 33. 1, but who has not yet produced a complete work. Saturninus is the literary Pompeius Saturninus of I. 8, 16 etc., still flourishing in VII. 7, 8, 15; see V. 7. 1 n. Zaranka (cf. *Lustrum*, vi. 286) identified Rufus with Octavius Rufus, and the verses with his book of poems mentioned in II. 10. The letter would then with Ep. 26 belong to the period of I–II.

39. *To Mustius*

Date. There is no precise clue to the date of the letter or the locality of the shrine in question. Pliny is writing from his estates to the architect Mustius who is apparently at Rome (s. 5 *istinc* n.), either during his well-authenticated visit to Tifernum in 107 (Epp. 15, 37 prefs.) or during the visit to Comum that seems to be indicated in Ep. 7, which is also concerned with building operations, but of a different sort, s. 2 n.

Address. Mustius is not identifiable, but a praetorian senator of this name occurs at Patavium; *PIR*¹ M 556.

1. haruspicum monitu reficienda est mihi aedes Cereris in praediis in melius et in maius. The last words show (Merrill, Guillemin, ad loc.)

that Pliny first decided to rebuild and then consulted the *haruspices*, who produced a sound pretext. Their duty was to approve, not to propose. Cf. Tac. *Hist.* 4. 53: 'haruspices monuere . . . nolle deos mutari veterem formam'. They give *responsa* when consulted; cf. Tac. *Ann.* 13. 24. For them at this period see II. 20. 4 n. There were local *haruspices* at Comum, *CIL* v. 5294.

Unlike the *aedes* at Tifernum in IV. 1 this shrine is on private land. Hence Pliny does not need to consult the municipality. It was a *res profana*; cf. Marcian, *Dig.* 1. 8. 6. 3: 'sacrae res . . . in nullius bonis sunt . . . si quis ergo privatim sibi sacrum constituerit sacrum non est sed profanum'.

For the Italian Ceres see *RE* iii. 1970 ff.; Wissowa, *Rel. Kult.*² 192 f.

1–2. sit alioqui stato die frequentissima. . . . sed nullum in proximo suffugium. This sounds as if Pliny had just witnessed the annual festival, and suffered its inconveniences; possibly this connects the letter with the Tuscan holiday of 107. The occasion is evidently a pre-vintage celebration (Merrill). It is not a country market.

Guillemin (*VL* 114) sees in this letter only the desire of Pliny to include something parallel to Cicero's letters about the shrine to Tullia (*ad Att.* 12. 19. 1, 35. 2, 37. 4). But the initial phrase of this paragraph is not there just because Cicero dilated on the desirability of *celebritas loci* for Tullia's shrine. The tone of this description recalls Pliny's own letter about the shrine of Clitumnus (VIII. 8) much more than Cicero's. This is not the only letter about a shrine in Pliny, as Guillemin maintained: see III. 6, IV. 1, VIII. 8. So Cicero need not be invoked to explain its inclusion.

multa vota. Cf. VIII. 8. 7.

3. addidero porticus aedi. In *CIL* v. (S.) 745 Caecilius Secundus of Comum, possibly the father of Pliny, built 'templum . . . cum porticibus et ornamentis' to the Eternity of Rome and Augustus (p. 732). Hartleben, ad loc., suggests the so-called 'triangular forum' at Pompeii as a similar establishment.

4. velim ergo emas quattuor marmoreas columnas. The shrine is to be rebuilt with a projecting tetrastyle porch. The earlier building was probably just a gabled box.

antiquum illud e ligno. The statue of Clitumnus was also of wood, cf. VIII. 8. 5.

5. nihil interim occurrit quod videatur istinc esse repetendum, nisi tamen ut formam . . . scribas. Mustius is at Rome where artistic treasures and exotic stone would be available, while Pliny is on his estates. The architect is to bring the plan with him complete. Hence

Pliny warns him about the site. The *nisi* clause follows a little awkwardly in logical construction. This may be due to the revision of the
original letter. The necessary detailed instructions and measurements
have been eliminated, as also in the similar letter III. 6.

   This is not the only business letter revised for publication, see I.
21, III. 6, 19, V. 7, VI. 3, VIII. 2 nn.

   solum templi hinc flumine et abruptissimis ripis hinc via cingitur.
The shrine seems to be sideways to the road and the river, hence the
difficulty, as Merrill suggested.

40. *To Pedanius Fuscus*

For the date and address see Ep. 36, which this continues.

1. scribis pergratas tibi fuisse litteras meas. This postscript is hardly
part of an entirely fictitious correspondence.

   in Laurentino. For his Laurentine villa see II. 17.

2. meridianus somnus eximitur. Mentioned in Ep. 36. 3. Cf. VII. 4. 4,
'meridie (erat enim aestas) dormiturus'.

   vel ante vel post diem. His uncle rose before dawn in winter for his
studies, preferring early rising to late bedding, III. 5. 8.

   agendi necessitas. Cf. Ep. 2. 1. Pliny is still busy with private
practice.

   non iam comoedo vel lyristae post cenam locus. Ep. 36. 4 n.

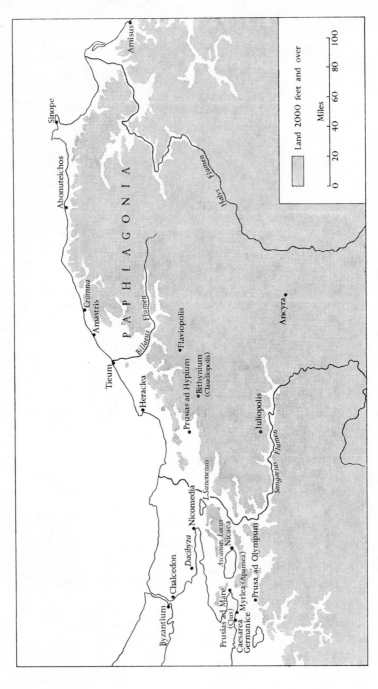

Fig. 1. The cities of Bithynia and proconsular Pontus, and adjacent areas

INTRODUCTION TO BOOK X

I. THE PROVINCE

I HAVE not included a detailed discussion of Bithynia-Pontus under Roman rule, because Pliny does not deal in the Letters with the whole area, and tends to raise very particular problems, most of which apply only to a single city. Those that affect the whole province are also very specific, and concern particular details of rules affecting certain topics, such as the admission of decurions to Councils, the treatment of long-term prisoners, the repayment of *alimenta* by foundlings, or the revocation of criminal sentences. Each precise problem requires its own introduction, and the area of common ground is limited. Any general introduction would amount to a discussion of the social and economic situation in the time of Augustus, as revealed in the main by Strabo and the material in the Elder Pliny. The amount of post-Augustan evidence down to the time of Trajan is remarkably small. Then some of the civic speeches of Dio Chrysostom cast an intense but narrow beam of light upon the internal politics of Prusa and the inter-city rivalries of Nicaea and Nicomedia, Prusa and Apamea, which is the theme of a small group of letters. Hence the commentary of each letter is intended to be self-sufficient. The exception which tests the rule is the pair of letters' about the Christians (Epp. 96–97). Here the considerable background has nothing to do with Bithynia-Pontus, and is accordingly treated in an Appendix, p. 772.

It may suffice to say that as in the other maritime provinces of Asia Minor the social and cultural life of Bithynia-Pontus depended upon the Greek cities, which administered the whole area as their separate civic territories, and controlled, so far as can be made out, such subordinate communities of villagers as did not possess civic rights in the Greek cities. But except at Nicomedia the existence and status of these is left in almost total obscurity by the sources. Pliny seldom concerns himself with anything but the affairs of the cities and of prominent individuals, for the reason that the city councils were the organs through which the governor dealt with his province. He had little occasion to deal directly with any parties except the magistracies and delegations of the cities, and with notable provincials who appeared before his tribunal on criminal charges or in civil suits. Hence the predominance in Pliny's letters of just these elements. Where minor characters emerge, as in the treatment of

servile recruits, and of the Christians, or in the affair of the foundlings, this is due to the reservation of certain subjects for the jurisdiction of the governor alone, notably capital offences and questions
of personal status. (Epp. 29, 65. 1, 72 nn.)

The interests of the Roman treasury do not appear in the Letters
with one doubtful exception (Ep. 84), because the collection of
tribute and the payment of the small band of officials and soldiers
were under the supervision of the quaestor in the previous proconsular régime, and of an independent imperial procurator during
Pliny's governorship (Ep. 27. 1 n.). Hence no discussion of Roman
imperial finances is here required. Financially Pliny was concerned
solely with overhauling municipal resources and expenditure (Ep.
18. 3 n.).

Another organ of government that is notably absent from the
Letters is the provincial Council or κοινοβούλιον—there was one for
each half of the province—and its deputies, the city representatives,
and their annual president, the Pontarchs and Bithyniarchs. None of
Pliny's problems arose from their activities, which were in this period
mostly concerned with the maintenance of the imperial cult of
Roma et Augustus, and the prosecution of offending governors if
occasion arose for extortion at the end of their term, as in VII.
6. 1–6 (nn.).

The province, unlike the other proconsular provinces of the eastern
empire, had a small force of at least two auxiliary cohorts, which was
under Pliny's command, and a coastal force of unknown size, under
the control of an equestrian *praefectus orae Ponticae*, which is to be
distinguished (it seems) from the main *classis Pontica* (Ep. 21. 1 n.).
A few letters concern the use of these troops.

The role of a general introduction is accordingly restricted.
Bithynia-Pontus had been administered by proconsuls under the
general supervision of the Senate, since the re-establishment of the
proconsular government in 27 B.C. But the Senate seldom exercised
this power in the century preceding Trajan. For Pliny only twice
quotes a *sensatusconsultum* in connexion with his problems (Epp.
56. 4, 72) against several citations of imperial enactments (Epp. 58,
72, 79, 112. 1, 118. 1). The history of the province's relations with
Rome in the past century seems to have been limited mostly to the
five occasions when Tacitus and Pliny note the prosecution of its
proconsuls (Tac. *Ann.* I. 74, 12. 22, 14. 46. Pliny, IV. 9, V. 20).
Bithynia hardly appears in any other connexion in the Annals of
Tacitus.

The reasons for Trajan's dispatch of Pliny to Bithynia are to be
gathered from the letters themselves. The intense inter-city rivalry,
documented by Dio's speeches, mostly focused on titles such as the

much-contested 'First City' and 'Neocoros' or 'temple-warden', which implied the management of a shrine of the imperial cult. But this rivalry existed as fiercely in the adjacent province of Asia without requiring the dispatch of an imperial commissioner like Pliny. The extravagance of the cities in public buildings seems to have been the main ground of Pliny's mission. This was certainly intensified by the inter-city rivalry, to judge by Dio's advocacy of a new building scheme at Prusa as a means of making Prusa the equal of her rivals (Ep. 23. I nn.). Pliny was sent, not to stop this orgy of construction, but to check its wastefulness (Epp. 18. 3 n., 23-24, 37-44, 47, 90-91, 98-99).

The existence of a turbulent element within the mass of the population, and of political intrigues within the governing class, can be detected from the Letters and from Dio. The popular disorders were directed against the civic authorities rather than the proconsuls, and the factions among the upper classes were concerned with personal feuds and ambitions within the civic framework, though on occasion cabals were formed within the provincial Council to secure the prosecution of unpopular proconsuls (Epp. 34. I n., 81. I n., IV. 9. 5, VII. 6. 1-6 nn.). Similar troubles in the province of Asia did not disturb the central government (VI. 31. 3 n.). Trajan seems to have given Pliny before he set out only a single directive on this matter—the instruction to suspend all 'clubs'—and possibly the general advice to maintain the *quies provinciae* (Epp. 34. 1, 96. 7, 117 nn.).

The determining factor in the dispatch of Pliny was Trajan's dislike of the waste of money by the cities. This was the reason for the invention at this time of the *curatores civitatium* in Italy, a sort of guardian appointed to license or veto extraordinary municipal expenditure. This paternalism appears also in the dispatch of Maximus to Achaea (VIII. 24. 2 n.). There is no sign of any economic malaise in Bithynia. The trouble sprang rather from an excess of prosperity. Though the evidence of Dio's speeches happens to indicate an outburst of municipal building at Prusa in the decade before Pliny's governorship (Ep. 23. I n.), it is perfectly possible that the various abuses in municipal finances which Pliny's letters reveal had been going on ever since the establishment of the Principate and of permanent peace restored the prosperity of this rich agricultural region. Trajan was the first emperor who cared to intervene. He could learn of the trouble from his various equestrian officials, whose presence in Bithynia is indicated as early as the time of Claudius (Tac. *Ann.* 12. 21). There is no reason to connect the prosecutions of Bassus and Varenus in 102-3 and 106-7 with the dispatch of Pliny. The facts of municipal expenditure would play no part in the evidence of an extortion trial.

The factor that made possible these municipal abuses was the lack of adequate counterchecks in the civic governments. There was no annually elected independent organ, such as the 'auditors' and the popular Council in classical Athens, to check the collusion between the local officers or magistrates and their kinsmen and friends in the local senates, whose members held their seats for life (Epp. 38. 2, 81. 1 nn.). The Romans themselves had brought this situation about by the reorganization of city government in Bithynia-Pontus through the *lex Pompeia* (in *c.* 62 B.C.), which established life-membership of the councils, and discouraged, though it did not abolish, the democratic organs that should have acted as a counterpoise. This basic weakness never presents itself to the mind of Pliny or Trajan, who were bent on the further discouragement of the popular element (Epp. 39. 5, 79. 1–3, 110. 1, 112–13 nn.). The technicalities of Pliny's appointment are discussed in the introduction to his career, p. 81.

BIBLIOGRAPHY

The province of Bithynia-Pontus has not been the subject of any lengthy monograph. The best discussions of its life and institutions in the Roman Empire are to be found in the articles concerning single cities, and related topics such as Pontarchs and Bithyniarchs, in Pauly-Wissowa, *Real-Encyclopädie*, in A. H. M. Jones, *Cities of the Eastern Roman Provinces*, (Oxford, 1937) ch. vi, and in relevant passages scattered through chs. viii, xi, xiii–xvi of his *Greek City* (Oxford, 1940). Much material is also to be collected in D. Magie, *Roman Rule in Asia Minor*, (Princeton, 1950) i–ii. Of special works there are only Cl. Bosch, *Die Kleinasiatischen Münzen der röm. Kaiserzeit*, (Stuttgart, 1935) Teil ii, which is devoted to Bithynia, and J. Solch, *Klio*, 1925, 'Bithynische Städte in Altertum', 165 f. Archaeological monographs on single cities, including articles in *RE*, will be mentioned in their place in the notes. Except for the superb walls and part of the theatre at Nicaea, and for the antiquities of *Prusias ad Hypium*, a city not mentioned in the Letters, this region is notably lacking in major monuments surviving above the ground.

The inscriptions of Bithynia-Pontus are not all readily accessible. There is a numerous selection down to 1906 in *Inscriptiones Graecae ad Res Romanas pertinentes* (*IGRR*). But the modern collections of *Tituli Asiae Minoris* and *Monumenta Asiae Minoris Antiqua*, and the modern edition of *Inscriptiones Graecae* do not cover this region as yet. Hence many are found only in the ancient *Corpus Inscriptionum Graecarum* (*CIG*), or in the books and journals in which they were originally published. These will be cited as required. *RE* xxiii. 1. 1075 f. lists all the inscriptions of Prusa.

Book X itself despite its exceptional value has attracted few general studies, E. G. Hardy's commentary remains outstanding despite its age: *Pliny's Correspondence with Trajan* (London, 1889). The dissertation of Joh. Meyer, *Der Briefwechsel des Plinius und Traianus als Quelle römischer Kaisergeschichte* (Straßburg, 1908), which dealt with formal aspects of the correspondence, seems not available in England. Hardy has been substantially supplemented only by L. Vidman's general study, 'Étude sur la correspondance de Pline le Jeune avec Trajan' (*Rozpravy Ceskoslovenské akadamie Věd*. S. 14, R. 70, Prague, 1960), which is not a continuous commentary. Other discussions of the style and form of the correspondence are given on pp. 536 f.

II. CHRONOLOGY OF THE LETTERS FROM BITHYNIA AND THE ORDER OF PLINY'S JOURNEYS

It has usually been accepted that the correspondence with Trajan is in its original sequence, and that an order of time can be established by Pliny's references to certain dates and annual festivals: his arrival on 17 September, that of his legate on 24 November, Trajan's birthday, 18 September (Epp. 17 A. 2, 25, 88–89), the New Year celebrations on 1 or more probably 3 January (Epp. 35–36, 100–1),[1] and Trajan's *dies imperii* on 28 January (Epp. 1 pref., 52, 102–3). These dates divide the correspondence into six blocks covering parts of three calendar years, or into two seasons from September to September, of which the second is incomplete. The letters in each block are commonly taken to be consecutive.[2] Certainly the letters about the canal project (41–42, 61–62), the bath at Prusa (23–24, 70–71), and the emissaries from Bosporus (63–64, 67) are in serial order in each case. So too the references to the municipal censors: *destinati* in 79. 4, some time before September (Ep. 88), after January (Ep. 100) they are in office (Ep. 114. 2). The query about out-of-date *diplomata* in Ep. 45 is neatly placed in the middle of January (Epp. 35 and 52). The main question about *liberi expositi* in Ep. 65 appropriately precedes a subsidiary inquiry *de agnoscendis liberis* in Ep. 72. Trajan's replies are grouped with the correct letters of Pliny, though they must often have arrived later than the next letter of Pliny to Trajan in the series.[3]

[1] For the uncertainty see Ep. 35 nn.

[2] U. Wilcken, 'Plinius' Reisen in Bithynien und Pontus', *Hermes*, xlix, 1914, 120 ff., is the basic study after Mommsen, *GS* iv. 391 f. Cf. also H. G. Pflaum, 'Essai sur le cursus publicus', *Mem. Ac. Inscr. et B. Lett.* xiv (1940), 189 ff.

[3] Cf. the sequence of the canal letters. Ep. 41 is dispatched in early January

If the letters of Pliny are in chronological order, they should give the order of Pliny's movements from city to city in each section. An apparent difficulty arises from this assumption in connexion with Epp. 58, 70, and 81, but disappears on close examination. These three fall between 28 January and 18 September of the first season (Epp. 52 and 88). Pliny seems to visit Prusa three times in this period. This is surprising in a single half year when he had a busy series of assizes in addition to his special mission. The three Prusan letters are separated by others referring to visits to the neighbourhood of Nicomedia (Ep. 61), to Nicaea (Ep. 67), and to Juliopolis (Epp. 67. 1, 77. 2). In Ep. 83 he is again at Nicaea. Now in Epp. 58. 1 and 81. 1 he refers to the opening and the closing phases of assizes at Prusa which can quite well belong to the same visit. In 58 he is certainly at Prusa,[1] opening the assize, and hears the case against Flavius Archippus. In 81, writing from Nicaea, he refers back to the initiation of charges against Dio brought by Archippus and his friends on the last day of a visit to Prusa, and transferred for further hearing to Nicaea. In Ep. 70 he discusses legal difficulties that had arisen over his plan for using a certain site for the new baths at Prusa. He had examined the site when at Prusa (s. 1), but the information about the legal difficulty may only have been brought to his notice after he had left the city: hence the apparent dislocation of Ep. 70. All these three letters then refer to a single visit early in the second calendar year of his first 'season'.

It has been suggested by Wilcken (art. cit. 122 ff.) that Pliny only sent off urgent problems straightway from the city where they arose, and that inquiries of longer term and less urgency, such as building problems, were sometimes held back for later dispatch. This is possible, though the reference to Claudiopolis in 39. 5 is the only clear case. But the distinction between urgent and non-urgent is difficult to draw, and though the assumption might help to eliminate minor difficulties,[2] it also eliminates altogether the solid basis of any account of Pliny's movements by introducing an unnecessary element of doubt about many of the fixed points. The difficulties are not such as to require this solution, which does not help at all with the threefold visit to Prusa. It is also very improbable that Pliny waited at cities for the replies to his queries from Rome.

(Ep. 52) and Pliny must have received Trajan's reply, Ep. 42, after the visits to Prusa (Ep. 58) and other business recorded in Epp. 54, 56, which are placed after the end of January, and before Ep. 61, Pliny's reply to Trajan's reply.

[1] Vidman's doubts are groundless: Ep. 58. 1 n.

[2] e.g. Vidman would make the Prusan Ep. 23 retrospective, putting the visit of Virdius (Ep. 21) at Nicomedia. The military matters of Epp. 27–30 may well have been settled at Nicomedia (Vidman), but there is no reason to remove Epp. 19–22 from the connexion with Prusa given by Epp. 17 and 23.

Otherwise the scheme of Pliny's travels set forth by U. Wilcken, improving on Mommsen's account, is generally convincing, with a few corrections (art. cit. 120 ff., cf. Vidman, *Étude*, 64 f.). In his first season, from September to September, Pliny confines himself to Bithynia. Before his first January he visits Prusa (Epp. 17–18, 23) Nicomedia (Epp. 25, 31, 33) and Nicaea (Ep. 31), and makes a special journey to Claudiopolis in eastern Bithynia at the time of the great fire at Nicomedia (Ep. 33. 1 with 39. 5). Claudiopolis lay on a direct route from Nicomedia. During his first January (Epp. 35–52) Pliny passes on from Nicomedia and Nicaea (Epp. 37, 39) to visit Byzantium (Ep. 43) and, apparently, Apamea (Ep. 47), returning thence to Nicomedia (Ep. 49), where, as Vidman suggests, the military celebrations of Trajan's birthday in Ep. 52—and the arrival of Clemens in Ep. 51—are best placed. Wilcken assumes that these last three journeys were made by sea, the obvious means of communication to such scattered goals if the visits were in the order of the letters. But the sea journeys and the number of visits in January are odd. It is possible that Pliny did not go to Apamea at the time of Ep. 47, which deals with a technical objection to his visit, but, having heard of this in advance, while still in Byzantium, postponed his visit to Apamea until he received Trajan's reply.[2] He may have gone to Byzantium by land and ferry at that time of year.

In the third part of his first season, from February to September (Ep. 52 to Ep. 88), the first located occasion is the visit to Prusa of Epp. 50, 70, 81, discussed above. He then, apparently, moves to the neighbourhood of Nicomedia, to inspect the canal site (Ep. 61), and thence to Nicaea (Epp. 63. 1, 67. 1). The canal visit is out of geographical order, since Nicomedia lies beyond Nicaea to one coming from Prusa. Pliny stresses his personal inspection—'in re praesenti invenisse videor'—but this knowledge may be derived from his visit in the previous autumn. The placing of Pliny's letter, which is a reply to Trajan's Ep. 42, may have been fixed by the date when he received Ep. 42. From Nicaea he goes off to *diversam provinciae partem* (Ep. 67. 1), which turns out to be Juliopolis (Ep. 77. 2) in eastern Bithynia, on a direct route from Nicaea. The reference in 77. 2 is an afterthought, though not 'held back' in Wilcken's sense. Pliny is not still at Juliopolis when he is prompted by an unexpected action of Trajan at Byzantium to make a recommendation on its behalf. The visit to Juliopolis may precede the tour of the unnamed locality (or localities) of Epp. 68, 72, 74, 75, which is not Nicomedia in 74 at least, and may be Nicaea, to which he has returned in Epp. 81 and 83. A journey from Nicaea to

---

[1] Cf. p. 530 n. 2.
[2] See Ep. 47, pref. The use of the locative rather favours his actual presence.

Juliopolis and back would make good sense. This concludes the first season, in which he seems to have used Nicaea and Nicomedia as bases for forays into the rest of Bithynia. Wilcken (art. cit. 123 f.) rightly argues against Mommsen that there is no evidence for a journey of Pliny into Paphlagonia, this season, where the freedman Maximus went on a special assignment (Ep. 27). The wording of Pliny's recommendation (Ep. 85)—'per omne tempus quo fuimus una'—does not imply that Pliny had gone with Maximus into inner Paphlagonia, which was not part of his own province, but that Maximus was away for part of the period.

In the second season, September of Ep. 88 through January of Epp. 100-3 onwards, only three places are named: Sinope (Ep. 90), Amisus (Ep. 92), Amastris (Ep. 90), and again Amisus (Ep. 110). The first three occur in the period September–January, with the second reference to Amisus coming later. The order is odd, since Amastris lies towards the western and Bithynian end of Pontus, and Amisus at the extreme east, with Sinope between them. Wilcken thought Pliny sailed along the coast, visiting Amastris first, but delaying the letter as non-urgent. Unfortunately on his principle it was neither less nor more urgent than that concerning Sinope which considerably precedes it. Both were about building permits. Perhaps Pliny was based at Sinope, which as the chief maritime centre was a suitable station for coastal journeys. There is no indication that Pliny visited Heraclea and Tium, which lie to the west of Amastris, to settle the affair of the memorial to Julius Largus which had been raised in Ep. 75, before he went to Amastris. There is no clear indication, also, whether the affair of the Christians (Ep. 96) was raised at Amisus, visited in Ep. 92, or at Amastris (Ep. 98).

It fits the serial order of the letters that the points affecting municipal constitutions raised in Ep. 79—during the first season—concern Bithynia alone, while those discussed in Epp. 108 and 112 concern both Bithynia and Pontus, even if there is no reference to Pontus in Ep. 114 on the same subject. This omission does not prove that Pliny had returned to Bithynia by that time (Ep. 114. 1 n.).

The serial order thus provides a consistent pattern for the journeys in a rational geographical order, with only two awkward points in the placing of the second visit to the lake of Nicomedia and of the visit to Amastris. Neither difficulty is insuperable or even severe. But it is only too often forgotten that five cities of Bithynia, whose finances Pliny must have regulated, are not even mentioned in Book x—Chalcedon, Cius or Prusias ad Mare, Caesarea Germanice, Creteia-Flaviopolis, and Prusias ad Hypium. Equally, in coastal Pontus no visit is recorded to Heraclea, Tium, and Abonuteichos, though anticipated for the first two in Ep. 75.[1] It is implied in Ep. 54 that the financial mission has been largely completed in Bithynia proper. When did Pliny visit the missing five cities? They would not be hard to fit in—Chalcedon with Byzantium, Caesarea with adjacent Apamea, Cius with Nicaea, Flaviopolis and Prusias with Claudiopolis. This is conjecture. But twice Pliny mentions visits to *diversam partem* and it is only probable cross-references that identify one with Juliopolis and the other with Claudiopolis (Epp. 33. 1, 39. 5, 67. 1, 77. 2).

III. THE COMPLETENESS OF BOOK X AND ITS PURPOSE

O. Kunz first suggested that certain letters were missing from the collection, in support of his improbable theory (Ep. 63 n.) connecting Pliny's mission with the Parthian war. There are no replies to Pliny's notes about the emissaries from the Bosporan kingdom and the runaway slave: Epp. 63, 64, 67, 74. Kunz failed to notice that seven other letters of Pliny lack a reply: 25, 26, 51, 85, 86A, 86B, 87. L. Vidman (*Listy Filologicke*, 1957, 21 ff.; *Étude*, 29 ff.) and K. U. Instinsky (*Philologus*, 1948, 193) have suggested that these various letters received no reply because they needed none, being either factual reports about movements of persons, or formal commendations of officials leaving the province. Further, the Bosporan letters involved the use of the imperial post, about which Trajan was fussy and Pliny scrupulous. But this does not account for the absence of replies to Epp. 26 and 87, which are recommendations of personal friends not apparently serving with Pliny. In three other examples, including the request of a serving centurion, Epp. 94–95, 104–7, Trajan informs Pliny of his decision as an act of courtesy, though the required favour was granted by other means. Vidman observed that in the pre-Bithynian section of Book x Trajan replies to Pliny's requests (Epp. 3B, 79) only when technical questions made a reply necessary (*Étude*, 35–36). Normally a rescript to the beneficiary, or to the appropriate official, sufficed (Epp. 2. 1, 6. 2, 7 nn.). Hence replies to Epp. 26 and 87 likewise may never have been written rather than lost. But the argument is perhaps circular. Besides in Ep. 10. 1 Pliny speaks of letters of Trajan in the plural (*epistulae tuae*) in the Harpocras affair, though only one occurs in the collection (Ep. 7). It seems unlikely that Trajan would fail to reply to so grave a

---

[1] For the cities see A. H. M. Jones, *CERP* 159 f., 165 f.; possibly Flaviopolis went with Pontus.

recommendation as that in Ep. 4, of a distinguished provincial for a seat in the Senate. Hence it remains probable that the replies to 26 and 87 have been lost, and those to some of the pre-Bithynian Letters.

A lesser doubt concerns three or four reports that are promised or requested but do not appear. In Epp. 38 and 40 Trajan asks for reports on building affairs, in Ep. 57 he promises to send Pliny information from a former proconsul of Bithynia about certain convicts, and in Ep. 73 he promises advice if Pliny sends him a certain document. The absence of the first of these requested reports, and of the fourth, is surprising because Trajan underlined his interest in the matter. The other two, at least, may never have been written, as Vidman argues, because in Ep. 40 Trajan disclaims interest, and the inquiry promised in Ep. 57 was perhaps in vain.

In Ep. 27 the instructions given to Pliny by Trajan (*iussisti*) about distribution of troops come not from a lost letter but from the *mandata*, as in Epp. 21–22 (Vidman). But in Ep. 77 it is possible that Pliny received news of Trajan's dispatch of a centurion to Byzantium in a letter that is not included in the collection. The puzzling condition of the opening of the present Ep. 86B, which some editors have wrongly amalgamated with Ep. 86A, suggests that the introduction to Ep. 86B has been lost, and possibly the whole of a second similar letter (nn.). But this occurs in the middle of a section containing a number of short letters of commendation which belong chronologically together, and does not suggest that there is a great gap in the original text. It is also possible that something has been lost from the middle of Ep. 41, about the canal at Nicomedia. But other solutions of the obscurity in this letter are possible.

With these few exceptions the 'Bithynian' collection appears to be complete. The inclusion of two sets of annual letters of greetings, phrased in similar terms (Epp. 35–36, 52–53, and 100–3), and of several examples of letters dealing with the same category of problem —e.g. five or six pairs about building questions, three pairs about the recruitment of municipal councillors—and of several personal recommendations of friends and dependants, a type already well represented in the pre-Bithynian section of x, all these taken together suggest that the book is intended not as a special selection of typical letters, but as a complete record. Even without Epp. 1–14 it considerably exceeds the average page-length of the books of private letters. In the Teubner text the excess is about a third: 51:35 for the Bithynian letters and 59:35 for the whole book. A few replies and reports may be missing, just as in the pre-Bithynian section a second letter of congratulation to Trajan on the Dacian victories is missing. But it seems unlikely that any serious inquiries of Pliny to

Trajan have been purposely omitted, and improbable that any such
have been accidentally lost where so much minor material has been
preserved.

An argument for incompleteness has been based on the omission
of official documents and various petitions (*libelli*) which Pliny
cites as attached to his letters in Epp. 47. 2, 56. 5, 59, 70. 4, etc.,
whereas a regular dossier is published in Ep. 58, though this too is
incomplete. In this letter Pliny states that he has attached the documents quoted by both sides, yet in our texts eight documents are
mentioned of which only four appear. The technical terms used by
Pliny to note the inclusion of documents with his letter—*iunxi*,
subieci—have been explained to mean that original petitions were
sent attached to Pliny's letter to be subsequently detached for action
(*iunxi*), while copies of official documents were written out on the
same papyrus as the letter (*subieci*) Epp. 22. 1, 107. 1 nn., Vidman).
Hence Pliny's own files might include the copied documents but
omit the petitions. It is the copied documents alone that appear in
the Archippus archive of Ep. 58. The selection chosen may be
explained by the supposition that Pliny's editor included only the
essential documents on which the issue depended, and aimed at
providing a balanced dossier (Ep. 58. 4 n.). As it stands the archive
is twice the length of the letter which it accompanied. To have
included all such documents throughout would have made the collection intolerably long and have swamped Pliny's own contribution.

The collection has been characterized as a special register of extraordinary reports excluding routine affairs (W. Weber, *Festgabe . . . K.
Müller*, 1922, 27 f.; P. Pflaum, *Mém. Ac. Inscr. B. L.* xiv. 235 f.).
But it includes numerous routine reports of brief character, and
private recommendations. The book is certainly not a handbook
of provincial law, as suggested by Durry (ed. Budé, iv, p. ix), for the
good reason that the rescripts of emperors were not yet regarded
as having universal validity (Ep. 65. 2 n.). Hence the book only
makes sense as intended to be the complete publication of Pliny's
letters to Trajan of all sorts, so far as these survived, including the
pre-Bithynian letters. The notion that Pliny, or any governor, sent
long annual or seasonal reports to Rome on his work in general is
not supported by any evidence, and may be discarded. The suggestion of Weber (loc. cit.) that the letters were extracted from the
files of imperial archives in Bithynia is excluded by the mixture of
official and unofficial letters. It is unlikely for the same reason that
they came from imperial archives at Rome, whether or not they
would there be distributed in different *scrinia* as Weber supposed.

IV. THE DRAFTING OF TRAJAN'S
REPLIES TO PLINY

The contemporary evidence of Suetonius, confirmed by a statement in Pliny, tells how Vespasian and his co-regent Titus dealt with their official correspondence.[1] Vespasian, rising before dawn, studied the documents submitted by his secretaries, and discussed them, if he thought fit, with his advisers, the *amici* who formed his *consilium*. He would then dictate a written reply to a secretary, if what Suetonius says about Titus may be transferred to his father: 'patris nomine et epistulas ipse dictaret'. Suetonius adds that Titus used also to compose edicts for his father, using the word *conscriberet*. This should not be pressed to mean that he wrote with his own hand. The procedure resembles Pliny's description of his own method of composition in IX. 36. 2: 'cogito si quid in manibus . . . ad verbum scribenti . . . similis . . . notarium voco et . . . quae formaveram dicto'. It is difficult to accept the literal implication of SHA, *Commodus*, 13. 6–7 that the emperors wrote their letters in their own hand, though they may have personally signed certain documents and written brief *subscriptiones*, as Nero is recorded to have done.[2] Over a century later the emperor Severus followed the same procedure as Vespasian.[3] Whether Trajan followed the same method is not stated or implied directly in any place. But the normal use of dictation by the wealthy classes should be borne in mind throughout the following discussion.

The documents themselves are *epistulae*, the regular form of correspondence between the Princeps and his senior administrators, as between fellow senators, not *libelli*. The technical language of Pliny and Trajan in several passages makes this clear: 'libellus . . . quem epistulae tuae iunxeras'.[4] As such, they passed through the hands of the secretary *ab epistulis*. H. Peter briefly stated the reasonable opinion that Trajan did not draft the rescripts himself or manage the details of law and administration which they involve, that being the work of the secretary.[5] This widely accepted view was established

[1] Suet. *Vesp.* 21; *Titus* 6. 1; Pliny, III. 5. 9 n. This introduction is reprinted, with a few alterations and additions, from the *Journal of Roman Studies*, 1962, by the courtesy of the Society for the Promotion of Roman Studies.

[2] Suet. *Nero* 10. 2. Cf. Hirschfeld, *Verwaltungsbeamten*, 327 n. 1, 328 n. 1, citing also SHA, *Carinus*, 16. 8. See text cited in Ep. 107 n.

[3] See III. 5. 9 n., 'Career'.

[4] Ep. 48. 1; cf. 60. 2, 83. W. Weber, *Festgabe . . . K. Müller* (Tübingen, 1922), 26. For the *libellus* system see Ep. 107 nn.

[5] H. Peter, 'Der Brief in der römischen Litteratur', *Abh. Sächs. Akad. d. Wiss. phil.-hist. Klasse*, xx (1903), 123. The secretary's identity is not known. He probably succeeded Titinius Capito, 1. 17. 1 n.

on a firmer basis by the investigations of A. Henneman into the
'outer and inner style' of the rescripts. His general conclusion was
that Trajan settled the more important problems himself from
material prepared by his secretariat, by giving a verbal decision
which the secretary worked up into the drafts which we have. These
were written in a uniform chancery style, but personal interventions
and comments of Trajan are recognizable within the formal texts.
Henneman used two main arguments to establish the secretarial
manner. First, he detected and tabulated a considerable body of
recurrent vocabulary and phraseology, both of common terms and of
administrative jargon.[1] The following few examples may suffice:

Ep. 30. 1. secundum mandata mea.
     34. 1. secundum exempla complurium.
     76.   secundum cuiusque loci condicionem.

Ep. 115.   merito haesisti.
    117.   merito vereris.
    121.   merito habuisti fiduciam.

Ep. 30. 1. de quibus cognosci oportebit.
     32. 2. hos oportebit poenae suae reddi.
     40. 1. quid oporteat fieri circa theatrum.
    109.   id dari a me non oportebit.
    111.   retractari a me non oportet.

Ep. 78. 2. onerabimus nos exemplo.
     82. 2. etiamsi exemplis adiuvaretur.
     97. 2. pessimi exempli . . . est.
     34. 1. secundum exempla complurium.
     69.   sequenda . . . exempla sunt eorum qui isti provinciae
             praefuerunt.

Ep. 76.   secundum cuiusque loci condicionem.
     80.   in curiam loci cuiusque.
    111.   hominibus cuiusque loci.

Ep. 78. 1. ea condicio est civitatis Byzantiorum.
     30. 2. cum haberent condicionis suae conscientiam.
     95.   ea condicione qua adsuevi.
    119.   mutata . . . condicione certaminum.

This argument fairly demonstrates the uniformity of the style of the
rescripts, and suggests the conventions of a bureau, and perhaps of a
single author. The second argument is based on the observation that
frequently the rescripts largely follow the wording of the letters of
Pliny which they are answering. Henneman tabulated some fifty

---

[1] A. Henneman, *Der äußere und innere Stil in Traians Briefen* (Diss.
Gießen, 1935), 28–33. U. Rangone, 'Traianea I. La lingua e lo stile', *Studia
Ghisleriana*, i, 1950, 243 ff., who seems not to have read Henneman, reaches
similar conclusions from a more superficial examination.

examples drawn from as many pairs of letters, in which short phrases of Pliny are repeated in practically the same words.[1] Thus:

Pliny 23.	desiderio eorum indulgere posse.
Trajan 24.	possumus desiderio eorum indulgere.
Pliny 54.	dispice ergo domine.
Trajan 55.	non aliud dispicio.
Pliny 77. 2.	quanto est infirmior (*sc.* civitas).
Trajan 78. 2.	quanto infirmiores erunt (*sc.* cives).

This habit may well be held to be the trait of a secretary set to draft his principal's replies. The argument might have been fortified by a more extensive comparison of certain pairs of letters as a whole. In some letters concerned with rather technical problems the reply is not only couched in Pliny's vocabulary but follows narrowly the form in which Pliny put the problem. This is most notable in the letters concerned with fine points of municipal constitutions: 79–80, 108–9, 112–13, 114–15, 116–17. The reply to Pliny's query about 'iselastic games' (118–19) is an extreme example of close correspondence between letter and rescript. The problems put forward by Pliny in these letters are such that one expects Trajan to lean heavily on his secretariat. The tendency is less marked, for example, in the earlier letters about building policy and the rescript about the Christians (38, 40, 97). But it reappears in other rescripts where one might expect Trajan's personal interest to be shown. The reply about the sewer at Amastris provides a brief and outstanding example:

Pliny 98. 1–2. Amastrianorum civitas . . . habet . . . plateam . . . cuius . . . per spatium . . . porrigitur . . . flumen . . . . quibus ex causis non minus salubritatis quam decoris interest eam contegi; quod fiet si permiseris, curantibus nobis ne desit quoque pecunia operi tam magno quam necessario.

Trajan 99. rationis est mi Secunde carissime contegi aquam istam quae per civitatem Amastrianorum fluit, si intecta salubritati obest. pecunia ne huic operi desit curaturum te secundum diligentiam tuam certum habeo.

Rescript 121, approving the use of the imperial post-wagons by Pliny's wife, follows its counterpart even more closely. But this may be grouped with the obviously formal notes in which Pliny transmits and Trajan nominally accepts the seasonal prayers and congratulations of the governor and the province (52–53, 88–89, 100–1, 102–3). The hand of the secretariat appears also in the formality by which grants of privilege are notified:

Ep. 95. dedisse me ius trium liberorum . . . referri in commentarios meos iussi.

Ep. 105. dedisse me ius Quiritium referri in commentarios meos iussi.

[1] Ibid. 33–37.

These arguments indicate the formal hand of the secretariat. To determine how much the rescripts owe to the mind and tongue of Trajan himself is less easy, though his intervention can be detected in a few obvious instances. When Trajan refuses a reasonable request rather sharply (40. 3) or snaps at Pliny for countenancing a charge of *maiestas*, or for not making his own decision (Epp. 82, 117), or when Trajan is enraged by scandalous corruptions or wanton disobedience, as in 38, 57. 2, the language is not that of an equestrian or freedman assistant to a consular legate. 'sed medius fidius ad eandem diligentiam tuam pertinet inquirere quorum vitio . . . tantam pecuniam Nicomedenses perdiderunt'. 'sed ego ideo prudentiam tuam elegi ut formandis istius provinciae moribus ipse moderaris'. It is equally unlikely that the various commendations of Pliny's actions derive merely from the secretary, even if they are expressed in stereotyped terms, e.g. 'merito haesisti' (above, p. 537), 'optime fecisti' (44), 'recte renuntiasti' (16).

Such instances cover only a small number of letters. Henneman tried to detect the hand of Trajan by comparing the language used in other official documents of Trajan with that of the rescripts to Pliny.[1] He found some twenty-two parallel usages, but these were mostly very short phrases. The longest, which all come from citations in the *Digest*, are as follows:

Ep. 82. 2.	cum et utilitas civitatis exigat.
Dig. 48. 18. 1. 19.	prout causa exegerit.
Ep. 97. 2 *et al.*	pessimi exempli . . . est.
Dig. 29. 1. 24.	eiusmodi exemplum non admitti.
,, 48. 22. 1.	hoc quoque remisi exemplum.
Ep. 38.	perfer in notitiam meam.
Dig. 29. 1. 1.	cum in notitiam meam perlatum sit.
Ep. 78. 1.	honoribus eius . . . consulendum habuerimus.
Dig. 29. 1. 1.	simplicitati eorum consulendum existimavi.

The shortest instances include:

Ep. 34. satius enim est.	*Dig.* 48. 19. 5. satius enim esse.
Ep. 113. id ergo.	,, 29. 1. 24. si ergo.

Henneman argued that since the juristic texts come through diverse hands the common vocabulary was due to the influence of Trajan. But the opposite is more likely to be the case. The richest source of these parallels, providing fourteen out of the twenty-two instances, consists of two related texts, a *caput ex mandatis* and a rescript (*Dig.* 29. 1. 1 and 24), about the wills of legionary soldiers. Trajan had evidently insisted upon a ruling contrary to the general principles of

---

[1] Op. cit. 3–18, 25–26.

Roman law—that the intention of soldiers making wills should prevail irrespective of the form. This is expressed tersely in the Trajanic words 'ut quoquo modo testati fuissent rata esset eorum voluntas. faciant igitur testamenta quo modo volent faciant quomodo poterunt'. The rest of the first document is concerned with formulating the rule suitably for the *mandata legatorum*. Most of the rescript is concerned with explanations of the application of the rule to prevent abuses which the horrified lawyer expects to arise from the emperor's Gordian solution. The common vocabulary in these documents is more likely to come from the lawyers and secretaries than from Trajan, whose own words are probably limited to the sentence quoted. Pliny himself, who had spent several years in the central administration, uses set forms in his short letters of commendation and official notes of congratulation.[1] He also uses the common official vocabulary in his major letters to Trajan. Thus he twice uses the term *perferre in notitiam* (Epp. 67. 2, 75) which recurs in Rescript 38. 2, and in the *caput ex mandatis*. This is likely to be official jargon, contrasting with the crisp *notum facies . . . mihi scribes* of Rescript 38—a passage dealing with military discipline. Both also use, for example, the phrase *in re praesenti*, 'on the spot'—Pliny in Epp. 61. 1, 81. 3; Trajan in 40. 1, 78. 3—which recurs in an official document of the period.[2]

The freedom with which the rescripts follow the terminology of Pliny generally suggests that the similarities of language between the external documents and the rescripts, and between these and Pliny's own letters, are due to the use of a common bureaucratic language, and not to the influence of Trajan. Henneman had rightly noted the general similarity in crispness of style between the Trajanic documents of all sorts and the similar documents from the Flavian and Hadrianic periods, though specific parallels are few because this material is scanty in Latin.[3]

The hand of Trajan cannot easily be detected by formal stylistic analysis, except for the few strong outbursts noted above. But a deeper examination of the material content of the letters may give better results. Henneman touched on this in a few pages devoted to the *innerer Stil* of the rescripts. By this he meant the principles that underlie the decisions of the Emperor. He detected the following: Equity towards the material interests of provincials (55, 69, 81,

---

[1] Especially the terminal 'ea fide quam tibi debeo': 85, 86A, 86B. Also the formal wording of Epp. 35, 52, 100, 102, echoed in the replies.

[2] *ILS* 5947 A. But cf. also Livy 40. 17. 1.

[3] e.g. the rescripts of Vespasian, Domitian, and Nerva in *FIRA* i. 72–77 and Ep. 58. 5–6, 10. Also McCrum and Woodhead, *Select Documents of the Flavian Emperors*, nn. 442, 458.

111, 115). Severity towards malingerers (32, 57, 119). A preference for flexible local rules rather than general enactments (59, 66, 97, 109, 113). Avoidance of dangerous precedents (24, 55, 78. 2, 82, 97. 2). Strictness of military discipline, combined with consideration for the troops (20, 22, 28, 30, 78). Suspicion of corporate bodies (34, 93, 96. 7, 117). A desire to preserve the 'justice of the age' (55, 97, cf. 115). A general interest in schemes of public building (38, 40, 42, 62, etc.).

These principles or policies can be readily discerned in the rescripts to Pliny, and a few of them recur in the other official documents of Trajan, or are attributed to Trajan in the historical sources for the period.[1] But these similarities do not suffice to prove that the decisions emanate in all cases, or even in most, from Trajan rather than from his advisers. A different approach is needed. Henneman made no use of Pliny's account in his private letters of proceedings before Trajan and his *consilium* in IV. 22, VI. 22, and VI. 31. These suggest that Trajan regularly consulted his advisers and followed their advice, unless he was strongly moved by some particular aspect of a problem to make a personal intervention. In the first of these sessions no intervention of Trajan is mentioned. In the second he refused to hear a malicious charge against a certain proconsul. In the third he indicated, after a sharp remark about the influence of his freedman, that he was dissatisfied with the proceedings of one party, and his assessors framed their advice accordingly. He accepted another case only because it involved a serious point of military discipline in the officer corps. It is likely that Trajan acted similarly when dealing with Pliny's problems, for which he may have used the help of his secretaries instead of his cabinet of 'friends' or *amici principis*; there is nothing in the letters to suggest that any of these matters was—or was not—referred to the *consilium principis*. The consiliar letters also show that the relative, or apparent, un-importance of a matter did not prevent Trajan from giving it personal consideration—a quarrel over competency between a local magistrate and his town council, or criminal charges against persons of high estate.

The onus of proof is on those who would maintain that Trajan's replies were concocted by the secretariat without reference to the emperor. Pliny certainly assumed that his problems reached Trajan himself, as Henneman noted (e.g. Epp. 31. 1, 56. 1, 81. 8, 96. 1), unless his language is all an elaborate pretence. Pliny as an experienced official of the bureaux at Rome knew the usages. Some of his

---

[1] Equity, in general, *Dig.* 48. 22. 1; 49. 14. 13; Eutropius VIII. 4. Humanity in judicial matters, *Dig.* 48. 18. 1. 21, 48. 19. 5, 49. 14. 13. Severity, *Dig.* 29. 5. 10. 1, 48. 18. 11–12. Care for troops, *Dig.* 2. 12. 9, 29. 1. 1, and 24; *Pan.* 18.

requests were carefully baited to attract Trajan's attention, notably in building projects (Epp. 41, 61, 90, 98). To assess Trajan's contribution to the rescripts each must be judged by itself, in its historical and legal context, with due attention to verbal style and the bias of policy. Apart from the obvious personal outbursts noted already, and the expressions of praise and blame, there are some tart comments in otherwise bureaucratic replies which suggest the tongue of Trajan. A judicial answer to the question of retrospective application of a certain rule is followed by the remark: 'non minus enim hominibus cuiusque loci quam pecuniae publicae consultum volo' (Ep. 111). The technical reply to the technical question about 'iselastic games' is sharpened by the addition: 'mutata enim condicione certaminum nihilo minus quae ante peregerant non revocantur' (Ep. 119). This would give the impudent petitioners— who were asking for more—a flea in the ear. So too the famous comment on the refusal of anonymous accusations is political not administrative in intention: 'pessimi exempli nec nostri saeculi est' (Ep. 97. 2). This notion recurs in Ep. 55 in conjunction with another barbed shaft: 'invitos ad accipiendum compellere (sc. pecuniam) quod fortasse ipsis otiosum futurum sit non est ex iustitia nostrorum temporum'. Pliny had complained that the moneys in question lay idle in the municipalities, and the reply turns his own argument against him. The emperor rather than the secretary speaks. There is a touch of satire in the reply to the fussiness of the colony of Apamea that also suggests the master's voice. Trajan had in effect said that the lengthy petition of the Apameans was superfluous because they were not in fact objecting to Pliny doing what he proposed to do (Ep. 48). The secretary put this into diplomatic language and then added the words: 'remuneranda est igitur probitas eorum ut iam nunc sciant hoc quod inspecturus es ex mea voluntate salvis privilegiis esse facturum'. The diplomatic language continues but scarcely veils the Emperor's impatience.

It is difficult to avoid subjective judgement of this question. Much depends upon a detailed understanding of each problem. When an unusual decision is made, when precedent is not followed, or a new one is set, it is likely that Trajan himself settled the issue with his characteristic independence of mind. The discussion of the problem of foundlings in Rescript 66 is revealing. The rescript opens with a definition of the problem, evidently summarizing a secretarial minute which explained for Trajan's benefit what had not been made clear in Pliny's somewhat allusive letter. There follows the summary of a vain search through the imperial archives for a relevant precedent. Finally a new solution was offered. This decision was based, not on Western usages which might be familiar to Trajan, but upon the practice of the Hellenistic provinces, which differed from the Western practice in the very point at issue.[1] This solution can only have come from a specialist, and is unlikely to be due to Trajan, who at this date had not visited the Eastern provinces since his boyhood.

Trajan had given Pliny particular instructions, *mandata*, on such subjects as military discipline, the banning of social and political clubs, and the control of municipal building operations.[2] It is likely that when Pliny submitted questions under these heads Trajan would give them more than usual attention. Most of the earlier rescripts about public building contain personal touches (Epp. 38. 2, 40. 2–3, 42, 62), but this declines in later examples (Epp. 71, 91, 99), as might be expected when the new controls were working smoothly. The last has already been seen to be very secretarial in style (p. 538). These, and the earliest of such rescripts (Ep. 24), are brief replies granting permission while underlining the principle that the project must be within the resources of the municipality. The similarity is striking:

> Ep. 24. si instructio novi balnei oneratura vires Prusensium non est...
> Ep. 91. aqua perducenda sit in coloniam . . . si modo et viribus suis adsequi potest.
> Ep. 99. pecunia ne huic operi desit curaturum te . . . .

Yet the point of financial caution is not made in reply to the most ambitious and unusual of all the schemes put forward—the canal project at Nicaea—which was nicely calculated to catch Trajan's personal interest in the improvement of communications. His rescripts 42 and 62 are solely concerned with the practicability of the scheme.

Two queries arising from the *mandatum* about clubs brought strong replies from Trajan, but the knowledge of oriental affairs that they reveal is likely to be derived from the secretariat and the archives, as with the case of the foundlings (Epp. 34, 93).[3]

Certain other turns of language may indicate the hand of the secretary. Rescript 32, about the release of prisoners under sentence, which is one of the most colourless and technical in form and substance, begins with a rather portentous opening phrase: 'meminerimus idcirco te in istam provinciam missum quoniam multa in ea emendanda apparuerint. erit autem vel hoc maxime corrigendum' etc. The very next rescript begins in similar fashion, but inverted: 'tibi quidem secundum exempla complurium in mentem venit . . .

---

[1] Ep. 66. 2 n. [2] Below, p. 547, for a fuller discussion.
[3] The curious suspicion of fire brigades, which lasted into the Late Empire, was already established before Pliny: 'secundum exempla complurium'. Cf. Epp. 33. 2, 34. 2 nn.

sed meminerimus provinciam istam' etc. The arrangement of the two rescripts is similar, and in each the use of the plural verb is maintained throughout. Pliny's question is first restated, and then the decision is formulated. This may be chancery technique, and *meminerimus* may be a secretarial word, used because the secretary is assuming the person of the emperor.

The plural is not necessarily significant. Generally verbs in the first person plural, like *nos* and *noster*, refer, as they should, to 'me Trajan and you Pliny': as in Epp. 20. 2, 22, 42, 71, 89, 93. But they are not common, and in several passages the use is ambiguous, or positively excludes reference to Pliny and tends to suggest the governmental 'we'.[1] This is clear in Rescript 78. 1, where 'honoribus eius consulendum habuerimus' refers to a decision in which Pliny had no part. The same may hold for the following sentence: 'si Iuliopolitanis succurrendum . . . putaverimus, onerabimus nos exemplo.' The precedent would affect provinces other than Pliny's Bithynia: hence *nos*. Trajan's decision is given in the following section, using singular verbs: 'tibi . . . fiduciam habeo . . . notum facies . . . mihi scribes'. In Rescript 111, where the issue concerns a fine point of law, the decision is given by a plural verb—'quidquid . . . actum ante viginti annos erit omittamus'—followed by a comment of Trajan in the first singular. Of three other instances of plural verbs two are unambiguous,[2] but Rescript 115, where the issue is again technical, recalls 78 and 111: 'mihi hoc temperamentum . . . placuit ut ex praeterito nihil moveremus . . . in futurum autem lex Pompeia observaretur; cuius vim si retro velimus custodire multa necesse est perturbari'. The influence of the secretary may be suspected in these three cases.

The use of initial summaries, which is perhaps the commonest form of opening in the rescripts, may be a secretarial device. It is very frequent in rescripts dealing with technical aspects of municipal government—notably in Epp. 109, 111, 113, 115, and less markedly in Epp. 80 and 119. For example:

> Ep. 109. quo iure uti debeant Bithynae vel Ponticae civitates in iis pecuniis quae ex quaque causa reipublicae debebuntur....
>
> Ep. 113. honorarium decurionatus omnes qui in quaque civitate Bithyniae decuriones fiunt, inferre debeant necne ....

It might be held that those rescripts which depart most widely from this type of opening, and show least repetition of Pliny's terminology,

---

[1] In Ep. 40. 3, *ad nos venire* means 'us at Rome'. In 62 'in usu *nobis* futurus sit (*sc*. lacus) ' refers to the province or the empire but not to Pliny.

[2] Ep. 42. 1, 'potest nos sollicitare lacus iste ut committere illum mari velimus'; 71, 'possumus area . . . uti', refer to joint decisions of Trajan and Pliny.

owe most to Trajan. The rescript about the Christians, though it contains certain repetitions, is an outstanding example, and carries other signs of Trajan's attention in the note of approbation at the beginning and in the concluding formula *nec nostri saeculi*. The rescripts about the canal project (42, 62), the punishment of servile recruits (30), the aqueduct at Nicomedia (38), the buildings at Nicaea and Claudiopolis (40) and the charges against Archippus and Dio (60, 82) are other clear instances. But the openings of many letters cannot easily be assigned to one or other category.

Contrasts exist between adjacent passages where the secretary has expressed the final view partly in polite and somewhat verbose chancery style and partly in the original abruptness, as it may seem, of Trajan's own words. In Ep. 78 the style changes from a ponderous opening, quoted below, to the abruptness of: 'si qui autem se contra disciplinam meam gesserint . . . mihi scribes'. In Ep. 40. 3, dismissing Pliny's request for the dispatch of experts from Rome, the scribe first smoothly remarks 'nulla provincia est quae non peritos et ingeniosos homines habeat', and then trenchantly adds: 'modo ne existimes brevius esse ab urbe mitti' etc.

In Ep. 30, on the punishment of servile recruits to the army, there is an odd mixture of the formal and the informal, of abstract and concrete. But a caution must be added even against the natural assumption that the long-winded style of vocabulary and construction is the monopoly of the secretariat. The brevity of Trajan's few recorded *ipsissima dicta* encourages the assumption. The preference for combinations of abstract nouns and similar periphrases, and for superfluous verbosity generally, may seem the characteristic of the professional clerk. Such a sentence as the opening of Rescript 78. 1 may reek of the inkpot: 'ea condicio est civitatis Byzantiorum confluente undique in eam commeantium turba ut secundum consuetudinem praecedentium temporum honoribus eius praesidio centurionis legionarii consulendum habuerimus'. But the rescripts of Domitian and Nerva quoted in Ep. 58 are in a succinct style, while the actual edict of Nerva there cited is notably verbose. Changes of style are possible for emperor and secretary alike, with changes of occasion. The difficulty about the rescripts to Pliny is that the style changes from sentence to sentence within single letters. There can be no final certainty in pinning down the responsibility for the variations.

The use of the opening formula *mi Secunde carissime* is not significant.[1] It appears in most routine acknowledgements of congratulations, but not in Ep. 103. It ushers in the rescript about the Christians, but also the formal notes of permission for buildings at Sinope and Amastris (Epp. 97, 91, 99). Once only it appears late, in

[1] Cf. Henneman, op. cit. 38 f.

Rescript 60, to introduce a postscript.[1] The omission of the address in several rescripts of substance is probably due to the compilers of the collection.

There is direct reference to the personnel of the secretariat only in one of the private letters of Pliny to Trajan (Ep. 6): 'annos eius et censum . . . libertis tuis quibus iusseras misi'. Such direct references are absent from the official letters, although the use of assistants is implied very distinctly in Rescript 22—'quae rescripsissem ut notum haberes his litteris subici iussi', in the hunt through the archives of Rescript 66, and in the formula already quoted from 95, 105, 'referri in commentarios meos iussi'. But even these references are only to the work of clerks. Nowhere in the drafting of the rescripts is it ever clearly admitted that a 'senior civil servant' was involved. Pains are taken to give the opposite impression. The curt and official notification added to Rescript 60 is very characteristic: 'libellos Furiae Primae accusatricis, item ipsius Archippi, quos alteri epistulae tuae iunxeras, legi'. Yet this pretty certainly means that the chief secretary has read them, and advised Trajan, as the previous sentence indicates, to leave the matter in Pliny's hands. The short rescripts about the use of diplomata of the imperial postal service equally avoid referring to the directorate of the *cursus publicus*, although this important executive office was in the hands of equestrians by the time of Hadrian if not earlier. In Rescripts 46 and 121 Trajan writes as if he dispatched the bundles of tickets with his own hands. This reticence is the more curious in that even freedman procurators involved in direct provincial administration are freely mentioned. In Rescript 84 Trajan instructs Pliny to take not only an equestrian procurator but his freedman assistant also into his deliberations. It was, then, the convention for the Princeps to write to his legates as if the formulation of policy and decisions was done by himself alone. The influence of professional advisers and the share of the Princeps in the final decisions is to be detected and determined, if at all, only by the analysis of style and content together.

V. TRAJAN AND PLINY: THE NECESSITY OF PLINY'S REQUESTS

So far Trajan's rescripts have been considered somewhat formally and in isolation from Pliny's letters of consultation. The content of these taken together may suggest that Trajan had a good deal to do with the management of his rescripts. The theme is allied to the

---

[1] Possibly this is an addition to the original draft, but whether by the secretary or, as seems more probable, by Trajan cannot be determined.

somewhat misprised question of Pliny's function and efficacy in
Bithynia-Pontus. Pliny has frequently been criticized harshly for
ineffectuality and lack of decision. It is alleged that he referred to
Trajan numbers of unimportant and even absurd problems which as a
governor with *imperium* he could have settled out of hand. Recently
L. Vidman has justly observed that Pliny was bound by his *mandata*,
which contained several new rules of Trajan's own devising, and that
many of his queries arose from gaps and ambiguities in his *mandata*.[1]
The influence of the mandatory system upon the centralization of
the government of the provinces has not been much considered, and
Vidman did not attempt a detailed analysis of the letters of Pliny
from this aspect. They are the principal, and almost the sole body of
evidence for the period before Hadrian. The *mandata* limit the free
use of *imperium*, and are bound to encourage, and as Vidman
implied, were possibly meant to encourage the system of reference
back to the centre when doubt arose over interpretations. It may
be added that if a governor wished to act contrary to his *mandata*
for some good reason, he had no choice but to consult the emperor.[2]

Several of the headings of Pliny's *mandata*, and something of the
contents, are directly mentioned in the Letters. They cover military
discipline and disposition of troops (Epp. 22, 30), municipal finances
(Epp. 110. 1, 111. 1), the veto on *hetaeriae* (Ep. 96. 7) and relegation
of criminals (Ep. 56. 3). The rules quoted are detailed and specific,
though it is fair to assume that Pliny's general instructions about
overhauling the civic finances and improving the *mores* and *quies*
provinciae were included in mandatory form (Epp. 18. 3, 21. 1, 43. 2,
117).[3] Careful examination of the letters about municipal building
operations suggests that Pliny was also instructed to allow no new
works without sanction from Trajan. On each occasion he uses a
phrase asking for consent, such as *si permiseris* or *si indulseris*,[4]
but omits to do so in letters about the continuation of works begun
before he took over the province; and Trajan gives formal consent.

There are thirty-nine letters in which Pliny submitted problems
for solution or actions for approval, apart from short notes of commendation and congratulation, personal requests, and formal
reports.[5] Of these thirty-nine consultations, fifteen arose from the
mandata, and hence required the explicit sanction of the emperor,

---

[1] L. Vidman, 'Die Mission Plinius etc.', *Klio* 1959, 217 ff.

[2] For *mandata* see Ep. 22. 1 n.

[3] Vidman (art. cit. 223) takes *memor propositi tui* in 43. 2 to refer to a *mandatum*. But in Ep. 82. 1 the term is not used in this sense.

[4] Ep. 23. 1 'indulgere posse' n.

[5] i.e. Epp. 15–17A, 25–26, 35, 63–64, 67, 83–89, 94, 100–7. In Ep. 84 Trajan
took the initiative in referring a certain arbitration at Nicaea to Pliny, who
had not consulted him.

even if in some cases this might be nominal. Five arose from the instructions about his armed forces: Epp. 19, 21, 27, 29, 77. Two were connected with the veto on clubs and assemblies: 33, 92. Five were applications for building permits: 23, 41, 70, 90, 98. Two concerned financial rules, and one arose from the rule about *relegati*: 43, 110, 56. In no instance does Trajan criticize Pliny for consulting him, though one or two were small matters, and twice he refuses to grant the exemption requested (34, 78).

In four letters (79, 108, 112, 114) Pliny proposes to extend or to amend the basic *lex provinciae*, which had been established by a law of the Republic and amended only by imperial edicts. He twice drew attention to the fact that changes effected by the decrees of ordinary governors lacked permanent force, and were liable to be forgotten or superseded. Permanence required an act of legislation, in effect a decree of the emperor, or a *senatus consultum*.[1] He gives the same reason for referring to Trajan the question of the legal status of foundlings.[2] This was a major problem in Asia Minor and required a permanent solution. But Pliny could discover no general regulation except for the province of Achaea. Volterra has shown that Pliny followed the normal administrative usage of the empire in assuming that rules established for other provinces should not be automatically applied to different regions.[3] Trajan and his advisers shared Pliny's doubts. The same grounds account for Ep. 72, where a similar difficulty occurs about another class of foundlings.

There was a parallel reason for the submission of the problems contained in Epp. 31 and 96. In each case Pliny was in no doubt about the literal application of law and usage: *damnati ad opus* ought to be kept at their punishments until the end of their sentences and confessed or proved *Christiani* should be executed.[4] In each case he suggests a partial remission of the law's severity, and seeks authority for such exemptions.

A kindred difficulty, but different in scale, arose when Pliny or a third party challenged the privileges of individuals, groups, or communities which had been granted by imperial decrees, and in two instances by Trajan himself. There are four such cases, concerning the status of the colony of Apamea and the free or federate city of Amisus, the rights of iselastic victors, and the standing of a Roman citizen, Flavius Archippus.[5] Here valid action was clearly possible only after a ruling by the central government.

---

[1] Epp. 108. 2, 112. 3. For the alternative cf. 72.
[2] Ep. 65. 1–2 n.   [3] Ep. 65. 2 n.
[4] Ep. 31. 3: 'reddere poenae post longum tempus . . . nimis severum arbitrabar.' Ep. 96. 10: 'si sit paenitentiae locus' etc.
[5] Epp. 47, 92, 118, and 58–59.

These three categories account for twenty-seven out of the thirty-nine letters of consultation. All of them are considered seriously by Trajan and his advisers. None of them could be absolutely delegated to a minor official save possibly those about the movement of small detachments of troops; it is remarkable—and has often been remarked—that even in these last the 'soldier emperor' has intervened with characteristic observations.[1] The analogy of the consiliar debates, reported in Pliny's private letters, where the topics are not more—or less—substantial,[2] suggests that Trajan had a fair share in most of the decisions, apart from his obvious personal comments in certain rescripts—and those not the most 'important'.

Of the twelve queries that do not fall within the three categories that certainly required imperial authorization, five were straightforward requests for technical assistance or advice not available in Bithynia. In 17B, 37, and 39 he asks for the loan of Roman-trained architects and surveyors, because he does not trust the corrupt local experts. This sort of request might well have been settled by a lesser official at Rome, yet the rescripts contain manifest evidence of the personal attention of Trajan.[3] Elsewhere Pliny asks for information about the use of diplomata of the imperial post (Ep. 45), and the legal rules affecting consecrated buildings (Ep. 49). The absence of any imperial archives or permanent bureau in this formerly senatorial province made these applications to Rome inevitable and is an additional reason for some of the consultations included in the first three categories. In every case but one the official documents quoted in Pliny's letters have been produced by the interested parties who appeared before him, sometimes in imperfect copies: 'recitabatur apud me edictum' is the usual formula.[4]

Of the remaining seven miscellaneous letters, Ep. 81, about the accusation of Cocceianus Dio, involved as in Ep. 58 the status and *caput* of a Roman citizen, and a reference to 'Caesar' was almost inevitable.[5] Ep. 120 is an explanation *post eventum* of an irregular use of the imperial post. It is well known—and recently fresh evidence in the shape of rescripts of Vespasian and Domitian has confirmed it[6]—that the emperors were particularly interested in trying to prevent abuse of this service, and Rescript 78 is partly concerned with that.

---

[1] Epp. 20. 2, 'haereat nobis quam paucissimos a signis avocandos'; 22. 2, 78. 3. Cf. above, pp. 539, 545.

[2] IV. 22, a question of municipal rules; VI. 31. 3, accusation of local notable (as in Epp. 58, 81), and 4–6, difficult point of criminal law, all referred from provinces to Rome.

[3] Especially 40. 3, 'modo ne existimes brevius esse ab urbe mitti'.

[4] See Ep. 31. 4 n. for this remarkable state of affairs.

[5] See below, p. 553.

[6] Ep. 45 n.

Pliny sent similar reports on the unusual use of diplomata in Epp. 63 and 64. It may well be a normal formality. Ep. 75 is little more than an act of courtesy on Pliny's part to his chief. An establishment in honour of Trajan was being promoted at two cities, and its form was left to the discretion of Pliny, who asked Trajan if he had any preference in the matter. Trajan as courteously left it to Pliny. Three more interesting letters remain: Epp. 54, 68, 117. In the first Pliny sought to impose a severe and novel financial burden on the upper classes of the whole province. The proposal was probably within his competence, but he is hardly to be criticized for seeking higher approval in this matter, since it was in fact refused. In Ep. 68 Pliny refers to Trajan as *pontifex maximus* for approval of the transfer of interments from site to site in cases where tombs have been damaged by natural causes, on the ground that this was a matter of sacral law. This may seem absurd, and is perhaps the oddest of Pliny's submissions, though basically, like Ep. 49 (on the transfer of a temple), it was a request for technical information. But Trajan did not find the proposal absurd, though he thought it involved undue difficulties for the provincials.[1] A fuller knowledge of the background makes the submission more understandable. The question was much discussed by lawyers in this period. Gaius gave it as the opinion of the majority that tombs *in solo provinciali* were not *loca religiosa*, and hence were not *divini iuris* and subject to the jurisdiction of the pontiffs.[2] But other views were also maintained, and the pontiffs were certainly consulted when bodies were transferred from provinces to Italy.[3] So Pliny's doubts were not so silly as they have been thought. Similar investigations frequently place Pliny's consultations in a more favourable light.[4]

Finally in this miscellaneous group comes Ep. 117. It is the last but two of Pliny's consultations, and it gave rise to the only rebuke that Trajan inflicted on him on purely administrative grounds.[5] Trajan thought Pliny's question unnecessary. It concerned the grant of permission for large private assemblies of a social sort. Pliny's reason for asking was that he wanted to grant the permission, but evidently felt that the occasion came within the scope of Trajan's mandatory veto on 'clubs'. Technically this was probably not so, since the assemblies were not formal societies, but Trajan's rescript virtually concedes the point.[6] Pliny was unlucky to be criticized,

---

[1] Partly because he misunderstood Pliny's question—see below, p. 551.

[2] Ep. 68 nn.   [3] Ibid., n.

[4] In addition to topics discussed in this section see the notes on the following: 29. 2, 31. 3, 47. 1, 49. 1, 54. 2, 56. 3, 58. 4, 71, 72 (*ad fin.*), 77. 1, 96. 10 *ad fin.*, 108. 1, 118.

[5] On Ep. 82. 1 see below, p. 553.

[6] Ep. 116. 2, 117 nn.

and might have replied in Trajan's words of another occasion: 'onerabimus nos exemplo'.

In this miscellaneous group then, which has needed lengthy treatment just because it is heterogeneous, most of the questions and reports were technical, and all but one of the rest were on serious issues. In all groups the problems, except the purely technical questions, required the consideration and assent of the head of the state, according to the contemporary usage shown in the rescripts of Vespasian and Domitian (cited p. 540 n. 3). This is borne out by the wording of the directive formulas employed in the rescripts, though the argument from wording cannot be conclusive. Generally the first person is used. But by use of impersonal formulas, avoiding the direct address—the gerund or gerundive, verbs such as *oportet*, and the subjunctive imperative—the decision is sometimes given without direct ascription to the emperor. These cases are rare—seven at most—and all but one of these brings in the 'first person' of a verb or the personal *meus/noster* in the adjacent comments.[1] Very subsidiary questions receive or lack the honour of a *mihi videtur*, while the rescript about the Christians, which involved a major issue for the *quies provinciae*, employed indirect forms throughout Ep. 97. The scribe was satisfied here with 'neque . . . in universum aliquid . . . constitui potest', yet in Ep. 113, on the fees of decurions, wrote 'in universum *a me* non potest statui'—indifferently, if one may trust the text so far.

Rescript 69 opens up another aspect of the secretarial question. Pliny in Ep. 68 had not asked for the authority of the College of Pontiffs in the matter of transferred burials, but of Trajan as *pontifex maximus*, citing the function of the College *in urbe nostra* as an analogy.[2] The whole sentence seems to be merely a courtly variation for the various formulas in which he invokes the 'virtues' of the emperor, his *providentia* in Ep. 108. 2; his *aeternitas* in 112. 3; his *indulgentia* in 120. 2, and so on. In any case Trajan has misunderstood Pliny's mention of the College. He did not suggest that anyone should consult it. This is not the only occasion when Pliny's letters have been read carelessly. The long report on building operations at Nicaea and Claudiopolis was intended to bolster up the hitherto rejected request for technical assistants to be sent from Rome: 'ergo

---

[1] Epp. 30. 2, 69, 97, 99, 109, 111, 117. Only Ep. 69 absolutely manages without even *meus*; Ep. 84 is very impersonal but uses *meus* in the middle of the directive. Epp. 50 and 76 are excluded as using the direct address *potes, dispice*, etc.

[2] 'quia sciebam in urbe nostra ex eiusmodi causa collegium pontificum adiri solere, te . . . maximum pontificem consulendum putavi quid observare me velis.' Cf. n. ad loc.

cum timeam ne illic publica pecunia hic . . . munus tuum collocetur, cogor petere a te non solum ob theatrum verum etiam ob haec balinea mittas architectum', and Pliny continues at some length on the technical issue.[1] Trajan proceeded to give Pliny advice which he had not asked for, and to refuse him the architect, on whose advice, and not the emperor's, he hoped to make his local decisions. In the same rescript Trajan seems to muddle what Pliny had said about exacting payments from decurions at Claudiopolis with what he said about promises of money due at Nicaea.[2] Earlier, in Ep. 24, Trajan warns Pliny not to allow the creation of a new local tax at Prusa, but Pliny had not suggested any such thing.[3]

In Ep. 38. 2 Trajan neglects the text of Pliny's letter in a curious fashion. Pliny had requested technical assistance, which was a main point in his letter. Trajan fails to answer the request at all, but bursts out in indignation at Pliny's report of corruption among the contractors, and needlessly demands that Pliny investigate this as a crime and send him a full account of his discoveries. This was pointless because any necessary punishments were entirely within Pliny's competence.

Possibly some of these examples have been pressed too hard. But a certain carelessness is apparent in the reading of Pliny's letters which is more likely to be due to the impatient Trajan than to the secretary who so carefully sorted out the issues about foundlings in Ep. 66. There is an odd parallel in Epp. 47–48: Trajan seizes on Pliny's statement that the Apameans were willing to let him inspect their accounts as an excuse to avoid the necessity of digesting the long petition which they had sent to prove that this was unprecedented.[4] The combined effect of these instances suggests that Trajan gave more than nominal attention to the papers laid before him, even if he sometimes did his work carelessly.

It has now been argued that the great majority of Pliny's consultations were necessary in the stage of centralized administration which the Empire had then reached, and that the rest were mostly inevitable technical inquiries, requests, or reports, and that both received the attention of Trajan himself to a surprising extent. Vidman justly

---

[1] Epp. 39. 5. *haec balinea* refers to both the bath at Claudiopolis and the gymnasium at Nicaea. It is used in the singular by Pliny, Ep. 23. 1, 70. 1, 3. Cf. II. 17. 11, 26, v. 6. 27.

[2] In Ep. 39. 3 and 5 Pliny only proposed exaction in the latter case, *nobis exigentibus*. But in 40. 1 *exigi opera* refers to the former. Cf. n. ad loc.

[3] Ep. 23. 2 suggested the transfer of an existing source of revenue.

[4] Ep. 48. 1, 'libellus . . . remisit mihi necessitatem perpendendi qualia essent . . . cum ipse ut eas inspiceres non recusaverint', merely repeats what Pliny said about the *libellus* in 47. 1–2. Cf. Ep. 48. 1 n.

remarked that if Pliny consulted Trajan with relative frequency, the
responsibility is Trajan's, who chose and encouraged him.[1] Trajan
is a much admired emperor, not least by those historians who are
most critical of Pliny. Yet this Trajan, who was far from being a
tolerant man, only twice objected to Pliny's consultations, once on
political and once on administrative grounds.[2] On the first occasion
a charge of *maiestas minuta* was made against a notable Roman
citizen of Prusa.[3] Capital charges against provincial Romans were
by this time normally referred to the court of the emperor, as in
the similar case against Claudius Ariston, a leading politician of
Ephesus, before Trajan and his *consilium* in 107.[4] Trajan's objection
was to the disfavour of such cases at Rome, and was hardly a reason
for rebuking Pliny in the context. The second occasion concerned an
administrative matter—the licensing of large private assemblies
discussed above.[5] It was the last but two of Pliny's administrative
consultations, and the first such in some eighteen months to draw
hostile fire from Trajan. It might not seem, even to modern criticism,
the most questionable and petty of Pliny's references back. Otherwise Trajan was content with the system followed by Pliny, and
very rarely if ever tosses any problems back without a serious
answer, though on occasion he turns down a comprehensive proposal
and substitutes for it the local usage.[6] At most two matters of local
building policy were 'tossed back' like the affair of the assemblies,
and one of these was due to a misunderstanding of Pliny's letter.[7]

Conversely it might have, but never has, been noted that Pliny
rarely consulted Trajan about the principal and most novel part of
his mission—the examination and control of the municipal finances.
The reason is simple and revealing. In this sphere Pliny was a master;
he had spent four or five years at the head of the Roman treasuries
and needed no guidance. He reports progress from time to time as he
goes along, making his decisions as he goes: Epp. 17A, 23, 39. 3 and
5, 47. 1, 54. 1. The latter is characteristic: 'pecuniae publicae domine
providentia tua et ministerio meo et iam exactae sunt et exiguntur'.
He submitted only three particular decisions or problems to Trajan
about finance as such.[8] One was an economy carried out in accordance with his *mandata*, which, however, affected the *dignitas* of the
emperor and a consular legate. Hence he reported it, but after, and
not before, taking action. The second was the serious and novel

---

[1] art. cit. 225.

[2] For Trajan's sharpness see Ep. 57. 2 nn. and VI. 22. 5, 31. 9–11. The rebuke
in Ep. 40. 3 should not be counted here because it was due to a misunderstanding of Pliny's argument in Ep. 39, above, p. 552.

[3] Epp. 81–82.   [4] VI. 31. 3.   [5] Epp. 116–17.

[6] Epp. 109, 113.   [7] Epp. 40. 1, 76. Above, p. 552.

[8] Epp. 43, 54, 118.

proposal about obligatory loans, considered above. The third was the dispute about the dating of grants to iselastic victors, which arose from Trajan's own arrangements earlier in this matter. In three other letters where financial dispositions are concerned, Trajan is being consulted not on the financial but on the constitutional or legal aspect: the question of *protopraxia* in Ep. 108, the *honorarium decurionatus* in 112, and the appeal of Julius Piso against the ruling of the *mandata Caesaris* in 110. It is noteworthy that Pliny never reports his decision in the arbitration between the city and the citizens of Nicaea, referred to him by Trajan (Ep. 84).

Pliny's credit would have ranked a great deal higher in the past if we had the record of the mass of business transacted without reference to Trajan against which his procedures in Book x should be judged. Five of the twelve cities of Bithynia whose finances he must have regulated before passing on to Pontus are not even mentioned in Book x. Others are mentioned, like Juliopolis, only in connexion with a single improvement or alteration which he thought desirable.[1] In Pontus much must have needed doing at the great city of Sinope, but we hear only of its aqueduct.

Something emerges also from the chronology of the letters, which is established from the references to certain periodic festivals in them. Between 18 September and 28 January of his first season Pliny sent fifteen of his serious queries or reports to Trajan. In the rest of that year to his second 18 September another twelve queries followed.[2] But in the first part of his second season, from 18 September to 28 January again, he consulted Trajan only four times. The rate of diminution is interesting. Pliny, like the rest of us, became more independent as he worked his way into the job. But the qualitative analysis is even more interesting. In his second and incomplete season there are eleven consultations in all, and they contain the weightiest and the most inevitable in the collection. Three concern the amendment of the *Lex Pompeia*.[3] Two arise from appeals against the *mandata*.[4] The affair of the Christians is the sixth. Two are straight applications for building permits.[5] The remaining three include a technical report on the use of the imperial post, the intelligible if unfortunate application about private assemblies and the 'iselastic' business.[6] In all, there are hardly two 'unnecessary' consultations. Pliny was decidedly learning his job. His was after all

---

[1] Cf. Introduction, p. 532. Only Prusa, Nicaea, Nicomedia, Juliopolis, Claudiopolis, Apamea, and Byzantium appear in Pliny.

[2] The dates come at Ep. 17A. 2, 17–18 September; Ep. 52, 28 January; Ep. 88, second 18th September; Ep. 102, second 28 January. I have ignored the breaks at New Year for this count. See Introduction, p. 529.

[3] Epp. 108, 112, 114.   [4] Epp. 92, 110.

[5] Epp. 90, 98.   [6] Epp. 116, 118, 120.

a special mission of reconstruction. If the central government had to concern itself once a month or every three weeks with Bithynian affairs, for the first time in over a century, it had nothing to grumble about.

If Trajan and Pliny between them were governing the Empire in an odd fashion by modern standards—which is by no means so certain now as it may have seemed in the nineteenth century—and if the Whitehall clerks were not quite so dominant as nowadays, it would be more profitable to inquire into the reasons why the best of emperors liked doing things this way, than to make sharp quips at the expense of Pliny, which catch Trajan on the ricochet. Least of all should those who complain of the arbitrariness and corruption of provincial government find fault with the man who tried to secure to the best of his ability, and in advance of the emperor's ideas, the reign of universal law.

COMMENTARY ON BOOK X

THE TEXT

FOR the reconstruction of the text from the early printed editions see p. 83.

THE PRIVATE LETTERS

1. *To Trajan*

Written shortly after the death of Nerva on 27 or 28 January A.D. 98. The *Feriale Cumanum* gives 28 January for a festival of Trajan which is restored as his *dies imperii*: *Yale Cl. St.* vii. 78–79. Dio dates Nerva's death a year, four months, nine days after his succession, which should count from his salutation as *imperator* on 18 September 96. This gives either 27 or 28 January, by inclusive or exclusive reckoning. (Cf. Garzetti, *Nerva*, 94 ff.; Dio 68. 4. 2; *FO* for 96; Pliny, *Pan.* 92. 4; Suet. *Dom.* 17. 3; *Ep. de Caes.* 12. 1.) The date 25 January given by the *Chronicon Paschale*, ol. 219, is evidently to be discarded, as that in *Chron. Min.* i. 117 (Frick).

1. **imperator sanctissime.** Cf. Ep. 3A. 3, 'sanctissimis moribus tuis', and IX. 28. 1, 'Plotinam, sanctissimam feminam'. The epithet never became a title. It connotes excellence of behaviour, not divinity. Only thrice does Pliny address Trajan as *imperator*, here because of his recent salutation, in Ep. 14 for his military victories, and in Ep. 4. 1 for no clear reason. Elsewhere Pliny uses *domine*, even when, as in Ep. 13, he is not holding an imperial appointment. Ep. 2. 1 n.

ut quam tardissime succederes patri. For Nerva's adoption of Trajan see *Pan.* 8, Dio 68. 3. 4. The statement that it took place three months before Nerva's death does not necessarily date it precisely to 27–28 October (*Ep. de Caes.* 12. 9, Hammond, *Mem. Am. Ac. Rome*, 1938, 39 n. 176). For theories about the adoption see R. Syme, *Tacitus*, 206 f., 233 f., III. 10. 2 'philosophi' n.

2. **precor ergo ut tibi et per te generi humano prospera omnia . . . contingant.** For the prayers appropriate to the *dies imperii* see Epp. 52, 102 nn. For *generi humano* cf. *Pan.* 80. 5, 'te dedit (sc. Juppiter) qui erga omne hominum genus vice sua fungereris'. Also Ep. 52. 1, 'generi humano cuius tutela et securitas saluti tuae innisa est'. The assumption is that the Roman Empire includes the whole οἰκουμένη and covers the *orbis terrarum*. Cf. Vogt, *Orbis Terrarum*, Tübingen, 1929. More briefly, Sherwin-White, *Roman Citizenship*, 270 f.

saeculo tuo. Though in Book X, and in some passages of the *Panegyricus*, Pliny's use of *saeculum* tends to approximate to the sense of 'reign', that is not (*pace* Merrill, ad loc.) the intended connotation. The exact sense is 'the present age' or 'generation', as frequently in I–IX. Cf. especially II. I. 6 n., 'magnum ornamentum principi, magnum saeculo'. VII. 33. 9, 'saeculo est gratulatus' etc., IV. 15. 3, V. 17. 6 *et al.* So too in *Pan.* 6. 1, 18. 1, 46. 4.

fortem te et hilarem, imperator optime et privatim et publice opto. Trajan was hailed from the beginning of his reign as *optimus*, *Pan.* 2. 7: 'illud additum a nobis Optimi cognomen'. The term *optimus princeps* appears on coins from 104 on; *RIC* ii, p. 235. But the cognomen *Optimus* was not added to his official titles by the Senate until his first successes in the East in 114; Dio 68. 23. 1. Thereafter it appears usually in conjunction with *Parthicus* on coins and public records; cf., for example, *ILS* 295–303, with 293 n. 1.

privatim et publice. The phrase is stereotyped, cf. Ep. 86B, 'milites et pagani . . . qua privatim qua publice testimonium . . . pertribuerunt'. Also Ep. 58. 9, III. 9. 4. So it does not mean that Pliny was speaking officially as prefect of Saturn. The term *publice* simply means 'in a public capacity' or 'for the sake of the State', as in II. 7. 6, V. 14. 6. Pliny had 'public' interests simply as a senator.

2. *To Trajan*

Date. Early 98, to judge by s. 2, 'inter initia felicissimi principatus tui'.

1. domine. The establishment of *dominus* as the usual form of personal address to the Princeps was slow. Augustus, Tiberius, and Claudius avoided it, because of its connotation of autocratic power; Suet. *Aug.* 53.1; *Tib.* 27; Tac. *Ann.* 2. 87, 12. 11. Domitian seems to have insisted on its use by his equestrian procurators in official documents, either alone or in the yet more objectionable form of 'dominus ac deus noster'; Suet. *Dom.* 13. 2. Cf. Juv. 4. 96. Martial addresses Domitian thus in verse (5. 8. 1, 9. 66), and he and Pliny celebrate the decline of this usage after Domitian's death; Martial 10. 72. 3, 8; Pliny, *Pan.* 2. 3, 7. 6, 45. 3. But the title *dominus* by itself remained in social, if not official, use. It was a common form of polite address between inferiors and superiors of free birth, not only between masters and slaves. So from child to parent (Suet. *Aug.* 53. 1), from brother to brother (Sen. *Ep.* 104. 1), and from junior senator to senior in the contemporary Will of Dasumius (*FIRA* 3 n. 48, 110 f.). So too in vulgar Latin, from son to father, and soldier to N.C.O.; *P. Mich.* viii. 467–8, 472. Hence it was a natural term of address from the equestrian procurators to the Princeps, and easily adopted by the legates. The intermixture of equestrian and freedmen officials in the various offices would encourage the usage; cf. Ep. 28 n. But the term did not become an official title of the emperor until the age of the Severi. See Friedlaender, *SG* (Eng. tr.) iv. 81 ff.; *CAH* xii. 35, 359 f.

me dignum putasti iure trium liberorum. The social legislation of Augustus sought to encourage marriage and large families among the wealthy classes by creating penalties for the childless and privileges for parents. Bachelors and childless persons were restricted in their rights of inheritance from strangers and remoter relatives, though there was a generous table of kinship within which there was no bar to inheritance. Thus fathers of a family could claim succession to an inheritance left to a childless man if they were mentioned in the will in certain circumstances, and they secured exemption from the onerous duties of compulsory guardianship. In public life they had preference in standing for magistracies, both Roman and municipal, in seniority in office, and in the allocation of proconsulships. They even had special seats at the Roman theatres. Women secured release from the condition of wardship, and freedmen from certain privileges due to their patrons. See in general *CAH* x. 450 ff. For public privileges, Tac. *Ann.* 15. 19; Dio 53. 13. 2; Gellius, *NA* 2. 15. 4–7; *Lex Malacitana* 56; Ulpian, *D.* iv. 4. 2. For private privileges Gaius 1. 194; 2. 206, 286; 3. 42–44; *Gnomon idiologi*, 27–32; Paulus, *Dig.* 38. 1. 37 pref.; Modestinus, ibid. 27. 1. 2. 3; *Fr. Vat.* 216.

The degree of privilege varied with the number of children, but benefits seem to have been maximal for free-born Italians with three children. The exact benefits of the *ius trium liberorum* are not fully known; it is first documented in the Flavian *Lex Malacitana*. For freedmen and provincial citizens the requisite number of children was increased, for some but not all benefits, from three to four or five. The notion of a sliding scale appears in some of the legal texts; cf. Paulus and *Lex Mal.*, loc. cit., *Tit. Ulp.* 29. 3–7; Gaius 3. 42, 44, 50. So the 'right of three children' refers to a series of privileges mainly concerning free-born Romans of Italy and the law of succession; it was largely created by the *Lex Papia Poppaea* of A.D. 9. It early became customary to grant these privileges in deserving cases to married men or women without children through natural causes, as to Pliny in this instance and to Voconius in II. 13. 8. Control of the grant passed from the Senate to the Princeps, perhaps before the Flavian period; Dio 55. 2. 6, 60. 24. 3; Suet. *Claud.* 19; *Galba* 14. 3; Martial 2. 92. 1–3. For the caution of the emperors in making such grants see II. 13. 8 n., Ep. 95. In form the grant was an exemption from the application of a statute such as the Senate had customarily controlled in the late Republic.

Iuli Serviani. For Pliny's connexion with this great consular see
III. 17 pref. At this time he was a legate in either Upper Germany or
Pannonia, VIII. 23. 5 n.

etiam ex rescripto intellego libentius hoc ei te praestitisse. Trajan's
reply to Servianus was probably much like Ep. 95, on a similar
occasion. The title to the privilege consisted not in the rescript but
in the entry of the name in the imperial *commentarii*, ibid. n.; cf.
Epp. 105, 107. Ordinary petitioners approached the emperor by a
libellus, which he answered by a brief *subscriptio*; this is the 'libellum
rescriptum quem illi redderes' of Ep. 107. So too in Epp. 47. 2, 48. 1.
But distinguished men wrote and received in reply an *epistula*, as
Servianus here and Pliny in Epp. 94–95. The distinction is made
clear in Ep. 48. 1: 'libellus . . . quem epistulae tuae iunxeras'.
But the terms *rescribere* and *rescriptum* are less technical, and are
used for the replies of the emperors to *libelli* and *epistulae* alike, as
here and in Ep. 107. For the *libellus* organization see Ep. 107 n. In
this correspondence documents of previous emperors, both to communities and to proconsuls, are called *epistulae* or *litterae* (Epp. 58,
65. 3, 66. 2, 72), but Trajan's own replies are described by *rescribere*,
rescripta, Epp. 27, 43. 4, 57. 1, 107. Ulpian in *Dig.* 1. 4. 1. 1 summarizes
technically 'quodcumque imperator per epistulam et subscriptionem
statuit', but writes in *Dig.* 49. 1. 1 'si praeses provinciae . . . con-
suluerit et ad consultationem eius fuerit rescriptum'. See Ep. 58. 4 n.

**2. eoque magis liberos concupisco quos habere etiam illo tristissimo
saeculo volui sicut potes duobus matrimoniis meis credere. sed di
melius qui omnia integra bonitati tuae reservarunt. malui hoc potius
tempore me patrem fieri.** What were the two marriages and when did
they take place? Otto, whose arguments have been expanded by
by S. Monti (IV. 1 pref.) refused to believe that Pliny had three wives.
They make the daughter of Pompeia Celerina, who died in early 97,
Pliny's first wife (I. 4, IV. 19 prefs., IX. 13. 4 n.), and date Pliny's
marriage to Calpurnia to 97–98. They explain 'quos . . . volui' as a
parenthesis, and construe 'sicut . . . credere' with 'liberos concupisco'. (Otto, art. cit. 36 n. 1, cf. IV. 1 pref.) This destroys the run of
the whole paragraph, and reduces the force of 'sed di melius' etc.
which contrasts the new times with the gloomy days of Domitian.
Besides, the gods have hardly had time to do anything about
Calpurnia, if Pliny married her after the death of his first wife
in 97.

Pliny's technique of parenthesis is quite different. Most commonly
he uses a short clause tied in by *enim*, or else an asyndeton. Compare
the following examples, chosen at random: v. 6. 8, 33, 42, 46, 7. 2,
8. 1, 13. 3, 14. 8, or from this book, Epp. 39. 1, 41. 5, 75. 1. The recent

death of a *second* wife, when the husband was aged only 35 or 36, gave a stronger claim to the *ius liberorum* than a recent second marriage to a young girl. Natural misfortune was the normal ground for the grant of this privilege, cf. Ep. 94. 2, 'parum felix matrimonium', and Martial 2. 91. 5–6: 'quod fortuna vetat fieri permitte videri', about his own lack of issue. The grant was sometimes made for limited periods to younger men; Suet. *Galba* 14. 3.

tristissimo saeculo. For the supposed reluctance to have children at that time see IV. 15. 3, 'eo saeculo quo plerisque etiam singulos filios orbitatis praemia graves faciunt'.

3. bonitati tuae. A courtly word, not used in I–IX. Cf. Epp. 4. 2, 8. 5, 11. 1, 94. 2.

malui. Commentators have misplaced much ingenuity in mistranslating this. Hardy paraphrased it as 'to be a father now will be a still greater blessing' and remarked that Pliny preferred to become a fictitious father by Trajan's favour than a real father under Domitian. But even Martial did not identify the *ius liberorum* with paternity (2. 91. 5–6, 3. 95. 5–6, 8. 31. 5–6, etc.). Pliny uses *malo* to express a choice between present possibilities; cf. III. 3. 1, 18. 5, VI. 27. 1. Here he uses the perfect tense naturally because the choice has been made, though not fulfilled; cf. I. 23. 4, IV. 3. 5, 14. 6. There is a contrast between *reservarunt* and *malui*; 'the gods have acted thus, but my preference was for real paternity' etc. The subjunctive *essem* equally expresses the unfulfilled element. So there is no need to emend the text with Ernesti and Merrill, whose *maluere* does not meet the objections raised above. In V. 4. 4 Pliny uses a nominative and infinitive after *malo*, but in I. 23. 4 he has the accusative construction just as here. Cf. *Thes. L.L.* s.v.

Monti (art. cit.) failed to ponder the last of Pliny's sentences in this paragraph. His argument that Pliny's remarks were absurd on the lips of a widower fails to take account of the varying tenses. His best argument—that Pliny was already married to the daughter of Celerina, his 'second' wife, in the year 81, on the strength of I. 18. 3—is not established (ibid. nn.). But Pliny's 'first' marriage may well have been short-lived. Sudden death of the young stalks through the Letters.

3A. *To Trajan*

Date. This letter is dated to the second half of 98 partly by the argument that the lengthy proceedings against Marius Priscus require that his proconsulship belongs to 97–98, and his indictment to late 98 (II. 11 pref.), and partly by the argument from the chronological order of Epp. 1–14. If Epp. 4 and 5 belong to late 98 and

early 99, then Ep. 3A must belong to 98. It is likely that the indictment of Priscus here mentioned would be made in middle or late
summer after his return from his proconsulship in June–July.
See pp. 56 f. and IV. 26 pref.

1. **ut primum me domine indulgentia vestra promovit ad praefecturam
aerarii Saturni.** This should be taken with Ep. 8. 3, 'primum mea
deinde patris tui valetudine postea curis delegati a vobis officii
retentus', and *Pan.* 91. 1, 'nondum biennium compleveramus in
officio laboriosissimo . . . cum tu nobis . . . consulatum obtulisti'.
Pan. 90. 6, 'habuerat hunc honorem periculis nostris divus Nerva ut
nos . . . promovere vellet'. Elsewhere in Book X Pliny always uses
tuus of the single, and living, emperor; and *tuus* is used throughout
I–IX of the single addressee; III. 10. 1–2 nicely tests the rule, where
vos and *vestra* refer to two personages. So Pliny was made prefect,
along with Tertullus, by the conjoint action of Nerva and Trajan.
Otto, art. cit. 59, rightly remarks that *promovit* means 'appoint' not
'designate to future office'; cf. Ep. 4. 2, 'ut illum in amplissimum
ordinem promoveret', and VII. 31. 3, 'promotus ad amplissimas
procurationes'. There was no regular interval between appointment
and entry on office for imperial appointments, such as there was
between election and tenure of an annual magistracy. So Pliny was
appointed prefect of Saturn before the death of Nerva, not quite
two full years before his designation to a suffect consulship in
January 100. Cf. pp. 75 f.

promovit. The word is used technically thus in military inscriptions
about the advancement of centurions; e.g. *ILS* 2656; Domaszewski,
Rangordnung, 95.

advocationibus quibus alioqui numquam eram promiscue functus.
In I. 23 Pliny remarks that he refused all advocacy when tribune
of the plebs, because of the special character of the tribunate, not
just because it was a magistracy. Otto, art. cit. 44, tried to maintain
that *alioqui* here means 'in other posts and offices', and hence that
Pliny did not act as advocate when praetor; cf. p. 765. But Pliny
uses the word elsewhere in the most general sense that the context
allows; cf. for example, II. 15. 2, V. 13. 2, VI. 6. 3. In I. 7 Pliny refuses
a brief even when out of any office. He seldom accepted a criminal or
political case before the Priscus case, perhaps only that against
Baebius Massa; III. 4. 8, VI. 29. 8, VII. 6. 8–9 nn. His Centumviral
practice kept him busy, but he could pick and choose because he took
no fees for advocacy; II. 14. 1, V. 13. 8 nn. Pliny certainly took briefs
during his *cura alvei Tiberis*, V. 9, VI. 33. For the needlessly long
controversy between Baerhens and Otto over this passage see Bursian, *Jahresbericht*, 1929, 2. 59 ff.

praefecturam aerarii Saturni. There were two prefects, and Cornutus Tertullus was Pliny's colleague; v. 14. 5 n.; *Pan.* 90–91. After various experiments with annual praetors and triennial quaestors in the early Principate the headship of the *aerarium Saturni* was vested, from Nero onwards, in two *praefecti* of praetorian rank who held office usually for three years (Tac. *Ann.* 13. 29; Dio 60. 24. 1–3; Tac. *Hist.* 4. 9. 1, 'nam tum a praetoribus tractabatur aerarium', seems to be a slip; cf. *ILS* 1005). Men of experience were chosen, usually after one or more legionary legateships or proconsulships, or as with Pliny and his junior contemporary Catilius Severus, after the prefecture of the *aerarium militare* (*ILS* 1005, 1041, 1047, 1057). The post is often followed directly by the consulship in a man's career, as with Pliny and Tertullus, IX. 13. 23 n. See Mommsen, *DPR* v. 307. After the consolidation of the imperial *fiscus* by Vespasian the treasury of Saturn ceased in practice to be the central bank of the whole Empire, but it continued to handle the funds of the surviving senatorial administration in Italy and the public provinces. See A. H. M. Jones, 'Aerarium and Fiscus', *JRS*, 1950, 22 ff., for the most convincing of various discussions on the emergence of the *fiscus*. Against this, F. Miller, *JRS* 1963, 29 f.

The prefects were also concerned with State claims to *bona vacantia* and *bona damnatorum*, and to inheritances and legacies forfeited under the Augustan social legislation as in II. 16. 4; cf. IV. 12. 3. The burden of this work increased with the growing complexity of governmental regulations. Trajan himself issued an edict designed to simplify matters by encouraging the voluntary surrender of illegal legacies, *Dig.* 49. 14. 13–16. The prefects had jurisdiction in many of these cases. Cf. Pliny's summary of his own activities in I. 10. 9–10: 'sedeo pro tribunali subnoto libellos conficio tabulas... cognoscere iudicare'.

2. petii veniam huius muneris. For the procedure see III. 4. 2–3 nn. Pliny invoked his privilege of exemption as a holder of public office.

pateremurque nomina nostra in urnam conici. So too in the Classicus case Pliny though exempt agreed to act at the request of the provincials (loc. cit.). In II. 11. 2 Pliny describes himself and Tacitus as *adesse provincialibus iussi.* It is not clear why the lot was used. Perhaps other advocates had demanded to have a hand in the affair, and the 'urn' takes the place of the Republican procedure known as *divinatio*, by which the Senate used to decide between advocates in such cases. Cf. Cicero's *Divinatio in Caecilium*.

The consul designate might be one of the two consuls of November–December 98: Bittius Proculus and Iulius Lupus, IX. 13. 23 n.

tranquillitati saeculi tui. See Ep. I. 2 n.

4. To Trajan

The letter belongs to the beginning of Trajan's reign. It is later than Epp. 1–2 but earlier than Ep. 5, s. 1 n. Some months might elapse before Pliny was emboldened to renew his request on behalf of Voconius to the new Princeps.

1. **ut audeam tibi etiam pro amicis obligari.** The *etiam* has suggested to most commentators that this letter contains Pliny's first request to Trajan on behalf of his friends, and hence that the letter is earlier than Ep. 5. 2, where he intervenes for a lady of rank, and Ep. 12 where he commends a junior senator. Since Ep. 5 carries with it the sequence 5–7, 10–11, about Pliny's medical attendants, whom he would count only as 'lesser *amici*', the chronological order of Epp. 1–14 is thus largely established.

Voconius Romanus ab ineunte aetate condiscipulus et contubernalis. This man was a Spanish dignitary, formerly *flamen provinciae*, from Saguntum, for whom Pliny had already secured from Nerva the *ius trium liberorum*, and from a consular legate a post in the *militia equestris*, II. 13 nn. He is evidently a man of Pliny's own age, who attended the same schools of rhetoric at Rome, VI. 6. 3 n.

2. **a divo patre tuo petieram ut illum in amplissimum ordinem promoveret.** There is not a word of this in II. 13, and the request must have been made at the very end of Nerva's reign. The Princeps by his censorial power, which the Flavians had assumed openly, could admit men to the Senate by adlection at a ranking appropriate to their age, or else by their power of *commendatio* they could secure them an entry through the quaestorship: II. 9. 2 n., Ep. 12. 1, 'cum locus vacet' n. Adlection as *praetorius* would be appropriate to a man of Voconius' age. Schuster (*RE* (2) 9. 1. 701) suggested that Pliny was only seeking for the *latus clavus* for Romanus. A distinction between the stages is clear in II. 9. 2 and VIII. 23. 2, though *amplissimus ordo* means the Senate itself in Epp. 3A. 2, 95, and Suet. *Otho*, 8. 1, *Vesp*. 2. 3.

mater Romani liberalitatem sestertii quadragies . . . nondum satis legitime peregerat. The endowment is over three times the minimal property qualification fixed by Augustus, which by this time was quite inadequate to maintain the state of a Roman senator; Pliny reckoned his much larger fortune moderate for the task: 'sunt . . . nobis modicae facultates, dignitas sumptuosa', II. 4. 3 n. Provincials were required to be 'boni viri ac locupletes' in the words of Claudius, *ILS* 212; Tac. *Ann*. II. 24, cf. *Hist*. 4. 74. Nerva had evidently replied that he could not act until the legal formalities were completed. Before this transaction Romanus had only his father's estate, which may not have exceeded the equestrian franchise. But there is nothing to suggest, with Hardy, that Nerva insisted on a particular sum.

sestertii quadragies. This figure, from the Bodleian reading, is greatly preferable to the Aldine *quadringenties*, which would imply immense wealth.

codicillis. For this form of document, sometimes used for testamentary purposes, see II. 16. I n., III. 18. 4, VI. 16. 8.

3. fundos emancipavit. The Roman law of gift, derived from the *Lex Cincia* of 204 B.C., originally forbade gifts save between relatives within certain grades, and also required formal execution of the gift. These restrictions were greatly relaxed in the classical law, which allowed objections under the *Lex Cincia* only in the period before the formal completion of the legal transaction. Paulus, *Fr. Vat.* 302–10, shows that the permitted grades were steadily widened, and dates back to Antoninus Pius the rule that gifts within the permitted grades were completed 'sola mancipatione vel permissione'. Some texts suggest that in classical law a valid gift of money and of other movable goods could be made outside the permitted grades with remarkable informality by a simple written statement, *codicilli* or *epistula*, as here; but other texts provide stricter rules in such cases. See Buckland, *Handbook*[3] etc., 25 ff.; Roby, *Roman Private Law*, i. 525; Schulz, *Roman Classical Law*, 566 ff. For the early form of the law see Paulus, *Fr. Vat.* 298; Papinian, ibid. 294. 1; *Tit. Ulp.* pref. 1. For gifts to strangers in later law see Paulus, *Fr. Vat.* 311, and citations in *Dig.* 39. 5. See also V. 1. 2–3 n., VII. 18. 2.

The necessity for ceremonial transfer by *mancipatio* was particularly retained when the gift was, as here and in VII. 18. 2, in the form of land, in order to establish full ownership. But this is Roman law applicable only to Italian land. Texts of Gaius and later lawyers show that the gift of provincial land did not require *mancipatio* (Gaius 1. 120; Paulus, *Fr. Vat.* 259, 293. 1, 313). Possibly the farms in question were in the territory not of Saguntum, but of neighbouring Valentia, a commune which possessed the legal status of *ius Italicum* (*Dig.* 50. 15. 8 pref.).

Pliny's information helps to date a stage in the development of the law of gifts. The less formal procedure seems to be established for gifts of certain kinds, including ordinary provincial land, between relatives within the permitted grades. Hence the mistake made by the lady. For epigraphical examples of *mancipatio* of gifts see *ILS* 7313, 7912.

emancipavit. So too in VII. 18. 2 Pliny mentions the *mancipatio* of another gift of land in Italy. The formalities of the archaic transfer or imaginary sale, *per aes et libram*, necessary for the transfer of ownership of land, slaves, and cattle, are described by Gaius I. 119–22. Pliny here uses the less technical word, *emancipavit*, usually confined to the freeing of sons from *patria potestas*, instead of the correct *mancipavit*, used in VII. 18. 2. Compare his reversal of the terms in IV. 2. 2 (n.), 'filium . . . emancipavit . . . mancipatum . . . captabat'. Also Cic. *Phil.* 2. 51, 'venditum atque emancipatum'.

4. eximia pietas, quae hanc ipsam matris liberalitatem et statim patris hereditatem et adoptionem a vitrico meruit. In II. 13. 4 Pliny stresses that Voconius no sooner succeeded to his father's estate than he was adopted by his stepfather. The point should be the same here. There is no force in a rapid sequence between the liberality of his mother and the paternal inheritance. Hence *statim* seems out of place, and oddly used with the sense of *simul*. Everywhere Pliny uses it normally, with a retrospective reference, to modify immediately a verb, except perhaps in IX. 37. 1: 'nisi te kalendis statim consulem videro'. Cf. II. 17. 23, III. 9. 32, V. 21. 1 (*statim ut*), VI. 16. 19, 22. 5, VII. 33. 8, VIII. 23. 3, IX. 13. 19, 28. 2, 4. (The word is not indexed by Longolius.) Hence it is worth noting the corruption in IX. 40. 3: 'inter hiemem [statim] aestatemque'. The present textual setting of *statim* is similar, between *liberalitatem* and *hereditatem*. The word may be a ghost, and should not be pressed, as by Schuster (*RE* (2) 9. 1. 699), for chronological refinements. None of the letters in Book X are textually above suspicion, and this very sentence contains a meaningless reading—*adit te, adverte* for *apud te*—only corrected in the second Aldine edition. Besides, the sentence is mainly concerned to list the proofs of the man's *pietas*, not to make their order clear.

liberalia studia. For Romanus as a man of letters and law see II. 13. 7, IX. 28. 5. Pliny says less about this to the uncultured Trajan than to Priscus.

5. auget haec et natalium et paternarum facultatium splendor. This is the usual term for equestrian standing in birth and wealth. Cf. I. 19. 2 n., 'equestres facultates', and in general Stein, *Römischer Ritterstand*, 97 f. The term *splendor* denoted equestrian rank from Cicero onwards. Unlike Minicius Macrinus and Cornelius Minicianus, of whom it could be said that 'natus splendide abundat facultatibus', (I. 14. 9, VII. 22. 2), the elder Voconius seems to have been a man of limited means who married well, though he probably owned more than the minimum equestrian census of S.400,000. Cf. II. 13. 4, 'pater ei in equestri gradu clarus clarior vitricus . . . mater e primis'. So too the senator Accius Sura in Ep. 12: 'natalium splendor et summa integritas in paupertate'.

6. ut non in me tantum verum et in amico gloriari iudiciis tuis possum. Syme suggests that Trajan refused Pliny's request (*Tac.* 83 n. 5), since there is no clear indication in the Letters that Romanus became a senator. This is very improbable in view of Pliny's own high standing, and of the rule that Nerva had recently established that beneficial grants of all sorts given by the preceding emperor, whether completed or not, should be confirmed *en bloc*, Ep. 58, 7–10. Voconius may have failed to secure election, or have preferred *quies*. See I. 14. 5 n., II. 13. 10 n., and Ep. 12. 1 n.

iudiciis tuis. Cf. IV. 15. 5 n., 'tibi ominamur . . . consulatum. ita iudicia principis augurari volunt'.

5. *To Trajan*

The four letters 5, 6, 7, and 10 about the citizenship of Harpocras, which must have been written within a few months of each other, are dated by the reference to Pliny's illness 'proximo anno', s. 1. This is mentioned in Ep. 8. 3 as occurring before the illness and death of Nerva. Any time between mid-98 and mid-99 would fit Ep. 5. The phrase may mean either 'a year ago' or 'last calendar year'. The assumption both of Stobbe, who dated the whole series to 99 (art. cit. 356), and of his opponents who dated them all to 98 (Otto, art. cit. 66 f.), that they must all fall in the same calendar year is unnecessary. Ep. 10 is dated to 99—and probably to the latter half of 99—by the news of Trajan's proposed return to Italy. The reference to Pompeius Planta as Prefect of Egypt in Ep. 7 excludes a date earlier than July 98. So the group is probably spread out between the end of 98 and the late summer of 99, with the intervening letters 8–9 coming in July–August 99.

1. gravissima valetudine. Pliny only once refers to a serious illness in the private Letters, when in VII. 1. 4–6 he describes his former recovery on the twentieth day from a violent fever.

iatralipten. This specialist, sometimes called simply *aliptes*, was concerned with convalescence rather than cures. He directed a course of exercise and massage intended for wealthy convalescents, *malades imaginaires*, and health fiends. The elder Pliny, who regarded the genus as money-making quacks, refers to the system in *NH* 29. 4 f. Three such attend Trimalchio, *Cena* 28. Spurinna's routine in III. 1. 3–8 nn. is characteristic of such courses. See *RE* ix. 800 f., and for doctors in general, Friedlaender, *SG* (Eng. tr.), i. 167 ff. They appear as one of the two main divisions of the medical practitioners in Vespasian's rescript, W-C 458. 2.

2. rogo des ei civitatem Romanam. est enim peregrinae condicionis manumissus a peregrina. There would be no difficulty in giving Roman status to an ordinary free-born *peregrinus*. But this man was only the freedman of a *peregrinus*, and in many communes of the Greek-speaking provinces freedmen did not acquire the citizenship of their local city. The condition of an Egyptian was still more peculiar, Ep. 6 nn. Yet Pliny seems quite unaware of any difficulty in his request. He mentions the death of the patron, but ignores the rights of her heirs. At least in Roman law direct heirs inherited in some degree the rights of the patron over his freedmen; Gaius 3. 42, 45–46, 53. Volterra (*Studi . . . Paoli*, 1955, 715) notes that Pliny assumes that the Roman rule applies to peregrine freedmen—that they acquire the status of their liberator. The power of the Princeps to give Roman citizenship to provincials derives from the power given to military commanders in the crises of the later Republic to reward faithful allies thus. The earliest document comes from the Social War, *ILS* 8888. Cf. Cic. *pro Balbo* 19, 46. Octavian received the power under the *Lex Munatia Aemilia*, as triumvir *FIRA*, i. 55. ii. 10 f.

Thermuthin Theonis. The names are characteristic of the usage of hellenized Egyptians, though *Theonis* could be an error for 'Thonis'; cf. *Chrestomathie*, ii. 2. 304.

item rogo des ius Quiritium libertis Antoniae Maximillae. Like the Valerii of Ep. 104, for whom he makes the same request, these are freedmen of the inferior grade known as *Latini Iuniani*. By the *ius Quiritium* they would secure the standing and privileges of an ordinary Roman freedman; cf. Gaius 1. 32–35; *Tit. Ulp.* 3. 1–5. In legal contexts the *ius Quiritium* refers especially to the property rights of Roman citizens, the most absolute right of ownership being *ex iure Quiritium*; cf. Gaius 1. 54; *Tit. Ulp.* 1. 16, 23; Jolowicz, *Hist. Intro. Roman Law*, 268 ff. But in contexts about Junian status the term refers to the whole complex of civil law rights that Junians lacked and ordinary freedmen enjoyed. The most severe of their limitations was the lack of any power of testamentary disposition. See Ep. 104 nn. The term *ius Quiritium* is apparently only used for grants of citizenship when persons of Latin status are concerned. F. de Visscher, *Studi . . . Paoli*, 240.

item. Pliny makes his request with more brusqueness than in Ep. 104. Such requests seem to have been granted as a matter of course. Junian status was more of an advantage to the owner than to the State.

petente patrona. Her consent was essential, since the patron of Junians succeeded to their property.

Antoniae Maximillae. In Ep. 6. 1 she is called *necessariae mihi feminae*, a term which includes *adfines* as well as *cognati*; Paulus in *Festus* s.v. Nothing else is known of her, but her rare *nomen* might connect her interestingly with the Domitianic rebel Antonius Saturninus. Women, unless freed from *tutela*, could not manumit formally (*legitime*), so that their freedmen were normally Junians (*Tit. Ulp.* I. 17). Hence the application to the Princeps (ib. III. 1. Cf. VII. 16. 4 n.).

Hediae. A preceding *Antoniae* must have dropped out. For the cognomen see *ILS* 9032.

Harmeridi. This is odd. Hermeros is a common *cognomen* among freedmen, and would provide a better correction than Mommsen's *Agathemeridi*.

6. To Trajan

Date shortly after Ep. 5, which it continues.

1. **cum annos eius et censum sicut praeceperas ederem.** For Roman citizens the registration of births and a system of birth-certificates was established by Augustus, and is well documented. Cf. F. Schulz, 'Roman Registers', *JRS*, 1942, 78 ff.; 1943, 55 ff. But for *peregrini* nothing seems to be known of any such system, which should have been in the hands of the municipalities. In Egypt the non-Roman population appears to have registered its male children in public archives for taxation, but this was not a birth registration; Schulz, art. cit., 1942, 83. The phrase *annos et censum* suggests that the only legal source of documentation was in the census lists of each province, which were made periodically, not annually. The statement of wealth and age was required because these provided the qualifications for *munera* and *honores*, municipal and Roman, and for the exercise of sundry privileges under the Roman social legislation. The registration of property was also required by the bureau of the inheritance tax on Roman citizens. See further Ep. 79. 4, 'a censoribus' n.

ante ei Alexandrinam civitatem impetrare, deinde Romanam, quoniam esset Aegyptius. The passage supports the disputed opinion that the population of Egypt was sharply divided between the Greek citizens of Alexandria, in various grades, together with those of Naucratis and Ptolemais, and the inhabitants of the villages and towns of the χώρα, including the hellenized descendants of the scattered colonists of the hellenistic period. Egypt differed from all other provinces in that the vast mass of its inhabitants were not organized into self-governing *civitates stipendiariae* possessing a local citizenship. There is no juridical commune between the three 'cities' and the mass of *Aegyptii* to which candidates like Harpocras may be assigned; the *Gnomon idiologi* (*FIRA* i, n. 99) 39, 46 summarizes the population as Romani, Aegyptii, and ἀστοί. Josephus, *c. Apionem* 2. 41, says that the Egyptians are the only people whom the Romans have not allowed to 'share in any form of citizenship'. Tacitus, *Hist.* I. 11, describes Egypt as *insciam legum ignaram magistratuum*—unacquainted with municipal institutions. See A. H. M. Jones, *JRS*, 1936, 232 f., and I. Bell in *CAH* x. 297 ff.

The general inability of Egyptians to become Romans is shown by the rule barring them from legionary service, *Gnomon idiologi*, 55. Jones, art. cit., has suggested that this inability was merely technical, and due to the fact that after the conquest Augustus left the population in the status of *dediticii* permanently, instead of authorizing a civic organization for the new province in the usual manner such as that provided by the *Lex Pompeia* for Bithynia and Pontus; Ep. 79. 1 n. But there is only tenuous support for the view that *dediticii* in the normal sense were incapable of becoming Roman citizens; Gaius 1. 26, 67–68, *Tit. Ulp.* 7. 4 are talking of the special penal category, invented by the social laws of Augustus, of *ei qui in numero dediticiorum sunt*; cf. Suet. *Aug.* 40. 4. In the Republican period the bestowal of Roman citizenship on 'surrendered enemies' was normal, notably after the Social War; see Sherwin-White, *RC* 131. Probably the real ground for the disability of the Egyptians was not technical but moral—their lack of any tradition of self-government and the peculiarity, as with Druids and Jews, of their religious customs (pp. 780 f.). Tacitus conjoins the two disqualifications in the passage cited above—'Aegyptum . . . superstitione ac lascivia discordem et mobilem, insciam legum' etc. Hence they were unsuitable candidates for the Roman citizenship, and the grant of Alexandrine status was originally intended not to circumvent a technical difficulty but to ensure that the person and his descendants should acquire some knowledge of the cultural values of the Graeco-Roman world. Cf. the lengthy discussion of the *dediticii* and of this passage in C. Sasse, *Die Constitutio Antoniniana* (Wiesbaden, 1958), 70 ff., 76 f.

Alexandrinam civitatem. The city of *Alexandria ad Aegyptum* contained at least two distinct grades of local citizens: those registered in the civic tribes and demes, and those not so registered. These are called by terms of which the connotations are not yet quite clear—'Alexandrines', 'citizens', and 'townsmen' or ἀστοί. Pliny's letter does not show whether the highest grade was necessary for the acquisition of Roman citizenship. Cf. *CAH* x. 294 f. with bibliography ibid. 928–9; H. Musurillo, *Acts of the Pagan Martyrs* (Oxford, 1958), 88 f.; Jones, *Cities*, 311 f.

a peritioribus. Pliny's ignorance would be general among senators, since none were allowed to visit Egypt without the permission of the Princeps, or employed there: Tac. *Hist.* 1. 11, *Ann.* 2. 59; Dio 51. 17. 1. Probably Pliny's learned friend was Titius Aristo, 1. 22. 1–2 nn., VIII. 14. 1.

2. rogo itaque, ut beneficio tuo legitime frui possim, tribuas ei et Alexandrinam civitatem [et Romanam]. R. Böhm, *Aegyptus*, 1958, 11 f., reasonably suggests the deletion of the last two words, so that the sentence is parallel to that in Ep. 10. 1: 'te . . . et Alexandrinam civitatem tribuisse'. The man already had the Roman citizenship, though irregularly. To regularize the position he required the Alexandrine in addition. Hence *et*, emphatic. Böhm insists that it is incorrect to speak of Harpocras or anyone else being given the two citizenships at the same time, cf. s. 1: 'ante . . . deinde'.

libertis tuis . . . misi. The principal secretaries of the *a libellis* and *a censibus* departments may have been equestrians in status by this time, but their executive staff continued to be filled by imperial freedmen: I. 17. 1 n., Ep. 27. 1 n., 'libertus et procurator tuus'.

7. To Pliny

This continues the series 5–6, and is shown to be later than June 98 by the reference to Pompeius Planta as Prefect of Egypt, n. below.

civitatem Alexandrinam secundum institutionem principum non temere dare proposui. Böhm (art. cit., Ep. 6. 2 n.) argues that Trajan could not give away the Alexandrine citizenship without consulting the Alexandrines through the Prefect, and inviting them to enrol Harpocras in their lists. Hence he suggests that Trajan is not the subject of *dare*, and that the meaning is: 'I have published in Egypt an instruction that they are not to give . . .'. But the intervention of *secundum institutionem principum* before *dare*, and the absence of *debere*, or something similar, is decisively against Böhm's version. The supposed parallel in *Dig.* 48. 3. 6. 1 does not help much, since it refers to an action of Pius as proconsul, not as emperor: 'caput mandatorum quod divus Pius cum provinciae Asiae praeerat sub edicto proposuit ut eirenarchae . . . interrogarent'. Böhm's idea would be valid for any other city of the Empire, but Alexandria lacked any civic body with the power to make decisions of this kind (Jones, *Cities*, 312). Hence the usual interpretation should stand, that such matters were under the administrative control of the Prefect, to whom Trajan sends his recommendation for implementation. Doubtless technically Harpocras did not become an Alexandrine until duly enrolled by the appropriate scribe in Alexandria.

Claudius earlier refused to allow the Jews who lived as metics in Alexandria to acquire its citizenship: *P. Lond.* 1912, 70 f.; Charlesworth, *Documents*, C. 2, p. 5; *CAH* x. 311. The emperors did not use the franchise of Naucratis and Ptolemais, which also were full cities, in this manner, probably for the very reason that their local autonomy, unlike that of Alexandria, was unimpaired (Jones, *Cities* 303, 306).

huic quoque petitioni tuae negare non sustineo. In Ep. 10. 1 Pliny takes this to mean that Trajan has given the man the required franchise. According to Böhm, Pliny misunderstood Trajan, who merely agreed to forward Pliny's request for the consideration of the Alexandrines. This is made improbable by the particle *quoque*. The phrase is a variant of, for example, 'tuo . . . desiderio subscripsi', in Ep. 95.

tu ex quo nomo sit notum mihi facere debebis ut epistulam tibi ad Pompeium Plantam praefectum Aegypti amicum meum mittam. Egypt was divided into forty-seven nomes, each under a στρατηγός who was immediately responsible to the ἐπιστράτηγος of one of the three regions of the Delta, the Thebaid, and 'the Seven Nomes with Arsinoite', and to the prefect, who ruled Egypt with powers equivalent to those of a *legatus Augusti propraetore*; *CAH* x. 288. It would be necessary for the new status of Harpocras to be entered on the register of the ἐπίκρισις, or census of Romans and Alexandrines; ibid. 300.

epistulam. Cf. Ep. 2. 1 n., 'ex rescripto'.

Pompeium Plantam. Junius Rufus was still prefect in office on 21 June 98 and Planta held office after him until summer 100. Stein, *Die Präfekten von Aegypten* (Bern, 1950), 47–48. Planta may be the man of letters mentioned in IX. 1. 1 n. Of his earlier career only the post of procurator of Lycia and Pamphylia under Vespasian is known, *c.* 75–76. *PIR*[1] P 483; Pflaum, n. 58.

amicum meum. The formal title was early given to equestrian officials. Claudius thus designates his agent in *ILS* 206, and Vespasian his procurator of Corsica in A–J 59. In the Alexandrine letter, cited above, Claudius thus calls his private friend Claudius Balbillus ἑταῖρος ἐμός. By itself the term does not mean that Planta belongs to the inner circle of the régime, as *CAH* xi. 198 suggests. See I. 18. 3 n.

8. *To Trajan*

The letter was written sometime in June–August (s. 3 n.) of either 98 or 99, when Pliny was prefect of Saturn and Trajan was still on the northern frontiers. The exact year depends partly on the placing of this letter in the middle of the series about the doctors; the placing after Ep. 7 points to 99, which year also better fits the chronology of the periodic *locatio agrorum* mentioned in s. 5 n. The leave here granted was the occasion when, as similarly described in III. 4. 2, he received the invitation to prosecute the associates of Caecilius

Classicus for extortion, s. 2 n. The later date well fits the circumstances of the Classicus affair (III. 9 pref. and 3 n.), but must be
settled independently of that, s. 3 n.

**1. cum divus pater tuus . . . honestissimo exemplo omnes cives ad
munificentiam esset cohortatus.** Nerva's building activities at Rome
were limited to the extension of granaries and aqueducts, and the
completion of the Forum Transitorium. He also initiated agricultural
settlement in depopulated parts of Italy and the charitable foundations known as *alimenta*; VII. 18, 31. 4 nn.; *CAH* xi. 192 f.

**petii ab eo ut statuas principum quae in longinquis agris per plures
successiones traditas mihi quales acceperam custodiebam, permitteret
in municipium transferre adiecta sua statua.** Pliny was wisely cautious.
Men who disposed of statues of dead emperors had in the past found
themselves in serious trouble, like Granius Marcellus (Tac. *Ann.* 1.
74). Gamurrini, who identified Pliny's estate with that of the same
Granius, on incomplete epigraphical evidence, and this passage,
suggested that the statues involved included those of Granius,
though Tacitus says nothing about their locality, v. 6. 1, 10 nn.

in longinquis agris. Sirago suggested that Pliny was transferring
the statues from Comum to Tifernum (*It. agr.* 28 n. 6). This is based
on a simple error. The *agri* of ss. 1, 5, and 6 are the same. The distance,
as in s. 6, is what Pliny, not the statues, has to travel.

permitteret. Cf. below, s. 4, 'rogo . . . permittas . . . exornare et tua
statua'. Why was permission necessary? Building operations in
Italy had not in the past been subject to any control but that of the
local council. The recent creation of the overseers of local finances
known as *curatores reipublicae* had not involved any reference to the
Princeps in such matters; VII. 15. 2 n. Such permission seems to have
come gradually to be required for the erection of public statues of
the emperor, especially if they were connected with the worship of
the imperial *numen* or *genius*. In the Julio-Claudian period such
permission was sometimes asked as an act of grace, but was not
compulsory. Thus Pisa asked Augustus to approve its honours in this
style of the dead L. Caesar in 3–2 B.C., but did not seek his approval
again for the honours paid to the dead C. Caesar in A.D. 4; *ILS*
139–40. Forum Clodii sought no permission to erect its shrine of
imperial statues in A.D. 18; *ILS* 154. There is stricter control in the
provinces. Claudius refuses to allow the erection of certain imperial
statues at Alexandria, but it is the proconsul who in the *lex de
flaminio* licenses such statues in Narbonensis: Charlesworth,
Documents, C. n. 2; *ILS* 6964; A–J 62 l. 25. Later, Domitian and
Nerva control the form and style of imperial statues at Rome; Suet.
Dom. 13; Dio 68. 1. 2. This control probably arose gradually from

the custom of inviting the Princeps, like any other citizen, to accept honours which he might politely refuse, as did Tiberius on occasion (E.–J., n. 102). Hence Trajan's reply, that he is 'eiusmodi honorum parcissimus'.

municipium. Tifernum Tiberinum, as appears from IV. 1. 4–5.

2. ego statim decurionibus scripseram ut adsignarent solum in quo templum pecunia mea exstruerem. In III. 4. 2, referring to the present occasion, he sums up his task as 'publicum opus . . . incohaturus'. In IV. 1 he records the completion of the task and the dedication of the temple. The latter is to be municipal property, but paid for by Pliny. As in the common epigraphical formula 'locus datus decurionum decreto', the site is on common land, and maintenance rests with the municipality. The arrangements are much as in the document from Forum Clodii, where an *aedicula* housing *statuae Caesarum* and an *ara numinis Augusti* form a single complex, with provision for sacrifices on various festivals, authorized by a decree of the council; *ILS* 154.

decurionibus. Cf. IV. 7. 2: 'scripsit publice ut a decurionibus eligeretur.' The councils rather than the annual magistrates were the effective organ of local government in Italy, just as in the provinces; Ep. 79 nn., IV. 22. 1 n.

3. primum mea deinde patris tui valetudine postea curis delegati a vobis officii retentus. The illnesses of Pliny and Nerva evidently belong to the end of 97 and January 98. Nerva, who suffered from gastric troubles, died on 27 or 28 January; Ep. 1 n., Dio 68. 1. 3. Thereafter Pliny was busy as prefect of Saturn, Ep. 3A. 1 n. If this letter belongs to July–August 99, Pliny has delayed the matter a longish while; but if he wrote in July 98 there would be nothing to apologize about in this fashion. The whole business of this shrine was conducted in a leisurely fashion, cf. IV. 1. 4–6 nn.

delegati a vobis officii. See Ep. 3A. 1 n.

menstruum meum kalendis Septembribus finitur, et sequens mensis complures dies feriatos habet. The two prefects of Saturn shared the duty on a rota of one or more months each, from Kalends to Kalends, according to this passage, but the prefect not on duty was expected to stand by, and not to leave Rome without permission. Since it is unlikely that Pliny would ask to be absent from stand-by duty for a whole *menstruum*, the period is likely to be of two months or even three; the period might correspond to the normal tenure of suffect consuls. A date not later than July is indicated to allow Trajan's reply to reach Rome from Pannonia in time.

complures dies feriatos. The number of public holidays in September was considerable, though only seven or eight were technically *feriae*, and two *dies nefasti*. The first nineteen days were effectively occupied by the festival of Juppiter Tonans on the first, the Actium festival on 2–3, then Ludi Romani, 4–12 and 15–19, overlapping with such occasions as the Arrest of Seianus, 10, and the birthday of Trajan, 18. There were festivals of Augustus on 23–24. So the duty prefect hardly needed his colleague in this month. See *CIL*, I² pp. 328–30. *D–S* I. 848, or the Augustan *Fasti Maffeiani, ILS* 8744.

4. indulgeas commeatum. Cf. III. 4. 2, 'accepto ut praefectus aerarii commeatu', and for a later leave when Pliny was *curator Tiberis*, v. 14. 9.

5. agrorum enim quos in eadem regione possideo locatio cum alioqui CCCC excedat adeo non potest differri ut proximam putationem novus colonus facere debeat. For Pliny's Tuscan estates at Tifernum Tiberinum and his life there see III. 19, v. 6. 7–13, IX. 15, 36, 40. The *locatio*, or letting of lands on short leases to peasant cultivators, took place at regular intervals of four or five years, IX. 37. 2 n. If the *locatio* of 107, ibid., was on his Tuscan estates, then the previous letting must have been either in 97 or 99; but 97 is excluded by the circumstances of this letter. Hardy, ad loc., took the dates for change of leases given by Suet. *Tib.* 35. 2, *ILS* 5723, Martial 12. 32 (Kalends of July and Ides of August) to mean that the new tenant took the harvest. But those dates refer to urban leases. Naturally the outgoing tenant had the harvest. Otherwise he could not pay his rent, and would lack any inducement to work during his last year. The new tenants take over when the harvest has been gathered in, and prune the vines for the next year. Such a date also fitted the ploughing of the arable lands in this estate, v. 6. 10.

CCCC excedat. The yield on agricultural investment seems to have been reckoned about 5 or 6 per cent., VII. 18. 2 n. So the capital value of this estate would be about S.8,000,000. The figure of 12 per cent. quoted in IX. 28. 5 applies to short-term loans.

colonus. For the system of tenancy see III. 19. 6, IX. 37. 2–4 nn.

continuae sterilitates cogunt me de remissionibus cogitare. For the question of an agricultural crisis in Italy in these years see III. 19. 7 n., IX. 37 nn. The continuing difficulties of Pliny's tenants over three *lustra* points to some serious difficulties.

remissionibus. Cf. III. 19. 6, IX. 37. 2 nn.

nisi praesens. For Pliny's careful attention to his private business see III. 19, VIII. 2, IX. 37.

6. et municipium et agri . . . sint ultra centesimum et quinquagesimum lapidem. For the route to Tifernum see I. 4. 1, VIII. 8. 1 nn. The distance agrees with that from Rome to Città di Castello. Pliny seems

to have covered about 30 to 35 miles a day on his journeys, II. 17. 2 n.,
VI. 10 pref., and to have taken not less than five days to reach
Tifernum, I. 4. I. So a third of his time was required for travelling.

Pliny does not name the *municipium* in this letter, although he is
requesting a licence of sorts from Trajan. The casualness of information in some of the business letters in I–IX may not be entirely due
to the excisions of a reviser; cf. III. 6. 5, IX. 39.

9. *To Pliny*

et multas et omnes publicas causas petendi commeatus reddidisti.
The opening words have been much amended; cf. O.C.T. *apparatus.*
Brakman proposed 'et multas proprias' and Schuster 'et multas
privatas' on the analogy of Epp. 1. 2 and 13 ad fin. Merrill and
Stout (*T.A. Ph. A.* 86. 238) defended the text. Pliny's estate manage-
ment contributed to the *restitutio Italiae* promised on the coins of
Nerva and Trajan: *RIC.* ii, Nerva, n. 92; Trajan, nn. 470, 472–3.
Hence his 'private' reasons were of 'public' interest.

**statuam poni mihi . . . quamquam eiusmodi honorum parcissimus,
tamen patior.** The imperial tone of deprecating such honours while
accepting them was first set by Tiberius and Claudius; Ep. 8. 1 n.;
Tac. *Ann.* 4. 37–38. For Trajan's moderation at this time see *Pan.*
52. 3. He maintained Nerva's ban on the use of precious metals for
imperial statues.

10. *To Trajan*

This continues the series about Harpocras, Epp. 5–7, and is dated
to the second part of 99 by the reference to the return of Trajan,
s. 2 n.

1. te Harpocrati . . . et Alexandrinam civitatem tribuisse. See Ep. 6.
1–2, 7 nn.

esse autem Harpocran νομοῦ Μεμφίτου indico tibi. Ep. 7. 1 n.
Memphis, in the *epistrategia* of the 'Seven Nomes with Arsinoite',
was the capital of the like-named nome. *RE* xv. 666.

2. indulgentissime imperator. Ep. 1. 1 n. For Pompeius Planta see
Ep. 7 n.

quo maturius . . . exoptatissimi adventus tui gaudio frui possim.
Otto and company, art. cit. 69 n. 1, in a desperate attempt to maintain the date of 98 for all these letters, pretended that this did not
refer to the actual return of Trajan in 99, but to a rumour in 98.
Stobbe, art. cit. 356, justly insisted that Pliny was officially able to
know the correct facts. Martial 10. 7. 8–9 is too vague to fix the

precise moment. In any case these letters need not be confined to a single calendar year, Ep. 5 pref.

The month of Trajan's return is not known. He was in Italy by the Ides of November 99 because a fragmentary rescript to the city of Delphi was dated from Antium before then (Henneman, *Der . . . Stil in T. Briefen*, 14, fr. 34; dated *cos. II*). Pliny knows nothing of the return in Ep. 8, written in June or July. A month later than September is probable because Pliny already had leave of absence for September. October would suit, since the activities of Trajan between his return and January 100, recorded in *Pan.* 22–63, do not require a great stretch of time. His return was after the failure of the Egyptian harvest was known, ibid. 30–31. P. L. Strack (*R. Reichsprägungen des II. Jahrhunderts*, i. 79, 88–89) finds no evidence in the coins to fix the exact moment, but suggests that he returned before the *congiarium* (*Pan.* 41. 1), dated *cos. II.* on the coins, which precedes the consular election of late 99, described in *Pan.* 61, 63–64.

quam longissime. Pliny is not asking for permission to leave Italy. Pannonia, whence Trajan was coming, was adjacent. There is no trace of any such journey in 1–11, and in *Pan.* 22–23 Pliny speaks as an eye-witness of Trajan's entry into Rome. Probably Trajan discouraged such attentions out of *civilitas*. The elderly Silius Italicus did not leave Campania for the occasion, III. 7. 6.

11. *To Trajan*

The last of the medical series. The *medicus* Marinus may have been stirred up to make his request after the success of Harpocras. Hence the delay in order of requests.

1. proxima infirmitas mea, domine, obligavit me Postumio Marino medico. Stobbe, art. cit. 365, doubted the identity of this illness with the *gravissima valetudo* of late 97, Ep. 5. 1, because of the plurality of doctors (cf. Otto, art. cit. 68–69). But the *medicus* treated the sick man, the *iatraliptes* looked after the convalescent; Ep. 5. 1 n., VII. 1. 4.

proxima. No longer *proximo anno* as in Ep. 5. 1. This, with *ex consuetudine . . . tua*, tends to support the serial order of the letters. This is now the seventh *beneficium* received by Pliny from Trajan.

2. rogo ergo ut propinquis eius des civitatem. By their names, in the form a single *nomen* with patronymic, they were free-born persons from any of the eastern provinces. Pliny doubtless enclosed a *libellus* for the archivist with the details of age and status required, as in Ep. 6. 1. Postumius was already a Roman, and required no such privilege.

item liberis eiusdem Chrysippi . . . ita ut sint in patris potestate
utque iis in libertos servetur ius patronorum. This request is in conformity with Gaius 1. 93: 'si peregrinus sibi liberisque suis civitatem
Romanam petierit, non aliter filii in potestate eius fient quam si
imperator eos in potestatem redegerit'. For a similar rule cf. *Lex
Salpensana* 22. The reason for the rule is that there was no *iustum
matrimonium* between the two former *peregrini*, who were not under
Roman civil law, and hence the *patria potestas* did not arise. Gaius
1. 67, 75 ff., 108; *Tit. Ulp.* 5. 1–4.

The sons required a separate grant of citizenship, not as Hardy
supposed to secure the *patria potestas*, but because only children
born after the grant would become Romans automatically.

utque iis. From the context it is clear that *iis* means 'to the
parents', not, as Hardy took it, 'to the children'. If Chrysippus
wanted his sons to enjoy property rights of this sort he need not
have asked for *patria potestas* in the first place. It would seem that his
children were still quite young. The provision is like that in the
Lex Salpensana 23: 'ut qui c. R. consequentur iura libertorum
retineant'. This clause laid down that enfranchised persons should
enjoy all the rights over their freedmen that they would have had if
they had not changed their status. In both cases, the freedmen were
non-Romans under local law, which would not apply automatically
to persons who changed their status. Down to the late Republican
period local law was not enforceable on enfranchised *peregrini*, who
were no longer members of their former juridical commune. In the
Principate a series of legal provisions, such as this instance, tended
to render the tenure of local and Roman citizenship compatible.
But in marriage and personal status the enfranchised provincial was
isolated from his former fellows by the operation of the Roman civil
law. Hence it was more convenient to enfranchise families rather
than individuals, which thenceforward were confined by their legal
status to relationships with other Roman citizens within their local
community. A general grant of legal *conubium cum peregrinis
uxoribus*, such as Claudius made to the enfranchised community of
Volubilis, was a rarity (*ILA* 634, or Charlesworth, C. n. 36); Gaius 1.
56. See Sherwin-White, *RC* 189, 213; de Visscher, *Édits d'Auguste*,
ch. iv.

ius patronorum. The traditional right of the *patronus* to *obsequium*
and *officium* gravely limited the ability of a freedman to prosecute
his *patronus*, and hence to protect himself against abuses; more
valuable were the *operae*, services imposed as a condition of manumission, and the patronal claim on the estate of a freedman at death,
which might rise to half the whole. Cf. A. M. Duff, *Freedmen in the
early Roman Empire*, ch. iii; Gaius 3. 39–53; *Tit. Ulp.* 29.

item rogo indulgeas ius Quiritium. See Ep. 5. 2. These persons are Junian Latins.

Panchariae Soteridi. The text may conceal the name Ancharia, but not P. Ancharia, as women do not have the *praenomen*.

quod a te volentibus patronis peto. Cf. Ep. 5. 2 n. The male patron could technically complete the manumission of Latins into Roman freedmen by carrying out the formal procedure of *manumissio iusta*. But this needed the presence of all parties before a Roman magistrate, frequently inconvenient, cf. VII. 16. 4 n. Hence, as in Ep. 104, the request is made to the emperor for the grant 'in absence'.

12. *To Trajan*

The letter is datable, by close attention to the meaning and implication of the opening formula, to a period when Trajan was again absent from Rome after his return to Italy in 99. Hence, assuming that the letters are still in correct order, the period of the first Dacian war is indicated, i.e. 101–2.

1. scio, domine, memoriae tuae . . . preces nostras inhaerere. quia tamen in hoc quoque indulsisti, admoneo simul ut Attium Suram praetura exornare digneris, cum locus vacet. The opening clauses have not received the notice that they deserve. Yet *tamen* and *quoque* should put readers on their guard, and *admoneo* is not a word with which Pliny exhorts Trajan elsewhere. He means: 'I have recommended Sura to you already. I know you do not forget my requests. But as you have granted me this kind of request before, I am now reminding you . . . .' Pliny is using *admoneo* not as an equivalent of *praemoneo* (II. 6. 6; cf. I. 19. 3), but in its primary meaning of calling to mind past events. It follows that Pliny had already recommended Sura to Trajan. Since the custom was that senators presented requests in writing only when the emperor was absent from Italy (Tac. *Ann.* 4. 39, cf. Ep. 94. 3), Pliny must have recommended Sura orally in the period 99–101, and is now pressing his suit on Trajan during his absence at (presumably) the first Dacian war.

in hoc quoque. This may refer specifically to the promotion of Voconius Romanus, Ep. 4, or of Erucius Clarus, if that was Trajanic, II. 9 nn. Evidently a praetor designate died suddenly. Pliny asked Trajan to give the vacant place to Sura by virtue of his *commendatio*. Pliny indicates in several letters that senatorial elections outside the list of *commendati Caesaris* were still actively contested, even for the praetorship; I. 14. 7 n., II. 9, VI. 6, 9; cf. *Pan.* 69. 1.

After the transfer of magisterial elections to the Senate in A.D. 14 the emperors seem not to have extended their control over the praetorian elections beyond what was already customary, i.e. the commendation of four candidates, 'sine repulsa et ambitu designandos' (Tac. *Ann.* I. 15); Vespasian's *lex de imperio* says more technically 'uti quos magistratus . . . petentes senatui populoque Romano commendaverit . . . eorum comitiis quibusque extra ordinem ratio habeatur'. If one of the ordinary designates died, a by-election normally took place, as in Tac. *Ann.* 2. 51; Mommsen, *DPR* v. 200 f. Possibly one of the *commendati* of this year had died.

Accius or Attius (*I*) Sura is not known: for the confusion see Tuccius/Tullius in II. II. 9 n. He is not likely to be a relation of the powerful Attius Suburanus, who could look after his own (VII. 6. 10 n.). Possibly he is connected with Accius or Attius Clemens of I. 10, IV. 2 (prefs.), or the equestrian officer of Nerva, Q. Attius Priscus from Cisalpine, *CIL* v. 7425 (Libarna). *PIR²* A 28.

exornare. The word is semi-technical of promotion: Epp. 13, 26. 3.

2. ad quam spem alioqui quietissimum hortatur et natalium splendor et summa integritas in paupertate. For political *quies* see I. 14. 5 n. The man is not inactive, but inoffensive. For the equestrian connotation of *splendor* see Ep. 4. 5 n. Like Voconius, Sura is the son of an equestrian of moderate wealth. But he has already reached the stage before the praetorship by his own means.

bonam conscientiam civium tuorum. For the curious phrase *cives tui* see Ep. 58. 7 n.

13. To Trajan

Otto, art. cit. 94 ff., argued from the order of letters in x that Pliny received his augurate *c.* 101, and not *c.* 103–4 as IV. 8 suggests. But it is possible that Pliny wrote to Trajan during the second year of the first Dacian war, received the honour in 103, and was duly congratulated by Arrianus, who was absent in Egypt, rather late. This letter must belong to a period of Trajan's absence from Rome; Ep. 12. 1 n. Otto assumed that Ep. 14 was written at the close of the first Dacian war, but the second war is possible also.

rogo dignitati ad quam me provexit indulgentia tua, vel auguratum vel septemviratum, quia vacant, adicere digneris. His *dignitas* is his consular rank, which he owed to Trajan, not a particular office (as Otto). Pliny is *privatus* now: 'pietate privata'. Cf. Ep. 26. 2–3. For the conditions and methods of appointment to the great priesthoods see IV. 8. 1–3 nn. Pliny secured the augurship left vacant by the death of Julius Frontinus. This letter was probably written then, because while Frontinus lived Pliny did not need to canvass in person, ibid. The septemvirate cannot be that lost by Marius Priscus in 99, because of the time interval, on any view (II. II. 12 n.).

14. *To Trajan*

victoriae tuae . . . maximae, pulcherrimae, antiquissimae . . . gratulor . . . cum virtutibus tantis gloria imperii et novetur et augeatur. On Pliny's lips this might refer to either the first or the second Dacian war. The latter alone was impressive enough to secure clear mention in the private letters; VIII. 4. 1–2 (cf. VI. 31. 8). But Trajan celebrated a triumph and took the title of *Dacicus* after the first war; the omission from the collection of a second letter of congratulation may be because it was couched in very similar terms. The final phrase may contain an oblique reference to the reversal of Domitian's disasters and inadequate successes in Dacia. So a date in 102 is preferable to one in 106.

optime. See Ep. 1. 2 n.

cum. The Budaean correction *cum* for *ut* of Aldus is preferable, because a double *ut* is not used by Pliny after *precor* in similar contexts, Epp. 35, 52, 100. It also gives a more specific sense.

THE BITHYNIAN LETTERS

Throughout, the letters of Pliny only are given dates. Trajan's replies must be assumed to be several weeks later in each case. See pp. 529 f. for the dates.

15. *To Trajan*

The first of the Bithynian series. After 17 September, first year.

nuntio tibi me Ephesum cum omnibus meis ὑπὲρ Μαλέαν navigasse quamvis contrariis ventis retentum. Pliny took the route south of the Peloponnese instead of that through the Corinthian gulf, because the Etesians blow mainly from the north-east in the Corinthian and Saronic gulfs in July–September, but along the west and south coast of the Peloponnese and in the south-west Aegean they blow from the north-west. In the central and eastern Aegean the prevailing direction is north to north-east, though local winds among the islands assist from other directions. (*Admiralty Geographical Handbook of Greece* (1944), i. 84, 87–88). Thus Pliny could hope to be carried well east of the longitude of Athens instead of being held up in the Gulf at Patras, but when he came to make his northing up to Ephesus he would meet the contrary winds here mentioned. Hence the reading of Stephanus—*retentum*—is preferable to *retentus* of the prototype, which is otiose with the final sentence of the letter. Ep. 17A. 2 shows that the adverse winds of the latter were experienced

in the coastal voyage between Ephesus and Pergamum, and beyond.
Pliny is referring to two phases of delay, one before and the other
after reaching Ephesus.

Ancient sources often refer to the difficulty of rounding Cape
Malea, which roughly marked the transition from the zone of pre-
dominant north-westerly to that of north-easterly winds. See Cic.
ad Fam. 4. 12. 1 for a parallel case, and compare the proverb:
Μαλέας δὲ κάμψας ἐπιλάθου τῶν οἰκάδε. For a discussion see *RE* xiv.
861 f.

**nunc destino partim orariis navibus partim vehiculis provinciam
petere. nam . . . continuae navigationi etesiae reluctantur.** He proceeded first by land from Ephesus to Pergamum, and thence by sea,
Ep. 17A, for lack of local winds to break the Etesians. Cf. Fronto,
ad M. Caesarem 1. 6. 4 (H.): 'navibusne an equis . . . facit haec tam
velocia stativa?' He could use the *cursus publicus* (Ep. 45) where it
existed along this route.

etesiae. The northerly winds become established in the area about
mid-June and prevail until September (*Handbook*, loc. cit.), but the
most intense period was reckoned to be the forty days following the
rising of the Dog Star, (20–21 July), according to Pliny, *NH* 2. 123.
Our Pliny probably started his journey at the end of this period,
and hence took three or four weeks to travel from Italy to Bithynia,
where he arrived on 17 September (Ep. 17A. 2). For a recent discussion of merchant routes in the eastern Mediterranean see Casson,
'Speed of Ships', *Trans. Am. Phil. Ass.*, 1951, 136 f. and articles
there cited.

16. *To Pliny*

mi Secunde carissime. The personal vocative is frequent but not
universal in Trajan's replies: Epp. 18, 20, 36, 44, 50, 53, etc., but does
not appear in the three private rescripts, Epp. 3B, 7, 9. Pliny only
twice uses it in the published version of his private letters, III. 10. 1,
VII. 21. 1. Cicero seems to use it rarely in the letters *ad familiares;*
cf. ibid. 4. 6. 1, 9. 14. 1, 11. 14. 1.

17A. *To Trajan*

Date. After 17 September, first year: s. 2.

**1–2. febriculis vexatus Pergami substiti. rursus cum transissem in
orarias naviculas contrariis ventis retentus . . . Bithyniam intravi.**
What was he doing at Pergamum? It lay in the Caicus valley some
80 miles north of Ephesus, and to a traveller from Ephesus about

25 miles inland beyond its port Elaeus. (Strabo 13. 1. 67, p. 615; cf. Magie's description of the road, *Romans in Asia*, 41 n. 19.) Pliny must have originally intended to make his way overland by the inland route from Pergamum to Cyzicus or Prusa, and then turned back from Pergamum to Elaeus when he decided to take to the sea. He stayed for the fever, not for the winds, took ship and was again held up. The northerlies were still against him, and the passage depended upon making use of the off-shore breeze that usually blows between 8 p.m. and 6 a.m. (*Admiralty Handbook of Turkey*, 1942, i. 207). Though the land route was very direct, Pliny preferred the delays of sea travel to the discomfort of the road.

2. tardius quam speraveram. Pliny must have left Rome at least two months later than the day—1 June—by which proconsuls were expected to arrive in and leave their provinces. Yet one would expect his appointment to be timed for him to take over from the previous proconsul conveniently, and also to avoid any awkwardness over the normal *sortitio provinciarum*. Possibly Pliny's departure was delayed by ill-health—whence his stress on the question of health in this letter—or accelerated by the death of his predecessor in office, whom he never mentions. The late and irregular arrival of Pliny's assistant legate supports the latter. The ordinary rule was for the governor in office to wait for his successor, who was required to forward the date of his arrival, and for legates to arrive with their chief, though the texts refer properly to proconsuls only, not imperial legates. *Dig.* 1. 16. 4–5, 10 pref., 48. 4. 2–3. Cf. Ep. 25 n.

Bithyniam intravi. He must, as Hardy suggested, have left ship at Cyzicus, the great port of the region, and travelled through the coastal lowland by Apollonia, round the northern end of Mt. Olympus, to Prusa, because he reached Prusa without passing through Apamea, the Bithynian port for Prusa (Dio, *Or.* 40. 30–31; Magie, op. cit. 306 n. 17; Dascylium was not counted as a port by Strabo, 12. 8. 10, p. 575). In some provinces particular cities had the right, by custom, that the governor should enter the province through their territory (*Dig.* 1. 16. 4. 5). But there is no evidence that Prusa held this privilege. The passage in Dio, *Or.* 48. 2–3 (cited by von Arnim, *Dio von Prusa*, 376) does not prove that the proconsul Varenus entered Bithynia by Prusa.

natalem tuum in provincia celebrare. Imperial birthdays became public festivals, with sacrifices and games, from Augustus onward; Suet. *Aug.* 57; Dio 51. 19. 2, 56. 25. 3. Trajan's birthday was the day following Pliny's entry, *xiv Kal. Oct.*, or 18 September, according to the Calendar of Philocalus—the same day as the murder of Domitian; Pliny, *Pan.* 92. 4; Suet. *Dom.* 17. 3.

3. nunc reipublicae Prusensium impendia reditus debitores excutio. The local politics of Prusa ad Olympum at this period are well known from the civic speeches of Dio Chrysostom who was a native. The city territory, so named from its Hellenistic founder Prusias I or II, was all inland, on the northern flank and western end of the Olympus massif. (Jones, *Cities*, 152 n. 9; Magie, *Romans*, 306 nn. 16–18, with fuller discussion; Strabo 12. 4. 3, p. 564; Pliny, *NH* v. 148.) It was an unprivileged *civitas stipendiaria* at this time, but had recently become the capital of an administrative *conventus*, and hence the seat of the governor's assizes; von Arnim, op. cit. 315, 328; Dio, *Or.* 44. 11; cf. 40. 10, 48. 11. For an exhaustive account of what is known of Prusa see *RE* xxiii. 1. 1075 ff. (Dörner).

excutio. For the financial aspect of Pliny's mission see Ep. 18. 3 n.

multae enim pecuniae variis ex causis a privatis detinentur. The first of these malpractices is illustrated by several passages in speeches of Dio, datable between 100 and 106, especially *Or.* 48. 9: ἐν πάσαις ταῖς πόλεσίν ἐστι χρήματα δημόσια καὶ ταῦτα ἔχουσιν ἔνιοι, τινὲς μὲν δι' ἄγνοιαν τινὲς δὲ ἄλλως. Those in charge of public works were very apt to embezzle the building funds, *Or.* 47. 19, as Pliny remarks in Ep. 17B; cf. Ep. 38. A similar charge was made against Dio himself in Ep. 81. 1. Sometimes contributions were promised but not paid up. A check on abuses lay in the system of public accounting; but it was easy to delay or avoid this. *Or.* 47. 19, 48. 9–11 and Ep. 81. 1 n.

quaedam minime legitimis sumptibus erogantur. In Ep. 24 Trajan is anxious to see that public money was spent only on *necessariae erogationes*. The only example of improper payments in the Letters is the gift of 40,000 *denarii* from Amisus to a local politician, Ep. 110. 1 n.

4. in ipso ingressu meo scripsi. A few days must have elapsed since his actual arrival. The term *ingressus* is technical, Ulpian, *Dig.* 1. 16. 4. It is noteworthy that Pliny does not report to Trajan the routine publication of his 'edictum . . . quo . . . hetaerias esse vetueram' (Ep. 96. 7), which belongs to this moment, and doubtless contained other matters too.

17B. *To Trajan*

Date. Between 17 September and 24 November, first year.

This is not separated in the Aldine edition from the previous letter. But the repetition of the statement about his entry, and of *domine*, just after *domine* in 17A. 4, shows that the note is a postscript dispatched some days later, when the need for a *mensor* occurred to Pliny, by a separate messenger who might happen to arrive earlier than the messenger of Ep. 17A.

2. **dispice, domine, an necessarium putes mittere huc mensorem. videntur enim non mediocres pecuniae posse revocari a curatoribus operum si mensurae fideliter agantur.** The request was not unusual, despite Trajan's reply. Vespasian sent a *mensor* to help the procurator of Corsica in a boundary dispute; *FIRA* i. 72, A–J 59. Properly a quantity surveyor was required to check the buildings erected against the contracts. Ulpian and Paulus, *Dig.* 11. 6, 5. 2 and 6, dealing with frauds by *agrimensores*, briefly mention frauds 'in aedificii mensura' and 'tignum vel lapidem metiendo'. The *mensor*, in several varieties, is distinguished, ibid. 7, from the *architectus*; there were the *mensor agrorum*, the *mensor machinarius*, and others; cf. Frontinus, *de aquis* 119. Pliny, like the Hadrianic proconsul in *ILS* 5947A, needed a legionary *mensor* with an all-round training: 'adhibito a me Iulio Victore evocato Augusti mensore'.

a curatoribus operum. Cf. *Ep.* 81. 1: 'exigendam esse a Dione rationem operis . . . quod aliter fecisset ac debuisset'. Such a *curator*, or ἐπιμελήτης ἔργων, was appointed for each specific job, as a liturgy. Dio, *Or.* 40. 7, describes himself as worn out with 'measurements and estimates and calculations', and with visiting the quarries in the mountains. But the duty was supervisory, not executive. The work was done by contract, or by a multiplicity of contracts for each part of a building. The *curator* supervises the contractors. See *Dig.* 50. 10. 2. 1; Jones, *Greek City*, 237 f. and nn. 50–51; Plutarch, *Praecepta rei publicae gerendae* 15. 811 C.

pecuniae posse revocari. Pliny is not expected to take criminal proceedings against offenders. Roman public law controlled such malpractices through the *Lex Iulia peculatus* and *de residuis*. But these laws applied only to the magistrates of the Roman State, and were first extended to Roman municipalities at this very time; cf. Paulus, *Dig.* 48. 13. 5. 4: 'sed et si de re civitatis aliquid subripiat, constitutionibus . . . Traiani . . . cavetur peculatus crimen'. In unprivileged communes the offence might be regulated by the local municipal charter, and the *ecdicus* of the city might initiate a suit, *Ep.* 110. 1 n., or he might bring the matter to the attention of the governor to deal with it as he thought fit. Evidently the usual custom was to regard such matters as involving a financial suit rather than a criminal charge.

dispice, domine. A favourite formula, cf. Epp. 33. 3, 49. 2, 54. 2, 75. 2, 77. 2.

ex ratione Prusensium, quam cum maxime tracto. Aldus printed 'cum Maximo'. But the freedman of *Ep.* 27 was not a subordinate of Pliny. The correction comes from the Bodleian copy. It is a Plinian usage, cf. VI. 31. 15, 'fit cum maxime portus'. It means not 'with all one's effort' but rather 'at this very moment'; cf. A. J. Dorjahn, *Cl. Phil.* 1927, 313 f.

18. To Pliny

1. **cuperem . . . simile tibi iter ab Epheso ⟨ei⟩ navigationi fuisset, quam expertus usque illo eras.** The reading of *et*—from the Bodleian copy—is pointless. Possibly it is due to a misconstruction for *ac* after *simile*. The correction of Catanaeus—*ei*—is preferable. For *ab* with a place-name compare Ep. 63, 'a Bosporo venisset', Ep. 67. 2, 'venisset a Bosporo'. The usage is not uncommon in Cicero and Caesar even where there is no ambiguity in the plain ablative, as even *Lewis and Short* s.v. *ab* reveals.

sine querela corporis tui. Not so much of a formality as it sounds. Lucian states that the first item in the book of imperial *mandata* issued to governors was an instruction to take care of their health (*pro lapsu inter salutandum* 13).

2. **ut manifestum sit illis electum te esse qui ad eosdem mei loco mittereris.** The long phrase emphasizes Pliny's special position and contrasts him with the proconsuls chosen by lot; cf. VIII. 24. 9: 'nitendum est ne . . . sorte quam iudicio missus . . . melior . . . fuisse videaris'.

ad eosdem mei. The suggestion of Müller—'ad eos domini loco'—was monstrous.

3. **rationes autem in primis tibi rerum publicarum excutiendae sunt.** For this aspect of his mission compare Ep. 47. 1: 'cum vellem . . . Apameae cognoscere publicos debitores et impendia'. He is concerned with financial questions at different cities in Epp. 37, 39, 43, 47, 77, 90, 92, 98. In Ep. 43. 1 his survey is defined as concerning *impendia maxima*, which covers sums as low as S.3,000. But Pliny is not merely a financial *corrector civitatium* in the later style. In Ep. 32. 1 his mission is more widely defined: 'idcirco te in istam provinciam missum quoniam multa in ea emendanda apparuerint'. He was particularly instructed to diminish the political faction which disturbed the province, Ep. 117: 'ut formandis istius provinciae moribus ipse moderareris et ea constitueres quae ad perpetuam eius . . . quietem essent profutura'. Cf. Epp. 34. 1 and Ep. 22. 1 n. on *mandata*.

satis constat. The notion that Bithynian conditions only became known at Rome through the extortion trials of Bassus and Varenus is unsatisfactory. These may have revealed the extent of municipal intrigue (IV. 9. 5, VII. 6. 1–7), but were not concerned with the civic finances. Trajan's procurators could have reported on Bithynia at any time.

mensores vix etiam iis operibus quae aut Romae aut in proximo fiunt sufficientes habeo. No wonder. Trajan was a tremendous builder. His great Baths were ready in 109, with the Aqua Traiana and the Naumachia. In January 112 the vast new Forum and the Basilica Ulpia were finished. In 113 his column was set up, and the Aedes Veneris in the Forum Julium was complete. His new harbour at Ostia is shown on a coin of 112. That at Centum Cellae was under way in 107, and that at Ancona was finished in 115. (See *CAH* xi. 206–8; *ILS* 298; *FO*, p. 736; *Roman Imp. Coin.* ii. 240 f.; Strack, *R. Reichsprägung*, i. 202 f.) Trajan's remark supports the earlier date, 109–10, for Pliny's mission (pp. 80 f.). By late 111 the demand for technicians at Rome should have begun to slacken.

sed in omni provincia inveniuntur quibus credi possit. Trajan touches on Pliny's unexpressed reason for the request, but as in Ep. 40. 3—'nulla provincia non . . . peritos . . . homines habet'—and Ep. 62—'neque provinciae istae his artificibus carent'—overestimates the trustworthiness of the technicians in Bithynia. Pliny returns to the charge in Ep. 39. 6.

19. *To Trajan*

Date. Between 17 September and 24 November, first year.

1. Rogo domine consilio me regas haesitantem, utrum per publicos civitatium servos, quod usque adhuc factum, an per milites adservare custodias debeam. Characteristically the duty of guarding prisoners awaiting trial by the proconsul—*custodiae*—was thrust by the Republican method of administration upon the municipalities. In the Asiatic provinces municipal *irenarchae* and *paraphylaces*, assisted by patrols of *diogmitae*, were responsible for arresting malefactors and sending them with a report to the proconsul. This system leaves its traces in the chapter 'de custodia et exhibitione reorum', *Dig.* 48. 3. Cf. ibid. 3. 10: 'si quos . . . sine causa solutos a magistratibus cognoveris . . . multam dices', from Venuleius, *de off. procons*. But the use of soldiers was also common, both in public and imperial provinces, ibid. 3. 1, 3, 12–14. Municipal custody meant the *carcer* and chains, and was thought more severe than detention *per milites*, though release on bail was allowed; ibid., citations from Hadrian, Ulpian. See Hirschfeld, *Kl. Sch.* 602 f.; Jones, *Greek City*, 212 f.; Magie, *Romans*, 647 nn. 46–47.

publicos servos. These were commonly used in routine and menial tasks of Roman and municipal administration as clerks and labourers, though senior clerks were freeborn men of respectable status. Even the slaves had a regular salary (Ep. 31. 2) and might be assigned a house. See *ILS*, Index vi, p. 432, and xi D; *Lex Ursonensis* 62; *Tab. Her.* 82; Frontinus *de aquis* 100; *RE* (S) vi. 967 f.; Mommsen,

DPR i. 406 nn. 2–3, 412 n. 1. For public slaves in Greek provinces see also W. Liebenam, *Städteverwaltung*, 296 n. 2. The suggestion that slaves were in short supply, and hence treated on an equality with free men by the cities, is not borne out by anything in Epp. 19–20, 31–32. Pliny's question concerns discipline (Vidman, *Étude* 83).

custodias. The term is first so used in Seneca. *Thes. L.L.* 3. 2, s.v.

per milites. For the troops at Pliny's command see Ep. 21. 1 n. Vidman's comment, that Pliny's decision amounted to a military interference in civic affairs, is inexact (op. cit. 60), since the custody of prisoners and convicted persons was not properly a municipal interest.

2. communem culpam hi in illos . . . regerere posse confidunt. The local magistrates would be technically responsible, cf. above. Dig. 48. 3. 12 gives regulations of Hadrian for the punishment of soldiers in cases of escape.

20. *To Pliny*

1. commilitones. The word here and in Epp. 52, 53, 100, 103 means little more than 'the men', as in later usage; e.g. Arrius and Macer, *Dig.* 49. 16. 6. 6 and 12. 2. But in contemporary usage it often retains its full force, as in Ep. 87. 1; VII. 31. 2, VIII. 23. 5. Tac. *Hist.* I. 35; Suet. *Claudius* 10. 2; *Galba* 20. 1.

perseveremus in ea consuetudine quae isti provinciae est. This principle, with its correlate 'secundum legem cuiusque civitatis', is in favour with Trajan, contrasting with the post-Hadrianic lawyers' desire to lay down general rules for the whole Empire. Cf. Epp. 65. 2, 69, 93, 109, 113.

2. quam paucissimos a signis avocandos esse. So too in Ep. 22. 2. In imperial provinces soldiers from the garrison, or that of a neighbouring armed province, were used sparingly in the administration. The legates had a small administrative staff, or *officium*, of *beneficiarii*, soldiers below the rank of centurion, whose appointment, carrying freedom from fatigues and higher pay, was a 'benefit', Ep. 21. 1. In Africa the proconsul drew *beneficiarii* from the Numidian legion (Tac. *Hist.* 4. 48) even after it was withdrawn from his control. Such *beneficiarii* were not normally available in a proconsular province, but Pliny would draw them from his auxiliary units. These staffs seem to have been kept to a minimal size, a dozen or a score at most. See Domaszewski, *Rangordnung*, 63–67; *RE* iii. 271. A single *cornicularius*, or chief clerk at headquarters, is known from Bithynia (*IGR* 3, 59: Prusias).

21. *To Trajan*

Date. Between 17 September and 24 November, first year.

1. **Gavius Bassus praefectus orae Ponticae et reverentissime et officiosissime, domine, venit ad me.** Rostovtzeff (*BSA* xxii. 10 ff.) connected this official with the *classis Pontica*, taken over *c.* A.D. 64 from the last king of Pontus Polemoniacus when this region was provincialized. (*CAH* x. 774 n. 1; Tac. *Hist.* 3. 47.) But it now seems that the Pontic fleet remained at its original port of Trapezus until the late second century, when it was transferred to Cyzicus. (J. C. Starr, *The Roman Imperial Fleet*, Ithaca 1941, 127 f.) Hence its sphere of operations lay outside Pliny's province, as it was mainly concerned with keeping the wild tribesmen of the Colchis coasts in order. (Cf. Jos. *BJ* 2. 16. 4, s. 367.) Gavius' post may be akin to that of the better-documented *praefectus orae maritimae* of the Spanish provinces, who controlled a military rather than a naval force (*RE* xxii. 2. 1333; Vidman, *Étude* 53–54). But why he needed *beneficiarii* from Pliny if he had troops of his own is not clear. Only two commanders of the Pontic fleet are known in epigraphy, both from the later period (*IGR* 4, 150; *ILS* 1327). Bassus must have done the work of the *praefectus classis* in a more westerly area, and the identity remains a possibility. Hardy's suggestion that Bassus was in charge of the Customs will not do. The *portoria* of all the Asian provinces were still collected by a farmer-in-chief acting for a company of tax-farmers (S. de Laet, *Portorium*, 273 f.; *AE*, 1924, n. 80).

This letter with Ep. 86A does not prove that Bassus was directly dependent on Pliny. Both Bassus and the procurator Virdius were provided with troops by Pliny because the command of the cohorts could not be divided (Ep. 27 n.). Like Virdius in Epp. 27, 28, 84, Bassus may be an independent collaborator, but being junior to Pliny in the hierarchy he owes Pliny respect, which is stressed here and in Ep. 86A, rather than *obsequium*. If he was prefect of the Fleet his immediate superior was the legate of Cappadocia-Galatia-Pontus Polemoniacus rather than Pliny. The procurator is certainly independent, like all procurators, despite much that has been written about the 'special circumstances' of Pliny's appointment (e.g. Vidman, op. cit. 42 f., 53–54, 61 f.), and the fact that Pliny assists both Bassus and the freedman adjutant of Virdius with testimonials, Epp. 85–86. The network of officials consists of a pattern of overlapping rather than concentric circles: even the *stationes* of gendarmerie are appointed independently of the governor by the emperor, Epp. 77–78 nn. Pflaum (*Proc. équestres*, 157 ff.) suggested that a principal function of procurators was to spy on the senatorial governors.

But Pliny seems to be on very good terms with these colleagues: 'procul a contentione adversus procuratores' (Tac. *Agric.* 9. 5). The relationship was not always as strained as that between the legate of Britain and Classicianus in Tac. *Ann.* 14. 38.

Gavius Bassus. The reading of the editions, *Gabius*, here and in 22 and 86, must be corrected by epigraphical usage; cf. *ILS* Index. The man is not otherwise known, *PIR²* G 96.

praecepisse te ut ex cohortibus quibus me praeesse voluisti contentus esset beneficiariis decem equitibus duobus centurione uno. This implies a surprisingly large force for a peaceful province from which the only troubled area, Pontus Polemoniacus, had been detached. In the previous period security forces for the Pontic area came from Moesia, and there was no standing force in western Pontus; cf. *ILS* 986; Tac. *Ann.* 12. 15. Possibly these cohorts were part of the former royal army of eastern Pontus, taken over at the provincialization (Tac. *Hist.* 3. 47), and transferred to the western province when it ceased to be proconsular. Two old proconsular provinces, Baetica and Africa, are known to have had a single cohort as garrison in the first century, and Macedonia seems to have had a similar unit in the second century (III. 9. 18 n.; Cheeseman, *Auxilia*, 159).

Of these cohorts only the *c. sexta equestris* is known, Ep. 106 n. Cheeseman, op. cit. 162 n. 1, and Cumont, *Studia Pontica*, iii n. 5, quote evidence for the *ala Claudia nova* and *ala I Flavia Aug. Brittonum* at Amasia under Trajan, outside Pliny's province. Military inscriptions of any date are very rare in Bithynia-Pontus; cf. the indexes of Dörner, *Inschriften* and *Reise*.

praecepisse te. i.e. in Pliny's *mandata*, below, Ep. 22. 1 n.

vir egregius. See IX. 23. 4 n. for Pliny's use of this term.

beneficiariis decem. For the use of military personnel in the administration see Ep. 20. 2 n. The detail casts light on the workings of the bureaucracy. The number is evidently the regular establishment for such a post as this, and was accordingly put forward by the appropriate secretary for insertion in Pliny's instructions. So too the procurator of the province is given an establishment of ten in Ep. 27.

equitibus duobus. A certain number of *equites singulares*, drawn from *auxilia*, appear in the *officia* of most officials. They acted as the personal guard of their office, cf. Ep. 27, 'tutelae causa . . . addidi duos equites'. Domaszewski, *Rangordnung*, 35 f.

22. *To Pliny*

1. **et mihi scripsit Gavius Bassus non sufficere sibi eum militum numerum qui ut daretur illi mandatis meis complexus sum.** There are references to the *mandata* of Trajan in Epp. 30, 56. 3, 96. 7,

110. 1, with 111 and indirectly perhaps in 27, 32. 1, and 43. 2. The *mandata quae praesidibus dantur* (*Dig.* 48. 19. 35) contained a series of instructions issued to each legate on his appointment. Systematic information is not found before Pliny, though there are casual references in Tacitus. Dio 53. 15. 4 attributes the usage to Augustus, but wrongly includes proconsuls among the recipients, judging by the custom of his own day. (Tac. *Hist.* 4. 48 about the proconsul's special relationship to the African legion does not support Dio.) *Mandata* are distinguished from *rescripta* issued on particular occasions. The classical lawyers often quote regulations about criminal law with the phrase 'mandatis cavetur' or 'mandatis continetur' or 'caput mandatorum exstat' (e.g. *Dig.* 48. 19. 27. 1-2, 47. 11. 6). Lucian once refers to the 'book of instructions issued to governors' (*pro Lapsu* 12). A large body of administrative law was steadily built up in the *mandata*, which must have contained ultimately considerable sections common to the whole Empire, such as the rules given in Epp. 30. 1, 56. 3, 110. 1. Ulpian writes of a rule that Titus, Domitian, and Nerva allowed: 'eamque et Traianus secutus est et exinde mandatis inseri coepit caput tale'. *Dig.* 29. 1. 1 pref. Some instructions would be limited to a particular province or emergency, such as the veto on clubs in Bithynia, Ep. 96. 7. Foreign policy and diplomacy must have bulked large in the instructions to governors of border provinces, cf. Tac. *Ann.* 15. 17: 'respondit (sc. Paetus) ... iuncti invaderent Armeniam ... non ea imperatoris habere mandata Corbulo'. A story in Tac. *Ann.* 12. 48 suggests that these were often incomplete: 'ne tamen adnuisse facinori viderentur et diversa Caesar iuberet'. Pliny seems to have had no instructions about relations with the Bosporan kingdom, which caused him some trouble, Epp. 63, 64, 67. But Bithynia was not a frontier region. The *mandata* seem to have contained not a comprehensive code but a mixture of guiding principles, innovations, and occasional instructions. By the third century a degree of codification was possibly secured, cf. Callistratus, *Dig.* 48. 19. 27. 2: 'alio quoque capite mandatorum in haec verba cavetur'. The most detailed collection of rules issued to an official, the Egyptian *Gnomon idiologi* (*FIRA* i, n. 99), is not so much a set of *mandata principum* as a collection of legal rules. For a brief discussion see *RE* xiv. 1023 f., L. Vidman, 'Die Mission Plinius in B.', *Klio*, 1959, 221 ff.; *Étude*, 45 f.; Th. Mayer-Maly, *Studia et Doc. Hist. Jur.* 1956, 313.

Pliny's *mandata* contained instructions about the disposition and control of his troops (22, 27, 30), administrative rules about relegation (56. 3) and *collegia* (96. 7), directions about the control of municipal expenditure, which were both particular (110–11, vetoing *donationes*) and general, e.g. 'ut sumptus levaretur', if 17A. 3, 18. 3, 43. 2, 47. 1 refer technically to the *mandata*. (Vidman, art. cit. 222;

but see Ep. 43. 2 n.) There may also have been a general instruction
to correct abuses of all sorts after consultation with Trajan, of which
Epp. 31. 1 and 32. 1 may echo the wording: 'cum ius mihi dederis
referendi ad te de quibus dubito', 'quoniam multa in ea (sc. provincia) emendanda apparuerint'. It is also likely that there was a
clause strictly controlling the initiation of projects of municipal
building, Ep. 23. 1 n. The *mandata* were for the legate's private
instruction, and were not officially published. The legate issued his
own edicts in accordance with them (Ep. 96. 7). But their contents
came to be known to the provincials, as in Ep. 110, possibly by
unauthorized means (Vidman).

cui quae rescripsissem ut notum haberes his litteris subici iussi.
This remark provides a clue to the question of the immediate authorship of the Letters (pp. 536 ff.). Routine answers and technical information were supplied by the Secretariat, but Trajan supervised
the correspondence. Cf. Ep. 6. 2: 'libertis tuis quibus iusseras misi'.

his litteris subici. Pliny and Trajan use three terms for the forward-
ing of documents: *subicere, iungere, mittere*. Vidman (*Étude*, 36–37),
following a suggestion of Wilcken, argues that *subicere* is properly
used for copies of documents of all sorts written out on the same
'sheet' at the end of the *epistula*, and *iungere* solely for original
libelli of petitioners, attached to the *epistula* by glue, instead of a
paper-clip. This distinction is clear for *iungere* in Epp. 48. 1, 59, 60. 2,
81. 6, 83, 93 and for *subicere* in 22. 1, 56. 5, 58. 4, 79. 5, 114. 3, while
mittere is used as a non-technical alternative in Epp. 47. 2, 65. 3,
70. 4, 73, 106–7, as also *perferre*, Ep. 83. But in Ep. 92 Pliny writes
libellum . . . his litteris subieci of an original petition. The secretariat,
however, never confuses the terms (Epp. 22. 1, 48. 1, 60. 2, 93)
though it too uses *mittere* for both (Epp. 73, 107 twice). Wilcken
(*Hermes*, 55. 25 n. 2) was applying to Pliny the terminology of the
heading of a file from the records of the prefect of Egypt (*P. Hamburg*
18, A.D. 220–1): συγκολλήσιμον ἐπιστολῶν αὐθεντικῶν καὶ βιβλιδίων
ὑποκεκολλημένων, 'the file of original letters and attached petitions'.
An instruction from the prefect to the officer of a cavalry unit in
A.D. 103 (*P.Ox.* vii. 1022) uses *subieci* for the addition of information
in the same document. This supports the notion that it is used for
additions in the same hand, including copies of documents.

multum interest †te† poscat an †homines in se ut† latius velint. So
the prototypes, with variant *velit* in I. Schuster and Kukula, following
Catanaeus and Orelli, read 'res poscat an homines iure uti' etc. Keil
and Hardy: 'in tempus poscat an hoc munere uti' etc. Either *res* or
in tempus would fit the context, and the latter is neatly extracted
from the text. Trajan licenses a temporary loan of soldiers in Ep. 28.
But *homines*, as Hardy saw, is inappropriate. So too is *iure*. Hardy's

munere is not perfect, because unlike the man in Ep. 28, where the word is used, Gavius is not employed on a special mission. But *homines* might conceal *hoc nomine* and *in se* could conceal *eis*: 'an hoc nomine eis uti latius velit' would give relevant sense and be nearer the prototype than anything else. Cf. Ep. 34. 2: 'si res poposcerit accursu populi ad hoc uti'; Ep. 62: 'res ipsa suaserit'. Both are from rescripts of Trajan. Also in a newly found rescript of Titus: 'ne quid hoc nomine reipublicae absit' (*Madrider Mitteilungen*, i. 148 f.).

23. *To Trajan*

Date. Between 17 September and 24 November, first year.

1. **Prusenses, domine, balineum habent et sordidum et vetus. itaque †tamen aestimans† novum fieri, quod videris mihi desiderio eorum indulgere posse.** This is the reading of the Bodleian supplement; the text of Aldus is an evident reconstruction: 'id itaque indulgentia tua restituere desiderant' etc. Modern editions reprint the emendation of Cuntz (*Hermes*, 1926, 206) as a matter of course: 'tamiae aestimant'. This was clever, but will not do. Pliny never uses *aestimo*, when followed by an infinitive as here, without a genitive of price or value. His favourite phrase is *magni aestimo*, cf. III. 2. 5, 4. 1; IV. 28. 1; VI. 23. 3. Cuntz's reading requires either *oportere* or *faciendum esse* to follow, as Schuster admits in his *apparatus*. Besides, it attributes a function to municipal *tamiae* which was not theirs. The formulation of building policy was done by the councils and magistrates. The 'stewards' were minor executive officials whose duties were mechanical. (Jones, *GC* 241; Magie, *Romans*, 61 n. 34, 646 n. 45.) Best read boldly: 'itaque magni aestimant novum fieri'. This fits *desiderio eorum*, sc. *Prusensium*. The general sense is that 'the Prusans have a bad bath and very much want a new one. You can easily grant their desire.' Stout (*T.A.Ph.A.* 86) produced *debere* not very probably out of T N, the presumed abbreviation of *tamen* in error for DRE. This was an improvement, but not Plinian in usage or word order.

sordidum et vetus. Dio describes the mean and sordid ruins that disfigured Prusa in *Or.* 47. 15. He had himself pulled down some shacks to improve the city, *Or.* 40. 9, and he mentions the baths in *Or.* 46. 9. In Ep. 70. 1 Pliny describes a palace at Prusa as *nunc deformis ruinis*. Perhaps, as at Claudiopolis, Ep. 39. 5 n., the citizens were tired of the simple Greek style of *thermae*, and keen to possess an establishment in the elaborate Roman manner, characteristic of the *saeculi nitor*, s. 2. For the place of baths in city life see Jones, op. cit. 219. For their ubiquity, II. 17. 26.

There were and still are hot-springs about two kilometres to the north-west of Prusa, but the baths of Pliny must be different, since Ep. 70 shows that they are inside the city and their location could be changed. Dörner (*RE* xxiii. 1. 1082–3) did not observe this.

The question of the baths is continued in Ep. 70.

novum fieri. Dio initiated a building plan for the modernization of Prusa about A.D. 97–103. This was submitted to a proconsul, who attended a special meeting of the city assembly (*Or.* 40. 5–10, 45. 15–16, 47. 11–15; Magie, *Romans*, 589–90 n. 60; Arnim, *Dio*, 314 f., 340 f.). Dio stresses the desirability of grand buildings to maintain the prestige of the city.

indulgere posse. Here, as in Epp. 70. 3, 90. 2, 98. 2, using *si permiseris* and *si indulseris*, Pliny explicitly asks permission for the erection of new public buildings. In Ep. 37. 3 he asks less explicitly for permission to replace an unsuccessful aqueduct by a new structure, and in Ep. 41. 1 he uses an elaborate formula to recommend the canal scheme. Trajan grants permission in each case. In Epp. 39 and 49 (nn.) Pliny reports the condition of buildings already half built, and makes no request for building permission, but puts forward other demands. In each case Pliny explains or Trajan insists that the work can be done out of local resources. Before this date it appears from Dio that only the proconsul's permission was needed for such operations. (*Or.* 40. 6, 45. 5–6, cf. Jones, op. cit. 136.) Now Macer, *de officio praesidis* (*Dig.* 50. 10. 3, 6, 7), quoted the rule already formulated by Pius and Marcus Aurelius, that no public buildings should be erected out of municipal funds without the emperor's licence, though private persons were mostly free from this restriction. It seems that Trajan had instructed Pliny, in his *mandata*, that no new public buildings were to be erected without reference to him. In two cases—of buildings already in hand—he refers the decision back to Pliny, Ep. 40. 1 and 3, and in no others.

This ruling explains a considerable part of Pliny's supposed tendency to consult the emperor to excess over minor matters. The rule, of course, did not have the effect of stopping new building either now or later; cf. Magie, *Romans*, 657 n. 62. Vidman (*Étude* 47, 76) rightly maintained that it was great expense and not building itself that Trajan seeks to control, and objects to the suggestion (A–J 81) that other financial expenditure of any size required the governor's approval before this time. Cassius Dio, a century later, similarly advised that the cities should be discouraged from extravagant building 'lest they exhaust themselves in futile exertions' (52. 30. 3).

Prusenses. Ep. 17A. 3 n.

2. erit enim pecunia ex qua fiat primum ea quam revocare a privatis et exigere iam coepi ; deinde quam ipsi erogare in oleum soliti parati sunt in opus balinei conferre. For the first fund see Epp. 17A. 3, B. 2 nn. The oil-money seems to be meant in Trajan's reply by the phrase *ad necessarias erogationes*. If so, Hardy was right in referring the oil-money not to that supplied free in the gymnasium (as Jones, op. cit. 221 f., n. 23), but to a dole of edible oil given by the city to the poorer citizens, and provided by a liturgy of the rich, as *ipsi . . . conferre* suggests. Magie (op. cit. 646 n. 44, 654 n. 58) collects evidence for the existence of oil funds and oil commissioners in Asiatic cities, including ταμίαι τῶν ἐλαιωνικῶν χρημάτων (*IGR*, iii. 60, 68) at Prusias ad Hypium. According to Jones oil was not usually provided free in the baths, though it was so given at the gymnasium out of liturgies or endowments. At Prusa there was a public liturgy concerned with the control of market prices and supplies, Dio, *Or.* 46. 14, 48. 17. The population had already rioted over bread, and might do so again over oil; hence Trajan's caution, Ep. 24; Dio, *Or.* 46. 8 f. Bithynia was not a great olive zone, though olives flourished around Prusa (Ep. 41. 2 n.)

quod alioqui et dignitas civitatis et saeculi tui nitor postulat. Cf. Dio, *Or.* 40. 10, 'the spirit of cities is apt to be exalted by buildings and festivals'. For *saeculi tui* see Ep. 1. 2 n.

24. *To Pliny*

si instructio novi balinei oneratura vires Prusensium non est. A similar formula is used in Ep. 91 to grant permission for works at Sinope. Trajan speaks of 'fitting out'—*instructio*—perhaps taking Pliny's *novum fieri* as *renovare*, cf. Epp. 28, 62.

ne quid ideo intribuatur aut minus illis in posterum fiat ad necessarias erogationes. The second proviso refers to the proposed diversion of the oil fund, but the reference of the first is not entirely in line with Pliny's letter. Pliny had made no such suggestion. Trajan or his secretary may have misunderstood *exigere iam coepi* in Ep. 23. 2.

25. *To Trajan*

Date. Just after 24 November, first year.

Servilius Pudens legatus, domine, viii kal. Decembres Nicomediam venit meque longae expectationis sollicitudine liberavit. Pudens is Pliny's assistant, as the sentence indicates. There has been a curious misunderstanding over this. Mommsen in the 'Life' (*GS* iv. 431 n. 3) maintained that a *legatus Augusti propraetore* could not have an assistant legate, and hence that Pudens was on his way to another province. But in *DPR* iii. 281–2 he later correctly held that an imperial legate could not *appoint* subordinate legates, and hence

that the assistant *legati iuridici*, who first appear in imperial provinces under the Flavians (e.g. *ILS* 1011, 1015–16), were appointed
by the emperor. Hardy saw the truth, but others have continued to
repeat Mommsen's earlier view, as in *PIR*¹ S 423. Cf. Vidman, *Étude*,
62. In the praetorian public provinces the proconsuls had a single
assistant *legatus propraetore*, appointed by the Senate (Dio 53. 14. 7;
cf. II. 11. 23, IX. 33. 9). Pliny refers to those of Bithynia in Ep. 31. 5.
He, as their successor, has the same, appointed by Trajan.

Such legates were mainly concerned with civil jurisdiction, and
lacked the full power of capital condemnation, which was reserved
for the proconsul or the *legatus Augusti propraetore*. Cf. Dio l.c. 5.
Dig. I. 16. 6. 1, 11–13. The earliest text asserting this limitation is a
citation of Pomponius (ibid. 13) from the middle of the second
century: 'legati proconsulis nihil proprium habent nisi a proconsule
eius mandata fuerit iurisdictio'. That this covers the powers of
governors over *peregrini* is confirmed by Ep. 29. 1 n. The assistant
legates in Bithynia had been concerned with criminal sentences, but
only below the level of capital punishment: Ep. 31. 5 n. See also my
Roman Society and Roman Law in the New Testament (Oxford, 1963),
4 n. 1. Pliny seems to have left the bulk of the civil jurisdiction to
Pudens. Only three rather difficult cases occur in the Letters, Epp.
65, 72, 110, whereas Pliny is concerned with criminal cases in Epp.
29, 31, 56, 58, 74, 81, 96. See in general Mommsen, *DPR* i. 263 ff.;
D. Pen. R. i. 288. For the assize tours of the legates see Ep. 58. 1,
'conventum incohaturus' n.

Servilius is otherwise unknown. Usually, but not always, such
legates were of praetorian rank. He may be grandfather of the consular Q. Servilius Pudens, brother-in-law of the emperor Verus. The
collocation of names is otherwise unknown among senators. *PIR*¹ S
423, 424, 425; Lambrechts, *Composition*, nn. 213, 278. The recent
proconsul of Bithynia Servilius Calvus might be connected, Ep. 56.
2 n. It is not unusual to find persons employed in provinces with which
they have a previous family connexion, cf. Gemellinus, Ep. 27 n.

longae expectationis. Cf. Ep. 17A. 2 n., 'Bithyniam intravi'. The
custom was for a legate to arrive with, if not before, his superior;
Dig. loc. cit. 10. 1. This man is at least two months late.

26. *To Trajan*

Date. Between 24 November and 3 January, first year.

1. Rosianum Geminum . . . habui enim illum quaestorem in consulatu.
For Pliny's young friend, T. Prifernius Paetus Rosianus Geminus,
possibly the adopted son of a consul of A.D. 96, and his subsequent
career see VII. 1 pref. For the consular quaestors see IV. 15. 8 n.

2. cui et si quid mihi credis indulgentiam tuam dabis ; dabit ipse operam ut in iis quae ei mandaveris maiora mereatur. This is a rather obscurely worded recommendation of Rosianus for any posts in the emperor's service to which his present rank qualifies him. It would seem from the next sentence that Rosianus had served as either a military tribune or a legionary legate, and passed through the senatorial career as far as the praetorship, but had not yet held an imperial governorship (s. 2). The request is too loosely worded to refer to an annual magistracy or priesthood, as in Epp. 12–13. Syme (*Historia* 1960, 369) even suggested the consulship, for which *mandaveris* is inappropriate. A provincial legateship or senatorial *praefectura* or *cura* is more probably intended, as in v. 14. 2: 'mandatum officium'. The length of Pliny's commendation may suggest that he was pleading for an unpopular man.

apud te. Cf. Tac. *Dial.* 7. 1, 'apud principem . . . procuratores . . . tueri', i.e. 'in your cabinet'.

integritatem eius . . . non solum ex eius honoribus . . . sed etiam ex commilitio esse notissimam. His military career seems to be more remote than his magistracies (*honores*). Possibly he served as military tribune under Trajan in Germany or Pannonia *c*. 97–99, though this would be unusually close to his quaestorship in 100. A legionary legateship in the Dacian wars is not excluded, either before his praetorship, which was presumably *c*. 105, or after it, as was more normal. His presence at Lugdunum in IX. 11 hardly proves that he was then *legatus propraetore* of Lugdunensis, as has sometimes been assumed, in face of the silence of Pliny here: *commilitium* means actual service, as in Ep. 86B. His consulship under Hadrian is belated: VII. 1 pref.

integritatem. For the qualities required in imperial servants see Epp. 12, 85–87 nn., III. 2. 2 n. Pliny does not commend Rosianus for literary qualities to the unliterary Trajan; cf. Ep. 4. 4 n. His *integritas* is much stressed, perhaps for its rarity, cf. Ep. 86B. n., and Tac. *Ann.* 16. 17, 'adquirendae pecuniae brevius iter credebat per procurationes administrandis principis negotiis'. Pflaum, *Proc. Eq.* 169.

3. exornata quaestoris mei dignitate. Pliny uses *exornare* alike of personal appointments and annual magistracies, II. 13. 2, 10, Ep. 12. 1.

27. To Trajan

Date. Between 24 November and 3 January, first year.

Maximus libertus meus et procurator tuus, domine, praeter decem beneficiarios quos adsignari a me Gemellino optimo viro iussisti, sibi

quoque confirmat necessarios esse milites. †ex his† interim sicut inveneram in ministerio eius relinquendos existimavi. Maximus, like Epimachus, Ep. 84, and Lycormas, Epp. 63, 67, is a freedman assistant of the equestrian 'procurator Augusti Ponti et Bithyniae', who, since the province became imperial, was concerned both with the ordinary revenues from taxation, in place of the quaestor, and with his former task, the management of the private estates of the emperor which fed the special *patrimonium* account. Cf. Ep. 58. 5 n. This procurator had formerly acted as the imperial representative in these parts for foreign affairs concerning the Crimean region; Tac. *Ann.* 12. 21; Rostovtzeff, *BSA* xxii. 15 ff. His authority at this time seems to cover a wider area than the proconsular province. There is no evidence for other equestrian procurators operating in Pliny's province. The agents of the indirect taxes, quoted by Hardy, belong to a later age: *ILS* 1330, 1359, 9490, cf. Ep. 21. 1 n. Their work at this time was done, if at all, by freedmen procurators like Maximus; cf. *ILS* 1396: 'Marianus Aug. n. lib. p(rae)p(ositus) xx lib(ertatis) Bithyniae Ponti Paphlag(oniae)', assistant of a procurator of Galatia.

There is nothing in Book x, except the allocation of troops, to suggest that the procurator and his staff were subordinate to Pliny, as argued by Vidman (*Étude* 42 f., 61 f.). Their operations appear to be quite independent in Epp. 28, 63, 67, 84. Cf. Ep. 21. 1 n.

Gemellino. Cf. Ep. 84. This man, Virdius Gemellinus, should be the son of the centurion Virdius Geminus, sent by Vespasian to protect eastern Pontus from brigands in A.D. 69, Tac. *Hist.* 3. 48; cf. Rostovtzeff, art. cit. 20; *PIR*¹ V 473. Similarly the Neronian procurator of Bithynia, C. Julius Aquila, also active in the affairs of the Crimean Bosporus, had local connexions, being a native of Amastris. (*CIL* 3. 6983; Tac. *Ann.* 12. 15.)

iussisti. i.e. in the *mandata*, Ep. 22. 1.

†ex his† interim. Mommsen ingeniously restored the text usually printed: 'necessarios esse milites *sex. tris* interim'. That means that he now had 3 plus 2 soldiers from Pliny's force on his own account. But Trajan's reply suggests that Maximus had more than this, since he orders a final reduction to 2 plus 2. It might be better to read 'milites. sex interim', or 'milites sex. hos interim'. Either would give a reduction in Ep. 28 from 8 to 4.

praesertim cum ad frumentum comparandum iret in Paphlagoniam. This, with the reference to the job as 'extraordinario munere' in Ep. 28, is the main prop of the theory of O. Cuntz (*Hermes*, 1926, 193) based on Rostovtzeff (art. cit. 22), that Pliny's governorship was part of a plan of preparation for Trajan's eastern campaigns of 113–17. Gemellinus and Maximus are supposed to be storing corn to feed legions on a march from the Danube to the Armenian frontier. A recently found inscription of the Severan age refers to a private citizen of Nicomedia who fed two legions thus, passing through Bithynia to a Persian war (Dörner, *Inschriften* n. 121). But there is no sign of any such intention here or elsewhere in Book X: for further adverse comments on this theory see Epp. 63, 67, 74, 78. 2 nn. The special duty may well have been concerned with corn shortage in any part of the eastern empire, or they may have been acting for the *praefectus annonae* at Rome. Hardy quotes a later procurator 'ad annonam provinciae Narbonensis et Liguriae', *ILS* 1432, and a post-Flavian *dispensator ad frumentum* has left his record at Cius, *CIL* 3. 333. Trajan's anxiety for the urban supply is shown by *Pan.* 29–30.

tutelae causa . . . addidi duos equites. Ep. 21. 1 n. for *equites singulares.*

in futurum quid servari velis rogo rescribas. Would those who criticize Pliny adversely for referring this type of question to Rome be so moved if the notes were formally addressed to a minor official of the secretariat instead of nominally to the emperor? This type of paper fussiness is characteristic of services at a certain stage of development, and of all modern armies. The criticism might be better directed against the 'establishment' rules of the empire and Trajan, than at Pliny. The chancellery does not reprove Pliny for asking.

28. To Pliny

fungebatur enim et ipse extraordinario munere. cum ad pristinum actum reversus fuerit sufficient illi duo a te dati milites et totidem a Virdio Gemellino procuratore meo, quem adiuvat. The two men were not in Bithynia just for this special job. It was added to their routine duties. Like Gavius Bassus, Ep. 21. 1 n., they are not under the direct orders of Pliny.

actum. A rare usage, 'rerum actus' usually refers to judicial sessions, as in Ep. 97. 1; cf. Suet. *Claud.* 15. 1, 23. 1.

totidem a Virdio. Presumably out of his allocation of ten *beneficiarii.*

quem adiuvat. The term *adiutor* is frequently used as the official title of the freedman or equestrian assistant of a senior procurator, *ILS*, Index vi B. Cf. vii. 6. 10 n., Suburanus.

29. To Trajan

Date. Between 24 November and 3 January, first year.

1. Sempronianus Caelianus egregius iuvenis repertos inter tirones duos servos misit ad me. Levies were carried out on imperial orders by special officers, *dilectatores*, who were senators in public provinces and recruited legionaries or equestrians in imperial provinces, recruiting both for legions and for auxiliary troops. (Mommsen, *GS* vi. 67, 72; *RE* v, s.v. 'dilectus', 618 f.; cf. Dio 53. 15. 6; *Dig.* 48. 4. 3.) It is disputed whether Caelianus is levying legionaries or auxiliaries. Mommsen (op. cit. 36), took the recruits to be legionary, but most moderns have taken them for auxiliary (Hardy, ad loc.; Vidman, *Étude* 57–59). Caelianus, since he is called *egregius*, like Gavius Bassus (Ep. 21. 1) and the leading centurion in Ep. 87. 3, is hardly a senator. (But cf. IX. 23. 4 n. for Pliny's unofficial usage.) No auxiliary units of Bithynian origin or title are known, but at this date recruitment for existing auxiliary units already took place in their area of service without regard to their place of origin. (Cheeseman, *Auxilia* 77, and App. ii; G. Forni, *Il reclutamento delle legioni* (Milan, 1953), 100 f.) The method of levy, partly voluntary, suits either arm (Ep. 30. 1 n.). The allocation to units apparently within Bithynia points to the auxiliary service, or possibly the *classis Pontica*. But numerous Bithynians appear among the soldiers of the African *legio III Augusta*, in a list of Trajanic date (*CIL* viii. 18084), in which no less than 25 out of 98 men give Bithynian cities as their domicile, including Nicomedia (7), Prusias (4), Apamea (4). Forni (op. cit. 29 n. 2, 96) assigns the African troops to the period of Trajan's oriental wars, and takes the present levy to be auxiliary. But the closest parallel is the equestrian officer of Flavian date, who recruits in Numidia—a district which like Bithynia had close affiliations with a 'public' province—for several legions (*ILS* 9195 nn.).

servos. Slaves were barred from all forms of military service, with death as the penalty, Marcianus, *Dig.* 49. 16. 11. Augustus had recruited freedmen in the crisis of the Illyrian and Germanic disasters, but they were mostly confined to special *cohortes civium Romanorum*. (Cf. Cheeseman, op. cit. 65–66; Vell. Pat. 2. 111. 1; Tac. *Ann.* 1. 31; Suet. *Aug.* 25. 2; Dio 55. 31. 1, 56. 23. 3.) The crime of false declaration involved an attempt to secure the Roman citizenship by illegal means. Vidman argues from the lack of reference to freedmen here that *auxilia* alone are in question, for which they were qualified to serve (op. cit. 58). But Pliny had no occasion to mention them.

conditorem disciplinae militaris. Twice in the Panegyric, 6. 2 and 18. 1, Pliny speaks of Trajan restoring military discipline from the slackness of the previous régime in passages which, though aimed against Domitian, are coloured by memory of the rebellion of the praetorian guard against Nerva. The sloth mentioned in VIII. 14. 7 refers to the notoriously slack legions of Syria, which Domitian never visited. It is hard to believe that legionary discipline in the armies of the North was bad under Domitian, an active military emperor who increased legionary pay substantially. However, Trajan publicly contrasted the cost of his provincial journeys with those of Domitian,

Pan. 20, and made a point of discipline, Ep. 78. 3 n., VI. 31. 4–6 nn. Alone of the early emperors he is cited three times as author of special regulations in the Digest title *de re militari* (49. 16. 4 pref., 5, 12, cf. also 2. 12. 9). For the writer of SHA, *M. Ant.* 11. 7, 'praecepta Traiani' were traditional.

2. iam dixerant sacramentum. The military oath was administered by the legionary officer to levies on enlistment. It was now an oath sworn to the emperor, and its general tenor is represented by Livy 22. 38. 4: 'sese fugae atque formidinis ergo non abituros neque ex ordine recessuros nisi teli sumendi aut petendi aut hostis feriendi aut civis servandi causa'. It is quite distinct from the oath of loyalty taken at accession and renewed annually by soldiers and civilians alike (Ep. 52 n.). See *RE* i. 2. 1667, and vi, 'dilectus', 598. Caesar, *BG* 6. 1. 2; *BC* 1. 23. 5; Polyb. 6. 21. 2; Dion. Hal. *Ant.* 11. 43. 2.

nondum distributi in numeros erant. Cf. III. 8. 4, 'neque . . . adhuc nomen in numeros relatum est', of the appointment of a military tribune, and the instructions of a prefect of Egypt to an auxiliary officer in A.D. 103 (*P. Ox.* vii. 1022): 'tirones sex probatos a me in cohorte cui praees in numeros referri . . . xi Kal. Mart.' Probably the term here refers to the official lists of men kept in the files of the unit concerned. (Cf. J. F. Gilliam, *Eos*, 48. 2, cited by Vidman, loc. cit.) The term can also refer to larger units, either standard formations or special detachments, cf. Tac. *Hist.* 1. 87: 'reliquos caesorum . . . in numeros legionis composuerat'; also, e.g., *Agric.* 18. 2, *Hist.* 1. 6; Ulpian, *Dig.* 3. 2. 2. 1: 'exercitum . . . non unam cohortem neque unam alam dicimus sed numeros multos militum'. Pliny seems to imply that the men are to be enrolled within the province, but the language is ambiguous. (Cf. also Arrius cited below, Ep. 30. 1 n., for *numeri*.)

Sempronianus Caelianus is not otherwise known, *PIR*¹ S 262.

cum pertineat ad exemplum. Pliny's problem is as in Ep. 65. 1 (n.): 'neque putavi posse me in eo quod auctoritatem tuam posceret exemplis esse contentum'. Much of the ordinary government followed the system of discretionary precedents, which lacked binding force. Cf. Epp. 72. 1, 97. 2. But Pliny does not regard Trajan's rescript as a mere *exemplum*, either here or in Ep. 81. 5, 'in re ad exemplum pertinenti' (contra, Vidman, op. cit. 86).

30. *To Pliny*

1. Secundum mandata mea fecit Sempronius Caelianus mittendo ad te eos de quibus cognosci oportebit an capitale supplicium meruisse videantur. This statement confirms the impression given by the

legal texts that all capital jurisdiction not only over Roman citizens
but also over *peregrini* was reserved for the *imperium*-holder (Ep.
25 n.). For the penalty, Ep. 29. 1 n. Vidman (*Étude* 56–57) oddly
took this sentence to mean that the instructions about the levy in
general were included in Pliny's *mandata*.

mandata. If Caelianus had separate *mandata* he must have been an
independent official. But Trajan may mean that these rules were laid
down in his instructions to Pliny, with which Caelianus was familiar.

**refert autem voluntarii se obtulerint an lecti sint vel etiam vicarii
dati.** The latter possibilities imply compulsion. Forni, op. cit. 28 f.,
asserts that voluntary enlistment was the rule in the Principate. But
the literary sources do not support this for the earlier period, when
the compulsory levy seems to have been much used, except in Italy.
Cf. Velleius 2. 130. 2; Tac. *Ann.* 13. 7, 35, 16. 13. Tiberius himself
stresses the worthlessness of volunteers, Tac. *Ann.* 4. 4: 'dilectibus
supplendos exercitus. nam voluntarium militem deesse, ac si sup-
peditet non eadem virtute ac modestia agere quia plerumque inopes
ac vagi sponte militiam sumant'. But not all the soldiers enlisted by
these large-scale levies were conscripts, and this letter indicates the
combination of both systems. The voluntary system eventually
prevailed with the recruitment of those born in the *canabae legionum*.
Cf. Fronto, *ad M. Ant.* 1. 2 (H.): 'non tantum voluntarios legimus sed
etiam latentes . . . conquirimus'. To the classical lawyers voluntary
recruitment is the norm, e.g. Arrius, *Dig.* 49. 16. 4. 10: 'qui ad
dilectum *olim* non respondebant . . . in servitutem redigebantur sed
mutato statu militiae recessum a capitis poena est, quia *plerumque*
voluntario milite numeri supplentur'. In general see *RE* v. 615 f.

vicarii dati. This seems to be the earliest allusion to the custom of
substitutes in the Roman army. There is no symptom of decay here,
since substitutes had to be up to the stringent standard of all recruits
(s. 2 n.), and servile persons were excluded. But the levy could be
used for corrupt purposes, cf. Tac. *Hist.* 4. 14: 'senes aut invalidos
conquirendo quos pretio dimitteret'.

2. inquisitio peccavit. For the abstract form cf. *custodiae*, Ep. 19. 1.
Curtius Rufus, 4. 6. 30, uses the term; which is also once used of the
selection of candidates for equestrian status, *I.L.Al.* 2145. Cf.
Dörner, *Reise* n. 19; *Dig.* 50. 8. 12. 4 (7).

**ille enim dies quo primum probati sunt veritatem ab iis originis suae
exegit.** Cf. *RE* art. cit. 619 f. The recruits in *P. Ox.* VII. 1022 registered their names and ages and distinguishing marks. There were
conditions of minimum age and of height, which was known as the
incomma, apparently 1·725 metres. Veg. *RM* 1. 5. Slaves and
ignominiosi were excluded from legions. So too were Egyptians,

perhaps because of their status as *dediticii*. *Dig.* 49. 16. 4. 1–9; Ep. 6.
1–2 nn. Trajan also barred *rei*, *Dig.* loc. cit. 16. 5. Northern Gauls also
seem not to have been regularly recruited for legionary service; Syme,
Latomus, 1953, 30 n. 4.

probati. For the term cf. *ILS* 2333, 'tiro probatus annorum xvi',
and *P. Ox.* VII. 1022 above. The accepted recruit was given a token
to wear round his neck like a modern identity disk; *Acta Martyrum*,
ed. Ruinart, p. 300 (A.D. 195). He was then sent to his permanent
unit for training, as this passage suggests. It is commonly assumed
that legionary recruits from the eastern provinces were given the
Roman franchise on enlistment, and such was doubtless often the
case; Mommsen, *GS* vi. 32 f.; Aristides, *Pan. Romae* 1. 352 (D); *RE*
art. cit. 621 f. But in the African service list cited above, Ep.
29. 1 n., the rarity of imperial *nomina* among the Bithynians and the
diversity of their gentile names suggest that most of that enlistment
were provincial Romans by descent, possibly scions of the numerous
Italian business men of the Republican period and their freedmen.

quo primum probati sunt. In *P. Ox.* VII. 1022 only five days intervene between the *probatio* by the prefect of Egypt and the receipt
of the men by their unit. Vidman concludes by analogy that Sempronius Caelianus had only recently commenced operations, after
Pliny's arrival, and acting under his orders. But this conclusion
does not follow, since Caelianus only referred a special case to Pliny.

31. To Trajan

Date. Between 24 November and 3 January, first year.

1. ius mihi dederis referendi ad te de quibus dubito. The phrase
suggests that Trajan had encouraged Pliny, because of the special
circumstances of his mission, to refer to the Princeps on matters
which ordinarily a legate might decide for himself. The present query
raised no problem that might not have been solved on the spot if
Pliny had been satisfied to apply the rigour of the law. He refers to
Trajan, as in the matter of the Christians, Ep. 96, because he wants to
innovate by dealing gently with these cases.

**2. in plerisque civitatibus . . . quidam vel in opus damnati vel in ludum
similiaque his genera poenarum publicorum servorum officio mini-
sterioque funguntur.** Various forms of detention in bonds with hard
labour in mines and quarries, or service in the amphitheatre, appear
as penalties in provincial jurisdiction over *peregrini*. The severest
forms, *damnatio ad metallum, in ludum, ad gladium*, replaced the
capital sentence, and entailed perpetual sentence and loss of civic
rights. The condemned person was defined in status, ultimately, as

servus poenae, though the origins of this are obscure. Condemnation *in opus publicum*, either *in tempus* or perpetual, was less severe, since the prisoner did not lose his civic status. This letter and Ep. 58. 2–3 dimly illuminate the early history of these penalties. (Brasiello, *Diritto penale*, 361 f., 373 f., 382 f., 419 f. Ulpian, *Dig.* 48. 19. 8, is the most coherent and informative of many confusing and confused texts collected in the title *de poenis*.)

in opus damnati. Pliny's brevity causes a difficulty. All these prisoners were evidently under life sentence and had lost civic status. But even in later law, which tended to increase in severity, the sentence to *opus publicum* did not have this effect. So Pliny is using the term to cover all forms of *damnatio in metallum*; for which see Ulpian, loc. cit. 10. He may include the mild penalty *in opus metalli* which originally did not have the severer consequences associated with the sentence *in metallum*: *Dig.* 48. 19. 28. 6; Brasiello, op. cit. 379 f.

publicorum servorum officio. Though released from the mines these persons have not recovered their civic status, unlike Archippus in Ep. 58. Their employment suggests that some form of the theory of *servus poenae* was already established. Brasiello, op. cit. 377, 419 f., argues that *damnati ad metallum* became *servi metalli* or *servi Caesaris* until Pius finally defined *servitus poenae*. But the passages cited seem only to show that the institution existed by the time of Pius: *Dig.* 34. 8. 3 pref., 49. 14. 12, *et al.*

Nicomediae et Nicaeae. Pliny has been in this locality since the date of Ep. 25 and remains there some time, Epp. 33–41, 49.

Of the two chief cities of Bithynia, Nicomedia was the provincial capital and Nicaea its close rival. Nicaea, now Iznik, the elder by a generation, was founded by the Successor Antigonus at the end of the fourth century B.C. with Macedonian and Hellenic colonists, in the rich plain at the eastern end of Lake Ascanias. It was soon incorporated in the new Bithynian kingdom, probably by Nicomedes I, and thereafter played little part in history. It flourished exceedingly from its agricultural products, despite its inland situation, using Cius as its port and having good communications with the interior. After the Roman conquest Pompeius attributed a large territory to Nicaea, which retained it till late in the empire. Strabo describes the great circuit of the city wall in his day. (Jones, *Cities*, 151, 160–2, 165–7; Magie, *Romans*, 305 nn. 13–14; Strabo, xii. 4. 7, p. 565.) This survives in its magnificent late-empire and Byzantine form: see the panoramic photograph in A. M. Schneider, *Istanbuler Forschungen*, ix, p. 56. Iznik is at present a large village with certain remains of its ancient buildings, hardly excavated: Ep. 39. 1 n. The authoritative account of ancient Nicaea is now *RE* xvii. 1. 226 f. (Ruge).

Nicomedia, now Izmit, was founded as his capital by Nicomedes I of Bithynia *c.* 264 B.C., on the site of one former Greek colony, Olbia, with the inhabitants of another, Astacus; it had a fine maritime and commercial position, at the head of the Gulf of Izmit and of the great highway that traversed northern Asia Minor from the Propontis to Armenia. Its subsequent history and prosperity resemble that of Nicaea. As capital of the Roman province, centre of the provincial council and imperial cult, and garrison city of the provincial forces (Ep. 21. 1), it had the precedence. But Nicaea kept up a long feud for the primacy, claiming the title of First City of Bithynia, perhaps on grounds of greater antiquity. Dio's oration xxxviii, *ad Nicomedenses de concordia*, documents this theme. But the doubts of Wilcken (*Hermes* 49. 129) as to which was the seat of the Roman governor seem unnecessary. (Jones, *Cities*, 151 f.; Magie, op. cit. 305 nn. 10–12, 451 n. 62, 589, n. 58; *RE* xvii. 1. 468 ff. is the most recent general account; cf. Strabo, xii. 4. 2, p. 563; Memnon 20. 1.)

annua accipiunt. See Ep. 19. 1 n. for servile officials. For the term cf. Suet. *Tib.* 50. 1, *Vesp.* 18. 1; Frontinus, *de aquis*, 2. 100.

3. reddere poenae post longum tempus plerosque iam senes . . . nimis severum arbitrabar. Pliny continues to apply as an official the canons which he observed in private life towards his own slaves (v. 19 nn.)

in publicis officiis retinere damnatos. It was the confidential nature of the work often performed by public slaves that was unsuitable, cf. Ep. 19. 1, VI. 22. 4—custody of prisoners, keeping of records. There was no reason why *damnati* should not work outside the mines at menial tasks, as Trajan concedes.

4. ut decreta quibus damnati erant proferebantur, ita nulla monumenta quibus liberati probarentur. erant tamen qui dicerent deprecantes iussu proconsulum legatorumve dimissos. There seem to have been no organized public archives in the province at this time. Official documents, decrees, edicts, and rescripts of emperors and proconsuls are produced in evidence by the interested parties: Epp. 47, 56. 2, 5, 58. 3, 65. 3, 72 nn. In Ep. 65. 3 Pliny applies to Trajan for accurate copies of imperial rescripts produced by plaintiffs, though in Ep. 72 he seems to have direct access to a *SC.*, and in Ep. 70. 4 a faulty copy of a will comes apparently from municipal archives. These could contain the charters and regulations quoted in Epp. 79, 92–93, 112, 114. The existence of a provincial record office, *tabularium*, with a staff of *tabularii* and *commentarienses* is well documented not only in imperial but in some public provinces, notably at Carthage for Africa Proconsularis and at Ephesus for Asia. But these served only the purposes of the imperial procurators. (See O. Hirschfeld, *Verwaltungsbeamten*, 59 f.; *RE* s.v. 'tabularium', (2) iv. 1966 f.)

Proconsular archives are less well documented. From VI. 22. 4 it seems that the *scribae* kept a record, *commentarii*, of the proconsuls' 'acts', and the citation of the decree of a proconsul of Sardinia *c.* A.D. 68 shows that such 'acts' were eventually filed in the senatorial archives at Rome. (*FIRA* i. 59; Mommsen, *GS* v. 343 f.) If the proconsuls took their records back to Rome it is not surprising that the provincial archives were inefficient or non-existent, as was certainly the case in the late Republic (*Cic. ad Fam.* 5. 20. 2) when a law of 59 B.C. required governors to leave a copy of their accounts in two cities of their province. But there is a reference to the proconsular archives at Ephesus in Eusebius, *HE* 5. 18. 235. How far this lack of good records in public provinces was general remains uncertain. The frequency with which in the Digest imperial decisions had to be reaffirmed by rescripts to the inquiries of successive proconsuls suggests that public archives continued to be ill maintained even in the later second century. The imperial legates, with adequate military personnel to man their *officia*, may have been more efficient: the proconsul of Africa exceptionally had the services of *beneficiarii* from the legion in Numidia to help him (Ep. 20. 2 n.). Elsewhere the system of annual change of proconsul, quaestor, and their attendant *scribae*, must have continued to militate against efficiency. J. N. Hough complained of this inefficiency, without observing its causes or even noting that most of the documents cited in the Letters did not come from official sources (*Cl. Journal*, xxxv. 1939, 25–26).

5. iussu proconsulum legatorumve. The spoken word of the *imperium*-holder sufficed for action without the need for documentation. Hence in part the lack of records. For the proconsular legates see Ep. 25 n. They evidently dealt with some forms of criminal jurisdiction for which penalties less than the capital sentence were given.

32. *To Pliny*

1. Meminerimus idcirco te in istam provinciam missum quoniam multa in ea emendanda apparuerint. For the terms of Pliny's mission see Epp. 18. 3 n., 22, 1 n. The plural verb ordinarily refers to Pliny and Trajan, e.g. Ep. 20. 1, but here, and in Epp. 34. 1, 78. 1—where *meminerimus* recurs—111 and 115, it may reflect the collaboration of the secretary. See pp. 543 f.

2. qui igitur intra . . . decem annos damnati nec ullo idoneo auctore liberati sunt, hos oportebit poenae suae reddi ; si qui vetustiores invenientur, et senes ante annos decem damnati, distribuamus illos in ea ministeria quae non longe a poena sint. Trajan anticipates the ruling of Pius, *Dig.* 48. 19. 22, that the aged and infirm might be released from service in the mines if they had served not less than ten years. Pius left such persons to the custody of their relatives, whereas Trajan retains them in servile work. Evidently a predecessor of Pliny had the same notion. None of these persons claimed, like those in Epp. 56. 2, 58. 3, that their sentences had been cancelled. Vidman (*Étude*, 86) suggests that Trajan's rescript acted as an *exemplum* to Pius.

vetustiores, etc. This clause apparently covers persons condemned more than ten years ago and improperly released, and aged persons condemned more than ten years ago who are still serving their official punishment.

ea ministeria. The cities saved money by using convicts instead of buying expensive slaves from dealers for these jobs.

solent enim eiusmodi [homines] ad balineum ad purgationes cloacarum item munitiones viarum et vicorum dari. These tasks fell under the supervision of the municipal officials called commonly ἀστυνόμοι, who either used *servi publici* or let the work out on contract. Jones, *Greek City*, 213 f. The *vici* are properly the blocks of urban houses to which there was access only from the roads on which they were built. Hence *vicus* came to be used for an urban street while the *viae* were the thoroughfares.

cloacarum. Strabo, xiv, p. 646, indicates that drainage and sewerage did not exist even in up-to-date eastern cities. The municipalities of Italy and the west were more systematic in the matter. Cf. Ep. 98; Jones, loc. cit.

solent enim eiusmodi homines. The insertion of *homines* seems essential, though editors have generally been content with the Aldine reading. The phrase is in chancellery style, cf. Ep. 34. 1, 'eiusmodi factionibus', 42, 'eiusmodi operum', 93, 'res huiusmodi'. The Budaean text, preferred by O.C.T., leaves the sense slightly obscure 'solent et ad . . .'—since the verb lacks a clear subject.

33. To Trajan

Date. Between 24 November and 31 December, first year.

1. diversam partem provinciae circumirem. His absence from Nicomedia was presumably during his visit to Claudiopolis, Ep. 39. 5, which therefore falls before January (Ep. 35).

Nicomediae vastissimum incendium . . . duo publica opera . . . Gerusian et Iseon absumpsit. Gerusiae were institutions found in many Hellenistic cities, and known in Bithynia-Pontus at Nicaea, Prusias, Amastris, and Sinope (*CIG* 3749, 3754, 4157; *IGR* iii. 42, 65, 95, *et al.*). Primarily they were civic centres for the elder men of substance, organized often around a *gymnasium*. They had officers, entrance fees, property, and regulations, and might also receive a subsidy from the civic revenues. Their members tended to be aristocratic, but were not always members of the decurional class. They meddle with politics, and have various religious functions, sometimes including care of the imperial cult. But whether the Gerusiae had a specific administrative function beside the councils is in dispute. Their standing was superior to that of a *collegium* or ἑταιρία. See Jones, *Greek City*, 225 f., 353 n. 31; Magie, *Romans*, 63 n. 38, 855–60; J. H. Oliver, *Historia*, vii. 472 ff. for their relations to councils. Vidman, *Étude* 73–74, correctly rejects their connexion with civic πρυτάνεις and πρυτανεῖον.

Iseon. The cult of Isis was well established in Bithynia in the pre-Roman period, and was apparently given an official organization at Nicomedia, with Sarapis, under Hadrian (Bosch). Her representation appears also on many civic coins from the time of Pius onwards. In an inscription (Dörner, *Inschriften*, n. 123) from Prusa of the second century a characteristic association of μύσται makes thank-offerings to Isis and Sarapis. See D. Magie, *AJA* lvii (1953) 176 f.; Bosch, *Münzen*, 150, 273 f.; or Waddington, *Recueil général*², 408 f., 527 f., 579 f., etc. For the cult in the Roman world at large see F. Cumont, *Les Religions orientales* etc. (Paris, 1929), ch. iv.

vastissimum incendium. The cities of the Empire suffered much from great fires. Tacitus in the period of the *Annals* records two conflagrations at Rome in addition to the Neronian fire, and others at Lugdunum, Oppidum Ubiorum, and Bononia; *Ann.* 4. 64, 6. 45, 12. 58, 13. 57, 15. 38, 16. 13, while Rome had another bad blaze under Titus, Suet. *Tit.* 8. 3. All this at Rome despite the organization of the *vigiles*, some 7,000 strong. In the municipalities of Italy and the Latin-speaking provinces there were organized bodies of firemen known from their apparatus as *fabri centonarii, f. dendrophori*, and *f. tignarii*, associated in *collegia*. But in the eastern Greek provinces the scanty evidence of these letters, and a passage in the *Vita S. Polycarpi* (Ep. 34. 2 n.), suggested to Jones (op. cit. 215) that there was a uniform ban on such brigades. This is confirmed by a passage from Isidore's *Origines*, quoted below, s. 2, and by the total absence of any epigraphical record of such organizations in the East. It seems that the cities of the East had to manage without any organized fire service. For the *collegia fabrorum* see Walzing, *Les Corporations* etc. ii. 193 f., and for their distribution ibid. 196–7, and iv. 78 ff.; also *RE* vi. 1905 f.

2. inertia hominum quos satis constat otiosos . . . perstitisse. Perhaps the masses were not sorry to see the palaces of the wealthy burning.

Dio *Or.* 46. 5–6, 11–13 tells of a bread riot at Prusa when the mob
tried to burn down his house. Cf. Rostovtzeff, *SEHRE*,[1] 111, 169,
188, on such riots, and Magie, *Romans*, 581 n. 37. See Ep. 34. 1 n.

**nullus usquam in publico sipo nulla hama nullum denique instru-
mentum.** The *sipo* was a regular stirrup-pump capable of raising
water to a fair elevation. Ulpian, *Dig.* 33. 7. 12. 18, lists the fire-
fighting equipment usually kept in a private house as: 'acetum . . .
centones sifones perticae . . . scalae et formiones et spongias et amas
et scopas'. Isidore, *Orig.* 20. 6. 9, in a passage cited by Merrill, gives a
remarkable description of the methods practised in eastern cities:
'sifon vas . . . quod aquas sufflando fundat. utuntur enim hoc
orientales. nam ubi senserint domum ardere currunt cum sifonibus
plenis aquis et exstinguunt incendia, sed et camaras ad superiora
aquis emundunt.'

**3. dispice an instituendum putes collegium fabrorum dumtaxat
hominum CL. ego attendam ne quis nisi faber recipiatur neve iure
concesso in aliud utatur.** Pliny suggests the normal means used in
Italy, but this conflicts with Trajan's *mandata* (Ep. 96. 7). Hence this
consultation. The Roman policy towards social clubs and guilds was
formulated gradually in the early Principate. The evidence, which is
scrappy and obscure, has been much discussed in recent years,
particularly the main legal text in *Dig.* 47. 22. The present account
follows in the main the exhaustive discussion of de Robertis (below).
In Italy a Caesarean or Augustan *Lex Iulia de collegiis* had subjected
all such clubs to a system of licence by the Senate, in order to prevent
a recrudescence of the turbulent political clubs of the late Republic
(Suet. *Aug.* 32. 1; *ILS* 4966). This was amended by a *SC.* of Claudian
or Neronian date which distinguished professional clubs from the
type known as *collegia tenuiorum*. These were clubs of poor men
organized around some form of religious cult, *religionis causa*, often
combining the functions of a burial and a dining club; cf. Ep. 93 n.
These were set free from the control of the *Lex Iulia*, and allowed to
form at will; de Robertis, op. cit. 247 f., 269 f. The law itself was
thus primarily concerned with organizations that might become a
political nuisance, as Trajan's reply shows. Under Nero the local
politics of Pompeii were much disturbed by unlicensed clubs of that
kind, and measures were taken to suppress them, Tac. *Ann.* 14. 17.

How far this legislation was applied to the provinces is disputed.
The Italian type of professional club is found all over the western
provinces (above, 1 n., and *ILS*, index xii). There is some evidence
that in the second century the licensing system was applied to them
in public provinces; (de Robertis, op. cit. 195 f., 219 f.). In Bithynia
Trajan had ordered a general suppression of clubs of all types,

Ep. 96. 7, only permitting *collegia tenuiorum* to function in special circumstances at Amisus, Ep. 93. This was a new ruling. Hitherto in Bithynia the right of association had been free, as the evidence of Dio Chrysostom shows, Ep. 34. 1 n. Trajan's rule was gradually extended to other provinces, cf. Marcian, *Dig.* loc. cit. 1: 'mandatis principalibus praecipitur praesidibus provinciarum ne patiantur esse collegia sodalicia'. This ruling was understood not to affect the *collegia tenuiorum*, ibid. But Vespasian's decree about the privileges of doctors implies that normally teachers required a licence to assemble audiences (W–C 458).

See especially F. de Robertis, *Il Diritto associativo Romano* (Bari, 1938); G. Bovini, *Proprietà ecclessiastica* etc. (Milan, 1949); P. W. Duff, *Personality in Roman Private Law* (Cambridge, 1938), ch. v.

ne quis nisi faber recipiatur. No honorary members and trouble-makers are to be admitted, cf. Callistratus, *Dig.* 50. 6. 6. 12: 'nec omnibus promiscue qui adsumpti sunt in his collegiis immunitas datur sed artificibus dumtaxat'.

34. *To Pliny*

1. Sed meminerimus provinciam istam et praecipue †eas† civitates eiusmodi factionibus esse vexatas. Thus O.C.T. Schuster follows Keil in amending the text of Aldus and Budaeus to *eam civitatem*, because only Nicomedia has been mentioned. But Trajan means that the cities are disturbed rather than the villages. Troubles in the villages are mentioned in Ep. 96. 9 and distinguished from the cities: 'neque civitates tantum sed vicos etiam et agros ...'. So too Ep. 41. 2, 'et in agris ... et ... in civitate'. Pliny uses *civitas* in x normally in this restricted sense (n. ibid.). A better emendation would be simply *ipsas*. The syllable *ip* could be lost after *praecipue*, and the correction of *sas* to *eas* would follow. In Ep. 62, also a letter of Trajan, 'praecipue res ipsa' is used. Only once elsewhere does Trajan have the demonstrative *is* without a correlative—Ep. 91, *ea res*, though in 78. 1 and 2 he uses *ea, eam, ... ut*. But in these three instances *is* is emphatic, at the beginning of a sentence or clause.

factionibus ... vexatas. The violent factions of Bithynia played a part in the fortunes of the proconsuls Bassus and Varenus, IV. 9. 5, VII. 6. 1, 6 nn., and are described in the civic speeches of Dio. In *Or.* 45. 7–10 he tells how the elections to the council of Prusa were managed by cabals, and summarizes the system as καθ' ἑταιρείας πολιτεύεσθαι. He claims in *Or.* 50. 3 never to have had a hand in such factions. His own schemes for the improvement of Prusa were opposed by a group of this kind, *Or.* 40. 8–15. Cf. Ep. 58. 2 n., 81. 1 n.

In *Or.* 43. 6–7 and 11 he claims to have resisted such conspiracies of delators as troubled Bassus, and which sometimes, in collusion with the proconsuls, perverted justice at the expense of their rivals or of the masses. In *Or.* 39 he talks of similar rivalries at Nicaea. Another source of trouble lay in the strong municipal feuds, as between Prusa and Apamea, Nicaea and Nicomedia. *Or.* 40. 16–31; 39. All this took place against the general background of strife between rich and poor. At Prusa the poorer classes were much victimized by the council, and a proconsul intervened to suspend the popular assembly. *Or.* 43. 1–2, 48. 1, 4–9, 50. 3–4. The upper classes, organized in their clubs, had the advantage. Cf. Rostovtzeff, op. cit.¹ 519 n. 16, and Ep. 33. 2 n. A tantalizingly incomplete inscription from Nicomedia, of the proconsular period, mentions riots over the high rate of prices, which the council had difficulty in controlling, until apparently it invoked the aid of the proconsul. F. K. Dörner, *Inschriften . . . aus Bithynien* (Berlin, 1941), n. 24.

quodcunque nomen ex quacumque causa dederimus iis qui in idem contracti fuerint, hetaeriae †quae breves† fient. Schuster's emendation *eaeque brevi* is ingenious and more convincing than the older *praegraves*. The general meaning is not in doubt. Lightfoot's equally ingenious *aeque* does not appear elsewhere in x, and is always used in i–ix by Pliny with expressed comparisons, here lacking; cf., for example, VIII. 5. 3, 20. 10; IX. 7. 3.

hetaeriae. The term is frequently used by Dio in passages cited above. Gaius, *Dig.* 47. 22. 4, gives the Latin equivalent as *collegium* and *sodales*. de Robertis, op. cit. 347 ff., holds that properly *collegium* is reserved for a professional and *sodalitas* for a social association.

2. admonerique dominos praediorum ut et ipsi inhibeant, ac si res poposcerit accursu populi ad hoc uti. Compare the regulations made after the Neronian fire, Tac. *Ann.* 15. 43: 'subsidia reprimendis ignibus in propatulo quisque haberet'. Trajan's preference for private enterprise is not so silly as it sounds. The close building and crowded streets of the ancient cities must have made it difficult to bring fire-brigades into action. Concentration on house-brigades and dispersal of instruments might be more effective than centralization.

accursu populi. This resembles the passage from Isidore, above, Ep. 33. 2. n. In the fourth-century life of Polycarp (Lightfoot, *Apostolic Fathers*,² ii. 2, p. 1042) during a great fire at Smyrna the people 'ran together' and the municipal magistrate ordered that 'the engines kept for this purpose' should be brought out, including *sipones*, and the citizens set to work.

dominis praediorum. Trajan may be thinking of the large *insulae* familiar at Rome.

35. To Trajan

Date. 3 January, second year.

In Epp. 35–36 and 100–1 Pliny records the public prayers made annually at the New Year, on behalf of the Princeps, throughout the Empire. In Epp. 52–53 and 102–3 he records the *vota* and the oath taken annually on the emperor's *dies imperii*, 28 January (Ep. 1 pref.). In Epp. 88–89 he congratulates Trajan privately on his birthday, 18 September, the second time since his arrival, cf. Ep. 17A. 2. These ceremonial letters provide fixed points for the chronology of the letters, if these are in serial order, as is argued in Introduction, pp. 529 f. If Epp. 35 and 52 belong to a single month, Pliny must have been very active in his first January, visiting Nicomedia, Nicaea, Byzantium, and Apamea (Epp. 37, 39, 43, 47), though the visit to Claudiopolis was before the New Year (Ep. 33. 1 n., 39, 5), and he may not yet have gone to Apamea (Ep. 47 pref.).

sollemnia vota pro incolumitate tua qua publica salus continetur et suscepimus, domine, pariter et solvimus. Vows or prayers for the well-being of the emperor and his family were made, *suscepta, nuncupata*, and paid, *soluta*, annually at Rome on 3 January, by the Senate, the pontifical college, and other priesthoods, and by the proconsuls and legates in the provinces. Plut. *Cic.* 2. 1; Dio 59. 24. 6, the *Feriale Duranum*, and Arval *Acta* (*ILS* 5033–4) give the date. These vows are described somewhat vaguely in *Pan.* 67. 3–68. 5. The records of the Arvals frequently minute the ceremonies of the *vota*, and preserve the formula of the prayer *pro incolumitate* used in the Flavian period. For the ceremonies see *D–S* v. 971 ff. The contractual nature of the prayer appears clearly: 'cum di ... propitiato numine suo vota orbis terrarum quae pro salute imperatoris ... suscepta erant exaudierunt, convenire collegio priora solvere et nova nuncupare'. The discovery of epigraphical fragments in Cyrene and Ptolemais has shown rather surprisingly that the formula of the vows used in the provinces was identical with that of the Arval Brothers. Cf. J. M. Reynolds, *BSR* xxx. 33 f. Evidently Epp. 35 and 100 mark 3 January and not New Year's Day.

It is doubtful whether an oath of loyalty was also taken in the provinces on 1 or 3 January at this period. Pliny mentions such an oath only in connexion with the ceremonies of the *dies imperii*, 28 January (Ep. 52 pref.). The evidence about the January oaths is slightly confusing for the first century A.D. Dio makes it plain in several passages that at Rome the Senate swore an oath *in acta Caesarum*, to uphold the *acta* of the living and the dead Augusti on 1 January. To this oath Gaius added the different oath of personal loyalty, connected originally with the *dies imperii* and the succession (Ep. 52 n.). But Claudius restored the pre-Gaian usage. Dio 57. 8. 4–5; 58. 17. 1–3; 59. 9. 1–3, 13. 1; 60. 10. 1–2, 25. 1–2. Tacitus, like Dio, refers to the oath in *acta* alone in *Ann.* 1. 72. 1, 4. 42, 13. 11. 1, 16. 22. 1. But an oath of loyalty was taken by the provincial armies regularly in the pre-Flavian period on 1 January: Tac. *Hist.* 1. 55. 1. Pliny in *Pan.* 68. 4 refers to this briefly in the midst of his account of the ceremonies of 3 January in 100 at Rome: 'scis tibi ubique iurari cum ipse iuraveris', where he conflates a reference to the senatorial oath *in acta Caesarum*, which alone Trajan himself could take, with one to the provincial oaths of loyalty (*ubique*). Epp. 35, 100 are wrongly combined with Epp. 52, 102 by the authors of 'Feriale Cumanum' (*Yale Cl. Stud.* vii. 65 f.) for the taking of oaths at the New Year. They have no such statement. Equally Tertullian, *de cor. mil.* 12, a century later refers only to *vota publica* of provincial armies and populace at the New Year: 'annua vota nuncupata prima in principiis . . . secunda in capitoliis'. Hence it seems that Trajan dropped the New Year oaths of loyalty after A.D. 100, and conflated them with those of his *dies imperii* four weeks later. But at Rome it is probable that there never was a New Year oath other than the Senate's oath *in acta*, except under Gaius.

There is further obscurity in Pliny's account in *Pan.* 67–68, which does not affect the above argument. He seems to pass from a description of Trajan's entry into office and his speech to the Senate on 1 January (66. 2) to the taking of the *vota* by the Senate on 3 January (67. 3), without explanation. It has even been suggested that ch. 68 is describing the ceremonies of 28 January, the *dies imperii*. See *Lustrum*, vi (1961), 291, for a summary of opinions. But it is possible that the *vota* of the Senate, as distinct from those of the priestly colleges, took place on 1 January, not 3 January. Dio 59. 24. 5 speaks of prayers for the Princeps taken on 1 January, though ibid. 6 he calls 3 January 'the day of prayers'. This seems to be the only evidence for the date of the Senate's prayers, outside the *Pan.*, in which Pliny seems to be talking about a single day, not two days: cf. 66. 2 and 68. 2.

suscepimus. The plural in these formal letters refers to Pliny's staff and to the municipal authorities present at the ceremony; cf. Trajan's reply: 'cum provincialibus'. In Ep. 88 Pliny uses the singular for his private greetings on Trajan's birthday.

signari. The record of the vow was sealed and kept, to be exactly paid the next year (*solvimus*).

36. To Pliny

et solvisse vos cum provincialibus dis immortalibus vota. At the next renewal, Epp. 100–1, soldiers take part. Here they are absent. The ceremonies at which Pliny presided evidently took place at Nicomedia, the capital, mentioned in Epp. 34 and 37, possibly at a meeting of the provincial council, composed of civic deputies. For this see VII. 6. 1 n.

37. To Trajan

Date. Between 3 January and 27 January, second year.

1. **in aquae ductum domine Nicomedenses impenderunt HS $\overline{\text{XXX}}$ $\overline{\text{CCCXVIII}}$, qui imperfectus adhuc †relictus ac etiam destructus† est. rursus in alium ductum erogata sunt $\overline{\text{CC}}$. hoc quoque relicto novo impendio est opus ut aquam habeant.** In the doubtful phrase the Bodleian copy (I) reads *emissum* (and *emissus*) *destructus etiam est.* From this Schuster produced his *omissus,* quoting Suet. *Claud.* 20. 1— 'ductum aquarum . . . omissum'. That is better than Merrill's *remissus,* for which VII. 27. 8 is no parallel. But compare Ep. 39. 2, where the texts do not vary, 'sitne faciendum an sit relinquendum an etiam destruendum'. The obelized Aldine version may be preferable, though O.C.T. follows I.

Both at the capital Nicomedia and at the great city of Sinope, Ep. 90, there was apparently till Pliny's time no external supply of water. Pliny's schemes for aqueducts at both, and that for a canal at Nicomedia, Epp. 41–42, alone of his building projects are strongly approved by Trajan, s. 3 n. In the rest of Asia Minor, lengthy aqueducts seem to be an introduction of the Roman period, cf. Jones, *GC* 214 f. Even Alexandria Troas, a favoured city, had only wells and cisterns until the time of Hadrian. The technical development of the aqueduct had taken place in Italy, even if some of the architects were Greek; cf. Frontinus *de aquis* I. 4–8, 16. This may be one reason for the persistent failure of the Nicomedian architects, s. 3 n. Dio of Prusa, on his return from Rome, built 'waters' for his native city, *Or.* 45. 12, and Hadrian was apparently responsible for a great *aqua* at Nicaea. (*Ist. Forsch.* 9, inscr. 10, 18.) Even in the later empire the provision of a regular water supply had the interest of novelty in the East, cf. Libanius, *Or* 11. 246–7, Aelius Aristides 17. 11 (K.).

The earlier visitors to Izmit found the remains of ancient drainage channels, including a water channel in the hills to the north of the city, which might be Pliny's duct, and also a large reservoir, but no aqueduct inside the city earlier than the Turkish period. (Texier, *Description de l'Asie Mineure*, Paris, 1839, i. 18; cf. Solch, *Klio* 19, 169.) But Dörner found the remains of baths and water channels, of the third century, in a building site within the ancient city (*Arch. Anzeiger* 1939, 163 f., figs. 27–32). The statement of Libanius about the abundance of water supplies in the late Empire at Nicomedia is thus borne out. (Or. 61. 7, 18; cf. Vidman, *Étude*, 78–79.)

Water was brought by the ducts to *castella* and delivered thence to public *lacus* and *nymphaea*; house-supply was the height of luxury (Jones, loc. cit.). The care of the mains was a public service under the *curator aquarum* at Rome, whose functions are described in detail by Frontinus in his book. In the municipalities the duty was often a liturgy if not done by magistrates, *Dig.* 50. 4. 18. 6. But the distribution of water from the mains, by *rivi, canales*, and *fistulae*, was made by private enterprise under the control, at Rome, not of imperial regulations but of the civil law; cf. *Dig.* 43. 21. 1. 39–43 and ib. 3. 4 on a rule of the praetorian edict which applied 'sive in publico sive in privato sunt constituti rivi (omnes)'. State or municipal action was necessary for building and maintaining the great ducts, but distribution remained in private hands even at Rome. The officials of the *cura aquarum* simply licensed the owners of the distributaries to draw water from the mains, cf. Frontinus, op. cit. 2. 103. 105–6. At Nicaea a schedule of regulations protects the new aqueduct of Hadrian under the sanction of fines (*Ist. Forsch.* 9 n. 10).

HS. The sums are considerable but not enormous. The S.200,000 was, as Hardy suggested, for a first instalment of the second work. Compare the aqueduct at Troas that cost seven million drachmas in the time of Hadrian—nearly ten times the cost of the first effort here. Friedlaender, *SG* (Eng. tr.), ii. 253.

2. videtur aqua debere perduci . . . erat arcuato opere ne tantum ad plana civitatis et humilia perveniat. Hardy criticised Pliny for not knowing, as his uncle knew (*NH.* xxxi. 57), that water in a closed pipe finds its own level. But if the water channel was open Pliny would be right. By maintaining the level on elevated ducts the engineers avoided the problem of high pressure within the pipes. So Frontinus, who understood hydraulics (op. cit. 1. 35), says that arcading was used to bring the Anio Vetus to the higher parts of Rome, 1. 18–19.

possunt et erigi quidam lapide quadrato qui ex superiore opere detractus est ; aliqua pars operis ut mihi videtur testaceo opere agenda erit. Hardy supposed that Pliny refers to the facing of the arches only, which normally, as in Ep. 39. 4, 'caemento . . . farti . . . testaceo opere praecincti', have a concrete core (Frontinus, op. cit. 2. 123), though at Rome all the piers were of solid stonework within the seventh milestone, ibid. 124. More likely plain brickwork is meant here. In either case this is an example of the spread of Roman technique through official guidance; cf. Ep. 39. 4 n.

3. necessarium est mitti a te vel aquilegem vel architectum ne rursus eveniat quod accidit. Trajan ignores this request, which he refuses in Epp. 18, 3 and 40. 3; though he promises experts for the canal work in Ep. 42, he withdraws the promise in Ep. 62 (n.). The local architects lacked experience in the peculiar problems of aqueducts, of which Frontinus (op. cit. 2. 119) drily remarks: 'non semper opus aut facere aut ampliare credentibus credendum est'.

aquilegem. The normal meaning of this term at this period seems to be water-diviner, *Thes. L.L.* s.v.; e.g. Pliny *NH* 26. 30. Sen. *Q. Nat.* 3. 15. 7. But Pliny evidently means a water engineer, as does Tarrutenus in a list of craftsmen (*Dig.* 50. 6. 7). Cf. *CIL* ii. 5726.

adfirmo et utilitatem operis et pulchritudinem saeculo tuo esse dignissimam. Cf. similar remarks in Epp. 23. 2, 41. 1, 90. 2 nn. This appears to be a request for approval. Unlike the projects in Ep. 39 a virtually new building is required here, and hence permission is sought. Cf. Ep. 23. 1 n.

38. To Pliny

credo te ea qua debebis diligentia hoc opus adgressurum. This *diligentia* is a virtue of the age, cf. Frontinus, *de aquis* 2. 89. Epp. 20. 2, 42, 78. 2 *et al.*

sed medius fidius ad eandem diligentiam tuam pertinet inquirere quorum vitio ad hoc tempus tantam pecuniam Nicomedenses perdiderint. This characteristic outburst must be attributed to Trajan himself, and not to the prosy clerk who penned such efforts as Epp. 30, 32, 78, 117, 119. So too Epp. 32. 1, 57. 2, 82. 1, 97. 2, and possibly 40. 1, 55 *ad fin.*, 111 *ad fin.*, and 119 *ad fin.* should be Trajanic, though style alone is not a safe guide for distinguishing routine answers from Trajan's own interventions. See Introduction, pp. 536 f. The letter ending has a chancellery ring; cf. Epp. 67. 2, 86B. 2, for the term *in notitiam perferre*. Yet here, as in Ep. 57. 2, the injunction is superfluous, since Pliny was armed with full powers.

dum. Gronovius' emendation of *cum* in the prototypes is required by sense. Cf. Ep. 39. 6: 'ne dum servare volumus quod impensum est, male impendamus quod addendum est'.

quorum vitio. The real weakness lay in the constitutional arrangements. The control over the execution of building contracts depended upon the efficiency of the checking of the *ratio operis* submitted by the *curator operum* to whom supervision of the contract was entrusted, as in Ep. 81. 1 (n.) Cf. 17B. 2 n. But this depended upon the honesty of the city councils of which the *curatores* were themselves members. Since the councillors were life-members closely connected with the annual magistrates (Ep. 79. 1-3 nn.) who should initiate objections and inquiries, it was inevitable, in the absence of democratic counterchecks, that collusion prevailed. This appears clearly in the affair of Dio's *cura* in Ep. 81, and in his own account of the malpractices of other curators (ibid. nn.).

perfer in notitiam meam. Here and in Epp. 40. 1, 57. 1 Trajan requests or promises information which does not appear in the Letters. Possibly the letters were omitted by the compilers, if not lost, if they were ever written, which Vidman doubts. (Introduction, pp. 533 f.; *Étude*, 35.)

39. *To Trajan*

Date. Between 3 January and 27 January, second year.

From Nicaea or Claudiopolis, named in the letter, or from Nicomedia, whence Epp. 37 and 41 derive.

This letter, with Ep. 49, differs from other reports to Trajan about building projects in that Pliny is not seeking approval for new construction. The three buildings were under way or half finished before Pliny's appointment. Hence there was no need for imperial sanction under the new rule which required it for municipal works, Ep. 23. 1 n. The purpose of Pliny's long report was to reinforce his request for the dispatch of a technician from Rome, since Trajan had refused or ignored his earlier requests in Epp. 18. 3 and 37. 3.

1. theatrum domine Nicaeae . . . sestertium (ut audio ; neque enim ratio †plus† excussa est) amplius centies hausit. The building, which eats up thrice the cost of the Nicomedian aqueduct (Ep. 37. 1), seems from its elaborate appendages, s. 3 n., to have been in the Roman style, in which the auditorium and the stage buildings were united into a continuous D-shaped block, like the theatre at Aspendus built later in the century. Robertson, *Handbook of Greek and Roman Architecture*, 271 ff. It or a successor survives, ruined and hardly excavated, built of stone and *opus incertum*, and measuring 80 metres in full width. C. Texier, op. cit. (Ep. 37. 1), 47-48; T.-Rice, *Antiquity*, iii. 63; A. M. Schneider, *Ist. Forsch.* xvi (1943), figs. 2-3, pp. 8-9.

plus. This reading, retained by Schuster, is meaningless. Yet the general sense is clear—Pliny had not yet audited the account. Mueller's *operis* is sensible, which O.C.T. prints, while *eius* might be more plausible still. Or the syllable might be deleted as an intrusion from the following *amplius*. The sense requires something like *adhuc*.

2. **ingentibus enim rimis desedit et hiat, sive in causa . . . lapis ipse gracilis.** The theatre, like that at Aspendus, was of stone, not concrete. No such cracks are visible in the surviving structure, which doubtless succeeded this. Pliny does not suggest that earthquakes were responsible, though Nicaea is in the quaking zone of Turkey. His informants should have known if it were so. Hence the fault lies with the architect.

fulturae ac substructiones . . . non tam firmae mihi quam sumptuosae videntur. He means the lower arcades that carried the terraces of seats. Perhaps the architect was attempting in stone a grandiose scheme better suited to Roman concrete, s. 3 n. Vitruvius 5. 3. 3 remarks on the danger of subsidence when theatres are built on marshy sites, and the need for extensive *substructiones*.

3. **huic theatro . . . multa debentur, ut basilicae circa, ut porticus supra caveam.** The *porticus* must be a colonnaded way round the topmost semicircle of the auditorium (*cavea*) as in the Aspendus theatre. Vitruvius 5. 6. 4 also refers to the use of a *porticus in summa gradatione*. It would be fed by the usual series of corridors at different levels interconnected by staircases; Robertson, op. cit. 276 ff. The reference to *basilicae* is odd. These properly were large covered halls, and no part of a theatre; op. cit. 267, cf. v. 9. 1. Pompey's theatre at Rome was served by the Porticus Pompeii as a public shelter, which was a colonnaded square not unlike a basilica in design; Ashby, *Top. Dict. Rome*, s.v. Something similar might be meant. But *circa* then must mean *circa theatrum*, not *circa caveam*.

pollicitationibus. See Ep. 40. 1 n.

4. **Nicaeenses gymnasium incendio amissum ante adventum meum restituere coeperunt.** According to Strabo, xii, p. 566, the gymnasium lay at the centre of the rectangular walled city of Nicaea, as a principal feature. Nothing survives except possibly the traces of a monumental gateway. Schneider, art. cit. 9 n. 2, pl. 4 *b*.

In Hellenistic cities the *gymnasium* was a complex of changing-rooms, exercise rooms, lecture halls, and porticoes around an open space, which acted as a wrestling ground and running track. The whole was used for the athletic and intellectual pursuits that formed a large part of Hellenistic culture; Vitruvius 5. 11; Jones, *GC* 220 ff. and nn.; Magie, *Romans* 62 n. 36, 652 n. 55. Some cities possessed several such entities. Something unusually elaborate was intended at Nicaea. But Pliny's adjectives show that the plan was for an interconnected group of buildings rather than a single pile: 'laxius . . . incompositum . . . et sparsum', numerosius. To contain more people, cf. Ep. 40. 2, 'quod possit illis sufficere'.

praeterea architectus sane aemulus ... adfirmat parietes quamquam viginti et duos pedes latos imposita onera sustinere non posse quia sint caemento medii farti nec testaceo opere praecincti. It is hard to understand why the buildings of a *gymnasium* required so vast a wall. Such a group should need only a narrow precinct-wall, and the individual halls should be of no immensity, unless, as was sometimes done, the *gymnasium* included *thermae*. But that is not stated. Presumably the wall is to carry a barrel vault—it is too early for great domes in Asia Minor. If the text is sound the principal building must be meant, but the breadth—22 Roman feet—exceeds even that of the wall of the Pantheon at Rome, which carried a dome of 141 feet span on a wall of 20·3 feet. The Roman 'palace of Domitian' had walls only 10 feet wide to carry a vault spanning 105 feet. Robertson, op. cit. 245, 249; Ashby, op. cit. 382 f. The arches of the outer wall of the Flavian amphitheatre were not more than 8·8 feet thick, ibid. 7. For a large *gymnasium* of the second century see F. Miltner, *Ephesus* (Wien, 1958), p. 76–77.

The reference to *caementum*—which means the filling material of roughcut stone, not the mortar (Vitruvius 2. 5. 3, 7. 1, 8. 1–3)—and to a brick facing indicate that the construction is in Roman concrete. As Pliny does not mention the mortar filling, it could be that the walls, presumably of stone, were filled with unmortared rubble, but the reference to *opus testaceum* would then lose its point. The language recalls Vitruvius 2. 4. 3, discussing the effect of weak mortar: 'non possunt contineri caementa sed ea ruunt et labuntur oneraque parietes non possunt sustinere'. The rival architect's criticism betrays ignorance of the principles of Roman construction; cf. Robertson, op. cit. 232 f.: 'The mixture was so strong that the external facing could be omitted or reduced to a mere studding of the surface with stone or brick.' This man thinks that the brick bonding is necessary to hold the mass together, within an outer facing of stone (*medii farti*). The original architect must have been very timid to design so thick a wall—even if the text is altered to *duodecim pedes*. It seems from this letter, as also from Ep. 37 about the aqueduct, that the Roman techniques were new to the Bithynian architects, who were making bad mistakes in applying them. A triumphal arch in the Roman style and good Greek stonework was built at Nicaea in the time of Vespasian, which survives. (A. M. Schneider, *Istanbuler Forschungen*, 'Die Stadtmauer von Iznik', ix. 24, pl. 18, Inscr. 45 n. 11.) It contrasts magnificently with the walls in late Roman and Byzantine brick and concrete. That Roman methods should be coming into use in Asia Minor at this period fits with the general picture of Graeco-Roman cultural relations. This is the age of Plutarch's *Quaestiones Romanae*, and of the admission of Asiatic Greeks to the equestrian order and even the Senate, VI. 19. 4 n. The Greeks were also acquiring the Roman taste for gladiators (L. Robert, *Les Gladiateurs dans l'Orient grec* (Paris, 1940), 263 f.). The Roman colonies of Asia Minor, such as Sinope and Apamea, Epp. 47, 90, are the probable local source of these influences.

viginti et duos pedes latos. Even if the numeral is corrupt the difficulty remains, since Pliny insists on the great width. The lowest reasonable correction would be from XXII to XII. Hartleben's drastic reduction to *duos* does not meet the context.

caemento medii farti nec testaceo opere praecincti. Is this whole sentence in its right place? Neither Pliny himself, nor Trajan in his reply, raises doubts about the strength of the structure, though Trajan deals briefly with every other point raised in Ep. 39. This sentence might have been transposed from the end of s. 2, and refer to the theatre. It would fit that context as confirmation of Pliny's own view by an expert if biased witness: the outer walls, though thick, are criticized (wrongly) as merely decorative because there is no brick binding behind the stone surfacing. It would then seem that the theatre was a stone building with a concrete core. The *parietes* would be the great outer wall of the complex of internal passages and arcades supported on the *substructiones* of s. 2. The only other letter where the order of sentences may be suspected is Ep. 41. 2 n.

The topic requires local archaeological investigation. For Roman concrete see N. Davey, *A History of Building Materials* (London, 1961), 120 f. H. Plommer, *Ancient and Classical Architecture* (London, 1956), 290 f.

5. Claudiopolitani quoque in depresso loco, imminente etiam monte, ingens balineum defodiunt magis quam aedificant. Pliny does not criticize the structure, only the site; cf. Ep. 40. 3, 'parum . . . idoneo loco'. Here too the city architect seems to be under Roman influence. As at Prusa (Ep. 24) something more grandiose than a bath of Greek style was required by the spirit of the age. For the elaboration in Italy of the Roman *thermae* out of Greek elements see Robertson, op. cit. 243. The Romans had combined the threefold bath—*frigidarium, tepidarium, caldarium*—with a *palaestra* and colonnades, elements of the Greek gymnasium, to form a complex whole. At Prusias ad Hypium a thermal establishment built out of funds left by a military tribune may have been in the new style; *IGRR* iii. 56, 66; Magie, op. cit. 590 n. 61.

Claudiopolis, modern Bolu, formerly Bithynium, was founded by a Bithynian king at an uncertain date, as the civic centre of the

fertile plain of Salona. It was technically a 'city' in the Republican
period, and has at this time a council, while other civic institutions
are named in inscriptions of the Hadrianic period and later, including
tribes, 'Great Claudian Games', and gymnasiarchs: F. K. Dörner,
Reise in Bithynien, nn. 83–84, 134, and 74 (after A.D. 212). Hence the
doubts of Magie about its status are void. No other commune is
mentioned in the Letters that is not a full 'city'. For what reason it
took the title Claudiopolis—which also implies civic rank—and held
Claudian Games is unknown. (Strabo xii, p. 505; Pliny *NH* 5. 149;
Jones, *Cities*, 151, 160 f.; Magie, *Romans*, 307 n. 22. Dörner, op. cit.
32 f., describes the territory and its antiquities.)

The hot springs discovered an hour's journey to the south of Bolu,
with no trace of ancient structures, may be the site of the civic baths,
but despite similarities of topography and the approval of modern
scholars, the buildings in this Letter seem all to be inside the towns.
A site by the acropolis of Bolu is more likely. (Cf. Dörner, op. cit.
32 n. 6; Vidman, *Étude* 82.)

**ex ea pecunia quam buleutae additi beneficio tuo . . . obtulerunt ob
introitum . . . conferent.** For the recent introduction into Bithynia of
the Italian *honorarium decurionatus*, and for the increase of the size
of the councils, see Ep. 112. 1 n. The payment amounted to S.4,000
or S.8,000. and was regarded as optional.

**cogor petere a te non solum ob theatrum verum etiam ob haec
balinea mittas architectum dispecturum.** This is the whole point of
the letter. Pliny had not asked for the advice which Trajan gives,
and did not use any of the customary formulas for taking advice,
such as *dispice an* (17B. 2, 33. 3) *rogo consilio me regas* (19. 1), or
quid debeam sequi rogo . . . scribas (29). Equally he has not used a
formula for requesting building permission, such as *videris indulgere
posse* (23. 1).

balinea. A true plural covering the gymnasium of Nicaea and the
baths of Claudiopolis. Cf. Ep. 23. 1, 70. 1, 3; II. 17. 26, 'balinea tria'.

40. *To Pliny*

1. **in re praesenti optime deliberabis et constitues. mihi sufficiet
indicari cui sententiae accesseris.** This kind of remark is absent from
the other replies about building, where new projects are concerned
(Epp. 24, 38, 62, 91, 99). No such report of Pliny survives, so that a
loss or omission may be suspected, or neglect on Pliny's part. Cf.
Ep. 38, 'perfer' n. and pp. 533 f.

**tunc autem a privatis exige opera cum theatrum propter quod illa
promissa sunt factum erit.** This corresponds to Ep. 39. 3, but Trajan's
advice is otiose. Pliny said nothing about pressing these donors at

Nicaea, but had suggested pressing the decurions of Claudiopolis, ibid. 5. Trajan or his secretary has been inattentive, as in Ep. 69. For his impatience see Ep. 48. 1 n.

exige opera. Rules were gradually established that made such promises enforceable in some circumstances. The first step was taken by Trajan; Pomponius, *Dig.* 50. 12. 14: 'si quis sui . . . honoris causa opus facturum se in aliqua civitate promiserit, ad perficiendum . . . ex constitutione divi Traiani obligatus est'. This recalls Trajan's extension to Bithynia of the *honorarium decurionatus*, Ep. 39. 5, 112. 1 n. The Aldine gives *exigi opera tibi curae sit*. The Bodleian copy reads *operactum* in place of the last four words. Hardy suggested 'exigere opera tempus cum'. Better simplify to 'exige opera cum'. Trajan occasionally uses the imperative to Pliny, even in clear chancellery style. Cf. Epp. 38. 2, 62, 76.

2. gymnasiis indulgent Graeculi. Surely another Trajanism. The tone is patronizing. Compare Juvenal's attack on the *Graeculus esuriens* 3. 66 ff., esp. 114–15, 'et quoniam coepit Graecorum mentio, transi gymnasia'. The attitude, echoed by Tacitus, *Hist.* 3. 47, 'desidiam licentiamque Graecorum', was traditional; cf. Livy 9. 18. 6, 36. 17. 5. *Auctor de bello Alexandrino* 15. 1. Cf. Sherwin-White, *RC* 255. Yet Trajan admitted some Greeks to the Senate, VI. 19. 4 n.

3. architecti tibi deesse non possunt. Cf. Epp. 18. 3, 62. Trajan again misses the cautious Pliny's point, that he cannot trust the local men, who were involved in the civic factions (Ep. 39. 4 'aemulus'). He needs the comfort of an independent opinion. Oddly, Bithynia provides several instances, elsewhere rare, of architects' names in building inscriptions, thus bearing out Trajan's remark. L. Robert, *REA*, xlii. 315 n. 12.

ex Graecia etiam ad nos venire soliti sint. Hardy quotes the discussion of Friedlaender (*SG*, Eng. tr., ii. 324 f.) to the effect that architects with Latin names were numerous amongst those used by emperors; e.g. Severus and Celer used by Nero, Rabirius by Domitian. But Trajan for his great schemes at Rome used Apollodorus of Damascus. The Roman army also had its own *architecti* attached to each legion, who were responsible for many engineering works throughout the Empire, such as bridges, aqueducts, and stone camps; and these were more than jobbing builders. Cf. Domaszewski, *Rangordnung*, 25.

41. *To Trajan*

Date. Between 3 January and 28 January, second year.

The topic of this letter is continued in Ep. 61.

1. opera . . . quantum . . . pulchritudinis tantum utilitatis habitura.

For the phraseology cf. Ep. 37. 3. The bait was well cast. Trajan was a great builder of the useful as well as of the beautiful, e.g. VI. 31. 15 n.

aeternitate tua. Cf. Epp. 59, 83, 112. 3. The term *a. Augusti* is on the coins: *RIC* ii, p. 250 etc.

2. est in Nicomedensium finibus amplissimus lacus. per hunc marmora fructus ligna materiae . . . usque ad viam navibus inde . . . vehiculis ad mare devehuntur. The city lies at the head of the narrow gulf of Izmid, with a fine natural harbour. The western end of Sabanja Göl or Lake Sophon, called *Sunonensis* in Ammianus (26. 8. 3), is some 18 miles to the east. This lake drains north-east to the Euxine, not to the gulf, by a tributary of the Sangarius, called anciently the Melas, now the Tshach Su. Pliny's project is to link the upper end of the lake by canal to a navigable river flowing into the gulf, reversing its natural outlet, and so provide a waterway for the trade of the hinterland to its market centre. This emerges eventually from s. 4: 'fossam . . . ad committendum flumini lacum'. But as the text stands Pliny's meaning only becomes clear with the help of Ep. 61. Scholars have suggested that there is a lacuna after the present sentence. But the trouble may be healed by a transposition of s. 4 (n.). The absurdity of the suggestion of Soelch (*Klio* xix. 169 f.) that the Ascanias lake in the territory of Nicaea was meant, has been shown by F. G. Moore, 'Three Canal Projects, etc.', *Am. J. Arch.* liv. 110. The topography of Ascanias in no way fits Pliny's description (despite L-H ad loc.).

marmora fructus ligna materiae. The timber and marble came from the foothills north and south of the lake, and the crops from the well-watered lowlands between the Sangarius and the gulf. Xeno-phon, *Anab.* 6. 4. 6, names ship-timber, grapes, and cereals as the products of the northern part of this region in his day. Strabo is less specific (12. 4. 7, 8. 8). The olive, which flourishes in the plain of Prusa, was rare: *Ec. Survey*, iv. 602 f., 611 f.; *Admiralty Geog. Handbook of Turkey*, ii. 143 f. All these materials were for export: 'ad mare'. Dio, *Or.* 38. 32, emphasizes the position of Nicomedia as a regional entrepôt.

ad viam navibus inde magno labore maiore impendio vehiculis. The economic advantage of water over road transport in antiquity has seldom been more clearly expressed. The great Roman roads did little to diminish the cost of wheeled transport. Yet the road transit here, along the first section of the highway from Nicomedia to Ancyra, was a mere 20 miles over level plain. Magie, op. cit., 304 n. 11. For the southern branch of this route through Juliopolis see Ep. 77. 3.

hoc opus multas manus poscit. at eae porro non desunt. The *opus* is left obscure. Hence Ernesti suggested the insertion of 'itaque mari committere cupiunt' before *hoc opus*. Rather more is in fact wanted. Possibly Pliny has simply failed to cope with the common difficulty of explaining a geographical situation without maps, though elsewhere his topographical explanations are excellent, e.g. v. 6. 7–13, VIII. 8, IX. 33. 2. Trajan in his brief reply refers to nothing which is not in the present text, and has made sense of it. See s. 4 n.

manus. The problem is one of excavation rather than construction. So Pliny deals with the question of labour rather than that of expense. He expects the work to be done by a municipal corvée. Usually municipal works were undertaken by contractors, Ep. 81. 1 n. But the use of direct labour, *operae*, is known from the western provinces in the charter of Urso c. 98 (*ILS* 6087). This allows the municipality to exact five days' work, and the service of wagons for three days a year, from adults between the ages of 14 and 60 for any *munitio*. Much more would be needed to dig a canal. Liebenam, *Städteverwaltung*, 402 nn. 2–3, 423, gives other examples.

This scheme is not for military purposes, and certainly not intended to help in Trajan's Parthian campaigns. Pliny says nothing about military supplies using the canal, and Trajan did not initiate the scheme. See Ep. 63. 1 n.

et in agris magna copia est hominum et maxima in civitate. By *civitas* Pliny means not the body of citizens, the properly classical meaning, but the urban centre—*città*—as the contrast with *agris* shows. This secondary meaning preponderates in Book x. Cf. Epp. 34. 1 n., 38. 1, 70. 1, 78. 1, 81. 3, 96. 9, 98, 99. *Thes. L.L.* s.v. Evidently the capital city collected an excessive population.

agris. The obscure life of the villagers in Bithynia has been illuminated by a series of inscriptions from the territory of Nicomedia recording the biennial festivals of certain rural communes with non-Greek names, such as Gauriani, Baiteni, Zbaleni. These had local officers called ἐπιμελητής, ἔκδικος, γραμματεύς, like the *magistri pagi* of the Gallic provinces, but more complicated, and forming a *cursus honorum*. F. K. Dörner, *Inschriften . . . aus Bithynia*, nn. 31–33. In certain tomb inscriptions of this area fines for violation are payable to the village (κώμη) instead of to the city, ibid. nn. 78, 81.

3. superest ut tu libratorem vel architectum si tibi videbitur mittas. So, when a water-tunnel went astray at Numidian Saldae a *librator* was summoned from the staff of the African legion to set things right, *ILS* 5795. This request, as in Ep. 39. 6, is a main point of Pliny's letter, though in this case he also needs official sanction for new construction work, Ep. 23. 1 n. For the technique of the *librator* see Vitruvius 8. 5.

altior. Above sea-level. Since Pliny was proposing to reverse the drainage system, the new cut might have a much steeper gradient than the natural outflow by the Sangarius tributary. The lake is today about 120 feet, twice Pliny's estimate, above sea-level. The gradient along the level plain to the sea is very slight, but the lake is separated by a low col from the plain. Hence the doubts (*Admiralty Handbook of Turkey*, i. 105). Pliny's device for dealing with the problem emerges in Ep. 61. 4.

4. ego per eadem loca invenio fossam a rege percussam, sed incertum utrum ad colligendum umorem circumiacentium agrorum an ad committendum flumini lacum. More obscurity. What are the *loca*? If ss. 4–5 were transferred to follow the first part of s. 2, after 'ad mare devehuntur', sense would emerge. The *loca* would be those of the *via* between *lacus* and *mare*, in the immediate context. Pliny's main plan would appear with reasonable clarity. The *opus* of s. 2 would gain a precise meaning, and the *superest* of s. 3 would be used more appropriately for the concluding request of the letter, as in Ep. 112. 3. In Epp. 37. 3 and 39. 6 the similar request for technical aid is kept to the end, after the reason for it has been given. In its present place s. 4 seems otiose, obscurely explaining the possibility of the drainage scheme from the previous attempt.

Nothing is known of this canal, which dates back to the regal period before 75 B.C. Hardy thought that the lake was in the nineteenth century connected with the Gulf of Izmid and with the Sangarius, and that this might be the result of Pliny's work. But he seems to have been misled by bad maps, according to Moore, art. cit. 110 n. 54. Magie (588 n. 57) quotes E. Naumann, *Vom Goldnen Horn zu den Quellen d. Euphrates* (Munich, 1893), 27 f., for similar projects. Moore connects the ruins of a great bridge over the Melas, and a notice in Procopius, *de aedificiis* 5. 3. 8–10, of Justinian's proposal to bridge the Sangarius, with a scheme to divert the Sangarius itself to the Gulf. Anna Comnena, *Alexiad*, 10. 5 B–C, reports a great dyke in the territory of Nicomedia near a Lake Banaa, attributed to Anastasius. But this can hardly be the remnants of Pliny's scheme.

42. *To Pliny*

potest nos sollicitare lacus iste ut committere illum mari velimus, sed plane explorandum est diligenter ne si emissus in mare fuerit totus effluat. None of the readings of the early editors—*dimissus, demissus, immissus*—is satisfactory. Pliny thrice uses parts of *emissus* in the required sense in Ep. 61. 2, 'lacus . . . in flumen emitti', and ibid. 3 and 4, probably echoing this letter. The Aldine reading may have arisen from the proximity of *in mare*, producing *immissus*, corrected subsequently to *dimissus*. It is odd that no editor has made this obvious suggestion.

nos. Simply 'you and me', rather than 'me and mine', or the administrative 'we', as in Epp. 32. 1, 78. 2 n.

poteris a Calpurnio Macro petere libratorem. For Macer see Epp. 61. 5, 77. 1. Addressed in v. 18 and probably vi. 24 nn., he is P. Calpurnius Macer Caulius Rufus, suffect consul in 103, and named in documents of 112–13 as legate of Moesia Inferior, the nearest armed province to Bithynia, since Thrace lacked legionary troops. *CIL* iii. 777, xvi. 58; *AE*, 1954, n. 223; *PIR²* C 273. He is a Cisalpine, but not of Comum, according to vi. 24. 5 n. The reference to Macer provides the only direct evidence for the date of Pliny's mission.

hinc aliquem . . . mittam. Trajan tacitly withdraws this offer in Ep. 62. It is notable that Trajan makes no proviso about expense as in Epp. 24, 91, 99.

43. *To Trajan*

Date. Between 3 January and 28 January, second year.

1. requirenti mihi Byzantiorum reipublicae impendia quae maxima fecit. The position of Byzantium, which lies across the Bosporus from Chalcedon, is in the provincial system peculiar. Its province was not Thrace—a kingdom till Claudius—but Bithynia, where it owned lands around L. Dascylitis, Strabo xii, p. 576. When Trajan reorganized Thrace as a praetorian legateship, between 106 and 114, it was left under Bithynia. (Jones, op. cit. 18 f.; *RE* (2) vi. 454; A. Stein, *Röm. Reichsbeamten des p. Thracia*, 10.) Apparently it had the beneficial status of a *civitas libera* in the early Principate and under Nero, though not under Claudius, and was again reduced to provincial status by Vespasian; Tac. *Ann.* 12. 62–63; Pliny, *NH* 4. 46; Suet. *Vesp.* 8. 4; Jones, *Cities*, 164, 556.

quae maxima. The qualification, with *memor propositi tui* below, casts a little light on Pliny's method and Trajan's instructions, Ep. 18. 3 n. He regards sums of S.3,000 (s. 3) and upwards as coming under this heading. Cf. Ep. 110, where D.40,000 is at stake. His instructions are to deal with major expenses and reduce them without impairing local efficiency (s. 2).

legatum ad te salutandum. To answer these formal letters of goodwill with scholarly grace the emperors created the equestrian office of *ab epistulis Graecis et ad responsa Graeca*, commonly held by men of erudition. Dionysius of Alexandria held this post, with the headship of the imperial libraries, from Nero to Trajan, 1. 18 pref.

cum psephismate. Byzantium presumably had the normal Hellenistic style of constitution based on council and assembly. The word
suggests that the latter was less moribund than in the cities subject to
the *Lex Pompeia*, from which Byzantium had been exempt as a
civitas libera, Epp. 79–80 nn.

Jones, *GC* 243, discusses the extent of these missions, which often
had the practical purpose of seeking privileges or redress. Cf. Plut.
Praecepta r.p. gerendae 10 A. Dio *Or.* 40. 13–14; Cassius Dio 52. 30. 9
advised their abolition except in judicial cases, and the substitution
of the governor as an intermediary, as Pliny here proposes. Nicaea
seeks to exploit this example in Ep. 83.

nummorum duodena milia. The *viaticum* was officially allowed,
and is often mentioned in inscriptions, though patriots paid their
own expenses. Vespasian limited such embassies to three persons a
city, throughout the Empire. Jones, *GC* 358 n. 60; *Dig.* 50. 4. 18. 12,
7. 3, 7. 5. 6.

**2. memor . . . propositi tui legatum quidem retinendum psephisma
autem mittendum putavi.** Pliny means, as Trajan understands him
below (*per te*), that he sent the missive by the *cursus publicus*. It was
the lack of a really public postal service that made these expensive
embassies unavoidable, unless the emperor made the imperial post
available, cf. Ep. 45 nn. Only when a claim was being submitted
through the governor could a municipality dispense with the formal
mission to carry its official letters to Rome or elsewhere; cf. Ep. 83,
also, for a Bithynian example, VII. 6. 1: 'provinciae legatus attulit
decretum concilii ad Caesarem'. Hence the office of municipal
emissary was sometimes a compulsory *munus*, *Lex Ursonensis* 92.

propositi tui. Perhaps this is not here used technically for the
mandata principis (Ep. 22. 1 n.) because in Ep. 82. 1 the term is
used by Trajan of his general policy. It indicates his more general
instructions.

3. annua dabantur legato eunti ad eum qui Moesiae praeest. For the
close connexion between the great port of Byzantium and the military
province of Lower Moesia see Epp. 42, 77. 1. Before Thrace became a
province the legate of Moesia would, as Hardy suggested, have been
responsible for the protection of Byzantium.

circumcidenda existimavi. Nowhere else in references to his financial
audit is it suggested that Trajan instructed Pliny to cut down routine
expenditure, cf. Epp. 17A. 3, B. 2, 18. 3, 23. 2, 54. 1.

viatici. Cf. *AE*, 1916, 120, for an emissary of Sinope who thrice
went to Rome on the city's business, to Hadrian and Pius, *sine viatico*.

4. quid sentias rescribendo. The alteration, though petty, affected the
dignity of the emperor; hence Pliny's report. Would any legate have

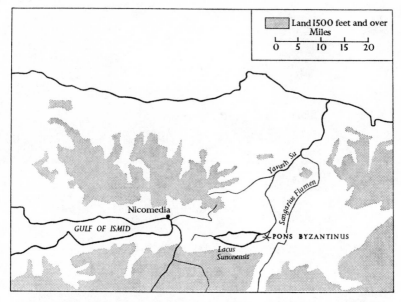

FIG. 2. The setting of Pliny's canal scheme in Epp. 41–42 and 61–62

failed to seek approval? Only twice again does Pliny consult Trajan on a purely financial question, Epp. 54, 118, each time with good reason. (Cf. Introduction, p. 553.) In Epp. 108, 110 the point at issue is constitutional, and in Ep. 110, an appeal against the *mandata*.

44. *To Pliny*

fungentur his partibus, etsi solum psephisma per te missum fuerit. ignoscet illis et Moesiae praeses. The correction of the prototype reading *fungetur* is necessary, as *illis* confirms. Schuster oddly defended the singular, understanding *respublica Byzantiorum* from the previous letter as if they were a continuous composition. To suppose that *psephisma* is the subject is grotesque.

45. *To Trajan*

Date. Between 3 January and 28 January, second year.

diplomata domine quorum dies praeterita an omnino observari et quam diu velis rogo scribas. The courier service, *cursus publicus* or *vehiculatio*, first organized by Augustus, consisted of a series of stations (*mansiones*) along the military highways at which relays of transport were kept by and at the expense of the provincials for the use of officials, soldiers on special duty, and messengers, when properly provided with a ticket or *diploma*. Cf. in general Suet. *Aug.* 49. 3; Dio 79 (78). 11. 3, 39. 3; Ep. 15 n. For users: Epp. 43. 2, 78. 3 nn.; Suet. *Gai.* 44; Tac. *Hist.* 2. 54; tickets: Epp. 64, 120; Plut. *Galba* 8. 4; *OGIS* 665. 25. It was not normally used by private persons, municipalities, or even client kings: Epp. 43, 64, 83, 120 nn. The system was a burden on the communes along the highways, un-equally distributed, like ship-money in seventeenth-century Eng-land. An enigmatic Bithynian inscription of later date connects two soldiers of the unit mentioned in Ep. 106 with the organization of the *mansiones* and the supply of mules from imperial herds. (*AE*, 1955, n. 266.) Otherwise there is little evidence that the government helped in the supply of material, and this inscription may refer to the army remount service (as Rostovtzeff, *BSA* xxii. 12 n. 4).

Emperors from Claudius onwards sought to check abuses, and a series of documents of Claudius, Nero, Vespasian, and Domitian marks their efforts: *ILS* 214; *OGIS* 665 (A-J 51, 163); W-C 457, 466. Nerva and Trajan showed like zeal, *RIC* ii, 'Nerva', n. 93; Victor, *de Caes.* 13. 5–6. There were apparently no controlling officers till the late Flavian period, when freedmen officials of the *vehicula* first appear, *CIL* vi. 8542–3. Hadrian centralized control under a *prae-fectus vehiculorum*, but abuses continued despite attempts to transfer the charges to the Fiscus: SHA *Pius* 12. 3; *Severus* 14. 2; *Dig.* 50. 4. 18. 4. For the general organization see the long article in *Diz. Epigr.* ii. 1405 ff. More briefly, *RE* iv. 1846 f. For recent theories: Magie, *Romans*, 487 n. 56, 628 n. 58; H. G. Pflaum, 'Essai sur le *cursus publicus*', *Mem. Ac. inscr. et b. lettres*, xiv (1940), 189 ff., 217 ff.

dies praeterita. O.C.T. prefers *praeterit*. The document, originally of parchment and later a waxed tablet, was a diptych like the military *diplomata* of discharge, dated by the consular year from Kalends to Kalends, and bearing the name and seal of the issuing emperor; Tac. *Hist.* 2. 54, 65; Suet. *Aug.* 50; Plut. *Galba* 8. 4; *Otho* 3. 2. There must have been a formula of authority 'to the bearer of these presents', or else, as Hardy suggested, the name of the user was added by the issuing officer in a blank space. Ep. 120. 1, 'neque cuiquam diplomata commodavi', suits either explanation. In the later Empire the diploma specified the route to be followed and the vehicles to be used: *Diz. Epig.* loc. cit. 1418. Their validity ended as here indicated, or else at the death of the issuing emperor. In the civil wars of 68–69 governors and consuls issued them independently: Tac. *Hist.* loc. cit., Plut. loc. cit.

Pliny's worry may be due to knowledge of Trajan's special interest in the courier service. He thrice sends reports on special uses of the service, and may have been instructed to do so (Epp. 64, 83, 120).

It is remarkable that no member of Pliny's staff could answer this query which arose when Pliny was asked 'inlicita confirmem'. Pflaum (op. cit. 233) suggests that Pliny was running out of the last year's supply, and assumes that the ration ran from January to January, which is now in mid course (Epp. 35, 52).

46. *To Pliny*

per omnes provincias ante mittam diplomata quam desiderari possint. Cf. Ep. 121, 'diplomatibus quae officio tuo dedi'. A freedman in charge of distribution is known, *ILS* 1677–8. Pflaum (op. cit. 231 ff.) notes that Pliny sent roughly the same number of letters each twelve months—forty-three between the first and second September 18, Epp. 17A to 88, and forty from New Year to New Year, Epp. 35 to 100. Hence he argues that Pliny was given some fifty tickets a year. But since the two years overlap, the argument is fortuitous. Also it is not certain or likely that each letter was sent by a separate *tabellarius*. Epp. 58 and 59 seem to have gone together, so too 63 and 64, and possibly the letters of commendation Epp. 85–87. Besides, officials not mentioned in the Letters would be using tickets.

Trajan's answer is presumably a formal chancellery note; was Pliny's question also only nominally addressed to Trajan? If so, Pliny is not to be castigated for inept use of the information service placed at his disposal. See Introduction, p. 543.

47. To Trajan

Date. Between 3 January and 28 January, second year.

Pliny seems to have gone to Apamea from Byzantium (Ep. 43), probably by sea, if the order of letters is correct, and thence back to Nicomedia (Ep. 49), in his first January (Ep. 52). Possibly he had prior knowledge of the objections of the Apameans, and delayed his visit to find out Trajan's opinion. But the locative *Apameae* should mean that he was or had been at the city: cf. *Prusae*, Epp. 70. 1, 81. 1, *Nicomediae*, Ep. 31. 2.

1. cum vellem domine Apameae cognoscere publicos debitores . . . responsum est mihi cupere quidem universos ut a me rationes coloniae legerentur. Pliny's mission evidently gave him, as here and at the free city of Amisus (Ep. 92), general authority over the privileged communities. His query, as in Epp. 58, 92, 118, arose out of particular privileges which he hesitated, perhaps rightly, to set aside.

The ancient Myrlea was refounded by Nicomedes II in the second century B.C. as Apamea. Later it was one of a number of Greek cities of Asia Minor on whose land veteran colonies were settled in the Late Republic and Early Principate. In Bithynia there were two others at Heraclea and Sinope, Epp. 75. 2 n., 90. 2 n. The colony of Julia Concordia at Apamea seems by its names to have been due to Julius Caesar rather than to the second Triumvirate; Jones, *Cities*, 152, 420 n. 9, 425 n. 30; Magie, *Romans*, 306 n. 20, 415 n. 34; M. Grant, *Imperium* etc. 256; Strabo xii, p. 564; *ILS* 314. The previous Greek city, as at Sinope and Heraclea, was not eliminated by the Roman settlement, but remained in a part of its former territory, like other dual communities of the Roman world; cf. A. N. Sherwin-White, *RC* 210 f. From Dio, *Or.* 41. 5–6, it is clear that two grades of local citizens existed in Apamea at this date, Greeks of the city and Romans of the colony. The gulf was bridged by the increasing number of Greeks given Roman citizenship as individuals. The practical difference between the two communes was probably fast disappearing, though Pliny's silence about the Greek city is inconclusive.

publicos debitores et reditum. Cf. Epp. 17A. 3, 18. 3 nn., 39. 3, 5 nn.

numquam tamen esse lectas ab ullo proconsulum. This statement eliminates by implication the notion that Bithynia had been a procuratorial province under Vespasian. Cf. Rostovtzeff, *BSA* xxii, art. cit. 16 f. The coin series of the procurator Antonius Naso, cited for the notion, seems to be contemporary with the coinage of two proconsuls, cf. Waddington, *Recueil*,[1] I, 'Bithynia', nn. 7–26, pp. 236 f. Bosch, *Münzen*, 85–87. Earlier a Neronian procurator features on coins contemporary with proconsuls, ibid. 83.

habuisse privilegium . . . arbitrio suo rem publicam administrare. The colony should have received at its foundation a *lex coloniae*, like that of Urso in Spain, *ILS* 6087 (A–J, n. 26), which regulated in detail all aspects of municipal life. Within the scope of its charter a colony enjoyed in practice rights similar to those of a *civitas libera* (Ep. 92 n.). But serious criminal cases and civil suits above a certain amount were reserved for proconsular jurisdiction. It is unlikely that Apamea had as a Roman colony a chartered right to absolute independence from proconsular interference. Normally proconsuls would be glad to leave them alone, within the field of their charter. Apamea also possessed the special privilege of *ius Italicum*, whereby its territory was exempt from direct taxation, like that of Italy. *Dig.* 50. 15. 1. 10. Hence the proconsuls would have no ground to concern themselves with its finances.

2. exegi ut quae dicebant . . . libello complecterentur, . . . quamvis intellegerem pleraque ex illo ad id de quo quaeritur non pertinere. Probably their charter contained no reference at all to proconsular control of local finance, since that was not envisaged in the Late Republic. *Lex Ursonensis* 96 implies that the local council had the last word in financial matters.

quaeque recitabant. The absence of official records is apparent here as elsewhere, Ep. 31. 4 n.

libello. The *libellus* was the form in which private persons, soldiers up to centurions, and villages petitioned the emperor, Epp. 58. 3, 59, 81. 5, 106. It might be occasionally used by municipalities in the submission of a claim, as here and in 92. But normally they, like persons of senatorial and equestrian rank, communicated with the emperor by an *epistula*; cf. Statius, *Silvae* 5. 1. 83 ff. Hirschfeld, *Verwaltungsbeamten*, 322 ff. The secretary *a libellis* normally handled the former type of request, but the *libelli* mentioned by Pliny evidently went forward with his own reports to the secretary *ab epistulis*, cf. Epp. 59–60, 106. The exact line of demarcation between use of *libellus* and *epistula* is not always clear, but a statement in SHA *Macrinus* 13. 1 suggests that an *epistula* with rescript was properly used for decisions which might become legal precedents, and a *libellus* with *subscriptio* for concession of benefits or appointments: 'cum Traianus numquam libellis responderit ne ad alias causas

facta praeferrentur quae ad gratiam composita viderentur'. Hirschfeld, op. cit. 328 n. 2.

For the organization of the bureaux see Epp. 2. 1, 'rescripto' n.,
65. 3, 'scriniis' n., 95 nn., 107, 'libellum rescripti' n.

48. To Pliny

1. **libellus Apamenorum . . . remisit mihi necessitatem perpendendi
qualia essent propter quae videri volunt eos, qui proconsulibus hanc
provinciam obtinuerunt, abstinuisse inspectatione rationum suarum,
cum ipse ut eas inspiceres non recusaverint.** Hardy, pressing *videri
volunt* and *salvis quae habent privilegiis* below, thought that Trajan
did not accept the claim but preferred not to make an issue of it.
But nothing in this rescript suggests that Trajan had read the whole
libellus. He seizes on Pliny's statement 'cupere quidem universos'
and its repetition at the beginning of the *libellus*, as an excuse for
ignoring the document. Pliny's inspection is to be done on this present
occasion without detriment to the rights of Apamea against the
proconsuls when proconsular government is restored: *salvis privilegiis*.
Trajan's impatience over paper work appears also in Ep. 40. 1 n.
The emperor certainly seems to have given personal attention to
this query of Pliny, if not to the Apameans' arguments.

iunxeras. For the technicality see Ep. 22. 1 n.

2. **ex mea voluntate.** The implied distinction appears in the Flavian
lex de imperio: 'ex voluntate auctoritateve iussu mandatuve eius'.
ILS 244, 7–8.

49. To Trajan

Date. Between 3 January and 28 January, second year.

1. **ante adventum meum, domine, Nicomedenses priori foro novum
adicere coeperunt.** This letter should be read with Epp. 68–69, 70–71,
on similar topics.

Since work on this new Forum had begun before Pliny's appointment no licence was necessary for it, or for moving the temple, under
the new rule, Ep. 23. 1 n. Dio, *Or.* 47. 16, refers briefly to the building
plans of Nicomedia *c.* A.D. 96–100, including a *stoa*, which involved
the removal of certain tombs. Cf. their half-finished aqueduct, Ep.
37. The site of the Forum, probably by the Turkish citadel, is unex-
cavated. Bosch attempted to reconstruct its layout from the illustrations on coins (*Münzen*, 216 f.).

aedes . . . Matris Magnae. For the popularity of alien cults in the
Greek cities see Ep. 33. 1, 'Iseon' n., Ep. 96. Dörner discovered a
statue of the Great Mother in his local excavations—apparently the

first yet found in Bithynia—but not the main shrine (*Arch. Anzeiger*, 1939, 166, fig. 34). Pliny's mention adds nothing to the history of the great Mother-Goddess of pre-Greek Anatolia. The importance of the temple is shown by its appearance on the local coinage. Bosch, op. cit. 121 f., 251 f.; Waddington, *Recueil*,[1] i, nn. 116, 350, etc.

2. cum quaererem num esset aliqua lex dicta templo. In Roman usage the dedication of a temple was a solemn act carried out by public authority, whereby the site was rendered sacred, as Pliny well knew from the dedication of his shrine at Tifernum, IV. 1. 5–6, Ep. 8. 2. Cf. Gaius 2. 5, 7 a; *Dig.* I. 8. 6. 3, 9 pref. In general *D–S*, 'Dedicatio', 43 f. The terms of the dedication were set down by the dedicant, normally a magistrate, in a formula which determined the area of the shrine, its administration, privileges, and ceremonies. The known examples tend to be stereotyped, and doubtless were provided by the pontifical college; cf. *ILS* 112, the *lex arae Narbonensis* and others in *ILS* 4906–14 (*FIRA* iii. 71–75). A dedication could be annulled by decree of the *Pontifices* if it had been performed improperly or unofficially, as in the famous case of Clodius and the house of Cicero; *pro domo* 50, 53; *ad Att.* 4. 2. 2–3. Otherwise a solemn *evocatio dei* was necessary, with ancient rites like those described in Livy I. 55, 5. 54; cf. Ulpian, *Dig.* I. 8. 9. 2; V. Busanoff, *Evocatio Dei* (Paris, 1947). Pliny, with some knowledge of these customs and the conscience of a Roman augur, did not take the matter lightly. But at Nicomedia and other Asian cities a vote of the popular assembly apparently sufficed for the transfer of sacred buildings, Dio, *Or.* 47. 16.

dispice ergo domine. Pliny does not appeal to Trajan as Pontifex Maximus, as in Ep. 68, and has not been given any precedents in the matter, as then. His request is for technical information, not available in Bithynia.

50. *To Pliny*

potes . . . sine sollicitudine religionis . . . aedem . . . transferre. Trajan is more complaisant than at the proposed alteration of the shrine of Divus Claudius in Ep. 71. But this answer is clearly the work of a legal adviser in the secretariat.

solum peregrinae civitatis capax non sit dedicationis quae fit nostro iure. Roman pontifical law had never extended its sway beyond Italy (Epp. 68–69 nn.), but provincial municipalities of Roman status in the western provinces used the Roman forms of dedication, Ep. 49. 2 n. Later in the century Gaius 2. 5–7a defines the matter thus: 'sacrum quidem hoc solum existimatur quod ex auctoritate populi Romani consecratum est. . . . quod in provinciis . . . consecratum est proprie sacrum non est, tamen pro sacro habetur',

51. To Trajan

Date. Close to 28 January, second year.

1. socrui. Pompeia Celerina, his former wife's mother, I. 4 pref.

adfinem eius Caelium Clementem in hanc provinciam transferres.
For a similar transfer of a legate's friend from province to province,
serving as Clemens must have been as military tribune or prefect,
see VIII. 23. 5. Clemens is otherwise unknown, *PIR*² C 127.

**2. cui referre gratiam parem nec audeo quidem, quamvis maxime
possim.** A rather nauseating phrase for the age of restored liberty.
The Latinity and logic of the last clause have bothered editors. The
logical flaw lies in *possim* rather than *maxime*. Catanaeus altered to
debeam, and has not been bettered. But sense might be given by
correcting to *cum maxime*, as in Ep. 49. I (O.C.T.). The phrase is a
favoured usage, cf. VI. 31. 15, Ep. 17B. 2 n. In the latter, as here,
the Aldine absurdly read *Maximo*.

52. To Trajan

Date, on or after 28 January, second year.

From the placing of Epp. 35–36 and 52–53 it should follow that
the intervening letters all belong to the month of January following
Pliny's arrival. These two letters, with Epp. 102–3, record the annual
repetition of prayers for the emperor and of the oath of loyalty taken
on the *dies imperii*, which for Trajan was 28 January (Ep. I pref.),
by the governor, the provincial authorities, and the troops. This
occasion is distinct from the proceedings on 3 January, Ep. 35 n.
Trajan seems to have transferred the oath-taking from the New
Year to the *dies imperii* (ibid.).

1. diem, domine, quo servasti imperium . . . celebravimus, precati deos.
The *dies imperii* is that on which the emperor was first saluted
imperator by the troops. The salutation was followed closely, but not
always on the same day, by the taking of the oath of loyalty; cf.
Suet. *Claud.* 10. 4; Jos. *Ant.* 19. 4. 2. The sources do not always mention both ceremonies, e.g. Tac. *Hist.* 2. 79: 'Kalendis Iuniis sacramento eius (sc. Vespasiani) legiones adegit. isque primus principatus
dies in posterum celebratus'. Vitellius changed his 'day' from that
of his initial salutation in Germany to the day on which the urban
troops and the Senate recognized him; Tac. *Hist.* I. 55 with *ILS* 241.
l. 85–86. The festival of Trajan's 'day' continued to be kept in the
later Empire as a great occasion, cf. 'Feriale Duranum', *Yale Class.
Stud.* vii. 77.

The formal vote of powers in the Senate might be separated by a long interval from the *dies imperii*, as with Nero, whose tribunician power dated from 4 December though his *dies imperii* was 13 October (*ILS* 229. 10 f., 20 f.), and with Vespasian, by force of circumstances, Suet. *Vesp.* 12. But for Trajan the powers which he already held as *consors imperii* were probably conferred on the same or the following day, as for Nerva (*FO* for A.D. 96).

precati deos. For these prayers, similar to those of 3 January, see Ep. 35 n. They are less often mentioned than the oath, but cf. Ep. 102, and Tac. *Hist.* 2. 74: 'praeeuntem sacramentum et fausta Vitellio omnia precantem'.

praeivimus et commilitonibus iusiurandum more sollemni. Cf. Tac. *Hist.* 1. 55. 1. 'legiones sollemni . . . sacramento . . . adactae'. This oath is distinct both from the senatorial oath *in acta Caesaris*, taken annually on New Year's Day (Ep. 35 n.) and from the old military oath, for which see Ep. 29. 2 n. This is the oath of personal loyalty to the family and interests of the Princeps. Its formula is known from three early provincial documents: A-J 37 (*OGIS* 532), from Paphlagonia; A-J 47 (*ILS* 190), from Aricia in Spain; A-J 48 (*FIR*[7] 102), from Assos in the Troad. The last named combines the elements of the other two in a formula showing Hellenistic influence that may well have been used in Bithynia, though the Latin formula from Aricia is likely to be the oldest, going back to the *coniuratio Italiae* that preceded the campaign of Actium. The principal sentence is as follows: 'we swear by Zeus the Saver, by the Divus Caesar Augustus, and by our own Holy Lady, that we will be loyal to Gaius Caesar Augustus and all his house, and will consider as friends whom he chooses and as enemies whom he declares. If I keep my oath may all be well with me. If I break it then may all be ill to me.' For a general discussion see A. von Premerstein, *Vom Werden und Wesen des Prinzipäts* (Munich, 1937), 27, 32 f., 45 f.; Syme, *Roman Revolution*, 288. S. Weinstock, 'Treue des und Kaiserkult', *Mitteil. D. Arch. Inst.* (Ath. Abt.), 1962, 306 f.

eadem provincialibus certatim pietate iurantibus. Here the provincial governor carries through the ceremony in his locality, as in Tac. *Ann.* 1. 34: 'Germanicus . . . Belgarum civitates in verba eius adigit'; cf. Jos. *Ant.* 18. 5. 3. Elsewhere the local authorities, the council at Assos, and the *magistri oppidi* at Aricia, administer the oath, apparently to a mass meeting of the inhabitants, as in Paphlagonia, where the officiants are not named. Perhaps by this time the oath was taken only by the provincial council in public session in the way described by Dio (58. 17. 1–3) for the senatorial oath, a single representative taking the oath and the rest saying 'amen'.

54. To Trajan

Date. Between 28 January and 18 September, second year.

1. **Pecuniae publicae . . . et iam exactae sunt et exiguntur. quae vereor ne otiosae iaceant.** For this part of Pliny's commission see Ep. 17A. 3, 18. 3 n. He does not mean that he has completed his task, since he is still busy with accountancy problems in Epp. 108, 110. Possibly he has completed it in the western part of his province, i.e. in Bithynia, though Ep. 77 suggests that he has not yet reached Julio-polis. Pliny's dislike of moneys lying idle is characteristic of his attitude to his own investments and endowments, IV. 13. 5–9, VII. 18. It leads him into an unfortunate suggestion that Trajan rejects. There was no reason why these funds should not have remained in store in the municipal treasuries.

praediorum comparandorum . . . rarissima occasio est. For land as the standard form of investment see III. 19. 8 n., VI. 19. 4–6. For an example of municipal investment in land in Asia see *IGRR*, iv. 915. B (Magie, *Romans*, 591). It is characteristic of antiquity that the only alternative envisaged is the personal short-term loan. Any other form of investment called for the active participation of the investor. Hence land was in great demand and short supply; cf. Heitland, *Agricola*, 106, 289 f. The existence of large estates in private owner-ship is well documented in Bithynia. (L. Robert, *Études anatoliennes*, 240 f. Cf. *IGRR*, iii. 17.)

nec inveniuntur. Because the municipality was stringent in its demand for security, and had priority in enforcing payment, as in Ep. 108. 1 n.

praesertim duodenis assibus. The phrase is surprising. Roman rates of interest were usually quoted at monthly rates, and one expects *assibus* or *centesimis*, as in IX. 28. 5, i.e. 12 per cent. a year, which is undoubtedly what Pliny meant (below). The words cannot be entirely omitted, as earlier editors suggested. Probably *duodenis* was inserted by a hand that did not understand *assibus* alone.

In the Empire 12 per cent. appears as the legal maximum rate of interest in Egypt (*Gnomon idiologi* 105), though up to 18 and 24 per cent. was sometimes secured. In Africa and Asia 12 is the highest rate paid on charitable and municipal endowments, for which the rate often ranges between 5 and 9. In Italy Columella assumes a rate of 6 per cent. for loans on good security: cf. VII. 18. 4 n. A rescript of Pius lays down 6 as the rate to be paid on certain municipal bequests, *Dig.* 50. 10. 5. The rate charged on the non-redeemable loans under Trajan's alimentary schemes was 5 per cent. at Veleia, and even lower elsewhere. So the rate in Bithynia seems to agree

with practice outside Italy for short-term loans. For further documentation see *Ec. Survey*, ii. 450 f., iv. 79, 491, 900. Also G. Billeter,
Geschichte des Zinsfußes (Leipzig, 1898), 103 ff.

**2. distribuendam inter decuriones pecuniam ita ut recte reipublicae
caveant.** The novelty of this suggestion is shown by *Dig.* 50. 1. 24,
a rescript of Marcus and Verus, to the effect that municipal magistrates should not be held responsible for interest on the surplus of
municipal income. Merrill's suggestion that Pliny had a Domitianic
precedent—based on Trajan's reference to *iustitia nostrorum temporum*
—is most unlikely, since he would have quoted it, as elsewhere.
The legate of Galatia who in *c.* A.D. 93 enforced the sale of corn by
hoarders at a reasonable price was dealing with a crisis, not a routine
problem; A-J 65 A. The novelty of the idea accounts for the reference
to Trajan; as in Ep. 65. 2, 108. 2, Pliny seeks a permanent rule.

caveant. The charter of Malaca in Spain gives the rules about
personal guarantees—*praedes, cognitores*—and *cautiones* in real estate
required from those who handled municipal monies. Similar rules
were probably introduced into Bithynia by the *Lex Pompeia. ILS*
6089: cc. 60, 63–65, 67, 89 (A-J 65).

55. *To Pliny*

**invitos ad accipiendum compellere quod fortassis ipsis otiosum
futurum sit, non est ex iustitia nostrorum temporum.** So too the
rescript quoted above of Marcus is motivated by the notion *humanum
est*. The ground for rejection is not legalist, and suggests the voice of
the emperor. The fact that he rejected the proposal is more important
than that Pliny proposed it. Too much weight has been given to
Pliny's idea, both by Merrill ad loc., and by Abbot and Johnson,
op. cit. 150, as foreshadowing the later system by which decurions
were made responsible, on the security of their estates, for the collection of imperial taxes. Even Pliny only suggested compulsion as a
pis aller.

ipsis otiosum. This neatly turns Pliny's argument against himself.
The vigour of the reply again suggests the emperor's own hand.

ex iustitia. Cf. Ep. 1. 2, 'saeculo' n., and Ep. 97. 2, 'nam et
pessimi exempli nec nostri saeculi est'.

56. *To Trajan*

Date. Between 28 January and 18 September, second year.

Letters 56–60 deal with similar problems about persons who claimed
that their penal sentences had been remitted.

2. adiit enim me quidam indicavitque adversarios suos a Servilio Calvo clarissimo viro in triennium relegatos in provincia morari. For the proconsular power of relegation and its effects see II. II. 8, III. 9. 31 nn. Provincial factions are at work again; Epp. 34. 1, 58. 1–3, 81. 1–2, 110. 1 nn.

Servilius Calvus is at present unknown, possibly related to Servilius Pudens, Ep. 25. It would seem from the tense of *morari* that their sentence was within the *triennium*, and hence that Calvus was a recent predecessor of Pliny; Garzetti, *Inc.* 132.

clarissimo viro. Pliny uses this honorary title also for the consular legate of Moesia, Ep. 61. 5, and it is so used of a consular in a contemporary inscription, *ILS* 6106. The term gradually came into use long before it was made formal by a regulation of Marcus and Verus. Two documents of A.D. 56 and 69 are the earliest examples; *ILS* 5947. 13, 6043. 24; Mommsen, *DPR* vi. 2. 62.

ab eodem se restitutos. This implies that they were restored within the single year of Calvus' proconsulship.

edictumque recitaverunt. Cf. Ep. 31. 4 n. on the absence of archives.

3. sicut mandatis tuis cautum est ne restituam ab alio aut a me relegatos. There was a general dislike in earlier Roman practice of the reversal of judicial decisions, whether civil or criminal, as in the rescript of Marcus and Verus to a provincial governor: 'non solere praesides provinciarum ea quae pronuntiaverunt ipsos rescindere', *Dig.* 48. 19. 27 pref. But exceptions were allowed, ibid., as when fresh evidence appeared, or perjury was proved, though this needed imperial sanction; cf. the Trajanic case quoted by Pliny, VII. 6. 10 nn. In the later second century there was a development of appeal from sentences of provincial and other magistrates to the Princeps, until in the late empire the pre-classical principle was reversed. But it was still the rule that a judge might not alter his own decision. *RE* ii. 196 ff. for civil appeals, 208 ff. for criminal appeals.

mandatis tuis. See Ep. 22. 1 n.

de iis quos alius et relegaverit et restituerit nihil comprehensum est. Was Pliny's question necessary? It is a lawyer's, and especially an advocate's, point. Pliny's predecessors, being proconsuls, had no *mandata* from the Princeps; cf. Ep. 57. 1. But Pliny might well consider that Trajan's instructions had retrospective force, as in the affair of forbidden gifts, Ep. 110, and that of the *iselastica*, Epp. 118–19. Trajan in his reply does not object to the retrospective principle. It had been common enough in the political legislation of the late Republic; the *Lex Pompeia* of 52 B.C. extended its scope *de ambitu* backwards to 70 B.C., Appian, *BC* 2. 23.

**4. quia sciebam acta Bassi rescissa datumque a senatu ius omnibus . . .
ex integro agendi.** For the proconsulship and condemnation of Julius
Bassus for extortion in 103 see IV. 9 nn. The second part of the
sentence is precise, and gives the ruling of the *SC*. If the acts of
Bassus had been automatically reversed there would have been no
case against this man. The Senate took a lenient view of Bassus'
conduct, who had much trouble in curbing the civic discord in
Bithynia, and hence made his sentences merely subject to revision;
IV. 9. 5 n. Pliny does not mention this provision there.

per biennium. Since each proconsul governed his province for a
biennium, in the narrower sense a part of each of two consular years,
the *SC*. confined appeals to the succeeding proconsular year.

**5. reddendum eum poenae suae an gravius aliquid . . . constituendum
putares.** Hadrian made a general ruling by edict that met this
problem, *Dig*. 48. 19. 28. 13. He substituted the next severer grade of
penalty in each case: 'ut qui ad tempus relegatus est si redeat, in
insulam relegetur; qui relegatus in insulam excesserit, in insulam
deportetur' and so on. No such rule was known to Pliny, and this
second query to Trajan was reasonable in the circumstances. As in
the affair of the prisoners who had been released from the mines,
Ep. 31, Pliny finds Trajan more severe than he expected.

decretum Calvi et edictum. The decree contained the original
sentence, the latter the administrative act recalling the man.

57. *To Pliny*

1. proxime tibi rescribam cum causas eius facti a Calvo requisiero.
Calvus as proconsul had been free to do as he pleased, not being
bound by *mandata*.

**2. si existimat se iniuria relegatum . . . atque in provincia morari
perseverarit, vinctus mitti ad praefectos praetorii mei debet.** The man
might have been a victim of the *conspiratio delatorum* which then
flourished in Bithynia, IV. 9. 5.

Trajan's instruction is very odd, and illuminates his personality.
Pliny had power to inflict the severest penalties, including death,
except on Roman citizens, who would be sent to Rome for trial;
Epp. 30. 1, 96. 3–4. It has been assumed that this man was a Roman,
but nothing in Ep. 56 suggests this, though Trajan could infer that
he was of the upper classes, since he had not been condemned to
one of the degrading penalties, such as *metallum*. Trajan was enraged
at the flagrant *contumacia*, and decided to sort the case out himself.
He thus anticipated, for a different reason, the later tendency to treat
honestiores in criminal jurisdiction as Roman citizens; cf. II. 11. 8 n.

The man was presumably named in the decree of Bassus (56. 5), but the name alone would not prove citizen status.

vinctus mitti. The praetorian prefect was responsible for keeping prisoners in custody while awaiting trial by the emperor, like St. Paul, *Ep. Phil.* 1. 13. The earliest example of a Roman sent in chains to Rome for an imperial inquiry comes from the second of the edicts of Augustus to Cyrene; E-J, n. 311, ii. l. 46 f. So too the consular Valerius Asiaticus, Tac. *Ann.* 11. 1: 'vinclis inditis in urbem raptus est'. Cf. Mommsen, *D.Pen.R.* i. 312 n. 4. This passage casts no light on the growth of the judicial power of the praetorian prefects. The only early trace of this seems to be found in an anecdote of Seneca, *de Clem.* 2. 1. 2, about the punishment of highwaymen. But in VII. 6. 10 (n.) Trajan delegates jurisdiction to Suburanus when he may have been praetorian prefect. Cf. *RE* xxii. 2, 2412 ff. Crook, *Consilium* etc. 70. Sherwin-White, *Roman Society* etc., 108 n. 1.

neque enim sufficit eum poenae suae restitui quam contumacia elusit. Trajan took a similar line when consulted about persons who failed to answer a summons on a criminal charge, *Dig.* 48. 19. 5: 'absentem in criminibus damnari non debere divus Traianus Iulio Frontoni rescripsit, sed nec de suspicionibus debere aliquem damnari. satius enim esse impunitum relinqui facinus nocentis quam innocentem damnari. adversus contumaces vero qui neque denuntiationibus neque edictis praesidum obtemperasset etiam absentes pronuntiari oportet.' Ulpian is here reproducing the substance of Trajan's words, since he goes on to criticize the decision as contradictory. Trajan shows in both cases the same illogicality or incoherence that pervades his rescript about the Christians, Ep. 97. Here he seems to regard the man's claim to justification as aggravating the offence. Compare also his sharp attitude in the incidents at trials reported by Pliny in VI. 22. 5, 31. 9–11.

58. *To Trajan*

Date. Between 28 January and 18 September, second year.

This query arose from the complicated judicial and legal situation affecting the status of a Roman citizen, resting on imperial rescripts.

1. **Cum citarem iudices, domine, conventum incohaturus.** Pliny is at Prusa, on his second visit, to hold the judicial assizes. Ep. 81. 1–3 describes another incident of this visit. There is no reason to doubt the locality, with Vidman, who supposes it to be Nicomedia. For Prusa had recently been made an assize city, at the request of a municipal embassy led by Dio; *Or.* 40. 10, 33; 44. 11; von Arnim, *Dio von Prusa*, 328. The reference to *iudices* has been taken to refer

only to a roll of *iudices privati* for civil cases, but it is unlikely that
there was a local *album* of this sort (*numero*, s. 2) for 'formulary'
jurisdiction; the governor would find his Roman *iudices* among his
comites (for whom cf. VI. 22. 2 n.). The first edict of Augustus from
Cyrene has revealed, contrary to the supposition of Mommsen, that
there existed a provincial system of criminal juries similar to the
quaestiones at Rome, as Hardy almost guessed from this passage.
It was introduced into Crete-and-Cyrene in the Republic and
remodelled by Augustus, who laid down minimum qualifications of
age and wealth for jurors—twenty-five years and S.25,000. They
were to be drawn in equal numbers from Roman citizens and Greeks
of the province. Hitherto it was held that all criminal jurisdiction in
provinces was decided by the personal *cognitio* of the governor sitting
with the usual *consilium* of officials and *comites*, the system which
finally prevailed in the Principate. The jury system can now be
detected in three provinces if the Augustan *praefectus fabrum iuri
dicundo et sortiendis iudicibus in Asia*, *ILS* 6286, was concerned with
a similar *album* to that in Cyrene; civil *iudices privati* were not
chosen by lot. *ILS* 7789 may also refer to a jury system in Asia under
Trajan: *custodiar . . . in urna iudicum*. See E-J., n. 311, i. 15–20; F.
de Visscher, *Les Édits d'Auguste* etc., ch. ii; Mommsen, *D.Pen.R.* i.
274, 278 f. It may be that this jury system, so far as it existed, was
limited to offences defined by the *leges publicae*, cf. II. 11. 8 n.

conventum incohaturus. Each year the governor and his *legatus
iuridicus* made a regular tour of his province; cf. Strabo 3. 4. 20, p. 167
on Hispania Tarraconensis. At each assize city he dealt with such
serious criminal and civil cases as could not be handled by the
municipal magistrates, with problems of administration (Ep. 81. 1,
'publicis negotiis . . . vacarem'), and with manumissions (VII. 16. 4
n.; Suet. *Galba* 10. 1). Cf. *RE* iv. 1173 ff. The assize cities of Bithynia
are not known apart from the evidence of Pliny and Dio, which is
indecisive in some cases because of the special circumstances of Pliny's
mission. Apart from the capital, Nicomedia, and Prusa (above) in
Bithynia, Amastris, and Sinope in Pontus are likely to have been
assize towns, Epp. 90, 98 nn. Byzantium across the water can hardly
have managed without an assize when it lost its *libertas*, Ep. 43. 1 n.

Flavius Archippus is known only from Pliny (*PIR²*, F 216). In
Ep. 81, where this feud is continued, he appears as an enemy of Dio,
and von Arnim identified him with an anonymous opponent of Dio
indicated rather indirectly in *Or.* 43. 5–6, 11–12 as 'one of those
condemned and disfranchised', and as a *delator* and a henchman of a
certain corrupt proconsul. Dio does not say that his enemy claimed
to be a philosopher.

vacationem . . . ut philosophus. Teachers of philosophy, though unwelcome at Rome when they intervened in politics, belonged to the group of professional men to whom special privileges were given by the Flavian emperors. An inscription contains fragmentary edicts of Vespasian and Domitian about the *immunitas* granted to *medici* and *praeceptores*, and measures taken to control it. Cf. IV. 13. 5 n., *AE* 1936, n. 128 (W-C 458). Arcadius *Dig.* 50. 4. 18. 30 states: 'grammaticis et oratoribus et medicis et philosophis ne hospitem reciperent a principibus fuisse immunitatem indultam et divus Vespasianus et divus Hadrianus rescripserunt'. The new edict mentions various freedoms. Later Pius and Commodus confirmed professional men in a general freedom from most types of provincial and municipal liturgies, *Dig.* 27. 1. 6. 2–9. The system was that a decree of the local council registered the various practitioners entitled to immunities. Numbers were limited according to the size of the cities, except for philosophers, because as Pius said, 'there are not many of *them*'. The freedom from jury service here mentioned is only one of these privileges. For bibliography see IV. 13. 5 n.

2. tollendum de iudicum numero. By *numerus* Pliny refers to something like the Italian system of *decuriae iudicum* from which the annual *album* was compiled, cf. IV. 29. 2 n.

3. recitata est sententia Veli Pauli proconsulis qua probabatur Archippus crimine falsi damnatus in metallum. The affair is over a quarter of a century old. Cf. the vendetta of Ep. 110. The trial must have been no later than 83–84, to fit in the proconsulships of Velius Rufus and Lappius Maximus before the consulship of the latter in 86, s. 6 n. Martial mentions a Velius who served with Domitian on Rhine and Danube, and an orator Paulus. These might be identical with our man, Mart. 7. 72, 9. 31; Garzetti, *Inc.* 155.

This letter, with Epp. 56, 72, 112, adds six Flavian and Trajanic proconsuls to the Fasti of Bithynia, all omitted by Magie, *Romans*, App. I, 1590 f.

It is notable that Archippus, though a Roman citizen and a person of some standing, was sentenced not to some form of exile but to a menial punishment involving some loss of civil rights; such punishments from Hadrian onwards tended to be reserved for *humiliores*, II. 11. 8 n. Yet in Ep. 96. 4 Pliny sends Roman citizens charged with a capital offence to Rome for trial. A possible explanation is that the distinction depended on the particular charge, and that the governor was free to sentence Roman citizens on capital charges only under the *leges publicae* II. 11. 8 n.

crimine falsi. The normal punishment under the *Lex Cornelia de falsis*, which the proconsul would tend to follow in his own jurisdiction, was capital, though certain lesser crimes of forgery came to be punished, in *cognitio extra ordinem*, by relegation alone; *Dig.* 48. 10. 13. Brasiello, op. cit. 75. The charge was extended from the forgery of wills, by a *SC. Libonianum* and imperial edicts, to cover false witness, corruption of witnesses, falsification of documents, and personification. Cf. VI. 22. 4, VII. 6. 8 nn. Since the accuser of Archippus was a woman, Ep. 60. 2, it is likely that, as in VII. 6, it was a testamentary affair, though Archippus might have been charged with suborning witnesses in a *conspiratio delatorum*, cf. IV. 9. 5.

in metallum. For variations of this punishment see Ep. 31. 2 n. Such convicts were always kept in chains, cf. *Dig.* 48. 19. 8. 6.

ille nihil proferebat quo restitutum se doceret. An edict of restitution was necessary to re-establish his civic status and property rights, as in Ep. 56. 2, if these had been affected. Cf. *Dig.* 48. 23. 2–3; Ulpian, Papinian. Since Archippus did not quote a grant of citizenship in proof, he must have become a citizen before his troubles; he is unlikely to have been a citizen by birth because of his *nomen* and the dates.

decretum Prusensium. The decree was one of the council of Prusa offering him a public statue, Ep. 60. 1. Cf. Dio, *Or.* 44. 3–4, recording his own family's honours from the borough.

4. donec te consulerem de eo quod mihi constitutione tua dignum videbatur. The fact that Trajan had confirmed the *beneficia* of Domitian to Archippus (below) justified Pliny's query on this occasion. In fact Trajan stood by his word, Ep. 60.

The term *constitutio* is the most general and least technical word for an imperial decision. Gaius 1. 5: 'constitutio principis est quod imperator decreto vel edicto vel epistula constituit'. So too Ulpian, for whom such decisions, when of a general nature, had the force of law, *Dig.* 1. 4. 1. 1. Decisions on particular cases were not so regarded, and did not form precedents: 'quaedam . . . sunt personales nec ad exemplum trahuntur . . . si cui sine exemplo subvenit personam non egreditur'.

ea quae sint utrimque recitata his litteris subieci. The selection of documents published is interesting, and may cast light on the purpose of the compilation of Book X. It omits the sentence of condemnation, which was not in dispute, the petition of Archippus and the decree of Prusa, which two would have avoided the delicate question of status, and the letter of Trajan, which would merely repeat the Nervan documents. The substantial evidence lay in the implications of Domitian's letters and their confirmation by Nerva. Both Nervan documents were necessary because the first was general and the second specific for Bithynia. So the dossier has been limited to the perfect presentation of a problem.

subieci. See Ep. 22. 1 n. These copies should be continuous in the original draft with Pliny's letter.

5. ad Terentium Maximum. This should be the procurator in charge of imperial domains in Bithynia-Pontus, not the proconsul since he is concerned with payments and lands. He is otherwise unknown, *PIR*[1] T 61, but could be a brother of Terentius Junior, VII. 25. 2 n., also a procurator.

ut agrum ei ad C̄ circa †Prusiadam† patriam suam emi iuberem cuius reditu suos alere posset. Editors rightly prefer the Bodleian correction *C* to the *DC* of Aldus—the D comes from the preceding *ad*. An estate of S.100,000 would keep a man in Italy in modest municipal comfort, I. 19, 2, VI. 3. 1. This sum seems to be have been named in the *Lex Pompeia* as the financial qualification for a decurion in Bithynia, Ep. 110. 2 n. Archippus was destitute after his escape from the mines. Vespasian was more generous to the Roman poet Saleius Bassus, Tac. *Dial.* 9. 5.

Prusiadam. The reading of Aa is at fault. Archippus is a citizen of *Prusa ad Olympum*, where he is now apparently a decurion, Ep. 81. 1 n., and not of the like-named and adjacent *Prusias ad mare* at the head of the gulf of Cius (for which see Strabo, XII pp. 563-4). *Prusiadam* and *Prusiadem* (Cellarius) are taken as adjectival forms of *Prusa* with *regionem* or *agrum* 'understood'. Yet Pliny always uses *Prusensis*, cf. s. 3, Ep. 17A. 3, etc. Varro, cited by Nonius 345. 23, used *Prusiades* as a proper name. A similar difficulty occurs in Ep. 81. 6, where *Prusiade* can only stand for *Prusae*. In both cases a nearby *ad* may have caused the distortion of the normal form. *Prusam* should be read here. *Prusiacus* is known, but has not been pressed into service by editors, wisely.

summam expensam liberalitati meae feres. Domitian refers to the *ratio liberalitatum*, testified, for example, in Suet. *Claud.* 29. 1; *Galba* 15. 1. Cf. the anecdote in Suet. *Vesp.* 22, 'adamato Vespasiano'. The item is transferred from the local account to that of the personal expenses; cf. Hiltbrunner, *Hermes*, 1942, 381.

6. Eiusdem ad Lappium Maximum. This is A. Bucius Lappius Maximus Norbanus, who suppressed the revolt of Saturninus against Domitian. He was *cos. I* late in 86, legate of lower Germany in 89, and of Syria in 92, and *cos. II* in 95. Hence his proconsulship cannot be later than 85-86. The correct name, long read as L. Appius Maximus from Dio 67. 11. 1 and *Ep. de Caes.* 11. 10, is now known from the Ostian Fasti (p. 734) and a new diploma. Garzetti, *C.* 86, with *AE*, 1961, n. 319.

professioni suae etiam moribus respondentem. Like Euphrates, I. 10. 2, he is 'plenus . . . humanitate quam praecipit' and similarly successful in his imposition.

7. quaedam sine dubio Quirites ipsa felicitas temporum edicit. This turgid document is an extract, it seems, from a general statement of Nerva, issued to or even before an assembly of the Roman people, soon after he became Princeps. Nerva is known to have carried at least one measure in the form of a *lex* before the *comitia*, Dio 68. 2. 2; *CAH* xi. 192 f.

The term *edictum* was used for any official pronouncement of a Roman magistrate, especially for declarations of policy, as here; the classical example is the annual 'praetorian edict'. Cf. de Visscher, op. cit. 38 f. on the terminology of the edicts from Cyrene.

The phrase *felicitas temporum* is associated with the restoration of 'liberty' after Domitian in Tac. *Hist.* I. 1, *Agr.* 3. 1.

hoc sibi civium meorum spondere possit vel non admonita persuasio. Cf. Ep. 12. 2, 'civium tuorum'. So too Pliny, *Pan.* 21. 4, 'cum civibus tuis quasi . . . parens vivis'. The use of *cives mei* after *Quirites* is curious. It anticipates the terms used in edicts of Caracalla, τοὺς ἐμοὺς ἀνθρώπους, οἱ κατὰ τὴν οἰκουμένην, A–J, n. 192; P. Giessen, 40. But the word has the connotation of order and legality, cf. Tac. *Ann.* 12. 11: 'non dominationem et servos sed rectorem et cives cogitaret'. (Cf. also Vespasian's usage in W–C 458. 6.)

ante me concessa servarem. Titus had initiated the custom of confirming his predecessor's *beneficia* in a block, Domitian followed suit, and so evidently did Nerva and Trajan, as later Hadrian and Pius. Suet. *Tit.* 8. 1; Dio 67. 2. 1; *Dig.* 27. 1. 6. 8; Mommsen, *DPR* v. 438. Previously some proof of title was required at the accession of a new Princeps, Suet. loc. cit. Proof of confirmation could not prevent a faulty title from being upset, cf. A–J n. 130. The *damnatio memoriae* of Domitian called in question his *acta* based on *imperium*, but did not affect *SC* passed on his *auctoritas*. It excluded him from the list of those to whose *acta* the January oath was taken (Ep. 52 nn.); Dio, 60. 4. 6; Mommsen, op. cit. 442. In practice the *actorum rescissio* tended to be limited to a review of the emperor's criminal jurisdiction and the restoration of political victims; genuine malefactors like Valerius Licinianus were left in their mines and islands. IV. 11. 14–15 n.; Dio 65. 9. 1, 68. 1. 2; Suet. *Claud.* 11. 3. Pliny twice elsewhere cites administrative acts of Domitian as precedents, Epp. 65. 3, 72. and they were accepted by Nerva and Trajan, s. 10, Ep. 66. 2.

9. quod alio principe vel privatim vel publice consecutus sit. Personal gifts at the expense of the *patrimonium* and favours to communities or persons involving the rights of the Roman State are here distinguished.

10. epistula eiusdem ad Tullium Iustum. This must be the proconsul of Bithynia for 96–97 or 97–98, rather than a procurator, as *PIR*¹

276 had it. He is not otherwise known, Garzetti, op. cit. *Inc.* 145. Possibly a brother of the consular Tullius Cerealis, II. II. 9 n.

The relative brevity of this rescript may derive from the official style of the *ab epistulis* office, at this time held by Pliny's friend Titinius Capito, I. 17. I n. The verbosity of Nerva derives from the difficulty of his situation.

rerum omnium ordinatio, quae prioribus temporibus incohatae . . . sunt. Incomplete transactions are to be honoured automatically. This may echo the political situation, in which it was desirable not to provoke the supporters of the Flavian régime, amongst whom Nerva himself had a conspicuous place. Cf. Ep. 4. 1–4, IV. 22. 4, VII. 33. 9 nn.

Domitiani. In I–IX Pliny once calls Domitian *Caesar*, I. 18. 3, unless the reference is to Titus. Elsewhere he is simply Domitianus, cf. I. 12. 6; III. 9. 31, 33; IV. 9. 2 *et al.*

59. *To Trajan*

This continues Ep. 58, at the same date.

Flavius Archippus per salutem tuam aeternitatemque petit a me ut libellum quem mihi dedit mitterem tibi. The same formula is used for a similar purpose in Ep. 83. Archippus wants to send his petition free of charge by the *cursus publicus* in Pliny's bag. Cf. Ep. 43. 2 n.

accusatrici eius. The lady Furia (Ep. 60. 2) is the prime mover in the affair and evidently a former victim of Archippus. At Rome, under the *ordo* system, she would be unable to prosecute, VII. 6. 8 n.

iunxi. For the technique see Ep. 22. 1 n.

60. *To Pliny*

1. tam multa ad honorem eius pertinentia scriberet. This need not mean that the editor of Book X cut down the length of the letters of Domitian in Ep. 58. 5–6.

statuarum ei honor totiens decretus. The decree of Prusa must have listed these occasions.

2. si quid illi novi criminis obicitur. This means that Furia was bringing fresh charges in connexion with the original offence, rather as in VII. 6. 8–10, since Pliny could not refuse to admit an entirely new charge.

libellos Furiae accusatricis, item ipsius Archippi . . . legi. This unusual postscript answers Pliny's insistence at the end of Ep. 59. Trajan evidently received Epp. 58–59 together.

mi Secunde. The exceptional placing of the address late in the
note suggests that this sentence is an addition of Trajan's to the
secretarial draft.

61. *To Trajan*

This letter continues at a later date the discussion in Epp. 41–42
about the linking of Lake Sabanja to the sea, initiated in January of
the second year, after the receipt of Ep. 42, between 29 January and
18 September (Ep. 88). The placing of the letter suggests an interval
of not many months.

2. contineri . . . et dirimi. No emendation is required. Cf. II. II. 18,
'nocte dirimi . . . triduo contineri'.

**sic consequemur ut †nec vacuo videatur† flumini mixtus, et sit
perinde ac si misceatur.** The text is trying to say; 'the waters will
not run away, but the channels will be as good as joined'. None of the
corrections so far proposed makes perfect sense. But Madvig's
vacuetur was a great advance on Keil's *vacuari videatur*. The root of
the trouble lies in *videatur*—'seems emptied' or 'seems not joined'
is merely inept. I suggest: 'ut neque aqua viduetur flumini immixtus',
or else *mixtus* (as in O.C.T.) This is nearer to the prototype than the
other emendations. NEQUE AQUA could easily produce NEC UACUA,
and the correction of *viduetur* to *videatur* would follow. Either *flumine*
or less commonly *flumini* is possible with *mixtus*. But *immixtus*
might be better amid all these compounds; cf. *commissus, emitti,
emittit*, ss. 1, 2, 3. It is in the style of Pliny to repeat a compound
verb by its simple form—*misceatur*, IV. 2. 2 n.

advecta fossa onera transponere. The goods, not the barges. Hence
the use of a *diolcos*, suggested by Moore (art. cit. below) is not
required.

3. est enim et lacus ipse satis altus. He means 'depth' here, not height
above sea-level, as in Ep. 41. 3. The lake is deep enough not to flow
away when a channel is provided as Trajan feared in Ep. 42.

**flumen emittit quod interclusum inde . . . tantum aquae quantum
nunc portat effundet.** Pliny obscures his meaning for the sake of
stylistic effect. This river is to be blocked up, while the *fossa* is to
carry off the equivalent of its outflow.

**per id spatium . . . incidunt rivi qui . . . augebunt illud quod lacus
dederit.** Pliny takes up Trajan's inquiry of Ep. 42. The idea is that
the canal should be filled without drawing excessively from the lake.

**4. si placeat fossam . . . artius pressam mari aequare . . . in ipsum mare
emittere.** Another scheme for conserving the water. The meaning
seems to be not only (as Hardy) to make the channel narrower, but to
excavate it down to sea-level. Unless this was done throughout its

length—which would empty the lake anyway—the gradient would still defeat Pliny's hopes. Compare Pliny's speculation about the action of water in IV. 30. 5–10.

expeditum tamen erat catarractis aquae cursum temperare. The word *catarracta* means a descending gate or portcullis used in fortifications (Livy 27. 28. 10; Veget. 4. 4; Dion. Hal. *Ant.* 8. 67. 7). Similarly the word is used by Ammianus (24. 1. 11) in connexion with weirs on the great canals of Babylonia: 'avulsis catarractis ad diffundendas reprimendasque aquas rigare suetas opere saxeo structis'. (Cf. ibid. 3. 10, 6. 2; Rut. Nam. 1. 481.) Evidently the stone weirs had gates in them, which properly were the *catarractae*. F. G. Moore (*AJA*, liv. 97 ff.) has argued that the use of the modern double or 'pound' lock was known in antiquity, and that *catarractae* are lock-gates operated by windlass, similar to a type first known in use in the late fourteenth century A.D. on the Naviglio Grande between Lake Maggiore and Milan. He finds evidence for the use of locks in antiquity in three places. In Tac. *Ann.* 13. 53 the legates of Nero commanding the Rhine armies proposed to build a canal linking the upper Saône and the Moselle across their water-shed. This evidently could not be done without the use of locks. But the plan was not carried out. Next, the Elder Pliny describes a method of controlling the waters of the upper Tiber in the low-water season, which would be known to Pliny as landlord of Tifernum, and which might refer to a primitive lock (*NH* 3. 53): '(Tiberis) tenuis primo nec nisi piscinis corrivatus emissusque navigabilis, sicuti Tinia et Clanis influentes in eum, novenorum ita conceptu dierum si non adiuvent imbres. sed Tiberis propter aspera et confragosa ne sic quidem praeterquam trabibus verius quam ratibus longe meabilis fertur, per C̄L̄ p. non procul Tiferno.' But this refers rather to the use of fish-weirs, doubtless with gates (*emissus*), which slowly raise the level in a long reach of the river. Shallow craft then ride the flood down to the next *piscina*, shooting the rapids as best they can. Moore objected to the risks involved, but the Elder Pliny implies that it was hazardous. A very similar method of navigation was in use in medieval Europe and China before the invention of pound locks. The great fish-weirs and mill-weirs of the upper Thames contained gates called 'stanches', which were lifted, like the *catarractae*, to admit the passage of vessels. These rode down on the flood or 'flash' of water released and thus crossed the weirs downstream so long as the 'flash' maintained the necessary depth. Passage upstream was effected by haulage, with windlasses, across the weirs, and by portages where necessary. The system, though risky and wasteful of water, had a long period of use from the fourteenth to the eighteenth century. Hence the stanch lock is much more likely to be of ancient derivation than the pound-lock. See T. S. Willan, *River*

Navigation in England (Oxford, 1936), 86 f.; *History of Technology*
(Oxford), 1957, iii. 440 f. Trajan's reply is against Moore's suggestion.
If he had known the use of pound-locks, he would not have been
concerned about the danger of emptying the lake. Pliny speaks only
of controlling the rate of flow. He might well have in mind the
piscinae of the upper Tiber, since he mentions its navigation in the
region of his estates at Tifernum (v. 6. 12).

Water-gates are said to have controlled the exit from the Nile–Red
Sea canal at Arsinoe, built by the Ptolemies, and are described
briefly in Strabo 17. 1. 25 (p. 804), Diodorus 1. 33. 11. But the
authors do not clearly mention double gates, and the problem of
differing levels may have been obviated by the use of the slight tides.

62. *To Pliny*

Calpurnium Macrum credo facturum ut te libratore instruat. Trajan
tacitly withdraws his offer of an expert from Rome, Ep. 42. Cf.
Epp. 18. 3, 40. 3.

neque provinciae istae his artificibus carent. Not the two Moesiae,
but the Asiatic provinces, where Pliny was.

63. *To Trajan*

Pliny is now at Nicaea; 'in eam civitatem' n. This pair of letters is
continued in Ep. 67. *Date*, between 28 January and 18 September,
second year.

**scripsit mihi . . . Lycormas libertus tuus ut si qua legatio a Bos-
poro venisset urbem petitura, usque in adventum suum retineretur.**
This is an obscure affair. A dispute had arisen between the freedman and the client king of the Crimean principality. This can
hardly be personal. The freedman would not venture to hold up
the king's messages to Trajan, who was severe with his freedmen,
except on grounds of State (cf. VI. 31. 8–10). Even the whereabouts of
Lycormas are not clear: cf. *ex itinere* below. He may be coming from
the Crimea after discussions with Sauromates, in which he acted for
his superior, the equestrian procurator Virdius Geminus; Ep. 27,
'Gemellinus' n. Since Lucian, *Alex.* 57, indicates that the king paid
tribute to Rome,—contrary to the usual custom of client kingdoms—
and sent it to Bithynia, the dispute may be fiscal rather than diplomatic. (Rostovtzeff, *BSA* xxii. 21, suggests this was a subsidy paid
to the king by Rome; the text is ambiguous.)

The suggestion of O. Cuntz, *Hermes*, lxi. 193 ff., that these messages
contained secret information affecting the plans of Trajan for
Partho-Armenian affairs, has been effectively criticized by R. P.

Longden, *JRS* xxi. 19 ff., and F. Lepper, *Trajan's Parthian War* (Oxford, 1948), 165 ff. Cf. also L. Vidman, *Listy filologiké*, 1957, 21 ff. A legation would not be a suitable vehicle for such dispatches, and one may add that the Crimea was outside the orbit of the Romano-Parthian conflict, even if this was in prospect at this time, which is far from certain. Cuntz suggested that the replies of Trajan to this series and also to Ep. 74 were suppressed for 'security reasons'. But what could there be to suppress? Here and elsewhere replies are missing only when Pliny's letters are formal reports or recommendations requiring merely formal acknowledgement: Epp. 25, 26, 83, 85–87. Cf. Introduction, pp. 533 f. No advice or comment was required from Trajan about the Bosporan reports, except possibly that Pliny had acted correctly. Of this group, Ep. 64 is a report on a special use of the public post, like Epp. 83, 120, of which only the latter receives a direct reply. Trajan's indifference to the traffic problem at the route centre Juliopolis also tells against Cuntz's theory, Ep. 78 nn.; see also Ep. 74 nn. The notion that Pliny's canal project was part of a military supply plan is shown to be false by Pliny's own account, Ep. 41. 2 n.

in eam civitatem in qua ipse sum. Nicaea, according to Ep. 67. 1, and not the capital Nicomedia, which the embassy would be expected to visit.

sed venit tabellarius Sauromatae regis. The principality that occupied the south-eastern Crimea, including the cities of Pantica-paeum, Theudosia, and Phanagorias, and controlled the folks of the coastal region north of the Caucasus, remained in client relationship to Rome without becoming a province. At this period there was a steady infiltration of Sarmatian elements from the adjacent steppes, as the use of Sauromates as a royal name indicates. See *CAH* x. 265 f., xi. 96 f. For Crimea as a source of corn, Rostovtzeff, *SEHRE*[1], 239 f. The name of the king, who seems to have reigned from 92–93 to 124, occurs in full on his coins as Ti. Iulius Sauromates. The house used grandiloquent titles, such as 'King of Kings', and made much of their loyalty to Rome and the emperor. Cf. *ILS* 851 nn.; *PIR*[1], S 179–81.

regis. For the restoration of this word see O.C.T., apparatus.

64. *To Trajan*

Date. Between 28 January and 18 September, second year, a little later than Ep. 63.

Rex Sauromates scripsit mihi esse quaedam quae deberes quam maturissime scire. Cuntz assumed that the contents of the various messages were concealed from Pliny. Possibly—but Pliny would not recount what Trajan could read for himself in the original version. So too in Ep. 59 he does not summarize the *libellus* of Archippus, or that of Apamea in Ep. 47, which he had certainly read.

maturissime. If foreign affairs were involved, it is more likely to concern the activities of the adjacent Alan hordes, which it was the proper business of Sauromates to contain, than Parthia.

qua ex causa festinationem tabellarii quem ad te cum epistulis misit diplomate adiuvi. This should be the original *tabellarius* of Ep. 63, who had not yet departed. So Hardy. Pliny speeds him thus on receipt of a second messenger with a message to himself, and explains to Trajan why he let Sauromates use the *cursus publicus*, which normally he had not the right to use, Cf. Epp. 45–46 nn. Lepper's suggestion, loc. cit., that Trajan had written to object and that Pliny is apologizing is not necessary.

65. *To Trajan*

Date. Between 28 January and 18 September, second year.

1. Magna domine et ad totam provinciam pertinens quaestio est de condicione et alimentis eorum quos vocant θρεπτούς. For once Pliny fails to put a clear and specific question to Trajan. The problem only emerges clearly for the modern reader from Ep. 66, but the *ab epistulis* did not doubt what was in Pliny's mind, because Pliny in effect referred the emperor to the existing documents, as in Ep. 72, and asked if they were valid.

The term θρεπτός and its correlates, θρέψας, τροφεύς, σύντροφος, which are well known from inscriptions of Asia Minor, have been discussed by A. Cameron, 'θρεπτός, and related terms' etc. *Anatolian Studies, presented to W. H. Buckler* (Manchester, 1939), 27 ff., and by T. G. Nani, *Epigraphica*, v–vi (1943–4), 45 f. Cameron distinguishes three types: the ordinary free-born foster-child, the adopted child, and persons of servile status. The latter may be either house-born slaves or as here (Ep. 66. 1): 'liberi nati expositi deinde sublati . . . et in servitute educati'. This third category were usually favourites brought up within the family of the *dominus* as companions to his legitimate children—hence called σύντροφος. The class of *expositi* tends also to occur among folk of humble station, and with professional slave-dealers. All types appear in the inscriptions of Bithynia and Pontus. For examples see Cumont, *Stud. Pont.* iii, nn. 5, 7b, 33, 44b., etc.; Dörner, *Inschriften . . . aus Bithynien*, 90. The common formula is, for example, Αὐρηλία Πρόκλα τῷ κυρίῳ καὶ θρέψαντι Φαρνάκῃ.

The term θρεπτός is social rather than legal, and the custom is deeply rooted in Asian history. The servile form appears in the code of Hammurabi, in the story of Eumaeus in the Odyssey (15. 361 ff.), and in documents of the Hellenistic and Roman period. In the western provinces the institution of *alumni* may be due to oriental influence (Cameron, art. cit. 52 f.). But the term in Roman legal texts covers a wider field than that of *expositi* (Volterra, *Studi . . . Besta* (Milan 1937–9), i. 451 f.). The reason for the present spurt of interest in the matter was not any economic crisis affecting individuals in Bithynia, but rather the opportunity offered by Pliny's mission. The fosterers might hope that Pliny would reverse the local custom in favour of the Roman rule which enabled them to recover their costs when θρεπτοί were claimed; Ep. 66. 2 n. (Cameron, art. cit. 50; Vidman, *Étude*, 85.)

2. quia nihil inveniebam aut proprium aut universale quod ad Bithynos referretur, consulendum te existimavi . . . neque putavi posse me in eo quod auctoritatem tuam posceret exemplis esse contentum. Though the question was *saepe tractata* (66. 1) no general ruling had yet been given in Bithynia, because the proconsuls proceeded by the method of individual judgments which lacked the compulsion of genuine case-law. Pliny, like Ulpian (Ep. 58. 4 n.), was not content with isolated judgments, *exempla*, and wanted a general ruling, partly because like Trajan he was personally much moved by *favor libertatis*, II. 6. 3 n., Ep. 66. 2. The basic point, assumed by both Pliny and Trajan's advisers, in Ep. 66, is that the imperial edicts do not have universal application. They are valid only for the area and persons for whom they have been issued. This is a principle of considerable importance, though seldom recognized, in the understanding of the development of administrative, civil, and criminal law in the provinces. The opposite assumption has vitiated many inquiries, such as the investigation into the development of *collegia* and the procedure of Christian persecution. Cf. Appendix V, p. 779. Hence Pliny was in no way absurd in sending this query to Rome. Cf. Volterra, art. cit. 450 ff. A century later the centralizing tendency was in control at Rome, and lawyers like Ulpian maintained that imperial rescripts, though particular in origin, were of universal validity. *Dig.* 47. 12. 3. 5, 1. 4. 1. 1.

exemplis esse contentum. So in Epp. 108. 2, 112. 3: 'quod in perpetuum mansurum est a te constitui decet'. So far as other provinces are concerned, and later times, Trajan's rescripts are themselves only *exempla*, as Vidman remarks (*Étude*, 85–86); the rescript about the Christians is the great instance of this (App., pp. 782 f.). But Pliny regards them as having permanent validity for Bithynia, which is half-way towards the final position taken by Ulpian.

The *exempla* are the decisions of the proconsuls, as in Ep. 72. But it seems from s. 3 that in Achaea many such cases were settled in municipal courts. The term is applied in its normal sense to administrative and judicial actions of Trajan and Pliny in Epp. 29. 2 n., 78. 2, 81. 5, 97. 2.

3. recitabatur autem apud me edictum . . . ad 'Andaniam' pertinens. The emendation of O. Cuntz (*Hermes*, lxi. 202) for *Anniam* (Aa), fits the context of Achaea and Lacedaemon, and is better than the *Asiam* of previous editors. Andania was a small city of Messenia, near a shrine of Demeter, which owned a right of asylum, and may have sheltered a community of θρεπτοί. Pausanias 4. 33. 4 (6); Ditt. *Syll.*³ 2. 735–6.

recitatae et epistulae divi Vespasiani ad Lacedaemonios, et divi Titi ad eosdem et Achaeos, et Domitiani ad Avidium Nigrinum et Armenium Brocchum proconsules. At first the question came from the cities and provincial council of Achaea. Only later was the proconsul involved. Cf. the affair of Vienna and Trajan, IV. 22 nn. Sparta as a *civitas libera* would negotiate with the Senate or Princeps, ignoring the proconsul. Sparta retained this status after Vespasian's general cancellation of the freedom given to Greece by Nero, cf. VIII. 24. 4 n., *RE* (2) iii. 1449.

proconsules. Hardy took both to be proconsuls of Achaea, as the context suggests. But Trajan uses the plural, *inter eas provincias*, Ep. 66. 4.

Avidium Nigrinum. Little is known of his career. For the family see v. 13. 6, VI. 29. 1 nn. He was brother of T. Avidius Quietus, a consul of 93, and father of the well-known consul of 110. His proconsulship of Achaea cannot be exactly dated. He is mentioned with his brother as friend and patron of Plutarch, *de fraterno amore*, I. 1, p. 478 B, but the passage does not prove their joint presence in Achaea (as Groag, *Reichsbeamten von Achaea*, 42, n. 167). Garzetti, *Inc.* 24.

Armenius Brocchus is not known, *PIR²*, A 1057. But the cognomen Brocchus occurs among the many names of an active praetorian senator from Nemausus who served in Domitian's Dacian wars, *ILS* 1016. It has strong Celtic and Illyrian affiliations, but appears in Italy also. Cf. *ILS*, Index ii. Armenius is rare, and has a Celtic ring also, cf. Arminius.

vera et emendata in scriniis tuis esse credebam. This passage demonstrates the lack of effective archives in Bithynia, cf. Ep. 31. 4 n. The secretaries *ab epistulis* and *a libellis* kept copies of all official documents in their 'cabinets', *scrinia*, though usually Pliny sends the relevant documents for convenience, cf. Epp. 58, 79. 5.

The term *scrinium* came into official use for the departments of the imperial administration in the Diocletianic administration. Earlier the term is rarely used in such contexts. But servile *scriniarii ab epistulis* are known in the Julio-Claudian period, *ILS* 1671, 1675, *RE* (2) ii. 894 f.

66. *To Pliny*

1. **nec quicquam invenitur in commentariis . . . quod ad omnes provincias sit constitutum.** Trajan, true to his general doctrine of preferring *cuiusque loci leges*, Epp. 109, 113 nn.,—or else the secretariat, which has evidently looked out the legal definitions and precedents for Trajan's benefit—is unwilling to apply to Bithynia rules proper to another region, and has caused a hunt to be made. Since neither a general nor a particular precedent can be found Trajan pronounces: 'et ideo . . .', s. 2.

    commentariis. Cf. Tac. *Ann.* 13. 43: 'compertum sibi referens ex commentariis patris sui' etc. Suet. *Dom.* 20, 'praeter commentarios et acta Tiberii Caesaris nihil lectitabat'. Ep. 95, 'referri in commentarios meos iussi'. The *commentarii* contained all the *constitutiones* of whatever type of each Princeps arranged according to their appropriate *scrinium* (Ep. 65. 3), and must have resembled the minute book of an Oxford college in the diversity of their material. Secretaries entitled *a commentariis Augusti*, assisted by clerks—*tabularii*, *scriniarii*, *exceptores*—organized the archives, known collectively as *tabularium principis*, or occasionally as *sanctuarium*, and located in the Palatium. Dio 60. 4. 5, 78 (79). 21. 1; Hirschfeld, *Verwaltungsbeamten*, 325, nn. 1–3. Cf. A. H. M. Jones, JRS 1949, 43 f.

2. **epistulae sane sunt Domitiani . . . quae fortasse debeant observari ; sed inter eas provincias de quibus rescripsit non est Bithynia.** The Aldine reading is clearly preferable to that of the other early editions: 'rescripsit inter quas (*non*) est Bithynia'. These made 'sed inter eas . . .' construe with *observari*, in the supposed sense that Domitian's rescripts should apply only to those provinces. But *in* or *intra* (Keil) not *inter* would be required. Trajan is not reversing but extending Domitian's ruling. This is shown by the following *et ideo*, which links *debeant observari* to *puto* etc.

    nec adsertionem denegandam iis qui ex eiusmodi causa in libertatem vindicabuntur puto. Trajan is true to the tendency, *favor libertatis*, underlying imperial legislation about manumission and freedom, expressed in his Principate by the *SC. Rubrianum, Dig.* 40. 5. 26. 7, which protected fideicommissary bequests of freedom. So too Nerva had discouraged posthumous suits against the free status of dead persons, ibid. 15. 4. The notion that Roman legal opinion and the great jurists were hostile to the interests of the freedmen class (Syme, *Tacitus*, 447, 533) makes too much of the debate, on a very special aspect of the matter, in Tac. *Ann.* 14. 42–45. See VIII. 14. 12 n.

adsertionem. In Roman law such cases were amongst those protected by the action known as *causa liberalis*, in which the representative of the claimant, who as a slave could not appear in person, championed his freedom against the *dominus* or *possessor*, who acted as *adsertor in servitutem*. Under this procedure the successful claimant of liberty recovers his liberty (but not his *ingenuitas*), and his former owner has no claim over him. Trajan's legal adviser is applying these principles within the domain of Hellenistic custom. See Buckland, *Roman Law of Slavery*, 653 ff.; Paulus, *Dig.* 40. 12. 24 pref.; P. F. Girard, *Manuel de droit romain*[3] (Paris, 1901), 99 f.

vindicabuntur. It has been suggested that Pliny's cases concern not the claim of parents over exposed children, but the children's own claims (Bonner, *Roman Declamation*, 126 n. 1, citing Cornil, *NRH* xxi (1897), 430–1), because the claim is *in libertatem* not *in potestatem*. This is wrong: the slave could not claim (cf. below), and *peregrini* did not have *patria potestas* (Gaius, 1. 55). The passive indicates the bringing of the action by third parties, i.e. parents.

neque ipsam libertatem redimendam pretio alimentorum. The legal background has been clarified by Volterra (art. cit. 450 ff.). Rules of law from the early Principate onwards protected the freedom of the exposed freeborn child—and equally the rights of a master over an exposed slave-child—subject to the payment of costs of upbringing to the fosterer. An early instance appears in a Neronian lawsuit recorded in Tablet xvi from Herculaneum (Piganiol, *Studi . . . Paoli*, 563 f., *Parola del Passato* (1948), 171) and the rule appears in non-juridical texts (e.g. Sen. *Controv.* 9. 3 (26); Pseudo-Quint. *Decl.* 278; Quint. 7. 1. 14–15; later Paulus. *Dig.* 41. 7. 8; *Cod. Iust.* 8. 51. 1, A.D. 224). Greek usage, while protecting the rights of the exposed child, did not allow the claim for *alimenta*. The Greek custom is widely documented in literature, notably in Menander's *Epitrepontes* and in various passages of Plautus (Volterra, art. cit. 462 ff., citing Taubenschlag's commentary on Menander, *ZS. Sav.* 46, 48). Hence Trajan applies the Greek, not the Roman, rule in the Hellenistic land of Bithynia, true to his preference for local usage. Cameron (art. cit. 50) seems to assume, wrongly, that the Asiatic custom favoured the fosterer rather than the *alumnus*. The texts in *Cod. Theod.* 5. 7, which refuse recovery and protect the rights of the fosterer, represent the views of a different age and moral climate. Even L. Mitteis seems to have been astray over this, in *Reichsrecht und Volksrecht* (1891), 107, 127–8. (Cf. Vidman, *Étude*, 85.)

In this letter the machinery behind the emperor's activity becomes apparent. The information is organized by the secretariat. The jurisprudents advise on law. But Trajan himself takes the decision to give Greek usage priority over Roman custom.

67. *To Trajan*

Date. Between 28 January and 18 September, second year, later than Ep. 64. Written from Nicaea before his departure to Juliopolis, s. 1. For the persons and circumstances see Epp. 63–64 nn.

1. ipse proficiscebar in diversam provinciae partem. This should mean his visit to Juliopolis, Ep. 77. 2. Cf. Ep. 33. 1 for the phrase. Pliny is not at Prusa at the moment of Ep. 70, which, besides, is not in a corner remote from Nicaea.

2. epistulae Lycormae quas detinere, ut ante praedixi, nolui, aliquot diebus hinc legatum antecessurae viderentur. In Ep. 63 he says that he sent the *tabellarii* of Sauromates and Lycormas on together, so that the first messages of Sauromates should arrive together with those of Lycormas.

68. *To Trajan*

Date. Between 28 January and 18 September, second year.

Petentibus quibusdam ut sibi reliquias suorum aut propter iniuriam vetustatis aut propter fluminis incursum aliaque his similia quaecumque secundum exemplum proconsulum transferre permitterem. Here, as in Ep. 49, Pliny wants to apply pontifical law to a provincial problem. In Roman usage the burial of a body, even illegally interred, rendered the site *religiosum*. Thereafter any interference, as, for example, for rebuilding or transfer of a corpse, within Italy or from a province to Italy, required the authorization of the pontiffs; Gaius 2. 6: 'religiosum . . . facimus (sc. locum) mortuum inferentes'. For the procedure see *Dig.* 1. 8. 6. 4, 11. 7. 2. 7–8, and in general Mommsen-Marquardt, *Ant. Rom.* xii. 1. 371 f. Instances of such reburials and transfers in Italy, or from a province to Italy are not uncommon in inscriptions, cf. *ILS* 1792, 8380–1, 8390, and occasionally the Princeps acts instead of the pontiffs, ibid. 1593, 1685. Within a province the pontiffs were not concerned, because sacral law did not operate outside Italy, cf. Ep. 50 n., Gaius 2. 7, Mommsen-Marquardt, op. cit. 383 f. But Gaius adds of such a case: 'etiamsi non sit religiosum pro religioso habetur'. The Roman rule came to be applied to provinces by its inclusion in the provincial edicts of governors, who acted as the licensing authority; Gaius, *Dig.* 11. 7. 7–9. Ulpian, ibid. 7. 38, quoting an edict of M. Aurelius. *ILS* 7742a. This is just what had been happening in Bithynia before Pliny: 'secundum exemplum proconsulum'.

petentibus quibusdam. Vidman (*Étude* 76) doubts whether proconsular permission was really necessary, and attributes the requests to local vanity and ambition, as in Plut. *Praecept. rp. gerundae* 19, cf. Epp. 81. 1, 110. 1 nn. But the custom had become a rule before Pliny's governorship.

propter iniuriam vetustatis. Cf. *Sent. Pauli* i. 21. 1: 'ob incursum fluminis aut metum ruinae corpus iam . . . sepulturae traditum . . . in alium locum transferri potest'.

exemplum proconsulum. Epp. 65. 2, 72.

quaecumque. The word seems otiose, and O.C.T. *quocumque* from Kukula gives the required sense. For the purely adjectival use in Pliny, who very seldom uses the word at all, cf. VIII. 20. 2, IV. 15. 13.

quia sciebam in urbe nostra ex eiusmodi causa collegium pontificum adiri solere, te domine maximum pontificem consulendum putavi. It is difficult at first to see why Pliny bothered Trajan with this case. But there was a legal point at issue (above) and his superficial knowledge of the law in the matter apparently worried him into believing, as in Ep. 49, that such problems were beyond his legal competence; his friend Titius Aristo had discussed problems of this kind, and even Gaius, loc. cit., gave the opinion that sacral law did not apply to provincial burials only as the opinion of the majority. But Pliny was not suggesting that the matter should be referred to the pontiffs; Trajan misunderstands him on this, Ep. 69 n. As in Ep. 72, he is not happy to apply the rulings of proconsuls in what is now an imperial province, and the long formula is just a variant of his other ways of putting the question to the Princeps, cf. Ep. 41. 1.

sciebam. Pliny rarely quotes his own experience, cf. Epp. 49. 2 n., 96. 1.

collegium pontificum adiri. Two such pontifical decrees are summarized in *ILS* 8380–1. The formula runs: 'si ea ita sunt ut libello continentur, placet fieri' etc. The decree was dated and countersigned by the presiding *promagister collegii*.

69. *To Pliny*

iniungere necessitatem provincialibus pontificum adeundorum. This had not been suggested by Pliny, who only asked 'quid observare me velis'. His letter has been read hastily, as in Ep. 40. 1 n.

70. To Trajan

Date. Between 28 January and 18 September, second year. The contents refer to the visit to Prusa recorded in Ep. 58. 1.

1. quaerenti mihi domine Prusae ubi posset balineum quod indulsisti fieri placuit locus. See Epp. 23–24. Trajan's reply hardly took six months to arrive, yet nothing has apparently been done about the Baths since the previous autumn. The explanation is that Pliny settled the site during the visit of Ep. 58, and subsequent difficulties prompted this letter, sent after he had left Prusa. See Introduction, p. 530.

consequemur ut foedissima facies civitatis ornetur. Pliny appeals to Trajan's passion for architectural improvements, as in Epp. 37. 3, 41. 1, 98.

nec ulla aedificia tollantur. There were ancient rules preventing the destruction of houses in the republican *Lex Tarenti municipi* 33–36 and *Lex coloniae Ursonensis* c. 75, in the Flavian *Lex Malacitana* 62, and later recurring in Hadrian's rescript about a house at Stratonicaea (A–J 20, 26, 65, 83, or *FIRA*. II. 18, 21, 24, 80). The common form is 'ne quis aedificia quae restiturius non erit destruat'.

For *civitas* in the sense of *urbs* or *oppidum* see Ep. 41. 2 n.

2. legaverat eam Claudius Polyaenus Claudio Caesari iussitque in peristylio templum ei fieri, reliqua ex domo locari. . . . reditum aliquamdiu civitas percepit. The terms of the bequest are obscure. The testator meant to endow the shrine out of the rent of the house, and to charge the city with the duty of maintenance. Hence the building never passed into the *patrimonium Caesaris*, and the city received the rent but did not own the house. This would explain the surprising failure of the imperial procurator of Bithynia to intervene; contrast Ep. 84.

deinde paulatim . . . cum peristylio domus tota collapsa est. The result of this complicated scheme could have been foreseen. Since neither the *patrimonium* nor the city benefited materially, neglect was inevitable; cf. IV. 13. 6, VII. 18. 2.

iam paene nihil ex ea nisi solum superest. The total ruin in some sixty years is surprising, unless the earth had quaked.

Claudius Polyaenus was probably a local aristocrat who had received citizenship from Claudius, rather than an imperial freedman. Other wealthy Polyaeni are known later in Bithynia with Roman status, being Julii, Claudii, and Aelii, at Prusa and the small city of Hadriani adjacent. The envoy of the provincial council in VII. 6. 6 is one of them. L. Robert regards them as forming a large clan (*BCH* xxxiii. 406).

peristylio. For the spacious courts of the Hellenistic houses see D. S. Robertson, *Greek and Roman Architecture*[2] (1959), 300 f. The house must have been on the scale of the larger houses at Pompeii, such as the House of the Faun, which had a separate peristyle court beyond the main building, ibid. 306.

3. **ego si permiseris cogito in area vacua balineum collocare, eum autem locum in quo aedificia fuerunt exedra et porticibus amplecti atque tibi consecrare.** There is an ambiguity in *area*, as Hartleben saw (ad loc.). He took it to be the peristyle, perhaps wrongly. The term is commonly used with or without *vacua* to denote a cleared site (Suet. *Vesp.* 8. 5; Tac. *Ann.* 15. 43. 1–3; *Dig.* 50. 16. 211). But Pliny uses *area* alone to mean the open courts within buildings (Ep. 81. 7, VI. 20. 4, VII. 27. 10). The *area vacua* must be of considerable extent to contain a set of *thermae*—cf. Ep. 23. 1 n. The *locum in quo aedificia fuerunt* should refer to the main building excluding the open court. Pliny may mean: 'I will build the baths on the cleared site as a whole and erect a shrine around (sc. *amplecti*) that part which was covered before, instead of the shrine in the court'. Compare the plan for Dio's library, Ep. 81. 7: 'id (monumentum) . . . in area collocatum quae porticibus includitur'.

si permiseris. Ep. 23. 1 n.

exedra. For a grandiose example see the plan of Trajan's new Forum at Rome, *CAH* xi. 775. Vitruvius 5. 11. 2: 'constituantur... in porticibus exedrae spatiosae habentes sedes in quibus philosophi rhetores . . . sedentes disputare possint'. Also 1. 13. 2, 'stationibus' n. Hartleben compares the *House of the Vigiles* at Ostia for an *exedra* on a court, dedicated to the imperial cult. (R. Calza–E. Nash, *Ostia*, fig. 129).

consecrare. Cf. Ep. 75. 2, 'opera . . . quae honori tuo consecrarentur'. The cult of the living emperor had been part of the paraphernalia of politics and government in Bithynia since the beginning of the Principate. The rule that Roman citizens should not take part in it had doubtless long been a dead letter in the Orient. Cf. Dio 51. 20. 7.

exemplar testamenti . . . misi tibi, ex quo cognosces multa Polyaenum . . . reliquisse quae . . . perierunt. One would expect the procurator Augusti to be involved at this point to hunt for the lost treasures. Pliny suspects a tenant of making away with everything.

The will might have been kept in the municipal archives, χρεω-φυλάκιον or ἀρχεῖον, in such a case, cf. Ep. 31. 4 n. Liebenam, *Städteverwaltung*, 278 f., 290.

71. *To Pliny*

illud tamen parum expressisti an aedes . . . facta esset. Cf. Ep. 70. 2. Pliny had only said what Polyaenus proposed to have done, though his own intended dedication of that part of the site suggests that the Claudian shrine had been built.

si facta est, licet collapsa sit, religio eius occupavit solum. Cf. Marcian, *Dig.* 1. 8. 6. 3: 'semel . . . aede facta etiam diruto aedificio locus sacer manet'. Hardy contrasts Trajan's attitude in Ep. 50, where he refuses to apply Roman sacral law to provincial territory. But here he is less concerned for legal technicality than for respect to the memory of Claudius, for which Vespasian also had shown some concern; cf. *CAH* xi. 19, 408.

72. To Trajan

Date. Between 28 January and 18 September, second year.

Postulantibus quibusdam ut de agnoscendis liberis restituendisque natalibus . . . ipse cognoscerem, respexi ad senatusconsultum pertinens ad eadem genera causarum. As Hardy saw, during the inquiry into the status of θρεπτοί, Ep. 65, cases of another sort had arisen, in which the parents of children who had been born free and reduced to slavery, but who were not in the class of θρεπτοί, claimed their freedom. The action is against the will of the *domini*, who dispute the facts, which the owners of the θρεπτοί did not. But Hardy, followed by Durry, ad loc., confused the issue by invoking the *SC. Plancianum* '*de agnoscendis liberis*', which has nothing to do with the case; it regulated the status of children born after divorce, and was concerned with legitimacy, Ulpian, *Dig.* 25. 3. 1–3. Pliny is referring to a procedure akin to the system of *restitutio natalium* known from texts of Ulpian and others, *Dig.* 40. 11. This was a special administrative act limited to the Princeps at Rome whereby freedmen, not slaves, were declared to be *ingenui*, either fictitiously or after submitting proofs. The later law also knew a civil suit, akin to the *causa liberalis* (Ep. 66. 2 n.) whereby a freedman might sue for recognition of his original *ingenuitas*, which the *causa liberalis* did not restore; Gaius 4. 44; *Dig.* 40. 14. Tac. *Ann.* 13. 27. 7 is an early example. Buckland, *Slavery* etc. 672 f. None of these exactly fits Pliny's cases, where the persons are still in servile status and hope to recover *ingenuitas*. The present procedure is nearer to that followed in the early Principate for redressing the wrongs of persons improperly enslaved and imprisoned in *ergastula*; cf. Suet. *Aug.* 32. 1; *Tib.* 8; Duff, *Freedmen* etc. 86 ff. The *SC.* quoted by Pliny may well have regulated both this kind of problem and that of the *causa liberalis* for Bithynia: 'eadem genera causarum'. The procedure was evidently more familiar and better documented than for the case of θρεπτοί. The type quoted by Pliny is only one of many forms that a *causa liberalis* might assume, in Roman law, and only twice mentioned in the lengthy passage of the *Digest*, 40. 12. 1, 3 pref.

Minicio Rufo. This should be L. Minicius Rufus, praetorian legate

of Lugdunensis after 83, and consul in 88; *ILS* 2118. *F. Pot.* The
like-named proconsul of Crete-and-Cyrene in 71 (*AE* 1951, n. 209)
should be another person, despite *PIR*¹, M 442–3 and Garzetti, *C.*
102. Rufus' proconsulship of Bithynia, implied by Pliny, must fall
before 88, close to that of Lappius Maximus, Ep. 58. 6 n.

ipse cognoscerem. This is the only question. He is not asking, as
in Ep. 65, for details of law and procedure, cf. Ep. 73.

respexi. For once Pliny quotes a document not produced by the
litigants. Ep. 31. 4 n.

de iis tantum provinciis loquitur quibus proconsules praesunt,
ideoque rem integram distuli. Durry is very severe with Pliny for
refusing to act on the apparently frivolous ground that he was not a
proconsul but a legate with proconsular powers, although he took
Hardy's view that the form of restitution in question was an imperial
monopoly. Pliny's problem arose reasonably, as in the case of the
θρεπτοί, from the principle that regulations applied only to the area
for which they were formulated: Ep. 65, 2 n. If the *SC.* omitted
reference to the inperial provinces, there might be good reason for
the distinction. This passage shows more clearly than Epp. 65 and
68 that Trajan in his *mandata* had not instructed Pliny normally to
apply *SC.* and *exempla proconsulum* of the previous period to problems
of his administration.

73. *To Pliny*

si mihi senatusconsultum miseris. Pliny had given no means of
identifying the document. Hence it was quicker for Pliny to send
the copy than the reference, as Hardy saw and J. N. Hough did not
(*Cl. J.* xxxv (1939), 25–26). Presumably the decrees of the Senate
were stored in the *tabularium* under the consular years by which the
lawyers cite them in the *Digest*. This is the only *SC.* mentioned by
Pliny about the administration of Bithynia, a proconsular province,
for nearly one hundred and forty years of the Principate, apart from
that concerning the acts of Bassus, Ep. 56. 4. Yet decisions of
Augustus and Domitian occur five times, though two of these are
personal: Epp. 58, 72, 79, 84. It seems that the proconsuls were very
much left to themselves in the century before Nerva's accession.

74. *To Trajan*

Date. Between 28 January and 18 September, second year.

1. Appuleius domine miles, qui est in statione Nicomedensi, scripsit mihi. Appuleius is serving in a post like those established at

Byzantium and proposed for Juliopolis under the control of a centurion in Ep. 77 nn., though he does not seem to have a superior officer. Such *stationes* acted as indicated in Ep. 77–78 and in Tertullian, *Apol*. 2. 8: 'latronibus vestigandis per universas provincias militaris statio sortitur'. They provided a link between the municipal security services and the governor, and enabled him to carry out his duty, enjoined later in the *mandata*, 'sacrilegos latrones plagiarios fures conquirere debent' (Ulpian, *Dig*. 1. 18. 13 pref.). Cf. Suet. *Aug*. 32. 1, *Tib*. 37. 2. For other such posts known in Bithynian cities see Ep. 77. 1 n. These *stationes* are distinct from the control-points of the Customs organized by the publicans concerned, and from the posting-stations of the imperial post, also known as *stationes*, though military and customs posts occur together in some localities. Nicomedia as a great port would have a *statio* of the *quadragesima portuum Bithyniae*, and as a provincial capital it had a military guard, drawn from the auxiliary forces (cf. Epp. 19. 1, 21. 1 nn.); the single nomen of *Appuleius* shows that he was not a legionary soldier. See Mommsen, *D. Pen. R.* i. 364 f.; *RE* (2) iii. A 2213, s.v. 'stationarius'.

The *stationarii* are concerned with the recovery of runaway slaves in conjunction with the municipal magistrates and the provincial governor, in a regulation of Marcus Aurelius and in citations of Ulpian and Paulus, just as in Pliny's letter (*Dig*. 11. 4. 1. 2, 4). Vidman and others, following a hint of Mommsen, have assumed that the officers of *stationes* already enjoyed the minor jurisdiction which they certainly possessed, in a restricted form, in the third century (Vidman, op. cit. 55, 60; Mommsen, op. cit. 368–9, citing esp. *Cod*. 9. 2. 8). But there is no trace of this in Pliny and the passages of Ulpian and Paulus cited above. The authority in the matter of fugitive slaves comes from the municipal magistrates and the provincial governors. (Cf. esp. Ulpian, loc. cit. 3, citing Pius.) Vidman stressed the lack of mention of municipal police, or *irenarchae*, in Pliny. But they are implied in the reference in s. 1: 'perductum ad magistratus'. Cf. Ulpian (loc. cit. 1. 6): 'in publicum deduci (sc. fugitivi) intelliguntur qui municipalibus magistratibus traditi sunt *vel publicis ministeriis*'.

operas locaverat. His employers, discovering his secret, forced Callidromus to work for nothing, but he preferred to take his chance as a confessed runaway with a good story to tell.

ad tuam statuam. Cf. Callistratus, *Dig*. 48. 19. 28. 7: 'ad statuas confugere vel imagines principum . . . prohibitum est . . . nisi si quis ex vinculis vel custodia detentus a potentioribus ad huiusmodi praesidium confugerit'. The practice began early, and abuses soon arose; Tac. *Ann*. 3. 36, 4. 67; Suet. *Aug*. 17. 5.

perductumque ad magistratus indicasse ⟨se⟩ servisse aliquando

Laberio Maximo captumque a Susago in Moesia et a Decibalo muneri missum Pacoro Parthiae regi. The story, with the slave's final return from somewhere in the mountains of Iran (s. 3) beyond Mesopotamia, took in Cuntz more effectively than it did Pliny. Cuntz (art. cit. Ep. 63. 1 n.) saw in this yarn serious evidence of Daco-Parthian co-operation, and of Trajan concocting secret plans for his Parthian campaigns at this moment; so too Hardy, in part, ad loc., Paribeni, *Ottimo Principe*, i. 237, 244, J. Guey, *Essai sur la Guerre parthique de Trajan*, 27 (Bucharest, 1937). But Longden (*JRS* xxi. 19 f.) and Lepper, op. cit. 168 (Ep. 63. 1 n.), were more sceptical. There is no proof of the truth of the man's story, which Pliny did not take on trust: 'attulisse dicebat', s. 3. Callidromus produced the ring and the nugget to bolster up his story, and to put off the evil day of punishment. Pliny does not regard the man as a secret agent with the latest news from the Parthian front. He is in no hurry to dispatch the fellow, s. 2. The legate of Syria was a more likely source for Trajan's 'intelligence service'.

⟨**se**⟩. Madvig's correction is necessary, and easy. Cf. s. 3, 'se . . . attulisse dicebat'.

Laberio Maximo. Presumably son of the like-named Prefect of Egypt in 83, *ILS* 1996. M'. Laberius Maximus was consul in 89, and legate of Lower Moesia by October 100. He commanded an army in Trajan's first Dacian war with success, and was given a second consulship in 103. This puffed him up to conspire against Trajan, for which he was exiled to an island, perhaps late in the reign—if he was in fact depicted on Trajan's Column. This letter casts no light on the date of his disgrace. Callidromus' adventures must have begun in 101–2. (*F. Pot.*; A-J n. 68; Dio 68. 9. 4; SHA, *Hadr.* 5. 5; Garzetti, *C.* 85; *RE* xii. 250 f.; Stuart-Jones, *BSR* v. 443.)

a Susago in Moesia. The invasion of Moesia by Sarmatian, not Dacian, forces is shown on the column; Cichorius, *Reliefs der Trajanssäule*, ii. 150 f. This passage is the only literary evidence for an invasion of Moesia in the first war, cf. Dio 68. 6–10. Susagus is unknown.

deinde fugisse atque ita in Nicomediam pervenisse. How did the man manage this journey? He could hardly have turned up in a more improbable port or province, or one more suspiciously close to Moesia and the Black Sea. Cf. Epp. 42, 43. 1, 77. 1.

muneri missum. The story, if not true, is *bien trouvé*. It might be evidence, not of a connexion between the Dacian and the Parthian, but of Roman suspicion that such a thing was possible. Just how such a mission found its way through the net of Roman dependencies round the Black Sea coasts is best left undiscussed. At this period Armenia was under effective Parthian control. The date of this remarkable journey must be placed, as Hardy saw, in 103–5 between the two Dacian wars. For Decibalus see VIII. 4. 2 n. Pacorus was dead by about 112–13, Dio 68. 17. 2.

2. gemmam . . . habentem imaginem Pacori. The coins of Pacorus II give some idea of this representation, *BMC* 'Parthia', pl. xxx.

3. glebulam misi quam se ex Parthico metallo attulisse dicebat. Cuntz did not stop to consider what this ingot could be. No precious metals are mined in the western and central areas of the Parthian empire, i.e. in Iraq, Iran, or the fringes of Armenia, though base metals are worked, including lead. There are famous and ancient turquoise pits near Nishapur. *Admiralty Geographical Handbook of Iran*, 464 ff.; idem, *Turkey*, ii. 124 f., fig. 23.

signata est anulo meo. For the sealing and witnessing of non-oral evidence cf. Cic. *ii in Verr.* 1. 50; *pro Clu.* 185; *RE* v A 1051 f.

75. To Trajan

Date. Between 28 January and 18 September, second year.

1. Iulius domine Largus ex Ponto, nondum mihi visus ac ne auditus quidem. A Roman citizen, whose family may have acquired their status through the short-lived Roman colony established at Heraclea by Julius Caesar, s. 2 n., he made his will according to Roman civil law. He is otherwise unknown, *PIR*[1] J 253.

2. rogavit enim testamento ut hereditatem suam adirem cerneremque. The heir is required to make known his acceptance of an inheritance within a certain period, using a fixed formula, Gaius: 2. 165–6. 'quod me . . . testamento suo heredem instituit eam hereditatem adeo cernoque'.

ac deinde praeceptis quinquaginta milibus nummum reliquum omne Heracleotarum et Tianorum civitatibus redderem. Largus is using the formula of the *fidei commissum*; Gaius 2. 249–50. He wished to make over the greater part of his estate to the two cities. But in Roman usage municipalities were not capable of ordinary inheritance. This disability was modified by two concessions. A Nervan *SC.* allowed legacies, and a Hadrianic *SC.* allowed *fidei commissa* to pass validly to such corporations. Largus was anticipating the Hadrianic legislation. His choice of Pliny as his agent suggests that he was aware of the difficulties, and wanted to ensure that his will would not be upset. It was in the nature of the *fidei commissum* that its use should tend to outstrip the law of the moment. For documentation see v. 7. 1 n. Duff, cited ibid., does not discuss this letter.

In the principal texts of Ulpian and Paulus, ibid., the privileges are said to have been granted 'omnibus civitatibus quae sub imperio populi Romani sunt', whereas in other relevant texts the term *municipia* is used, once with clear reference to Italian jurisdiction; *Tit. Ulp.* 22. 5; Maecianus, *Dig.* 36. 4. 12; cf. 38. 3. 1. 1. *Cod. Iust.* 7. 9. 3 brings out the distinction, with reference to the right of Roman *municipia* to enfranchise freedmen, which was extended from Italian to provincial *municipia*, not to all *civitates*, by *SC.* in A.D. 129. Hence it is questionable whether the concessions of Nerva and Hadrian concerned peregrine *civitates* at all; Hadrian forbade the leaving of *fidei commissa* to individual *peregrini* altogether, Gaius 2. 285. In any case the *SC.* refer only to bequests made under the civil law, i.e. by Roman citizens. Bequests by *peregrini* came under local law, unless modified by the jurisdiction of the proconsuls. The phrase quoted above may represent a reinterpretation of the law after the *Constitutio Antoniniana*. Pliny's letter does not solve the problem because it is earlier than Hadrian's ruling about individuals. But neither Pliny, who knew the law (v. 7. 1), nor Trajan's advisers question the bequest to two Greek cities. With the steady increase in the number of wealthy Roman citizens within provincial communes such bequests must have become rather frequent. Pliny's letter shows that the legislation of Nerva and Hadrian sought to regulate an existing practice of which simple points of procedure were still obscure in the time of Pius; Gaius 2. 195.

praeceptis quinquaginta milibus nummum. For inheritance by *praeceptio* see v. 7. 1 n. Pliny would have this sum free of encumbrances, whereas the ordinary heir was responsible for his share of the liabilities of what he inherited. The fideicommissary rules limited the share of the beneficiary to three-quarters (Gaius 2. 254). Hence the bequest amounted to S.150,000 at most for the proposed objects.

Neither Pliny nor Trajan notices that Pliny was exposing himself to a formal charge under the extortion law, much like Julius Bassus, IV. 9. 7 n. The extension of the equestrian class throughout the provinces tended to render out of date the old regulation which forbade any kind of private increment to public officials.

Heracleotarum et Tianorum. Heraclea was once the most powerful republic of the Pontic area, and remained independent until annexed by Mithridates Eupator *c.* 74 B.C. It was one of the eleven civic centres of the province of Pontus created by Pompey. But its sufferings in the Mithridatic wars and under local dynasts in the triumviral period, who destroyed a Roman colony established there by Julius Caesar, reduced its importance. In the Principate it was a plain *civitas stipendiaria*. By the third century or earlier it had become 'metropolis of Pontus' and seat of the provincial council. Strabo 12. 3. 6, pp. 542–3; Memnon, *FHG* iii, fr. 42; *IGGR* iii. 79; Jones, *Cities*, 151, 154, 163, 421 n. 13; Magie, *Romans*, 307, n. 23.

nondum mihi visus. Pliny has not yet visited Pontus, and does not in the remaining letters mention Heraclea, though he visits Pontic Amastris, Sinope, and Amisus.

Tium, famous only as birthplace of the Attalid dynasty, had been a dependency of Heraclea until it fell into the power of the Bithynian kings *c.* 179 B.C. Hence it became part of the Bithynian province at the time of its original annexation in 74. Strabo 12. 3. 8, p. 543; Jones, op. cit. 149, 152 f., 160; Magie, *Romans*, 308–9 n. 28.

utrum opera facienda quae honori tuo consecrarentur putarem, an instituendos quinquennales agonas. By the first suggestion was meant some public building or colonnade with a shrine of Trajan, as in Ep. 70. 3 n. For the popularity of festivals of games, and for the similar Trajanic Games at Pergamum, see Ep. 118. 1 n. Such festivals, on the Olympian model, spread throughout the Hellenistic world. It had been customary to associate them with the name of a popular Roman governor even in the Republican period, as with the *Mucia* at Ephesus in memory of the proconsul Mucius Scaevola (Magie, *Romans*, 174 n. 48). Augustus' foundation of *Quinquennalia* at Actium led to a fresh multiplication of games, Suet. *Aug.* 59. The Actian games included, like the *Neronia* at Rome, a 'certamen . . . musicum gymnicum equestre'. Suet. *Nero* 12. 3.

ut dispiceres quid eligere debeam. Pliny does not ask for a building licence, because the project was not municipal but private, Ep. 23. 1 n. It was reasonable to ask Trajan which he preferred in his own honour. The reference to Trajan is merely courteous, and treated as such by Trajan.

76. *To Pliny*

secundum cuiusque loci condicionem ipse dispice. For the principle see Epp. 65. 2, 66. 2 nn., 109, 111, 113. For the use of *locus* in the sense of *civitas* cf. Ep. 80, 'curiam . . . loci cuiusque', Ep. 111, 'hominibus cuiusque loci'. It goes back in legal terminology to the Republic, cf. *Lex de Gallia Cisalpina*, xx l. 43 (A–J. n. 27; *FIRA* I, n. 19).

77. *To Trajan*

Date. Between 28 January and 18 September, second year.

1. praecepisti Calpurnio Macro clarissimo viro ut legionarium centurionem Byzantium mitteret. Centurions were commonly used on special missions, or as district commissioners, where direct exercise of military discipline was required, cf. Tac. *Ann.* 14. 31, *ILS* 1349. This man was to organize a *statio* of traffic-control, as at Nicomedia

(Ep. 74. 1 n.), for the reasons given in Trajan's reply. It seems that the Byzantines had approached Trajan directly, and he had informed Pliny of his action. This centurion would have a small force under him; cf. Ep. 21. 1. Pliny writes to Trajan because he has been firmly instructed not to dissipate his own forces, Epp. 20. 2, 22. 2.

Other centurions are known later in the territory of Prusias, Claudiopolis, Sinope, and a *stationarius* at Tium, though only one of the centurions seems to have official connexions. (Vidman, op. cit. 54–56; *IGRR* iii. 74, 1390, 1426; L. Robert, *Ét. Anatol.* 285; Dörner, *Reise*, n. 11.) Vidman and others have made much of these centurions on special duties as foreshadowing the militarization of the civil government. But there is no sign in Pliny that they do more than control the traffic of the great highways and deal with problems arising thence outside the competence of the civic authorities, Ep. 74. 1 n. Vidman (op. cit. 60) speaks of the cities ceaselessly pressing for such intervention, and stresses the absence of mention of civic police in the Letters. But the present request came not from Juliopolis but from Pliny himself. In Ep. 74 the slave is first arrested by the civic authorities and only transferred to the military *stationarius* when he claims to have information for the emperor. Cf. also Epp. 19. 1 n., 86B n. See also my *Roman Society* etc. p. 98.

For Macer and his titles see Epp. 42 n., 56. 2 n.

2. an etiam Iuliopolitanis simili ratione consulendum putes, quorum civitas, cum sit perexigua, onera maxima sustinet. Hardy erred in suggesting that the problem arose from the bulk of civilian trade and travellers—though these contributed to it, s. 3 n.—and that the *onera* were those of the imperial customs. Trajan's reply shows that the main trouble arose from military transports, exaggerating the usual difficulties of the *cursus publicus* (Ep. 45 nn.). The relevant parallel is not Tac. *Ann.* 13. 50, concerning complaints about the *portoria*, but Tac. *Ann.* 12. 62, which Hardy did not quote: 'Byzantii . . . magnitudinem onerum apud senatum deprecarentur . . . ea loca insiderent quae transmeantibus terra marique ducibus exercitibusque simul vehendo commeatu opportuna forent'. Ibid. 63, they were 'Thraecio Bosporanoque bello recens fessos'. So too after the Balkan wars of Augustus the provinces of Achaea and Macedonia appealed for relief to Tiberius: 'onera deprecantes', ibid. 1. 76. The collection of customs, in any case, was not controlled by military personnel (Ep. 74. 1 n.) though it is likely that there was a customs station at Juliopolis, controlling traffic with Galatia. It was not till the time of Severus that Bithynia was combined with Asia in a customs union; cf. *RE* xxii. 1, 372 f., correcting de Laet, *Portorium*, 274 f., from a Trajanic inscription, *AE* 1920, n. 80.

Juliopolis, old Gordiucome, market town of the royal lands of the Bithynian kingdom, became the capital of a local brigand leader, Cleon, in the Triumviral period, who gave it the status of a city and its new name when he came over to Octavian. Strabo, xii, p. 574; Jones, *Cities*, 165 and n. 32.

3. sunt enim in capite Bithyniae plurimisque per eam commeantibus transitum praebent. The main east–west highway of northern Anatolia, from the military camps of Cappadocia, passed through the road centres of Sebastea, Tavium, and Ancyra, whence its southern branch entered Bithynia some 50 miles east of Juliopolis, which lies in the eastern part of the upper Sangarius basin: 'in capite Bithyniae'. Thence on to Nicaea and Nicomedia. Cf. Magie, *Romans*, 305 n. 14.

commeantibus. The career of Cleon shows the value of the situation as a trade centre. But the brigandage endemic in the time of Strabo, loc. cit., no longer troubles the city. The verb *commeare* seems not to be limited to the military connotation that dominates the noun *commeatus*, 'leave' or 'supplies'.

78. *To Pliny*

1. ea condicio est civitatis Byzantiorum confluente in eam commeantium turba. Trajan's Dacian wars may well have added, as in the time of Claudius (above 77. 2 n.), to the troubles of Byzantium. It was now the main entrepôt for the trade from the Mediterranean to the Euxine, and also canalized much of the traffic, both civil and military, in supplies and persons, between the provinces of the lower Danube, the wealthy lands of western Asia Minor, and the Euphrates frontier, as its connexion with the legate of Moesia indicates (Ep. 43. 3). Cf. in general E. Gren, *Kleinasien und der Ost-Balkan* etc. (Uppsala, 1941), and E. Gray's review, *JRS*, 1947, 212 f.

praecedentium temporum. This may mean the period since Vespasian made Byzantium part of a province, Ep. 43. 1 n.

2. ⟨si⟩ Iuliopolitanis succurrendum eodem modo putaverimus onerabimus nos exemplo. The imperial machine that in the later empire exploited and crushed the prosperity of the provincials is still welcomed as a protection, and its intervention invited. Cf. Rostovtzeff, *SEHRE*[1] 422 ff.

nos. A classical precaution of all civil servants—*nos* is 'the government', 'myself and my advisers'. Here the preceding 'habuerimus' shows that he does not mean 'you and me' as in Ep. 42: 'potest nos sollicitare lacus iste'. Cf. Ep. 32. 1 n. Pliny had no hand in the dispatch of the centurion. Trajan is quick enough to say 'me' when he means it, as in the last paragraph of this letter, or in Ep. 82. 1. This letter illustrates very nicely the combination of the somewhat pompous chancellery manner of the Secretary, in ss. 1–2, followed by the crisp intervention of the Princeps on a point that interests him in s. 3. See Ep. 32. 1 n. Introduction, p. 545.

3. si qui autem se contra disciplinam meam gesserint statim coerceantur ; aut si plus admiserint . . . si milites erunt, legatis eorum . . . notum facies, aut si in urbem versus venturi erunt mihi scribes. The *autem* marks a contrast which Hardy missed, and hence interpreted the sentence as referring to civilians except for the clause *si milites*. In s. 2 Trajan instructed Pliny to deal with civilian misbehaviour by himself. Now he turns to the question of soldiers and officials from outside Bithynia. Pliny can deal with minor offences—*statim coerceantur*—but in serious cases he is to notify their army commanders, in the case of soldiers, and the emperor himself in the case of functionaries, such as freedmen or equestrian procurators, returning to Rome. Pliny could not deal with serious offences by himself because he had no capital jurisdiction over Roman citizens, not even the *ius gladii* needed for the control of legionary troops, since his own troops were auxiliaries. Cf. Epp. 30. 1, 96. 4 nn., II. II. 8 n. Compare the instructions later given by Modestinus, *Dig.* 49. 16. 3 pref.: 'desertorem . . . ad suum ducem cum elogio praeses mittet praeterquam si quid gravius . . . in ea provincia . . . admiserit: ibi enim eum plecti debet ubi facinus admissum est'. An inscription from Euhippe in Caria, of the third century, tells how the city appealed to Caracalla for protection from the exactions of soldiers and *officiales* straying from the 'imperial and public routes'. They were referred back to the proconsul, much as here. *AE* 1953, n. 90. But there is no question yet of the later municipal burden of supplying Roman armies on the march, as suggested tentatively by Vidman (op. cit. 60) and Rostovtzeff (*BSA* xxii. 14, 20). The *prosecutio exercituum* first appears in Bithynian inscriptions of the Severan period, when the armies took the northern route by Nicomedia and Claudiopolis. *IGR* iii. 60, 62, 66–67. Dörner, *Inschriften*, n. 121, from Nicomedia; *Reise*, n. 10, from Prusias ad Hypium.

contra disciplinam meam. See Ep. 29. 1 n. for Trajan's insistence on discipline. He had taken special care to reduce the burden of the imperial post, Ep. 45 nn., and to avoid outrages in his own journeys, *Pan.* 20. 3–5. All service under the emperor was *militia* and hence subject to *disciplina*. In Ep. 85 a freedman procurator is *disciplinae tenacissimum*: cf. Ep. 86B. Hence the curious usage by which the domestic bursar of the Palace at Rome was called *procurator castrensis*. *ILS* 1567–9; Hirschfeld, *Verwaltungsbeamten*, 312 ff.

This reply of Trajan tells against the theory of Cuntz that Pliny was involved in secret preparations for the Parthian war. Epp. 63, 67. 74 nn. Trajan is not concerned about this traffic centre on the road to the East.

79. *To Trajan*

Date. Between 28 January and 18 September, second year, probably after midsummer.

Epp. 79 and 80, with 112–15, raise problems put by municipal magistrates in charge of the periodic census. The questions affecting *ingenuitas* in Epp. 65 and 72, and also the affair of Ep. 81, may also have been precipitated by the activity of the census.

1. **Cautum est domine Pompeia lege quae Bithynis data est ne quis capiat magistratum neve sit in senatu minor annorum triginta.** Pompeius after the final elimination of Mithridates Eupator reorganized the former kingdoms of Bithynia and Pontus as a Roman province, and settled the status of the communes by this law. Its name shows that by origin it was an ordinance issued by Pompeius in virtue of his *imperium* under the *Lex Manilia*; it was presumably among the *acta* of Pompeius ratified by the legislation of Caesar in 59 B.C. (Dio 37. 20; cf. Magie *Romans*, 369 n. 34). Earlier *leges provinciarum* were issued *ex senatusconsulto*, like the Sicilian *Lex Rupilia*, Cic. *ii in Verr.* 2. 90, 125; Mommsen, *DPR* vi. 1. 354. They usually settled the basis of taxation and military obligations, and defined the limits of local self-government, though great latitude in jurisdiction was left to the future proconsuls. Usually few changes were made in the existing pattern of city or tribal government. But Pompeius, faced by a region which had been largely administered by royal officials and Hellenistic bureaucratic methods, greatly enlarged the number, territory, and competence of the Greek cities, especially in Pontus. The arrangements of his *lex* were more detailed than was necessary in areas with a firmer tradition of Hellenistic city-government, such as Syria at the same time or Asia in 133. (Jones, *Cities*, 159–62, 170 ff.; Strabo, xii. 3. 1. p. 541 in particular.) The general rules of the *lex provinciae* seem to have been supplemented by local city charters (Epp. 109, 113), though these were often modified by later changes, as at Claudiopolis, Byzantium, Amisus, Heraclea (Epp. 39. 5, 43. 1, 75. 1, 92 nn.), and at the Roman colonies of Apamea and Sinope, Epp. 47. 1, 90 nn. In his organization Pompeius introduced Roman ideas of local government into the Greek city system, particularly in the organization of the local councils, in the qualifications for magistracies, and in the census

arrangements. Such changes were apt to favour an oligarchy of wealth. Gaius 1. 193, quoting the *Lex Bithynorum*, notes that it contained a rule about the status of women that was closely akin to the Roman principle of *tutela*. Possibly this too was a Pompeian innovation.

ne quis capiat magistratum. The qualifications for local office are better known from the Latin charters of the western provinces than from the Greek east. The similarity of the Bithynian rules to these is remarkable. The Flavian *Lex Malacitana* 54, and the Caesarean *Tabula Heracleensis* 89 ff., require free birth and a minimum age of 30, as here, for decurions and magistrates, with no wealth qualification in the extant chapters, though this is known elsewhere in Italy (1. 19, 2 n.). A wealth qualification is known for certain in the Greek area only in Achaea and Thessaly, and was probably not common. The Greek system of liturgies, and the Roman custom of *honorarium decurionatus*, which was introduced into Bithynia long after the time of Pompey (Ep. 113 n.), effectively excluded men of no property; Jones, *Greek City*, 170; Magie, *Romans*, 651 n. 54; A–J 79 ff., 84 ff. But there is a hint in Ep. 110, 2 that a census qualification existed at Amisus, and perhaps throughout the province; cf. also Ep. 58. 5 n.

For other grounds of exclusion see Ep. 114. 1 n.

eadem lege comprehensum est ut qui ceperint magistratum sint in senatu. This rule derives from the Roman custom codified finally in the Sullan law by which the Senate was recruited automatically from ex-quaestors, who became members for life. It was normal in the western municipalities, cf. *Tab. Her.* 135 ff. This provision, with the use of censorial adlection, s. 3 n., changed the principle of Greek city-government. The yearly elective and nominally democratic councils were supplanted by oligarchical corporations of life-members. The assemblies lost their power to the councils, which became the cornerstone of local government. (Jones, *Greek City*, 170 ff.; Magie, *Romans*, 642 n. 33. Cf. Ep. 110. 1 n.)

sint in senatu. In the western system a man entered his council after his first magistracy, and had the power to speak, *sententiam dicere*, but was not technically a decurion until placed on the roll at the next census. For the distinction see *Tab. Her.* 109 f., 126 ff., *Lex municipi Tarentini* 26 f. (A–J n. 20).

annorum triginta. Merrill, *Cl. Rev.* xvii. 54, suggested that Pompey followed the Sullan rule for the minimum age of the Roman quaestors; for which see *CAH*, ix. 290 n. 1.

2. secutum est deinde edictum divi Augusti quo permisit minores magistratus ab annis duobus et viginti capere. Augustus was twice active in Bithynian affairs, in 29 B.C. when the province was re-established, and during his eastern journey of 20 B.C., when Dio mentions a financial reorganization. Dio. 51. 20. 6, 54. 7. 5. Strabo, xii. p. 547. Cf. Ep. 84 n.

The prototypes give the numeral thus (or as *XXII*), both here and in Ep. 80, which should stand. The alteration to *XXV* was proposed by Merrill (art. cit.), following Nipperdey. He assumed that Augustus lowered the age limit in all provinces when he set the age for the Roman quaestorship at 25. This minimum age appears in the Spanish *Lex Malacitana* 54, and in citations from the lawyers covering Italy and the provinces generally, *Dig.* 50. 2. 6. 1, 2. 11, 4. 8. But Callistratus noted (ibid. 2. 11) that Nicomedia maintained an ancient custom of creating decurions (not magistrates) below the normal age (Ep. 80 n.). So low a figure as 22 years is allowed by the rules of the *Tab. Her.* 89 ff., by which those who had done military service could hold office at ages that work out at 21–22 for cavalry-men and 24–25 for infantry. Conditions in Bithynia *c.* 29 B.C. may have made it necessary to lower the age limits considerably in order to fill the councils.

Youths were often made decurions far below the legal age, as a compliment, but the lawyers ruled that such persons had not the right of voting, *Dig.* loc. cit.; Magie, *Romans*, 650 n. 51.

minores magistratus. The phrase implies that the typically Roman idea of the *cursus honorum* was introduced into Bithynia, character-istic of most fully documented municipal careers, and implied in such texts as *Lex Malacitana* 54, finally to be enshrined in the rules of the classical lawyers, e.g. Callistratus, *Dig.* 50. 4. 14. 5: ' gerendorum honorum . . . ordo certus . . . est; nam neque prius maiorem magi-stratum quisquam nisi minorem susceperit gerere potest neque ab omni aetate neque continuare quisque honores potest'. A fixed order may be discovered at Prusa in the career of the son of Cocceianus Dio, who advanced from minor offices concerned with the *ephebi* to be chief magistrate; *Or.* 51, 8 with 50. 6–10; Arnim, op. cit. 386 f. But frequent repetition of magistracies was common. Dio's father almost monopolized the archonship, *Or.* 44. 3. Hadrian later ob-jected to such repetitions, *Dig.* loc. cit.

The titles and order of local magistracies in Bithynia and Pontus are not well known except at Prusias ad Hypium. Στρατηγοί are testified at five cities including Nicaea and Nicomedia, mostly by coins; Magie, *Romans*, 643 n. 36; *RE* (S), vi. 1122. Πρῶτοι ἄρχοντες are known at Prusa, Prusias, and Claudiopolis, Ep. 81. 1 n. At Prusias six inscriptions generally confirm the order: γραμματεύς, ἔκδικος, ἀγορανόμος, πρῶτος ἄρχων, τιμητής though the place of ἔκδικος varies (Ep. 110. 1 n.); Dörner, *Reisen*, nn. 4, 5, 10; *IGRR*, iii. 64, 65, 68. Others (ibid. 60–63, 67, 69) are less orderly.

3. **quaeritur ergo an . . . ii quoque qui non gesserint possint . . . senatores legi.** So too *Tab. Her.* 105 ff., 126 ff. provides for direct co-optation of part of the decurions from private citizens. Recruitment from ex-magistrates alone would not provide enough annual recruits to maintain the councils at strength. In other regions even small cities such as Oenoanda might number up to 500 or 600 decurions, Jones, *Greek City*, 176; *IGRR* iii. 492. Pliny and Trajan take co-optation after the age of 30 as normal.

a censoribus. The *Lex Pompeia* evidently introduced the Roman five-yearly census just as the *Lex Rupilia* had done in Sicily, Cic. *ii in Verr.* 2. 131 ff., 139, and provided special magistrates, τιμῆται, to carry it out. Twenty years later the Caesarean *Tabula Heracleensis*, 141 ff., assigned the census duty to the ordinary chief magistrates of Italian municipalities in a census year. Mommsen, *DPR* iv. 100 n. 1, did not observe the parallel. The censors, as at Rome, maintained the roll of the local council by striking out the names of dead or disqualified persons and adding new names from the ex-magistrates of the past quinquennium and from private citizens; cf. *Tab. Her.* 85 ff., Epp. 112–15 nn. Dio attests censorial adlection at Prusa, *Or.* 48. 9, but when Trajan increased the number of decurions the extra members seem to have been chosen by popular election; *Or.* 45. 7–10, cf. ἐχειροτονήσατε, ibid. 9.

The municipal censors also maintained lists of citizens and property for the use of imperial officials, *censitores*, *procuratores ad census accipiendos*, who were responsible for the province as a whole. These were the basis of the taxation system. Ulpian, *Dig.* 50. 15. 3–4, describes the procedure. Each citizen made a detailed *professio* of his estates: 'nomen fundi cuiusque et in qua civitate et in quo pago sit et quos vicinos proximos habeat . . . vinea quot vites habeat, olivae quot iugerum et quot arbores habeant' etc. Cf. also Hyginus, *Agrimensores Rom.*, p. 205 La.; *RE* iii. 1921.

Two Greek titles for *censores* appear in Bithynia and adjacent regions, πολιτογράφος and τιμητής. Both are well testified at Prusias ad Hypium within roughly the same period, from the middle of the second to the middle of the third century (*IGR* iii. 60, 63–65 ; *SEG* xiv. 773–4 *et al.*). The *timetes* appears at Prusa and Dia, but the *politographos* is not yet known elsewhere in Bithynia (Le Bas-Waddington, *Voyage en . . . Asie* 1111; *BCH* 25, 54 n. 198). Since the two offices are never known to have been held by the same man, either one is the assistant of the other, or one title is a substitute for the other, possibly as variant translations of the same Latin term, as suggested by Vidman (*Étude*, 70). It has been suggested that the *timetes* was concerned only with the recruitment of the councils, like the βουλογράφος who appears yet later (*OGIS* 549; *IGR* iii. 1397), and his colleague with the lists of citizens. The *politographos* office is sometimes held for life, but not that of *timetes*. Pliny indicates that the censorship was an elective office at this time, and mentions only the function of recruiting the council, here and in Epp. 112, 114. But the close connexion of the office with the *Lex Pompeia* suggests that the same *censores*, whatever their Greek title, performed all the functions done by their Italian municipal equivalent. At Sinope the normal *duoviri quinquennales* of a Roman colony appear (*CIL* iii. 6980).

For the controversy and full documentation see Vidman's summary, *Étude*, 69–71; Dörner, *RE* xxiii. 1. 1142–3; L. Robert, *BCH* lii. 410–11; Jones, *Greek City*, 171; Magie, *Romans*, 641 n. 31. For the census generally see *Diz. Epigr.* ii. 176 ff.

esse necessarium dicitur quia sit aliquando melius honestorum hominum liberos quam e plebe in curiam admitti. Cf. Ep. 116. 1, 'solent totam bulen atque etiam e plebe non exiguum numerum vocare. This interesting statement is given not as Pliny's own opinion (as Jones, *Greek City*, 181 takes it), but as his consultants' notion, though Pliny seems to accept it as valid. It is the earliest direct evidence of that cleavage between *honestiores* and *plebeii* or *humiliores* that set the social pattern of the later empire. The *honestiores* became a hereditary and privileged aristocracy monopolizing municipal office, but were ground to dust in the decline of the Empire by the burden of their duties when the central government made them personally responsible for the payment of the revenues which it was their duty as decurions to collect. See Jones, op. cit. 179 ff.; Rostovtzeff, *SEHRE*[1] 468 ff.; Magie, *Romans*, 648 n. 48; A-J 197 ff. Such troubles lay in the future. Pliny's subjects suffered only from their own extravagance (Ep. 110. 2 n.), and go out of their way to encourage exclusiveness. Jones, loc. cit., quotes this passage as evidence of a difficulty in filling the councils, but the difficulty arose only from this prejudice. There were evidently plenty of *plebeii* available.

For the origins of the distinction between *humiliores* and *honestiores* in the sphere of criminal law under Hadrian see II. 11. 8, Ep. 58. 3 nn.

4. destinatis. The censors were elected in the summer of Pliny's second calendar year, before September (Ep. 88), and appear in office after the following January, Epp. 100, 112, 114. So much the serial order shows. Hence the magisterial year instituted by the *Lex Pompeia* ran from January to January as in the Roman system, rather than from midsummer to midsummer as in many Greek civic calendars. In either case Pliny's second year corresponds to the

last year of a censorial cycle. This would fix the date of Pliny's
governorship if the dates of the Bithynian system were known. In
Italy new *lustra* began in III and 116 (*FO*). But in the earlier
Principate the censorial period was not uniform throughout the
provinces. Even in Italy not all municipalities followed a common
system, though most did so. The Syrian census of A.D. 6 coincided
with the Italian, but the Gallic census was spread over several years
and held at long intervals. Ulpian, *Dig.* 50. 15. 4 pref., implies that
by his day the census was established universally on a ten-year cycle.
Perhaps the quinquennial period was retained for the rolls of
decurions, and the longer interval sufficed for the registration of
property. In general see *RE* iii. 1918; *Diz. Epigr.* ii. 176 ff.;
Mommsen, *DPR* iv. 99 f., v. 400 f. For the Italian exceptions, *CIL*
x. 5405 n. (Mommsen), to which add Aquinum with census in
A.D. 3 and Pompeii in A.D. 5 instead of A.D. 6. For Gaul cf. Tac.
Ann. I. 31, 33, 2. 6, A.D. 14–16. ibid. 14. 46, A.D. 61. Frontinus,
Strat. I. I. 8, *c.* A.D. 82–83.

5. capita legis tum edictum Augusti litteris subieci. The cities kept
copies of these basic documents, Ep. 31. 4 n.

The question could have been settled by Pliny if it had not been
for the imperial edict in the case. He hesitates to amend an imperial
decision, and thinks, as in Epp. 108. 2, 112. 3, that any amendment
of the basic statutes should be done by a more permanent enactment
than the decree of a governor—perhaps rightly.

subieci. For the method of attachment see Ep. 22. I n.

80. *To Pliny*

**non capto magistratu eos qui minores triginta annorum sint, quia
magistratum capere possint, in curiam etiam loci cuiusque non
existimo legi posse.** This does not support Hardy's contention, based
on a misapplication of Suet. *Aug.* 38. 2, which concerns only the
Roman Senate, that young *honestiores* were slipping into the local
councils by adlection, and avoiding the magistracies. Membership
of the council did not exclude a further magisterial career. Pliny and
Trajan merely insist that if a man wants to start his career early he
must first hold a magistracy. Nothing prevents those who have not
yet held office from becoming decurions at the age of 30. Trajan's
veto was not maintained, for *Dig.* 50. 2. 11 quotes a rescript of
Severus and Caracalla approving the ancient custom at Nicomedia of
adlecting decurions below the then prescribed age of 25.

curiam. This is the earliest instance of this term in an official
document in place of *ordo*, the normal word in the classical lawyers,

which only yields to *curia* in post-classical texts such as the *Sententiae Pauli* (E. Levy, *Studia Gaiana* (Leiden, 1956), iv. 73). But the secretary is only echoing Pliny's literary usage, Ep. 79. 3.

81. *To Trajan*

Date. Between 28 January and 18 September, second year.

Written like Ep. 67 from Nicaea, whither he has returned from a journey to Juliopolis (ss. 3–4 n., Epp. 67. 1, 77. 2). The visit to Prusa is probably that of Ep. 58. The reference is retrospective, cf. p. 530.

1. **Cum Prusae ad Olympum, domine, publicis negotiis intra hospitium eodem die exiturus vacarem.** Pliny held assizes at Prusa earlier in this his second season, which was his first full summer in Bithynia, Ep. 58. 1, many months after his first visit to Prusa in the previous autumn, when he dealt with its finances, Ep. 17A. 3–4. Arnim, op. cit. 508, thinks the question might have been raised the previous autumn—for no good reason.

Asclepiades magistratus indicavit appellatum me a Claudio Eumolpo. Asclepiades is evidently the πρῶτος ἄρχων of Prusa. The single magistracy is implied by references in Dio, *Or.* 44. 3, 50. 9–10; Arnim, op. cit. 386. For the title see Ep. 79. 2 n. The term is used in other provinces for πρῶτος στρατηγός, but in Bithynia it is the correct title; cf. Magie, *Romans*, 644 n. 37. The name Asclepiades was borne by a clan of healers at Prusa: Pliny, *NH* 7. 124; *ILS* 7789 names a younger Asclepiades. Our man and Eumolpus are unknown otherwise.

Evidently there was a majority of the council in favour of Dio's request, which Eumolpus frustrated by appealing to the governor. The matter was within the council's competence since it did not concern a new construction; hence a secondary issue of *maiestas* was raised, s. 2. For the tendency of local politicians to involve the governors unnecessarily in municipal affairs see Ep. 110. 1 n.

cum Cocceianus Dion in bule adsignari civitati opus cuius curam egerat vellet, tum Eumolpus adsistente Flavio Archippo dixit exigendam esse a Dione rationem operis antequam reipublicae traderetur. Archippus was evidently bent on paying out Dio for the attack made recently on his civic status, which if not due to Dio himself was initiated by his côterie: Ep. 58 nn. Arnim, op. cit. 509, identifies Archippus with an unnamed enemy of Dio mentioned in *Or.* 43. 5. The request was fair, and Trajan was surprised that Dio resisted it; perhaps the fuss was only about the second charge. Dio himself criticized a man who gave no account of his stewardship of a similar project, *Or.* 47. 19. Ep. 17B shows that the tendency was widespread. Hardy, writing before Arnim, identified the *opus* with the *stoa*, built partly at Dio's expense, in fulfilment of a long-standing promise, yet subjected to much local criticism: *Or.* 40. 5–9, 45. 11–15, 47. 8–19. But Arnim's analysis shows that this was under construction in about 100, and nearly completed by the proconsulship of Varenus, i.e. not later than 105–6 (v. 20, 1 n.). It was no longer an issue a little later in *Or.* 47. 6–7, 48. 11 (Arnim, op. cit. 344 ff., 357). Hence the present work appears distinct. This building is a library with a colonnaded court (s. 7), like that of Athena Polias at Pergamum, or the library of Trajan in his new Forum at Rome (Hartleben, ad loc.). Dio's description of the *stoa* fits a colonnaded street better than an enclosed building, such as this was, s. 7 n. *Or.* 47. 15.

G. Sautel (*Rév. Int. Dr. Ant.* 1956, 422 ff.) also connected this *cura* with the *stoa* operation, and suggested that Dio was involved not only as *curator operum* but in virtue of a technical *pollicitatio reipublicae*. But of this there is no word in the present letters, and nothing in Dio suggests that his promise extended beyond the *stoa*. The enforcement of such promises is first documented in a regulation of Trajan at this time, Ep. 40. 1 n.

traderetur. The ἐπιμελητὴς ἔργων, often appointed for a particular operation, is a familiar feature of Asian cities: Liebenam, *Städteverwaltung,* 384 f. This method of regulating the liturgy may have been laid down in the *Lex Pompeia*; it occurs in Italian practice at an early date, cf. *FIRA* iii, no. 153 with Cic. *ii in Verr.* 1. 129 f.

adsistente. See s. 6 n.

aliter fecisset. In building the *stoa* Dio was in trouble for knocking down an old smithy, *Or.* 40. 8–9, 47. 11–12. Earlier he was unpopular for building a private establishment on a public site which he claimed to have bought, *Or.* 46. 9.

Cocceianus Dion. His Roman names are not otherwise known. His by-name Chrysostomos was a grammarian's name to distinguish him from the historian. His mother was a Roman citizen by birth, but his father Pasicrates was a plain *peregrinus*. Hence by the Roman rule Dio took the inferior status (Gaius 1. 75–77), unless the Prusenses possessed the rare privilege of *conubium*. Dio, *Or.* 41. 6, 44. 5, 46. 2–5. Arnim, op. cit. 122 f. *PIR²* D 93, wrongly makes the father a Roman, but this did not follow from his honorary citizenship of the colony of Apamea. Dio must have acquired his Roman status later from a Flavian emperor, possibly Domitian, since he never mentions its origin, and claims to have had no personal benefits from Nerva, *Or.* 45. 3. The second *cognomen* Cocceianus may mark his much advertised connexion with Nerva: *Or.* 44. 12, 45. 2–3, 47. 22. His full names might be T. Flavius Dion Cocceianus. His age must have been in the forties or fifties at this time. The outline of his life down to about 100 is fairly clear thanks to the labours of Arnim. Born at Prusa, he went to Italy in the Flavian period to try his luck as a showman orator in the style of Isaeus (II. 3 nn.). He was not yet a philosopher. He was relegated early in Domitian's reign for some criticism of the emperor, and as a friend of a Domitianic victim, perhaps the consular T. Flavius Sabinus, c. 83–84. (*Or.* 44. 6–8, 45. 1; Suet. *Dom.* 10. 3. Cf. *Or.* 13. 1; *CAH* xi. 24 n. 1; Arnim, op. cit. 122 ff., 223 ff., at great length.) Nerva cancelled his sentence, and he returned to Bithynia c. 98. (*Or.* 44. 12, 45. 2–3; Arnim, op. cit. 312 ff.) He visited Rome as a municipal emissary about 100. (*Or.* 40. 1–4, 13–15, 44. 11–12, 45. 7–9, 48. 11; Arnim, op. cit. 312 ff., 322 ff.) Returning to Prusa, he sponsored a project of public works, including his *stoa*, which involved him in controversy; above, and Ep. 23. 1 n. Later he was concerned in the troubles that revolved around the actions of an unpopular proconsul, who may have been either Julius Bassus or Varenus (IV. 9. 1, 5 nn.; *Or.* 13, 43. 11, 50. 3–4; Arnim, op. cit. 369 ff.). After this the facts are less certain. He may have toured Italy and the provinces for a year or two after the proconsulship of Varenus, a plan mentioned in *Or.* 47. 22, 49. 14–15. (Arnim, op. cit. 407, 507.) By Pliny's governorship he was back at Prusa, where he had long been a decurion; cf. *Or.* 40. 6, 50. 9–10.

2. in eodem positam tuam statuam et corpora sepultorum. The provincial politicians were now trying the same tricks as had been developed so successfully at Rome, under Tiberius and Domitian, of involving their rivals in charges of *maiestas* on frivolous or technical grounds. For similar charges of disrespect to the effigy of the emperor see Tac. *Ann.* 1. 74; Suet. *Tib.* 58; *Dom.* 10; Dio 67. 12. 2. But Dio is not directly charged with treason on the score of burying his family in sacred ground. The procedure shows the difference between the Roman system of delation under a *lex publica* and provincial *cognitio extra ordinem*. Eumolpus alleges the facts themselves without citing a statute, and leaves it to the governor to decide whether they constitute a particular offence. Cf. Ep. 96. 1, 'cognitionibus' n. But probably the *Lex Pompeia*, like the contemporary *Lex Ursonensis c.* 73, forbade any burial within the city precincts, and this is the basis of the prosecution.

3. utque in alia civitate cognoscerem petiit. This is an act of courtesy to Pliny who was ready to leave Prusa, not, as Hardy suggested, a trick to prevent Pliny from investigating the facts himself, which he did, s. 7. Pliny appoints Nicaea, as convenient for Prusans, and, if he visited it after Juliopolis (Ep. 77. 2), allowing fair time.

4. ubi cum consedissem cogniturus. Stout (*T.A.Ph.A.* 86. 243) followed by O.C.T., rightly preferred 'consedissem' from A to 'sedissem' of Aldus, comparing VI. 31. 9: 'consederat auditurus'. The term is technical, and means that Pliny used an advisory *consilium* on this occasion, as was normal.

5. dicta sunt utrimque multa, etiam de causa. This is not satirical. Pliny means 'arguments about the hearing, and also about the substance of the case'.

dixi utrique parti ut . . . libellos darent. For the procedure cf. Ep. 59 n.

6. Archippus cui Eumolpus sicut †Prusiade† adsistebat, dixit se libellum daturum. This reverses the roles of the two at Prusa, where Archippus was the *adsistens*, s. 1. Hence Catanaeus, followed by O.C.T., there read *adsistens* for *adsistente*, unnecessarily. For the principal charge, 'quae reipublicae petebat', Eumolpus was the leader, but reversed his role for the subsidiary charge about the tomb, made by Archippus; s. 2, 'adiecit etiam'. Eumolpus was now becoming uneasy about the treason charge. (Similarly, Sautel, art. cit. 437 f.) Both men were evidently decurions, and Eumolpus, not Archippus, had appealed to Pliny. Pliny's compression rather than the text is at fault.

Prusiade. See Ep. 58. 5, 'Prusiadem' n. This form can only mean the city of Prusias. *Prusae* is required, as in s. 1 and Ep. 70. 1.

ita nec . . . adhuc mihi libellos dederunt. They behave like the delators to whom Claudius objected: 'inimicos suos reos fecerunt, relincunt eos in albo pendentes et ipsi tamquam nihil egerint peregrinantur'. *BGU* 611 (2). Charlesworth, *Documents*, Cl. 3.

iunxi. See Ep. 22, 1.

7. id autem in quo dicuntur sepulti filius et uxor Dionis in area collocatum quae porticibus includitur. The building consisted of a colonnaded court with a library set in an *exedra*, cf. Ep. 70. 3 n. The *monumentum* was in the centre of the court.

Dio mentions a living grown-up son in several speeches, Ep. 79. 2 n. His wife is unknown; Arnim, op. cit. 386.

8. in hoc praecipue genere cognitionis regere. Pliny's request reflects the condition of public life after Domitian rather than Pliny's timidity—even under the 'best' emperor only the action of the emperor himself could disallow a charge involving *maiestas minuta*.

magna sit exspectatio, ut necesse est in ea re quae et in confessum venit et exemplis defenditur. The defence claimed that the precedents were on their side. Hardy rightly defended the text against Mommsen's *nec exemplis*. Trajan's reply—'quaestione quam non admitterem etiamsi exemplis adiuvaretur'—means that he would not accept the charge even if the *exempla* were on the side of the prosecution. There is 'great expectation' because if Dio lost many others would stand in the same condemnation. Pliny's consultation of Trajan was all the more necessary. Besides, the charge verged on a capital offence, if treated seriously, and Dio was a Roman citizen, with right of appeal to the emperor. There was a tendency to use the *maiestas* law to cover otherwise undefined offences. In the Flavian rescript *de medicorum commodis* violation of the privileges of doctors is assimilated to an action against the *domus Augusta* (W–C 458. 17–18).

82. *To Pliny*

1. potuisti non haerere. Pliny is unlucky to be snubbed for consulting the emperor on a matter which any governor might have thought it wise to refer to him. Hence when next he makes a similar inquiry, in the Christian affair, he apologizes, Ep. 96. 1.

propositum meum optime nosses non ex metu nec terrore hominum aut criminibus maiestatis reverentiam nomini meo adquiri. Pliny's own account in the *Panegyric*, 34–35, 42. 1, shows Trajan's care to check frivolous charges of treason. More recently he had heard Trajan dismiss the interest of his freedmen with the comment: 'non curo . . . an isti suspicionibus relinquantur, ego relinquor'. VI. 31. 11.

2. ratio totius operis effecti sub cura Cocceiani Dionis excutiatur. Hardy alone among modern editors did not like Orelli's emendation *curatura* of the prototype, *cura tua*, and deleted *tua*. The word is rare and archaic, not appearing in classical Latin after Terence, and hence is out of place in a chancellery letter. *Thes. L.L.* s.v. It is, however, used in the required meaning in an inscription of the Principate, *CIL* vi. 21383. O.C.T. follows Hardy, and also neatly alters *totius*, which seems inept, to *potius*. But Trajan may have in mind the objection in Ep. 81. 1, that the work was contrary to the original plan, rather than that the finance was at fault.

83. *To Trajan*

Date. Between 28 January and 18 September, second year, probably late summer. Written from Nicaea, like Ep. 81.

rogatus domine a Nicaeensibus publice . . . ut preces suas ad te perferrem. The municipality through its chief magistrate has asked Pliny to send their petition by the *cursus publicus*, instead of dispatching a costly legation; cf. Epp. 43. 1–2 nn., 45 nn. The cities had direct access to the Princeps both from public and from imperial provinces, cf. IV. 22. 1–3 nn.; *FIRA* i, nn. 72, 74 (A–J nn. 59, 61).

per aeternitatem tuam. Cf. Epp. 41. 1 n., 59. 1, 112. 3.

84. To Pliny

Date, several weeks after Ep. 83, but before 18 September, second year.

Nicaeensibus qui intestatorum civium suorum concessam vindicationem bonorum a divo Augusto adfirmant debebis vacare. This letter contains another reminder that Roman and provincial law were often very different, cf. Epp. 49, 66. 2, 68 nn. The Roman law made every effort to secure that *bona intestatorum* found an heir among the agnate relatives, including female connexions; Gaius 3. 25–27; *Tit. Ulp.* 28. 7. Failing this they were assimilated to *bona caduca*, inheritances that had not been accepted and could be claimed by the *aerarium* for the 'Roman people' (*not* the *fiscus*). Cf. Hirschfeld, *Verwaltungsbeamten* 46, nn. 1–2. *Tit. Ulp.* loc. cit.: 'si nemo sit ad quem bonorum possessio pertinere possit . . . *populo* bona deferuntur ex lege Iulia caducaria'. Gaius 2. 150, 286a. Contrast the later form of the rule given in *Tit. Ulp.* 17. 2: 'ex constitutione imp. Antonini omnia caduca *fisco* vindicantur'. See *RE* iii. 685–6.

In Egypt the *Gnomon idiologi* shows that the Roman principle was applied in that the provincial treasury claimed intestate estates when there was no legal heir, though this is considered Alexandrine law by the editors of *FIRA* i. p. 471 n. 8. But at Nicaea the municipality, taking the place of the Roman treasury, claims intestate goods without any consideration for the legal heirs under the rules of intestate succession. This is so surprising that one wonders whether some qualification such as 'quibus heredes non sunt' has fallen out, or should be taken as implied, after *civium suorum*.

Trajan's reference to the procurators (below) does not imply, as Hardy assumed, that such goods in Bithynia would normally go, as in Egypt, to the provincial treasury. In the earlier Principate the Roman government would hardly so interfere with the property rights of *peregrini* and peregrine communities, who were not even subject to the Roman *vicesima hereditatum*. Egypt as always, with its general lack of municipal autonomy, is a special case.

a divo Augusto. Probably during the financial reorganization of 20 B.C. Ep. 79. 2 n.

contractis omnibus personis ad idem negotium pertinentibus, adhibitis Virdio Gemellino et Epimacho liberto meo procuratoribus, ut aestimatis etiam iis quae contra dicuntur, quod optimum credideritis statuatis. The contestant parties—*personis*—are the municipality and aggrieved citizens. The procurators are to act, not as claimants, but as members of Pliny's *consilium*. The technical word *adhibitis* and the plural *statuatis* show this; cf. V. I. 5; VI. 11. 1, 15. 3–4; cf. Suet. *Claud.*

35. 2, *FIRA* i. n. 75. 11–12, quoted IV. 22. 1 n. Trajan refers the claim
back to Pliny because it is local, and is covered by Pliny's commission. He is not to arbitrate between the emperor and the municipality, though the procurators would doubtless look after any
imperial interest that might arise. Vespasian similarly referred back
to the proconsul of Baetica the request of a municipality to raise new
local taxes (*FIRA* i. 74; A–J n. 61) with the remark: 'ego . . . nullo
respondente constituere nil possum'.

For Virdius Gemellinus see Ep. 27. 1 n. Epimachus was the
successor as *adiutor procuratoris* of Maximus, who left the province
at this time, Ep. 85. This passage shows that the legates and procurators did not ordinarily work together, though they were usually
on good terms, cf. Ep. 21. 1 n.

etiam iis quae contra dicuntur. Trajan assumes that the municipality
has a good case, but justice must be seen to be done. He would
hardly have written *etiam* if the counterclaimant had been the procurator, though his administration was particularly sharp in fiscal
matters; *Gnomon* 1; *Fr. de iure fisci* 1. 6 (*FIRA* ii. p. 628).

85. *To Trajan*

Date. Shortly before 18 September, second year.

This and the following three letters illustrate the system of official
testimonials and preferment in the imperial service, studied by
H. G. Pflaum, *Les Procurateurs* etc. (Paris, 1950), 198 f., and by E. G.
Birley, *Roman Britain and the Roman Army* (Kendal, 1953), Paper
xiii. Pflaum argued, mainly from Suet. *Dom.* 4, that there was a fixed
annual season for promotions: 'cur sibi visum esset ordinatione
proxima Aegypto praeficere Mettium Rufum', and from Fronto's
insistence that he had twice recommended a certain man for a post in
two years (*ad Ant. Pium* 9, p. 170 N.). From the dating of the anecdote
in Suetonius by the quaestorian games Pflaum suggested November
as the season of promotions. The serial placing of these letters confirms Pflaum's suggestion, since Ep. 88 was written on the occasion
of Trajan's birthday, 18 September (Ep. 17A. 2 n.), and two at least,
Epp. 85 and 86A, concern men leaving the province. U. Instinsky
(*Philologus*, 1948, 193) suggests that the men took their certificates
with them, and hence there was no need for Trajan to reply; cf. Ep.
88. 3. Or else all these testimonials were sent to the secretariat
together, for the files.

Maximum libertum et procuratorem tuum. See Ep. 27 n.

**per omne tempus quo fuimus una probum et industrium et diligen-
tem.** Pliny uses stock epithets, but qualifies or varies them, so that

Trajan can read between the lines, as in Ep. 26. 2. Maximus is
accorded neither the *integritas* of Bassus (Ep. 86A) and Rosianus
Geminus (Ep. 26. 2), nor the *reverentissimus mei* of the former, which
quality Ep. 27 suggests that he lacked. But he is allowed other
qualities. The younger Lupus, who had not served under Pliny, is
given the minimum, Ep. 87. 3. None of these are commended as
strongly as the subject of Ep. 86B.

apud te testimonio prosequor. The phrase indicates that he, like
Bassus below, was vacating his post. They had both been appointed
before Pliny, and were leaving at the same season as Pliny arrived,
Epp. 17A, 21. 1, 28.

86A. *To Trajan*

Date, as Ep. 85.

Gavium Bassum. See Ep. 21. 1 n.

voto pariter et suffragio prosequor. Cf. II. 1. 8 n. for the metaphorical use of *suffragium*. This is a positive recommendation for
preferment.

86B. *To Trajan*

Date, as Ep. 85.

**Fabium Valentem ⟨domine⟩ instructum commilitio tuo valde
probo.** This is the reading of Catanaeus' first edition, altered in his
second edition to 'quem abunde conspexi instructum' etc., but
repeated in the marginal correction of the Bodleian copy (i²). If the
latter is independent of Catanaeus, this would be valuable confirmation. It is hard to see why Catanaeus, if inventing, picked this obscure
name out of the heading of IV. 24, where alone it reappears. The other
prototypes join 86A and B together with meaningless phrases in place
of this sentence of Catanaeus's, having *abunde instructum* as a common
element: 'quam abunde ea quae speret instructum' etc. is the fullest.
Avantius omits *abunde*, which, however, reappears in Cat.². Beroaldus
had 'quem ad ea . . .'. Stout (*T.A.Ph.A.* 86. 245 f.) endeavoured to
make sense of 86A and B by omitting the concluding *ea fide quam
tibi debeo* from A, as an editorial addition, and continuing 'prosequor
ea quae speret'. But this still is not sense.

Stout did not realize the formal character of Epp. 85–86B. Comparison with Ep. 85 shows that the phrase 'expertus . . . debeo' in
86A is a unity, and a technical formula. Hence 86A is complete.
As an official testimonial was evidently expected to begin with the
name and ranking of the commended person and to end with the
'ea fide' formula, there is no reason to doubt that the present text is

nearly complete, and that Catanaeus's first thoughts are still the best reconstruction. But the meaningless words may represent a lost letter, additional to 86B, as Professor Mynors has suggested in discussion.

commilitio tuo. Ep. 26. 2 n.

indulgentia tua dignum est. The term is used of promotion, Epp. 26. 2, 87. 3.

et milites et pagani a quibus iustitia eius et humanitas penitus inspecta est. Pflaum sardonically remarks that the numerous inscriptions praising the *abstinentia* or *integritas* of officials are a proof of the rarity of such qualities (op. cit. 169). Valens alone is commended by Pliny for the philanthropic virtues, but he may select the attribute appropriate to each man's duty. Cf. Ep. 26. 2 n.

et milites et pagani. This is a variant for *commilitones et provinciales*, used in Epp. 100–4. The term *pagani* properly means the country folk as opposed to the *oppidani*, but it is commonly used in a derivative sense to distinguish the civilian from the military man, even in an urban setting. Cf. VII. 25. 6: 'sunt . . . ut in castris . . . plures cultu pagano'. This usage is common in contemporary literature, though it may have a colloquial origin: Tac. *Hist.* I. 53, 2. 88; Suet. *Galba* 19. 2. But the original meaning persists, and both occur in the lawyers later: Tac. *Hist.* 2. 14; Ulpian, *Dig.* 11. 4. 1. 2, 3; 29. 1. 9. 1. See *RE* xviii. 2. 2295 f.; Forcellini, s.v.

publice. By municipal decree. Ep. 83, III. 9. 4.

quod in notitiam tuam perfero. The formula suggests that this is a special citation for merit rather than a testimonial at the end of Valens' appointment, as Birley takes it (op. cit. 142).

87. To Trajan

Date, as Ep. 85.

1. **Nymphidium Lupum, domine, primipilarem commilitonem habui, cum ipse tribunus ille praefectus.** For Pliny's military service in Syria, about A.D. 82, see I. 10. 2 n., III. 11. 5, and VII. 31. 1–2, where a *praefectus alae* is mentioned. Lupus cannot have been prefect of an auxiliary unit, as Durry suggests ad loc., since these were commanded in this period by men of equestrian rank, which Lupus evidently lacks. Hardy suggested that he had been *praefectus castrorum*, a post which in and after the Flavian period was held generally by plain *primipilares*; cf. Domaszewski, *Rangordnung*, 120 f., where only two out of numerous examples suggest equestrian status. Parker, *Roman Legions*, 191. Hence Pliny uses no equestrian epithet, cf. Ep. 106. The *praefecti civitatium et levis armaturae* also were equestrian at this period. Sherwin-White, *BSR* xv. 12 f. An able man could reach the

primipilate in twenty years from enlistment, Ep. 5. 2 n. Lupus now retired and *senex* could have been forty years of age in A.D. 81–82.

primipilarem. The leading centurions, who commanded the first century of a legion's first cohort, frequently continued in service in a special corps of *primipilares* for secondment to staff duties at Rome or in the provinces, as *primus pilus bis*; Domaszewski, op. cit., 112 f., 116 f. But Pliny's friend was in retirement, s. 2.

2. quieti eius inieci manum et exegi ut me in Bithynia consilio instrueret. Legates and proconsuls, like urban magistrates, chose the unofficial members of their staffs, who formed an unofficial committee to advise them in administration and jurisdiction. The governor was expected, by custom but not by law, to act *e consili sententia*. Cf. VI. 11. 1, 15. 3. Ep. 84, ' adhibitis' nn.; Mommsen, *DPR* i. 351 f., 364 f., *D. Pen. R.* i. 171, 278 ff. In *FIRA* i, n. 59 (*ILS* 5947) a proconsul of Sardinia adjudicates a boundary dispute in A.D. 69 with a *consilium* composed of his legate, quaestor, and six other persons.

senectutis ratione postposita. A man might reach the primipilate between the ages of 40 and 50, though there are many exceptions. In *ILS* 2118 a man enlisted in 73 becomes junior centurion in 90. In *ILS* 2648 a man enlisted in 42 is already procurator by 66. The age of enlistment was 18 or later. Cf. Birley, op. cit. 135 ff.

3. iuvenem probum industrium et egregio patre dignissimum. For the qualities see Ep. 85 n. For *egregius* cf. Epp. 21. 1, 29. 1 where it is used of equestrian officials.

praefectus cohortis plenissimum testimonium meruerit. A son of an established man, Nymphidius Lupus, like Virdius Gemellinus and many others, passed straight into the *militia equestris* with good prospects of rapid advancement in the procuratorial career. Thereafter his own son could easily secure senatorial status. This social pattern is well documented. In Pliny's letters Julius Servianus (Ep. 2. 1) and himself are examples. Though the influence of powerful friends counted for much, most families trace their rise back to the reputation of some effective *vir militaris* such as the elder Lupus, or such a procurator as the Elder Pliny, III. 5 nn. See in general Stein, *Römische Ritterstand*, chs. iii–iv.

praefectus cohortis. Such a man would usually secure this first step in the *militia equestris* about the age of 30; earlier appointment seems rare, cf. Birley, op. cit. 139.

testimonium meruerit. Evidently it was normal for governors to make such reports, cf. Epp. 85–86. Birley, op. cit. 142, thinks that Pliny has seen these documents, and hence that copies were given to the officer himself. But Pliny may be relying on the word of the elder Lupus.

For the two consulars Ferox and Salinator see II. II. 5, VI. 26. I nn. Apparently they were successive commanders of the unknown province where young Lupus served. Salinator was much the senior. A consular legateship presumably *c.* 107–9 is surprising for a man who was consul before 86. Syme, *Tac.* 232 n. 5.

clarissimorum virorum. For the title see Ep. 56. 2 n.

meamque gratulationem filii honore continebis. Lupus needs a military tribunate, or the right to seek one from an imperial legate, II. 13. 2, III. 8. I nn. For *honos* of an equestrian post see VII. 22. 3.

Though personal influence counted for much in promotion, yet it was always within the framework of the system. Even the influential Fronto could not always secure a friend promotion at his first request, and remarks: 'petit nunc procurationem ex forma suo loco ac iusto tempore' (*ad M. Caes.* 5. 37, p. 87 N.). Cf. Pflaum, op. cit. 198 ff. Ep. 85 pref.

continebis. O.C.T. prefers Maguinness's *cumulabis,* for which Ep. 26. I is the nearest support. But cf. Ep. 35 for *contineri* as 'maintain'.

88. *To Trajan*   89. *To Pliny*

Date. 18 September, second year.

hunc natalem. For Trajan's birthday, 18 September, see Ep. 17A. 2 n. No official celebrations, like those of the *dies imperii* or New Year's Day, are mentioned, cf. Epp. 35, 52.

florente statu reipublicae nostrae. Trajan's change of emphasis from Pliny's 'virtutis tuae gloriam' is characteristic. Cf. Ep. 9. For *nostra* cf. Ep. 42, 'nos' n. 58. 7, 'civium meorum' n. 97. 2, 'nostri saeculi'. Here as in the last citation it just means 'thine and mine'.

90. *To Trajan*

From Sinope. Pliny has now moved from Bithynia to Pontus. The date is on or after 18 September of his second year, Ep. 88, and before his second January, Epp. 100–2.

1. Sinopenses domine aqua deficiuntur. There was a similar lack at Nicomedia itself, which like other Greek cities also set about provision of water supplies on the Roman model in this period, Ep. 37. I nn.

Sinope, for long the chief trading centre of the eastern Euxine, occupied a peninsular site with a double harbour like Amastris, Ep. 98. It was an early Greek settlement which in later days passed under the control of the Pontic kings. Mithridates Eupator made it his capital. At the Roman conquest Lucullus gave it the status of a *civitas libera.* Pompey extended its territory to the Halys, so that it became conterminous with Amisus (Ep. 92). Julius Caesar confiscated part of its territory to establish a colony of veterans, 'colonia Iulia Felix Sinope', apparently in 46–45 B.C. The colony had the *ius Italicum*, which made it immune from provincial taxation. The régime was that of a dual community, a Greek city existing beside the Roman colony, as at Apamea: Ep. 47. 1 n.; *IGRR* iii. n. 94; *Am. J. Arch.* (1905) 309 n. 36; Strabo xii p. 546. In Strabo's day Sinope was the greatest city of Pontus, with fine walls and public buildings. The nearer territory was very fertile, and the hinterland produced timber for export. Strabo xii pp. 544–6; Arrian, *Periplus*, 22 M; *Dig.* 50. 15. 1. 10; Jones, *Cities*, 148 f., 159 n. 22, 167 n. 38; Magie, *Romans*, 183 ff. nn. 18–21, 342 n. 42, 414 n. 33. For the local topography see also D. M. Robinson (below), pp. 126 ff.

an recipere et sustinere opus possit. i.e. an *opus arcuatum*. Cf. the difficulties at Nicomedia, Ep. 37. 1–2 nn.

2. pecunia curantibus nobis contracta non deerit. Pliny has in mind the financial arrangements which he made at Prusa, Nicaea, and Claudiopolis, Epp. 23. 2, 39. 3, 5.

curantibus nobis. For Pliny's 'we', which seems to mean merely 'I and my staff', see Epp. 39. 5, 54. 1, 98. 2. Sinope, unlike Apamea, Ep. 47. 1, did not object to Pliny's review of their finances here implied.

indulseris. See Ep. 23. 1 n. for Trajan's ruling about new buildings.

91. *To Pliny*

si modo et viribus suis adsequi potest, cum plurimum ea res et salubritati et voluptati eius collatura sit. The rescript follows the wording of Ep. 90 closely, and shows no personal touch. Cf. Epp. 98–99. As at Prusa financial self-sufficiency comes first, but Trajan seldom resists the appeal to amenity, whether accompanied by *pulchritudo* or not. Epp. 37. 3, 41. 1, 98. 2, 99. The scanty remains of what seemed to be an aqueduct, formerly visible at Sinope, were noted by D. M. Robinson, *Am. J. Phil.* xxvii. 131, 264.

92. *To Trajan*

Date. Between 18 September and 3 January, second year. Written from Amisus, as *in hac* shows.

Amisenorum civitas libera et foederata beneficio indulgentiae tuae legibus suis utitur. This query arises both from the special privilege of Amisus, and from the *mandatum* about *collegia* (below).

Amisus, an old Greek settlement, had long been part of the Pontic kingdom, when captured by the army of Lucullus. In Pompey's reorganization its territory finally stretched along the coast from the Halys eastward beyond the Lycus to Themiscyra, and inland up to forty miles. Julius Caesar added the privilege of *libertas* for the city's resistance to Pharnaces of Bosporos. M. Antonius made the area over to a local dynast, whom Augustus deposed, while restoring its 'freedom' to Amisus within the provincial system, with an era that dated from 31 B.C. Strabo, xii p. 547; Pliny, *NH* 6. 7; Arrian, *Periplus* 22 M; Jones, *Cities*, 159 ff., 167 ff.; Magie, *Romans*, 185 f. n. 24, 337 n. 33; Waddington, *Recueil*[2], 52 ff. For the city's prosperity in the Principate see Cumont, *Stud. Pont.* iii. 2–3.

When Vespasian established an army command within Galatia-Cappadocia, Amisus, having easy access by the central Asian highway to Satala, became a port of entry for military supplies. Inscriptions attest among other units an auxiliary *ala* on its way to or from Trajan's Parthian campaigns. Cuntz, *Hermes* 61. 200 f.; Rostovtzeff, art. cit. *BSA* xxii. 14 f.; *CIL* iii. 6748, 13635.

libera et foederata. In the Principate *libertas* chiefly denoted freedom from the intervention of the governor in local administration and jurisdiction. The formulation is given in the letter of an Augustan proconsul to Chios, A–J n. 40. 15–17 (Ditt. *Syll.*[3], n. 785): ὅπως νόμοις τε καὶ ἔθεσιν καὶ δικαίοις χρῶνται ἃ ἔσχον ὅτε τῇ Ῥωμαίων [φι]λίᾳ προσῆλθον ἵνα τε ὑπὸ μήθ' ᾧτινι [οὖν] τύπῳ ὦσιν ἀρχόντων ἢ ἀνταρχόντων. Two Republican charters of *libertas* also envisaged local legislative activity; A–J n. 17. 47–50; 19. 31–35. Other privileges, such as freedom from billeting, tended to be eliminated during the later Republic. Freedom from taxation depended on a separate grant of *immunitas*, rarely given. Freedom was a revocable grant, made by the Senate or the Princeps, of a charter that fixed the privileges of the community concerned.

A *civitas foederata* was one that had, usually in the pre-provincial phase of Roman expansion, made a formal treaty of alliance with Rome, which subjected only its foreign policy to Roman control. Very few such survived the wars and rebellions of the late Republic in the eastern provinces. See A–J ch. v; Sherwin-White, *RC* ch. vi; Jones, *Greek City*, 129 ff.

beneficio indulgentiae tuae. A minor enigma arises. There is no evidence for more than *libertas* before Trajan. These words imply that Trajan had granted treaty-status to Amisus, an odd thing at this period. Hardy's suggestion that Pliny was speaking loosely, of the reference of all *beneficia* to the living Princeps, will not do, since the terms *beneficium* and *indulgentia* are technical, cf. Epp. 3A. 1, 23. 1, 26. 1, 94. 3. Jones, op. cit. 131 n. 67, refers the *foedus* to

Augustus, who granted *foedera* to two Greek cities in Asia. Cuntz, art. cit., adduced the titles of Amisus in an inscription of A.D. 131–2, *OGIS* 530: ἐλευθέρας καὶ αὐτονόμου καὶ ὁμοσπόνδου. This inscription dates the *libertas* alone, by an era-date, to the year of Actium, ἔτος ρξγ τῆς ἐλευθερίας. The coins of Amisus, not fully known to Cuntz, bear the title ἐλευθέρα only on a single Augustan issue, and then lack it on later issues, including some under Vespasian. It reappears on issues of 98–99, 106–7, and 113–14, and then continues until 257–8. Waddington, *Recueil*², nn. 52–54, 68, 74a–d, 77, etc. (*pace* Magie, *Romans*, 594 n. 3). The first of the Trajanic series repeats the type of the Augustan coin just mentioned. Trajan evidently confirmed some privilege which could be described as a *foedus*. Yet it is unlikely that he would revive the archaic procedure in full. He was more apt to increase than to diminish central control. Possibly he reconfirmed the *libertas* of Amisus after a temporary lapse, with the nominal title of *foedus*. The city of Tyre seems to have enjoyed the same, Jones, op. cit. 118 n. 41; *Dig.* 50. 15. 1. The distinction between *foedus* and *libertas* is blurred in other contemporary sources. Cf. Suet. *Aug.* 47: 'urbium quasdam foederatas . . . libertate privavit'. Tac. *Ann.* 2. 53 erroneously speaks of Athens as *foederata*.

legibus suis utitur. Every municipal unit in a Roman province, whatever its status, could be said to 'enjoy its own laws', in that it governed itself in most matters according to custom or its own charter, *lex cuiusque civitatis*; Ep. 113 n. Cf. *Dig.* 50. 4. 3, 4. 18, 27, 6. 6. 1. But these rights depended on the *lex provinciae* and could be modified only by the Roman authority. A *civitas libera* would usually retain its previous organization, as at Chios (above), and, as Ep. 93 implies, could modify this by its own legislation. At Amisus, since the city was not originally 'free', the local rules would derive from the *Lex Pompeia*.

in hac datum mihi libellum ad ἐράνους pertinentem his litteris subieci. Pliny does not explain how he came to be dealing with the affairs of a *civitas libera*. His mission presumably included the power to deal with their finances but was not *ad ordinandum statum liberarum civitatum*, like that of Maximus in VIII. 24. Hence his reference to Trajan. The question arose out of Pliny's edict suppressing clubs, Epp. 33. 3 n., 96. 7. Only Trajan could alter his own *mandatum* in the matter. It is remarkable that the authorities of Amisus despite their *libertas* went out of their way in the affair of Julius Piso to provoke the intervention of Pliny, Ep. 110. 1 n. Plutarch, *Praec. rep. ger.* 19, deplores this tendency in Greek cities to refer their affairs to the governors.

ἐράνους. Trajan in his reply takes this to refer to a Greek equivalent of the *collegia tenuiorum*, social clubs which existed in the western

empire to promote the welfare of their members. They usually
provided common dinners and often funeral expenses, out of communal subscriptions, and were nominally connected with a religious
cult. See Ep. 33. 3 n. Walzing, *Les Corporations*, i. 141 ff. These were
replaced in Hellenistic practice by trade-guilds of workmen, which
may ultimately have been assimilated to *collegia tenuiorum*; cf.
Rostovtzeff, *SEHRE* 168 n. 42. Walzing, op. cit. iv. 2 B, lists no
eastern *collegia* as such. But a Hellenistic ἔρανος was more of a
temporary arrangement for subscription dinners than a regular club.
RE iv. 387. Walzing, op. cit. i. 146. Generally the entertainment of
the poor in the eastern provinces was done, if at all, by the benefactions of the rich in the form of διανομαί, Epp. 116–17 nn.

93. *To Pliny*

⌐ **si legibus istorum quibus de officio foederis utuntur concessum est
eranum habere possumus . . . non impedire.** The known charters of
'freedom' include a general provision that the city should form its
own laws or enjoy its previous laws, Ep. 92, *libera* n., but do not
descend to details of internal organization, except in matters affecting
the paramount interests of Rome, such as military operations. The
comment of Jones (*Greek City*, 132) that Trajan was only prepared to
allow the practice in question if it was expressly allowed in the constitution as guaranteed by the charter—and hence that 'the scope
for interference was enormous'—presses the wording too hard.
Trajan is not prepared to allow any fresh development contrary to
Roman policy, but accepts the existing rules and established practices
as they stand, not just those existing at the moment of the grant.

   si tali collatione . . . ad sustinendam tenuiorum inopiam utuntur.
For the normal exemption of *collegia tenuiorum* from the control
exercised over other forms of social organisation see Epp. 33. 3 n.,
34. 1 n.

94. *To Trajan*

Date. Between 18 September and 31 December, second year.

**1. Suetonium Tranquillum probissimum honestissimum eruditissimum
virum.** For his career and literary abilities see I. 18 pref., III. 8. 1 n.,
v. 10. Pliny's silence about any public service may suggest that
Suetonius had not yet nerved himself to take up any public post; but
see III. 8 pref. It appears from the reading 'quanto *nunc* propius
inspexi' below that he accompanied Pliny to Bithynia as a member of
his *cohors*, like Nymphidius Lupus, Ep. 87. 2 n.

iam pridem domine in contubernium adsumpsi tantoque magis
diligere coepi quanto nunc propius inspexi. The *contubernium* is
metaphorical, as often, of literary friendships, cf. I. 2. 5. There is a
contrast between Pliny's former acquaintance—*iampridem*—and
more recent knowledge of Suetonius; cf. Schuster, *app. crit.* The
prototypes read *hunc*, which is redundant. The alternative emendation *tunc* does not make any good sense after 'tanto magis coepi'.
With *tunc* Suetonius' presence in Bithynia remains possible but
unproven; cf. Weber, *Festgabe . . . K. Müller*, 40 n. 2; Syme, *Tacitus*,
779. Vidman (*Étude*, 63) thinks Suetonius was not in Bithynia, even
with *nunc*.

**2. huic ius trium liberorum necessarium faciunt duae causae : nam
et iudicia amicorum promeretur et parum felix matrimonium expertus
est.** For the *ius trium liberorum* see Ep. 2. 1 n. Pliny secured it also
for Voconius Romanus, II. 13. 8. For the phrase *iudicia amicorum*
cf. IV. 15. 5. Pliny presses this because, as the privilege was restricted,
it could not be earned by misfortune alone. Pliny himself secured it
through the influence of Servianus, Ep. 2. 1.

By *parum felix* is meant infertile, as the next sentence shows;
cf. Ep. 2. 2.

impetrandumque a bonitate tua per nos habet. At first sight this
seems to be a genuine 'plural for singular'. But he means 'I and his
other friends'; *nos* picks up *iudicia amicorum*, and *fortunae malignitas*
repeats *parum felix matrimonium*. Cf. Ep. 90. 2 n.

3. quod non rogarem absens si mediocriter cuperem. Pliny made very
few such requests in absence, if Epp. 2–13 represent the total for
the years 98–109. It was not the custom for a senator to write to the
Princeps when both were in Rome, Ep. 13 pref. At this period Pliny
makes only three such requests, cf. Epp. 26, 87.

95. *To Pliny*

**etiam in senatu adfirmare soleam non excessisse me numerum
quem apud amplissimum ordinem suffecturum mihi professus sum.**
The passage implies that Trajan made a statement of his require-
ments in the matter at the beginning of his Principate and regularly
reported consumption thereafter. This is a curious remnant of the
Senate's original control of these grants, which had passed to the
Princeps by the Flavian period, Ep. 2. 2 n. Exemptions of individuals
from existing statutes had been made in the later Republic by the
Senate, and this was an exemption from the social legislation. Under
Nero the Senate still regulated the application of the *Lex Papia
Poppaea*: Tac. *Ann.* 15. 19.

quam parce. Cf. 11. 13. 8, 'ius . . . parce et cum delectu daret', of Nerva. Suet. *Galba* 14. 3: 'dedit iura trium liberorum vix uni atque alteri ac ne id quidem nisi ad certum praefinitumque tempus'.

tuo tamen desiderio subscripsi. Cf. Ep. 2. 1 'ex rescripto' n.

ea condicione qua adsuevi. Perhaps the grant was limited in time, as above, or revocable if the holder omitted certain opportunities, e.g. of remarriage on the death or divorce of a wife. Martial received the grant separately from Titus and Domitian; 2. 92. 1–3, 3. 95. 5–6.

in commentarios meos. Cf. Ep. 66. 1 n.

96. *To Trajan*

Date. Between 18 September and 3 January, second year, written from Amastris (Ep. 98) or Amisus (Ep. 92).

Preface. It is hardly necessary to defend the genuine character of these two letters. The curious may refer to Durry's summary of that unnecessary controversy, in the Budé edition ad loc., and the consensus of opinion may be found in Mayer-Maly, *Studia et Doc. Hist. et Iuris*, 1956, 312; Vidman, *Étude*, 87–88. The letters were known to Tertullian, who summarizes them in *Apology* 2. 6. In style they exactly fit Book x and have many touches characteristic of Pliny, cf. s. 1, 'quid et quatenus' n.; s. 3, 'pertinaciam certe' etc. n.; s. 8, 'superstitionem pravam' n.; s. 9, 'civitates' n. Also they are exact in technical language and usage; s. 2, 'flagitia cohaerentia' n. s. 3, 'duci' n.; s. 4, 'quia cives Romani' etc. n.; 'adnotavi', 'species' nn.; s. 5, 'praeeunte me' n.; s. 7, 'edictum . . . secundum mandata tua' n. Above all, where could a forger have learned about the special edict against *collegia* in s. 7, which is not specified elsewhere in Book x even in Ep. 33? It would need a forger with a more accurate knowledge of Roman procedure and usage in the second century than Tertullian himself.

Equally improbable is the attempt of L. Hermann (*Latomus*, 1954, 343 ff., 'Les interpolations de la lettre de Pline' etc.) to show that the two letters contain large interpolations, made by a second-century Christian, whom Hermann actually identifies with the martyr Apollonius. This gentleman is supposed to have concocted most of ss. 4–8, parts of ss. 9–10, and two phrases in Ep. 97, out of Tacitus, *Ann.* 15. 44 (for tone and phraseology), the *Acts of the Apostles* (for the sending of Roman citizens to Rome), Justin's *Apology* (for the blaspheming of Christ), and Book x itself (for the attitude to *collegia*). Just how the interpolations were inserted into all texts of Book X between Pliny's death and the date of Tertullian's *Apology*, which knows the 'interpolated version', is not explained. Hermann's only serious grounds are the unusual length of Ep. 96, which is in fact only seven or eight Teubnerian lines longer than Ep. 81, and a third longer than Ep. 58, and the incorrect belief that Trajan did not answer all the questions put by Pliny in the 'interpolated' text; for this see Ep. 97. 1 n. This type of theory, like the notion that Tacitus' account of the Neronian affair is a forgery, raises greater difficulties than it solves, by neglecting (amongst other things) the subtlety and accuracy of knowledge shown in the documents, and by implying an improbable literary skill on the part of the forger.

The more subversive criticism of R. Grant, *Theol. Rev.* (Harvard, 1948), 273 f., calls for more serious comment. He suggests that Pliny wrote up his account not so much from the evidence of the witnesses, as in terms and style borrowed from Livy's narrative of the Bacchanalian scandal. What of the rest of Book X? The supposition must be that the book was a literary compilation like Books I–IX, which is clearly false. It is true that Pliny never quite shakes himself free in X from the literary and oratorical training to which he had devoted his previous life. But this letter like all others in X is a factual report to the Princeps, however well written, and whatever the literary echoes. (See also Introduction, pp. 538 f.) The similarities with Livy, which are not nearly so striking as they seemed to Grant, are due to the similarity of the material treated by two men of letters; cf. s. 7, 'carmen' n. Compare VI. 31. 15–17 nn., for another example of this problem. The immediate influence may be not Livy but an account, in any of the annalists of the Julio-Claudian period, of measures taken to repress Druids, Magians, or Jews.

Tertullian's close summary of Epp. 96–97 in *Apology* 2. 6–7 differs from the narrative of Pliny in some details. He adds the words *quibusdam gradu pulsis*, after his summary *damnatis quibusdam Christianis*. This might be due to a faulty recollection, or to a misinterpretation of the sentence in s. 4 about Roman citizens. He uses *inquirendos, inquisitio* in place of Trajan's *conquirendi*, and substitutes *homicidium* for Pliny's *furta . . . latrocinia* in s. 7. He somewhat misinterprets Pliny's *obstinationem* in s. 3 as *obstinationem non sacrificandi*, in the light of his own times. Evidently Tertullian reproduced the substance of the Letters from memory.

Pliny's narrative is summarized more briefly, and as accurately, by Eusebius 3. 33. 128–9, who quotes Tertullian. The tradition is given with various inaccuracies by Jerome, *Chron.* s. *Ol.* 221; Sulpicius Severus, *Chron.* 2. 31. 2; Orosius 7. 12. 3; Zonaras 11. 22 C–D.

Method. These two letters contain the earliest and fullest pagan account of Roman conflict with Christians in the first century of their existence—earlier by five or more years than Tacitus' briefer and obscurer account of the Neronian affair. The letters touch also on some aspects of early Christian organization. Their main value lies in their evidence about the causes and legal forms of Christian 'persecution', all the more valuable because of the judicial and factual nature of the document. All these topics have been discussed repeatedly by the past two generations of scholars, and have a vast bibliography, to which additions are continuously being made. The present commentary is concentrated on the political and legal problems arising immediately from the text. It is to be read with Appendix V, where an attempt is made to summarize the controversy that has raged over the legal aspects of the early persecutions as a whole, and to restate the problem in relation to the present state of cognate Roman studies. The Appendix contains a bibliography of most of the relevant works written since 1914, which are cited here only by their authors' names. The principal works of the period 1890–1914 will be quoted as required, and are cited in *CAH* xii. 775 n. Vidman, *Étude*, 87 f., contains a useful criticism of recent views. For a survey of judicial procedure see also Th. Mayer-Maly, 'Der rechtsgeschichtliche Gehalt der Christenbriefen von Plinius', *Studia et Doc. Hist. et Iuris*, 1956, 311 ff.

An attempt is made (below, s. 7 nn.) to place Pliny's references to Christian liturgy and usage in the context of Christian evidence, with a separate commentary and bibliography.

Setting. The serial order of the letters puts Pliny's encounter with Christians in Pontus and during his second year of office, between 18 September and New Year; cf. Epp. 88, 100. The city where the trouble first arose cannot be determined. Epp. 96–97 are sandwiched between letters concerning the affairs of Amisus (Ep. 92) and of Amastris (Ep. 98), with Amisus recurring in Ep. 110 and Sinope also in the offing (Ep. 90). Wilcken (art. cit. 133–4) favoured Amisus, but his argument depends largely on his doubtful theory that this was an 'urgent' letter dispatched from the scene of action. (Cf. p. 530.) But there was no reason why Pliny should not keep the Christians languishing under arrest for many months, like St. Paul, while he consulted Trajan. Weber (art. cit. 31–32) preferred Amastris, because he reckoned that Sinope and Amisus were excluded by their autonomous status from Pliny's judicial activity (Epp. 90, 92 nn.). None of these cities, except possibly Amastris, is known to have been an assize city, or *conventus* centre (*Ec. Survey*, iv. 709, 741; Lucian, *Alex.* 57). Amisus, though a free city, might have sought out the

jurisdiction of Pliny, as it did in the affair of Ep. 110. But since the
governor alone could exercise capital jurisdiction over ordinary
provincials, the charges could have been referred to Pliny's tribunal
from any city in Pontus. Amastris may be preferred as the chief
Christian centre of Pontus later in the century.

The early establishment of Christianity in Pontus is known from
the address of 1 Peter (i. 1) to 'the elect in Pontus ... and Bithynia',
and a passing reference to Aquila of Pontus in Acts (xviii. 2). Later in
the century, Lucian indicates that Christians were very numerous in
Pontus (*Alex.* 25, 38.) and Dionysius, bishop of Corinth in the middle
of the century, addresses one letter to 'the church at Amastris and
others in Pontus', and another to the church of Nicomedia. The
notorius Marcion, his contemporary, came from Sinope (Eusebius, *HE*
4. 23. 185–6; cf. Harnack, *Die Mission*, etc., 754 f.). It is noteworthy
that Pliny had trouble with Christians only in Pontus—the common
reference of the affair to Bithynia is misleading. But the suggestion
of Ramsay (*The Church in the R. Empire*, 224 f.) that Pliny had
earlier been executing Christians in Bithynia without hesitation,
because no apostates occurred until he reached Pontus, ignores the
clear indications of the letter that the affair came to a head fairly
quickly, in two main stages, marked by *interim* (s. 2) and *mox* (s. 4),
and that Pliny had doubts from the beginning, and not only about
apostates (s. 2). The lack of charges against Christians earlier is not
surprising in view of the sporadic nature of persecution at all times.
(Appendix, pp. 775, 782.)

1. **sollemne est mihi, domine, omnia de quibus dubito ad te referre.**
Pliny makes it clear that the present trials arose from the action
of private prosecutors, and were not stirred up by him, s. 2, 'deferebantur' n. But it is apparent that he has taken the advice of interested parties about the method of trial, s. 3, 'iterum' n., s. 5,
'dicuntur' n., and that there had been previous trials in Pontus,
s. 6 n. It is also apparent that Pliny knows of no specific
enactment, rescript, or edict of Trajan affecting the treatment of
Christians in his province or elsewhere. The only ruling of Trajan
which he quotes is the *mandatum* about social clubs, s. 7. Cf. Appendix, p. 775. Contrast his quotation of legislation and directives in
other affairs; Epp. 56, 58, 65, 72. Pliny has been urged to deal with
the Christians as in Ep. 72, 'ut ... secundum exempla proconsulum
ipse cognoscerem'.

cognitionibus de Christianis interfui numquam. This implies that
Pliny knew that such trials had taken place within the period of his
public career, and hence at Rome.

The term *cognitio* confirms what the later evidence indicates, that the form of trial was the personal judgement of the holder of *imperium* sitting formally *pro tribunali* to hear charges made in due form, and assisted by his *consilium*. He may be the proconsul or the imperial legate in provinces, or the city prefect who exercised the main police supervision at Rome with capital powers. Cf. Appendix, p. 782. For the working of *cognitio* see VI. 22, 31 nn. The jury courts of the *quaestio* system are never associated with the trial of Christians. Pliny had some experience of *cognitio* procedure when prefect of Saturn, I. 10. 10 n., and as assessor in Trajan's personal court, IV. 22, VI. 22, 31.

Pliny's lack of previous provincial experience explains his ignorance of Christian trials, though he sometimes acted as assessor to the city prefect, VI. 11. 1 n. His statement does little to confirm the vague generalization of Eusebius, *HE* 3 (17–18) 108–9, about Christian persecutions under Domitian. The one person named by Eusebius, Flavia Domitilla, was condemned with her husband the consular Flavius Clemens in 95 on a political charge that involved ἀθεότης and Judaic practices according to Dio's obscure phrase; Dio 67. 14. 2; Suet. *Dom.* 15. 1. The trial took place either before the Princeps or, like other political trials of the time, before the Senate, whence Pliny could hardly have been absent; III. 10. 3, VII. 19. 5–6 nn. For the controversy over the religion of Clemens and Domitilla see Hardy, *Christianity and the Roman Government*, ch. v; E. T. Merrill, *Essays in Early Christian History*, ch. vi. The evidence of Eusebius is not lightly to be set aside when he names a particular person, even if the archaeological evidence of the catacombs can no longer be invoked to support his tradition about Domitilla; cf. briefly, H. M. Last, *JRS*, 1937, 90.

Two other persons are known on good evidence to have been condemned as Christians elsewhere under Trajan, Cleophas, reputed cousin of Christ, at Jerusalem by the legate 'Atticus', and Ignatius the *episcopos* of Antioch in Syria, who was sent by an unknown legate to Rome, where he perished in the Flavian amphitheatre. Eusebius, op. cit. iii. 127, 130; for a discussion see Lightfoot, *Apostolic Fathers*, I. 21 ff., II. i. 446 f. E. M. Smallwood, *JRS* 1962, 131 f.

ideo nescio quid et quatenus aut puniri solet aut quaeri. Merrill, ad loc., perversely construed *quid* with *puniri* and *quatenus* with *quaeri*, to mean 'what punishment should be inflicted, and how far should the investigation be pushed?' But the order is chiasmatic. The questions expanded in the following sentence are *quatenus puniri* and *quid quaeri*. Durry, ad loc., rightly compared Ep. 92 'quid et quatenus aut permittendum aut prohibendum putares', where the order is also chiasmatic. Pliny here does not doubt that convicted Christians are liable to the maximum penalty, but is aware that in *cognitio extra ordinem* the governor was free to vary the penalty (Appendix, p. 782).

2. nec mediocriter haesitavi sitne aliquod discrimen aetatum. Whole families might be accused, as in the persecution at Lyons under Marcus, where a boy of 15 perished, Eusebius, op. cit. 5. 1. 209. The lawyers occasionally allow for *aetatis excusatio* when considering criminal penalties: Ulpian, *Dig.* 29. 5. 1. 32; Maecianus, ibid. 14. Cf. 48. 19. 16. 3.

detur paenitentiae venia an ei qui omnino Christianus fuit desisse non prosit. This suggestion renders untenable for this period the 'common law' theory of the persecutions, that the Christians were accused of specific crimes, such as violation of the edict *de collegiis* (s. 7), or of treason (Appendix, p. 775). There could be no pardon for such offences in the ordinary course.

nomen ipsum si flagitiis careat an flagitia cohaerentia nomini puniantur. This question covers the whole problem of the attitude of the Roman government to the Christians in the period before the Decian persecutions. It is apparent that Pliny has been following the procedure known from the Christian apologists as *accusatio nominis*, Appendix, p. 780. Trajan's too brief reply confirms this procedure without explaining the grounds for it.

The phrase *flagitia cohaerentia nomini* gives the grounds on which the Roman government in the late Republic and early Principate had normally taken proceedings against sectaries of cults alien to the Roman State, such as those of Bacchus, Isis, Druidism, and Magism. Religious persecution as such had no place in such action, which was directed against the criminal by-products of the sects, *flagitia, scelera*. When the practice of a sect was banned, either by *SC* or by an imperial or proconsular edict, indictment of the *nomen*, i.e. of membership of a cult group, sufficed to secure conviction. This looked uncommonly like religious persecution to the victims themselves, but the underlying ground remained the *flagitia* supposed to be inseparable from the practice of the cult. Appendix, pp. 780 f. Trajan's reply suggests that he or his advisers believed, despite Pliny's plea, that Christians tended to commit the *scelera* which their enemies alleged against them—the 'Thyestian banquets' and 'Oedipodean marriages' alleged against the martyrs of Lyons; Eusebius, op. cit. 5. 1. 201; cf. 4. 7. 149. Justin, *Apology.* 2. 12. So too Tacitus, *Ann.* 15. 44, reckons the sect 'exitiabilis' and 'novissima exempla meritos', and Suetonius, *Nero* 16. 2, calls them 'genus hominum superstitionis novae et *maleficae*'. But late in the second century the indifferent Lucian, in his satirical account of the Christians and their tribulations, says nothing to suggest that he had ever heard of any Christian 'crimes' except 'atheism', though he knows something of their 'brotherly love', community of goods, and abstention from certain foods. Like Pliny he regards them as foolish zealots whose way of life is morally blameless: *de morte Peregrini* 11–13, 16; cf. s. 5 n.

The passage in 1 Peter iv. 15–16 may be mentioned here: 'Let none among you suffer as a murderer or a thief or an evildoer . . . but if as a Christian, then do not be ashamed but glorify God in this name.' Possibly the author is insisting that Christians should see to it that they could only be charged *ob nomen* and not *ob scelera*, and so create the impression that Pliny here receives of their innocence of life. The theory raises a question of dates, which this is not the place to discuss. (J. Knox, *J.Bibl. Lit.* 1953, 187 f.)

interim ⟨in⟩ iis qui ad me tamquam Christiani deferebantur hunc sum secutus modum. The initiative comes from the provincials, not from the governor. So too in all instances from the second century where the evidence is at all clear, the prosecution is initiated by private prosecutors: Appendix, p. 778. In Eusebius, op. cit. 4. 16. 174, Justin is accused by Crescens, and ibid. 17. 177 Ptolomaeus and his convert are accused by her husband. In the Scillitan *Acta* the martyrs were arrested in their municipality and sent to the proconsul at Carthage who had not taken the initiative, though not all details are clear; Appendix, p. 784. This usage follows the general ruling of Paulus, *Dig.* 48. 18. 18. 9 and *Sent. Paul.* 5. 16. 14–15: 'reis suis edere crimina accusatores cogendi sunt . . . cogniturum de criminibus praesidem oportet ante diem palam facere custodias se auditurum, ne hi qui defendendi sunt subitis accusatorum criminibus opprimantur'. The Apologists complain of delation rather than of official inquisition (Appendix, p. 778). This latter, which Trajan forbids, was apt to occur when popular clamour was stirred up to demand victims, as in the condemnation of Polycarp, and at Lyons: Eusebius, op. cit. 4. 15. 164, 5. 1. 199, 201. There, first the populace began to hound down Christians, then the municipal magistrates arrested and charged numbers of them. These had to await trial by the legate, who finally ordered that Christians should be 'sought out publicly'. In Pontus the first accusation was brought presumably by the civic magistrates interested in the sales of sacrificial meat (s. 10 n.), but later other parties took up the game of baiting Christians (s. 4 n.).

3. interrogavi ipsos an essent Christiani. confitentes iterum ac tertio interrogavi supplicium minatus ; perseverantes duci iussi. This procedure of the repeated question with threats followed by sentence appears in the trials of Ptolomaeus, the Lyons martyrs, the Scillitan

martyrs, and of Polycarp; cf. Eusebius, loc. cit. and 4. 15. 167–8. The proconsul of Africa offered the men of Scilli thirty days' grace, and the proconsul of Asia tried hard to induce Polycarp to take the oath to the Fortune of Caesar. Pliny did not put an oath to the accused at this stage, but was satisfied with the admission of guilt. Roman lawyers seem not to have questioned the validity of the confession as proof of guilt until the Severan period: *Dig.* 48. 18. 1. 17 and 27; Mayer-Maly, art. cit. 317.

By *supplicium* Pliny means punishment, not torture (despite Brasiello, op. cit. 248), though the threat or use of torture occurs in other martyr trials. Cf. VIII. 14. 12: 'post quaestionem supplicio liberandos'; II. 11. 8, IV. 11. 8, VIII. 14. 15, 24 for Pliny's usage. In s. 8 he only uses torture (*tormenta*) to test evidence.

iterum ac tertio. The double question recurs in the most primitive version of the trial of Christ (Mark xv. 2–4, Matt. xxvii. 11–15), and the triple question occurs in a form of procedure quoted by the classical lawyers for dealing with absent parties. *Dig.* 48. 1. 10. This is no normal trial, but an attempt to secure submission to the governor's will.

duci. They are led off to immediate execution by the sword, like the men of Scilli. This use of *duci* is common enough: Sen. *de ira* I. 18. 4; Suet. *Cal.* 27. 1; at the end of the trial of Ptolomaeus 'κελευσάντος αὐτὸν ἀχθῆναι', Justin *Ap.* 2. 2; *Acta Ap.* 12. 19. Pliny did not reserve them for a death in the amphitheatre, like that of Ignatius under Trajan, or Polycarp and the Lyons martyrs later in the century. Eusebius, op. cit. 3. 36. 130, 5. 1. 207. For Romans and *honestiores* accused of Christian practices execution by the sword was normal, ibid. 2. 25. 83; 5. 1. 207, 21. 240. Grades of capital punishment came to be defined clearly in the later second century, the age of the classical lawyers. Then it appears that *bestiis obici* was regarded as a useful alternative to the *summum supplicium* of fire or crucifixion for certain special crimes, in the case of *humiliores*, for which decapitation was thought inadequate. These crimes include murder, treason, magic, and 'impious rites'. This appears most clearly in Paulus and Ulpian as cited in *Mos. et Rom. legum collatio* I. 2. 2, 8. 4. 1, 12. 5. 1; *Sent. Pauli* 5. 23. 1 and 15–17, 29. 1. Cf. Callistratus, *Dig.* 48. 19. 28 pref. and 10–12; Paulus, ibid. 38. 2; Brasiello, op. cit. 247 f. Ulpian, *Dig.* 48. 19. 8. 1, indicates that the normal death sentence was decapitation by the sword, and that the sentence, once pronounced, could not be carried out by any other method. Evidently the severer penalties could only be inflicted by formal sentence. But how far these distinctions were defined in provincial usage before the age of the Antonines can hardly now be determined. Pliny appears to be unaware of any alternatives. Proconsuls were probably free to follow their own devices, short of *saevitia*. See also Ep. 58. 3 n.

neque enim dubitabam . . . pertinaciam certe et inflexibilem obstinationem debere puniri. A fresh ground of objection to the Christian
nomen is here revealed, which tended in time to underline the
supposed hostility of Christians to the Roman government. See
Appendix, pp. 784 f. In the Scillitan Acts the proconsul, who like Pliny
showed consideration for the accused, says: 'Since they remained
unbending in opinion I have condemned them to be slain by the
sword', and earlier, 'Take no part in such folly and obstinacy'.
Sanctus, before the legate at Lyons, refused to give his name,
domicile, or status, or to give any other answer save that he was
a Christian; Eusebius, op. cit. 5. 1. 202. This attitude was summarized by Marcus Aurelius as ψιλὴ παράταξις, *Med.* 11. 3, i.e. *mera
contumacia*. Pliny's comment would be echoed by any Roman
magistrate so defied by a provincial, cf. III. 9. 15: 'esse . . . se
provinciales et ad omne proconsulum imperium metu cogi'. A
proconsul of Sardinia in A.D. 69 threatens punishment for *contumacia*
to those communities who fail to observe a certain regulation about
their civic boundaries (*ILS* 5947). The *Lex Iulia de vi* cancelled even
the right of the Roman citizen to *provocatio* in the case of those 'qui
ideo in carcerem duci iubentur quod ius dicenti non obtemperaverint';
Sent. Pauli 5. 26. 2. Ulpian comments on the *obstinata persuasio* and
contumacia of Chaldaean and other magicians who practised their
black arts in open defiance of imperial regulations; *Collatio* 15. 2. 1, 2,
cf. Appendix, p. 785. Trajan was particularly incensed against a man
who sought to evade a judicial sentence, an offence which the lawyers later regulated, as a type of *contumacia*, with stiffened penalties
on the principle that *contumacia cumulat poenam*; Ep. 57. 2 n. Pliny's
point is similar—the Christians were wantonly defying a magistrate
bidding them abandon an undesirable cult (above, *iterum* n.). That
there was no specific legislation was irrelevant within the sphere
of magisterial *coercitio* and *cognitio extra ordinem*; Appendix, p. 782.
The terms used by Pliny recur in the imperial rulings of the later
empire instead of the lawyer's term *contumacia*; cf. Mayer-Maly,
art. cit. 318 n. 43, citing e.g. *Codex* 7. 14. 5. 2; 10. 32. 33. 1.

**4. fuerunt alii similis amentiae quos quia cives Romani erant adnotavi
in urbem remittendos.** So too the legate of Lugdunensis hesitated to
deal with Roman Christians, and referred to Marcus Aurelius for
instructions, who bade him execute them by the sword. Eusebius,
op. cit. 5. 1. 207. The circumstances in which a provincial governor
could execute a Roman citizen without appeal to the Princeps were
extremely limited, cf. II. 11. 8 n. For Roman citizens among the
provincial proletariat see Ep. 29. 1 n. Some might hail from the colony
of Sinope, Ep. 90.

The accusation against Romans raises the legal question in the form that was favoured by Mommsen. Action was taken at times in the later Republic and early Principate to forbid the practice of certain religions by Roman citizens, and to enforce the principle that a Roman citizen might not introduce an alien cult into the Roman state without public authority; Appendix, p. 776. For example, a *SC* of A.D. 16 made the practice of Magian arts by Romans a capital offence, p. 785. Cicero expressed this notion in ideal terms, *de leg.* 2. 19: 'separatim nemo habessit deos... novos... nisi publice adscitos'. This principle could be the basis of charges against Roman citizens, or even of other persons inside Italy, and in a later age anywhere in the Empire. It is expressed in legal form in a rescript of Marcus, *Dig.* 48. 19. 30: 'si quis aliquid fecerit quo leves hominum animi superstitione numinis terrentur... in insulam relegari'. This is elaborated in *Sent. Pauli* 5. 21. 2: 'qui novas sectas vel ratione incognitas religiones inducunt ex quibus animi hominum moveantur, honestiores deportantur humiliores capite puniuntur'. But in both cases the penalty, being below that customary, under the charge of Christian practices, for Roman citizens and *honestiores* alike in the later second century, shows that these texts are not those on which the punishment of Christians was immediately based. Pliny's affair may be the first occasion that Roman citizens were condemned for the 'name', and the question for Trajan was whether to extend to provincial Romans a punishment already fixed for *peregrini*. Possibly Ignatius (above) was a Roman citizen, though his name alone does not prove it.

adnotavi. Technical term for the registration of official decisions, cf. *Dig.* 48. 17 *passim.*

mox ipso tractatu ut fieri solet diffundente se crimine plures species inciderunt. Different sets of interested parties take the matter up after the persons indicated by s. 2, 10 (nn.), who are probably civic priestly authorities, had initiated the denunciations, as was to be expected in a *provincia factionibus vexata*, as it was at all levels. Cf. Epp. 34. 1, 81. 1, 93, 117; IV. 9. 5 nn.

For *species* cf. Ep. 56. 4, 'haec... species incidit in cognitionem'; 116. 2; Gaius, *Inst.* 2. 79; Ulpian, *Dig.* 47. 20. 3. 1, 'hae omnes species stellionatum continent'.

5. qui negabant esse se Christianos aut fuisse, cum praeeunte me deos adpellarent et imagini tuae, . . . ture ac vino supplicarent, praeterea maledicerent Christo, . . . dimittendos putavi. Pliny applies this test only to those who deny the charge. In the later records the governors try to induce those who admit the charge to make the sacrifices—Polycarp, Lyons, and Scillitan martyrs, above. Neither Pliny nor

Trajan, who approves the test, seeks to compel conformity to the state religion or the imperial cult as such, or regards the Christian ἀθεότης as an offence in itself. The imperial cult was a voluntary institution, and involved the upper classes of the provinces rather than the masses: Appendix, p. 783. The punishment of Christians at this time cannot be related to the crime of *maiestas*. Those condemned had shown no active disrespect to *di nostri*. Pliny uses no suggestive term such as *impietas*, nothing beyond *amentia, obstinatio*, and *prava superstitio*, ss. 3–4, 8. Besides, Trajan refuses to countenance charges of *maiestas* in other contexts, Ep. 82. 1 n.

praeeunte me. Pliny spoke the formula, cf. Ep. 52, 'praeivimus'.

deos. The inclusion of the Capitoline deities in the test is not mentioned in other trials of the second century, but the Christians were generally regarded as 'godless' by their opponents. Hence the shout αἶρε τοὺς ἀθέους at the trial of Polycarp, Eusebius 4. 15. 167; cf. *id.* 5. 1. 200. So too the philosopher Demonax in Lucian had to face at Athens a popular charge of taking no part in the civic cults (*Dem.* 11), and Lucian asserts generally that Christians 'deny the Hellenic gods' (*de morte Peregrini* 13).

ture ac vino supplicarent. Pliny has in mind the indirect cult of the *numen Augusti* which had republican precedents at Rome itself. Cf. the story of Gratidianus in 86 B.C.: Cic. *Off.* 3. 80.

maledicerent Christo. Cf. Eusebius, loc. cit. ὄμοσον καὶ ἀπολύσω σε· λοιδόρησον τὸν Χριστόν. In the Scillitan Acts the prisoners were urged to abandon their religion altogether.

dicuntur. Pliny quotes his informants without comment. The similar phrase in Justin, *Ap.* 2. 2 is used of those denying the charge itself: ὧν οὐδὲν πρόσεστι τῷ ἀληθίνῳ Χριστιανῷ.

dimittendos. For this technical sense cf. Modestinus, *Dig.* 48. 1. 12. 1: 'innoxios dimittant', Tertullian, *Scap.* 4. 3. It commonly has the sense 'let off' rather than 'acquit', when the judge is not fully satisfied of guilt. The dismissal may then be accompanied by a beating. Cf. *Dig.* 47. 11. 7, 48. 19. 28. 3.

6. alii ab indice nominati esse se Christianos dixerunt et mox negaverunt. At Lyons the pagan servants of the Christians laid information against them, Eusebius, op. cit. 5. 1. 201. There also a number denied the charge, of whom some affirmed their faith later, ibid. 204, 208. Doubtless the most stalwart leaders were attacked first. K. Müller ingeniously suggested that these apostates were not lapsed Christians but persons excommunicated for mortal sins, who thought to redeem themselves as martyrs but lacked the courage to persist. But the parallel from Lyons does not support this (*Zeit. N.T. Wiss.* 1924, 214 f.).

fuisse quidem sed desisse quidam ante triennium . . . non nemo etiam ante viginti. This might support the case for earlier troubles under Domitian and recently, ss. 1–2 nn. There evidently had been previous trials in the area. But Pliny gives no reason for the recantations, and is not talking about a multitude. Merrill, *Essays*, ch. vi, and Hardy, op. cit., ch. v, failed to notice the implication. This text supports the evidence of 1 Peter i. 1 that the evangelization of Pontus goes back to the apostolic age (cf. p. 694).

7. **hance fuisse summam vel culpae suae vel erroris.** Lawyer's language, e.g. *Cod*. 10. 32. 33 'sub qualibet culpae vel erroris offensa'. Paulus, *Dig*. 9. 2. 31, defines *culpa* as involving negligence or *dolus*.

The Christian Liturgy

The following notes on s. 7 are concerned with the contribution of Pliny to the early history of the organized 'services' of the Church. Almost every word is charged with liturgical significance.

essent soliti stato die ante lucem convenire carmenque Christo quasi deo dicere secum invicem seque sacramento non in scelus aliquod obstringere . . . quibus peractis morem sibi discedendi fuisse rursusque coeundi ad capiendum cibum, promiscuum tamen et innoxium. quod ipsum facere desisse post edictum meum.

This passage, properly understood, neatly fills a gap in the Christian documentary evidence for the development of the 'services' of the primitive church, between the Apostolic age and the latter part of the second century, when Tertullian and Justin provide a relatively clear picture. Yet church historians on the whole have not made effective use of it. There are three elements to be distinguished in the regular occasions of the church: the meeting for instruction by preaching and reading, diversified by prayer and singing—connected with the Jewish morning service of prayers and readings; the assembly for the *Agape* or fellowship meal of the 'brethren'; and, third, what came to be known as the Eucharist, the solemn breaking of bread and taking of wine on the model of the Last Supper. In the apostolic period the *Agape* and the Eucharist were conjoined, and took place at the end of the day, though St. Paul's animadversions on misconduct at the *Agape* foreshadowed the ultimate separation (1 Cor. xi. 29–34). But the service of instruction had no set time. In the middle second century, the detailed account of Justin, *Ap*. 1. 65–67, confirmed later by sundry passages in Tertullian, notably *De Cor*. 3 and *Ap*. 39, shows that the Eucharist had been separated from the *Agape* and joined to the service of instruction to make a single occasion, which took place at dawn on the 'Sunday' of each week, while the *Agape* remained in the evening.

The evidence of the *Didache* (9–10, 14), which may be earlier than Pliny's letter by twenty years, and of his contemporary Ignatius, in *ad Smyrnaeos* (8. 1–2) and *ad Romanos* (7), has been taken to date the separation to an early date, especially the distinction in Ignatius between the 'corruptible' and 'incorruptible' *Agape*. But these texts are ambiguous, and have been interpreted both as proving and as disproving the separation, though the most recent investigations have tended to reaffirm the separation and date it back to the age of Paul (Pera, Allo). Vidman justly remarks that Tertullian's brief account of the Eucharist as a dawn service is given as part of an already traditional usage (*De Cor.* 3, quoted below; *Étude*, 105–6). But this need not carry the separation further back than the date already given by Justin.

So much seems to be fairly common ground between those who have contributed in the present century to the vast bibliography of this subject. For a summary of controversies see *Encyclopaedia of Religion and Ethics (ERE)*, i, 'Agape', 167–75 (A. S. Maclean); v, 'Eucharist', 546–8 (J. H. Srawley); and more recently, Vidman, *Étude*, 98 f. Lightfoot, *Apostolic Fathers²*, 1. 50 f., still useful. More recent contributions, cited in the following notes, include:

E. B. Allo, 'S. Paul', *Première épître aux Corinthiens* (Paris², 1935).

F. L. Cirlot, *The Early Eucharist* (London, 1939), chs. ii–iii.

C. C. Coulter, *Class. Phil.* xxxv (1940), 60 f.

F. J. Dölger, 'Sol salutis', *Liturgiegeschichtliche Forsch.* (Münster, 1920).

M. Goguel, *L'Église primitive* (Paris, 1947), 272 ff.

R. Hanslik, *Bursians Jahrbuch*, 1943 (282), 67 f.

J. A. Jungman, *Missarum Sollemnia*, i³ (1952).

C. J. Kraemer, 'Pliny and the early church service', *Cl. Phil.* xxix (1934), 293 f.

A. Kurfess, *Zeitschr. neuetest. Wiss.* xxxv. 215 f.; *Mnemos.* N.S., vii (1939), 238.

H. Lietzmann, *Beginnings of the Christian Church* (London, 1949), 1. 147 f.; *Gesch. Stud. Hauck* (1916), 34 f.: 'Carmen-Taufsymbol', *Rhein. Mus.* lxxi (1916), 281 f.; *Messe und Herrenmahl* (Bonn, 1926), 257–60.

C. Mohlberg, 'Carmen Christo', *Riv. Arch. Christ.* xiv. 93 f.

S. L. Mohler, 'Bithynian Christians', *Cl. Phil.* xxx (1935), 167 f.

C. Pera, 'Eucharistia Fidelium', *Salesianum*, 3–5, 1941–3.

J. H. Srawley, *Early History of the Liturgy* (Cambridge, 1947).

Hitherto insufficient attention has been paid to the 'service of instruction' in interpreting Pliny's letter. The first meeting, at dawn, with its hymns or prayers and exhortations, fits best with what is known of the 'service of the word', and the second fits best, at first sight, with the combined Eucharistic *Agape*. Scholars have confused the issue by identifying the first service with that of baptism, because of the list of renunciations. But the baptismal service was an occasional, not a regular service in the post-apostolic age. By Tertullian's time it was normally held at Easter and Pentecost (*De Bapt.* 19). Pliny's evidence implies that the Eucharistic *Agape*, if still united, was held in the evening until his time, and the 'service of the word' at dawn, and that as a result of his edict *de hetaeriis* a change then took place in the usage of the churches of Pontus. This change could be that the *Agape* was abandoned and the Eucharist was transferred to the dawn service (Srawley, Cirlot). Since it is impossible that the Christians abandoned the Eucharist, Pliny's phrase, 'quod ipsum facere desisse', must refer to the *Agape* alone, if, as is argued on pp. 707 f., this sentence describes the action taken by all Christians, and not just the apostates. Alternatively it has been argued from the term *sacramento* that the Eucharist itself is being described in connexion with the dawn service (Mohlberg, Pera). But this goes beyond the obvious meaning of Pliny's words (below).

soliti essent stato die ante lucem convenire. This phrase fits exactly what Justin, op. cit. I. 67, says about the regular meeting for the weekly Eucharist held on the 'day of Saturn', i.e. the day after the Jewish Sabbath. The prisoners were describing the regular routine of the Christians, not special occasions. For 'Sunday' see also *Acta Ap.* 20. 7; *Didache* 14. 1; Ignatius, *Magn.* 9; Jungman, art. cit. 23.

ante lucem. Comparison with III. 5. 9, 'ante lucem ibat ad Vespasianium', and III. 12. 2, 'officia antelucana', shows that the hour was chosen not for secrecy, but because this was the ordinary beginning of the day, when men hurried to work or to the early levées of their patrons. Cf. also III. 1. 4, IX. 36. 1 nn. For working folk in the big Hellenistic cities it was the only free time before the end of working hours. Cf. Goguel, op. cit. 281. Eusebius, *HE* 3. 33. 128, renders the words ἅμα τῇ ἕῳ. It may be remarked that from what is known of the eating habits of the Roman world it follows that the Christians went fasting to this early service, III. 1. 8–9, 5. 10 nn.

carmenque Christo quasi deo dicere secum invicem seque sacramento non in scelus aliquod obstringere. Very different explanations have been given of these words, which are at the heart of the liturgical dispute. The *carmen* has been identified with an antiphonal hymn, with a prayer followed by a liturgical response of the type *Christe eleeson* or *maranatha* (Mohlberg, Coulter), and with a baptismal formula of confession, in a pattern of question and answer (Lietzmann). The last view depends largely on the assumption that antiphonal hymns were unknown before the second century, the invention of the antiphon being attributed to Ignatius by Socrates, *Hist.*

Eccles. 6. 8, possibly because of allusions to 'song' in his *Ephes.* 4 and *Rom.* 2 (Lightfoot). The Christian use of metrical forms dated from the apostolic age, as E. G. Selwyn (*First Epistle of S. Peter* (London, 1946), 273 f.) showed from Col. iii. 16, Eph. v. 19, 1 Cor. 14. 15, though Paul does not speak of responses. Mohler argued that antiphonal responses were used in the Judaic *shemaʿ* service, and Dölger and Mohlberg that such responses, if not antiphonal hymns, go back to the earliest period of the church. Coulter found a prototype of hymns praising Christ in 1 Tim iii. 16, which is a hymn but not antiphonal, and Phil. ii. 9–11, which is neither. So the proof does not seem to be definitive.

The short answer is that *carmen dicere* is ordinary Latin for to sing a song or to intone verses, frequent in Augustan authors, and recurring with the same meaning in Seneca (*Ep.* 108. 11) and the *Acta Arvalium* of A.D. 219. (*ILS* 5040. *Thes. L.L.* s.v.) Tertullian took the words at face value: 'canendum Christo'. It is true that *carmen* may mean the set formula of, for example, an oath, as in *Pan.* 92. 3, and *carmen dicere* might mean an invocation as in a magical rite. But the normality of the phrase from the pen of a literary man, the contrast with *maledicerent Christo* in s. 5, and the conjunction of *quasi deo*, all favour the original interpretation as a hymn of praise. Nothing forbids belief that this was antiphonal. It is at least perverse to regard the *carmen* rather than the *sacramentum* as a formula of baptism.

The *carmen* as a hymn fits what is known of the 'service of the word'. The connexion of hymns with the later term χαριστήρια has been urged to suggest that the dawn service already contained the Eucharist. It was to discredit the interpretation of the *carmen* as a hymn of this sort that Grant suggested that Pliny's terminology was drawn from Livy's account of the Bacchanal affair. But the supposed parallels are weak, and the differences are more striking than the resemblances in the passage concerned (Livy 39. 18. 3): 'ex carmine sacro praeeunte verba sacerdote precationes fecerant quibus nefanda coniuratio in omne facinus ac libidinem continebatur'. Pliny's account of *carmen* and *sacramentum* hardly echo this, and the 'commandments' cited by Pliny refer to very different crimes from those cited in Livy, ibid. 8. 7. Pliny does not once use the word *coniuratio*, so frequent in the Livian passage, and Livy's single use of *sacramentum* (ibid. 15. 13) is due to the mention of soldiers: 'hoc sacramento initiatos iuvenes milites faciendos censetis?' Pliny hardly reproduced this one term from the rhetorical mass of Livy's story. Equally, *non in scelus aliquod* is but a remote cousin of *in omne facinus*.

quasi deo. The particle has no strong effect. Cf. Ep. 97. 1, 'quasi certam formam'. The doctrinal idea recurs in Clement, *Ep.* 2. 1: φρονεῖν περὶ 'Ιησοῦ . . . ὡς περὶ θεοῦ (Herman, art. cit.).

seque sacramento . . . obstringere. The most general opinion connects this with the baptismal vow or promise to 'renounce the world', first mentioned in Justin, op. cit. 65, with the words οὕτω . . . βιοῦν ὑπισχνοῦμαι, and indicated by Tertullian (*De Cor.* 3, *De Bapt.* 20) as involving confession and renunciation (*ERE*, ii, 'Baptism', 384 ff.). But the *sacramentum* need not be the baptismal oath, which was taken once and for all, not repeated at regular intervals. Mohlberg connected it with the Eucharistic confession in *Didache* 14: 'on the day of the Lord meet together and break bread and give thanks, after first confessing your sins, that your sacrifice may be holy'. This interpretation still assumes that the word means 'oath'. But whence does it come? If Pliny's prisoners spoke Greek, without using an interpreter, the choice of word is due to Pliny, who should intend the meaning 'oath', as in Ep. 29. 2. But if the prisoners spoke Latin, or were correctly interpreted into Latin, the word may be intended in the later Christian sense of a sacred institution, which first appears in Tertullian, and is thought to be derived from a popular and non-legal usage of the word (*Ad Marc.* 4. 34; *De Cor.* 3; *De Praes.* 20, 40; *De Bapt.* 5; *ERE*, x, 'Sacraments', 903). The reference could then be to the Eucharist rather than to baptism, as in Tertullian (*De Cor.* 3): 'eucharistiae sacramentum . . . omnibus mandatum a domino . . . antelucanis coetibus . . . sumimus'. If the Eucharist is not contained in the *Agape*, some reference to it is required here. It is unlikely that the apostates would all conceal its existence from Pliny as an *arcanum*. But if the Eucharist was not yet separate, then the *sacramentum* must be connected with baptism. But the suggestion of Lightfoot (1.² 52), and others, that the prisoners described the conjoint baptism and Eucharist as in Justin (loc. cit.), and that this confused Pliny, is unnecessary. Any confusion is due only to Pliny's habitual rapidity and compression in narrative. Cf. IV. 9. 2 n.

ne fidem fallerent, ne depositum adpellati abnegarent. A third opinion about this whole passage is that the Ten Commandments are meant, and that this usage is connected with the influence of the Jewish service of prayer, in which they seem to have played a part. The developed Judaic *shemaʿ*, which may have included the commandments, benedictions, and certain responses, is the basis of the 'service of the word' (Kraemer, art. cit., Mohler, art. cit.). But the last two vows do not correspond exactly to anything in the Commandments. As they stand the vows are closer to the catalogues of sins in 1 Thess. iv. 3–6 and 1 Pet. iv. 15 than even to Christ's version of the Decalogue in Mark x. 19. Coulter (art. cit.) suggested that the addition in Mark, μὴ ἀποστερήσῃς, provides a link with the present text.

A. D. Nock compared the remarkable oath of a private 'mystery cult' at Philadelphia, of the pre-Christian era, which prohibits a long list of crimes and sins to the faithful. But this proves nothing about the Christian rites here described (*Cl. Rev.* xxxviii. 58 f.; Ditt. *Syll.*³ 985). Early Christian practice in taking oaths varied considerably, despite the scriptural veto in Matt. v. 33–37. Cf. *ERE* ix, 'Oath', 434 f.

rursusque coeundi ad capiendum cibum, promiscuum tamen et innoxium. The prisoners are describing the habitual Christian usage before the edict of Pliny against clubs. The last four words should represent their reply to the charge of 'Thyestean banquets', made against the Eucharist rather than the *Agape*. Hence this meal could be the Eucharistic *Agape* in its original form, first mentioned in Jude 12 and discussed in 1 Cor. 11. 19 f. The argument of Vidman, that it was mainly the 'love feast' that was the cause of scandal to pagans, is not quite just: it could suggest Oedipodean rather than Thyestean crimes. But the *Agape* certainly needed explanation to a Roman governor. The prisoners were at pains to show that this was a meal similar, by the official standard, to those associated with the hitherto legal clubs and guilds.

There is no indication of the time of the *Agape*. The ordinary evening meal was taken during the last hours of daylight, and extended on occasion into the night. But this was rare, even among the wealthy, because of the expense and inefficiency of lighting: cf. III. 1. 9, 5. 13 nn. The extension of Paul's discourse and of the *Agape* in Acts xx. 7–8 into the night, and the bringing in of lights, is noted because it was unusual.

quod ipsum facere desisse post edictum meum, quo secundum mandata tua hetaerias esse vetueram. Those who identify the dawn service with that of baptism, and the meal with the Eucharistic *Agape* are compelled to maintain that *desisse* refers only to the lapsed Christians, from whom the information came, since the same scholars are mostly unwilling to accept the transfer of the Eucharist to the dawn service as a consequence of Pliny's edict. But Pliny puts this evidence forward as describing the common practice of the Christians (*morem fuisse, soliti*), and reckons that it was confirmed by the evidence of the *ministrae*, taken under torture. Those apostates who were still attending the *Agape* until Pliny's edict cannot have been among those who abandoned the sect three or more years previously. They are describing what the general community of Christians including themselves did on hearing of Pliny's edict, and their apostasy is very recent. The common meal was characteristic of the social club, and politically its most equivocal feature (Ep. 93). Pliny is satisfied that the Christians are not at fault under his edict.

The examination of the *ministrae* had shown nothing except a *superstitionem pravam*, naturally, since the dawn service alone had very little in common with the activities of a *collegium*. It follows that all Christians have abandoned the *Agape*, and that the Eucharist, if not previously separate, has been transferred to the service at dawn.

On the liturgical issue the most faithful interpretation of Pliny's words would suggest that the witnesses were describing in the dawn service primarily the 'service of the word', complete with antiphonal hymns and a confessional protestation, and certainly not the great seasonal baptisms, and that the Eucharist, if not previously separated, was so separated at this time from the *Agape*. Any other view involves attributing an uncharacteristic inaccuracy to Pliny's report of his findings, or an unnecessary misunderstanding.

---

hetaerias esse vetueram. The theory that the edict against clubs was the basis of Pliny's procedure, and that of other governors, breaks down (Appendix, p. 779). Pliny could not condone, or Trajan approve, the violation of the new policy, which was essential for the situation in Bithynia-Pontus. Cf. Epp. 33–34, 92–93 nn. For *mandata*, Ep. 22. 1 n.

8. quo magis necessarium credidi ex duabus ancillis . . . et per tormenta quaerere. Pliny treats the *diakonoi*, as these 'servants' evidently were, as slaves, whose evidence was commonly taken under torture. The torture of free-born witnesses in ordinary criminal procedure was an innovation of the Late Empire, approved first in a restricted field by a Severan text: Callistratus, *Dig.* 22. 5. 21. 2; Mommsen, *D.Pen.R.* ii. 83. But torture was used in trials of treason and magic in the earlier Principate; ibid. 81; Mayer-Maly, art. cit. 325. At Lyons it was used before the sentence, Euseb. *HE*, 5. 1. 201–2. There 'gentile' servants of the Christians were arrested and gave evidence against their masters. Sanctus the Deacon and Pothinos the Episcopos were among the prisoners at Lyons. But here the Christian leaders escape special notice.

ministrae. This passage suggests that Pliny or his interpreter was translating Christian terms literally into Latin. Cf. *sacramento*, s. 7 n. Women as 'deacons' appear first in Romans xvi. 1. Pliny adds nothing of value, except their continued existence.

nihil aliud inveni quam superstitionem pravam. So too Tacitus on the Christians, *Ann.* 15. 44. 4: *exitiabilis superstitio*, and Suetonius, *Nero* 16. 2: *superstitionis . . . maleficae.* The word is regularly used at this time for private and foreign cults, Tac. *Ann.* 11. 15. 1, 13. 32. 3. Cf. also Ep. VI. 2. 2, 'semper haruspices consulebat . . . a nimia superstitione'.

9. **multi enim omnis aetatis omnis ordinis utriusque sexus etiam vocantur in periculum et vocabuntur.** So too at Lyons, where some forty-eight persons were accused, women and children were involved. Lucian noted the role of old women, widows, and young orphans among Christians, *De morte Peregrini* 12.

neque civitates tantum sed vicos etiam atque agros superstitionis istius contagio pervagata est. For the contrast, and the use of *civitas* for *oppidum*, see Ep. 41. 2 n.

10. **certe satis constat prope iam desolata templa coepisse celebrari.** Pliny is reporting the allegations of others—hence the evident exaggeration, often taken as an eyewitness assertion of fact by historians of religion. No doubt not only the municipal priests, who belonged to the magisterial class, but the tradesmen involved in the losses mentioned below stirred up the trouble (s. 2: *deferebantur*).

sacra sollemnia diu intermissa repeti passimque venire victimarum ⟨carnem⟩ cuius adhuc rarissimus emptor inveniebatur. With *passim* from the Aldine prototype instead of Avantius's *pastum* Körte's addition of *carnem* greatly improves the text. Its syllables could disappear after the preceding *-arum*. The sale of sacrificial meat must have been a far more extensive interest than that of fodder for the vendors of sacrificial animals—most improbably supposed to be stabled in the cities instead of marketed—if that is what is intended by the Avantius reading. The identity and function of the *emptor* in Avantius' text is obscure, and the phrase *pastum victimarum* is hardly intelligible in the context. Stout (*T.A.Ph.A.* lxxxvi. 246) vainly defends it by citing the repeated use of *pastus* for the food of ordinary animals, not 'victims', in Cic. *De nat. deor.* 2. 121–2. Besides, there is a rhetorical balance and contrast throughout this sentence, which *passim* preserves—answering to *adhuc rarissimus* as *prope iam* to *diu*—and *pastum* destroys. The separation of the dependent genitive from its noun is contrary to usage in the rest of this letter. In favour of *carnem* is the notorious fact that Christians refused to eat sacrificial meat. Lucian was aware of this (*De morte Peregrini* 16), apart from the numerous Christian statements: 1 Cor. x. 20 f.; *Didache* 6. 3; Aristides, *Ap.* 15. 5 (p. 20). The parallel with the outcry raised against Paul by the silversmiths of Ephesus is obvious (Acts xix. 23). But the interested parties are the civic priests or their agents and assistants, deprived of a lucrative privilege. Plankl's objection that the civic officials would not need to use anonymous accusations is pointless, because ss. 4–5 make it clear that the later accusations came from different quarters (W. Plankl, *B. Gymnas.*, 1953, 54 f.).

W. Schmid, *Vigiliae Christianae*, 1953, 75 f., has suggested *prosiciem* instead of *passim*, and L. Wickert (*Rhein. Mus.*, 1957, 100) wants to bring both in, to preserve the balance noted above. The noun, or the adjective *prosicius*, is known in connexion with sacrificial meats from Varro, *Rer. Div.* 11 (Nonius 220 M), Festus 225 M, and Arnobius, 7. 25: 'si omnes has partes quas prosicias dicitis dii amant'. But this is altogether too rare and odd a word for Pliny, whose vocabulary is prosaic and conventional, especially in Book x. He would not have used such a word without an apology; cf. s. 8, 'quae ministrae dicebantur', Ep. 65, 1, 'quos vocant θρεπτούς'. He uses technical terms such as *sipo* and *catarracta* (Epp. 33. 2, 61. 4) without explanation, but there is no reason to think that those words were rare in themselves, any more than the terminology of the villa letters. But Arnobius had to explain *prosicius* even to a religious audience.

sacra sollemnia. More exaggeration. The great municipal offerings financed out of rates and liturgies would not be affected. Only the small offerings of individuals and families on personal occasions would be reduced.

adhuc rarissimus emptor. Vidman (*Étude* 98) suggested that the Christians followed Paul's advice (1 Cor. x. 27–29) to turn a blind eye on occasion, to avoid giving offence. But this dispensation was strictly limited: the Christian need not inquire rigorously about the origin of his meat, but if he knows that it is from the temples he must refuse it.

facile est opinari quae turba hominum emendari possit si sit paenitentiae locus. Merrill, op. cit. 195, thought that Pliny was pleading for a general revision of the anti-Christian policy. But in ss. 6–10 Pliny is concerned only with lapsed Christians and the possibility of increasing their number. It was only such cases that he had postponed. In ss. 1–4 he concedes that the determined sectary must be punished, but inquires into the grounds of punishment. Here he is enlarging on the theme 'quatenus puniri?', s. 1 n. Cf. also Ep. 39. 6 n.

97. *To Pliny*

1. actum quem debuisti . . . secutus es. Trajan approves Pliny's general procedure—*actum*—in punishing confessed Christians, for the *nomen* alone. The question *quatenus* therefore falls, and Trajan barely answers the questions asked in Ep. 96. 1–2, but corrects Pliny on two points, inquisition and anonymous accusations, and confirms his method of dealing with 'penitents', which was an innovation. Pliny had asked no other questions. The length of his letter, as in Ep. 39, is due to the necessity of explanation.

neque enim in universum aliquid quod quasi certam formam habeat constitui potest. conquirendi non sunt. si deferantur et arguantur puniendi sunt. This is Trajan's reply to the main question in 96. 1, 'quid et quatenus aut puniri soleat aut quaeri'. He specifies no punishment, leaving this to *arbitrium iudicantis*; Appendix, p. 782. He does not answer the question about *flagitia cohaerentia nomini* because he approves the 'accusation of the name'. For the rest of Pliny's letter he meets the main point urged in ss. 6–10 successfully, and deserves some credit for the limitation in scale and frequency of Christian persecutions in the following century, when his ruling was closely followed.

in universum. The formula is used again by Trajan in Ep. 113, where as usual he insists on following local custom. His answer, despite the carping of the Apologists, was exact enough, and generally applied later. But it was not a law for the whole empire, though it might be followed as an *exemplum* by governors of other provinces as they saw fit, cf. Appendix, p. 783, and Vidman, *Étude*, 94–95. For the non-universality of imperial rulings issued to particular provinces see Ep. 65. 2 n.

There is administrative genius in Trajan's solution. He insists on the principle when presented in due form of law, but avoids mass persecutions. No manifest violation of this rule can be proved in the following century, except for the isolated action of the legate at Lyons, who bade the Christians to be 'sought out' after local agents had initiated the persecution; Eusebius, loc. cit. Cf. Hardy, op. cit. 116. These words do not prove, as Ramsay held in the extreme form of the *coercitio* theory, that hitherto it had been customary to hunt Christians out, or that such inquisition was covered by the standing orders of governors as given by Ulpian, *de officio proconsulis* (*Dig.* 1. 18. 13): 'sacrilegos latrones plagiarios fures conquirere debet et prout quisque deliquerit in eum animadvertere . . . receptoresque eorum coercere', and in a more generalized form by Paulus, ibid. 18. 3. This text refers solely to thieves, including *sacrilegi* in its technical sense of temple robbers. Besides, it is extremely doubtful whether in the period down to Trajan any standing orders were issued to proconsular governors who ruled those provinces—apart from Syria—where Christian troubles mostly arose. Trajan uses this word *conquirere* because Pliny evidently (s. 6) had sought out those named in the anonymous indictments and the informer's list, and was prepared to go on doing so: 'vocantur . . . et vocabuntur', s. 9.

certam formam. For the term cf. A-J 139, iv (Gordian), with similar implication: 'rescripto principali certam formam reportare'.

deferantur. The ordinary form of *cognitio extra ordinem* is to be followed—private accusation by third parties, and formal trial before the governor, cf. Appendix, p. 777. This principle underlies the rescript of Hadrian to Minicius Fundanus about the trial of Christians (Justin, *Ap*. 1. 69; Euseb. *HE* 4. 9; see Appendix, p. 780, with Lightfoot, op. cit.² 1. 461 f.). Despite its present corrupt form in both known versions, the Latin of Rufinus' translation of Eusebius, and the Greek of Eusebius and Justin, so much is clear, cf.: 'si provinciales . . . adesse volent adversus Christianos ut pro tribunali eos in aliquo arguant, hoc eos exsequi non prohibeo. precibus autem . . . et acclamationibus uti eis non permitto.' Hadrian also reinforced Trajan's rule by subjecting such accusation to the procedure of *calumnia*, ibid. Tertullian, *Ap*. 5. 6, says that this was strictly applied in the time of Marcus: 'poenam . . . dispersit . . . adiecta etiam accusatoribus damnatione'. Melito (apud Eusebium, op. cit. iv. 26. 189) blames delators for the resurgence of persecution in proconsular Asia at that period.

ita tamen ut qui negaverit . . . veniam ex paenitentia impetret. Trajan confirms the details of Pliny's procedure of remission at some length (though he does not insist on *Christo maledicere*), because this is the first time that the exception has been ratified. This ruling allows a procedure otherwise unknown in Roman criminal law. The exceptional measure indicates the peculiarity of the situation, and possibly the desire of the government to weaken the movement by undermining it from within (Mayer-Maly, art. cit. 327).

2. sine auctore vero propositi libelli ⟨in⟩ nullo crimine locum habere debent. nam et pessimi exempli nec nostri saeculi est. Tertullian *(ad Scap.* 4. 4), tells of a proconsul who refused to accept a written, but not anonymous, accusation, against a Christian: 'sine accusatione negavit se auditurum hominem'. Rescripts of Hadrian and Pius (*Dig.* 48. 3. 6) required municipal officials from distant areas to put the case in person even against brigands arrested and charged by the summary procedure mentioned above, s. 1 n. But a veto against anonymous accusations is otherwise unknown until the time of Constantine. *Cod. Th.* 9. 34. 4; Mayer-Maly, art. cit. 319.

et pessimi exempli nec nostri saeculi est. See Ep. 1. 2, 'saeculi' n. and Epp. 29. 2 n. and 65. 2 n., 'exemplis'.

98. *To Trajan*

Date. Between 18 September and 3 January, second year.

1. Amastrianorum civitas domine et elegans et ornata habet inter praecipua opera pulcherrimam eandemque longissimam plateam. The city, built like Sinope (Ep. 90. 1 n.) on a peninsular site with a double harbour, was formed at the end of the fourth century B.C. out of the synoecism of the smaller Greek settlements of Sesamus, Cromna, and Cytorus, by Amastris, queen of the then tyrant of Heraclea. Later it became part of the great Pontic kingdom and remained a city without a history, prosperous from its timber trade, then and later under the Romans. Cf. Strabo, XII, p. 544; Memnon, 4. 10. 7. 1 (*F.H.G.* Müller); Lucian, *Toxaris*, 59–60; Jones, *Cities*, 150, 153, 157, 159; Magie, *Romans*, 309 n. 29. At the end of the second century A.D. Amastris was metropolis of the Pontic κοινόν, *CIG* 4149; Jones's argument (op. cit. 154 n. 13) in favour of Heraclea is not proven by *IGRR* iii. 79 or the coin titles. In Head, *Hist. Numm.*² 516, the word μητρόπολις refers to colonization. Cf. *RE* (S), iv. 932.

civitas. For the sense of *urbs* see Ep. 41. 2 n.

plateam. The principal street of the city—the ordinary meaning of the word—not a square.

nomine quidem flumen, re vera cloaca foedissima. The former superintendent of the Roman sewers speaks his mind.

2. non minus salubritatis quam decoris interest eam contegi. See Ep. 91 n.

quod fiet si permiseris curantibus nobis ne pecunia desit. Cf. Epp. 23. 1 n., 90. 2 n.

99. *To Pliny*

No fresh comment is needed. The rescript like Ep. 92, another building permit, follows its original very closely.

100. *To Trajan*   101. *To Pliny*

Date. 3 January, third year.

For the annual ceremonies at the New Year, on 3 January, see Ep. 35 nn. This year Pliny is in Pontus, either at Amastris, Ep. 98, or less probably the free city Amisus (Ep. 110), since soldiers are present.

vota priore anno nuncupata alacres laetique persolvimus. This is Mommsen's emendation, printed by O.C.T. Schuster retained the prototype reading *priorum annorum*. But the vows were repaid each year, so that the plural is not possible. The source of error is obvious: ANNO NUN- would easily produce ANNORUM. A quantitative genitive of time is possible in dependence on a bare noun, 'puer tredecim annorum', but hardly with a passive participle. Cf. *Handbuch des Altertums-Wiss.* ii. 2, 'Lat. Gramm.'³, 236–7.

commilitonum et provincialium pietate. The presence of soldiers was not mentioned the previous year, Ep. 35.

102. To Trajan   103. To Pliny

Date. 28 January, third year.

For the annual prayers and oath at the anniversary of Trajan's
dies imperii at the end of January see Epp. 52–53 nn.

Pliny in this note mentions only the prayers, *vota publica*. Trajan's
formal reply also assumes the presence of soldiers, mentioned in
Ep. 100 but not in Ep. 102.

104. To Trajan

Date, after 28 January, third year.

**Valerius domine Paulinus excepto Paulino ius Latinorum suorum
mihi reliquit.** For the class of enfranchised slaves known as *Latini
Juniani* see VII. 16. 4 n. Though free and capable of contracts in their
lifetime they had no right of testamentation, and hence their goods
passed back to their *patronus*, like the *peculium* of a slave. The
patronal rights over Latins could be transferred by a will to heirs,
whether members of the family or not. Duff, *Freedmen*, 78; Gaius 1.
23–24, 3. 56; *Tit. Ulp.* 19. 4, 20. 14, 22. 3. So the patron had a freer
hand than he had over the disposition of that part of the inheritance
of a full freedman which fell to him, since the latter could be be-
queathed freely only to 'natural heirs'; Gaius 3. 58.

Pliny means that the dead Paulinus had used his right to exclude
his son, the younger Valerius Paulinus, from the succession to this
part of his estate, and left it to Pliny instead. But Pliny does not
say, as Hardy took it, that Paulinus had disinherited his son. Hence
the text is sound, and emendations such as Aldus' *excepto uno* (sc.
Latino) are not wanted. The latter is inept, since Pliny would not
need to inform Trajan of that. For *excipere* cf. Cic. *Leg. Ag.* 2. 21;
Gaius 2. 225.

reliquit. Pliny must be among the heirs, not a legatee, since Latins
could not be left by legacy; the patronal relationship could descend
by its nature only to an heir. Cf. the long discussion in Gaius 3.
57–73; Duff, op. cit. 79. But an heir could not be left a particular
object except by the special form known as *praeceptio*: cf. V. 7. 1 n.
Hence Pliny received the Latins *per praeceptionem*.

ius Quiritium des. For the granting of full freedman-citizenship
to a Junian Latin in the lifetime of his patron see VII. 16. 4 n., Epp.
5. 2, 11. 2 n. After the patron's death recourse had to be made to the
beneficium principis. Cf. Gaius 3. 72; *Tit. Ulp.* 3. 2. Otherwise they
could secure citizenship under certain enactments in return for

public services, such as enlistment in the Roman *vigiles*, or activity in the food supply of Rome, including the bakery business. Gaius I. 29–34; *Tit. Ulp.* 3. 1–6.

For *ius Quiritium* see Ep. 5. 1 n. Application is made to the Princeps when the patron is unable to carry out the rite of full enfranchisement in person, Ep. 11.2 n. Valerius Paulinus is presumably the consular of 107; cf. IV. 9. 20 n. IX. 37 pref. For his care for his slaves see V. 19. His son is not known.

105. *To Pliny*

qui apud fidem tuam . . . depositi sunt. This does not mean that Pliny was left the Latins under a *fideicommissum* requiring him to set them fully free, as Hardy seemed to think, though this was a customary practice. Trajan could not gather that from Pliny's letter. The reference in *fidem* is simply to the patronal relationship.

referri in commentarios meos iussi. See Epp. 66. 1, 95 nn. Also Ep. 2. 1 n.

106. *To Trajan*

Date. After 28 January, third year.

Rogatus domine a P. Accio Aquila, centurione cohortis sextae equestris, ut mitterem tibi libellum, per quem indulgentiam pro statu filiae suae implorat. The man is evidently a Roman citizen, as his names suggest. His status had not been acquired, as Hardy thought, by *diploma* as a time-expired auxiliary, since the auxiliaries received citizenship both for themselves and for all children, existing or future, and also for their wives; the status of a legitimate daughter would not be questionable in such a case. Hardy's suggestion that the daughter came from a former marriage is no more helpful; such were equally covered by the 'diploma'. More probably Aquila, himself a Roman, married to a 'peregrine' (as was possible in auxiliary service), is seeking to anticipate the grant of family privileges usual on the retirement of auxiliaries. Or else the child was simply an illegitimate 'peregrine'. Cf. in general Cheeseman, *Auxilia*, 32 ff. Normally the children of mixed marriages took the status of the inferior parent. Gaius I. 75.

centurione. Most centurions and decurions of auxiliary units were promoted from the ranks, and hence of peregrine status until the end of their service; cf. *CIL* xvi, n. 48. But examples are known of legionaries, or others of Roman status, becoming auxiliary centurions. Cf. in A.D. 83, *ILS* 1996, Cheeseman, op. cit. 38.

cohortis sextae equestris. The title is strange. It lacks the usual ethnic or imperial title, e.g. *c. prima Hispanorum* or *Ulpia equitata*, and *equestris* replaces the normal *equitata*. Cheeseman, op. cit. 161 n. 1, 189, compared the *cohors secunda equitum* known from Syria in *CIL* iii. 600. Mommsen amended the text to *campestris*, a title known elsewhere (Cheesman, op. cit. 187). But a Greek inscription from the road between Nicomedia and Chalcedon, of later date, gives what is evidently the same title as Pliny: *IGRR* iii. 2; *AE*, 1955, n. 266; Magie, *Romans*, 603 n. 21.

The *cohortes equitatae* were devised to meet the need for mixed units containing a proportion of mounted men. They were composed of four *turmae* each of thirty mounted infantry, and six centuries of infantry; or if at double strength, i.e. as *c. miliariae*, they had eight squadrons and ten centuries. The strength of the centuries is uncertain. Cheeseman, op. cit. 27 ff.

mitterem. i.e. by the imperial post. Cf. Ep. 83 n.

107. *To Pliny*

libellum rescriptum quem illi redderes misi tibi. Trajan notifies the soldier by a rescript to his *libellus*, recording the entry of the item in the imperial *commentarii*, as in Epp. 2. 1 n., 105. He did not send the soldier's daughter a *diploma civitatis*, as Hardy thought. A military *diploma* was not a rescript, but a copy of an excerpt from a lengthy imperial edict or *constitutio* published at Rome. (Cf. Nesselhauf in *CIL* xvi. 147 ff.; Gaius 1. 57.) Suet. *Nero* 12. 1 records the grant of *diplomata civitatis* to civilians as unusual.

This is the only occasion that the Letters deal with the formalities of the *libellus* system. These are given most clearly in Gordian's rescript *ad Scaptoparenos* (*IGRR* i. 674; A–J, n. 139). The petition of the villagers is followed by a brief reply in the form 'imp. Caesar vicanis dicit' which ends with the formula 'rescripsi recognovi signa'. A preface states that the *libellus* was a faithful copy made from the 'liber libellorum rescriptorum a domino nostro', and published in a public place at Rome, much as the military *diplomata* were published. Cf. also the rescript of Commodus to the *coloni* of the *Saltus Burunitanus* (A–J, n. 111) c. iv, and with minor variations the rescript of Pius to a representative of Zmyrna (*FIRA* i. 82), in which a filing numeral replaces the reference to the *liber libellorum*.

That method appears to be post-Trajanic. Wilcken has been generally followed in using Pliny's statement as evidence that in the previous period the beneficiary was notified directly by the return (*redderes*) of his original petition through the hands of the governor. This interpretation assumes the emendation *libellum rescriptum*, for

l. rescripti, which in itself seems doubtful Latin. But too much
weight has been put on Pliny, whose intervention in this affair was
informal, and mainly concerned with the use of the postal service
for the *libellus* (Ep. 106 n.). Dessau objected that Wilcken's view
requires *libellum subscriptum* rather than *rescriptum*, and that
reddere means to hand *over* as well as to give *back* (as in Ep. 9. 1;
but cf. Epp. 31. 3, 32. 2, 56. 5, 58. 2). If *rescripti* is read, only the
imperial reply was sent back, and the system is the same as later.
It seems essential that a copy of the decision should be sent to the
interested party in the later system also.

For this controversy summarized by Vidman, *Étude*, 37–38, see
U. Wilcken, 'Zu den Kaiserreskripten', *Hermes*, lv. 1 ff., esp. 19–20;
F. Schwind, *Zur Frage der Publikation im r. Recht* (Munich, 1940),
168; *RE* vi. 209 (Brasloff); H. Dessau, *Hermes*, lxii. 208.

A full account of the *libellus* organization is given by Wilcken,
art. cit., or briefly in Hirschfeld, *Verwaltungsbeamten*, 327 n. 2, 328
n. 1. He suggests that the emperors wrote the original subscript in
their own hand, quoting SHA, *Commodus*, 13. 6–8, *Carinus*, 16. 8,
'in subscribendo tardus . . . ut libellis una forma multis subscriberet'.

108. *To Trajan*

Date, after 28 January, third year.

1. **Quid habere iuris velis . . . civitates in exigendis pecuniis . . . rogo
domine rescribas.** The cities had perpetual difficulty in making private
contractors pay up, as sundry passages in Dio's speeches show; cf.
Or. 47. 19, 48. 9. Also Ep. 110. 1.

ego inveni a plerisque proconsulibus concessam iis protopraxian.
In provincial finances the imperial treasury normally had first claim
on a debtor's resources, as is stated generally by *Sententiae Pauli* 5.
12. 10; this appears already in Egypt in an edict of A.D. 68, *OGIS*
669, ii. 3. 17 ff. (But cf. ib. 25 f.) Municipalities had similar rights
only exceptionally; cf. the later generalization of Marcianus, *Dig.*
50. 1. 10: 'simile privilegium fisco nulla civitas habet in bonis
debitoris nisi nominatim id a principe datum est'. Thus Syrian Antioch
had the right of preference only on the goods of a dead debtor; *Dig.*
42. 5. 37. The contrary generalization of Paulus (ibid. 38. 1)—'respublica creditrix omnibus chirographariis debitoribus praefertur'—
appears in the context of the sale of goods of a dead man, and may
be more limited than it seems. So the independent proconsuls of
Bithynia-Pontus had been more generous than the later imperial
administration in this matter.

2. quae sunt ab aliis instituta sint licet sapienter indulta brevia tamen et infirma sunt nisi illis tua contingat auctoritas. Here, as in Epp. 65. 2, 68, 72, 112. 3, Pliny feels that the *exempla proconsulum* are not enough in a province transferred to imperial control. These passages show a weakness of proconsular government. A continuous policy was not necessarily maintained, because precedents were not binding on successive proconsuls, although Pliny admits that the system generally worked well: 'pro lege valuisse'.

109. *To Pliny*

ex lege cuiusque animadvertendum est. Trajan, closer than Pliny to the spirit of the early empire, frequently prefers local custom to a general rule for the whole province—let alone the whole empire. Cf. Epp. 65–66, 69, 97. 1, 111, 113. But on occasion he is impatient of local privilege: Epp. 48, 93.

These passages show that the *Lex Pompeia* had imposed a uniformity on the cities only in the main fabric of their constitutions. There was much variety in the detail of each city's arrangements.

in iniuriam privatorum id dari a me non oportebit. So too in Epp. 55, 111, 113, 115. Trajan protects individuals against excessive pressure from the central and municipal government, in a manner very different from the oppression of the *curiales* in the third century; for which see Ep. 79. 3 n. Trajan here is in full agreement with his advisers, whose somewhat legal phraseology is apparent, and reinforces their arguments with a certain breezy force of his own, with his usual care for *iustitia nostrorum temporum* (Ep. 55).

110. *To Trajan*

Date. After 27 January, third year.

1. Ecdicus, domine, Amisenorum civitatis petebat apud me a Iulio Pisone denariorum circiter quadraginta milia donata ei publice . . . bule et ecclesia consentiente, utebaturque mandatis tuis. It is remarkable that the authorities of a 'free city' like Amisus (Ep. 92) should invoke the intervention of the governor, and base a case on imperial regulations which had no legal force in their instance. This is all the odder in that the proposed application would be retrospective, since under the previous proconsular régime imperial *mandata* were not issued for Bithynia-Pontus (Ep. 22. 1 n.). As in the attacks on Dio (Ep. 81. 1), Flavius Archippus (Ep. 58), and the anonymous persons in Ep. 56. 2, there is probably a political motive, inspired by the violent political jealousies of the province; cf. IV. 9. 5 for the 'conspiracy of delators' in Bithynia.

Dio and Plutarch, both contemporaries of Pliny, protest against the habit of referring to the proconsul disputes arising out of local faction, especially about the detention of municipal monies, such as could readily be settled by local tribunals. This led to the weakening of local independence. Dio, *Or.* 45. 8, 47. 18, 48. 3, 9, cited Ep. 17B. 2 n., Plut. *Praecepta reipublicae gerendae* 19, p. 815 A.

Elsewhere appeals from a *civitas libera* to the Princeps are mentioned at Cnidos under Augustus, who avoided the appearance of giving a direct order (*IGRR* iv. 1031; A–J n. 36); at Sparta, where the Princeps regulates the rules of appeal; and at Cos, where the proconsul claims the right of vetoing such appeals (*IG* v. 21, *IGRR* iv. 1044; both undated). For appeals to the proconsul at Athens, see *IG* ed. min. ii–iii. 1100 (A–J 90, l. 55) Hadrianic.

The *ecdicus* or *syndicus* of the cities was not a financial officer but a municipal advocate, concerned with civic rights in financial matters. The terms of appointment varied from city to city. The post was sometimes created *ad hoc*, when *syndicus* was the usual term, and sometimes, as at Amisus, was a regular office. At Prusias ad Hypium the two terms appear synonymous (Dörner, *Reise*, nn. 4, 10; *IGRR* iii. 64). At Nicaea the office was later perpetual, *Ist. Forsch.* ix, n. 30. In the village inscriptions of Bithynia published by Dörner the *ecdicus* appears as the local *quaestor. Inschriften aus B.*, nn. 32, 33. Cf. Jones, *Greek City*, 244, and n. 61; Magie, *Romans*, 648 n. 49; Liebenam, *Städteverwaltung*, 303 ff.

Iulio Pisone. He is not otherwise known. The names are rare, but recur for a *vir egregius* at Ephesus. *PIR¹* J 311–12.

bule et ecclesia consentiente. For the formula cf. (e.g.) *IGRR* iii. 74–75, and for a *psephisma*, Ep. 43. 1. The popular assemblies retained some liveliness at this time, since Plutarch, op. cit. 24 c, discusses as living issues the management of assemblies and the activities of radical demagogues (Jones, *Greek City*, 271). Nine out of the eleven political speeches of Dio delivered at Prusa were addressed to the assembly on matters of public policy, such as securing an increase in the size of the council, or a petition for *libertas* (*Or.* 40, 42–47, 51). Dio ventilated his building schemes at an assembly summoned by the proconsul himself (*Or.* 45. 15–16). The assembly retained some control over elections (*Or.* 45. 7–9, 46. 14, 48. 17, 51. 6), though these were sometimes arranged by the council (*Or.* 49. 15). Plutarch, loc. cit., discusses the influence of the assembly in financial affairs at this period. But the suspension of the Prusan assembly after political disturbances by the predecessor of the proconsul Varenus showed

which way the wind was blowing (*Or.* 48. 1). The effective power lay
with the city councils, even if the assembly provided a useful
sounding board for public opinion; cf. *Or.* 50 in general, and 48. 17:
τὴν βουλὴν παρακαλεῖν πρὸς ταῦτα ἵνα ὥσπερ εἴωθε προνοῇ τῆς πόλεως.
Cf. Ep. 79. 1 n. The provincial governors seem regularly to exercise
a right of ratification over decrees of the Asian assemblies; Magie,
Romans, 641 n. 29. Jones remarks, op. cit. 177 f., that most surviving
psephismata of the imperial period were concerned with grants of
civic distinction—as in Ep. 43. 1. The forms of Hellenistic democracy
continued to be observed long after the reality had perished. Yet
Cassius Dio, a century later, still thought it necessary to recommend
the suppression of civic assemblies and of their deliberations on 'any
matter' (52. 30. 2). For epigraphical references to assemblies and lists
of decrees from the Asiatic provinces see Magie, *Romans*, 640, nn.
26, 28.

mandatis. See Ep. 22. 1 n.

eiusmodi donationes vetantur. Despite many prohibitions the
practice continued. Ulpian (*Dig.* 50. 9. 4) speaks of such *customary*
gifts (*ut solent*) being invalid.

2. Piso contra plurima se in rem publicam contulisse ac prope totas
facultates erogasse dicebat. Plutarch, op. cit. 31, speaks of men who
borrowed from friends to make a great show of liturgies. Hermo-
genian later records the rule that decurions who spent their substance
on their city, *ob munificentiam*, might receive a civic pension (*Dig.*
50. 2. 8). The extravagance which public service involved was
still willingly borne: Jones, op. cit. 180 f.; Magie, op. cit. 650 f., nn.
52–54. The grandfather of Dio, like Piso, spent his whole fortune
on his city, and Dio himself, after exile and partial ruin, involved
himself in fresh liturgies; *Or.* 40. 5–8; 46. 3; 47. 8, 19–21. But
occasionally he records a meaner tendency, *Or.* 47. 6, 14, 19;
48. 10.

ne id quod pro multis et olim accepisset cum eversione reliquae
dignitatis reddere cogeretur. This implies that at Amisus there existed
a social classification based on a wealth qualification. The social class
can hardly be anything other than membership of the council. Piso
would cease to be a decurion if he lost his remaining fortune. This
passage is evidence of a census qualification for the decurionate in
Bithynia not otherwise testified. (Cf. Ep. 79. 1 n.) Domitian presented Archippus with an estate worth S.100,000 perhaps for
precisely this reason (Ep. 58. 5). The sum is very close to that required
in Italy at Comum, (1. 19. 2 n.), and may have been introduced by the
Lex Pompeia before Amisus became a 'free city'. For the technical
sense of *dignitas* see 1. 19. 1: 'augere dignitatem tuam'; Ep. 26. 3.

111. *To Pliny*

quidquid ergo ex hac causa actum ante viginti annos erit omittamus.
Jones, *Greek City*, 135, suggests that this clause of the *mandata* was
of long standing. But this passage hardly proves it, since the figure
of twenty years was chosen to cover Piso's particular case. Trajan
and his secretaries have carelessly forgotten that the *mandata* were
an innovation in Bithynia, and do not hold a general objection to
retrospective legislation; cf. Ep. 56. 3 n. Trajan's attitude is practical
as in Ep. 115.

non minus enim hominibus cuiusque loci . . . consultum volo. For
Trajan's protection of private interests cf. Ep. 109 n. For *homines* cf.
cives mei, Ep. 58. 7 n.

112. *To Trajan*

Date. After 28 January, third year.

**1. Lex Pompeia domine . . . eos qui in bulen a censoribus leguntur dare
pecuniam non iubet.** This passage, with Epp. 79, 1 and 114. 1, shows
how drastically the democratic organization of the Hellenistic cities
was altered by Pompeius in Bithynia-Pontus to suit Roman ideas.
Membership is for life, and is regulated by censors created on the
Roman model, who make up the roll, first with ex-magistrates and
then from private citizens, enforcing age limits and wealth qualifications. Epp. 79. 1, 3, 110. 2, 114. 1 nn.; Jones, *Greek City*, 170 ff.

The custom of the *honorarium decurionatus*, a substantial subscription paid on enrolment, was commoner in the western than in
the eastern provinces, where the onerous system of liturgies effectively mulcted the rich throughout their lives for the benefit of the
whole community. Here, as at Claudiopolis (below), the Roman
governors favour the system of *honorarium*.

**sed ii quos indulgentia tua quibusdam civitatibus super legitimum
numerum adicere permisit, et singula milia denariorum et bina
intulerunt.** At Claudiopolis and at Prusa Trajan and Nerva increased
the size of the councils, and the new members paid a *honorarium*,
which Pliny regarded as obligatory: 'aut iam obtulerunt aut nobis
exigentibus conferent' (Ep. 39. 5; Dio, *Or.* 45. 7–10, 48. 11). The
councils of several hundred members varied in size from city to city;
at Prusa Nerva raised it by one hundred. Cf. Ep. 79. 3 n. The distinction between the extra councillors and those appointed by the
censors is not quite clear. At Prusa it seems that the extra members
were elected, not chosen by censors, Dio, *Or.* 45. 9. Such decurions are
distinguished here and in Trajan's reply from the routine members,

as a special group. These honorary members may include the category mentioned in Ep. 114.3 of decurions who were not natives of the city concerned. The suggestion that the emperors by increasing the councils sought to secure a controlling majority (Vidman, *Étude*, 68) ignores the fact that such increases were made at the request of the local authorities, probably out of civic pride.

et singula milia . . . et bina. Hardy suggested that the sum paid depended on the rank accorded within the council, assuming that there were distinctions like those drawn in the western municipalities between *quaestorii* and *duoviralicii*. The system is best illustrated by the *Album* of Canusium, *ILS* 6121; A–J n. 136. But it is more likely that different cities had different rates according to the local standard of wealth. In the west the rate varied considerably, cf. A–J, p. 66; Liebenam, *Städteverwaltung*, 238. A similar distinction of rate appears in Anicius' ruling, s. 2 n. and in Ep. 116. 1, both probably referring to different cities. Vidman (*Étude*, 68) notes an Egyptian parallel whereby honorary priests paid an *honorarium*, but not the regulars, quoting S. L. Wallace, *Taxation in Egypt*, 119, 407 nn. 22–23.

2. Anicius . . . Maximus proconsul eos etiam qui a censoribus legerentur, dumtaxat in paucissimis civitatibus, aliud aliis iussit inferre. Hardy saw rightly that the difference was from city to city; *aliis* takes up *civitatibus*.

A senator of this name from Pisidian Antioch is known under Hadrian, *PIR*² A, n. 663. But Pliny's man may have been proconsul before the accession of Trajan. This proconsul also is omitted from Magie's list, cf. Ep. 58. 1 n.

3. an in omnibus civitatibus certum aliquid omnes . . . debeant . . . dare. For Pliny's liking and Trajan's dislike of general rules see see Ep. 109 n.

debetur aeternitas. Ep. 41. 1 n.

113. *To Pliny*

Honorarium decurionatus omnes . . . inferre debeant necne, in universum a me non potest statui. For the closing formula cf. Ep. 97. 1: 'neque . . . in universum aliquid . . . constitui potest'. What was impossible was not the framing of such a rule, but framing a single rule that would work in the differing circumstances of each city.

sequendam cuiusque civitatis legem puto. See Ep. 112. 3 n.

sed verius eos qui invitati fiunt decuriones id existimo acturos ut praestatione ceteris praeferantur. The reader will perceive a new solution of an old crux. The prototypes read: 'scilicet ("sed" in *i* only)

adversus eos qui inviti fiunt decuriones id existimo acturos ut praefatio (*Cat.* "erogatio") ceteris praeferantur (or "-atur")." The
sentence contains the most notorious crux of historical importance in
the Letters. Editors since Mommsen have been bemused by the
words *inviti fiunt decuriones* into amending the following phrase so
as to support the notion that Trajan was dealing with a class of
persons who were trying to dodge public service. Mommsen, perceiv-
ing the contradiction between the apparent sense of the two clauses,
punctuated after *decuriones*, construing the first clause with 'sequendam . . . legem'. He then boldly inserted the words 'qui sponte fiunt'
before *id*. This might do if Trajan were still discussing the category
of ordinary councillors. But, as Jones saw (*Greek City*, 343 n. 64),
Trajan's reply must be closely related, as always, to Pliny's question.
Pliny said nothing about reluctant decurions. Trajan has answered
Pliny's main question about decurions in general: *omnes* in 113. 1
corresponds to *omnes* in 112. 3. Now he adds a note about super-
numerary decurions, who are also mentioned in 112. 1.

Since both the opening and the closing words of the sentence are
manifestly corrupt (below), there is no reason to assume that the
middle words are absolutely sound. The simplest emendation is to
read *invitati* for *inviti*. This has never yet been proposed. Then one
may accept Schuster's text for the meaningless closing words of the
prototype. The sense fits the context: 'Supernumeraries, I am sure,
will see to it that by offering donations they stand out from the
rest.' The use of *invito* is much as in Ep. 54. 2, 'per hoc . . . debitores
invitandos'; or VII. 25. 3, 'invitatus hospitio'. There is a Ciceronian
parallel, *ad Att.* 2. 18. 3, 'a Caesare liberaliter invitor ad legationem'.
The word is more explicit than the colourless technical term *adsciti*
used in Ep. 115—'contra legem adsciti sc. decuriones'—which is
hardly admissible here as an emendation. The prototypes have a
similar error in Ep. 17A. 3, where the Aldine reads *tractu* and the
Budean correction gives *tractatu*. In Ep. 96. 4 both read *tractatu*,
but Catanaeus printed *tractu*.

The corruption in the opening words seems hardly to have been
noticed. Yet *adversus* is nonsense, though less so in Mommsen's
drastic reconstruction than in the modern versions. It is required to
mean 'in regard to' instead of 'against' or 'opposite', its proper
meaning; cf. II. 17. 4, V. 20. 1, VI. 16. 16. All the early editors
read *sed*, which is restored by the Budean correction, as *scilicet*;
Catanaeus repeats the error in 75. 1. What was read as *scilicet adversus*
is likely to have been *sed* followed by some part of *verus*. Hence I
suggest *sed verius . . . existimo* as closer to the prototypes than *sed
vere*, and meaning 'but I really rather think . . .'. In Ep. 38 Trajan
uses *vere credo*, and *sed verius* is good lawyers' Latin, used, for example,

by Julianus in mid-second century: *Dig.* 41. 7. 7. The comparative is latent in the opposition of *existimo* and *puto*.

For the closing words Hardy's text, followed by Schuster and O.C.T., makes good sense, perhaps better than Stout's ingenious *praefati ceteris praeferantur* (*T.A.Ph.A.* lxxvi. 247). A correlate is required to *dare* in 112. 3, and *promises* are not apt, despite the parallel in Cic. *ii in Verr.* 3. 80, 'praefatio donationis'. To make sense of the mangled text some have supposed that *censores* was to be understood, from Pliny's letter, as the subject of *acturos*. Guillemin ineptly inserted *duumviros* before *acturos*, where *magistratus* would have been more probable, as in Epp. 79 and 81. 1. But the present proposal, already accepted by the editor of O.C.T., avoids all these difficulties, and creates none of its own.

This sentence is no longer to be regarded as an early document of the decline of zeal for municipal service among the wealthy classes. The passage might have been suspected earlier, since Pliny and Dio of Prusa otherwise indicate an excess rather than a decline of such zeal. Cf. Ep. 114. 1 n. But it was supposed to be supported by clause 51 of the *Lex Malacitana*, which provides for the compulsory nomination of candidates for annual magistracies if there were insufficient volunteers. That passage also appears insignificant when related to its historical context. Remote and backward Spanish communities at the time of Vespasian's large-scale grant of Latin rights might not be capable of maintaining the machinery of government without this protective clause. Cf. Sherwin-White, *RC* 198. For the older view, *CAH* xi. 465–6. Besides, why should Nerva and Trajan have increased the size of the councils if men were reluctant to serve on the existing bodies?

114. *To Trajan*

Date, after 28 January, third year.

1. **Lege domine Pompeia permissum ⟨est⟩ Bithynicis civitatibus adscribere sibi quos vellent cives dum ne quem earum civitatium quae sunt in Bithynia.** Passages from Dio of Prusa cited below indicate the extent to which the law was being disregarded. Hardy suggested that the Pompeian rule was derived from the Republican principle that no Roman could become a citizen of another state without forfeiting his Roman citizenship; cf. Sherwin-White, *RC* 54, 134. The *Lex Pompeia* certainly ignored the widespread Hellenistic custom of *isopoliteia*, by which not only single persons but whole communities exchanged citizenship (Jones, *Greek City*, 170). Hardy's assumption that the persons concerned were resident strangers, μέτοικοι, is inexact. Grants of honorary citizenship were commonly made to

inhabitants of other municipalities. Dio, resident at Prusa, held the franchise of Nicomedia and Apamea, and 'very many' other cities adopted him as a citizen and decurion. *Or.* 38. 1, 41. 1–2. He also indicates that grants of citizenship to resident or non-resident strangers were valid only for the lifetime of the holder, and were not inheritable. His father and grandfather had each received the franchise of Apamea, he himself received it before his exile, and after his exile Apamea urged him to settle in the city. His children lived there during his exile, but were not citizens. *Or.* 41. 1–2, 5–6; Von Arnim, *Dio*, 122 ff. So there seems to be no legal distinction between the kinds of local franchise granted to resident strangers and to non-residents.

Dual local citizenship led later in the Empire to disputes about liability for municipal liturgies and magistracies, such as figure in *Dig.* 50. 1. The usual rule was that a man was liable for the *munera* but not the magistracies of his place of domicile, if it was not his native city, ibid. 17. 11. The earliest legal texts dealing with these problems seems to be a passage of Gaius *ad edictum provinciale* quoted in *Dig.* 50. 1. 29, and a rescript of Hadrian ibid. 37 pref.; cf. *Cod. Iust.* 10. 40 (39). 7. Since neither Trajan nor Pliny seems to be concerned about this aspect of the question, the passage confirms the impression that reluctance to hold office was not yet a feature of public life in Bithynia, cf. Ep. 113 n.

ne quem earum. The early editors rewrote or interpolated this sentence, as also the next and the opening of Ep. 115. Both letters were evidently hard to decipher in the manuscript. The sound text, as printed in modern editions, comes from the Budean supplements.

in Bithynia. The absence of reference to Pontus should not be pressed to suggest with Wilcken (art. cit. 133–4) that Pliny had returned to Bithynia since writing Ep. 112. For Pontus is named by Pliny in Ep. 112. 1 but omitted in the text of Trajan's reply, 113.

quibus de causis e senatu a censoribus eiciantur. The Roman rules are known from the Caesarean *Tabula Heracleensis* 105–25 and *Lex coloniae Ursonensis* 105, the Flavian *Lex Malacitana* 54, which are all concerned with municipal organization on the Italian model, and from later texts of Ulpian and Papinian (*Dig.* 50. 3. 3, 5, 6. 3), which affirm similar principles for the whole empire. Grounds of exclusion cover criminal condemnation for a variety of offences, pursuit of ignoble trades, and expulsion from the army, all of which in Roman law rendered a man liable to loss of personal status, cf. II. 11. 12 n.

3. in omni civitate plurimos esse buleutas ex aliis civitatibus. Cf. Dio, *Or.* 41. 10, on Apamea and Prusa: πλείστους τῶν ἐκεῖθεν καὶ πολίτας πεποίησθε καὶ βουλῆς μετεδώκατε. Epigraphical examples occur infrequently, e.g. *IGRR* iii. 96, *CIG* 4150 b, *AE* 1960, n. 81.

futurumque ut multi homines multaeque civitates concuterentur ea
parte legis ⟨reducta⟩ quae iampridem . . . exolevisset. Avantius read
read *ea pars*. The Aldine text here printed does not make clear sense
without the addition of some such passive participle as is here suggested. Hence Cataneaus printed '*si* ea pars legis *revocaretur*', and
Keil, less well, '*cum* ea pars legis [quae] . . . exolevisset'. Some addition is essential. For *futurum ut . . . concuterentur* leads one to expect
some positive statement about the *lex*, which did not include a direct
order of expulsion in these cases.

The long period in s. 3 is unusual as an introduction to the formula
of consultation. Cf. Epp. 56. 3, 58. 4, 72, 79. 5, 110. 2. But Epp.
65. 2 and 68 are parallel, though shorter.

capita legis his litteris subieci. Cf. Ep. 22. 1 n., 31. 4 n.

115. *To Pliny*

merito haesisti . . . quid a te rescribi oporteret. This at least must
be allowed to be one of Pliny's more necessary questions, on the
authority of Trajan himself.

**censoribus consulentibus an ⟨manere deberent⟩ in senatu aliarum
civitatium eiusdem tamen provinciae cives.** A lacuna in the archetype
is preserved by Avantius' version: 'an in senatum' etc. Hardy's
supplement, out of Cataneaus and accepted by Schuster and O.C.T.,
fits better with the question put in Ep. 114. 2 than the *legerent* of
Aldus and the Budean supplement.

ut ex praeterito nihil novaremus. Here the reading of Aldus and
the Budean supplement is supported by Ep. 80, 'hactenus . . .
novatam esse legem', against the *moveremus* of Beroaldus.

**cuius vim si retro quoque velimus custodire multa necesse est
perturbari.** In Ep. 111 Trajan is moved by a similar consideration
against retrospective rulings, 'ne multorum securitas subruatur'.
Cf. Epp. 56. 3 n., 119 n.

116. *To Trajan*

Date. After 28 January, third year.

1. Qui virilem togam sumunt vel . . . opus publicum dedicant. For
these various occasions see I. 5. 11, 9. 2; IV. 1. 5–6; IX. 37. 1 nn. Pliny
refers to the Greek equivalents, such as enrolment among the ἔφηβοι.
Attendant feasts are well documented in inscriptions of the western
provinces, e.g. *ILS* 5494, 5570, but Pliny does not here mention
feasts.

etiam e plebe. For the distinction and its implications see Ep. 79.
3 n., 'quia sit . . . melius honestorum hominum liberos quam e plebe
in curiam admitti'. Jones (*Greek City*, 180) remarks, without noticing
this passage, that at public distributions of this kind councillors
commonly received much larger sums than plebeians.

binosque denarios vel singulos. Cf. Ep. 112. 1, 'singula milia' n.
Hardy quoted Apuleius, *Apol.* 88, for *sportulae* on such occasions,
but that refers to the western provinces, where the custom of
sportulae was well established, cf. 11. 14. 4 n. For a list of public
banquets and distributions testified in Asian provinces see Magie,
Romans, 654 n. 58.

**2. ipse enim, sicut arbitror praesertim ex sollemnibus causis conceden-
dum ius istud invitationis, ita vereor ne . . .** This is Postgate's neat
emendation, out of Scheffer, and accepted by Schuster and O.C.T.,
of the variants of the prototypes: *concedendum iussi* (*A a*) or *iussisti*
(*i*), *invitationes* (*a i*) or *immutationes* (*A*). Hardy, faithful to the
Budean copy, awkwardly bracketed *sicut arbitror* as a parenthesis,
and read 'concedendas iussisti invitationes', which is not very
probable Latin, and is contradicted by Pliny's implication that he
knew of no ruling of Trajan in the matter. Besides, *sicut* goes with
ita, as in Ep. 118. 2.

ius istud. At Rome Nero's government had limited and Domitian
restored the custom of great public feasts, but this did not affect
provincial usage. Cf. Suet. *Nero* 16, *Dom.* 7.

sollemnibus causis. Cf. Epp. 52, 96. 10 for the sense of 'formal
and customary' rather than 'usual and ordinary', *pace* Hardy who
thought Pliny wished to exclude magisterial occasions.

**ne ii qui mille homines . . . vocant . . . in speciem διανομῆς incidere
videantur.** Hardy saw here a reference to political bribery, but his
Ciceronian references to electioneering are irrelevant. Pliny means
that these private functions were developing into rowdy public
occasions which ought to be controlled, like the subscription dinners
at Amisus, Ep. 93. Trajan understands him so. The term διανομή is
in common epigraphical usage for distributions of money, cf. Magie,
loc. cit. For a distribution of this sort at Prusias see Dörner, *Reise*,
n. 5. Paulus refers to the thing as proper in itself on a limited scale,
Dig. 30. 122 pref.: 'quod ad divisionem singulorum civium vel
epulum relictum fuerit'. Cf. ibid. 33. 1. 23. The vast imperial banquets at Rome cited by Hardy, such as Suet. *Claud.* 32, were for the
senatorial order only, though Caesar once entertained the whole
Roman *plebes*, ibid. *Caes.* 26. 2. Banquets on a municipal scale were
common in Greek cities, cf. Magie, loc. cit. *Diz. Epig.* 'cena publica',
ii. 154. But banquets are not here in question.

speciem. Cf. Epp. 56. 4, 96. 4 n., a legal term. It is possible that there was a heading in the *mandatum* about clubs concerning this 'category', since Trajan agrees (below) that there is an infraction of some rule.

117. *To Pliny*

invitatio quae . . . quasi per corpora . . . contrahit. The reference in *corpora* is not to *collegia*, which Trajan had suspended in this province (Epp. 33. 3, 96. 7 nn.), and which Pliny had not mentioned, but to the two classes of society, *ordo* and *plebes*, Ep. 116. 1.

merito. Cf. Ep. 115. 1, 121.

sed ego ideo prudentiam tuam elegi ut formandis istius provinciae moribus ipse moderareris. Trajan snaps slightly at Pliny, but less severely than in Ep. 82. 1. He had recently given Pliny a clear lead over the similar problem at Amisus, Ep. 93, if that rescript had yet reached Pliny. At Amisus a violation of the rule about clubs was involved, here only private occasions were in doubt, which nominally did not constitute an illicit public assembly. But that is precisely the reason for Pliny's doubts. He consults because he does not want to veto the custom altogether by making rules. Pliny and Trajan take it for granted that the 'species διανομῆς' is contrary to administrative law, but there are few indications about this in legal sources, cf. above, Ep. 116. 2 n. If it is the Roman *lex ambitus* that is in their minds it is odd that Pliny and Trajan used the Greek word instead of some Latin technical term, such as *divisio*. It is possible that there was a ruling in Pliny's *mandata* about this *species*: otherwise, they must mean here and above (Ep. 116. 2) that this was an offence commonly recognized in *cognitio extra ordinem* (Ep. 96. 1 n.).

et ea constitueres quae ad perpetuam eius provinciae quietem essent profutura. Cf. Ep. 32. 1: 'idcirco te in istam provinciam missum quoniam multa in ea emendanda apparuerint'. This, if part of Pliny's original instructions, is very vaguely worded. In later times imperial legates were somewhat similarly instructed: 'ut curet is qui provinciae praeest malis hominibus provinciam purgare'. Paulus, *Dig.* 1. 18. 3. Ulpian comments, ibid. 13 pref.: 'congruit bono et gravi praesidi curare ut pacata atque quieta provincia sit quam regit'.

118. *To Trajan*

Date. After 28 January, and probably in summer, third year, after the 'games'.

Hardy rescued the text of this pair of letters from a sad state of confusion partly due to the failure of an early editor or copyist to

understand the somewhat condensed arguments. The general drift
is clear enough, but one of Hardy's readings involves an historical
improbability. Schuster printed two nonsensical phrases, and
Guillemin one, unobelized, through excessive conservatism.

1. **Athletae, domine, ea quae pro iselasticis certaminibus constituisti
deberi sibi putant.** The custom was that victors in the great pan-
hellenic contests should on returning home ride into their cities in
a chariot through a breach in the walls, and thereafter receive a
pension at the city's expense. Plut. *Q. Conv.* 2. 5. 2; Vitruvius 9 pref.;
Suet. *Nero* 25; Dio 52. 30. 4–6, 63. 20. Trajan had evidently revised
the list of games that qualified as 'iselastic', and the scale of rewards;
a document shows that a new 'iselastic' *certamen Iovis et Traiani*
was established at Pergamum in or after A.D. 112; *IGRR* iv. 336;
A–J n. 73; Magie, *Romans*, 594 n. 7. Claims for such status were
evidently put forward through municipal ambition, and the official
list was revised as the reputation of festivals waxed or waned. Thus
the *Pythia* of Tralles lost and regained this status in the second and
third centuries, *CIG* 2932; see briefly, *RE* v. 2141; Jones, *Greek
City*, 232–3.

Whether Trajan increased the iselastic rewards, as Hardy suggested, is uncertain. Probably he standardized them so far as possible.
At Pergamum he apparently ruled that the new prizes should be the
same as for an earlier foundation. Hardy also assumed that the
prizes were paid out of the imperial treasury. This is certainly wrong.
In Vitruvius' time they were paid from the municipal funds (loc.
cit.), so too in that of Cassius Dio (52. 30. 6), who wished to restrict
the payment to a short list of festivals, so as to save the cities'
finances. So too at Pergamum, a special endowment paid the pensions.
Even in third-century Egypt victors were paid from civic funds at
Hermoupolis (below). The emperor had no reason to take over what
was a municipal project in this age of lavish civic philanthropy.

Details of pensions are known from Egyptian documents of the
Roman period. At Hermoupolis iselastic victors received 180
drachmae a month. In A.D. 266–7 the city disbursed over eight talents
on such payments, but the triumphal entry was by then abandoned.
Victors also received exemption from civic liturgies. The formula of
application was: αἰτοῦμαι ἐπισταλῆναι ἐκ τοῦ πολιτικοῦ λόγου ὑπὲρ
ὀψωνίων μου ὧν ἐνίκησα κτλ. See G. Méautis, *Hermoupolis la Grande*,
153 ff., 174, 199 ff.; Wilcken, *Chrestomathie* I. 2. 156–7; *Cod. Iust.*
10. 54. 1.

ego contra praescribo iselastici nomen[e]. itaque [eorum] vehementer addubitem an sit potius id tempus quo εἰσήλασαν intuendum.
Hardy, following Orelli, read *contrascribo* as a single word. The verb

is rare, but *contrascriptor* is common in epigraphy for a tally clerk,
cf. *ILS* index vi B. Hardy took the clause to mean 'I countersign
drafts for payment under the heading of iselastic money'. But this
attributes the payment to the imperial treasury, which is against
usage (above), and introduces the improbability of the legate acting
as the procurator's clerk. The words *ego contra* should introduce
Pliny's reply to the argument of the athletes. This is his ordinary use
of *contra* in such contexts. Cf. Ep. 110. 1: 'ecdicus . . . petebat. . . .
Piso contra . . . dicebat'. Also Epp. 56. 2, 81. 4. Plain *scribo* gives a
feeble sense. A compound is required. *Praescribo* would fit either in
the sense 'put forward an excuse or objection' (as in Tac. *Ann.* 4. 52,
11. 16; Quint. 7. 5. 3; Macer in *Dig.* 47. 15. 3; the latter two intransitive), or in the sense 'put forward a title', as in Frontinus, *De
Aquis* 93; Tac. *Hist.* 2. 65; Pliny, *Pan.* 92. 2; Forcellini, *Lexicon*, s.v.
Alternatively *transcribo*, in its ordinary meaning of 'copy out', as in
IV. 7. 2, would fit. The disappearance of the preposition *prae* or
trans after *contra* is easy.

There remains *itaque eorum* of Avantius and Aldus. Catanaeus
read, or printed, this as *ita tamen ut*. Possibly there was a repetition
of *nomen*, e.g.: *praescribo iselastici nomen. itaque nomine* . . . . Or: . . .
nomen. Quorum nomine . . . . A separation of the parts of *quorum*, like
that of *qui ierant* in 119, might produce *que eorum*. For *dubito* with
a plain ablative cf. I. 22. 3.

Gruter cut it all, as a passage 'defiled with glosses', to 'ego contra
iselastici nomine vehementer . . .'. Perhaps rightly.

119. *To Pliny*

nec proficere pro desiderio athletarum potest quod eorum (*sc.*
certaminum) **quae postea iselastica non esse constitui, quam
vicerunt, accipere** (*sc.* opsonia) **desierunt.** So Hardy and Scheffer
improving on Catanaeus's *vincerent*. The prototypes read *lege* for *esse*
and *quierant* or *qui ierant* for *vicerunt*. Schuster and Guillemin print
those readings in blind faith, without even a mention of Hardy. But
Hardy rightly insisted that the rescript follows the wording of Ep.
118. 2 very closely—and indeed of all Pliny's letter. This sentence is
parallel to : 'sicut non detur pro iis certaminibus quae esse iselastica
postquam vicerunt desierunt'. Trajan (or his secretary) having used
placuit in his first sentence substitutes *constitui* here. The notion of
'retired champions'—*quierant*—and of an 'iselastic law' are absurd
intrusions, defensible only if the text of these two letters were generally sound. All that is wanted here is a negative version of the preceding sentence, without the addition of alien matter. At least *vicerunt*
is essential, and easy. The intrusion of *lege* is odd, but not so odd as

the word order according to Guillemin: 'iselastica non lege'. No-where else does Trajan, or Pliny, speak of an imperial edict or rescript as a *lex*, though the phrase *lex iselastica* for a schedule of rules is not impossible.

mutata enim condicione certaminum nihilominus quae ante perceperant non revocantur. Trajan is rather sharp, as Hardy remarked. He may well have been provoked by the sophistical insolence of the requests. Cf. Ep. 57. 2 n.

perceperant. So Aldus and the Budean copy (*i*). Schuster oddly preferred to print the senseless *peregerant* from Avantius, which could only refer to the contests, not the perquisites.

120. *To Trajan*

Date. After 28 January, third year.

1. Usque in hoc tempus domine neque cuiquam diplomata commodavi neque in rem ullam nisi tuam misi. Pliny several times goes out of his way to explain what he considered an irregular use of the *cursus publicus*, Epp. 43. 2, 59, 64, 83, 106 nn. For the system see Ep. 45 nn. The issue of passes to private persons is implied to be exceptional in Sen. *De Clem*. 1. 10. 3; Fronto, *Ep*. 1. 6, p. 15 (N); Venuleius, *Dig*. 45. 137. 2.

2. uxori . . . meae. For Calpurnia see IV. 1 pref., 19 pref.

audita morte avi. For Calpurnius Fabatus see ibid. He was an extremely old man by now, and likely to die while Pliny was away. One wonders at this lengthy journey in the circumstances of the ancient world, even if Calpurnia Hispulla was *parentis loco* to Pliny's wife. But Trajan takes it all for granted.

amitam suam. For Calpurnia Hispulla see IV. 19 pref.

121. *To Pliny*

diplomatibus quae officio tuo dedi. For the issue of passes to the governors see Ep. 45 n.

APPENDIX I

THE PERSONAL INSCRIPTIONS OF PLINY

1. From Comum, *CIL* v. 5262, printed also in *ILS* 2927.

C. PLINIUS L.F. OUF. CAECILIUS   [SECUNDUS   COS.]
AUGUR. LEGAT. PRO PR. PROVINCIAE. PON[TI ET BITHYNIAE]
CONSULARI. POTESTA[T.] IN EAM PROVINCIAM. E[X S.C. MISSUS AB]
IMP. CAESAR. NERVA TRAIANO. AUG. GERMAN[ICO DACICO P.P.]
CURATOR. ALVEI. TI[B]ERIS. ET. RIPARUM E[T CLOACARUM URB,]
PRAEF. AERARI. SATU[R]NI. PRAEF. AERARI. MIL[IT. PR. TRIB. PL.]
QUAESTOR. IMP. SEVIR. EQUITUM. [ROMANORUM]
TRIB. MILIT. LEG. [III] GALLICA[E] [X VIR STLI-]
TIB. IUDICAND. THERM[AS   ] ADIECTIS IN
ORNATUM. HS $\overline{\text{CCC}}$ [. . . ET EO AMP]LIUS IN TUTELA[M]
HS. $\overline{\text{CC}}$. T.F.I. [ITEM IN ALIMENTA] LIBERTOR. SUORUM HOMIN. C.
HS. | $\overline{\text{XVIII}}$ | $\overline{\text{LXVI}}$ DCLXVI. REI [P. LEGAVIT QUORUM INC]REMENT
    POSTEA AD EPULUM
[PL]EB. URBAN. VOLUIT PERTIN[ERE ITEM VIVU]S DEDIT IN. ALIMENT.
    PUEROR.
ET. PUELLAR. PLEB. URBAN. HS [D. ITEM BYBLIOTHECAM ET] IN TUTE-
    LAM. BYBLIOTHECAE. HS. $\overline{\text{C}}$.

The last lines are in smaller capitals than the rest.

2. From Comum, before the mission to Bithynia. *CIL* v. 5263.

C. Plinio L.f. Ouf. Caecilio Secundo cos. aug. cur. alvei Tiber(is) et
rip[arum et cloac]a[r,] urb . . ..

3. From Fecchio, set up by the people of Vercellae. Also before the
mission to Bithynia. *CIL* v. 5667.

    C. Plini[o L.f.] Ouf. Caec[ilio] Secundo. [c]os. augur. cur. alv. Tib.
e[t ri]p. et cloac. urb. p[raef. a]er. Sat. praef. aer. mil. . . . . q. imp.
sevir. eq. R. tr. m[i]l. leg. III Gall. Xviro stl. iud. fl. divi. T. Aug.
Vercellens[es].

4. From Comum. The person honoured may be Pliny's father, the
lady his sister, and the dedicator himself. *CIL* v, *Suppl. Italica I*,
745.

CAECI]LIAE. F. SUAE NOMINE. L. CAE
CILIU]S. C.F. OUF. SECUNDUS. PRAEF.
FABR] A. COS. IIIIVIR I. D. PONTIF. TEM
PLUM] AETERNITATI. ROMAE. ET. AUGU[STI
   C]UM PORTICIBUS. ET. ORNAMEN
      TIS. INCOHAVIT
CAECI]LIUS. SECUNDUS. F. DEDIC

5. From Comum. Cilo may be a grandfather or grand-uncle of Pliny. *CIL* v. 5279, *ILS* 6728.

L. Caecilius L.f. Cilo IIIvir a(edilicia) p(otestate) qui testamento suo HS. n. X̄X̄X̄X̄ municipibus Comensibus legavit, ex quorum reditu quot annis per Neptunalia oleum in campo et in thermis et balineis omnibus quae sunt Comi populo praeberetur, t(estamento) f(ieri) i(ussit) et L. Caecilio L.f. Valenti et P. Caecilio L.f. Secundo et Lutullae Picti f. contubernali.

Aetas properavit, faciendum fuit. noli plangere mater. mater rogat quam primum ducatis se ad vos.

6. The fragment *CIL* xi. 5272 from Hispellum of a testamentary inscription covering Pliny's whole career adds nothing to *CIL* v. 5262 except the formal record of his praetorship and tribunate, which are there missing. But it confirms the reading *Ex SC*, ibid., l. 3.

APPENDIX II

THE CONSULAR *FASTI*, 94–117

THE following list is presented for the convenience of the reader
It is compiled from Degrassi, *I Fasti Consulari* (Rome, 1952), with
additions from the subsequently discovered *Fasti* of Potentia, published by N. Alfieri, *Athenaeum*, 1948, 110 ff., with corrections and
additions due to R. Syme, *JRS*, 1946, 159 f.; 1954, 81; and *Tacitus*,
637 f. Some of the additional information included in the *Fasti* of
Ostia has been included, for which see *Inscriptiones Italicae*, vol.
'Fasti Consulares', and for the latest additions *AE*, 1954, 220–3. For
the *Fasti* of Potentia see also *AE*, 1949, 23. Syme, *Tacitus*, 639–40,
prints the list of the Domitianic consuls from 85 to 96. Here, as
there, names are given without epigraphical indications of incompleteness, unless identifications are in serious doubt, and only the
attested short form is used for persons who have numerous additional
names.

94 L. Nonius Asprenas. T. Sextius Magius Lateranus.
    k. Mai. D. Valerius Asiaticus. A. Julius Quadratus.
    k. Sept. L. Silius Decianus. T. Pomponius Bassus.

95 Imp. Domitianus XVII. T. Flavius Clemens.
    id. Ian. L. Neratius Marcellus.
    k. Mai. A. Lappius Maximus II. P. Ducenius Verus.
    k. Sept. Q. Pomponius Rufus. L. Baebius Tullus.

96 C. Manlius Valens. C. Antistius Vetus.
    k. Mai. Q. Fabius Postuminus. T. Prifernius [Paetus?].
    k. Sept. Ti. Caesius Fronto. M. Calpurnius [Flac]cus.

    XIIII k. Oct. Domitianus occisus. eodem die M. Cocceius Nerva
      imperator appellatus est.
    XIII k. Oct. S.C. factum est . . .

97 Imp. Nerva Caesar III. L. Verginius Rufus III.
    M. Annius Verus. L. Neratius Priscus.
    L. Domitius Apollinaris. Se[. . . . . .]
    Q. (Glitius) Atilius Agricola. P. Cornelius Tacitus (?).
    (L. Licinius Sura?)

98 Imp. Nerva Caesar Aug. IV. Imp. Nerva Traianus II.
    id. Ian. Cn. Domitius [Tullus II].
    k. Febr. Sex. Julius Frontinus II.

k. Mart. L. Julius Ursus [II ?]
k. April. T. Vestricius Spurinna II.
k. Mai. C. Pomponius Pius.
k. Iul. A. Vicirius Martialis. L. Maecius Postumus.
[k. Sept.] C. Pomponius Rufus. Cn. Pompeius Ferox.
k. Nov. [Q. Fulvius . . . Bittius Proculus. P. Julius Lupus.]

99 A. Cornelius Palma. Q. Sosius Senecio.
Sulpicius Lucretius Barba. Senecio Memmius Afer.
Q. Fabius Barbarus. A. Caecilius Faustinus.

100 Imp. Nerva Traianus III. Sex. Julius Frontinus III.
                             T. Vestricius Spurinna III.
Q. Acutius Nerva. [Calpurn ?]ius Piso.
L. Herennius Saturninus. T. Pomponius Mamilianus.
C. Plinius Secundus. C. Julius Cornutus Tertullus.
L. Roscius Aelianus etc. Ti. Claudius Sacerdos
and possibly others, cf. *AE*, 1954, 221.

101 Imp. Nerva Traianus IV. Q. Articuleius Paetus.
Sex. Attius Suburanus Aemilianus.
Q. Servaeus Innocens. M. Maecius Celer.
[M. Eppulei]us Procul[us T]i. C[aepio Hispo ?]

102 L. Julius Servianus II. L. Licinius Sura II.
[k. Mart. L. Fabius] Justus.
[k. Mai. L. Publi]lius Celsus.
[k. Sept.] L. Antonius Albus. M. Junius Homullus.

103 Imp. Nerva Traianus V. M'. Laberius Maximus II.
id. Ian. Q. Atilius Agricola II.
[P. M]etilius [Sabinus]. Q. Baebius [Macer].
[   ]er. C. Mettius Modestus.
[   ]nnius Mela. P. Calpurnius [Macer].
[Fe]br. Imp. Nerva Traianus [congiarium dedit ?].

104 Sex. Attius Suburanus II. M. Asinius Marcellus.
No others certain. Cornelius Priscus ? Herennius Pollio ?
D. Terentius Scaurianus ? P. Valerius Priscus ?

105 Ti. Julius Candidus II. A. Julius Quadratus II.
k. Mai. C. Julius Bassus. Cn. Afranius Dexter.
XVI k. Aug. Q. Caelius Honoratus loco Dextri.
k. Sept. M. Vitorius Marcellus. C. Caecilius Strabo.
pr. non. Iun. imp. Nerva Traianus Aug. in Moesia[m] profectus.
VIII k. Iul. Afranius Dexter cos. in domo sua exanimis inventus.

106 L. Ceionius Commodus. Sex. Vettulenus Civica Cerealis
Decibali . . . in scalis Gemoniis . . . .
L. Minicius Natalis. Q. Licinius Silvanus.
            ?   ?

107 L. Licinius Sura III. Q. Sosius Senecio II
    [k. Mart.] [L. Acilius] Rufus.
    [k. Mai.] C. Minicius Fundanus. Vettenius Severus.
    [k. Sept.] C. Julius Longinus. C. Valerius Paulinus.
    VII k. I[un. ? . . . Traianus] congiarium dedit.

108 Ap. Annius Gallus. M. Atilius Bradua.
    [k. Mai.] P. Aelius Hadrianus. M. Trebatius Priscus.
    [k. Sept.] . . .   [Q. Pompe]ius F[alco].

109 A. Cornelius Palma II. P. Calvisius Tullus Ruso.
    k. Mart. L. Annius Largus.
    k. Mai. Cn. Antonius Fuscus. C. Julius Philopappus.
    k. Sept. C. Aburnius Valens. C. Julius Proculus.
    X k. Iul. imp. Nerva Traianus . . . Dacicus thermas suas dedicavit
    et publicavit.
    VIII k. Iul. aquam suo nomine tota urbe salientem dedicavit.

110 M. Peducaeus Priscinus. Ser. Scipio Orfitus.
    C. Avidius Nigrinus. Ti. Julius Aquila.
    L. Catilius Severus. C. Erucianus Silo.
    A. Larcius Priscus. Sex. Marcius Honoratus.

111 C. Calpurnius Piso. M. Vettius Bolanus.
    [k. Ma]i. T. Avidius Quietus. L. Eggius Marullus.
    [k. Sept.] L. Octavius Crassus. P. Coelius Apollinaris.

112 Imp. Nerva Traianus VI. T. Sextius Africanus.
    [id. Ian. M.] Licinius Ruso.
    Cn. Cornelius Severus. Q. Valerius Vegetus.
    P. Stertinius Quartus. T. Julius Maximus.
    C. Claudius Severus. T. Settidius Firmus.
    k. Ianuar. imp. Traianus forum suum et basilicam Ulpiam dedicavit
    etc.

113 L. Publilius Celsus II. C. Clodius Crispinus.
    [k. Mart] Ser. Cornelius Dolabella.
    [k. Mai.] L. Stertinius Noricus. L. Fadius Rufinus.
    [k. Sept.] Cn. Cornelius Urbicus. T. Sempronius Rufus.
    . . . . IIII id. Mai. imp. Traianus templum Veneris in foro Caesaris
    et columnam in foro suo dedicavit pr. id. Mai.

114 Q. Ninnius Hasta. P. Manilius Vopiscus.
    C. Clodius Nummus.
    L. Lollianus Avitus. L. Messius Rusticus.

115 L. Vipstanus Messala. M. Pedo Vergilianus.
    L. Julius Se[ ]. [T. Statilius Maximus Severus].
    M. Pomp[eius]. . . .

116 L. Fundanius Lamia Aelianus. Sex. Carminius [Vetus]
    Ti. Julius Secundus. M. Egnatius [Marcellinus].
    D. Terentius Gentianus. Q. Cor[nelius Annianus].
    L. Statius Aquila. C. Julius Berenicianus.

117 Q. Aquilius Niger. M. Rebilus Apronianus.
    Sex. Erucius Clarus. Ti. Julius Alexander.
    Cn. Minicius Faustinus. Lusius Quietus?

APPENDIX III

GENERAL LIST OF CONTEMPORARY PERSONS

THIS list contains a summary account of the recipients of the letters and the contemporary persons mentioned in them. Persons dead before Pliny's manhood are excluded, except for close connexions. Fuller discussion and documentation will be found in the notes cited in each case. A list of the letters addressed to each person is given with a brief note of contents. The list is intended only for the convenience of the less experienced reader, to facilitate study of the correspondents as a group.

Persons are cited under the form of name commonly used in the Letters. Where double names are the norm the alphabetical citation is by the gentile name, but the correspondents are listed under both forms. Additional names known from external sources are printed in capitals and small letters, and the forms used by Pliny in capitals and small capitals; italics are used in cases of doubt.

P. ACCIUS AQUILA, centurion in Bithynia, seeks citizenship for his daughter. X. 106.

ACCIUS SURA, junior senator recommended by Pliny to Trajan for the praetorship *c.* 101. X. 12 n. Possibly his name was *Attius*, and he was related to Attius Clemens, q.v.

ACILIUS, recipient of III. 14, on the murder of Larcius Macedo, is uncertain. Possibly P. Acilius of Patavium (I. 14. 6) rather than the senator L. Acilius Rufus (V. 20. 6). III. 14 pref.

L. ACILIUS RUFUS, consul suffect in 106 or 107, who opposes the request of Varenus at his preliminary accusation, is an undistinguished senator from Sicily. V. 20. 6 n., VI. 13. 5.

Q. ACUTIUS NERVA, consul suffect in 100, gives the leading opinion in the trial of Hostilius Firminus, legate of Marius Priscus. Soon after he became legate of Lower Germany. II. 12. 2 n.

AEFULANUS MARCELLINUS, unknown, possibly connected with Minicius Fundanus. V. 16 pref. Receives two long letters: V. 16, death of Fundanus' daughter. VIII. 23, death of Junius Avitus.

AFRANIUS DEXTER, proposes reproval of Tuscilius Nominatus, erring advocate, when consul designate 105 (V. 13. 4), and is murdered by his slaves when in office in June 105. VIII. 14. 12 n.

ALBINUS, *see* LUCCEIUS.

AMMIUS FLACCUS, unknown praetorian senator, speaks in debate on Publicius Certus. IX. 13. 13 n.

ANICIUS MAXIMUS, proconsul of Bithynia of uncertain date, possibly from Ephesus. X. 112. 2.

ANNIANUS, *see* ANNIUS SEVERUS.

ANNIUS BASSUS, supporter of Vespasian, cos. suff. in 70, protector of the equestrian Claudius Pollio. VII. 31. 5 n.

ANNIUS SEVERUS, Pliny's agent at Comum, receives II. 16, an unsigned codicil, III. 6, a bronze statue for Comum, V. 1, a disputed inheritance. II. 16 pref.

ANTEIA, widow of younger Helvidius Priscus, probably of consular family. IX. 13. 5 n.

ANTONIA MAXIMILLA, Pliny's kinswoman; her freed women. X. 5, 2, 6. 1.

APER, *see* FLAVIUS.

APOLLINARIS, *see* DOMITIUS.

M. AQUILIUS REGULUS, advocate and former *delator*, who secured condemnation of three aristocratic consulars in Nero's last years when *adulescentulus*, and narrowly escaped punishment in 70. Thereafter became leader of the Centumviral bar, making a large fortune, until his death *c.* 104. I. 5. 1 n. Apparently only a praetorian senator (II. 11. 22 n.). Pliny describes his methods in court, I. 5. 4–7, 20. 14, IV. 7. 3–5, VI. 2; his feud with Herennius Senecio and Arulenus Rusticus, I. 5. 2–5, IV. 7. 5; his alarm after the death of Domitian, I. 5. 8–11; his behaviour in Senate under Trajan, II. 11. 22; his superstition and wealth, II. 20. 13, VI. 2. 2; his efforts at captation, II. 20; his behaviour towards his son, IV. 2, 7. Pliny considered prosecuting Regulus in 97, I. 5. 15.

ARISTO, *see* TITIUS.

ARMENIUS BROCCHUS, Flavian proconsul of Achaea, with Gallic connexions. X. 65. 3.

ARRIA, younger daughter of Caecina Paetus and the elder Arria, and wife of the Neronian statesman Thrasea Paetus, was exiled with her daughter Fannia in 93, in connexion with the condemnation of Herennius Senecio and the younger Helvidius, returned in 97 and with Fannia stirred Pliny up against Publicius Certus. III. 11. 3 n., 16. 10, IX. 13. 3–5, 15–16.

ARRIANUS MATURUS, equestrian man of letters from Altinum, for whom Pliny secures an administrative post in Egypt *c.* 103. I. 2 pref., III. 2 nn. Receives letters on books, courts, and politics: I. 2, Attic style II. 11–12, trial of Marius Priscus, IV. 8 Pliny's augurate, IV. 12, a good quaestor, VI. 2, Regulus in court, VIII. 21, Pliny's second book of verses.

ARRIONILLA, wife of Timon, possibly connected with Thrasea Paetus. I. 5. 5 n.

ARRIUS ANTONINUS, elder statesman eminent under Nerva, probably *cos*. II in 97, but his public career is little known (*cos. suff.* 69, proconsul of Asia *c.* 78). IV. 3 pref. Pliny exchanges brief letters about versification, IV. 3, 18, V. 15.

ARTEMIDORUS, Stoic philosopher from Syria, pupil and son-in-law of Musonius Rufus, admired by Pliny, and assisted at time of expulsion of philosophers from Rome in 93. III. 11 n.

Q. Iunius ARULENUS RUSTICUS, senator of Cisalpine origin and Stoic opinions, tribune in 66, praetor in 69, and apparently consul in 92, devoted follower of Thrasea Paetus and the elder Helvidius, the defenders of senatorial *libertas* under Nero and Vespasian. As praetor he tried to arrange an armistice after the defeat of Vitellius. Under Domitian was involved with his brother Junius Mauricus and others on charge of criticism of the régime in his biography of the elder Helvidius; was executed. I. 5. 2, 4. 4 nn., III. 11. 3 n. Pliny, an old friend (I. 14. 1), mentions his feud with Regulus, I. 5. 2–4, defended Arrionilla at his request, ibid. 5, and under Nerva found a husband for his daughter, I. 14, and a tutor for his sons, II. 18.

ASCLEPIADES, chief magistrate of Prusa *c.* 110. X. 81. 1.

ASINIUS BASSUS, unknown quaestor commended to Minicius Fundanus. IV. 15. 3–10 n.

L. ASINIUS RUFUS, praetorian senator, father of Pliny's protégé Asinius Bassus. IV. 15. 1 n.

ASUDIUS CURIANUS, of uncertain rank, disinherited by his mother Pomponia Galla. V. 1. 1 n.

ATILIUS CRESCENS, scholar and wit from Cisalpine, friend of Pliny, Minicius Fundanus, and the Elder Maximus, VI. 8. 1 n., I. 9. 8, II. 14. 2. His poverty and character, VI. 8. Surprisingly, no letters, unless perhaps III. 14, murder of Macedo.

ATILIUS SCAURUS, unknown person, witness to the disappearance of a traveller. VI. 25. 1 n.

ATRIUS, who receives brief note IX. 35, is probably Attius Clemens, q.v.

ATTIA VIRIOLA, sister rather than daughter of the former praetorian prefect and consular Attius Suburanus. Disinherited, she sues her father's heirs. VI. 33. 2 n.

ATTIUS CLEMENS. Career unknown, a man of letters. Receives I. 10, Euphrates the philosopher. IV. 2, death of son of Regulus. Possibly IX. 35, revision of books.

ATTIUS, *see* ACCIUS, SUBURANUS.

AUGURINUS, *see* SENTIUS.

AVIDIUS NIGRINUS the elder, father of C. Avidius Nigrinus, and brother of Avidius Quietus, friend of Plutarch and proconsul of Achaea under Domitian. X. 65. 3 n.

T. Avidius Quietus, senator from Faventia, *cos. suff.* 93 and legate of Britain 98–*c.* 101, moralist and friend of Plutarch and Thrasea Paetus, advised the young Pliny on choice of cases. Uncle of C. Avidius Nigrinus. Speaks in debate on Publicius Certus, IX. 13. 15. Dead by 107, VI. 29. 1 n.

Avitus, *see* Julius, Junius.

Aurelia, lady with consular relatives. II. 20. 10 n. Her legacy to Regulus ibid.

Baebius Hispanus, man of business, possibly police official. I. 24 pref. Receives I. 24, sale of farm. VI. 25, murder story.

Baebius Macer, senator with active career under Domitian and Trajan, but out of favour with Hadrian. Curator of Appian Way and proconsul of Baetica before 100, *cos. suff.* in 103, city prefect *c.* 117. III. 5 pref. Twice speaks in Senate, IV. 9. 16, 12. 4. Receives III. 5, life of Elder Pliny, and possibly VI. 24, suicide of married couple.

Baebius Massa, former procurator, supporter of Vespasian in civil wars, promoted to be senator and proconsul of Baetica *c.* 91–92. Active *delator*. Accused of extortion in Spain by Pliny and Herennius Senecio in 93, and condemned. VII. 33. 4 n. His counter-accusation against Senecio fails, ibid. 7–8 n.

Baebius Probus, accessory of Caecilius Classicus in extortion, III. 9. 12–17; is exiled, despite plea of 'superior orders'.

Bittius Priscus, client of Pliny in a Centumviral case. VI. 12, 2 n.

Q. Fulvius Gillo Bittius Proculus, Pliny's predecessor as prefect of treasury of Saturn. *Cos. suff.* 98. Speaks as praetorian in debate on Publicius Certus, his colleague. Second husband of Pliny's mother-in-law Pompeia Celerina, survives till 120. IX. 13. 13, 23 nn.

Caecilius Celer, *see* Celer.

Caecilius Classicus, praetorian senator of African origin, proconsul of Baetica, prosecuted for extortion in 98, but died before trial. III. 4. 2 n., 7–8. His associates tried, III. 9, VI. 29. 8.

Caecilius Macrinus. The *nomen* occurs only in the preface of III. 4. He is probably the recipient of all the letters—mostly on public affairs—addressed to Macrinus, rather than Minicius Macrinus of Brixia, q.v. His wife's death may be mentioned in VIII. 5. He receives II. 7, honours of Spurinna. III. 4, indictment of Classicus. VII. 6, 10, Varenus' inquiry. VIII. 17, Tiber floods. IX. 4, dispatch of a speech (about extortion?). II. 7 pref.

C. Caecilius Strabo, *cos. suff.* 105, dead by 117. IV. 12. 4 n. He speaks to a financial point, ibid. His suit against Corellia, IV. 17.

Caelius Clemens, relation of Pompeia Celerina, joins Pliny's staff, X. 51.

Ti. Caepio Hispo Galleo Severus M. Eppuleius Proculus, consular senator (suff. 101 ?), proposes mild sentence at the trial of Julius Bassus.

IV. 9. 16 n. Probably father-in-law or brother-in-law of Aquilius Regulus.

CAESENNIUS SILVANUS, equestrian friend of Suetonius, possibly from Lanuvium. Given a military tribunate, III. 8. 1 n.

P. CAESIUS, protégé of Pliny; his slave manumitted, X. 11. 2.

CALESTRIUS TIRO, senator, possibly from Picenum, colleague of Pliny as quaestor and praetor, proconsul of Baetica in 107/8 or 108/9. VII. 16 nn. Receives I. 12, death of Corellius Rufus. VI. 1, a brief note. VI. 22, trial of a proconsul's *comes*. IX. 5, advice about his proconsulship. In VII. 16, 23, 32 Pliny arranges for him to manumit the Latin freedmen of Calpurnius Fabatus.

CALPURNIA, Pliny's last wife, granddaughter of Calpurnius Fabatus of Comum, married between 100 and 104, IV. 1 pref. Described in IV. 19. Her abortion, VIII. 10–11. Receives only VI. 4, 7. VII. 5, about her convalescence in Campania. Goes with Pliny to Bithynia, X. 120.

CALPURNIA HISPULLA, daughter of Calpurnius Fabatus, and aunt of Pliny's third wife. Possibly related to the Corellii, IV. 19 pref. Receives IV. 19, education of her niece. VIII. 11, her niece's abortion.

L. CALPURNIUS FABATUS, grandfather of Pliny's third wife Calpurnia, equestrian magnate of Comum owning land also in Tuscany and Campania, after a short official career was involved in a political affair, and retired *c.* 65. Dies at great age when Pliny is in Bithynia. IV. 1 pref., X. 120. Receives eight shorter letters on family affairs. IV. 1, Pliny's visit to Comum. V. 11, Fabatus' memorial to his dead son. VI. 12, his frankness to Pliny. VI. 30, his villa in Campania. VII. 11, Pliny's sale of land to Corellia. VII. 16, 23, 32, manumission of his Latin freedmen. VIII. 10, Calpurnia's abortion.

Calpurnius Fabatus, son of the preceding, died before Pliny married his daughter, V. 11, 2 n.

CALPURNIUS FLACCUS, probably the like-named suffect consul of 96, and one of Pliny's Spanish friends, receives a brief note, V. 2.

P. CALPURNIUS MACER Caulius Rufus, consular senator, possibly from Cisalpine (suff. 103), governs Moesia Inferior *c.* 109–12, when Pliny is in Bithynia. X. 42, 62, 77, V. 18 pref. Receives brief note V. 18, and possibly VI. 24, suicide of devoted couple at Comum.

CALPURNIUS PISO, writer of poem on astronomy, member of old nobility, *cos. ord.* in 111, V. 17. 1 n.

CALVINA, unknown lady, to whom Pliny remits a debt, II. 4.

CALVISIUS RUFUS, decurion of Comum and Roman knight. Possibly military tribune in Britain. Gossip and business consultant of Pliny, II. 20 pref. Receives II. 20, social tricks of Regulus. III. 1, daily life of Spurinna. III. 19, buying an estate. V. 7, a legacy for Comum. VIII. 2, sale of vintage. IX. 6, chariot races.

CANINIUS RUFUS, landowner of Comum, devoted to his estates and to literature. Pliny urges him to write, I. 3 pref. Receives I. 3, his occupations. II. 8, the same. III. 7, death of Silius Italicus. VI. 21, recitation of Vergilius Romanus. VII. 18, his municipal benefaction. VIII. 4, his proposed poem on the Dacian war. IX. 33, the dolphin story. Possibly also VII. 25, an educated procurator.

CASTA, wife of Caecilius Classicus, acquitted of complicity in his crimes, III. 9. 19, 34.

L. CATILIUS SEVERUS Iulianus Claudius Reginus, notable senator, of uncertain origin, in the clique of Hadrian. He held numerous praetorian posts including the prefecture of both treasuries before his suffect consulship in 110, fought as legate in the Parthian war, governed Cappadocia with Armenia Major and then Syria between 116 and 120, was *cos. II* in 120, and *praefectus urbi* in 137–8. Intermarries with family of wealthy Domitius Lucanus. I. 22 pref., VIII. 18. 2 n. Receives I. 22, illness of Titius Aristo and brief note III. 12, invitation to dinner. Possibly IX. 22, illness of poet Passenus Paulus.

Ti. CATIUS Caesius FRONTO, suffect consul in 96 at time of Domitian's murder, advocate and cautious politician, probably a patron of Martial, II. 11. 3 n. He checks attacks on former delators in 96–97, IX. 13. 4 n., and defends, on charges of extortion, Marius Priscus, Julius Bassus, and Varenus Rufus, II. 11. 3, IV. 9. 15, VI. 13. 2.

CATIUS LEPIDUS, apparently councillor of an unknown municipality in Cisalpine. Receives IV. 7, Regulus' biography of his son.

L. Valerius CATULLUS MESSALINUS, consular senator (*ord. 73, suff. II* 85) who acted as Domitian's tool in senatorial trials, though not a *delator*. Dead by 97. IV. 22. 5 n.

CELER, an older man to whom Pliny defends his custom of reciting speeches, VII. 17. Possibly Caecilius Celer, friend of Pliny and Regulus, who may be a senator from Spain, I. 5. 8 n.

CERIALIS, *see* TULLIUS or VELIUS CERIALIS.

CLAUDIUS ARISTION, magnate of Ephesus, and President of the Council of Asia, acquitted on charge of subversive activity before Trajan, VI. 31. 3 n.

CLARUS, *see* ERUCIUS, SEPTICIUS.

CLAUDIUS CAPITO, emissary of Bithynia against Varenus Rufus. VI. 13. 2 n.

CLAUDIUS EUMOLPUS, attacks Dio at Prusa with Archippus, X. 81.

CLAUDIUS FUSCUS, son-in-law of Caecilius Classicus, not yet a senator, acquitted of complicity in extortion, III. 9. 18.

CLAUDIUS MARCELLINUS, defends Flavius Marcianus in case of Marius Priscus, II. 11. 16 n. Not to be identified with Aefulanus Marcellinus.

Ti. CLAUDIUS POLLIO, Flavian equestrian officer, who served with Pliny in Syria *c.* 81, and after a procuratorial career acted as assistant to Corellius Rufus on Nerva's agrarian commission. Wrote life of his patron Annius Bassus. Pliny commends him to Cornutus Tertullus, VII. 31 nn.

CLAUDIUS RESTITUTUS, advocate in trial of associates of Classicus, known to Martial, possibly from Africa, III. 9. 16 n. Receives VI. 17, on bad audiences.

CLEMENS, *see* ATTIUS, CAELIUS.

CLUSINIUS GALLUS. Possibly two Galli appear in Pliny's letters: Clusinius, recipient of three letters, and the man involved in a provincial lawsuit from Baetica, I. 7. 4. The *nomen* appears only in the Index for IV. 17. One or other may be connected with Pliny's friend Pomponia Galla, V. I. 1 n., and the praetorian senator Pomponius Gallus Didius Rufus, II. 17 pref. Gallus receives two scenic descriptions—II. 17, the Laurentine villa, and VIII. 20, the lake Vadimon—and IV. 17, Corellia's lawsuit.

COLONUS, possibly son of equestrian Peducaeus Colonus, receives IX. 9, note on death of Pompeius Quintianus.

T. FLAVIUS(?) COCCEIANUS DION, orator and philosopher, politician and benefactor of Prusa, accused by Archippus, X. 81 nn.

CORELLIA HISPULLA, daughter of the consular Corellius Rufus, III. 3 pref. Pliny finds a schoolmaster for her son, ibid., and represents her in court, IV. 17. Receives only III. 3.

CORELLIA, sister of Corellius Rufus, and husband of Minicius Justus, VII. 11. 3 n. Buys land cheap from Pliny, ibid. and VII. 14. Receives only VII. 14. To be distinguished from her niece Corellia Hispulla.

CORELLIUS PANSA, consular (*ord.* 122), may be the unnamed son of Corellia, III. 3. 1 n.

Q. CORELLIUS RUFUS, a Cisalpine senator possibly from Ateste, was consul (*suff.*) in 78 and legate of Upper Germany *c.* 82. He apparently held no other office until Nerva's reign, when he served on the Land Commission until his philosophical suicide. He hated Domitian, perhaps on personal grounds. I. 12 nn., VII. 31. 4. Pliny, who was his protégé and a friend of his son, IV. 17. 6–8, V. 1. 5, later finds a tutor for his grandson, protects his daughter's interests in a lawsuit, and sells land to his sister cheaply; III. 3, IV. 17, VII. 11, 14. Pliny describes Corellius' death in I. 12 and his character in IV. 17.

CORNELIA Cossa, senior Vestal Virgin, after twenty-eight years' service executed on just charge of unchastity after two trials, *c.* 90. IV. 11. 6–7 nn.

CORNELIANUS. The name in the MS. of VI. 31 is probably a misreading for *Cornelius Minicianus*, q.v.

C. CORNELIUS MINICIANUS, equestrian and municipal magnate from Bergomum, honoured also at Mediolanum and Otesia, is given post as *praefectus cohortis* by Pompeius Falco, legate of Judaea, *c.* 107, later *trib. mil.* and *praefectus fabrorum*. III. 9 pref., VII. 22 n. Receives III. 9, the Classicus case. IV. 11, story of the Vestal. VIII. 12, recitation of Titinius Capito. Possibly also I. 17, character of Titinius Capito. VII. 12, on rhetorical style. VI. 31, the Court at Centum Cellae. See prefs.

CORNELIUS PRISCUS, suffect consul *c.* 103 and proconsul of Asia *c.* 120, III. 21 pref. Speaks in Varenus debate, V. 20. 7. Receives III. 21, death of Martial, and possibly VII. 8, introduction of Pompeius Saturninus (cf. VII. 7. 1, 15. 3), VI. 8, debt due to Atilius, VII. 19, sickness of Fannia.

CORNELIUS TACITUS, the historian, is a consular senator (*pr.* 88, *cos. suff.* 97) from Cisalpine or Narbonensis, of whose other posts only a probable junior legateship (89–93) and the proconsulship of Asia (*c.* 112–13) can be certainly traced, I. 6 pref., IV. 13. 1 n. Incidental references in Pliny to Tacitus' *laudatio* of Verginius Rufus (II. 1. 6), his part in the prosecution of Marius Priscus (II. 11. 2), and to his numerous pupils (IV. 13. 10), show his standing as an advocate. Of his books, the *Agricola* was probably published before Book I (I. 6 pref.), the *Dialogus* and *Historiae* are dated to the period of V–IX by the evidence of V. 8. 12, VI. 16. 1, VII. 20. 1, 33, VIII. 7 nn. The *Annales* are a decade later. Of eleven letters, I. 6. IX. 10, on hunting and books, VI. 9, on the election of Julius Naso, VIII. 7, on exchange of unpublished books, and IX. 14, on their mutual praises, are brief notes. Of the longer letters, I. 20 is about style, and IV. 13 is about a schoolmaster for Comum, but VI. 16 and 20, the death of the Elder Pliny and Vesuvius, and VII. 33, the trial of Baebius Massa, contain contributions to the *Historiae*. VII. 20 and IX. 23 (to Maximus), compare the literary reputations of Pliny and Tacitus.

CORNELIUS TITIANUS, whose *nomen* is known only from I. 17, if the text is sound, receives this letter, about the *pietas* of Titinius Capito, and IX. 32, a brief note.

CORNELIUS URSUS, a literary equestrian receives IV. 9, the defence of Julius Bassus, V. 20, VI. 5, 13, the accusation of Varenus Rufus, and VIII. 9, brief note on *studia* and business.

C. IULIUS CORNUTUS TERTULLUS, a senator possibly from Perge in Pamphylia, was promoted to be *praetorius* by Vespasian in 73–74, thereafter proconsular legate of Crete-Cyrene and proconsul of Narbonensis, but his career was checked under Domitian, after whose death he held, with Pliny as colleague, the prefecture of the treasury of Saturn (98–100) and the suffect consulship in 100. Later, *c.* 104–5, he became curator of the Aemilian Way, in special circumstances, perhaps in charge of the *alimenta* of the region, was director of the census of Aquitania, succeeded Pliny in Bithynia-Pontus, and held the proconsulship of either Asia or Africa. V. 14 nn. He was a friend of Corellius Rufus and the Helvidian family, IV. 17. 9, IX. 13. 16 nn. Not a man of letters or an advocate, he proposed the decisive sentence against Marius Priscus, II. 11. 19. Pliny describes his career and character in V. 14, but addresses to him only a brief note, VII. 21, on sickness, and the longer account of the procurator Claudius Pollio, VII. 31, both in the same book.

COTTIA, wife of Vestricius Spurinna, may be a descendant of the Julii Cottii, who once ruled the Cottian Alps, II. 7. 3 n. Mentioned III. 1. 5, and joint recipient with Spurinna of III. 10, about their son's biography.

Vestricius COTTIUS, son of Vestricius Spurinna, and a senator of unknown rank. The Senate erects his statue after his sudden death, II. 7. 3–7 n. Pliny writes his biography, III. 10.

CREMUTIUS RUSO, well-born young advocate and pupil of Pliny, whose affiliation is uncertain. VI. 23. 2 n. Receives probably IX. 19, on funeral monuments of Julius Frontinus and Verginius Rufus.

DIO, *see* COCCEIANUS.

L. DOMITIUS APOLLINARIS, fellow advocate of Pliny, and Martial's patron, a consular senator (suff. 97) whose earlier career is known, spoke against Pliny in the debate about Publicius Certus. But Pliny afterwards sought his support for the candidature of Erucius Clarus. II. 9 pref., IX. 13. 13. Their friendship appears in the villa letter, V. 6. 1–3. Receives II. 9, Erucius Clarus, and V. 6, the Tuscan villa.

Cn. DOMITIUS Afer Titius Marcellus Curvius LUCANUS, Flavian consular and administrator, adopted son of the orator Domitius Afer, brother of Domitius Tullus. His family affairs, VIII. 18. 4 n.

Domitia Lucilla, adopted daughter of Domitius Tullus, and natural daughter of Domitius Lucanus. See VIII. 18. 2 n.

Cn. DOMITIUS Afer Titius Marcellus Curvius TULLUS, Flavian consular and administrator, possibly *cos. II* in 98, brother of Cn. Domitius Lucanus, whose daughter Lucilla he adopted. His financial intrigues and sordid old age, VIII. 18 nn.

Sextus ERUCIUS CLARUS, son of an equestrian advocate. Pliny secures him senatorial magistracies in *c.* 97–101. II. 9. 1 n. Later he served in the Parthian wars and gained a consulship in 117. As nephew of a praetorian prefect dismissed by Hadrian he was not further promoted, until he became consul II and city prefect in 146, when he died. He or his father receives I. 16, the account of Saturninus' writings, but does not recur in the Letters.

ERUCIUS CLARUS, the Elder, an equestrian advocate and father of the consular Sextus Erucius Clarus, and brother-in-law of the equestrian official Septimius Clarus. I. 16 pref., II. 9. 4 n. Receives (probably) I. 16, description of works of Pompeius Saturninus.

M. EGNATIUS MARCELLINUS, quaestor of an unknown province and later suffect consul in 116, IV. 12 nn.; his honest conduct, ibid.

ENCOLPIUS, Pliny's professional reader, a slave or freedman. VIII. 1, his illness.

EUPHRATES, Stoic philosopher from Syria, pupil of Musonius Rufus, protégé of Flavians, and enemy of Apollonius of Tyana, but leaves Rome 93–96, returning in 97–98. Dies in 119. I. 10 nn.

M. ULPIUS EURYTHMUS, freedman and procurator of Trajan, accused of forgery, VI. 31. 8.

M. ULPIUS EPIMACHUS, freedman assistant to the procurator of Bithynia, X. 84.

FABATUS, *see* CALPURNIUS.

FABIUS APER, *see* FLAVIUS.

FABIUS HISPANUS, accessory of Caecilius Classicus in extortion, relegated for five years. III. 9. 12–17.

FABIUS POSTUMINUS, consular (suff. 96), mentioned in debate on Publicius Certus, IX. 13. 13.

FABIUS VALENS, possibly an equestrian officer who served with Pliny in Bithynia, IV. 24 pref., X. 86B n. Receives IV. 24, the advocates of the Centumviral Court.

L. FABIUS IUSTUS, senator, probably from Spain, advocate and man of letters to whom Tacitus addressed his *Dialogus*. Suffect consul in 102 and later legate of Syria and perhaps Lower Moesia. I. 5. 8 n. Receives I. 11, VII. 2, brief notes.

L. FADIUS RUFINUS, consular senator (suff. 113), mentioned as guest in anecdote (IX. 23. 4), is probably recipient of VIII. 18, on the habits of Domitius Tullus, ibid. pref.

A. Didius Gallus FABRICIUS VEIENTO, a court figure, disgraced under Nero when a praetorian senator, influential under the Flavians and Nerva, becoming *cos. III* by 90. IV. 22. 4 n. He dines with Nerva, IV. 22. 4, and defends Publicius Certus, IX. 13. 13, 19.

FALCO, *see* POMPEIUS.

FANNIA, daughter of the Neronian senator P. Fannius Thrasea Paetus and the younger Arria, and wife of the elder Helvidius Priscus. She twice accompanied her husband into exile, under Nero and Vespasian, induced Herennius Senecio to write his biography, and was thereby involved in the prosecution of Senecio and Arulenus Rusticus for treason, and was exiled, in 93. III. 11. 3 n., VII. 19. 3–5 n. She returned in 97 and stirred Pliny to prosecute Publicius Certus, who assisted the condemnation of Helvidius the younger, her stepson. IX. 13. 3–5. Her illness, VII. 19.

C. FANNIUS, advocate and biographer of Neronian victims, possibly related to Thrasea Paetus. Dies *c.* 105. Described V. 5 nn.

FEROX, *see* IULIUS.

FLAVIUS APER, senator who proposed severer sentence against Tuscilius Nominatus, for defective advocacy. The name *Flavius* or *Fabius* is doubtful in the text. Possibly son of the orator M. Aper, V. 13. 5 n.

FLAVIUS MARCIANUS, decurion of Lepcis, involved in charges against Marius Priscus, II. 11. 8, 23.

FLAVIUS ARCHIPPUS, philosopher and politician of Prusa; his earlier disgrace and Domitian's favour, and quarrel with Dion, X. 58–60, 81.

FONTEIUS MAGNUS, representative of the council of Bithynia in prosecution of Varenus Rufus, V. 20. 4, VII. 6. 6.

FRONTO CATIUS, *see* CATIUS.

FUNDANUS, *see* MINICIUS.

Cn. Pedanius Fuscus Salinator, son of the like-named consular. His career though exalted is little known. He married Hadrian's niece, daughter of the consular Julius Servianus, before his quaestorship, *c.* 106, was *consul ord.* with Hadrian in 118, and had hopes of the succession. In 136 his son perished in a plot with Servianus. VI. 26. 1 n. Fuscus studied advocacy with Pliny, VI. 11. He receives two long letters and a postscript: VII. 9, on literary composition. IX. 36, 40, Pliny's country life.

Gallitta, wife of military tribune, condemned for adultery, VI. 31. 4–6.

Gallus, *see* Clusinius *or* Pomponius.

Gavius Bassus, equestrian *praefectus orae Ponticae*, commended by Pliny, X. 21–22, 86A.

C. Geminius, unknown friend of Corellius Rufus, I. 12. 9 n. Not to be confused with Rosianus Geminus.

Geminus, *see* Rosianus.

Genialis, unknown recipient of brief note on *studia*, VIII. 13.

Gratilla, apparently the wife of Arulenus Rusticus, and involved in his condemnation in 93. She may be Verulania Gratilla, a supporter of Vespasian in 69. III. 11. 3 n., v. 1. 8.

Harpocras, Pliny's Egyptian masseur. Difficulties over his citizenship, X. 5–7, 10.

Helvidiae, daughters of younger Helvidius Priscus, IV. 21, their death.

Helvidius Priscus, the elder, husband of Fannia, critic of Nero and Vespasian, first exiled in 66, then again *c.* 75, and later executed. Senator of praetorian rank. VII. 19. 4 n.

Helvidius Priscus the younger, son of the elder Helvidius by his first wife, and stepson of Fannia, held all offices up to the consulship (before 86). Accused of libelling Domitian, and executed, in 93. III. 11. 3 n., IX. 13. 2–3 n.

Herennius Senecio, advocate and senator from Spain, associate of Helvidius Priscus and Arulenus Rusticus, critic of the Flavians, refused further office after his quaestorship, prosecuted the *delator* Baebius Massa for extortion, represented Valerius Licinianus in the Vestal affair, and was condemned on a charge of treasonable libel arising from his biography of the elder Helvidius, in 93. 1. 5. 3, III. 11. 3, IV. 11. 12, VII. 19. 5, 33. 4 nn. His quips against Regulus, IV. 7. 5.

Herennius Severus, a scholar and apparently a consular senator. Requests portraits of two writers, IV. 28. 1 n. Possibly recipient of IX. 22, illness of poet Passenus Paulus.

Plinius Hermes, freedman and land-agent of Pliny, VII. 11. 1.

Hispanus, *see* Baebius.

Hispulla, wife of Corellius Rufus, possibly related to Calpurnia Hispulla, I. 12. 3 n.

M. Iunius Homullus, consular (suff. 102), later legate of Cappadocia, defends Julius Bassus and Varenus Rufus, IV. 9. 15 n., V. 20. 6, and intervenes in debate on *ambitus*, VI. 19. 3.

Hostilius Firminus, praetorian legate of Marius Priscus, condemned for complicity in his crimes. II. II. 23 n., 12.

L. Iavolenus Priscus Octavius Tidius Tossianus, a consular senator (suff. 86) and jurisprudent, counsellor of Trajan and Hadrian, and governor of three military provinces, including Syria *c.* 96–100. II. 13 pref. Anecdote about his oddity, VI. 15. 2. May receive II. 13, promotion of Voconius Romanus.

Isaeus, 'Sophistic' orator from Syria, admired by Pliny. II. 3 nn.

Iulia Serviana, daughter of Julius Ursus Servianus and niece of Hadrian, betrothed to the young Pedanius Fuscus Salinator. VI. 26. 1 n.

Iulius Africanus, young advocate. VII. 6. 11–12.

Iulius Atticus, friend of family of Corellius Rufus, of uncertain identification. I. 12. 10 n.

Iulius Avitus, dead quaestor, brother of Julius Naso, V. 21. 3 n. To be distinguished from Junius Avitus, dead when designated aedile, VIII. 23, 1, 8.

Iulius Bassus, praetorian senator, in perpetual difficulties under Flavians, returns from relegation in 97, proconsul of Bithynia in 101–2, defended by Pliny on an extortion charge in 103, and lightly sentenced. Probably of Asiatic origin, but not to be identified with the noted consular C. Julius Quadratus Bassus. IV. 9, 1 nn., VI. 29. 10, X. 56. 4.

Iulius Candidus, whose apophthegm is quoted by Pliny V. 20. 5 (n.), is probably the consular Ti. Julius Candidus Marius Celsus, *cos. II* in 105.

Ti. Iulius Ferox, consular senator (suff. in 98 or 99), predecessor of Pliny as *curator alvei Tiberis* (101–4), commands an army between 105 and 109, proconsul of Asia in *c.* 116–17, intervenes in trial of Marius Priscus. II. II. 5 n., X. 87. 3 n. Receives brief note VII. 13.

Sextus Iulius Frontinus, possibly Narbonese, a consular senator (suff. *c.* 74), legate of Britain *c.* 76–78, *curator aquarum c.* 96–97, then *cos. II* in 98 and *cos. III* in 100, elder statesman under Nerva and Trajan, perhaps had a hand in Trajan's succession. Author of the *de Aquis* and *Strategemata*. IV. 8. 3 n. He advises Pliny, and recommends him for promotion, ibid. and V. 1. 5. His refusal of a funerary memorial, IX. 19.

Iulius Genitor, a *rhetor Latinus* whom Pliny discovers and recommends to Corellia, III. 3. 5 n. Receives III. 11, the philosopher Artemidorus, VII. 30, death of a pupil, IX. 17, reproof for priggishness.

Iulius Largus, wealthy man from Pontus, leaves legacy to Pliny, X. 75.

Iulius Naso, brother of Julius Avitus who is recently dead, is commended by Pliny and Tacitus for the quaestorship. VI. 6, 9 nn. Receives IV. 6, crops and storms.

IULIUS PISO, benefactor of Amisus, sued by the city, X. 110.

Sextus IULIUS SPARSUS, consular senator (suff. 88), possibly friend of Martial. IV. 5 pref. Receives two shorter letters, IV. 5, VIII. 3, on speeches of Pliny.

IULIUS TIRO, testator whose will is said to have been forged by an imperial freedman, VI. 31. 7–12.

IULIUS VALERIANUS, a senator owning land in Marsian region. II. 15 pref. Receives II. 15, sale of land. V. 4, 13, misdemeanours of advocate Tuscilius.

IULIUS VALENS, unknown; his illness, V. 21. 2.

L. IULIUS Ursus SERVIANUS, consular pillar of Trajan and Hadrian, from Spain, born c. 46 and later adopted by Domitian's praetorian prefect Julius Ursus. Marries a sister of Hadrian before 90 when he was suffect consul. Afterwards legate of Upper Germany and Pannonia c. 98–101, and cos. II in 102. His daughter marries patrician Fuscus Salinator c. 106, for whose son he failed to secure the succession to Hadrian, perishing after a third consulship (134) in 136, VI. 26, VIII. 23. 5 nn. He acts for Trajan as special investigator (VII. 6. 8–9), and secures Pliny the ius III liberorum (X. 2. 1 n.). Receives two short notes, personal in tone: III. 17, his absence in danger, VI. 26, betrothal of his daughter.

IUNIOR, see TERENTIUS.

IUNIUS AVITUS, young senator, protégé of Pliny, served with Julius Servianus in Germany and Pannonia c. 98–100, died when aedile designate. To be distinguished from Julius Avitus, VIII. 23 nn. Receives II. 6, duties of a host.

IUNIUS MAURICUS, Cisalpine senator, born before 43, already in Senate by 68. His career is otherwise unknown. In politics more cautious than his brother Arulenus Rusticus, but involved in same treason charge in 93 and exiled. Returns in 97, and acts as counsellor to Nerva and Trajan. I. 5. 10 n., IV. 22. 3–4 nn. Pliny arranges betrothal of his niece, I. 14, and the education of his nephews, II. 18. Receives these letters, but later only VI. 14, brief reply to an invitation.

IUNIUS PASTOR, early client of Pliny in courts, possibly friend of Martial. I. 18. 3.

IUSTUS, see FABIUS, MINICIUS.

P. IUVENTIUS CELSUS, consular senator, jurisprudent and counsellor of Hadrian (suff. 115, cos. II 129). Speaks as praetor in 106–7 in debate on extortion law, VI. 5. 4–7 n.

M. LABERIUS MAXIMUS, consular legate in Dacian war, 101–2; his runaway slave, X. 74.

A. Bucius LAPPIUS MAXIMUS Norbanus, consular legate, twice consul (86, 95); earlier proconsul of Bithynia, when Domitian commends Archippus to him, X. 58. 6.

LARCIUS MACEDO, praetorian senator, son of freedman and father of a consular, is murdered by his slaves. Connexion with other Larcii uncertain. III. 14. I n.

LIBO FRUGI, consular of uncertain identity, attacks Norbanus at the Classicus trial. Friend of Salvius Liberalis. III. 9. 33 n.

LICINIUS NEPOS, praetor in 105, in charge of a criminal court, vigorously enforces rules of procedure and checks corruption. IV. 29. 2 n., V. 4, 9, 13. Proposes amendment to extortion law after his praetorship, VI. 5. 2 n.

L. LICINIUS SURA, advocate and senator from Spain, known to Martial. Trajan's closest friend and adviser. After promotion by Domitian to mostly civil offices, he distinguished himself in diplomacy in Trajan's first Dacian war, became thrice consul (II. 102, III. 107), and died c. 110, IV. 30 pref. Receives two long letters on curiosities of nature. IV. 30, water springs. VII. 27, ghosts.

LUCCEIUS ALBINUS, senator from Spain, accuses associates of Classicus, defends Julius Bassus, III. 9. 7, IV. 9. 13 nn.; receives VI. 10, memorial of Verginius Rufus.

LUPERCUS, unknown man of letters, receives two long letters. II. 5, Pliny's speech *pro patria*. IX. 26, on ornate style. Possibly Narbonese, II. 5 pref.

LUSTRICIUS BRUTTIANUS, praetorian senator, proconsul of unnamed province, accused by his *comes* and acquitted by Trajan, VI. 22.

MACER, *see* BAEBIUS, CALPURNIUS.

LYCORMAS, imperial freedman in dispute with king of Bosporus, X. 63, 67.

MACRINUS, *see* CAECILIUS, MINICIUS.

MAECILIUS NEPOS. The *nomen* which occurs only in IV. 26 is testified once among Trajanic senators, and twice earlier. Elsewhere the headings give only the *cognomen* Nepos. The text need not be altered to substitute the known consular *P. Metilius Sabinus Nepos* (q.v.), II. 3 pref., IV. 26 n. Maecilius, who is appointed to an unnamed proconsular province, IV. 26. 2 n., receives II. 3, the rhetor Isaeus. III. 16, anecdotes of Arria. IV. 26, loan of books. VI. 19, politics and land prices.

MAESIUS MAXIMUS, unknown, probably not a senator, III. 20 pref. Receives two letters about misconduct at elections. III. 20, IV. 25. He is not easily identified with other of Pliny's Maximi.

T. Pomponius MAMILIANUS, consular senator (suff. 100) and possibly legate of Britain c. 107–8. IX. 16 pref. Receives, on active service, IX. 16 and 25, brief notes on harvests, hunting, and poems.

MARCELLINUS, *see* AEFULANUS, CLAUDIUS, EGNATIUS.

MARIUS PRISCUS, senator of Spanish origin, consul before 86, proconsul of Africa in 97–98, accused of extortion in late 98 and condemned after protracted trials in January 100. II. 11. 2 n., III. 9. 2, VI. 29. 9, X. 3A.

MATURUS, *see* ARRIANUS.

Mauricus, *see* Iunius.

Maximus. For the distribution of letters between the various Maximi see II. 14 pref. Also Maesius, Novius, Valerius, Vibius, and *infra*.

Maximus the Elder, a man of Pliny's age, not definitely a senator, interested in literature and Pliny's career. May be Maesius or Novius Maximus, II. 14 pref. Receives II. 14, the Centumviral court. VI. 11, Pliny's pupils. VIII. 19, a literary consultation. IX. 1, his quarrel with Planta. IX. 23, comparison of Pliny and Tacitus.

Maximus the Younger, a praetorian senator without interest in literature. His wife comes from Verona, VI. 34, and he is appointed special commissioner to Achaea, VIII. 24. *See* also Quinctilius Valerius Maximus.

Valerius Maximus, from Alexandria Troas, or another Valerius Maximus from Cisalpine Gaul, VI. 8. 4 n., VIII. 24. 8 n. He receives VI. 34, funeral games for his wife. VII. 26, behaviour in illness. VIII. 24, his appointment to reorganize Achaea. *See Valerius Maximus.*

Ulpius Maximus. Freedman procurator in Bithynia. Disputes with Pliny, X. 27–28. Commended, X. 85.

Metilius Crispus, centurion from Comum, murdered. VI. 25. 2.

Metilius Nepos, *see* Maecilius.

Mettius Carus, apparently a senator, a formidable *delator* in Domitian's last years, of whom little is known in detail except his prosecution of Herennius Senecio and Fannia, I. 5, 3 n., VII. 19. 5. His information against Pliny, VII. 27. 14.

Trebonius Proculus Mettius Modestus, praetorian senator exiled under Domitian, father of like-named consular, I. 5. 5 n. His quip against Regulus, ibid. 14.

Minicia Marcella, well-educated daughter of consular Minicius Fundanus, dies at 15. V. 16. 2–6 nn.

Minicianus, *see* Cornelius.

Minicius Acilianus, praetorian senator from Brixia, son of Minicius Macrinus, suggested by Pliny as a husband for daughter of Arulenus Rusticus. I. 14. 3–8 n. Dies soon after, II. 16. 1 n.

Minicius Fundanus, senator possibly from Cisalpine, apparently legionary legate and prefect of treasury of Saturn before suffect consulship in 107. Proconsul of Asia *c.* 124–5, when he queries the treatment of Christians. Friend of Plutarch and student of philosophy. I. 9, IV. 15 prefs. Receives I. 9, the daily round. IV. 15, recommendation of a quaestor as his consular assistant. VI. 6, recommendation of Julius Naso for elections. In V. 16 Pliny describes the grief of Fundanus at his daughter's death. VII. 12, on rhetoric, may not be addressed to him.

Minicius Iustus, aged equestrian, husband of elder Corellia. VII. 11. 4 n.

Minicius Macrinus, elderly equestrian from Brixia, father of the senator Minicius Acilianus, was offered senatorial status by Vespasian.

I. 14. 5. His wife's death may be recorded in VIII. 5. Receives no letters: VII. 12 pref., VIII. 17 pref.

L. MINICIUS RUFUS, proconsul of Bithynia before his consulship in 88. Rescript of Domitian on enslaved children addressed to him. X. 72.

MONTANIUS ATTICINUS, assistant of proconsul Lustricius Bruttianus, forged a document against him, and was condemned by Trajan, VI. 22. 2 n.

MONTANUS, to whom the letters about the freedman Pallas are addressed, VII. 29, VIII. 6, may be the elderly consular T. Junius Montanus (cos. 81). VII. 29 pref.

MURENA, see Q. POMPEIUS FALCO.

C. MUSONIUS RUFUS, an equestrian from a Tuscan municipality, and the most influential Stoic philosopher and teacher of the period from Nero to Titus, exiled by Nero and Vespasian. Father-in-law of the Syrian philosopher Artemidorus. Probably the source of some of the political opinions of the resistance to the emperor Vespasian. III. 11. 5–7 nn.

MUSTIUS, Pliny's architect, receives IX. 39, instructions on building a shrine of Ceres.

NASO, see IULIUS.

NEPOS, see LICINIUS, MAECILIUS, SABINUS, STATIUS.

L. NERATIUS MARCELLUS, senator from Saepinum, brother of the jurist Neratius Priscus, was suffect consul in 95, curator aquarum before 101, and legate of Britain by 103 when Pliny secured from him a military tribunate for Suetonius. Later cos. II (129). III. 8. 1 n.

Neratius Priscus, see PRISCUS.

C. Avidius NIGRINUS, nephew of Pliny's friend Avidius Quietus, a distinguished senator under Trajan, consul in 110 and later legate of Dacia or Moesia, was among the four consulars executed at the beginning of Hadrian's reign. Speaks as tribune in debate of 105 on corruption of advocates, and later for Bithynia against Varenus. V. 13. 6 n., V. 20. 6, VII. 6. 2–4.

NONIUS, of uncertain identification, praised for generosity by Geminus, IX. 30. 1 n.

NONIUS CELER, unknown advocate, marries granddaughter of Tutilius, VI. 32. 1 n.

NOVIUS MAXIMUS, man of letters, son or brother of the consular Novius Priscus (suff. 78), may be the 'Elder Maximus' of the Letters, II. 14 pref. Receives IV. 20, criticisms of his book, V. 5, death of the writer Fannius, and probably IX. 1, his book against Planta. Possibly also VI. 11, VIII. 19, IX. 23. See s.v. MAXIMUS, MAXIMUS the Elder.

Novius PRISCUS, see PRISCUS.

NORBANUS LICINIANUS, leading provincial and advocate at Rome and in Baetica, enemy and accuser of Caecilius Classicus and Salvius Liberalis. III. 9. 29–35. His condemnation for praevaricatio, ibid.

3 C

NYMPHIDIUS LUPUS, served as military prefect with Pliny in Syria *c.* 81, acts as his adjutant in Bithynia. Pliny recommends his son, an equestrian officer, to Trajan, x. 87.

OCTAVIUS RUFUS, probably C. Marius Marcellus Octavius Publius Cluvius Rufus, suffect consul in 80, I. 7 pref. Receives I. 7, a lawsuit from Baetica. II. 10, advice on publishing his verses. Perhaps dead soon after. Possibly mentioned in IX. 38.

C. PASSENNUS PAULUS Propertius Blaesus, Roman knight and poet from Asisium, descendant of the Augustan poet Propertius, VI. 15. 1 n. His recitation ibid. IX. 22, his illness.

PATERNUS, *see* PLINIUS.

PAULINUS, *see* VALERIUS.

Pedanius FUSCUS SALINATOR, Flavian patrician and consul, apparently before 86, father of the younger Fuscus. VI. 26. 1 n., x. 87. 3 n., his army command, late in his career.

PLINIUS PATERNUS, an obscure man of letters possibly known to Martial, I. 21 pref. He receives I. 21, sale of slaves. IV. 14, Pliny's first volume of verse. VIII. 16, generosity to slaves. IX. 27, recitation of an historian, perhaps Tacitus.

C. PLINIUS SECUNDUS, the Elder Pliny, a Roman knight from Comum, born *c.* 24, was Pliny's uncle and adopted him in his will. He served as officer in Lower and Upper Germany between 47 and 51, probably held another post in Upper Germany *c.* 56, was procurator of Africa in the early years of Nero, and of Hispania Tarraconensis either before 66 or after 69. He was prefect of the *classis Misenensis* for some years before 79, and acted as adviser of Vespasian. He was a friend of Titus from earlier years. No more is certain or probable about his public career. III. 5, 'career' nn. The order and titles of his books are known from III. 5. 3–6. III. 5. 7–17 describes his daily routine and VI. 16 his death in the eruption of Vesuvius, in 79. For Pliny's relations with his uncle, see I. 19. 1, V. 8. 5, VI. 16. 7, 20. 2–5.

CLAUDIUS POLYAENUS, leader of mission from the council of Bithynia in favour of Varenus Rufus; possibly of Prusa. VII. 6. 6 n., 10. 1. His kinsman at Prusa, x. 70. 2.

POMPEIA CELERINA, wealthy mother of Pliny's second wife, later married the senator Bittius Proculus before 96, still alive *c.* 110; related to the consular L. Pompeius Celer. I. 4 pref., III. 19. 8, IX. 13. 13. Though very friendly to Pliny she receives only I. 4, Pliny's visit to her villas. Cf. I. 18. 3, VI. 10. 1. Her kinsman Clemens serves on Pliny's staff, x. 51.

Pompeia PLOTINA, Trajan's wife. Voconius Romanus sends her some literary letters, IX. 28. 1 n.

Sex. POMPEIUS COLLEGA, consular senator (*ord.* 93), proposes milder punishment for Marius Priscus, II. 11. 20–22 n.

Q. POMPEIUS FALCO, who was also named Q. Roscius Coelius Murena
Silius Decianus Vibullus Pius Iulius Eurycles, a noted officer and
administrator under Trajan and Hadrian, was already tribune in 97
when he supported Fabricius Veiento in the Senate, IX. 13. 19. He was
decorated as a legionary legate in the first Dacian war (101–2),
governed Lycia-Pamphylia and Judaea before his suffect consulship
in 108, later Moesia Inferior (c. 116), Britain, and Asia. His origin is
obscure, not Cisalpine. His names connect him with the leading states-
men Julius Frontinus and Sosius Senecio, whose daughter he married,
and the less influential consular Roscii and Silii. I. 23 pref. He receives
I. 23, advice on his tribunate. IV. 27, recitation of Sentius Augurinus.
VII. 22, recommendation of Cornelius Minicianus. IX. 15, brief note on
country life.

POMPEIUS IULIANUS, a notable of Syria, father-in-law of the philosopher
Euphrates. I. 10. 8 n.

C. POMPEIUS PLANTA, former procurator of Lycia, prefect of Egypt
(98–103) and author of a history of the civil wars of 69. Probably
mentioned in IX. 1 as the enemy of Novius (?) Maximus.

POMPEIUS QUINTIANUS, possibly a Roman knight from Antioch. IX. 9. 1.
His death, ibid.

POMPEIUS SATURNINUS, otherwise unknown advocate and writer of
verse and history, praised by Pliny as a new friend, I. 16, I. 8 pref.
He receives two long letters. I. 8, Pliny's library speech, V. 21, death
of Julius Avitus, and two brief notes, VII. 7, 15, introducing one
Priscus to him. To be distinguished from Saturninus of Comum,
V. 7. 1 n.

T. POMPONIUS BASSUS, an elderly senator who after a late consulship in
94 governed Cappadocia-Galatia c. 95–100, and in 101 organized the
alimenta in central Italy. IV. 23 pref. Receives IV. 23, on the pleasures
of retirement.

POMPONIA GALLA, lady of high rank, probably daughter of senator
Pomponius Gallus, and connexion of Fabricius Veiento. Disinherits
her son Asudius Curianus. Dead c. 94–96. V. 1. 1 n.

POMPONIANUS, friend of the Elder Pliny, VI. 16. 11, should be the same
as Tascius, ibid. 8.

C. POMPONIUS RUFUS Acilius Priscus Coelius Sparsus, consular senator
(suff. 98) and advocate, attacks the principal accuser in the Classicus
case (III. 9. 33 n.) and prosecutes Julius Bassus, IV. 9. 3.

PONTIUS ALLIFANUS, son of a praetorian senator, and connected with
Campania, V. 14 pref. Receives two long letters: V. 14, career of
Cornutus Tertullus, VII. 4, account of Pliny's verse experiments, and
brief note, VI. 28, on his hospitality.

POPILIUS ARTEMISIUS, freedman of the Voconii Romani, IX. 28. 2 n.

POSTUMIUS MARINUS, Pliny's doctor, receives citizenship, X. 11. 1.

C. Bruttius PRAESENS L. Fulvius Rusticus, senator with erratic career,
accepts no serious employment after his praetorship *c.* 104 (?), but
serves much later as legionary legate in the Parthian War, *c.* 114–15,
governs Cilicia in 117, and after consulship governs Moesia Inferior,
Cappadocia-Galatia, and *c.* 136 Syria. Is *cos. II* in 139. VII. 3 pref.
Receives only VII. 3, on his idleness, and perhaps IX. 29.

PRISCUS, an unidentified consular legate to whom Pliny commends
Voconius Romanus, is probably Javolenus Priscus, and not Neratius
Priscus, II. 13 pref. See also s.v. Cornelius, Helvidius, Iavolenus,
Marius, Neratius, Novius, Stilonius.

L. Neratius PRISCUS, jurisprudent, brother of consular Neratius Marcellus, was prefect of *aerarium Saturni*, consul in 97, and later legate
of Pannonia between 103 and 108. Hence not the recipient of II. 13
(pref.). Possibly receives VII. 8, introduction of Pompeius Saturninus.

Novius PRISCUS, consular (suff. 78), related to Novius Maximus, may
be the recipient of VI. 8 (pref.), Atilius Crescens' debt, VII. 8, introduction of Pompeius Saturninus, VII. 19, stories of Fannia. But see also
CORNELIUS PRISCUS, Neratius PRISCUS.

PUBLICIUS CERTUS, praetorian senator, prefect of treasury of Saturn
with Bittius Priscus before Pliny, accused of scandalous behaviour
at the trial of Helvidius Priscus, IX. 13. 2 n. His disgrace and death,
ibid. 22–24.

QUADRATUS, *see* UMMIDIUS.

QUINTILIANUS, unknown man, marries his daughter to the advocate
Nonius Celer, VI. 32.

RECTINA, wife of Tascius, friend of the Elder Pliny, possibly related to
Voconius Romanus, VI. 16. 8.

REGULUS, *see* AQUILIUS.

RESTITUTUS, *see* CLAUDIUS RESTITUTUS.

ROBUSTUS, unknown knight, supposed murdered, VI. 25. 1 n.

ROMANUS, *see* VOCONIUS.

ROMATIUS FIRMUS, a decurion of Comum, secures equestrian status and
a place on the jury panel, through Pliny's help. I. 19 pref. Receives
I. 19, Pliny's offer. IV. 29, severity of the praetor Nepos.

T. Prifernius Paetus ROSIANUS GEMINUS, Pliny's consular quaestor in
100, had served as military tribune or legate under Trajan and was a
praetorian senator *c.* 110, when recommended by Pliny to Trajan for
promotion. He was later, apparently, suffect consul *c.* 125 and proconsul of Africa *c.* 142, surviving until 150. Possibly adopted son of
consular T. Prifernius Paetus and father-in-law of jurisprudent Pactumeius Clemens. He is a *patronus* but not a native of Ostia. VII. 1 pref.,
X. 26 nn. A series of admonitory and exemplary letters is addressed to
him. VII. 1, on illness. VII. 24, Ummidia Quadratilla and her grandson.
VIII. 5, death of a wife. VIII. 22, on pardoning faults. IX. 11, Pliny's
books at Lugdunum. IX. 30, on liberality.

RUFINUS, *see* FADIUS.

RUFUS, *see* ACILIUS, ASINIUS, CALVISIUS, CANINIUS, CORELLIUS, MUSONIUS, OCTAVIUS, POMPONIUS, SEMPRONIUS, VARENUS, VERGINIUS.

RUSO, *see* CREMUTIUS.

RUSTICUS, recipient of a short note IX. 29 about Pliny's verses, is commonly identified with the Flavian historian Fabius Rusticus, a protégé of Seneca of uncertain status. But L. Messius Rusticus (*cos.* 114) is as probable, or a son of ARULENUS RUSTICUS.

SABINA, kinswoman of Statius Sabinus, leaves money to Pliny. IV. 10. 1 n.

SABINIANUS, unidentified recipient of two notes about his undutiful freedman. IX. 21, 24.

P. *Metilius* SABINUS *Nepos*, a consular, suffect in 91, probably legate of Britain *c.* 98, may be the recipient of IX. 2, 18, addressed to Sabinus, or of II. 3, etc., addressed to Nepos, but not of both series and probably of neither. See MAECILIUS, STATIUS.

SARDUS, unknown, receives IX. 31, brief note of thanks.

C. SALVIUS LIBERALIS Nonius Bassus, senator and advocate promoted by Vespasian, assistant legate in Britain *c.* 80–1, suffect consul before 86, accused of unknown charge and perhaps exiled *c.* 89. He defended Marius Priscus, and attacked the prosecutors in the Caecilius case, II. 11. 17, III. 9. 33, 36 nn. Possibly he is 'mean Nonius' of IX. 30.

L. SATRIUS, unknown protégé of Pliny, manumits slaves, X. 11. 2.

SATRIUS RUFUS, advocate and praetorian senator, senior to Pliny, supports Publicius Certus against Pliny. I. 5. 11, IX. 13. 17.

SATURIUS FIRMUS, son-in-law of Asinius Rufus, possibly a procurator from Asculum. IV. 15. 3 n.

SATURNINUS, of Comum, leaves property to Comum. V. 7, 1 n. *See* also POMPEIUS.

Ti. Iulius SAUROMATES, king of Bosporus; his messages to Trajan, X. 63–64, 67.

SEMPRONIUS RUFUS, suffect consul of 113, receives IV. 22, politics of Vienna in Trajan's *consilium*. V. 9, strictness of praetor Nepos, and possibly VII. 25, an educated procurator. IV. 22 pref.

SEMPRONIUS CAELIANUS, equestrian recruiting officer, X. 29–30.

SEMPRONIUS SENECIO, knight accused of forgery before Trajan, VI. 31. 8.

SENECIO, *see* HERENNIUS, SOSIUS.

Q. Gellius SENTIUS AUGURINUS, young senator, perhaps from Cisalpine, related to Spurinna or Arrius Antoninus, later proconsul of Macedonia. IV. 27. 1 n. His poems praised, ibid. Receives IX. 8, note of thanks.

C. SEPTICIUS CLARUS, a friend common to Pliny and Suetonius, who dedicated his *Lives* to him, and to the elder Erucius Clarus. His career is unknown until he became Hadrian's second praetorian prefect with Marcius Turbo in 119, from which post he was dismissed together with

Suetonius, then secretary *ab epistulis*. I. I pref., II. 9. 4 n. Receives I. I, the dedication, and other brief notes. I. 15, dinner party. VII. 28, excessive praise of friends. VIII. I, illness of Encolpius.

SERRANA PROCULA, stern grandmother of Minicius Acilianus, from Patavium. I. 14, 6 n.

SERTORIUS SEVERUS, praetorian senator, heir of Pomponia Galla. V. I. I n.

SERVIANUS, *see* IULIUS.

SERVILIUS CALVUS, proconsul of Bithynia shortly before Pliny, possibly related to Servilius Pudens, X. 56. 2.

SERVILIUS PUDENS, Pliny's assistant legate in Bithynia, X. 25.

SEVERUS, *see* ANNIUS, CATILIUS, HERENNIUS, VETTENIUS, VIBIUS, SERTORIUS.

Ti. Catius Asconius SILIUS ITALICUS (*cos. ord.* 68), a friend of Martial and possibly from northern Italy, was an advocate and *delator* under Nero, but later lived in retirement writing his *Punica*. His habits and suicide at the age of 76, *c.* 103, are described in III. 7.

SILIUS PROCULUS, unknown, submits his writings to Pliny, III. 15.

SOLLERS, praetorian senator, has dispute with the municipality of Vicetia. Probably he is Ti. Claudius Alpinus Augustanus L. Bellicius Sollers of Verona, and perhaps son-in-law of Claudius Marcellinus, V. 4. I n.

Q. SOSIUS SENECIO, influential senator under Trajan, *cos. ord.* in 99 and *cos. II* in 107. Son-in-law of Julius Frontinus, possibly a Cisalpine. His career is otherwise enigmatic. Apparently a consular legate *c.* 104–5, he may have served in the second Dacian war. A noted philhellene, friend of Plutarch, and probably a supporter of Hadrian. I. 13 pref. Receives I. 13, on literary salons. IV. 4, recommendation for a military tribunate. None later.

SPARSUS, *see* IULIUS.

SPURINNA, *see* VESTRICIUS.

STATIUS SABINUS, military man of uncertain rank from Firmum. The *nomen* appears only in IV. 10. Sabinus of the latter letters is not to be identified with P. Metilius Sabinus Nepos. VI. 18, IX. 2 prefs. Receives IV. 10, a freedman's legacy. VI. 18, lawsuit for Firmum. IX. 2, 18, dispatch of letters and books.

STILONIUS PRISCUS, military tribune involved in crimes of Caecilius Classicus. III. 9. 18 n.

SUBURANUS, son or brother of consular Attius Suburanus, and nephew or cousin of Attia Viriola, involved in lawsuit over will with her, VI. 33. 6 n.

Sex. Attius SUBURANUS, Flavian procurator, connected with family of Julius Ursus Servianus, was the first praetorian prefect of Trajan, promoted consul in 101, *cos. II* in 104. VII. 6. 10 n. Acts as arbitrator ibid. His kinsmen, VI. 33. 2–6 nn.

C. SUETONIUS TRANQUILLUS, the biographer, born *c.* 70–75, studied advocacy in the circle of Pliny, who assisted his equestrian career. He may have held a military tribunate *c.* 103–6 and accompanied Pliny to Bithynia *c.* 110. At the end of Trajan's reign and beginning of Hadrian's he held a series of secretariats—*a studiis, a bibliothecis, ab epistulis*—until he was involved in the fall of the praetorian prefect Septicius Clarus, his second protector (q.v.). His career is now partly known from an inscription found at Hippo Regius, which may be his home town. I. 18 pref., X. 94 n. Receives I. 18, difficulty over a brief. III. 8, transfer of his military tribunate to a friend. V. 10, his first book. IX. 34, on recitation. None of these are long. In I. 24 Pliny negotiates the buying of a farm for Suetonius, and secures him the *ius III liberorum* in X. 94.

SURA, *see* LICINIUS, also ACCIUS.

TACITUS, *see* CORNELIUS.

TASCIUS, friend of Elder Pliny, husband of Rectina, is probably Tascius Pomponianus, and a son of the Claudian consular Pomponius Secundus. Caught in Vesuvius eruption. VI. 16. 8 n.

TERENTIUS IUNIOR, Roman knight and former procurator of Narbonensis, probably from Perusia, lived in retirement after refusing senatorial status, devoted to literature and farming. His son became consul. VII. 25 nn. Receives VIII. 15, brief note on harvest. IX. 12, tiresome sons.

TERENTIUS MAXIMUS, Flavian procurator of Bithynia, possibly brother of Terentius Junior, X. 58. 5.

TERENTIUS SCAURUS, of uncertain identity. Either a contemporary grammarian, or a senator and relative of two Trajanic consular Terentii. V. 12 pref. Receives V. 12, recitation of a speech.

TERTULLUS, *see* CORNUTUS.

THEOPHANES, Bithynian politician, principal accuser of Julius Bassus, but suspected of corrupt practices. III. 9. 3 n., 20–21.

TIMON, husband of Arrionilla, connected with Arulenus Rusticus, perhaps a philosopher. I. 5. 5 n.

TIRO, *see* CALESTRIUS.

TITIANUS, *see* CORNELIUS.

C. Octavius TITINIUS CAPITO, equestrian officer and man of letters. He is the first known of the free-born secretaries of state (*a patrimonio* and *ab epistulis*), holding office from Domitian to *c.* 102, and later *praefectus vigilum*. I. 17 nn. Two letters (I. 17, VIII. 12) describe his loyalty to a dead friend and his biographies in prose and verse, but he receives only V. 8, on writing history.

TITIUS ARISTO, a great jurisprudent, not a senator, consultant of Trajan, and elder rival of Neratius Priscus and Juventius Celsus. Often quoted in legal sources. Described at length in I. 22 (nn.), on his illness.

Receives V. 3, on his reproof of Pliny's verse recitations. VIII. 14, rules of senatorial procedure.

TRANQUILLUS, *see* SUETONIUS.

TREBONIUS RUFINUS, magistrate of Vienna, quarrels with his council, IV. 22. 1 n., over abolition of gymnastic games.

TRIARIUS, unknown client of Pliny. Receives VI. 23, commending Cremutius Ruso as assistant advocate.

M. TULLIUS CERIALIS, consular senator (suff. 90), intervenes in trial of Marius Priscus, II. 11. 9 n. Possibly receives II. 19, on recitation of Pliny's speech in that trial. MSS. give his name as TUCCIUS.

M. TULLIUS IUSTUS, proconsul of Bithynia, probably related to Cerialis, X. 58. 10 n.

TUSCILIUS NOMINATUS, advocate of Vicetia, accused of abandoning clients. A knight from Ricina. V. 4. 1 n., 13.

TUTILIUS, whose granddaughter marries the advocate Nonius Celer, may be either a known acquaintance of Quintilian or a minor philosopher, VI. 32 nn.

VALERIANUS, *see* IULIUS.

VALERIUS LICINIANUS, praetorian senator and advocate, lover of the Vestal Cornelia, exiled on confession, becomes teacher of rhetoric; is not the Licinianus known from Martial. See IV. 11 nn.

VALERIUS MARTIALIS, the satirist from Bilbilis in Spain, whither he retired *c.* 98. III. 21 n. His death, ibid., not later than 103–4, and verses on Pliny.

Sextus Quinctilius *Valerius* MAXIMUS, a junior senator from Alexandria Troas and former quaestor of Bithynia-Pontus, has been identified with Maximus heir of Valerius Varus (VI. 8. 4 n.) and with the praetorian senator of VIII. 24, who after a normal career, including the quaestorship of Bithynia-Pontus, became special envoy for the reorganization of the free cities of Achaea. He may be the 'younger Maximus', q.v., but the identifications are far from certain. VIII. 24. 8 n.

VALERIUS PAULINUS, from Forum Julii, who speaks as a praetorian senator at the trial of Julius Bassus in 103, was suffect consul in 107 and dead by *c.* 110. II. 2 pref., X. 104. Receives II. 2, brief. IV. 16, a long speech of Pliny. V. 19, sickness of freedman Zosimus. IX. 3, fame versus leisure. IX. 37, reform of farm rents.

VALERIUS VARUS, possibly the father of the praetorian commissioner *Valerius* Maximus, owed a debt to Atilius Crescens, VI. 8. 4 n.

VARENUS RUFUS, appointed advocate of Bithynia against Julius Bassus, then proconsul of Bithynia, probably in 105–6, and prosecuted for extortion in 106–7. The action is apparently abandoned when the council of Bithynia disagrees. V. 20. 1–2 nn., VI. 13, VII. 6, 10.

VARISIDIUS NEPOS, obscure equestrian, recommended by Pliny to Sosius Senecio for a military tribunate. IV. 4. 1 n. Relative of Calvisius Rufus.

Velius Cerialis, unknown recipient of iv. 21 (pref.) on death of the sisters Helvidia, and possibly of ii. 19, on recitation of Pliny's *In Marium*.

Velius Paulus, proconsul of Bithynia before 85, sentenced Archippus, x. 58. 3.

Velleius Blaesus, consular of uncertain identification, perhaps known to Statius and Martial, and related to Sallustius Lucullus, a consular legate, tricks Regulus in his will, ii. 20. 7 n.

Venator, unknown recipient of brief note about harvest, ix. 20.

Verania, daughter of Neronian consular Q. Veranius, and wife of Calpurnius Piso, the adopted heir of Galba. ii. 20. 2 n. Regulus tricks her, ibid.

Vergilius Romanus, unknown writer of comedies and *mimiambi*. vi. 21. 2 n.

L. Verginius Rufus, a new senator from Mediolanum, *consul ord.* in 63, as legate of Upper Germany in 68 crushed the rising of Julius Vindex, and refused to be made emperor by his army. In 69 he was *cos. II* under Otho, and after Otho's defeat again refused the Principate. Lived in retirement under the Flavians, and was among the supporters of Nerva. He was *cos. III* in 97, refused a post on the 'Economy Commission', and died after an accident. He was legal guardian and political patron of Pliny. ii. 1. 8–9 nn., his death, reputation, and public funeral. v. 3. 5, his light verses. vi. 10, his monument at Alsium. ix. 19, comparison with Julius Frontinus, and his altercation with Cluvius Rufus.

Verus, a tenant farmer. Receives vi. 3, his farm.

T. Vestricius Spurinna, noted elder statesman of Nervan régime, whose son was a friend of Pliny. Served as praetorian legate for Otho in wars of 69, and under the Flavians won a victory over the Bructeri as legate of Lower Germany at uncertain date. Nerva gave him belated triumphal decorations. He served on the 'Economy Commission' and held second and third consulships in 98 and 100, possibly for promoting Nerva's adoption of Trajan. Of Narbonese or Cisalpine origin. Dabbled in literature. Pliny describes his honours and his daily life at length. ii. 7. 1–3 nn., iii. 1 nn., iv. 27. 5. He advised Pliny politically, i. 5. 8–9. He receives only two shorter letters, iii. 10, biography of his son. v. 17, poem of Calpurnius Piso on astronomy.

Vettenius Severus, suffect consul in 107, receives vi. 27, advice on proposals in honour of the Princeps.

C. Vibius Maximus, literary equestrian, possibly from Dalmatia, known to Statius and Martial. After posts in Dalmatia *c.* 95 he became prefect of Egypt from 103 to 107, when he was condemned for malpractices. iii. 2 pref. Receives iii. 2, commendation of Arrianus Maturus, and probably no other letters.

VIBIUS SEVERUS, man of letters from Mediolanum or Ticinum, otherwise unknown. Receives III. 18, recitation of the Panegyric. IV. 28, request for two portraits. Possibly IX. 22, sickness of poet Passennus.

VITELLIUS HONORATUS, provincial involved in charges against Marius Priscus, dead before the trial, II. 11. 8 n.

VIRDIUS GEMELLINUS, son of a centurion, and financial procurator of Bithynia-Pontus. His assistants, X. 26–27. Acts as assessor to Pliny, X. 84.

UMMIDIA QUADRATILLA, octogenarian daughter of a Neronian consular, from Casinum, and grandmother of Pliny's protégé Ummidius Quadratus. VII. 24 nn., her habits.

C. UMMIDIUS QUADRATUS, grandson, apparently by adoption, of Ummidia Quadratilla, and great-grandson of the like-named Neronian consular, is aged 23 c. 107, and already married and an advocate. His career is not known until his suffect consulship in 118. He was connected with Catilius Severus. The two were in favour under Hadrian until his later years. VII. 24. 2 nn. Pliny, who guides his studies, describes him twice, VI. 11. 1, VII. 24. 2–3. Quadratus receives two long letters: VI. 29, on choice of cases. IX. 13, Pliny's attack on Publicius Certus.

VOCONIUS ROMANUS, related to or identical with C. Licinius Macrinus Voconius Romanus, known from inscriptions of Saguntum in Spain, was a former president of the council of Hispania Tarraconensis. He was an advocate and man of letters, and fellow student with Pliny, who recommended him between 97 and 100 first for the *ius III liberorum* and for an equestrian appointment, and then for senatorial status, which he may not have taken up. II. 13 nn., X. 4 nn. He receives I. 5, Pliny's relations with Regulus in 97. III. 13, revision of the Panegyric. VI. 15, story about Iavolenus Priscus. VI. 33, Pliny's defence of Attia Viriola. VIII. 8, the fountain of Clitumnus. IX. 7, on building. IX. 28, exchange of correspondence.

URSUS, *see* CORNELIUS, IULIUS.

C. *Plinius* ZOSIMUS, Pliny's consumptive freedman and professional reader. V. 19. 2–3 nn.

APPENDIX IV[1]

THE DATE OF PLINY'S PRAETORSHIP

THERE are two main opinions about the date: Mommsen's, that Pliny was praetor in the known year of the trial of Baebius Massa, A.D. 93, and Otto's, that the praetorship must be later than this year, and belongs to A.D. 95. The suggestion of Harte, that it could have preceded the year of Massa's trial, has secured no support.[2]

The principal evidence is as follows. In III. 11 Pliny states that as praetor he befriended the philosopher Artemidorus, at a time when the philosophers had been expelled from Rome, by visiting him *in suburbano* and by giving him money, and he did this despite the fact that a group of his senatorial philosopher friends, including Herennius Senecio and Helvidius Priscus, had been condemned and sentenced on political charges. Tacitus in the *Agricola* 44–45 dates these trials as later than the death of Agricola in August 93, and remarks that at that moment Baebius Massa was still on trial. Pliny, in VII. 33, tells that Baebius Massa was prosecuted for extortion by Senecio and Pliny himself, as advocates assigned to the plaintiff province by the Senate, and adds that Massa after his condemnation brought a counter-charge of *impietas* against Senecio. From all this Mommsen not unnaturally concluded that the trials of the Senecio group, and the expulsion of the philosophers, took place in the last months of 93, and hence that Pliny was praetor in 93. The year 94 is not, however, excluded by the evidence so far adduced, since the praetorship is only connected with Pliny's visit to Artemidorus after the trials.

Xiphilinus (in Dio 67. 13–14) places his summary of the condemnations of Rusticus and Senecio, and of the expulsions of philosophers, in the period before certain events of 95, for which he gives a consular date, and after the last wars of Domitian *c.* 89–92. The late *Chronicon* of Eusebius, in both its versions (discussed below), agrees in placing a slaughter and exile of noble men in the thirteenth year of Domitian, which is 93–94. This evidence would place the praetorship of Pliny in

---

[1] This Appendix is reprinted in an amended form from *JRS*, 1957, by the kind permission of the Society for the Promotion of Roman Studies.

[2] Mommsen, 'Zur Lebensgeschichte des j. Plinius', *GS* iv. 414 ff.; W. Otto, 'Zur Lebensgeschichte' etc., *SB. Bayer. Ak. Wiss.* 1919, Abh. 10, 44 ff.; R. H. Harte, 'The praetorship of the younger Pliny', *JRS* xxv (1935), 51 ff.; F. Oertel, *Rhein. Mus.* 1939, 179 ff., restated Otto's case, and rejected Harte's.

either 93 or 94, and the *mox* in Tacitus' statement in the *Agricola*, might be thought to favour 94.

Otto objected that if Pliny were praetor in 93 then in undertaking the prosecution of Massa he violated the principle which he declares, in I. 23 and X. 3A, of not accepting briefs when holding public appointments. Next he inferred justly from Pliny's account of his early career in VII. 16 (nn.) that if Pliny were praetor in 94 he must have been tribune in 93 at the time of the prosecution of Massa. But I. 23 clearly states that as tribune he refused all advocacies. So the year 94 is excluded for the praetorship. In this Otto is evidently right. He then opted for the year 95, putting the tribunate in 94 and the quaestorship in 92.

Otto thought to confirm this scheme by invoking the evidence of the late chronographers for the expulsions of philosophers by Domitian. Here he, and later Harte, abandoned the path of caution. The more or less contemporary Latin sources, Pliny, Suetonius, and Aulus Gellius, give no exact dates for this action of Domitian, and do not suggest that there was more than one expulsion.[1] Xiphilinus, epitomizing Dio, records in a section between the last wars of Domitian and events of A.D. 95–96, that the condemnation of Senecio was followed by an expulsion of philosophers for a second time, αὖθις.[2] This may mean 'for a second time under Domitian', or less probably 'since Vespasian first so expelled them'. But the late chronographers give exact dates, for those that have unlimited faith. Jerome, in the Latin version of Eusebius' Chronicon, has the entry 'mathematicos et philosophos Romana urbe pepulit' under the year VIII of Domitian, i.e. A.D. 88–89, and a similar entry 'rursum . . . Roma per edictum extrudit' under year XV, i.e. A.D. 95–96, not 94–95 as Otto and others misrendered it. In the Armenian version of Eusebius, according to the translation of Karst, very similar entries appear under the years IX and XIII, i.e. 89–90 and 93–94, not 92–93 as Oertel has it.[3]

[1] Gellius, *NA* xv. 11. 4–5. Suet., *Dom.* 10. 3. Suetonius, like Pliny, puts the expulsion after the trial of Senecio. The epitomators Zonaras (xi. 19) and Syncellus (p. 343) add nothing to what they preserve of the Eusebian tradition.

[2] Xiphilinus is best found in the Loeb text of Dio 67. 13. 3. The statement is made in the passive: οἱ λοιποὶ πάντες (φιλόσοφοι) ἐξηλάθησαν αὖθις ἐκ τῆς Ῥώμης, and may refer back to that in 65. 13. 2, about Vespasian's expulsion.

[3] Eusebius, *Op.* v (Leipzig, 1911), p. 217. For Jerome, ibid. vii (ed. Helm), pp. 189 f.

The arrangement in Karst is clear enough. There is no doubt that these are regnal years, as Otto saw, op. cit. 50. Domitian rightly is given fifteen full years with a sixteenth of five days in the Armenian version (five months (!) in Jerome). The regnal years, which run from 13 Sept. (Suet. *Dom.* 17. 3. *Titus* 11), must take precedence over the years of Abraham with which they are

That Eusebius took some care over his Domitianic summary appears from his separation of the two sets of Vestal trials.[1] But his exact attributions are often unreliable. His Trajanic data are in a rare muddle,[2] and the Armenian version is better on the years XV–XVI of Domitian than Jerome, who turns the five days of year XVI into five months. There is nothing to justify a preference for the Latin version, and there is nothing in any source to suggest, as some have done, that there are three dates and three expulsion orders amongst which one may pick and choose. Xiphilinus may confirm belief in two expulsions, of which one was before 91 and the other after 92. No more is certain. For each expulsion there are, then, two alternative dates in the Eusebian sources, each covering parts of two calendar years from September to September. It may here be added that Philostratus, placing the misfortunes of Apollonius of Tyana at Rome in 92, might be held to point to 93–94 rather than to 95–96.[3] But evidently Eusebius cannot be used to determine a fluctuating and doubtful argument. The second date in Jerome, accepted by Otto, would put the expulsion in or after September 95, in the last twelve months of Domitian's reign. This hardly agrees with the indications of Xiphilinus noted above.

The assumptions of Otto, that there is not enough time in the last four months of 93 for the completion of the trials of Massa and the Senecio faction, and that Pliny would have refused on principle to act as advocate while praetor, are equally fragile. The latter argument will not stand up to the sort of minute criticism that Otto favoured. Pliny made it a matter of principle in his tribunate not to act as advocate because of the very special nature of the office, as he clearly states.[4] But as prefect of the treasury he only abandoned advocacy for reasons of convenience[5] which he was prepared to set aside, and did set aside, to conduct the prosecutions of Marius Priscus and Caecilius Classicus.[6] He felt no qualms as *curator alvei Tiberis*

equated, because they came ultimately from an historical source. Hence the lower dates, which ignore the regnal divisions, cannot be accepted.

[1] See IV. 11. 7 n.

[2] The Parthian campaigns are given twice, the first time in Years V and VI the second in XVI–XIX. Pliny's governorship of Bithynia is attributed to Year X, i.e. 107–8, which though near cannot be right.

[3] Philostratus, *Ap. Ty.* 8. 7. 11. Cf. Otto, op. cit. 48, n. 3; Mommsen, op. cit. 419, n. 2.

[4] I. 23. 2–4 n.

[5] x. 3A. I. 'ut toto animo delegato mihi officio vacarem.' Cf. III. 4. 2–4, 'de communis officii necessitatibus praelocuti excusare me . . . temptarunt'.

[6] There is no force in Otto's suggestion that in x. 3A. I, *alioqui* in 'omnibus advocationibus quibus alioqui numquam eram promiscue functus' means 'in other offices'. His usage of this adverb elsewhere shows that its effect is quite generalized, cf. II. 15. 2, V. 14. 3, VI. 6. 3, VII. 31. I. Besides, the

in representing Corellia against C. Caecilius Strabo or in defending Varenus in 105 and the following period.[1] As praetor he need feel such qualms only if he were one of the few praetors to whom a judicial province was assigned. His own silence might suggest that he was among the unoccupied praetors. Besides, if Domitian had turned to rend the erstwhile favoured Massa, it is unlikely that Pliny, who was ready to attack Regulus and Certus in favourable circumstances,[2] would have refused to lend a hand, when nominated by the Senate to do so, as he was.

To Otto's argument about the shortness of time there is a short answer. The trials of the numerous principals involved in the conspiracy of Piso against Nero were finished off in less than three weeks, as the indications of Tacitus make apparent. The plot was detected on the eve of the *Cereales Circenses*, 11 April, and the last major victim, Lucan, perished on 30 April.[3] If it is objected that imperial *cognitio* was swifter than trials before the Senate, then one may refer to the complicated case against the numerous friends of Caecilius Classicus, which was completed in three sessions of the Senate, that is, at most a month.[4] The delays in the extortion cases recorded by Pliny occur in the interval between indictment and hearing, not after the hearing had begun;[5] such delay cannot be presumed in cases of treason under the emperor's eye. There was, then, plenty of time in late 93 for the sevenfold accusation of the friends of Senecio.

But Otto was right in insisting that the scene described by Pliny at the end of the Massa trial does not contain the denunciation that ushered in the sevenfold trial, and hence that there may have been a further interval before the latter was set afoot. But what Massa brought against Senecio was not, as is commonly assumed from the phrase 'impietatis reum postulat', a charge of high treason, but a charge of misconduct in his duty as an advocate, akin to *calumnia*. This was the one move left to a *damnatus* to secure the reversal of his sentence.[6] It is clear from Pliny that the effect of his intervention was that Massa's charge was not accepted; that is why the judicious Nerva congratulated him. So this concession helps Otto little. Even if Senecio was not immediately charged by Massa there was plenty of

brief against Massa was not *promiscue*. Cf. Bursian, *JB*, 1929, ii. 59 ff., for this controversy.

[1] The Corellia case is dated by the consulship of Caecilius Strabo to 105 (IV. 17. 1). See v. 20 pref. for the date of the Varenus case.

[2] I. 5. 15–16, IX. 13.

[3] Tac., *Ann*. 15. 53 and 70, with Furneaux ad loc.

[4] III. 9. 18–19.

[5] Above, Introduction VII, pp. 57 f.

[6] Otto, op. cit. 45 f. VII. 33. 7–8 nn.

time left for the ruin of the seven in 93. Otto's thesis lies in ruins. That of Mommsen for 93 was always reasonable. Otto has assisted by showing the impossibility of 94 for Pliny's praetorship. A fresh argument can be found to clinch the matter.

There was always an objection to Otto's thesis in that it left Pliny very little time to hold the prefecture of the *aerarium militare* between the end of his praetorship in December 95, and his appointment to the treasury of Saturn in January, 98.[1] Such appointments were usually held for three years or longer.[2] Pliny's second prefecture lasted two years and eight months, and he comments in the Panegyricus on the exceptional distinction of his rapid promotion from it to the consulship. At the end of the Panegyric he also commits himself to the claim that when he saw that Domitian was going to extremes of iniquity, he himself desisted from the pursuit of fresh honours.[3] He would hardly have had the audacity to write this if he had not only taken a praetorship from the tyrant in 95 but at once advanced from it to the prefecture of the *aerarium militare* in 96 and continued to hold this office till the death of Domitian. The claim that his career suffered a check of sorts is repeated in sundry letters.[4] The claim may not amount to much, but is easier to understand if he had become a *privatus* again before the death of Domitian.

This argument can be pressed further. If Pliny were praetor in 95, only 96 and 97 are left for his military treasurership. Now in numerous letters of Book I Pliny appears as a man of unfettered leisure who has to account to no one for his absences from Rome, whereas when holding imperial appointments he could not quit Rome without an official leave or *commeatus* given by the emperor for limited periods, a month being the norm. Thus in I. 7. 4 he expects to be at Rome by the Ides of October, but the date is not firm. In I. 13 he protracts his stay in Rome during April of his own choice in order to hear poetical recitals. In I. 22 the illness of Titius Aristo keeps him for a long time in the city unexpectedly. He has also journeyed at leisure through the Tuscan estates of his friend Pompeia Celerina in I. 4

[1] Above, Introduction VI, pp. 75 f., for this date.

[2] Ibid.

[3] *Pan.* 95. 3–4: 'si cursu quodam provectus ab illo insidiosissimo principe antequam profiteretur odium bonorum, postquam professus est substiti, cum viderem quae ad honores compendia paterent longius iter malui'. But the only *honor* left to Pliny was the consulship. Otto, op. cit. 53, thought this a *suggestio falsi*, since Pliny could not expect the consulship by 96. But Pliny means only that he refused to take steps towards the consulship, i.e. he ceased to hold office.

[4] III. II. 2–3, IV. 24. 4–5, VII. 27. 14, 33. 8–9 nn. The praetorship, of course, is not culpable, since on any view the final 'reign of terror' begins after he became praetor. But this point does not help to decide between 93 and 95. The actual appointment would be in 92 or 94 (Oertel).

and visited Comum in I. 8, which he did not do when occupied at the *aerarium Saturni*.[1] In I. 9, an account of the daily round at Rome, he makes no mention of official tasks, but is busy only with social duties. Very different is the tone of I. 10, where he groans over his duties as treasurer, and his lack of leisure.[2]

There is then a year in the period covered by the letters of the first book—which the most ardent critics of Mommsen never sought to extend beyond the end of 98 or to push back before the death of Domitian—when Pliny was not limited by the claims of public office.[3] The April of the new age of revived literature described in I. 13 can only be that of 97, since Pliny was no longer a free man by 98, and the October when Pliny was out of Rome may be either 96 or more probably 97; for Pliny was not likely to leave Rome in the exciting weeks of Nerva's succession. Otto himself would have to admit on his own hypothesis that Pliny was not holding office when he meditated the prosecution of Regulus, and initiated his abortive attack on Certus, in January 97 and the following months.[4] For present purposes it does not matter much whether the free period falls in 96 or 97 or in 96–97. The first and third would make it impossible, and the second very difficult, to fit in the military treasurership between the end of 95, and the beginning of 98, whereas Mommsen's date runs into none of these difficulties. Again, if Pliny had been promoted by Nerva directly from the military treasury to that of Saturn—as is required if the free period is placed in 96—after only some twelve months' service under Nerva, not Domitian, he would not have passed it by in silence in the Panegyric, where he makes so much of his second promotion after a bare *biennium*. Everything— his recorded leisure in the Letters, and his remarks about his career in the Panegyric—combines to suggest that Pliny was a *privatus* through a part of 96 and all 97. A single empty year is fatal to the thesis of Otto, but it would agree with ordinary imperial practice that after a praetorship in 93 Pliny should have proceeded to a praetorian appointment for some three years, and that after a fairly short interval, which was normal in treasury appointments to

---

[1] No visit to Comum is recorded after that of I. 8. 2 until IV. I, 13. 3, 30. I. In II. 8. 2–3 he bewails his inability to visit Comum, and in III. 6 makes a tentative plan for a sudden visit—'si tamen officii ratio permiserit excurrere isto'—which may be that of IV. I.

[2] This office is shown to be the prefecture of the treasury of Saturn, not that of the *aerarium militare*, by the judicial duties which it involved, I. 10. 10 n. Hence the letter belongs to 98 or later.

[3] I. 5. 8–10 suggests that Pliny was not encumbered by a public office in late December 96 which would require him to be on his tribunal or in his bureau early in the morning. But perhaps the passage is too inexplicit to press.

[4] I. 5. II, 15, IX. 13. 13 nn.

enable the scrutiny of accounts and possible charges of *peculatus* to be made, he should advance to another office.[1] This interval of idleness would then justify in some measure his curious boast that he was out of favour in Domitian's last months.

A subsidiary argument can be found in Pliny's account of Minicius Acilianus of Brixia, whom he recommends as a prospective son-in-law to Junius Mauricus, when the returned exile was arranging his family affairs in 97 or at latest 98 (I. 14 nn.). Acilianus had completed his senatorial career up to the praetorship, so that, as Pliny remarks, there was no further necessity of canvassing for him at elections. He is a 'few years' younger than Pliny, and is depicted as looking up to Pliny not only *ut iuvenis iuvenem* but even *ut senem*, and he accepts the guidance of Pliny as his social mentor (ibid. 3). His praetorship can hardly be more recent than 96, or 97 at a pinch. If Pliny's praetorship was in 95, the whole careful structure of the situation would collapse as a manifest absurdity.

Something should be said of the ingenious attempt of Harte to place Pliny's praetorship, the expulsion of philosophers from Rome, and the visit to Artemidorus *in suburbano*, recorded in III. II. 2, before instead of after 93, and to separate these events by an interval of years from the expulsion of philosophers from Italy and the trial of Senecio, in 93 or 94. The commentary on III. II. 2–13 has shown the weakness of this theory. Harte connected Pliny's praetorship and his visit to Artemidorus *in suburbano* with an expulsion of philosophers from *Rome alone* in 88–89 or 89–90, and distinguished these events from Pliny's loan of money to Artemidorus after the Senecio trial, putting this at the time of a second expulsion of philosophers from Rome *and Italy* in 93–94 or 94–95. This ingeniously exploits Pliny's reference to an expulsion of philosophers *ab urbe*, but presses the evidence of the late chronographers beyond what they say to establish the distinction between an expulsion from Rome and an expulsion from Italy against the indications of the early sources Suetonius and Gellius, that there never was an expulsion from the city alone, which is not proved by Pliny's summary reference. But the principal objection is that the theory depends upon an improbable translation of Pliny, attributing a most uncharacteristic obscurity to his Latin, and a misuse of a particle of time.

Harte's solution, then, breaks down in its two main parts, and Pliny's praetorship returns to the niche where Mommsen lodged it. In this there are historical advantages. Tacitus stated that Agricola

---

[1] Pliny, *Pan.* 92. 2: 'tanta tibi integritatis nostrae fiducia fuit ut non dubitares te salva diligentiae tuae ratione facturum si nos post maximum officium privatos esse non sineres.' This is the exception which tests the rule.

by his opportune death escaped the worst period of Domitian's reign, and went on to enumerate the misfortunes of the Senecio faction. It is Pliny's praetorship alone that fixes the date of these trials, and the effect of Otto's date was to reduce the duration of the most notorious of all the 'terrors' of the earlier Empire to a mere twenty months' duration, or even as little as twelve if one presses the Eusebian date. That was hardly the implication of Tacitus, and very far from the underlying truth in the possibly exaggerated picture drawn by Pliny in VIII. 14. 8–9: 'proximus curiam sed curiam trepidam et elinguem cum dicere quod velles periculosum, quod nolles miserum esset . . . eadem mala iam senatores . . . multos per annos vidimus tulimusque'. This dates the troubled period back as far as Pliny's entry into the Senate in 90 or 92, according to the two theories. Even on Mommsen's chronology the 'many years' number no more than seven, with a peak of three for the worst phase, but Otto reduces them to scarcely five with a peak of less than two years.

Hanslik attempted to settle the date of Pliny's praetorship by an ingenious manipulation of the date of Domitian's Sarmatian war, commonly attributed to 92. Domitian, according to Martial (7. 6–8, 8. 2, 9. 31), was absent nearly eight months on this campaign, and returned from it to Rome at the beginning of a certain January. Hanslik sought to place the war in the year 93. Domitian would then be absent from the city from May to the end of the year, in the very months in which he should have been personally presiding over the trial of Senecio and Helvidius, if Pliny was praetor in 93[1] (Tac. *Agric.* 45. 2). But Tacitus implies the personal presence of the emperor in or near Rome throughout the summer months of 93 when Agricola was dying (ibid. 43–44). Hence Hanslik's theory does not start. Hanslik's argument rests upon a misunderstanding of the dates contained in military *diplomata*. The date of the Sarmatian war depends upon the evidence for the date of Domitian's last and isolated salutation as *imperator XXII*, which is commonly associated with that war. This appears on coins of the Roman mint and in the preamble of a military diploma (*CIL* xvi. 38) in association with Domitian's twelfth tribunician year: *tr. pot. xii.* This is the year 16 (or 30) September 92 to 15 (or 29) September 93[2]. The previous salutation, *imp. xxi*, is continuous on coins from 88–89 to the eleventh tribunician year, 91–92, and also appears on military *diplomata* within that period, of which the latest is dated to May 91.[3] In *CIL*

---

[1] *Wiener Studien*, lxiii (1948), 126–7. Cf. Vidman, *Étude*, 15.

[2] See M. Hammond, 'The tribunician day', *Mem. Am. Ac. Rome*, xix. 39 f., whose conclusions were strikingly confirmed by the subsequent discovery of the Fasti of Potentia. [3] See *RIC* ii. 170–4; *AE*, 1961, no. 319.

xvi. 38 the second section of the diploma, authorizing the award to the particular individual concerned, contains a dating in the usual style by suffect consuls known to be those of July 94, though the tribunician year is 92–93. Such discrepancies are not unknown in *diplomata*, and if not due to a mere error in the figure of the *tr. pot.* dating, may occur when the provincial distribution of the *diplomata* is postponed for reasons of policy to a year later than that of the enabling act at Rome given by the preamble.[1] The consular date does not affect the date and data in the preamble, and hence provides only a *terminus ante quem* for the imperial salutation. The determining date of that is the tribunician number, which occurs (with the present number of the emperor's consulships) in the preamble. The date of *imp. xxii* remains within the period September 92–September 93, and nothing in the *diploma* proves that it belongs to 93 rather than 92. Hence the argument that Domitian was away from Rome during the latter part of 93 does not hold.

An argument from the coinage suggests that the salutation belongs to the early part of the year 92–93, or even precedes it shortly. There exist coins of the Roman mint for Domitian's sixteenth tribunician year, September 96–September 97. They were presumably ready for issue when Domitian was murdered on 18 September 96, and were issued subsequently before the first coins of Nerva.[2] Hence it may be argued that *imp. xxii* was already known at the beginning of Domitian's twelfth tribunician year, in September 92, since it appears on all the dated issues of that year. This, rather than the uncertain chronology of Martial's books, is the reason for dating the Sarmatian campaign to 92. But it may be fairly noted that the indications in Martial favour the early date. The references to Domitian's return from the Sarmatian war form a major feature in Book 7. The return, anticipated in Poems 5–7, takes place in Poem 8. In Book 8 it is a past event in Poems 2, 11, and in Poem 65 an elaborate triumphal arch and a temple to Fortuna Redux have been erected on the site where Domitian was greeted by the populace on his famous return. The very next verses in 8, Poem 66, record the designation of a consul of 94, i.e. in late 93 or January 94. This is the latest date in these books. It is hard to believe that the return of Domitian, recorded a book earlier, belongs to the same moment. The theme of the return appears again in 9. 31 with other themes of several years earlier (cf. 5, 7, 84). Rather similarly the references to the Dacian victory are spread through several books, long past the actual moment (4. 11, 5. 3, 6. 4, 10, 76, 8. 11).

[1] Cf. F. Lepper, *Trajan's Parthian War*, 37 n. 2, and discussions cited. For an error in dating cf. *AE*, 1954, 10 a, *tr. pot. x* with *imp. xxii*.

[2] *RIC* ii. 176. Hammond, art. cit. 45. Mattingly, *JRS* xx. 80.

APPENDIX V[1]

THE EARLY PERSECUTIONS AND ROMAN LAW

SERIOUS discussion about the attitude of the Roman government to the Christian communities in the period before the Great Persecutions of the third century began in 1890 with the publication of Neumann's book and Mommsen's article on the central theme.[2] Some twenty years of controversy produced three main opinions. First, there is the theory, argued at length by Callawaert and held by most French and Belgian scholars, that there was a general enactment, precisely formulated and valid for the whole empire, which forbade the practice of the Christian religion. The origin of this is most commonly attributed to Nero, but sometimes to Domitian. Second, there is Mommsen's theory of *coercitio*, best known to English readers by Hardy's *Christianity and the Roman Government*—that the Christians were punished by the Roman governors in virtue of their ordinary power, derived from their *imperium*, of enforcing public order at their own discretion, without reference to specific legislation. The ground for such magisterial suppression in Mommsen is that the Christians offended against a canon of government in introducing an alien cult which induced 'national apostasy', the abandonment of the traditional Roman religion. Others substituted for this a general aversion to the established order and disobedience to constituted authority, but all of Mommsen's school seem to envisage the procedure as direct police action or inquisition against notable malefactors, arrest, and punishment without the ordinary forms of trial. A third school, led by Conrat, argued that the Christians were prosecuted simply under the known criminal laws for specific offences, such as child-murder, incest, magic, illegal assembly, and especially for treason—a charge based on their refusal to worship the divinity of the Roman emperor.[3] This third opinion, which may

---

[1] The greater part of Appendix V appeared in *J.T.S.*, N.S., iii (2), 1952, 199 ff. and is reprinted by the courtesy of the editor.

[2] For bibliography of works previous to 1914 cited in the first two paragraphs see *CAH*, xii. 775 (h). L. Vidman, *Étude*, 90–96, provides a good brief resumé of the controversy, and reaches conclusions similar to those propounded in this article, which he did not see. So too A. Ronconi, *Studi ... Paoli* (Florence, 1956), 615 ff. See also Th. Mayer-Maly, 'Der rechtsgeschichtliche Gehalt der Christenbriefen von Plinius', *Stud. et Doc. Hist. Iur.* 1956, 311 ff.

[3] To Conrat's book, cited ibid., add E. Le Blant, *Les Persécutions et les martyrs*, (Paris, 1893); A. Profumo, *Le fonti ed i tempi dell'incendio neroniano*

be called the 'common law' theory, has usually been combined with the *coercitio* theory, but some scholars have attributed all Christian persecution to a single criminal charge, notably treason, or illegal assembly, or the introduction of an alien cult.

The controversy had spent its force by about 1913, when the Italian Manaresi and the American Canfield in well-balanced summaries of the controversy favoured the *coercitio* theory, but admitted that Trajan's rescript to Pliny, endorsing his coercitial procedure, might have had the ultimate effect of a general law. Subsequently the controversy slumbered, save for a vigorous attempt of Merrill to revive the theory of a single crime in favour of the law against illegal assembly.[1] Yet strangely the two main schools of thought have persisted side by side without paying much attention to one another. Generally the French historians of the early church have taken for granted the theory of the 'general law',[2] while the Germans have been faithful to Mommsen's *coercitio*. W. Weber could dismiss the 'general law' as quite unproven in a brief footnote to a discussion of Pliny's Bithynian persecution, and H. Lietzman, summarizing the *coercitio* theory in his Church history, was similarly cavalier.[3]

Of recent years the controversy has flared up again. First M. Bourgéry, and then M. Dieu more effectively, reasserted the *coercitio* theory against the French school, and drove the present champion of the General Law, M. Zeiller, to modify it.[4] M. Grégoire, while avoiding the specific juridical point, has argued that any official enactment of a general nature was suspended during the reigns of Hadrian, Pius, and Marcus Aurelius.[5] Several scholars have discussed the basis of the Neronian persecution,[6] and a more promising presentation has been made of the core of Mommsen's theory of 'national apostasy' in this connexion.[7] Meanwhile in 1937 the then

(Rome, 1905) and P. Brezzi, *Cristianesimo ed impero romano* (ed. 2, Rome, 1944). Books and articles accrue, but generally present nothing new.

[1] E. T. Merrill, *Essays in Early Christian History* (London, 1924).

[2] Notably H. Leclercq, 'Droit persécuteur', *Dict. d'arch. chrét. et de liturg.* iv. 2, c. 1565; J. Zeiller–J. Lebreton, *Histoire de l'église* (Paris, 1946), i. 293 ff.

[3] H. Lietzman, *Founding of the Church Universal* (Eng. Tr.,[2] London, 1950), ii, ch. vi; W. Weber, *Festgabe von Fachgenossen v. K. Müller* (Tübingen, 1922), 37, n. 1.

[4] L. Dieu, *Rev. d'hist. ecclés.* (1942), 5 ff. A. Bourgéry, *Latomus* (1938), 106 ff. E. Griffe also, *Bull. litt. ecclés. de Toulouse* (1949), 131 ff., summarized in *Année philologique* (1949), 292, and B. Motzo, *Atene e Roma*, 1921. Contra: J. Zeiller, *Rev. d'hist. ecclés.* (1951), 521 ff., and in *Analecta Bollandia* (1949), 49 f.

[5] H. Grégoire, *Les Persécutions dans l'empire romain* (Brussels, 1951), 24 ff., 138 ff.   [6] Below, p. 781, nn. 2–4.

[7] S. L. Guterman, *Religious Toleration and Persecution in Ancient Rome* (London, 1951), 27–48. So too Griffe, apparently, in form of *coercitio*, art. cit.

Camden Professor amplified a hint of Hardy, that the Roman government only suppressed strange religions, such as Druidism and Christianity, when they were shown to give rise to scandalous behaviour.[1]

The position, then, is once more open, but it is noteworthy that Roman historians proper have shown a marked preference for some form of the *coercitio* theory, combined or not with that of the specific crime. No Roman historian seems to have supported wholeheartedly the notion of a general law of early date, for three main reasons. First, the limited and sporadic nature of the persecutions down to Tertullian's time and later is against it, while the evidence of the Apologists tends to deny official action under certain emperors. Secondly, the well-known passages in Pliny, Suetonius, and Tacitus do not require it. Thirdly, the specific references in Tertullian's *Apology* to *leges*, whereby *non licet esse Christianos*, are too forensic and rhetorical to prove it. The theory of a General Law was formulated at a time when the historical perspective of the early persecutions was barely becoming clear. The great works of Mommsen's school on the administration, local government, and social fabric of the Roman Empire, greatly expanded by detailed studies of single municipalities and provinces in the succeeding period, have shown the extreme insignificance of the Christian communities in the vast framework of the empire. Hence there arises a general improbability either that the Christians seemed important enough to the government of Nero and Domitian to require a measure of universal suppression, or that any action taken was more than local and temporary.

Meanwhile a separate investigation has been afoot into the legal status of the Christian associations as corporative bodies.[2] Though explanations differ widely, all scholars seem to be agreed that either *de iure* or *de facto* the churches enjoyed effective property rights before the Decian troubles, save in moments of active persecution. This offers no difficulty to the *coercitio* theory, but is hard to reconcile with the General Law.

Of recent years the discussion has mostly been out of the hands of Roman institutional historians, and the protagonists have worked on the same assumptions about Roman administration and public law as held good in Hardy's generation. For a restatement of the case for *coercitio* within these limits it would be hard to better the expositions of MM. Dieu and Grégoire. But in the last half century

---

[1] H. Last, 'The Study of the Persecutions', *JRS*, 1937, 80 ff.

[2] G. Bovini, *La proprietà ecclesiastica* etc. (Milan, 1949), surveys most previous work. The most substantial discussion of *collegia* in Roman Law is F. de Robertis, *Il diritto associativo romano* (Bari, 1938); cf. also P. W. Duff, *Personality in Roman Private Law* (Cambridge, 1938), ch. v.

developments in the study of imperial administration, particularly in the field of *cognitio* and criminal law, have altered the setting of the Christian problem. Hence it is possible to bring fresh objections against the General Law, and to restate the theory of *coercitio* in a more acceptable form.

The advocates of the General Law seem now to fall into two classes. First there are those who have realized that imperial edicts, especially of emperors who suffered *damnatio memoriae*, died with their authors, and that any general law can only have been a standing imperial edict renewed at the beginning of each Principate.[1] But the amended theory is more vulnerable than its predecessor. A new issue should have been more effective than an obsolescent rule; yet Grégoire rightly points out that on Tertullian's own evidence there had been no persecution in Africa down to the case of the Scillitan martyrs in the proconsulship of Saturninus, A.D. 180.[2] The evidence of the Apologists exculpating Vespasian, Hadrian, Pius, and Marcus Aurelius, is harder for the new version than the old to explain away.[3] Trajan certainly issued no edict in A.D. 98 for the Bithynian anti-Christians to quote to Pliny in 111–12, or for Trajan himself to reaffirm.[4] The rescript of Hadrian to the proconsul of Asia, even in its present rather garbled form, implies that there was no general edict known to the proconsul or approved by the emperor, and the document may mean that the Christians were henceforth to be prosecuted only for ordinary crimes.[5]

Then there are those who, adopting a form of the 'common law' theory, attribute great weight to Tertullian's description of 'accusation of the Name' as an *institutum Neronianum*, and now identify this with his *vetus decretum* forbidding the introduction of new religions, explaining the *institutum* as an application to the Christian sect of the Republican principle that it is a capital offence to introduce a *nova superstitio* unauthorized into the Roman state.[6] Dr. S. L. Guterman has recently shown that this principle was still sporadically enforced in the Julio-Claudian period.[7] But though this theory might explain persecution at Rome it fails to explain it in the provinces. In the study of the minor persecutions there has been too ready an assumption that any scrap of *ius publicum*, and especially the *leges*

---

[1] e.g. Zeiller, art. cit. (1951), 523–4.

[2] Grégoire, op. cit. 30 f.; Tert. *Scap.* 3. 4.

[3] Melito in Euseb. *HE* 4. 26 (190); Tert. *Ap.* 5.

[4] x. 96–97. Cf. Weber, art. cit. 36–37; Dieu, art. cit. 15.

[5] Euseb. *HE* 4. 9. Grégoire takes the extremer view, op. cit. 139 f.; but the interpretation is far from certain; cf. L. H. Canfield, *Early Persecutions of the Christians* (N.Y., 1913), pt. i, ch. v, and for the text, 193 ff.

[6] Tert. *Ap.* 5. 1; *Nat.* i. 7; cf. Zeiller, art. cit. (1951), 527 ff., on Griffe, art. cit.

[7] Op. cit. 27–40.

publicae of the Roman political and criminal law, can be transferred at will from a Roman or Italian to a provincial context. Of this more anon, but what applies in public law to Italy and Roman citizens is far from applying automatically to provinces and *peregrini*. In any case it requires no long demonstration that the Romans, who were remarkably tolerant of religious innovations in Italy, were indifferent to the religion of their subjects in the provinces.

A second form of the foregoing theory, originated by Profumo in 1905 and still maintained by some scholars, is that the *institutum Neronianum* is really an *institutum Tiberianum*, and means that the Christians were accused of a complex of offences, including some, such as the introduction of a new cult, that were construed as *maiestas*, and hence that the whole accusation was covered by the extension of the treason law as it operated in the senatorial court under Tiberius.[1] This involves a very improbable transfer of senatorial procedure—which the theory hardly interprets correctly—to the jurisdiction of the City Prefect, or whoever dealt with Christians at Rome, and thence to provincial jurisdiction. It has no better evidence to commend it than Tertullian's statements that Christians were in his day popularly regarded as *hostes publici* and *maiestatis rei*.[2] That provincial *peregrini* were accused directly on the grounds of *maiestas* certainly does not fit Pliny's letter to Trajan.

So much for the General Law. The weakness of the *coercitio* theory is that its earlier exponents failed to provide a satisfactory offence which should render the Christians liable to 'coercion'. Mommsen's theory of national apostasy, which is largely based on the charges brought popularly against Christians in the age of Tertullian and Celsus, does not fit a provincial context in the earlier Empire. It may account for action taken at Rome or against Romans under Nero, but Mommsen's own attempts to explain the extension to *peregrini* are unconvincing.[3] Others, as Ramsay and Hardy, dissatisfied with 'apostasy', have pressed the nuisance value of the Christians and reduced the matter to the repression of recalcitrant persons.[4] A plea made in Trajan's reign shows the extent of *coercitio*:[5] 'esse . . . se provinciales et ad omne proconsulum imperium metu cogi'. None the less, Christians did not provoke arrest by openly defying

---

[1] Profumo, op. cit., 197 ff.; Guterman, op. cit. 45; E. Wolf, 'Ecclesia pressa', *Theolog. Lit.-Zeit.* (1947), 223 ff.; U. Hüntemann, *Theol. Quartalschrift.*, 1932, 72 ff.   [2] Tert. *Ap.* 28. 3, 35–36.

[3] Cf. ibid. 24. 1, 'crimen laesae . . . Romanae religionis'. On Mommsen, *GS* iii. 395, 405–6; cf. Last, art. cit. 81. For the ordinary distinction cf. Acts xvi. 21. 'They teach customs which we, *as Romans*, may not practise.'

[4] W. Ramsay, *The Church in the Roman Empire* (London, 1893), 207 ff.; Hardy, op. cit. 62, 91 ff.

[5] III. 9. 15.

proconsular authority. Hence it is next shown from a passage of Ulpian's *De officio proconsulis* that the searching out and punishment of ordinary malefactors and robbers fell under *coercitio*.[1] The Christians are identified with these malefactors as sheer 'enemies of of society', *hostes humani generis*, activated by an *odium humani generis*, on the grounds of their religion, as in Ramsay, or as in Hardy's refinement, because their antisocial tendency involved a 'latent political disobedience'.[2] In either case the offence exists, not 'in the eyes of the law' but 'in the eyes of the police administration', and is curbed by direct police action. So too M. Dieu thinks that the Christians were coerced because they were the indirect cause of public disturbances.[3]

The weakness of such a theory lies partly in the implicit idea of a cultural nationalism alien to Roman provincial practice, but more seriously in its assumptions about police procedure and provincial jurisdiction. A police administration in the required sense hardly existed save in a few capital cities, such as Lyons, Carthage, and Alexandria, where it is known that armed forces were stationed which could be thus used. Elsewhere a most rudimentary police force was provided by the municipal authorities.[4] The irenarch, in the eastern cities, was supposed to cope with robbers and brigands. Prisoners whose offences were serious were sent with a statement of the charges, *elogium*, to the provincial governor, but even against manifest brigands the charges had to be properly presented in court.[5] The sphere of *animadversio* without formal trial, or *de plano*, was much more limited than the older expositions of *coercitio* allow.[6] Apart from manifest offenders the enforcement of law and order depended upon private initiative. The system can be seen at work in the adventures of St. Paul. At Philippi and Corinth he is brought before the municipal magistrates and the proconsul respectively by private enemies. At Ephesus the 'town clerk' advises St. Paul's enemies to charge him properly at the proconsular assizes. So too Festus: 'it is not the custom among the Romans to give up anyone

[1] *Dig*. 1. 18. 13.

[2] Hardy, loc. cit., confuses this *odium* with *contumacia*, on which see below, p. 784. For *odium humani generis* see H. Fuchs, 'Tacitus über die Christen', *Vigiliae Christianae* (1950), 82–88, who shows that it is a concept compounded of Hellenistic 'misanthropy', and Jewish exclusiveness.

[3] Hardy, op. cit. 63, 77, 91, following Mommsen, *GS* iii. 404–11. Dieu, art. cit. 14 ff. So too Lietzman, op. cit. ii. 158.

[4] Cf. W. Liebenam, *Städteverwaltung im r. Kaiserreiche* (Leipzig, 1900), 357 f.; A. H. M. Jones, *The Greek City* (Oxford, 1940), 212–13, 349, n. 4; G. Lopuszanski, 'La police romaine et les chrétiens', *Ant. Class.* (1951), 7, 46.

[5] *Dig*. 48. 3, 6, rescripts of Hadrian and Pius. Cf. Tert. *Ap*. 2. 4.

[6] *Dig*. 1. 16. 9. 3, 48. 2. 6, from Ulpian, *De off. proc.* Cf. Brasiello (cited p. 782 n. 1), p. 396. *RE* IV, s.v. 'cognitio', c. 214–15.

for punishment before the accused has had his accusers face to face, and has had an opportunity of defending himself'. Only in the special circumstances of turbulent Jerusalem does the police force of the governor intervene.[1]

There is evidence enough from Trajan onwards that the emperors insisted that all charges against Christians must be made in proper form by a private *accusator* or *delator*, who is not an informer, *index*, but a private prosecutor. No charge, then no case. In addition the letter of Hadrian extends to trials of Christians the ordinary protection of the *calumnia* process, which heavily discouraged vexatious prosecutions. Pliny as governor of Bithynia-Pontus became involved with Christians because they were prosecuted by others before his court: *ad me tamquam Christiani deferebantur*. He did not initiate action, though he must have 'sought out' the persons later named anonymously and by an informer. Trajan authorizes only private accusation. The Apologists too complain not of inquisition but of delation, though inquisition sometimes took place, as in the martyrdoms at Lyons, against orders.[2] Tertullian's complaint that the Christians were not allowed the ordinary forms of defence means not that the procedure was inquisitorial, but that the accused was only allowed to defend himself against the charge of Christianity; he was not allowed to defend Christianity itself any more than a murderer might defend murder. Similarly Tertullian objects to *accusatio nominis* as abnormal, simply because there was no detailed specification of a particular deed.[3]

Normally, then, the prosecution of Christians followed the forms of the *cognitio* system of penal jurisdiction in which proconsular *coercitio* finds its usual expression. Book XLVII sections 11–22 of the *Digest* defines a wide range of offences which gradually evolved in the empire, outside the schedule or *ordo* of the older criminal code of the *leges publicae*, and hence are known as the *crimina extra ordinem*. They cover many forms of wrongdoing, but not 'whatever was inconvenient to the police administration', and their mode of operation is not police action but private delation.[4] So too there must

---

[1] Acts xvi. 19–40, xvii. 6–8, xviii. 12–15, xix. 35–38, xxi. 31–40, xxii. 24–29, xxv. 15–16. Cf. A. N. Sherwin-White, *Roman Society and Roman Law in the New Testament*, 48 ff., 78 ff.

[2] x. 96–97; Euseb. *HE* 4. 9; Tert. *Fuga* 12. 12; *Scap.* 4. 4; Athenagoras, *Leg.* 1; Melito in Euseb. *HE* 4. 26. Cf. Wolf, art. cit. 225. For Lyons, Euseb. *HE* 5. 1.

[3] Tert. *Nat.* 1. 2–3. *Ap.* 2.

[4] *Dig.* 47. 17. 1, 19. 2, 20. 3 pref., for delation, all from Ulpian *De off. proc.*, more generally ibid. 47. 15. 6 (Paulus), 48. 2. 7. Cf. A. Beck, *Römisches Recht bei Tertullian und Cyprian* (Halle, 1930), 78–80, with bibliography ibid. 79, n. 2, and below, p. 782, n. 1. See for *cognitio* in the early Principate A. N. Sherwin-White, *Roman Society* etc. 13 ff.

be a specific malefaction that could be urged by a private prosecutor against Christians. Hardy's 'latent political disobedience', which would explain a police inquisition, will not fit here. This disobedience is first mentioned in Pliny's letter, where it appears not as the prime ground of the accusation and condemnation, but as a subsequent discovery. Pliny cut off the heads of the first batch because they were 'Christiani', not because they refused to sacrifice to *di nostri*—he did not require them to do so—nor because they obstinately refused to change their habits, when ordered to do so, though he thought the latter a good alternative reason for punishment when he began to have qualms about the formal charge.

Thus there is already in Pliny's time a specific charge which fits the 'General Law' better than the older *coercitio* theory. E. T. Merrill tried a short cut, the theory of the illicit *collegium*, holding that the Christian offence consisted simply in holding meetings contrary to imperial legislation about social clubs.[1] Recent investigations into this topic have tended to conclusions the very opposite of Merrill's. De Robertis has argued that there was a general enabling act of Julio-Claudian date which legitimized without further registration precisely such groups as the Christians would form, *collegia tenuiorum religionis causa*.[2] Others have argued for a yet wider freedom of association.[3] At most the limitation of free association was concerned with a different group, professional associations and the social clubs of the middle classes, types which might take on a political tone. For such there was in Italy, and later in some provinces, a system of licences controlled by the Senate or Princeps.[4] Apart from this consideration Merrill's argument illustrates the same weakness as is shown by the theory of national apostasy. He assumes the early and universal application throughout the Empire of a certain Augustan *Lex Iulia de collegiis*, because the lawyers quoted in the *Digest* title *de collegiis* speak as though control was—eventually—general. The topic is much more complex than Merrill realized, but even so one *Digest* text makes it clear that a crucial part of the legislation affecting *collegia tenuiorum* was not widely applied outside Rome before the time of Septimius Severus.[5] A long process of development may lie between the passing of an enactment affecting Italy and its adoption as a general canon of provincial administration. It is true that Pliny in Bithynia had decreed a general suppression of political

[1] Merrill, op. cit., ch. vii. So too Beck, op. cit., 77 f., 81–82.

[2] De Robertis, op. cit., esp. 371–4.

[3] e.g. Bovini, op. cit., ch. iv, esp. 135–42. Summary of other theories ibid., ch. iii. For a more cautious view cf. Wolf, art. cit. 223–4, Duff, op. cit., ch. v.

[4] De Robertis, op. cit. 195, 219 ff.

[5] *Dig.* 47. 22. 1 pref.: 'quod non tantum in urbe sed et in Italia et in provinciis locum habere divus *quoque* Severus rescripsit'.

clubs, which had recently been troublesome there.[1] But he himself did not connect it with the Christian offence, and admits that the Christians claimed to have obeyed it. Later, a passage in Tertullian shows that illegal association was one charge, not the sole charge, sometimes urged against Christians, but he also shows that it was easily disproved. This very passage is the main prop of those who argue that the Christians might legally establish *collegia*, provided that they were subject to no other ban.[2]

There remains the theory of the specific criminal charge, as expounded especially by Conrat, who argued that in many cases Christians were accused under the ordinary criminal law, e.g. of *maiestas* for refusing homage to Caesar, of 'apostasy' if they were Roman citizens, or of disregarding the laws of association. Such charges can be supported by literal interpretation of some passages in Tertullian's *Apology*, and may be the charges envisaged by Hadrian's rescript to Fundanus,[3] but they do not fit the evidence of Pliny's letter, in which it is plain that the persons were accused *tamquam Christiani*, or the preponderant complaints of the Apologists that Christians were normally accused of the 'name'.[4] Conrat's theory, however, does allow for Pliny's question to Trajan: 'Nomen ipsum si flagitiis careat an flagitia cohaerentia nomini puniantur?' He suggests that the Romans, instead of forbidding the general practice of Christianity, tended to particularize certain aspects of Christian behaviour as criminal.[5] If Conrat's argument is combined with the approach suggested by Mr. Last in *Journal of Roman Studies*, 1937, and with a proper appreciation of the *cognitio* system, a solution can be put forward which avoids the pitfalls both of the General Law and of the *coercitio* theories.

Mr. Last compared the Roman treatment of Christians with that of other forbidden sects. There is common ground between Livy's account, echoing Augustan ideas, of the repression of the Bacchanalian scandals in the second century B.C., the Julio-Claudian policy towards Druids, and the treatment of the Christians. The Romans ceased to tolerate these cults when they appeared to give rise to anti-social acts, *scelera* or *flagitia*. Bacchanals and Druids murdered men in secret rites, and Christians were believed to do similar things.

---

[1] Pliny, x. 96. 7. For the situation in Bithynia see x. 34, 93 nn.

[2] *Ap.* 38–39, on which see de Robertis, op. cit. 375–81, G. Krüger, *Die Rechtsstellung der vorkonstantinischen Kirchen* (Stuttgart, 1935), 91–107. Cf. also Mayer-Maly, art. cit. 325.

[3] *Ap.* 27–35, 38–39. Cf. above, p. 775, n. 5. Canfield, op. cit. 109, argues, with Ramsay, that Hadrian's rescript does not exclude 'accusatio nominis'.

[4] e.g. Justin, *Ap.* 1. 4; Athenagoras, *Leg.* 2; Tert. *Ap.* 2–3.

[5] M. Conrat, *Die Christenverfolgungen . . . vom Standpunkte des Juristen* (Leipzig, 1897), 76.

When cult and *scelera* appear inseparable, a total ban, or strict control, may be placed upon a particular cult. So because of the *flagitia*, the *nomen*, active membership of a criminal organization without further proof of individual guilt is constituted a capital charge, by direct magisterial action, that is, by an *edictum* with or without support of a senatorial decree. The charge is enforced by *coercitio*, normally through the procedural form of *cognitio*. The *nomen* then acts as a pointer to the magistrate, indicating a man whom it is proper for him to coerce as a malefactor, if accused: 'praesumatis de sceleribus nostris ex nominis confessione'.

This is certainly how the Julio-Claudians sought to deal with the Druids,[1] and it is the most obvious explanation of the evidence of Pliny and Tacitus about Christians. Tacitus believed in the *flagitia*, though he did not believe that the Christians fired Rome, and therefore reckoned them *sontes et novissima exempla meritos*.[2] Pliny, disproving the *flagitia*, could not believe that the *nomen* alone was punishable. The procedure before Nero's magistrate, so far as it can be disentangled from the brevity of Tacitus and Suetonius, seems to have involved both *flagitia* or *scelera*—charges of 'Thyestean banquets', of incendiarism and perhaps magic too—and the *nomen* principle: *primum correpti qui fatebantur* (sc. *se Christianos esse*).[3] There may have been a proscription of the sect on account of the *flagitia*, by a magisterial edict, either before or, more probably, after the establishment of the *incendium* charge.[4] How such proscription might be later extended to the provinces will be explained below.

Yet is not this to readmit the General Law by the backdoor after dismissing it by the front portal? The procedure may be 'coercitial', the religious aspect may not be the basis of the veto; yet this presentation seems to admit the principle of accusation by a standing

[1] The action against Druids seems to depend on an imperial edict reaffirming a former *SC.* against human sacrifice. Pliny, *NH* 29. 54, 30. 13; Suet. *Claudius* 25. 5. Also Pomponius Mela 3. 2. 18; Victor, *De Caes.* 4. 2; H. Last, 'Rome and the Druids', *JRS*, 1949, 1 ff. For previous citation see *Ap.* 2. 11.

[2] Fuchs's scholarly discussion, with full bibliography, of the problems arising from Tac. *Ann.* 15. 44, cited above, p. 777, n. 2, reasserts the fidelity of Tacitus' narrative, improving on A. G. Roos, 'Nero and the Christians', *Symbolae van Oven* (Leiden, 1946), 297 ff., against M. Dibelius's attempt to deny a connexion between the Fire and the Neronian trials (*Forschungen und Fortschritte*, xviii (1942), 189).

[3] Cf. Fuchs. art. cit. 77–78; the imperfect is decisive for the meaning. F. W. Clayton, *Cl. Q.* 1947, 81 ff., exaggerates the ambiguity of this and other phrases.

[4] Roos, art. cit. 302 and n. 13, followed by Fuchs, art. cit. 82, n. 31, shows that Tacitus' *crimen incendii* cannot be eliminated from the affair. But Suetonius' terms, *Nero* 16. 2, 'animadversa . . . et coercita', 'genus hominum superstitionis novae et maleficae', are more helpful for the technical aspect; cf. Bourgéry, art. cit. 106 f. For the connexion of *maleficium* with magic cf. Apuleius, *Apology*, 28–30; H. Janne, *Latomus*, 1937, 50 f.

edict, presumably Nero's *institutum* again. The answer lies in a consideration of jurisdiction *extra ordinem*. The charges and penalties for the major *crimina ordinaria*, fixed by Roman statutes for Italy, may often have provided the governors with a model for their provincial jurisdiction in this sphere. But everything else was left very largely to the discretion of the governor, whose *imperium* gave him power of life and death over all non-citizens, but did not compel him to use it. The more recent studies of the *cognitio* process have stressed the freedom enjoyed by governors during the first two centuries of the Principate in recognizing *crimina* and determining sentences *extra ordinem*.[1] It is only in and after the late second century that the government sought to limit this power and so to codify gradually the *crimina extra ordinem*.[2] The action of a magistrate of Nero in proscribing the Christian sect among the urban rabble constituted no general law, and was in no way, then or later, binding on provincial governors. Proconsuls, and City Prefects too, could take the same line on subsequent occasions, or not, as they thought fit. The evidence is that over large parts of the Empire for long periods they did not see fit. Suetonius' terms for the Neronian innovation—*animadversa . . . coercita . . . instituta*, and Tertullian's *institutum*, cannot be pressed beyond this.[3] Tertullian himself admits, in this very passage, that Nero's *acta* were technically cancelled. The knowledge of the Neronian precedent, however, could spread, after so famous an incident as the Fire, and local enemies of Christians could try it out with provincial governors. But it lay in the governor's discretion whether to accept or refuse accusations, how to manage the case if accepted, and how to sentence the guilty, whether to a particular form of death, or to the mines, or to relegation. Pliny's letter is evidence of just such a 'try out', in which the governor, though ignorant of the custom, first accepts local advice and later trusts to his coercive powers for justification.[4] Four out of six governors of Africa, mentioned by Tertullian, and a proconsul of Asia, refused prosecutions or devised new procedures favourable to the accused.[5] It is because the governors enjoyed such discretion that

---

[1] U. Brasiello's monumental *La repressione penale in diritto romano* (Naples, 1937), continually stresses the independence of the governors in the earlier period, e.g. 273 f., 292 f. Cf. also F. de Robertis, 'Arbitrium Iudicantis', *Z–S.* (1939), 219–60. G. Cardascia, 'L'apparition dans le droit des classes d'honestiores et d'humiliores', *Rev. hist. de droit fr. étr.* (1950), 305 ff., 461 ff.

[2] Cf. Cardascia, art. cit. 473, Brasiello, op. cit. 174.

[3] Cf. Motzo, art. cit. 2.

[4] Cf. Weber, art. cit. 34–36. The 'test' was suggested by others, x. 96. 5.

[5] Tert. *Scap.* 3–5. Cf. Gallio's refusal of jurisdiction, Acts xviii. 15; Beck, op. cit. 80, n. 1.

Tertullian addressed his *Apology* and *Ad Scapulam*, with their technical protests at the form of accusation, to the governors and not the emperor: the remedy lay in the governor's *arbitrium*. In Lucian the legate of Syria, understanding something of Christianity, releases Peregrinus, at that time a notable Christian leader, on the ground of expediency, because he wanted to be a martyr.[1]

Should a governor have doubts, he could consult the Princeps, who would advise him by a rescript. This then bound him, and might be invoked later in the same province to induce others to follow the same line. But the rescript would not be automatically applicable by later governors unless the emperor saw fit to include it in the general instructions, *mandata*, issued to them. The sporadic nature of the pre-Decian persecutions suggests that this was not commonly done. Still less likely is it that any such rescripts of the Flavio-Trajanic period, including Trajan's reply to Pliny, were generalized for the whole empire at an early date.[2] The statement of Lactantius, that Ulpian in his *De officio proconsulis*, Book VII, collected the rescripts affecting Christians, suggests that no generalization took place earlier.[3] Accordingly where the governor of a province refused to exercise *cognitio* against Christians, their communities could live freely and organize themselves openly under the laws permitting religious associations.

The objection arises: if the *nomen* was only proscribed on account of the *flagitia*, ought not complete toleration to have supervened when it was found, as Pliny began to find, that the *flagitia* did not exist? Here Conrat's thesis helps. As fast as one *crimen* proved baseless, another took its place, better substantiated, as the *cohaerens scelus*. Pliny thought the Christians virtuous men who deserved punishment for their excessive obstinacy in refusing to obey a reasonable order. This obstinacy came out particularly on the test requiring homage to the *di nostri*. This refusal did not render them guilty of *maiestas*. Neither Pliny nor Trajan takes that line in the letters, and Trajan is otherwise known to have been most averse to making his cult the basis of treason charges.[4] The common assumption that the provincials were compelled to take part in the ceremonies of the imperial cult is not well grounded. The cult was supposed to be voluntary, and its ceremonies were administered by and largely confined to the municipal and provincial aristocracies.[5]

[1] Lucian, *De Morte Peregrini*, 14.

[2] Cf. Pliny's reluctance to enforce earlier rescripts, x. 65–66, 72. See x. 97. 1 n. Vidman, *Étude*, 94–95.

[3] Lactantius, *Div. Inst.* 5. 11. 19.

[4] Cf. x. 82. 1; Weber, art. cit. 37.

[5] For the general organization cf. E. Beurlier, *Le Culte rendu aux empereurs romains* (Paris, 1890), pt. iii, chs. 1 and 2; L. R. Taylor, *Divinity of the Roman*

But the test was reasonable, and its refusal revealed what the lawyers called *contumacia*. For Trajan, the disciplinarian, that sufficed. There is evidence enough in the classical lawyers that *contumacia* was regarded very seriously. Earlier, under Nero, a remarkable document describes the indignation and severe threats of a proconsul of Sardinia at the *longa contumacia* of a community which had persistently failed to comply with an official decision in a dispute about boundaries.[1] Hardy rightly seized upon this point, though he wrongly made it the original ground of Christian persecution. Christians gained a name for wanton contumacy that proved their perpetual undoing. The better documented trials of the second and early third centuries show that, whatever the popular view of Christians might be, this *contumacia* was the core of the official objection. Marcus Aurelius says just this, for his ψιλὴ παράταξις is a literal translation of *mera contumacia*.[2] In addition to Pliny's letter and Tertullian's instances, Lucian's account of the acquittal of Peregrinus, Eusebius' description of the trial of Polycarp, the early Acts of the Scillitan martyrs, and the Acts of Apollonius, all show the remarkable reluctance of Roman officials to condemn Christians and their anxiety to induce them to withdraw from an unnecessary opposition to public authority.[3] They are only condemned when their *contumacia* has been proved. The proconsul says in the Scillitan Acts: 'though time was given to them to return to the Roman tradition, yet they remained obstinate in their will. Therefore I condemn them to death by the sword.' This change in the *cohaerens scelus* explains the old puzzle, that the official policy was to grant a *locus paenitentiae*. Had the old *flagitia* still been believed, or had the charge of *maiestas* been taken seriously, Christians could hardly have escaped punishment.

There may have been further changes in the interpretation of the *cohaerens scelus*. A wide interpretation could be given to *contumacia*, and in the age of Celsus the *scelus* could embrace what would have seemed less important at an earlier time, the Christian disregard for the religious tradition of Rome, Mommsen's national apostasy or

Emperor (Middletown, Conn., 1931), ch. viii. The Julio-Claudian attitude of official reluctance (cf. Claudius' letter to the Alexandrines and Tiberius' to Gytheum, Charlesworth, *Documents*, C2; *E-J* 102) was reaffirmed by Trajan (cf. n. 4, above) after the aberrations of Domitian, which are not known to have extended to the provinces, *pace* Ramsay, op. cit. 275, 295 f.; cf. *CAH* xi. 41–42. In the third century things were different, cf. D. V. Berchem, *Museum Helueticum*, 1944, 102.

[1] e.g. *Dig.* 48. 19. 4, 5 pref. *Coll. Mos. et Rom. leg.* 15. 2. 2. *FIRA*, i. n. 59.
[2] M. Antoninus, *Ad se ipsum*, 11. 3.
[3] Eusebius, *HE* 4. 15, 5. 21. For the *Acta* see conveniently Hardy, op. cit. 151 ff.; J. A. Robinson, *Texts and Studies* (Cambridge, 1891), i. 104 f. For Tertullian, above, p. 782 n. 5.

Hardy's antisocial tendency—in other words ἀθεότης and *odium humani generis*. In Lucian's well-informed account of the Church in *De Morte Peregrini* and in his brief reference in the *Alexander* there is no trace of the scandalous charges.[1] The *cohaerens scelus* in his opinion, which may well represent the popular view rather than the official standpoint, is ἀθεότης: the Christians deny the Hellenic gods. No doubt the official policy was far from clear to the persecuted, who, accused technically of the Name, did not perceive the underlying cause, and it did not suit the Apologists to be fair to the imperial policy on this point. It remains true that the Roman official is indifferent to the religious aspects in the known cases, provided that the Christian sheds his *contumacia*. But the sentence of the proconsul, above, illustrates the infiltration of a newer, more religious interpretation under cover of the old.[2]

A passage from Ulpian about the treatment of *Magi* and *Chaldaei* illuminates the treatment of Christians, though its starting-point is a kind of 'general law'.[3] A *Senatusconsultum* of A.D. 16 made it a capital offence under the *ordo* system for Romans to practise magical or prophetic arts in Italy, foreign practitioners being punished *extra ordinem*. This was enforced in different ways at different times. The question arose whether the offence consisted in giving audiences (*exercitio, professio*), or in mere knowledge of black arts (*scientia*). The earlier interpreters condemned only *professio*. One might study freely but was punished *pro mensura consultationis*. Under this partial toleration the *Magi* waxed insolent, and began to practise publicly. This, says Ulpian, was *contumacia*. Hence most emperors

---

[1] *De Morte Peregrini* 11–14, esp. 13. *Alexander* 25.

[2] I am in agreement with Mr. de Ste.-Croix in his view, expressed in a lecture at an Oxford congress in 1961 and later published, that the basic ground for the popular objection to the Christians was their otherness and exclusiveness. This is made very clear by Lucian, whom he did not quote. This objection was most easily reduced to a formal charge under the heading of ἀθεότης, or of *maiestas* if the imperial divinity was taken into account. The question is, when did the popular become the official view? The evidence makes it clear that there is no trace of an official charge of 'atheism' in the period before Hadrian, and suggests that these religious charges were frequently not approved by governors in the later second century. Vidman (*Étude*, 95–96) distinguishes too abruptly between *flagitia* as the cause of popular feeling and *obstinatio* as the official ground. Equally his distinction between 'superstition' which the Romans repress for non-religious reasons, and 'religion' of which they are tolerant, conceals a fallacy. For one of the effects of a *superstitio* was to withdraw men from due observance of their obligations to the civic gods, as in the Bacchanalian affair. For Mr. de Ste.-Croix's article see further p. 787.

[3] From *De off. proc.* 3 cited in *Coll. Mos. et Rom. Leg.* xv. ii. For the occasion see Dio 47. 15. 8; Tac. *Ann.* 2. 27–32; Suet. *Tib.* 36. For commentary see Brasiello, op. cit. 231 ff., who suggests that the *SC.* brought the offence under the *Lex Cornelia de veneficiis*.

3 E

imposed a total ban: 'Ne quis omino huiusmodi ineptiis se immis-ceret.' Ulpian makes it clear that this took effect not by a general ordinance for the whole Empire, but by a series of rescripts answering the queries of provincial governors couched in terms like Pliny's *quid et quatenus puniri soleat ?*[1] He then gives his own opinion that all such persons should be punished 'because they practise wicked arts against the peace of the State'. One here discerns most aspects of the Christian persecutions. The *cohaerens scelus*, which in its extreme form is *consultatio de salute principis*, leads to a ban on the *nomen*, limited at first to Italy but later spreading to all provinces by proconsular imitation and rescript. There is, in the earlier age, no objection to beliefs as such. Later, aggressive *contumacia* produces an unfavourable reaction, and the basis of the objection is widened: ultimately the idea of universal suppression occurs, but always sub-ject to the rules of private delation.

The limitation of the early persecutions is thus partly the result of official policy, a determination not to take the matter too seriously, as evinced in Trajan's and Hadrian's rescripts, and to confine the issues to real offences (*flagitia, contumacia*). But it results also from the Roman system of jurisdiction, the wide latitude allowed to the provincial governor, and partly again from the checks imposed by the Roman system of private delation. To bring a capital charge was both dangerous and difficult, dangerous because the *calumnia* process enabled the wrongly accused to turn the tables on his accuser,[2] difficult because of the practical limitations on the frequency of capital charges. The *calumnia* process may have checked the prosecu-tion of members of an unobtrusive and even secretive sect about whom evidence to justify prosecution must have been rare, and who only had to take the oath in order to expose the accusation. The difficulty arose because in each province there was only one man who had power to pass capital sentences. This power, unlike the civil jurisdiction, could not be delegated.[3] To bring such charges one must either visit the provincial capital or else await the governor's visit on assize to the regional capitals of the province. Such visits were not always annual. Pliny in Bithynia-Pontus took two seasons to work through a rather small province. This forgotten factor, calling for leisure and money, acted as yet another check on the extent of the early persecutions. It is no accident that the known cases outside

---

[1] Loc. cit. 3, 'saepissime . . . interdictum est fere ab omnibus principibus': ibid. 4, a rescript of Pius.
[2] For a Christian instance cf. Euseb. *HE* 5. 21. See VI. 31. 10 n.
[3] Venuleius, *De off. proc.*, in *Dig.* I. 16. 11: 'legatus (proconsulis) . . . neque . . . animadvertendi coercendi vel atrociter verberandi ius habet'. Cf. i. 16. 6 pref. (Ulpian), 1. 21. 1. 1 (Papinian), and ibid. 5 (Paul). See X. 30. 1 n.

Rome occur in the great provincial cities, Lugdunum and neighbouring Vienna, Antioch, Carthage, Smyrna, Pergamum.[1] The number of
'hanging judges' in all Asia Minor would hardly exceed five in the
mid-second century.[2]

[1] Thysdrus, Tert. *Scap.* 4. 3, was the chief city of Africa Byzacene. The Scillitan
martyrs were tried at Carthage.

[2] The proconsul of Asia, proconsul or imperial legate of Pontus-Bithynia,
imperial legates of Cilicia, Lycia, and Galatia-Cappadocia.

ADDENDUM

In an article in *Past and Present* 1963, followed by a reply on my
part and a rejoinder of his own (ib. 1964), Mr. de Ste.-Croix argued
that at all times the prosecution of Christians was based on the in-
compatibility of the *nova superstitio* with Roman or civic religious
duties. He surprisingly maintained this even for the earliest period
when the Roman evidence clearly indicates that *cohaerentia scelera*
were the starting-point. He also argued, with more plausibility,
against my suggestion that *contumacia* was the principal ground of
official objection in the second century. His argument is based, fairly
enough, on the analogy of 'contempt of court'. *Contumacia* can occur
only when a person defies the orders of a magistrate or governor concerning some specific issue. A man cannot be punished for *contumacia*
in isolation, and Pliny (he holds) had given no specific orders to the
Christians. But this argument ignores the peculiar character of the
procedure in these trials. The whole purpose was to compel the
Christian to give up his profession. The *reus* is required under threat
of punishment to answer *no* to the question thrice put: 'tertio
interrogavi supplicium minatus: perseverantes duci iussi'. Tertullian understood the procedure in just this sense (*Apol.* 2. 10–13).
So too the proconsul in the Scillitan *acta*. The requirement of the
magistrate is revealed by the test of sacrifice put to the *negantes*.
An order is implied, and hence *contumacia* is involved in refusal to
recant. That Pliny prefers the literary words *obstinatio, pertinacia,*
does not mean that he did not have *contumacia* in mind. He uses
perseverare in the context, and this turns up in the formula *perseverare*
in contumacia in official documents of A.D. 69 and 170 (*FIRA* i, no.
59. 10–15, no. 61. 23).

INDEX

This index is selective. It aims at giving references to all terms and topics about which the commentary provides information of substance. It should be used in conjunction with the list of Contents and the catalogue of Persons.

3 F

INDEX OF DISPUTED READINGS IN PLINY'S TEXT DISCUSSED IN THE COMMENTARY

INDEX OF GREEK TERMS

INDEX OF PASSAGES IN OTHER
AUTHORS SPECIALLY DISCUSSED

Though the private letters of Pliny lie at the centre of the social and political history of the Principate, and many have frequently been studied in small groups or in isolation, there has been no general commentary on the whole collection since the eighteenth century. Meanwhile new inscriptions accumulate yearly to illuminate the contents and chronology of the letters. This book tries to set each letter in its social, political, legal or literary context, and to present a conspectus of modern opinion about them, though grammatical and philological questions are considered only when relevant to the general interpretation. The composition, distribution, and chronology of the letters, and questions about the career of Pliny, are discussed in introductory chapters. The second part of the commentary, dealing with the Bithynian correspondence of Pliny and Trajan, should replace that of E. G. Hardy, published in 1889.